# Directory of
# Financial Aids
# for Women
# 2014-2016

# RSP FINANCIAL AID DIRECTORIES
# OF INTEREST TO WOMEN

### College Student's Guide to Merit and Other No-Need Funding
Selected as one of the "Outstanding Titles of the Year" by *Choice,* this directory describes 1,300 no-need funding opportunities for college students. 490 pages. ISBN 1588412350. $32.50, plus $7 shipping.

### Directory of Financial Aids for Women
There are nearly 1,500 funding programs set aside for women described in this biennial directory, which has been called "the cream of the crop" by *School Library Journal* and the "best available reference source" by *Guide to Reference.* 504 pages. ISBN 1588412504. $45, plus $7 shipping.

### Financial Aid for African Americans
Nearly 1,300 funding opportunities open to African American college students, professionals, and postdoctorates are described in this award-winning directory. 481 pages. ISBN 1588412423. $42.50, plus $7 shipping.

### Financial Aid for Asian Americans
This is the source to use if you are looking for funding for Asian Americans, from college-bound high school seniors to professionals and postdoctorates; more than 900 sources of free money are described here. 341 pages. ISBN 1588412431. $40, plus $7 shipping.

### Financial Aid for Hispanic Americans
The 1,100 biggest and best sources of free money available to undergraduates, graduates students, professionals, and postdoctorates of Mexican, Puerto Rican, Central American, or other Latin American heritage are described here. 437 pages. ISBN 158841244X. $42.50, plus $7 shipping.

### Financial Aid for Native Americans
Detailed information is provided on nearly 1,400 funding opportunities open to American Indians, Native Alaskans, and Native Pacific Islanders for college, graduate school, or professional activities. 499 pages. ISBN 1588412458. $45, plus $7 shipping.

### Financial Aid for Research and Creative Activities Abroad
Described here are more than 1,000 scholarships, fellowships, grants, etc. available to support research, professional, or creative activities abroad. 413 pages. ISBN 1588412512. $45, plus $7 shipping.

### Financial Aid for Study and Training Abroad
This directory, which the reviewers call "invaluable," describes nearly 1,000 financial aid opportunities available to support study abroad. 353 pages. ISBN 1588412520. $40, plus $7 shipping.

### Financial Aid for Veterans, Military Personnel, & Their Families
According to *Reference Book Review,* this directory (with its 1,100 entries) is "the most comprehensive guide available on the subject." 429 pages. ISBN 1588412482. $40, plus $7 shipping.

### High School Senior's Guide to Merit and Other No-Need Funding
Here's your guide to 1,100 funding programs that *never* look at income level when making awards to college-bound high school seniors. 411 pages. ISBN 1588412369. $29.95, plus $7 shipping.

### Money for Graduate Students in the Arts & Humanities
Use this directory to identify 1,000 funding opportunities available to support graduate study and research in the arts/humanities. 287 pages. ISBN 1588412296. $42.50, plus $7 shipping

### Money for Graduate Students in the Biological Sciences
This unique directory focuses solely on funding for graduate study/research in the biological sciences (800+ funding opportunities). 241 pages. ISBN 158841230X. $37.50, plus $7 shipping.

### Money for Graduate Students in the Health Sciences
Described here are 1,000+ funding opportunities just for students interested in a graduate degree in dentistry, medicine, nursing, nutrition, pharmacology, etc. 313 pages. ISBN 1588412318. $42.50, plus $7 shipping.

### Money for Graduate Students in the Physical & Earth Sciences
Nearly 900 funding opportunities for graduate students in the physical and earth sciences are described in detail here. 280 pages. ISBN 1588412326. $40, plus $7 shipping.

### Money for Graduate Students in the Social & Behavioral Sciences
Looking for money for a graduate degree in the social/behavioral sciences? Here are 1,100 funding programs for you. 319 pages. ISBN 1588412334. $42.50, plus $7 shipping.

# Directory of Financial Aids for Women 2014-2016

**Gail Ann Schlachter**
**R. David Weber**

A Listing of Scholarships, Fellowships, Grants, Awards, Internships, and Other Sources of Free Money Available Primarily or Exclusively to Women, Plus a Set of Six Indexes (Program Title, Sponsoring Organization, Residency, Tenability, Subject, and Deadline Date)

**Reference Service Press**
El Dorado Hills, California

**Library of Congress Cataloging in Publication Data**

Schlachter, Gail A.
    Directory of financial aids for women, 2014-2016
    Includes indexes.
    1. Women—United States—Scholarships, fellowships, etc.—Directories.  2.  Grants-in-aid—United  States—Directories.  3. Credit—United States—Directories. I. Title.
LB2338.5342 2014          378'.30'2573
ISBN 10: 1588412504
ISBN 13: 9781588412508
ISSN 0732-5215


10 9 8 7 6 5 4 3 2 1

**Reference Service Press (RSP)** began in 1977 with a single financial aid publication *(The Directory of Financial Aids for Women)* and now specializes in the development of financial aid resources in multiple formats, including books, large print books, print-on-demand reports, eBooks, and online sources. Long recognized as a leader in the field, RSP has been called "a true success in the world of independent directory publishers" by the *Simba Report on Directory Publishing*  Both Kaplan Educational Centers and Military.com have hailed RSP as "the leading authority on scholarships."

**Reference Service Press**
**El Dorado Hills Business Park**
**5000 Windplay Drive, Suite 4**
**El Dorado Hills, CA 95762-9319**
        **(916) 939-9620**
        **Fax: (916) 939-9626**
        **E-mail: info@rspfunding.com**
**Visit our web site: www.rspfunding.com**


Manufactured in the United States of America
Price: $45, plus $7 shipping

**ACADEMIC INSTITUTIONS, LIBRARIES, ORGANIZATIONS, AND OTHER QUANTITY BUYERS:**
Discounts on this book are available for bulk purchases. Write or call for information on our discount programs.

# Contents

# Introduction

## HOW THE DIRECTORY HAS GROWN IN THE PAST 35 YEARS

In 1977 and 1978, while we were furiously researching, writing, editing, and updating entries for the very first edition of the *Directory of Financial Aids for Women,* major events were occurring that would have a lasting effect on the role of women in American society:

- The first National Women's Conference was held in Houston, Texas, attended by 20,000 women who passed the landmark National Plan of Action.

- The National Coalition Against Domestic Violence was established.

- The Air Force graduated its first women pilots.

- Congress passed the Pregnancy Discrimination Act, prohibiting discrimination against pregnant women in all areas of employment.

- Congress allocated $5 million to the Department of Labor to set up centers for displaced homemakers.

- The Philadelphia Mint began stamping the Susan B. Anthony dollar.

- Dianne Feinstein became the first female mayor of San Francisco, replacing the assassinated George Moscone.

- Margaret Thatcher was chosen to become Britain's first female prime minister.

- Hanna Gray was named president of the University of Chicago, becoming the first woman to lead a major America university.

But, from our point of view, the most significant development occurred in the field of higher education. In 1978, for the first time ever, more women than men entered American colleges and universities. We knew these women would face many challenges, particularly financial ones. Numerous studies had shown that, historically, when women competed again men for college aid, they were notably unsuccessful. We believed we could help to level this funding playing field by compiling the first-ever listing of financial aid opportunities open primarily or exclusively to women. And, so, the *Directory of Financial Aids for Women* was launched. Finally, women could find out about the hundreds of funding opportunities that were available just for them!

We were right. The directory did make a difference. Orders poured in. Women wrote to us about their successes. The book was featured in numerous magazines, television shows, bibliographic guides, and reviewing sources. It became clear to us at Reference Service Press that there was an continuing need for this type of compilation. So, in 1980, we made a commitment to collect, organize, and disseminate—on an on-going basis—the most current and accurate information available on all types of funding opportunities open to women.

To accomplish this goal over the years, we have had to become sophisticated information sleuths, tracking down all possible leads, identifying even the slightest changes to existing programs, finding new sources of funding opportunities for women, and constantly expanding and updating the electronic database used to prepare each new biennial edition of the *Directory of Financial Aids for Women.* The results have been dramatic, especially when the first (1978) edition is compared, side-by-side, to this issue (2014-2016). In the past 35 years, the directory has increased fivefold in size, growing from a modest 300 programs (200 pages) to the staggering 1,486 opportunities described in the 2014-2016 edition's more than 500 pages. Access to the information has advanced significantly as well, going beyond the simple program title listing in the first edition (with basic subject, geographic, and sponsor indexes) to a user-friendly grouping of records by recipient category (undergraduates, graduate students, and professionals/postdoctorates) and six detailed and sub-divided indexes in the latest edition, making it possible to search the information by all current, variant, and former program titles; every sponsor and administering organization; each location where an applicant must live; every place where the money can be spent; hundreds of specific subject fields; and month-by-month deadline dates.

Even the physical appearance of the two editions is strikingly different. In 1978, we laboriously photocopied program information, cut and pasted the draft, and then produced the final "camera-ready" version on an IBM Selectric typewriter. If you look carefully in the first edition, you'll be able to see where we used White-Out and correction tape! In contrast, the entries in the 2014-2016 edition have been carefully selected from our database of 45,000 unique funding records, extensively reviewed electronically by editors in geographically-dispersed locations, formatted using a layout and font chosen specifically for maximum utility, and produced simultaneously in both book and electronic versions.

One thing that hasn't changed during the past 35 years, however, is our passionate commitment to making a difference. Little did we realize, when we first published the *Directory of Financial Aids for Women* in 1978, that we had taken the initial steps on what would become a life-long search for unique funding opportunities available specifically to special needs groups. And though our focus has broadened beyond women and our output has expanded beyond books, we have never lost sight of the fact that financial need is not just one of our publishing interests. It is and will be our only business. Perhaps that's why *The Simba Report on Directory Publishing* called Reference Service Press "a true success in the world of independent directory publishers" and why both Kaplan Educational Centers and Military.com have hailed the company as "the leading authority on scholarships."

## WHY THIS DIRECTORY IS NEEDED

Currently, billions of dollars in financial aid are available primarily or exclusively for women. In fact, more money is available today than ever before. This funding is open to applicants at any level (high school through postdoctoral and professional) for study, research, travel, training, career development, or innovative efforts. While numerous directories have been prepared to identify and describe general financial aid programs (those open to both men and women), they have never covered more than a small portion of the programs designed primarily or exclusively for women. As a result, many advisors, librarians, scholars, researchers, and students have not been aware of the impressive array of financial aid programs established with women in mind. Now, with the 2014-2016 edition of the *Directory of Financial Aids for Women,* up-to-date and comprehensive information is available in a single source about the special resources set aside for women. No other source, in print or online, comes anywhere close to matching the extensive coverage provided by this publication.

The unique value of the *Directory* has been highly praised by the reviewers. Here are just some of the rave reviews:

- "The title is a must-purchase guide." —*American Reference Books Annual*

- "Nobody does a better job...a great resource and highly recommended." —*College Spotlight*

- "The only current source of information on financial aid specifically for women...an essential and reasonably priced purchase." —*Reference Books Bulletin*

- "The quintessential acquisition for public libraries of all sizes...feminists, homemakers, and women everywhere will welcome this book, since it is so well-done and simple to use." —*Small Press*

- "The variety of programs is amazing...an essential purchase...has become the standard source for information on scholarships, fellowships, loans, grants, awards, and internships available primarily to women." —*Library Journal*

## SAMPLE ENTRY

(1) **[114]**

(2) **CAROLYN B. ELMAN NATIONAL UNDERGRADUATE SCHOLARSHIP**

(3) American Business Women's Association
11050 Roe Avenue, Suite 200
Overland Park, KS 66211
Toll Free: (800) 228-0007
Web: www.sbmef.org/Scholarships.cfm

(4) **Summary** To provide financial assistance to female undergraduate students who are working on a degree in a specified field (the field changes each year).

(5) **Eligibility** This program is open to women who have completed at least 60 credit hours of work on an undergraduate degree. Applicants are not required to be members of the American Business Women's Association. Along with their application, they must submit a 250-word biographical sketch that includes information about their background, activities, honors, work experience, and long-term educational and professional goals. Financial need is not considered in the selection process. Annually, the trustees designate an academic discipline for which the scholarship will be presented that year. U.S. citizenship is required.

(6) **Financial data** The stipend is $5,000 per year. Funds are paid directly to the recipient's institution to be used only for tuition, books, and fees.

(7) **Duration** 2 years.

(8) **Additional information** This program began in 2011 as part of ABWA's Stephen Bufton Memorial Education Fund. The ABWA does not provide the names and addresses of local chapters; it recommends that applicants check with their local Chamber of Commerce, library, or university to see if any chapter has registered a contact's name and number.

(9) **Number awarded** 1 each odd-numbered year.

(10) **Deadline** May of each odd-numbered year.

## DEFINITION

(1) **Entry number:** The consecutive number assigned to the references and used to index the entry.

(2) **Program title:** Title of the scholarship, fellowship, grant, award, internship, or other source of free money described in the directory.

(3) **Sponsoring organization:** Name, address, and telephone number, toll-free number, fax number, e-mail address, and/or web site (when information was supplied) for organization sponsoring the program.

(4) **Summary:** Identifies the major program requirements; read the rest of the entry for additional detail.

(5) **Eligibility:** Qualifications required of applicants, plus information on application procedure and selection process.

(6) **Financial data:** Financial details of the program, including fixed sum, average amount, or range of funds offered, expenses for which funds may and may not be applied, and cash-related benefits supplied (e.g., room and board).

(7) **Duration:** Period for which support is provided; renewal prospects.

(8) **Additional information:** Any unusual (generally nonmonetary) benefits, features, restrictions, or limitations associated with the program.

(9) **Number awarded:** Total number of recipients each year or other specified period.

(10) **Deadline:** The month by which applications must be submitted.

Previous editions of the directory were selected as the "cream of the crop" in *School Library Journal's* "Reference Round-Up;" were included in *Recommended Reference Books for Small and Medium-sized Libraries and Media Centers;* were featured in *Glamour, Good Housekeeping, New Woman,* and *Teen* magazines; and were selected as the "Best of the Best" in education and career information print materials by members of the National Education and Information Center Advisory Committee. In the view of The Grantsmanship Center, "No organization interested in serving women should be without this directory!" Want to read more reviews? Go to: www.rspfunding.com/reviews.html.

## WHAT'S UPDATED?

The preparation of each new edition of the *Directory of Financial Aids for Women* involves extensive updating and revision. To make sure that the information included here is both reliable and current, the editors at Reference Service Press 1) reviewed and updated all relevant programs covered in the previous edition of the directory, 2) collected information on all programs open primarily or exclusively to women that were added to Reference Service Press' funding database since the last edition of the directory, and then 3) searched extensively for new program leads in a variety of sources, including printed directories, news reports, journals, newsletters, house organs, annual reports, and sites on the Internet. We only include program descriptions in the *Directory* that are written directly from information supplied by the sponsoring organization in print or online (no information is ever taken from secondary sources). When that information could not be found, we sent up to four data collection letters (followed by up to three telephone or email inquiries, if necessary) to those sponsors. Despite our best efforts, however, some sponsoring organizations still failed to respond and, as a result, their programs are not included in this edition of the *Directory.*

The 2014-2016 edition of the *Directory of Financial Aids for Women* completely revises and updates the previous (16th) edition. Programs that have ceased operations have been dropped. Similarly, programs that have broadened their focus to include men have also been removed from the listing. Profiles of continuing programs have been rewritten to reflect operations in 2014-2016; more than 70 percent of the continuing programs reported substantive changes in their locations, requirements (particularly application deadline), benefits, or eligibility requirements since 2012. In addition, more than 450 new entries have been added to the program section of the *Directory.* The resulting listing describes the close to 1,500 biggest and best sources of free money available to women, including scholarships, fellowships, grants, awards, and internships.

## WHAT MAKES THIS DIRECTORY UNIQUE?

The 2014-2016 edition of the *Directory of Financial Aids for Women* identifies billions of dollars available for study, research, creative activities, past accomplishments, future projects, professional development, and work experience. The listings cover every major subject area, are sponsored by more than 900 different private and public agencies and organizations, and are open to women at any level—from high school through postdoctorate and professional. This approach is unique. No other source, in print or online, provides this type of comprehensive and current coverage of funding opportunities available primarily or exclusively to women.

Not only does the *Directory of Financial Aids for Women* provide the most comprehensive coverage of available funding (1,486 entries), but it also displays the most informative program descriptions (on the average, more than twice the detail found in any other listing). In addition to this extensive and focused coverage, the directory also offers several other unique features. First of all, hundreds of funding opportunities listed here have never been covered in any other source. So, even if you have checked elsewhere, you will want to look at the *Directory of Financial Aids for Women* for additional leads. And, here's another plus: all of the funding programs in this edition of the directory offer "free" money; not one of the programs will ever require you to pay anything back (provided, of course, that you meet the program requirements).

Further, unlike other funding directories, which generally follow a straight alphabetical arrangement, the *Directory of Financial Aids for Women* groups entries by intended recipients (undergraduates, graduate students, or professionals/postdoctorates), to make it easy for you to search for appropriate programs.

This same convenience is offered in the indexes, where program title, sponsoring organization, geographic, subject, and deadline date entries are each subdivided by recipient group.

Finally, we have tried to anticipate all the ways you might wish to search for funding. The volume is organized so you can identify programs not only by intended recipient, but also by subject focus, sponsoring organization, program title, residency requirements, where the money can be spent, and even deadline date. Plus, we've included all the information you'll need to decide if a program is right for you: purpose, eligibility requirements, financial data, duration, special features, limitations, number awarded, and application date. You even get fax numbers, toll-free numbers, e-mail addresses, and web sites (when available), along with complete contact information.

## WHAT'S EXCLUDED?

While this book is intended to be the most comprehensive source of information on funding available to women, there are some programs we've specifically excluded from the directory.

- *Programs that do not accept applications from U.S. citizens or residents.* If a program is open only to foreign nationals or excludes Americans from applying, it is not covered.

- *Programs that are open equally to men and women:* Only funding opportunities set aside primarily or exclusively for women are included here.

- *Money for study or research outside the United States.* Since there are comprehensive and up-to-date directories that describe the available funding for study, research, or other activities abroad (see the list of Reference Service Press publications opposite the directory's title page), only programs that fund activities in the United States are covered here.

- *Very restrictive programs.* The emphasis here is on the biggest and best funding available. In general, programs are excluded if they are open only to a limited geographic area (less than a state) or offer limited financial support (less than $1,000). Note, however, that the majority of programs award considerably more than the $1,000 minimum requirement, paying up to full tuition or stipends that exceed $25,000 a year!

- *Programs administered by individual academic institutions solely for their own students.* The directory identifies "portable" programs—ones that can be used at any number of schools. Financial aid administered by individual schools specifically for their own students is not covered. Write directly to the schools you are considering to get information on their offerings.

- *Money that must be repaid.* Only "free money" is identified here. If a program requires repayment or charges interest, it's not listed. Now you can find out about billions of dollars in aid and know (if you meet the program requirements) that not one dollar of that will ever need to be repaid.

## HOW THE DIRECTORY IS ORGANIZED

The *Directory* is divided into two sections: 1) a detailed list of financial aid programs available to women and 2) a set of six indexes to help you pinpoint appropriate funding programs.

**Financial Aid Programs Open Primarily or Exclusively to Women.** The first section of the *Directory* describes the nearly 1,500 biggest and best sources of free money aimed primarily or exclusively at women. These programs are sponsored by government agencies, professional organizations, corporations, sororities and social groups, foundations, religious groups, educational associations, and military/veterans organizations. They are open to women at any level (high school through postdoctoral) for study, research, travel, training, career development, personal needs, or creative activities. All areas of the sciences, social sciences, and humanities are covered in the awards listed. The focus is on programs tenable in the United States that are open to women who are U.S. citizens or permanent residents

To help you focus your search, the entries in this section are grouped in the following three chapters:

- **Undergraduates:** Included here are more than 700 scholarships, grants, awards, internships, and other sources of free money that support women's undergraduate study, training, research, or creative activities. These programs are open to high school seniors, high school graduates, currently-enrolled college students, and students returning to college after an absence. Money is available to support these students in any type of public or private postsecondary institution, ranging from technical schools and community colleges to major universities in the United States.

- **Graduate Students:** Described here nearly 500 fellowships, grants, awards, internships, and other sources of free money that support women's post-baccalaureate study, training, research, and creative activities. These programs are open to students applying to, currently enrolled in, or returning to a master's, doctoral, professional, or specialist program in public or private graduate schools in the United States.

- **Professionals/Postdoctorates:** Included here are more than 275 funding programs for women who are U.S. citizens or residents and 1) are in professional positions (e.g., artists, writers), whether or not they have an advanced degree; 2) are master's or professional degree recipients; 3) have earned a doctoral degree or its equivalent (e.g., Ph.D., Ed.D., M.D.); or 4) have recognized stature as established scientists, scholars, academicians, or researchers.

Within each chapter in the *Directory,* entries appear alphabetically by program title. Since some of the programs supply assistance to more than one specific group, those are listed in all relevant chapters. For example, the Amelia Earhart Memorial Academic Scholarship supports both undergraduate or graduate study, so the program is described in both the Undergraduates *and* Graduate Students chapters.

Each program entry has been designed to give you a concise profile that, as the sample on page 7 illustrates, includes information (when available) on organization address and telephone numbers (including toll-free and fax numbers), e-mail addresses and web site, purpose, eligibility, money awarded, duration, special features, limitations, number of awards, and application deadline.

The information reported for each of the programs in this section was gathered from research conducted through the end of 2013. While the listing is intended to cover as comprehensively as possible the biggest and best sources of free money available to women, some sponsoring organizations did not post information online or respond to our research inquiries and, consequently, are not included in this edition of the directory.

**Indexes.** To help you find the aid you need, we have constructed six indexes; these will let you access the listings by program title, sponsoring organization, residency, tenability, subject focus, and deadline date. These indexes use a word-by-word alphabetical arrangement. Note: numbers in the index refer to entry numbers, not to page numbers in the book.

**Program Title Index.** If you know the name of a particular funding program and want to find out where it is covered in the *Directory,* use the Program Title Index. To assist you in your search, every program is listed by all its known names, former names, and abbreviations. Since one program can be included in more than one place (e.g., a program providing assistance to both undergraduate and graduate students is described in both the first and second chapter), each entry number in the index has been coded to indicate the intended recipient group ("U" = Undergraduates; "G" = Graduate Students; "P" = Professionals/Postdoctorates). By using this coding system, you can avoid duplicate entries and turn directly to the programs that match your eligibility characteristics.

**Sponsoring Organization Index.** This index makes it easy to identify agencies that offer funding primarily or exclusively to women. More than 900 organizations are listed alphabetically, word by word. As in the Program Title Index, we've used a code to help you determine which organizations sponsor programs that match your educational level.

**Residency Index.**  Some programs listed in this book are restricted to women in a particular state, region, or other geographic location. Others are open to women wherever they live. This index helps you identify programs available only to residents in your area as well as programs that have no residency requirements. Further, to assist you in your search, we've also indicated the recipient level for the funding offered to residents in each of the areas listed in the index.

**Tenability Index.**  This index identifies the geographic locations where the funding described in the *Directory* may be used. Index entries (city, county, state, province, region) are arranged alphabetically (word by word) and subdivided by recipient group. Use this index when you are looking for money to support your activities in a particular geographic area.

**Subject Index.**  This index allows you to identify the subject focus of each of the financial aid opportunities described in the *Directory*. More than 250 different subject terms are listed. Extensive "see" and "see also" references, as well as recipient group subdivisions, will help you in your search for appropriate funding opportunities.

**Calendar Index.**  Since most financial aid programs have specific deadline dates, some may have closed by the time you begin to look for funding. You can use the Calendar Index to determine which programs are still open. This index is arranged by recipient group (Undergraduates, Graduate Students, and Professionals/Postdoctorates) and subdivided by month during which the deadline falls. Filing dates can and quite often do vary from year to year; consequently, this index should be used only as a guide for deadlines beyond the end of 2016.

## HOW TO USE THE DIRECTORY

Here are some tips to help you get the most out the funding opportunities listed in the *Directory of Financial Aids for Women.*

**To Locate Funding by Recipient Group.**  To bring together programs with a similar educational focus, this directory is divided into three chapters: Undergraduates, Graduate Students, and Professionals/Postdoctorates. If you want to get an overall picture of the sources of free money available to women in any of these categories, turn to the appropriate chapter and then review the entries there. Since each of these chapters functions as a self-contained entity, you can browse through any of them without having to first consulting an index.

**To Locate a Particular Women's Financial Aid Program.**  If you know the name of a particular financial aid program, and the group eligible for that award, then go directly to the appropriate chapter in the directory (e.g., Undergraduates, Graduate Students), where you will find the program profiles arranged alphabetically by title. To save time, though, you should always check the Program Title Index first if you know the name of a specific award but are not sure in which chapter it has been listed. Plus, since we index each program by all its known names and abbreviations, you'll also be able to track down a program there when you only know the popular rather than official name.

**To Locate Programs Sponsored by a Particular Organization.**  The Sponsoring Organization Index makes it easy to identify agencies that provide financial assistance to women or to target specific financial aid programs for women offered by a particular organization. Each entry number in the index is coded to identify recipient group (Undergraduates, Graduate Students, Professionals/Postdoctorates), so that you can easily target appropriate entries.

**To Browse Quickly Through the Listings.**  Look at the listings in the chapter that relates to you (Undergraduates, Graduate Students, or Professionals/Postdoctorates) and read the "Summary" paragraph in each entry. In seconds, you'll know if this is an opportunity that you might want to pursue. If it is, be sure to read the rest of the information in the entry, to make sure you meet all of the program requirements before writing or going online for an application form. Please save your time and energy. Don't apply if you don't qualify!

**To Locate Funding Open to Women from or Tenable in a Particular Geographic Location.**
The Residency Index identifies financial aid programs open to women in a particular geographic loca-

tion. The Tenability Index shows where the money can be spent. In both indexes, "see" and "see also" references are used liberally, and index entries for a particular geographic area are subdivided by recipient group (Undergraduates, Graduate Students, and Professionals/Postdoctorates) to help you identify the funding that's right for you. When using these indexes, always check the listings under the term "United States," since the programs indexed there have no geographic restrictions and can be used in any area.

**To Locate Financial Aid for Women in a Particular Subject Area.**    Turn to the Subject Index first if you are interested in identifying financial aid programs for women in a particular subject area (more than 250 different subject fields are listed there). To make your search easier, the intended recipient groups (Undergraduates, Graduate Students, Professionals/Postdoctorates) are clearly labeled in each of the subject listings. Extensive cross-references are also provided. As part of your search, be sure to check the listings in the index under the heading "General Programs;" those programs provide funding in any subject area (although they may be restricted in other ways).

**To Locate Financial Aid Programs for Women by Deadline Date.**   If you are working with specific time constraints and want to weed out the financial aid programs whose filing dates you won't be able to meet, turn first to the Calendar Index and check the program references listed under the appropriate recipient group and month. Note: not all sponsoring organizations supplied deadline information; those programs are listed under the "Deadline not specified" entries in the index. To identify every relevant financial aid program, regardless of filing date, go the appropriate chapter and read through all the entries there that match your educational level.

**To Locate Financial Aid Programs Open to Both Men and Women.**   Only programs designed with women in mind are listed in this publication. There are thousands of other programs that are open equally to men and women. To identify these programs, talk to your local librarian, check with your campus financial aid office, look at the list of RSP print resources on the page opposite the title page in this directory, or see if your library subscribes to Reference Service Press' interactive online funding database (for more information on that resource, go online to: www.rspfunding.com/esubscriptions.html).

## PLANS TO UPDATE THE DIRECTORY

This volume, covering 2014-2016, is the 17th edition of the *Directory of Financial Aids for Women.* The next biennial edition will cover the years 2016-2018 and will be released in the Fall of 2016.

## OTHER RELATED PUBLICATIONS

In addition to the *Directory of Financial Aids for Women,* Reference Service Press publishes dozens of other titles dealing with fundseeking, including the *High School Senior's Guide to Merit and Other No-Need Funding; Money for Christen College Students; How to Pay for Your Degree in Education; Financial Aid for the Disabled and Their Families; Financial Aid for Study and Training Abroad;* and *Financial Aid for Veterans, Military Personnel, and Their Dependents.* Since each of these titles focuses on a separate population group, there is very little duplication in the listings. For more information on all of Reference Service Press' award-winning publications, write to the company at 5000 Windplay Drive, Suite 4, El Dorado Hills, CA 95762, give us a call at (916) 939-9620, fax us at (916) 939-9626, send us an e-mail at info@rspfunding.com, or visit our expanded web site: www.rspfunding.com.

## ACKNOWLEDGEMENTS

A debt of gratitude is owed all the organizations that contributed information to the 2014-2016 edition of the *Directory of Financial Aids for Women.* Their generous cooperation has helped to make this publication the most current and comprehensive survey of awards.

# ABOUT THE AUTHORS

**Dr. Gail Ann Schlachter** has worked for more than three decades as a library administrator, a library educator, and an administrator of library-related publishing companies. Among the reference books to her credit are the biennially-issued *College Student's Guide to Merit and Other No-Need Funding* (named by *Choice* as one of the outstanding reference titles of the year) and two award-winning bibliographic guides: *Minorities and Women: A Guide to Reference Literature in the Social Sciences* (which also was chosen as an "Outstanding Reference Book of the Year" by *Choice*) and *Reference Sources in Library and Information Services* (which won the first Knowledge Industry Publications "Award for Library Literature"). She was the reference book review editor for *RQ* (now *Reference and User Services Quarterly*) for 10 years, is a past president of the American Library Association's Reference and User Services Association, is the former editor-in-chief of the *Reference and User Services Association Quarterly,* and is currently serving her sixth term on the American Library Association's governing council. In recognition of her outstanding contributions to reference service, Dr. Schlachter has been named the University of Wisconsin School of Library and Information Studies "Alumna of the Year" and has been awarded both the Isadore Gilbert Mudge Citation and the Louis Shores/Oryx Press Award.

**Dr. R. David Weber** taught history and economics at Los Angeles Harbor College (in Wilmington, California) for many years and continues to teach there as an emeritus professor. During his years of full-time teaching at Harbor College, and at East Los Angeles College, he directed the Honors Program and was frequently chosen "Teacher of the Year." He has written a number of critically-acclaimed reference works, including *Dissertations in Urban History* and the three-volume *Energy Information Guide.* With Dr. Schlachter, he is the author Reference Service Press's award-winning *Financial Aid for the Disabled and Their Families* and dozens of other distinguished financial aid titles, including the highly-acclaimed *Money for Graduate Students in the Social & Behavioral Sciences* and *Financial Aid for Hispanic Americans.*

# Financial Aid Programs Primarily or Exclusively for Women

*Undergraduates* ●

*Graduate Students* ●

*Professionals/Postdoctorates* ●

# Undergraduates

---

Listed alphabetically by program title and described in detail here are 723 scholarships, grants, awards, internships, and other sources of "free money" set aside for females who are college-bound high school seniors, high school graduates who haven't started college yet, and continuing or returning undergraduate students. This funding is available to support study, training, research, and/or creative activities in the United States.

## [1]
## AAJUW SCHOLARSHIP PROGRAM

American Association of Japanese University Women
Attn: Scholarship Committee
3543 West Boulevard
Los Angeles, CA 90016
E-mail: scholarship@aajuw.org
Web: www.aajuw.org/scholarship.php

**Summary**  To provide financial assistance to female students (any ethnicity) currently enrolled in upper-division or graduate classes in California.

**Eligibility**  This program is open to women enrolled at accredited colleges or universities in California as juniors, seniors, or graduate students. Applicants must be involved in U.S.-Japan relations, cultural exchanges, and leadership development in the areas of their designated field of study. Along with their application, they must submit a current resume, an official transcript of the past 2 years of college work, 2 letters of recommendation, and an essay (up to 2 pages in English or 1,200 characters in Japanese) on what they hope to accomplish in their field of study and how that will contribute to better U.S.-Japan relations.

**Financial data**  The stipend is $2,000.

**Duration**  1 year.

**Additional information**  The association was founded in 1970 to promote the education of women as well as to contribute to U.S.-Japan relations, cultural exchanges, and leadership development.

**Number awarded**  1 to 3 each year. Since this program was established, it has awarded more than $100,000 worth of scholarships to nearly 100 women.

**Deadline**  October of each year.

## [2]
## AAU HIGH SCHOOL SULLIVAN SCHOLARSHIP AWARD

Amateur Athletic Union of the United States
1910 Hotel Plaza Boulevard
P.O. Box 22409
Lake Buena Vista, FL 32830
(407) 934-7200                    Toll Free: (800) AAU-4USA
Fax: (407) 934-7242          E-mail: pam@aausports.org
Web: highschoolsullivan.org

**Summary**  To provide financial assistance for college to outstanding high school athletes (females and males compete separately).

**Eligibility**  This program is open to seniors graduating from high schools in the United States and planning to attend a college or university. Applicants must have a record of outstanding participation in sports. Men and women are judged separately. Selection is based on athletic accomplishments, leadership, character, and academic performance.

**Financial data**  Stipends are $10,000 for winners and $2,500 for other finalists.

**Duration**  1 year.

**Additional information**  This program, which began in 2011, is sponsored by Eastbay.

**Number awarded**  8 each year: 1 male winner, 1 female winner, 3 male finalists, and 3 female finalists.

**Deadline**  February of each year.

## [3]
## AAUW CAREER DEVELOPMENT GRANTS

American Association of University Women
Attn: AAUW Educational Foundation
301 ACT Drive, Department 60
P.O. Box 4030
Iowa City, IA 52243-4030
(319) 337-1716, ext. 60               Fax: (319) 337-1204
E-mail: aauw@act.org
Web: www.aauw.org

**Summary**  To provide financial assistance to women who are seeking career advancement, career change, or reentry into the workforce.

**Eligibility**  This program is open to women who are U.S. citizens or permanent residents, have earned a bachelor's degree, received their most recent degree more than 4 years ago, and are making career changes, seeking to advance in current careers, or reentering the workforce. Applicants must be interested in working toward a master's degree, second bachelor's or associate degree, professional degree (e.g., M.D., J.D.), certification program, or technical school certificate. They must be planning to undertake course work at an accredited 2- or 4-year college or university (or a technical school that is licensed, accredited, or approved by the U.S. Department of Education). Primary consideration is given to women of color and women pursuing their first advanced degree or credentials in nontraditional fields. Support is not provided for prerequisite course work or for Ph.D. course work or dissertations. Selection is based on demonstrated commitment to education and equity for women and girls, reason for seeking higher education or technical training, degree to which study plan is consistent with career objectives, potential for success in chosen field, documentation of opportunities in chosen field, feasibility of study plans and proposed time schedule, validity of proposed budget and budget narrative (including sufficient outside support), and quality of written proposal.

**Financial data**  Grants range from $2,000 to $12,000. Funds may be used for tuition, fees, books, supplies, local transportation, dependent child care, or purchase of a computer required for the study program.

**Duration**  1 year, beginning in July; nonrenewable.

**Additional information**  The filing fee is $35.

**Number awarded**  Varies each year; recently, 63 of these grants, with a value of $670,000, were awarded.

**Deadline**  December of each year.

## [4]
## ACADEMIC EXCELLENCE SCHOLARSHIPS

Delta Sigma Theta Sorority, Inc.-Federal City Alumnae
   Chapter
Attn: Educational Development Committee
P.O. Box 1605
Washington, DC 20013
(202) 545-1913                E-mail: thefcacdst@yahoo.com
Web: thefcacdst.org

**Summary**  To provide financial assistance to high school seniors (especially female African Americans) in Washington, D.C. who plan to attend a 4-year college or university in any state.

**Eligibility**  This program is open to seniors graduating from public or charter high schools in the District of Columbia and planning to enroll full time at an accredited 4-year college or university in any state. Applicants must have a GPA of 3.3 or higher. Along with their application, they must submit a 500-word essay on either how they plan to use their education to make the world a better place or why they should be selected to receive this scholarship.

**Financial data**   The stipend is $5,000.

**Duration**   1 year.

**Additional information**   The sponsor is the local alumnae chapter of a traditionally African American social sorority.

**Number awarded**   2 each year.

**Deadline**   February of each year.

## [5]
## ACCELERATOR APPLICATIONS DIVISION SCHOLARSHIP

American Nuclear Society
Attn: Scholarship Coordinator
555 North Kensington Avenue
La Grange Park, IL 60526-5535
(708) 352-6611                    Toll Free: (800) 323-3044
Fax: (708) 352-0499               E-mail: outreach@ans.org
Web: www.new.ans.org/honors/scholarships

**Summary**   To provide financial assistance to women and other undergraduate students who are interested in preparing for a career dealing with accelerator applications aspects of nuclear science or nuclear engineering.

**Eligibility**   This program is open to students entering their junior year in physics, engineering, or materials science at an accredited institution in the United States. Applicants must submit a description of their long- and short-term professional objectives, including their research interests related to accelerator aspects of nuclear science and engineering. Selection is based on that statement, faculty recommendations, and academic performance. Special consideration is given to members of underrepresented groups (women and minorities), students who can demonstrate financial need, and applicants who have a record of service to the American Nuclear Society (ANS).

**Financial data**   The stipend is $1,000 per year.

**Duration**   1 year (the junior year); may be renewed for the senior year.

**Additional information**   This program is offered by the Accelerator Applications Division (AAD) of the ANS.

**Number awarded**   1 each year.

**Deadline**   January of each year.

## [6]
## ADA I. PRESSMAN SCHOLARSHIP

Society of Women Engineers
Attn: Scholarship Selection Committee
203 North LaSalle Street, Suite 1675
Chicago, IL 60601-1269
(312) 596-5223                    Toll Free: (877) SWE-INFO
Fax: (312) 644-8557               E-mail: scholarships@swe.org
Web: societyofwomenengineers.swe.org

**Summary**   To provide financial assistance to women working on an undergraduate or graduate degree in engineering or computer science.

**Eligibility**   This program is open to women who will be sophomores, juniors, seniors, or graduate students at ABET-

accredited colleges and universities. Applicants must be U.S. citizens or permanent residents working full time on a degree in computer science or engineering and have a GPA of 3.0 or higher. Selection is based on merit.

**Financial data**   The stipend is $5,000.

**Duration**   1 year.

**Number awarded**   7 each year.

**Deadline**   February of each year.

## [7]
## ADMIRAL GRACE MURRAY HOPPER MEMORIAL SCHOLARSHIPS

Society of Women Engineers
Attn: Scholarship Selection Committee
203 North LaSalle Street, Suite 1675
Chicago, IL 60601-1269
(312) 596-5223                    Toll Free: (877) SWE-INFO
Fax: (312) 644-8557               E-mail: scholarships@swe.org
Web: societyofwomenengineers.swe.org

**Summary**   To provide financial assistance to women who will be entering college as freshmen and are interested in studying engineering or computer science, particularly computer-related engineering.

**Eligibility**   This program is open to women who are entering college as freshmen with a GPA of 3.5 or higher. Applicants must be U.S. citizens or permanent residents planning to enroll full time at an ABET-accredited 4-year college or university and major in computer science or engineering. Selection is based on merit. Preference is given to students in computer-related engineering.

**Financial data**   The stipend is $1,500.

**Duration**   1 year.

**Additional information**   This program, established in 1992, is named for the "mother of computerized data automation in the naval service."

**Number awarded**   3 each year.

**Deadline**   May of each year.

## [8]
## ADULT STUDENTS IN SCHOLASTIC TRANSITION (ASIST) PROGRAM

Executive Women International
Attn: Scholarship Coordinator
3860 South 2300 East
Salt Lake City, UT 84109
(801) 355-2800                    Toll Free: (877) 4EWI-NOW
Fax: (801) 355-2852               E-mail: ewi@ewiconnect.com
Web: ewiconnect.com

**Summary**   To provide financial assistance to adults (particularly those responsible for small children) who are interested in pursuing additional education to improve their life status.

**Eligibility**   This program is open to adult students at transitional points in their lives. Applicants may be persons who are 1) past high school age and entering a college, university, trade school, and/or the workforce for the first time; 2) already enrolled in a college, university, or trade program as nontraditional students; 3) re-training due to changes in the workplace; or 4) otherwise finished with high school but not the traditional college or trade school student. They must utilize reentry programs available through colleges and universities, community agencies, and service groups or career professionals; be 18 years of age or older; have clearly defined career goals and objectives; and specify the educational requirements to attain their goals and objectives. Priority is given to applicants who are responsible for small children; are socially, physically, or economically challenged adults; and can demonstrate financial need. The program is conducted by local chapters of Executive Women International (EWI). Chapters that participate establish their own requirements for applicants. From among the pool of applicants for chapter scholarships, high-ranking individuals are selected to receive corporate (national) scholarships.

**Financial data**   The stipend at the corporate level ranges from $2,000 to $10,000. Individual chapters established their own funding level.

**Duration**   1 year.

**Additional information**   For a list of participating chapters, contact EWI.

**Number awarded**   Varies each year; recently, 13 corporate scholarships were awarded: 1 at $10,000, 2 at $5,000, and 10 at $2,000. In addition, 42 chapters awarded scholarships. A total of $250,000 is distributed through this program each year.

**Deadline**   Each participating chapter sets its own application deadline.

## [9]
## ADVANCING ASPIRATIONS GLOBAL SCHOLARSHIPS

Womenetics
Attn: Advancing Aspirations Global Scholarships
99 West Paces Ferry Road, N.W., Suite 200
Atlanta, GA 30305
(404) 816-7224   E-mail: scholarships@womenetics.com
Web: www.womenetics.com

**Summary**   To recognize and reward undergraduates who submit outstanding essays on topics related to the global advancement of women.

**Eligibility**   This competition is open to U.S. citizens and permanent residents who are currently enrolled as undergraduates at accredited colleges and universities. Applicants must submit an essay of up to 2,500 words on assigned topics; recently, those were 1) gender stereotypes in film and other media; and/or 2) women in media leadership. They must also submit a "works cited" page to document any research they conducted to write the essay and a 200-word essay on what they plan to do with the prize money if they win.

**Financial data**   For each topic, the winner receives a $5,000 prize and other essayists each receive $1,500 prizes. Funds may be used to finance education, travel, or other opportunities that may lead to further understanding of the global issues raised in the essays.

**Duration**   The competition is held annually.

**Additional information**   Recently, prizes for the first topic were sponsored by U.S. Bank and prizes for the second topic were sponsored by Discover. Winners are also invited to conferences of the sponsor, which covers all expenses of the first-place winners.

**Number awarded**   10 each year: 1 first-place winner and 4 additional essayists for each of the sponsors' topics.

**Deadline**   July of each year.

## [10]
## ADVANCING WOMEN IN ACCOUNTING SCHOLARSHIP

Illinois CPA Society
Attn: CPA Endowment Fund of Illinois
550 West Jackson, Suite 900
Chicago, Il 60661-5716
(312) 993-0407        Toll Free: (800) 993-0407 (within IL)
Fax: (312) 993-9954
Web: www.icpas.org/hc-students.aspx?id=2724

**Summary**   To provide financial assistance to female residents of Illinois who will be enrolled as seniors or graduate students in an accounting program in the state.

**Eligibility**   This program is open to women in Illinois who plan to enroll as seniors or graduate students in an accounting program at a college or university in the state. Applicants must be planning to complete the educational requirements needed to sit for the C.P.A. examination in Illinois. They must have at least a 3.0 GPA and be able to demonstrate financial need or special circumstances; the society is especially interested in assisting students who, because of limited options or opportunities, may not have alternative means of support. U.S. citizenship or permanent resident status is required. Selection is based on academic achievement and financial need.

**Financial data**   The maximum stipend is $4,000 for payment of tuition and fees. Awards include up to $500 in expenses for books and required classroom materials.

**Duration**   1 year (fifth year for accounting students planning to become a C.P.A.).

**Additional information**   This program was established by the Women's Executive Committee of the Illinois CPA Society. The scholarship does not cover the cost of C.P.A. examination review courses. Recipients may not receive a full graduate assistantship, fellowship, or scholarship from a college or university, participate in a full-tuition reimbursement cooperative education or internship program, or participate in an employee full-tuition reimbursement program during the scholarship period.

**Number awarded**   Varies each year; recently, 3 of these scholarships were awarded.

**Deadline**   March of each year.

## [11]
## AEPHI FOUNDATION SCHOLARSHIPS

Alpha Epsilon Phi
Attn: AEPhi Foundation
11 Lake Avenue Extension, Suite 1A
Danbury, CT 06811
(203) 748-0029                        Fax: (203) 748-0039
E-mail: aephifoundation@aephi.org
Web: www.aephi.org/foundation/scholarships

**Summary**   To provide financial assistance for undergraduate or graduate education to Alpha Epsilon Phi members or alumnae.

**Eligibility**   This program is open to active and alumnae members of the sorority who are either full-time rising juniors or seniors or graduate students who have completed at least 1 year of graduate study. Applicants must have a GPA of 3.0 or higher. Along with their application, they must submit a letter describing 1) their activities in their chapter, on campus, and in the general community; 2) what they have done to supplement their parents' contribution toward their education; and 3) their need for scholarship consideration.

**Financial data** Stipends range from $1,000 to $2,000 per year.

**Duration** 1 year; may be renewed.

**Additional information** This program includes the following named scholarships: the 1909 Scholarships (established in 2009 to celebrate the sorority's centennial), the Anne Klauber Berson Memorial Scholarship, the Edith Hirsch Miller Memorial Scholarship (preference to Jewish applicants who are members of Nu Chapter at the University of Pittsburgh or residents of Pittsburgh), the Irma Loeb Cohen Scholarship (preference to members of Rho Chapter at Ohio State University), the Constance Bauman Abraham Scholarship (preference to members of Eta Chapter at SUNY Albany or at universities in other northeastern states), and the Shonnette Meyer Kahn Scholarship (preference to members of Rho Chapter at Ohio State University or Epsilon Chapter at Tulane University). Recipients must be willing to remain active in the sorority and live in the sorority house (if any) for the entire year the scholarship covers.

**Number awarded** Several each year.

**Deadline** March of each year.

## [12]
## AGI/AAPG SEMESTER INTERNSHIPS IN GEOSCIENCE PUBLIC POLICY

American Geological Institute
Attn: Government Affairs Program
4220 King Street
Alexandria, VA 22302-1502
(703) 379-2480                    Fax: (703) 379-7563
E-mail: govt@agiweb.org
Web: www.agiweb.org/gap/interns/index.html

**Summary** To provide work experience to women, minority, and other geoscience students who have a strong interest in federal science policy.

**Eligibility** This program is open to geoscience undergraduate and master's degree students who are interested in working with Congress and federal agencies to promote sound public policy in areas that affect geoscientists, including water, energy, and mineral resources; geologic hazards; environmental protection, and federal funding for geoscience research and education. Applicants must submit official copies of college transcripts, a resume with the names and contact information for 2 references, and a statement of their science and policy interests and what they feel they can contribute to the program. Women and minorities are especially encouraged to apply.

**Financial data** The stipend is $5,000.

**Duration** 14 weeks, during the fall or spring semester.

**Additional information** This program is jointly funded by the American Geological Institute (AGI) and the American Association of Petroleum Geologists (AAPG). Activities for the interns include monitoring and analyzing geoscience-related legislation in Congress, updating legislative and policy information on AGI's web site, attending House and Senate hearings and preparing summaries, responding to information requests from AGI's member societies, and attending meetings with policy-level staff members in Congress, federal

agencies, and non-governmental organizations. The sponsor also offers a similar internship program for 12 weeks during the summer (with a $5,000 stipend).

**Number awarded** 1 each semester.

**Deadline** April of each year for fall internships; October of each year for spring internships.

## [13]
## AHIMA FOUNDATION DIVERSITY SCHOLARSHIPS

American Health Information Management Association
Attn: AHIMA Foundation
233 North Michigan Avenue, 21st Floor
Chicago, IL 60601-5809
(312) 233-1175                    Fax: (312) 233-1475
E-mail: info@ahimafoundation.org
Web: www.ahimafoundation.org

**Summary** To provide financial assistance to women and other members of the American Health Information Management Association (AHIMA) who are interested in working on an undergraduate or graduate degree in health information management (HIM) or health information technology (HIT) and will contribute to diversity in the profession.

**Eligibility** This program is open to AHIMA members who are enrolled at least half time in a program accredited by the Commission on Accreditation for Health Informatics and Information Management Education (CAHIM). Applicants must be working on a degree in HIM or HIT at the associate, bachelor's, post-baccalaureate, master's, or doctoral level. They must have a GPA of 3.5 or higher and at least 1 full semester remaining after the date of the award. To qualify for this support, applicants must demonstrate how they will contribute to diversity in the health information management profession; diversity is defined as differences in race, ethnicity, nationality, gender, sexual orientation, socioeconomic status, age, physical capabilities, and religious beliefs. Selection is based on GPA and academic achievement, volunteer and work experience, commitment to the HIM profession, quality and relevance of references, and completeness and clarity of thought.

**Financial data** Stipends are $1,000 for associate degree students, $1,500 for bachelor's degree or post-baccalaureate certificate students, $2,000 for master's degree students, or $2,500 for doctoral degree students.

**Duration** 1 year.

**Number awarded** Varies each year; recently, 9 of these scholarships were awarded: 6 to undergraduates and 3 to graduate students.

**Deadline** September of each year.

## [14]
## AKA ENDOWMENT AWARDS

Alpha Kappa Alpha Sorority, Inc.
Attn: Educational Advancement Foundation
5656 South Stony Island Avenue
Chicago, IL 60637
(773) 947-0026                    Toll Free: (800) 653-6528
Fax: (773) 947-0277               E-mail: akaeaf@akaeaf.net
Web: www.akaeaf.org/fellowships_endowments.htm

**Summary** To provide financial assistance to undergraduate and graduate students (especially African American women) who meet designated requirements.

**Eligibility** This program is open to undergraduate and graduate students who are enrolled full time as sophomores or higher in an accredited degree-granting institution and are planning to continue their program of education. Applicants may apply for scholarships that include specific requirements established by the donor of the endowment that supports it. Along with their application, they must submit 1) a list of honors, awards, and scholarships received; 2) a list of organizations in which they have memberships, especially minority organizations; and 3) a statement of their personal and career goals, including how this scholarship will enhance their ability to attain those goals. The sponsor is a traditionally African American women's sorority.

**Financial data** Award amounts are determined by the availability of funds from the particular endowment. Recently, stipends averaged more than $1,700 per year.

**Duration** 1 year or longer.

**Additional information** Each endowment establishes its own requirements. Examples of requirements include residence of the applicant, major field of study, minimum GPA, attendance at an Historically Black College or University (HBCU) or member institution of the United Negro College Fund (UNCF), or other personal feature. For further information on all endowments, contact the sponsor.

**Number awarded** Varies each year; recently, 32 of these scholarships, with a total value of nearly $76,00, were awarded.

**Deadline** April of each year.

## [15]
## AKA UNDERGRADUATE SCHOLARSHIPS

Alpha Kappa Alpha Sorority, Inc.
Attn: Educational Advancement Foundation
5656 South Stony Island Avenue
Chicago, IL 60637
(773) 947-0026          Toll Free: (800) 653-6528
Fax: (773) 947-0277          E-mail: akaeaf@akaeaf.net
Web: www.akaeaf.org/undergraduate_scholarships.htm

**Summary** To provide financial assistance to students (especially African American women) who are working on an undergraduate degree in any field.

**Eligibility** This program is open to undergraduate students who are enrolled full time as sophomores or higher in an accredited degree-granting institution and are planning to continue their program of education. Applicants may apply either for a scholarship based on merit (requires a GPA of 3.0 or higher) or on financial need (requires a GPA of 2.5 or higher). Along with their application, they must submit 1) a list of honors, awards, and scholarships received; 2) a list of organizations in which they have memberships, especially minority organizations; and 3) a statement of their personal and career goals, including how this scholarship will enhance their ability to attain those goals. The sponsor is a traditionally African American women's sorority.

**Financial data** Stipends range up to $2,500.

**Duration** 1 year; nonrenewable.

**Number awarded** Varies each year; recently, 133 of these scholarships, with a total value of $69,950 were awarded.

**Deadline** April of each year.

## [16]
## AKASH KURUVILLA MEMORIAL SCHOLARSHIPS

Akash Kuruvilla Memorial Scholarship Fund
P.O. Box 140900
Gainesville, FL 32614-0900
E-mail: info@akmsf.com
Web: www.akmscholarship.com

**Summary** To provide financial assistance to entering or continuing undergraduates who demonstrate qualities of leadership, diversity, integrity, and academia.

**Eligibility** This program is open to graduating high school seniors who have a GPA of 3.5 or higher and continuing full-time undergraduates who have a GPA of 3.0 or higher. Applicants must be able to demonstrate the qualities of the young man after whom this program is named: leadership, diversity, integrity, and academia. Along with their application, they must submit 1) a 750-word essay on what the phrase "The American Dream" means to them; and 2) a 500-word personal statement about themselves. Other factors considered in the selection process include financial need, character, and the applicants' potential to make an impact on their peers and community. Male and female applicants are considered separately.

**Financial data** The stipend is $1,000.

**Duration** 1 year.

**Additional information** This program began in 2007 to honor a young man of Indian ancestry who immigrated from England as a child and who impacted the lives of many people before his untimely death.

**Number awarded** 2 each year: 1 to a male and 1 to a female.

**Deadline** May of each year.

## [17]
## ALABAMA GOLF ASSOCIATION WOMEN'S SCHOLARSHIP FUND

Alabama Golf Association
1025 Montgomery Highway, Suite 210
Birmingham, AL 35216
(205) 979-1234          Toll Free: (800) 783-4446
Fax: (205) 979-1602          E-mail: alyson@bamagolf.com
Web: www.bamagolf.com/womens-scholarship-fund

**Summary** To provide financial assistance to female high school seniors in Alabama who can demonstrate an interest in golf and plan to attend college in the state.

**Eligibility** This program is open to women who are graduating from high schools in Alabama and planning to attend a college or university in the state. Applicants must be able to demonstrate an interest in the game of golf and financial need. They must have an ACT score of 22 or higher. Along with their application, they must submit a 200-word statement on why a college education is important to them, their goals, and how they hope to achieve those goals. Selection is based on academic excellence, citizenship, sportsmanship, community involvement, and financial need.

**Financial data** The stipend is $3,000 per year.

**Duration** 1 year; may be renewed up to 3 additional years if the recipient maintains a GPA of 2.4 or higher during her freshman year and 2.8 or higher during subsequent years.

**Additional information** This program, established in 1993, includes the Stone Hodo Scholarship and the Ann Samford Upchurch Scholarship.

**Number awarded** 1 each year.

**Deadline** March of each year.

## [18]
## ALBERTA E. CROWE STAR OF TOMORROW AWARD

United States Bowling Congress
Attn: Youth Department
621 Six Flags Drive
Arlington, TX 76011
Toll Free: (800) 514-BOWL, ext. 3168
Fax: (817) 385-8262
E-mail: usbcyouth@bowl.com
Web: www.bowl.com

**Summary** To provide financial assistance for college to outstanding women bowlers.

**Eligibility** This program is open to women amateur bowlers who are current members in good standing of the United States Bowling Congress (USBC) Youth organization and competitors in its sanctioned events. Applicants must be high school seniors or college students and have a GPA of 3.0 or higher. They may not have competed in a professional bowling tournament. Along with their application, they must submit a 500-word essay on how the lessons they have learned through academics, community involvement, and bowling have influenced their life and their goals for the future. Selection is based on bowling performances on local, regional, state, and national levels; academic achievement; and extracurricular involvement.

**Financial data** The stipend is $1,500 per year.

**Duration** 1 year; may be renewed for 3 additional years.

**Number awarded** 1 each year.

**Deadline** November of each year.

## [19]
## ALICE T. SCHAFER MATHEMATICS PRIZE

Association for Women in Mathematics
11240 Waples Mill Road, Suite 200
Fairfax, VA 22030
(703) 934-0163            Fax: (703) 359-7562
E-mail: awm@awm-math.org
Web: sites.google.com

**Summary** To recognize and reward undergraduate women who have demonstrated excellence in mathematics.

**Eligibility** Women may not apply for this award; they must be nominated by a member of the mathematical community. The nominee may be at any level in her undergraduate career. She must be a U.S. citizen or attending school in the United States. Selection is based on the quality of the student's performance in advanced mathematics courses and special programs, demonstration of real interest in mathematics, ability for independent work in mathematics, and performance in mathematical competitions at the local or national level.

**Financial data** The prize is $1,000.

**Duration** The prize is presented annually.

**Additional information** This prize was first presented in 1990.

**Number awarded** 1 each year.

**Deadline** Nominations must be submitted by September of each year.

## [20]
## ALPHA CHI OMEGA EDUCATIONAL ASSISTANCE GRANTS

Alpha Chi Omega Foundation
Attn: Educational Assistance Grants Committee
5939 Castle Creek Parkway North Drive
Indianapolis, IN 46250-4343
(317) 579-5050, ext. 265            Fax: (317) 579-5051
E-mail: alatta@alphachiomega.org
Web: www.alphachiomega.org/index.aspx?id=1031

**Summary** To provide financial assistance to members of Alpha Chi Omega sorority who are interested in continuing education, including study abroad.

**Eligibility** This program is open to members of the sorority at the undergraduate and graduate school levels. Applicants must be seeking funding for continuing education and related expenses. They may be interested in studying abroad if the credits earned will be included with credits needed to earn a degree. Along with their application, they must submit documentation of financial need, an outline of their future career goals, a description of their participation in sorority activities, transcripts, and (if studying abroad) confirmation that credits earned will be included with credits needed to earn a degree.

**Financial data** Grants range from $500 to $2,000.

**Duration** 1 year.

**Additional information** This program includes the Alpha Zeta Undergraduate Member Assistance Grant in Memory of Kay Roh, the Anne Folrath Gerhart/Carla Henke Mattson Educational Assistance Grant the Carol Edmundson Hutcheson Education Assistance Fund, the Florence Staiger Lonn Educational Grants, the Lisa Hancock Rehrig Educational Assistance Grants, and the Mary Frances-Guilbert Mariani-Bigler Continuing Education Grant.

**Number awarded** Varies each year; recently, 30 of these grants, worth $19,621, were awarded.

**Deadline** April of each year for spring applications; September of each year for fall applications.

## [21]
## ALPHA CHI OMEGA FOUNDATION SCHOLARSHIPS

Alpha Chi Omega Foundation
Attn: Assistant Director-Grants and Stewardship
5939 Castle Creek Parkway North Drive
Indianapolis, IN 46250-4343
(317) 579-5050, ext. 265            Fax: (317) 579-5051
E-mail: alatta@alphachiomega.org
Web: www.alphachiomega.org/index.aspx?id=1030

**Summary** To provide financial assistance for college to undergraduate and graduate members of Alpha Chi Omega.

**Eligibility** This program is open to women attending college full time who are members of Alpha Chi Omega. Applicants must be sophomores, juniors, seniors, or graduate students working on a degree in any field. Selection is based on academic achievement, chapter involvement, campus and community service, and financial need.

**Financial data** A stipend is awarded (amount not specified).

**Duration** 1 year.

**Additional information** This program includes more than 80 separate funds, many of which give preference to members of specified chapters of the sorority or are limited to students majoring in specified fields.

**Number awarded** Varies each year; recently, 111 of these scholarships, worth $103,581, were awarded.

**Deadline** February of each year.

## [22]
## ALPHA GAMMA CHAPTER RECRUITMENT GRANT

Delta Kappa Gamma Society International-Mississippi
  Alpha Gamma Chapter
c/o Donna Matthews
910 South 34th Avenue
Hattiesburg, MS 39402
(601) 268-6987  E-mail: donnamatthews527@gmail.com
Web: www.alphagammachapter.com/scholarship.htm

**Summary** To provide financial assistance to women enrolled at colleges in Mississippi and majoring in education, library science, or a related field.

**Eligibility** This program is open to women currently enrolled as juniors at colleges and universities in Mississippi. Applicants must be majoring in education, library science, or a related field. Along with their application, they must submit a brief autobiography that includes career plans and any unique financial needs. Preference is given to applicants planning to teach in Lamar, Forrest, Covington, or Perry counties in Mississippi.

**Financial data** The stipend is $1,000.

**Duration** 1 year.

**Number awarded** 1 each year.

**Deadline** December of each year.

## [23]
## ALPHA GAMMA DELTA FOUNDATION SCHOLARSHIPS

Alpha Gamma Delta Foundation, Inc.
Attn: Scholarship Committee
8710 North Meridian Street
Indianapolis, IN 46260
(317) 663-4242                    Fax: (317) 663-4244
E-mail: jmores@alphagammadeltafoundation.org
Web: alphagammadelta.org

**Summary** To provide financial assistance to members of Alpha Gamma Delta who are interested in continuing undergraduate or graduate study.

**Eligibility** This program is open to 1) collegiate members of Alpha Gamma Delta who are entering their junior or senior year of full-time undergraduate study; and 2) alumnae members entering or enrolled in a full-time graduate program. Applicants must submit a 1-page narrative on their reasons for requesting a scholarship, why they have chosen their field of study, and their special qualifications for it. Financial need is considered in the selection process.

**Financial data** A stipend is awarded (amount not specified).

**Duration** 1 year.

**Number awarded** Varies each year.

**Deadline** February of each year.

## [24]
## ALPHA OMICRON PI DIAMOND JUBILEE FOUNDATION SCHOLARSHIPS

Alpha Omicron Pi Foundation
Attn: Scholarship Committee
5390 Virginia Way
Brentwood, TN 37027
(615) 370-0920                    Fax: (615) 370-4424
E-mail: foundation@alphaomicronpi.org
Web: www.alphaomicronpi.org

**Summary** To provide financial assistance for college or graduate school to collegiate and alumnae members of Alpha Omicron Pi.

**Eligibility** This program is open to members of Alpha Omicron Pi who are 1) full-time undergraduates entering their sophomore, junior, or senior year; 2) seniors applying to graduate school or alumnae of 2 years or less already enrolled in graduate school; or 3) returning alumnae reentering college after an absence of 3 or more years. Applicants must submit brief essays about themselves. Selection is based on those essays, academic achievement, Alpha Omicron Pi leadership and honors, campus and community involvement, letters of recommendation, and financial need.

**Financial data** Stipend amounts vary; recently, the average value of each scholarship provided by this foundation was approximately $1,200.

**Duration** 1 year.

**Additional information** This program began in 1962. It includes the Muriel T. McKinney Scholarship, awarded to the top-ranked undergraduate applicant.

**Number awarded** Varies each year; recently, 20 of these scholarships were awarded (11 to undergraduates, 7 to graduate students, and 2 to a returning alumna).

**Deadline** February of each year.

## [25]
## ALPHA SIGMA TAU SCHOLARSHIPS

Alpha Sigma Tau National Foundation
Attn: Scholarships
3334 Founders Road
Indianapolis, IN 46268
(317) 613-7575                    Fax: (317) 613-7111
E-mail: melinda@alphasigmataufoundation.org
Web: www.alphasigmataufoundation.org/scholarships

**Summary** To provide financial assistance to members of Alpha Sigma Tau sorority interested in continuing undergraduate or graduate study.

**Eligibility** This program is open to members of Alpha Sigma Tau who are sophomores, juniors, seniors, or graduate students. Applicants must have a GPA of 3.0 or higher. Along with their application, they must submit a 1-page essay on how their involvement in the sorority has impacted them personally and professionally. Selection is based on academic achievement, service to Alpha Sigma Tau, academic honors, university or community service, and financial need.

**Financial data**    Stipends range from $200 to $2,550.

**Duration**    1 year.

**Number awarded**    Varies each year; recently, 26 of these scholarships were awarded.

**Deadline**    January of each year.

## [26]
## ALPHA STATE ASPIRING EDUCATOR AWARDS

Delta Kappa Gamma Society International-Alpha State Organization
Attn: State Headquarters
6220 Campbell Road, Suite 204
P.O. Box 797787
Dallas, TX 75379-7787
(972) 930-9945       Toll Free: (800) 305-3525
Fax: (972) 447-0471    E-mail: alphasttx@sbcglobal.net
Web: www.alphastatetexas.org/scholarships.html

**Summary**    To provide financial assistance to female residents of Texas who are working on an undergraduate degree or certificate in education at a school in any state.

**Eligibility**    This program is open to female residents of Texas who are attending a college or university in any state and working on an undergraduate degree in education or taking courses for certification. Applicants need not be members of Delta Kappa Gamma (an honorary society for women educators), but they must be recommended by a member of its Alpha State Organization. Along with their application, they must submit a statement of their specific goals, how they plan to achieve their goals, why they want to pursue those goals, and where they aspire to teach after completing certification. Financial need is not considered in the selection process.

**Financial data**    Stipends are $1,000 for students enrolled in at least 6 hours or $500 for students enrolled in at least 3 hours.

**Duration**    1 year.

**Number awarded**    1 or more each year.

**Deadline**    February of each year.

## [27]
## AMELIA EARHART MEMORIAL ACADEMIC SCHOLARSHIPS

Ninety-Nines, Inc.
4300 Amelia Earhart Road, Suite A
Oklahoma City, OK 73159
(405) 685-7969       Toll Free: (800) 994-1929
Fax: (405) 685-7985    E-mail: AEChair@ninety-nines.org
Web: www.ninety-nines.org/index.cfm/scholarships.htm

**Summary**    To provide funding to members of the Ninety-Nines (an organization of women pilots) who are enrolled in academic study related to aviation or aerospace.

**Eligibility**    This program is open to women from any country who have been members of the organization for at least 1 year. Applicants must be currently enrolled at an accredited college or university and working on an associate, bachelor's, master's, or doctoral degree in such fields as aerospace engineering, aviation technology, aviation business management, air traffic management, or professional pilot. They must have a GPA of 3.0 or higher and be able to demonstrate financial need.

**Financial data**    The stipend is $5,000 per year.

**Duration**    1 year; may be renewed.

**Additional information**    This program began in 1941.

**Number awarded**    Varies each year; recently, 7 of these scholarships were awarded: 5 to undergraduates and 2 to graduate students.

**Deadline**    Applications must be submitted to the chapter scholarship chair by November of each year; those chairs must forward the applications from their chapter to the designated trustee by January of each year. At-large numbers (those who do not belong to a specific chapter) must submit their application to their section by December of each year.

## [28]
## AMELIA KEMP MEMORIAL SCHOLARSHIP

Women of the Evangelical Lutheran Church in America
Attn: Scholarships
8765 West Higgins Road
Chicago, IL 60631-4101
(773) 380-2741       Toll Free: (800) 638-3522, ext. 2741
Fax: (773) 380-2419    E-mail: valora.starr@elca.org
Web: www.womenoftheelca.org

**Summary**    To provide financial assistance to lay women of color who are members of Evangelical Lutheran Church of America (ELCA) congregations and who wish to study on the undergraduate, graduate, professional, or vocational school level.

**Eligibility**    This program is open to ELCA lay women of color who are at least 21 years of age and have experienced an interruption of at least 2 years in their education since high school. Applicants must have been admitted to an educational institution to prepare for a career in other than ordained ministry. U.S. citizenship is required.

**Financial data**    The maximum stipend is $1,000.

**Duration**    Up to 2 years.

**Number awarded**    1 or more each year.

**Deadline**    February of each year.

## [29]
## AMERICAN AIRLINES AND AMERICAN EAGLE ENGINEERING SCHOLARSHIP

Women in Aviation, International
Attn: Scholarships
Morningstar Airport
3647 State Route 503 South
West Alexandria, OH 45381-9354
(937) 839-4647       Fax: (937) 839-4645
E-mail: scholarships@wai.org
Web: www.wai.org/education/scholarships.cfm

**Summary**    To provide financial assistance to members of Women in Aviation, International (WAI) who are studying aeronautical, electrical, or mechanical engineering in college.

**Eligibility**    This program is open to WAI members who are currently enrolled in an accredited U.S. engineering program and have "a passion to work in the airline/aviation industry." Applicants must be working on a degree in aeronautical, electrical, or mechanical engineering. They must be U.S. citizens or permanent residents and have a GPA of 3.0 or higher. Along with their application, they must submit an essay of 500 to 1,000 words on who or what inspired them to prepare for a career in engineering, their greatest life challenge, their greatest strength and strongest characteristic, their most memorable academic experience, and why they are the most qualified candidate for this scholarship. Selection is based on achievements, attitude toward self and others, commitment to success, dedication to career, financial need, motivation, reliability, responsibility, and teamwork.

**Financial data** The stipend is $5,000.

**Duration** 1 year.

**Additional information** WAI is a nonprofit professional organization dedicated to encouraging women to consider an aviation career and to providing educational outreach activities and networking resources to women active in the industry. This program is sponsored by American Airlines and its regional subsidiary, American Eagle.

**Number awarded** 1 each year.

**Deadline** November of each year.

## [30]
## AMERICAN AIRLINES VETERAN'S INITIATIVE SCHOLARSHIP

Women in Aviation, International
Attn: Scholarships
Morningstar Airport
3647 State Route 503 South
West Alexandria, OH 45381-9354
(937) 839-4647                    Fax: (937) 839-4645
E-mail: scholarships@wai.org
Web: www.wai.org/education/scholarships.cfm

**Summary** To provide financial assistance to veterans who are members of Women in Aviation, International (WAI) and interested in attending college, flight school, or other institution.

**Eligibility** This program is open to veterans of the U.S. military who are WAI members and interested in studying aviation or aeronautics at an accredited college, flight school, or other institution of higher education. Along with their application, they must submit 2 letters of recommendation, a 500-word essay on their aviation history and goals, a resume, copies of all aviation licenses and medical certificates, and the last 3 pages of their pilot logbook (if applicable). Selection is based on achievements, attitude toward self and others, commitment to success, dedication to career, financial need, motivation, reliability, responsibility, and teamwork.

**Financial data** The stipend is $5,000. Funds are paid directly to the college, flight school, or other institution.

**Duration** 1 year.

**Additional information** WAI is a nonprofit professional organization dedicated to encouraging women to consider an aviation career and to providing educational outreach activities and networking resources to women active in the industry. This program was established in 2011 by American Airlines.

**Number awarded** 1 each year.

**Deadline** November of each year.

## [31]
## AMERICAN BAPTIST WOMEN'S MINISTRIES OF COLORADO STUDENT GRANTS

American Baptist Churches of the Rocky Mountains
Attn: American Baptist Women's Ministries
9085 East Mineral Circle, Suite 170
Centennial, CO 80112
(303) 988-3900                    E-mail: web@abcrm.org
Web: www.abcrm.org

**Summary** To provide financial assistance to women who are members of churches affiliated with the American Baptist Churches (ABC) USA in Colorado, New Mexico, and Utah and interested in attending an ABC college or seminary in any state.

**Eligibility** This program is open to women older than 26 years of age who are active members of churches cooperating with ABC in Colorado, New Mexico, or Utah. Applicants must be enrolled or planning to enroll at an ABC college, university, or seminary in any state. Along with their application, they must submit a personal letter describing their Christian experience; their participation in the life of their church, school, and community; and their goals for the future. Selection is based on academic performance, Christian participation in church and school, and financial need.

**Financial data** A stipend is awarded (amount not specified). Funds are sent directly to the recipient's school.

**Duration** 1 year; recipients may reapply.

**Number awarded** 1 or more each year.

**Deadline** March of each year.

## [32]
## AMERICAN BAPTIST WOMEN'S MINISTRIES OF NEW YORK STATE SCHOLARSHIPS

American Baptist Women's Ministries of New York State
c/o Rebecca Walters, Scholarship Committee
7 Sealy Drive
Potsdam, NY 13676
(315) 265-5309                    E-mail: ontiptoe20@gmail.com
Web: www.abwm-nys.org/scholarship

**Summary** To provide financial assistance to women who are members of American Baptist Churches in New York and interested in attending college in any state.

**Eligibility** This program is open to women who are residents of New York and active members of an American Baptist Church. Applicants must be enrolled or planning to enroll full time at a college or university in any state. While in college, they must maintain Christian fellowship, preferably with the American Baptist Church (although any Protestant church or campus ministry is acceptable). Along with their application, they must submit a 1-page essay on an event that occurred in their life during the past year and how it has impacted their faith. Women may be of any age; graduate students are considered on an individual basis. Financial need is considered in the selection process.

**Financial data** A stipend is awarded (amount not specified).

**Duration** 1 year.

**Number awarded** Varies each year.

**Deadline** February of each year.

## [33]
## AMERICAN LEGION AUXILIARY EMERGENCY FUND

American Legion Auxiliary
Attn: AEF Program Case Manager
8945 North Meridian Street
Indianapolis, IN 46260
(317) 569-4544                    Fax: (317) 569-4502
E-mail: aef@alaforveterans.org
Web: www.alaforveterans.org

**Summary**   To provide funding to members of the American Legion Auxiliary who need educational training or are facing temporary emergency needs.

**Eligibility**   This program is open to members of the American Legion Auxiliary who have maintained their membership for the immediate past 2 consecutive years and have paid their dues for the current year. Applicants must need emergency assistance for the following purposes: 1) food, shelter, and utilities during a time of financial crisis; 2) food and shelter because of weather-related emergencies and natural disasters; or 3) educational training for eligible members who lack the necessary skills for employment or to upgrade competitive workforce skills. They must have exhausted all other sources of financial assistance, including funds and/or services available through the local Post and/or Unit, appropriate community welfare agencies, or state and federal financial aid for education. Grants are not available to settle already existing or accumulated debts, handle catastrophic illness, resettle disaster victims, or other similar problems.

**Financial data**   The maximum grant is $2,400. Payments may be made directly to the member or to the mortgage company or utility. Educational grants may be paid directly to the educational institution.

**Duration**   Grants are expended over no more than 3 months.

**Additional information**   This program began in 1969. In 1981, it was expanded to include the Displaced Homemaker Fund (although that title is no longer used).

**Number awarded**   Varies each year.

**Deadline**   Applications may be submitted at any time.

## [34]
## AMERICAN METEOROLOGICAL SOCIETY NAMED SCHOLARSHIPS

American Meteorological Society
Attn: Development and Student Program Manager
45 Beacon Street
Boston, MA 02108-3693
(617) 227-2426, ext. 3907        Fax: (617) 742-8718
E-mail: dFernandez@ametsoc.org
Web: www.ametsoc.org

**Summary**   To provide financial assistance to undergraduates (particularly women, minorities, and individuals with disabilities) who are majoring in meteorology or an aspect of atmospheric sciences.

**Eligibility**   This program is open to full-time students entering their final year of undergraduate study and majoring in meteorology or an aspect of the atmospheric or related oceanic and hydrologic sciences. Applicants must intend to make atmospheric or related sciences their career. They must be U.S. citizens or permanent residents enrolled at a U.S. institution and have a cumulative GPA of 3.25 or higher. Along with their application, they must submit 200-word essays on 1) their most important attributes and achievements that qualify them for this scholarship; and 2) their career goals in the atmospheric or related sciences. Financial need is considered in the selection process. The sponsor specifically encourages applications from women, minorities, and students with disabilities who are traditionally underrepresented in the atmospheric and related sciences.

**Financial data**   Stipend amounts vary each year.

**Duration**   1 year.

**Additional information**   All scholarships awarded through this program are named after individuals who have assisted the sponsor in various ways.

**Number awarded**   Varies each year; recently, 20 of these scholarships were awarded.

**Deadline**   February of each year.

## [35]
## AMERICAN NUCLEAR SOCIETY DELAYED EDUCATION SCHOLARSHIP FOR WOMEN

American Nuclear Society
Attn: Scholarship Coordinator
555 North Kensington Avenue
La Grange Park, IL 60526-5535
(708) 352-6611                    Toll Free: (800) 323-3044
Fax: (708) 352-0499              E-mail: outreach@ans.org
Web: www.new.ans.org/honors/scholarships

**Summary**   To provide financial assistance to mature women whose formal studies in nuclear science or nuclear engineering have been delayed or interrupted.

**Eligibility**   Applicants must be mature women who have experienced at least a 1-year delay or interruption of their undergraduate studies and are returning to school to work on an undergraduate or graduate degree in nuclear science or nuclear engineering. They must be members of the American Nuclear Society (ANS), but they may be citizens of any country. Along with their application, they must submit an essay on their academic and professional goals, experiences that have affected those goals, and other relevant information. Selection is based on that essay, academic achievement, letters of recommendation, and financial need.

**Financial data**   The stipend is $5,000. Funds may be used by the student to cover any educational expense, including tuition, books, room, and board.

**Duration**   1 year; nonrenewable.

**Number awarded**   1 each year.

**Deadline**   January of each year.

## [36]
## AMERICA'S NATIONAL TEENAGER SCHOLARSHIP PROGRAM

America's National Teenager Scholarship Organization
1132 Frenchtown Lane
Franklin, TN 37067
(615) 771-7478                    Toll Free: (866) NAT-TEEN
Fax: (888) 370-2075             E-mail: jennytelwar@mac.com
Web: www.nationalteen.com/pageants

**Summary**   To recognize (locally and nationally) the scholastic and leadership achievements of America's teenage girls and to provide cash, tuition scholarships, and awards to the participants.

**Eligibility** Girls who are 13 to 15 years of age are eligible to enter the Miss Junior National Teenager competition and girls who are 16 to 18 may enter the Miss National Teenager competition. Entrants must have no children and never have been married. Selection is based on academic excellence (15%), school and community involvement (15%), social and conversational skills in an interview (30%), poise and personality in an evening gown (15%), personal expression (15%), and response to an on-stage question (10%). There is no swimsuit competition.

**Financial data** This program awards approximately $100,000 in scholarships at state and national levels each year.

**Duration** The contest is held annually.

**Additional information** The contest began in 1971, to recognize the leadership achievements of America's teenagers and to provide travel, entertainment, and scholarships for their college education. The application fee is $25.

**Number awarded** Varies each year.

**Deadline** Deadline dates vary. Check with the sponsors of your local and state pageant.

## [37]
## AMS FRESHMAN UNDERGRADUATE SCHOLARSHIPS

American Meteorological Society
Attn: Development and Student Program Manager
45 Beacon Street
Boston, MA 02108-3693
(617) 227-2426, ext. 3907          Fax: (617) 742-8718
E-mail: dFernandez@ametsoc.org
Web: www.ametsoc.org

**Summary** To provide financial assistance to high school seniors (particularly women, minorities, and individuals with disabilities) who are planning to attend college to prepare for a career in the atmospheric or related oceanic or hydrologic sciences.

**Eligibility** This program is open to high school seniors entering their freshman year of college to work on a bachelor's degree in the atmospheric or related oceanic or hydrologic sciences. Applicants must be U.S. citizens or permanent residents planning to enroll full time. Along with their application, they must submit a 500-word essay on how they believe their college education, and what they learn in the atmospheric and related sciences, will help them to serve society during their professional career. Selection is based on performance in high school, including academic records, recommendations, scores from a national examination, and the essay. Financial need is not considered. The sponsor specifically encourages applications from women, minorities, and students with disabilities who are traditionally underrepresented in the atmospheric and related oceanic sciences.

**Financial data** The stipend is $2,500 per academic year.

**Duration** 1 year; may be renewed for the second year of college study.

**Number awarded** Varies each year; recently, 14 of these scholarships were awarded.

**Deadline** February of each year.

## [38]
## AMVETS NATIONAL LADIES AUXILIARY SCHOLARSHIPS

AMVETS National Ladies Auxiliary
Attn: Scholarship Officer
4647 Forbes Boulevard
Lanham, MD 20706-4380
(301) 459-6255          Fax: (301) 459-5403
E-mail: auxhdqs@amvets.org
Web: amvetsaux.org/scholarship.html

**Summary** To provide financial assistance to members and certain dependents of members of AMVETS National Ladies Auxiliary who are already enrolled in college.

**Eligibility** Applicants must belong to AMVETS Auxiliary or be the child or grandchild of a member. They must be in at least the second year of undergraduate study at an accredited college or university. Applications must include 3 letters of recommendation and an essay (from 200 to 500 words) about their past accomplishments, career and educational goals, and objectives for the future. Selection is based on the letters of reference (15%), academic record (15%), the essay (25%), and financial need (45%).

**Financial data** Scholarships are $1,000 or $750 each.

**Duration** 1 year.

**Number awarded** Up to 7 each year: 2 at $1,000 and 5 at $750.

**Deadline** June of each year.

## [39]
## ANDY STONE SCHOLARSHIPS

US Youth Soccer-Region III
c/o Janice Drimer, Director of Operations
105 Citrus Place
Cary, NC 27519
(919) 414-4300          E-mail: hagfishin@gmail.com
Web: regioniii.usyouthsoccer.org/awards

**Summary** To provide financial assistance for college to high school seniors in selected southern states (females and males are judged separately) who have been active in soccer.

**Eligibility** This program is open to seniors graduating from high schools in states that are part of Region III of US Youth Soccer (Alabama, Arkansas, Florida, Georgia, Louisiana, Mississippi, North Carolina, Oklahoma, South Carolina, Tennessee, and Texas). Applicants must have been an active member of Region III as a player, coach, and/or referee. Selection is based on years and depth of involvement in US Youth Soccer and soccer in general, academic achievement, financial need, citizenship, and extracurricular activities. Boys and girls and considered separately.

**Financial data** The stipend is $1,500. The first $1,000 is issued at the beginning of the school year and the second $500 is issued upon receipt of proof of an overall "C" average for the first grading period.

**Duration** 1 year.

**Additional information** This program began in 1999 and limited to applicants from Mississippi. In subsequent years, it has rotated among the states that comprise Region III in alphabetical order. Applicants must be from South Carolina in 2014, Tennessee in 2015, North Texas in 2016, South Texas in 2017, etc.

**Number awarded**    2 each year: 1 to a boy and 1 to a girl.
**Deadline**    April of each year.

## [40]
## ANITA BORG MEMORIAL SCHOLARSHIPS

Google Inc.
Attn: Scholarships
1600 Amphitheatre Parkway
Mountain View, CA 94043-8303
(650) 253-0000                    Fax: (650) 253-0001
E-mail: anitaborgscholarship@google.com
Web: www.google.com/anitaborg/us

**Summary**    To provide financial assistance to women working on a bachelor's or graduate degree in a computer-related field.

**Eligibility**    This program is open to women who are entering their senior year of undergraduate study or are enrolled in a graduate program in computer science, computer engineering, or a closely-related field. Applicants must be full-time students at a university in the United States and have a GPA of 3.5 or higher. They must submit essays of 400 to 600 words on 1) a significant technical project on which they have worked; 2) their leadership abilities; 3) what they would do if someone gave them the funding and resources for a 3- to 12-month project to investigate a technical topic of their choice; and 4) what they would do if someone gave them $1,000 to plan an event or project to benefit women in technical fields. Citizens, permanent residents, and international students are eligible. Selection is based on academic background and demonstrated leadership.

**Financial data**    The stipend is $10,000 per year.
**Duration**    1 year; recipients may reapply.
**Additional information**    These scholarships were first offered in 2004.
**Number awarded**    Varies each year; recently, 25 of these scholarships were awarded.
**Deadline**    February of each year.

## [41]
## ANNA GEAR JUNIOR SCHOLARSHIP

American Legion Auxiliary
Department of Virginia
Attn: Education Chair
1708 Commonwealth Avenue
Richmond, VA 23230
(804) 355-6410                    Fax: (804) 353-5246
Web: vaauxiliary.org/Education.php

**Summary**    To provide financial assistance to junior members of the American Legion Auxiliary in Virginia who plan to attend college in any state.

**Eligibility**    This program is open to seniors graduating from high schools in Virginia and planning to attend college in any state. Applicants must have been junior members of the American Legion Auxiliary for at least the 3 previous years. They must have completed at least 30 hours of volunteer service within their community and submit a 500-word article on "The Value of Volunteering in the Community."

**Financial data**    The stipend is $1,000.
**Duration**    1 year.
**Number awarded**    1 each year.
**Deadline**    March of each year.

## [42]
## ANNALEY NAEGLE REDD STUDENT AWARD IN WOMEN'S HISTORY

Brigham Young University
Attn: Charles Redd Center for Western Studies
366 Spencer W. Kimball Tower
Provo, UT 84602
(801) 422-4048                    Fax: (801) 422-0035
E-mail: redd_center@byu.edu
Web: reddcenter.byu.edu/Pages/Apply-for-an-Award.aspx

**Summary**    To provide funding to undergraduate and graduate students interested in conducting research on women in the West.

**Eligibility**    This program is open to undergraduate and graduate students who are interested in conducting a research project related to women in the American West (defined as west of the Mississippi). Applicants may be proposing any kind of project, including seminar papers, theses, or dissertations. Along with their application, they must submit brief statements on the central research question and conceptual framework, how the project will increase understanding of the American West, where they plan to conduct research and the resources available there, other research that has been conducted on the topic, what makes this study and approach unique and important, the planned use of the research, and a detailed budget.

**Financial data**    The grant is $1,500. Funds may be used for research support (supplies, travel, etc.) but not for salary or capital equipment.
**Duration**    Normally work is to be undertaken during the summer.
**Number awarded**    1 each year.
**Deadline**    March of each year.

## [43]
## ANNE MAUREEN WHITNEY BARROW MEMORIAL SCHOLARSHIP

Society of Women Engineers
Attn: Scholarship Selection Committee
203 North LaSalle Street, Suite 1675
Chicago, IL 60601-1269
(312) 596-5223                    Toll Free: (877) SWE-INFO
Fax: (312) 644-8557              E-mail: scholarships@swe.org
Web: societyofwomenengineers.swe.org

**Summary**    To provide financial assistance to women interested in studying engineering or computer science in college.

**Eligibility**    This program is open to women who are enrolled or planning to enroll full time at an ABET-accredited 4-year college or university. Applicants must be planning to major in engineering or computer science. Entering freshmen must have a GPA of 3.5 or higher; current undergraduates must have a GPA of 3.0 or higher. Selection is based on merit.

**Financial data**    The stipend is $7,000 per year.
**Duration**    1 year; may be renewed for 4 additional years.
**Additional information**    This program began in 1992.
**Number awarded**    1 every 5 years.
**Deadline**    May of the years in which it is offered.

## [44]
## APPLIED COMPUTER SECURITY ASSOCIATES CYBERSECURITY SCHOLARSHIP

Society of Women Engineers
Attn: Scholarship Selection Committee
203 North LaSalle Street, Suite 1675
Chicago, IL 60601-1269
(312) 596-5223          Toll Free: (877) SWE-INFO
Fax: (312) 644-8557          E-mail: scholarships@swe.org
Web: societyofwomenengineers.swe.org

**Summary**  To provide financial assistance to women working on an undergraduate or graduate degree in a field of engineering related to cybersecurity.

**Eligibility**  This program is open to women who will be juniors, seniors, or graduate students at ABET-accredited colleges and universities. Applicants must be U.S. citizens or permanent residents working full time on a degree in computer science, cybersecurity, computer security, or software engineering. They must have a GPA of 3.0 or higher and a demonstrated interest in security, as evidenced by course work, outside study, and work experience. Selection is based on merit.

**Financial data**  The stipend is $10,000.

**Duration**  1 year.

**Additional information**  This program, which began in 2011, is sponsored by Applied Computer Security Associates.

**Number awarded**  1 each year.

**Deadline**  February of each year.

## [45]
## APPRAISAL INSTITUTE MINORITIES AND WOMEN EDUCATIONAL SCHOLARSHIP PROGRAM

Appraisal Institute
Attn: Appraisal Institute Education Trust
200 West Madison Street, Suite 1500
Chicago, IL 60606
(312) 335-4133          Fax: (312) 335-4134
E-mail: educationtrust@appraisalinstitute.org
Web: www.appraisalinstitute.org

**Summary**  To provide financial assistance to women and minority undergraduate students majoring in real estate or allied fields.

**Eligibility**  This program is open to members of groups underrepresented in the real estate appraisal profession. Those groups include women, American Indians, Alaska Natives, Asians and Pacific Islanders, Blacks or African Americans, and Hispanics. Applicants must be full- or part-time students enrolled in real estate courses within a degree-granting college, university, or junior college. They must have a GPA of 2.5 or higher and be able to demonstrate financial need. U.S. citizenship is required.

**Financial data**  The stipend is $1,000. Funds are paid directly to the recipient's institution to be used for tuition and fees.

**Duration**  1 year.

**Number awarded**  At least 1 each year.

**Deadline**  April of each year.

## [46]
## APS/IBM RESEARCH INTERNSHIP FOR UNDERGRADUATE WOMEN

American Physical Society
Attn: Committee on Status of Women in Physics
One Physics Ellipse
College Park, MD 20740-3844
(301) 209-3232          Fax: (301) 209-0865
E-mail: apsibmin@us.ibm.com
Web: www.aps.org

**Summary**  To provide an opportunity for undergraduate women to participate in a summer research internship in science or engineering at facilities of IBM.

**Eligibility**  This program is open to women currently enrolled as sophomores or juniors and majoring in biology, chemistry, chemical engineering, computer science or engineering, electrical engineering, materials science or engineering, mechanical engineering, or physics. Applicants are not required to be U.S. citizens, but they must be enrolled at a college or university in the United States or Puerto Rico. They must be interested in working as a research intern at a participating IBM laboratory. A GPA of at least 3.0 is required. Selection is based on commitment to and interest in their major field of study.

**Financial data**  Interns receive a competitive salary of approximately $8,000 for the summer.

**Duration**  10 weeks during the summer.

**Additional information**  Participating IBM laboratories are the Almaden Research Center in San Jose, California, the Watson Research Center in Yorktown Heights, New York, or the Austin Research Laboratory in Austin, Texas.

**Number awarded**  3 each year: 1 at each laboratory.

**Deadline**  January of each year.

## [47]
## AREMA PRESIDENTIAL SPOUSE SCHOLARSHIP

American Railway Engineering and Maintenance-of-Way Association
Attn: AREMA Educational Foundation Scholarship Committee
10003 Derekwood Lane, Suite 210
Lanham, MD 20706
(301) 459-3200, ext. 706          Fax: (301) 459-8077
E-mail: sspaulding@arema.org
Web: www.arema.org/arema_foundation.aspx

**Summary**  To provide financial assistance to female undergraduate students who are interested in majoring in engineering or engineering technology and preparing for a career in railway engineering.

**Eligibility**  This program is open to women who have completed at least 1 quarter or semester at an ABET-accredited 4- or 5-year program (or a comparably accredited program in Canada or Mexico). Applicants must be working on a bachelor's degree in engineering or engineering technology and have a GPA of 2.0 or higher. They must be interested in a career in railway engineering. Along with their application, they must submit a 350-word cover letter explaining why they believe they are deserving of this scholarship and identifying the areas of railroading in which they are particularly interested. Financial need is not considered in the selection process.

**Financial data** The stipend is $1,000.

**Duration** 1 year.

**Number awarded** 1 each year.

**Deadline** March of each year.

## [48]
## ARFORA UNDERGRADUATE SCHOLARSHIP FOR WOMEN

Association of Romanian Orthodox Ladies Auxiliaries of
North America
Attn: Scholarship Committee
222 Orchard Park Drive
New Castle, PA 16105
(724) 652-4313          E-mail: adelap@verizon.net
Web: www.arfora.org/scholarships.htm

**Summary** To provide financial assistance to women who are members of a parish of the Romanian Orthodox Episcopate of America and currently enrolled in college.

**Eligibility** This program is open to women who have been voting communicant members of a parish of the Romanian Orthodox Episcopate of America for at least 1 year or are daughters of a communicant member. Applicants must have completed at least 1 year of undergraduate study at a college or university. Along with their application, they must submit a 300-word statement describing their personal goals; high school, university, church, and community involvement; honors and awards; and why they should be considered for this award. Selection is based on academic achievement, character, worthiness, and participation in religious life.

**Financial data** The stipend is $1,000.

**Duration** 1 year; nonrenewable.

**Additional information** This program began in 1994. The Association of Romanian Orthodox Ladies Auxiliaries (ARFORA) was established in 1938 as a women's organization within the Romanian Orthodox Episcopate of America.

**Number awarded** 1 or more each year.

**Deadline** May of each year.

## [49]
## ARIZONA BPW FOUNDATION SCHOLARSHIPS

Arizona Business and Professional Women's Foundation
Attn: Administrator
P.O. Box 32596
Phoenix, AZ 85064
Web: www.arizonabpwfoundation.com/scholarships.html

**Summary** To provide financial assistance to women in Arizona who are attending or interested in attending a community college in the state.

**Eligibility** This program is open to women, at least 25 years of age, who are attending a community college or trade school in Arizona. Applicants must fall into 1 of the following categories: women who have been out of the workforce and wish to upgrade their skills; women with no previous experience in the workforce who are seeking a marketable skill; and women who are currently employed who are interested in career advancement or change. Along with their application, they must submit 2 letters of recommendation, a statement of financial need (latest income tax return must be provided), a career goal statement, and their most recent transcript (when available). Selection is based on financial need, field of study, and possibility of success.

**Financial data** The stipend is $1,000 per year.

**Duration** 1 year; renewable for up to 3 consecutive semesters if the recipient maintains a GPA of 2.0 or higher.

**Additional information** In addition to the general scholarship, there are 3 named endowments: Dr. Dorine Chancellor (established in 1990 and open to students at any community college in Arizona, although 1 is set aside specifically for a student at Eastern Arizona College), Lynda Crowell (established in 1999 and open to students at community colleges in Maricopa County), and Muriel Lothrop-Ely (established in 2006 and open to students at any community college in Arizona).

**Number awarded** Varies each year; recently, 10 of these scholarships were awarded.

**Deadline** February of each year.

## [50]
## ARKANSAS SINGLE PARENT SCHOLARSHIPS

Arkansas Single Parent Scholarship Fund
Attn: Executive Director
614 East Emma Avenue, Suite 119
Springdale, AR 72764
(479) 927-1402          Fax: (479) 927-0755
E-mail: rhill@aspsf.org
Web: www.aspsf.org/students_spscholarships.html

**Summary** To provide financial assistance to single parents in Arkansas who plan to attend college in any state.

**Eligibility** This program is open to single parents in Arkansas who have custodial care of 1 or more children younger than 18 years of age. Applicants must reside in 1 of the 70 counties in which a Single Parent Scholarship Fund has been established; for a list of these counties, contact the sponsor. They must be planning to attend a college or university in any state. Financial need is considered in the selection process in most counties, and students are expected to qualify for a federal Pell Grant.

**Financial data** Each participating county organization establishes its own stipend. Most are in the range of $500 per semester ($1,000 for the academic year).

**Duration** 1 semester or year.

**Additional information** This program was established in 1990.

**Number awarded** Varies each year.

**Deadline** Each participating county organization establishes its own deadline.

## [51]
## ARKANSAS STATE FARM SCHOLAR-ATHLETE PROGRAM

Arkansas Activities Association
Attn: Wadie Moore
3920 Richards Road
North Little Rock, AR 72117
(501) 955-2500          Fax: (501) 955-2600
Web: www.ahsaa.org/activities/32/scholarship

**Summary** To provide financial assistance to high school seniors in Arkansas who have participated in athletics (females and males are judged separately) and are interested in attending college in any state.

**Eligibility** This program is open to seniors graduating from high schools in Arkansas who have a GPA of 3.5 or higher and scores of at least 21 on the ACT or 900 on the mathematics and critical reading SAT. Boys must have participated in the following sports: football, basketball, baseball, track and field, or other sports; girls must have participated in volleyball, basketball, softball, track and field, or other sports. Applicants must be interested in attending college in any state. Along with their application, they must submit an essay on the reasons they believe they qualify for this scholarship and why they want to receive it. Selection is based on the essay, academic achievement, citizenship in school and in the community, leadership traits, and participation in other school activities.

**Financial data** The stipend is $1,000.

**Duration** 1 year; nonrenewable.

**Additional information** This program is sponsored by State Farm Insurance Companies and its Arkansas agents.

**Number awarded** 10 each year: 1 boy in each of the 5 qualifying sports and 1 girl in each of the 5 qualifying sports.

**Deadline** March of each year.

## [52]
## ARLENE JOHNS ENDOWMENT SCHOLARSHIP

Girl Scouts of Oregon and Southwest Washington
Attn: Shannon Shea, Portland Service Center Office
9620 S.W. Barbur Boulevard
Portland, OR 97219
(503) 977-6813                    Fax: (503) 977-6801
E-mail: sshea@girlscoutsosw.org
Web: www.girlscoutsosw.org/girls/scholarships

**Summary** To provide financial assistance to high school seniors in Oregon and southwestern Washington who are Ambassador Girl Scouts and planning to attend college in any state.

**Eligibility** This program is open to seniors graduating from high schools in Oregon and southwestern Washington who are Ambassador Girl Scouts and have earned their Gold Award. Applicants must be planning to enroll at an accredited university, college, technical school, vocational school, or trade school in any state. Along with their application, they must submit 1) a 1,000-word essay on how Girl Scouts has impacted their life and how that will impact them in the future; 2) a 500-word description of their Gold Award project; and 3) a 500-word essay on how they have made the world a better place by being a Girl Scout.

**Financial data** A stipend is awarded (amount not specified).

**Duration** 1 year.

**Number awarded** 1 each year.

**Deadline** May of each year.

## [53]
## ARMENIAN INTERNATIONAL WOMEN'S ASSOCIATION SCHOLARSHIPS

Armenian International Women's Association
65 Main Street, Room 3A
Watertown, MA 02472
(617) 926-0171                    E-mail: aiwainc@aol.com
Web: aiwainternational.org/initiatives/scholarships

**Summary** To provide financial assistance to Armenian women who are upper-division and graduate students.

**Eligibility** This program is open to full-time women students of Armenian descent attending an accredited college or university. Applicants must be full-time juniors, seniors, or graduate students with a GPA of 3.2 or higher. They must submit an essay, up to 500 words, describing their planned academic program, their career goals, and the reasons why they believe they should be awarded this scholarship. Selection is based on financial need and merit.

**Financial data** Stipends are $1,000 or $500.

**Duration** 1 year.

**Additional information** This program includes the following named scholarships: the Ethel Jafarian Duffett Scholarships, the Zarouhi Y. Getsoyan Scholarship, the Rose "Azad" Hovannesian Scholarship, the Agnes Missirian Scholarship, and the Dr. Carolann S. Najarian Scholarships.

**Number awarded** Varies each year; recently, 15 of these scholarships were awarded: 12 at $1,000 and 3 at $500.

**Deadline** April of each year.

## [54]
## ART STUDIO INTERNSHIPS

Women's Studio Workshop
722 Binnewater Lane
P.O. Box 489
Rosendale, NY 12472
(845) 658-9133                    Fax: (845) 658-9031
E-mail: info@wsworkshop.org
Web: www.wsworkshop.org/program/internships

**Summary** To provide internship opportunities in the arts at the Women's Studio Workshop (WSW) in Rosendale, New York.

**Eligibility** This program is open to young women artists interested in working with the staff at the studio on projects including papermaking, book arts, and arts administration. Applicants should send a resume, 10 to 20 images of recent works, 3 letters of reference, and a letter of interest. They should have studio experience, be hard-working, and have a desire and ability to live in a close-knit community of women artists. Along with their application, they must submit a letter of interest explaining why an internship at WSW is important to them and why type of experiences they would bring to the position, 3 letters of reference, a resume, and a CD with 10 images of recent work.

**Financial data** Interns receive on-site housing and a stipend of $250 per month.

**Duration** Approximately 6 months, either as winter-spring interns (beginning in January) or as summer-fall interns (beginning in June). Interns may reapply for a second 6-month assignment.

**Additional information** Tasks include (but are not limited to) maintaining the studios; assisting in the production of artists' books; administrative duties (including data entry and web maintenance); designing, printing, and distributing brochures and posters; assisting in all aspects of the exhibition program; preparing the apartments for visiting artists; setting up evening programs; managing the set up and break down of lunch each day; and working as studio assistants in all classes.

**Number awarded**  2 to 3 each term (winter-spring or summer-fall).

**Deadline**  October of each year for winter-spring internships; February of each year for summer-fall internships.

## [55]
## ARTHUR H. GOODMAN MEMORIAL SCHOLARSHIPS

CDC Small Business Finance
Attn: Scholarship Program
2448 Historic Decatur Road, Suite 200
San Diego, CA 92106
(619) 291-3594  Toll Free: (800) 611-5170
Fax: (619) 291-6954
Web: cdcloans.com/scholar.htm

**Summary**  To provide financial assistance to women and minority college students from California or Arizona who are transitioning from a 2-year to a 4-year college and are interested in preparing for a career related to community development.

**Eligibility**  This program is open to women and minorities who are residents of or attending school in California or Arizona. Applicants must have completed 2 years of community college study with a GPA of 3.0 or higher and be ready to transfer to a 4-year college or university in those states. They must be interested in preparing for a career in business, government, nonprofit, public service, or other profession that will improve3their community. Along with their application, they must submit a 3-page personal statement on their community involvement and volunteerism, why they volunteer, how it has influenced them personally and their career goals, how their volunteerism has impacted individuals or the community, an individual or event that has influenced their decision to attend college and/or select their desired career, their future goals and how they include community involvement, and why they feel they are a strong candidate for this scholarship. Financial need is considered in the selection process.

**Financial data**  Stipends range from $1,500 to $3,000.

**Duration**  1 year.

**Additional information**  This program began in 1998 with a fund administered through the San Diego Foundation.

**Number awarded**  Approximately 4 each year.

**Deadline**  May of each year.

## [56]
## ARTTABLE MENTORED INTERNSHIPS FOR DIVERSITY IN THE VISUAL ARTS PROFESSIONS

ArtTable Inc.
137 Varick Street, Suite 402
New York, NY 10013
(212) 343-1735, ext. 24  Fax: (866) 363-4188
E-mail: ebround@arttable.org
Web: www.arttable.org

**Summary**  To provide an opportunity for women who are from diverse backgrounds to gain mentored work experience during the summer and to prepare for a career as an art professional.

**Eligibility**  This program is open to women who are college seniors, recent graduates, or graduate students and interested in preparing for a career as a visual arts professional (including administrative director, art adviser, art appraiser, art critic, art dealer, art librarian, arts funder, arts lawyer, conservator, curator, editor, educator, fundraiser, management consultant, public relations consultant, writer). Applicants must be from a cultural or ethnic background that is underrepresented in the field. They must be interested in working during the summer with a mentor at an art museum or similar facility. U.S. citizenship or permanent resident status is required.

**Financial data**  The stipend is $3,000. The hosting institution or mentor receives $500 for administrative and other costs.

**Duration**  8 weeks during the summer.

**Additional information**  This program began in 2000.

**Number awarded**  Varies each year; recently, 4 of these internships were awarded.

**Deadline**  February of each year.

## [57]
## ASHADO SCHOLARSHIP

The Race for Education
Attn: Student Services Manager
1818 Versailles Road
P.O. Box 11355
Lexington, KY 40575
(859) 252-8648  Fax: (859) 252-8030
E-mail: info@raceforeducation.org
Web: raceforeducation.org/scholarships

**Summary**  To provide financial assistance to female undergraduate students working on an equine-related degree.

**Eligibility**  This program is open to female undergraduate students under 24 years of age working on an equine-related degree, including (but not limited to) pre-veterinary medicine (equine practice only), equine science, equine business management, racetrack management, or other equine- or agriculture-related program. Applicants must have a GPA of 2.85 or higher and a household income of less than $50,000 per year. Along with their application, they must submit a 500-word essay on 1 of the following topics: 1) the last book they read for enjoyment only, why they chose it, and what they learned from it; 2) a facet of thoroughbred racing that interests them and why; or 3) their interests outside the equine industry or chosen career field.

**Financial data**  The stipend covers payment of tuition, to a maximum of $6,000 per year. The student is responsible for all other fees.

**Duration**  1 year; may be renewed up to 3 additional years, provided the recipient maintains a GPA of 3.0 or higher.

**Additional information**  This program began in 2002 with funding from the Racehorse Nomination Program, to which horse owners donate a percentage of their race horses' earnings.

**Number awarded**  1 or more each year.

**Deadline**  February of each year.

## [58]
## ASIAN WOMEN IN BUSINESS SCHOLARSHIP FUND

Asian Women in Business
42 Broadway, Suite 1748
New York, NY 10004
(212) 868-1368                    Fax: (877) 686-6870
E-mail: info@awib.org
Web: www.awib.org

**Summary**   To provide financial assistance to women of Asian ancestry who are currently in college and have demonstrated community or entrepreneurial achievement.

**Eligibility**   This program is open to women who are of at least 50% Asian or Pacific Island ancestry and are U.S. citizens or permanent residents. Applicants must be enrolled full time at an accredited 4-year undergraduate institution in the United States and have a GPA of 3.0 or higher. They must be able to demonstrate either 1) a leadership role in a community endeavor; or 2) a record of entrepreneurial achievement (e.g., founded their own business). Additional funding is available to applicants who can demonstrate financial need.

**Financial data**   The stipend is $2,500. Recipients who demonstrate financial need are eligible for an additional $2,500. Funds are paid directly to the recipient.

**Duration**   1 year.

**Additional information**   This program began in 2006.

**Number awarded**   6 each year.

**Deadline**   September of each year.

## [59]
## ASSE DIVERSITY COMMITTEE SCHOLARSHIP

American Society of Safety Engineers
Attn: ASSE Foundation
Scholarship Award Program
1800 East Oakton Street
Des Plaines, IL 60018
(847) 699-2929                    Fax: (847) 768-3434
E-mail: bzylstra@asse.org
Web: www.asse.org

**Summary**   To provide financial assistance to women and other upper-division and graduate students working on a degree related to occupational safety who come from diverse groups.

**Eligibility**   This program is open to students who are working on an undergraduate or graduate degree in occupational safety, health, environment, industrial hygiene, occupational health nursing, or a closely-related field (e.g., industrial or environmental engineering). Applicants must be full-time students who have completed at least 60 semester hours with a GPA of 3.0 or higher as undergraduates or at least 9 semester hours as graduate students. A goal of this program is to encourage diversity within the field. U.S. citizenship is not required. Membership in the American Society of Safety Engineers (ASSE) is not required, but preference is given to members.

**Financial data**   The stipend is $1,000 per year.

**Duration**   1 year; recipients may reapply.

**Number awarded**   1 each year.

**Deadline**   November of each year.

## [60]
## ASSOCIATION FOR WOMEN IN AVIATION MAINTENANCE SCHOLARSHIP PROGRAM

Association for Women in Aviation Maintenance
Attn: World Headquarters
P.O. Box 1030
Edgewater, FL 32132-1030
(386) 416-0248                    Fax: (386) 236-0517
E-mail: scholarships@awam.org
Web: www.awam.org/Scholarships.aspx

**Summary**   To provide financial assistance to members of the Association for Women in Aviation Maintenance (AWAM) who are interested in preparing for a career as an aviation mechanic.

**Eligibility**   Applicants for all awards included in this program must be AWAM members (membership in the association is open to both men and women). Some awards specify that applicants must be women, and others impose additional requirements. Most provide support for study at a particular aviation maintenance school or training program, although some offer cash awards that recipients can use at the school or program of their choice. All applicants must submit a resume describing their education, work experience, qualifications, and honors; a 200-word essay on their interest in aviation; and at least 2 letters of recommendation.

**Financial data**   Cash awards are $1,000 or $500. Other awards provide full or partial payment of tuition and/or other program expenses.

**Duration**   Awards are offered annually.

**Additional information**   The cash awards offered through this program are named the Aircraft Electronics Association Avionics Technician Scholarship, Aviation Student Entrepreneur Scholarship, the "Helping Hand" from Rice Family Scholarships, the "Taking It to the Sky" Scholarship, and the "Tools Beneath Your Wings" Scholarship. Other programs are offered by Abaris Training Resources, CAE SimuFlite, American Eurocopter, FlightSafety International, Baker School of Aeronautics, Nolan Avionics, Pittsburgh Institute of Aeronautics, Southwest Airlines, JetBlue Airways, Horizon Air Alaska Airlines, Pratt & Whitney, UPS, and Global Jet Services.

**Number awarded**   Varies each year; recently, 29 scholarships with a value in excess of $72,000 were awarded, but most of those were for specified schools or training programs. The cash awards for use at any maintenance training program were 1 at $1,000 and 5 at $500.

**Deadline**   November of each year.

## [61]
## ASSOCIATION FOR WOMEN IN SPORTS MEDIA SCHOLARSHIP/INTERNSHIP PROGRAM

Association for Women in Sports Media
Attn: Scholarship and Internship Coordinator
161 West Sylvania Avenue
Neptune City, NJ 07753
E-mail: lindsay.jones@awsmonline.org
Web: awsmonline.org/internship-scholarship

**Summary**   To provide financial assistance and work experience to women undergraduate and graduate students who are interested in preparing for a career in sports writing.

**Eligibility**   This program is open to women who are enrolled in college or graduate school full time and preparing for a career in sports writing, sports copy editing, sports broadcasting, or sports public relations. Applicants must submit a 750-word essay describing their most memorable experience in sports or sports media, a 1-page resume highlighting their journalism experience, a letter of recommendation, up to 5 samples of their work, and a $20 application fee. They must apply for and accept an internship with a sports media organization.

**Financial data**　Winners receive a stipend up to $1,000 and placement in a paid internship.

**Duration**　1 year; nonrenewable.

**Additional information**　This program, which began in 1990, includes the Jackie and Gene Autry Memorial Scholarship, the Jim Brennan Scholarship, the Betty Brennan Scholarship, the Mike Roberts Memorial Scholarship, the Katie Jackson Morrison Memorial Scholarship, and the Leah Siegel Scholarship.

**Number awarded**　Varies each year; recently, 6 students received support from this program.

**Deadline**　October of each year.

## [62]
## ASSOCIATION ON AMERICAN INDIAN AFFAIRS DISPLACED HOMEMAKER SCHOLARSHIPS

Association on American Indian Affairs, Inc.
Attn: Director of Scholarship Programs
966 Hungerford Drive, Suite 12-B
Rockville, MD 20850
(240) 314-7155　　　　　　Fax: (240) 314-7159
E-mail: general.aaia@indian-affairs.org
Web: www.indian-affairs.org

**Summary**　To provide financial assistance to Native American displaced homemakers who are trying to complete their college education.

**Eligibility**　This program is open to full-time college students who are Native Americans and have special needs because of family responsibilities. Examples of displaced homemakers include students who are attending college for the first time, usually between the ages of 30 and 35, because they have put off higher education to raise their children, students who are entering or returning to college after their children enter elementary school, and men or women who have been divorced and had to leave college to care for children and are now returning. Applicants must submit documentation of financial need, a Certificate of Degree of Indian Blood (CDIB) showing at least one-quarter Indian blood, proof of tribal enrollment, an essay on their educational goals and family responsibilities, 2 letters of recommendation, and their most recent transcript.

**Financial data**　The stipend is $1,500. Awards are intended to assist recipients with child care, transportation, and some basic living expenses as well as educational costs.

**Duration**　1 year; recipients may reapply.

**Number awarded**　Varies each year; recently, 2 of these scholarships were awarded.

**Deadline**　June of each year.

## [63]
## ATKINS TRANSPORTATION YOU HIGH SCHOOL SCHOLARSHIP

Women's Transportation Seminar
Attn: WTS Foundation
1701 K Street, N.W., Suite 800
Washington, DC 20006
(202) 955-5085　　　　　　Fax: (202) 955-5088
E-mail: wts@wtsinternational.org
Web: www.wtsinternational.org/education/scholarships

**Summary**　To provide financial assistance to female high school seniors who are studying fields of science, technology, engineering, or mathematics (STEM) and planning to attend college to prepare for a career in transportation.

**Eligibility**　This program is open to women who are high school seniors with a GPA of 3.0 or higher. Applicants must be studying STEM fields in high school and be planning to attend college to prepare for a career in transportation (e.g., civil engineering, city planning, logistics, automotive engineering, truck repair). Along with their application, they must submit a 500-word statement about their career goals after graduation and why they think they should receive the scholarship. Applications must be submitted first to a local chapter; the chapters forward selected applications for consideration on the national level. Minority women are especially encouraged to apply. Selection is based on transportation involvement and goals, job skills, academic record, and leadership potential; financial need is not considered.

**Financial data**　The stipend is $1,000.

**Duration**　1 year.

**Additional information**　Local chapters may also award additional funding to winners for their area.

**Number awarded**　1 each year.

**Deadline**　Applications must be submitted by November to a local WTS chapter.

## [64]
## AURA NEELY-GARY MEMORIAL SCHOLARSHIP

Community Foundation of Greater Jackson
525 East Capitol Street, Suite 5B
Jackson, MS 39201
(601) 974-6044　　　　　　Fax: (601) 974-6045
E-mail: info@cfgj.org
Web: www.cfgreaterjackson.org/scholarships.html

**Summary**　To provide financial assistance to students at colleges and universities in Mississippi (especially young women) who have resumed their studies after an absence.

**Eligibility**　This program is open to residents of any state who are enrolled or planning to enroll at a college or university in Mississippi. Preference is given to students who desire to resume their education following a period of personal difficulties. Special consideration is given to young women who had previously dropped out of school and are now enrolled at a postsecondary institution. Applicants must be able to demonstrate financial need and potential contribution to society.

**Financial data**　The stipend is $2,000.

**Duration**　1 year.

**Additional information**　This program began in 2007.

**Number awarded**　1 each year.

**Deadline**　June of each year.

## [65]
## AUTOMOTIVE WOMEN'S ALLIANCE FOUNDATION SCHOLARSHIPS

Automotive Women's Alliance Foundation
Attn: Scholarship
P.O. Box 4305
Troy, MI 48099
Toll Free: (877) 393-AWAF          Fax: (248) 239-0291
E-mail: admin@AWAFoundation.org
Web: www.awafoundation.org/pages/Scholarships

**Summary** To provide financial assistance to women who are interested in attending college or graduate school to prepare for a career in the automotive industry.

**Eligibility** This program is open to women who are entering or enrolled in an undergraduate or graduate program that will prepare them for a career in the automotive industry. Applicants must be citizens of Canada or the United States. They must have a GPA of 3.0 or higher. Along with their application, they must submit a 1-page cover letter explaining their automotive-related career aspirations.

**Financial data** The stipend is $2,500.

**Duration** 1 year.

**Additional information** This program began in 2001.

**Number awarded** Varies each year; recently, 5 of these scholarships were awarded.

**Deadline** Deadline not specified.

## [66]
## AWA SCHOLARSHIPS

Association for Women in Architecture
Attn: Scholarship Chair
22815 Frampton Avenue
Torrance, CA 90501-5034
(310) 534-8466          Fax: (310) 257-1942
E-mail: scholarships@awa-la.org
Web: awa-la.org/scholarships

**Summary** To provide financial assistance to women undergraduates in California who are interested in preparing for a career in architecture.

**Eligibility** This program is open to women who have completed at least 18 college units of study in any of the following fields: architecture; civil, structural, mechanical, or electrical engineering as related to environmental design; landscape architecture; urban and/or land planning; interior design; architectural rendering and illustration; or environmental design. Applicants must be residents of California or attending school in the state. Students in their final year of study are also eligible and may use the funds for special projects (such as a trip abroad). Selection is based on grades, a personal statement, recommendations, and the quality and organization of materials submitted; financial need is not considered.

**Financial data** The stipend is $1,000.

**Duration** 1 year.

**Number awarded** 5 each year.

**Deadline** April of each year.

## [67]
## AWARDS FOR UNDERGRADUATE PERFORMANCE

Sigma Alpha Iota Philanthropies, Inc.
One Tunnel Road
Asheville, NC 28805
(828) 251-0606          Fax: (828) 251-0644
E-mail: nh@sai-national.org
Web: www.sai-national.org

**Summary** To recognize and reward, with scholarships for additional study, outstanding performances in vocal and instrumental categories by undergraduate members of Sigma Alpha Iota (an organization of women musicians).

**Eligibility** This competition is open to undergraduate student members of the organization who are vocalists or instrumentalists. Entrants must be younger than 25 years of age. Selection is based on taped auditions in 4 categories: voice, piano or percussion, strings or harp, and winds or brass.

**Financial data** The awards are $1,500. Funds must be used for continued study.

**Duration** The competition is held triennially.

**Additional information** This program consists of the following named awards: the Blanche Z. Hoffman Memorial Award for Voice, the Mary Ann Starring Memorial Award for Piano and Percussion, the Dorothy E. Morris Memorial Award for Strings or Harp, and the Mary Ann Starring Memorial Award for Woodwinds or Brass.

**Number awarded** 4 every 3 years: 1 in each of the 4 categories.

**Deadline** March of the year of the awards (2015, 2018, etc.).

## [68]
## AWG MINORITY SCHOLARSHIP

Association for Women Geoscientists
Attn: AWG Foundation
12000 North Washington Street, Suite 285
Thornton, CO 80241
(303) 412-6219          Fax: (303) 253-9220
E-mail: minorityscholarship@awg.org
Web: www.awg.org/EAS/scholarships.html

**Summary** To provide financial assistance to underrepresented minority women who are interested in working on an undergraduate degree in the geosciences.

**Eligibility** This program is open to women who are African American, Hispanic, or Native American (including Eskimo, Hawaiian, Samoan, or American Indian). Applicants must be full-time students working on, or planning to work on, an undergraduate degree in the geosciences (including geology, geophysics, geochemistry, hydrology, meteorology, physical oceanography, planetary geology, or earth science education). They must submit a 500-word essay on their academic and career goals, 2 letters of recommendation, high school and/or college transcripts, and SAT or ACT scores. Financial need is not considered in the selection process. U.S. citizenship is required.

**Financial data** A total of $6,000 is available for this program each year.

**Duration** 1 year; may be renewed.

**Additional information** This program, first offered in 2004, is supported by ExxonMobil Foundation.

**Number awarded** 1 or more each year.

**Deadline** June of each year.

## [69]
## B. JUNE WEST RECRUITMENT GRANT

Delta Kappa Gamma Society International-Theta State Organization
c/o Sharron Stepro, Committee on Professional Affairs Chair
10038 San Marcos Court
Las Cruces, NM 88007-8954
Web: thetastatenmdkg.weebly.com/award-forms-html

**Summary** To provide financial assistance to women in New Mexico who are interested in preparing for a career as a teacher.

**Eligibility** This program is open to women residents of New Mexico who are 1) graduating high school seniors planning to go into education; 2) college students majoring in education; or 3) teachers needing educational assistance. Applicants must submit a list of activities in which they are involved, 3 letters of recommendation, a list of achievements and awards, and a statement of their educational goal and how this grant would be of assistance to them. Financial need is not considered in the selection process.

**Financial data** A stipend is awarded (amount not specified).

**Duration** 1 year.

**Number awarded** 1 or more each year.

**Deadline** February of each year.

## [70]
## BANNER ENGINEERING MINNESOTA SWE SCHOLARSHIP

Society of Women Engineers-Minnesota Section
Attn: Scholarship Committee
P.O. Box 582813
Minneapolis, MN 55458-2813
E-mail: scholarships@swe-mn.org
Web: www.swe-mn.org/scholarships.html

**Summary** To provide financial assistance to women from any state working on an undergraduate or graduate degree in electrical or mechanical engineering at colleges and universities in Minnesota, North Dakota, and South Dakota.

**Eligibility** This program is open to female undergraduate and graduate students at ABET-accredited engineering programs in Minnesota, North Dakota, or South Dakota. Applicants must be working full time on a degree in electrical or mechanical engineering. Along with their application, they must submit a short paragraph describing how they plan to utilize their engineering skills after they graduate. Selection is based on potential to succeed as an engineer (20 points), communication skills (10 points), extracurricular or community involvement and leadership skills (10 points), demonstrated successful work experience (10 points), and academic success (5 points).

**Financial data** The stipend is $2,000.

**Duration** 1 year.

**Additional information** This program is sponsored by Banner Engineering Corporation.

**Number awarded** 1 each year.

**Deadline** March of each year.

## [71]
## BARBARA ALICE MOWER MEMORIAL SCHOLARSHIP

Barbara Alice Mower Memorial Scholarship Committee
c/o Nancy A. Mower
1536 Kamole Street
Honolulu, HI 96821-1424
(808) 373-2901          E-mail: nmower@hawaii.edu

**Summary** To provide financial assistance to female residents of Hawaii who are interested in women's studies and are attending college on the undergraduate or graduate level in the United States or abroad.

**Eligibility** This program is open to female residents of Hawaii who are at least juniors in college, are interested in and committed to women's studies, and have worked or studied in the field. Selection is based on interest in studying about and commitment to helping women, previous work and/or study in that area, previous academic performance, character, personality, and future plans to help women (particularly women in Hawaii). If there are several applicants who meet all these criteria, then financial need may be taken into consideration.

**Financial data** The stipend ranges from $1,000 to $3,500.

**Duration** 1 year; may be renewed.

**Additional information** Recipients may use the scholarship at universities in Hawaii, on the mainland, or in foreign countries. They must focus on women's studies or topics that relate to women in school.

**Number awarded** 1 or more each year.

**Deadline** April of each year.

## [72]
## BARBARA JEAN BARKER MEMORIAL SCHOLARSHIP FOR A DISPLACED HOMEMAKER

General Federation of Women's Clubs of Vermont
c/o Betty Haggerty, Scholarship Chair
16 Taylor Street
Bellows Falls, VT 05101
(802) 463-4159          E-mail: hubett@hotmail.com

**Summary** To provide financial assistance to displaced homemakers in Vermont who are interested in attending college in any state.

**Eligibility** Applicants must be Vermont residents who have been homemakers (primarily) for at least 15 years and have lost their main means of support through death, divorce, separation, spouse's long-time illness, or spouse's long-time unemployment. Applicants must be interested in upgrading their skills so they can work outside the home. As part of the application process, they must submit a completed application form and a letter of recommendation (from a personal friend or their postsecondary school). Selection is based on the information provided in the application form and a personal interview (finalists only).

**Financial data** The stipend ranges from $500 to $1,500.

**Duration** 1 year.

**Additional information** This program began in 1993.

**Number awarded** 1 to 3 each year.

**Deadline** March of each year.

## [73]
## BARBARA MCBRIDE SCHOLARSHIP

Society of Exploration Geophysicists
Attn: SEG Foundation
8801 South Yale, Suite 500
P.O. Box 702740
Tulsa, OK 74170-2740
(918) 497-5500                   Fax: (918) 497-5557
E-mail: scholarships@seg.org
Web: www.seg.org/web/foundation/programs/scholarship

**Summary**  To provide financial assistance to women who are interested in studying applied geophysics or a related field on the undergraduate or graduate school level.

**Eligibility**  This program is open to women who are 1) high school students planning to enter college in the fall; or 2) undergraduate or graduate students whose grades are above average. Applicants must intend to work on a degree directed toward a career in applied geophysics or a closely-related field (e.g., energy, environmental sciences, geology, geoscience, mathematics, physics, or seismology). Along with their application, they must submit a 150-word essay on how they plan to use geophysics in their future. Financial need is not considered in the selection process.

**Financial data**  Stipends provided by this sponsor average $3,000 per year.

**Duration**  1 academic year; may be renewable, based on scholastic standing, availability of funds, and continuance of a course of study leading to a career in applied geophysics.

**Number awarded**  1 each year.

**Deadline**  February of each year.

## [74]
## BASIC MIDWIFERY STUDENT SCHOLARSHIPS

American College of Nurse-Midwives
Attn: ACNM Foundation, Inc.
8403 Colesville Road, Suite 1550
Silver Spring, MD 20910-6374
(240) 485-1850                   Fax: (240) 485-1818
E-mail: fdn@acnm.org
Web: www.midwife.org

**Summary**  To provide financial assistance for midwifery education to student members of the American College of Nurse-Midwives (ACNM).

**Eligibility**  This program is open to ACNM members who are currently enrolled in an accredited basic midwife education program and have successfully completed 1 academic or clinical semester/quarter or clinical module. Applicants must submit a 150-word essay on their midwifery career plans and a 100-word essay on their intended future participation in the local, regional, and/or national activities of the ACNM. Selection is based on leadership potential, financial need, academic history, and potential for future professional contribution to the organization.

**Financial data**  The stipend is $3,000.

**Duration**  1 year.

**Number awarded**  Varies each year; recently, 4 of these scholarships were awarded.

**Deadline**  March of each year.

## [75]
## BECHTEL CORPORATION SCHOLARSHIP

Society of Women Engineers
Attn: Scholarship Selection Committee
203 North LaSalle Street, Suite 1675
Chicago, IL 60601-1269
(312) 596-5223                   Toll Free: (877) SWE-INFO
Fax: (312) 644-8557              E-mail: scholarships@swe.org
Web: societyofwomenengineers.swe.org

**Summary**  To provide financial assistance to undergraduate women who are members of the Society of Women Engineers and majoring in engineering.

**Eligibility**  This program is open to SWE members who are entering their sophomore, junior, or senior year at an ABET-accredited college or university. Applicants must be working full time on a degree computer science or architectural, civil, electrical, environmental, or mechanical engineering or equivalent fields of engineering technology. They must have a GPA of 3.0 or higher. Only members of the society are considered for this award. Selection is based on merit.

**Financial data**  The stipend is $1,400.

**Duration**  1 year.

**Additional information**  This program, established in 2000, is sponsored by Bechtel Group Foundation.

**Number awarded**  2 each year.

**Deadline**  February of each year.

## [76]
## BERNICE F. ELLIOTT MEMORIAL SCHOLARSHIP

Baptist Convention of New Mexico
Attn: Missions Mobilization Team WMU
5325 Wyoming Boulevard, N.E.
P.O. Box 94485
Albuquerque, NM 87199-4485
(505) 924-2316                   Toll Free: (800) 898-8544
Fax: (505) 924-2320             E-mail: ktreece@bcnm.com
Web: www.bcnm.com

**Summary**  To provide financial assistance to women who are Southern Baptists from New Mexico and interested in attending a college or seminary in any state.

**Eligibility**  This program is open to women college and seminary students who are members of churches affiliated with the Baptist Convention of New Mexico. Preference is given to applicants who are committed to full-time Christian service, have a background in the Woman's Missionary Union, and can demonstrate financial need.

**Financial data**  A stipend is awarded (amount not specified).

**Duration**  1 year; may be renewed.

**Number awarded**  1 or more each year.

**Deadline**  March of each year.

## [77]
## BERNICE MURRAY SCHOLARSHIP

Vermont Student Assistance Corporation
Attn: Scholarship Programs
10 East Allen Street
P.O. Box 2000
Winooski, VT 05404-2601
(802) 654-3798                   Toll Free: (888) 253-4819
Fax: (802) 654-3765        TDD: (800) 281-3341 (within VT)
E-mail: info@vsac.org
Web: services.vsac.org

**Summary**   To provide financial assistance for child care to single parents in Vermont who wish to improve their education or skills.

**Eligibility**   Applicants must be Vermont residents, single parents with primary custody of at least 1 child 12 years of age or younger, able to demonstrate financial need (expected family contribution of $23,360 or less), and enrolled in a full- or part-time degree program at an approved postsecondary school. Along with their application, they must submit 1) a 100-word essay on any significant barriers that limit their access to education; 2) a 250-word essay on their short- and long-term academic, educational, career, vocational, and/or employment goals; and 3) a 100-word essay on how the program in which they will be enrolled will enhance their career or vocation. Selection is based on their essays, a letter of recommendation, financial need (expected family contribution of $23,360 or less), and a personal interview.

**Financial data**   The maximum stipend is $2,000; funds must be used to pay for child care services while the recipient attends an approved postsecondary institution.

**Duration**   1 year; recipients may reapply.

**Additional information**   This program is sponsored by U.S. Senator James Jeffords and the Federal Executives' Association.

**Number awarded**   1 or 2 each year.

**Deadline**   March of each year.

## [78]
## BERTHA LAMME MEMORIAL SCHOLARSHIP

Society of Women Engineers
Attn: Scholarship Selection Committee
203 North LaSalle Street, Suite 1675
Chicago, IL 60601-1269
(312) 596-5223                   Toll Free: (877) SWE-INFO
Fax: (312) 644-8557        E-mail: scholarships@swe.org
Web: societyofwomenengineers.swe.org

**Summary**   To provide financial assistance to women who will be entering college as freshmen and are interested in studying electrical engineering.

**Eligibility**   This program is open to women who are entering college as freshmen with a GPA of 3.5 or higher. Applicants must be U.S. citizens or permanent residents planning to enroll full time at an ABET-accredited 4-year college or university and major in electrical engineering. Selection is based on merit.

**Financial data**   The stipend is $1,200.

**Duration**   1 year.

**Number awarded**   1 each year.

**Deadline**   May of each year.

## [79]
## BERTHA PITTS CAMPBELL SCHOLARSHIP PROGRAM

Delta Sigma Theta Sorority, Inc.
Attn: Scholarship and Standards Committee Chair
1707 New Hampshire Avenue, N.W.
Washington, DC 20009
(202) 986-2400                   Fax: (202) 986-2513
E-mail: dstemail@deltasigmatheta.org
Web: www.deltasigmatheta.org

**Summary**   To provide financial assistance to members of Delta Sigma Theta who are working on an undergraduate degree in education.

**Eligibility**   This program is open to current undergraduate students who are working on a degree in education. Applicants must be active, dues-paying members of Delta Sigma Theta. Selection is based on meritorious achievement.

**Financial data**   The stipends range from $1,000 to $2,000. The funds may be used to cover tuition, fees, and living expenses.

**Duration**   1 year; may be renewed for 1 additional year.

**Additional information**   This sponsor is a traditionally-African American social sorority. The application fee is $20.

**Number awarded**   1 or more each year.

**Deadline**   April of each year.

## [80]
## BESSIE BARROW MEMORIAL FOUNDATION SCHOLARSHIPS

Baptist Convention of Maryland/Delaware
Attn: United Baptist Women of Maryland, Inc.
10255 Old Columbia Road
Columbia, MD 21046
(410) 290-5290                   Toll Free: (800) 466-5290
E-mail: gparker@bcmd.org
Web: www.bcmd.org/wmu

**Summary**   To provide financial assistance to women who are members of Baptist churches associated with an affiliate of United Baptist Women of Maryland and interested in working on an undergraduate degree at a college in any state.

**Eligibility**   This program is open to women who are enrolled or planning to enroll full time at an accredited college or university in any state to work on an undergraduate degree in any field. Applicants must be a member in good standing of a Baptist church associated with an affiliate of United Baptist Women of Maryland. They must have a grade average of "C" or higher and be able to demonstrate financial need. Along with their application, they must submit brief statements on their Christian experience, school activities, church and community activities, and career goals.

**Financial data**   A stipend is awarded (amount not specified).

**Duration**   1 year.

**Number awarded**   Varies each year.

**Deadline**   June of each year.

## [81]
## BETSY B. AND GAROLD A. LEACH SCHOLARSHIP FOR MUSEUM STUDIES

Delta Zeta Sorority
Attn: Foundation Coordinator
202 East Church Street
Oxford, OH 45056
(513) 523-7597                    Fax: (513) 523-1921
E-mail: DZFoundation@dzshq.com
Web: www.deltazeta.org

**Summary**   To provide financial assistance to members of Delta Zeta Sorority working on an undergraduate or graduate degree to prepare for a career in museum work.

**Eligibility**   This program is open to upper-division and graduate members of the sorority who have a GPA of 3.0 or higher. Applicants must be working on a degree in a field that will prepare them for a career in museum work, including library science, archaeology, geology, or art history. Along with their application, they must submit an official transcript, a statement of their career goals, information on their service to the sorority, documentation of campus activities and/or community involvement, a list of academic honors, and an explanation of their financial need.

**Financial data**   The stipend ranges from $500 to $2,500 for undergraduates or from $1,000 to $15,000 for graduate students, depending on the availability of funds.

**Duration**   1 year; nonrenewable.

**Number awarded**   1 each year.

**Deadline**   February of each year.

## [82]
## BETTY HANSEN NATIONAL SCHOLARSHIPS

Danish Sisterhood of America
c/o Connie Schell, Scholarship Chair
246 Foster Road
Fort Covington, NY 12937
(518) 358-4686              E-mail: cschell4dss@aol.com
Web: www.danishsisterhood.org/DanishHTML/rschol.asp

**Summary**   To provide financial assistance for educational purposes in the United States or Denmark to members or relatives of members of the Danish Sisterhood of America.

**Eligibility**   This program is open to members or the family of members of the sisterhood who are interested in attending an accredited 4-year college or university as a full-time undergraduate or graduate student. Members must have belonged to the sisterhood for at least 1 year. They must have a GPA of 2.5 or higher. Selection is based on academics (including ACT or SAT scores), academic awards or honors, other special recognition and awards, employment record, special talents or hobbies, and participation in Danish Sisterhood and other civic activities. Upon written request, the scholarship may be used for study in Denmark.

**Financial data**   The stipend is $1,000.

**Duration**   1 year; nonrenewable.

**Number awarded**   Up to 8 each year.

**Deadline**   February of each year.

## [83]
## BETTY LOU BAILEY SWE REGION F SCHOLARSHIP

Society of Women Engineers
Attn: Scholarship Selection Committee
203 North LaSalle Street, Suite 1675
Chicago, IL 60601-1269
(312) 596-5223                 Toll Free: (877) SWE-INFO
Fax: (312) 644-8557        E-mail: scholarships@swe.org
Web: societyofwomenengineers.swe.org

**Summary**   To provide financial assistance to members of the Society of Women Engineers (SWE) working on an undergraduate or graduate degree in engineering or computer science at a school in its Region F (states in New England and upstate New York).

**Eligibility**   This program is open to members of the society who will be sophomores, juniors, seniors, or graduate students at ABET-accredited colleges and universities. First preference is given to applicants who attend college or graduate school in the New England states or upstate New York; second preference is given to students who reside in New England or upstate New York. Applicants must be working full time on a degree in computer science or engineering and have a GPA of 3.0 or higher. Financial need is considered in the selection process. U.S. citizenship or permanent resident status is required.

**Financial data**   The stipend is $1,500.

**Duration**   1 year.

**Number awarded**   1 each year.

**Deadline**   February of each year.

## [84]
## BETTY MCKERN SCHOLARSHIP

Association for Iron & Steel Technology-Midwest Chapter
c/o Love Kalra, Scholarship Chair
ArcelorMittal
Number 3 Steel Producing, Door 438
3001 Dickey Road
East Chicago, IN 46312
(219) 399-2259        E-mail: love.kalra@arcelormittal.com
Web: www.aist.org/chapters/midwest_scholarship.htm

**Summary**   To provide financial assistance to women who are members or dependents of members of the Midwest Chapter of the Association for Iron & Steel Technology (AIST) and plan to study engineering at a college in any state to prepare for a career in the iron and steel industry.

**Eligibility**   This program is open to women who are members or dependents of members of the AIST Midwest Chapter and are graduating high school seniors or currently enrolled full time in the first, second, or third year at an accredited college or university in any state. Applicants must be studying or planning to study engineering and have an interest in preparing for a career in the iron and steel industry. Along with their application, they must submit a letter of recommendation, a current transcript (including SAT/ACT scores), and a 1- to 2-page essay describing their objectives for college and career. Selection is based on merit.

**Financial data**   The stipend is $3,000.

**Duration**   1 year.

**Additional information**   The AIST was formed in 2004 by the merger of the Iron and Steel Society (ISS) and the Association of Iron and Steel Engineers (AISE). The Midwest Chapter replaced the former AISE Chicago Section in northern Illinois and northwestern Indiana and also includes the states of Wisconsin, Minnesota, Iowa, Nebraska, South Dakota, and North Dakota.

**Number awarded** 1 each year.

**Deadline** March of each year.

## [85]
## BETTY MULLINS JONES SCHOLARSHIP

National Panhellenic Conference
Attn: NPC Foundation
3901 West 86th Street, Suite 398
Indianapolis, IN 46268
(317) 872-3185                    Fax: (317) 872-3192
E-mail: npcfoundation@npcwomen.org
Web: www.npcwomen.org/foundation/scholarships.aspx

**Summary** To provide financial assistance to undergraduate women who are members of Greek-letter societies.

**Eligibility** This program is open to Greek-affiliated women at colleges and universities in the United States. Applicants must be able to demonstrate that they have worked to further their fraternal community's reputation on their campus. In the selection process, emphasis is placed on financial need and participation in university, Panhellenic, chapter, and other activities.

**Financial data** The stipend is $1,000.

**Duration** 1 year.

**Number awarded** 1 each year.

**Deadline** January of each year.

## [86]
## BETTY RENDEL SCHOLARSHIPS

National Federation of Republican Women
Attn: Scholarships and Internships
124 North Alfred Street
Alexandria, VA 22314-3011
(703) 548-9688                    Fax: (703) 548-9836
E-mail: mail@nfrw.org
Web: www.nfrw.org/programs/scholarships.htm

**Summary** To provide financial assistance to undergraduate Republican women who are majoring in political science, government, or economics.

**Eligibility** This program is open to women who have completed at least 2 years of college. Applicants must be majoring in political science, government, or economics. Along with their application, they must submit 3 letters of recommendation, an official transcript, a 1-page essay on why they should be considered for the scholarship, and a 1-page essay on career goals. Applications must be submitted to the Republican federation president in the applicant's state. Each president chooses 1 application from her state to submit for scholarship consideration. Financial need is not a factor in the selection process. U.S. citizenship is required.

**Financial data** The stipend is $1,000.

**Duration** 1 year; nonrenewable.

**Additional information** This program began in 1995.

**Number awarded** 3 each year.

**Deadline** Applications must be submitted to the state federation president by May of each year.

## [87]
## BILLINGS CHAPTER AFWA TWO-YEAR COLLEGE SCHOLARSHIP

Accounting and Financial Women's Alliance-Billings Chapter
Attn: Scholarship Chair
P.O. Box 20593
Billings, MT 59104-0593
E-mail: aswabillings@gmail.com
Web: www.billingsafwa.org/scholarship

**Summary** To provide financial assistance to women working on an associate degree in accounting at a 2-year or community college in Montana.

**Eligibility** This program is open to women working on an associate degree in accounting or finance at a 2-year or community college in Montana. Applicants must have completed at least 15 semester hours and have a GPA of 3.0 or higher. Along with their application, they must submit an essay of 150 to 250 words on their career goals and objectives, the impact they want to have on the accounting world, their community involvement, and leadership examples. Selection is based on leadership, character, scholastic average, communication skills, and financial need.

**Financial data** The stipend is $1,000.

**Duration** 1 year.

**Additional information** The application of the recipient is forwarded to the American Society of Women Accountants (ASWA) Educational Foundation for consideration for a national scholarship.

**Number awarded** 1 each year.

**Deadline** October of each year.

## [88]
## BILLINGS CHAPTER AFWA UNDERGRADUATE SCHOLARSHIPS

Accounting and Financial Women's Alliance-Billings Chapter
Attn: Scholarship Chair
P.O. Box 20593
Billings, MT 59104-0593
E-mail: aswabillings@gmail.com
Web: www.billingsafwa.org/scholarship

**Summary** To provide financial assistance to women working on an bachelor's degree in accounting at a college or university in Montana.

**Eligibility** This program is open to women working on a bachelor's degree in accounting or finance at a college or university in Montana. Applicants must have completed at least 60 semester hours and have a GPA of 3.0 or higher. Along with their application, they must submit an essay of 150 to 250 words on their career goals and objectives, the impact they want to have on the accounting world, their community involvement, and leadership examples. Selection is based on leadership, character, scholastic average, communication skills, and financial need.

**Financial data** The stipend is $1,500.

**Duration** 1 year.

**Additional information** The application of 1 of the recipients is forwarded to the American Society of Women Accountants (ASWA) Educational Foundation for consideration for a national scholarship.

**Number awarded** 2 each year.

**Deadline** October of each year.

## [89]
## BIRMINGHAM SECTION SWE SCHOLARSHIP

Society of Women Engineers-Birmingham Section
c/o Shunna Cannon, Scholarship Chair
P.O. Box 361311
Birmingham, AL 35236
E-mail: smcannon@southernco.com
Web: www.swebham.org/Default.aspx?pageId=979915

**Summary** To provide financial assistance to female high school seniors planning to study engineering at a college or university in Alabama.

**Eligibility** This program is open to women graduating from high schools in any state and planning to enter a college or university in Alabama that has an ABET-accredited engineering program. Applicants must submit an essay about their career goals and why they need this scholarship. Selection is based on that essay (10 points); SAT or ACT test scores (10 points); GPA, honors received, and early college courses completed (10 points); high school science and mathematics courses completed by date of graduation (10 points); leadership and extracurricular activities (10 points); community and civic activities and employment (10 points); communication skills (10 points); and financial need (5 points). U.S. citizenship or permanent resident status is required.

**Financial data** A stipend is awarded (amount not specified).

**Duration** 1 year.

**Number awarded** 1 or more each year.

**Deadline** July of each year.

## [90]
## B.J. HARROD SCHOLARSHIPS

Society of Women Engineers
Attn: Scholarship Selection Committee
203 North LaSalle Street, Suite 1675
Chicago, IL 60601-1269
(312) 596-5223          Toll Free: (877) SWE-INFO
Fax: (312) 644-8557      E-mail: scholarships@swe.org
Web: societyofwomenengineers.swe.org

**Summary** To provide financial assistance to women who will be entering college as freshmen and are interested in studying engineering or computer science.

**Eligibility** This program is open to women who are entering college as freshmen with a GPA of 3.5 or higher. Applicants must be planning to enroll full time at an ABET-accredited 4-year college or university and major in computer science or engineering. Selection is based on merit.

**Financial data** The stipend is $1,500.

**Duration** 1 year.

**Additional information** This program began in 1999.

**Number awarded** 2 each year.

**Deadline** May of each year.

## [91]
## B.K. KRENZER MEMORIAL REENTRY SCHOLARSHIP

Society of Women Engineers
Attn: Scholarship Selection Committee
203 North LaSalle Street, Suite 1675
Chicago, IL 60601-1269
(312) 596-5223          Toll Free: (877) SWE-INFO
Fax: (312) 644-8557      E-mail: scholarships@swe.org
Web: societyofwomenengineers.swe.org

**Summary** To provide financial assistance to women interested in returning to college or graduate school to study engineering or computer science.

**Eligibility** This program is open to women who are planning to enroll at an ABET-accredited 4-year college or university. Applicants must have been out of the engineering workforce and school for at least 2 years and must be planning to return as an undergraduate or graduate student to work on a degree in computer science or engineering. They must have a GPA of 3.0 or higher. Selection is based on merit. Preference is given to engineers who already have a degree and are planning to reenter the engineering workforce after a period of temporary retirement.

**Financial data** The stipend is $2,000.

**Duration** 1 year.

**Additional information** This program began in 1996.

**Number awarded** 1 each year.

**Deadline** February of each year.

## [92]
## BOB RAPP MEMORIAL ASA SCHOLARSHIP

Oregon Amateur Softball Association
c/o Joe Driggers
972 N.E. 12th Place
Canby, OR 97013
(503) 226-3696          E-mail: jdcanby@aol.com
Web: www.oregon-asa.com/rapp

**Summary** To provide financial assistance to female high school seniors in Oregon who have played softball and plan to attend college in any state.

**Eligibility** This program is open to female seniors graduating from high schools in Oregon who plan to attend a college or university in any state. Applicants must have played for an American Softball Association (ASA) team at some time. Along with their application, they must submit an essay on how ASA softball impacted their life. Financial need is not considered in the selection process.

**Financial data** Stipends are $1,000 or $500.

**Duration** 1 year.

**Number awarded** 4 each year: 2 at $1,000 and 2 at $500.

**Deadline** June of each year.

## [93]
## BOBBI MCCALLUM MEMORIAL SCHOLARSHIP

Seattle Foundation
Attn: Scholarship Administrator
1200 Fifth Avenue, Suite 1300
Seattle, WA 98101-3151
(206) 622-2294          Fax: (206) 622-7673
E-mail: scholarships@seattlefoundation.org
Web: www.seattlefoundation.org

**Summary** To provide financial assistance to women college students in Washington who are interested in preparing for a career in journalism.

**Eligibility** This program is open to female residents of Washington who are entering their junior or senior year and studying print journalism at a 4-year public college or university in the state. Applicants must submit 5 samples of news writing (published or unpublished); brief essays on topics related to their interest in journalism; 2 letters of recommendation; and documentation of financial need. Selection is based on need, talent, and motivation to prepare for a career in print journalism.

**Financial data** The stipend is $3,000 per year.

**Duration** 1 year; may be renewed.

**Additional information** This scholarship was established in 1970 by the late Dr. Walter Scott Brown in memory of Bobbi McCallum, a prizewinning reporter and columnist for the *Seattle Post-Intelligencer* who died in 1969 at age 25 while a patient of Dr. Brown. The scholarship was administered by the newspaper until it suspended publication in 2010 and the program was transferred to the Seattle Foundation.

**Number awarded** 2 each year.

**Deadline** February of each year.

## [94]
## BOSTON AFFILIATE AWSCPA SCHOLARSHIP

American Woman's Society of Certified Public
  Accountants-Boston Affiliate
c/o Andrea Costantino
Oxford Bioscience Partners
222 Berkeley Street, Suite 1650
Boston, MA 02116
(617) 357-7474        E-mail: acostantino@oxbio.com
Web: www.awscpa.org/affiliate_scholarships/boston.html

**Summary** To provide financial assistance to women from any state who are working on an undergraduate or graduate degree in accounting at a college or university in New England.

**Eligibility** This program is open to women from any state who are attending a college in New England and majoring in accounting. Applicants must have completed at least 12 semester hours of accounting or tax courses and have a cumulative GPA of 3.0 or higher. They must be planning to graduate between May of next year and May of the following year or, for the 15-month graduate program, before September of the current year. Along with their application, they must submit a brief essay on why they feel they would be a good choice for this award. Selection is based on that essay, academic achievement, work experience, extracurricular activities, scholastic honors, career plans, and financial need.

**Financial data** The stipend is $1,000.

**Duration** 1 year.

**Number awarded** 2 each year.

**Deadline** September of each year.

## [95]
## BOSTON SCIENTIFIC SCHOLARSHIPS

Society of Women Engineers
Attn: Scholarship Selection Committee
203 North LaSalle Street, Suite 1675
Chicago, IL 60601-1269
(312) 596-5223        Toll Free: (877) SWE-INFO
Fax: (312) 644-8557        E-mail: scholarships@swe.org
Web: societyofwomenengineers.swe.org

**Summary** To provide financial assistance to upper-division women majoring in computer science or designated engineering specialties at designated universities.

**Eligibility** This program is open to women who are entering their senior year at a designated ABET-accredited college or university. Applicants must be working full time on a degree in computer science or chemical, computer, electrical, industrial, manufacturing, materials, or mechanical engineering and have a GPA of 3.5 or higher. Selection is based on merit.

**Financial data** The stipend is $5,000.

**Duration** 1 year.

**Additional information** This program, established in 2004, is supported by Boston Scientific Corporation. For a list of the designated colleges and universities, contact the sponsor.

**Number awarded** 2 each year.

**Deadline** February of each year.

## [96]
## BPW/WA PAST PRESIDENT MEMORIAL SCHOLARSHIP

Washington State Business and Professional Women's
  Foundation
Attn: Virginia Murphy, Scholarship Committee Chair
P.O. Box 631
Chelan, WA 98816-0631
(509) 682-4747        E-mail: vamurf@nwi.net
Web: www.bpwwa.org/foundation_apps.htm

**Summary** To provide financial assistance to mature women in Washington who are interested in continuing their education.

**Eligibility** This program is open to women who have been residents of Washington for 2 or more years and have been accepted into a program or course of study at an accredited school in the state. Applicants must be 30 years of age or older. They must be able to demonstrate scholastic ability and financial need. Along with their application, they must submit a 500-word essay on their specific short-term goals and how the proposed training will help them accomplish those goals and make a difference in their professional career. U.S. citizenship is required.

**Financial data** The stipend is $1,000.

**Duration** 1 year.

**Number awarded** Varies each year; recently, 4 of these scholarships were awarded.

**Deadline** April of each year.

## [97]
## BRADFORD GRANT-IN-AID

Delta Kappa Gamma Society International-Delta State Organization
c/o Sharon Hardecke, Scholarship Committee Chair
3864 North Franklin Avenue
Springfield, MO 65803
(417) 833-0788          E-mail: hardebest@aol.com
Web: www.dkgmissouri.com/resources.html

**Summary** To provide financial assistance to upper-division women who are residents of Missouri and attending college in any state to prepare for a career in education.

**Eligibility** This program is open to female residents of Missouri who are preparing for a career in education through a teacher preparation program at a college or university in any state. Applicants must have completed at least 75 college hours. Preference is given to relatives (e.g., daughter, granddaughter, niece, sister) of members of Delta Kappa Gamma (an honorary society of women educators). Financial need is not considered in the selection process.

**Financial data** The stipend is $1,000.

**Duration** 1 year.

**Number awarded** Up to 2 each year.

**Deadline** February of each year.

## [98]
## BRILL FAMILY SCHOLARSHIP

Society of Women Engineers
Attn: Scholarship Selection Committee
203 North LaSalle Street, Suite 1675
Chicago, IL 60601-1269
(312) 596-5223          Toll Free: (877) SWE-INFO
Fax: (312) 644-8557          E-mail: scholarships@swe.org
Web: societyofwomenengineers.swe.org

**Summary** To provide financial assistance to undergraduate women majoring in designated engineering specialties.

**Eligibility** This program is open to women who are entering their sophomore, junior, or senior year at an ABET-accredited 4-year college or university. Applicants must be working full time on a degree in computer science or aeronautical or biomedical engineering and have a GPA of 3.0 or higher. Selection is based on merit.

**Financial data** The stipend is $1,000.

**Duration** 1 year.

**Number awarded** 1 each year.

**Deadline** February of each year.

## [99]
## BROOKHAVEN NATIONAL LABORATORY SCIENCE AND ENGINEERING PROGRAMS FOR WOMEN AND MINORITIES

Brookhaven National Laboratory
Attn: Diversity Office, Human Resources Division
Building 400B
P.O. Box 5000
Upton, New York 11973-5000
(631) 344-2703          Fax: (631) 344-5305
E-mail: palmore@bnl.gov
Web: www.bnl.gov/diversity/programs.asp

**Summary** To provide on-the-job training in scientific areas at Brookhaven National Laboratory (BNL) during the summer to underrepresented women and minority students.

**Eligibility** This program at BNL is open to women and underrepresented minority (African American/Black, Hispanic, Native American, or Pacific Islander) students who have completed their freshman, sophomore, or junior year of college. Applicants must be U.S. citizens or permanent residents, at least 18 years of age, and majoring in applied mathematics, biology, chemistry, computer science, engineering, high and low energy particle accelerators, nuclear medicine, physics, or scientific writing. Since no transportation or housing allowance is provided, preference is given to students who reside in the BNL area.

**Financial data** Participants receive a competitive stipend.

**Duration** 10 to 12 weeks during the summer.

**Additional information** Students work with members of the scientific, technical, and professional staff of BNL in an educational training program developed to give research experience.

**Number awarded** Varies each year.

**Deadline** April of each year.

## [100]
## BUICK ACHIEVERS SCHOLARSHIP PROGRAM

Scholarship America
Attn: Scholarship Management Services
One Scholarship Way
P.O. Box 297
St. Peter, MN 56082
(507) 931-1682          Toll Free: (866) 243-4644
Fax: (507) 931-9168
E-mail: buickachievers@scholarshipamerica.org
Web: www.buickachievers.com

**Summary** To provide financial assistance to students (particularly women, minorities, and those with ties to the military) who are entering college for the first time and planning to major in specified fields related to engineering, design, or business.

**Eligibility** This program is open to high school seniors and graduates who are planning to enroll full time at an accredited 4-year college or university as first-time freshmen. Applicants must be planning to major in fields of engineering (chemical, computer, controls, electrical, energy, environmental, industrial, manufacturing, materials, mechanical, plastic/polymers, or software); technology (automotive technology, computer science, engineering technology, information technology); design (graphic, industrial, product, transportation); or business (accounting, business administration, ergonomics, finance, industrial hygiene, international business, labor and industrial relations, management information systems, marketing, mathematics, occupational health and safety, production management, statistics, or supply chain/logistics). U.S. citizenship or permanent resident status is required. Selection is based on academic achievement, financial need, participation and leadership in community and school activities, work experience, educational and career goals, and other unusual circumstances. Special consideration is given to first-generation college students, women, minorities, military veterans, and dependents of military personnel.

**Financial data** Stipends are $25,000 or $2,000 per year.

**Duration** 1 year. The $25,000 awards may be renewed up to 3 additional years (or 4 years for students entering a 5-year engineering program), provided the recipient remains enrolled full time, continues to major in an eligible field, and maintains a GPA of 3.0 or higher. The $2,000 awards are non-renewable.

**Additional information** This program, which began in 2011, is funded by the General Motors Foundation.

**Number awarded** 1,100 each year: 100 at $25,000 and 1,000 at $2,000.

**Deadline** February of each year.

## [101]
## BUSINESS AND PROFESSIONAL WOMEN OF IOWA FOUNDATION EDUCATIONAL SCHOLARSHIP

Business and Professional Women of Iowa Foundation
c/o DiAnne Lerud-Chubb, Scholarship Chair
2429 Gnahn Street
Burlington, IA 52601
(319) 759-3896                    E-mail: lerud2@mchsi.com

**Summary** To provide financial assistance for college to female and other nontraditional students who reside in Iowa.

**Eligibility** Applicants must be Iowa residents (although they may be currently attending school in another state) who have completed at least 1 year of education beyond high school. They must be nontraditional students who 1) have been out of the workforce and need additional education to go back to work or 2) completed high school 5 or more years ago and now want to restart their college education. Along with their application, they must submit essays on why they think they should receive this scholarship and how they expect to use the training. Financial need is considered in the selection process. U.S. citizenship is required.

**Financial data** The stipend is $1,000. Funds are sent directly to the recipient's school.

**Duration** 1 year.

**Additional information** Recipients may attend school in any state.

**Number awarded** 1 or more each year.

**Deadline** March of each year.

## [102]
## BUSINESS AND PROFESSIONAL WOMEN'S FOUNDATION OF MARYLAND SCHOLARSHIP

Business and Professional Women of Maryland
Attn: BPW Foundation of Maryland
c/o Joyce Draper, Chief Financial Officer
615 Fairview Avenid=316ue
Frederick, MD 21701
Web: bpwmd2.timberlakepublishing.com

**Summary** To provide financial assistance for college to mature women in Maryland.

**Eligibility** This program is open to women who are at least 25 years of age and who are interested in working on undergraduate studies to upgrade their skills for career advancement, to train for a new career field, or to reenter the job market. Applicants must be residents of Maryland or, if a resident of another state, a member of Business and Professional Women of Maryland. They must have been accepted into an accredited program or course of study at a Maryland aca-

demic institution and be able to demonstrate critical financial need. U.S. citizenship is required.

**Financial data** The stipend is $1,400.

**Duration** 1 year.

**Number awarded** 1 or more each year.

**Deadline** April of each year.

## [103]
## BUSINESS WOMEN IN MISSOURI GENERAL SCHOLARSHIPS

Business Women of Missouri Foundation, Inc.
Attn: Scholarship Committee Chair
P.O. Box 28243
Kansas City, MO 64188
(816) 333-6959                    Fax: (816) 333-6959
E-mail: jo.mofedbpw@gmail.com
Web: www.businesswomenmo.org/foundation/index.html

**Summary** To provide financial assistance to women in Missouri who plan to attend college in any state.

**Eligibility** This program is open to women in Missouri who have been accepted into an accredited program or course of study in any state to upgrade their skills and/or complete education for career advancement. Along with their application, they must submit brief statements on the following: their achievements and/or specific recognitions in their field of endeavor; professional and/or civic affiliations; present and long-range career goals; how they plan to participate in and contribute to their community upon completion of their program of study; why they feel they would make a good recipient; and any special circumstances that may have influenced their ability to continue or complete their education. They must also demonstrate financial need and U.S. citizenship.

**Financial data** The stipend is $1,000.

**Duration** 1 year.

**Number awarded** Varies each year; recently, 4 of these scholarships were awarded.

**Deadline** January of each year.

## [104]
## CADY MCDONNELL MEMORIAL SCHOLARSHIP

National Society of Professional Surveyors
Attn: Scholarships
5119 Pegasus Court, Suite Q
Frederick, MD 21704
(240) 439-4615, ext. 105              Fax: (240) 439-4952
E-mail: trisha.milbun@nsps.us.com
Web: www.acsm.net

**Summary** To provide financial assistance for undergraduate study in surveying to female members of the National Society of Professional Surveyors (NSPS) from designated western states.

**Eligibility** This program is open to women who are NSPS members and enrolled full or part time at a 2- or 4-year college or university in any state. Applicants must be residents of Alaska, Arizona, California, Colorado, Hawaii, Idaho, Montana, Nevada, New Mexico, Oregon, Utah, Washington, or Wyoming. They must be majoring in surveying or a closely-related program (e.g., mapping, surveying engineering, geographic information systems, geodetic science). Along with their application, they must submit a statement describing their educational objectives, future plans for study or research, professional activities, and financial need. Selection is based on that statement (30%), academic record (30%), letters of recommendation (20%), and professional activities (20%); if 2 or more applicants are judged equal based on those criteria, financial need might be considered.

**Financial data** The stipend is $1,000.

**Duration** 1 year.

**Additional information** This program was previously offered by the American Congress on Surveying and Mapping (ACSM), which merged with the NSPS in 2012.

**Number awarded** 1 each year.

**Deadline** February of each year.

## [105]
## CALDER SUMMER UNDERGRADUATE RESEARCH PROGRAM

Fordham University
Attn: Louis Calder Center Biological Field Station
53 Whippoorwill Road
P.O. Box 887
Armonk, NY 10504
(914) 273-3078, ext. 10          Fax: (914) 273-2167
E-mail: REUatCalder@fordham.edu
Web: www.fordham.edu

**Summary** To provide an opportunity for undergraduates (particularly women, underrepresented minorities, and individuals with disabilities) to pursue summer research activities in biology at Fordham University's Louis Calder Center Biological Field Station.

**Eligibility** This program is open to undergraduates interested in conducting a summer research project of their own design at the center. Applicants must be U.S. citizens, nationals, or permanent residents. Fields of interest must relate to the activities of staff who will serve as mentors on the projects; those include forest ecology, limnology, wildlife ecology, microbial ecology, Lyme disease, insect-plant interactions, evolutionary ecology, and the effects of urbanization on ecosystem processes. Applications from underrepresented minorities (African Americans, Hispanics, American Indians, Native Hawaiians, Pacific Islanders, and Alaska Natives), persons with disabilities, and women are especially encouraged.

**Financial data** The program provides a stipend of $5,000, housing on the site, and support for research supplies and local travel.

**Duration** 10 weeks during the summer.

**Additional information** This program has operated since 1967 with support from the Research Experience for Undergraduates (REU) program of the National Science Foundation.

**Number awarded** Up to 10 each year.

**Deadline** February of each year.

## [106]
## CALIFORNIA LEGION AUXILIARY PAST DEPARTMENT PRESIDENT'S JUNIOR SCHOLARSHIP

American Legion Auxiliary
Department of California
205 13th Street, Suite 3300
San Francisco, CA 94103-2461
(415) 861-5092          Fax: (415) 861-8365
E-mail: calegionaux@calegionaux.org
Web: www.calegionaux.org/scholarships.htm

**Summary** To provide financial assistance for college to the daughters and other female descendants of California veterans who are active in the American Legion Junior Auxiliary.

**Eligibility** This program is open to the daughters, granddaughters, and great- granddaughters of veterans who served during wartime. Applicants must be in their senior year at an accredited high school, must have been members of the Junior Auxiliary for at least 3 consecutive years, and must be residents of California (if eligibility for Junior Auxiliary membership is by a current member of the American Legion or Auxiliary in California, the applicant may reside elsewhere). They must be planning to attend college in California. Selection is based on scholastic merit (20%); active participation in Junior Auxiliary (15%); record of service or volunteerism within the applicant's community, school, and/or unit (35%); a brief description of the applicant's desire to pursue a higher education (15%); and 3 letters of reference (15%).

**Financial data** The stipend depends on the availability of funds but ranges from $300 to $1,000.

**Duration** 1 year.

**Number awarded** 1 each year.

**Deadline** April of each year.

## [107]
## CALIFORNIA P.E.O. SELECTED SCHOLARSHIPS

P.E.O. Foundation-California State Chapter
c/o Lynne Miller, Scholarship Committee Chair
1875 Los Altos
Clovis, CA 93611
(559) 709-6123          E-mail: peoca.rgw@gmail.com
Web: www.peocalifornia.org

**Summary** To provide financial assistance to female residents of California attending college or graduate school in any state.

**Eligibility** This program is open to female residents of California who have completed 4 years of high school (or the equivalent); are enrolled at or accepted by an accredited college, university, vocational school, or graduate school in any state; and have an excellent academic record. Selection is based on financial need, character, academic ability, and school and community activities. Some awards include additional requirements.

**Financial data** Stipends recently ranged from $400 to $2,500.

**Duration** 1 year; may be renewed for up to 3 additional years.

**Additional information** This program includes the following named scholarships: the Barbara Furse Mackey Scholarship (for women whose education has been interrupted); the Beverly Dye Anderson Scholarship (for the fields of teaching or health care); the Marjorie M. McDonald P.E.O. Scholarship (for women who are continuing their education after a long hiatus from school); the Ora Keck Scholarship (for women who are preparing for a career in music or the fine arts); the Phyllis J. Van Deventer Scholarship (for women who are preparing for a career in music performance or music education); the Jean Gower Scholarship (for women preparing for a career in education); the Helen D. Thompson Memorial Scholarship (for women studying music or fine arts); the Stella May Nau Scholarship (for women who are interested in reentering the job market); the Linda Jones Memorial Fine Arts Scholarship (for women studying fine arts); the Polly Thompson Memorial Music Scholarship (for women studying music); the Ruby W. Henry Scholarship; the Jean W. Gratiot Scholarship; the Pearl Prime Scholarship; the Helen Beardsley Scholarship; the Chapter GA Scholarship; and the Nearly New Scholarship.

**Number awarded** Varies each year; recently, 43 of these scholarships were awarded.

**Deadline** January of each year.

## [108]
## CAMMER-HILL GRANT

Wisconsin Women of Color Network, Inc.
Attn: Scholarship Committee
P.O. Box 2337
Madison, WI 53701-2337
E-mail: contact@womenofcolornetwork-wis.org
Web: www.womenofcolornetwork-wis.org/scholarship.html

**Summary** To provide financial assistance for vocation/technical school or community college to adult women of color from Wisconsin.

**Eligibility** This program is open to residents of Wisconsin who are adult women of color planning to continue their education at a vocational/technical school or community college in any state. Applicants must be a member of 1 of the following groups: African American, Asian, American Indian, or Hispanic. They must be able to demonstrate financial need. Along with their application, they must submit a 1-page essay on how this scholarship will help them accomplish their educational goal. U.S. citizenship is required.

**Financial data** A stipend is awarded (amount not specified).

**Duration** 1 year.

**Additional information** This program began in 1994.

**Number awarded** 1 each year.

**Deadline** May of each year.

## [109]
## CAPTAIN SALLY TOMPKINS NURSING AND APPLIED HEALTH SCIENCES SCHOLARSHIP

United Daughters of the Confederacy-Virginia Division
c/o Barbara Joyner, Second Vice President
8219 Seaview Drive
Chesterfield, VA 23838-5163
E-mail: bobbielou-udc@comcast.net
Web: vaudc.org

**Summary** To provide financial assistance for college to women who are Confederate descendants from Virginia and working on a degree in nursing at a school in the state.

**Eligibility** This program is open to women residents of Virginia interested in working on a degree in nursing at a school in the state. Applicants must be 1) lineal descendants of Confederates; or 2) collateral descendants and also members of the Children of the Confederacy or the United Daughters of the Confederacy. They must submit proof of the Confederate military record of at least 1 ancestor, with the company and regiment in which he served. They must also submit a personal letter pledging to make the best possible use of the scholarship; describing their health, social, family, religious, and fraternal connections within the community; and reflecting on what a Southern heritage means to them. They must have a GPA of 3.0 or higher and be able to demonstrate financial need.

**Financial data** The amount of the stipend depends on the availability of funds. Payment is made directly to the college or university the recipient attends.

**Duration** 1 year; may be renewed up to 3 additional years if the recipient maintains a GPA of 3.0 or higher.

**Number awarded** This scholarship is offered whenever a prior recipient graduates or is no longer eligible.

**Deadline** April of the years in which a scholarship is available.

## [110]
## CAPTURE THE DREAM SINGLE PARENT SCHOLARSHIP

Capture the Dream, Inc.
Attn: Scholarship Program
484 Lake Park Avenue, Suite 15
Oakland, CA 94610
(510) 343-3635        E-mail: info@capturethedream.org
Web: www.capturethedream.org/programs/scholarship.php

**Summary** To provide financial assistance to residents of California who are single parents and planning to attend college in any state.

**Eligibility** This program is open to California residents who are graduating high school seniors or current full-time undergraduates at 2- or 4-year colleges and universities in any state. Applicants must be U.S. citizens or permanent residents and have at least 1 birth child in their custody. Along with their application, they must submit a 1,000-word essay on why they should be selected to receive this scholarship, using their experiences within school, work, and home to display the challenges they have faced as a single parent and how they overcame adversity to exemplify a leader. They should also explain how their career goals and future aspirations will build them as a future community leader. Selection is based on academic performance, community service, leadership history, professional recommendations, and financial need.

**Financial data** The stipend is $1,000.

**Duration** 1 year.

**Additional information** This program is sponsored by the PG&E Women's Network Employee Association.

**Number awarded** 1 or more each year.

**Deadline** July of each year.

## [111]
## CAREER ADVANCEMENT SCHOLARSHIPS

Business and Professional Women's Foundation
Attn: Scholarship Program
1718 M Street, N.W., Suite 148
Washington, DC 20036
(202) 293-1100 Fax: (202) 861-0298
E-mail: foundation@bpwfoundation.org
Web: www.bpwfoundation.org/index.php/about/scholarships

**Summary** To provide financial assistance for college to mature women who are interested in completing a bachelor's degree in a field of science, technology, engineering, or mathematics (STEM).

**Eligibility** This program is open to women who are at least 25 years of age, citizens of the United States, and within 2 years of completing a bachelor's degree in a field of STEM. They must apply through a participating partner organization of the Business and Professional Women's (BPW) Foundation at the state or local level. Selection is based on academics (20%), career objectives (25%), responsibility and involvement, e.g., paid employment, domestic or family responsibilities (15%), disadvantage, e.g., financial, situational, physical or mental, medical (35%), and special considerations, e.g., military veteran (5%).

**Financial data** Stipends are at least $1,000.

**Duration** 1 year.

**Additional information** This program began in 1969. For a list of partner organizations, contact the BPW Foundation.

**Number awarded** Varies each year; recently, 12 of these scholarships (including 1 for a veteran) were awarded.

**Deadline** Each partner organization sets its own deadline.

## [112]
## CARLOZZI FAMILY SCHOLARSHIP

New York Women in Communications, Inc.
Attn: NYWICI Foundation
355 Lexington Avenue, 15th Floor
New York, NY 10017-6603
(212) 297-2133 Fax: (212) 370-9047
E-mail: nywicipr@nywici.org
Web: www.nywici.org/foundation/scholarships

**Summary** To provide financial assistance to female residents of designated eastern states who are working on an undergraduate degree in communications at a college in any state.

**Eligibility** This program is open to women who are residents of New York, New Jersey, Connecticut, or Pennsylvania and currently enrolled as undergraduates at a college or university in any state. Also eligible are women who reside outside the 4 states but are currently enrolled at a college or university within 1 of the 5 boroughs of New York City. All applicants must be working on a degree in a communications-related field (e.g., advertising, broadcasting, communications, English, film, journalism, marketing, digital media, public relations) and be an accomplished writer. They must have a GPA of 3.2 or higher. Along with their application, they must submit a 2-page resume; a personal essay of 300 words on an assigned topic that changes annually; 2 letters of recommendation; and an official transcript. Selection is based on academic record, need, demonstrated leadership, participation in school and community activities, honors and other awards or recognition, work experience, goals and aspirations, and unusual personal and/or family circumstances. U.S. citizenship is required.

**Financial data** The stipend ranges up to $10,000.

**Duration** 1 year.

**Number awarded** 1 each year.

**Deadline** January of each year.

## [113]
## CAROL STEPHENS REGION F SCHOLARSHIP

Society of Women Engineers
Attn: Scholarship Selection Committee
203 North LaSalle Street, Suite 1675
Chicago, IL 60601-1269
(312) 596-5223 Toll Free: (877) SWE-INFO
Fax: (312) 644-8557 E-mail: scholarships@swe.org
Web: societyofwomenengineers.swe.org

**Summary** To provide financial assistance to members of the Society of Women Engineers (SWE) working on an undergraduate or graduate degree in engineering or computer science at a school in its Region F (New England states and eastern New York).

**Eligibility** This program is open to members of the society who will be sophomores, juniors, seniors, or graduate students at ABET-accredited colleges and universities. First preference is given to applicants who attend college or graduate school in the New England states or upstate New York; second preference is given to students who reside in New England or upstate New York. Applicants must be working full time on a degree in computer science or engineering and have a GPA of 3.0 or higher. Financial need is considered in the selection process. U.S. citizenship or permanent resident status is required.

**Financial data** The stipend is $1,000.

**Duration** 1 year.

**Number awarded** 1 each year.

**Deadline** February of each year.

## [114]
## CAROLYN B. ELMAN NATIONAL UNDERGRADUATE SCHOLARSHIP

American Business Women's Association
Attn: Stephen Bufton Memorial Educational Fund
11050 Roe Avenue, Suite 200
Overland Park, KS 66211
Toll Free: (800) 228-0007
Web: www.sbmef.org/Scholarships.cfm

**Summary** To provide financial assistance to female undergraduate students who are working on a degree in a specified field (the field changes each year).

**Eligibility** This program is open to women who have completed at least 60 credit hours of work on an undergraduate degree. Applicants are not required to be members of the American Business Women's Association. Along with their application, they must submit a 250-word biographical sketch that includes information about their background, activities, honors, work experience, and long-term educational and professional goals. Financial need is not considered in the selection process. Annually, the trustees designate an academic discipline for which the scholarship will be presented that year. U.S. citizenship is required.

**Financial data** The stipend is $5,000 per year. Funds are paid directly to the recipient's institution to be used only for tuition, books, and fees.

**Duration** 2 years.

**Additional information** This program began in 2011 as part of ABWA's Stephen Bufton Memorial Education Fund. The ABWA does not provide the names and addresses of local chapters; it recommends that applicants check with their local Chamber of Commerce, library, or university to see if any chapter has registered a contact's name and number.

**Number awarded** 1 each odd-numbered year.

**Deadline** May of each odd-numbered year.

## [115]
## CATERPILLAR SWE SCHOLARSHIPS

Society of Women Engineers
Attn: Scholarship Selection Committee
203 North LaSalle Street, Suite 1675
Chicago, IL 60601-1269
(312) 596-5223          Toll Free: (877) SWE-INFO
Fax: (312) 644-8557          E-mail: scholarships@swe.org
Web: societyofwomenengineers.swe.org

**Summary** To provide financial assistance to women who are working on an undergraduate or graduate degree in selected fields of engineering or computer science.

**Eligibility** This program is open to women who are sophomores, juniors, seniors, or graduate students at ABET-accredited 4-year colleges and universities. Applicants must be working full time on a degree in computer science or agricultural, chemical, electrical, industrial, manufacturing, materials, or mechanical engineering. They must be U.S. citizens or authorized to work in the United States and have a GPA of 3.0 or higher. Selection is based on merit.

**Financial data** The stipend is $2,400.

**Duration** 1 year.

**Additional information** This program is sponsored by Caterpillar, Inc.

**Number awarded** 3 each year.

**Deadline** February of each year.

## [116]
## CENTRAL INDIANA SECTION SWE SCHOLARSHIPS

Society of Women Engineers-Central Indiana Section
Attn: Scholarship Coordinator
P.O. Box 44450
Indianapolis, IN 46244
E-mail: swe-ci_scholarship@swe.org
Web: www.swe-ci.com/page_id=19

**Summary** To provide financial assistance to women who live or attend college in Indiana and are studying engineering or computer sciences.

**Eligibility** This program is open to women who are residents of Indiana or attending a college or university in the state. Applicants must be sophomores, juniors, or seniors and working full time on a bachelor's degree in an ABET/CSAB-accredited program in engineering or computer sciences. They must have a GPA of 3.0 or higher. Along with their application, they must submit a 500-word essay on the ways in which they are fulfilling the mission of the Society of Women Engineers (SWE): to stimulate women to achieve full

potential in careers as engineers and leaders, expand the image of the engineering profession as a positive force in improving the quality of life, and demonstrate the value of diversity. Financial need may be considered in the selection process.

**Financial data** Stipends are $1,000, $750, or $500.

**Duration** 1 year.

**Additional information** This program began in 2007. The 2 smaller scholarships are sponsored by Rolls-Royce Corporation.

**Number awarded** 3 each year: 1 each at $1,000, $750, and $500.

**Deadline** July of each year.

## [117]
## CENTRAL NEW MEXICO RE-ENTRY SCHOLARSHIP

Society of Women Engineers
Attn: Scholarship Selection Committee
203 North LaSalle Street, Suite 1675
Chicago, IL 60601-1269
(312) 596-5223          Toll Free: (877) SWE-INFO
Fax: (312) 644-8557          E-mail: scholarships@swe.org
Web: societyofwomenengineers.swe.org

**Summary** To provide financial assistance to members of the Society of Women Engineers (SWE) from any state who are reentering college or graduate school in New Mexico to work on a degree in engineering or computer science.

**Eligibility** This program is open to members of the society who are sophomores, juniors, seniors, or graduate students at an ABET-accredited college, university, or 4-year engineering technology program in New Mexico. Applicants must be returning to college or graduate school after an absence of several years to work on a degree in computer science or engineering. They must have a GPA of 3.0 or higher. Selection is based on merit. U.S. citizenship or permanent resident status is required.

**Financial data** The stipend is $1,250 per year.

**Duration** 1 year; may be renewed up to 5 additional years.

**Additional information** This program began in 2005 by the Central New Mexico section of SWE.

**Number awarded** 1 each year.

**Deadline** February of each year.

## [118]
## CHARLIE ADAMS ENDOWED STUDENT SCHOLARSHIPS

North Carolina High School Athletic Association
Attn: Assistant Director Grants and Fundraising
222 Finley Golf Course Road
P.O. Box 3216
Chapel Hill, NC 27515-3216
(919) 240-7371          Fax: (919) 240-7399
E-mail: mary@nchsaa.org
Web: www.nchsaa.org

**Summary** To provide financial assistance to high school seniors in North Carolina who have participated in female cross country or male wrestling and plan to attend college in any state.

**Eligibility** This program is open to seniors graduating from high schools that are members of the North Carolina High

School Athletic Association (NCHSAA). Males must have participated on their varsity wrestling team; females must have participated on their varsity cross country team. Applicants must have a clean disciplinary record (both school and athletics related) and demonstrated athletic success. They must be planning to attend an accredited college, university, or community college in any state. Along with their application, they must submit a 2-page essay addressing how athletic participation has influenced their decision-making and the importance of athletics in teaching independence, unselfishness, and honesty. Financial need is not considered in the selection process.

**Financial data** The stipend is $1,500.

**Duration** 1 year; nonrenewable.

**Additional information** This program began in 2010.

**Number awarded** 2 each year: 1 to a male and 1 to a female.

**Deadline** March of each year.

## [119]
## CHARLINE CHILSON SCHOLARSHIPS

Delta Zeta Sorority
Attn: Foundation Coordinator
202 East Church Street
Oxford, OH 45056
(513) 523-7597                    Fax: (513) 523-1921
E-mail: DZFoundation@dzshq.com
Web: www.deltazeta.org

**Summary** To provide financial assistance to members of Delta Zeta Sorority working on an undergraduate or graduate degree in science.

**Eligibility** This program is open to upper-division and graduate members of the sorority who have a high GPA in their major. Applicants must be working on a degree in science. Along with their application, they must submit an official transcript, a statement of their career goals, information on their service to the sorority, documentation of campus activities and/or community involvement, a list of academic honors, and an explanation of their financial need.

**Financial data** The stipend ranges from $500 to $2,500 for undergraduates or from $1,000 to $15,000 for graduate students, depending on the availability of funds.

**Duration** 1 year; nonrenewable.

**Number awarded** Varies each year; recently, 12 of these scholarships were awarded: 6 to undergraduates and 6 to graduate students.

**Deadline** February of each year.

## [120]
## CHERYL A. RUGGIERO SCHOLARSHIP

Rhode Island Society of Certified Public Accountants
45 Royal Little Drive
Providence, RI 02904
(401) 331-5720                    Fax: (401) 454-5780
E-mail: info@riscpa.org
Web: student.riscpa.org

**Summary** To provide financial assistance to female undergraduate and graduate students from Rhode Island who are working on a degree in accounting at a school in any state.

**Eligibility** This program is open to female residents of Rhode Island who are working on an undergraduate or grad-

uate degree in public accounting at a school in any state. Applicants must be U.S. citizens who have a GPA of 3.0 or higher. Selection is based on demonstrated potential to become a valued member of the public accounting profession. Finalists are interviewed.

**Financial data** The stipend is $1,250.

**Duration** 1 year.

**Additional information** This program began in 2005.

**Number awarded** 1 each year.

**Deadline** January of each year.

## [121]
## CHERYL DANT HENNESY SCHOLARSHIP

National FFA Organization
Attn: Scholarship Office
6060 FFA Drive
P.O. Box 68960
Indianapolis, IN 46268-0960
(317) 802-4419                    Fax: (317) 802-5419
E-mail: scholarships@ffa.org
Web: www.ffa.org

**Summary** To provide financial assistance to female FFA members from Kentucky, Georgia, or Tennessee who plan to attend college in any state.

**Eligibility** This program is open to female members who are seniors graduating from high schools in Kentucky, Georgia, or Tennessee. Applicants must be interested in working on a 2- or 4-year degree in any area of study at a college or university in any state. They must demonstrate financial need and personal motivation. Selection is based on academic achievement (10 points for GPA, 10 points for SAT or ACT score, 10 points for class rank), leadership in FFA activities (30 points), leadership in community activities (10 points), and participation in the Supervised Agricultural Experience (SAE) program (30 points). U.S. citizenship is required.

**Financial data** The stipend is $1,250 per year.

**Duration** 1 year; may be renewed up to 3 additional years if the recipient maintains a GPA of 2.0 or higher.

**Number awarded** Approximately 3 each year.

**Deadline** February of each year.

## [122]
## CHERYL KRAFF-COOPER, M.D. GIRAFFE FUND EMERGENCY GRANTS FOR UNDERGRADUATES

Alpha Epsilon Phi
Attn: AEPhi Foundation
11 Lake Avenue Extension, Suite 1A
Danbury, CT 06811
(203) 748-0029                    Fax: (203) 748-0039
E-mail: aephifoundation@aephi.org
Web: www.aephi.org/foundation/scholarships

**Summary** To provide assistance to undergraduate members of Alpha Epsilon Phi who are facing severe financial emergencies and need money to continue their education.

**Eligibility** This program is open to undergraduate members of the sorority who can demonstrate that they will be forced to withdraw from school if they do not receive emergency assistance. Applicants must submit statements on their career and professional objectives, academic or professional honors, other honors received, scholarships and loans received, Alpha Epsilon Phi activities, college and community activities, work experience, and why they are in need of emergency assistance.

**Financial data** Stipends are $1,000; funds may be used only for tuition, fees, and books.

**Duration** These are 1-time grants.

**Number awarded** Several each year.

**Deadline** Applications may be submitted at any time.

## [123]
## CHUNGHI HONG PARK SCHOLARSHIPS

Korean-American Scientists and Engineers Association
Attn: Scholarship Committee
1952 Gallows Drive, Suite 300
Vienna, VA 22182
(703) 748-1221          Fax: (703) 748-1331
E-mail: admin@ksea.org
Web: scholarship.ksea.org/InfoUndergraduate.aspx

**Summary** To provide financial assistance to women who are undergraduate student members of the Korean-American Scientists and Engineers Association (KSEA).

**Eligibility** This program is open to women who are Korean American undergraduate students, are KSEA members, have completed at least 2 semesters as a college student, and are majoring in science, engineering, or a related field. Along with their application, they must submit an essay on a topic that changes annually but relates to science or engineering. Selection is based on the essay (20%), KSEA activities and community service (30%), recommendation letters (20%), and academic performance (30%).

**Financial data** The stipend is $1,000.

**Duration** 1 year.

**Number awarded** 2 each year.

**Deadline** March of each year.

## [124]
## CINCH ACADEMIC FINALS COWBOY AND COWGIRL SCHOLARSHIPS

National High School Rodeo Association
Attn: NHSR Foundation
4503 Sheila Court
Lilburn, GA 30047
(404) 386-2564          Fax: (770) 279-0972
E-mail: info@nhsrfoundation.com
Web: www.nhsrfoundation.com/scholarship.aspx

**Summary** To provide financial assistance for college to high school seniors who compete in the National High School Rodeo Association's (NHSRA) national rodeo (females and males are judged separately).

**Eligibility** This program is open to high school seniors who have qualified for the NHSRA finals by winning, first, in their state rodeos and then presenting a scholarship application in person prior to the national rodeo. Along with their application, they must also present a copy of their high school transcript and a 100-word description of why this scholarship would make a difference to them. In addition, applicants must appear before an interview committee during the national rodeo. They are asked to answer questions on estimated school expenses, where they want to be in 5 years, their need for this scholarship, and other related topics. Boys and girls are judged separately for these scholarships.

**Financial data** The stipend is $3,000.

**Duration** 1 year.

**Additional information** This program is sponsored by Cinch Jeans and Shirts.

**Number awarded** 2 each year: 1 for a boy and 1 for a girl.

**Deadline** July of each year.

## [125]
## CISCO/UNCF SCHOLARS PROGRAM

United Negro College Fund
Attn: Scholarships and Grants Department
8260 Willow Oaks Corporate Drive
P.O. Box 10444
Fairfax, VA 22031-8044
(703) 205-3466          Toll Free: (800) 331-2244
Fax: (703) 205-3574
Web: www.uncf.org

**Summary** To provide financial assistance and work experience to African American students (especially women) who are majoring in electrical engineering or computer science at designated colleges and universities, including members of the United Negro College Fund (UNCF).

**Eligibility** This program is open to African American students in their sophomore year at designated colleges and universities. Applicants must be majoring in electrical engineering or computer science and have a GPA of 3.2 or higher. Special consideration is given to women and to students who have demonstrated leadership through community service. Along with their application, they must submit a current academic transcript, current resume, nomination letter from a member of the faculty, financial need statement, and 1-page essay of career interest and personal goals. Selection is based on strength of the essays, nominations, community service record, and academic profile. Final selection is made by advisers from Cisco Systems, the program's sponsor.

**Financial data** The scholarship stipend is $4,000. Recipients may also be offered paid internships.

**Duration** 2 years (the junior and senior years).

**Additional information** Currently, the designated UNCF institutions are Claflin University, Clark Atlanta University, Dillard University, Jarvis Christian College, Johnson C. Smith University, Livingstone College, Morehouse College, Morgan State University, Paul Quinn College, Rust College, Shaw University, Spelman College, St. Augustine's College, Wiley College, and Xavier University. The other participating universities are California Polytechnic State University at San Luis Obispo, Georgia Institute of Technology, Grambling State University, Massachusetts Institute of Technology, North Carolina Central University, North Carolina State University, North Carolina A&T State University, Prairie View A&M University, San Jose State University, Stanford University, University of California at Berkeley, University of Illinois at Urbana-Champaign, University of Michigan, and University of Texas at Austin. This program is sponsored by Cisco Systems, Inc.

**Number awarded** 10 each year.

**Deadline** April of each year.

**[126]**
## CISCO'S FUTURE SCHOLARSHIPS

Society of Women Engineers
Attn: Scholarship Selection Committee
203 North LaSalle Street, Suite 1675
Chicago, IL 60601-1269
(312) 596-5223           Toll Free: (877) SWE-INFO
Fax: (312) 644-8557      E-mail: scholarships@swe.org
Web: societyofwomenengineers.swe.org

**Summary** To provide financial assistance to undergraduate women, especially members of underrepresented groups, who are members of the Society of Women Engineers (SWE) and majoring in designated engineering specialties.

**Eligibility** This program is open to SWE members who are entering their sophomore or junior year at a 4-year ABET-accredited college or university. Preference is given to members of underrepresented ethnic or racial groups, candidates with disabilities, and veterans. Applicants must be working full time on a degree in computer science or computer or electrical engineering and have a GPA of 3.0 or higher. They must be U.S. citizens or permanent residents. Financial need is considered in the selection process.

**Financial data** The stipend is $5,000.

**Duration** 1 year.

**Additional information** This program is sponsored by Cisco Systems.

**Number awarded** 5 each year.

**Deadline** February of each year.

**[127]**
## CLOROX SUENA SIN LIMITES MOTHERS SCHOLARSHIPS

Hispanic Scholarship Fund
Attn: Selection Committee
1411 West 190th Street, Suite 325
Gardena, CA 90248
Toll Free: (877) HSF-INFO      E-mail: scholar1@hsf.net
Web: www.hsf.net/Scholarship-Programs.aspx

**Summary** To provide financial assistance to Hispanic college students who are mothers and majoring in any field.

**Eligibility** This program is open to U.S. citizens and permanent residents (must have a permanent resident card or a passport stamped I-551) who are of Hispanic heritage. Applicants must be mothers between 25 and 45 years of age who have completed at least 6 units as a part-time or full-time undergraduate at a 2- or 4-year college, university, or online accredited institution in the United States, Puerto Rico, Guam, or the U.S. Virgin Islands. They must have a GPA of 3.0 or higher, but they may be majoring in any field. Along with their application, they must submit an essay describing how the scholarship will make their biggest dreams a reality and how that will allow them to give back to their family and community. Selection is based on academic achievement, personal strengths, leadership, and financial need.

**Financial data** The stipend is $10,000.

**Duration** 1 year.

**Additional information** This program began in 2012 by the Clorox Company as part of its "Sueña Sin Lìmites" (Dream Without Limits) program.

**Number awarded** 6 each year.

**Deadline** December of each year.

**[128]**
## COCHRAN/GREENE SCHOLARSHIP

National Naval Officers Association-Washington, D.C. Chapter
Attn: Scholarship Program
2701 Park Center Drive, A1108
Alexandria, VA 22302
(703) 566-3840           Fax: (703) 566-3813
E-mail: Stephen.Williams@Navy.mil
Web: dcnnoa.memberlodge.com

**Summary** To provide financial assistance to female minority high school seniors from the Washington, D.C. area who are interested in attending college in any state.

**Eligibility** This program is open to female minority seniors graduating from high schools in the Washington, D.C. metropolitan area who plan to enroll full time at an accredited 2- or 4-year college or university in any state. Applicants must have a GPA of 2.5 or higher and be U.S. citizens or permanent residents. Selection is based on academic achievement, community involvement, and financial need.

**Financial data** The stipend is $1,500.

**Duration** 1 year; nonrenewable.

**Additional information** Recipients are not required to join or affiliate with the military in any way.

**Number awarded** 1 each year.

**Deadline** March of each year.

**[129]**
## COLDER PRODUCTS COMPANY MINNESOTA SWE SCHOLARSHIP

Society of Women Engineers-Minnesota Section
Attn: Scholarship Committee
P.O. Box 582813
Minneapolis, MN 55458-2813
E-mail: scholarships@swe-mn.org
Web: www.swe-mn.org/scholarships.html

**Summary** To provide financial assistance to women from any state working on an undergraduate or graduate degree in mechanical engineering at colleges and universities in Minnesota, North Dakota, and South Dakota.

**Eligibility** This program is open to female undergraduate and graduate students at ABET-accredited engineering programs in Minnesota, North Dakota, or South Dakota. Applicants must be working full time on a degree in mechanical engineering. Along with their application, they must submit a short paragraph describing how they plan to utilize their engineering skills after they graduate. Selection is based on potential to succeed as an engineer (20 points), communication skills (10 points), extracurricular or community involvement and leadership skills (10 points), demonstrated successful work experience (10 points), and academic success (5 points).

**Financial data** The stipend is $1,000.

**Duration** 1 year.

**Additional information** This program is sponsored by Colder Products Company.

**Number awarded** 1 each year.

**Deadline** March of each year.

## [130]
## COLLABORATIVE RESEARCH EXPERIENCE FOR UNDERGRADUATES IN COMPUTER SCIENCE AND ENGINEERING

Computing Research Association
1828 L Street, N.W., Suite 800
Washington, DC 20036-5104
(202) 234-2111      Fax: (202) 667-1066
E-mail: creu@cra.org
Web: cra-w.org/undergraduate

**Summary** To provide funding to female and underrepresented minority undergraduate students who are interested in conducting a research project in computer science or engineering.

**Eligibility** This program is open to teams of 2 or 4 undergraduates who have completed 2 years of study, including at least 4 courses in computer science or computer engineering, at a college or university in the United States. Applicants must be interested in conducting a research project directly related to computer science or computer engineering. They must apply jointly with 1 or 2 sponsoring faculty members. Teams consisting of all women or all underrepresented minorities are especially encouraged to apply; teams may also include students from non-underrepresented groups, but financial support is available only to underrepresented students. U.S. citizenship or permanent resident status is required.

**Financial data** The program provides a stipend of $3,000 for the academic year. Students who wish to participate in an optional summer extension receive an additional stipend of $4,000. Additional funding up to $1,500 per team may be available for purchase of supporting materials and/or travel to conferences to present the work.

**Duration** 1 academic year plus an optional summer extension.

**Additional information** This program is sponsored by the Computing Research Association's Committee on the Status of Women in Computing Research (CRA-W) and the Coalition to Diversify Computing (CDC) in cooperation with the National Science Foundation.

**Number awarded** Varies each year; recently, 21 teams of students received support from this program.

**Deadline** May of each year.

## [131]
## COLLEEN CONLEY MEMORIAL SCHOLARSHIP

New Mexico Engineering Foundation
Attn: Scholarship Chair
P.O. Box 3828
Albuquerque, NM 87190-3828
(505) 615-1800      E-mail: info@nmef.net
Web: www.nmef.net/?section=scholarship

**Summary** To provide financial assistance to female high school seniors in New Mexico who plan to study engineering at a college or university in any state.

**Eligibility** This program is open to female seniors graduating from high schools in New Mexico who are planning to enroll at a college or university in any state and major in engineering, engineering technology, or a related field (including scientific disciplines). Applicants must have a GPA of 3.0 or higher. Along with their application, they must submit a 300-

word letter discussing their interest in science or engineering and their future plans. Financial need is not considered in the selection process. Preference is given to applicants who are the first member of their family to attend college.

**Financial data** The stipend is $1,000.

**Duration** 1 year; may be renewed up to 3 additional years, provided the recipient remains enrolled at least half time and maintains a GPA of 2.5 or higher.

**Additional information** This program is sponsored by the Central New Mexico Section of the Society of Women Engineers.

**Number awarded** 1 each year.

**Deadline** February of each year.

## [132]
## COLORADO LEGION AUXILIARY DEPARTMENT PRESIDENT'S SCHOLARSHIP FOR JUNIOR AUXILIARY MEMBERS

American Legion Auxiliary
Department of Colorado
7465 East First Avenue, Suite D
Denver, CO 80230
(303) 367-5388      Fax: (303) 367-5388
E-mail: dept-sec@alacolorado.com
Web: www.alacolorado.com/Forms.html

**Summary** To provide financial assistance to junior members of the American Legion Auxiliary in Colorado who plan to attend college in the state.

**Eligibility** This program is open to seniors at high schools in Colorado who have been junior members of the auxiliary for the past 3 years. Applicants must be Colorado residents planning to attend college in the state. Along with their application, they must submit a 1,000-word essay on the topic, "My Obligations as an American." Selection is based on character (20%), Americanism (20%), leadership (20%), scholarship (20%), and financial need (20%).

**Financial data** The stipend is $1,000.

**Duration** 1 year; nonrenewable.

**Number awarded** 1 each year.

**Deadline** March of each year.

## [133]
## COLORADO WOMEN'S EDUCATION FOUNDATION SCHOLARSHIPS

Colorado Federation of Business and Professional Women
Attn: Colorado Women's Education Foundation
P.O. Box 1189
Boulder, CO 80306-1189
(303) 443-2573      Fax: (720) 564-0397
E-mail: office@cwef.org
Web: cwef.org/scholarships/how-to-apply

**Summary** To provide financial assistance for college to mature women residing in Colorado.

**Eligibility** This program is open to women 25 years of age and older who are enrolled at an accredited Colorado college, university, or vocational school. Applicants must be U.S. citizens who have resided in Colorado for at least 12 months. They must have a GPA of 3.0 or higher. Along with their application, they must submit a copy of their most recent high school or college transcript, proof of Colorado residency and

U.S. citizenship, a statement of their educational and career goals, 2 letters of recommendation, and documentation of financial need.

**Financial data** Stipends range from $250 to $1,000. Funds are to be used for tuition, fees, or books.

**Duration** 1 semester; recipients may reapply.

**Number awarded** Varies each year; recently, 22 of these scholarships were awarded.

**Deadline** May of each year for fall semester; October of each year for spring semester.

## [134]
## COMPUTING RESEARCH ASSOCIATION OUTSTANDING UNDERGRADUATE RESEARCH AWARD

Computing Research Association
1828 L Street, N.W., Suite 800
Washington, DC 20036-5104
(202) 234-2111          Fax: (202) 667-1066
E-mail: awards@cra.org
Web: www.cra.org/awards/undergrad

**Summary** To recognize and reward undergraduate students (females and males are judged separately) who show exceptional promise in an area of importance to computing research.

**Eligibility** This award is available to undergraduates at colleges and universities in North America who show outstanding research potential in computing research. Students must be nominated by 2 faculty members and recommended by their department chair. Nomination packages must include the nominee's resume (up to 2 pages), the nominee's transcript, a verification statement signed by the department chair, 2 letters of support, and a 1-page description of the student's research or other achievements. Selection is based primarily on the significance of the student's research contributions; consideration is also given to academic record and service to the computing or broader community. Women and men are judged separately.

**Financial data** The award is $1,000.

**Duration** The awards are presented annually.

**Additional information** This award is sponsored by Microsoft (in odd-numbered years) and Mitsubishi Electric Research Labs (in even-numbered years). The 2 first-prize winners also receive financial assistance to attend a major computing research conference, where the prizes are awarded.

**Number awarded** 2 cash prizes (1 to a woman and 1 to a man) and a number of certificates of honorable mention are presented each year.

**Deadline** March of each year.

## [135]
## CONGRESSIONAL BLACK CAUCUS FOUNDATION ENVIRONMENTAL STUDIES SCHOLARSHIPS

Congressional Black Caucus Foundation, Inc.
Attn: Director, Educational Programs
1720 Massachusetts Avenue, N.W.
Washington, DC 20036
(202) 263-2800          Toll Free: (800) 784-2577
Fax: (202) 775-0773     E-mail: scholarships@cbcfinc.org
Web: www.cbcfinc.org/scholarships.html

**Summary** To provide financial assistance to minority and female upper-division students who are working on a degree in environmental science.

**Eligibility** This program is open to minorities and women who are currently enrolled as full-time juniors at a 4-year college or university. Applicants must be working on a degree in environmental science and have a GPA of 2.5 or higher. They must be able to demonstrate understanding and acceptance of ServiceMaster's core values. Along with their application, they must submit a personal statement of 500 to 1,000 words on 1) their future goals, major field of study, and how that field of study will help them to achieve their future career goals; 2) involvement in school activities, community and public service, hobbies, and sports; 3) how receiving this award will affect their current and future plans; and 4) other experiences, skills, or qualifications. They must also be able to demonstrate financial need, leadership ability, and participation in community service activities. Preference is given to students who plan to complete a 4-year degree and work in an underserved community. U.S. citizenship or permanent resident status is required.

**Financial data** The stipend is $10,000. Funds are paid directly to the student's institution.

**Duration** 1 year.

**Additional information** This program is sponsored by ServiceMaster.

**Number awarded** 2 each year.

**Deadline** March of each year.

## [136]
## CONNECTICUT CHAPTER AFWA SCHOLARSHIP

Accounting and Financial Women's Alliance-Connecticut Chapter
c/o Jenna Bennetti, Scholarship Committee Chair
Whittlesey & Hadley, P.C.
147 Charter Oak Avenue
Hartford, CT 06106-5100
(860) 522-3111          E-mail: scholarship@aswact.org
Web: www.aswact.org

**Summary** To provide financial assistance to women from Connecticut working on an undergraduate degree in accounting at a school in the state.

**Eligibility** This program is open to women who are residents of Connecticut and enrolled at a college or university in the state as a sophomore, junior, or senior. Applicants must be preparing for a career in accounting. Along with their application, they must submit a short statement on their career goals and objectives. Financial need is considered in the selection process.

**Financial data**   Stipends range from $500 to $1,500. Funds are paid directly to the student.

**Duration**   1 year.

**Number awarded**   Varies each year; recently, 2 of these scholarships were awarded.

**Deadline**   October of each year.

## [137]
## CONNECTICUT ELKS ASSOCIATION GIRL SCOUT GOLD AWARD SCHOLARSHIP

Girl Scouts of Connecticut
Attn: Program Department
20 Washington Avenue
North Haven, CT 06437
(203) 239-2922, ext. 3310
Toll Free: (800) 922-2770 (within CT)
E-mail: program@gsoft.org
Web: www.gsoft.org

**Summary**   To provide financial assistance to Girl Scouts in Connecticut who plan to attend college in any state.

**Eligibility**   This program is open to high school seniors who are registered Girl Scouts in Connecticut and planning to attend college in any state. Applicants must have earned the Gold Award. They must be able to demonstrate leadership ability and a strong record of participation in activities in and outside of Girl Scouts.

**Financial data**   The stipend is $1,000.

**Duration**   1 year.

**Additional information**   This program is sponsored by the Connecticut Elks Association.

**Number awarded**   1 each year.

**Deadline**   March of each year.

## [138]
## CONTINUING EDUCATION FOR ADULT WOMEN SCHOLARSHIP

American Baptist Women's Ministries of Wisconsin
c/o Nancy Byleen, Scholarship Committee Chair
9322 West Garden Court
Hales Corners, WI 53130
Web: www.abcofwi.org/abwinfo.htm

**Summary**   To provide financial assistance to adult female members of American Baptist Churches in Wisconsin who are interested in attending college in any state.

**Eligibility**   This program is open to adult women who are residents of Wisconsin and attending or planning to attend college in any state. Applicants must have been an active member of an American Baptist Church in Wisconsin for the preceding 3 years. The college does not need to be affiliated with the American Baptist Churches USA. Financial need is considered in the selection process.

**Financial data**   A stipend is awarded (amount not specified).

**Duration**   2 or 4 years.

**Number awarded**   1 or more each year.

**Deadline**   February of each year.

## [139]
## CORINNE JEANNINE SCHILLINGS FOUNDATION ACADEMIC SCHOLARSHIPS

Corinne Jeannine Schillings Foundation
10645 Nebraska Street
Frankfort, IL 60423-2223
(815) 534-5598          E-mail: dschillings1@comcast.net
Web: www.cjsfoundation.org/html/academic_study.html

**Summary**   To provide financial assistance to Girl Scouts who plan to study a foreign language in college.

**Eligibility**   This program is open to members of the Girl Scouts who have earned the Silver or Gold Award. Applicants must be enrolled or planning to enroll full time at a 4-year college or university and major or minor in a foreign language. They must have a GPA of 3.0 or higher. Along with their application, they must submit a 5-page essay about themselves, including the impact of Girl Scouting on their life, why they have chosen to major or minor in a foreign language, how they plan to utilize their language skills, and why they feel they should receive this scholarship. Financial need is not considered in the selection process.

**Financial data**   The stipend is $1,500 per year.

**Duration**   1 year; may be renewed up to 3 additional years, provided the recipient maintains a GPA of 3.0 or higher, both overall and in foreign language classes.

**Additional information**   This program began in 2005.

**Number awarded**   Varies each year; recently, this program awarded 13 new and renewal scholarships.

**Deadline**   May of each year.

## [140]
## CORNELL UNIVERSITY SUMMER PROGRAM IN ASTRONOMY AND ASTROPHYSICS

Cornell University
Department of Astronomy
Attn: REU Astronomy Coordinator
510 Space Sciences Building
Ithaca, NY 14853-6801
(607) 255-0288                    Fax: (607) 255-1767
E-mail: pf46@cornell.edu
Web: www.astro.cornell.edu/specialprograms/reu/reu.html

**Summary**   To provide an opportunity for undergraduate students (particularly women, minorities, and persons with disabilities) to work as student assistants on astronomy research projects at Cornell University during the summer.

**Eligibility**   This program is open to undergraduate students who have completed at least 1 year of academic training. Applicants must be interested in working with Cornell University faculty and research staff on projects covering a wide range of disciplines in radio, infrared, and radar astronomy and related theoretical topics. They must be U.S. citizens, nationals, or permanent residents. Applications are especially encouraged from underrepresented minorities, persons with disabilities, and women.

**Financial data**   The stipend is $6,200. Other support includes $1,000 for relocation and housing and up to $1,000 round-trip transportation to Ithaca, New York.

**Duration**   8 weeks during the summer.

**Additional information**   This program is funded by the National Science Foundation as part of its Research Experiences for Undergraduates (REU) Program.

**Number awarded** 8 each year.

**Deadline** February of each year.

## [141]
## CREW NETWORK SCHOLARSHIPS

Commercial Real Estate Women (CREW) Network
1201 Wakarusa Drive, Suite C3
Lawrence, KS 66049
(785) 832-1808                    Fax: (785) 832-1551
E-mail: crewnetwork@crewnetwork.org
Web: crewnetwork.org/CZ_scholarships.aspx?id=257

**Summary** To provide financial assistance to women who are attending college to prepare for a career in commercial real estate.

**Eligibility** This program is open to women who are enrolled as full-time juniors, seniors, or graduate students at a college or university that has an accredited real estate program. If their institution does not have a real estate program, they may be studying another field, as long as they are preparing for a career in commercial real estate. They must have a GPA of 3.0 or higher and be U.S. or Canadian citizens. Along with their application, undergraduates must submit a brief statement about their interest in commercial real estate and their career objectives; graduate students must submit a statement that explains why they are interested in the commercial real estate industry, their experiences and insights into that industry and how those have impacted them, the impact they expect to make in the commercial real estate industry, and how their long-term career objectives make them uniquely qualified for this scholarship. Financial need is not considered in the selection process.

**Financial data** The stipend is $5,000.

**Duration** 1 year.

**Number awarded** 10 each year.

**Deadline** April of each year.

## [142]
## CUMMINS SCHOLARSHIPS

Society of Women Engineers
Attn: Scholarship Selection Committee
203 North LaSalle Street, Suite 1675
Chicago, IL 60601-1269
(312) 596-5223                    Toll Free: (877) SWE-INFO
Fax: (312) 644-8557        E-mail: scholarships@swe.org
Web: societyofwomenengineers.swe.org

**Summary** To provide financial assistance to women working on an undergraduate or graduate degree in computer science or designated engineering specialties.

**Eligibility** This program is open to women who are sophomores, juniors, seniors, or graduate students at 4-year ABET-accredited colleges and universities. Applicants must be working full time on a degree in computer science or automotive, chemical, computer, electrical, industrial, manufacturing, materials, or mechanical engineering and have a GPA of 3.5 or higher. Preference is given to members of groups underrepresented in engineering or computer science. Selection is based on merit. U.S. citizenship or permanent resident status is required.

**Financial data** The stipend is $1,000.

**Duration** 1 year.

**Additional information** This program is sponsored by Cummins, Inc.

**Number awarded** 2 each year.

**Deadline** February of each year.

## [143]
## CYNTHIA HUNT-LINES SCHOLARSHIP

Minnesota Nurses Association
Attn: Minnesota Nurses Association Foundation
345 Randolph Avenue, Suite 200
St. Paul, MN 55102-3610
(651) 414-2822        Toll Free: (800) 536-4662, ext. 122
Fax: (651) 695-7000   E-mail: linda.owens@mnnurses.org
Web: www.mnnurses.org

**Summary** To provide financial assistance to members of the Minnesota Nurses Association (MNA) and the Minnesota Student Nurses Association (MSNA) who are single parents and interested in working on a baccalaureate or master's degree in nursing.

**Eligibility** This program is open to MNA and MSNA members who are enrolled or entering a baccalaureate or master's program in nursing in Minnesota or North Dakota. Applicants must be single parents, at least 21 years of age, with at least 1 dependent. Along with their application, they must submit: a current transcript; a short essay describing their interest in nursing, their long-range career goals, and how their continuing education will have an impact on the profession of nursing in Minnesota; a description of their financial need; and 2 letters of support.

**Financial data** The stipend is $2,000 per year.

**Duration** 1 year; may be renewed.

**Number awarded** 1 each year.

**Deadline** May of each year.

## [144]
## D. ANITA SMALL SCIENCE AND BUSINESS SCHOLARSHIP

Business and Professional Women of Maryland
Attn: BPW Foundation of Maryland
c/o Joyce Draper, Chief Financial Officer
615 Fairview Avenue
Frederick, MD 21701
Web: bpwmd2.timberlakepublishing.com

**Summary** To provide financial assistance to women in Maryland who are interested in working on an undergraduate or graduate degree in a science or business-related field.

**Eligibility** This program is open to women who are at least 21 years of age and have been accepted to a bachelor's or advanced degree program at an accredited Maryland academic institution. Applicants must be preparing for a career in 1 of the following or a related field: business administration, computer sciences, engineering, mathematics, medical sciences (including nursing, laboratory technology, therapy, etc.), or physical sciences. They must have a GPA of 3.0 or higher and be able to demonstrate financial need.

**Financial data** The stipend is $1,500.

**Duration** 1 year.

**Number awarded** 1 or more each year.

**Deadline** April of each year.

## [145]
## DAGMAR JEPPESON GRANT

Delta Kappa Gamma Society International-Alpha Rho
  State Organization
c/o Jill Lang, State Scholarship Chair
16301 S.E. Katie Court
Milwaukie, OR 97267-5198
(503) 786-7268          E-mail: jaceel@comcast.net
Web: www.deltakappagamma.org

**Summary** To provide financial assistance to women from
Oregon who are enrolled as upper-division students at a college in any state and preparing for a career in early childhood
or elementary education.

**Eligibility** This program is open to female residents of Oregon who are at least juniors at a college in any state and interested in preparing for a career in early childhood or elementary education. Applicants may not be members of Delta
Kappa Gamma (an honorary society of women educators),
but they must be sponsored by a local chapter of the society.
Along with their application, they must submit a summary of
their education from high school through the present, high
school and college activities and achievements, community
service, employment history, career goals, and financial
need.

**Financial data** A stipend is awarded (amount not specified).

**Duration** 1 year.

**Additional information** Recipients may not accept a
scholarship from the Alpha Rho state organization and from
Delta Kappa Gamma International in the same year.

**Number awarded** 1 or more each year.

**Deadline** February of each year.

## [146]
## DASSAULT FALCON JET CORPORATION
## SCHOLARSHIP

Women in Aviation, International
Attn: Scholarships
Morningstar Airport
3647 State Route 503 South
West Alexandria, OH 45381-9354
(937) 839-4647          Fax: (937) 839-4645
E-mail: scholarships@wai.org
Web: www.wai.org/education/scholarships.cfm

**Summary** To provide financial assistance to women who
are working on an undergraduate or graduate degree in a
field related to aviation.

**Eligibility** This program is open to women who are working
on an undergraduate or graduate degree in an aviation-
related field. Applicants must be U.S. citizens, be fluent in
English, and have a GPA of 3.0 or higher. Along with their
application, they must submit 2 letters of recommendation; a
1-page essay on their current educational status, what they
hope to achieve by working on a degree in aviation, and their
aspirations in the field; a resume; copies of all aviation
licenses and medical certificates; and the last 3 pages of their
pilot logbook (if applicable). Selection is based on achievements, attitude toward self and others, commitment to success, dedication to career, financial need, motivation, reliability, responsibility, and teamwork.

**Financial data** The stipend is $1,000.

**Duration** 1 year.

**Additional information** WAI is a nonprofit professional
organization dedicated to encouraging women to consider an
aviation career and to providing educational outreach activities and networking resources to women active in the industry. This program is sponsored by Dassault Falcon Jet Corporation.

**Number awarded** 1 each year.

**Deadline** November of each year.

## [147]
## DAUGHTERS OF PENELOPE UNDERGRADUATE
## SCHOLARSHIPS

Daughters of Penelope
Attn: Daughters of Penelope Foundation, Inc.
1909 Q Street, N.W., Suite 500
Washington, DC 20009-1007
(202) 234-9741          Fax: (202) 483-6983
E-mail: president@dopfoundationinc.com
Web: dopfoundationinc.com/scholarships/apply

**Summary** To provide financial assistance for college to
women of Greek descent.

**Eligibility** This program is open to women who have been
members of the Daughters of Penelope or the Maids of
Athena for at least 2 years, or whose parents or grandparents
have been members of the Daughters of Penelope or the
Order of AHEPA for at least 2 years. Applicants must be 1)
high school seniors or recent high school graduates applying
to a college, university, or accredited technical school; or 2)
current undergraduates at the college level. They must have
taken the SAT or ACT (or Canadian, Greek, or Cypriot equivalent) and must write an essay (in English) about their educational and vocational goals. Selection is based on academic
merit only.

**Financial data** Stipends are $1,500 or $1,000.

**Duration** 1 year; nonrenewable.

**Additional information** This program includes the follow-
ing endowed awards: the Daughters of Penelope Past Grand
Presidents' Memorial Scholarship, the Alexandra Apostolides
Sonenfeld Scholarship, the Helen J. Beldecos Scholarship,
the Hopewell Agave Chapter 224 Scholarship, the Kottis
Family Scholarship, the Mary M. Verges Scholarship, the
Joanne V. Hologgitas Ph.D. Scholarship, the Eos #1 Mother
Lodge Chapter Scholarship, the Barbara Edith Quincey
Thorndyke Memorial Scholarship, and the Paula J. Alexander
Memorial Scholarship.

**Number awarded** Varies each year; recently, 19 of these
scholarships were awarded: 6 at $1,500 and 13 at $1,000.

**Deadline** May of each year.

## [148]
## DAUGHTERS OF THE CINCINNATI
## SCHOLARSHIP PROGRAM

Daughters of the Cincinnati
Attn: Scholarship Administrator
20 West 44th Street, Suite 508
New York, NY 10036
(212) 991-9945 E-mail: scholarships@daughters1894.org
Web: www.daughters1894.org/scholarship.htm

**Summary** To provide financial assistance for college to high school seniors who are the daughters of active-duty, deceased, or retired military officers.

**Eligibility** This program is open to high school seniors who are the daughters of career commissioned officers of the regular Army, Navy, Air Force, Coast Guard, or Marine Corps on active duty, deceased, or retired. Applicants must be planning to enroll at a college or university in any state. Along with their application, they must submit an official school transcript, SAT or ACT scores, a letter of recommendation, and documentation of financial need.

**Financial data** Scholarship amounts have recently averaged $4,000 per year. Funds are paid directly to the college of the student's choice.

**Duration** 1 year; may be renewed up to 3 additional years, provided the recipient remains in good academic standing.

**Additional information** This program was originally established in 1906.

**Number awarded** Approximately 12 each year.

**Deadline** March of each year.

## [149]
## DAVID EVANS AND ASSOCIATES SCHOLARSHIPS

David Evans and Associates, Inc.
2100 S.W. River Parkway
Portland, OR 97201
(503) 223-2701          Toll Free: (800) 721-1916
Fax: (503) 223-6663
Web: www.deainc.com/scholarships.aspx

**Summary** To provide financial assistance to women and minority undergraduates working on a degree in civil engineering or geomatics at colleges in designated states.

**Eligibility** This program is open to women and minority undergraduates majoring in civil engineering (including transportation, structural, land development, or environmental) or geomatics. Applicants must be enrolled at a college or university in Arizona, California, Colorado, Idaho, New York, Oregon, or Washington. They must have a GPA of 3.0 or higher.

**Financial data** The stipend is $3,000.

**Duration** 1 year; nonrenewable.

**Number awarded** 2 each year.

**Deadline** April of each year.

## [150]
## DAVIS & DAVIS SCHOLARSHIP

National Naval Officers Association-Washington, D.C.
   Chapter
c/o LCDR Stephen Williams
P.O. Box 30784
Alexandria, VA 22310
(703) 566-3840          Fax: (703) 566-3813
E-mail: Stephen.Williams@navy.mil
Web: dcnnoa.memberlodge.com

**Summary** To provide financial assistance to female African American high school seniors from the Washington, D.C. area who are interested in attending college in any state.

**Eligibility** This program is open to female African American seniors graduating from high schools in the Washington, D.C. metropolitan area who plan to enroll full time at an accredited 2- or 4-year college or university in any state.

Applicants must have a GPA of 2.5 or higher and be U.S. citizens or permanent residents. Selection is based on academic achievement, community involvement, and financial need.

**Financial data** The stipend is $1,000.

**Duration** 1 year; nonrenewable.

**Additional information** Recipients are not required to join or affiliate with the military in any way.

**Number awarded** Varies each year; recently, 2 of these scholarships were awarded.

**Deadline** March of each year.

## [151]
## DEALER DEVELOPMENT SCHOLARSHIP PROGRAM

General Motors Corporation
Women's Retail Network
c/o Charitable Management Systems, Inc.
P.O. Box 648
Naperville, IL 60566
(630) 428-2412          Fax: (630) 428-2695
E-mail: wrnscholarshipinfo@gmsac.com
Web: www.gmsac.com

**Summary** To provide financial assistance to women attending college or graduate school to prepare for a retail automotive career.

**Eligibility** This program is open to women who are enrolled full time in undergraduate, graduate, and nontraditional continuing education institutions that offer degrees in the automotive retail and/or automotive service field. Applicants must be interested in preparing for a career in automotive retail and/or service management. They must be citizens of the United States or have the ability to accept permanent employment in the United States without the need for visa sponsorship now or in the future. Along with their application, they must submit an essay of 500 to 750 words on their interest and motivation for a career in the automotive retail and/or automotive service sector. Selection is based on that statement, academic performance, leadership and participation in school and community activities, work experience, career and educational aspirations, and financial need.

**Financial data** The stipend is $5,000 per year.

**Duration** 1 year; recipients may reapply.

**Additional information** This program began in 2011.

**Number awarded** Varies each year; recently, 6 of these scholarships were awarded.

**Deadline** April of each year.

## [152]
## DEAN WEESE SCHOLARSHIP

University Interscholastic League
Attn: Texas Interscholastic League Foundation
1701 Manor Road
Austin, TX 78722
(512) 232-4937          Fax: (512) 232-7311
E-mail: tilf@uiltexas.org
Web: tilf.uiltexas.org/scholarships/list

**Summary** To provide financial assistance to high school seniors who participate in programs of the Texas Interscholastic League Foundation (TILF), have competed in girls' high school varsity basketball, and plan to attend college in the state.

**Eligibility** This program is open to seniors graduating from high schools in Texas who have competed in a University Interscholastic League (UIL) academic state meet and have participated in girls' high school varsity basketball. Applicants must be planning to attend a college or university in the state and major in any field. Along with their application, they must submit high school transcripts that include SAT and/or ACT scores and documentation of financial need.

**Financial data** The stipend is $1,000.

**Duration** 1 year; nonrenewable.

**Additional information** This program is sponsored by Whataburger Inc. and Southwest Shootout Inc.

**Number awarded** 1 each year.

**Deadline** May of each year.

## [153]
## DEFENSE INTELLIGENCE AGENCY UNDERGRADUATE TRAINING ASSISTANCE PROGRAM

Defense Intelligence Agency
Attn: Human Resources, HCH-4
200 MacDill Boulevard, Building 6000
Bolling AFB, DC 20340-5100
(202) 231-2736　　　　　　　Fax: (202) 231-4889
TDD: (202) 231-5002　　　　　E-mail: staffing@dia.mil
Web: www.dia.mil/careers/students

**Summary** To provide loans-for-service and work experience to high school seniors and lower-division students (particularly women, minorities, and persons with disabilities) who are interested in majoring in specified fields and working for the U.S. Defense Intelligence Agency (DIA).

**Eligibility** This program is open to graduating high school seniors and college freshmen and sophomores interested in working full time on a baccalaureate degree in 1 of the following fields in college: biology, chemistry, computer science, engineering, foreign area studies, intelligence analysis, international relations, microbiology, pharmacology, physics, political science, or toxicology. High school seniors must have a GPA of 2.75 or higher and either 1) an SAT combined critical reading and mathematics score of 1000 or higher plus 500 or higher on the writing portion or 2) an ACT score of 21 or higher. College freshmen and sophomores must have a GPA of 3.0 or higher. All applicants must be able to demonstrate financial need (household income ceiling of $70,000 for a family of 4 or $80,000 for a family of 5 or more) and leadership abilities through extracurricular activities, civic involvement, volunteer work, or part-time employment. Students and all members of their immediate family must be U.S. citizens. Minorities, women, and persons with disabilities are strongly encouraged to apply.

**Financial data** Students accepted into this program receive tuition (up to $18,000 per year) at an accredited college or university selected by the student and endorsed by the sponsor; reimbursement for books and needed supplies; an annual salary to cover college room and board expenses and for summer employment; and a position at the sponsoring agency after graduation. Recipients must work for DIA after college graduation for at least 1 and a half times the length of study. For participants who leave DIA earlier than scheduled, the agency arranges for payments to reimburse

DIA for the total cost of education (including the employee's pay and allowances).

**Duration** 4 years, provided the recipient maintains a GPA of 2.75 during the freshman year and 3.0 or higher in subsequent semesters.

**Additional information** Recipients are provided a challenging summer internship and guaranteed a job at the agency in their field of study upon graduation.

**Number awarded** Only a few are awarded each year.

**Deadline** October of each year.

## [154]
## DEGENRING SCHOLARSHIP FUND

American Baptist Women's Ministries of New Jersey
36-10 Garden View Terrace
East Windsor, NJ 08520
Web: www.abwminnj.org/custom.html

**Summary** To provide financial assistance to Baptist women in New Jersey who are interested in attending college in any state to prepare for a career in Christian service.

**Eligibility** This program is open to Baptist women in New Jersey who are at least sophomores at postsecondary institutions in any state and preparing for a career involving Christian work. Applicants must be members of an American Baptist Church in New Jersey. Selection is based on financial need and career goals.

**Financial data** The amount awarded varies, depending upon the need of the recipient and her career goals in Christian work.

**Duration** 1 year.

**Number awarded** 1 or more each year.

**Deadline** February of each year.

## [155]
## DELL COMPUTER CORPORATION SCHOLARSHIPS

Society of Women Engineers
Attn: Scholarship Selection Committee
203 North LaSalle Street, Suite 1675
Chicago, IL 60601-1269
(312) 596-5223　　　　　　Toll Free: (877) SWE-INFO
Fax: (312) 644-8557　　　　E-mail: scholarships@swe.org
Web: societyofwomenengineers.swe.org

**Summary** To provide financial assistance to upper-division women majoring in computer science or designated engineering specialties.

**Eligibility** This program is open to women who are entering their junior or senior year at an ABET-accredited college or university. Applicants must be working full time on a degree in computer science or electrical, computer, or mechanical engineering and have a GPA of 3.0 or higher. Financial need is considered in the selection process.

**Financial data** The stipend is $2,250.

**Duration** 1 year.

**Additional information** This program, established in 1999, is sponsored by Dell Inc.

**Number awarded** 2 each year.

**Deadline** February of each year.

## [156]
## DELLA VAN DEUREN MEMORIAL SCHOLARSHIPS

American Legion Auxiliary
Department of Wisconsin
Attn: Education Chair
2930 American Legion Drive
P.O. Box 140
Portage, WI 53901-0140
(608) 745-0124                Toll Free: (866) 664-3863
Fax: (608) 745-1947     E-mail: alawi@amlegionauxwi.org
Web: www.amlegionauxwi.org/Scholarships.htm

**Summary** To provide financial assistance to Wisconsin residents who are members or children of members of the American Legion Auxiliary and interested in attending college in any state.

**Eligibility** This program is open to members and children of members of the American Legion Auxiliary in Wisconsin. Applicants must be high school seniors or graduates attending or planning to attend a college or university in any state. They must have a GPA of 3.5 or higher and be able to demonstrate financial need. Along with their application, they must submit a 300-word essay on "Education—An Investment in the Future."

**Financial data** The stipend is $1,000.

**Duration** 1 year; nonrenewable.

**Number awarded** 2 each year.

**Deadline** March of each year.

## [157]
## DELMAR SECTION SCHOLARSHIP AWARD

Delaware Engineering Society
c/o Stacy Ziegler
Duffield Associates, Inc.
5400 Limestone Road
Wilmington, DE 19808
(302) 239-6634                Fax: (302) 239-8485
E-mail: sziegler@duffnet.com
Web: www.desonline.us

**Summary** To provide financial assistance to female high school seniors in the DelMar area who are interested in majoring in engineering in college.

**Eligibility** This program is open to female high school seniors in Delaware and Maryland who will be enrolling in an engineering program at an ABET-accredited college or university. Applicants must have SAT scores of 600 or higher in mathematics, 500 or higher in critical reading, and 500 or higher in writing (or ACT scores of 29 or higher in mathematics and 25 or higher in English). They must submit an essay (up to 500 words) on their interest in engineering, their major area of study and area of specialization, the occupation they propose to pursue after graduation, their long-term goals, and how they hope to achieve them. Selection is based on the essay, academic record, honors and scholarships, volunteer activities, work experience, and letters of recommendation. Financial need is not required.

**Financial data** A stipend is awarded (amount not specified).

**Duration** 1 year (freshman year); nonrenewable.

**Additional information** This program is sponsored jointly by the Delaware Engineering Society and the DelMar Section of the Society of Women Engineers.

**Number awarded** Varies each year.

**Deadline** December of each year.

## [158]
## DELTA AIR LINES AVIATION MAINTENANCE MANAGEMENT/AVIATION BUSINESS MANAGEMENT SCHOLARSHIPS

Women in Aviation, International
Attn: Scholarships
Morningstar Airport
3647 State Route 503 South
West Alexandria, OH 45381-9354
(937) 839-4647                Fax: (937) 839-4645
E-mail: scholarships@wai.org
Web: www.wai.org/education/scholarships.cfm

**Summary** To provide financial assistance to members of Women in Aviation, International (WAI) who are interested in a career in aviation management.

**Eligibility** This program is open to WAI members who are full-time students with at least 2 semesters of study remaining. Applicants must be working on an associate or baccalaureate degree in aviation maintenance management or aviation business management and have a cumulative GPA of 3.0 or higher. They must be U.S. citizens or eligible noncitizens. Along with their application, they must submit an essay of 500 to 1,000 words on who or what inspired them to prepare for a career in aviation maintenance management or aviation business management, their greatest life challenge, their greatest strength and strongest characteristic, their most memorable academic experience, and why they are the most qualified candidate for this scholarship. Selection is based on achievements, attitude toward self and others, commitment to success, dedication to career, financial need, motivation, reliability, responsibility, and teamwork.

**Financial data** The stipend is $5,000.

**Duration** 1 year.

**Additional information** WAI is a nonprofit professional organization dedicated to encouraging women to consider an aviation career and to providing educational outreach activities and networking resources to women active in the industry. This program is sponsored by Delta Air Lines. In addition to the scholarship, recipients are reimbursed for up to $2,000 in travel and lodging expenses to attend the WAI annual conference.

**Number awarded** 1 each year.

**Deadline** November of each year.

## [159]
## DELTA AIR LINES ENGINEERING SCHOLARSHIP

Women in Aviation, International
Attn: Scholarships
Morningstar Airport
3647 State Route 503 South
West Alexandria, OH 45381-9354
(937) 839-4647                Fax: (937) 839-4645
E-mail: scholarships@wai.org
Web: www.wai.org/education/scholarships.cfm

**Summary** To provide financial assistance to members of Women in Aviation, International (WAI) who are studying engineering in college.

**Eligibility** This program is open to WAI members who are full-time juniors or seniors with at least 2 semesters of study remaining. Applicants must be working on a baccalaureate degree in aerospace, aeronautical, electrical, or mechanical engineering and have a cumulative GPA of 3.0 or higher. They must be U.S. citizens or eligible noncitizens. Along with their application, they must submit an essay of 500 to 1,000 words on who or what inspired them to prepare for a career in engineering, their greatest life challenge, their greatest strength and strongest characteristic, their most memorable academic experience, and why they are the most qualified candidate for this scholarship. Selection is based on achievements, attitude toward self and others, commitment to success, dedication to career, financial need, motivation, reliability, responsibility, and teamwork.

**Financial data** The stipend is $5,000.

**Duration** 1 year.

**Additional information** WAI is a nonprofit professional organization dedicated to encouraging women to consider an aviation career and to providing educational outreach activities and networking resources to women active in the industry. This program is sponsored by Delta Air Lines. In addition to the scholarship, recipients are reimbursed for up to $2,000 in travel and lodging expenses to attend the WAI annual conference.

**Number awarded** 1 each year.

**Deadline** November of each year.

## [160]
## DELTA DELTA DELTA UNRESTRICTED UNDERGRADUATE SCHOLARSHIPS

Delta Delta Delta
Attn: Tri Delta Foundation
2331 Brookhollow Plaza Drive
P.O. Box 5987
Arlington, TX 76005-5987
(817) 633-8001                    Fax: (817) 652-0212
E-mail: fdnscholarship@trideltaeo.org
Web: www.tridelta.org/Foundation/Scholarships

**Summary** To provide financial assistance for undergraduate study to women students who are members of Delta Delta Delta.

**Eligibility** This program is open to undergraduate women, majoring in any field, who are current members of the sorority. Applicants must be entering their junior or senior year and planning to remain enrolled full time. Selection is based on academic achievement, past and present involvement in the sorority, community and campus involvement, and financial need.

**Financial data** The stipends range from $500 to $1,500. Funds are sent directly to the financial aid office of the recipient's college or university.

**Duration** 1 year.

**Additional information** This program, originally established in 1942, includes the following named scholarships: the Zoe Gore Perrin Scholarship, the Luella Atkins Key Scholarship, the Sarah Shinn Marshall Scholarship, the Martha Sale Ferman Scholarship, the Sisterhood Scholarship, and the Martin Sisters Scholarship.

**Number awarded** Varies each year; recently, a total of 62 undergraduate scholarships were awarded.

**Deadline** February of each year.

## [161]
## DELTA GAMMA SCHOLARSHIPS

Delta Gamma Foundation
Attn: Director of Scholarships, Fellowships and Loans
3250 Riverside Drive
P.O. Box 21397
Columbus, OH 43221-0397
(614) 481-8169                    Toll Free: (800) 644-5414
Fax: (614) 481-0133
E-mail: scholarshipfellowship@deltagamma.org
Web: www.deltagamma.org

**Summary** To provide financial assistance for college to members of Delta Gamma sorority who have made a significant contribution to both their chapter and their campus.

**Eligibility** This program is open to initiated members of a collegiate chapter of Delta Gamma in the United States or Canada who have completed 3 semesters or 4 quarters of their college course and have maintained a GPA of 3.0 or higher. Applicants must submit a 1- to 2-page essay in which they introduce themselves, including their career goals, their reasons for applying for this scholarship, and the impact Delta Gamma has had on their life. Selection is based on scholastic excellence and participation in chapter, campus, and community leadership activities.

**Financial data** The stipend is $1,000. Funds are sent directly to the university or college to be used for tuition, books, laboratory fees, room, and board. They may not be used for sorority dues, house fees, or other chapter expenses.

**Duration** 1 year.

**Additional information** This program includes several special endowment scholarships that give preference to members of specified chapters. Recipients are expected to remain active participating members of their collegiate chapter throughout the following academic year.

**Number awarded** At least 200 each year.

**Deadline** February of each year.

## [162]
## DELTA KAPPA GAMMA NATIVE AMERICAN PROJECT GRANTS

Delta Kappa Gamma Society International-Mu State
 Organization
c/o Joann Higgins, Native American Project
1386 Craleigh Street
North Port, FL 34288
E-mail: charlygrll496@yahoo.com
Web: dkgmustateflorida.weebly.com

**Summary** To provide financial assistance to female Native Americans from Florida who are working on a degree in education or conducting research into the history of Native Americans at a college or university in the state.

**Eligibility** This program is open to women who are members of a recognized Native American tribe in Florida. Applicants must be enrolled at an accredited college or university in the state and either working on a degree in education or conducting research into the history of Native Americans in Florida. Along with their application, they must submit a brief statement with details of the purpose of the grant, a letter of recommendation from a tribal official, and a copy of high school or college transcripts.

**Financial data** The stipend is $1,000.

**Duration** 1 year.

**Number awarded** 6 each year: 1 in each of the districts of the sponsoring organization in Florida.

**Deadline** May of each year.

## [163]
## DELTA PHI EPSILON UNDERGRADUATE SCHOLARSHIPS

Delta Phi Epsilon Educational Foundation
Attn: Executive Director
251 South Carnac Street
Philadelphia, PA 19107
(215) 732-5901                    Fax: (215) 732-5906
E-mail: info@dphie.org
Web: www.dphie.org

**Summary** To provide financial assistance for college to Delta Phi Epsilon Sorority members.

**Eligibility** This program is open to undergraduate Delta Phi Epsilon sorority sisters (not pledges). Applicants must submit a 250-word essay on how this scholarship will benefit the continuation of their educational pursuits. Selection is based on service and involvement, academics, and financial need.

**Financial data** The stipend is $1,000.

**Duration** 1 year.

**Number awarded** Varies each year; recently, 10 of these scholarships were awarded.

**Deadline** March of each year.

## [164]
## DELTA SIGMA THETA SORORITY GENERAL SCHOLARSHIPS

Delta Sigma Theta Sorority, Inc.
Attn: Scholarship and Standards Committee Chair
1707 New Hampshire Avenue, N.W.
Washington, DC 20009
(202) 986-2400                    Fax: (202) 986-2513
E-mail: dstemail@deltasigmatheta.org
Web: www.deltasigmatheta.org

**Summary** To provide financial assistance to members of Delta Sigma Theta who are working on an undergraduate or graduate degree in any field.

**Eligibility** This program is open to active, dues-paying members of Delta Sigma Theta who are currently enrolled in college or graduate school. Applicants must submit an essay on their major goals and educational objectives, including realistic steps they foresee as necessary for the fulfillment of their plans. Financial need is considered in the selection process.

**Financial data** The stipends range from $1,000 to $2,000. The funds may be used to cover tuition, fees, and living expenses.

**Duration** 1 year; may be renewed for 1 additional year.

**Additional information** This sponsor is a traditionally-African American social sorority. The application fee is $20.

**Number awarded** Varies each year.

**Deadline** April of each year.

## [165]
## DELTA ZETA GENERAL UNDERGRADUATE SCHOLARSHIPS

Delta Zeta Sorority
Attn: Foundation Coordinator
202 East Church Street
Oxford, OH 45056
(513) 523-7597                    Fax: (513) 523-1921
E-mail: DZFoundation@dzshq.com
Web: www.deltazeta.org

**Summary** To provide financial assistance for continued undergraduate study to members of Delta Zeta Sorority.

**Eligibility** This program is open to members of the sorority who are entering their junior or senior year and have a GPA of 3.0 or higher. Applicants must submit an official transcript, a statement of their career goals, information on their service to the sorority, documentation of campus activities and/or community involvement, a list of academic honors, and an explanation of their financial need.

**Financial data** The stipend ranges from $500 to $2,500, depending on the availability of funds.

**Duration** 1 year; nonrenewable.

**Number awarded** Varies each year; recently, 6 of these scholarships were awarded.

**Deadline** February of each year.

## [166]
## DENVER CHAPTER AFWA SCHOLARSHIPS

Accounting and Financial Women's Alliance-Denver
  Chapter
c/o Sandy Purdy, President
P.O. Box 2234
Denver, CO 80201-2234
(303) 489-9021          E-mail: president@afwadenver.org
Web: www.aswadenver.org/scholarship.html

**Summary** To provide financial assistance to women working on a degree in accounting at a college or university in Colorado.

**Eligibility** This program is open to women who have completed at least 60 semester hours toward a degree in accounting with a GPA of 3.0 or higher. Applicants must be attending a college or university in Colorado. Membership in the Accounting and Financial Women's Alliance (AFWA) is not required. Selection is based on academic achievement, extracurricular activities and honors, a statement of career goals and objectives, 3 letters of recommendation, and financial need.

**Financial data** A stipend is awarded (amount not specified).

**Duration** 1 year.

**Number awarded** Several each year; a total of $7,000 is available for this program annually.

**Deadline** June of each year.

## [167]
## DESK AND DERRICK EDUCATION TRUST SCHOLARSHIPS

Association of Desk and Derrick Clubs
Attn: Desk and Derrick Educational Trust
3930 Waverly Bend
Katy, TX 77450
(281) 392-7181                         Fax: (318) 671-8887
E-mail: info@theeducationaltrust.org
Web: www.theeducationaltrust.org/scholarships

**Summary**   To provide funding (some just for women) to currently-enrolled college students who are planning a career in the petroleum or an allied industry.

**Eligibility**   This program is open to full-time undergraduate and graduate students who have completed at least 2 years of college or are currently enrolled in the second year of undergraduate study. Applicants must have a GPA of 3.2 or higher and be able to demonstrate financial need. They must be preparing for a career in the petroleum, energy, or an allied industry; qualifying majors include geology, geophysics, petroleum engineering, chemical engineering, mechanical engineering, nuclear engineering, and energy management. Students working on degrees in research and development of alternate energy sources (e.g., coal, electric, solar, wind, hydroelectric, nuclear, ethanol) are also eligible. U.S. or Canadian citizenship is required. Some of the awards are designated for women.

**Financial data**   Stipends range from $1,000 to $1,500.

**Duration**   1 year.

**Additional information**   This program, established in 1982, includes the following named awards designated for women: the Bettie Conley Helis Scholarship, the Lois G. Johnston Scholarship, the Edith Snizek Scholarship, the Gladys Watford Scholarship, and the Paula Mace Scholarship.

**Number awarded**   Varies each year; recently, 12 of these scholarships (including 9 designated for women) were awarded.

**Deadline**   March of each year.

## [168]
## DETROIT SECTION SCHOLARSHIPS

Society of Women Engineers-Detroit Section
Attn: Scholarship Chair
P.O. Box 2978
Southfield, MI 48037-2978
(586) 453-3745          E-mail: Shannon.atchison@swe.org
Web: www.swe.org/SWE/RegionH/Detroit/student.html

**Summary**   To provide financial assistance to female high school seniors in Michigan who are interested in studying engineering at a school in any state.

**Eligibility**   This program is open to female seniors at high schools in Michigan who are planning to enroll the following fall at a university or college in any state that has an ABET-accredited engineering program. Along with their application, they must submit a 1-page essay on why they want to be an engineer. Selection is based on that essay (40%); awards and honors received in high school (20%); leadership, activities (community, church, school, etc.), and employment (30%); and academic performance (10%).

**Financial data**   The stipend is $1,000.

**Duration**   1 year.

**Number awarded**   Varies each year; recently, 2 of these scholarships were awarded.

**Deadline**   February of each year.

## [169]
## DEXTER/USBC HIGH SCHOOL ALL-AMERICAN TEAM

United States Bowling Congress
Attn: USBC High School
621 Six Flags Drive
Arlington, TX 76011
Toll Free: (800) 514-BOWL, ext. 3168
Fax: (817) 385-8262
E-mail: usbchighschool@bowl.com
Web: www.bowl.com

**Summary**   To recognize and reward, with college scholarships, high school students who are affiliated with the United States Bowling Congress (USBC) and are selected for its All-American Team (females and males compete separately).

**Eligibility**   This program is open to high school students who participate on a high school bowling team that has USBC membership or is registered in the Coaches Registration Program. Candidates must be nominated by their high school coach or athletic director. They must have a GPA of 3.0 or higher. Nominees must submit a 500-word essay on the life lesson they have learned through high school bowling. Selection is based on the essay, bowling accomplishments in the current school year, academic achievement, recommendations, extracurricular and community involvement, and a resume.

**Financial data**   Awards, in the form of college scholarships, are $1,000.

**Duration**   Awards are presented annually.

**Additional information**   Nominees must submit a fee of $20 along with their application.

**Number awarded**   10 each year: 5 boys and 5 girls.

**Deadline**   Nominations must be submitted by March of each year.

## [170]
## DIAMONDS IN THE ROUGH MINISTRY SCHOLARSHIP

Diamonds in the Rough Ministry International
Attn: Scholarship Fund
2414 East Highway 80, Suite 302
Mesquite, TX 75150
(972) 288-0112 E-mail: aparker@diamondsntherough.org
Web: diamondsntherough.org/scholarship.html

**Summary**   To provide financial assistance to female high school seniors from Texas who are allowing God to develop them into "precious diamonds" by attending college in any state.

**Eligibility**   This program is open to women who are graduating from high schools in Texas and planning to attend college in any state. Applicants must be able to demonstrate that they understand the goal of the sponsoring organization to "empower women down the road of self-discovery and self-worth in Jesus Christ." They must have a GPA of 2.5 or higher. Along with their application, they must submit a 500-

word essay on how they see God using a challenging situation or circumstance to polish them into a precious diamond.

**Financial data** A stipend is awarded (amount not specified).

**Duration** 1 year.

**Additional information** This program began in 2011.

**Number awarded** 1 or 2 each year.

**Deadline** April of each year.

## [171]
## DINAH SHORE SCHOLARSHIP

Ladies Professional Golf Association
Attn: LPGA Foundation
100 International Golf Drive
Daytona Beach, FL 32124-1082
(386) 274-6200            Fax: (386) 274-1099
E-mail: foundation.scholarships@lpga.com
Web: www.lpgafoundation.org/scholarships?

**Summary** To provide financial assistance for college to female graduating high school seniors who played golf in high school.

**Eligibility** This program is open to female high school seniors who have a GPA of 3.2 or higher. Applicants must have played in at least 50% of their high school golf team's scheduled events or have played golf "regularly" for the past 2 years. They must be planning to enroll full time at a college or university in the United States, but they must not be planning to play collegiate golf. Along with their application, they must submit a letter that describes how golf has been an integral part of their lives and includes their personal, academic, and professional goals; chosen discipline of study; and how this scholarship will be of assistance. Financial need is not considered in the selection process.

**Financial data** The stipend is $5,000.

**Duration** 1 year.

**Additional information** This program, established in 1994, is supported by Kraft Foods, Inc.

**Number awarded** 1 each year.

**Deadline** May of each year.

## [172]
## DISABLED AMERICAN VETERANS AUXILIARY NATIONAL EDUCATION SCHOLARSHIP FUND

Disabled American Veterans Auxiliary
Attn: National Education Scholarship Fund
3725 Alexandria Pike
Cold Spring, KY 41076
(859) 441-7300        Toll Free: (877) 426-2838, ext. 4020
Fax: (859) 442-2095        E-mail: dava@davmail.org
Web: auxiliary.dav.org/membership/Programs.aspx

**Summary** To provide financial assistance to members of the Disabled American Veterans (DAV) Auxiliary who are interested in attending college or graduate school.

**Eligibility** This program is open to paid life members of the auxiliary who are attending or planning to attend a college, university, or vocational school as a full- or part-time undergraduate or graduate student. Applicants must be at least seniors in high school, but there is no maximum age limit. Selection is based on academic achievement; participation in DAV activities; participation in other activities for veterans in their school, community, or elsewhere; volunteer work; membership in clubs or organizations; honors and awards; a statement of academic goals; and financial need.

**Financial data** Stipends are $1,500 per year for full-time students or $750 per year for part-time students.

**Duration** 1 year; may be renewed for up to 4 additional years, provided the recipient maintains a GPA of 2.5 or higher.

**Additional information** Membership in the DAV Auxiliary is available to extended family members of veterans eligible for membership in Disabled American Veterans (i.e., any man or woman who served in the armed forces during a period of war or under conditions simulating war and was wounded, disabled to any degree, or left with long-term illness as a result of military service and was discharged or retired from military service under honorable conditions). This program was established in September 2010 as a replacement for the educational loan program that the DAV Auxiliary operated from 1931 until August 2010.

**Number awarded** Varies each year.

**Deadline** March of each year.

## [173]
## DISTINGUISHED YOUNG WOMEN SCHOLARSHIPS

Distinguished Young Women
Attn: Foundation Administrator
751 Government Street
Mobile, AL 36602
(251) 438-3621            Fax: (251) 431-0063
E-mail: foundation@distinguishedyw.org
Web: www.distinguishedyw.org/about/scholarships

**Summary** To recognize and reward, with college scholarships, female high school seniors who participate in the Distinguished Young Women competition.

**Eligibility** This competition is open to girls who are seniors in high school, are U.S. citizens, have never been married, and have never been pregnant. Contestants first enter local competitions, from which winners advance to the state level. The winner in each state is invited to the national competition, held in Mobile, Alabama in June of each year. Prior to the contestants' arrival for the national competition, the judges evaluate their high school academic records and test scores for the scholastics score (20% of the overall score). At the competition, girls are given scores on the basis of their personality, ability to relate to others, maturity, and ability to express themselves in an interview (25% of overall score); their performing arts talent presented during a 90-second audition on stage in front of an audience (25% of overall score); their fitness as demonstrated during a choreographed group aerobic routine (15% of overall score); and their self-expression, grace, poise, demeanor, carriage, posture, and speaking ability (15% of overall score). The girls with the highest scores in each of the 5 categories receive awards. Overall scores are used for selection of 10 finalists, from whom the "Distinguished Young Woman of America" and 2 runners-up are selected. In addition, "satellite awards" are presented to girls who excel in special activities.

**Financial data** The "Distinguished Young Woman of America" receives a $30,000 scholarship; other scholarships are $15,000 for the first runner-up, $10,000 for the second runner-up, $2,500 for each of the 7 other finalists, $1,000 for each of the category winners, and "satellite awards" ranging from $500 to $1,500 for other activities.

**Duration** The competition is held annually.

**Additional information** This program began in 1958 as America's Junior Miss. It acquired its current name in 2010.

**Number awarded** More than $140,000 in scholarships is awarded at the national finals each year.

**Deadline** Each local competition sets its own deadline.

## [174]
## DISTRIBUTED RESEARCH EXPERIENCES FOR UNDERGRADUATES (DREU)

Computing Research Association
1828 L Street, N.W., Suite 800
Washington, DC 20036-5104
(202) 234-2111                    Fax: (202) 667-1066
E-mail: dreu@cra.org
Web: cra-w.org/undergraduate

**Summary** To provide an opportunity for female and under-represented minority undergraduate students to work on a summer research project in computer science or engineering.

**Eligibility** This program is open to members of underrepresented groups (women, Hispanics, African Americans, and American Indians) who are entering their junior or senior year of college. Applicants must be interested in conducting a summer research project directly related to computer science or computer engineering under the mentorship of a faculty member at the mentor's home university. They must be U.S. citizens or permanent residents. Selection is based on the student's potential for success in graduate school, the match between the student's experience and skills and the needs of a participating professor's research project, the student's potential gain from the experience, and the possibility that the student's participation will advance the goals of the program.

**Financial data** Students receive a stipend of $600 per week plus relocation travel assistance up to $500.

**Duration** 10 weeks during the summer.

**Additional information** This program began in 1994 as the Distributed Mentor Project (DMP) by the Computing Research Association's Committee on the Status of Women in Computing Research (CRA-W). In 2007, the Coalition to Diversify Computing (CDC) became a cosponsor of the program and in 2009 it was given its current name. From the beginning, funding has been provided by the National Science Foundation. Other sponsors have included the Henry Luce Foundation (current), USENIX, and AAAI.

**Number awarded** Varies each year; recently, 53 students were selected to participate in this program.

**Deadline** February of each year.

## [175]
## DISTRICT OF COLUMBIA AREA AFWA CHAPTER SCHOLARSHIPS

Accounting and Financial Women's Alliance-District of
   Columbia Area Chapter
c/o Rebecca Boland, Scholarship Committee Chair
BDO
7101 Wisconsin Avenue, Suite 800
Bethesda, MD 20814-4827
(301) 770-4490
Web: aswadc.org/page/scholarship-information

**Summary** To provide financial assistance to women from any state working on an undergraduate degree in accounting or finance at a college or university in the Washington, D.C. area.

**Eligibility** This program is open to female residents of any state who are working on a bachelor's degree in accounting or finance at a college or university in the Washington, D.C. area. Applicants must be entering their third, fourth, or fifth year of study and have a GPA of 3.0 or higher. Along with their application, they must submit an essay of 150 to 250 words on their career goals and objectives, the impact they want to have on the accounting world, community involvement, and leadership examples. Membership in the Accounting and Financial Women's Alliance (AFWA) is not required. Selection is based on leadership, character, communication skills, scholastic average, and financial need.

**Financial data** The stipend is $1,500.

**Duration** 1 year.

**Number awarded** 1 each year.

**Deadline** April of each year.

## [176]
## DIXIE SOFTBALL SCHOLARSHIPS

Dixie Softball, Inc.
Attn: President
1101 Skelton Drive
Birmingham, AL 35224
(205) 785-2255                    Fax: (205) 785-2258
E-mail: OBIEDSI@aol.com
Web: softball.dixie.org/page/scholarships

**Summary** To provide financial assistance for college to high school senior women who have participated in the Dixie Softball program.

**Eligibility** This program is open to high school senior women who played in the Dixie Softball program for at least 2 seasons. Applicants must submit academic data (GPA, SAT/ACT scores, class rank), a letter explaining why they are seeking this assistance, verification from a Dixie Softball local official of the number of years the applicant participated in the program, and documentation of financial need. Ability as an athlete is not considered in the selection process.

**Financial data** The stipend is $1,500.

**Duration** 1 year.

**Additional information** This program, established in 1979, includes the following named scholarships: the Billy Adkins Memorial Scholarship, the Frank L. Baxter Honorary Scholarship, the R.T. Adams Memorial Scholarship, the Helen Louise Jordan Memorial Scholarship, the George D. Matthews, Sr. Honorary Scholarship, the Tim Neely Memorial Scholarship, the Aubrey Tapley Honorary Scholarship, and the Charles "Buddy" Wade Memorial Scholarship. Dixie Softball operates in Alabama, Arkansas, Florida, Georgia, Louisiana, Mississippi, North Carolina, South Carolina, Tennessee, Texas, and Virginia.

**Number awarded** 8 each year.

**Deadline** February of each year.

## [177]
## DOE/MICKEY LELAND ENERGY FELLOWSHIPS

Department of Energy
Office of Fossil Energy
1000 Independence Avenue, S.W., FE-6
Washington, DC 20585
(202) 586-4484          E-mail: alan.perry@hq.doe.gov
Web: energy.gov/fe/mickey-leland-energy-fellowship

**Summary**  To provide summer work experience at fossil energy sites of the Department of Energy (DOE) to female and underrepresented minority students or postdoctorates.

**Eligibility**  This program is open to U.S. citizens currently enrolled full time at an accredited college or university. Applicants must be undergraduate, graduate, or postdoctoral students in fields of science, technology (IT), engineering, or mathematics (STEM) and have a GPA of 3.0 or higher. They must be interested in a summer work experience at a DOE fossil energy research facility. Along with their application, they must submit a 100-word statement on why they want to participate in this program. A goal of the program is to recruit women and underrepresented minorities into careers related to fossil energy, although all qualified students are encouraged to apply.

**Financial data**  Weekly stipends are $600 for undergraduates, $750 for master's degree students, or $850 for doctoral and postdoctoral students. Travel costs for a round trip to and from the site and for a trip to a designated place for technical presentations are also paid.

**Duration**  10 weeks during the summer.

**Additional information**  This program began as 3 separate activities: the Historically Black Colleges and Universities Internship Program established in 1995, the Hispanic Internship Program established in 1998, and the Tribal Colleges and Universities Internship Program, established in 2000. Those 3 programs were merged into the Fossil Energy Minority Education Initiative, renamed the Mickey Leland Energy Fellowship Program in 2000. Sites to which interns may be assigned include the Albany Research Center (Albany, Oregon), the National Energy Technology Laboratory (Morgantown, West Virginia and Pittsburgh, Pennsylvania), Pacific Northwest National Laboratory (Richland, Washington), Rocky Mountain Oilfield Testing Center (Casper, Wyoming), Strategic Petroleum Reserve Project Management Office (New Orleans, Louisiana), or U.S. Department of Energy Headquarters (Washington, D.C.).

**Number awarded**  Varies each year; recently, 30 students participated in this program.

**Deadline**  January of each year.

## [178]
## DOMINIQUE LISA PANDOLFO SCHOLARSHIP

Community Foundation of New Jersey
Attn: Chief Operating Officer
35 Knox Hill Road
P.O. Box 338
Morristown, NJ 07963-0338
(973) 267-5533, ext. 227          Toll Free: (800) 659-5533
Fax: (973) 267-2903          E-mail: fkrueger@cfnj.org
Web: www.cfnj.org/funds/scholarship/all.php

**Summary**  To provide financial assistance to female residents of New Jersey who demonstrate outstanding scholarship, character, personality, and leadership qualities.

**Eligibility**  This program is open to women graduating from high schools in New Jersey who have already been accepted at a postsecondary educational institution in any state. Applicants may not necessarily be the top student in their class, but they must have shown outstanding potential, merit, and/or improvement. Selection is based primarily on financial need, but academic performance, extracurricular activities, and work experience are also considered.

**Financial data**  The stipend is $1,250 per year. Funds are made payable jointly to the recipient and her educational institution.

**Duration**  4 years, provided the recipient maintains a GPA of 2.8 or higher.

**Additional information**  This program was established after September 11, 2001 to honor a student who was killed in the attack on the World Trade Center.

**Number awarded**  1 each year.

**Deadline**  March of each year.

## [179]
## DONALD AND ITASKER THORNTON MEMORIAL SCHOLARSHIP

Thornton Sisters Foundation
P.O. Box 21
Atlantic Highlands, NJ 07716-0021
(732) 872-1353          E-mail: tsfoundation2001@yahoo.com
Web: www.thornton-sisters.com/ttsf.htm

**Summary**  To provide financial assistance for college to women of color in New Jersey.

**Eligibility**  This program is open to women of color (defined as African Americans, Latino Americans, Caribbean Americans, and Native Americans) who are graduating from high schools in New Jersey. Applicants must have a grade average of "C+" or higher and be able to document financial need. They must be planning to attend an accredited 4-year college or university. Along with their application, they must submit a 500-word essay describing their family background, personal and financial hardships, honors or academic distinctions, and community involvement and activities.

**Financial data**  A stipend is awarded (amount not specified). Funds are to be used for tuition and/or books.

**Duration**  1 year; nonrenewable.

**Number awarded**  1 or more each year.

**Deadline**  May of each year.

## [180]
## DONNA REIFSCHNEIDER SCHOLARSHIP

Delta Zeta Sorority
Attn: Foundation Coordinator
202 East Church Street
Oxford, OH 45056
(513) 523-7597          Fax: (513) 523-1921
E-mail: DZFoundation@dzshq.com
Web: www.deltazeta.org

**Summary**  To provide financial assistance for continued undergraduate or graduate study in music or music education to members of Delta Zeta Sorority.

**Eligibility**  This program is open to upper-division and graduate members of the sorority who have a GPA of 3.0 or higher. Applicants must be working on a degree in music or music education. Along with their application, they must submit an official transcript, a statement of their career goals, information on their service to the sorority, documentation of campus activities and/or community involvement, a list of academic honors, and an explanation of their financial need. Preference is given to members of the Iota Upsilon chapter at California State University at Fullerton or Iota Iota chapter at Middle Tennessee State University.

**Financial data** The stipend ranges from $500 to $2,500 for undergraduates or from $1,000 to $15,000 for graduate students, depending on the availability of funds.

**Duration** 1 year; nonrenewable.

**Number awarded** 1 each year.

**Deadline** February of each year.

## [181]
## DORIS HERTSGAARD SCHOLARSHIP

Fargo-Moorhead Area Foundation
Attn: Finance/Program Assistant
502 First Avenue North, Suite 202
Fargo, ND 58102-4804
(701) 234-0756          Fax: (701) 234-9724
E-mail: Cher@areafoundation.org
Web: areafoundation.org/index.php/scholarships

**Summary** To provide financial assistance to women from any state who are working on an undergraduate or graduate degree in a mathematics-related field at specified colleges and universities in Minnesota or North Dakota.

**Eligibility** This program is open to women from any state who are currently enrolled at Concordia University, Minnesota State University at Moorhead, or North Dakota State University. Applicants must be working on an undergraduate or graduate degree with a mathematics component (e.g., computer science, engineering, mathematics, physical science, statistics). Along with their application, they must submit a 2-page essay on their professional goals and how those relate to their academic interest in their mathematical field of study. Financial need is considered in the selection process, but greater emphasis is placed on academic achievement. Preference is given to women who are single parents with pre-teenage children.

**Financial data** A stipend is awarded (amount not specified).

**Duration** 1 year.

**Number awarded** 1 or more each year.

**Deadline** April of each year.

## [182]
## DOROTHY ANDREWS KABIS MEMORIAL INTERNSHIPS

National Federation of Republican Women
Attn: Scholarships and Internships
124 North Alfred Street
Alexandria, VA 22314-3011
(703) 548-9688          Fax: (703) 548-9836
E-mail: mail@nfrw.org
Web: www.nfrw.org/programs/scholarships.htm

**Summary** To provide summer work internships to undergraduate women interested in working at the headquarters of the National Federation of Republican Women.

**Eligibility** This program is open to women who are at least juniors in college but have not graduated. Applicants may be

majoring in any field, but they should have a general knowledge of government and a keen interest in politics, including campaign experience and clerical office skills. Along with their application, they must submit 3 letters of recommendation, an official transcript, a 1-page essay on their interest in the internship, and a 1-page description of a particular political, extracurricular, or community activity in which they have been involved, including an account of their personal contribution to the activity. Applications must be submitted to the federation president in the applicant's state. Each president chooses 1 application from her state to submit for scholarship consideration. U.S. citizenship is required.

**Financial data** Interns receive housing in the Washington, D.C. metropolitan area, round-trip airfare, and a small stipend.

**Duration** 6 weeks during the summer.

**Number awarded** 3 each year.

**Deadline** February of each year.

## [183]
## DOROTHY C. WISNER SCHOLARSHIP

P.E.O. Foundation-California State Chapter
c/o Lynne Miller, Scholarship Committee Chair
1875 Los Altos
Clovis, CA 93611
(559) 709-6123          E-mail: peoca.rgw@gmail.com
Web: www.peocalifornia.org

**Summary** To provide financial assistance to women from California who are interested in working on an undergraduate degree in the medical field at a school in any state.

**Eligibility** This program is open to female residents of California who have completed at least their first year of undergraduate work in the broad field of medicine. Graduate students are not eligible. Applicants may be studying in any state. They must submit a personal narrative that describes their background, interests, scholastic achievements, extracurricular activities, service, talents, and goals. Selection is based on character, integrity, academic excellence, and financial need.

**Financial data** The stipend ranges from $500 to $1,000 per year.

**Duration** 1 year; recipients may reapply.

**Additional information** This fund was established in 1990.

**Number awarded** 1 each year.

**Deadline** January of each year.

## [184]
## DOROTHY CAMPBELL MEMORIAL SCHOLARSHIP

Oregon Student Access Commission
Attn: Grants and Scholarships Division
1500 Valley River Drive, Suite 100
Eugene, OR 97401-2146
(541) 687-7395      Toll Free: (800) 452-8807, ext. 7395
Fax: (541) 687-7414      TDD: (800) 735-2900
E-mail: awardinfo@osac.state.or.us
Web: www.oregonstudentaid.gov/scholarships.aspx

**Summary** To provide financial assistance to women in Oregon who are interested in golf and planning to attend college in the state.

**Eligibility** This program is open to residents of Oregon who are U.S. citizens or permanent residents. Applicants must be female high school seniors or graduates with a cumulative GPA of 2.75 or higher and a strong continuing interest in golf. They must be enrolled or planning to enroll full-time at an Oregon 4-year college. Along with their application, they must submit a 1-page essay on the contribution that golf has made to their development. Financial need is considered in the selection process.

**Financial data** Stipends for scholarships offered by the Oregon Student Access Commission (OSAC) range from $200 to $10,000 but recently averaged $2,300.

**Duration** 1 year; may be renewed up to 3 additional years.

**Additional information** This program is administered by the OSAC with funds provided by the Oregon Community Foundation.

**Number awarded** Varies each year; recently, 2 of these scholarships were awarded.

**Deadline** February of each year.

## [185]
## DOROTHY COOKE WHINERY MUSIC BUSINESS/ TECHNOLOGY SCHOLARSHIP

Sigma Alpha Iota Philanthropies, Inc.
One Tunnel Road
Asheville, NC 28805
(828) 251-0606                    Fax: (828) 251-0644
E-mail: nh@sai-national.org
Web: www.sai-national.org

**Summary** To provide financial assistance to members of Sigma Alpha Iota (an organization of women musicians) working on a degree in music, business, or technology.

**Eligibility** This program is open to members of the organization entering their junior or senior year of college. Applicants must be working on a degree in the field of music business or music technology, including music marketing, music business administration, entertainment industry, commercial music, recording and production, music management, or other related fields. They must have a GPA of 3.0 or higher. Along with their application, they must submit a statement of purpose that includes their career goals.

**Financial data** The stipend is $2,000.

**Duration** 1 year.

**Additional information** This program began in 2003.

**Number awarded** 1 each year.

**Deadline** March of each year.

## [186]
## DOROTHY E. SCHOELZEL MEMORIAL SCHOLARSHIP

General Federation of Women's Clubs of Connecticut
c/o Nancy Kalyan, President
4 Mulberry Lane
Enfield, CT 06082
E-mail: KalyanGFWCC@aol.com
Web: www.gfwcct.org

**Summary** To provide financial assistance to women in Connecticut who are working on an undergraduate or graduate degree in education.

**Eligibility** This program is open to female residents of Connecticut who have completed at least 3 years of college.

Applicants must have a GPA of 3.0 or higher and be working on a bachelor's or master's degree in education. They must be U.S. citizens. Selection is based on academic ability, future promise, and financial need.

**Financial data** The stipend is $2,000.

**Duration** 1 year.

**Number awarded** 1 each year.

**Deadline** February of each year.

## [187]
## DOROTHY L. WELLER PEO SCHOLARSHIP

P.E.O. Foundation-California State Chapter
c/o Lynne Miller, Scholarship Committee Chair
1875 Los Altos
Clovis, CA 93611
(559) 709-6123                    E-mail: peoca.rgw@gmail.com
Web: www.peocalifornia.org

**Summary** To provide financial assistance for law school or paralegal studies to women in California.

**Eligibility** This program is open to female residents of California who have been admitted to an accredited law school or a licensed paralegal school. Applicants must have completed 4 years of high school and be able to demonstrate excellence in academic ability, character, integrity, and school activities. Financial need is also considered in the selection process.

**Financial data** Recently, the stipend was $2,500.

**Duration** 1 year.

**Number awarded** Varies each year; recently, 4 of these scholarships were awarded.

**Deadline** January of each year.

## [188]
## DOROTHY LEMKE HOWARTH SCHOLARSHIPS

Society of Women Engineers
Attn: Scholarship Selection Committee
203 North LaSalle Street, Suite 1675
Chicago, IL 60601-1269
(312) 596-5223                    Toll Free: (877) SWE-INFO
Fax: (312) 644-8557              E-mail: scholarships@swe.org
Web: societyofwomenengineers.swe.org

**Summary** To provide financial assistance to lower-division women majoring in computer science or engineering.

**Eligibility** This program is open to women who are entering their sophomore year at a 4-year ABET-accredited college or university. Applicants must be U.S. citizens or permanent residents who are working full time on a degree in computer science or engineering and have a GPA of 3.0 or higher. Selection is based on merit.

**Financial data** The stipend is $2,500.

**Duration** 1 year.

**Additional information** This program began in 1991.

**Number awarded** 6 each year.

**Deadline** February of each year.

## [189]
## DOROTHY M. AND EARL S. HOFFMAN SCHOLARSHIPS

Society of Women Engineers
Attn: Scholarship Selection Committee
203 North LaSalle Street, Suite 1675
Chicago, IL 60601-1269
(312) 596-5223　　　　　　Toll Free: (877) SWE-INFO
Fax: (312) 644-8557　　　　E-mail: scholarships@swe.org
Web: societyofwomenengineers.swe.org

**Summary** To provide financial assistance to women who will be entering college as freshmen and are interested in studying engineering or computer science.

**Eligibility** This program is open to women who are entering college as freshmen with a GPA of 3.5 or higher. Applicants must be planning to enroll full time at an ABET-accredited 4-year college or university and major in computer science or engineering. Selection is based on merit. Preference is given to students at Bucknell University and Rensselaer Polytechnic Institute.

**Financial data** The stipend is $3,000 per year.

**Duration** 1 year; may be renewed for up to 3 additional years.

**Additional information** This program began in 1999.

**Number awarded** Varies each year; recently, 8 of these scholarships were awarded.

**Deadline** May of each year.

## [190]
## DOROTHY P. MORRIS SCHOLARSHIP

Society of Women Engineers
Attn: Scholarship Selection Committee
203 North LaSalle Street, Suite 1675
Chicago, IL 60601-1269
(312) 596-5223　　　　　　Toll Free: (877) SWE-INFO
Fax: (312) 644-8557　　　　E-mail: scholarships@swe.org
Web: societyofwomenengineers.swe.org

**Summary** To provide financial assistance to undergraduate women majoring in computer science or engineering.

**Eligibility** This program is open to women who are entering their sophomore, junior, or senior year at a 4-year ABET-accredited college or university. Applicants must be U.S. citizens or permanent residents working full time on a degree in computer science or engineering and have a GPA of 3.0 or higher. Financial need is considered in the selection process.

**Financial data** The stipend is $1,500.

**Duration** 1 year.

**Number awarded** 1 each year.

**Deadline** February of each year.

## [191]
## DOT SUMMER TRANSPORTATION INTERNSHIP PROGRAM FOR DIVERSE GROUPS

Department of Transportation
Attn: Summer Transportation Internship Program for Diverse Groups
HAHR-40, Room E63-433
1200 New Jersey Avenue, S.E.
Washington, DC 20590
(202) 366-2907　　　　　E-mail: lafayette.melton@dot.gov
Web: www.fhwa.dot.gov/education/stipdg.cfm

**Summary** To enable female, minority, and disabled undergraduate, graduate, and law students to gain work experience during the summer at facilities of the U.S. Department of Transportation (DOT).

**Eligibility** This program is open to all qualified applicants, but it is designed to provide women, persons with disabilities, and members of diverse social and ethnic groups with summer opportunities in transportation. Applicants must be U.S. citizens currently enrolled in a degree-granting program of study at an accredited institution of higher learning at the undergraduate (community or junior college, university, college, or Tribal College or University) or graduate level. Undergraduates must be entering their junior or senior year; students attending a Tribal or community college must have completed their first year of school; law students must be entering their second or third year of school. Students who will graduate during the spring or summer are not eligible unless they have been accepted for enrollment in graduate school. The program accepts applications from students in all majors who are interested in working on transportation-related topics and issues. Preference is given to students with a GPA of 3.0 or higher. Undergraduates must submit a 1-page essay on their transportation interests and how participation in this program will enhance their educational and career plans and goals. Graduate students must submit a writing sample representing their educational and career plans and goals. Law students must submit a legal writing sample.

**Financial data** The stipend is $4,000 for undergraduates or $5,000 for graduate and law students. The program also provides housing and reimbursement of travel expenses from interns' homes to their assignment location.

**Duration** 10 weeks during the summer.

**Additional information** Assignments are at the DOT headquarters in Washington, D.C., a selected modal administration, or selected field offices around the country.

**Number awarded** 80 to 100 each year.

**Deadline** December of each year.

## [192]
## DR. BEA OKWU GIRL SCOUT GOLD AWARD SCHOLARSHIP

Girl Scouts of Connecticut
Attn: Program Department
20 Washington Avenue
North Haven, CT 06437
(203) 239-2922, ext. 3310
Toll Free: (800) 922-2770 (within CT)
E-mail: program@gsoft.org
Web: www.gsoft.org

**Summary** To provide financial assistance to Girl Scouts in Connecticut who plan to attend college in any state.

**Eligibility** This program is open to high school seniors who are registered Girl Scouts in Connecticut and planning to attend college in any state. Applicants must have earned the Gold Award. Selection is based primarily on achievement in the completion of the Gold Award requirements.

**Financial data** The stipend is $1,000.

**Duration** 1 year.

**Number awarded** 1 each year.

**Deadline** March of each year.

## [193]
## DR. BLANCA MOORE-VELEZ WOMAN OF SUBSTANCE SCHOLARSHIP

National Association of Negro Business and Professional Women's Clubs
Attn: Scholarship Committee
1806 New Hampshire Avenue, N.W.
Washington, DC 20009-3206
(202) 483-4206                    Fax: (202) 462-7253
E-mail: education@nanbpwc.org
Web: www.nanbpwc.org/scholarship_applications0.aspx

**Summary** To provide financial assistance to mature African American women from Nevada who are interested in working on an undergraduate degree at a college in any state.

**Eligibility** This program is open to African American women over 35 years of age who are residents of Nevada. Applicants must be working on an undergraduate degree at an accredited college or university in any state. They must have a GPA of 3.0 or higher. Along with their application, they must submit a 500-word essay on "Challenges to the Mature Student and How I Overcame Them." Financial need is not considered in the selection process. U.S. citizenship is required.

**Financial data** A stipend is awarded (amount not specified).

**Duration** 1 year.

**Number awarded** 1 each year.

**Deadline** February of each year.

## [194]
## DR. IVY M. PARKER MEMORIAL SCHOLARSHIP

Society of Women Engineers
Attn: Scholarship Selection Committee
203 North LaSalle Street, Suite 1675
Chicago, IL 60601-1269
(312) 596-5223                    Toll Free: (877) SWE-INFO
Fax: (312) 644-8557          E-mail: scholarships@swe.org
Web: societyofwomenengineers.swe.org

**Summary** To provide financial assistance to upper-division women majoring in computer science or engineering.

**Eligibility** This program is open to women who are entering their junior or senior year at an ABET-accredited college or university. Applicants must be working full time on a degree in computer science or engineering and have a GPA of 3.0 or higher. Financial need is considered in the selection process.

**Financial data** The stipend is $1,500.

**Duration** 1 year.

**Additional information** This program began in 1986.

**Number awarded** 1 each year.

**Deadline** February of each year.

## [195]
## DR. JULIANNE MALVEAUX SCHOLARSHIP

National Association of Negro Business and Professional Women's Clubs
Attn: Scholarship Committee
1806 New Hampshire Avenue, N.W.
Washington, DC 20009-3206
(202) 483-4206                    Fax: (202) 462-7253
E-mail: education@nanbpwc.org
Web: www.nanbpwc.org/scholarship_applications0.aspx

**Summary** To provide financial assistance to African American women studying journalism, economics, or a related field in college.

**Eligibility** This program is open to African American women enrolled at an accredited college or university as a sophomore or junior. Applicants must have a GPA of 3.0 or higher and be majoring in journalism, economics, or a related field. Along with their application, they must submit an essay, up to 1,000 words in length, on their career plans and their relevance to the theme of the program: "Black Women's Hands Can Rock the World." U.S. citizenship is required.

**Financial data** The stipend is $1,000.

**Duration** 1 year.

**Number awarded** 1 or more each year.

**Deadline** February of each year.

## [196]
## DR. SHARON WIBER YOUNG CAREERIST SCHOLARSHIP

Kansas Federation of Business & Professional Women's Clubs, Inc.
Attn: Kansas BPW Educational Foundation, Inc.
c/o Kathy Niehoff, Executive Secretary
605 East 15th
Ottawa, KS 66067
(785) 242-9319                    Fax: (785) 242-1047
E-mail: kathyniehoff@sbcglobal.net
Web: kansasbpw.memberlodge.org

**Summary** To provide financial assistance for college to residents of Kansas who have participated in the Young Careerist Program of the Kansas BPW Educational Foundation.

**Eligibility** This program is open to members of the Kansas BPW between 21 and 35 years of age who have represented their local BPW organization in district, regional, or state Young Careerist competitions and are majoring in a subject that will increase their employable skills. Applicants must submit 1) proof of participation in the Young Careerist program; and 2) a 3-page personal biography in which they express their career goals, the direction they want to take in the future, their proposed field of study, their reason for selecting that field, the institutions they plan to attend and why, their circumstances for reentering school (if a factor), and what makes them uniquely qualified for this scholarship. They must also be able to document financial need. Applications must be submitted through a local unit of the sponsor.

**Financial data** A stipend is awarded (amount not specified).

**Duration** 1 year.

**Number awarded** 1 or more each year.

**Deadline** December of each year.

## [197]
## DUPONT SCHOLARSHIPS

Society of Women Engineers
Attn: Scholarship Selection Committee
203 North LaSalle Street, Suite 1675
Chicago, IL 60601-1269
(312) 596-5223          Toll Free: (877) SWE-INFO
Fax: (312) 644-8557          E-mail: scholarships@swe.org
Web: societyofwomenengineers.swe.org

**Summary**  To provide financial assistance to women interested in studying chemical or mechanical engineering at a college or university in the East or Midwest.

**Eligibility**  This program is open to women entering their sophomore, junior, or senior year as a full-time student at an ABET-accredited 4-year college or university in an eastern or midwestern state. Applicants must have a GPA of 3.0 or higher and be planning to major in chemical or mechanical engineering. Selection is based on merit.

**Financial data**  The stipend is $1,000.

**Duration**  1 year.

**Additional information**  This program, established in 2000, is sponsored by E.I. duPont de Nemours and Company.

**Number awarded**  2 each year.

**Deadline**  February of each year.

## [198]
## DWIGHT F. DAVIS MEMORIAL SCHOLARSHIPS

United States Tennis Association
Attn: USTA Serves
70 West Red Oak Lane
White Plains, NY 10604
(914) 696-7223          Fax: (914) 697-2307
E-mail: foundation@usta.com
Web: www.ustaserves.com

**Summary**  To provide financial assistance to female and male high school seniors (judged separately) who have participated in an organized community tennis program and plan to attend college in any state.

**Eligibility**  This program is open to high school seniors who have excelled academically, demonstrated achievements in leadership, and participated extensively in an organized community tennis program. Applicants must be planning to enroll as a full-time undergraduate student at a 4-year college or university. They must have a GPA of 3.0 or higher and be able to demonstrate financial need. Along with their application, they must submit an essay of 1 to 2 pages about how their participation in a tennis and education program has influenced their life, including examples of special mentors, volunteer service, and future goals. Women and men are judged separately in the selection process.

**Financial data**  The stipend is $2,500 per year. Funds are paid directly to the recipient's college or university.

**Duration**  4 years.

**Number awarded**  2 each year: 1 to a woman and 1 to a man.

**Deadline**  February of each year.

## [199]
## DWIGHT MOSLEY SCHOLARSHIPS

United States Tennis Association
Attn: USTA Serves
70 West Red Oak Lane
White Plains, NY 10604
(914) 696-7223          Fax: (914) 697-2307
E-mail: foundation@usta.com
Web: www.ustaserves.com

**Summary**  To provide financial assistance to female and male high school seniors (judged separately) who are from diverse ethnic backgrounds, have participated in an organized community tennis program, and plan to attend college in any state.

**Eligibility**  This program is open to high school seniors from diverse ethnic backgrounds who have excelled academically, demonstrated achievements in leadership, and participated extensively in an organized community tennis program. Applicants must be planning to enroll as a full-time undergraduate student at a 4-year college or university. They must have a GPA of 3.0 or higher and be able to demonstrate financial need and sportsmanship. Along with their application, they must submit an essay of 1 to 2 pages about how their participation in a tennis and education program has influenced their life, including examples of special mentors, volunteer service, and future goals. Females and males are considered separately.

**Financial data**  The stipend is $2,500 per year. Funds are paid directly to the recipient's college or university.

**Duration**  4 years.

**Number awarded**  2 each year: 1 female and 1 male.

**Deadline**  February of each year.

## [200]
## E. WAYNE COOLEY SCHOLARSHIP AWARD

Iowa Girls High School Athletic Union
Attn: Scholarships
5000 Westown Parkway
West Des Moines, IA 50266
(515) 288-9741          Fax: (515) 284-1969
E-mail: jasoneslinger@ighsau.org
Web: www.ighsau.org/aspx/cooley_award.aspx

**Summary**  To provide financial assistance to female high school seniors in Iowa who have participated in athletics and plan to attend college in the state.

**Eligibility**  This program is open to women graduating from high schools in Iowa who have a GPA of 3.75 or higher and an ACT score of 23 or higher. Applicants must have earned a varsity letter in at least 2 different sports and have participated in at least 2 sports each year of high school. They must be planning to attend a college or university in Iowa. Each high school in the state may nominate 1 student. Selection is based on academic achievements, athletic accomplishments, non-sports extracurricular activities, and community involvement.

**Financial data**  The winner's stipend is $3,750 per year. Finalists receive a $1,000 scholarship.

**Duration**  4 years for the winner, provided she maintains at least a 2.5 GPA while enrolled in college. The scholarships for finalists are for 1 year.

**Additional information**  This program began in 1993.

**Number awarded** 6 each year: 1 winner and 5 finalists.

**Deadline** December of each year.

## [201]
## ECL CAREER IN TEACHING SCHOLARSHIPS

American Baptist Churches of the Rocky Mountains
Attn: American Baptist Women's Ministries
9085 East Mineral Circle, Suite 170
Centennial, CO 80112
(303) 988-3900 E-mail: web@abcrm.org
Web: abcrm.org/ministries/women_scholarships_co.htm

**Summary** To provide financial assistance to women who are members of churches affiliated with the American Baptist Churches (ABC) USA in Colorado, New Mexico, and Utah and interested in attending college in Colorado to prepare for a career as a teacher.

**Eligibility** This program is open to women under 26 years of age who are active members of churches cooperating with ABC in Colorado, New Mexico, or Utah. Applicants must be enrolled or planning to enroll full time at a 4-year college or university in Colorado. They must be preparing for a career in teaching. Along with their application, they must submit a personal letter describing their Christian experience; their participation in the life of their church, school, and community; and their goals for the future. Selection is based on academic performance, Christian participation in church and school, and financial need.

**Financial data** The stipend is $1,000 per year.

**Duration** 1 year; recipients may reapply.

**Number awarded** 1 or more each year.

**Deadline** March of each year.

## [202]
## EDITH B. WONNELL SCHOLARSHIP

American College of Nurse-Midwives
Attn: ACNM Foundation, Inc.
8403 Colesville Road, Suite 1550
Silver Spring, MD 20910-6374
(240) 485-1850 Fax: (240) 485-1818
E-mail: fdn@acnm.org
Web: www.midwife.org

**Summary** To provide financial assistance for midwifery education to student members of the American College of Nurse-Midwives (ACNM) who plan to work in a home or birth center midwifery practice after graduation.

**Eligibility** This program is open to ACNM members who are currently enrolled in an accredited basic midwife education program and have successfully completed 1 academic or clinical semester/quarter or clinical module. Applicants must be planning to work in an out-of-hospital setting, either in a birth center or home birth practice. Along with their application, they must submit a 150-word essay on their midwifery career plans; a 100-word essay on their intended future participation in the local, regional, and/or national activities of the ACNM; and a 300-word statement about their goals in choosing to work in a home or birth center as a midwife. Selection is based on leadership potential, financial need, academic history, and potential for future professional contribution to the organization.

**Financial data** A stipend is awarded (amount not specified).

**Duration** 1 year.

**Number awarded** 1 or more each year.

**Deadline** March of each year.

## [203]
## EDITH GREEN GRANT

Delta Kappa Gamma Society International-Alpha Rho State Organization
c/o Jill Lang, State Scholarship Chair
16301 S.E. Katie Court
Milwaukie, OR 97267-5198
(503) 786-7268 E-mail: jaceel@comcast.net
Web: www.deltakappagamma.org

**Summary** To provide financial assistance to women from Oregon who are enrolled as upper-division students at a college in any state and preparing for a career in secondary education.

**Eligibility** This program is open to female residents of Oregon who are at least juniors at a college in any state and interested in preparing for a career in secondary education. Applicants may not be members of Delta Kappa Gamma (an honorary society of women educators), but they must be sponsored by a local chapter of the society. Along with their application, they must submit a summary of their education from high school through the present, high school and college activities and achievements, community service, employment history, career goals, and financial need.

**Financial data** A stipend is awarded (amount not specified).

**Duration** 1 year.

**Additional information** Recipients may not accept a scholarship from the Alpha Rho state organization and from Delta Kappa Gamma International in the same year.

**Number awarded** 1 or more each year.

**Deadline** February of each year.

## [204]
## EDITH HEAD SCHOLARSHIP

Delta Zeta Sorority
Attn: Foundation Coordinator
202 East Church Street
Oxford, OH 45056
(513) 523-7597 Fax: (513) 523-1921
E-mail: DZFoundation@dzshq.com
Web: www.deltazeta.org

**Summary** To provide financial assistance for continued undergraduate or graduate study in fashion design to members of Delta Zeta Sorority.

**Eligibility** This program is open to upper-division and graduate members of the sorority who have a GPA of 3.0 or higher. Applicants must be juniors, seniors, graduate students, or students at a professional school that offers fashion merchandising, textiles, and clothing and costume design. Along with their application, they must submit an official transcript, a statement of their career goals, information on their service to the sorority, documentation of campus activities and/or community involvement, a list of academic honors, and an explanation of their financial need.

**Financial data** The stipend ranges from $500 to $2,500 for undergraduates or from $1,000 to $15,000 for graduate students, depending on the availability of funds.

**Duration** 1 year; nonrenewable.

**Number awarded** 1 each year.

**Deadline** February of each year.

## [205]
## EDUCATIONAL FOUNDATION FOR WOMEN IN ACCOUNTING IMA UNDERGRADUATE SCHOLARSHIP

Educational Foundation for Women in Accounting
Attn: Foundation Administrator
136 South Keowee Street
Dayton, OH 45402
(937) 424-3391                    Fax: (937) 222-5749
E-mail: info@efwa.org
Web: www.efwa.org/scholarships.php

**Summary** To provide financial support to women who are working on an undergraduate accounting degree.

**Eligibility** This program is open to women who are enrolled at any stage in an accounting bachelor's degree program at an accredited college or university. Selection is based on aptitude for accounting and business, commitment to the goal of working on a degree in accounting (including evidence of continued commitment after receiving this award), clear evidence that the candidate has established goals and a plan for achieving those goals (both personal and professional), and financial need. U.S. citizenship is required.

**Financial data** The stipend is $2,000. Winners also receive a CMA Learning System kit (worth $745) and a complimentary 1-year students membership to the Institute of Management Accountants (IMA).

**Duration** 1 year.

**Additional information** This program is funded by the IMA.

**Number awarded** 2 each year.

**Deadline** April of each year.

## [206]
## EDWIN G. AND LAURETTA M. MICHAEL SCHOLARSHIP

Christian Church (Disciples of Christ)
Attn: Disciples Home Missions
130 East Washington Street
P.O. Box 1986
Indianapolis, IN 46206-1986
(317) 713-2652                    Toll Free: (888) DHM-2631
Fax: (317) 635-4426        E-mail: mail@dhm.disciples.org
Web: www.discipleshomemissions.org

**Summary** To provide financial support to ministers' wives whose basic education was interrupted to enable their husbands to complete their theological education.

**Eligibility** This program is open to ministers' wives who are working on an undergraduate degree and whose husbands have completed their basic theological education, are employed full time in ministry, and hold standing in the ministry of the Christian Church (Disciples of Christ) in the United States or Canada. Primary consideration is given to ministers' wives who will be in institutions of higher education accredited by 1 of the major regionally accrediting bodies for secondary schools and colleges. Evidence of financial need is required.

**Financial data** The stipend is $1,000.

**Duration** 1 year.

**Number awarded** A limited number are awarded each year.

**Deadline** March of each year.

## [207]
## ELIZABETH AHLEMEYER QUICK/GAMMA PHI BETA SCHOLARSHIP

National Panhellenic Conference
Attn: NPC Foundation
3901 West 86th Street, Suite 398
Indianapolis, IN 46268
(317) 872-3185                    Fax: (317) 872-3192
E-mail: npcfoundation@npcwomen.org
Web: www.npcwomen.org/foundation/scholarships.aspx

**Summary** To provide financial assistance to undergraduate women who are members of Greek-letter societies.

**Eligibility** This program is open to women enrolled full time as juniors or seniors at colleges and universities in the United States. Applicants must have a GPA of 3.0 or higher and be able to demonstrate financial need. They must be nominated by their college Panhellenic and have demonstrated outstanding service to that organization. Selection is based on campus, chapter, and community service; financial need; academic standing; and nomination by the applicant's college Panhellenic.

**Financial data** The stipend is $2,000.

**Duration** 1 year.

**Number awarded** 1 each year.

**Deadline** January of each year.

## [208]
## ELIZABETH BANTA MUELLER SCHOLARSHIPS

Kappa Delta Sorority
Attn: Foundation Project Manager
3205 Players Lane
Memphis, TN 38125
(901) 748-1897, ext. 203        Toll Free: (800) 536-1897
Fax: (901) 748-0949
E-mail: caroline.cullum@kappadelta.org
Web: www.kappadelta.org/scholarshipapplications_1

**Summary** To provide financial assistance to members of Kappa Delta Sorority who are majoring in speech and communications.

**Eligibility** This program is open to undergraduate members of Kappa Delta Sorority. Applicants must submit a personal statement giving their reasons for applying for this scholarship, an official undergraduate transcript, and 2 letters of recommendation. Special consideration is given to members majoring in speech and communications. Selection is based on academic excellence; service to the chapter, alumnae association, or national Kappa Delta; service to the campus and community; personal objectives and goals; potential; recommendations; and financial need.

**Financial data** The stipend is $2,000 per year. Funds may be used only for tuition, fees, and books, not for room and board.

**Duration** 1 year; may be renewed.

**Number awarded** 3 each year: 2 to speech and communication majors and 1 to a member with any major.

**Deadline** November of each year.

## [209]
## ELIZABETH LOWELL PUTNAM PRIZE

Mathematical Association of America
1529 18th Street, N.W.
Washington, DC 20036-1358
(202) 387-5200          Toll Free: (800) 741-9415
Fax: (202) 265-2384          E-mail: maahq@maa.org
Web: www.maa.org/awards/putnam.html

**Summary**  To recognize and reward outstanding women participants in a mathematics competition.

**Eligibility**  This program is open to women at colleges and universities in Canada and the United States. Entrants participate in an examination containing mathematics problems designed to test originality as well as technical competence. The woman with the highest score receives this prize.

**Financial data**  The prize is $1,000.

**Duration**  The competition is held annually.

**Additional information**  This program began in 1992.

**Number awarded**  1 each year.

**Deadline**  Deadline not specified.

## [210]
## ELIZABETH M. SMITH MEMORIAL SCHOLARSHIP

Delta Sigma Theta Sorority, Inc.-Boston Alumnae Chapter
Attn: Scholarship Committee
P.O. Box 51424
Boston, MA 02205
(617) 548-3642          E-mail: bac_dst@yahoo.com
Web: www.cityofboston.gov

**Summary**  To provide financial assistance to African American women from Massachusetts interested in working on a degree in social sciences.

**Eligibility**  This program is open to African American women who either live or attend an accredited college or university in Massachusetts. Applicants must be sophomores, juniors, or seniors who are majoring in the social sciences and have a GPA of 3.0 or higher. They must be able to demonstrate academic achievement, commitment to community service, motivation, character, and ability to overcome adversity and meet challenges.

**Financial data**  The stipend is $1,000.

**Duration**  1 year.

**Additional information**  The sponsor is the local alumnae chapter of a traditionally African American social sorority.

**Number awarded**  1 each year.

**Deadline**  February of each year.

## [211]
## ELIZABETH MCLEAN MEMORIAL SCHOLARSHIP

Society of Women Engineers
Attn: Scholarship Selection Committee
203 North LaSalle Street, Suite 1675
Chicago, IL 60601-1269
(312) 596-5223          Toll Free: (877) SWE-INFO
Fax: (312) 644-8557          E-mail: scholarships@swe.org
Web: societyofwomenengineers.swe.org

**Summary**  To provide financial assistance to undergraduate women majoring in civil engineering.

**Eligibility**  This program is open to women who are entering their sophomore, junior, or senior year at an ABET-accredited 4-year college or university. Applicants must be working full time on a degree in civil engineering and have a GPA of 3.0 or higher. Selection is based on merit.

**Financial data**  The stipend is $1,500.

**Duration**  1 year.

**Number awarded**  1 each year.

**Deadline**  February of each year.

## [212]
## ELKS NATIONAL FOUNDATION "MOST VALUABLE STUDENT" SCHOLARSHIP AWARD

Elks National Foundation
Attn: Scholarship Department
2750 North Lakeview Avenue
Chicago, IL 60614-2256
(773) 755-4732          Fax: (773) 755-4729
E-mail: scholarship@elks.org
Web: www.elks.org/ENF/scholars/mvs.cfm

**Summary**  To provide financial assistance to outstanding high school seniors who can demonstrate financial need and are interested in attending college (females and males are judged separately).

**Eligibility**  This program is open to graduating high school students (or the equivalent) who are U.S. citizens residing within the jurisdiction of the B.P.O. Elks of the U.S.A. Applicants must be planning to work on a 4-year degree on a full-time basis at a college or university within the United States. Along with their application, they must submit 1) a 500-word essay on their choice of 3 assigned topics; and 2) exhibits, up to 20 pages, on their achievements in scholarship, leadership, athletics, performing arts, community service, or other activities. Selection is based on that essay and exhibits, transcripts, SAT and/or ACT scores, a report from their school counselor, letters of recommendation, and financial need. Male and female students compete separately.

**Financial data**  First place is $12,500 per year; second place is $10,000 per year; third place is $7,500 per year; fourth place is $5,000 per year; and runners-up receive $1,000 per year. Nearly $2.3 million is distributed through this program each year.

**Duration**  4 years.

**Additional information**  In addition to this program, established in 1931, many Elks State Associations and/or Lodges also offer scholarships. Applications must be submitted to an Elks Lodge in your community.

**Number awarded**  500 each year: 2 first awards (1 male and 1 female), 2 second awards (1 male and 1 female), 2 third awards (1 male and 1 female), 14 fourth awards (7 males and 7 females), and 480 runners-up (240 males and 240 females).

**Deadline**  December of each year.

## [213]
## ELLIS/CORLEY SCHOLARSHIP

National Naval Officers Association-Washington, D.C.
  Chapter
c/o LCDR Stephen Williams
P.O. Box 30784
Alexandria, VA 22310
(703) 566-3840                    Fax: (703) 566-3813
E-mail: Stephen.Williams@navy.mil
Web: dcnnoa.memberlodge.com

**Summary** To provide financial assistance to female African American high school seniors from the Washington, D.C. area who are interested in attending an Historically Black College or University (HBCU) in any state.

**Eligibility** This program is open to female African American seniors graduating from high schools in the Washington, D.C. metropolitan area who plan to enroll full time at an HBCU in any state. Applicants must have a GPA of 2.5 or higher and be U.S. citizens or permanent residents. Selection is based on academic achievement, community involvement, and financial need.

**Financial data** The stipend is $1,000.

**Duration** 1 year; nonrenewable.

**Additional information** Recipients are not required to join or affiliate with the military in any way.

**Number awarded** 1 each year.

**Deadline** March of each year.

## [214]
## ELSIE G. RIDDICK SCHOLARSHIP

North Carolina Federation of Business and Professional
  Women's Club, Inc.
Attn: BPW/NC Foundation
175 BPW Club Road
P.O. Box 276
Carrboro, NC 27510
Web: www.bpw-nc.org/Default.aspx?pageId=837230

**Summary** To provide financial assistance to women attending North Carolina colleges, community colleges, or graduate schools.

**Eligibility** This program is open to women who are currently enrolled in a community college, 4-year college, or graduate school in North Carolina. Applicants must be endorsed by a local BPW unit. Along with their application, they must submit a 1-page statement that summarizes their career goals, previous honors, or community activities and justifies their need for this scholarship. U.S. citizenship is required.

**Financial data** The stipend is $1,000. Funds are paid directly to the recipient's school.

**Duration** 1 year; recipients may reapply.

**Additional information** This program began in 1925 as a loan fund. Since 1972 it has been administered as a scholarship program.

**Number awarded** 1 each year.

**Deadline** April of each year.

## [215]
## EMERGE SCHOLARSHIPS

Emerge Scholarships, Inc.
3525 Piedmont Road
Building Five, Suite 30305
Atlanta, GA 30305
(404) 477-5808      E-mail: info@emergescholarships.org
Web: www.emergescholarships.org

**Summary** To provide financial assistance to women interested in returning to college or graduate school after a delay or interruption.

**Eligibility** This program is open to women who are at least 25 years of age and who have interrupted or delayed their education because they are changing careers, seeking advancement in their career or work life, looking for personal growth, or returning to school after caring for children. Applicants must have been accepted as an undergraduate or graduate student at an educational institution. They must be current residents of the United States or Puerto Rico (including foreign nationals who plan to study in the United States) or U.S. citizens living abroad applying to study in the United States. Along with their application, they must submit a 2-page essay on how beginning or continuing their education will positively impact their life. Selection is based on that essay, leadership and participation in community activities, honors and awards received, career and life goals, financial need, and other funding received. Preference is given to women pursuing their education in Georgia.

**Financial data** Stipends range from $2,000 to $5,000. funds may be used only for tuition, books, and fees at the recipient's educational institution.

**Duration** 1 year.

**Additional information** This program began in 2001. Winners are invited to Atlanta to accept their scholarships; the sponsor pays all travel expenses.

**Number awarded** Varies each year; recently, 13 of these scholarships were awarded.

**Deadline** October of each year.

## [216]
## EMIL SLAVIK MEMORIAL SCHOLARSHIPS

Slovak Catholic Sokol
Attn: Membership Memorial Scholarship Fund
205 Madison Street
P.O. Box 899
Passaic, NJ 07055-0899
(973) 777-2605                    Toll Free: (800) 886-7656
Fax: (973) 779-8245  E-mail: life@slovakcatholicsokol.org
Web: www.slovakcatholicsokol.org/grantsscholarships.asp

**Summary** To provide financial assistance to female and male members (judged separately) of the Slovak Catholic Sokol who are working on a degree in specified fields at a college or graduate school in any state.

**Eligibility** This program is open to members of the Slovak Catholic Sokol who have completed at least 1 semester of college and are currently enrolled full time as an undergraduate or graduate student at an accredited college, university, or professional school in any state with a GPA of 2.5 or higher. Applicants must have been a member for at least 5 years, have at least $3,000 permanent life insurance coverage, have both parents who are members, and have at least 1 parent who is of Slovak descent. They must be working on a degree in the liberal arts, the sciences, pre-law, pre-medicine, or business. Males and females are judged separately.

**Financial data** The stipend is $2,500 per year.

**Duration** 1 year; may be renewed 1 additional year.

**Additional information** Slovak Catholic Sokol was founded as a fraternal benefit society in 1905. It is licensed to operate in the following states: Connecticut, Illinois, Indiana, Massachusetts, Michigan, New Jersey, New York, Ohio, Pennsylvania, and Wisconsin.

**Number awarded** 2 each year: 1 for a male and 1 for a female.

**Deadline** March of each year.

## [217]
## EMILY CHAISON GOLD AWARD SCHOLARSHIP

Girl Scouts of Connecticut
Attn: Program Department
20 Washington Avenue
North Haven, CT 06437
(203) 239-2922, ext. 3310
Toll Free: (800) 922-2770 (within CT)
E-mail: program@gsoft.org
Web: www.gsoft.org

**Summary** To provide financial assistance to Girl Scouts in Connecticut who plan to attend college in any state.

**Eligibility** This program is open to high school seniors who are registered Girl Scouts in Connecticut and planning to attend college in any state. Applicants must have earned the Gold Award. Along with their application, they must submit essays on 1) how they will embody Girl Scout value in the future; and 2) the involvement they intend to have with Girl Scouts and why. Selection is based on the essays, community service, and commitment to Girl Scouting.

**Financial data** The stipend is $1,000.

**Duration** 1 year.

**Additional information** This program began in 1985.

**Number awarded** 1 each year.

**Deadline** March of each year.

## [218]
## EMILY SCHOENBAUM RESEARCH AND COMMUNITY DEVELOPMENT GRANTS

Tulane University
Newcomb College Institute
Attn: Assistant Director for Administration and Programs
200 Caroline Richardson Hall
62 Newcomb Place
New Orleans, LA 70118
(504) 314-2721          Toll Free: (888) 327-0009
Fax: (504) 862-8589        E-mail: lwolford@tulane.edu
Web: tulane.edu/newcomb/grants.cfm

**Summary** To provide funding to scholars and students in Louisiana interested in conducting research or other projects related to women and girls.

**Eligibility** This program is open to students, faculty, and staff of primary and secondary schools, colleges, and universities in Louisiana, as well as community scholars and activists. Applicants must be interested in conducting a project with potential to bring about change in women's lives or effect

public policy so as to improve the well-being of women and girls, particularly those in the New Orleans area.

**Financial data** The grant is $2,000.

**Duration** 1 year.

**Additional information** This program began in 1999.

**Number awarded** 1 or 2 each year.

**Deadline** April of each year.

## [219]
## EMMA HARPER TURNER FUND

Pi Beta Phi
Attn: Pi Beta Phi Foundation
1154 Town and Country Commons Drive
Town and Country, MO 63017
(636) 256-1357          Fax: (636) 256-8124
E-mail: fndn@pibetaphi.org
Web: www.pibetaphifoundation.org/emma-harper-turner

**Summary** To provide assistance to alumnae of Pi Beta Phi Sorority who are in extreme need of college funding or personal financial assistance.

**Eligibility** Any member of Pi Beta Phi needing financial assistance is eligible to be considered for this funding. Each potential recipient must be sponsored by 3 Pi Beta Phi alumnae who are aware of the candidate's need and are personally acquainted with her. Applicants must submit a confidential financial information form to validate their need. The program includes 3 types of grants: collegian (for college students who have experienced a life change that jeopardizes their ability to stay in school), alumna (for college graduates who are experiencing financial difficulties), and immediate needs (for alumnae who are victims of a natural disaster).

**Financial data** Small monthly gifts are awarded.

**Duration** Awards are provided for 1 year; the recipient's application is then reviewed to determine if the "gifts of love" should continue.

**Additional information** This fund was established in 1946.

**Number awarded** Varies each year. A total of $100,000 is available for these grants annually.

**Deadline** Applications may be submitted at any time.

## [220]
## ERIN MARIE EMERINE MEMORIAL SCHOLARSHIP

Columbus Foundation
Attn: Scholarship Manager
1234 East Broad Street
Columbus, OH 43205-1453
(614) 251-4000          Fax: (614) 251-4009
E-mail: dhigginbotham@columbusfoundation.org
Web: tcfapp.org

**Summary** To provide financial assistance to women working on an undergraduate or graduate degree at a college or university in Ohio.

**Eligibility** This program is open to women currently attending an accredited 4-year college or university in Ohio. Applicants may be residents of any state, although preference may be given to Ohio residents. They must meet 1 of the following stipulations: 1) returned to college as an undergraduate or graduate student after an extended absence of at least 2 years; 2) 23 years of age or older and in college for the first time or applying for graduate school for the first time with a GPA of 3.0 or higher; or 3) has completed the freshman year with a GPA of 3.0 or higher. Along with their application, they must submit their most recent transcript, 2 letters of recommendation, a list of volunteer activities, a list of extracurricular activities, a personal essay on how volunteering has impacted their life, and information on financial need.

**Financial data** The stipend is $1,500.

**Duration** 1 year.

**Number awarded** 1 or more each year.

**Deadline** April of each year.

## [221]
## ERMA METZ BROWN SCHOLARSHIP

Kappa Delta Sorority
Attn: Foundation Project Manager
3205 Players Lane
Memphis, TN 38125
(901) 748-1897, ext. 203        Toll Free: (800) 536-1897
Fax: (901) 748-0949
E-mail: caroline.cullum@kappadelta.org
Web: www.kappadelta.org/scholarshipapplications_1

**Summary** To provide financial assistance to members of Kappa Delta Sorority who are majoring in elementary education.

**Eligibility** This program is open to undergraduate members of Kappa Delta Sorority. Applicants must submit a personal statement giving their reasons for applying for this scholarship, an official undergraduate transcript, and 2 letters of recommendation. They must be majoring in elementary education. Selection is based on academic excellence; service to the chapter, alumnae association, or national Kappa Delta; service to the campus and community; personal objectives and goals; potential; recommendations; and financial need.

**Financial data** The stipend is $2,000 per year. Funds may be used only for tuition, fees, and books, not for room and board.

**Duration** 1 year; may be renewed.

**Additional information** This program began in 2005.

**Number awarded** 3 each year.

**Deadline** November of each year.

## [222]
## ESPERANZA SCHOLARSHIP

New York Women in Communications, Inc.
Attn: NYWICI Foundation
355 Lexington Avenue, 15th Floor
New York, NY 10017-6603
(212) 297-2133                Fax: (212) 370-9047
E-mail: nywicipr@nywici.org
Web: www.nywici.org/foundation/scholarships

**Summary** To provide financial assistance to Hispanic women who are residents of designated eastern states and interested in preparing for a career in communications at a college or graduate school in any state.

**Eligibility** This program is open to Hispanic women who are seniors graduating from high schools in New York, New Jersey, Connecticut, or Pennsylvania or undergraduate or graduate students who are permanent residents of those states; they must be attending or planning to attend a college

or university in any state. Graduate students must be members of New York Women in Communications, Inc. (NYWICI). Also eligible are Hispanic women who reside outside the 4 states but are currently enrolled at a college or university within 1 of the 5 boroughs of New York City. All applicants must be working on a degree in a communications-related field (e.g., advertising, broadcasting, communications, English, film, journalism, marketing, digital media, public relations) and have a GPA of 3.2 or higher. Along with their application, they must submit a 2-page resume; a personal essay of 300 words on an assigned topic that changes annually; 2 letters of recommendation; and an official transcript. Selection is based on academic record, need, demonstrated leadership, participation in school and community activities, honors and other awards or recognition, work experience, goals and aspirations, and unusual personal and/or family circumstances. U.S. citizenship is required.

**Financial data** The stipend ranges up to $10,000.

**Duration** 1 year.

**Additional information** This program is funded by Macy's and Bloomingdale's.

**Number awarded** 1 each year.

**Deadline** January of each year.

## [223]
## ETHEL B. LYNCH MEMORIAL SCHOLARSHIP

National Association of Women in Construction-
   Wilmington Chapter 96
Attn: Gladys King, Scholarship Chair
P.O. Box 96
Montchanin, DE 19710
(302) 285-3630
Web: www.nawicde.org/scholarships-block-kids

**Summary** To provide financial assistance to female residents of Delaware who are interested in attending college in any state to prepare for a career in construction.

**Eligibility** This program is open to female residents of Delaware who are interested in working full or part time on an associate or bachelor's degree in a construction-related program, including engineering, at a school in any state. Applicants may be high school seniors, high school graduates, or currently-enrolled college students. Selection is based on GPA, interest in construction, extracurricular activities, employment experience, academic adviser evaluation, and financial need.

**Financial data** Stipends range from $500 to $1,000.

**Duration** 1 year; may be renewed, provided the recipient maintains a GPA of 2.5 or higher.

**Number awarded** 1 or more each year.

**Deadline** March of each year.

## [224]
## ETHEL LEE HOOVER ELLIS SCHOLARSHIP

National Association of Negro Business and Professional
   Women's Clubs
Attn: Scholarship Committee
1806 New Hampshire Avenue, N.W.
Washington, DC 20009-3206
(202) 483-4206                Fax: (202) 462-7253
E-mail: education@nanbpwc.org
Web: www.nanbpwc.org/scholarship_applications0.aspx

**Summary** To provide financial assistance to African American women from designated southern states studying business at a college in any state.

**Eligibility** This program is open to African Americans women who are residents of Alabama, Florida, Georgia, Mississippi, North Carolina, South Carolina, Tennessee, or West Virginia. Applicants must be enrolled at an accredited college or university in any state as a sophomore or junior. They must have a GPA of 3.0 or higher and be majoring in business. Along with their application, they must submit an essay, up to 750 words in length, on the topic, "Business and Community United." U.S. citizenship is required.

**Financial data** A stipend is awarded (amount not specified).

**Duration** 1 year.

**Number awarded** 1 or more each year.

**Deadline** February of each year.

## [225]
## ETHEL O. GARDNER PEO SCHOLARSHIP

P.E.O. Foundation-California State Chapter
c/o Lynne Miller, Scholarship Committee Chair
1875 Los Altos
Clovis, CA 93611
(559) 709-6123　　　　E-mail: peoca.rgw@gmail.com
Web: www.peocalifornia.org

**Summary** To provide financial assistance to women from California who are upper-division or graduate students at a school in any state.

**Eligibility** This program is open to female residents of California who have completed at least 2 years at a college or university in any state. Applicants must be enrolled as full-time undergraduate or graduate students. Selection is based on financial need, character, and a record of academic and extracurricular activities achievement.

**Financial data** Stipends range from $500 to $1,500.

**Duration** 1 year.

**Number awarded** Varies each year; recently, 69 of these scholarships were awarded.

**Deadline** January of each year.

## [226]
## EUGENIA VELLNER FISCHER AWARD FOR THE PERFORMING ARTS

Miss America Pageant
Attn: Scholarship Department
222 New Road, Suite 700
Linwood, NJ 08221
(609) 653-8700, ext. 127　　　　Fax: (609) 653-8740
E-mail: info@missamerica.org
Web: www.missamerica.org/scholarships/eugenia.aspx

**Summary** To provide financial assistance to women who are working on an undergraduate or graduate degree in the performing arts and who, in the past, competed at some level in the Miss America competition.

**Eligibility** This program is open to women who are working on an undergraduate, master's, or higher degree in the performing arts and who competed at the local, state, or national level in a Miss America competition within the past 10 years. Applicants may be studying dance, instrumental, monologue, or vocal. They must submit an essay, up to 500 words, on the

factors that influenced their decision to enter the field of performing arts, what they consider to be their major strengths in the field, and how they plan to use their degree in the field. Selection is based on GPA, class rank, extracurricular activities, financial need, and level of participation within the system.

**Financial data** The stipend is $2,000.

**Duration** 1 year; renewable.

**Additional information** This scholarship was established in 1999.

**Number awarded** 1 each year.

**Deadline** June of each year.

## [227]
## EUNICE RIGGINS MEMORIAL SCHOLARSHIP

Alpha Delta Kappa-North Carolina Chapter
c/o Renee Friday, Scholarship Chair
1240 Branson Road
Concord, NC 28027
(704) 793-9540　　　　E-mail: renfriday@yahoo.com
Web: www.alphadeltakappa.org

**Summary** To provide financial assistance to female high school seniors in North Carolina who plan to attend college in the state.

**Eligibility** This program is open to women graduating from high schools in North Carolina and planning to enroll at a 4-year college or university in the state. Applicants must rank in the top 10% of their class and have scores of at least 1650 on the SAT or 20 on the ACT. Along with their application, they must submit a letter on their plans, career goals, and reasons for wanting this scholarship. Selection is based on character and participation in extracurricular activities; financial need is not considered.

**Financial data** The stipend is $2,000.

**Duration** 1 year; nonrenewable.

**Number awarded** 1 each year.

**Deadline** January of each year.

## [228]
## EVE KRAFT EDUCATION AND COLLEGE SCHOLARSHIPS

United States Tennis Association
Attn: USTA Serves
70 West Red Oak Lane
White Plains, NY 10604
(914) 696-7223　　　　Fax: (914) 697-2307
E-mail: foundation@usta.com
Web: www.ustaserves.com

**Summary** To provide financial assistance to female and male high school seniors (judged separately) who have participated in an organized community tennis program, reside in an economically disadvantaged community, and plan to attend college in any state.

**Eligibility** This program is open to high school seniors who have excelled academically, demonstrated achievements in leadership, and participated extensively in an organized community tennis program. Applicants must be planning to enroll as a full-time undergraduate student at a 4-year college or university. They must reside in an economically disadvantaged community. Along with their application, they must submit an essay of 1 to 2 pages about how their participation in a tennis and education program has influenced their life, including examples of special mentors, volunteer service, and future goals. Females and males are considered separately.

**Financial data**   The stipend is $2,500. Funds are paid directly to the recipient's college or university.

**Duration**   1 year; nonrenewable.

**Number awarded**   2 each year: 1 female and 1 male.

**Deadline**   February of each year.

## [229]
## EXELON SCHOLARSHIPS

Society of Women Engineers
Attn: Scholarship Selection Committee
203 North LaSalle Street, Suite 1675
Chicago, IL 60601-1269
(312) 596-5223                    Toll Free: (877) SWE-INFO
Fax: (312) 644-8557              E-mail: scholarships@swe.org
Web: societyofwomenengineers.swe.org

**Summary**   To provide financial assistance to women who will be entering college as freshmen and are interested in studying electrical or mechanical engineering or computer science.

**Eligibility**   This program is open to women who are entering college as freshmen with a GPA of 3.5 or higher. Applicants must be planning to enroll full time at an ABET-accredited 4-year college or university and major in computer science, electrical engineering, or mechanical engineering. Selection is based on merit.

**Financial data**   The stipend is $1,000.

**Duration**   1 year.

**Additional information**   This program is sponsored by Exelon Corporation, parent of ComEd and PECO, the electric utilities for northern Illinois and southeastern Pennsylvania, respectively.

**Number awarded**   5 each year.

**Deadline**   May of each year.

## [230]
## EXERCISE FOR LIFE ATHLETIC SCHOLARSHIPS

Boomer Esiason Foundation
c/o Jerry Cahill
483 Tenth Avenue, Suite 300
New York, NY 10018
(646) 292-7930                    Fax: (646) 292-7945
E-mail: jcahill@esiason.org
Web: esiason.org/thriving-with-cf/scholarships.php

**Summary**   To provide financial assistance for college to female and male high school seniors (judged separately) who have been involved in athletics and who have cystic fibrosis (CF).

**Eligibility**   This program is open to CF patients who are college-bound high school seniors. Applicants must have been involved in athletics. They should be jogging on a regular basis and training for a 1.5 mile run. Along with their application, they submit a letter from their doctor confirming the diagnosis of CF and a list of daily medications, information on financial need, a detailed breakdown of tuition costs from their academic institution, a completed running log, transcripts, and a 2-page essay on 1) their postgraduation goals; and 2) the importance of compliance with CF therapies and what they practice on a daily basis to stay healthy. Selection

is based on academic ability, athletic ability, character, leadership potential, service to the community, financial need, and daily compliance to CF therapy. Male and female students compete separately.

**Financial data**   The stipend is $10,000. Funds are paid directly to the academic institution to assist in covering the cost of tuition and fees.

**Duration**   1 year; nonrenewable.

**Number awarded**   2 each year: 1 to a male and 1 to a female.

**Deadline**   June of each year.

## [231]
## EXXONMOBIL BERNARD HARRIS MATH AND SCIENCE SCHOLARSHIPS

Council of the Great City Schools
1301 Pennsylvania Avenue, N.W., Suite 702
Washington, DC 20004
(202) 393-2427                    Fax: (202) 393-2400
Web: www.cgcs.org/Page/47

**Summary**   To provide financial assistance to African American and Hispanic high school seniors interested in studying science, technology, engineering, or mathematics (STEM) in college (females and males are judged separately).

**Eligibility**   This program is open to African American and Hispanic seniors graduating from high schools in a district that is a member of the Council of the Great City Schools, a coalition of 65 of the nation's largest urban public school systems. Applicants must be planning to enroll full time at a 4-year college or university and major in a STEM field of study. They must have a GPA of 3.0 or higher. Along with their application, they must submit 1-page essays on 1) how mathematics and science education has impacted their lives so far; and 2) why they have chosen to prepare for a career in a STEM field. Selection is based on those essays; academic achievement; extracurricular activities, community service, or other experiences that demonstrate commitment to a career in a STEM field; and 3 letters of recommendation. Financial need is not considered. Males and females are judged separately.

**Financial data**   The stipend is $5,000.

**Duration**   1 year; nonrenewable.

**Additional information**   This program, which began in 2010, is sponsored by the ExxonMobil Corporation and The Harris Foundation.

**Number awarded**   4 each year: an African American male and female and an Hispanic male and female.

**Deadline**   May of each year.

## [232]
## FANNIE WILDER EDUCATIONAL FUND SCHOLARSHIP

Center for Scholarship Administration, Inc.
Attn: Wells Fargo Accounts
4320 Wade Hampton Boulevard, Suite G
Taylors, SC 29687
Toll Free: (866) 608-0001
E-mail: allisonlee@bellsouth.net
Web: www.csascholars.org/wilder/index.php

**Summary**   To provide financial assistance to women from Georgia who plan to attend college in any state.

**Eligibility** This program is open to female residents of Georgia who have a cumulative GPA of 2.5 or higher. Applicants must be attending or planning to attend an accredited 4-year college or university in any state. Selection is based on academic ability, educational goals, participation in extracurricular activities, career ambitions, and financial need.

**Financial data** A stipend is awarded (amount not specified).

**Duration** 1 year; may be renewed up to 3 additional years or until completion of a bachelor's degree (whichever comes first).

**Number awarded** 1 or more each year.

**Deadline** April of each year.

## [233]
## FAY H. SPENCER MEMORIAL SCHOLARSHIPS IN ARCHITECTURE

Texas Society of Architects
Attn: Texas Architectural Foundation
500 Chicon Street
Austin, TX 78702
(512) 478-7386        Fax: (512) 478-0528
E-mail: jallison@texasarchitect.org
Web: texasarchitects.org/v/scholarships

**Summary** To provide financial assistance to women from any state who are entering their fifth or sixth year of study at designated schools of architecture in Texas.

**Eligibility** This program is open to women from any state who are entering their fifth or sixth year of study at the school of architecture at the University of Houston, Rice University, Texas A&M University, or the University of Texas. Applicants must submit their application to the office of the dean of their school. Financial need is considered in the selection process.

**Financial data** A stipend is awarded (amount not specified).

**Duration** 1 year.

**Number awarded** 2 each year.

**Deadline** Deadline not specified.

## [234]
## FEDERALLY EMPLOYED WOMEN NATIONAL COLLEGIATE SCHOLARSHIPS

Federally Employed Women
Attn: Scholarships
700 North Fairfax Street, Suite 510
Alexandria, VA 22314
(202) 898-0994        E-mail: scholarships@few.org
Web: www.few.org

**Summary** To provide financial assistance for college to members of Federally Employed Women (FEW) and their immediate family members.

**Eligibility** This program is open to 1) members of FEW who have actively participated in the organization for 3 years or more; and 2) the children and grandchildren of FEW members. Applicants must be enrolled or planning to enroll at a college or university. Along with their application, members must submit information on their involvement in FEW, accomplishments, special honors and awards, and potential major or field of study; family members must submit an original essay.

**Financial data** A stipend is awarded (amount not specified).

**Duration** 1 year.

**Number awarded** Varies each year; recently, 3 of these scholarships (1 for a member and 2 for family) were awarded.

**Deadline** April of each year.

## [235]
## FEDERATION OF HOUSTON PROFESSIONAL WOMEN EDUCATIONAL FOUNDATION SCHOLARSHIPS

Federation of Houston Professional Women
Attn: Educational Foundation
P.O. Box 27621
Houston, TX 77227-7621
E-mail: educationalfoundation@fhpw.org
Web: www.fhpw.org/the_foundation.html

**Summary** To provide financial assistance for college or graduate school to women from Texas.

**Eligibility** This program is open to women who are residents of Texas and have completed at least 30 semesters hours of work on an associate, bachelor's, or graduate degree at an accredited college or university in the state. Applicants must be U.S. citizens or permanent residents and have a GPA of 3.0 or higher. Along with their application, they must submit 1) a 200-word statement on their short- and long-term goals; 2) a 400-word essay on either the experiences that have helped determine their goals or the avenues that can help determine their goals; and 3) a 100-word biographical sketch. Financial need is considered in the selection process.

**Financial data** Stipends are $2,000 for students at 4-year colleges and universities or $1,000 for students at community colleges. Funds are issued payable jointly to the student and the educational institution.

**Duration** 1 year.

**Additional information** This program began in 2000.

**Number awarded** Varies each year; recently, 18 of these scholarships were awarded. Since this program began, it has awarded more than $275,000 in scholarships.

**Deadline** March of each year.

## [236]
## FINANCIAL WOMEN INTERNATIONAL OF HAWAII SCHOLARSHIP

Hawai'i Community Foundation
Attn: Scholarship Department
827 Fort Street Mall
Honolulu, HI 96813
(808) 566-5570        Toll Free: (888) 731-3863
Fax: (808) 521-6286
E-mail: scholarships@hcf-hawaii.org
Web: www.hawaiicommunityfoundation.org/scholarships

**Summary** To provide financial assistance to women in Hawaii who are studying business on the upper-division or graduate school level at a school in any state.

**Eligibility** This program is open to female residents of Hawaii who are working on a degree in business or a business-related field as a junior, senior, or graduate student at a school in any state. Applicants must be able to demonstrate academic achievement (GPA of 3.5 or higher), good moral character, and financial need. Along with their application, they must submit a short statement indicating their reasons for attending college, their planned course of study, their career goals, and what community service means to them.

**Financial data**   The amounts of the awards depend on the availability of funds and the need of the recipient. Recently, the average value of each of the scholarships awarded by the foundation was more than $2,000.

**Duration**   1 year.

**Additional information**   This program was established in 1992 by the Hawaii chapter of Financial Women International.

**Number awarded**   1 or more each year.

**Deadline**   February of each year.

## [237]
## FIRST LIEUTENANT MICHAEL L. LEWIS, JR. MEMORIAL FUND SCHOLARSHIP

American Legion Auxiliary
Department of New York
112 State Street, Suite 1310
Albany, NY 12207
(518) 463-1162                    Toll Free: (800) 421-6348
Fax: (518) 449-5406     E-mail: alanysandy@nycap.rr.com
Web: www.deptny.org/scholarships.htm

**Summary**   To provide financial assistance to members of the American Legion Auxiliary in New York who plan to attend college in any state.

**Eligibility**   This program is open to 1) junior members of the New York Department of the American Legion Auxiliary who are high school seniors or graduates younger than 20 years of age; and 2) senior members who are continuing their education to further their studies or update their job skills. Applicants must be attending or planning to attend college in any state. Along with their application, they must submit a 200-word essay on "Why a college education is important to me," or "Why I want to continue my post high school education in a business or trade school." Selection is based on character (25%), Americanism (25%), leadership (25%), and scholarship (25%).

**Financial data**   A stipend is awarded (amount not specified).

**Duration**   1 year.

**Number awarded**   2 each year: 1 to a junior member and 1 to a senior member. If no senior members apply, both scholarships are awarded to junior members.

**Deadline**   March of each year.

## [238]
## FLORENCE A. COOK RECRUITMENT GRANTS

Delta Kappa Gamma Society International-Lambda State
  Organization
c/o Becky Retzer, Educational Excellence Committee
  Chair
P.O. Box 24
Wood River, IL 62095-0024
(618) 610-3062                    E-mail: Baretz1@yahoo.com
Web: www.deltakappagamma.org/IL/profaffairs.htm

**Summary**   To provide financial assistance to female residents of Illinois who are studying education at a college in any state.

**Eligibility**   This program is open to female residents of Illinois who are enrolled in a certified teacher education program at a college or university in any state. Each chapter of the sponsoring organization in Illinois may nominate 1 student for this scholarship. Nominees must submit a 2-page personal essay on their career goals and interests within the field of education. Selection is based on the essay, academic excellence, leadership qualities, participation in school activities, contribution to the community and church, and letters of recommendation.

**Financial data**   The stipend is $1,000.

**Duration**   1 year.

**Additional information**   The sponsor is an honorary society of women educators.

**Number awarded**   6 each year.

**Deadline**   January of each year.

## [239]
## FLORENCE ALLEN SCHOLARSHIPS

The Allen Endowment
c/o Holly S. Goodyear
3500 Granger Road
Medina, OH 44256-8602
(330) 725-3333          E-mail: allenendowmen@gmail.com

**Summary**   To provide financial assistance to women from Ohio who are interested in attending college in any state.

**Eligibility**   This program is open to women from Ohio who are either traditional students (graduating high school seniors or recent GED recipients) or nontraditional students (at least 30 years of age). Traditional students must be enrolled or planning to enroll full time at a 4-year college or university in Ohio; nontraditional students must also attend a 4-year college or university in Ohio, but they are not required to enroll full time. All applicants must submit a 500-word essay describing their short-term goals and how the proposed training will help them to accomplish those goals and make a difference in their professional career. Selection is based on that essay; academic, employment, and/or volunteer record; and financial need. Special consideration is given to members of the Ohio Federation of Business and Professional Women (BPW/Ohio) and/or applicants endorsed by a BPW/Ohio local organization. U.S. citizenship is required.

**Financial data**   A stipend is awarded (amount not specified).

**Duration**   1 year.

**Additional information**   This program was originally established in 1924, but became a tax-exempt endowment fund in 1988; since that time, it has awarded more than $79,200 in scholarships.

**Number awarded**   1 or more each year.

**Deadline**   March of each year.

## [240]
## FLORIDA BOARD OF ACCOUNTANCY MINORITY SCHOLARSHIPS

Florida Department of Business and Professional
Regulation
Attn: Division of Certified Public Accounting
240 N.W. 76th Drive, Suite A
Gainesville, FL 32607-6656
(850) 487-1395          Fax: (352) 333-2508
Web: www.myfloridalicense.com/dbpr/cpa

**Summary**  To provide financial assistance to female and minority residents of Florida who are entering the fifth year of an accounting program.

**Eligibility**  This program is open to Florida residents who have completed at least 120 credit hours at a college or university in the state and have a GPA of 2.5 or higher. Applicants must be planning to remain in school as a full-time student for the fifth year required to sit for the C.P.A. examination. They must be members of a minority group, defined to include African Americans, Hispanic Americans, Asian Americans, Native Americans, or women. Selection is based on scholastic ability and performance and financial need.

**Financial data**  The stipend is $3,000 per semester.

**Duration**  1 semester; may be renewed 1 additional semester.

**Number awarded**  Varies each year; a total of $100,000 is available for this program annually.

**Deadline**  May of each year.

## [241]
## FLORIDA LEGION AUXILIARY MEMORIAL SCHOLARSHIP

American Legion Auxiliary
Department of Florida
1912A Lee Road
P.O. Box 547917
Orlando, FL 32854-7917
(407) 293-7411          Toll Free: (866) 710-4192
Fax: (407) 299-6522     E-mail: contact@alafl.org
Web: alafl.org/index.php/scholarships

**Summary**  To provide financial assistance to members and female dependents of members of the Florida American Legion Auxiliary who are interested in attending college in any state.

**Eligibility**  Applicants must be members of the Florida Auxiliary or daughters or granddaughters of members who have at least 3 years of continuous membership. They must be sponsored by their local units, be Florida residents, and be enrolled or planning to enroll full time at a college, university, community college, or vocational/technical school in any state. Selection is based on academic record and financial need.

**Financial data**  The stipends are up to $2,000 for a 4-year university or up to $1,000 for a community college or vocational/technical school. All funds are paid directly to the institution.

**Duration**  1 year; may be renewed if the recipient needs further financial assistance and has maintained at least a 2.5 GPA.

**Number awarded**  Varies each year, depending on the availability of funds.

**Deadline**  January of each year.

## [242]
## FLORIDA P.E.O. SCHOLARSHIPS

P.E.O. Sisterhood-Florida Chapters
c/o Donna Beckwith
2 Holly Circle
Indialantic, FL 32903-4112
(321) 723-1813
Web: peoflorida.org/peo/index.php

**Summary**  To provide financial assistance to women from Florida who will be entering their freshman or sophomore year at a college in the state.

**Eligibility**  This program is open to women who are residents of Florida and entering their freshman or sophomore year as full-time students at an accredited college or university in the state. Applicants must have a GPA of 3.0 or higher and be planning to work on a bachelor's or associate degree. They must be sponsored by a Florida P.E.O. chapter. Selection is based on scholarship, character, and financial need.

**Financial data**  Stipends are $2,000 for students at 4-year institutions or $1,500 for students at 1-year institutions.

**Duration**  1 year; recipients who enroll as freshmen may apply for renewal for their sophomore year.

**Additional information**  This program began in 1994.

**Number awarded**  Varies each year.

**Deadline**  December of each year.

## [243]
## FODALE ENERGY SCHOLARSHIP

Louisiana High School Athletic Association
Attn: Commissioner
12720 Old Hammond Highway
Baton Rouge, LA 70816
(225) 296-5882          Fax: (225) 296-5919
E-mail: lhsaa@lhsaa.org
Web: www.lhsaa.org

**Summary**  To provide financial assistance to student-athletes in Louisiana who plan to study business at a college in any state (females and males are judged separately).

**Eligibility**  This program is open to student-athletes who are seniors graduating from high schools that are members of the Louisiana High School Athletic Association. Applicants must be planning to attend a college or university in any state and work on a degree in business. They must have a GPA of 3.5 or higher and be nominated by their principal. Females and males are considered separately.

**Financial data**  The stipend is $2,500.

**Duration**  1 year.

**Additional information**  This program is sponsored by J.C. Fodale Energy Services.

**Number awarded**  2 each year: 1 for a female and 1 for a male.

**Deadline**  April of each year.

**[244]**
## FORD MOTOR COMPANY SWE UNDERGRADUATE SCHOLARSHIPS

Society of Women Engineers
Attn: Scholarship Selection Committee
203 North LaSalle Street, Suite 1675
Chicago, IL 60601-1269
(312) 596-5223          Toll Free: (877) SWE-INFO
Fax: (312) 644-8557     E-mail: scholarships@swe.org
Web: societyofwomenengineers.swe.org

**Summary**  To provide financial assistance to undergraduate women majoring in designated engineering specialties.

**Eligibility**  This program is open to women who are entering their sophomore or junior year at a 4-year ABET-accredited college or university. Applicants must be working full time on a degree in automotive, electrical, industrial, or mechanical engineering and have a GPA of 3.5 or higher. Selection is based on merit and leadership potential.

**Financial data**  The stipend is $1,000.

**Duration**  1 year.

**Additional information**  This program, established in 2002, is sponsored by the Ford Motor Company.

**Number awarded**  3 each year: 1 to a sophomore and 2 to juniors.

**Deadline**  February of each year.

**[245]**
## FORD OPPORTUNITY PROGRAM SCHOLARSHIP

Oregon Student Access Commission
Attn: Ford Family Foundation
440 East Broadway, Suite 200
Eugene, OR 97401
(541) 485-6211          Toll Free: (877) 864-2872
Fax: (541) 485-6223     E-mail: fordscholarships@tfff.org
Web: www.tfff.org

**Summary**  To provide financial assistance to residents of Oregon and Siskiyou County, California who are single parents working on a college degree at a school in Oregon or California.

**Eligibility**  This program is open to residents of Oregon and Siskiyou County, California who are U.S. citizens or permanent residents. Applicants must be single heads of household with custody of a dependent child or children. They must have a cumulative high school or college GPA of 3.0 or higher or a GED score of 2650 or higher, and they must be planning to earn a bachelor's degree. Students from Oregon must attend a college or university in the state; students from Siskiyou County, California must attend a college or university in California. Selection is based on leadership ability through participation in school and community activities, concern for others and contribution of time and energy to volunteer projects and/or service organizations, contribution to personal success through paid work experience, ability to succeed in college, ability to communicate personal strengths and goals clearly, and financial need.

**Financial data**  This program provides up to 90% of a recipient's unmet financial need, to a maximum of $25,000 per year.

**Duration**  1 year; may be renewed for up to 3 additional years.

**Additional information**  This program, funded by the Ford Family Foundation, began in 1996.

**Number awarded**  55 each year: 50 from Oregon and 5 from Siskiyou County.

**Deadline**  February of each year.

**[246]**
## FRAMELINE COMPLETION FUND

Frameline
Attn: Completion Fund
145 Ninth Street, Suite 300
San Francisco, CA 94103
(415) 703-8650          Fax: (415) 861-1404
E-mail: info@frameline.org
Web: www.frameline.org/filmmaker-support

**Summary**  To provide funding to lesbian, gay, bisexual, and transgender (LGBT) film/video artists (priority is given to women and people of color).

**Eligibility**  This program is open to LGBT artists who are in the last stages of the production of documentary, educational, narrative, animated, or experimental projects about or of interest to LGBT people and their communities. Applicants may be independent artists, students, producers, or nonprofit corporations. They must be interested in completion work and must have 90% of the production completed; projects in development, script-development, pre-production, or production are not eligible. Student projects are eligible only if the student maintains artistic and financial control of the project. Women and people of color are especially encouraged to apply. Selection is based on financial need, the contribution the grant will make to completing the project, assurances that the project will be completed, and the statement the project makes about LGBT people and/or issues of concern to them and their communities.

**Financial data**  Grants range from $1,000 to $5,000.

**Duration**  These are 1-time grants.

**Additional information**  This program began in 1990.

**Number awarded**  Varies each year; recently, 5 of these grants were awarded. Since this program was established, it has provided $389,200 in support to 118 films.

**Deadline**  October of each year.

**[247]**
## FRAN O'SULLIVAN WOMEN IN LENOVO LEADERSHIP (WILL) SCHOLARSHIP

Society of Women Engineers
Attn: Scholarship Selection Committee
203 North LaSalle Street, Suite 1675
Chicago, IL 60601-1269
(312) 596-5223          Toll Free: (877) SWE-INFO
Fax: (312) 644-8557     E-mail: scholarships@swe.org
Web: societyofwomenengineers.swe.org

**Summary**  To provide financial assistance to women working on an undergraduate or graduate degree in computer science or engineering.

**Eligibility**  This program is open to women who are entering full-time freshmen, sophomores, juniors, seniors, or graduate students at an ABET-accredited 4-year college or university. Applicants must be interested in studying computer science or engineering and have a GPA of 3.5 or higher (for entering freshmen) or 3.0 or higher (for all other students). Selection is based on merit.

**Financial data** The stipend is $7,500. The award includes a travel grant for the recipient to attend the national conference of the Society of Women Engineers.

**Duration** 1 year.

**Additional information** This program began in 2011.

**Number awarded** 1 each year.

**Deadline** February of each year for continuing students; May of each year for entering freshmen.

## [248]
## FRANCIS M. KEVILLE MEMORIAL SCHOLARSHIP

Construction Management Association of America
Attn: CMAA Foundation
7926 Jones Branch Drive, Suite 800
McLean, VA 22101-3303
(703) 356-2622          Fax: (703) 356-6388
E-mail: foundation@cmaanet.org
Web: www.cmaafoundation.org

**Summary** To provide financial assistance to female and minority undergraduate and graduate students working on a degree in construction management.

**Eligibility** This program is open to women and members of minority groups who are enrolled as full-time undergraduate or graduate students. Applicants must have completed at least 1 year of study and have at least 1 full year remaining for a bachelor's or master's degree in construction management or a related field. Along with their application, they must submit essays on why they are interested in a career in construction management and why they should be awarded this scholarship. Selection is based on that essay (20%), academic performance (40%), recommendation of the faculty adviser (15%), and extracurricular activities (25%); a bonus of 5% is given to student members of the Construction Management Association of America (CMAA).

**Financial data** The stipend is $3,000. Funds are disbursed directly to the student's university.

**Duration** 1 year.

**Number awarded** 1 each year.

**Deadline** June of each year.

## [249]
## FRESH START SCHOLARSHIP

Wilmington Women in Business
Attn: Fresh Start Scholarship Foundation, Inc.
P.O. Box 7784
Wilmington, DE 19803
(302) 656-4411          E-mail: fsscholar@comcast.net
Web: www.wwb.org?page_id=11

**Summary** To provide financial assistance to women from any state who have experienced an interruption in their education and are interested in attending college in Delaware.

**Eligibility** This program is open to women from any state who are at least 20 years of age, have a high school diploma or GED, and have been admitted to an accredited Delaware college in a 2- or 4-year undergraduate degree program. Applicants must have had at least a 2-year break in education either after completing high school or during college studies. They must have at least a "C" average if currently enrolled in

college and be recommended by a social service agency (or a college representative if a social service agency is not available). U.S. citizenship or permanent resident status is required. Financial need is considered in the selection process.

**Financial data** The stipend varies annually, depending on the availability of funds. Awards are paid to the college at the beginning of each semester.

**Duration** 1 year.

**Additional information** This program began in 1996.

**Number awarded** Varies each year. Since the program was established, it has awarded close to $500,000 to 150 women.

**Deadline** May of each year.

## [250]
## FUTURAMA FOUNDATION CAREER ADVANCEMENT SCHOLARSHIP

Maine Federation of Business and Professional Women's
  Clubs
Attn: BPW/Maine Futurama Foundation
c/o Marilyn V. Ladd, Office Manager
103 County Road
Oakland, ME 04963
Web: www.bpwmefoundation.org/files/index.php?id=10

**Summary** To provide financial assistance to Maine women over 30 years of age who are continuing a program of higher education.

**Eligibility** This program is open to women who are older than 30 years of age and residents of Maine. Applicants must be continuing in, or returning to, an accredited program of higher education or job-related training, either full or part time. They must have a definite plan to use the desired training in a practical and immediate way to improve chances for advancement, train for a new career field, or enter or reenter the job market. Along with their application, they must submit a statement describing their educational, personal, and career goals, including financial need, expectations of training, and future plans for using this educational program. Preference is given to members of Maine Federation of Business and Professional Women's Clubs.

**Financial data** The stipend is $1,200. Funds are paid directly to the school.

**Duration** 1 year.

**Number awarded** 1 or more each year.

**Deadline** April of each year.

## [251]
## GAIL BURNS-SMITH "DARE TO DREAM" SCHOLARSHIPS

Hartford Foundation for Public Giving
Attn: Donor Services Officer
10 Columbus Boulevard, Eighth Floor
Hartford, CT 06106
(860) 548-1888          Fax: (860) 524-8346
E-mail: scholarships@hfpg.org
Web: www.hfpgscholarships.org

**Summary** To provide financial assistance to residents of Connecticut who have participated in sexual violence prevention activities and are interested in attending college in any state to continue their involvement in the field.

**Eligibility** This program is open to Connecticut residents who are attending a high school or college in the state. Applicants must have paid or volunteer work experience in the field of women's issues or sexual violence prevention or advocacy. They must be planning to continue work in the field of sexual violence prevention or advocacy.

**Financial data** The stipend is $1,000.

**Duration** 1 year.

**Additional information** This program is sponsored by Connecticut Sexual Assault Crisis Services, Inc.

**Number awarded** 1 each year.

**Deadline** February of each year.

## [252]
## GE WOMEN'S NETWORK MINNESOTA SWE SCHOLARSHIP

Society of Women Engineers-Minnesota Section
Attn: Scholarship Committee
P.O. Box 582813
Minneapolis, MN 55458-2813
E-mail: scholarships@swe-mn.org
Web: www.swe-mn.org/scholarships.html

**Summary** To provide financial assistance to women from any state working on an undergraduate or graduate degree in biomedical engineering at colleges and universities in Minnesota, North Dakota, and South Dakota.

**Eligibility** This program is open to female undergraduate and graduate students at ABET-accredited engineering programs in Minnesota, North Dakota, or South Dakota. Applicants must be working full time on a degree in biomedical engineering. Along with their application, they must submit a short paragraph describing how they plan to utilize their engineering skills after they graduate. Selection is based on potential to succeed as an engineer (20 points), communication skills (10 points), extracurricular or community involvement and leadership skills (10 points), demonstrated successful work experience (10 points), and academic success (5 points).

**Financial data** The stipend is $1,500.

**Duration** 1 year.

**Additional information** This program is sponsored by the General Electric Women's Network.

**Number awarded** 2 each year.

**Deadline** March of each year.

## [253]
## GENERAL ELECTRIC WOMEN'S NETWORK SCHOLARSHIPS

Society of Women Engineers
Attn: Scholarship Selection Committee
203 North LaSalle Street, Suite 1675
Chicago, IL 60601-1269
(312) 596-5223          Toll Free: (877) SWE-INFO
Fax: (312) 644-8557     E-mail: scholarships@swe.org
Web: societyofwomenengineers.swe.org

**Summary** To provide financial assistance to undergraduate members of the Society of Women Engineers (SWE) majoring in computer science or specified fields engineering.

**Eligibility** This program is open to members of the society who are entering their sophomore or junior year at a 4-year ABET-accredited college or university. Applicants must be

working full time on a degree in computer science or aeronautical, civil, electrical, industrial, or mechanical engineering and have a GPA of 3.0 or higher. Along with their application, they must submit an essay on why they want to be an engineer or computer scientist, how they believe they will make a difference as an engineer or computer scientist, and what influenced them to study engineering or computer science. Selection is based on merit. Preference is given to students attending selected schools; for a list, contact the sponsor. U.S. citizenship or permanent resident status is required.

**Financial data** The stipend is $5,000.

**Duration** 1 year.

**Additional information** This program, established in 2002, is sponsored by the General Electric Women's Network of the General Electric Company.

**Number awarded** 15 each year.

**Deadline** February of each year.

## [254]
## GENERATION GOOGLE SCHOLARSHIPS

Google Inc.
Attn: Scholarships
1600 Amphitheatre Parkway
Mountain View, CA 94043-8303
(650) 253-0000          Fax: (650) 253-0001
E-mail: generationgoogle@google.com
Web: www.google.com

**Summary** To provide financial assistance to women and members of other underrepresented groups planning to work on a bachelor's degree in a computer-related field.

**Eligibility** This program is open to high school seniors planning to enroll full time at a college or university in the United States or Canada. Applicants must be members of a group underrepresented in computer science: African Americans, Hispanics, American Indians, women, or people with a disability. They must be interested in working on a bachelor's degree in computer science, computer engineering, software engineering, or a related field. Selection is based on academic achievement (GPA of 3.2 or higher), leadership, commitment to and passion for computer science and technology through involvement in their community, and financial need.

**Financial data** The stipend is $10,000 per year for U.S. students or $C5,000 for Canadian students.

**Duration** 1 year; may be renewed for up to 3 additional years or until graduation, whichever comes first.

**Additional information** Recipients are also invited to attend Google's Computer Science Summer Institute at either Mountain View, California or Cambridge, Massachusetts in the summer.

**Number awarded** Varies each year.

**Deadline** February of each year.

## [255]
## GFWC/OHIO FEDERATION OF WOMEN'S CLUBS CLUBWOMAN SCHOLARSHIP

GFWC/Ohio Federation of Women's Clubs
c/o Sharon Pervo, Scholarship Chair
208 Cherry Lane
Avon Lake, OH 44012
E-mail: pervo208@oh.rr.com
Web: www.gfwcohio.org/scholarships.html

**Summary** To provide financial assistance members of the GFWC/Ohio Federation of Women's Clubs who wish to return to college.

**Eligibility** This program is open to members of a federated club who wish to return to college in Ohio. Applicants must be able to demonstrate that they need additional education or training in order to join the work force or to help to provide for themselves and/or their families.

**Financial data** A stipend is awarded (amount not specified).

**Duration** 1 year.

**Number awarded** 1 each year.

**Deadline** February of each year.

## [256]
## GFWC-MFWC HEBRON MEMORIAL SCHOLARSHIP

GFWC/Mississippi Federation of Women's Clubs, Inc.
c/o Ione Bond, Scholarship Committee Chair
224 Beverly Hills Loop
Petal, MS 39465
E-mail: info@gfwc-mfwc.org
Web: www.gfwc-mfwc.org

**Summary** To provide financial assistance to women in Mississippi who are interested in attending college or graduate school in the state.

**Eligibility** This program is open to women who are residents of Mississippi and are high school seniors, high school graduates, or graduates of a college in the state. Applicants must be planning to enroll at a Mississippi institution of higher learning as an undergraduate or graduate student. They may be planning to work on a degree in any field, but preference is given to applicants in areas of service where it is felt there is a need in the state.

**Financial data** The stipend is $1,000. Funds are sent directly to the recipient's institution.

**Duration** 1 year.

**Number awarded** 1 each year.

**Deadline** January of each year.

## [257]
## GIFT FOR LIFE SCHOLARSHIPS

United States Bowling Congress
Attn: Youth Department
621 Six Flags Drive
Arlington, TX 76011
Toll Free: (800) 514-BOWL, ext. 3168
Fax: (817) 385-8262
E-mail: usbcyouth@bowl.com
Web: www.bowl.com

**Summary** To provide financial assistance for college to members of the United State Bowling Congress (USBC) who demonstrate financial hardship (females and males are judged separately).

**Eligibility** This program is open to USBC members who are high school students (grades 9-12) with a GPA of 2.5 or higher. Applicants must be able to demonstrate a financial hardship, defined as residing in a household where the number of children, the income level of their parents, and possible extenuating circumstances make obtaining a college education financially unlikely. They must submit 1) an essay explaining how their financial situation could hinder or stop them from achieving their educational goals; and 2) an essay of up to 500 words on a topic of their choice. Other factors considered in the selection process include academic achievements, community service, scholastic honors, and extracurricular activities. Applications from males and females are evaluated separately. In honor of the heroes of September 11, 2001, 2 scholarships are reserved for an eligible son or daughter of fire/police/emergency rescue personnel.

**Financial data** The stipend is $1,000.

**Duration** Scholarships are presented annually. Students may apply each year they are eligible and may win 1 scholarship each year before their high school graduation.

**Number awarded** 12 each year: 6 specifically for females and 6 for males. That total includes 2 awards reserved for children (1 daughter and 1 son) of fire/police/emergency rescue department employees.

**Deadline** November of each year.

## [258]
## GILBERT G. POMPA MEMORIAL ENDOWED SCHOLARSHIP

¡Adelante! U.S. Education Leadership Fund
8415 Datapoint Drive, Suite 400
San Antonio, TX 78229
(210) 692-1971                    Toll Free: (877) 692-1971
Fax: (210) 692-1951        E-mail: info@adelantefund.org
Web: www.adelantefund.org/adelante/Scholarships1.asp

**Summary** To provide financial assistance to undergraduates at colleges in Texas, especially Hispanic women enrolled in a pre-law program.

**Eligibility** This program is open to full-time students who have completed at least 90 credit hours at an accredited college or university in Texas. Preference is given to women of Hispanic descent. Applicants may be majoring in any field, but preference is given to those enrolled in a pre-law program and/or planning to attend law school. They must be U.S. citizens or permanent residents and have a GPA of 2.75 or higher.

**Financial data** The stipend is $1,000.

**Duration** 1 year.

**Additional information** This fund was established by the Hispanic Association of Colleges and Universities in 1997 and became a separate organization in 1999.

**Number awarded** Varies each year.

**Deadline** May of each year.

## [259]
## GIRL SCOUT COUNCIL OF THE NATION'S CAPITAL GOLD AWARD SCHOLARSHIPS

Girl Scout Council of the Nation's Capital
Attn: Gold Award Scholarship Committee
4301 Connecticut Avenue, N.W.
Washington, DC 20008
(202) 534-3776                        Fax: (202) 274-2161
Web: www.gscnc.org/teen_scholarships.html

**Summary** To provide financial assistance to high school seniors in the Washington, D.C. area who are Girl Scouts and planning to attend college in any state.

**Eligibility** This program is open to seniors graduating from high schools in the Washington, D.C. area and planning to attend a college or university in any state. Applicants must be Girl Scouts who have earned their Gold Award. Along with their application, they must submit essays describing their activities in Girl Scouts and other community organizations.

**Financial data** The stipend is $1,000.

**Duration** 1 year.

**Additional information** This program includes the Sara and Lawrence Phillips Girl Scout Gold Award Scholarships, the Gold Award Scholarship in Honor of Marilynn Carr, and the Shenandoah Region Gold Award Scholarships.

**Number awarded** 17 each year.

**Deadline** March of each year.

## [260]
## GLADYS ANDERSON EMERSON SCHOLARSHIP

Iota Sigma Pi
c/o Jill Nelson Granger, National Director for Student
  Awards
Sweet Briar College
Department of Chemistry
134 Chapel Road
Sweet Briar, VA 24595
(434) 381-6166                E-mail: granger@sbc.edu
Web: www.iotasigmapi.info

**Summary** To provide financial assistance to women undergraduates who have achieved excellence in the study of chemistry or biochemistry.

**Eligibility** The nominee must be a female chemistry or biochemistry student who has attained at least junior standing but has at least 1 semester of work to complete. Both the nominator and the nominee must be members of Iota Sigma Pi, although students who are not members but wish to apply for the scholarship may be made members by National Council action. Selection is based on transcripts; a list of all academic honors and professional memberships; a short essay by the nominee describing herself, her goals in chemistry, any hobbies or talents, and her financial need; and letters of recommendation.

**Financial data** The stipend is $2,000.

**Duration** 1 year.

**Additional information** This program began in 1987.

**Number awarded** 1 or 2 each year.

**Deadline** February of each year.

## [261]
## GLADYS BALES SCHOLARSHIP FOR MATURE WOMEN

Idaho State Business and Professional Women
Attn: Scholarship Committee
P.O. Box 804
Mountain Home, ID 83647
E-mail: idahostatebpw@yahoo.com
Web: www.idahostatebpw/Scholarship.html

**Summary** To provide financial assistance to mature women in Idaho who are interested in majoring in any field at a college in any state.

**Eligibility** This program is open to women in Idaho who are 25 years of age or older. Applicants must be enrolled or planning to enroll full or part time at a community college, techni-

cal school, or 4-year university in any state. They must have a GPA of 2.5 or higher. Along with their application, they must submit brief essays on 1) their career objectives; 2) why the sponsor should consider them for this scholarship, including their financial need; and 3) the challenges they anticipate in reaching their career goal and their plan to address those challenges. Priority is given to women who are 1) returning to the workforce; 2) unemployed or in a job with limited pay, limited growth opportunities, and limited benefits; or 3) raising another family member's child (e.g., grandparents raising grandchildren). U.S. citizenship is required.

**Financial data** The stipend is $1,000. Funds are issued payable to both the educational institution and the recipient and are to be used for tuition, fees, and books.

**Duration** 1 year.

**Number awarded** 1 each year.

**Deadline** June of each year.

## [262]
## GLADYS C. ANDERSON MEMORIAL SCHOLARSHIP

American Foundation for the Blind
Attn: Scholarship Committee
2 Penn Plaza, Suite 1102
New York, NY 10121
(212) 502-7661                Toll Free: (800) AFB-LINE
Fax: (888) 545-8331           E-mail: afbinfo@afb.net
Web: www.afb.org/Section.asp?Documentid=2962

**Summary** To provide financial assistance to legally blind women who are studying classical or religious music on the undergraduate or graduate school level.

**Eligibility** This program is open to women who are legally blind, U.S. citizens, and enrolled in an undergraduate or graduate degree program in classical or religious music. Along with their application, they must submit 200-word essays on 1) their past and recent achievements and accomplishments; 2) their intended field of study and why they have chosen it; and 3) the role their visual impairment has played in shaping their life. They must also submit a sample performance tape or CD of up to 30 minutes. Financial need is considered in the selection process.

**Financial data** The stipend is $1,000.

**Duration** 1 academic year.

**Number awarded** 1 each year.

**Deadline** April of each year.

## [263]
## GLADYS L. MERSEREAU GRANTS-IN-AID

Delta Kappa Gamma Society International-Pi State
  Organization
c/o Jeanne M. Schenk, Grants-in-Aid Committee Chair
7835 County Road 12
Naples, NY 14512
E-mail: jmos29@aol.com
Web: www.deltakappagamma.org/NY/ASaGiA.html

**Summary** To provide financial assistance to women in New York whose education was interrupted and who now need help to become teachers.

**Eligibility** This program is open to women in New York who are interested in completing teacher certification requirements but whose education has been interrupted. Along with their application, they must submit a statement on their educational philosophy, documentation of their financial need, and 3 letters of recommendation (including at least 1 from a member of the sponsoring organization). Members of that organization are not eligible.

**Financial data** The amounts of the grants depend on the availability of funds.

**Duration** 1 year.

**Additional information** This program began in 1975.

**Number awarded** Varies each year; recently, 5 of these grants were awarded.

**Deadline** February of each year.

## [264]
## GLAMOUR'S TOP TEN COLLEGE WOMEN COMPETITION

Glamour Magazine
4 Times Square, 16th Floor
New York, NY 10036-6593
Toll Free: (800) 244-GLAM          Fax: (212) 286-6922
E-mail: TTCW@glamour.com
Web: www.glamour.com/about/top-10-college-women

**Summary** To recognize and reward outstanding college women.

**Eligibility** This competition is open to women enrolled full time in their junior year at accredited colleges and universities in the United States and Canada. Applications must be approved and signed by the appropriate members of the school's faculty and administration (i.e., faculty adviser, the director of public relations, the director of student activities, or the dean of students). There is no limit on the number of applicants from any 1 school. Applicants must submit an essay (up to 500 words) describing their most meaningful achievements and how those relate to their field of study and future goals. Selection is based on leadership experience (34%), personal involvement in campus and community affairs (33%), and academic excellence (33%).

**Financial data** The grand prize is $20,000 and other prizes are $3,000. Each winner also receives a trip to New York City and recognition in the October issue of *Glamour* magazine.

**Duration** The competition is held annually.

**Additional information** The first competition was held in 1990.

**Number awarded** 10 each year: 1 grand prize and 9 other prizes.

**Deadline** July of each year for the early deadline; September of each year for the final deadline.

## [265]
## GO RED MULTICULTURAL SCHOLARSHIP FUND

American Heart Association
Attn: Go Red for Women
7272 Greenville Avenue
Dallas, TX 75231-4596
Toll Free: (800) AHA-USA1
E-mail: GoRedScholarship@heart.org
Web: www.goredforwomen.org/goredscholarship.aspx

**Summary** To provide financial assistance to women from multicultural backgrounds who are preparing for a career in a field of health care.

**Eligibility** This program is open to women who are currently enrolled at an accredited college, university, health care institution, or program and have a GPA of 3.0 or higher. Applicants must be undergraduates of Hispanic, African American, or other minority origin. They must be preparing for a career as a nurse, physician, or allied health care worker. Selection is based on community involvement, a personal letter, transcripts, and 2 letters of recommendation.

**Financial data** The stipend is $2,500.

**Duration** 1 year.

**Additional information** This program, which began in 2012, is supported by Macy's.

**Number awarded** Varies each year; recently, 16 of these scholarships were awarded.

**Deadline** November of each year.

## [266]
## GOLDMAN SACHS SCHOLARSHIPS

Society of Women Engineers
Attn: Scholarship Selection Committee
203 North LaSalle Street, Suite 1675
Chicago, IL 60601-1269
(312) 596-5223          Toll Free: (877) SWE-INFO
Fax: (312) 644-8557     E-mail: scholarships@swe.org
Web: societyofwomenengineers.swe.org

**Summary** To provide financial assistance to upper-division women who are members of the Society of Women Engineers (SWE) and majoring in designated engineering specialties.

**Eligibility** This program is open to members of the society who are entering their junior or senior year at an ABET-accredited 4-year college or university. Applicants must be working full time on a degree in computer science or electrical or computer engineering and have a GPA of 3.2 or higher. They must be SWE members. Selection is based on merit.

**Financial data** The stipend is $2,000. The award includes a travel grant for the recipient to attend the SWE national conference.

**Duration** 1 year.

**Additional information** This program is sponsored by Goldman Sachs.

**Number awarded** 2 each year.

**Deadline** February of each year.

## [267]
## GOOGLE ANITA BORG MEMORIAL SCHOLARSHIPS FOR FIRST YEARS

Google Inc.
Attn: Scholarships
1600 Amphitheatre Parkway
Mountain View, CA 94043-8303
(650) 253-0000          Fax: (650) 253-0001
E-mail: anitaborgscholars@google.com
Web: www.google.com/anitaborg/junior-anita-borg.html

**Summary** To provide financial assistance to female high school seniors planning to attend college and major in a computer-related field.

**Eligibility** This program is open to women who are graduating from high schools in the United States and planning to enroll full time at a college or university. Applicants must be planning to attend a college that has a computer science department and take at least 1 computer science course during their first year. They must intend to work on a baccalaureate degree in computer science, computer engineering, software engineering, or a related field. Along with their application, they must submit 3 essays of 200 words each and 3 short answer questions. International students are eligible if they intend to enroll at a university in the United States. Selection is based on academic background, passion for computer science, community service, and leadership.

**Financial data**   The stipend is $10,000.

**Duration**   1 year.

**Number awarded**   Varies each year; recently, 7 of these scholarships were awarded.

**Deadline**   January of each year.

## [268]
## GRADY-RAYAM PRIZE IN SACRED MUSIC

"Negro Spiritual" Scholarship Foundation
P.O. Box 547728
Orlando, FL 32854-7728
(407) 841-NSSF
Web: www.negrospiritual.org/competition

**Summary**   To recognize and reward, with college scholarships, African American high school students in selected eastern states who excel at singing "Negro spirituals" (females and males are judged separately).

**Eligibility**   This competition is open to high school juniors and seniors of Afro-ethnic heritage in 6 districts: 1) Florida; 2) Southeast (Georgia, North Carolina, and South Carolina); 3) Mid-south (Alabama, Arkansas, Louisiana, Mississippi, and Tennessee); 4) Northeast (New Jersey, New York, and Pennsylvania; 5) New England (Connecticut, Maine, Massachusetts, New Hampshire, Rhode Island, and Vermont); and 6) Capital (Delaware, Maryland, Virginia, Washington, D.C., and West Virginia). Participants must perform 2 "Negro spiritual" songs, 1 assigned and 1 selected. Selection is based on technique (tone quality, intonation, and vocal production), musicianship and artistry (inflection, diction, authenticity, rhythmic energy, and memorization), and stage presence (demeanor, posture, and sincerity of delivery). U.S. citizenship or permanent resident status is required.

**Financial data**   Winners earn tuition assistance grants for college of $3,000 and cash prizes of $300. Other finalists receive cash prizes of $100.

**Duration**   The competition is held annually at a site in each of the 5 regions.

**Additional information**   This program began in Florida in 1997, in the Mid-south district in 2006, in the New England and Capital districts in 2008, in the Southeast district in 2010, and in the Northeast district in 2012. The entry fee is $20.

**Number awarded**   12 tuition assistance grants and cash prizes (1 to a male and 1 to a female in each of the 6 districts) are awarded each year. The number of other cash prizes awarded to finalists varies each year.

**Deadline**   December of each year.

## [269]
## GRANDMA MOSES SCHOLARSHIP

Western Art Association
Attn: Foundation
13730 Loumont Street
Whittier, CA 90601

**Summary**   To provide financial assistance for art school to female high school seniors whose art demonstrates a "congruence with the art of Grandma Moses."

**Eligibility**   This program is open to female graduating high school seniors. Applicants must be planning to study art in a college, university, or specialized school of art. Preference is given to applicants from the western United States. Candidates must submit samples of their artwork; selection is based on the extent to which their work "manifests a congruence with the work of the famed folk artist, Grandma Moses." Financial need is not considered.

**Financial data**   The stipend is $3,000 per year.

**Duration**   1 year; may be renewed up to 3 additional years.

**Additional information**   Requests for applications should be accompanied by a self-addressed stamped envelope, the student's e-mail address, and the source where they found the scholarship information.

**Number awarded**   1 each year.

**Deadline**   March of each year.

## [270]
## GREATLAND SWE SECTION SCHOLARSHIPS

Society of Women Engineers-Greatland Section
c/o Maria Kampsen, Scholarship Chair
DOWL HKM
4041 B Street
Anchorage, AK 99503
(907) 562-2000                      Fax: (907) 563-3953
E-mail: mkampsen@dowlhkm.com
Web: www.swealaska.org/scholarships.html

**Summary**   To provide financial assistance to female high school seniors in Alaska who plan to major in engineering at a college in any state.

**Eligibility**   This program is open to women graduating from high schools in Alaska and planning to enroll in an ABET-accredited engineering program at a 4-year college or university in any state. Applicants must submit a 2-page essay discussing their interest in engineering, their major area of study or specialization, the job they wish to pursue after receiving their college degree, their long-term goals, and how they hope to achieve those. Selection is based on that essay, academic performance, activities and work experience, recommendations, honors and awards, application presentation, and financial need.

**Financial data**   The stipend is $1,500 or $1,000.

**Duration**   1 year.

**Number awarded**   3 each year: 2 at $1,500 and 1 at $1,000.

**Deadline**   February of each year.

## [271]
## GROTTO/JOB'S DAUGHTERS SCHOLARSHIP

International Order of Job's Daughters
c/o Betty Klotz, Educational Scholarships Committee
  Chair
1228 Moss Rock Court
Santa Rosa, CA 95404
(707) 462-6834          E-mail: bettyklotz@gmail.com
Web: www.jobsdaughtersinternational.org

**Summary**  To provide financial assistance to members of Job's Daughters who are working on an undergraduate or graduate degree in a dental field.

**Eligibility**  This program is open to high school seniors and graduates; students in early graduation programs; junior college, technical, and vocational students; and college and graduate students. Applicants must be Job's Daughters in good standing in their Bethels; unmarried majority members under 30 years of age are also eligible. They must be working on a degree in a dental field, preferably with some training in the field of disabilities. Selection is based on scholastic standing, Job's Daughters activities, recommendation by the Executive Bethel Guardian Council, faculty recommendations, and achievements outside Job's Daughters.

**Financial data**  The stipend is $1,500.

**Duration**  1 year.

**Number awarded**  1 or more each year.

**Deadline**  April of each year.

## [272]
## HADASSAH-BRANDEIS INSTITUTE UNDERGRADUATE INTERNSHIPS

Brandeis University
Hadassah-Brandeis Institute
Attn: Program Manager
515 South Street
Mailstop 079
Waltham, MA 02454-9110
(781) 736-8113                    Fax: (781) 736-2078
E-mail: dolins@brandeis.edu
Web: www.brandeis.edu/hbi/internship/undergraduate.html

**Summary**  To provide summer work experience to undergraduate students in the field of Jewish women's studies at the Hadassah-Brandeis Institute of Brandeis University.

**Eligibility**  This program is open to undergraduate students attending universities in the United States and abroad. Applicants must have a demonstrated interest in women's studies, Jewish women's studies, or issues relating to Jewish women around the world. They must be interested in working at the institute with Brandeis staff and scholars on new and established research projects. Applicants must select 2 of the supervised projects operating each year and write a brief explanation of why they would like to assist on it. They must also submit a 1-page essay explaining their interest in Jewish gender studies and 1 or 2 ideas for an independent project. Selection is based on intellectual promise, independence, originality, initiative, capacity for growth, enthusiasm, unique skills, and strengths and weaknesses.

**Financial data**  Interns receive subsidized housing on the Brandeis campus and a weekly stipend.

**Duration**  8 weeks during the summer.

**Additional information**  The Hadassah-Brandeis Institute was formerly the Hadassah International Research Institute on Jewish Women at Brandeis University.

**Number awarded**  6 each year.

**Deadline**  March of each year.

## [273]
## HARVARD-SMITHSONIAN CENTER FOR ASTROPHYSICS SOLAR REU PROGRAM

Harvard-Smithsonian Center for Astrophysics
Attn: Solar REU Program
60 Garden Street, Mail Stop 70
Cambridge, MA 02138
(617) 496-7703    E-mail: dnickerson-at-cfa@harvard.edu
Web: www.cfa.harvard.edu/opportunities/solar_reu

**Summary**  To enable undergraduates (particularly women, minorities, and persons with disabilities) to participate in a summer research program at the Harvard-Smithsonian Center for Astrophysics (CfA).

**Eligibility**  This program is open to U.S. citizens, nationals, and permanent residents who are full-time undergraduates, preferably those entering their junior or senior year. Applicants must be interested in working during the summer on a project in either of 2 CfA divisions: high energy astrophysics (which focuses on X-ray astronomy) or solar, stellar, and planetary sciences (which focuses on understanding star and planet formation and the physical processes in the Sun, stars, and stellar systems). Applications from underrepresented minorities, persons with disabilities, and women are encouraged.

**Financial data**  The stipend is $5,000. Housing and travel expenses are also covered.

**Duration**  10 weeks during the summer.

**Additional information**  This program is supported by the National Science Foundation as part of its Research Experiences for Undergraduates (REU) Program.

**Number awarded**  8 each year.

**Deadline**  February of each year.

## [274]
## HASMIK MGRDICHIAN SCHOLARSHIP

Armenian International Women's Association-Los
  Angeles Affiliate
c/o Lily Ring Balian
2311 Roscomare Road, Number 10
Los Angeles, CA 90077
(310) 472-2454                    E-mail: hyelil@aol.com
Web: www.aiwala.org/index.php/projects

**Summary**  To provide financial assistance to Armenian women from California who are interested in attending college in any state.

**Eligibility**  This program is open to female residents of California who are of Armenian descent. Applicants must be enrolled or planning to enroll full time at an accredited college or university in any state. They must have a GPA of 3.5 or higher and be able to demonstrate financial need. Along with their application, they must submit a 500-word statement describing their planned academic program, their career goals, and the reasons why they believe they should be awarded this scholarship.

**Financial data**  The stipend is $2,500.

**Duration**　1 year.

**Additional information**　This program began in 2011.

**Number awarded**　4 each year.

**Deadline**　March of each year.

## [275]
## HATTIE J. HILLIARD SCHOLARSHIP

Wisconsin Women of Color Network, Inc.
Attn: Scholarship Committee
P.O. Box 2337
Madison, WI 53701-2337
E-mail: contact@womenofcolornetwork-wis.org
Web: www.womenofcolornetwork-wis.org/scholarship.html

**Summary**　To provide financial assistance to women of color from Wisconsin who are interested in studying art at a school in any state.

**Eligibility**　This program is open to residents of Wisconsin who are women of color enrolled or planning to enroll at a college, university, or vocational/technical school in any state. Applicants must be a member of 1 of the following groups: African American, Asian, American Indian, or Hispanic. Their field of study must be art, graphic art, commercial art, or a related area. They must be able to demonstrate financial need. Along with their application, they must submit a 1-page essay on how this scholarship will help them accomplish their educational goal. U.S. citizenship is required.

**Financial data**　A stipend is awarded (amount not specified).

**Duration**　1 year.

**Additional information**　This program began in 1995.

**Number awarded**　1 each year.

**Deadline**　May of each year.

## [276]
## HAZEL BEARD LEASE SCHOLARSHIP

Kappa Alpha Theta Foundation
Attn: Manager of Programs
8740 Founders Road
Indianapolis, IN 46268-1337
(317) 876-1870　　　　　Toll Free: (800) KAO-1870
Fax: (317) 876-1925
E-mail: gmerritt@kappaalphatheta.org
Web: www.kappaalphathetafoundation.org

**Summary**　To provide financial assistance to members of Kappa Alpha Theta who are working on an undergraduate or graduate degree in speech therapy or speech communication.

**Eligibility**　This program is open to members of Kappa Alpha Theta who are full-time sophomores, juniors, seniors, or graduate students at a college or university in Canada or the United States. Applicants must be working on a degree in speech therapy or speech communication. Along with their application, they must submit an official transcript, personal essays on assigned topics related to their involvement in Kappa Alpha Theta, and 2 letters of reference. Financial need is not considered in the selection process.

**Financial data**　The stipend is $1,940.

**Duration**　1 year.

**Number awarded**　1 each year.

**Deadline**　January of each year.

## [277]
## HEARST SCHOLARSHIP OF NEW YORK WOMEN IN COMMUNICATIONS

New York Women in Communications, Inc.
Attn: NYWICI Foundation
355 Lexington Avenue, 15th Floor
New York, NY 10017-6603
(212) 297-2133　　　　　Fax: (212) 370-9047
E-mail: nywicipr@nywici.org
Web: www.nywici.org/foundation/scholarships

**Summary**　To provide financial assistance to female residents of designated eastern states who are enrolled as undergraduates at a college in any state and preparing for a career in magazines or digital media.

**Eligibility**　This program is open to women who are residents of New York, New Jersey, Connecticut, or Pennsylvania and currently enrolled as sophomores, juniors, or seniors at a college or university in any state. Also eligible are women who reside outside the 4 states but are currently enrolled at a college or university within 1 of the 5 boroughs of New York City. Applicants must be able to demonstrate a commitment to a career in magazines (editorial or advertising sales) or digital media. They must have a GPA of 3.2 or higher. Along with their application, they must submit a 2-page resume; a personal essay of 300 words on an assigned topic that changes annually; 2 letters of recommendation; and an official transcript. Selection is based on academic record, need, demonstrated leadership, participation in school and community activities, honors and other awards or recognition, work experience, goals and aspirations, and unusual personal and/or family circumstances. U.S. citizenship is required.

**Financial data**　The stipend ranges up to $10,000.

**Duration**　1 year.

**Additional information**　This program is sponsored by the Hearst Corporation, which may invite the recipient to apply for a summer internship at its New York City headquarters.

**Number awarded**　1 each year.

**Deadline**　January of each year.

## [278]
## HEATHER WESTPHAL MEMORIAL SCHOLARSHIP AWARD

International Association of Fire Chiefs
Attn: IAFC Foundation
4025 Fair Ridge Drive, Suite 300
Fairfax, VA 22033-2868
(703) 896-4822　　　　　Fax: (703) 273-9363
E-mail: Sbaroncelli@iafc.org
Web: www.iafc.org/Scholarship.htm

**Summary**　To provide financial assistance to female firefighters, especially members of the International Association of Fire Chiefs, who wish to further their academic education.

**Eligibility**　This program is open to women who are active members of state, county, provincial, municipal, community, industrial, or federal fire departments in the United States or Canada and have demonstrated proficiency as members for at least 2 years of paid or 3 years of volunteer service. Dependents of members are not eligible. Applicants must be planning to attend a recognized institution of higher education. Along with their application, they must submit a 250-word essay that includes a brief description of the course work, how the course work will benefit their fire service career and department and improve the fire service, and their financial need. Preference is given to members of the International Association of Fire Chiefs (IAFC).

**Financial data** A stipend is awarded (amount not specified).

**Duration** Up to 1 year.

**Additional information** This program began in 2009 with support from the International Association of Women in Fire and Emergency Service.

**Number awarded** 1 each year.

**Deadline** May of each year.

## [279]
## HECKSEL-SUTHERLAND SCHOLARSHIP

Ninety-Nines, Inc.-Michigan Chapter
c/o Rosemary Sieracki, Administrator
41490 Hanford Road
Canton, MI 48187-3512
(734) 981-4787          E-mail: sierackr@att.net
Web: michigan99s.info/node/4

**Summary** To provide financial assistance to women in Michigan who are interested in attending a school in any state to prepare for a career in aviation.

**Eligibility** This program is open to women who live in Michigan and are interested in preparing for a career in aviation or aeronautics. Applicants must be enrolled or planning to enroll in private pilot training, additional pilot certificate or rating, college education in aviation, technical training in aviation, or other aviation-related training. Along with their application, they must submit 1) a 1-page essay on how the money will be used; 2) documentation from the training or academic institution verifying the cost of the training; 3) copies of all aviation and medical certificates and the last 3 pages of the pilot logbook (if applicable); and 4) an essay that covers their aviation history, short- and long-term goals, how the scholarship will help them achieve those goals, any educational awards and honors they have received, their significant or unique achievements, where training would be received and the costs involved, their involvement in aviation activities, and their community involvement. Selection is based on motivation, willingness to accept responsibility, reliability, and commitment to success.

**Financial data** The stipend is $1,500.

**Duration** 1 year.

**Additional information** This program began in 2012.

**Number awarded** 1 each year.

**Deadline** October of each year.

## [280]
## HELEN MUNTEAN EDUCATION SCHOLARSHIP FOR WOMEN

Association of Romanian Orthodox Ladies Auxiliaries of
   North America
Attn: Scholarship Committee
222 Orchard Park Drive
New Castle, PA 16105
(724) 652-4313          E-mail: adelap@verizon.net
Web: www.arfora.org/scholarships.htm

**Summary** To provide financial assistance to women who are members of a parish of the Romanian Orthodox Episco-

pate of America and interested in working on a degree in education in college.

**Eligibility** This program is open to women who have been voting communicant members of a parish of the Romanian Orthodox Episcopate of America for at least 1 year or are daughters of a communicant member. Applicants must have completed at least 1 year of work on a baccalaureate degree in education at a college or university. Along with their application, they must submit a 300-word statement describing their personal goals; high school, university, church, and community involvement; honors and awards; and why they should be considered for this award. Selection is based on academic achievement, character, worthiness, and participation in religious life.

**Financial data** The stipend is $1,000.

**Duration** 1 year; nonrenewable.

**Additional information** The Association of Romanian Orthodox Ladies Auxiliaries (ARFORA) was established in 1938 as a women's organization within the Romanian Orthodox Episcopate of America.

**Number awarded** 1 or more each year.

**Deadline** May of each year.

## [281]
## HELEN TRUEHEART COX ART SCHOLARSHIP

National League of American Pen Women
1300 17th Street, N.W.
Washington, DC 20036-1973
(202) 785-1997          Fax: (202) 452-8868
E-mail: contact@nlapw.org
Web: www.nlapw.org/competitions

**Summary** To provide financial assistance to Native American women interested in studying art in college.

**Eligibility** This program is open to women between 17 and 24 years of age who are members of a Native American tribe. Applicants must be interested in attending a college or university and majoring in art. They must submit 3 prints (4 by 6 inches) in any media (e.g., oil, water color, original works on paper, mixed media, acrylic) or 3 prints (4 by 6 inches) of artwork, sculpture, or photographic works. U.S. citizenship is required. Financial need is considered in the selection process.

**Financial data** A stipend is awarded (amount not specified).

**Duration** 1 year.

**Number awarded** 1 each even-numbered year.

**Deadline** January of even-numbered years.

## [282]
## HELOISE WERTHAN KUHN SCHOLARSHIP

Community Foundation of Middle Tennessee
Attn: Scholarship Committee
3833 Cleghorn Avenue, Suite 400
Nashville, TN 37215-2519
(615) 321-4939          Toll Free: (888) 540-5200
Fax: (615) 327-2746          E-mail: grants@cfmt.org
Web: www.cfmt.org/request/scholarships/allscholarships

**Summary** To provide financial assistance to residents of Tennessee who are pregnant or parenting teens and interested in attending college in any state.

**Eligibility** This program is open to residents of middle Tennessee who are pregnant or parenting teens. Applicants must be attending or planning to attend an accredited college, university, junior college, technical school, or job training program in any state to increase their job skills and become more employable. Along with their application, they must submit an essay describing their educational plans and how those plans will help them reach their career goals. Financial need is considered in the selection process.

**Financial data** Stipends range from $500 to $2,500 per year. Funds are paid to the recipient's school and must be used for tuition, fees, books, supplies, room, board, or miscellaneous expenses.

**Duration** 1 year; recipients may reapply.

**Additional information** This program began in 2001.

**Number awarded** 1 or more each year.

**Deadline** March of each year.

## [283]
## HELPING HANDS OF WSC ENDOWMENT SCHOLARSHIP

Epsilon Sigma Alpha International
Attn: ESA Foundation
363 West Drake Road
Fort Collins, CO 80526
(970) 223-2824 Fax: (970) 223-4456
Web: www.epsilonsigmaalpha.org/scholarships-and-grants

**Summary** To provide financial assistance for college to female members of the Western States Council (WSC) of Epsilon Sigma Alpha (ESA).

**Eligibility** This program is open to female ESA members from its WSC (Alaska, Arizona, Australia, California, Oregon, or Washington). Applicants must be 1) graduating high school seniors with a GPA of 3.0 or higher or with minimum scores of 22 on the ACT or 1030 on the combined critical reading and mathematics SAT; 2) enrolled in college with a GPA of 3.0 or higher; 3) enrolled at a technical school or returning to school after an absence for retraining of job skills or obtaining a degree; or 4) engaged in online study through an accredited college, university, or vocational school. They may be majoring or planning to major in any field at an institution in any state. Selection is based on service and leadership (30 points), financial need (30 points), and scholastic ability (30 points). A $5 processing fee is required.

**Financial data** The stipend is $1,000.

**Duration** 1 year; nonrenewable.

**Additional information** Epsilon Sigma Alpha (ESA) is a women's service organization. This program began in 2006. Completed applications must be submitted to the ESA state counselor who then verifies the information before forwarding them to the scholarship director.

**Number awarded** 1 each year.

**Deadline** January of each year.

## [284]
## HERMINE DALKOWITZ TOBOLOWSKY SCHOLARSHIP

Texas Business Women
Attn: Texas Business and Professional Women's Foundation
2637 Pine Springs Drive
Plano, TX 75093
(972) 822-1173 E-mail: info@texasbusinesswomen.org
Web: www.texasbpwfoundation.org/scholarships.php

**Summary** To provide financial assistance to women from any state who are attending college in Texas to prepare for a career in selected professions.

**Eligibility** This program is open to women from any state who are interested in preparing for a career in law, public service, government, political science, or women's history. Applicants must have completed at least 2 semesters of study at an accredited college or university in Texas, have a GPA of 3.0 or higher, and be U.S. citizens. Selection is based on academic achievement and financial need.

**Financial data** A stipend is awarded (amount not specified).

**Duration** 1 year.

**Additional information** This program began in 1995 when Texas Business Women was named Texas Federation of Business and Professional Women's Clubs.

**Number awarded** 1 or more each year.

**Deadline** December of each year.

## [285]
## HONEYWELL INTERNATIONAL SCHOLARSHIPS

Society of Women Engineers
Attn: Scholarship Selection Committee
203 North LaSalle Street, Suite 1675
Chicago, IL 60601-1269
(312) 596-5223 Toll Free: (877) SWE-INFO
Fax: (312) 644-8557 E-mail: scholarships@swe.org
Web: societyofwomenengineers.swe.org

**Summary** To provide financial assistance to women interested in studying specified fields of engineering in college.

**Eligibility** This program is open to women who are graduating high school seniors or rising college sophomores, juniors, or seniors. Applicants must be enrolled or planning to enroll full time at an ABET-accredited 4-year college or university and major in computer science or aerospace, chemical, computer, electrical, industrial, manufacturing, materials, or mechanical engineering. They must have a GPA of 3.5 or higher. Preference is given to members of groups underrepresented in computer science and engineering. U.S. citizenship or permanent resident status is required. Financial need is considered in the selection process.

**Financial data** The stipend is $5,000.

**Duration** 1 year.

**Additional information** This program is sponsored by Honeywell International Inc.

**Number awarded** 3 each year.

**Deadline** February of each year for current college students; May of each year for high school seniors.

## [286]
## HONOLULU ALUMNAE PANHELLENIC ASSOCIATION COLLEGIATE SCHOLARSHIPS

Honolulu Alumnae Panhellenic Association
Attn: Vice President Scholarship
94-253 Hokulewa Loop
Mililani, HI 96789
E-mail: honoluluhapa@yahoo.com
Web: www.greekhawaii.com

**Summary**   To provide financial assistance to female college student from Hawaii who are members of a National Panhellenic Conference (NPC) sorority.

**Eligibility**   This program is open to women who are initiated and active members of an NPC-affiliated sorority at a college or university where they are working on an undergraduate degree. Their permanent home address or college address must be in Hawaii. Along with their application, they must submit 1) a brief essay on the part sorority membership has played in their life and why they feel this scholarship will benefit their future goals; 2) a list of all school, sorority, and community activities and offices; and 3) letters of recommendation from a professor, sorority officer, and another person in the community. Financial need is not considered in the selection process.

**Financial data**   A stipend is awarded (amount not specified).

**Duration**   1 year.

**Number awarded**   1 or more each year.

**Deadline**   March of each year.

## [287]
## HONOLULU ALUMNAE PANHELLENIC ASSOCIATION HIGH SCHOOL SCHOLARSHIPS

Honolulu Alumnae Panhellenic Association
Attn: Vice President Scholarship
94-253 Hokulewa Loop
Mililani, HI 96789
E-mail: honoluluhapa@yahoo.com
Web: www.greekhawaii.com

**Summary**   To provide financial assistance to female high school seniors in Hawaii who are interested in going to a college with National Panhellenic Conference (NPC) sororities on campus.

**Eligibility**   This program is open to females graduating from high schools in Hawaii. Applicants must be interested in attending 1 of the more than 500 colleges and universities with NPC sororities. Along with their application, they must submit 1) a brief essay on the expectations they have of becoming part of a sorority and the qualities they can bring to the sisterhood; 2) SAT and/or ACT scores; 3) a list of all class and school offices, other offices and responsibilities, school and athletic activities, extracurricular and community activities, honors, and awards; and 4) letters of recommendation from their high school senior counselor and another person in the community. Financial need is also considered in the selection process, but the program gives priority to well-rounded students who have balanced scholastics with school and/or community activities. Interviews are included.

**Financial data**   A stipend is awarded (amount not specified).

**Duration**   1 year.

**Number awarded**   1 or more each year.

**Deadline**   February of each year.

## [288]
## HONOLULU BRANCH AAUW UNDERGRADUATE SCHOLARSHIP

American Association of University Women-Honolulu Branch
Attn: Scholarship Committee
1802 Ke'eaumoku Street
Honolulu, HI 96822
(808) 537-4702                              Fax: (808) 537-4702
E-mail: aauwhnb@hawaii.rr.com
Web: honolulu-hi.aauw.net/scholarships

**Summary**   To provide financial assistance to women in Hawaii who are working on an undergraduate degree in any field at a school in the state.

**Eligibility**   This program is open to female residents of Hawaii who have completed at least 48 credits of undergraduate study in any field at an accredited university in the state. Applicants must be able to demonstrate academic excellence, leadership in community and school activities, and financial need. They must be U.S. citizens. Along with their application, they must submit a personal statement that includes information on their educational goals.

**Financial data**   Stipends range up to $10,000.

**Duration**   1 year.

**Number awarded**   1 or more each year.

**Deadline**   April of each year.

## [289]
## HONOLULU CHAPTER ADULT STUDENTS IN SCHOLASTIC TRANSITION (ASIST) SCHOLARSHIP PROGRAM

Executive Women International-Honolulu Chapter
Attn: Karen Mendes
P.O. Box 2295
Honolulu, HI 96804-2295
(808) 723-4577                     E-mail: mendeskp@gmail.com
Web: www.ewihonolulu.org/scholarships.asist.html

**Summary**   To provide financial assistance to nontraditional students from Hawaii who wish to attend college in any state.

**Eligibility**   This program is open to nontraditional students who are residents of Hawaii and socially, physically, or economically challenged adults with small children. Applicants must be planning to enter a college, university, or other institution of higher education in any state as a reentry student. They must be able to demonstrate clearly defined career goals and objectives, specific educational requirements to attain those goals and objectives, and financial need. U.S. citizenship or permanent resident status is required.

**Financial data**   Stipends range from $1,000 to $3,500.

**Duration**   1 year.

**Number awarded**   Varies each year; recently, 4 of these scholarships were awarded: 1 at $3,500, 1 at $2,500, 1 at $1,500, and 1 at $1,000.

**Deadline**   April of each year.

## [290]
## HORIZONS FOUNDATION SCHOLARSHIP PROGRAM

Women in Defense
c/o National Defense Industrial Association
2111 Wilson Boulevard, Suite 400
Arlington, VA 22201-3061
(703) 247-2552                    Fax: (703) 522-1885
E-mail: wid@ndia.org
Web: wid.ndia.org/horizons/Pages/default.aspx

**Summary** To provide financial assistance to women who are upper-division or graduate students engaged in or planning careers related to the national security interests of the United States.

**Eligibility** This program is open to women who are already working in national security fields as well as women planning such careers. Applicants must 1) be currently enrolled at an accredited college or university, either full time or part time, as graduate students or upper-division undergraduates; 2) demonstrate financial need; 3) be U.S. citizens; 4) have a GPA of 3.25 or higher; and 5) demonstrate interest in preparing for a career related to national security. The preferred fields of study include business (as it relates to national security or defense), computer science, cyber security, economics, engineering, government relations, international relations, law (as it relates to national security or defense), mathematics, military history, political science, physics, and security studies; others are considered if the applicant can demonstrate relevance to a career in national security or defense. Selection is based on academic achievement, participation in defense and national security activities, field of study, work experience, statements of objectives, recommendations, and financial need.

**Financial data** The stipend ranges up to $10,000.

**Duration** 1 year; renewable.

**Additional information** This program began in 1988.

**Number awarded** Varies each year; recently, 6 of these scholarships were awarded: 1 at $10,000, 1 at $7,000, 1 at $5,000, 1 at $3,000, and 2 at $2,500. Since the program was established, 116 women have received more than $180,000 in support.

**Deadline** June of each year.

## [291]
## HORIZONS-MICHIGAN SCHOLARSHIP

Women in Defense-Michigan Chapter
Attn: Scholarship Director
P.O. Box 4744
Troy, MI 48099
E-mail: scholarships@wid-mi.org
Web: www.wid-mi.org/scholarships.aspx

**Summary** To provide financial assistance to women in Michigan who are upper-division or graduate students working on a degree related to national defense.

**Eligibility** This program is open to women who are residents of Michigan and enrolled either full or part time at a college or university in the state. Applicants must be juniors, seniors, or graduate students and have a GPA of 3.25 or higher. They must be interested in preparing for a career related to national security or defense. Relevant fields of study include security studies, military history, government

relations, engineering, computer science, physics, mathematics, business (as related to national security or defense), law (as related to national security or defense), international relations, political science, or economics; other fields may be considered if the applicant can demonstrate relevance to a career in national security or defense. Along with their application, they must submit brief statements on their interest in a career in national security or defense, the principal accomplishments in their life that relate to their professional goals, and the objectives of their educational program. Selection is based on those statements, academic achievement, participation in defense and national security activities, field of study, work experience, recommendations, and financial need. U.S. citizenship is required.

**Financial data** Stipends have averaged at least $3,000.

**Duration** 1 year.

**Additional information** This program began in 2009.

**Number awarded** Varies each year; recently, 6 of these scholarships were awarded.

**Deadline** August of each year.

## [292]
## HOUSTON AREA SECTION FIRST SCHOLARSHIP

Society of Women Engineers-Houston Area Section
Attn: Vice President Outreach
P.O. Box 1355
Houston, TX 77251-1355
E-mail: VP_Outreach@swehouston.org
Web: www.swehouston.org/education/Scholarships.php

**Summary** To provide financial assistance to high school women, especially those in Texas, interested in studying engineering at a college in any state.

**Eligibility** This program is open to female high school seniors planning to attend an ABET-accredited 4-year college or university to major in engineering. Preference is given to students attending high school in Texas, but applicants may be planning to enroll at a college in any state. They must have completed at least 1 regional FIRST (For Inspiration and Recognition of Science and Technology) competition. Along with their application, they must submit transcripts; a 1-page essay on why they would like to be an engineer, how they believe they will make a difference as an engineer, and what influenced them to study engineering; a letter of reference regarding their scholastic ability, general character, attitude, ambition, motivation, and leadership characteristics; and a resume. Information on financial situation is purely voluntary and is not used in the selection process.

**Financial data** The stipend is $1,000.

**Duration** 1 year; nonrenewable.

**Additional information** This organization is not currently offering scholarships.

**Number awarded** 1 each year.

**Deadline** February of each year.

## [293]
## HOUSTON/NANCY HOLLIMAN SCHOLARSHIP

Delta Zeta Sorority
Attn: Foundation Coordinator
202 East Church Street
Oxford, OH 45056
(513) 523-7597          Fax: (513) 523-1921
E-mail: DZFoundation@dzshq.com
Web: www.deltazeta.org

**Summary** To provide financial assistance for continued undergraduate study to members of Delta Zeta Sorority who are majoring in a field related to hearing and speech.

**Eligibility** This program is open to members of the sorority who are entering their junior or senior year and have a GPA of 3.0 or higher. Applicants must be working on a degree in hearing and speech, audiology, or a related field. Along with their application, they must submit an official transcript, a statement of their career goals, information on their service to the sorority, documentation of campus activities and/or community involvement, a list of academic honors, and an explanation of their financial need.

**Financial data** The stipend ranges from $500 to $2,500, depending on the availability of funds.

**Duration** 1 year; nonrenewable.

**Number awarded** 1 each year.

**Deadline** February of each year.

## [294]
## H.S. AND ANGELINE LEWIS SCHOLARSHIPS

American Legion Auxiliary
Department of Wisconsin
Attn: Education Chair
2930 American Legion Drive
P.O. Box 140
Portage, WI 53901-0140
(608) 745-0124          Toll Free: (866) 664-3863
Fax: (608) 745-1947     E-mail: alawi@amlegionauxwi.org
Web: www.amlegionauxwi.org/Scholarships.htm

**Summary** To provide financial assistance for college or graduate study in any state to the wives, widows, and children of Wisconsin residents who are veterans or members of the American Legion Auxiliary.

**Eligibility** This program is open to the children, wives, and widows of veterans who are high school seniors or graduates and have a GPA of 3.5 or higher. Grandchildren and great-grandchildren of members of the American Legion Auxiliary are also eligible. Applicants must be residents of Wisconsin and interested in working on an undergraduate or graduate degree at a school in any state. Along with their application, they must submit a 300-word essay on "Education—An Investment in the Future." Financial need is considered in the selection process.

**Financial data** The stipend is $1,000.

**Duration** 1 year; nonrenewable.

**Number awarded** 6 each year: 1 to a graduate student and 5 to undergraduates.

**Deadline** March of each year.

## [295]
## HUENEFELD/DENTON SCHOLARSHIP

Delta Zeta Sorority
Attn: Foundation Coordinator
202 East Church Street
Oxford, OH 45056
(513) 523-7597          Fax: (513) 523-1921
E-mail: DZFoundation@dzshq.com
Web: www.deltazeta.org

**Summary** To provide financial assistance for continued undergraduate study to members of Delta Zeta Sorority who are majoring in child development or library science.

**Eligibility** This program is open to members of the sorority who are entering their junior or senior year. Applicants must be working on a degree in child development (including kindergarten through primary education) or library science. Along with their application, they must submit an official transcript, a statement of their career goals, information on their service to the sorority, documentation of campus activities and/or community involvement, a list of academic honors, and an explanation of their financial need.

**Financial data** The stipend ranges from $500 to $2,500, depending on the availability of funds.

**Duration** 1 year; nonrenewable.

**Number awarded** 1 each year.

**Deadline** February of each year.

## [296]
## HUMBLE ARTESIAN CHAPTER ABWA
## SCHOLARSHIP GRANTS

American Business Women's Association-Humble Artesian Chapter
c/o Caroline Smith, Education Committee
1702 Baldsprings Trail
Kingwood, TX 77345-1997
(281) 360-6226     E-mail: californiasmith@earthlink.net
Web: abwahumble.org/scholarship

**Summary** To provide financial assistance to women from any state who have completed at least the sophomore year of college.

**Eligibility** This program is open to all women who are U.S. citizens. Applicants must be enrolled as juniors, seniors, or graduate students at a college or university in any state and have a GPA of 2.5 or higher.

**Financial data** The stipend is $2,000.

**Duration** 1 year.

**Number awarded** 1 each year.

**Deadline** January of each year.

## [297]
## IBM CORPORATION SWE SCHOLARSHIPS

Society of Women Engineers
Attn: Scholarship Selection Committee
203 North LaSalle Street, Suite 1675
Chicago, IL 60601-1269
(312) 596-5223          Toll Free: (877) SWE-INFO
Fax: (312) 644-8557     E-mail: scholarships@swe.org
Web: societyofwomenengineers.swe.org

**Summary** To provide financial assistance to undergraduate women majoring in designated engineering specialties.

**Eligibility** This program is open to women who are entering their sophomore or junior year at a 4-year ABET-accredited college or university. Applicants must be working full time on a degree in computer science or electrical or computer engineering and have a GPA of 3.4 or higher. Preference is given to members of groups underrepresented in engineering or computer science. Selection is based on merit. U.S. citizenship or permanent resident status is required.

**Financial data** The stipend is $1,000.

**Duration** 1 year.

**Additional information** This program is sponsored by the IBM Corporation.

**Number awarded** 5 each year.

**Deadline** February of each year.

## [298]
## IDA M. POPE MEMORIAL SCHOLARSHIPS

Hawai'i Community Foundation
Attn: Scholarship Department
827 Fort Street Mall
Honolulu, HI 96813
(808) 566-5570          Toll Free: (888) 731-3863
Fax: (808) 521-6286
E-mail: scholarships@hcf-hawaii.org
Web: www.hawaiicommunityfoundation.org/scholarships

**Summary** To provide financial assistance to Native Hawaiian women who are interested in working on an undergraduate or graduate degree in designated fields at a school in any state.

**Eligibility** This program is open to female residents of Hawaii who are Native Hawaiian, defined as a descendant of the aboriginal inhabitants of the Hawaiian islands prior to 1778. Applicants must be enrolled at a school in any state in an accredited associate, bachelor's, or graduate degree program and working on a degree in health, science, mathematics, or education (including counseling and social work). They must be able to demonstrate academic achievement (GPA of 3.5 or higher), good moral character, and financial need. Along with their application, they must submit a short statement indicating their reasons for attending college, their planned course of study, their career goals, and what community service means to them.

**Financial data** The amounts of the awards depend on the availability of funds and the need of the recipient. Recently, the average value of each of the scholarships awarded by the foundation was more than $2,000.

**Duration** 1 year; may be renewed.

**Number awarded** Varies each year; recently, 61 of these scholarships were awarded.

**Deadline** February of each year.

## [299]
## ILLINOIS SCHOLARSHIPS FOR JUNIOR MEMBERS

American Legion Auxiliary
Department of Illinois
2720 East Lincoln Street
P.O. Box 1426
Bloomington, IL 61702-1426
(309) 663-9366          Fax: (309) 663-5827
E-mail: karen.boughan@ilala.org
Web: www.ilala.org/education.html

**Summary** To provide financial assistance to high school seniors or graduates in Illinois who are junior members of the American Legion Auxiliary and planning to attend college in any state.

**Eligibility** This program is open to junior members of the Illinois American Legion Auxiliary who are daughters, granddaughters, great-granddaughters, or sisters of veterans who served during eligibility dates for membership in the American Legion. Applicants must have been members for at least 3 years. They must be high school seniors or graduates who have not yet attended an institution of higher learning and are planning to attend college in any state. Along with their application, they must submit a 1,000-word essay on "The Veteran in My Life." Selection is based on that essay (25%) character and leadership (25%), scholarship (25%), and financial need (25%).

**Financial data** The stipend is $1,000.

**Duration** 1 year.

**Number awarded** Varies each year.

**Deadline** March of each year.

## [300]
## INDIANA AMERICAN LEGION AMERICANISM AND GOVERNMENT TEST

American Legion
Department of Indiana
777 North Meridian Street, Suite 104
Indianapolis, IN 46204
(317) 630-1200          Fax: (317) 630-1277
Web: www.hoosierlegionnaire.org

**Summary** To recognize and reward, with college scholarships, high school students in Indiana who score highest on a test on Americanism (females and males compete separately.

**Eligibility** All Indiana students in grades 10-12 are eligible to take a written test on Americanism and government. Scholarships are awarded to the students with the highest scores. Girls and boys compete separately.

**Financial data** The award is a $1,000 scholarship.

**Duration** The awards are presented annually.

**Additional information** The test has been given during National Education Week in November of every year since 1984.

**Number awarded** 6 each year: 3 are set aside for girls in grades 10, 11, and 12 respectively and 3 to a boy in each of the participating grades.

**Deadline** Schools that wish to have their students participate must order the tests by October of each year.

## [301]
## INDIANA AMERICAN LEGION GOLD AWARD GIRL SCOUT OF THE YEAR SCHOLARSHIP ACHIEVEMENT AWARD

American Legion
Department of Indiana
777 North Meridian Street, Suite 104
Indianapolis, IN 46204
(317) 630-1200                    Fax: (317) 630-1277
Web: www.hoosierlegionnaire.org

**Summary** To recognize and reward, with scholarships to attend college in any state, members of the Girl Scouts in Indiana who have received the Gold Award.

**Eligibility** This program is open to high school seniors in Indiana who plan to attend college in any state. Applicants must be registered Girl Scouts who have received the Gold Award; are active members of their religious institution and have received the appropriate religious emblem at the Ambassador or Senior Scout level; have demonstrated good and practical citizenship in their Girl Scouting, school, religious institution, and community; are U.S. citizens; and submit letters of recommendation from a leader in each of the following groups: Scouting, school, religious institution, and community.

**Financial data** The awards are a $1,000 scholarship for the state winner and $200 scholarships for each district winner.

**Duration** The awards are presented annually.

**Additional information** Winners must utilize their awards within 1 year of graduating from high school as full-time students at an accredited institution of higher education in the United States.

**Number awarded** 12 each year: 1 state winner and 11 district winners.

**Deadline** April of each year.

## [302]
## INDIANA BPW GIRL SCOUT SCHOLARSHIP

Indiana Women's Education Foundation, Inc.
P.O. Box 33
Knightstown, IN 46148-0033
(765) 345-9812                    Fax: (765) 345-9812
E-mail: infbpw@centurylink.net
Web: www.inwomeneducation.org/index.php/scholarships

**Summary** To provide financial assistance to Girl Scout members in Indiana who are interested in attending college, preferably in the state.

**Eligibility** This program is open to Girl Scouts who have completed the Business and Professional Women (BPW) patch and have been residents of Indiana for at least 1 year. Applicants must be between their senior year of high school and their senior year of college in any state; preference is given to students at schools in Indiana. Along with their application, they must submit a statement (up to 200 words) on their career goals and how their education relates to those goals. Financial need is not considered in the selection process.

**Financial data** A stipend is awarded (amount not specified). Funds are paid directly to the recipient's school.

**Duration** 1 year; recipients may reapply.

**Additional information** This program began in 2008. The Indiana Women's Education Foundation was formerly named the Indiana Business and Professional Women's Foundation.

**Number awarded** 1 each year.

**Deadline** February of each year.

## [303]
## INDIANA WOMEN IN PUBLIC FINANCE SCHOLARSHIP

Indiana Women in Public Finance
c/o Katie Aeschliman, Scholarship Committee
BMO Harris Bank
135 North Pennsylvania Street, Ninth Floor
Indianapolis, IN 46204
(317) 269-1376            E-mail: indianawpf@gmail.com
Web: www.indianawpf.com/scholarship

**Summary** To provide financial assistance to women from Indiana who are working on a degree in a field related to public finance at a college in the state.

**Eligibility** This program is open to women who are residents of Indiana and currently enrolled as juniors at a college or university in the state. Applicants must be majoring in finance, public finance, law, government accounting, public policy, public management, or a closely-related field. Along with their application, they must submit 500-word essays on 1) any extracurricular activities in which they have participated; and 2) their post-collegiate work plans.

**Financial data** The stipend is $1,000.

**Duration** 1 year.

**Additional information** Indiana Women in Public Finance was organized in 2009.

**Number awarded** 1 each year.

**Deadline** September of each year.

## [304]
## INDIANA WOMEN IN TRANSITION SCHOLARSHIP

Indiana Women's Education Foundation, Inc.
P.O. Box 33
Knightstown, IN 46148-0033
(765) 345-9812                    Fax: (765) 345-9812
E-mail: infbpw@centurylink.net
Web: www.inwomeneducation.org/index.php/scholarships

**Summary** To provide financial assistance for college to mature women in Indiana.

**Eligibility** This program is open to women who are 30 years of age or older and have been an Indiana resident for at least 1 year. Applicants must be reentering the workforce, be changing careers, or be a displaced worker. They must have applied to a postsecondary institution for at least part-time attendance. Along with their application, they must submit 1) a statement (up to 200 words) on their career goals and how their education relates to those goals; and 2) documentation of financial need.

**Financial data** The stipend is $1,000. Funds are paid directly to the recipient's school.

**Duration** 1 year; recipients may reapply.

**Additional information** This program began in 1995, when the Indiana Women's Education Foundation was named the Indiana Business and Professional Women's Foundation.

**Number awarded** 1 each year.

**Deadline** February of each year.

## [305]
## INDIANA WORKING WOMAN SCHOLARSHIP

Indiana Women's Education Foundation, Inc.
P.O. Box 33
Knightstown, IN 46148-0033
(765) 345-9812          Fax: (765) 345-9812
E-mail: bpwin@msn.com
Web: indianawomensfoundation.org/scholarships.htm

**Summary** To provide financial assistance for college to women in Indiana who are also working at least part time.

**Eligibility** This program is open to women who are 25 years of age or older and have been an Indiana resident for at least 1 year. Applicants must be employed at least 20 hours per week and must have applied to or be attending a postsecondary institution on at least a part-time basis. Along with their application, they must submit 1) a statement (up to 200 words) on their career goals and how their education relates to those goals; and 2) documentation of financial need.

**Financial data** The stipend is $1,000. Funds are paid directly to the recipient's school.

**Duration** 1 year; recipients may reapply.

**Additional information** This program began in 1995, when the Indiana Women's Education Foundation was named the Indiana Business and Professional Women's Foundation.

**Number awarded** 1 each year.

**Deadline** February of each year.

## [306]
## INTERPUBLIC GROUP SCHOLARSHIP AND INTERNSHIP

New York Women in Communications, Inc.
Attn: NYWICI Foundation
355 Lexington Avenue, 15th Floor
New York, NY 10017-6603
(212) 297-2133          Fax: (212) 370-9047
E-mail: nywicipr@nywici.org
Web: www.nywici.org/foundation/scholarships

**Summary** To provide financial assistance and work experience to women from ethnically diverse groups who are residents of designated eastern states and enrolled as juniors at a college in any state to prepare for a career in advertising or public relations.

**Eligibility** This program is open to female residents of New York, New Jersey, Connecticut, or Pennsylvania who are from ethnically diverse groups and currently enrolled as juniors at a college or university in any state. Also eligible are women who reside outside the 4 states but are currently enrolled at a college or university within 1 of the 5 boroughs of New York City. Applicants must be preparing for a career in advertising or public relations and have a GPA of 3.2 or higher. They must be available for a summer internship with Interpublic Group (IPG) in New York City. Along with their application, they must submit a 2-page resume; a personal essay of 300 words on an assigned topic that changes annually; 2 letters of recommendation; and an official transcript. Selection is based on academic record, need, demonstrated leadership, participation in school and community activities, honors and other awards or recognition, work experience, goals and aspirations, and unusual personal and/or family circumstances. U.S. citizenship is required.

**Financial data** The scholarship stipend ranges up to $10,000; the internship is salaried (amount not specified).

**Duration** 1 year.

**Additional information** This program is sponsored by IPG, a holding company for a large number of firms in the advertising industry.

**Number awarded** 2 each year.

**Deadline** January of each year.

## [307]
## IOTA SIGMA PI MEMBERS-AT-LARGE REENTRY AWARD

Iota Sigma Pi
c/o Gail Blaustein, MAL National Coordinator
West Liberty University
208 University Drive
College Union Box 139
West Liberty, WV 26074
(304) 336-8539       E-mail: gail.blaustein@westliberty.edu
Web: www.iotasigmapi.info

**Summary** To provide financial assistance to women who are reentering college to work on an undergraduate or graduate degree in chemistry.

**Eligibility** This program is open to women who have returned to academic studies after an absence of 3 or more years and have completed at least 1 academic year of college chemistry since returning. Students must be working on an undergraduate or graduate degree in chemistry or a related field at a 4-year college or university. They must be nominated by a member of Iota Sigma Pi or by a member of the faculty at their institution. Nominees must submit a short essay describing their goals, pertinent experiences that influenced their choice of major, any interests or talents that will assist them in succeeding in their professional career, and how the scholarship will benefit them in meeting their goals. Financial need is not considered in the selection process.

**Financial data** The winner receives a stipend of $1,500, a certificate, and a 1-year waiver of Iota Sigma Pi dues.

**Duration** 1 year.

**Additional information** This award was first presented in 1991.

**Number awarded** 1 each year.

**Deadline** March of each year.

## [308]
## IRENE AND LEETA WAGY MEMORIAL SCHOLARSHIP

Daughters of the American Revolution-Missouri State Society
Attn: State Scholarship Chair
821 Main Street
P.O. Box 297
Boonville, MO 65233
(660) 882-5320          E-mail: missouridar@gmail.com
Web: www.mssdar.org

**Summary** To provide financial assistance to female high school seniors in Missouri who plan to study education at a college or university in the state.

**Eligibility** This program is open to female seniors graduating from high schools in Missouri in the top 10% of their class. Applicants must be planning to attend an accredited college or university in Missouri to major in education. They must be sponsored by a chapter of the Daughters of the American Revolution in Missouri and able to demonstrate financial need. U.S. citizenship is required.

**Financial data** A stipend is awarded (amount not specified).

**Duration** 1 year.

**Number awarded** 1 or more each year.

**Deadline** January of each year.

## [309]
## ITW SCHOLARSHIPS

Society of Women Engineers
Attn: Scholarship Selection Committee
203 North LaSalle Street, Suite 1675
Chicago, IL 60601-1269
(312) 596-5223             Toll Free: (877) SWE-INFO
Fax: (312) 644-8557        E-mail: scholarships@swe.org
Web: societyofwomenengineers.swe.org

**Summary** To provide financial assistance to undergraduate women majoring in designated engineering specialties.

**Eligibility** This program is open to women who are entering their junior year at a 4-year ABET-accredited college or university. Applicants must be working full time on a degree in computer science, electrical or mechanical engineering, or polymer science. They must have a GPA of 3.0 or higher. Preference is given to members of groups underrepresented in engineering or computer science. Selection is based on merit. U.S. citizenship or permanent resident status is required.

**Financial data** The stipend is $2,500 per year.

**Duration** 1 year; may be renewed 1 additional year.

**Additional information** This program is sponsored by Illinois Tool Works, Inc.

**Number awarded** 2 each year.

**Deadline** February of each year.

## [310]
## JAMES J. WYCHOR SCHOLARSHIPS

Minnesota Broadcasters Association
Attn: Scholarship Program
3033 Excelsior Boulevard, Suite 440
Minneapolis, MN 55416
(612) 926-8123             Toll Free: (800) 245-5838
Fax: (612) 926-9761
E-mail: llasere@minnesotabroadcasters.com
Web: www.minnesotabroadcasters.com/membership

**Summary** To provide financial assistance to female, minority, and other residents of Minnesota who are interested in studying broadcasting at a college in any state.

**Eligibility** This program is open to residents of Minnesota who are accepted or enrolled at an accredited postsecondary institution in any state offering a broadcast-related curriculum. Applicants must have a high school or college GPA of 3.0 or higher and must submit a 500-word essay on why they wish to prepare for a career in broadcasting or electronic media. Employment in the broadcasting industry is not required, but students who are employed must include a letter

from their general manager describing the duties they have performed as a radio or television station employee and evaluating their potential for success in the industry. Financial need is not considered in the selection process. Some of the scholarships are awarded only to minority or women candidates.

**Financial data** The stipend is $1,500.

**Duration** 1 year; recipients who are college seniors may reapply for an additional 1-year renewal as a graduate student.

**Number awarded** 10 each year, distributed as follows: 3 within the 7-county metro area, 5 allocated geographically throughout the state (northeast, northwest, central, southeast, southwest), and 2 reserved specifically for women and minority applicants.

**Deadline** June of each year.

## [311]
## JAN GWATNEY SCHOLARSHIP

United Daughters of the Confederacy
Attn: Second Vice President General
328 North Boulevard
Richmond, VA 23220-4008
(804) 355-1636             Fax: (804) 353-1396
E-mail: jamieretired@sbcglobal.net
Web: www.hqudc.org/Scholarships/index.htm

**Summary** To provide financial assistance to female lineal descendants of Confederate Veterans, especially those from designated southern states.

**Eligibility** Eligible to apply for these scholarships are female lineal descendants of worthy Confederates or collateral descendants who are current or former members of the Children of the Confederacy or current members of the United Daughters of the Confederacy. Applicants must submit a family financial report and certified proof of the Confederate record of 1 ancestor, with the company and regiment in which he served. They must have at least a 3.0 GPA in high school. Preference is given to residents of Georgia, Louisiana, or Texas.

**Financial data** The amount of this scholarship depends on the availability of funds.

**Duration** 1 year; may be renewed.

**Number awarded** 1 each year.

**Deadline** April of each year.

## [312]
## JANE LORING JONES SCHOLARSHIPS

American Baptist Churches of the Rocky Mountains
Attn: American Baptist Women's Ministries
9085 East Mineral Circle, Suite 170
Centennial, CO 80112
(303) 988-3900             E-mail: web@abcrm.org
Web: abcrm.org/ministries/women_scholarships_co.htm

**Summary** To provide financial assistance to women who are members of churches affiliated with the American Baptist Churches (ABC) USA in Colorado, New Mexico, and Utah and interested in attending an ABC college in any state.

**Eligibility** This program is open to women under 26 years of age who are active members of churches cooperating with ABC in Colorado, New Mexico, or Utah. Applicants must be enrolled or planning to enroll full time at an ABC college or university in any state. They are not required to enter Christian service as a vocation, but they must have a real desire to prepare themselves for Christian leadership in the home, church, and community. Along with their application, they must submit a personal letter describing their Christian experience; their participation in the life of their church, school, and community; and their goals for the future. Selection is based on academic performance, Christian participation in church and school, and financial need. Preference is given to women entering their first or second year at an ABC school.

**Financial data**   The stipend is $2,000 per year.

**Duration**   1 year; recipients may reapply.

**Number awarded**   1 or more each year.

**Deadline**   March of each year.

## [313]
## JANE M. KLAUSMAN WOMEN IN BUSINESS SCHOLARSHIPS

Zonta International
Attn: Foundation
1211 West 22nd Street, Suite 900
Oak Brook, IL 60523-3384
(630) 928-1400                    Fax: (630) 928-1559
E-mail: programs@zonta.org
Web: www.zonta.org

**Summary**   To provide financial assistance to women working on an undergraduate or master's degree in business at a school in any country.

**Eligibility**   This program is open to women who are working on a business-related degree at a college or university anywhere in the world at the level of the second year of an undergraduate program through the final year of a master's degree program. Applicants first compete at the club level, and then advance to district and international levels. Along with their application, they must submit a 500-word essay that describes their academic and professional goals, the relevance of their program to the business field, and how this scholarship will assist them in reaching their goals. Selection is based on that essay, academic record, demonstrated intent to complete a program in business, achievement in business-related subjects, and 2 letters of recommendation.

**Financial data**   District winners receive a $1,000 scholarship; the international winners receive a $7,000 scholarship.

**Duration**   1 year.

**Additional information**   This program began in 1998.

**Number awarded**   The number of district winners varies each year; recently, 12 international winners (including 5 from the United States) were selected. Since this program was established, it has awarded more than 300 of these scholarships to women from 44 countries.

**Deadline**   Clubs set their own deadlines but must submit their winners to the district governor by May of each year.

## [314]
## JANE RING/SUE RING-JARVI GIRLS'/WOMEN'S HOCKEY SCHOLARSHIP

Scholarship America
Attn: Scholarship Management Services
One Scholarship Way
P.O. Box 297
St. Peter, MN 56082
(507) 931-1682                    Toll Free: (800) 537-4180
Fax: (507) 931-9168

**Summary**   To provide financial assistance to female high school seniors in Minnesota who have played hockey in high school and plan to attend college in any state.

**Eligibility**   This program is open to women graduating from high schools in Minnesota who have played varsity hockey or equivalent. Applicants must have a GPA of 3.0 or higher and be planning to enroll full time at an accredited college, university, or vocational/technical school in any state. Along with their application, they must submit a 2-page personal statement describing how hockey has affected their life, the contributions they have made to hockey in high school, and what role they expect hockey to play in their future. Selection is based on academic achievement, demonstrated leadership and participation in school and community activities, honors, work experience, a statement of goals and aspirations, an outside appraisal, contributions to girls' hockey, and skill level.

**Financial data**   The stipend is $2,500.

**Duration**   1 year; nonrenewable.

**Additional information**   This program began in 1996.

**Number awarded**   2 or 3 each year.

**Deadline**   April of each year.

## [315]
## JANE WALKER SCHOLARSHIP

United Methodist Church-Alabama-West Florida
    Conference
Attn: Commission on the Status and Role of Women
100 Interstate Park Drive, Suite 120
Montgomery, AL 36109
(334) 356-8014                    Toll Free: (888) 873-3127
Fax: (334) 356-8029              E-mail: awfcrc@awfumc.org
Web: www.awfumc.org/news/detail/547

**Summary**   To provide financial assistance to female residents of the Alabama-West Florida Conference of the United Methodist Church (UMC) who are undergraduate or seminary students preparing for a church-related career.

**Eligibility**   This program is open to women who are residents of the Alabama-West Florida Conference of the UMW and who affirm, represent, and advocate women's leadership in the church. Applicants must be accepted or enrolled at an approved UMC seminary or working on an undergraduate degree in Christian education at an approved UMC institution in any state. They must be a candidate for ministry or preparing for a UMC church-related career. Along with their application, they must submit a 500-word essay on why they are preparing for full-time Christian ministry and how they can promote the cause of women through this ministry. Financial need is considered in the selection process.

**Financial data**   The stipend is $1,000.

**Duration**   1 year.

**Number awarded** 1 each year.

**Deadline** May of each year.

## [316]
## JANET CULLEN TANAKA SCHOLARSHIP

Association for Women Geoscientists
Attn: AWG Foundation
12000 North Washington Street, Suite 285
Thornton, CO 80241
(303) 412-6219                    Fax: (303) 253-9220
E-mail: scholarship@awg-ps.org
Web: www.awg.org/EAS/scholarships.html

**Summary** To provide financial assistance to women from any state who are working on an undergraduate degree in geoscience at a college or university in Oregon or Washington.

**Eligibility** This program is open to undergraduate women from any state who are working on a bachelor's degree and committed to preparing for a career or graduate work in the geosciences, including geology, environmental or engineering geology, geochemistry, geophysics, hydrogeology, or hydrology. Applicants must be currently enrolled in a 2- or 4-year college or university in Oregon or Washington and have a GPA of 3.2 or higher. Along with their application, they must submit a 1-page essay summarizing their commitment to a career in the geosciences. Selection is based on potential for professional success, academic achievements, and financial need.

**Financial data** The stipend is $1,000.

**Duration** 1 year.

**Additional information** This program is sponsored by the Pacific Northwest Chapter of the Association for Women Geoscientists.

**Number awarded** 1 each year.

**Deadline** November of each year.

## [317]
## JANET H. GRISWOLD PEO SCHOLARSHIP

P.E.O. Foundation-California State Chapter
c/o Lynne Miller, Scholarship Committee Chair
1875 Los Altos
Clovis, CA 93611
(559) 709-6123          E-mail: peoca.rgw@gmail.com
Web: www.peocalifornia.org

**Summary** To provide financial assistance to women from California who are undergraduate or graduate students at a school in any state.

**Eligibility** This program is open to female residents of California who are attending an accredited college or university in any state. Applicants must be enrolled as full-time undergraduate or graduate students. Selection is based on financial need, character, and a record of academic and extracurricular activities achievement.

**Financial data** Stipends range from $500 to $1,500.

**Duration** 1 year.

**Number awarded** Varies each year.

**Deadline** January of each year.

## [318]
## JAZZ PERFORMANCE AWARDS

Sigma Alpha Iota Philanthropies, Inc.
One Tunnel Road
Asheville, NC 28805
(828) 251-0606                    Fax: (828) 251-0644
E-mail: nh@sai-national.org
Web: www.sai-national.org

**Summary** To provide financial assistance to members of Sigma Alpha Iota (an organization of women musicians) who are interested in working on an undergraduate or graduate degree in jazz performance.

**Eligibility** This program is open to members of the organization who are enrolled in an undergraduate or graduate degree program in jazz performance or studies. Applicants must be younger than 32 years of age. Along with their application, they must submit a CD recording of a performance "set" of 30 to 45 minutes.

**Financial data** Stipends are $2,000 for the winner or $1,500 for the runner-up.

**Duration** 1 year.

**Additional information** These awards were first presented in 2006.

**Number awarded** 2 every 3 years.

**Deadline** March of the year of the awards (2015, 2018, etc.).

## [319]
## JAZZ STUDIES SCHOLARSHIP

Sigma Alpha Iota Philanthropies, Inc.
One Tunnel Road
Asheville, NC 28805
(828) 251-0606                    Fax: (828) 251-0644
E-mail: nh@sai-national.org
Web: www.sai-national.org

**Summary** To provide financial assistance to members of Sigma Alpha Iota (an organization of women musicians) who are interested in working on an undergraduate degree in jazz studies.

**Eligibility** This program is open to members of the organization who are working on an undergraduate music degree with an emphasis in jazz studies. Applicants must submit a 500-word essay on their career plans and professional goals in jazz studies and why they feel they are deserving of this scholarship. Financial need is not considered in the selection process.

**Financial data** The stipend is $1,500.

**Duration** 1 year.

**Number awarded** 1 each year.

**Deadline** March of each year.

## [320]
## JEAN E. LYONS MEMORIAL SCHOLARSHIP

New Hampshire Women's Golf Association
c/o Rowena Wilks, Scholarship Committee
1098 Route 103A
New London, NH 03257-5670
(603) 763-9945                    E-mail: nhwga@aol.com
Web: www.nhwga.org

**Summary** To provide financial assistance to women in New Hampshire who have played golf and are interested in attending college in any state.

**Eligibility** This program is open to women who are residents of New Hampshire or playing members at New Hampshire golf clubs. Applicants must be enrolled or planning to enroll at a college or university in any state; preference is given to candidates enrolled in a 4-year undergraduate program. They must play golf; preference is given to applicants who play golf competitively in high school and/or who plan to play golf competitively in college. Along with their application, they must submit an essay describing their education and career goals, why they have chosen their course of study, and the job or career they are considering. Selection is based on academic success (as measured by grades and test scores) and character (as measured by extracurricular activities).

**Financial data** The stipend is $1,500. Funds are sent directly to the recipient's school.

**Duration** 1 year.

**Additional information** This scholarship, first awarded in 2009, is endowed through the New Hampshire Charitable Foundation.

**Number awarded** 1 each year.

**Deadline** April of each year.

## [321]
## JEAN FITZGERALD SCHOLARSHIP

Hawai'i Community Foundation
Attn: Scholarship Department
827 Fort Street Mall
Honolulu, HI 96813
(808) 566-5570          Toll Free: (888) 731-3863
Fax: (808) 521-6286
E-mail: scholarships@hcf-hawaii.org
Web: www.hawaiicommunityfoundation.org/scholarships

**Summary** To provide financial assistance to women tennis players in Hawaii who are entering freshmen at a college in any state.

**Eligibility** This program is open to female Hawaiian residents who are active tennis players entering their freshman year at a college or university in any state as full-time students. Preference may be given to members of the Hawai'i Pacific Section of the United States Tennis Association (USTA). Applicants must be able to demonstrate academic achievement (GPA of 2.7 or higher), good moral character, and financial need. Along with their application, they must submit a short statement indicating their reasons for attending college, their planned course of study, their career goals, and what community service means to them.

**Financial data** The amounts of the awards depend on the availability of funds and the need of the recipient. Recently, the average value of each of the scholarships awarded by the foundation was more than $2,000.

**Duration** 1 year.

**Number awarded** Varies each year; recently, 2 of these scholarships were awarded.

**Deadline** February of each year.

## [322]
## JEAN TUCKER STRADLEY SCHOLARSHIP

Kappa Delta Sorority
Attn: Foundation Project Manager
3205 Players Lane
Memphis, TN 38125
(901) 748-1897, ext. 203          Toll Free: (800) 536-1897
Fax: (901) 748-0949
E-mail: caroline.cullum@kappadelta.org
Web: www.kappadelta.org/scholarshipapplications_1

**Summary** To provide financial assistance to members of Kappa Delta Sorority who are majoring in elementary education.

**Eligibility** This program is open to undergraduate members of Kappa Delta Sorority. Applicants must submit a personal statement giving their reasons for applying for this scholarship, an official undergraduate transcript, and 2 letters of recommendation. They must be majoring in elementary education. Selection is based on academic excellence; service to the chapter, alumnae association, or national Kappa Delta; service to the campus and community; personal objectives and goals; potential; recommendations; and financial need.

**Financial data** The stipend is $2,000 per year. Funds may be used only for tuition, fees, and books, not for room and board.

**Duration** 1 year; may be renewed.

**Number awarded** 1 each year.

**Deadline** November of each year.

## [323]
## JEANNE L. HAMMOND MEMORIAL SCHOLARSHIP

Maine Federation of Business and Professional Women's Clubs
Attn: BPW/Maine Futurama Foundation
c/o Marilyn V. Ladd, Office Manager
103 County Road
Oakland, ME 04963
Web: www.bpwmefoundation.org/files/index.php?id=10

**Summary** To provide financial assistance to female high school seniors and recent graduates in Maine who plan to attend college in any state.

**Eligibility** This program is open to women who are seniors graduating from high schools in Maine or recent graduates of those schools. Applicants must be planning to enroll at least half time for their first year of postsecondary study at an accredited college or university in any state. They must have a realistic goal for the educational plans. Along with their application, they must submit a statement describing their educational and personal goals, including their financial need. First priority is given to women who can demonstrate a record of school and/or community involvement. Second priority is given to applicants who are interested in working on a journalism degree, members of the Maine Federation of Business and Professional Women's Clubs (BPW/Maine) and their dependents, and members of the American Association of University Women (AAUW) and their dependents.

**Financial data** The stipend is $1,200. Funds are paid directly to the recipient's school.

**Duration** 1 year.

**Number awarded** 1 or more each year.

**Deadline** April of each year.

## [324]
## JEANNETTE RANKIN AWARD

Jeannette Rankin Foundation, Inc.
1 Huntington Road, Suite 701
Athens, GA 30606
(706) 208-1211                    Fax: (706) 548-0202
E-mail: info@rankinfoundation.org
Web: www.rankinfoundation.org

**Summary** To provide financial assistance for college to women who are 35 years of age or older.

**Eligibility** This program is open to women who are 35 years of age or older and working on a technical or vocational certificate, associate degree, or first bachelor's degree. Applicants must meet standards of a low-income household, currently defined as net income less than $14,593 for a family of 1, rising to $55,923 for a family of 6. Along with their application, they must submit a 2-page essay that includes a description of their academic and career goals, what they have done of which they are the most proud, and how their education will benefit themselves, their family, and their community. Selection is based on the applicants' goals, plan for reaching those goals, challenges they have faced, and their financial situation. U.S. citizenship is required.

**Financial data** The stipend is $2,000.

**Duration** 1 year; nonrenewable.

**Additional information** This program began in 1978. Awards are not given to students enrolled in graduate courses or working on a second undergraduate degree.

**Number awarded** Varies each year; recently, 87 of these scholarships were awarded. Since the program began, it has awarded more than $1.8 million in scholarships to more than 700 women.

**Deadline** February of each year.

## [325]
## JENNY LIND COMPETITION FOR SOPRANOS

Barnum Festival Foundation
Attn: Director
1070 Main Street
Bridgeport, CT 06604
(203) 367-8495                    Toll Free: (866) 867-8495
Fax: (203) 367-0212      E-mail: barnumfestival@aol.com
Web: barnumfestival.com

**Summary** To recognize and reward outstanding young female singers who have not yet reached professional status.

**Eligibility** This program is open to sopranos between 20 and 30 years of age who have not yet attained professional status. They must be U.S. citizens. Past finalists may reapply, but former first-place winners and mezzo-sopranos are not eligible. Applicants must submit a CD or audio cassette tape with 2 contrasting arias and 1 art song. Based on the CD or tape, 12 semifinalists are selected for an audition at the Barnum Festival in Bridgeport, Connecticut every April. From that audition, 6 finalists are chosen. Selection of the winner is based on technique, musicianship, diction, interpretation, and stage presence.

**Financial data** The winner receives a $2,000 cash prize and is featured in a concert in June with the Swedish Jenny Lind. The runner-up receives a $500 prize.

**Duration** The competition is held annually.

**Additional information** The winner of this competition serves as the American Jenny Lind, a 21st-century counterpart of the Swedish Nightingale brought to the United States for a successful concert tour in 1850 by P.T. Barnum. There is a $35 application fee.

**Number awarded** 2 each year: 1 winner and 1 runner-up.

**Deadline** April of each year.

## [326]
## JESSICA POWELL LOFTIS SCHOLARSHIP FOR ACTEENS

Woman's Missionary Union
Attn: WMU Foundation
100 Missionary Ridge
Birmingham, AL 35242
(205) 408-5525                    Toll Free: (877) 482-4483
Fax: (205) 408-5508      E-mail: wmufoundation@wmu.org
Web: www.wmufoundation.com

**Summary** To provide financial assistance for college or other activities to female high school seniors who have been active in the Southern Baptist Convention's Acteens (Academic/Events/Training).

**Eligibility** This program is open to female high school seniors who are members of a Baptist church and active in Acteens. Applicants must 1) be planning to attend college and have completed *Quest for Vision* in the MissionsQuest program or StudiAct; 2) have been an Acteen for at least 1 year and be planning to attend an Acteens event; or 3) be an Acteens leader who is pursuing academic or leadership training to lead an Acteens group. Along with their application, they must submit an essay listing their major accomplishments and missions activities.

**Financial data** A stipend is awarded (amount not specified).

**Duration** 1 year.

**Additional information** This program began in 1995 by Woman's Missionary Union, an Auxiliary to Southern Baptist Convention.

**Number awarded** 1 or more each year.

**Deadline** February of each year.

## [327]
## JESSICA REDFIELD GHAWI SCHOLARSHIP

San Antonio Area Foundation
Attn: Scholarship Funds Program Officer
303 Pearl Parkway, Suite 114
San Antonio, TX 78215-1285
(210) 228-3759                    Fax: (210) 225-1980
E-mail: buresti@ssafdn.org
Web: www.saafdn.org

**Summary** To provide financial assistance to upper-division women from any state working on a degree in sports journalism or broadcasting.

**Eligibility** This program is open to women entering their junior or senior year of full-time study at a college or university in any state. Applicants must be preparing for a career in journalism, preferable sports journalism or broadcasting. They must have a GPA of 2.5 or higher. Along with their application, they must submit brief statements on what sports provides to society, their short-term career goals in the field of journalism, an experience from their own life and how it has influenced them, and their favorite sport or sports personality.

**Financial data** Stipends vary; recently, they averaged $2,000.

**Duration** 1 year; may be renewed.

**Additional information** This program began in 2012 to honor a woman killed in the Aurora, Colorado theater shooting of July 20 of that year.

**Number awarded** 1 each year.

**Deadline** February of each year.

## [328]
## JILL S. TIETJEN P.E. SCHOLARSHIP

Society of Women Engineers
Attn: Scholarship Selection Committee
203 North LaSalle Street, Suite 1675
Chicago, IL 60601-1269
(312) 596-5223           Toll Free: (877) SWE-INFO
Fax: (312) 644-8557      E-mail: scholarships@swe.org
Web: societyofwomenengineers.swe.org

**Summary** To provide financial assistance to women working on an undergraduate degree in engineering or computer science.

**Eligibility** This program is open to women who will be sophomores, juniors, or seniors at ABET-accredited colleges and universities. Applicants must be U.S. citizens or permanent residents working full time on a degree in computer science or engineering and have a GPA of 3.0 or higher. Selection is based on merit.

**Financial data** The stipend is $1,500.

**Duration** 1 year.

**Additional information** This program began in 2004.

**Number awarded** 1 each year.

**Deadline** February of each year.

## [329]
## JOHN AND MURIEL LANDIS SCHOLARSHIPS

American Nuclear Society
Attn: Scholarship Coordinator
555 North Kensington Avenue
La Grange Park, IL 60526-5535
(708) 352-6611           Toll Free: (800) 323-3044
Fax: (708) 352-0499      E-mail: outreach@ans.org
Web: www.new.ans.org/honors/scholarships

**Summary** To provide financial assistance to undergraduate or graduate students (especially women and minorities) who are interested in preparing for a career in nuclear-related fields and can demonstrate financial need.

**Eligibility** This program is open to undergraduate and graduate students at colleges or universities located in the United States who are preparing for, or planning to prepare for, a career in nuclear science, nuclear engineering, or a nuclear-related field. Qualified high school seniors are also eligible. Applicants must have greater than average financial need and have experienced circumstances that render them disadvantaged. Along with their application, they must submit an essay on their academic and professional goals, experiences that have affected those goals, etc. Selection is based

on that essay, academic achievement, letters of recommendation, and financial need. Women and members of minority groups are especially urged to apply. U.S. citizenship is not required.

**Financial data** The stipend is $5,000, to be used to cover tuition, books, fees, room, and board.

**Duration** 1 year; nonrenewable.

**Number awarded** Up to 9 each year.

**Deadline** January of each year.

## [330]
## JOHN EDGAR THOMSON FOUNDATION AID

John Edgar Thomson Foundation
Attn: Director
201 South 18th Street, Suite 318
Philadelphia, PA 19103
(215) 545-6083           Toll Free: (800) 888-1278
Fax: (215) 545-5102      E-mail: sjethomson@aol.com

**Summary** To provide financial assistance for education or maintenance to daughters of railroad employees who died while employed by a railroad in the United States.

**Eligibility** This program is open to women whose parent died in the active employ of a railroad in the United States, although the cause of death need not be work related. Applicants must live in the home of the surviving parent or guardian (unless attending college full time and living on campus), be in good health, and receive satisfactory academic grades. Eligibility of the daughter is also dependent upon the parent's remaining unmarried. Consideration is given to other factors as well, including the financial status of the family.

**Financial data** Payments are made on a monthly basis to assist with the education or maintenance of eligible daughters. The payment is available from infancy to age 18 or, under certain circumstances, to age 24 (for pursuit of higher education). This supplement to family income is to be used in its entirety for the benefit of the recipient. The grant may be terminated at any time if the financial need ceases or the daughter or surviving parent is either unable or fails to meet the eligibility requirements.

**Duration** Monthly payments may be made up to 24 years.

**Additional information** This foundation was established in 1882. Grantees are encouraged to participate in religious services of their faith.

**Number awarded** Varies; generally, 100 or more each year.

**Deadline** Deadline not specified.

## [331]
## JOSEPHINE AND BENJAMIN WEBBER TRUST SCHOLARSHIPS

Arizona Association of Family and Consumer Sciences
Attn: Webber Educational Grant Committee
Kathryn L. Hatch
4843 North Via Sonrisa
Tucson, AZ 85718-5724
(502) 577-6109           E-mail: klhatch@u.arizona.edu
Web: ag.arizona.edu/webbertrusts

**Summary** To provide financial assistance to Hispanic women from mining towns in Arizona who are interested in working on an undergraduate or graduate degree in a field related to family and consumer sciences at a school in the state.

**Eligibility** This program is open to Hispanic women who reside in the following Arizona mining towns: Ajo, Arizona City, Bisbee, Clifton, Douglas, Duncan, Globe, Green Valley, Hayden, Kingman, Kearny, Mammoth, Morenci, Prescott, Safford, Sahuarita, San Manuel, Seligman, Superior, or Winkelman. If too few female Hispanic residents of those towns apply, the program may be open to 1) non-Hispanic women who live in those towns, and/or 2) Hispanic women who currently live elsewhere in Arizona and whose parents or grandparents had lived or continue to live in those communities. Applicants must be enrolled or planning to enroll at a college or university in Arizona to work on an undergraduate or graduate degree. Eligible fields of study include those in the following categories: foods, nutrition, and/or dietetics; restaurant and food service management; culinary arts; family studies; interior design; family and consumer science education; dietetic education; early childhood education; or apparel and clothing. Financial need is considered in the selection process.

**Financial data** Funding at public colleges and universities provides for payment of tuition and fees, books, educational supplies, housing, food, and transportation to and from campus. At private institutions, stipend amounts are equivalent to those at public schools.

**Duration** 1 year; may be renewed for a total of 8 semesters and 2 summers of undergraduate study or 4 semesters and 2 summers of graduate study.

**Additional information** This program began in 1980.

**Number awarded** Varies each year; recently, 5 of these scholarships were awarded.

**Deadline** March of each year.

## [332]
## JUANITA KIDD STOUT SCHOLARSHIP PROGRAM

Delta Sigma Theta Sorority, Inc.
Attn: Scholarship and Standards Committee Chair
1707 New Hampshire Avenue, N.W.
Washington, DC 20009
(202) 986-2400                    Fax: (202) 986-2513
E-mail: dstemail@deltasigmatheta.org
Web: www.deltasigmatheta.org

**Summary** To provide financial assistance to members of Delta Sigma Theta who are working on an undergraduate degree in criminal justice.

**Eligibility** This program is open to current undergraduate students who are working on a degree in criminal justice. Applicants must be active, dues-paying members of Delta Sigma Theta. Selection is based on meritorious achievement.

**Financial data** The stipends range from $1,000 to $2,000. The funds may be used to cover tuition, fees, and living expenses.

**Duration** 1 year; may be renewed for 1 additional year.

**Additional information** This sponsor is a traditionally-African American social sorority. The application fee is $20.

**Number awarded** 1 or more each year.

**Deadline** April of each year.

## [333]
## JUDGE HAZEL PALMER GENERAL SCHOLARSHIP

Business Women of Missouri Foundation, Inc.
Attn: Scholarship Committee Chair
P.O. Box 28243
Kansas City, MO 64188
(816) 333-6959                    Fax: (816) 333-6959
E-mail: jo.mofedbpw@gmail.com
Web: www.businesswomenmo.org/foundation/index.html

**Summary** To provide financial assistance to women in Missouri who are interested in working on a college degree leading to public service at a school in any state.

**Eligibility** This program is open to women in Missouri who have been accepted into an accredited program or course of study in any state to work on a degree leading to public service. Along with their application, they must submit brief statements on the following: achievements and/or specific recognitions in their field of endeavor; professional and/or civic affiliations; present and long-range career goals; how they plan to participate in and contribute to their community upon completion of their program of study; why they feel they would make a good recipient; and any special circumstances that may have influenced their ability to continue or complete their education. They must also demonstrate financial need and U.S. citizenship.

**Financial data** The stipend is $1,000.

**Duration** 1 year.

**Number awarded** Varies each year; recently, 2 of these scholarships were awarded.

**Deadline** January of each year.

## [334]
## JUDITH MCMANUS PRICE SCHOLARSHIPS

American Planning Association
Attn: Leadership Affairs Associate
205 North Michigan Avenue, Suite 1200
Chicago, IL 60601
(312) 431-9100                    Fax: (312) 786-6700
E-mail: fellowship@planning.org
Web: www.planning.org/scholarships/apa

**Summary** To provide financial assistance to women and underrepresented minority students enrolled in undergraduate or graduate degree programs at recognized planning schools.

**Eligibility** This program is open to undergraduate and graduate students in urban and regional planning who are women or members of the following minority groups: African American, Hispanic American, or Native American. Applicants must be citizens of the United States and able to document financial need. They must intend to work as practicing planners in the public sector. Along with their application, they must submit a 2-page personal and background statement describing how their education will be applied to career goals and why they chose planning as a career path. Selection is based (in order of importance), on: 1) commitment to planning as reflected in their personal statement and on their resume; 2) academic achievement and/or improvement during the past 2 years; 3) letters of recommendation; 4) financial need; and 5) professional presentation.

**Financial data** Stipends range from $2,000 to $4,000 per year. The money may be applied to tuition and living expenses only. Payment is made to the recipient's university and divided by terms in the school year.

**Duration** 1 year; recipients may reapply.

**Additional information** This program began in 2002.

**Number awarded** Varies each year; recently, 3 of these scholarships were awarded.

**Deadline** April of each year.

## [335]
## JUDITH RESNIK MEMORIAL SCHOLARSHIP

Alpha Epsilon Phi
Attn: AEPhi Foundation
11 Lake Avenue Extension, Suite 1A
Danbury, CT 06811
(203) 748-0029                    Fax: (203) 748-0039
E-mail: aephifoundation@aephi.org
Web: www.aephi.org/foundation/scholarships

**Summary** To provide financial assistance to Alpha Epsilon Phi members or alumnae who are working on an undergraduate or graduate degree, especially in science, engineering, or a related field.

**Eligibility** This program is open to active and alumnae members of the sorority who are either full-time rising juniors or seniors or graduate students who have completed at least 1 year of graduate study. Preference is given to applicants who are working on a degree in science, engineering, or a related field and have a GPA of 3.5 or higher. Along with their application, they must submit a letter describing 1) their activities in their chapter, on campus, and in the general community; 2) what they have done to supplement their parents' contribution toward their education; and 3) their need for scholarship consideration.

**Financial data** Stipends range from $1,000 to $2,000 per year.

**Duration** 1 year; may be renewed.

**Additional information** Recipients must be willing to remain active in the sorority and live in the sorority house (if any) for the entire year the scholarship covers.

**Number awarded** 1 or more each year.

**Deadline** March of each year.

## [336]
## JUDITH RESNIK MEMORIAL SWE SCHOLARSHIP

Society of Women Engineers
Attn: Scholarship Selection Committee
203 North LaSalle Street, Suite 1675
Chicago, IL 60601-1269
(312) 596-5223                    Toll Free: (877) SWE-INFO
Fax: (312) 644-8557          E-mail: scholarships@swe.org
Web: societyofwomenengineers.swe.org

**Summary** To provide financial assistance to undergraduate members of the Society of Women Engineers (SWE) who are majoring in designated engineering specialties.

**Eligibility** This program is open to society members who are entering their sophomore, junior, or senior year at an ABET-accredited 4-year college or university. Applicants must be working full time on a degree in aerospace, aeronautical,

astronautical, or other space-related field of engineering and have a GPA of 3.0 or higher. Selection is based on merit.

**Financial data** The stipend is $3,000.

**Duration** 1 year.

**Additional information** This award was established in 1988 to honor society member Judith Resnik, who was killed aboard the Challenger space shuttle.

**Number awarded** 1 each year.

**Deadline** February of each year.

## [337]
## JUDY CORMAN MEMORIAL SCHOLARSHIP AND INTERNSHIP

New York Women in Communications, Inc.
Attn: NYWICI Foundation
355 Lexington Avenue, 15th Floor
New York, NY 10017-6603
(212) 297-2133                    Fax: (212) 370-9047
E-mail: nywicipr@nywici.org
Web: www.nywici.org/foundation/scholarships

**Summary** To provide financial assistance and work experience to female residents of designated eastern states who are interested in preparing for a career in communications and media relations at a college or graduate school in any state.

**Eligibility** This program is open to women who are seniors graduating from high schools in New York, New Jersey, Connecticut, or Pennsylvania or undergraduate or graduate students who are permanent residents of those states; they must be attending or planning to attend a college or university in any state. Graduate students must be members of New York Women in Communications, Inc. (NYWICI). Also eligible are women who reside outside the 4 states but are currently enrolled at a college or university within 1 of the 5 boroughs of New York City. Applicants must be preparing for a career in communications and media relations and be interested in a summer internship with Scholastic. They must have a GPA of 3.2 or higher. Along with their application, they must submit a 2-page resume; a personal essay of 300 words on an assigned topic that changes annually; 2 letters of recommendation; and an official transcript. Selection is based on academic record, need, demonstrated leadership, participation in school and community activities, honors and other awards or recognition, work experience, goals and aspirations, and unusual personal and/or family circumstances. U.S. citizenship is required.

**Financial data** The scholarship stipend ranges up to $10,000; the internship is salaried (amount not specified).

**Duration** 1 year.

**Additional information** This program is sponsored by Scholastic, Inc.

**Number awarded** 1 each year.

**Deadline** January of each year.

## [338]
## JULIA H. DODDS JUNIOR GIRL'S AWARD

Illinois Women's Golf Association
c/o Marlene Miller
11683 Wimbledon Circle
Wellington, FL 33414
(561) 333-3014          E-mail: mememiller@aol.com
Web: iwga.org/?page_id=88

**Summary** To provide financial assistance to women in Illinois who have participated in golf and are interested in attending college in any state.

**Eligibility** This program is open to female high school seniors in Illinois who have played in the Illinois Women's Golf Association (IWGA) State Junior Tournament. Nominations may be submitted by anyone with knowledge of qualified girls. Nominees must arrange for 2 letters of recommendation, 1 from their high school golf coach and 1 from a teacher or principal at their high school. Selection is based on character, scholarship, leadership, sportsmanship, and love for the game of golf.

**Financial data** The stipend is $2,000. Funds are paid directly to the recipient's college.

**Duration** 1 year.

**Additional information** This program began in 1992.

**Number awarded** 1 each year.

**Deadline** March of each year.

## [339]
## JULIETTE MATHER SCHOLARSHIP

Woman's Missionary Union
Attn: WMU Foundation
100 Missionary Ridge
Birmingham, AL 35242
(205) 408-5525          Toll Free: (877) 482-4483
Fax: (205) 408-5508     E-mail: wmufoundation@wmu.org
Web: www.wmufoundation.com

**Summary** To provide financial assistance to female Southern Baptist undergraduate or graduate students preparing for a career in Christian ministry.

**Eligibility** This program is open to female Southern Baptist undergraduate and graduate students who are preparing for a career in Christian ministry and service. They must be interested in preparing to become the Baptist leaders of the future.

**Financial data** A stipend is awarded (amount not specified).

**Duration** 1 year.

**Number awarded** Varies each year.

**Deadline** January of each year.

## [340]
## JUNIOR GIRLS SCHOLARSHIPS

Ladies Auxiliary to the Veterans of Foreign Wars
c/o National Headquarters
406 West 34th Street
Kansas City, MO 64111
(816) 561-8655          Fax: (816) 931-4753
E-mail: info@ladiesauxvfw.org
Web: www.ladiesauxvfw.org/programs/scholarships.html

**Summary** To provide financial assistance for college to outstanding members of a Junior Girls Unit of the Ladies Auxiliary to the Veterans of Foreign Wars.

**Eligibility** Applicants must have been active members of a unit for 1 year, have held an office in the unit, and be between 13 and 16 years of age. Previous winners are not eligible, although former applicants who did not receive scholarships may reapply. Selection is based on participation in the Junior Girls Unit (40 points), school activities (30 points), and academic achievement (30 points).

**Financial data** The winner receives a $7,500 scholarship. Funds are paid directly to the college of the recipient's choice. In addition, $100 is awarded to each Junior Girl who is selected as the department winner and entered in the national competition.

**Duration** 1 year.

**Number awarded** 1 each year.

**Deadline** March of each year.

## [341]
## KA'IULANI HOME FOR GIRLS TRUST SCHOLARSHIP

Hawai'i Community Foundation
Attn: Scholarship Department
827 Fort Street Mall
Honolulu, HI 96813
(808) 566-5570          Toll Free: (888) 731-3863
Fax: (808) 521-6286
E-mail: scholarships@hcf-hawaii.org
Web: www.hawaiicommunityfoundation.org/scholarships

**Summary** To provide financial assistance to women of Native Hawaiian ancestry who are attending college in any state.

**Eligibility** This program is open to women of Native Hawaiian ancestry who are full-time freshmen or sophomores at a college or university in any state. Applicants must demonstrate academic achievement (GPA of 3.3 or higher), good moral character, and financial need. Along with their application, they must submit a short statement indicating their reasons for attending college, their planned course of study, their career goals, and what community service means to them.

**Financial data** The amounts of the awards depend on the availability of funds and the need of the recipient. Recently, the average value of each of the scholarships awarded by the foundation was more than $2,000.

**Duration** 1 year; may be renewed.

**Additional information** This fund was established in 1963 when the Ka'iulani Home for Girls, formerly used to provide boarding home facilities for young women of Native Hawaiian ancestry, was demolished and the property sold.

**Number awarded** Varies each year.

**Deadline** February of each year.

**[342]**
## KAPPA ALPHA THETA UNDERGRADUATE SCHOLARSHIPS

Kappa Alpha Theta Foundation
Attn: Manager of Programs
8740 Founders Road
Indianapolis, IN 46268-1337
(317) 876-1870                    Toll Free: (800) KAO-1870
Fax: (317) 876-1925
E-mail: gmerritt@kappaalphatheta.org
Web: www.kappaalphathetafoundation.org

**Summary**   To provide financial assistance for college in the United States or abroad to members of Kappa Alpha Theta.

**Eligibility**   This program is open to members of Kappa Alpha Theta who are enrolled full time at a college or university in Canada or the United States. Along with their application, they must submit an official transcript, personal essays on assigned topics related to their involvement in Kappa Alpha Theta, and 2 letters of reference. Financial need is not considered in the selection process.

**Financial data**   Stipends range from $1,000 to $7,100. Recently, the average was $2,700.

**Duration**   1 year. Recipients may reapply, but they may receive a maximum lifetime amount of $20,000 from the foundation.

**Additional information**   Recipients may study abroad, provided they do so as part of a program leading to a degree from an institution in the United States or Canada.

**Number awarded**   Varies each year; recently, the organization scholarships to 131 undergraduate members.

**Deadline**   February of each year.

**[343]**
## KAPPA DELTA SORORITY UNDERGRADUATE SCHOLARSHIPS

Kappa Delta Sorority
Attn: Foundation Project Manager
3205 Players Lane
Memphis, TN 38125
(901) 748-1897, ext. 203         Toll Free: (800) 536-1897
Fax: (901) 748-0949
E-mail: caroline.cullum@kappadelta.org
Web: www.kappadelta.org/scholarshipapplications_1

**Summary**   To provide financial assistance to members of Kappa Delta Sorority who are interested in continuing their undergraduate education.

**Eligibility**   This program is open to undergraduate members of Kappa Delta Sorority. Applicants must submit a personal statement giving their reasons for applying for this scholarship, an official undergraduate transcript, and 2 letters of recommendation. Most scholarships are available to all undergraduate members, but some restrict the field of study and others are limited to members at specified chapters. Selection is based on academic excellence; service to the chapter, alumnae association, or national Kappa Delta; service to the campus and community; personal objectives and goals; potential; recommendations; and financial need.

**Financial data**   Stipends range from $1,000 to $4,000 per year. Funds may be used only for tuition, fees, and books, not for room and board.

**Duration**   1 year; may be renewed.

**Additional information**   This program includes the following named scholarships that have no additional restrictions: the Kappa Delta Founders' Scholarships, the Grayce Chase Scholarship, the Grace Follmer Scholarship, the M. Amanda Gordon Scholarships, the Margaret Budd Haemer Scholarship, the Muriel Johnstone Scholarships, the Phyllis M. Meisner Kappa Delta President's Risk Management Scholarship, the Marilyn Mock Scholarship, the Ernestine L. Newman Scholarship, the Minnie Mae Prescott Kappa Delta Staff Risk Management Scholarship, and the Dorothy Ramage Scholarship.

**Number awarded**   Varies each year; recently, the sorority awarded a total of 31 scholarships: 4 at $4,000, 1 at $2,500, 22 at $2,000, 2 at $1,250, and 2 at $1,000.

**Deadline**   November of each year.

**[344]**
## KAPPA KAPPA GAMMA UNDERGRADUATE SCHOLARSHIPS

Kappa Kappa Gamma Fraternity
Attn: Foundation Administrator
530 East Town Street
P.O. Box 38
Columbus, OH 43216-0038
(614) 228-6515                    Toll Free: (866) KKG-1870
Fax: (614) 228-6303              E-mail: kkghq@kappa.org
Web: www.kappakappagamma.org

**Summary**   To provide financial assistance for college to members of Kappa Kappa Gamma.

**Eligibility**   This program is open to members of Kappa Kappa Gamma who are enrolled full time and have a GPA of 3.0 or higher for each academic term. Applicants must be initiated members; associate members are not eligible. Along with their application, they must submit a personal essay or letter describing their educational and career goals and financial need. Selection is based on merit, academic achievement, participation in sorority activities, and financial need.

**Financial data**   Stipends average $3,000.

**Duration**   1 year.

**Number awarded**   Varies each year; recently, the foundation awarded a total of 152 undergraduate and graduate scholarships with a value of $466,812.

**Deadline**   January of each year.

**[345]**
## KATE GLEASON SCHOLARSHIP

ASME International
Attn: Centers Administrator
Two Park Avenue
New York, NY 10016-5675
(212) 591-8131                    Toll Free: (800) THE-ASME
Fax: (212) 591-7143              E-mail: LefeverB@asme.org
Web: www.asme.org

**Summary**   To provide financial assistance to female undergraduate and graduate students from any country who are working on a degree in mechanical engineering.

**Eligibility**   This program is open to women who are enrolled in an ABET-accredited or equivalent mechanical engineering, mechanical engineering technology, or related undergraduate or graduate program. Applicants must submit a nomination from their department head, a recommendation from a faculty member, and an official transcript. Only 1 nomination may be submitted per department. There are no citizenship requirements, but study must be conducted in the United States. Selection is based on academic ability and potential contribution to the mechanical engineering profession.

**Financial data**  The stipend is $3,000.

**Duration**  1 year.

**Number awarded**  1 each year.

**Deadline**  February of each year.

## [346]
## KATHLEEN BARRA MEMORIAL SCHOLARSHIP

American Association of University Women-Northern
  Ocean County Branch
P.O. Box 608
Manasquan, NJ 08736
E-mail: AAUW-NOCB@hotmail.com

**Summary**  To provide financial assistance to women who are friends or relatives of members of the American Association of University Women (AAUW) in New Jersey and working on a degree in a business-related field at a school in any state.

**Eligibility**  This program is open to women who are a friend or relative of a current member of the AAUW in any of the New Jersey branches. Applicants must be enrolled or planning to enroll full time at a college or university in any state and working on a degree in a business-related field (e.g., marketing, economics, business). Along with their application, they must submit a 2-page essay on their educational and career goals and personal ambitions. Financial need is not considered in the selection process.

**Financial data**  The stipend is $1,000.

**Duration**  1 year.

**Number awarded**  1 each year.

**Deadline**  May of each year.

## [347]
## KATHY KARDISH WILSON MEMORIAL EDUCATIONAL FUND

Chautauqua Region Community Foundation
Attn: Scholarship Coordinator
418 Spring Street
Jamestown, NY 14701
(716) 661-3394                    Fax: (716) 488-0387
E-mail: llynde@crcfonline.org
Web: www.crcfonline.org

**Summary**  To provide financial assistance to married women in New York, Ohio, and Pennsylvania who are interested in returning to school to complete an undergraduate or graduate degree.

**Eligibility**  This program is open to women who live and attend college or graduate school in New York, Ohio, or Pennsylvania. Applicants must be mothers of school-aged children, part of a 2-income family in which tuition would be a burden on the family, able to complete the educational and career goals set for themselves, community-minded and considerably involved in at least 1 community organization, and giving of themselves and their talents to help others reach their potential. Along with their application, they must submit

a 1-page essay describing their past achievements, career goals, and reasons for returning to school or training.

**Financial data**  A stipend is awarded (amount not specified).

**Duration**  1 year.

**Number awarded**  1 or more each year.

**Deadline**  May of each year.

## [348]
## KATHY LOUDAT MUSIC SCHOLARSHIP

New Mexico Baptist Foundation
5325 Wyoming Boulevard, N.E.
P.O. Box 16560
Albuquerque, NM 87191-6560
(505) 332-3777                    Toll Free: (877) 841-3777
Fax: (505) 332-2777              E-mail: foundation@nmbf.com
Web: www.bcnm.com

**Summary**  To provide financial assistance to female members of Southern Baptist churches in New Mexico who are attending college in any state to prepare for a career in church music.

**Eligibility**  This program is open to full-time female college, university, and seminary students who are preparing for a career in church music. Applicants must have a GPA of 3.0 or higher and be able to demonstrate financial need. They must be members of Southern Baptist churches in New Mexico or former members in good standing with the Southern Baptist Convention.

**Financial data**  A stipend is awarded (amount not specified).

**Duration**  1 year.

**Number awarded**  1 or more each year.

**Deadline**  April of each year.

## [349]
## KATIE ROSE MARTIN SCHOLARSHIP

Community Foundation of Middle Tennessee
Attn: Scholarship Committee
3833 Cleghorn Avenue, Suite 400
Nashville, TN 37215-2519
(615) 321-4939                    Toll Free: (888) 540-5200
Fax: (615) 327-2746              E-mail: grants@cfmt.org
Web: www.cfmt.org/request/scholarships/allscholarships

**Summary**  To provide financial assistance to female residents of any state attending a school of cosmetology in Tennessee.

**Eligibility**  This program is open to women who are high school graduates or second career adults. Applicants must be attending an accredited cosmetology school in Tennessee. Along with their application, they must submit an essay describing their educational plans and how those plans will help them reach their career goals. Financial need is considered in the selection process.

**Financial data**  Stipends range from $500 to $2,500 per year. Funds are paid to the recipient's school and must be used for tuition, fees, books, supplies, room, board, or miscellaneous expenses.

**Duration**  1 year.

**Additional information**  This program began in 2010.

**Number awarded** 1 or more each year.

**Deadline** March of each year.

## [350]
## KELLI STATHEROS RE-ENTRY SCHOLARSHIP

Daughters of Penelope-District 11
Attn: AHEPA Buckeye Scholarship Foundation
25590 West County Line Road
Sunman, IN 47041
(513) 310-5299
Web: www.ahepabuckeye.org

**Summary** To provide financial assistance to women who wish to reenter the workforce and are members of the Daughters of Penelope in its District 11 (Kentucky, Ohio, and parts of Pennsylvania and West Virginia).

**Eligibility** This program is open to residents of Kentucky, Ohio, and parts of Pennsylvania and West Virginia who have been members of the Daughters of Penelope for the past 2 years and the current year. Applicants must be women entering an accredited college, vocational school, or university in any state to obtain training necessary to prepare for a career in the field of her choice. Financial need is considered in the selection process.

**Financial data** A stipend is awarded (amount not specified).

**Duration** 1 year.

**Additional information** This program began in 1987.

**Number awarded** 1 or more each year.

**Deadline** April of each year.

## [351]
## KELLOGG SCHOLARSHIPS

Society of Women Engineers
Attn: Scholarship Selection Committee
203 North LaSalle Street, Suite 1675
Chicago, IL 60601-1269
(312) 596-5223          Toll Free: (877) SWE-INFO
Fax: (312) 644-8557     E-mail: scholarships@swe.org
Web: societyofwomenengineers.swe.org

**Summary** To provide financial assistance to undergraduate members of the Society of Women Engineers (SWE) who are majoring in designated engineering specialties.

**Eligibility** This program is open to society members who are entering their sophomore or junior year at an ABET-accredited 4-year college or university. Applicants must be working full time on a degree in computer science or biosystems, chemical, or mechanical engineering and have a GPA of 3.0 or higher. Preference is given to students attending designated universities and to those who can demonstrate financial need.

**Financial data** The stipend is $3,000 or $1,000.

**Duration** 1 year.

**Additional information** For a list of the designated universities, contact SWE.

**Number awarded** 3 each year: 1 at $3,000 and 2 at $1,000.

**Deadline** February of each year.

## [352]
## KENTUCKY COLONELS BETTER LIFE SCHOLARSHIPS

Kentucky Community and Technical College System
Attn: Financial Aid
300 North Main Street
Versailles, KY 40383
(859) 256-3100     Toll Free: (877) 528-2748 (within KY)
Web: www.kctcs.edu

**Summary** To provide financial assistance to single parents attending or planning to attend 1 of the schools within the Kentucky Community and Technical College System (KCTCS).

**Eligibility** This program is open to Kentucky residents who are single working parents with at least 1 child under 12 years of age. Applicants must be attending or planning to attend a KCTCS institution and able to demonstrate unmet financial need. Selection is based on demonstrated enthusiasm for learning and potential for academic success.

**Financial data** The stipend is $2,500 per year.

**Duration** 1 year; may be renewed 1 additional year if the recipient maintains full-time enrollment and satisfactory academic progress.

**Additional information** This program began in 2004.

**Number awarded** 32 each year: 2 in each of the KCTCS districts.

**Deadline** Deadline not specified.

## [353]
## KENTUCKY WOMEN IN AGRICULTURE SCHOLARSHIP

Kentucky Women in Agriculture
Attn: Scholarship
P.O. Box 4409
Lexington, KY 40544-4409
Toll Free: (877) 266-8823
E-mail: info@kywomeninag.com
Web: www.kywomeninag.com/scholarship.php

**Summary** To provide financial assistance to female residents of Kentucky enrolled as upper-division or graduate students at colleges in the state and working on a degree in agriculture.

**Eligibility** This program is open to women who are residents of Kentucky and enrolled full time as juniors, seniors, or graduate students at a college or university in the state. Applicants must be working on a degree in a field related to agriculture and have a GPA of 2.5 or higher. Along with their application, they must submit a 500-word essay on their career goals for working in agriculture and how this scholarship will support them in their academic pursuits. Selection is based on desire to work in the field of agriculture (40 points), financial need (30 points), academic record (20 points), and extracurricular activities (10 points).

**Financial data** The stipend is $1,000 per year.

**Duration** 1 year.

**Number awarded** 1 each year.

**Deadline** May of each year.

## [354]
## KIM MILLER SYNCHRONIZED SWIMMING SCHOLARSHIP

Community Foundation of Greater New Britain
Attn: Scholarship Manager
74A Vine Street
New Britain, CT 06052-1431
(860) 229-6018, ext. 305    Fax: (860) 225-2666
E-mail: cfarmer@cfgnb.org
Web: www.cfgnb.org

**Summary** To provide financial assistance for college to female high school seniors who are registered members of United States Synchronized Swimming (USSS) East Zone.

**Eligibility** This program is open to graduating high school seniors who are members of USSS East Zone. Applicants must be planning to attend a college or university in any state and participate in synchronized swimming at the collegiate level. They must have a GPA of 3.0 or higher. Along with their application, they must submit an essay explaining why they feel they should be awarded this scholarship.

**Financial data** A stipend is awarded (amount not specified).

**Duration** 1 year.

**Additional information** This program began in 2007 by the Hamden Heronettes Synchronized Swim Team of Hamden, Connecticut.

**Number awarded** 1 each year.

**Deadline** February of each year.

## [355]
## LA FRA SCHOLARSHIP

Ladies Auxiliary of the Fleet Reserve Association
Attn: Membership Service Administrator
P.O. Box 2086
Shingle Springs, CA 95682-2086
(530) 677-3925    E-mail: laframsa@att.net
Web: www.la-fra.org/scholarship.html

**Summary** To provide financial assistance for college to the daughters and granddaughters of naval personnel.

**Eligibility** Eligible to apply for these scholarships are the daughters and granddaughters of Navy, Marine, Coast Guard, active Fleet Reserve, Fleet Marine Corps Reserve, and Coast Guard Reserve personnel on active duty, retired with pay, or deceased while on active duty or retired with pay. Applicants must submit an essay on their life experiences, career objectives, and what motivated them to select those objectives. Selection is based on academic record, financial need, extracurricular activities, leadership skills, and participation in community activities. U.S. citizenship is required.

**Financial data** The stipend is $2,500.

**Duration** 1 year; may be renewed.

**Number awarded** 1 each year.

**Deadline** April of each year.

## [356]
## LAMBDA THETA NU SORORITY LATINA SCHOLARSHIP PROGRAM

Lambda Theta Nu Sorority, Inc.
Attn: Director of Community Service
1220 Rosecrans, Suite 543
San Diego, CA 92106
E-mail: community@lambdathetanu.org
Web: www.lambdathetanu.org

**Summary** To provide financial assistance for college to female high school seniors with a connection to the Latino community.

**Eligibility** This program is open to female graduating high school seniors who are either of Latino heritage or able to demonstrate dedication to community service and empowerment of the Latino community. Applicants must be planning to attend an accredited community college, university, or vocational/technical school. Along with their application, they must submit a personal statement that covers their family background, academic achievements, educational and career goals, commitment to the Latino community, and financial need.

**Financial data** A stipend is awarded (amount not specified).

**Duration** 1 year.

**Number awarded** Approximately 35 each year (1 selected by each chapter of the sorority).

**Deadline** April of each year.

## [357]
## LAO AMERICAN WOMEN ASSOCIATION OF WASHINGTON D.C. METROPOLITAN AREA VOCATIONAL TRAINING/GED SCHOLARSHIP FUND

Lao American Women Association
Attn: Scholarship Committee
3908 Carroll Court
Chantilly, VA 20151
(703) 283-8698    E-mail: info@lawadc.org
Web: www.lawadc.org

**Summary** To provide financial assistance to women of Lao ancestry in the Washington, D.C. area who need additional training to find a job.

**Eligibility** This program is open to women in the Washington, D.C. metropolitan area who are of Lao parentage. Applicants must be in need of additional training to find a job, to obtain work at a higher level, or to complete a GED certificate. They must provide information on their personal situation, proposed training program, work experience, family and community activities, and financial situation. They must also submit a 150-word personal statement on their family and community activities. Financial need is considered in the selection process (must have family income less than $75,000 per year).

**Financial data** The stipend is $1,000 for vocational training or $500 for GED completion.

**Duration** 1 year.

**Number awarded** Either 1 scholarship for vocational training or 2 for GED completion are awarded each year.

**Deadline** April of each year.

## [358]
## LARONA J. MORRIS SCHOLARSHIP

Sigma Gamma Rho Sorority, Inc.
Attn: National Education Fund
1000 Southhill Drive, Suite 200
Cary, NC 27513
(919) 678-9720          Toll Free: (888) SGR-1922
Fax: (919) 678-9721          E-mail: info@sgrho1922.org
Web: www.sgrho1922.org/nef

**Summary** To provide financial assistance to African American women and other undergraduate students working on a degree in hotel and restaurant management.

**Eligibility** This program is open to undergraduates working on a degree in hotel and restaurant management. The sponsor is a traditionally African American sorority. Applicants must have a GPA of "C" or higher and be able to demonstrate financial need.

**Financial data** A stipend is awarded (amount not specified).

**Duration** 1 year.

**Additional information** A processing fee of $20 is required.

**Number awarded** 1 each year.

**Deadline** April of each year.

## [359]
## LCDR EIFFERT FOSTER STUDENT SCHOLARSHIP

National Naval Officers Association-Washington, D.C.
  Chapter
c/o LCDR Stephen Williams
P.O. Box 30784
Alexandria, VA 22310
(703) 566-3840          Fax: (703) 566-3813
E-mail: Stephen.Williams@navy.mil
Web: dcnnoa.memberlodge.com

**Summary** To provide financial assistance to female African American high school seniors from the Washington, D.C. area who have been in foster care and are interested in attending college in any state.

**Eligibility** This program is open to female African American seniors graduating from high schools in the Washington, D.C. metropolitan area who plan to enroll full time at an accredited 2- or 4-year college or university in any state. Applicants must have lived in a foster home. They must have a GPA of 2.5 or higher and be U.S. citizens or permanent residents. Selection is based on academic achievement, community involvement, and financial need.

**Financial data** The stipend is $1,000.

**Duration** 1 year; nonrenewable.

**Additional information** Recipients are not required to join or affiliate with the military in any way.

**Number awarded** 1 each year.

**Deadline** March of each year.

## [360]
## LEMIEUX-LOVEJOY YOUTH SCHOLARSHIP

Maine Federation of Business and Professional Women's
  Clubs
Attn: BPW/Maine Futurama Foundation
c/o Marilyn V. Ladd, Office Manager
103 County Road
Oakland, ME 04963
Web: www.bpwmefoundation.org/files/index.php?id=10

**Summary** To provide financial assistance to female high school seniors and recent graduates in Maine who plan to attend college in any state.

**Eligibility** This program is open to women who are seniors graduating from high schools in Maine or recent graduates of those schools. Applicants must be planning to attend an accredited college or university in any state. They must have a realistic goal for the educational plans. Along with their application, they must submit a statement describing their educational and personal goals, including their financial need. Other criteria being equal, preference is given to members of the Maine Federation of Business and Professional Women's Clubs and their relatives.

**Financial data** The stipend is $1,200. Funds are paid directly to the recipient's school.

**Duration** 1 year.

**Number awarded** 1 or more each year.

**Deadline** April of each year.

## [361]
## LEROY APKER AWARD

American Physical Society
Attn: Honors Program
One Physics Ellipse
College Park, MD 20740-3844
(301) 209-3268          Fax: (301) 209-0865
E-mail: honors@aps.org
Web: www.aps.org/programs/honors/awards/apker.cfm

**Summary** To recognize and reward undergraduate students (particularly women and underrepresented minorities) for outstanding work in physics.

**Eligibility** This program is open to undergraduate students at colleges and universities in the United States. Nominees should have completed or be completing the requirements for an undergraduate degree with an excellent academic record and should have demonstrated exceptional potential for scientific research by making an original contribution to physics. Each department of physics in the United States may nominate only 1 student. Each nomination packet should include the student's academic transcript, a description of the original contribution written by the student (such as a manuscript or reprint of a research publication or senior thesis), a 1,000-word summary, and 2 letters of recommendation. Nominations of qualified women and members of underrepresented minority groups are especially encouraged.

**Financial data** The award consists of a $5,000 honorarium for the student, a certificate citing the work and school of the recipient, and an allowance for travel expenses to the meeting of the American Physical Society (APS) at which the prize is presented. Each of the finalists receives an honorarium of $2,000 and a certificate. Each of the physics departments whose nominees are selected as recipients and finalists receives a certificate and an award; the departmental award is $5,000 for recipients and $1,000 for finalists.

**Duration** The award is presented annually.

**Additional information** This award was established in 1978.

**Number awarded** 2 recipients each year: 1 to a student at a Ph.D. granting institution and 1 at a non-Ph.D. granting institution.

**Deadline** June of each year.

## [362]
## LESLIE S. PARKER MEMORIAL SCHOLARSHIP

Order of the Eastern Star-Grand Chapter of Oregon
c/o Marymargaret Holstein, Scholarship Committee Chair
161 S.E. 118th Street
South Beach, OR 97366-9732
E-mail: mholstein@charter.net
Web: www.oregonoes.org/scholarships/index.html

**Summary** To provide financial assistance to women who are residents of Oregon and attending college or graduate school in the state.

**Eligibility** This program is open to female residents of Oregon who have completed at least 2 years of undergraduate or graduate study at an accredited non-sectarian college or university in the state. Applicants must be able to demonstrate financial need.

**Financial data** Stipends are approximately $1,000. Funds are sent directly to the recipient's college or university to be used for books, tuition, room and board, clothing, or medical aid.

**Duration** 1 year.

**Number awarded** 1 or more each year.

**Deadline** April of each year.

## [363]
## LETA ANDREWS SCHOLARSHIP

University Interscholastic League
Attn: Texas Interscholastic League Foundation
1701 Manor Road
Austin, TX 78722
(512) 232-4937                    Fax: (512) 232-7311
E-mail: tilf@uiltexas.org
Web: tilf.uiltexas.org/scholarships/list

**Summary** To provide financial assistance to high school seniors who participate in programs of the Texas Interscholastic League Foundation (TILF), have competed in girls' high school varsity basketball, and plan to attend college in the state.

**Eligibility** This program is open to seniors graduating from high schools in Texas who have competed in a University Interscholastic League (UIL) academic state meet and have participated in girls' high school varsity basketball. Applicants must be planning to attend a college or university in the state and major in any field. Along with their application, they must submit high school transcripts that include SAT and/or ACT scores and documentation of financial need.

**Financial data** The stipend is $1,000.

**Duration** 1 year; nonrenewable.

**Additional information** This program is sponsored by Whataburger Inc. and Southwest Shootout Inc.

**Number awarded** 1 each year.

**Deadline** May of each year.

## [364]
## LIBRARY OF CONGRESS JUNIOR FELLOWS PROGRAM

Library of Congress
Library Services
Attn: Junior Fellows Program Coordinator
101 Independence Avenue, S.E., Room LM-642
Washington, DC 20540-4600
(202) 707-6610                    Fax: (202) 707-6269
E-mail: jrfell@loc.gov
Web: www.loc.gov/hr/jrfellows/index.html

**Summary** To provide summer work experience at the Library of Congress (LC) to upper-division students, graduate students, and recent graduates (particularly women, minorities, and persons with disabilities).

**Eligibility** This program is open to U.S. citizens with subject expertise in the following areas: collections preservation; geography and maps; humanities, art, and culture; information technology; library science; or chemistry and science. Applicants must 1) be juniors or seniors at an accredited college or university; 2) be graduate students; or 3) have completed their degree in the past year. Women, minorities, and persons with disabilities are strongly encouraged to apply. Selection is based on academic achievement, letters of recommendation, and an interview.

**Financial data** Fellows are paid a taxable stipend of $3,000.

**Duration** 10 weeks, beginning in either May or June. Fellows work a 40-hour week.

**Additional information** Fellows work with primary source materials and assist selected divisions at LC in the organization and documentation of archival collections, production of finding aids and bibliographic records, preparation of materials for preservation and service, completion of bibliographical research, and digitization of LC's historical collections.

**Number awarded** Varies each year; recently, 38 of these internships were awarded.

**Deadline** January of each year.

## [365]
## LIFE TECHNOLOGIES SCHOLARSHIPS

Society of Women Engineers
Attn: Scholarship Selection Committee
203 North LaSalle Street, Suite 1675
Chicago, IL 60601-1269
(312) 596-5223                    Toll Free: (877) SWE-INFO
Fax: (312) 644-8557              E-mail: scholarships@swe.org
Web: societyofwomenengineers.swe.org

**Summary** To provide financial assistance to undergraduate women who are majoring in designated engineering specialties.

**Eligibility** This program is open to society members who are entering their sophomore, junior, or senior year at an ABET-accredited 4-year college or university. Applicants must be working full time on a degree in computer science or biomedical, chemical, civil, computer, electrical, industrial, manufacturing, materials, mechanical, or software engineering and have a GPA of 3.0 or higher. They must be U.S. citizens or permanent residents. Selection is based on merit. Preference is given to groups underrepresented in computer science and engineering.

**Financial data**   The stipend is $7,500 or $2,500.

**Duration**   1 year.

**Number awarded**   3 each year: 1 at $7,500 and 2 at $2,500.

**Deadline**   February of each year.

## [366]
## LILLIAN MOLLER GILBRETH MEMORIAL SCHOLARSHIP

Society of Women Engineers
Attn: Scholarship Selection Committee
203 North LaSalle Street, Suite 1675
Chicago, IL 60601-1269
(312) 596-5223                Toll Free: (877) SWE-INFO
Fax: (312) 644-8557          E-mail: scholarships@swe.org
Web: societyofwomenengineers.swe.org

**Summary**   To provide financial assistance to upper-division women majoring in computer science or engineering.

**Eligibility**   This program is open to women who are entering their junior or senior year at an ABET-accredited 4-year college or university. Applicants must be working full time on a degree in computer science or engineering and have a GPA of 3.0 or higher. Selection is based on merit.

**Financial data**   The stipend is $10,000 per year.

**Duration**   1 year; may be renewed 1 additional year.

**Additional information**   This program began in 1958.

**Number awarded**   1 each year.

**Deadline**   February of each year.

## [367]
## LILLIAN WALL SCHOLARSHIP

Zonta Club of Bangor
c/o Barbara A. Cardone
P.O. Box 1904
Bangor, ME 04402-1904
Web: www.zontaclubofbangor.org/?area=scholarship

**Summary**   To provide financial assistance to women attending or planning to attend college in Maine and major in special education or a related field.

**Eligibility**   This program is open to women who are attending or planning to attend an accredited 2- or 4-year college in Maine. Applicants must major in special education or a related field. Along with their application, they must submit brief essays on 1) their goals in seeking higher education and their plans for the future; and 2) any school and community activities that have been of particular importance to them and why they found them worthwhile. Financial need may be considered in the selection process.

**Financial data**   The stipend is $1,000.

**Duration**   1 year.

**Number awarded**   1 each year.

**Deadline**   March of each year.

## [368]
## LILLIE LOIS FORD SCHOLARSHIPS

American Legion
Department of Missouri
3341 American Avenue
P.O. Box 179
Jefferson City, MO 65102-0179
(573) 893-2353                Toll Free: (800) 846-9023
Fax: (573) 893-2980          E-mail: info@missourilegion.org
Web: www.missourilegion.org/default_016.htm

**Summary**   To provide financial assistance for college to descendants of Missouri veterans who have participated in specified American Legion programs (females and males are considered separately).

**Eligibility**   This program is open to the unmarried children, grandchildren, and great-grandchildren under 21 years of age of honorably-discharged Missouri veterans who served at least 90 days on active duty. Applicants must be enrolled or planning to enroll at an accredited college or university in any state as a full-time student. Boys must have attended a complete session of Missouri Boys State or Cadet Patrol Academy. Girls must have attended a complete session of Missouri Girls State or Cadet Patrol Academy. Financial need is considered in the selection process.

**Financial data**   The stipend is $1,000.

**Duration**   1 year (the first year of college).

**Number awarded**   2 each year: 1 for a boy and 1 for a girl.

**Deadline**   April of each year.

## [369]
## LINCOLN COMMUNITY FOUNDATION MEDICAL RESEARCH SCHOLARSHIP

Lincoln Community Foundation
215 Centennial Mall South, Suite 100
Lincoln, NE 68508
(402) 474-2345                Toll Free: (888) 448-4668
Fax: (402) 476-8532          E-mail: lcf@lcf.org
Web: www.lcf.org/page.aspx?pid=477

**Summary**   To provide financial assistance to residents of Nebraska (preference given to women) who are interested in working on an advanced degree in a medical field at a school in any state.

**Eligibility**   This program is open to residents of Nebraska who are working on an advanced degree in a medical field (nursing students may apply as undergraduates or graduate students). Applicants must submit an essay explaining their progress toward completing their education, why they have chosen to prepare for a career in a medical field, and their future career goals once they complete their degree. Preference is given to 1) female applicants; 2) students preparing for careers as physicians and nurses; and 3) applicants who demonstrate financial need.

**Financial data**   The stipend is $2,000.

**Duration**   1 year; may be renewed up to 3 additional years.

**Additional information**   This program began in 2005.

**Number awarded**   2 each year.

**Deadline**   March of each year.

## [370]
## LINDA LAEL MILLER SCHOLARSHIPS FOR WOMEN

Linda Lael Miller Scholarships
P.O. Box 19461
Spokane, WA 99219
Toll Free: (800) 308-3169
E-mail: NBPR@nancyberland.com
Web: www.lindalaelmiller.com/lindas-scholarship

**Summary**  To provide financial assistance for college to mature women.

**Eligibility**  This program is open to women who are 25 years of age or older and citizens of the United States or Canada. Applicants must be enrolled or planning to enroll at a college, university, or other postsecondary institution. Along with their application, they must submit a 500-word essay on why they are applying for this scholarship, how achieving their educational goals will enhance their and their family's future, the specific purpose for which they would use the funds, and the dollar amount they are requesting. Selection is based on the essay's readability, demonstration of commitment to education and/or career, and the possible impact of the scholarship on the life of the recipient, her family, and/or her community.

**Financial data**  Stipend amounts vary; recently, they averaged $1,500. Funds are disbursed to the registrar of the recipient's college for payment of tuition, and/or the college bookstore for purchase of books and other supplies, and/or the accredited child care facility that the recipient's children will attend.

**Duration**  1 year.

**Additional information**  This program began in 2001.

**Number awarded**  Varies each year; recently, 11 of these scholarships were awarded.

**Deadline**  August of each year.

## [371]
## LINDA RIDDLE/SGMA ENDOWED SCHOLARSHIPS

Women's Sports Foundation
Attn: Award and Grant Programs Manager
Eisenhower Park
1899 Hempstead Turnpike, Suite 400
East Meadow, NY 11554-1000
(516) 307-3915          Toll Free: (800) 227-3988
E-mail: lflores@womenssportsfoundation.org
Web: www.womenssportsfoundation.org

**Summary**  To provide financial assistance to female high school seniors who have participated in athletics and plan to attend college in any state.

**Eligibility**  This program is open to women who are graduating high school seniors planning to enroll full-time at an accredited 2- or 4-year college or university. Applicants must have participated on an officially recognized high school athletic team and maintained a GPA of 3.5 or higher. They must be U.S. citizens or permanent residents and able to demonstrate financial need.

**Financial data**  The stipend is $3,000.

**Duration**  1 year.

**Additional information**  This program, which began in 1996, is sponsored by the Sporting Goods Manufacturers Association (SGMA), which recently changed its name to the Sports and Fitness Industry Association.

**Number awarded**  At least 2 each year.

**Deadline**  May of each year.

## [372]
## LINDY CALLAHAN SCHOLAR ATHLETE

Mississippi High School Activities Association
1201 Clinton/Raymond Road
P.O. Box 127
Clinton, MS 39060
(601) 924-6400          Fax: (601) 924-1725
E-mail: mhsaa@netdoor.com
Web: http:

**Summary**  To provide financial assistance to graduating high school scholar-athletes in Mississippi (females and males are judged separately) who plan to attend college in any state.

**Eligibility**  This program is open to seniors graduating from high schools that belong to the Mississippi High School Activities Association. Applicants must have won at least 1 varsity letter prior to their senior year and have a GPA of 3.3 or higher. They must be planning to attend a college or university in any state. Along with their application, they must submit a 500-word essay on how athletics and other extracurricular activities have influenced their life. Selection is based on academic achievement, involvement in sports, leadership in school and community, and volunteerism. Males and females compete separately.

**Financial data**  The stipend is $1,500.

**Duration**  1 year.

**Number awarded**  16 each year: 1 female and 1 male graduating high school senior in each of the association's 8 districts.

**Deadline**  February of each year.

## [373]
## LINLY HEFLIN SCHOLARSHIP

Linly Heflin Unit
c/o Caroline Thomas, Scholarship Committee Co-Chair
13 Office Park Circle, Suite 8
Mountain Brook, AL 35223-2520
(205) 871-8171     E-mail: LHScholarship@Bellsouth.net
Web: www.linlyheflin.org/scholarship-information

**Summary**  To provide financial assistance to women attending colleges and universities in Alabama.

**Eligibility**  This program is open to female residents of Alabama entering or attending accredited 4-year colleges in the state. Applicants must have an ACT score of 23 or higher. U.S. citizenship is required. Selection is based on academic proficiency and financial need.

**Financial data**  The stipend is $3,000 per year.

**Duration**  1 year; may be renewed until completion of an undergraduate degree, provided the recipient remains enrolled full time, continues to demonstrate financial need, and maintains a GPA of 2.5 or higher.

**Additional information**  The Linly Heflin Unit was founded in 1919 as an organization of 125 women who raise funds for these scholarships.

**Number awarded** Approximately 20 to 25 of these scholarships are awarded each year.

**Deadline** January of each year.

## [374]
## LISA SECHRIST MEMORIAL FOUNDATION SCHOLARSHIP

Lisa Sechrist Memorial Foundation
Attn: Kim Mackmin, Scholarship Selection Committee
Brookfield Homes
8500 Executive Park Avenue, Suite 300
Fairfax, VA 22031-2225
(703) 270-1400
Web: lisasechrist.com/scholarship.html

**Summary** To provide financial assistance to female high school seniors from Virginia who come from disadvantaged backgrounds and plan to attend college in any state.

**Eligibility** This program is open to women graduating from high schools in Virginia who come from a disadvantaged background. Applicants must be planning to attend an accredited college, university, community college, or technical school in any state. Preference is given to applicants who are members of honor societies, participate in sports or other extracurricular activities, demonstrate citizenship and service within the community, and/or exhibit leadership skills within the school or community. Selection is based on merit, integrity, academic potential, and financial need.

**Financial data** The stipend is $2,500 per year.

**Duration** 4 years, provided the recipient maintains a GPA of 2.5 or higher.

**Number awarded** 1 each year.

**Deadline** March of each year.

## [375]
## LOCKHEED MARTIN SCHOLARSHIPS

Society of Women Engineers
Attn: Scholarship Selection Committee
203 North LaSalle Street, Suite 1675
Chicago, IL 60601-1269
(312) 596-5223          Toll Free: (877) SWE-INFO
Fax: (312) 644-8557     E-mail: scholarships@swe.org
Web: societyofwomenengineers.swe.org

**Summary** To provide financial assistance to women working on an undergraduate or graduate degree in computer science, computer engineering, or electrical engineering.

**Eligibility** This program is open to women who are entering full-time freshmen, sophomores, juniors, seniors, or graduate students at an ABET-accredited 4-year college or university. Applicants must be interested in studying computer science, computer engineering, or electrical engineering and have a GPA of 3.5 or higher (for entering freshmen) or 3.2 or higher (for all other students). Selection is based on merit.

**Financial data** The stipend is $2,000. The award includes a travel grant for the recipient to attend the national conference of the Society of Women Engineers.

**Duration** 1 year.

**Additional information** This program, established in 1996, is supported by Lockheed Martin Corporation.

**Number awarded** 4 each year: 2 for entering freshmen and 2 for other students.

**Deadline** February of each year for continuing students; May of each year for entering freshmen.

## [376]
## LODINE ROBINSON NATIONAL ASSOCIATION OF WOMEN IN CONSTRUCTION SCHOLARSHIP

Arizona Community Foundation
Attn: Education and Scholarships Manager
2201 East Camelback Road, Suite 405B
Phoenix, AZ 85016
(602) 682-2040          Toll Free: (800) 222-8221
Fax: (602) 381-1575     E-mail: jmedina@azfoundation.org
Web: azfoundation.academicworks.com/?page=4

**Summary** To provide financial assistance to women from Arizona who are working on a degree in a field related to construction at a public university in the state.

**Eligibility** This program is open to women who are residents of Arizona and entering their junior or senior year at a public university in the state (University of Arizona, Northern Arizona University, Arizona State University). Applicants must be majoring in architecture, construction, engineering (architectural, civil, electrical, or mechanical), or construction management. They must have a GPA of 2.5 or higher and a record of participation in volunteer organizations.

**Financial data** The stipend is $2,000.

**Duration** 1 year; nonrenewable.

**Additional information** This program is sponsored by Greater Phoenix Chapter 98 of National Association of Women in Construction.

**Number awarded** 3 each year: 1 at each of the 3 public universities in the state.

**Deadline** May of each year.

## [377]
## LORAM MINNESOTA SWE SCHOLARSHIP

Society of Women Engineers-Minnesota Section
Attn: Scholarship Committee
P.O. Box 582813
Minneapolis, MN 55458-2813
E-mail: scholarships@swe-mn.org
Web: www.swe-mn.org/scholarships.html

**Summary** To provide financial assistance to women from any state working on an undergraduate or graduate degree in mechanical engineering at colleges and universities in Minnesota, North Dakota, and South Dakota.

**Eligibility** This program is open to female undergraduate and graduate students at ABET-accredited engineering programs in Minnesota, North Dakota, or South Dakota. Applicants must be working full time on a degree in mechanical engineering. Along with their application, they must submit a short paragraph describing how they plan to utilize their engineering skills after they graduate. Selection is based on potential to succeed as an engineer (20 points), communication skills (10 points), extracurricular or community involvement and leadership skills (10 points), demonstrated successful work experience (10 points), and academic success (5 points).

**Financial data** The stipend is $1,000.

**Duration** 1 year.

**Additional information** This program is sponsored by Loram Maintenance of Way.

**Number awarded** 1 each year.

**Deadline** March of each year.

## [378]
## LOUISE MORITZ MOLITORIS LEADERSHIP AWARD

Women's Transportation Seminar
Attn: WTS Foundation
1701 K Street, N.W., Suite 800
Washington, DC 20006
(202) 955-5085      Fax: (202) 955-5088
E-mail: wts@wtsinternational.org
Web: www.wtsinternational.org/education/scholarships

**Summary** To provide financial assistance to undergraduate women interested in a career in transportation.

**Eligibility** This program is open to women who are working on an undergraduate degree in transportation or a transportation-related field (e.g., transportation engineering, planning, finance, or logistics). Applicants must have a GPA of 3.0 or higher. Along with their application, they must submit a 500-word statement about their career goals after graduation and why they think they should receive the scholarship award; their statement should specifically address the issue of leadership. Applications must be submitted first to a local chapter; the chapters forward selected applications for consideration on the national level. Minority women are especially encouraged to apply. Selection is based on transportation involvement and goals, job skills, academic record, and leadership potential; financial need is not considered.

**Financial data** The stipend is $5,000.

**Duration** 1 year.

**Additional information** Local chapters may also award additional funding to winners for their area.

**Number awarded** 1 each year.

**Deadline** Applications must be submitted by November to a local WTS chapter.

## [379]
## LOUISIANA WOMAN ZONTA SCHOLARSHIP

Zonta Club of Lafayette
c/o Lisa LeBlanc
175 Antigua Drive
Lafayette, LA 70503
(337) 984-4197      E-mail: lisa.leblanc@lusfiber.net
Web: zontalafayette.com/scholarships.html

**Summary** To provide financial assistance to female residents of Louisiana who are attending college in the state.

**Eligibility** This program is open to female residents of Louisiana who are the major wage earner of their family. Applicants must be enrolled at a Louisiana university, college, or vocational/technical school in non-remedial courses and have minimum ACT scores of 18 in English and 19 in mathematics or SAT scores of at least 450 in critical reading and 460 in mathematics. They must apply to Zonta Clubs in Lafayette, Shreveport, and New Orleans. Each of those 3 clubs nominates a woman for this scholarship. U.S. citizenship and evidence of financial need are required.

**Financial data** The stipend of the state scholarship is $1,500. If the nominee of the Lafayette club is not chosen as the state winner, she receives a $500 scholarship.

**Duration** 1 year.

**Number awarded** 1 each year.

**Deadline** September of each year.

## [380]
## LUBRIZOL CORPORATION SCHOLARSHIP PROGRAM

College Now Greater Cleveland, Inc.
Attn: Managed Scholarships
200 Public Square, Suite 3820
Cleveland, OH 44114
(216) 241-5587      Fax: (216) 241-6184
E-mail: info@collegenowgc.org
Web: www.collegenowgc.org

**Summary** To provide financial assistance to women and minorities working on a degree in specified fields of science and business at college in any state.

**Eligibility** This program is open to members of minority ethnic groups (American Indians, African Americans, Asian Pacific Americans, and Hispanic Americans) and women. Applicants must be enrolled full time at a 4-year college or university in any state and majoring in chemistry, computer information systems, computer science, engineering (chemical, computer, or mechanical), business, marketing, accounting, or finance. They must have a GPA of 3.0 or higher and be able to demonstrate financial need. Along with their application, they must submit a 500-word essay describing their academic and career goals.

**Financial data** The stipend is $4,000 per year.

**Duration** 1 year; may be renewed, provided the recipient maintains a GPA of 3.0 or higher.

**Additional information** This program is sponsored by the Lubrizol Corporation.

**Number awarded** Varies each year.

**Deadline** March of each year.

## [381]
## LUCENT TECHNOLOGIES BELL LABORATORIES SUMMER RESEARCH PROGRAM FOR MINORITIES AND WOMEN

Lucent Technologies
Attn: Special Programs Manager
283 King George Road, Room B1-D32
Warren, NJ 07059
(732) 559-4267      E-mail: summersearch@lucent.com
Web: www.bell-labs.com/employment/srp/info.html

**Summary** To provide technical work experience at facilities of Bell Laboratories during the summer to women and underrepresented minority undergraduate students.

**Eligibility** This program is open to women and members of minority groups (African Americans, Hispanics, and Native American Indians) who are underrepresented in the sciences. Applicants must be interested in pursuing technical employment experience in research and development facilities of Bell Laboratories. The program is primarily directed at undergraduate students who have completed their second or third year of college. Emphasis is placed on the following disciplines: chemistry, communications science, computer science and engineering, data networking, electrical engineering, information science, materials science, mathematics, optics, physics, statistics, and wireless and radio engineering. U.S. citizenship or permanent resident status is required. Selection is based on academic achievement, personal motivation, and compatibility of student interests with current Bell Laboratories activities.

**Financial data** Salaries are commensurate with those of regular Bell Laboratories employees with comparable education. Interns are reimbursed for travel expenses up to the cost of round-trip economy-class airfare.

**Duration** 10 weeks during the summer.

**Additional information** This program is sponsored by Lucent Technologies and Bell Laboratories.

**Number awarded** Varies each year.

**Deadline** November of each year.

## [382]
## LUCILE B. KAUFMAN WOMEN'S SCHOLARSHIPS

Society of Manufacturing Engineers
Attn: SME Education Foundation
One SME Drive
P.O. Box 930
Dearborn, MI 48121-0930
(313) 425-3300        Toll Free: (800) 733-4763, ext. 3300
Fax: (313) 425-3411        E-mail: foundation@sme.org
Web: www.smeef.org/scholarships

**Summary** To provide financial assistance to undergraduate women enrolled in a degree program in manufacturing engineering or manufacturing engineering technology.

**Eligibility** This program is open to women enrolled full time at a degree-granting institution in North America and preparing for a career in manufacturing engineering. Applicants must have completed at least 30 units in a manufacturing engineering or manufacturing engineering technology curriculum and have a GPA of 3.0 or higher. Along with their application, they must submit a 300-word essay that covers their career and educational objectives, how this scholarship will help them attain those objectives, and why they want to enter this field. Financial need is not considered in the selection process.

**Financial data** Stipend amounts vary; recently, the value of all scholarships provided by this foundation averaged approximately $2,330.

**Duration** 1 year; may be renewed.

**Number awarded** Varies each year; recently, 3 of these scholarships were awarded.

**Deadline** January of each year.

## [383]
## LUCILE MILLER WRIGHT SCHOLARS PROGRAM

Girls Incorporated
Attn: Scholarships and Awards
120 Wall Street, Third Floor
New York, NY 10005-3902
(212) 509-2000        Toll Free: (800) 374-4475
Fax: (212) 509-8708
E-mail: communications@girlsinc.org
Web: www.girlsinc.org/about/national-scholars.html

**Summary** To provide financial assistance for college to Girls Incorporated members.

**Eligibility** This program is open to members of Girls Incorporated affiliates who are currently in high school (in grades 11 or 12) and have been members of the association for at least 2 years. They must have a GPA of 2.8 or higher. Selection is based on extracurricular activities, goals and objectives, soundness of ideas, motivation, communication skills, and presentation. Financial need is not considered. Academic record is of secondary importance.

**Financial data** The scholarships are either $15,000 or $2,500. Funds are held in escrow and paid directly to the recipient's college, professional school, or technical institute.

**Duration** Up to 5 years.

**Additional information** This program began in 1992. Funds may not be used for education at a vocational or technical school.

**Number awarded** Varies each year; recently, 28 of these scholarships were awarded: 10 at $15,000 and 18 at $2,500. Since this program was established, it has awarded $3.3 million in scholarships to 413 high school women.

**Deadline** Deadline not specified.

## [384]
## LUCY KASPARIAN AHARONIAN SCHOLARSHIPS

Armenian International Women's Association
65 Main Street, Room 3A
Watertown, MA 02472
(617) 926-0171        E-mail: aiwainc@aol.com
Web: aiwainternational.org/initiatives/scholarships

**Summary** To provide financial assistance to Armenian women who are upper-division or graduate students working on a degree in specified fields.

**Eligibility** This program is open to full-time women students of Armenian descent attending an accredited college or university. Applicants must be full-time juniors, seniors, or graduate students with a GPA of 3.2 or higher. They must be working on a degree in architecture, computer science, engineering, mathematics, science, or technology. Selection is based on financial need and merit.

**Financial data** Stipends are $4,000 or $1,000.

**Duration** 1 year.

**Additional information** This program, established in 2008, is offered in conjunction with the Boston Section of the Society of Women Engineers.

**Number awarded** Varies each year; recently, 4 of these scholarships were awarded: 2 at $4,000 and 2 at $1,000.

**Deadline** April of each year.

## [385]
## LUELLA AND GEORGE SHAVER FAMILY SCHOLARSHIP

Girl Scouts of Oregon and Southwest Washington
Attn: Shannon Shea, Portland Service Center Office
9620 S.W. Barbur Boulevard
Portland, OR 97219
(503) 977-6813        Fax: (503) 977-6801
E-mail: sshea@girlscoutsosw.org
Web: www.girlscoutsosw.org/girls/scholarships

**Summary** To provide financial assistance to high school seniors in Oregon and southwestern Washington who are

Ambassador Girl Scouts and planning to attend college in any state.

**Eligibility** This program is open to seniors graduating from high schools in Oregon and southwestern Washington who are Ambassador Girl Scouts and have earned their Gold Award. Applicants must be planning to enroll at an accredited college, vocational training program, or apprenticeship program in any state. Along with their application, they must submit 1) a 1,000-word essay on how Girl Scouts has impacted their life and how that will impact them in the future; and 2) a 500-word essay on how they have made the world a better place by being a Girl Scout.

**Financial data** A stipend is awarded (amount not specified).

**Duration** 1 year.

**Number awarded** 1 each year.

**Deadline** April of each year.

## [386]
## LYDIA PICKUP MEMORIAL SCHOLARSHIP

Society of Women Engineers-Pacific Northwest Section
Attn: Scholarship Committee
P.O. Box 1601
Bellevue, WA 98009
E-mail: pnw@swe.org
Web: www.swe-pnw.org/scholarship.html

**Summary** To provide financial assistance to women from any state studying engineering at a university in Montana or western Washington.

**Eligibility** This program is open to women from any state who have, at the time of application, completed at least 50% of the requirements toward college graduation in an engineering field. Applicants must be attending an ABET-accredited engineering school in Montana or western Washington. They must be U.S. citizens and members of the Society of Women Engineers (SWE) student section at their school or, if no student section exists, of the national SWE organization. Along with their application, they must submit 1) a 300-word essay on their educational and career goals; and 2) a 500-word essay describing why they have chosen their particular field of engineering; the person, event, or job experience influencing their decision to work on an engineering degree; and the most and least favorite courses they have taken and which course they are most looking forward to and why. Selection is based on the essays, academic achievement, extracurricular and community service activities, and financial need.

**Financial data** The stipend is $1,000.

**Duration** 1 year.

**Number awarded** 1 each year.

**Deadline** November of each year.

## [387]
## M. JOSEPHINE O'NEIL ARTS AWARD

Delta Kappa Gamma Society International-Lambda State Organization
c/o Sue Dion
139 Barrington Lane
East Peoria, IL 61550-9438
(309) 694-1157          E-mail: sddion@gmail.com
Web: www.deltakappagamma.org

**Summary** To provide financial assistance to female residents of Illinois who are studying an arts-related field at a college in any state.

**Eligibility** This program is open to female residents of Illinois who are in or approaching junior standing at an accredited college or university in any state. Applicants must be majoring in 1 or more areas of the arts, including music, visual arts, dance, or theater. Along with their application, they must submit 1) evidence of the quality and extent of accomplishment in the arts, such as programs of performances, catalogs, articles from the media, published reviews of their work, listings of awards and prizes, or other recognition; 2) samples of their work on DVD, 35mm slides, CD, videotapes, or audio tapes; 3) college transcripts; 4) letters of recommendation; 5) a statement on the use of the award for continued involvement in their selected area of the arts; and 6) a personal essay on their family, personal interests, awards, achievements, goals (short- and long-term), and philosophy. Selection is based on the statement on the use of the award (15 points), the personal essay (15 points), letters of recommendation (20 points), academic achievement (20 points), work samples (25 points), and application appearance (5 points).

**Financial data** The stipend ranges up to $6,000.

**Duration** 1 year.

**Additional information** The sponsor is an honorary society of women educators.

**Number awarded** 1 each year.

**Deadline** January of each year.

## [388]
## M. LOUISE CARPENTER GLOECKNER, M.D. SUMMER RESEARCH FELLOWSHIP

Drexel University College of Medicine
Attn: Archives and Special Collections
2900 West Queen Lane
Philadelphia, PA 19129
(215) 991-8340          Fax: (215) 991-8172
E-mail: archives@drexelmed.edu
Web: archives.drexelmed.edu/fellowship.php

**Summary** To provide funding to scholars and students interested in conducting research during the summer on the history of women in medicine at the Archives and Special Collections on Women in Medicine at Drexel University in Philadelphia.

**Eligibility** This program is open to students at all levels, scholars, and general researchers. Applicants must be interested in conducting research utilizing the archives, which emphasize the history of women in medicine, nursing, medical missionaries, the American Medical Women's Association, American Women's Hospital Service, and other women in medical organizations. Selection is based on research background of the applicant, relevance of the proposed research project to the goals of the applicant, overall quality and clarity of the proposal, appropriateness of the proposal to the holdings of the collection, and commitment of the applicant to the project.

**Financial data** The grant is $4,000.

**Duration** 4 to 6 weeks during the summer.

**Number awarded** 1 each year.

**Deadline** February of each year.

## [389]
## MABEL HEIL SCHOLARSHIP

United Methodist Church-Wisconsin Conference
Attn: United Methodist Women
750 Windsor Street
P.O. Box 620
Sun Prairie, WI 53590-0620
(608) 837-7328                Toll Free: (888) 240-7328
Fax: (608) 837-8547
Web: www.wisconsinumc.org

**Summary**   To provide financial assistance to United Methodist women from Wisconsin who are interested in attending college or graduate school in any state.

**Eligibility**   This program is open to women who are members of congregations affiliated with the Wisconsin Conference of the United Methodist Church and attending or planning to attend college or graduate school in any state. Applicants must submit an essay on why they consider themselves a worthy student and a letter of recommendation from their pastor or the president of the local United Methodist Women. Preference is given to women who are responsible for others and are returning to the employment field.

**Financial data**   A stipend is awarded (amount not specified).

**Duration**   1 semester; recipients may reapply.

**Number awarded**   1 or more each year.

**Deadline**   April of each year for the first semester; September of each year for the second semester.

## [390]
## MAHINDRA USA WOMEN IN AG SCHOLARSHIPS

National FFA Organization
Attn: Scholarship Office
6060 FFA Drive
P.O. Box 68960
Indianapolis, IN 46268-0960
(317) 802-4419                Fax: (317) 802-5419
E-mail: scholarships@ffa.org
Web: www.ffa.org

**Summary**   To provide financial assistance to female FFA members interested in studying fields related to agriculture in college.

**Eligibility**   This program is open to female members from 38 designated states who are graduating high school seniors or currently-enrolled college students. Applicants must be working on or planning to work on a 2- or 4-year degree in agriculture (excluding food service, packaging, biosciences or technology, marine biology, natural resource management, parks and recreation studies, public service, or dietetics). They must have a GPA of 3.0 or higher. Selection is based on academic achievement (10 points for GPA, 10 points for SAT or ACT score, 10 points for class rank), leadership in FFA activities (30 points), leadership in community activities (10 points), and participation in the Supervised Agricultural Experience (SAE) program (30 points). Financial need is also considered. U.S. citizenship is required.

**Financial data**   The stipend is $2,500. Funds are paid directly to the recipient.

**Duration**   1 year; nonrenewable.

**Additional information**   This program is sponsored by Mahindra USA, Inc. For a list of the designated 38 states, contact FFA.

**Number awarded**   4 each year.

**Deadline**   February of each year.

## [391]
## MAIDS OF ATHENA SCHOLARSHIPS

Maids of Athena
1909 Q Street, N.W., Suite 500
Washington, DC 20009-1007
(202) 232-6300                Fax: (202) 232-2145
E-mail: MOAHeadquarters@gmail.com
Web: www.maidsofathena.org

**Summary**   To provide financial assistance for undergraduate and graduate education to women of Greek descent.

**Eligibility**   This program is open to women who are members of the Maids of Athena. Applicants may be a graduating high school senior, an undergraduate student, or a graduate student. Selection is based on academic merit, financial need, and participation in the organization.

**Financial data**   The stipend is $1,000.

**Duration**   1 year.

**Additional information**   Membership in Maids of Athena is open to unmarried women between 14 and 24 years of age who are of Greek descent from either parent.

**Number awarded**   At least 2 each year.

**Deadline**   May of each year.

## [392]
## MAINE BPW CONTINUING EDUCATION SCHOLARSHIP

Maine Federation of Business and Professional Women's Clubs
Attn: BPW/Maine Futurama Foundation
c/o Marilyn V. Ladd, Office Manager
103 County Road
Oakland, ME 04963
Web: www.bpwmefoundation.org/files/index.php?id=10

**Summary**   To provide financial assistance to women in Maine who are attending college in any state.

**Eligibility**   This program is open to women who are residents of Maine. Applicants must have completed at least 1 year of college or an accredited training program in any state requiring attendance for more than a year. They must have a definite plan to complete the educational program, regardless of whether it leads to an associate or bachelor's degree or other certificate. Along with their application, they must submit a statement describing their educational, personal, and career goals, including their financial need. Preference is given to members of Maine Federation of Business and Professional Women's Clubs.

**Financial data**   The stipend is $1,200.

**Duration**   1 year.

**Number awarded**   1 or more each year.

**Deadline**   April of each year.

## [393]
## MAKING A DIFFERENCE LEADER SCHOLARSHIP

Royal Neighbors of America
Attn: Fraternal Services
230 16th Street
Rock Island, IL 61201-8645
(309) 788-4561          Toll Free: (800) 627-4762
E-mail: contact@royalneighbors.org
Web: www.royalneighbors.org

**Summary**   To provide financial assistance to female members of the Royal Neighbors of America (RNA) who are high school seniors planning to attend college in any state.

**Eligibility**   This program is open to female high school seniors who are beneficial members of RNA and rank in the top quarter of their senior class. Applicants must have an outstanding record of volunteerism. They must be planning to enroll full time at an accredited college, university, or junior college to work eventually on a bachelor's degree.

**Financial data**   The stipend is $5,000 per year.

**Duration**   1 year; may be renewed up to 3 additional years.

**Number awarded**   1 each year.

**Deadline**   Requests for applications must be submitted by December of each year.

## [394]
## MAMIE W. MALLORY NATIONAL SCHOLARSHIP PROGRAM

National Black Coalition of Federal Aviation Employees
Attn: Tamisha Thomas
P.O. Box 87216
Atlanta, GA 30337
E-mail: tlarue@gmail.com
Web: www.nbcfae.org

**Summary**   To provide financial assistance to undergraduate students, especially women and those from other underrepresented groups, who are interested in preparing for a career in a field related to aviation.

**Eligibility**   This program is open to undergraduate students preparing for a career in aviation, science, or technology. The program encourages applications from women, minorities, and people with disabilities. Selection is based on academic achievement, leadership, community involvement, and financial need.

**Financial data**   The stipend is $2,000.

**Duration**   1 year.

**Additional information**   This program began in 2005.

**Number awarded**   24 each year: 3 in each of the sponsor's regions.

**Deadline**   April of each year.

## [395]
## MANAHAN-BOHAN AWARD

Philanthrofund Foundation
Attn: Scholarship Committee
1409 Willow Street, Suite 109
Minneapolis, MN 55403-2241
(612) 870-1806          Toll Free: (800) 435-1402
Fax: (612) 871-6587          E-mail: info@PfundOnline.org
Web: www.pfundonline.org/scholarships.html

**Summary**   To provide financial assistance to lesbian students from rural Minnesota.

**Eligibility**   This program is open to residents of Madelia, Minnesota; if no resident of Madelia applies, the award is available to residents of any rural area in Minnesota. Applicants must be self-identified as lesbian. They may be attending or planning to attend trade school, technical college, college, or university in any state (as an undergraduate or graduate student). Selection is based on the applicant's 1) affirmation of GLBT or allied identity; 2) evidence of experience and skills in service and leadership; and 3) evidence of service, leading, and working for change in GLBT communities, including serving as a role model, mentor, and/or adviser.

**Financial data**   The stipend is $1,000. Funds must be used for tuition, books, fees, or dissertation expenses.

**Duration**   1 year.

**Number awarded**   1 each year.

**Deadline**   January of each year.

## [396]
## MARA CRAWFORD PERSONAL DEVELOPMENT SCHOLARSHIP

Kansas Federation of Business & Professional Women's Clubs, Inc.
Attn: Kansas BPW Educational Foundation, Inc.
c/o Kathy Niehoff, Executive Secretary
605 East 15th
Ottawa, KS 66067
(785) 242-9319          Fax: (785) 242-1047
E-mail: kathyniehoff@sbcglobal.net
Web: kansasbpw.memberlodge.org

**Summary**   To provide financial assistance to women in Kansas who are already in the workforce but are interested in pursuing additional education.

**Eligibility**   This program is open to women residents of Kansas who graduated from high school more than 5 years previously and are already in the workforce. Applicants may be seeking a degree in any field of study and may be attending a 2-year, 4-year, vocational, or technological program. They must submit a 3-page personal biography in which they express their career goals, the direction they want to take in the future, their proposed field of study, their reason for selecting that field, the institutions they plan to attend and why, their circumstances for reentering school (if a factor), and what makes them uniquely qualified for this scholarship. Preference is given to applicants who demonstrate they have serious family responsibilities and obligations. Applications must be submitted through a local unit of the sponsor.

**Financial data**   A stipend is awarded (amount not specified).

**Duration**   1 year.

**Number awarded**   1 or more each year.

**Deadline**   December of each year.

## [397]
## MARGARET ABEL SCHOLARSHIP

Delta Kappa Gamma Society International-Alpha Zeta
  State Organization
c/o Marilyn Gonyo, State Scholarship Chair
22 Chichester Road
Monroe Township, NJ 08831
E-mail: mgony1063@aol.com
Web: www.deltakappagamma.org/NJ/scholarships.html

**Summary** To provide financial assistance to women who are residents of New Jersey working on an undergraduate or graduate degree in education at a school in the state.

**Eligibility** This program is open to women who residents of New Jersey and enrolled as juniors, seniors, or graduate students at a 4-year college or university in the state. Applicants must be preparing for a career as a teacher and have a GPA of 3.0 or higher. They must be U.S. citizens. Along with their application, they must submit a 500-word essay and their desire to become a teacher and the attributes that make them worthy to receive this scholarship.

**Financial data** The stipend is $1,000.

**Duration** 1 year; recipients may reapply.

**Number awarded** 1 or more each year.

**Deadline** November of each year.

## [398]
## MARGARET KELDIE SCHOLARSHIP

Accounting and Financial Women's Alliance-Chicago
  Chapter
c/o Pamela Metz, Scholarship Fund Secretary
1957 North Dayton Street, Number 1
Chicago, IL 60614
(312) 480-8566          E-mail: MKSF_aswa@yahoo.com

**Summary** To provide financial assistance to women from any state working on an undergraduate or graduate degree in accounting at a college or university in Illinois.

**Eligibility** This program is open to women from any state who are currently enrolled full or part time at an accredited 4-year college or university in Illinois. Applicants must be working on an undergraduate or graduate degree in accounting and have a cumulative grade average of "B" or higher. They must have indicated an intention to prepare for an accounting career. Undergraduates must have completed at least 60 semester hours. Financial need is not considered in the selection process.

**Financial data** Stipends are $1,500 for full-time students or $800 for part-time students.

**Duration** 1 year.

**Additional information** This program began in 1956.

**Number awarded** 1 or more each year. Since the program was established, it has awarded nearly $135,000 in scholarships to more than 250 women.

**Deadline** February of each year.

## [399]
## MARIAN NORBY SCHOLARSHIP

Society for Technical Communication
Attn: Scholarships
9401 Lee Highway, Suite 904
Fairfax, VA 22031-1822
(703) 522-4114                    Fax: (703) 522-2075
E-mail: stc@stc.org
Web: www.stc.org

**Summary** To provide financial assistance to female employees of the federal government who are interested in additional study related to technical communications.

**Eligibility** This program is open to women who working full or part time for the federal government as a secretary or administrative assistant. Applicants must be interested in enrolling in a training or academic class related to technical communication, including technical writing, editing, graphical design, interface design, or web design. Along with their application, they must submit a 1- to 3-page description of their career goals and significant achievements to date. Financial need is not considered in the selection process.

**Financial data** The stipend is $2,500.

**Duration** 1 academic year.

**Number awarded** 1 each year.

**Deadline** May of each year.

## [400]
## MARILYNN SMITH SCHOLARSHIP

Ladies Professional Golf Association
Attn: LPGA Foundation
100 International Golf Drive
Daytona Beach, FL 32124-1082
(386) 274-6200                    Fax: (386) 274-1099
E-mail: foundation.scholarships@lpga.com
Web: www.lpgafoundation.org/scholarships?

**Summary** To provide financial assistance to female graduating high school seniors who played golf in high school and plan to continue playing in college.

**Eligibility** This program is open to female high school seniors who have a GPA of 3.2 or higher. Applicants must have played in at least 50% of their high school golf team's scheduled events or have played golf "regularly" for the past 2 years. They must be planning to enroll full time at a college or university in the United States and play competitive golf. Along with their application, they must submit a letter that describes how golf has been an integral part of their lives and includes their personal, academic, and professional goals; their chosen discipline of study; and how this scholarship will be of assistance. Financial need is not considered in the selection process.

**Financial data** The stipend is $5,000.

**Duration** 1 year.

**Additional information** This program began in 1999.

**Number awarded** 10 each year.

**Deadline** May of each year.

## [401]
## MARION DAY MULLINS SCHOLARSHIP

Kappa Delta Sorority
Attn: Foundation Project Manager
3205 Players Lane
Memphis, TN 38125
(901) 748-1897, ext. 203          Toll Free: (800) 536-1897
Fax: (901) 748-0949
E-mail: caroline.cullum@kappadelta.org
Web: www.kappadelta.org/scholarshipapplications_1

**Summary**  To provide financial assistance to members of Kappa Delta Sorority who are majoring in business.

**Eligibility**  This program is open to undergraduate members of Kappa Delta Sorority. Applicants must submit a personal statement giving their reasons for applying for this scholarship, an official undergraduate transcript, and 2 letters of recommendation. They must be majoring in business, including accounting, economics, finance, and marketing. Selection is based on academic excellence; service to the chapter, alumnae association, or national Kappa Delta; service to the campus and community; personal objectives and goals; potential; recommendations; and financial need.

**Financial data**  The stipend is $1,000 per year. Funds may be used only for tuition, fees, and books, not for room and board.

**Duration**  1 year; may be renewed.

**Number awarded**  1 each year.

**Deadline**  November of each year.

## [402]
## MARJORIE BOWENS-WHEATLEY SCHOLARSHIPS

Unitarian Universalist Association
Attn: UU Women's Federation
25 Beacon Street
Boston, MA 02108-2800
(617) 948-4692                    Fax: (617) 742-2402
E-mail: uuwf@uua.org
Web: www.uuwf.org

**Summary**  To provide financial assistance to women of color who are working on an undergraduate or graduate degree to prepare for Unitarian Universalist ministry or service.

**Eligibility**  This program is open to women of color who are either 1) aspirants or candidates for the Unitarian Universalist ministry; or 2) candidates in the Unitarian Universalist Association's professional religious education or music leadership credentialing programs. Applicants must submit a 1- to 2-page narrative that covers their call to UU ministry, religious education, or music leadership; their passions; how their racial/ethnic/cultural background influences their goals for their calling; and how the work of the program's namesake relates to their dreams and plans for their UU service.

**Financial data**  Stipends from $1,500 to $2,000.

**Duration**  1 year.

**Additional information**  This program began in 2009.

**Number awarded**  Varies each year; recently, 4 of these scholarships were awarded.

**Deadline**  March of each year.

## [403]
## MARTHA DROUYOR BELKNAP DECAMP SCHOLARSHIP

Alpha Sigma Tau National Foundation
Attn: Scholarships
3334 Founders Road
Indianapolis, IN 46268
(317) 613-7575                    Fax: (317) 613-7111
E-mail: melinda@alphasigmataufoundation.org
Web: www.alphasigmataufoundation.org/scholarships

**Summary**  To provide financial assistance to undergraduate members of Alpha Sigma Tau who have been involved in philanthropic service.

**Eligibility**  This program is open to members of Alpha Sigma Tau who are entering their sophomore, junior, or senior year. Applicants be able to demonstrate a desire to "contribute to the progress of mankind." They must have a GPA of 3.0 or higher and a record of leadership ability to involve others in philanthropic endeavors. Along with their application, they must submit academic transcripts and 4 letters of recommendation.

**Financial data**  The stipend is $1,175.

**Duration**  1 year.

**Number awarded**  1 each year.

**Deadline**  January of each year.

## [404]
## MARTHA GUERRA-ARTEAGA SCHOLARSHIP

National Organization of Professional Hispanic Natural
  Resources Conservation Service Employees
c/o Jessie Howard, Scholarship and Endowment
  Committee
Natural Resources Conservation Service
Bedford Service Center
1031 Turnpike Road
Bedford, VA 24523
(540) 586-9195                    Fax: (540) 586-4638
E-mail: scholarships@nophnrcse.org
Web: www.nophnrcse.org

**Summary**  To provide financial assistance to Hispanic women interested in working on a bachelor's degree in a field related to public affairs or natural resources conservation.

**Eligibility**  This program is open to Hispanic women who are graduating high school seniors or current full-time college students with at least 1 year remaining before graduation. Applicants must be interested in working on a bachelor's degree in public affairs, communications, or natural resources conservation. They must have a GPA of 2.75 or higher. Along with their application, they must submit a personal statement (in English) of 350 to 500 words on their background, name of school they attend or plan to attend, personal and career goals, extracurricular activities, and interest in preparing for a career related to natural resources conservation. Financial need is not considered in the selection process. U.S. citizenship is required.

**Financial data**  The stipend is $1,000.

**Duration**  1 year.

**Additional information**  The National Organization of Professional Hispanic Natural Resources Conservation Service Employees (NOPRNRCSE) is comprised of Hispanic employees of the Natural Resources Conservation Service of the U.S. Department of Agriculture (USDA-NRCS).

**Number awarded**   1 each year.

**Deadline**   February of each year.

## [405]
## MARY BARRETT MARSHALL SCHOLARSHIP

American Legion Auxiliary
Department of Kentucky
P.O. Box 5435
Frankfort, KY 40602-5435
(502) 352-2380                    Fax: (502) 352-2381
Web: www.kyamlegionaux.org

**Summary**   To provide financial assistance to female dependents of veterans in Kentucky who plan to attend college in the state.

**Eligibility**   This program is open to the daughters, wives, sisters, widows, granddaughters, or great-granddaughters of veterans eligible for membership in the American Legion who are high school seniors or graduates and 5-year residents of Kentucky. Applicants must be planning to attend a college or university in Kentucky.

**Financial data**   The stipend is $1,000. The funds may be used for tuition, registration fees, laboratory fees, and books, but not for room and board.

**Duration**   1 year.

**Number awarded**   1 each year.

**Deadline**   March of each year.

## [406]
## MARY BLACKWELL BARNES MEMORIAL SCHOLARSHIPS

Women in Public Finance-Virginia Chapter
Attn: Scholarship Committee
P.O. Box 129
Richmond, VA 23219
E-mail: info@virginiawpf.org
Web: www.virginiawpf.org/?page_id=202

**Summary**   To provide financial assistance to women from any state who are working on an undergraduate or graduate degree in a field related to public finance at a college in Virginia or Washington, D.C.

**Eligibility**   This program is open to women from any state who are enrolled at a college or university in Virginia or Washington, D.C. as a sophomore or higher undergraduate or a graduate student. Applicants must be preparing for a career in public finance, including work in government, nonprofits, law, or finance. Along with their application, they must submit essays on 1) their interested in preparing for a career in public finance, government, or public service; 2) their career goals and what has influenced those goals; and 3) their personal interests, activities, and achievements. Financial need is not considered.

**Financial data**   Stipends range from $1,000 to $3,000.

**Duration**   1 year.

**Additional information**   This program began in 2009.

**Number awarded**   Up to 5 each year.

**Deadline**   August of each year.

## [407]
## MARY ELLEN RUSSELL MEMORIAL SCHOLARSHIP

Society of Women Engineers-Pacific Northwest Section
Attn: Scholarship Committee
P.O. Box 1601
Bellevue, WA 98009
E-mail: pnw@swe.org
Web: www.swe-pnw.org/scholarship.html

**Summary**   To provide financial assistance to women from any state studying engineering at a university in Montana or western Washington.

**Eligibility**   This program is open to women from any state who, at the time of application, have completed at least 50% of the requirements toward college graduation in an engineering field. Applicants must be attending an ABET-accredited engineering school in Montana or western Washington. They must be U.S. citizens and members of the Society of Women Engineers (SWE) student section at their school or, if no student section exists, of the national SWE organization. Along with their application, they must submit 1) a 300-word essay on their educational and career goals; and 2) a 500-word essay describing why they have chosen their particular field of engineering; the person, event, or job experience influencing their decision to work on an engineering degree; and the most and least favorite courses they have taken and which course they are most looking forward to and why. Selection is based on the essays, academic achievement, extracurricular and community service activities, and financial need.

**Financial data**   The stipend is $1,000.

**Duration**   1 year.

**Number awarded**   1 each year.

**Deadline**   November of each year.

## [408]
## MARY GUNTHER MEMORIAL SCHOLARSHIP

Society of Women Engineers
Attn: Scholarship Selection Committee
203 North LaSalle Street, Suite 1675
Chicago, IL 60601-1269
(312) 596-5223                    Toll Free: (877) SWE-INFO
Fax: (312) 644-8557          E-mail: scholarships@swe.org
Web: societyofwomenengineers.swe.org

**Summary**   To provide financial assistance to women interested in studying engineering or computer science in college.

**Eligibility**   This program is open to women who are enrolled or planning to enroll full time at an ABET-accredited 4-year college or university. Applicants must be planning to major in engineering or computer science; preference is given to students majoring in architectural or environmental engineering. Entering freshmen must have a GPA of 3.5 or higher; current undergraduates must have a GPA of 3.0 or higher. Selection is based on merit.

**Financial data**   The stipend is $2,000.

**Duration**   1 year.

**Number awarded**   4 each year: 2 for entering freshmen and 2 for continuing undergraduates.

**Deadline**   February of each year for continuing undergraduates; May of each year for entering freshmen.

## [409]
## MARY LILY RESEARCH GRANTS

Duke University
David M. Rubenstein Rare Book and Manuscript Library
Attn: Sallie Bingham Center for Women's History and
   Culture
P.O. Box 90185
Durham, NC 27708-0185
(919) 660-5828               Fax: (919) 660-5934
E-mail: cwhc@duke.edu
Web: library.duke.edu

**Summary**  To provide funding to scholars at all levels who wish to use the resources of the Sallie Bingham Center for Women's History and Culture in the Special Collections Library at Duke University.

**Eligibility**  This program is open to undergraduates, graduate students, faculty members, and independent scholars in any academic field who wish to use the resources of the center for their research in women's studies. Applicants must reside outside a 100-mile radius of Durham, North Carolina. Undergraduate and graduate students must be currently enrolled, be working on a degree, and enclose a letter of recommendation from their adviser or thesis director. Faculty members must be working on a research project and enclose a curriculum vitae. Independent scholars must be working on a nonprofit project and enclose a curriculum vitae. Research topics should be strongly supported by the collections of the center.

**Financial data**  Grants up to $1,000 are available; funds may be used for travel, accommodations, meals, and photocopying and reproduction expenses.

**Duration**  Up to 1 year.

**Additional information**  The library's collections are especially strong in the history of feminist activism and theory, prescriptive literature, girls' literature, artists' books by women, lay and ordained church women, gender expression, women's sexuality, and the history and culture of women in the South. A number of prominent women writers have placed their personal and professional papers in the collections.

**Number awarded**  Varies each year; recently, 8 of these grants were awarded.

**Deadline**  January of each year.

## [410]
## MARY MACON MCGUIRE SCHOLARSHIP

General Federation of Women's Clubs of Virginia
Attn: Scholarship Committee
513 Forest Avenue
P.O. Box 8750
Richmond, VA 23226
(804) 288-3724           Toll Free: (800) 699-8392
Fax: (804) 288-0341
E-mail: scholarships@gfwcvirginia.org
Web: www.gfwcvirginia.org/forms.htm

**Summary**  To provide financial assistance to women heads of households in Virginia who have returned to school.

**Eligibility**  This program is open to women residents of Virginia who are heads of households. Applicants must be currently enrolled in a course of study (vocational or academic) at an accredited Virginia school. They must have returned to school to upgrade their education and employment skills in order to better provide for their families. Selection is based on 3 letters of recommendation; a resume of educational and employment history, financial circumstances, and community activities; and an essay up to 2,000 words that outlines the financial need for the grant as well as the reasons for entering the field of study selected.

**Financial data**  The stipend is $2,500. Funds are paid directly to the recipient's college or university.

**Duration**  1 year.

**Additional information**  This program began in 1929 as a loan fund. It was converted to its current form in 2000.

**Number awarded**  2 each year.

**Deadline**  March of each year.

## [411]
## MARY PAOLOZZI MEMBER'S SCHOLARSHIP

Navy Wives Clubs of America
c/o NSA Mid-South
P.O. Box 54022
Millington, TN 38054-0022
Toll Free: (866) 511-NWCA
E-mail: nwca@navywivesclubsofamerica.org
Web: www.navywivesclubsofamerica.org/scholarships

**Summary**  To provide financial assistance for undergraduate or graduate study to members of the Navy Wives Clubs of America (NWCA).

**Eligibility**  This program is open to NWCA members who can demonstrate financial need. Applicants must be 1) a high school graduate or senior planning to attend college full time next year; 2) currently enrolled in an undergraduate program and planning to continue as a full-time undergraduate; 3) a college graduate or senior planning to be a full-time graduate student next year; or 4) a high school graduate or GED recipient planning to attend vocational or business school next year. Along with their application, they must submit a brief statement on why they feel they should be awarded this scholarship and any special circumstances (financial or other) they wish to have considered. Financial need is also considered in the selection process.

**Financial data**  Stipends range from $500 to $1,000 each year (depending upon the donations from the NWCA chapters).

**Duration**  1 year.

**Additional information**  Membership in the NWCA is open to spouses of enlisted personnel serving in the Navy, Marine Corps, Coast Guard, and the active Reserve units of those services; spouses of enlisted personnel who have been honorably discharged, retired, or transferred to the Fleet Reserve on completion of duty; and widows of enlisted personnel in those services.

**Number awarded**  1 or more each year.

**Deadline**  May of each year.

## [412]
## MARY R. NORTON MEMORIAL SCHOLARSHIP AWARD

ASTM International
100 Barr Harbor Drive
P.O. Box C700
West Conshohocken, PA 19428-2959
(610) 832-9500
Web: www.astm.org/studentmember/Student_Awards.html

**Summary** To provide financial assistance to female undergraduate and graduate students working on a degree related to physical metallurgy.

**Eligibility** This program is open to women entering their senior year of college or first year of graduate study. Applicants must be working on a degree in physical metallurgy or materials science, with an emphasis on relationship of microstructure and properties.

**Financial data** The stipend is $1,000.

**Duration** 1 year.

**Additional information** This program, established in 1975, is administered by ASTM Committee CO4 on Metallography. ASTM International was formerly the American Society for Testing and Materials.

**Number awarded** 1 or more each year.

**Deadline** Deadline not specified.

## [413]
## MARY RUBIN AND BENJAMIN M. RUBIN SCHOLARSHIP FUND

Central Scholarship Bureau
1700 Reisterstown Road, Suite 220
Baltimore, MD 21208
(410) 415-5558          Toll Free: (855) 276-0239
Fax: (410) 415-5501
E-mail: gohigher@central-scholarship.org
Web: www.central-scholarship.org/scholarships/overview

**Summary** To provide financial assistance to women in Maryland who plan to attend college in any state.

**Eligibility** This program is open to women residents of Maryland who are attending or planning to attend a college or university in any state. Applicants must have been out of high school for at least 12 months. They must have a GPA of 3.0 or higher and a family income of less than $90,000 per year. Selection is based on academic achievement, extracurricular activities, and financial need. U.S. citizenship or permanent resident status is required.

**Financial data** Stipends range up to $2,500 per year. Funds may be used to pay tuition only.

**Duration** 1 year. May be renewed up to 4 additional years. Renewal applicants who maintain a GPA of 3.0 or higher are given preference over new applicants.

**Additional information** This non-sectarian fund, established in 1988, is administered by the Central Scholarship Bureau for the Jewish Community Federation of Baltimore.

**Number awarded** 1 or more each year.

**Deadline** March of each year.

## [414]
## MARY V. MUNGER MEMORIAL SCHOLARSHIP

Society of Women Engineers
Attn: Scholarship Selection Committee
203 North LaSalle Street, Suite 1675
Chicago, IL 60601-1269
(312) 596-5223          Toll Free: (877) SWE-INFO
Fax: (312) 644-8557     E-mail: scholarships@swe.org
Web: societyofwomenengineers.swe.org

**Summary** To provide financial assistance to undergraduate members of the Society of Women Engineers (SWE) who are majoring in computer science or engineering.

**Eligibility** This program is open to members of the society who are juniors, seniors, or reentry students at a 4-year ABET-accredited college or university. Applicants must be majoring in computer science or engineering and have a GPA of 3.0 or higher. Selection is based on merit. U.S. citizenship or permanent resident status is required.

**Financial data** The stipend is $4,000.

**Duration** 1 year.

**Number awarded** 1 each year.

**Deadline** February of each year.

## [415]
## MARYLAND LEGION AUXILIARY CHILDREN AND YOUTH FUND SCHOLARSHIP

American Legion Auxiliary
Department of Maryland
1589 Sulphur Spring Road, Suite 105
Baltimore, MD 21227
(410) 242-9519          Fax: (410) 242-9553
E-mail: hq@alamd.org
Web: www.alamd.org/Scholarships.html

**Summary** To provide financial assistance for college to the daughters of veterans who are Maryland residents and wish to study designated fields at a school in the state.

**Eligibility** This program is open to Maryland senior high school girls with a veteran parent who wish to study arts, sciences, business, public administration, education, or a medical field other than nursing at a college or university in the state. Preference is given to children of members of the American Legion or American Legion Auxiliary. Selection is based on character (30%), Americanism (20%), leadership (10%), scholarship (20%), and financial need (20%). U.S. citizenship is required.

**Financial data** The stipend is $2,000.

**Duration** 1 year; may be renewed up to 3 additional years.

**Number awarded** 1 each year.

**Deadline** April of each year.

## [416]
## MARYLAND LEGION AUXILIARY PAST PRESIDENTS' PARLEY NURSING SCHOLARSHIP

American Legion Auxiliary
Department of Maryland
1589 Sulphur Spring Road, Suite 105
Baltimore, MD 21227
(410) 242-9519          Fax: (410) 242-9553
E-mail: hq@alamd.org
Web: www.alamd.org/Scholarships.html

**Summary** To provide financial assistance to the female descendants of Maryland veterans who wish to study nursing at a school in any state.

**Eligibility** This program is open to Maryland residents who are the daughters, granddaughters, great-granddaughters, step-daughters, step-granddaughters, or step-great-grand-daughters of ex-servicewomen (or of ex-servicemen, if there are no qualified descendants of ex-servicewomen). Applicants must be interested in attending a school in any state to become a registered nurse and be able to show financial need. They must submit a 300-word essay on the topic "What a Nursing Career Means to Me."

**Financial data** The stipend is $2,000. Funds are sent directly to the recipient's school.

**Duration** 1 year; may be renewed for up to 3 additional years if the recipient remains enrolled full time.

**Number awarded** 1 each year.

**Deadline** April of each year.

## [417]
## MASWE SCHOLARSHIPS

Society of Women Engineers
Attn: Scholarship Selection Committee
203 North LaSalle Street, Suite 1675
Chicago, IL 60601-1269
(312) 596-5223　　　　Toll Free: (877) SWE-INFO
Fax: (312) 644-8557　　E-mail: scholarships@swe.org
Web: societyofwomenengineers.swe.org

**Summary** To provide financial assistance to undergraduate women majoring in computer science or engineering.

**Eligibility** This program is open to women who are entering their sophomore, junior, or senior year at a 4-year ABET-accredited college or university. Applicants must be working full time on a degree in computer science or engineering and have a GPA of 3.0 or higher. Financial need is considered in the selection process.

**Financial data** The stipend is $1,500.

**Duration** 1 year.

**Additional information** These scholarships were established by the Men's Auxiliary of the Society of Women Engineers (MASWE) in 1971 and are continued through a fund established by the organization when it disbanded in 1976 (effective with the opening of Society of Women Engineer's membership to men).

**Number awarded** 4 each year.

**Deadline** February of each year.

## [418]
## MATURE WOMAN EDUCATIONAL SCHOLARSHIP

Washington State Business and Professional Women's
　Foundation
Attn: Virginia Murphy, Scholarship Committee Chair
P.O. Box 631
Chelan, WA 98816-0631
(509) 682-4747　　　　　E-mail: vamurf@nwi.net
Web: www.bpwwa.org/foundation_apps.htm

**Summary** To provide financial assistance to mature women from Washington interested in attending postsecondary school in the state for retraining or continuing education.

**Eligibility** This program is open to women over 30 years of age who have been residents of Washington for at least 2

years. Applicants must be planning to enroll at a college or university in the state for a program of retraining or continuing education. Along with their application, they must submit a 500-word essay on their specific short-term goals and how the proposed training will help them accomplish those goals and make a difference in their professional career. Financial need is considered in the selection process. U.S. citizenship is required.

**Financial data** The stipend is $1,000.

**Duration** 1 year.

**Number awarded** 1 or more each year.

**Deadline** April of each year.

## [419]
## MCGRAW-HILL COMPANIES SCHOLARSHIP OF NEW YORK WOMEN IN COMMUNICATIONS

New York Women in Communications, Inc.
Attn: NYWICI Foundation
355 Lexington Avenue, 15th Floor
New York, NY 10017-6603
(212) 297-2133　　　　　　Fax: (212) 370-9047
E-mail: nywicipr@nywici.org
Web: www.nywici.org/foundation/scholarships

**Summary** To provide financial assistance to female residents of designated eastern states who are enrolled at a college in any state and preparing for a career in corporate communications and public relations.

**Eligibility** This program is open to women who are residents of New York, New Jersey, Connecticut, or Pennsylvania and currently enrolled as undergraduate or graduate students at a college or university in any state. Graduate students must be members of New York Women in Communications, Inc. (NYWICI). Also eligible are women who reside outside the 4 states but are currently enrolled at a college or university within 1 of the 5 boroughs of New York City. Applicants must be able to demonstrate a commitment to a career in corporate communications and public relations. They must have a GPA of 3.2 or higher. Along with their application, they must submit a 2-page resume; a personal essay of 300 words on an assigned topic that changes annually; 2 letters of recommendation; and an official transcript. Selection is based on academic record, need, demonstrated leadership, participation in school and community activities, honors and other awards or recognition, work experience, goals and aspirations, and unusual personal and/or family circumstances. U.S. citizenship is required.

**Financial data** The stipend ranges up to $10,000.

**Duration** 1 year.

**Additional information** This program is sponsored by McGraw-Hill Companies.

**Number awarded** 1 each year.

**Deadline** January of each year.

## [420]
## MEDTRONIC SWENET SCHOLARSHIP

Society of Women Engineers-Minnesota Section
Attn: Scholarship Committee
P.O. Box 582813
Minneapolis, MN 55458-2813
E-mail: scholarships@swe-mn.org
Web: www.swe-mn.org/scholarships.html

**Summary** To provide financial assistance to women from any state working on an undergraduate or graduate degree in specified fields of engineering at colleges and universities in Minnesota, North Dakota, and South Dakota.

**Eligibility** This program is open to female undergraduate and graduate students at ABET-accredited engineering programs in Minnesota, North Dakota, or South Dakota. Applicants must be working full time on a degree in biomedical, chemical, electrical, or mechanical engineering. Along with their application, they must submit a short paragraph describing how they plan to utilize their engineering skills after they graduate. Selection is based on potential to succeed as an engineer (20 points), communication skills (10 points), extracurricular or community involvement and leadership skills (10 points), demonstrated successful work experience (10 points), and academic success (5 points).

**Financial data** The stipend is $1,000.

**Duration** 1 year.

**Additional information** This program is sponsored by Medtronic, Inc.

**Number awarded** 3 each year.

**Deadline** March of each year.

## [421]
## MEREDITH CORPORATION SCHOLARSHIP AND INTERNSHIP

New York Women in Communications, Inc.
Attn: NYWICI Foundation
355 Lexington Avenue, 15th Floor
New York, NY 10017-6603
(212) 297-2133          Fax: (212) 370-9047
E-mail: nywicipr@nywici.org
Web: www.nywici.org/foundation/scholarships

**Summary** To provide financial assistance and work experience to female residents of designated eastern states who are interested in preparing for a career in publishing at a college or graduate school in any state.

**Eligibility** This program is open to women who are residents of New York, New Jersey, Connecticut, or Pennsylvania and enrolled as sophomores, juniors, seniors, or graduate students at a college or university in any state. Graduate students must be members of New York Women in Communications, Inc. (NYWICI). Also eligible are women who reside outside the 4 states but are currently enrolled at a college or university within 1 of the 5 boroughs of New York City. Applicants must be preparing for a career in publishing (print, digital, and/or marketing) and be interested in a summer internship with Meredith Corporation. They must have a GPA of 3.2 or higher. Along with their application, they must submit a 2-page resume; a personal essay of 300 words on an assigned topic that changes annually; 2 letters of recommendation; and an official transcript. Selection is based on academic record, need, demonstrated leadership, participation in school and community activities, honors and other awards or recognition, work experience, goals and aspirations, and unusual personal and/or family circumstances. U.S. citizenship is required.

**Financial data** The scholarship stipend ranges up to $10,000; the internship is salaried (amount not specified).

**Duration** 1 year.

**Additional information** This program is sponsored by Meredith Corporation.

**Number awarded** 1 each year.

**Deadline** January of each year.

## [422]
## MERIDITH THOMS MEMORIAL SCHOLARSHIPS

Society of Women Engineers
Attn: Scholarship Selection Committee
120 South LaSalle Street, Suite 1515
Chicago, IL 60603-3572
(312) 596-5223          Toll Free: (877) SWE-INFO
Fax: (312) 644-8557
E-mail: scholarshipapplication@swe.org
Web: societyofwomenengineers.swe.org

**Summary** To provide financial assistance to undergraduate women majoring in computer science or engineering.

**Eligibility** This program is open to women who are entering their sophomore, junior, or senior year at a 4-year ABET-accredited college or university. Applicants must be working full time on a degree in computer science or engineering and have a GPA of 3.0 or higher. Selection is based on merit.

**Financial data** The stipend is $2,000.

**Duration** 1 year.

**Additional information** This program began in 2001.

**Number awarded** 5 each year.

**Deadline** February of each year.

## [423]
## MHSAA SCHOLAR-ATHLETE AWARDS

Michigan High School Athletic Association
1661 Ramblewood Drive
East Lansing, MI 48823-7392
(517) 332-5046          Fax: (517) 332-4071
E-mail: afrushour@mhsaa.com
Web: www.mhsaa.com

**Summary** To provide financial assistance for college to seniors (females and males are judged separately) who have participated in athletics at high schools that are members of the Michigan High School Athletic Association (MHSAA).

**Eligibility** This program is open to seniors graduating from high schools that are members of the MHSAA. Applicants must be planning to attend an accredited college, university, or trade school and have a GPA of 3.5 or higher. They must have won a varsity letter in 1 of the sports in which post-season tournaments are sponsored by MHSAA: baseball, boys' and girls' basketball, boys' and girls' bowling, girls' competitive cheer, boys' and girls' cross country, football, boys' and girls' golf, girls' gymnastics, ice hockey, boys' and girls' lacrosse, boys' and girls' soccer, softball, boys' and girls' skiing, boys' and girls' swimming and diving, boys' and girls' tennis, boys' and girls' track and field, girls' volleyball, and wrestling. Along with their application, they must submit a long essay on the importance of sportsmanship in educational athletics and short essays on how they have benefited by activity in school sports and outside school activities. Selection is based on the long essay (40%), involvement in extracurricular activities (30%), the short essays (20%), and 2 letters of recommendation (10%).

**Financial data** The stipend is $1,000.

**Duration** 1 year; nonrenewable.

**Additional information** This program is sponsored by Farm Bureau Insurance.

**Number awarded** 32 each year: 12 from Class A schools (6 boys and 6 girls), 8 from Class B schools (4 boys and 4 girls), 6 from Class C schools (3 boys and 3 girls), 4 from Class D schools (2 boys and 2 girls), and 2 selected at large to minority students.

**Deadline** Students must submit applications to their school by November of each year. The number of nominations each school may submit depends on the size of the school; Class A schools may nominate 6 boys and 6 girls, Class B schools may nominate 4 boys and 4 girls, Class C schools may nominate 3 boys and 3 girls, and Class D schools may nominate 2 boys and 2 girls.

## [424]
## MICHAEL BAKER INC. SCHOLARSHIP FOR DIVERSITY IN ENGINEERING

Association of Independent Colleges and Universities of Pennsylvania
101 North Front Street
Harrisburg, PA 17101-1405
(717) 232-8649 Fax: (717) 233-8574
E-mail: info@aicup.org
Web: http:

**Summary** To provide financial assistance to women and minority students from any state enrolled at member institutions of the Association of Independent Colleges and Universities of Pennsylvania (AICUP) who are majoring in designated fields of engineering.

**Eligibility** This program is open to full-time undergraduate students from any state enrolled at designated AICUP colleges and universities who are women and/or members of the following minority groups: American Indians, Alaska Natives, Asians, Blacks/African Americans, Hispanics/Latinos, Native Hawaiians, or Pacific Islanders. Applicants must be juniors majoring in architectural, civil, or environmental engineering with a GPA of 3.0 or higher. Along with their application, they must submit a 2-page essay on what they believe will be the greatest challenge facing the engineering profession over the next decade, and why.

**Financial data** The stipend is $2,500 per year.

**Duration** 1 year; may be renewed 1 additional year if the recipient maintains appropriate academic standards.

**Additional information** This program, sponsored by the Michael Baker Corporation, is available at the 83 private colleges and universities in Pennsylvania that comprise the AICUP.

**Number awarded** 1 each year.

**Deadline** April of each year.

## [425]
## MICHELE L. MCDONALD SCHOLARSHIP

Educational Foundation for Women in Accounting
Attn: Foundation Administrator
136 South Keowee Street
Dayton, OH 45402
(937) 424-3391 Fax: (937) 222-5749
E-mail: info@efwa.org
Web: www.efwa.org/scholarships.php

**Summary** To provide financial support to women who are returning to college from the workforce or after raising their family to work on a degree in accounting.

**Eligibility** This program is open to women who are returning to college from the workforce or after raising children. Applicants must be planning to begin a program of study for a college degree in accounting. Selection is based on aptitude for accounting and business, commitment to the goal of working on a degree in accounting (including evidence of continued commitment after receiving this award), clear evidence that the candidate has established goals and a plan for achieving those goals (both personal and professional), and financial need. U.S. citizenship is required.

**Financial data** The stipend is $1,000 per year.

**Duration** 1 year; may be renewed 1 additional year if the recipient completes at least 12 hours each semester.

**Additional information** This program was established by the Albuquerque Chapter of the American Society of Women Accountants (ASWA) and transferred to the Educational Foundation for Women in Accounting in 2006.

**Number awarded** 1 each year.

**Deadline** April of each year.

## [426]
## MICHIGAN COUNCIL OF WOMEN IN TECHNOLOGY FOUNDATION SCHOLARSHIPS

Michigan Council of Women in Technology Foundation
Attn: Scholarship Committee
19011 Norwich Road
Livonia, MI 48152
(248) 654-3697 Fax: (248) 281-5391
E-mail: info@mcwtf.org
Web: www.mcwt.org/Scholarships_196.html

**Summary** To provide financial assistance to women from Michigan who are interested in working on an undergraduate or graduate degree in a field related to information technology at a school in any state.

**Eligibility** This program is open to female residents of Michigan who are graduating high school seniors, current undergraduates, or graduate students. Applicants must be planning to work on a degree in business applications, computer science, computer engineering, graphics design, health technology, information security, information systems, instructional technology, music technology, or software engineering at a college or university in any state. They must have a GPA of 2.8 or higher. Along with their application, they must submit an essay of 200 to 400 words on why they are preparing for a career in information technology, the accomplishments in which they take the most pride, why they should be selected for this scholarship, and what constitutes success for them in this program and/or their future career and life mission. Selection is based on that essay, GPA, technology related activities, community service, letters of recommendation, and completeness of the application. U.S. citizenship is required.

**Financial data** The stipend is $5,000 per year; funds are sent directly to the financial aid office at the college or university where the recipient is enrolled.

**Duration** 1 year; may be renewed for up to 3 additional years for high school seniors or 2 additional years for undergraduate and graduate students.

**Number awarded** 3 or more each year: at least each to a high school senior, an undergraduate, and a graduate student.

**Deadline** January of each year.

## [427]
## MIKE SHINN DISTINGUISHED MEMBER OF THE YEAR AWARDS

National Society of Black Engineers
Attn: Programs Department
205 Daingerfield Road
Alexandria, VA 22314
(703) 549-2207                Fax: (703) 683-5312
E-mail: scholarships@nsbe.org
Web: www.nsbe.org/Programs/Scholarships.aspx

**Summary** To provide financial assistance to male and female members of the National Society of Black Engineers (NSBE) who are working on a degree in engineering.

**Eligibility** This program is open to members of the society who are undergraduate or graduate engineering students. Applicants must have a GPA of 3.2 or higher. Selection is based on an essay; NSBE and university academic achievement; professional development; service to the society at the chapter, regional, and/or national level; and campus and community activities. The male and female applicants for the NSBE Fellows Scholarship Program who are judged most outstanding receive these awards.

**Financial data** The stipend is $7,500. Travel, hotel accommodations, and registration to the national convention are also provided.

**Duration** 1 year.

**Number awarded** 2 each year: 1 male and 1 female.

**Deadline** November of each year.

## [428]
## MILLIE GONZALEZ MEMORIAL SCHOLARSHIPS

Factor Support Network Pharmacy
Attn: Scholarship Committee
900 Avenida Acaso, Suite A
Camarillo, CA 93012-8749
(805) 388-9336                Toll Free: (877) 376-4968
Fax: (805) 482-6324
E-mail: Scholarships@FactorSupport.com
Web: www.factorsupport.com/scholarships.htm

**Summary** To provide financial assistance to women with a bleeding disorder.

**Eligibility** This program is open to women with hemophilia or von Willebrand Disease who are entering or attending a college, university, juniors college, or vocational school. Applicants must submit 3 short essays: 1) their career goals; 2) how hemophilia or von Willebrand Disease has affected their life; and 3) their efforts to be involved in the bleeding disorder community and what they can do to education their peers and others outside their family about bleeding disorders. Selection is based on academic goals, volunteer work, school activities, other pertinent experience and achievements, and financial need.

**Financial data** The stipend is $1,000. Funds are paid directly to the recipient.

**Duration** 1 year.

**Number awarded** 5 each year.

**Deadline** April of each year.

## [429]
## MILWAUKEE CHAPTER AFWA SCHOLARSHIPS

Accounting and Financial Women's Alliance-Milwaukee Chapter
c/o Sue Heaton, Scholarship Chair
9310 North 107th Street
Milwaukee, WI 53224
(414) 446-9098                Fax: (414) 365-9138
E-mail: scholarship@aswamilwaukee.org
Web: aswamilwaukee.org/scholarship

**Summary** To provide financial assistance to women from any state who are majoring in accounting at a college in Wisconsin.

**Eligibility** This program is open to women who are entering their second year at a 2-year college or their senior year at a 4-year college or university in Wisconsin. Applicants must be majoring in accounting. Along with their application, they must submit an essay of 150 to 250 words on their career goals and objectives, the impact they want to have on the accounting world, community involvement, and leadership examples. Selection is based on the essay, grades, extracurricular activities, life experience, and financial need.

**Financial data** The stipend is $1,500 for students in a 4-year program or $500 for students in a 2-year program.

**Duration** 1 year.

**Number awarded** 2 each year: 1 to a woman at a 2-year college and 1 to a woman at a 4-year college or university.

**Deadline** October of each year for students in a 2-year program or November of each year for students in a 4-year program.

## [430]
## MINNESOTA CHILD CARE GRANT PROGRAM

Minnesota Office of Higher Education
Attn: Manager of State Financial Aid Programs
1450 Energy Park Drive, Suite 350
St. Paul, MN 55108-5227
(651) 642-0567                Toll Free: (800) 657-3866
Fax: (651) 642-0675            TDD: (800) 627-3529
E-mail: info@ohe.state.mn.us
Web: www.ohe.state.mn.us/mPg.cfm?pageID=891

**Summary** To provide financial assistance for child care to students in Minnesota who are not receiving Minnesota Family Investment Program (MFIP) benefits.

**Eligibility** Minnesota residents who are working on an undergraduate degree or vocational certificate in the state and who have children age 12 and under (14 and under if disabled) may receive this assistance to help pay child care expenses. Recipients must demonstrate financial need but must not be receiving MFIP benefits. U.S. citizenship or eligible noncitizen status is required.

**Financial data** The amount of the assistance depends on the income of applicant and spouse, number of day care hours necessary to cover education and work obligations, student's enrollment status, and number of eligible children in applicant's family. The maximum available is $2,600 per eligible child per academic year.

**Duration** 1 year; may be renewed as long as the recipient remains enrolled on at least a half-time basis in an undergraduate program.

**Additional information** Assistance may cover up to 40 hours per week per eligible child.

**Number awarded** Varies each year; recently, a total of $1.1 million was provided for this program.

**Deadline** Deadline not specified.

## [431]
## MINNESOTA LEGION AUXILIARY PAST PRESIDENTS PARLEY HEALTH CARE SCHOLARSHIP

American Legion Auxiliary
Department of Minnesota
State Veterans Service Building
20 West 12th Street, Room 314
St. Paul, MN 55155-2069
(651) 224-7634                Toll Free: (888) 217-9598
Fax: (651) 224-5243      E-mail: deptoffice@mnala.org
Web: www.mnala.org/ala/scholarship.asp

**Summary** To provide financial assistance for education in health care fields to members of the American Legion Auxiliary in Minnesota.

**Eligibility** This program is open to residents of Minnesota who have been members of the American Legion Auxiliary for at least 3 years. Applicants must have a GPA of 2.0 or higher and be planning to study in Minnesota. Their proposed major may be in any phase of health care, including nursing assistant, registered nursing, licensed practical nurse, X-ray or other technician, physical or other therapist, dental hygienist, or dental assistant.

**Financial data** The stipend is $1,000. Funds are sent directly to the recipient's school after satisfactory completion of the first quarter.

**Duration** 1 year.

**Number awarded** Up to 10 each year.

**Deadline** March of each year.

## [432]
## MINNESOTA SECTION SWE SCHOLARSHIP

Society of Women Engineers-Minnesota Section
Attn: Scholarship Committee
P.O. Box 582813
Minneapolis, MN 55458-2813
E-mail: scholarships@swe-mn.org
Web: www.swe-mn.org/scholarships.html

**Summary** To provide financial assistance to upper-division women from any state studying engineering or computer science at colleges and universities in Minnesota, North Dakota, and South Dakota.

**Eligibility** This program is open to women entering their junior or senior year at an ABET-accredited engineering or computer science program in Minnesota, North Dakota, or South Dakota. Applicants must be full-time students majoring in engineering or computer science. Along with their application, they must submit a short paragraph describing how they plan to utilize their engineering skills after they graduate. Preference is given to student members of the Society of Women Engineers (SWE). Selection is based on potential to succeed as an engineer (20 points), communication skills (10

points), extracurricular or community involvement and leadership skills (10 points), demonstrated successful work experience (10 points), and academic success (5 points).

**Financial data** The stipend is $1,500.

**Duration** 1 year.

**Number awarded** 1 each year.

**Deadline** March of each year.

## [433]
## MISS AMERICA COMMUNITY SERVICE SCHOLARSHIPS

Miss America Pageant
Attn: Scholarship Department
222 New Road, Suite 700
Linwood, NJ 08221
(609) 653-8700, ext. 127           Fax: (609) 653-8740
E-mail: info@missamerica.org
Web: www.missamerica.org

**Summary** To recognize and reward, with college scholarships, women who participate in the Miss America Pageant at the state level and demonstrate outstanding community service.

**Eligibility** This competition is open to women who compete at the state level of the Miss America Pageant. Applicants must demonstrate that they have fulfilled a legitimate need in their community through the creation, development, and/or participation in a community service project. Selection is based on excellence of community service.

**Financial data** The stipend is $1,000.

**Duration** 1 year.

**Additional information** This program, established in 1998, is administered by Scholarship Management Services, a division of Scholarship America, One Scholarship Way, P.O. Box 297, St. Peter, MN 56082, (507) 931-1682, (800) 537-4180, Fax: (507) 931-9168, E-mail: smsinfo@csfa.org.

**Number awarded** Up to 52 each year: 1 for each of the states, the District of Columbia, and the Virgin Islands.

**Deadline** Varies, depending upon the date of local pageants leading to the state finals.

## [434]
## MISS AMERICA COMPETITION AWARDS

Miss America Pageant
Attn: Scholarship Department
222 New Road, Suite 700
Linwood, NJ 08221
(609) 653-8700, ext. 127           Fax: (609) 653-8740
E-mail: info@missamerica.org
Web: www.missamerica.org/scholarships

**Summary** To provide educational scholarships to participants in the Miss America Pageant on local, state, and national levels.

**Eligibility** To enter an official Miss America Preliminary Pageant, candidates must meet certain basic requirements and agree to abide by all the rules of the local, state, and national Miss America Pageants. Among the qualifications required are that the applicant be female, between the ages of 17 and 24, a resident of the town or state in which they first compete, in good health, of good moral character, and a citizen of the United States. A complete list of all eligibility requirements is available from each local and state pageant.

Separate scholarships are awarded to the winners of the talent competition and the lifestyle and fitness in swimsuit competition. Other special awards may be presented on a 1-time basis.

**Financial data** More than $45 million in cash and tuition assistance is awarded annually at the local, state, and national Miss America Pageants. At the national level, nearly $500,000 is awarded: Miss America receives $50,000 in scholarship money, the first runner-up $25,000, second runner-up $20,000, third runner-up $15,000, fourth runner-up $10,000, 5 other top 10 finalists $7,000 each, 2 other top 12 semifinalists $5,000 each, 3 other top 15 semifinalists $4,000 each, and other national contestants $3,000 each. Other awards include those for the 3 preliminary talent winners at $2,000 each, the 3 preliminary lifestyle and fitness in swimsuit winners at $1,000 each, and the 5 non-finalist talent winners at $1,000 each. Recent special awards included the Miracle Maker Award of $5,000, the Fourpoints Award of $2,000, the Miss Congeniality Award of $2,000, the Ric Ferentz Non-Finalist Interview Award of $2,000, the Louanne Gamba Instrumental Award of $1,000, and the Marion A. Crooker Award of $1,000.

**Duration** The pageants are held every year.

**Additional information** The Miss America Pageant has been awarding scholarships since 1945. Scholarships are to be used for tuition, room, board, supplies, and other college expenses. Use of the scholarships must begin within 4 years from the date of the award (5 years if the recipient is Miss America), unless a reasonable extension is requested and granted. Training under the scholarship should be continuous and completed within 10 years from the date the scholarship is activated; otherwise, the balance of the scholarship may be canceled without further notice.

**Number awarded** At the national level, 52 contestants (1 from each state, the District of Columbia, and the Virgin Islands) share the awards.

**Deadline** Varies, depending upon the date of local pageants leading to the state and national finals.

## [435]
## MISS AMERICA SCHOLAR AWARDS

Miss America Pageant
Attn: Scholarship Department
222 New Road, Suite 700
Linwood, NJ 08221
(609) 653-8700, ext. 127      Fax: (609) 653-8740
E-mail: info@missamerica.org
Web: www.missamerica.org/scholarships/missstate.aspx

**Summary** To recognize and reward, with college scholarships, women who participate in the Miss America Pageant at the state level and demonstrate academic excellence.

**Eligibility** This competition is open to women who compete at the state level of the Miss America Pageant. Selection is based on academic excellence (grades, course content, and academic standing of the institution).

**Financial data** The stipend is $1,000.

**Duration** 1 year.

**Additional information** This program, established in 1998, is administered by Scholarship Management Services, a division of Scholarship America, One Scholarship Way, P.O. Box 297, St. Peter, MN 56082, (507) 931-1682, (800) 537-4180, Fax: (507) 931-9168, E-mail: smsinfo@csfa.org.

**Number awarded** Up to 52 each year: 1 for each of the states, the District of Columbia, and the Virgin Islands.

**Deadline** Varies, depending upon the date of local pageants leading to the state finals.

## [436]
## MISS INDIAN USA SCHOLARSHIP PROGRAM

American Indian Heritage Foundation
P.O. Box 750
Pigeon Forge, TN 37868
(703) 819-0979      E-mail: MissIndianUSA@indians.org
Web: www.indians.org/miss-indian-usa-program.html

**Summary** To recognize and reward the most beautiful and talented Indian women.

**Eligibility** American Indian women between the ages of 18 and 26 are eligible to enter this national contest if they are high school graduates and have never been married, cohabited with the opposite sex, been pregnant, or had children. U.S. citizenship is required. Selection is based on public appearance (20%), a traditional interview (15%), a contemporary interview (15%), beauty of spirit (15%), a cultural presentation (10%), scholastic achievement (10%), a platform question (10%), and a finalist question (5%).

**Financial data** Awards vary each year; recently, Miss Indian USA received an academic scholarship of $4,000 plus a cash grant of $6,500, a wardrobe allowance of $2,000, appearance fees of $3,000, a professional photo shoot worth $500, gifts worth more than $4,000, honoring gifts worth more than $2,000, promotional materials worth more than $2,000, and travel to Washington, D.C. with a value of approximately $2,000; the total value of the prize was more than $26,000. Members of her court received scholarships of $2,000 for the first runner-up, $1,500 for the second runner-up, $1,000 for the third runner-up, and $500 for the fourth runner-up.

**Duration** This competition is held annually.

**Additional information** The program involves a week-long competition in the Washington, D.C. metropolitan area that includes seminars, interviews, cultural presentations, and many public appearances. The application fee is $100 if submitted prior to mid-April or $200 if submitted later. In addition, a candidate fee of $750 is required.

**Number awarded** 1 winner and 4 runners-up are selected each year.

**Deadline** May of each year.

## [437]
## MISS LATINA WORLD

Dawn Rochelle Models Agency
129 South Tennessee Street
McKinney, TX 75069
(469) 396-5670      E-mail: contact@dawnrochelle.com
Web: www.misslatina.com

**Summary** To recognize and reward young Latina women who compete in a national beauty pageant.

**Eligibility** This program is open to women between 18 and 28 years of age who are at least 25% Hispanic. Applicants may be single, married, or divorced, and they may have children. They appear in a nationally-televised pageant where selection is based on 3 categories: beauty/evening gown, fashion wear, and photogenic. Judges also interview each participant; the interview score may replace the fashion wear score. Height and weight are not factors, but contestants should be proportionate. Pageant experience and fluency in Spanish are not required.

**Financial data** Each year, prizes vary. The overall winner receives a $5,000 cash award.

**Duration** The pageant is held annually.

**Number awarded** 1 overall winner is selected each year.

**Deadline** April of each year.

## [438]
## MISS TEEN AMERICA

Miss Teen America, Inc.
P.O. Box 37
Getzville, NY 14068
(716) 629-3990          E-mail: info@missteenamerica.com
Web: www.missteenamerica.com

**Summary** To recognize and reward, with college scholarships, teen-age women who participate in a talent and beauty competition.

**Eligibility** This competition is open to females between 15 and 18 years of age who have never been to college, been married, or given birth to a child. Applicants must first apply for state or metropolitan area competitions by submitting a 1-page essay on why they want to represent their state. At the national level, they participate in talent, modeling, and photogenic competitions. Selection is based on a personal interview with judges (20%), talent or spokesmodel presentation (20%), physical fitness, in recommended swimsuit (20%), a formal eveningwear presentation (10%), a 30-second commercial or public service announcement about their state (10%), the photogenic competition (10%), and modeling (10%).

**Financial data** Cash scholarships, for use at an accredited college or university, range up to $5,000 for Miss Teen America. Other awards vary each year.

**Duration** The competition is held annually.

**Additional information** All participants are required to pay a total sponsorship fee of $1,195, including a deposit of $50 to accompany the application. They are also required to sell $400 worth of ads for the national program.

**Number awarded** 5 winners receive national scholarships each year.

**Deadline** Deadline not specified.

## [439]
## MISS TEEN USA

Miss Universe Organization
1370 Avenue of the Americas, 16th Floor
New York, NY 10019
(212) 373-4999          Fax: (212) 315-5378
E-mail: pr@missuniverse.com
Web: www.missuniverse.com/missteenusa

**Summary** To recognize and reward beautiful and talented women between 14 and 19 years of age in the United States.

**Eligibility** Some cities and all states have preliminary pageants. The winner of the city pageant goes on to compete in the state pageant for her home city. A delegate may also enter a state pageant without having won a city title. One delegate from each of the 50 states and the District of Columbia is selected to compete in the pageant. Participants must be between 14 and 19 years of age. They must never have been married or pregnant. Selection is based on beauty, intelligence, and ability to handle an interview.

**Financial data** Miss Teen USA receives cash and prizes whose value varies each year.

**Duration** The national pageant is held annually, usually at the end of the summer.

**Additional information** The competition began in 1983.

**Number awarded** 1 national winner each year.

**Deadline** June of each year.

## [440]
## MISS USA

Miss Universe Organization
1370 Avenue of the Americas, 16th Floor
New York, NY 10019
(212) 373-4999          Fax: (212) 315-5378
E-mail: pr@missuniverse.com
Web: www.missuniverse.com/missusa

**Summary** To identify and reward the most beautiful women selected in a competition among women from each state.

**Eligibility** This program is open to women between 18 and 27 years of age who have never been married or pregnant. Entrants are first selected in state competitions, and then 51 women (1 from each state and the District of Columbia) compete in the Miss USA Pageant. Selection of the winner is based on interviews by pageant judges (on successes, talents, goals, and ambitions), a swimsuit competition (with swimsuit styles provided by the pageant), and an evening gown competition (with gowns chosen by the competitors). The Photogenic Award is presented to the delegate voted on and selected by the television audience, and the Congeniality Award is presented to the delegate selected by her sister delegates as the most charismatic and inspirational.

**Financial data** Miss USA receives cash and prizes whose value varies each year.

**Duration** The national pageant is held annually, in February or March.

**Additional information** This pageant began in 1952. Miss USA competes for additional prizes in the Miss Universe Pageant.

**Number awarded** 1 each year.

**Deadline** January of each year.

## [441]
## MISSOURI STATE KNIGHTS OF COLUMBUS LADIES AUXILIARY SCHOLARSHIP

Knights of Columbus-Missouri State Council
c/o J.Y. Miller, Scholarship Committee Chair
322 Second Street
Glasgow, MO 65254
(660) 338-2105          E-mail: j.y.miller@sbcglobal.net
Web: www.mokofc.org

**Summary** To provide financial assistance to members of the Ladies Auxiliary of the Knights of Columbus in Missouri who are interested in attending college in the state.

**Eligibility** This program is open to residents of Missouri who are enrolled or planning to enroll at an accredited college, university, or trade school in the state. Applicants must be a member of the Ladies Auxiliary of the Knights of Columbus. Along with their application, they must submit a 200-

word statement explaining their goals for the future, their professional ambitions, and their Catholic life. Selection is based on Catholic citizenship, community service, scholarship, and financial need.

**Financial data** The stipend is $1,000.

**Duration** 1 year.

**Additional information** This program was originally established in 1971.

**Number awarded** 1 each year.

**Deadline** February of each year.

## [442]
## MISSOURI WOMEN'S GOLF EDUCATION ASSOCIATION SCHOLARSHIPS

Missouri Women's Golf Association
Attn: Scholarship Director
3401 Truman Boulevard, Suite 100
P.O. Box 104164
Jefferson City, MO 65110
(573) 636-8994                    Fax: (573) 636-4225
E-mail: Scholarship@mowomensga.org
Web: www.mowomensga.org/Scholarship

**Summary** To provide financial assistance to female high school seniors in Missouri who have been involved in golf and plan to attend college in any state.

**Eligibility** This program is open to women graduating from high schools in Missouri or Johnson County, Kansas and planning to attend college in any state. Applicants must submit a copy of their high school transcript, a statement of their involvement in golf, a description of their involvement in community and school activities, a statement indicating their reasons for wanting to further their education and their future career goals, 3 personal references, and a statement of their financial need. U.S. citizenship is required.

**Financial data** A stipend is awarded (amount not specified).

**Duration** 1 year; nonrenewable.

**Additional information** This program includes the Susan E. Shepherd Memorial Scholarship, funded by the Shepherd Foundation of St. Louis, and the Mary Jane Landreth Scholarship, established in 2006.

**Number awarded** Varies each year; recently, 5 of these scholarships were awarded.

**Deadline** March of each year.

## [443]
## MORGAN STANLEY SOPHOMORE INTERNSHIP PROGRAM

Morgan Stanley
Attn: Diversity Recruiting
1585 Broadway
New York, NY 10036
(212) 762-0211                    Toll Free: (888) 454-3965
Fax: (212) 507-4972
E-mail: mbafellowship@morganstanley.com
Web: www.morganstanley.com

**Summary** To provide summer work experience to female and other college sophomores from underrepresented groups who are interested in a career in the financial services business.

**Eligibility** This program is open to female, Black, Hispanic, and LGBT students who are currently enrolled as sophomores at a 4-year college or university. Applicants may be majoring in any field, but they must desire to work at Morgan Stanley in the following divisions: bank resource management, equity research, fixed income and commodities, fund services, global capital markets, institutional equity and equity financing products, investment banking, public finance, or internal audit. Selection is based on academic achievement, extracurricular activities, leadership qualities, and an on-site interview.

**Financial data** These are paid internships.

**Duration** 10 weeks during the summer.

**Number awarded** 1 or more each year.

**Deadline** December of each year.

## [444]
## MOSS ADAMS FOUNDATION SCHOLARSHIP

Educational Foundation for Women in Accounting
Attn: Foundation Administrator
136 South Keowee Street
Dayton, OH 45402
(937) 424-3391                    Fax: (937) 222-5749
E-mail: info@efwa.org
Web: www.efwa.org/scholarships_MossAdams.php

**Summary** To provide financial support to women, including minority women, who are working on an accounting degree.

**Eligibility** This program is open to women who are enrolled in an accounting degree program at an accredited college or university. Applicants must meet 1 of the following criteria: 1) women pursuing a fifth-year requirement either through general studies or within a graduate program; 2) women returning to school as current or reentry juniors or seniors; or 3) minority women. Selection is based on aptitude for accounting and business, commitment to the goal of working on a degree in accounting (including evidence of continued commitment after receiving this award), clear evidence that the candidate has established goals and a plan for achieving those goals (both personal and professional), financial need, and a demonstration of how the scholarship will impact her life. U.S. citizenship is required.

**Financial data** The stipend is $1,000.

**Duration** 1 year.

**Additional information** This program was established by Rowling, Dold & Associates LLP, a woman-owned C.P.A. firm based in San Diego. It was renamed when that firm merged with Moss Adams LLP.

**Number awarded** 1 each year.

**Deadline** April of each year.

## [445]
## MRS. DEXTER OTIS ARNOLD SCHOLARSHIP

General Federation of Women's Clubs of New Hampshire
c/o Edith Hogan, Scholarship Chair
34 Dearborn Street
Nashua, NH 03060
E-mail: info@gfwcnh.org
Web: www.gfwcnh.org

**Summary** To provide financial assistance to female high school seniors in New Hampshire who plan to attend college in the state.

**Eligibility** This program is open to female seniors graduating from high schools in New Hampshire and planning to attend an accredited college, university, or technical/specialty school in the state. Applicants must submit a 1-page essay on their reasons for pursuing further education, their intended major, and why they consider themselves a worthy applicant for this scholarship. Selection is based on academic achievement, community service, leadership, individual determination, school activities, and financial need.

**Financial data** The stipend is $1,200.

**Duration** 1 year.

**Number awarded** 1 each year.

**Deadline** March of each year.

## [446]
## MSCPA WOMEN IN ACCOUNTING SCHOLARSHIP

Massachusetts Society of Certified Public Accountants
Attn: MSCPA Educational Foundation
105 Chauncy Street, Tenth Floor
Boston, MA 02111
(617) 556-4000          Toll Free: (800) 392-6145
Fax: (617) 556-4126          E-mail: info@mscpaonline.org
Web: www.cpatrack.com/scholarships

**Summary** To provide financial assistance to women from Massachusetts working on an undergraduate or graduate degree in accounting at a college or university in the state.

**Eligibility** This program is open to female Massachusetts residents enrolled at a college or university in the state. Applicants must be undergraduates who have completed the first semester of their junior year or graduate students. They must be able to demonstrate financial need, academic excellence, and an intention to prepare for a career as a Certified Public Accountant (C.P.A.) at a firm in Massachusetts.

**Financial data** The stipend is $2,500.

**Duration** 1 year.

**Additional information** This program is sponsored by the Women's Golf Committee of the Massachusetts Society of Certified Public Accountants (MSCPA).

**Number awarded** Varies each year; recently, 4 of these scholarships were awarded.

**Deadline** March of each year.

## [447]
## MTS SYSTEMS CORPORATION SCHOLARSHIP

Society of Women Engineers-Minnesota Section
Attn: Scholarship Committee
P.O. Box 582813
Minneapolis, MN 55458-2813
E-mail: scholarships@swe-mn.org
Web: www.swe-mn.org/scholarships.html

**Summary** To provide financial assistance to women from any state working on an undergraduate or graduate degree in software or mechanical engineering at colleges and universities in Minnesota, North Dakota, and South Dakota.

**Eligibility** This program is open to female undergraduate and graduate students at ABET-accredited engineering programs in Minnesota, North Dakota, or South Dakota. Applicants must be working full time on a degree in software or mechanical engineering. Along with their application, they must submit a short paragraph describing how they plan to utilize their engineering skills after they graduate. Selection is based on potential to succeed as an engineer (20 points), communication skills (10 points), extracurricular or community involvement and leadership skills (10 points), demonstrated successful work experience (10 points), and academic success (5 points).

**Financial data** The stipend is $1,500.

**Duration** 1 year.

**Additional information** This program is sponsored by MTS Systems Corporation.

**Number awarded** 1 each year.

**Deadline** March of each year.

## [448]
## MUSEMECHE SCHOLARSHIP PROGRAM

Louisiana High School Athletic Association
Attn: Commissioner
12720 Old Hammond Highway
Baton Rouge, LA 70816
(225) 296-5882          Fax: (225) 296-5919
E-mail: lhsaa@lhsaa.org
Web: www.lhsaa.org

**Summary** To provide financial assistance to student-athletes in Louisiana who plan to attend college in the state (females and males are considered separately).

**Eligibility** This program is open to student-athletes who are seniors graduating from high schools in Louisiana. Applicants must be planning to attend a college or university in the state. They must be nominated by their principal. Females and males are considered separately. Selection is based primarily on financial need.

**Financial data** The stipend is $1,000.

**Duration** 1 year.

**Additional information** This program is sponsored by Musemeche Photography.

**Number awarded** 2 each year: 1 for a female and 1 for a male.

**Deadline** April of each year.

## [449]
## MUSIC THERAPY SCHOLARSHIP

Sigma Alpha Iota Philanthropies, Inc.
One Tunnel Road
Asheville, NC 28805
(828) 251-0606          Fax: (828) 251-0644
E-mail: nh@sai-national.org
Web: www.sai-national.org

**Summary** To provide financial assistance to members of Sigma Alpha Iota (an organization of women musicians) who are working on an undergraduate or graduate degree in music therapy.

**Eligibility** This program is open to members of the organization who have completed at least 2 years of study for an undergraduate or graduate degree in music therapy. Applicants must submit an essay that includes their personal definition of music therapy, their career plans and professional goals as a music therapist, and why they feel they are deserving of this scholarship. Selection is based on music therapy skills, musicianship, fraternity service, community service, leadership, self-reliance, and dedication to the field of music therapy as a career.

**Financial data** The stipend is $1,500.

**Duration** 1 year.

**Number awarded** 1 each year.

**Deadline** March of each year.

## [450]
## MUSICAL THEATER SCHOLARSHIP

Sigma Alpha Iota Philanthropies, Inc.
One Tunnel Road
Asheville, NC 28805
(828) 251-0606　　　　　　　Fax: (828) 251-0644
E-mail: nh@sai-national.org
Web: www.sai-national.org

**Summary** To provide financial assistance to members of Sigma Alpha Iota (an organization of women musicians) who are working on an undergraduate degree with an emphasis on musical theater.

**Eligibility** This program is open to members of the organization who are enrolled in an undergraduate degree program in music with an emphasis on musical theater. Applicants must be endorsed or recommended by a director of musical theater or major professor with whom they have worked for at least 6 months. Along with their application, they must submit a 15-minute performance DVD that includes a variety of styles and at least 2 monologues; a brief resume, including their musical experience; current academic transcripts; and a brief statement of their career goals and aspirations. Financial need is not considered in the selection process.

**Financial data** The stipend is $1,500.

**Duration** 1 year.

**Additional information** This program began in 2010.

**Number awarded** 1 each year.

**Deadline** March of each year.

## [451]
## MUSICIANS WITH SPECIAL NEEDS SCHOLARSHIP

Sigma Alpha Iota Philanthropies, Inc.
One Tunnel Road
Asheville, NC 28805
(828) 251-0606　　　　　　　Fax: (828) 251-0644
E-mail: nh@sai-national.org
Web: www.sai-national.org

**Summary** To provide financial assistance for college or graduate school to members of Sigma Alpha Iota (an organization of women musicians) who have a disability and are working on a degree in music.

**Eligibility** This program is open to members of the organization who either 1) have a sensory or physical impairment and are enrolled in a graduate or undergraduate degree program in music; or 2) are preparing to become a music teacher or therapist for people with disabilities. Performance majors must submit a 15-minute DVD of their work; non-performance majors must submit evidence of work in their area of specialization, such as composition, musicology, or research.

**Financial data** The stipend is $1,500.

**Duration** 1 year.

**Number awarded** 1 each year.

**Deadline** March of each year.

## [452]
## MYRT WILLEY SCHOLARSHIP

Zonta Club of Bangor
c/o Barbara A. Cardone
P.O. Box 1904
Bangor, ME 04402-1904
Web: www.zontaclubofbangor.org/?area=scholarship

**Summary** To provide financial assistance to women attending or planning to attend college in Maine and major in a business-related field.

**Eligibility** This program is open to women who are attending or planning to attend an accredited 2- or 4-year college in Maine. Applicants must major in a business-related field. Along with their application, they must submit brief essays on 1) their goals in seeking higher education and their plans for the future; and 2) any school and community activities that have been of particular importance to them and why they found them worthwhile. Financial need may be considered in the selection process.

**Financial data** The stipend is $1,000.

**Duration** 1 year.

**Number awarded** 1 each year.

**Deadline** March of each year.

## [453]
## NABA 20 PEARLS SCHOLARSHIP

National Association of Black Accountants
Attn: National Scholarship Program
7474 Greenway Center Drive, Suite 1120
Greenbelt, MD 20770
(301) 474-NABA　　　　　　　Fax: (301) 474-3114
E-mail: scholarships@nabainc.org
Web: www.nabainc.org

**Summary** To provide financial assistance to student members of the National Association of Black Accountants (NABA) who are also members of Alpha Kappa Alpha sorority and working on an undergraduate or graduate degree in a field related to accounting.

**Eligibility** This program is open to NABA members who are also Alpha Kappa Alpha members and enrolled full time as 1) an undergraduate freshman, sophomore, junior, or first-semester senior majoring in accounting, business, or finance at a 4-year college or university; or 2) a graduate student working on a master's degree in accounting. High school seniors are not eligible. Applicants must have a GPA of 3.5 or higher in their major and 3.3 or higher overall. Selection is based on grades, financial need, and a 500-word description of their involvement in NABA.

**Financial data** The stipend is $1,500.

**Duration** 1 year.

**Number awarded** 1 each year.

**Deadline** January of each year.

## [454]
## NACOPRW SCHOLARSHIP AWARD

National Conference of Puerto Rican Women-Miami
Chapter
c/o Elizabeth Baez, President
13381 S.W. 77th Street
Miami, FL 33183
(305) 338-1844    E-mail: NACOPRW.MIAMI@gmail.com
Web: www.nacoprwmiami.org/ScholarshipApp.htm

**Summary** To provide financial assistance for college to Puerto Rican women.

**Eligibility** This program is open to women who are Puerto Rican by birth or descent. Applicants must have been admitted to an accredited college or university in the United States or Puerto Rico. They must have a GPA of 3.0 or higher and be able to demonstrate financial need.

**Financial data** The stipend is approximately $1,000.

**Duration** 1 year.

**Additional information** The National Conference of Puerto Rican Women (NACOPRW) "promotes the full participation of Puerto Rican and other Hispanic women in the economic, social and political life of the United States and Puerto Rico.".

**Number awarded** 1 or more each year.

**Deadline** April of each year.

## [455]
## NAHB WOMEN'S COUNCIL STRATEGIES FOR SUCCESS SCHOLARSHIP

National Housing Endowment
1201 15th Street, N.W.
Washington, DC 20005
(202) 266-8069      Toll Free: (800) 368-5242, ext. 8069
Fax: (202) 266-8177      E-mail: nhe@nahb.com
Web: www.nationalhousingendowment.com

**Summary** To provide financial assistance to undergraduate students, especially women, who are interested in preparing for a career in the building industry.

**Eligibility** This program is open to current undergraduates who are enrolled full time at a 2- or 4-year college or university or a vocational program. Applicants must be working on or planning to work on a degree in a housing-related program, such as construction management, building, construction technology, civil engineering, architecture, design, or a trade specialty. They must have at least a 2.5 GPA in all courses and at least a 3.0 GPA in core curriculum classes. Preference is given to 1) women; 2) applicants who would be unable to afford college without financial assistance; and 3) students who are current members (or will be members in the upcoming semester) of a student chapter of the National Association of Home Builders (NAHB). Along with their application, they must submit an essay on their reasons for becoming a professional in the housing industry and their career goals. Selection is based on financial need, career goals, academic achievement, employment history, extracurricular activities, and letters of recommendation.

**Financial data** The stipend is $2,000. Funds are made payable to the recipient and sent to the recipient's school.

**Duration** 1 year; may be renewed.

**Additional information** The National Housing Endowment is the philanthropic arm of the National Association of Home Builders (NAHB). Its women's council established this scholarship in 2001.

**Number awarded** Varies each year; recently, 11 of these scholarships were awarded. Since this program began, it has awarded nearly $30,500 to 32 students.

**Deadline** March of each year.

## [456]
## NANCY ANNE WEINSTEIN SCHOLARSHIP

Accounting and Financial Women's Alliance-Richmond
Chapter
c/o Dionne Brice, Scholarship Coordinator
Brice Bookkeeping & Tax, LLC
P.O. Box 31
Goochland, VA 23063
E-mail: db.booksntax@yahoo.com
Web: www.aswarichmond.org/scholar.htm

**Summary** To provide financial assistance to nontraditional female students from any state who are enrolled at colleges in the Richmond area of North Carolina working on a degree in accounting or finance.

**Eligibility** This program is open to women from any state who have had to delay starting or completing a college degree. Applicants must be attending a college, university, or professional school of accounting in the Richmond area. They must be entering their third, fourth, or fifth year of study with a declared major in accounting or finance and a have GPA of 3.0 or higher. Along with their application, they must submit an essay of 150 to 250 words on their career goals and objectives, the impact they want to have on the accounting world, community involvement, and leadership examples. Selection is based on leadership, character, communication skills, scholastic average, and financial need. Membership in the Accounting and Financial Women's Alliance (AFWA) is not required.

**Financial data** A stipend is awarded (amount not specified).

**Duration** 1 year.

**Number awarded** 1 each year.

**Deadline** February of each year.

## [457]
## NANCY KELLY FEMALE WRITER AWARD

Philanthrofund Foundation
Attn: Scholarship Committee
1409 Willow Street, Suite 109
Minneapolis, MN 55403-2241
(612) 870-1806      Toll Free: (800) 435-1402
Fax: (612) 871-6587      E-mail: info@PfundOnline.org
Web: www.pfundonline.org/scholarships.html

**Summary** To provide financial assistance to female Minnesota students who have supported gay, lesbian, bisexual, and transgender (GLBT) activities and are interested in studying writing.

**Eligibility** This program is open to female residents of Minnesota and students attending a Minnesota educational institution. Applicants must be self-identified as GLBT or from a GLBT family. They may be attending or planning to attend trade school, technical college, college, or university (as an undergraduate or graduate student) to study writing. Selection is based on the applicant's 1) affirmation of GLBT or allied identity; 2) evidence of experience and skills in service and leadership; and 3) evidence of service, leading, and working for change in GLBT communities, including serving as a role model, mentor, and/or adviser.

**Financial data**   The stipend is $2,000. Funds must be used for tuition, books, fees, or dissertation expenses.

**Duration**   1 year.

**Number awarded**   1 each year.

**Deadline**   January of each year.

## [458]
## NANCY LORRAINE JENSEN MEMORIAL SCHOLARSHIP FUND

Sons of Norway
Attn: Foundation
1455 West Lake Street
Minneapolis, MN 55408-2666
(612) 821-4632                   Toll Free: (800) 945-8851
Fax: (612) 827-0658             E-mail: foundation@sofn.com
Web: www.sofn.com

**Summary**   To provide financial assistance to women who have a connection to the Sons of Norway and are interested in studying chemistry, physics, or engineering in college.

**Eligibility**   This program is open to women who are U.S. citizens between 17 and 35 years of age and members (or daughters or granddaughters of members) of the Sons of Norway; they must have been a member for at least 3 years. Applicants must have a combined SAT score of 1800 or higher, a mathematics score of 600 or higher, or an ACT score of 26 or higher. They must be full-time undergraduate students and have completed at least 1 quarter or semester of study in chemistry, physics, or chemical, electrical, or mechanical engineering. Selection is based on long-term career goals, clarity of study plan, academic potential, evidence of ability to succeed, and letters of recommendation attesting to good character, eagerness, earnestness, and ambition in the field of science or engineering.

**Financial data**   Stipends range from 50% of tuition for 1 quarter or semester to 100% for 1 year. Grants are issued jointly to the recipient and her institution.

**Duration**   Awards are made for either 1 term (quarter or semester) or 1 year; a student may receive up to 3 awards as an undergraduate.

**Additional information**   This fund was established in 1995 by Dr. and Mrs. Arthur S. Jensen in memory of their daughter, a chemical engineer whose work resulted in advances in the field of weather satellite photography and who died at the age of 35.

**Number awarded**   Varies each year; recently, 4 of these scholarships were awarded.

**Deadline**   March of each year.

## [459]
## NANNIE W. NORFLEET SCHOLARSHIP

American Legion Auxiliary
Department of North Carolina
P.O. Box 25726
Raleigh, NC 27611-5726
(919) 832-4051                   Fax: (919) 832-1888
E-mail: ala1_nc@bellsouth.net
Web: nclegion.org/auxil.htm

**Summary**   To provide financial assistance to members of the American Legion Auxiliary in North Carolina and their children and grandchildren who plan to attend college in any state.

**Eligibility**   This program is open to North Carolina residents who are either adult members of the American Legion Auxiliary or high school seniors (with preference to the children and grandchildren of members). Applicants must be interested in attending college in any state. They must be able to demonstrate financial need.

**Financial data**   The stipend is $1,000.

**Duration**   1 year.

**Number awarded**   1 each year.

**Deadline**   January of each year.

## [460]
## NASA UNDERGRADUATE STUDENT RESEARCH PROGRAM

Universities Space Research Association
Attn: NASA USRP Project Administrator
2101 NASA Parkway, AE2 Education Office
Houston, TX 77058
(281) 244-2036                   E-mail: garza@epo.usra.edu
Web: usrp.usra.edu

**Summary**   To provide an opportunity for undergraduate students (particularly female and other students from diverse backgrounds) to participate in a research project at centers of the U.S. National Aeronautics and Space Administration (NASA).

**Eligibility**   This program is open to sophomores, juniors, and seniors enrolled full time at accredited U.S. colleges and universities. Applicants must have a GPA of 3.0 or higher with an academic major or demonstrated course work concentration in engineering, mathematics, computer science, or physical/life sciences. They must be interested in participating in a mentored research experience at a designated NASA center. The program seeks participation from students who represent America's rich and diverse population: female and male students of all races, creeds, colors, national origins, ages, and disabilities. U.S. citizenship is required.

**Financial data**   The stipend is $6,500 for the summer session or $9,500 for the fall or spring semester. Participants also receive round-trip airfare or ground transportation costs to and from the NASA host center.

**Duration**   10 weeks during the summer or 15 weeks during the fall or spring semester.

**Additional information**   The participating NASA centers include Ames Research Center (Moffett Field, California), Dryden Flight Research Center (Edwards, California), Glenn Research Center (Cleveland, Ohio), Goddard Space Flight Center (Greenbelt, Maryland), Jet Propulsion Laboratory (Pasadena, California), Johnson Space Center (Houston, Texas), Kennedy Space Center (Florida), Langley Research Center (Hampton, Virginia), Marshall Space Flight Center (Huntsville, Alabama), Stennis Space Center (Mississippi), Wallops Flight Facility (Virginia), and White Sands Test Facility (Las Cruces, New Mexico).

**Number awarded**   Approximately 330 each year.

**Deadline**   Deadline not specified.

## [461]
## NATHALIE A. PRICE MEMORIAL SCHOLARSHIP

Ocean State Women's Golf Association
P.O. Box 597
Portsmouth, RI 02871-0597
(401) 683-6301                 E-mail: oswgari@aol.com
Web: oswga.org

**Summary**  To provide financial assistance to women in Rhode Island who have played golf and are interested in attending college in any state.

**Eligibility**  This program is open to women in Rhode Island who are graduating high school seniors or current students under 25 years of age at a college or university in any state. Applicants must have been active in golf, as a member of the Ocean State Women's Golf Association (OSWGA), as a member of another association, or on their school golf team. They must have a GPA of 2.5 or higher. Along with their application, they must submit a transcript, a list of their citizenship and community service activities, and letters of recommendation. Financial need is not considered.

**Financial data**  A stipend is awarded (amount not specified).

**Duration**  1 year; may be renewed.

**Additional information**  This program began in 1996.

**Number awarded**  Varies each year; recently, 11 of these scholarships were awarded.

**Deadline**  June of each year.

## [462]
## NATIONAL CO-OP SCHOLARSHIP PROGRAM

World Association for Cooperative Education (WACE)
600 Suffolk Street, Suite 125
Lowell, MA 01854
(978) 934-1870          E-mail: danielle.perry@uml.edu
Web: www.waceinc.edu/scholarship/index.htm

**Summary**  To provide financial assistance to female, minority, and other students participating or planning to participate in cooperative education projects at designated colleges and universities.

**Eligibility**  This program is open to high school seniors and community college transfer students entering 1 of the 10 partner colleges and universities. Applicants must be planning to participate in college cooperative education. They must have a GPA of 3.5 or higher. Along with their application, they must submit a 1-page essay describing why they have chosen to enter a college cooperative education program. Applications are especially encouraged from minorities, women, and students interested in science, mathematics, engineering, and technology. Selection is based on merit; financial need is not considered.

**Financial data**  The stipend is $6,000 per year.

**Duration**  1 year; may be renewed up to 3 additional years or (for some programs) up to 4 additional years.

**Additional information**  The schools recently participating in this program were Clarkson University (Potsdam, New York), Drexel University (Philadelphia, Pennsylvania), Johnson & Wales University (Providence, Rhode Island; Charleston, South Carolina; Norfolk, Virginia; North Miami, Florida; Denver, Colorado; and Charlotte, North Carolina), Kettering University (Flint, Michigan), Rochester Institute of Technology (Rochester, New York), State University of New York at Oswego (Oswego, New York), University of Cincinnati (Cincinnati, Ohio), University of Massachusetts at Lowell, University of Toledo (Toledo, Ohio), and Wentworth Institute of Technology (Boston, Massachusetts). Applications must be sent directly to the college or university.

**Number awarded**  Varies each year; recently, 195 of these scholarships were awarded: 10 at Clarkson, 30 at Drexel, 30 at Johnson & Wales, 20 at Kettering, 15 at Rochester Tech, 15 at SUNY Oswego, 15 at Cincinnati, 15 at UM Lowell, 15 at Toledo, and 30 at Wentworth Tech.

**Deadline**  February of each year.

## [463]
## NATIONAL HISPANIC BUSINESS WOMEN ASSOCIATION EDUCATIONAL SCHOLARSHIPS

National Hispanic Business Women Association
2024 North Broadway, Suite 100
Santa Ana, CA 92706
(714) 836-4042
Web: nationalhbwa.com/main/?page_id=367

**Summary**  To provide financial assistance to women in California who are working on an undergraduate or graduate degree at a school in any state and submit an essay related to Latinas in education.

**Eligibility**  This program is open to female residents of California who are currently enrolled as undergraduate or graduate students at a school in any state. Applicants must have a GPA of 3.0 or higher and be able to demonstrate financial need. They must also have a record of participation in some form of community service. Along with their application, they must submit 2 essays of 2 pages each on 1) their academic and professional goals; and 2) the importance or value of obtaining a higher education, the potential impacts or influences of a growing Latino population in relation to their field of interest, or the specific challenges faced by Latinas in pursuit of higher education.

**Financial data**  Stipends range from $500 to $1,000.

**Duration**  1 year.

**Number awarded**  Varies each year; recently, 13 of these scholarships were awarded.

**Deadline**  March of each year.

## [464]
## NATIONAL NETWORK OF PRESBYTERIAN COLLEGE WOMEN SCHOLARSHIP

Presbyterian Church (USA)
Attn: National Network of Presbyterian College Women
100 Witherspoon Street
Louisville, KY 40202-1396
(502) 569-5848          Toll Free: (800) 728-7228, ext. 5848
E-mail: HyoJin.Kang@pcusa.org
Web: www.presbyterianmission.org

**Summary**  To provide financial assistance to undergraduate women who are involved in a Christian church or campus ministry.

**Eligibility**  This program is open to women between 18 and 25 years of age who are currently enrolled as an undergraduate at an accredited college or university in the United States. Applicants must be members of the National Network of Presbyterian College Women and involved in a Christian church or campus ministry. Along with their application, they must submit essays of 300 to 400 words on 1) how their faith informs their studies and vocational choice; and 2) how they have integrated a commitment to feminism as part of their past and future activism on campus. Financial need is considered in the selection process.

**Financial data**   The stipend is $1,500.

**Duration**   1 year; nonrenewable.

**Number awarded**   1 each year.

**Deadline**   April of each year.

## [465]
## NATIONAL ORGANIZATION OF ITALIAN AMERICAN WOMEN SCHOLARSHIPS

National Organization of Italian American Women
25 West 43rd Street, Suite 1005
New York, NY 10036
(212) 642-2003         Fax: (212) 642-2006
E-mail: noiaw@noiaw.org
Web: www.noiaw.org

**Summary**   To provide financial assistance for college or graduate school to women of Italian descent.

**Eligibility**   This program is open to women who have at least 1 parent of Italian American descent and are working on an associate, bachelor's, or master's degree. Applicants must be enrolled full time and have a GPA of 3.5 or higher. Along with their application, they must submit a 2-page essay on how being an Italian American has impacted them personally and professionally. Financial need is considered in the selection process.

**Financial data**   The stipend is $2,000.

**Duration**   1 year; nonrenewable.

**Additional information**   A processing fee of $25 must accompany the application.

**Number awarded**   5 each year, including 1 reserved for an undergraduate or graduate student at the City University of New York system.

**Deadline**   March of each year.

## [466]
## NATIONAL PATHFINDER SCHOLARSHIPS

National Federation of Republican Women
Attn: Scholarships and Internships
124 North Alfred Street
Alexandria, VA 22314-3011
(703) 548-9688         Fax: (703) 548-9836
E-mail: mail@nfrw.org
Web: www.nfrw.org/programs/scholarships.htm

**Summary**   To provide financial assistance for college or graduate school to Republican women.

**Eligibility**   This program is open to women currently enrolled as college sophomores, juniors, seniors, or master's degree students. Recent high school graduates and first-year college women are not eligible. Applicants must submit 3 letters of recommendation, an official transcript, a 1-page essay on why they should be considered for the scholarship, and a 1-page essay on career goals. Applications must be submitted to the Republican federation president in the applicant's state. Each president chooses 1 application from her state to submit for scholarship consideration. Financial need is not a factor in the selection process. U.S. citizenship is required.

**Financial data**   The stipend is $2,500.

**Duration**   1 year; nonrenewable.

**Additional information**   This program, previously named the Nancy Reagan Pathfinder Scholarships, was established in 1985.

**Number awarded**   3 each year.

**Deadline**   Applications must be submitted to the state federation president by May of each year.

## [467]
## NATIONAL PRESS CLUB SCHOLARSHIP FOR JOURNALISM DIVERSITY

National Press Club
Attn: Executive Director's Office
529 14th Street, N.W., 13th Floor
Washington, DC 20045
(202) 662-7599
Web: www.press.org/about/students

**Summary**   To provide funding to high school seniors who are planning to major in journalism in college and will bring diversity to the field.

**Eligibility**   This program is open to high school seniors who have been accepted to college and plan to prepare for a career in journalism. Applicants must submit 1) a 500-word essay explaining how they would add diversity to U.S. journalism; 2) up to 5 work samples demonstrating an ongoing interest in journalism through work on a high school newspaper or other media; 3) letters of recommendation from 3 people; 4) a copy of their high school transcript; 5) documentation of financial need; 6) a letter of acceptance from the college or university of their choice; and 7) a brief description of how they have pursued journalism in high school.

**Financial data**   The stipend is $2,000 for the first year and $2,500 for each subsequent year. The program also provides an additional $500 book stipend, designated the Ellen Masin Persina Scholarship, for the first year.

**Duration**   4 years.

**Additional information**   The program began in 1990.

**Number awarded**   1 each year.

**Deadline**   February of each year.

## [468]
## NATIONAL SORORITY OF PHI DELTA KAPPA SCHOLARSHIPS

National Sorority of Phi Delta Kappa, Inc.
Attn: Perpetual Scholarship Foundation
8233 South King Drive
Chicago, IL 60619
(773) 783-7379         Fax: (773) 783-7354
E-mail: nspdkhq@aol.com

**Summary**   To provide financial assistance to African American high school seniors interested in studying education in college (females and males compete separately).

**Eligibility**   This program is open to African American high school seniors who are interested in working on a 4-year college degree in education. Men and women compete separately. Financial need is considered in the selection process.

**Financial data**   The stipend is $1,500 per year.

**Duration**   4 years, provided the recipient maintains a GPA of 2.5 or higher and a major in education.

**Additional information** The sponsor was founded in 1923 as an organization of female African American educators.

**Number awarded** 10 each year: 1 male and 1 female in each of the organization's 5 regions.

**Deadline** Applications must be submitted to a local chapter of the organization by January of each year.

## [469]
## NATIONAL SPACE GRANT COLLEGE AND FELLOWSHIP PROGRAM

National Aeronautics and Space Administration
Attn: Office of Education
300 E Street, S.W.
Mail Suite 6M35
Washington, DC 20546-0001
(202) 358-1069                    Fax: (202) 358-7097
E-mail: Diane.D.DeTroye@nasa.gov
Web: www.nasa.gov

**Summary** To provide financial assistance to undergraduate and graduate students (particularly women, underrepresented minorities, and persons with disabilities) interested in preparing for a career in a space-related field.

**Eligibility** This program is open to undergraduate and graduate students at colleges and universities that participate in the National Space Grant program of the U.S. National Aeronautics and Space Administration (NASA) through their state consortium. Applicants must be interested in a program of study and/or research in a field of science, technology, engineering, or mathematics (STEM) related to space. A specific goal of the program is to recruit and train U.S. citizens, especially underrepresented minorities, women, and persons with disabilities, for careers in aerospace science and technology. Financial need is not considered in the selection process.

**Financial data** Each consortium establishes the terms of the fellowship program in its state.

**Duration** 1 year; may be renewed.

**Additional information** NASA established the Space Grant program in 1989. It operates through 52 consortia in each state, the District of Columbia, and Puerto Rico. Each consortium includes selected colleges and universities in that state as well as other affiliates from industry, museums, science centers, and state and local agencies.

**Number awarded** Varies each year.

**Deadline** Each consortium sets its own deadlines.

## [470]
## NATIONAL STRENGTH AND CONDITIONING ASSOCIATION WOMEN'S SCHOLARSHIPS

National Strength and Conditioning Association
Attn: Grants and Scholarships Program
1885 Bob Johnson Drive
Colorado Springs, CO 80906-4000
(719) 632-6722, ext. 152        Toll Free: (800) 815-6826
Fax: (719) 632-6367        E-mail: foundation@nsca-lift.org
Web: www.nsca-lift.org/Foundation/grants-and-scholarships

**Summary** To provide financial assistance to women who are interested in working on an undergraduate or graduate degree in strength training and conditioning.

**Eligibility** This program is open to women who are 17 years of age or older. Applicants must have been accepted into an accredited postsecondary institution to work on an undergraduate or graduate degree in the strength and conditioning field. Along with their application, they must submit a 500-word essay on their personal and professional goals and how receiving this scholarship will assist them in achieving those goals. Selection is based on that essay, academic achievement, strength and conditioning experience, honors and awards, community involvement, letters of recommendation, and involvement in the National Strength and Conditioning Association (NSCA).

**Financial data** The stipend is $1,500.

**Duration** 1 year.

**Additional information** The NSCA is a nonprofit organization of strength and conditioning professionals, including coaches, athletic trainers, physical therapists, educators, researchers, and physicians. This program was first offered in 2003.

**Number awarded** Varies each year; recently, 12 of these scholarships were awarded.

**Deadline** March of each year.

## [471]
## NATIVE DAUGHTERS OF THE GOLDEN WEST SCHOLARSHIP PROGRAM

Native Daughters of the Golden West
Attn: Education and Scholarships
543 Baker Street
San Francisco, CA 94117-1405
(415) 563-9091        Toll Free: (800) 994-NDGW
Fax: (415) 563-5230        E-mail: ndgwgpo@att.net
Web: www.ndgw.org/edu.htm

**Summary** To provide financial assistance for college to members of the Native Daughters of the Golden West (NDGW) in California and their families.

**Eligibility** This program is open to members and their children who are attending or planning to attend an accredited university, college, or vocational school in California. Applicants must have been born in the state and be sponsored by a local parlor of the NDGW.

**Financial data** A stipend is awarded (amount not specified).

**Duration** 1 year; may be renewed if the recipient maintains a GPA of 3.0 or higher.

**Additional information** This program includes the Annie L. Adair Scholarship and the Sue J. Irwin Scholarship.

**Number awarded** Varies each year; recently, 4 of these scholarships were awarded.

**Deadline** April of each year.

## [472]
## NAVY/MARINE CORPS/COAST GUARD ENLISTED DEPENDENT SPOUSE SCHOLARSHIP

Navy Wives Clubs of America
c/o NSA Mid-South
P.O. Box 54022
Millington, TN 38054-0022
Toll Free: (866) 511-NWCA
E-mail: nwca@navywivesclubsofamerica.org
Web: www.navywivesclubsofamerica.org/scholarships

**Summary** To provide financial assistance for undergraduate or graduate study to spouses of naval personnel.

**Eligibility** This program is open to the spouses of active-duty Navy, Marine Corps, or Coast Guard members who can demonstrate financial need. Applicants must be 1) a high school graduate or senior planning to attend college full time next year; 2) currently enrolled in an undergraduate program and planning to continue as a full-time undergraduate; 3) a college graduate or senior planning to be a full-time graduate student next year; or 4) a high school graduate or GED recipient planning to attend vocational or business school next year. Along with their application, they must submit a brief statement on why they feel they should be awarded this scholarship and any special circumstances (financial or other) they wish to have considered. Financial need is also considered in the selection process.

**Financial data** The stipends range from $500 to $1,000 each year (depending upon the donations from chapters of the Navy Wives Clubs of America).

**Duration** 1 year.

**Number awarded** 1 or more each year.

**Deadline** May of each year.

## [473]
## NCAIAW SCHOLARSHIP

North Carolina Alliance for Athletics, Health, Physical Education, Recreation and Dance
Attn: Executive Director
1030 Washington Street
Raleigh, NC 27605
(919) 833-1219              Toll Free: (888) 840-6500
Fax: (888) 840-6FAX        E-mail: awards@ncaahperd.org
Web: www.ncaahperd.org/awards.html

**Summary** To provide financial assistance to women who are undergraduates involved in sports at an institution that is a member of the former North Carolina Association of Intercollegiate Athletics for Women (NCAIAW).

**Eligibility** This program is open to women who have been a participant on 1 or more varsity athletic teams either as a player or in the support role of manager, trainer, etc. Applicants must be attending 1 of the following former NCAIAW colleges or universities in North Carolina: Appalachian State, Belmont Abbey, Bennett, Campbell, Davidson, Duke, East Carolina, Gardner-Webb, High Point, Mars Hill, Meredith, North Carolina A&T, North Carolina State, Pembroke State, Salem, University of North Carolina at Ashville, University of North Carolina at Chapel Hill, University of North Carolina at Charlotte, University of North Carolina at Wilmington, Wake Forest, or Western Carolina. They must be majoring in health, physical education, recreation, and/or dance; be able to demonstrate high standards of scholarship; and show evidence of leadership potential (as indicated by participation in school and community activities).

**Financial data** The stipend is $1,000. Funds are sent to the recipient's school.

**Duration** 1 year.

**Additional information** This scholarship was established in 1983 when the NCAIAW dissolved and transferred its assets to the North Carolina Alliance for Athletics, Health, Physical Education, Recreation and Dance.

**Number awarded** 1 each year.

**Deadline** June of each year.

## [474]
## NEBRASKA RURAL COMMUNITY SCHOOLS ASSOCIATION SCHOLARSHIPS

Nebraska Rural Community Schools Association
Attn: Executive Director
455 South 11th Street, Suite B
Lincoln, NE 68508
(402) 440-4378              Fax: (402) 476-7740
E-mail: jhabben@nrcsa.net
Web: www.nrcsa.net/about/scholarshipsandawards.htm

**Summary** To provide financial assistance to seniors at high schools in Nebraska that are members of the Nebraska Rural Community Schools Association (NRCSA) who plan to attend college in the state and work on a degree in the field of education (females and males are considered separately).

**Eligibility** This program is open to seniors graduating from high schools that are NRCSA members. Applicants must have a GPA of 3.5 or higher, and either a composite ACT score of 22 or higher or a combined SAT mathematics and critical reading score of 1030 or higher. They must be planning to attend a college or university in Nebraska and prepare for a career as a teacher, media specialist, counselor, or other position related to education. Selection is based on academic achievement, level of involvement in activities, student goals, leadership, character, initiative, school and community involvement, quality and neatness of the application, and financial need. Males and females are considered separately.

**Financial data** The stipend is $1,000.

**Duration** 1 year.

**Additional information** This program is sponsored by NRCSA.

**Number awarded** 8 each year: 4 to females and 4 to males.

**Deadline** January of each year.

## [475]
## NETWORK OF EXECUTIVE WOMEN SCHOLARSHIP

Network of Executive Women
c/o Nathalia Granger, Director of Operations
Accenture
161 North Clark Street, 38th Floor
Chicago, IL 60601
(312) 693-6855              Fax: (312) 726-4704
E-mail: ngranger@newonline.org
Web: www.newonline.org

**Summary** To provide financial assistance to upper-division and graduate student women preparing for a career in the consumer products and retail industry.

**Eligibility** This program is open to women enrolled full time as juniors, seniors, or graduate students in a retail, food, or consumer packaged goods-related program at a U.S. college or university. Applicants must have a GPA of 3.0 or higher. Along with their application, they must submit a 1-page essay explaining why they merit this scholarship and outlining their food, retail, or consumer packaged goods industry interests. Selection is based on that essay, a current resume, a transcript, and 2 letters of recommendation; financial need is not considered. U.S. citizenship is required.

**Financial data** The stipend is $5,000.

**Duration** 1 year.

**Number awarded** Varies each year; recently, 5 of these scholarships were awarded.

**Deadline** April of each year.

## [476]
## NEW HORIZONS LEADER SCHOLARSHIP

Royal Neighbors of America
Attn: Fraternal Services
230 16th Street
Rock Island, IL 61201-8645
(309) 788-4561     Toll Free: (800) 627-4762
E-mail: contact@royalneighbors.org
Web: www.royalneighbors.org

**Summary** To provide financial assistance to women who are members of the Royal Neighbors of America and interested in attending college.

**Eligibility** This program is open to female beneficial members of the society who are 18 years of age or older and planning to enroll as a full- or part-time student at an accredited college, university, or junior college. They must have previously graduated from high school.

**Financial data** The stipend is $5,000 per year.

**Duration** 1 year; may be renewed up to 3 additional years.

**Number awarded** 1 each year.

**Deadline** Requests for applications must be submitted by December of each year.

## [477]
## NEW IMMIGRANT SCHOLARSHIPS

Presbyterian Church (USA)
Attn: National Network of Presbyterian College Women
100 Witherspoon Street
Louisville, KY 40202-1396
(502) 569-5848     Toll Free: (800) 728-7228, ext. 5848
E-mail: HyoJin.Kang@pcusa.org
Web: www.presbyterianmission.org

**Summary** To provide financial assistance to undergraduate women who are recent immigrants and involved in a Christian church.

**Eligibility** This program is open to women between 18 and 25 years of age who are entering or enrolled as an undergraduate at an accredited college, university, or trade school in the United States. Applicants must be new immigrants to the United States, defined as a noncitizen who has been living in the country for 5 years or less. They must be involved in and with a Christian church, preferably the Presbyterian Church (USA). Along with their application, they must submit essays of 300 to 400 words on 1) how their faith informs their studies and vocational choice; and 2) how they have integrated a commitment to feminism as part of their past and future activism on campus. Financial need is considered in the selection process.

**Financial data** The stipend is $1,500 per year.

**Duration** 1 year; may be renewed 1 additional year.

**Number awarded** 1 each year.

**Deadline** April of each year.

## [478]
## NEW JERSEY SCHOOLWOMEN'S CLUB SCHOLARSHIPS

New Jersey Schoolwomen's Club
c/o Arlene Rogers
13 Ryerson Drive
Hamilton, NJ 08690

**Summary** To provide financial assistance to female high school seniors in New Jersey who plan to attend college in any state to prepare for a career in education.

**Eligibility** This program is open to women graduating from high schools in New Jersey who plan to attend a college or university in any state to work on a baccalaureate degree and certification in education. Applicants must have a GPA of 2.5 or higher and scores of at least 1460 on the SAT or 24 on the ACT. Along with their application, they must submit 500-word essays on why they have chosen the field of education as a career, what they anticipate their area of concentration will be, and the contributions they expect to make to their students and to the profession during their career. Financial need is not considered in the selection process.

**Financial data** Stipends are $1,000 or $500.

**Duration** 1 year.

**Additional information** This program includes the Jeannette Hodge Scholarship and the Patricia Barber Scholarship.

**Number awarded** 4 each year: 2 at $1,000 (the 2 named scholarships) and 2 at $500.

**Deadline** February of each year.

## [479]
## NEW JERSEY STATE ELKS SPECIAL CHILDREN'S SCHOLARSHIP

New Jersey State Elks
Attn: Special Children's Committee
665 Rahway Avenue
P.O. Box 1596
Woodbridge, NJ 07095-1596
(732) 326-1300     E-mail: info@njelks.org
Web: www.njelks.org

**Summary** To provide financial assistance to high school seniors in New Jersey (girls and boys are judged separately) who have a disability and plan to attend college in any state.

**Eligibility** This program is open to seniors graduating from high schools in New Jersey who have a disability. Applicants must be planning to attend a college or university in any state. Selection is based on academic standing, general worthiness, and financial need. Boys and girls are judged separately.

**Financial data** The stipend is $2,500 per year. Funds are paid directly to the recipient's college or university.

**Duration** 4 years.

**Number awarded** 2 each year: 1 to a boy and 1 to a girl.

**Deadline** April of each year.

## [480]
## NEW JERSEY SWE SCHOLARSHIP

Society of Women Engineers
Attn: Scholarship Selection Committee
203 North LaSalle Street, Suite 1675
Chicago, IL 60601-1269
(312) 596-5223          Toll Free: (877) SWE-INFO
Fax: (312) 644-8557     E-mail: scholarships@swe.org
Web: societyofwomenengineers.swe.org

**Summary**  To provide financial assistance to women from New Jersey who will be entering freshmen at a college in any state and are interested in studying engineering or computer science.

**Eligibility**  This program is open to women who are entering college in any state as freshmen with a GPA of 3.5 or higher. Applicants must be residents of New Jersey planning to enroll full time at an ABET-accredited 4-year college or university in any state and major in computer science or engineering. Selection is based on merit.

**Financial data**  The stipend is $2,000.

**Duration**  1 year.

**Additional information**  This program began in 1998 by the New Jersey Section of the Society of Women Engineers (SWE).

**Number awarded**  1 each year.

**Deadline**  May of each year.

## [481]
## NEW JERSEY UTILITIES ASSOCIATION EXCELLENCE IN DIVERSITY SCHOLARSHIPS

New Jersey Utilities Association
50 West State Street, Suite 1117
Trenton, NJ 08608
(609) 392-1000          Fax: (609) 396-4231
E-mail: info@njua.com
Web: www.njua.com/html/njua_eeo_scholarship.cfm

**Summary**  To provide financial assistance to female, minority, and disabled high school seniors in New Jersey interested in attending college in any state.

**Eligibility**  This program is open to seniors graduating from high schools in New Jersey who are women, minorities (Black or African American, Hispanic or Latino, American Indian or Alaska Native, Asian, Native Hawaiian or Pacific Islander, or 2 or more races), and persons with disabilities. Applicants must be planning to work on a bachelor's degree at a college or university in any state. Along with their application, they must submit a 500-word essay explaining their career ambition and why they have chosen that career. Children of employees of any New Jersey Utilities Association-member company are ineligible. Selection is based on overall academic excellence and demonstrated financial need. U.S. citizenship or permanent resident status is required.

**Financial data**  The stipend is $1,500 per year. Funds are paid to the recipient's college or university.

**Duration**  4 years.

**Number awarded**  2 each year.

**Deadline**  March of each year.

## [482]
## NEW MEXICO ELKS ASSOCIATION CHARITABLE AND BENEVOLENT TRUST SCHOLARSHIPS

New Mexico Elks Association
Attn: Charitable and Benevolent Trust Commission
c/o Barbara Venturi, Scholarship Committee
407 Peggy Lane
Las Vegas, NM 87701
(505) 425-3110          Fax: (505) 425-6181
E-mail: bdvent@msn.com
Web: nmelks.org/projects.asp?WCI=scholars

**Summary**  To provide financial assistance for college to high school seniors in New Mexico (some awards are only for women).

**Eligibility**  Applicants must be seniors graduating from a high school in New Mexico. They must have exhibited outstanding scholastic and leadership ability, including extracurricular and civic activities. High school class rank, GPA, and standardized test scores must be validated by a school official. An endorsement from the local Elks Lodge is required. Financial need is also considered in the selection process. Some awards are designated for females and some for males.

**Financial data**  Stipends are either $2,000 or $1,000 per year.

**Duration**  1 or 4 years.

**Additional information**  Recipients may attend any level of academic institution and may major in any field. This program includes the following named awards: the Charles Mahr Memorial Scholarship, the Evelyn Boney Memorial Scholarships, the Howard Medlin Memorial Scholarship, and the Robert E. Boney Memorial Scholarship.

**Number awarded**  Varies each year; recently, 26 of these scholarships were awarded: 1 at $2,000 per year for 4 years to the top female applicant, 1 at $2,000 per year for 4 years to the top male applicant, 12 at $2,000 for 1 year (6 for females and 6 for males), and 12 at $1,000 for 1 year (6 for females and 6 for males).

**Deadline**  Applications must be submitted to local Elks Lodges by March of each year.

## [483]
## NEW MEXICO FEDERATION OF REPUBLICAN WOMEN SCHOLARSHIPS

New Mexico Federation of Republican Women
c/o Diana Billingsley, Scholarship Committee Chair
P.O. Box 987
Alto, NM 88312
(575) 336-7038          E-mail: dianalb@valornet.com
Web: nmfrw.com

**Summary**  To provide financial assistance for college in New Mexico to women who reside in the state and are Republicans or daughters of Republicans.

**Eligibility**  This program is open to women who are residents of New Mexico and either high school seniors or students already enrolled full time at a college, university, or vocational school in the state. Applicants must be registered Republicans or, if younger than 18 years of age, daughters of registered Republicans. They must have a GPA of 3.0 or higher and majoring or planning to major in government, history, international relations, or political science. Special consideration is given to students who have participated in political activities.

**Financial data** Stipends are $1,000 or $500.

**Duration** 1 year.

**Number awarded** 2 each year: 1 at $1,000 and 1 at $500.

**Deadline** March of each year.

## [484]
## NFMC BIENNIAL STUDENT/COLLEGIATE AUDITION AWARDS

National Federation of Music Clubs
1646 Smith Valley Road
Greenwood, IN 46142
(317) 882-4003                    Fax: (317) 882-4019
E-mail: info@nfmc-music.org
Web: nfmc-music.org

**Summary** To recognize and reward outstanding student musicians (some awards are only for women) who are members of the National Federation of Music Clubs (NFMC).

**Eligibility** This competition is open to instrumentalists and vocalists between 19 and 26 years of age. Student membership in the federation and U.S. citizenship are required. Competition categories include: women's voice, men's voice, piano, organ, harp, classical guitar, violin, viola, cello, double bass, orchestral woodwinds, orchestral brass, and percussion. Awards are presented at the national level after auditions at the state and district levels.

**Financial data** The winner in each category is awarded $1,100.

**Duration** The competition is held biennially, in odd-numbered years.

**Additional information** Students who enter this competition are also automatically considered for a number of supplemental awards. The entry fee is $30 for each category.

**Number awarded** 13 each year: 1 in each category.

**Deadline** January of odd-numbered years.

## [485]
## NFWL/NRA BILL OF RIGHTS ESSAY CONTEST

National Foundation for Women Legislators, Inc.
910 16th Street, N.W., Suite 100
Washington, DC 20006
(202) 293-3040                    Fax: (202) 293-5430
E-mail: events@womenlegislators.org
Web: www.womenlegistors.org

**Summary** To recognize and reward, with college scholarships, the best essays written by female high school juniors or seniors on a topic related to the Bill of Rights.

**Eligibility** This competition is open to female high school juniors or seniors. Applicants are invited to write an essay of 400 to 600 words on a topic (changes annually) related to the Bill of Rights; recently, the topic related to the impact public policies have on women and historically underrepresented populations as they are decided at the state versus federal level. In addition to the essay, candidates must submit 2 personal reference letters.

**Financial data** Each winner receives a $3,000 unrestricted scholarship to use toward college tuition at any U.S. college or university and an all-expense paid trip to the foundation's annual conference.

**Duration** The competition is held annually.

**Additional information** This essay competition is sponsored jointly by the National Foundation of Women Legislators (NFWL) and the National Rifle Association (NRA).

**Number awarded** Varies each year; recently, 7 of these scholarships were awarded.

**Deadline** June of each year.

## [486]
## NINA BELLE REDDITT MEMORIAL SCHOLARSHIP

American Business Women's Association-Pirate Charter
    Chapter
Attn: Scholarship Program
P.O. Box 20498
Greenville, NC 27858
E-mail: pirateabwascholarship@yahoo.com
Web: pirateabwa.org/scholarship.html

**Summary** To provide financial assistance to female residents of North Carolina interested in working on an undergraduate or graduate degree at a school in the state.

**Eligibility** This program is open to women who are residents of North Carolina and U.S. citizens. Applicants must be graduating high school seniors, undergraduates, or graduate students and have a GPA of 2.5 or higher. They must be attending or planning to attend an accredited college, university, community college, or technical/vocational school in North Carolina. Along with their application, they must submit a 2-page biographical sketch that includes information about their background, school activities, outside interests, honors and awards, work experience, community service, and long-term goals. Financial need is not considered in the selection process.

**Financial data** The stipend is $5,000.

**Duration** 1 year.

**Additional information** This program began in 1978.

**Number awarded** 2 each year.

**Deadline** May of each year.

## [487]
## NORMA ROSS WALTER SCHOLARSHIP PROGRAM

Willa Cather Pioneer Memorial and Educational
    Foundation
Attn: Scholarship Program
413 North Webster
Red Cloud, NE 68970
(402) 746-2653                    Toll Free: (866) 731-7304
Fax: (402) 746-2652
Web: www.willacather.org/education/scholarships

**Summary** To provide financial assistance to female graduates of Nebraska high schools who are or will be majoring in English at an accredited college or university in any state.

**Eligibility** This program is open to women who have graduated or plan to graduate from a Nebraska high school and enter a college or university in any state as a first-year student. Applicants must plan to continue their education as English majors (journalism is not acceptable). Along with their application, they must submit a 1,500-word essay on several of the short stories or a novel written by Willa Cather. Selection is based on intellectual promise, creativity, and character.

**Financial data** Stipends are $2,000, $1,000, or $500.

**Duration** 1 year; nonrenewable.

**Number awarded** 3 each year: 1 each at $2,000, $1,000, and $500.

**Deadline** January of each year.

## [488]
## NORTH CAROLINA BUSINESS AND PROFESSIONAL WOMEN'S FOUNDATION SCHOLARSHIPS

North Carolina Federation of Business and Professional
Women's Club, Inc.
Attn: BPW/NC Foundation
175 BPW Club Road
P.O. Box 276
Carrboro, NC 27510
Web: www.bpw-nc.org/Default.aspx?pageId=837230

**Summary** To provide financial assistance to women attending North Carolina colleges, community colleges, or graduate schools.

**Eligibility** This program is open to women who are currently enrolled in a community college, 4-year college, or graduate school in North Carolina. Applicants must be endorsed by a local BPW unit. Along with their application, they must submit a 1-page statement that summarizes their career goals, previous honors, or community activities and justifies their need for this scholarship. U.S. citizenship is required.

**Financial data** The stipend is $1,000. Funds are paid directly to the recipient's school.

**Duration** 1 year; recipients may reapply.

**Additional information** This program began in 1996.

**Number awarded** 2 each year: 1 for an undergraduate and 1 for a graduate student.

**Deadline** April of each year.

## [489]
## NORTH DAKOTA WOMEN'S OPPORTUNITY SCHOLARSHIP FUND

North Dakota Council on Abused Women's Services
Attn: Scholarship Review Committee
525 North Fourth Street
Bismarck, ND 58501
(701) 255-6240          Toll Free: (888) 255-6240
Fax: (701) 255-1904
Web: www.ndcaws.org/what_we_do/scholarships

**Summary** To provide financial assistance to women in North Dakota who are interested in attending a college or university in the state.

**Eligibility** This program is open to female residents of North Dakota who are enrolled or planning to enroll full time at a college, university, or certification program in the state. Applicants must be able to demonstrate income lower than established financial guidelines for 125% of poverty. Along with their application, they must submit an essay of 500 to 1,000 words on their motivation for attending college and their plans for the future. Priority is given to 1) first-time students and current students in special circumstances that may prevent them from completing a pending degree or program; and 2) students who may not be eligible for sources of funding normally available to low-income applicants.

**Financial data** A stipend is awarded (amount not specified).

**Duration** 1 year; may be renewed.

**Number awarded** Varies each year.

**Deadline** June of each year.

## [490]
## NORTH POINTE JUNIOR GOLD CHAMPIONSHIPS

United States Bowling Congress
Attn: Junior Gold Program
621 Six Flags Drive
Arlington, TX 76011
(817) 385-8426          Toll Free: (800) 514-BOWL, ext. 3171
Fax: (817) 385-8262   E-mail: USBCjuniorgold@bowl.com
Web: www.bowl.com

**Summary** To recognize and reward, with college scholarships, United States Bowling Congress (USBC) Junior Gold program members who achieve high scores in a national competition (females and males compete separately).

**Eligibility** This program is open to USBC members who qualify for the Junior Gold program by achieving top scores in qualifying events. Competitions for Junior Gold members are held throughout the season at bowling centers and in bowling leagues in the United States. Each approved competition may enter its top scorers in the Junior Gold Championships, held annually at a site in the United States. Competitions are held in 4 categories: boys from 12 to 15 years of age, girls from 12 to 15 years of age, boys from 16 through 20, and girls from 16 through 20. Scholarships are awarded solely on the basis of bowling performance in the national tournament.

**Financial data** Awards, in the form of college scholarships, vary each year, depending on the availability of funding from sponsors. Recently, in the boys under 15 division, stipends ranged from $250 to $6,000; in the girls under 15 division from $200 to $5,000; in the boys under 20 division from $200 to $15,000; and in the girls under 20 division from $200 to $10,000.

**Duration** The competition is held annually.

**Additional information** This competition was first held in 1998 and was previously known as the USBC Junior Gold Championships. The sponsoring league or center must pay a fee of $200 for each participant in the under 20 category or $150 in the under 15 category who advances to the national tournament.

**Number awarded** The number of scholarships depends on the number of participants in each category; recently, 32 boys under 15, 24 girls under 15, 150 boys under 20, and 81 girls under 20 won scholarships.

**Deadline** Applications must be submitted by May of each year. The national finals are held in July.

## [491]
## NORTHROP GRUMMAN FOUNDATION SCHOLARSHIP

Society of Women Engineers
Attn: Scholarship Selection Committee
203 North LaSalle Street, Suite 1675
Chicago, IL 60601-1269
(312) 596-5223          Toll Free: (877) SWE-INFO
Fax: (312) 644-8557     E-mail: scholarships@swe.org
Web: societyofwomenengineers.swe.org

**Summary** To provide financial assistance to female undergraduates at designated universities who are interested in studying specified fields of engineering.

**Eligibility** This program is open to women who entering their sophomore, junior, or senior year as a full time student at a designated ABET-accredited 4-year college or university. Applicants must have a GPA of 3.0 or higher and be majoring in computer science or aerospace, computer, electrical, industrial, mechanical, or systems engineering. Selection is based on merit. U.S. citizenship or permanent resident status is required.

**Financial data** The stipend is $5,000.

**Duration** 1 year.

**Additional information** This program, established in 1983, is sponsored by Northrup Grumman. Check the Society of Women Engineers web site for the list of designated universities.

**Number awarded** 5 each year.

**Deadline** February of each year.

## [492]
## NORTHWEST WOMEN IN EDUCATIONAL ADMINISTRATION SCHOLARSHIP

Confederation of Oregon School Administrators
Attn: Youth Development Program
707 13th Street, S.E., Suite 100
Salem, OR 97301-4035
(503) 581-3141          Fax: (503) 581-9840
Web: www.cosa.k12.or.us

**Summary** To provide financial assistance to women who are high school seniors in Oregon and interested in preparing for a teaching career at a community college, college, or university in the state.

**Eligibility** This program is open to women who are graduating from high schools in Oregon. Applicants must be interested in attending a community college, college, or university in the state to major in education. They must have been active in community and school affairs, have a GPA of 3.5 or higher, and be able to enroll in the fall term after graduating from high school. Along with their application, they must submit a 1-page statement on their background, influences, and goals. Financial need is not considered in the selection process.

**Financial data** The stipend is $1,000. Funds are paid directly to the recipient.

**Duration** 1 year; nonrenewable.

**Additional information** This program is offered through Northwest Women in Educational Administration.

**Number awarded** 2 each year.

**Deadline** February of each year.

## [493]
## NSPE AUXILIARY LEGACY SCHOLARSHIP

National Society of Professional Engineers
Attn: NSPE Educational Foundation
1420 King Street
Alexandria, VA 22314-2794
(703) 684-2833          Toll Free: (888) 285-NSPE
Fax: (703) 836-4875     E-mail: education@nspe.org
Web: www.nspe.org/Students/Scholarships/index.html

**Summary** To provide financial assistance to female members of the National Society of Professional Engineers (NSPE) who are entering their junior year at a college or university in any state.

**Eligibility** This program is open to women who are NSPE student members entering their junior year in an ABET-accredited engineering program. Applicants must submit a 500-word essay on their engineering career goals and aspirations and their plans to achieve them. Selection is based on that essay, GPA, internship and co-op experience, involvement in other activities, 2 faculty recommendations, and honors and awards since high school. U.S. citizenship is required.

**Financial data** The stipend is $2,000; funds are paid directly to the recipient's institution.

**Duration** 1 year.

**Number awarded** 1 each year.

**Deadline** February of each year.

## [494]
## NYWICI FOUNDATION SCHOLARSHIPS

New York Women in Communications, Inc.
Attn: NYWICI Foundation
355 Lexington Avenue, 15th Floor
New York, NY 10017-6603
(212) 297-2133          Fax: (212) 370-9047
E-mail: nywicipr@nywici.org
Web: www.nywici.org/foundation/scholarships

**Summary** To provide financial assistance to female residents of designated eastern states who are interested in preparing for a career in communications at a college or graduate school in any state.

**Eligibility** This program is open to women who are seniors graduating from high schools in New York, New Jersey, Connecticut, or Pennsylvania or undergraduate or graduate students who are permanent residents of those states; they must be attending or planning to attend a college or university in any state. Graduate students must be members of New York Women in Communications, Inc. (NYWICI). Also eligible are women who reside outside the 4 states but are currently enrolled at a college or university within 1 of the 5 boroughs of New York City. All applicants must be working on a degree in a communications-related field (e.g., advertising, broadcasting, communications, English, film, journalism, marketing, new media, public relations) and have a GPA of 3.2 or higher. Along with their application, they must submit a 2-page resume; a personal essay of 300 words on an assigned topic that changes annually; 2 letters of recommendation; and an official transcript. Selection is based on academic record, need, demonstrated leadership, participation in school and community activities, honors and other awards or recognition, work experience, goals and aspirations, and unusual personal and/or family circumstances. U.S. citizenship is required.

**Financial data** The maximum stipend is $10,000.

**Duration** 1 year; recipients may reapply.

**Number awarded** Varies each year; recently, 9 of these scholarships were awarded.

**Deadline** January of each year.

## [495]
## OHIO COUNCIL 8 AFSCME SCHOLARSHIPS

American Federation of State, County and Municipal
  Employees-Ohio Council 8
6800 North High Street
Worthington, OH 43085-2512
(614) 841-1918                    Fax: (614) 841-1299
Web: www.afscmecouncil8.org/node/1620

**Summary** To provide financial assistance to the children of members of Ohio Council 8 of the American Federation of State, County and Municipal Employees (AFSCME) who are high school seniors planning to attend college in any state (daughters and sons are considered separately).

**Eligibility** This program is open to graduating high school seniors whose parent has been a member of AFSCME for at least 1 year. Applicants must be planning to enroll full time at a 4-year college or university in any state. Along with their application, they must submit 2 essays of 350 to 500 words each on 1) what AFSCME means to their family; and 2) their reasons for seeking a college degree. Sons and daughters of members are considered separately.

**Financial data** The stipend is $2,500 per year.

**Duration** 1 year; may be renewed up to 3 additional years.

**Additional information** This program began in 1982. Each year, the scholarships are named in honor of 2 distinguished leaders of Ohio Council 8.

**Number awarded** 2 each year: 1 to a son and 1 to a daughter.

**Deadline** April of each year.

## [496]
## OKLAHOMA BW FOUNDATION SCHOLARSHIPS

Oklahoma Federation of Business Women, Inc.
Attn: Oklahoma Business Women's Foundation
P.O. Box 160
Maud, OK 74854-0160
(405) 374-2866                    Fax: (405) 374-2316
E-mail: askkathy@oklahomabusinesswomen.org
Web: www.oklahomabusinesswomen/obw_foundation.htm

**Summary** To provide financial assistance to women from any state who are working on an undergraduate or graduate degree in any field at a school in Oklahoma.

**Eligibility** This program is open to women from any state who are working on an undergraduate or graduate degree at a college, university, or technical school in Oklahoma. Applicants must submit a 500-word essay on their career goals and how receiving this scholarship will help them to accomplish those goals and make a difference in their professional career. Selection is based on that essay, academic record, employment and volunteer record, and financial need.

**Financial data** Stipends are $1,000, $750, or $500.

**Duration** 1 year.

**Additional information** This program includes the following named scholarships: the Jewell Russell Mann Scholarship, the Dorothy Dickerson Scholarship, the Ann Garrison/Delores Schofield Scholarship, and the Dr. Ann Marie Benson Scholarship.

**Number awarded** Varies each year; recently, 9 of these scholarships were awarded.

**Deadline** February of each year.

## [497]
## OKLAHOMA CITY CHAPTER AWC SCHOLARSHIPS

Association for Women in Communications-Oklahoma
  City Chapter
c/o Sunny Cearley, Scholarship Committee Chair
2728 Orlando Road
Oklahoma City, OK 73120
Web: www.awcokc.org/events-programs

**Summary** To provide financial assistance to women from any state working on an undergraduate or graduate degree in communications or a related field at a school in Oklahoma.

**Eligibility** This program is open to women who are residents of any state working full time on an undergraduate or graduate degree in a communications-related field (e.g., public relations, journalism, advertising, photography) at a 2- or 4-year college or university in Oklahoma. Applicants must submit a 250-word statement explaining why they are applying for the scholarship, why they chose to study communications, their goals after graduation, and related topics. Selection is based on aptitude, interest in a communications-related career, academic achievement, community service, and financial need.

**Financial data** Stipends range from $1,000 to $1,500.

**Duration** 1 year.

**Additional information** Recipients must enroll full time.

**Number awarded** Varies each year; recently, 5 of these scholarships were awarded: 1 at $1,500, 2 at $1,250, and 2 at $1,000.

**Deadline** March of each year.

## [498]
## OLIVE LYNN SALEMBIER MEMORIAL REENTRY SCHOLARSHIP

Society of Women Engineers
Attn: Scholarship Selection Committee
203 North LaSalle Street, Suite 1675
Chicago, IL 60601-1269
(312) 596-5223                    Toll Free: (877) SWE-INFO
Fax: (312) 644-8557           E-mail: scholarships@swe.org
Web: societyofwomenengineers.swe.org

**Summary** To provide financial assistance to women interested in returning to college or graduate school to study engineering or computer science.

**Eligibility** This program is open to women who are planning to enroll at an ABET-accredited 4-year college or university. Applicants must have been out of the engineering workforce and school for at least 2 years and must be planning to return as an undergraduate or graduate student to major in computer science or engineering. They must have a GPA of 3.0 or higher. Selection is based on merit.

**Financial data** The award is $1,500.

**Duration** 1 year; may be renewed up to 3 additional years.
**Additional information** This program began in 1978.
**Number awarded** 1 each year.
**Deadline** February of each year.

## [499]
## OMAHA CHAPTER AFWA SCHOLARSHIPS

Accounting and Financial Women's Alliance-Omaha
  Chapter
Attn: Scholarship Committee
P.O. Box 540345
Omaha, NE 68154
E-mail: aswaomaha@gmail.com
Web: www.aswaomaha.org

**Summary** To provide financial assistance to women from any state working on an undergraduate or graduate degree in accounting at a school in Nebraska.

**Eligibility** This program is open to women from any state enrolled part or full time in a bachelor's or master's degree program in accounting or finance at a college or university in Nebraska. Applicants must have completed at least 60 semester hours of a 4- or 5-year program. They must have a GPA of 3.0 or higher. Membership in the Accounting and Financial Women's Alliance (AFWA) is not required. Along with their application, they must submit an essay of 150 to 250 words on their career goals and objectives, the impact they want to have on the accounting world, community involvement, and leadership examples. Selection is based on leadership, character, communication skills, scholastic average, and financial need.

**Financial data** The stipend is $2,000.
**Duration** 1 year.
**Number awarded** Varies each year; recently, 3 of these scholarships (2 for undergraduates and 1 for a graduate student) were awarded.
**Deadline** March of each year.

## [500]
## ONE FAMILY SCHOLARS PROGRAM

One Family, Inc.
Attn: Director, One Family Scholars Program
186 South Street, Fourth Floor
Boston, MA 02111
(617) 423-0504          Fax: (617) 588-0441
E-mail: scholars@onefamilyinc.org
Web: www.onefamilyinc.org/scholar-application

**Summary** To provide financial assistance to residents of Massachusetts who are single heads of households and interested in attending college in the state.

**Eligibility** This program is open to residents of Massachusetts who are single heads of household with dependent children younger than 18 years of age. Applicants must be attempting to enter or reenter college in Massachusetts to work on an associate or bachelor's degree. They must apply through a participating social service organization at sites in Massachusetts. Along with their application, they must submit a personal essay and 3 letters of reference. They must also apply for financial aid and participate in an interview. U.S. citizenship or permanent resident status is required. Selection is based on financial need (family earnings below 200% of the federal poverty level), clear and realistic academic and

career goals, potential for success in chosen academic program, and desire to participate actively in all aspects of the program.

**Financial data** A stipend is awarded (amount not specified).
**Duration** 1 year; may be renewed until completion of a degree, provided the scholar successfully completes 6 to 9 credits per semester; participates in mandatory leadership development retreats, seminars, and activities; maintains a GPA of 3.0 or higher; remains a Massachusetts resident; and maintains contact with site coordinators.
**Additional information** This program began in 2000 by the Paul and Phyllis Fireman Charitable Foundation.
**Number awarded** Varies each year; recently, 23 scholars received support from this program.
**Deadline** July of each year for fall; November of each year for spring; April of each year for summer.

## [501]
## ONIPA'A CHAPTER ABWA SCHOLARSHIPS

American Business Women's Association-Onipa'a
  Chapter
c/o Julie Dugan, Education Committee Chair
P.O. Box 43
Waimanalo, HI 96795
Web: www.onipaa.hawaiiabwa.org/Scholarship.htm

**Summary** To provide financial assistance to female residents of Hawaii who are working on an undergraduate degree at a college or university in the state.

**Eligibility** This program is open to residents of Hawaii who have completed at least 2 semesters as a full-time undergraduate student at an accredited university, community college, or business school in the state. Applicants must have a GPA of 3.0 or higher. Along with their application, they must submit a 1-page biographical summary that includes educational background and career objective. Financial need is also considered in the selection process. U.S. citizenship is required.

**Financial data** The stipend is $1,000.
**Duration** 1 year.
**Number awarded** 2 each year.
**Deadline** April of each year.

## [502]
## OPTIMIST INTERNATIONAL ORATORICAL CONTEST

Optimist International
Attn: Programs Department
4494 Lindell Boulevard
St. Louis, MO 63108
(314) 371-6000          Toll Free: (800) 500-8130, ext. 235
Fax: (314) 371-6009          E-mail: programs@optimist.org
Web: optimist.org/e/member/scholarships4.cfm

**Summary** To recognize and reward, with college scholarships, outstanding orators at the high school or younger level (females and males may compete separately).

**Eligibility** All students in public, private, or parochial elementary, junior high, and senior high schools in the United States, Canada, or the Caribbean who are under 18 years of age may enter. All contestants must prepare their own orations of 4 to 5 minutes, but they may receive advice and make minor changes or improvements in the oration at any time. Each year a different subject is selected for the orations; a recent topic was "How my Optimism Helps me Overcome Obstacles." The orations may be delivered in a language other than English if that language is an official language of the country in which the sponsoring club is located. Selection is based on poise (20 points), content of speech (35 points), delivery and presentation (35 points), and overall effectiveness (10 points). Competition is first conducted at the level of individual clubs, with winners advancing to zone and then district competitions. At the discretion of the district, boys may compete against boys and girls against girls in separate contests.

**Financial data**   Each district awards either 2 scholarships of $2,500 (1 for a boy and 1 for a girl) or (if the district chooses to have a combined gender contest) a first-place scholarship of $2,500, a second-place scholarship of $1,500, and a third-place scholarship of $1,000.

**Duration**   The competition is held annually.

**Additional information**   This competition was first held in 1928. Nearly 2,000 Optimist International local clubs participate in the program each year. Entry information is available only from local Optimist Clubs.

**Number awarded**   Each year, more than $150,000 is awarded in scholarships.

**Deadline**   Each local club sets its own deadline. The district deadline is the end of June.

## [503]
## ORDER OF THE EASTERN STAR OF PENNSYLVANIA SCHOLARSHIPS

Pennsylvania Masonic Youth Foundation
Attn: Educational Endowment Fund
1244 Bainbridge Road
Elizabethtown, PA 17022-9423
(717) 367-1536     Toll Free: (800) 266-8424 (within PA)
Fax: (717) 367-0616     E-mail: pmyf@pagrandlodge.org
Web: www.pmyf.org/scholarships

**Summary**   To provide financial assistance to students from Pennsylvania who are members of Masonic youth organizations and are attending college in any state (females and males are considered separately).

**Eligibility**   This program is open to active Pennsylvania DeMolays, Rainbow Girls, and Job's Daughters who have completed at least 1 year in an accredited college or university in any state. Applicants must be enrolled full time in a program of at least 3 years' duration or an accredited nursing program leading to an R.N. degree. They must have a GPA of 2.5 or higher, good moral character, limited financial resources, and a willingness to help themselves.

**Financial data**   The stipend is $1,000 per year.

**Duration**   1 year; may be renewed 1 additional year.

**Additional information**   This program is sponsored by the Grand Chapter of Pennsylvania of the Order of the Eastern Star.

**Number awarded**   3 each year: 1 each to a member of DeMolay, Rainbow Girls, and Job's Daughters.

**Deadline**   March of each year.

## [504]
## OREGON LEGION AUXILIARY DEPARTMENT NURSES SCHOLARSHIP FOR DEPENDENTS OF DISABLED VETERANS

American Legion Auxiliary
Department of Oregon
30450 S.W. Parkway Avenue
P.O. Box 1730
Wilsonville, OR 97070-1730
(503) 682-3162          Fax: (503) 685-5008
E-mail: alaor@pcez.com
Web: www.alaoregon.org

**Summary**   To provide financial assistance to the wives and children of disabled Oregon veterans who are interested in studying nursing at a school in any state.

**Eligibility**   This program is open to Oregon residents who are the wives or children of veterans with disabilities. Applicants must have been accepted by an accredited hospital or university school of nursing in any state. Selection is based on ability, aptitude, character, determination, seriousness of purpose, and financial need.

**Financial data**   The stipend is $1,500.

**Duration**   1 year; may be renewed.

**Number awarded**   1 each year.

**Deadline**   May of each year.

## [505]
## OREGON LEGION AUXILIARY DEPARTMENT NURSES SCHOLARSHIP FOR WIDOWS

American Legion Auxiliary
Department of Oregon
30450 S.W. Parkway Avenue
P.O. Box 1730
Wilsonville, OR 97070-1730
(503) 682-3162          Fax: (503) 685-5008
E-mail: alaor@pcez.com
Web: www.alaoregon.org

**Summary**   To provide financial assistance to the widows of Oregon veterans who are interested in studying nursing at a school in any state.

**Eligibility**   This program is open to Oregon residents who are the widows of deceased veterans. Applicants must have been accepted by an accredited hospital or university school of nursing in any state. Selection is based on ability, aptitude, character, determination, seriousness of purpose, and financial need.

**Financial data**   The stipend is $1,500.

**Duration**   1 year; may be renewed.

**Number awarded**   1 each year.

**Deadline**   May of each year.

**[506]**
## OREGON LEGION AUXILIARY DEPARTMENT SCHOLARSHIPS FOR DEPENDENTS OF DISABLED VETERANS

American Legion Auxiliary
Department of Oregon
30450 S.W. Parkway Avenue
P.O. Box 1730
Wilsonville, OR 97070-1730
(503) 682-3162                    Fax: (503) 685-5008
E-mail: alaor@pcez.com
Web: www.alaoregon.org

**Summary**  To provide financial assistance to the dependents of disabled Oregon veterans who are interested in attending college in any state.

**Eligibility**  This program is open to Oregon residents who are children or wives of disabled veterans. Applicants must be interested in obtaining education beyond the high school level at a college, university, business school, vocational school, or any other accredited postsecondary school in the state of Oregon. Selection is based on ability, aptitude, character, seriousness of purpose, and financial need.

**Financial data**  The stipend is $1,000.

**Duration**  1 year; nonrenewable.

**Number awarded**  1 or more each year.

**Deadline**  March of each year.

**[507]**
## OREGON LEGION AUXILIARY DEPARTMENT SCHOLARSHIPS FOR WIDOWS OF VETERANS

American Legion Auxiliary
Department of Oregon
30450 S.W. Parkway Avenue
P.O. Box 1730
Wilsonville, OR 97070-1730
(503) 682-3162                    Fax: (503) 685-5008
E-mail: alaor@pcez.com
Web: www.alaoregon.org

**Summary**  To provide financial assistance to the widows of Oregon veterans who are interested in attending college in any state.

**Eligibility**  This program is open to Oregon residents who are widows of veterans. Applicants must be interested in obtaining education beyond the high school level at a college, university, business school, vocational school, or any other accredited postsecondary school in the state of Oregon. Selection is based on ability, aptitude, character, seriousness of purpose, and financial need.

**Financial data**  The stipend is $1,000.

**Duration**  1 year; nonrenewable.

**Number awarded**  1 or more each year.

**Deadline**  March of each year.

**[508]**
## OUTPUTLINKS WOMAN OF DISTINCTION AWARD

Electronic Document Systems Foundation
Attn: EDSF Scholarship Awards
1845 Precinct Line Road, Suite 212
Hurst, TX 76054
(817) 849-1145                    Fax: (817) 849-1185
E-mail: info@edsf.org
Web: www.edsf.org/what_we_do/scholarships/index.html

**Summary**  To provide financial assistance to female undergraduate and graduate students from any country interested in preparing for a career in document management and graphic communications.

**Eligibility**  This program is open to full-time female undergraduate and graduate students from any country who demonstrate a strong interest in preparing for a career in the document management and graphic communications industry, including computer science and engineering (e.g., web design, webmaster, software development, materials engineer, applications specialist, information technology designer, systems analyst); graphic and media communications (e.g., graphic designer, illustrator, color scientist, print production, prepress imaging specialist, workflow specialist, document preparation, production and/or document distribution, content management, e-commerce, imaging science, printing, web authoring, electronic publishing, archiving, security); or business (e.g., sales, marketing, trade shows, customer service, project or product development, management). Preference is given to graduate students and upper-division undergraduates, but freshmen and sophomores who can show interest, experience, and/or commitment to the document management and graphic communication industry are encouraged to apply. Applicants must have a GPA of 3.0 or higher. Along with their application, they must submit 2 essays on assigned topics that change annually but relate to the document management and graphic communication industries. Selection is based on the essays, academic excellence, participation in school activities, community service, honors and organizational affiliations, education goals, and recommendations; financial need is not considered.

**Financial data**  The stipend is $5,000.

**Duration**  1 year.

**Additional information**  This program is sponsored by OutputLinks Communications Group.

**Number awarded**  1 each year.

**Deadline**  April of each year.

**[509]**
## PAM BARTON STAPLES SCHOLARSHIP

Kappa Delta Sorority
Attn: Foundation Project Manager
3205 Players Lane
Memphis, TN 38125
(901) 748-1897, ext. 203          Toll Free: (800) 536-1897
Fax: (901) 748-0949
E-mail: caroline.cullum@kappadelta.org
Web: www.kappadelta.org/scholarshipapplications_1

**Summary**  To provide financial assistance to members of Kappa Delta Sorority who have served their campus Panhellenic association and are interested in continuing their undergraduate education.

**Eligibility** This program is open to members of Kappa Delta Sorority who are entering their junior or senior year. Applicants must submit a personal statement giving their reasons for applying for this scholarship, an official undergraduate transcript, and 2 letters of recommendation. They must have a GPA of 3.0 or higher and a record of outstanding service to the campus Panhellenic association. Selection is based on academic excellence; service to the chapter, alumnae association, or national Kappa Delta; service to the campus and community; personal objectives and goals; potential; recommendations; and financial need.

**Financial data** The stipend is $2,000 per year. Funds may be used only for tuition, fees, and books, not for room and board.

**Duration** 1 year; may be renewed.

**Number awarded** 1 each year.

**Deadline** November of each year.

## [510]
## PAT GAINEY STUDENT ATHLETE SCHOLARSHIP AWARD

North Carolina High School Athletic Association
Attn: Assistant Director Grants and Fundraising
222 Finley Golf Course Road
P.O. Box 3216
Chapel Hill, NC 27515-3216
(919) 240-7371                    Fax: (919) 240-7399
E-mail: mary@nchsaa.org
Web: www.nchsaa.org

**Summary** To provide financial assistance to seniors at high schools in North Carolina counties of limited financial resources who have participated in athletics and plan to attend college in any state (females and males are considered in alternating years).

**Eligibility** This program is open to seniors graduating from high schools that are members of the North Carolina High School Athletic Association (NCHSAA) and are located in the 84 counties in North Carolina classified as having limited financial resources. In even-numbered years, the award is limited to a male student who has played on the school baseball team; in odd-numbered years, the award is limited to a female student who has participated in school athletics. Applicants must have a GPA of 3.2 or higher, a clean disciplinary record (both school and athletics related), and demonstrated athletic success. They must be planning to attend an accredited college, university, or community college in any state. Along with their application, they must submit a 2-page essay addressing how athletic participation has influenced their decision-making and the importance of athletics in teaching independence, unselfishness, and honesty. Financial need is not considered in the selection process.

**Financial data** The stipend is $2,000.

**Duration** 1 year; nonrenewable.

**Additional information** This program began in 2007. For a list of the 84 (out of 100 in the state) eligible counties, contact NCHSAA.

**Number awarded** 1 each year.

**Deadline** March of each year.

## [511]
## PATRICIA CREED SCHOLARSHIP

Connecticut Women's Golf Association
c/o Karen Bunting, Scholarship Committee
615 Broad Swamp Road
Cheshire, CT 06410
(203) 272-4623                    E-mail: kkbunting@cox.net
Web: www.cwga.org/CWGA/index.php?section=16

**Summary** To provide financial assistance to women high school seniors from Connecticut who are golfers and planning to attend college in any state.

**Eligibility** This program is open to female high school seniors who are residents of Connecticut planning to attend a public college or university in any state. Applicants must be active golfers with a handicap. Along with their application, they must submit a 250-word essay on how golf has made an impact on their life. Selection is based on character, academic achievement, interest in golf, and financial need.

**Financial data** A stipend is awarded (amount not specified).

**Duration** 1 year.

**Additional information** This program began in 1997.

**Number awarded** 1 or 2 each year.

**Deadline** April of each year.

## [512]
## PATSY TAKEMOTO MINK EDUCATION FOUNDATION EDUCATION SUPPORT AWARD

Patsy Takemoto Mink Education Foundation for Low-
  Income Women and Children
P.O. Box 769
Granby, MA 01033
Web: www.patsyminkfoundation.org/edsupport.html

**Summary** To provide financial assistance for college or graduate school to low-income mothers.

**Eligibility** This program is open to women who are at least 17 years of age and are from a low-income family (less than $18,000 annually for a family of 2, $24,000 for a family of 3, or $27,000 for a family of 4). Applicants must be mothers with minor children. They must be 1) enrolled in a skills training, ESL, or GED program; or 2) working on a technical/vocational, associate, bachelor's, master's, professional, or doctoral degree. Along with their application, they must submit brief essays on what this award will help them accomplish, the program in which they are or will be enrolled, how they decided on that educational pursuit, their educational goals, their educational experience, and their personal and educational history.

**Financial data** The stipend is $3,000.

**Duration** 1 year.

**Additional information** This program began in 2003.

**Number awarded** Up to 6 each year.

**Deadline** July of each year.

## [513]
## PEDRO ZAMORA PUBLIC POLICY FELLOWSHIP

AIDS United
Attn: Fellowship Coordinator
1424 K Street, N.W., Suite 200
Washington, DC 20005
(202) 408-4848, ext. 248          Fax: (202) 408-1818
E-mail: Zamora@aidsunited.org
Web: www.aidsunited.org/about/jobs

**Summary** To provide work experience at AIDS United to female, minority, and other undergraduate and graduate students from diverse backgrounds who are interested in public policy.

**Eligibility** This program is open to undergraduate and graduate students who can demonstrate strong research, writing, and organizational skills and a willingness to work in a professional office. Familiarity with HIV-related issues and the legislative process is preferred. Applicants must 1) describe their participation in school or extracurricular activities related to HIV and AIDS (e.g., peer prevention programs, volunteer activities); 2) describe their participation in any school, work, or extracurricular activities related to advocacy (e.g., lobbying, political campaigns); 3) explain why they would be the best candidate for this fellowship; and 4) explain how they would use the skills they acquire from the fellowship. People of color, women, gay, lesbian, bisexual, transgender, and HIV-positive individuals are encouraged to apply.

**Financial data** A stipend is provided (amount not specified).

**Duration** From 8 to 26 weeks.

**Additional information** Responsibilities include assisting in researching a variety of public health and civil rights issues related to HIV prevention, treatment, and care; attending Congressional hearings and coalition meetings; monitoring voting records; reviewing the Federal Register and Congressional Record; and preparing correspondence, mailings, and briefing materials. AIDS United was formerly named AIDS Action. Fellows must commit to a minimum of 30 hours per week at AIDS United in Washington, D.C.

**Number awarded** Varies each year.

**Deadline** March of each year for summer; July of each year for fall; October of each year for spring.

## [514]
## PENNSYLVANIA BPW FOUNDATION SCHOLARSHIPS

Business and Professional Women of Pennsylvania
Attn: Pennsylvania BPW Foundation
c/o Liz Leeper, Vice Chair
1460 Gompers Avenue
Indiana, PA 15701
(724) 465-8692          E-mail: lleeper@digitalrazor.net
Web: www.bpwpa.org/downloads.htm

**Summary** To provide financial assistance to women from Pennsylvania who are interested in attending college in any state.

**Eligibility** This program is open to female residents of Pennsylvania who are attending or planning to attend a college or university in any state. Applicants must submit an essay that 1) discusses their specific short-term career goals and how the proposed training will help them accomplish

those goals; 2) explains how those short-term goals apply to their long-range career goals; and 3) includes a summary of issues that are important to working women in today's world. In the selection process, strong emphasis is placed on financial need.

**Financial data** The stipend is $2,500.

**Duration** 1 year.

**Number awarded** 6 each year: 3 in the fall semester and 3 in the spring semester.

**Deadline** April of each year for fall semester; October of each year for spring semester.

## [515]
## PENNSYLVANIA FEDERATION OF DEMOCRATIC WOMEN MEMORIAL SCHOLARSHIP

Pennsylvania Federation of Democratic Women
c/o Bonita Hannis, Scholarship Chair
36 Betts Lane
Lock Haven, PA 17745
(570) 769-7175          E-mail: behannis@kcnet.org
Web: www.pfdw.org

**Summary** To provide financial assistance to women from Pennsylvania who are registered Democrats and attending college in any state.

**Eligibility** This program is open to women who are residents of Pennsylvania and currently enrolled as juniors at an accredited college or university in any state. Applicants must be registered Democrats and an active participant in the Democratic Party with a Democratic Party family background. Along with their application, they must submit a 1-page essay describing their need for this scholarship, their professional goals, their Democratic Party activities, and their family Democratic Party involvement.

**Financial data** The stipend is $5,000.

**Duration** 1 year (the senior year of college).

**Number awarded** Varies each year; recently, 5 of these scholarships were awarded.

**Deadline** April of each year.

## [516]
## P.E.O. PROGRAM FOR CONTINUING EDUCATION

P.E.O. Sisterhood
Attn: Executive Office
3700 Grand Avenue
Des Moines, IA 50312-2899
(515) 255-3153          Fax: (515) 255-3820
Web: www.peointernational.org/peo-projectsphilanthropies

**Summary** To provide financial assistance to mature women interested in resuming or continuing their academic or technical education.

**Eligibility** This program is open to mature women who are citizens of the United States or Canada and have experienced an interruption in their education that has lasted at least 24 consecutive months during their adult life. Applicants are frequently single parents who must acquire marketable skills to support their families. They must be within 2 years of completing an academic or technical course of study and be sponsored by a local P.E.O. chapter. Students enrolled in a doctoral degree program are not eligible.

**Financial data** The maximum stipend is $3,000.

**Duration** 1 year; nonrenewable.

**Additional information** This program was established in 1973 by the Women's Philanthropic Educational Organization (P.E.O.).

**Number awarded** Varies each year; for a recent biennium, 3,242 of these awards, with a total value of nearly $4.3 million, were granted.

**Deadline** Applications may be submitted at any time.

## [517]
## P.E.O. STAR SCHOLARSHIPS

P.E.O. Sisterhood
Attn: Scholar Awards Office
3700 Grand Avenue
Des Moines, IA 50312-2899
(515) 255-3153                     Fax: (515) 255-3820
E-mail: psa@peodsm.org
Web: www.peointernational.org/peo-projectsphilanthropies

**Summary** To provide financial assistance for college to female high school seniors in the United States or Canada.

**Eligibility** This program is open to women who are graduating from high schools in the United States or Canada and planning to enroll full or part time at an accredited postsecondary educational institution. Applicants must have an unweighted GPA of 3.0 or higher. They must be sponsored by a local P.E.O. chapter. Selection is based on academic excellence, leadership, extracurricular activities, community service, and potential for success; financial need is not considered. U.S. or Canadian citizenship or permanent resident status is required.

**Financial data** The stipend is $2,500.

**Duration** 1 year; nonrenewable.

**Additional information** This program was established in 2009 by the Women's Philanthropic Educational Organization (P.E.O.).

**Number awarded** Varies each year.

**Deadline** October of each year.

## [518]
## PEPPY MOLDOVAN SCHOLARSHIP

Illinois Society of Professional Engineers
Attn: ISPE Foundation, Inc.
100 East Washington Street
Springfield, IL 62701
(217) 544-7424                     Fax: (217) 528-6545
E-mail: info@IllinoisEngineer.com
Web: www.illinoisengineer.com/scholarships.shtml

**Summary** To provide financial assistance to women from selected colleges in Illinois who are working on an engineering degree.

**Eligibility** This program is open to women currently enrolled as sophomore engineering students at the following institutions: Illinois Central College, Kaskaskia Community College, Rend Lake Community College, Bradley University, Southern Illinois University (SIU) at Carbondale, Southern Illinois University (SIU) at Edwardsville, or the University of Illinois at Urbana-Champaign (UIUC). Applicants must have been accepted for enrollment in an ABET-accredited engineering program at SIU Carbondale, SIU Edwardsville, or UIUC. Along with their application, they must submit a 500-word essay on their interest in engineering, their major area

of study and specialization, the occupation they propose to pursue after graduation, their long-term goals, and how they hope to achieve those. Selection is based on the essay, transcripts, work experience, extracurricular activities, honors and scholarships, and 2 letters of reference.

**Financial data** The stipend is $1,000.

**Duration** 1 year.

**Number awarded** 1 each year.

**Deadline** March of each year.

## [519]
## PEPSI USBC YOUTH BOWLING CHAMPIONSHIPS

United States Bowling Congress
Attn: Pepsi-Cola Youth Bowling Event Manager
621 Six Flags Drive
Arlington, TX 76011
(817) 385-8308          Toll Free: (800) 514-BOWL, ext. 8308
E-mail: USBCyouthchampionships@bowl.com
Web: www.bowl.com/pepsiyouth

**Summary** To recognize and reward (with college scholarships) members of the United States Bowling Congress (USBC) who achieve high scores in local competitions (females and males compete separately).

**Eligibility** This competition is open to USBC members in the United States, Puerto Rico, U.S. military zones, and Canada. Applicants enter in 1 of 8 categories based on age (from 6 through 8, from 9 through 11, from 12 through 15, and from 16 through 20) with separate categories for boys and girls. Based on their bowling scores in local competitions, the top bowlers advance to state competitions and qualify for scholarships.

**Financial data** Each state sets the level of its scholarships.

**Duration** The competition is held annually.

**Additional information** This competition is sponsored by PepsiCo, presented by Brunswick, and conducted by the USBC.

**Number awarded** Varies each year. More than $500,000 in scholarships is awarded annually.

**Deadline** Qualifying tournaments are held in bowling centers from October through February of each year.

## [520]
## PHIPPS MEMORIAL SCHOLARSHIP

General Federation of Women's Clubs of Connecticut
c/o Nancy Kalyan, President
4 Mulberry Lane
Enfield, CT 06082
E-mail: KalyanGFWCC@aol.com
Web: www.gfwcct.org

**Summary** To provide financial assistance to women in Connecticut who are working on an undergraduate or graduate degree.

**Eligibility** This program is open to female residents of Connecticut who have completed at least 2 years of college. Applicants must have a GPA of 3.0 or higher and be working on a bachelor's or master's degree. They must be U.S. citizens. Selection is based on academic ability, future promise, and financial need.

**Financial data** The stipend is $1,000.

**Duration** 1 year.

**Number awarded** 1 each year.

**Deadline** February of each year.

## [521]
## PHYLLIS DOBBYN HOLT SCHOLARSHIPS

Sigma Alpha Iota Philanthropies, Inc.
One Tunnel Road
Asheville, NC 28805
(828) 251-0606 Fax: (828) 251-0644
E-mail: nh@sai-national.org
Web: www.sai-national.org

**Summary** To provide financial assistance for undergraduate study to members of Sigma Alpha Iota (an organization of women musicians).

**Eligibility** This program is open to members of the organization in the first 3 years of undergraduate study. Candidates must be nominated by their chapter and their chapter adviser must submit a letter of recommendation. Nominees must submit a brief statement of career goals and aspirations. Selection is based on financial need, musical ability, scholarship, potential leadership, contribution to campus and community life, and exemplification of the ideals of the organization.

**Financial data** The stipend is $2,000.

**Duration** 1 year.

**Number awarded** 3 each year.

**Deadline** March of each year.

## [522]
## PHYLLIS G. MEEKINS SCHOLARSHIP

Ladies Professional Golf Association
Attn: LPGA Foundation
100 International Golf Drive
Daytona Beach, FL 32124-1082
(386) 274-6200 Fax: (386) 274-1099
E-mail: foundation.scholarships@lpga.com
Web: www.lpgafoundation.org/scholarships?

**Summary** To provide financial assistance to minority female graduating high school seniors who played golf in high school and plan to continue to play in college.

**Eligibility** This program is open to female high school seniors who are members of a recognized minority group. Applicants must have a GPA of 3.0 or higher and a background in golf. They must be planning to enroll full time at a college or university in the United States and play competitive golf. Along with their application, they must submit a letter that describes how golf has been an integral part of their lives and includes their personal, academic, and professional goals; their chosen discipline of study; and how this scholarship will be of assistance. Financial need is considered in the selection process. U.S. citizenship or legal resident status is required.

**Financial data** The stipend is $1,250.

**Duration** 1 year.

**Additional information** This program began in 2006.

**Number awarded** 1 each year.

**Deadline** May of each year.

## [523]
## PHYLLIS SANDERS SCHOLARSHIP

Business Women of Missouri Foundation, Inc.
Attn: Scholarship Committee Chair
P.O. Box 28243
Kansas City, MO 64188
(816) 333-6959 Fax: (816) 333-6959
E-mail: jo.mofedbpw@gmail.com
Web: www.businesswomenmo.org/foundation/index.html

**Summary** To provide financial assistance to members of Business Women in Missouri (BWM) who plan to attend college in any state.

**Eligibility** This program is open to BWM members who have been accepted into an accredited program or course of study in any state to upgrade their skills and/or complete education for career advancement. Along with their application, they must submit brief statements on the following: their achievements and/or specific recognitions in their field of endeavor; professional and/or civic affiliations; present and long-range career goals; how they plan to participate in and contribute to their community upon completion of their program of study; why they feel they would make a good recipient; and any special circumstances that may have influenced their ability to continue or complete their education They must also demonstrate financial need and U.S. citizenship.

**Financial data** The stipend is $1,000.

**Duration** 1 year.

**Number awarded** Varies each year; recently, 3 of these scholarships were awarded.

**Deadline** January of each year.

## [524]
## PI BETA PHI FRIENDSHIP FUND SCHOLARSHIPS

Pi Beta Phi
Attn: Pi Beta Phi Foundation
1154 Town and Country Commons Drive
Town and Country, MO 63017
(636) 256-1357 Fax: (636) 256-8124
E-mail: fndn@pibetaphi.org
Web: www.pibetaphifoundation.org/programs/scholarships

**Summary** To provide financial assistance to members of Pi Beta Phi who are working on an undergraduate degree.

**Eligibility** This program is open to women who are officially enrolled full time at a college or university where there is a Pi Beta Phi chapter. They must be active members in good standing in the sorority and have a GPA of 3.0 or higher (70% or higher for Canadian members). Selection is based on financial need, academic record, and service to the sorority, campus, and community.

**Financial data** The stipend is $1,000.

**Duration** 1 year.

**Number awarded** Varies each year; recently 16 of these scholarships were awarded.

**Deadline** February of each year.

## [525]
## PI BETA PHI UNDERGRADUATE SCHOLARSHIPS

Pi Beta Phi
Attn: Pi Beta Phi Foundation
1154 Town and Country Commons Drive
Town and Country, MO 63017
(636) 256-8124                    Fax: (636) 256-8124
E-mail: fndn@pibetaphi.org
Web: www.pibetaphifoundation.org/programs/scholarships

**Summary**  To provide financial assistance for college to members of Pi Beta Phi.

**Eligibility**  This program is open to women who are officially full time enrolled at a college or university where there is a Pi Beta Phi chapter. They must be active members in good standing in the sorority and have a GPA of 3.0 or higher (70% or higher for Canadian members). Selection is based on financial need, academic record, and service to the sorority, campus, and community.

**Financial data**  Stipends range from $1,000 to $10,000.

**Duration**  1 year.

**Additional information**  This program includes approximately 50 named scholarships. Many of those specify additional eligibility requirements, such as chapter, residence, or academic major. Recipients must use the funds during the immediately succeeding academic year and must be willing to write a brief report of their academic progress at the end of the school year.

**Number awarded**  Varies each year; recently, the sponsor awarded a total of 123 scholarships worth more than $324,000.

**Deadline**  February of each year.

## [526]
## PI STATE NATIVE AMERICAN GRANTS-IN-AID

Delta Kappa Gamma Society International-Pi State
 Organization
c/o Deborah Packard, Native American Committee Chair
232 Evergreen Road
Brockport, NY 14420-1140
(315) 657-2373          E-mail: dpackard@bataviacsd.org
Web: www.deltakappagamma.org/NY/ASaGiA.html

**Summary**  To provide funding to Native American women from New York who plan to work in education or another service field.

**Eligibility**  This program is open to Native American women from New York who are attending a 2- or 4-year college in the state. Applicants must be planning to work in education or another service field, but preference is given to those majoring in education. Both undergraduate and graduate students are eligible.

**Financial data**  The grant is $500 per semester ($1,000 per year). Funds may be used for any career-related purpose, including purchase of textbooks.

**Duration**  1 semester; may be renewed for a total of 5 years and a total of $5,000 over a recipient's lifetime.

**Number awarded**  Up to 5 each year.

**Deadline**  February of each year.

## [527]
## PNC/KHSAA SWEET 16 SCHOLARSHIPS

Kentucky High School Athletic Association
Attn: Assistant Commissioner
2280 Executive Drive
Lexington, KY 40505
(859) 299-5472                    Fax: (859) 293-5999
E-mail: bcope@khsaa.org
Web: www.khsaa.org

**Summary**  To provide financial assistance to student-athletes in Kentucky high schools who plan to attend college in the state (females and males compete separately).

**Eligibility**  This program is open to high school seniors in Kentucky who have participated in athletics or cheerleading and plan to attend college in the state. The awards are presented in conjunction with the state basketball tournament, but all student-athletes, not just basketball players, are eligible. Students must be nominated by a school representative. Letters of nomination must explain why the student is an exemplary leader and should receive the scholarship. Selection is based on academic achievement, leadership at school, and community service. Men and women are judged separately.

**Financial data**  The stipend is $1,000.

**Duration**  1 year; nonrenewable.

**Additional information**  This program is sponsored by PNC Bank.

**Number awarded**  32 each year: 1 female and 1 male in each of 16 regions in Kentucky.

**Deadline**  February of each year.

## [528]
## P.O. PISTILLI SCHOLARSHIPS

Design Automation Conference
c/o Andrew B. Kahng, Scholarship Director
University of California at San Diego-Jacobs School of
 Engineering
Jacobs Hall, EBU3B, Rpp, 2134
9500 Gilman Drive
La Jolla, CA 92093-0404
(858) 822-4884                    Fax: (858) 534-7029
E-mail: abk@cs.ucsd.edu
Web: www.dac.com

**Summary**  To provide financial assistance to female, minority, or disabled high school seniors who are interested in preparing for a career in computer science or electrical engineering.

**Eligibility**  This program is open to graduating high school seniors who are members of underrepresented groups: women, African Americans, Hispanics, Native Americans, and persons with disabilities. Applicants must be interested in preparing for a career in electrical engineering, computer engineering, or computer science. They must have at least a 3.0 GPA, have demonstrated high achievements in math and science courses, have demonstrated involvement in activities associated with the underrepresented group they represent, and be able to demonstrate significant financial need. U.S. citizenship is not required, but applicants must be U.S. residents when they apply and must plan to attend an accredited U.S. college or university. Along with their application, they must submit 3 letters of recommendation, official transcripts,

ACT/SAT and/or PSAT scores, a personal statement outlining future goals and why they think they should receive this scholarship, and documentation of financial need.

**Financial data** Stipends are $4,000 per year. Awards are paid each year in 2 equal installments.

**Duration** 1 year; may be renewed up to 4 additional years.

**Additional information** This program is funded by the Design Automation Conference of the Association for Computing Machinery's Special Interest Group on Design Automation.

**Number awarded** 2 to 7 each year.

**Deadline** January of each year.

## [529] POLL-ETTE FOUNDERS SCHOLARSHIPS

American Hereford Association
Attn: National Junior Hereford Association
1501 Wyandotte Street
P.O. Box 014059
Kansas City, MO 64101
(816) 842-3757          Fax: (816) 842-6931
E-mail: acowan@hereford.org
Web: www.hereford.org/node/1758

**Summary** To provide financial assistance to members of the National Junior Hereford Association (NJHA) who are interested in majoring in any field in college (females and males compete separately).

**Eligibility** This program is open to NJHA members who are between 17 and 22 years of age and currently enrolled as high school seniors or college undergraduates. Along with their application, they must submit an essay on what their involvement with Herefords has done for them. Selection is based on the essay, participation in state Junior Hereford Association activities, number of years they have shown Hereford cattle, participation in other (4-H, FCCLA, FFA) activities, and participation in other community and religious activities. Financial need is not considered. Males and females compete separately.

**Financial data** The stipend is $1,000.

**Duration** 1 year; nonrenewable.

**Additional information** This program, established in 2003, is funded by the Hereford Youth Foundation of America and managed by the National Organization of Poll-Ettes.

**Number awarded** 2 each year: 1 for a female and 1 for a male.

**Deadline** March of each year.

## [530] PRAXAIR SCHOLARSHIPS

Society of Women Engineers
Attn: Scholarship Selection Committee
203 North LaSalle Street, Suite 1675
Chicago, IL 60601-1269
(312) 596-5223          Toll Free: (877) SWE-INFO
Fax: (312) 644-8557     E-mail: scholarships@swe.org
Web: societyofwomenengineers.swe.org

**Summary** To provide financial assistance to undergraduate women who are majoring in chemical or mechanical engineering.

**Eligibility** This program is open to society members who are entering their sophomore, junior, or senior year at an

ABET-accredited 4-year college or university. Applicants must be working full time on a degree in computer science or chemical or mechanical engineering and have a GPA of 3.2 or higher. Selection is based on merit. Preference is given to groups underrepresented in computer science and engineering.

**Financial data** The stipend is $1,000.

**Duration** 1 year.

**Additional information** This program began in 2011 by Praxair, Inc.

**Number awarded** 10 each year.

**Deadline** February of each year.

## [531] PRISCILLA CARNEY JONES SCHOLARSHIP

American Chemical Society
Attn: Department of Diversity Programs
1155 16th Street, N.W.
Washington, DC 20036
(202) 872-6334          Toll Free: (800) 227-5558, ext. 6334
Fax: (202) 776-8003     E-mail: diversity@acs.org
Web: www.womenchemists.sites.acs.org

**Summary** To provide financial assistance to female upper-division students majoring in chemistry.

**Eligibility** This program is open to women entering their junior or senior year of full-time study with a major in chemistry or chemistry-related science. Students in pre-med programs who intend to go to medical school are not eligible. Applicants must have a GPA of 3.25 or higher and be able to demonstrate financial need. They must have completed research or plan to conduct research during their undergraduate years. Along with their application, they must submit brief statements on why they are a good candidate to receive this scholarship, their community service activities and related responsibilities, the key leadership roles they have fulfilled, any research presentations or publications, and their future plans and goals. U.S. citizenship or permanent resident status is required.

**Financial data** The stipend is at least $1,500.

**Duration** 1 year.

**Number awarded** 1 each year.

**Deadline** April of each year.

## [532] PRISCILLA MAXWELL ENDICOTT SCHOLARSHIPS

Connecticut Women's Golf Association
c/o Karen Bunting, Scholarship Committee
615 Broad Swamp Road
Cheshire, CT 06410
(203) 272-4623          E-mail: kkbunting@cox.net
Web: www.cwga.org/CWGA/index.php?section=16

**Summary** To provide financial assistance to women golfers from Connecticut who are interested in attending college in any state.

**Eligibility** This program is open to high school seniors and college students who are residents of Connecticut attending or planning to attend a 4-year college or university in any state. Applicants must be active women golfers with a handicap. Along with their application, they must submit a 250-word essay on how golf has made an impact on their life.

Selection is based on participation in golf programs, academic achievement, and financial need.

**Financial data**   The maximum stipend is $3,000 per year.

**Duration**   Up to 4 years.

**Additional information**   This program began in 1977.

**Number awarded**   Varies each year; recently, 5 of these scholarships were awarded.

**Deadline**   April of each year.

## [533]
## PROFESSIONAL BUSINESS WOMEN OF CALIFORNIA ACADEMIC SCHOLARSHIPS

Professional Business Women of California
c/o Rene Kim, Chair and President
886 Birdhaven Court
Lafayette, CA 94549
(415) 857-2923                    E-mail: info@pbwc.org
Web: www.pbwc.org/join-pbwc/scholarship-program

**Summary**   To provide financial assistance to female high school seniors in California who plan to attend college in any state.

**Eligibility**   This program is open to women who are graduating from high schools in California and planning to enroll as an undergraduate at an accredited college or university in any state. Applicants must submit a 2-page essay on their career plans, future goals, and why they believe they are a worthy recipient of this scholarship.

**Financial data**   A stipend is awarded (amount not specified). Funds are sent directly to the recipient's institution.

**Duration**   1 year.

**Number awarded**   At least 3 each year.

**Deadline**   March of each year.

## [534]
## PROVIDENCE ALUMNAE CHAPTER SCHOLASTIC ACHIEVEMENT AWARD

Delta Sigma Theta Sorority, Inc.-Providence Alumnae
   Chapter
Attn: Scholarship Committee
P.O. Box 40175
Providence, RI 02940-0175
(401) 351-1332                    E-mail: mestel@verizon.net
Web: www.dstprovidencealumnae.org

**Summary**   To provide financial assistance to female African American residents of Rhode Island who are attending college in any state.

**Eligibility**   This program is open to African American women who are residents of Rhode Island. Applicants must be attending a 4-year college or university in any state and have a GPA of 3.0 or higher. Along with their application, they must submit a current official transcript, a letter of recommendation, and an essay describing their career goals, community service activities, educational accomplishments, and personal interests and talents.

**Financial data**   The stipend is $1,000.

**Duration**   1 year.

**Number awarded**   1 or more each year.

**Deadline**   March of each year.

## [535]
## PROVIDENCE ALUMNAE MEMORIAL AWARD

Delta Sigma Theta Sorority, Inc.-Providence Alumnae
   Chapter
Attn: Scholarship Committee
P.O. Box 40175
Providence, RI 02940-0175
(401) 351-1332                    E-mail: mestel@verizon.net
Web: www.dstprovidencealumnae.org

**Summary**   To provide financial assistance to African American female high school seniors from Rhode Island who are planning to attend college in any state.

**Eligibility**   This program is open to African American women who are seniors graduating from high schools in Rhode Island. Applicants must be planning to enroll at a college in any state. Along with their application, they must submit a current official transcript, a letter of recommendation, and an essay describing their career goals, community service activities, educational accomplishments, and personal interests and talents.

**Financial data**   The stipend is $1,250.

**Duration**   1 year.

**Number awarded**   1 or more each year.

**Deadline**   March of each year.

## [536]
## QUALITY OF LIFE AWARDS

Miss America Pageant
Attn: Scholarship Department
222 New Road, Suite 700
Linwood, NJ 08221
(609) 653-8700, ext. 127                    Fax: (609) 653-8740
E-mail: info@missamerica.org
Web: www.missamerica.org/scholarships/quality.aspx

**Summary**   To recognize and reward, with college scholarships, women who participate in the Miss America Pageant at the national level and demonstrate outstanding community service.

**Eligibility**   This program is open to women who compete at the national level of the Miss America Pageant and demonstrate a commitment to enhancing the quality of life for others through volunteerism and community service. Applicants must demonstrate that they have fulfilled a legitimate need in their community through the creation, development, and/or participation in a community service project. Selection is based on the depth of service, creativity of the project, and effects on the lives of others.

**Financial data**   The awards are college scholarships of $6,000 for the winner, $4,000 for the first runner-up, and $2,000 for the second runner-up.

**Duration**   The awards are presented annually.

**Additional information**   This program began in 1988.

**Number awarded**   3 each year.

**Deadline**   Deadline not specified.

## [537]
## REAM'S FOOD STORES SCHOLARSHIPS

Utah Sports Hall of Fame Foundation
Attn: Scholarship Committee Chair
P.O. Box 95982
South Jordan, UT 84095
(801) 944-2379
Web: www.utahsportshalloffame.org/about.html

**Summary** To recognize and reward outstanding high school seniors in Utah who have been involved in athletics and are interested in attending college in the state (females and males are considered separately).

**Eligibility** Each high school in Utah may nominate 1 boy and 1 girl who are graduating this year. Nominees must be planning to attend college in the state. Selection is based on academic record (25%); personal character, including leadership and service (25%); financial need (25%); and involvement in athletics, including football, basketball, cross country, volleyball, tennis, track and field, soccer, rodeo, baseball, swimming, wrestling, officiating, community recreation, or intramural sports (25%).

**Financial data** The stipend is $3,000. Funds are paid to the recipient's institution.

**Duration** 1 year; nonrenewable.

**Additional information** Formerly, the sponsoring organization was known as the Old Time Athletes Association.

**Number awarded** 4 each year: 2 to boys and 2 to girls.

**Deadline** April of each year.

## [538]
## REED AND GLORIA PENNINGTON SCHOLARSHIP

Kappa Delta Sorority
Attn: Foundation Project Manager
3205 Players Lane
Memphis, TN 38125
(901) 748-1897, ext. 203          Toll Free: (800) 536-1897
Fax: (901) 748-0949
E-mail: caroline.cullum@kappadelta.org
Web: www.kappadelta.org/scholarshipapplications_1

**Summary** To provide financial assistance to members of Kappa Delta Sorority who are majoring in journalism or communications.

**Eligibility** This program is open to undergraduate members of Kappa Delta Sorority. Applicants must submit a personal statement giving their reasons for applying for this scholarship, an official undergraduate transcript, and 2 letters of recommendation. They must be majoring in journalism or communications. Selection is based on academic excellence; service to the chapter, alumnae association, or national Kappa Delta; service to the campus and community; personal objectives and goals; potential; recommendations; and financial need.

**Financial data** The stipend is $2,000 per year. Funds may be used only for tuition, fees, and books, not for room and board.

**Duration** 1 year; may be renewed.

**Number awarded** 1 each year.

**Deadline** November of each year.

## [539]
## REGION H SCHOLARSHIP

Society of Women Engineers
Attn: Scholarship Selection Committee
203 North LaSalle Street, Suite 1675
Chicago, IL 60601-1269
(312) 596-5223          Toll Free: (877) SWE-INFO
Fax: (312) 644-8557          E-mail: scholarships@swe.org
Web: societyofwomenengineers.swe.org

**Summary** To provide financial assistance to members of the Society of Women Engineers (SWE) working on an undergraduate or graduate degree in engineering or computer science at a school in the upper Midwest (Region H).

**Eligibility** This program is open to members of the society who will be sophomores, juniors, seniors, or graduate students at ABET-accredited colleges and universities in Illinois, Indiana, Iowa, Michigan, Minnesota, North Dakota, South Dakota, or Wisconsin. Applicants must have a record of active involvement in SWE, based on the amount of time spent volunteering, level of commitment, and years of service. They must be working full time on a degree in computer science or engineering and have a GPA of 3.0 or higher. Selection is based on merit and participation in SWE activities.

**Financial data** The stipend is $1,500 or $1,000.

**Duration** 1 year.

**Number awarded** 2 each year: 1 at $1,500 and 1 at $1,000.

**Deadline** February of each year.

## [540]
## REGIONAL SUMMER MUSIC SCHOLARSHIPS

Sigma Alpha Iota Philanthropies, Inc.
One Tunnel Road
Asheville, NC 28805
(828) 251-0606          Fax: (828) 251-0644
E-mail: nh@sai-national.org
Web: www.sai-national.org

**Summary** To provide financial assistance for summer study in music, in the United States or abroad, to members of Sigma Alpha Iota (an organization of women musicians).

**Eligibility** This program is open to undergraduate and graduate student members of the organization who are planning to study at a summer music program in the United States or abroad. Applicants must submit a complete resume (including musical studies and activities, academic GPA, community service record, and record of participation in Sigma Alpha Iota), supporting materials (recital and concert programs, reviews, repertoire list, etc.), a statement of why they chose this program and how it will aid their musical growth, a full brochure of information on the program (including cost and payment due dates), a copy of the completed summer school application and acceptance letter (when available), and a letter of recommendation from their major teacher.

**Financial data** The stipend is $1,000.

**Duration** Summer months.

**Number awarded** 10 each year: 2 from each region of Sigma Alpha Iota.

**Deadline** March of each year.

## [541]
## REJESTA V. PERRY SCHOLARSHIP

Sigma Gamma Rho Sorority, Inc.
Attn: National Education Fund
1000 Southhill Drive, Suite 200
Cary, NC 27513
(919) 678-9720                    Toll Free: (888) SGR-1922
Fax: (919) 678-9721              E-mail: info@sgrho1922.org
Web: www.sgrho1922.org/nef

**Summary** To provide financial assistance to undergraduate students (particularly African American women) working on a degree in education.

**Eligibility** This program is open to undergraduates working on a degree in education. The sponsor is a traditionally African American sorority. Applicants must have a GPA of "C" or higher and be able to demonstrate financial need.

**Financial data** A stipend is awarded (amount not specified).

**Duration** 1 year.

**Additional information** A processing fee of $20 is required.

**Number awarded** 1 each year.

**Deadline** April of each year.

## [542]
## RESEARCH AND ENGINEERING APPRENTICESHIP PROGRAM (REAP) FOR HIGH SCHOOL STUDENTS

Academy of Applied Science
Attn: REAP
1 Maple Street
Concord, NH 03301
(603) 228-4520                    Fax: (603) 228-0210
E-mail: renie@aas-world.org
Web: www.aas-world.org/interest-pages/for-students.html

**Summary** To provide an opportunity for high school students from groups historically underrepresented in science, technology, engineering, and science (STEM) to engage in a summer research apprenticeship.

**Eligibility** This program is open to high school students from groups historically underrepresented or underserved in STEM; that includes 1) Blacks/African Americans; 2) Hispanics; 3) Native Americans/Alaskan Natives; 4) low-income according to federal TRIO criteria; and 5) women in physical science, computer science, mathematics, or engineering. Applicants must be interested in working as an apprentice on a research project in the laboratory of a mentor scientist at a college or university near their home. Selection is based on demonstrated interests in STEM research and demonstrated potential for a successful career in STEM. They must be at least 16 years of age.

**Financial data** The stipend is $1,300.

**Duration** Summer months.

**Additional information** The program provides intensive summer training for high school students in the laboratories of scientists. The program, established in 1980, is funded by a grant from the U.S. Army Research Office. Students must live at home while they participate in the program and must live in the area of an approved college or university. The program does not exist in every state.

**Number awarded** Varies; recently, approximately 120 students were funded at 44 universities nationwide.

**Deadline** February of each year.

## [543]
## RESEARCH EXPERIENCES FOR UNDERGRADUATES PROGRAM IN SOLAR AND SPACE PHYSICS

University of Colorado
Attn: Laboratory for Atmospheric and Space Physics
1234 Innovation Drive
Boulder, CO 80303-7814
(303) 735-2143   E-mail: martin.snow@lasp.colorado.edu
Web: lasp.colorado.edu/home/education/reu

**Summary** To provide an opportunity for upper-division students (particularly women, underrepresented minorities, and persons with disabilities) to work on research projects related to solar and space physics at laboratories in Boulder, Colorado during the summer.

**Eligibility** This program is open to students currently enrolled as sophomores and juniors at colleges and universities in any state. Applicants must be interested in participating on a research project related to solar and space physics at a participating laboratory in Boulder, Colorado. They must be U.S. citizens, nationals, or permanent residents. Applications are especially encouraged from underrepresented minorities, persons with disabilities, and women.

**Financial data** The stipend is $500 per week. Students also receive dormitory housing, a food allowance, and a travel stipend of $500.

**Duration** 8 weeks, starting in June.

**Additional information** The participating laboratories are the Laboratory for Atmospheric and Space Physics (LASP) of the University of Colorado, the High Altitude Observatory (HAO) of the National Center for Atmospheric Research (NCAR), the Space Weather Prediction Center (SWPC) of the National Oceanic and Atmospheric Administration (NOAA), the Planetary Science Directorate of the Southwest Research Institute (SwRI), and NorthWest Research Associates (NWRA). This program is funded by the National Science Foundation as part of its Research Experiences for Undergraduates (REU) Program.

**Number awarded** Varies each year; recently, 16 of these internships were awarded.

**Deadline** January of each year.

## [544]
## RESOURCES FOR THE FUTURE SUMMER INTERNSHIPS

Resources for the Future
Attn: Internship Coordinator
1616 P Street, N.W., Suite 600
Washington, DC 20036-1400
(202) 328-5020                    Fax: (202) 939-3460
E-mail: IC@rff.org
Web: www.rff.org

**Summary** To provide internships to undergraduate and graduate students (especially women and minorities) who are interested in working on research projects in public policy during the summer.

**Eligibility** This program is open to undergraduate and graduate students (with priority to graduate students) interested in an internship at Resources for the Future (RFF). Applicants must be working on a degree in the social and natural sciences and have training in economics and quantitative methods or an interest in public policy. They should display strong writing skills and a desire to analyze complex environmental policy problems amenable to interdisciplinary methods. The ability to work without supervision in a careful and conscientious manner is essential. Women and minority candidates are strongly encouraged to apply. Both U.S. and non-U.S. citizens are eligible, if the latter have proper work and residency documentation.

**Financial data** The stipend is $375 per week for graduate students or $350 per week for undergraduates. Housing assistance is not provided.

**Duration** 10 weeks during the summer; beginning and ending dates can be adjusted to meet particular student needs.

**Number awarded** Varies each year.

**Deadline** February of each year.

## [545]
## RHODA D. HOOD MEMORIAL SCHOLARSHIP

Northwest Baptist Convention
Attn: Woman's Missionary Union
3200 N.E. 109th Avenue
Vancouver, WA 98682-7749
(360) 882-2100                    Fax: (360) 882-2295
Web: www.nwbaptist.org

**Summary** To provide financial assistance to women from the Northwest who are attending college or seminary in any state to prepare for a career in vocational ministry, preferably with a Southern Baptist Convention church.

**Eligibility** This program is open to women who have been active members of a church affiliated with the Northwest Baptist Convention and a member of the Woman's Missionary Union within their church. Special consideration is given to women who are the children of ministers from the Northwest. Applicants must be attending or planning to attend an accredited college, university, or Southern Baptist seminary in any state with the intention of serving in a vocational ministry position through a church or denomination; priority is given to applicants going into a mission vocation affiliated with the Southern Baptist Convention. Along with their application, they must submit 1) a written account of their conversion experience and their call to vocational ministry; and 2) a written endorsement from their church.

**Financial data** A stipend is awarded (amount not specified).

**Duration** 1 year; may be renewed if the recipient maintains a GPA of 2.5 or higher.

**Additional information** The Northwest Baptist Convention serves Oregon, Washington, and northern Idaho.

**Number awarded** 1 or more each year.

**Deadline** May of each year for fall term; October of each year for spring term.

## [546]
## RHODE ISLAND COMMISSION ON WOMEN/
## FREDA H. GOLDMAN EDUCATION AWARDS

Rhode Island Foundation
Attn: Funds Administrator
One Union Station
Providence, RI 02903
(401) 427-4017                    Fax: (401) 331-8085
E-mail: lmonahan@rifoundation.org
Web: www.rifoundation.org

**Summary** To provide supplemental funding to women in Rhode Island who are working on a degree or job training beyond high school.

**Eligibility** This program is open to women in Rhode Island who are 1) preparing for a nontraditional job or career through an educational program; 2) needing skills to reenter the job market; 3) seeking skills to improve their job status; 4) ex-offenders wishing to undertake vocational or career education and training; or 5) displaced homemakers and single mothers wishing to further their education. Applicants must be enrolled or registered in an educational or job skills training program and be able to demonstrate financial need. Preference is given to highly motivated, self-supporting, low-income women who are completing their first undergraduate degree or certificate program. Along with their application, they must submit an essay (up to 300 words) in which they explain their reasons for returning to school, how they chose their intended career or job training, how this scholarship can help them achieve their goals, and specifically how the money will be used.

**Financial data** Stipends range from $500 to $1,000; funds may be used for transportation, child care, introductory courses to a program, tutoring, educational materials, and related costs (not including tuition).

**Duration** 1 year; may be renewed.

**Additional information** This program, established in 1983 and transferred to the foundation in 1997, is supported by the Rhode Island Commission on Women.

**Number awarded** 2 each year.

**Deadline** June of each year.

## [547]
## RHODE ISLAND WOMEN'S GOLF ASSOCIATION
## SCHOLARSHIPS

Rhode Island Women's Golf Association
c/o Pat Davitt
17 Oak Manor Drive
Barrington, RI 02806
(401) 245-4959          E-mail: pdavitt@lincolnschool.org
Web: www.riwga.org/scholarships.html

**Summary** To provide financial assistance to female high school seniors in Rhode Island who have participated in golf and plan to attend college in any state.

**Eligibility** This program is open to women who are graduating high school seniors and have participated in the program of the Rhode Island Women's Golf Association. Applicants must be planning to attend a college or university in any state. Selection is based on academics, community service, recommendations, financial need, and participation in golf.

**Financial data** A stipend is awarded (amount not specified).

**Duration** 1 year; may be renewed up to 3 additional years, provided the recipient maintains a "C" average.

**Additional information** This program began in 1981.

**Number awarded** Varies each year; recently, 22 girls received a total of $11,650 in scholarships.

**Deadline** May of each year.

## [548]
## RHONDA J.B. O'LEARY MEMORIAL SCHOLARSHIP

Educational Foundation for Women in Accounting
Attn: Foundation Administrator
136 South Keowee Street
Dayton, OH 45402
(937) 424-3391                    Fax: (937) 222-5749
E-mail: info@efwa.org
Web: www.efwa.org/scholarships.php

**Summary** To provide financial support to women who are enrolled in an undergraduate or graduate accounting degree program at a school in Washington.

**Eligibility** This program is open to women from any state who are working on a bachelor's or master's degree in accounting at an accredited school in Washington. Selection is based on aptitude for accounting and business, commitment to the goal of working on a degree in accounting (including evidence of continued commitment after receiving this award), clear evidence that the candidate has established goals and a plan for achieving those goals (both personal and professional), and financial need. U.S. citizenship is required.

**Financial data** The stipend is $2,000 per year.

**Duration** 1 year; may be renewed 1 additional year if the recipient completes at least 12 hours each semester.

**Additional information** This program began in 2007 with funds provided by the Seattle Chapter of the American Society of Women Accountants (ASWA).

**Number awarded** 1 each year.

**Deadline** April of each year.

## [549]
## RICHARD J. PHELPS SCHOLAR-ATHLETE PROGRAM

Boston Globe
Attn: School Sports Editor
135 Morrissey Boulevard
P.O. Box 55819
Boston, MA 02205
(617) 929-2860
Web: www.bostonscholarshipguide.com

**Summary** To provide financial assistance to outstanding scholar-athletes from Massachusetts (females and males are judged separately) who plan to attend college in any state.

**Eligibility** This program is open to seniors graduating from high schools in Massachusetts who are nominated by their principals. Selection is based on academic and athletic excellence. Females and males are evaluated separately.

**Financial data** The stipend is $3,000.

**Duration** 1 year.

**Additional information** This program began in 1991 as an adjunct to the *Boston Globe's* All-Scholastic sports teams.

**Number awarded** 14 each year: 1 female and 1 male from each district of the Massachusetts Interscholastic Athletic Association (MIAA).

**Deadline** April of each year.

## [550]
## R.L. GILLETTE SCHOLARSHIPS

American Foundation for the Blind
Attn: Scholarship Committee
2 Penn Plaza, Suite 1102
New York, NY 10121
(212) 502-7661                    Toll Free: (800) AFB-LINE
Fax: (888) 545-8331               E-mail: afbinfo@afb.net
Web: www.afb.org/Section.asp?Documentid=2962

**Summary** To provide financial assistance to legally blind undergraduate women who are studying literature or music.

**Eligibility** This program is open to women who are legally blind, U.S. citizens, and enrolled full time in a 4-year baccalaureate degree program in literature or music. Along with their application, they must submit 200-word essays on 1) their past and recent achievements and accomplishments; 2) their intended field of study and why they have chosen it; and 3) the role their visual impairment has played in shaping their life. They must also submit a sample performance tape or CD (not to exceed 30 minutes) or a creative writing sample. Financial need is considered in the selection process.

**Financial data** The stipend is $1,000.

**Duration** 1 academic year.

**Number awarded** 2 each year.

**Deadline** April of each year.

## [551]
## ROBERT SMILEY SCHOLARSHIP

Iowa Girls High School Athletic Union
Attn: Scholarships
5000 Westown Parkway
West Des Moines, IA 50266
(515) 288-9741                    Fax: (515) 284-1969
E-mail: jasoneslinger@ighsau.org
Web: www.ighsau.org

**Summary** To provide financial assistance to female high school seniors in Iowa who have participated in athletics and plan to attend college in the state.

**Eligibility** This program is open to women graduating from high schools in Iowa who have lettered in 1 varsity sport sponsored by the Iowa Girls High School Athletic Union (IGHSAU) each year of high school and have a GPA of 2.5 or higher. Applicants must be planning to attend a college or university in Iowa. Each high school in the state may nominate 1 student. Selection is based on academic achievements, athletic accomplishments, non-sports extracurricular activities, and community involvement.

**Financial data** The stipend is $1,000.

**Duration** 1 year.

**Number awarded** 1 each year.

**Deadline** March of each year.

## [552]
## ROCK CATS SCHOLAR-ATHLETE AWARDS

New Britain Rock Cats Baseball Club
Attn: Rock Cats Foundation
230 John Karbonic Way
P.O. Box 1718
New Britain, CT 06050
(860) 224-8383, ext. 23        Fax: (860) 225-6267
E-mail: ahelbling@rockcats.com
Web: www.rockcats.com

**Summary**  To provide financial assistance to high school seniors in Connecticut who have participated in sports and plan to attend college in any state (females and males are considered separately).

**Eligibility**  This program is open to seniors graduating from high schools in Connecticut and planning to attend a college or university in any state. Applicants must be a member of at least 1 sports team at their high school and participate in extracurricular activities. They must have a GPA of 3.0 or higher and minimum scores of 1300 on the 2400-scale SAT, 850 on the 1600-scale SAT, or 19 on the ACT. Along with their application, they must submit a 500-word essay that describes who they are, how they view themselves, and any other information they wish to have considered. Males and females are judged separately. Financial need is not considered in the selection process.

**Financial data**  The stipend is $2,500.

**Duration**  1 year.

**Additional information**  This program began in 2007.

**Number awarded**  2 each year: 1 for a female and 1 for a male.

**Deadline**  May of each year.

## [553]
## ROCKWELL AUTOMATION SCHOLARSHIPS

Society of Women Engineers
Attn: Scholarship Selection Committee
203 North LaSalle Street, Suite 1675
Chicago, IL 60601-1269
(312) 596-5223        Toll Free: (877) SWE-INFO
Fax: (312) 644-8557        E-mail: scholarships@swe.org
Web: societyofwomenengineers.swe.org

**Summary**  To provide financial assistance to upper-division women majoring in computer science or selected engineering specialties.

**Eligibility**  This program is open to women who are entering their junior year at an ABET-accredited college or university. Applicants must be working full time on a degree in computer science or computer, electrical, industrial, manufacturing, mechanical, or software engineering and have a GPA of 3.0 or higher. Selection is based on merit and demonstrated leadership potential. Preference is given to students attending designated universities and to members of groups underrepresented in computer science and engineering.

**Financial data**  The stipend is $2,500.

**Duration**  1 year.

**Additional information**  This program, established in 1991, is supported by Rockwell Automation, Inc. For a list of the preferred universities, check the web site of the Society of Women Engineers.

**Number awarded**  2 each year.

**Deadline**  February of each year.

## [554]
## ROCKWELL COLLINS SWE SCHOLARSHIPS

Society of Women Engineers
Attn: Scholarship Selection Committee
203 North LaSalle Street, Suite 1675
Chicago, IL 60601-1269
(312) 596-5223        Toll Free: (877) SWE-INFO
Fax: (312) 644-8557        E-mail: scholarships@swe.org
Web: societyofwomenengineers.swe.org

**Summary**  To provide financial assistance to undergraduate members of the Society of Women Engineers (SWE) majoring in computer science or selected engineering specialties.

**Eligibility**  This program is open to members of the society who are entering their sophomore or junior year at a 4-year ABET-accredited college or university. Applicants must be working full time on a degree in computer science or computer, electrical, or software engineering and have a GPA of 3.0 or higher. Selection is based on merit. They must be available to accepted 1 Rockwell Collins co-op or internship prior to completing their degree. Preference is given to members of groups underrepresented in computer science and engineering.

**Financial data**  The stipend is $2,500.

**Duration**  1 year.

**Additional information**  This program, established in 1991, is supported by Rockwell Collins, Inc.

**Number awarded**  3 each year.

**Deadline**  February of each year.

## [555]
## ROCKY MOUNTAIN SECTION COLLEGE SCHOLARSHIPS

Society of Women Engineers-Rocky Mountain Section
Attn: Collegiate Scholarship Committee Chair
P.O. Box 260692
Lakewood, CO 80226-0692
(303) 751-0741        Fax: (303) 751-2581
E-mail: christi.wisleder@gmail.copm
Web: www.societyofwomenengineers.org

**Summary**  To provide financial assistance to women from any state who are working on an undergraduate or graduate degree in engineering at colleges and universities in Colorado and Wyoming.

**Eligibility**  This program is open to women from any state who are enrolled as an undergraduate or graduate engineering student in an ABET-accredited engineering or computer science program in Colorado or Wyoming (excluding zip codes 80800-81599). Applicants must have a GPA of 3.0 or higher. Along with their application, they must submit an essay on why they have chosen an engineering major, what they will accomplish or how they believe they will make a difference as an engineer, and who or what influenced them to study engineering. Selection is based on merit.

**Financial data**  The stipend is $1,250.

**Duration**  1 year.

**Additional information**  This program includes the following named scholarships: the Dorolyn Lines Scholarship, the

Lottye Miner Scholarship, and the Rocky Mountain Section Pioneer Scholarship.

**Number awarded**   3 each year.

**Deadline**   January of each year.

## [556]
## ROGER J. SHERIDAN MEMORIAL SCHOLARSHIPS

Vermont Elks Association, Inc.
c/o Roger J. Campo, Scholarship Chair
16 Windridge Drive
Barre, VT 05641-9748
(802) 479-1286                    E-mail: rcampo@aol.com

**Summary**   To provide financial assistance to high school seniors in Vermont who are interested in studying physical education at a college in any state (females and males are considered separately).

**Eligibility**   This program is open to seniors graduating from high schools in Vermont who plan to attend a college or university in any state. Applicants must be planning to major in physical education to prepare for a career as a teacher of physical education. Along with their application, they must submit transcripts, copies of their SAT or ACT scores, letters of recommendation, documentation of financial need, and an essay on their plans after graduation from college. Selection is based on commitment to chosen career and field of study, academic achievement, school and community involvement and/or service, and financial need. Females and males are considered separately.

**Financial data**   Stipends range up to $1,000.

**Duration**   1 year.

**Number awarded**   2 each year: 1 to a female and 1 to a male.

**Deadline**   January of each year.

## [557]
## ROLLIE HOPGOOD FUTURE TEACHERS AFT MEMBER SCHOLARSHIPS

AFT Michigan
Attn: Scholarship Committee
2661 East Jefferson Avenue
Detroit, MI 48207
(313) 393-2200                    Toll Free: (800) MFT-8868
Fax: (313) 393-2236      E-mail: ldoniver@aftmichigan.org
Web: aftmichigan.org/members/scholarships.html

**Summary**   To provide financial assistance to high school seniors in Michigan who are children of members of AFT Michigan and interested in attending college in any state to prepare for a career as a teacher (females and males compete separately).

**Eligibility**   This program is open to graduating high school seniors who are children of members of AFT Michigan. Applicants must be planning to enroll full time at a college or university in any state to prepare for a career as a teacher. Along with their application, they must submit a 500-word essay on why they want to become a teacher, why they should be considered for this scholarship, and the correlation between education and politics. Selection is based on the essay, GPA, extracurricular activities, community-related activities, and financial need. Female and male applicants compete separately.

**Financial data**   The stipend is $1,000.

**Duration**   1 year.

**Additional information**   AFT Michigan was formerly the Michigan Federation of Teachers & School Related Personnel.

**Number awarded**   2 each year: 1 female and 1 male.

**Deadline**   May of each year.

## [558]
## ROLLIE HOPGOOD FUTURE TEACHERS HIGH SCHOOL SENIOR SCHOLARSHIPS

AFT Michigan
Attn: Scholarship Committee
2661 East Jefferson Avenue
Detroit, MI 48207
(313) 393-2200                    Toll Free: (800) MFT-8868
Fax: (313) 393-2236      E-mail: ldoniver@aftmichigan.org
Web: aftmichigan.org/members/scholarships.html

**Summary**   To provide financial assistance to high school seniors in Michigan who are interested in attending college in any state to prepare for a career as a teacher (females and males compete separately).

**Eligibility**   This program is open to seniors graduating from high schools that are represented by AFT Michigan. Applicants must be planning to enroll full time at a college or university in any state to prepare for a career as a teacher. Along with their application, they must submit a 500-word essay on why they want to become a teacher, why they should be considered for this scholarship, and the correlation between education and politics. Selection is based on the essay, GPA, extracurricular activities, community-related activities, and financial need. Female and male applicants compete separately.

**Financial data**   The stipend is $1,000.

**Duration**   1 year.

**Additional information**   AFT Michigan was formerly the Michigan Federation of Teachers & School Related Personnel.

**Number awarded**   2 each year: 1 female and 1 male.

**Deadline**   May of each year.

## [559]
## RONALD N. DAVIS ACADEMIC ALL-STATE TEAM

Florida High School Athletic Association
Attn: Director of Special Programs
1801 N.W. 80th Boulevard
Gainesville, FL 32606
(352) 372-9551, ext. 170          Toll Free: (800) 461-7895
Fax: (352) 373-1528                E-mail: lring@fhsaa.org
Web: www.fhsaa.org

**Summary**   To provide financial assistance to student-athletes in Florida who have excelled in academics and athletics and plan to attend college in any state (females and males are judged separately).

**Eligibility**   This program is open to seniors graduating from high schools in Florida and planning to attend college in any state. Each high school in the state may nominate 1 boy and 1 girl. Nominees must have a cumulative unweighted GPA of 3.5 or higher and have earned a varsity letter in at least 2 different sports during each of their junior and senior years. Boys and girls are judged separately.

**Financial data** Each honoree receives a $1,000 award. From among those honorees, the Scholar-Athletes of the Year receive an additional $3,000 scholarship.

**Duration** The awards are presented annually.

**Number awarded** 24 honorees (12 boys and 12 girls) are selected each year. From among those, 2 Scholar-Athletes of the Year (1 boy and 1 girl) are selected annually.

**Deadline** Schools must submit nominations by February of each year.

## [560]
## ROSE MCGILL FUND UNDERGRADUATE CONFIDENTIAL AID GRANTS

Kappa Kappa Gamma Fraternity
Attn: Foundation Administrator
530 East Town Street
P.O. Box 38
Columbus, OH 43216-0038
(614) 228-6515          Toll Free: (866) KKG-1870
Fax: (614) 228-6303          E-mail: kkghq@kappa.org
Web: www.kappakappagamma.org

**Summary** To assist undergraduate members of Kappa Kappa Gamma who face serious financial problems.

**Eligibility** This program is open to Kappa Kappa Gamma college students facing a personal or family catastrophe of a financial nature. Applications may be submitted by an alumnae association, a Kappa sister, or the member herself.

**Financial data** Grants range up to $2,500 per year.

**Duration** These are 1-time grants.

**Additional information** The Rose McGill fund was established in 1922 to provide confidential aid to Kappa Kappa Gamma members. Requests for applications must be accompanied by a self-addressed stamped envelope and chapter membership identification.

**Number awarded** Varies each year; in a recent biennium, Rose McGill programs provided $696,424 in support.

**Deadline** January or September of each year.

## [561]
## ROSE SCHOLARSHIP

Zonta International District 10 Foundation
c/o Lisa LeBlanc
175 Antigua Drive
Lafayette, LA 70503
(337) 984-4197          E-mail: lisa.leblanc@lusfiber.net
Web: www.zontadistrict10.org

**Summary** To provide financial assistance to female nontraditional college students in designated states.

**Eligibility** This program is open to residents of Arkansas, Louisiana, New Mexico, Oklahoma, or Texas who are nontraditional students, female heads of households, and primary wage earners of their family. Applicants must be attending an accredited educational institution to obtain postsecondary training or certification in a program that does not require a baccalaureate degree. They must be able to document financial need, but other factors considered in the selection process include good citizenship, character, reputation, and moral and ethical standing. U.S. citizenship is required.

**Financial data** The stipend is $1,000. Funds are paid directly to the institution providing the certification or training.

**Duration** 1 year.

**Number awarded** 1 each year.

**Deadline** February of each year.

## [562]
## ROWDY AND LUCKY SHAIN SCHOLARSHIP

Chi Omega Fraternity
Attn: Chi Omega Foundation
3395 Players Club Parkway
Memphis, TN 38125
(901) 748-8600          Fax: (901) 748-8686
E-mail: foundation@chiomega.com
Web: www.chiomega.com/wemakeadifference/scholarships

**Summary** To provide financial assistance to women who are collegian or alumnae members of Chi Omega Fraternity studying animal welfare or veterinary medicine.

**Eligibility** This program is open to women who are collegian or alumnae members of Chi Omega Fraternity. Applicants must be working on an undergraduate or graduate degree in animal welfare or veterinary medicine. Selection is based on an essay, academic aptitude, service to Chi Omega, contributions to the university and community, personal and professional goals, and financial need.

**Financial data** The stipend is $1,000.

**Duration** 1 year.

**Additional information** This program began in 2012 with a gift from foundation trustee Melanie Maxwell Shain and her husband John who wished to honor their 2 cats.

**Number awarded** 1 each year.

**Deadline** April of each year.

## [563]
## RURAL MUTUAL INSURANCE COMPANY SCHOLARSHIPS

Wisconsin Towns Association
Attn: Scholarship Program
W7686 County Road MMM
Shawano, WI 54166-6086
(715) 526-3157          Fax: (715) 524-3917
E-mail: wtowns@frontiernet.net
Web: www.wisctowns.com/home/scholarship-program

**Summary** To provide financial assistance to high seniors in Wisconsin who submit outstanding essays on town government and plan to attend college in the state (females and males are judged separately).

**Eligibility** This program is open to seniors graduating from high schools in Wisconsin who plan to attend a college, university, or vocational/technical institute in the state. Applicants must live in a town or village that has insurance from Rural Mutual Insurance Company for its municipal government. Along with their application, they must submit an essay of 500 to 1,000 words on a topic that changes annually but relates to local government in Wisconsin; recently, students were asked to write on "How can towns and villages best protect their infrastructure and still provide other needed services such as fire and emergency services in tough economic times?" Selection is based primarily on the essay's originality and subject matter in relationship to the topic; financial need is not considered. Boys and girls are judged separately.

**Financial data** The stipend is $1,000.

**Duration** 1 year.

**Additional information** This program is supported by Rural Mutual Insurance Company.

**Number awarded** 2 each year: 1 to a boy and 1 to a girl.

**Deadline** May of each year.

## [564]
## RUTH ROSENBAUM GOLDFEDER MEMORIAL SCHOLARSHIP

Alpha Epsilon Phi
Attn: AEPhi Foundation
11 Lake Avenue Extension, Suite 1A
Danbury, CT 06811
(203) 748-0029                 Fax: (203) 748-0039
E-mail: aephifoundation@aephi.org
Web: www.aephi.org/foundation/scholarships

**Summary** To provide financial assistance for undergraduate or graduate education to Alpha Epsilon Phi members or alumnae, especially those at California universities.

**Eligibility** This program is open to active and alumnae members of the sorority who are either full-time rising juniors or seniors or graduate students who have completed at least 1 year of graduate study. Preference is given to members at universities in California. Applicants must have a GPA of 3.0 or higher. Along with their application, they must submit a letter describing 1) their activities in their chapter, on campus, and in the general community; 2) what they have done to supplement their parents' contribution toward their education; and 3) their need for scholarship consideration.

**Financial data** Stipends range from $1,000 to $2,000 per year.

**Duration** 1 year; may be renewed.

**Additional information** Recipients must be willing to remain active in the sorority and live in the sorority house (if any) for the entire year the scholarship covers.

**Number awarded** 1 or more each year.

**Deadline** March of each year.

## [565]
## RUTH ROUSE DOLBERG SCHOLARSHIP

Kappa Delta Sorority
Attn: Foundation Project Manager
3205 Players Lane
Memphis, TN 38125
(901) 748-1897, ext. 203       Toll Free: (800) 536-1897
Fax: (901) 748-0949
E-mail: caroline.cullum@kappadelta.org
Web: www.kappadelta.org/scholarshipapplications_1

**Summary** To provide financial assistance to members of Kappa Delta Sorority who are majoring in accounting.

**Eligibility** This program is open to undergraduate members of Kappa Delta Sorority. Applicants must submit a personal statement giving their reasons for applying for this scholarship, an official undergraduate transcript, and 2 letters of recommendation. They must be majoring in accounting. Selection is based on academic excellence; service to the chapter, alumnae association, or national Kappa Delta; service to the campus and community; personal objectives and goals; potential; recommendations; and financial need.

**Financial data** The stipend is $2,000 per year. Funds may be used only for tuition, fees, and books, not for room and board.

**Duration** 1 year; may be renewed.

**Number awarded** 1 each year.

**Deadline** November of each year.

## [566]
## RUTH WHITNEY SCHOLARSHIP

New York Women in Communications, Inc.
Attn: NYWICI Foundation
355 Lexington Avenue, 15th Floor
New York, NY 10017-6603
(212) 297-2133            Fax: (212) 370-9047
E-mail: nywicipr@nywici.org
Web: www.nywici.org/foundation/scholarships

**Summary** To provide financial assistance to female residents of designated eastern states who are interested in preparing for a career in magazine journalism or publishing at a college or graduate school in any state.

**Eligibility** This program is open to women who are residents of New York, New Jersey, Connecticut, or Pennsylvania and enrolled as undergraduate or graduate students at a college or university in any state. Graduate students must be members of New York Women in Communications, Inc. (NYWICI). Also eligible are women who reside outside the 4 states but are currently enrolled at a college or university within 1 of the 5 boroughs of New York City. Applicants must have some experience in writing, reporting, or design and be preparing for a career in magazine journalism or publishing. Along with their application, they must submit a 2-page resume; a personal essay of 300 words on an assigned topic that changes annually; 2 letters of recommendation; and an official transcript. Selection is based on academic record, need, demonstrated leadership, participation in school and community activities, honors and other awards or recognition, work experience, goals and aspirations, and unusual personal and/or family circumstances. U.S. citizenship is required.

**Financial data** The stipend ranges up to $10,000.

**Duration** 1 year.

**Additional information** This program is sponsored by *Glamour* magazine, which invites the recipient to visit its offices and spend a week with its editorial team.

**Number awarded** 1 each year.

**Deadline** January of each year.

## [567]
## RUTHANN FAIRBAIRN SCHOLARSHIP

Oklahoma Society of Certified Public Accountants
Attn: OSCPA Educational Foundation
1900 N.W. Expressway, Suite 910
Oklahoma City, OK 73118-1898
(405) 841-3811
Toll Free: (800) 522-8261, ext. 3811 (within OK)
Fax: (405) 841-3801       E-mail: hjared@oscpa.com
Web: www.oscpa.com/?524

**Summary** To provide financial assistance to female members of the Oklahoma Society of Certified Public Accountants (OSCPA) working on a bachelor's or advanced degree in accounting in Oklahoma.

**Eligibility** This program is open to female OSCPA members who are nominated by an accounting program at an Oklahoma college or university. Nominees must be working on a bachelor's or advanced degree in accounting and have successfully completed at least 6 hours of principles of accounting. As part of the selection process, they must submit a resume, a transcript, standardized test scores, and 3 letters of reference.

**Financial data** The stipend ranges from $250 to $1,500.
**Duration** 1 year.
**Number awarded** 1 each year.
**Deadline** March of each year.

## [568]
## S. EVELYN LEWIS MEMORIAL SCHOLARSHIP IN MEDICAL HEALTH SCIENCES

Zeta Phi Beta Sorority, Inc.
Attn: National Education Foundation
1734 New Hampshire Avenue, N.W.
Washington, DC 20009
(202) 387-3103                     Fax: (202) 232-4593
E-mail: scholarship@ZPhiBNEF.org
Web: www.zphib1920.org/nef

**Summary** To provide financial assistance to women interested in studying medicine or health sciences on the undergraduate or graduate school level.

**Eligibility** This program is open to women enrolled full time in a program on the undergraduate or graduate school level leading to a degree in medicine or health sciences. Proof of enrollment is required. Applicants need not be members of Zeta Phi Beta Sorority. Along with their application, they must submit a 150-word essay on their educational goals and professional aspirations, how this award will help them to achieve those goals, and why they should receive the award. Financial need is not considered in the selection process.

**Financial data** The stipend ranges from $500 to $1,000. Funds are paid directly to the college or university.
**Duration** 1 academic year.
**Number awarded** 1 or more each year.
**Deadline** January of each year.

## [569]
## SABAN MILITARY WIFE EDUCATIONAL SCHOLARSHIPS

Operation Homefront
8930 Fourwinds Drive, Suite 340
San Antonio, TX 78239
(210) 659-7756                     Toll Free: (800) 722-6098
Fax: (210) 566-7544
Web: www.operationhomefront.net/scholarship

**Summary** To provide financial assistance to wives of military personnel who are interested in studying a medical-related field at a vocational school.

**Eligibility** This program is open to wives of military members currently serving on active duty, including Reserve and National Guard members who have served at least 180 combined days of full-time military duty since January 1, 2008. Applicants must be enrolled or planning to enroll in a vocational training program as a dental assistance, medical assistant, medical billing and coding specialist, medical insurance technician, patient care assistant/technician, nurse assistant, vocational nurse, or medical transcriber. Along with their application, they must submit a 300-word essay on how, besides being a military wife, they have contributed to making

their community a better place. Selection is based on the essay and commitment to volunteerism.

**Financial data** Maximum stipends are $30,000, $10,000, or $8,500. Funds may be used for tuition only; books and other fees are not covered.
**Duration** The program of study must be completed within 48 months.
**Additional information** Recipients must perform at least 12 hours of community service in the year when they receive the scholarship.
**Number awarded** 22 each year: 2 at $30,000 (for nursing students only), 5 at $10,000, and 15 at $8,500.
**Deadline** April of each year.

## [570]
## SAE WOMEN ENGINEERS COMMITTEE SCHOLARSHIP

Society of Automotive Engineers
Attn: Scholarship Administrator
400 Commonwealth Drive
Warrendale, PA 15096-0001
(724) 776-4970                     Fax: (724) 776-3049
E-mail: scholarships@sae.org
Web: students.sae.org/awdscholar/scholarships/wec

**Summary** To provide financial support to female graduating high school seniors interested in studying engineering in college.

**Eligibility** This program is open to female U.S. citizens who intend to earn an ABET-accredited degree in engineering. Applicants must be high school seniors with a GPA of 3.0 or higher. Selection is based on high school transcripts; SAT or ACT scores; school-related extracurricular activities; non-school related activities; academic honors, civic honors, and awards; and a 250-word essay on their goals, plans, experiences, and interests in mobility engineering. Financial need is not considered.

**Financial data** The stipend is $2,000.
**Duration** 1 year; nonrenewable.
**Additional information** Funds for this scholarship are provided by Mercedes-Benz USA.
**Number awarded** 1 each year.
**Deadline** January of each year.

## [571]
## SANDRA SEBRELL BAILEY SCHOLARSHIP

Delta Zeta Sorority
Attn: Foundation Coordinator
202 East Church Street
Oxford, OH 45056
(513) 523-7597                     Fax: (513) 523-1921
E-mail: DZFoundation@dzshq.com
Web: www.deltazeta.org

**Summary** To provide financial assistance for continued undergraduate study to members of Delta Zeta Sorority, especially those planning to major in education.

**Eligibility** This program is open to members of the sorority who are entering their junior or senior year and have been an initiated member for at least 1 year. Applicants must submit an official transcript, a statement of their career goals, information on their service to the sorority, documentation of campus activities and/or community involvement, a list of academic honors, and an explanation of their financial need. Preference may be given to students entering the field of education, but that is not required.

**Financial data** The stipend ranges from $500 to $2,500, depending on the availability of funds.

**Duration** 1 year; nonrenewable.

**Number awarded** 1 each year.

**Deadline** February of each year.

## [572]
## SAO SUMMER INTERN PROGRAM

Harvard-Smithsonian Center for Astrophysics
Attn: Summer Intern Program
60 Garden Street, Mail Stop 70
Cambridge, MA 02138
(617) 496-7063          E-mail: intern-at-cfa@harvard.edu
Web: hea-www.harvard.edu/REU/REU.html

**Summary** To enable undergraduates interested in a physical science career or science education to obtain research experience at the Smithsonian Astrophysical Observatory (SAO) at Harvard University.

**Eligibility** This program is open to U.S. citizens, nationals, and permanent residents enrolled in a program leading to a bachelor's degree. Applicants must be interested in a career in astronomy, astrophysics, physics, or related physical sciences. Along with their application, they must submit an essay of 600 to 800 words describing academic and career goals, scientific interests, relevant work experience, why they would like to be in the program, and why they would be a good candidate. Graduating seniors are not eligible. Applications are especially encouraged from underrepresented minorities, persons with disabilities, and women.

**Financial data** The stipend is $4,500. Housing and travel expenses are provided.

**Duration** 10 weeks during the summer.

**Additional information** Each intern works with a scientist on an individual research project. Potential areas of research include observational and theoretical cosmology, extragalactic and galactic astronomy, interstellar medium and star formation, laboratory astrophysics, supernovae and supernova remnants, planetary science, and solar and stellar astrophysics. Also included in the program are weekly lectures, field trips, and workshops specifically designed for the participants. This program is supported by the National Science Foundation as part of its Research Experiences for Undergraduates (REU) Program.

**Number awarded** 10 each year.

**Deadline** January of each year.

## [573]
## SARAH E. HUNEYCUTT SCHOLARSHIP

Florida State Golf Association
Attn: Junior Girls' Scholarship Fund
12630 Telecom Drive
Tampa, FL 33637
(813) 632-3742          Fax: (813) 910-2129
E-mail: dgreen@fsga.org
Web: www.fsga.org

**Summary** To provide financial assistance to female high school seniors in Florida who have been involved in golf and are interested in attending college in any state.

**Eligibility** This program is open to women who are graduating seniors at high schools in Florida and have an interest or association with the game of golf. Applicants must be planning to attend a junior college, college, university, or technical school in any state but not be eligible for a golf scholarship. They must have a GPA of 3.0 or higher and be able to document financial need.

**Financial data** Stipends range up to $5,000 per year. Funds are paid directly to the recipient's school.

**Duration** 4 years.

**Additional information** This program was established by the Florida Women's State Golf Association (FWSGA) in 1994. When that organization merged with the Florida State Golf Association in 2012, the scholarship fund remained independent.

**Number awarded** 1 renewable scholarship at $5,000 per year and a varying number of nonrenewable smaller scholarships are awarded each year.

**Deadline** February of each year.

## [574]
## SARAH JANE HOUSTON SCHOLARSHIP

Delta Zeta Sorority
Attn: Foundation Coordinator
202 East Church Street
Oxford, OH 45056
(513) 523-7597          Fax: (513) 523-1921
E-mail: DZFoundation@dzshq.com
Web: www.deltazeta.org

**Summary** To provide financial assistance for continued undergraduate study to members of Delta Zeta Sorority who are majoring in English or a related field.

**Eligibility** This program is open to members of the sorority who are entering their junior or senior year and have a GPA of 3.0 or higher. Applicants must be working on a degree in English or a related field (e.g., speech, debate, drama, theater, education). Along with their application, they must submit an official transcript, a statement of their career goals, information on their service to the sorority, documentation of campus activities and/or community involvement, a list of academic honors, and an explanation of their financial need. Preference is given to members of chapters in Illinois.

**Financial data** The stipend ranges from $500 to $2,500, depending on the availability of funds.

**Duration** 1 year; nonrenewable.

**Number awarded** 1 each year.

**Deadline** February of each year.

## [575]
## SARAH PEUGH BUTTERFLY SCHOLARSHIP

GFWC/Mississippi Federation of Women's Clubs, Inc.
c/o Suzanne Poynor, President
225 Briarhill Cove
Florence, MS 39073
E-mail: info@gfwc-mfwc.org
Web: www.gfwc-mfwc.org

**Summary** To provide financial assistance to high school seniors in Mississippi who are members of a Juniorette club affiliated with the GFWC/Mississippi Federation of Women's Clubs and plan to attend college in any state.

**Eligibility** This program is open to women who are seniors graduating from high schools in Mississippi and members of a GFWC-MFWC Juniorette club. Applicants must be planning to major in any field at a college or university in any state. They must submit a list of their leadership activities, ACT score, and a letter of recommendation from a GFWS-MWFC sponsoring club.

**Financial data** The stipend is $1,000. Funds are sent directly to the recipient's institution.

**Duration** 1 year.

**Number awarded** 1 each year.

**Deadline** February of each year.

## [576]
## SCHOLARSHIP FOR WOMEN IN TRANSITION

Accounting and Financial Women's Alliance-Billings
   Chapter
Attn: Scholarship Chair
P.O. Box 20593
Billings, MT 59104-0593
E-mail: aswabillings@gmail.com
Web: www.billingsafwa.org/scholarship

**Summary** To provide financial assistance to women from any state who are returning to school to work on an undergraduate degree in accounting or finance at a college in Montana.

**Eligibility** This program is open to women from any state who have a gap of at least 4 years between high school and college or in college attendance. Applicants must be enrolled full time at an accredited college, university, or professional school of accounting in Montana and working on a degree in accounting or finance. They must have a GPA of 3.0 or higher. Along with their application, they must submit an essay of 150 to 250 words on their career goals and objectives, the impact they want to have on the accounting world, and their community involvement, extracurricular activities, applicable and current work experience, and leadership. Selection is based on that essay, academic average, leadership, character, communication skills, community service, extracurricular activities, and financial need.

**Financial data** The stipend is $1,000.

**Duration** 1 year.

**Number awarded** 2 each year.

**Deadline** October of each year.

## [577]
## SCHOLARSHIPS FOR ELCA SERVICE ABROAD

Women of the Evangelical Lutheran Church in America
Attn: Scholarships
8765 West Higgins Road
Chicago, IL 60631-4101
(773) 380-2741        Toll Free: (800) 638-3522, ext. 2741
Fax: (773) 380-2419        E-mail: valora.starr@elca.org
Web: www.womenoftheelca.org

**Summary** To provide financial assistance to lay women who are members of Evangelical Lutheran Church of America (ELCA) congregations and who wish to pursue postsecondary education for service abroad, either in general or in health fields.

**Eligibility** This program is open to ELCA lay women who are at least 21 years of age and have experienced an inter-ruption of at least 2 years in their education since high school. Applicants must have been admitted to an academic institution to prepare for a career other than the ordained ministry. This program is available only to women studying for ELCA service abroad, either in general or in health professions associated with ELCA projects abroad. U.S. citizenship is required.

**Financial data** The stipend ranges from $800 to $1,000 per year.

**Duration** Up to 2 years.

**Additional information** This program includes the following named scholarships: the Belmer Scholarship, the Flora Prince Scholarship, the Kahler Scholarship, the Vickers/Raup Scholarship, and the Emma Wettstein Scholarship.

**Number awarded** 1 or more each year.

**Deadline** February of each year.

## [578]
## SCHOLARSHIPS FOR WOMEN RESIDENTS OF THE STATE OF DELAWARE

American Association of University Women-Wilmington
   Branch
Attn: Scholarship Committee
1800 Fairfax Boulevard
Wilmington, DE 19803-3106
(302) 737-6447        E-mail: aauwwilm@gmail.com
Web: www.aauwwilmington.org/procedure.html

**Summary** To provide financial assistance to female residents of Delaware who plan to attend college in any state.

**Eligibility** This program is open to women who are U.S. citizens and 1) a Delaware resident and a high school graduate; 2) a Delaware resident and a senior at a high school in New Castle County; or 3) a resident of New Castle County, Delaware and a home-schooled student who can meet the admission requirements of the University of Delaware. Applicants must be attending or planning to attend a college or university in any state. Along with their application, they must submit a 150-word essay on what they plan to study and why. High school seniors must also submit a 150-word essay on either 1) what they would do and where they would do it if they had 4 hours to spend any place, either now or in history; or 2) the famous person, past or present, they would like to meet and why. Selection is based on scholastic standing, contributions to school and community, SAT scores, and financial need. An interview is required.

**Financial data** A stipend is awarded (amount not specified).

**Duration** 1 year.

**Number awarded** Varies each year; recently, 17 of these scholarships, worth $55,000, were awarded.

**Deadline** February of each year.

## [579]
## SCHOLARSHIPS SUPPORTING POST-SECONDARY EDUCATION FOR A CAREER IN THE AUDIOVISUAL INDUSTRY

InfoComm International
International Communications Industries Foundation
11242 Waples Mill Road, Suite 200
Fairfax, VA 22030
(703) 273-7200          Toll Free: (800) 659-7469
Fax: (703) 278-8082     E-mail: jhardwick@infocomm.org
Web: www.infocomm.org

**Summary**  To provide financial assistance to undergraduate and graduate students (especially women and minorities) who are interested in preparing for a career in the audiovisual (AV) industry.

**Eligibility**  This program is open to second-year students at 2-year colleges, juniors and seniors at 4-year institutions, and graduate students. Applicants must have a GPA of 2.75 or higher and be majoring or planning to major in audiovisual subjects or related fields, including audio, video, audiovisual, radio/television/film, or other field related to a career in the audiovisual industry. Students in other programs, such as journalism, may be eligible if they can demonstrate a relationship to career goals in the AV industry. Along with their application, they must submit 1) an essay of 150 to 200 words on the career path they plan to pursue in the audiovisual industry in the next 5 years; and 2) an essay of 250 to 300 words on the experience or person influencing them the most in selecting the audiovisual industry as their career of choice. Minority and women candidates are especially encouraged to apply. Selection is based on the essays, presentation of the application, GPA, AV-related experience, work experience, and letters of recommendation.

**Financial data**  The stipend is $4,000. Funds are sent directly to the school.

**Duration**  1 year.

**Additional information**  InfoComm International, formerly the International Communications Industries Association, established the International Communications Industries Foundation (ICIF) to manage its charitable and educational activities.

**Number awarded**  Varies each year.

**Deadline**  April of each year.

## [580]
## SEATTLE CHAPTER AFWA SCHOLARSHIPS

Accounting and Financial Women's Alliance-Seattle
  Chapter
Attn: Scholarships
800 Fifth Avenue, Suite 101
PMB 237
Seattle, WA 98104-3191
(206) 467-8645     E-mail: scholarship@aswaseattle.com
Web: www.aswaseattle.com/scholarships.cfm

**Summary**  To provide financial assistance to women from any state working on an undergraduate or graduate degree in accounting at a college or university in Washington.

**Eligibility**  This program is open to female residents of any state who are working part time or full time on an associate, bachelor's, or master's degree in accounting at a college or university in Washington. Applicants must have completed at least 30 semester hours and have maintained a GPA of at least 2.5 overall and 3.0 in accounting. Membership in the Accounting and Financial Women's Alliance (AFWA) is not required. Selection is based on career goals, communication skills, GPA, personal circumstances, and financial need.

**Financial data**  Stipends range from $1,500 to $5,000.

**Duration**  1 year.

**Additional information**  This program began in 1962.

**Number awarded**  Varies each year; recently, 8 of these scholarships were awarded: 1 at $5,000, 2 at $3,000, and 5 at $2,000. Since the program began, it has awarded nearly $250,000 in scholarships.

**Deadline**  June of each year.

## [581]
## SEATTLE PROFESSIONAL CHAPTER AWC SCHOLARSHIPS

Association for Women in Communications-Seattle
  Professional Chapter
Attn: Tina Christiansen, Vice-president of Student Affairs
P.O. Box 60262
Seattle, WA 98160
E-mail: tina@writeasrain.com
Web: www.seattleawc.org

**Summary**  To provide financial assistance to female upper-division and graduate students in Washington who are preparing for a career in the communications industry.

**Eligibility**  This program is open to female Washington state residents who are enrolled at a 4-year college or university in the state as a junior, senior, or graduate student (sophomores at 2-year colleges applying to a 4-year institution are also eligible). Applicants must be working on or planning to work on a degree in a communications program, including print and broadcast journalism, television and radio production, film, advertising, public relations, marketing, graphic design, multimedia design, photography, or technical communication. Selection is based on demonstrated excellence in communications, contributions made to communications on campus and/or in the community, scholastic achievement, financial need, and work samples.

**Financial data**  The stipend is $1,500. Funds are paid directly to the recipient's school and must be used for tuition and fees.

**Duration**  1 year.

**Number awarded**  2 each year.

**Deadline**  April of each year.

## [582]
## SEHAR SALEHA AHMAD AND ABRAHIM EKRAMULLAH ZAFAR FOUNDATION SCHOLARSHIP

Oregon Student Access Commission
Attn: Grants and Scholarships Division
1500 Valley River Drive, Suite 100
Eugene, OR 97401-2146
(541) 687-7395     Toll Free: (800) 452-8807, ext. 7395
Fax: (541) 687-7414     TDD: (800) 735-2900
E-mail: awardinfo@osac.state.or.us
Web: www.oregonstudentaid.gov/scholarships.aspx

**Summary** To provide financial assistance to female high school seniors in Oregon who are interested in studying English at a college in the state.

**Eligibility** This program is open to women who are graduating seniors from high schools in Oregon (including GED recipients and home-schooled students). Applicants must be planning to major in English at a 4-year college or university in the state. They must have a GPA of 3.5 or higher and be able to demonstrate financial need.

**Financial data** Stipends for scholarships offered by the Oregon Student Access Commission (OSAC) range from $200 to $10,000 but recently averaged $2,300.

**Duration** 1 year; may be renewed if the recipient shows satisfactory academic progress and continued financial need.

**Number awarded** 1 or more each year.

**Deadline** February of each year.

## [583]
## SENATOR SCOTT WHITE MEMORIAL SCHOLARSHIP

Women's Transportation Seminar-Puget Sound Chapter
c/o Jennifer Barnes, Scholarship Co-Chair
Heffron Transportation, Inc.
532 27th Avenue
Seattle, WA 98122
(206) 324-3623                          Fax: (877) 314-9959
E-mail: jennifer@hefftrans.com
Web: www.wtsinternational.org

**Summary** To provide financial assistance to women undergraduate and graduate students from Washington enrolled in a college in the state and working on a degree related to public policy or public administration in transportation.

**Eligibility** This program is open to women who are residents of Washington, studying at a college in the state, or working as an intern in the state. Applicants must be currently enrolled in an undergraduate or graduate degree program in public policy or public administration in a transportation-related field. They must have a GPA of 3.0 or higher and plans to prepare for a career in their field of study. Minority women are especially encouraged to apply. Along with their application, they must submit a 500-word statement about their career goals after graduation, how their goals are related to public policy or public administration, and why they think they should receive this scholarship award. Selection is based on that statement, academic record, financial need, and transportation-related activities or job skills.

**Financial data** The stipend is $2,500.

**Duration** 1 year.

**Number awarded** 1 each year.

**Deadline** November of each year.

## [584]
## SHANNON FUND

Episcopal Diocese of Bethlehem
Attn: Archdeacon Howard Stringfellow
333 Wyandotte Street
Bethlehem, PA 18015
(610) 691-5655, ext. 222
Toll Free: (800) 358-5655 (within PA)
E-mail: archdeacon@diobeth.org
Web: www.diobeth.org

**Summary** To provide financial assistance to residents of Pennsylvania who are daughters of Episcopal clergy and interested in working on a degree at a college in any state.

**Eligibility** Applicants must be 1) residents of 1 of the 5 dioceses of Pennsylvania; 2) daughters of an Episcopal priest; 3) younger than 20 years of age; and 4) interested in working on a degree at a college in any state. The clergy parent must live in Pennsylvania and must be canonically resident in 1 of its dioceses. Financial need is considered in the selection process.

**Financial data** A stipend is awarded (amount not specified).

**Duration** 1 year.

**Number awarded** 5 each year.

**Deadline** April of each year.

## [585]
## SHARON D. BANKS MEMORIAL UNDERGRADUATE SCHOLARSHIP

Women's Transportation Seminar
Attn: WTS Foundation
1701 K Street, N.W., Suite 800
Washington, DC 20006
(202) 955-5085                          Fax: (202) 955-5088
E-mail: wts@wtsinternational.org
Web: www.wtsinternational.org/education/scholarships

**Summary** To provide financial assistance to undergraduate women interested in a career in transportation.

**Eligibility** This program is open to women who are working on an undergraduate degree in transportation or a transportation-related field (e.g., transportation engineering, planning, finance, or logistics). Applicants must have a GPA of 3.0 or higher and be interested in a career in transportation. Along with their application, they must submit a 500-word statement about their career goals after graduation and why they think they should receive the scholarship award. Applications must be submitted first to a local chapter; the chapters forward selected applications for consideration on the national level. Minority women are especially encouraged to apply. Selection is based on transportation involvement and goals, job skills, and academic record; financial need is not considered.

**Financial data** The stipend is $5,000.

**Duration** 1 year.

**Additional information** This program began in 1992. Local chapters may also award additional funding to winners in their area.

**Number awarded** 1 each year.

**Deadline** Applications must be submitted by November to a local WTS chapter.

## [586]
## SHELLY SZEPANSKI MEMORIAL FLIGHT TRAINING SCHOLARSHIP

Alaska Community Foundation
Attn: Scholarships
3201 C Street, Suite 110
Anchorage, AK 99503
(907) 334-6700                          Toll Free: (855) 336-6701
Fax: (907) 334-5780                     E-mail: info@alaskacf.org
Web: www.alaskacf.org

**Summary** To provide financial assistance to female residents of Alaska who are interested in learning to fly as preparation for a science-related career.

**Eligibility** This program is open to women who are residents of Alaska and currently enrolled in a science-related degree program, preferably in wildlife biology or natural resources. Applicants must have passed their FAA written flight test and medical examination and be planning to earn a private or commercial/instrument rating, including a float rating, as part of a career in a science-related field. Along with their application, they must submit a 1,000-word essay describing their background, educational and professional goals, how flying is relevant to those goals, and specific qualifications for this scholarship. Preference is given to applicants attending college in Alaska and to those who can demonstrate financial need.

**Financial data** The stipend is $5,000 per year.

**Duration** 1 year; recipients may reapply.

**Number awarded** 1 or more each year.

**Deadline** February of each year.

## [587]
## SHERYL KRATZ MEMORIAL SCHOLARSHIP

California Groundwater Association
P.O. Box 14369
Santa Rosa, CA 95402
(707) 578-4408                    Fax: (707) 546-4906
E-mail: wellguy@groundh2o.org
Web: www.groundh2o.org/programs/scholarship.html

**Summary** To provide financial assistance to women in California who are interested in attending college in any state and either have a relationship to the California Groundwater Association (CGA) or plan to major in a field related to ground water.

**Eligibility** This program is open to female residents of California currently enrolled or accepted at a college or university in any state. Applicants must either 1) have a family affiliation with a CGA member (including employees of business members) and be interested in working on a degree in any field; or 2) be interested in working on a degree in a field of study related to ground water. Along with their application, they must submit a 500-word essay demonstrating their interest in either their chosen field of interest or in ground water technology. Financial need is not considered in the selection process.

**Financial data** The stipend is $1,000.

**Duration** 1 year.

**Number awarded** 1 each year.

**Deadline** March of each year.

## [588]
## SIEMENS AWARDS FOR ADVANCED PLACEMENT

Siemens Foundation
170 Wood Avenue South
Iselin, NJ 08830
Toll Free: (877) 822-5233          Fax: (732) 603-5890
E-mail: foundation.us@siemens.com
Web: www.siemens-foundation.org

**Summary** To recognize and reward high school students with exceptional scores on the Advanced Placement (AP) examinations in mathematics and the sciences (males and females are judged separately).

**Eligibility** All students in U.S. high schools are eligible to be considered for these awards (including home-schooled students and those in U.S. territories). Each fall, the College Board identifies the male and female seniors in each state who have earned the highest number of scores of 5 on 8 AP exams: biology, calculus BC, chemistry, computer science A, environmental science, physics C mechanics, physics C electricity and magnetism, and statistics. Males and females are considered separately. Students with the highest scores nationally receive separate awards. The program also provides awards to teachers who demonstrate excellence in teaching AP mathematics and science.

**Financial data** State scholarships are $2,000; in addition, national winners receive $5,000 scholarships. State awards for teachers high schools are $1,000; the National AP Teacher of the Year receives $5,000.

**Duration** The awards are presented annually.

**Additional information** Information from the College Board is available at (877) 358-6777.

**Number awarded** 100 state scholarships (1 female and 1 male from each state) and 2 national scholarships (1 female and 1 male) are awarded each year. In addition, 50 teachers (1 from each state) receive awards and 1 of those is designated the National AP Teacher of the Year.

**Deadline** There is no application or nomination process for these awards. The College Board identifies the students and teachers for the Siemens Foundation.

## [589]
## SIGMA ALPHA IOTA/KENNEDY CENTER INTERNSHIP

Sigma Alpha Iota Philanthropies, Inc.
One Tunnel Road
Asheville, NC 28805
(828) 251-0606                    Fax: (828) 251-0644
E-mail: nh@sai-national.org
Web: www.sai-national.org

**Summary** To provide summer internships at the Kennedy Center to members of Sigma Alpha Iota (an organization of women musicians).

**Eligibility** This program is open to student members of the organization who are interested in a summer internship at the Institute for Arts Management at the John F. Kennedy Center for the Performing Arts in Washington, D.C. Applicants must be juniors, seniors, graduate students, or graduates out of school for less than 2 years.

**Financial data** The stipend is $2,400.

**Duration** 10 weeks during the summer.

**Additional information** Assignments are full time, with possible college credit available.

**Number awarded** 1 or more each year.

**Deadline** February of each year.

## [590]
## SIGMA ALPHA IOTA UNDERGRADUATE SCHOLARSHIPS

Sigma Alpha Iota Philanthropies, Inc.
One Tunnel Road
Asheville, NC 28805
(828) 251-0606          Fax: (828) 251-0644
E-mail: nh@sai-national.org
Web: www.sai-national.org

**Summary**  To provide financial assistance for undergraduate study to members of Sigma Alpha Iota (an organization of women musicians).

**Eligibility**  This program is open to members of the organization in the first 3 years of undergraduate study. Candidates must be nominated by their chapter and their chapter adviser must submit a letter of recommendation. Nominees must submit a brief statement of career goals and aspirations. Selection is based on financial need, musical ability, scholarship, potential leadership, contribution to campus and community life, and exemplification of the ideals of the organization.

**Financial data**  The stipend is $1,500.

**Duration**  1 year.

**Number awarded**  12 each year.

**Deadline**  March of each year.

## [591]
## SIGMA GAMMA RHO SCHOLARSHIPS/ FELLOWSHIPS

Sigma Gamma Rho Sorority, Inc.
Attn: National Education Fund
1000 Southhill Drive, Suite 200
Cary, NC 27513
(919) 678-9720          Toll Free: (888) SGR-1922
Fax: (919) 678-9721          E-mail: info@sgrho1922.org
Web: www.sgrho1922.org/nef

**Summary**  To provide financial assistance for undergraduate or graduate study to African American women and other applicants who can demonstrate financial need.

**Eligibility**  This program is open to high school seniors, undergraduates, and graduate students who can demonstrate financial need. The sponsor is a traditionally African American sorority. Applicants must have a GPA of "C" or higher.

**Financial data**  A stipend is awarded (amount not specified).

**Duration**  1 year.

**Additional information**  This program includes the following named awards: the Lorraine A. Williams Scholarship, the Philo Sallie A. Williams Scholarship, the Cleo W. Higgins Scholarship (limited to doctoral students), the Angela E. Randall Scholarship, the Inez Colson Memorial Scholarship (limited to students majoring in education or mathematics at Savannah State University), and the Philo Geneva Young Scholarship. A processing fee of $20 is required.

**Number awarded**  Varies each year.

**Deadline**  April of each year.

## [592]
## SIGMA KAPPA FOUNDERS' SCHOLARSHIPS

Sigma Kappa Foundation Inc.
Attn: Scholarship Committee
8733 Founders Road
Indianapolis, IN 46268
(317) 872-3275          Fax: (317) 872-0716
E-mail: foundationscholarships@sigmakappa.org
Web: www.sigmakappafoundation.org/scholarships

**Summary**  To provide financial assistance to undergraduate members of Sigma Kappa sorority who have demonstrated leadership.

**Eligibility**  This program is open to undergraduate members of the sorority who have a GPA of 3.0 or higher. Applicants must be able to demonstrate a leadership role on campus (e.g., student government, chapter officer, Panhellenic). Along with their application, they must submit an essay describing themselves, their future career goals after graduation, and why they are qualified for this scholarship. Financial need is considered in the selection process. Preference is given to sophomores and juniors with at least 1 year's study remaining.

**Financial data**  The stipend is $1,000.

**Duration**  1 year.

**Number awarded**  4 each year.

**Deadline**  March of each year.

## [593]
## SIGN OF THE ARROW MELISSA SCHOLARSHIP

Pi Beta Phi
Attn: Pi Beta Phi Foundation
1154 Town and Country Commons Drive
Town and Country, MO 63017
(636) 256-1357          Fax: (636) 256-8124
E-mail: fndn@pibetaphi.org
Web: www.pibetaphifoundation.org/programs/scholarships

**Summary**  To provide financial assistance to members of Pi Beta Phi who are working on an undergraduate degree.

**Eligibility**  This program is open to women who are officially enrolled full time at a college or university where there is a Pi Beta Phi chapter. They must be active members in good standing in the sorority and entering their senior year as a full-time student with a GPA of 3.1 or higher. Applicants must commit to 1) continue a program of community service for the year the scholarship is applicable; 2) promote and inspire others to community service; and 3) write a reflective piece summarizing community service efforts during the award year. Financial need is not considered.

**Financial data**  Stipends up to $10,000 are available.

**Duration**  1 year.

**Additional information**  This program began in 2001.

**Number awarded**  Varies each year; recently, 3 of these scholarships were awarded.

**Deadline**  February of each year.

## [594]
## SIGNIFICANT OPPORTUNITIES IN ATMOSPHERIC RESEARCH AND SCIENCE (SOARS) PROGRAM

University Corporation for Atmospheric Research
Attn: SOARS Program Manager
3090 Center Green Drive
P.O. Box 3000
Boulder, CO 80307-3000
(303) 497-8622                    Fax: (303) 497-8629
E-mail: soars@ucar.edu
Web: www.soars.ucar.edu

**Summary** To provide summer work experience to undergraduate or graduate students, especially those from underrepresented groups (including women), who are interested in preparing for a career in atmospheric or a related science.

**Eligibility** This program is open to U.S. citizens or permanent residents who have completed their sophomore year of college and are majoring in atmospheric science or a related field (e.g., biology, chemistry, computer science, earth science, engineering, environmental science, the geosciences, mathematics, meteorology, oceanography, physics, or social science). Applicants must have a GPA of 3.0 or higher and be planning to prepare for a career in the field of atmospheric or a related science. The program especially encourages applications from members of groups that are historically underrepresented in the atmospheric and related sciences, including Blacks/African Americans, Hispanics/Latinos, American Indians/Alaskan Natives, women, first-generation college students, and students with disabilities. It also welcomes applications from students who are gay, lesbian, bisexual, or transgender; have experienced, and worked to overcome, educational or economic disadvantage; or have personal or family circumstances that may complicate their continued progress in research careers.

**Financial data** Participants receive a competitive stipend and a housing allowance. Round-trip travel between Boulder and any 1 location within the continental United States is also provided. Students who are accepted into a graduate program receive full scholarships (with SOARS and the participating universities each sharing the costs).

**Duration** 10 weeks during the summer. Students are encouraged to continue for 4 subsequent summers.

**Additional information** This program began in 1996. Students are assigned positions with a research project. They are exposed to the research facilities at the National Center for Atmospheric Research (NCAR), including computers, libraries, laboratories, and aircraft. NCAR is operated by the University Corporation for Atmospheric Research (a consortium of 40 universities) and sponsored by the National Science Foundation, the Department of Energy, the National Aeronautics and Space Administration, and the National Oceanic and Atmospheric Administration. Before completing their senior years, students are encouraged to apply to a master's or doctoral degree program at 1 of the participating universities.

**Number awarded** At least 12 each year.

**Deadline** January of each year.

## [595]
## SISTER ELIZABETH CANDON SCHOLARSHIP

Vermont Student Assistance Corporation
Attn: Scholarship Programs
10 East Allen Street
P.O. Box 2000
Winooski, VT 05404-2601
(802) 654-3798                    Toll Free: (888) 253-4819
Fax: (802) 654-3765      TDD: (800) 281-3341 (within VT)
E-mail: info@vsac.org
Web: services.vsac.org

**Summary** To provide financial assistance to single mothers in Vermont who plan to attend college in any state.

**Eligibility** This program is open to female residents of Vermont who are single parents with primary custody of at least 1 child 12 years of age or younger. Applicants must be enrolled at least half time in an accredited undergraduate degree program in any state. Along with their application, they must submit 1) a 250-word essay on their short- and long-term academic, educational, career, vocational, and/or employment goals; 2) a 100-word essay on how the program in which they will be enrolled will enhance their career or vocation; and 3) a 250-word essay on what they believe distinguishes their application from others that may be submitted. Selection is based on those essays, a letter of recommendation, and financial need (expected family contribution less than $23,360).

**Financial data** The stipend is $1,000 per year.

**Duration** 1 year; may be renewed up to 3 additional years.

**Number awarded** 1 each year.

**Deadline** March of each year.

## [596]
## SMART CHOICES SCHOLARSHIP PROGRAM

Washington Interscholastic Activities Association
435 Main Avenue South
Renton, WA 98057
(425) 687-8585                    Fax: (425) 687-9476
E-mail: smartchoices@wiaa.com
Web: www.wiaa.com/subcontent.aspx?SecID=959

**Summary** To provide financial assistance to high school seniors in Washington who have participated in athletics and plan to attend college in any state (females and males are considered separately).

**Eligibility** This program is open to seniors graduating from high schools that are members of the Washington Interscholastic Activities Association (WIAA) and planning to enroll at a college or university in any state. Applicants must have participated in a WIAA-sanctioned sport or activity during their senior year and have a GPA of 3.2 or higher. They must verify that they are a consumer of real dairy products and are not opposed to dairy production or practices based on their social or personal choice regarding animal welfare or nutritional benefits. Along with their application, they must submit a personal statement (as a 250-word essay or 5-minute video) on how they plan to use their education to benefit others. Selection is based on that statement (5%), athletic or activity excellence (35%), academic achievement (35%), leadership (15%), and citizenship and community service (10%). Male and female student WIAA participants are considered separately.

**Financial data** The stipend is $5,000.

**Duration** 1 year.

**Additional information** This program is sponsored by the Dairy Farmers of Washington and Les Schwab Tire.

**Number awarded** 2 each year: 1 male and 1 female.

**Deadline** March of each year.

## [597]
## SOCIETY OF DAUGHTERS OF THE UNITED STATES ARMY SCHOLARSHIPS

Society of Daughters of the United States Army
c/o Janet B. Otto, Scholarship Chair
7717 Rockledge Court
Springfield, VA 21152

**Summary** To provide financial assistance for college to daughters and granddaughters of active, retired, or deceased career Army warrant and commissioned officers.

**Eligibility** This program is open to the daughters, adopted daughters, stepdaughters, or granddaughters of career commissioned officers or warrant officers of the U.S. Army (active, regular, or Reserve) who 1) are currently on active duty; 2) retired after 20 years of active duty or were medically retired; or 3) died while on active duty or after retiring from active duty with 20 or more years of service. Applicants must have at least a 3.0 GPA and be studying or planning to study at the undergraduate level. Selection is based on depth of character, leadership, seriousness of purpose, academic achievement, and financial need.

**Financial data** Scholarships, to a maximum of $1,000, are paid directly to the college or school for tuition, laboratory fees, books, or other expenses.

**Duration** 1 year; may be renewed up to 4 additional years if the recipient maintains at least a 3.0 GPA.

**Additional information** Recipients may attend any accredited college, professional, or vocational school. This program includes named scholarships from the following funds: the Colonel Hayden W. Wagner Memorial Fund, the Eugenia Bradford Roberts Memorial Fund, the Daughters of the U.S. Army Scholarship Fund, the Gladys K. and John K. Simpson Scholarship Fund, and the Margaret M. Prickett Scholarship Fund. Requests for applications must be accompanied by a self-addressed stamped envelope.

**Number awarded** Varies each year.

**Deadline** February of each year.

## [598]
## SOCIETY OF WOMEN ENGINEERS MID-HUDSON SECTION SCHOLARSHIP

Society of Women Engineers
Attn: Scholarship Selection Committee
203 North LaSalle Street, Suite 1675
Chicago, IL 60601-1269
(312) 596-5223          Toll Free: (877) SWE-INFO
Fax: (312) 644-8557     E-mail: scholarships@swe.org
Web: societyofwomenengineers.swe.org

**Summary** To provide financial assistance to women, especially those from New York, who are working on an undergraduate or graduate degree in engineering or computer science.

**Eligibility** This program is open to women who will be full-time sophomores, juniors, seniors, or graduate students at

ABET-accredited colleges and universities. Applicants must be working on a degree in computer science or engineering and have a GPA of 3.0 or higher. Selection is based on merit. Preference is given to applicants who reside and attend school in New York.

**Financial data** The stipend is $1,000.

**Duration** 1 year.

**Additional information** This program is supported by the Mid-Hudson Section of the Society of Women Engineers.

**Number awarded** 1 each year.

**Deadline** February of each year.

## [599]
## SOCIETY OF WOMEN ENGINEERS PAST PRESIDENTS SCHOLARSHIPS

Society of Women Engineers
Attn: Scholarship Selection Committee
203 North LaSalle Street, Suite 1675
Chicago, IL 60601-1269
(312) 596-5223          Toll Free: (877) SWE-INFO
Fax: (312) 644-8557     E-mail: scholarships@swe.org
Web: societyofwomenengineers.swe.org

**Summary** To provide financial assistance to women working on an undergraduate or graduate degree in engineering or computer science.

**Eligibility** This program is open to women who will be sophomores, juniors, seniors, or graduate students at ABET-accredited colleges and universities. Applicants must be U.S. citizens or permanent residents working full time on a degree in computer science or engineering and have a GPA of 3.0 or higher. Along with their application, they must submit a 1-page essay on why they want to be an engineer or computer scientist, how they believe they will make a difference as an engineer or computer scientist, and what influenced them to study engineering or computer science. Selection is based on merit.

**Financial data** The stipend is $1,500.

**Duration** 1 year.

**Additional information** This program began in 1999 by an anonymous donor to honor the commitment and accomplishments of past presidents of the Society of Women Engineers (SWE).

**Number awarded** 2 each year.

**Deadline** February of each year.

## [600]
## SOLAR TURBINES SCHOLARSHIP

Society of Women Engineers
Attn: Scholarship Selection Committee
203 North LaSalle Street, Suite 1675
Chicago, IL 60601-1269
(312) 596-5223          Toll Free: (877) SWE-INFO
Fax: (312) 644-8557     E-mail: scholarships@swe.org
Web: societyofwomenengineers.swe.org

**Summary** To provide financial assistance to women who will be entering college as freshmen and are interested in studying computer science or specified fields of engineering.

**Eligibility** This program is open to women who are entering college as freshmen with a GPA of 3.5 or higher. Applicants must be planning to enroll full time at a designated ABET-accredited 4-year college or university and major in computer science or aeronautical, chemical, electrical, industrial, manufacturing, materials, mechanical, metallurgical, or petroleum engineering. Selection is based on merit.

**Financial data** The stipend is $1,000. The award includes a travel grant for the recipient to attend the national conference of the Society of Women Engineers (SWE).

**Duration** 1 year.

**Additional information** For the list of designated universities, check the SWE web site.

**Number awarded** 1 each year.

**Deadline** May of each year.

## [601]
## SOUTH CAROLINA COACHES ASSOCIATION OF WOMEN'S SPORTS AND TROPHIES BY "M" SCHOLARSHIP

South Carolina Coaches Association of Women's Sports
c/o Amy Boozer, Executive Secretary
P.O. Box 261
Newberry, SC 29108
(803) 321-2628          E-mail: amy_caws@yahoo.com
Web: www.hometeamsonline.com

**Summary** To provide financial assistance to female high school senior athletes in South Carolina who plan to study at medical field at a college in any state.

**Eligibility** This program is open to women graduating from high schools in South Carolina who have participated in at least 1 athletic team. Applicants must be planning to attend a college or university in any state to prepare for a career in medicine. They must have minimum scores of 1000 on the SAT and/or 22 on the ACT. Along with their application, they must submit a 1-page essay on why they want to enter the medical field and the area of specialization they plan to pursue. Selection is based on that essay, academic achievement, participation in athletic and non-athletic extracurricular activities, and financial need.

**Financial data** The stipend is $1,000.

**Duration** 1 year; nonrenewable.

**Additional information** Support for this program is provided by Trophies by "M."

**Number awarded** 1 each year.

**Deadline** March of each year.

## [602]
## SOUTH CAROLINA FARM BUREAU YOUTH AMBASSADOR SCHOLARSHIP PROGRAM

South Carolina Farm Bureau
Attn: Women's Program Coordinator
P.O. Box 754
Columbia, SC 29202-0754
(803) 936-4287          E-mail: flawrimore@scfb.com
Web: www.scfb.org

**Summary** To provide an opportunity for South Carolina residents who are interested in a career in agriculture to serve as a spokesperson for the state's farmers and earn a college scholarship (females and males are considered separately).

**Eligibility** This program is open to residents of South Carolina between 17 and 21 years of age who reside in a Farm Bureau member home. Applicants must be interested in serving as a Youth Ambassador for a year, during which time they

represent the Farm Bureau at a minimum of 6 official state functions to promote the bureau, the farmers of South Carolina, and their products. They must submit their application through their county farm bureau. Each county may nominate 1 male and 1 female, who compete separately for the state title of Youth Ambassador. Along with their application, they must submit a short paragraph on why they think they would make a good Youth Ambassador and a 500-word essay on a topic that changes annually but relates to agriculture. Semifinalists are invited to an interview, during which judges question them on their knowledge of agriculture. Selection is based on the essay (50 points), an interview (50 points), and responses to questions (100 points).

**Financial data** Following their year of service, the Youth Ambassadors receive a $2,000 college scholarship.

**Duration** The scholarships are for 1 year.

**Additional information** During their year of service, the Youth Ambassadors must give full priority to the South Carolina Farm Bureau, follow a code of conduct, not consume any alcoholic beverages or use illegal substances, and not get married.

**Number awarded** 2 each year: 1 male and 1 female.

**Deadline** September of each year.

## [603]
## SOUTH EASTERN REGION FELLOWSHIP FOR LIFE-LONG LEARNING

Alpha Kappa Alpha Sorority, Inc.
Attn: Educational Advancement Foundation
5656 South Stony Island Avenue
Chicago, IL 60637
(773) 947-0026          Toll Free: (800) 653-6528
Fax: (773) 947-0277          E-mail: akaeaf@akaeaf.net
Web: www.akaeaf.org/fellowships_endowments.htm

**Summary** To provide financial assistance to members of Alpha Kappa Alpha (a traditionally African American women's sorority) in southeastern states who are engaged in a program of lifelong learning.

**Eligibility** This program is open to sorority m who are enrolled full time as sophomores or higher in an accredited degree-granting institution and are planning to continue their program of education. Applicants must be residents of Alabama, Mississippi, or Tennessee and enrolled in a program of lifelong learning at a college or university in those states. Along with their application, they must submit 1) a list of honors, awards, and scholarships received; 2) a list of organizations in which they have memberships, especially minority organizations; and 3) a statement of their personal and career goals, including how this scholarship will enhance their ability to attain those goals. The sponsor is a traditionally African American women's sorority.

**Financial data** A stipend is awarded (amount not specified).

**Duration** 1 year.

**Number awarded** 1 each even-numbered year.

**Deadline** April of each even-numbered year.

## [604]
## SOUTHWEST IDAHO SECTION SWE SCHOLARSHIPS

Society of Women Engineers-Southwest Idaho Section
c/o Scholarship Committee Chair
11548 West Rader Drive
Boise, ID 83713
(208) 396-4458          E-mail: idahoswe@gmail.com
Web: www.swiswe.org/scholarships.html

**Summary** To provide financial assistance to female high school seniors in Idaho planning to enter an engineering school in any state.

**Eligibility** This program is open to women graduating from high schools in Idaho and planning to attend an ABET-accredited 4- or 5-year engineering program in any state. Applicants must submit an essay of 500 to 1,000 words on their desire to enter an engineering or engineering-related field, transcripts, SAT/ACT scores, and a letter of recommendation from a high school science or mathematics teacher. Selection is based on that essay, academic accomplishments (especially in science and mathematics), extracurricular accomplishments, and the letter of recommendation. Financial need is not considered.

**Financial data** Stipends are generally $2,000.

**Duration** 1 year.

**Number awarded** Varies each year; recently, 6 of these scholarships were awarded.

**Deadline** February of each year.

## [605]
## SPIE SCHOLARSHIP PROGRAM

SPIE-The International Society for Optical Engineering
Attn: Scholarship Committee
1000 20th Street
P.O. Box 10
Bellingham, WA 98227-0010
(360) 676-3290          Toll Free: (888) 504-8171
Fax: (360) 647-1445     E-mail: scholarships@spie.org
Web: spie.org/x7236.xml

**Summary** To provide financial assistance to entering or continuing undergraduate and graduate student members of SPIE-The International Society for Optical Engineering who are preparing for a career in optical science or engineering (particularly women, minorities, and veterans).

**Eligibility** This program is open to high school seniors planning to attend college, current undergraduate students, and current graduate students. Applicants must be society members majoring or planning to enroll full or part time and major in optics, optoelectronics, photonics, imaging, or a related discipline (e.g., physics, electrical engineering) at a college or university anywhere in the world. Along with their application, they must submit a 500-word essay on their academic work, career objectives, how this scholarship would help them attain their goals, and what they have achieved and learned through their studies and activities. Financial need is not considered in the selection process. Women, minorities, and veterans are encouraged to apply.

**Financial data** Stipends range from $2,000 to $11,000. Special awards include the D.J. Lovell Scholarship at $11,000; the John Kiel Scholarship at $10,000; the Laser Technology, Engineering, and Applications Scholarship at $5,000; the Optical Design and Engineering Scholarship at $5,000, and the BACUS Scholarship at $5,000.

**Duration** 1 year.

**Additional information** The International Society for Optical Engineering was founded in 1955 as the Society of Photo-Optical Instrumentation Engineers (SPIE). This program includes the following special named scholarships: the D.J. Lovell Scholarship, sponsored by SPIE (the most prestigious of the scholarships); the John Kiel Scholarship, awarded for a student's potential for long-term contribution to the field of optics and optical engineering; the Optical Design and Engineering Scholarship in Optical Engineering, established to honor Bill Price and Warren Smith and awarded to a full-time graduate or undergraduate student in the field of optical design and engineering; the Laser Technology, Engineering, and Applications Scholarship (formerly the F-MADE Scholarship), sponsored by the Forum for Military Applications of Directed Energy (F-MADE) in recognition of a student's scholarly achievement in laser technology, engineering, or applications; and the BACUS Scholarship, awarded to a full-time undergraduate or graduate student in the field of microlithography with an emphasis on optical tooling and/or semiconductor manufacturing technologies, sponsored by BACUS (SPIE's photomask international technical group).

**Number awarded** Varies each year; recently, this program awarded 140 scholarships with a value of $353,000. Since the program was established, it has awarded more than $3.8 million to nearly 2,000 students in 86 countries.

**Deadline** February of each year.

## [606]
## SPIRIT OF YOUTH SCHOLARSHIP FOR JUNIOR MEMBERS

American Legion Auxiliary
8945 North Meridian Street
Indianapolis, IN 46260
(317) 569-4500          Fax: (317) 569-4502
E-mail: alahq@alaforveterans.org
Web: www.alaforveterans.org

**Summary** To provide financial assistance for college to junior members of the American Legion Auxiliary.

**Eligibility** Applicants for this scholarship must have been junior members of the Auxiliary for at least the past 3 years. They must be seniors at an accredited high school in the United States, have a GPA of 3.0 or higher, and be planning to enroll full time at an accredited 4-year institution of higher education. Along with their application, they must submit a 1,000-word essay on a topic that changes annually; recently, students were asked to write on "How I Can Help Children of Military Families." Selection is based on that essay (30%), character and leadership (30%), and academic record (40%). Each unit of the Auxiliary may select a candidate for application to the department level, and each department submits a candidate for the national award.

**Financial data** The stipend is $1,250 per year.

**Duration** 4 years.

**Additional information** Applications are available from the president of the candidate's own unit, or from the secretary or education chair of the department.

**Number awarded** 5 each year: 1 in each division of the American Legion Auxiliary.

**Deadline** Applications must be submitted to the unit president by February of each year.

## [607]
## SPORTSMANSHIP RECOGNITION PROGRAM SCHOLARSHIP

Kentucky High School Athletic Association
Attn: Assistant Commissioner
2280 Executive Drive
Lexington, KY 40505
(859) 299-5472          Fax: (859) 293-5999
E-mail: bcope@khsaa.org
Web: www.khsaa.org/sportsmanship

**Summary** To recognize and reward, with college scholarships, outstanding student-athletes in Kentucky high schools (females and males compete separately).

**Eligibility** This program is open to high school seniors in Kentucky who have participated in athletics or cheerleading. Applicants must have at least a 2.5 GPA, 3 letters of recommendation from coaches and administrators illustrating the student's traits of good sportsmanship, demonstrated leadership within the school and the community, and a 2-page essay on a topic that changes annually (recently, students were asked to discuss why they play sports, how their participation prepares them for their future, and the impact of sports participation on themselves, their school, and their community). They must be planning to attend a college or university in Kentucky. A male and a female are recognized from each school in the state. They are chosen on the basis of these traits: playing the game by the rules; treating game officials, coaches, and competitors with due respect; shaking hands with opponents at the end of each contest; taking victory and defeat without undue emotionalism; controlling their tempers; being positive with officials, coaches, and competitors who criticize them; cooperating with officials, coaches, and fellow players in trying to promote good sportsmanship; being positive with opponents; letting student and adult audiences know that inappropriate behavior reflects poorly on the team; and serving as a role model for future student-athletes. These students are awarded a certificate and are entered into a regional competition. Males and females continue to compete separately. The regional winners are given a plaque and are considered for the Sportsmanship Recognition Program Scholarship. Selection is based on GPA, recommendations, leadership roles and honors, and the case study essay.

**Financial data** The stipend is $3,000.

**Duration** 1 year.

**Additional information** This program, instituted in 1997, is currently sponsored by Kentucky National Insurance Company and the Forcht Group of Kentucky.

**Number awarded** 2 each year: 1 for a female and 1 for a male.

**Deadline** Applications must be submitted to the school's athletic director in March.

## [608]
## SR EDUCATION GROUP SINGLE PARENT SCHOLARSHIP

SR Education Group
Attn: Contests
123 Lake Street South, Suite B-1
Kirkland, WA 98033
(425) 605-8898          E-mail: etana@sreducationgroup.org
Web: www.sreducationgroup.org/scholarships

**Summary** To recognize and reward, with scholarships for continuing study, single parents who submit outstanding essays on themselves and their status.

**Eligibility** This competition is open to full-time undergraduate students who are single parents (men and women) at least 16 years of age and legal residents of the United States. Applicants must submit 3 essays of 300 to 500 words each on the following questions: 1) their intended major and why they believe this is the right career path for them; 2) how they will apply their degree in the future and what they anticipate for their first 5 years outside of college; and 3) any special personal or family circumstances affecting their need for financial assistance.

**Financial data** The award is a $2,000 scholarship.

**Duration** The competition is held periodically.

**Additional information** This program began in 2012.

**Number awarded** In a recent year, this competition was held on 4 occasions.

**Deadline** Deadline dates are announced whenever a competition is being held.

## [609]
## SR EDUCATION GROUP WOMEN'S SCHOLARSHIP

SR Education Group
Attn: Contests
123 Lake Street South, Suite B-1
Kirkland, WA 98033
(425) 605-8898          E-mail: etana@sreducationgroup.org
Web: www.sreducationgroup.org/scholarships

**Summary** To recognize and reward, with scholarships for continuing study, female undergraduates who submit outstanding essays on themselves and their status.

**Eligibility** This competition is open to women currently enrolled full time at accredited institutions in the United States. Applicants must submit 3 essays of 300 to 500 words each on the following questions: 1) their intended major and why they believe this is the right career path for them; 2) how they will apply their degree in the future and what they anticipate for their first 5 years outside of college; and 3) any special personal or family circumstances affecting their need for financial assistance.

**Financial data** The award is a $2,000 scholarship.

**Duration** The competition is held periodically.

**Additional information** This program began in 2011.

**Number awarded** In a recent year, this competition was held on 7 occasions.

**Deadline** Deadline dates are announced whenever a competition is being held.

## [610]
## ST. JUDE MEDICAL MINNESOTA SWE SCHOLARSHIP

Society of Women Engineers-Minnesota Section
Attn: Scholarship Committee
P.O. Box 582813
Minneapolis, MN 55458-2813
E-mail: scholarships@swe-mn.org
Web: www.swe-mn.org/scholarships.html

**Summary** To provide financial assistance to women from any state working on an undergraduate or graduate degree in biomedical engineering at colleges and universities in Minnesota, North Dakota, and South Dakota.

**Eligibility** This program is open to female undergraduate and graduate students at ABET-accredited engineering programs in Minnesota, North Dakota, or South Dakota. Applicants must be working full time on a degree in biomedical engineering. Along with their application, they must submit a short paragraph describing how they plan to utilize their engineering skills after they graduate. Selection is based on potential to succeed as an engineer (20 points), communication skills (10 points), extracurricular or community involvement and leadership skills (10 points), demonstrated successful work experience (10 points), and academic success (5 points).

**Financial data** The stipend is $1,000.

**Duration** 1 year.

**Additional information** This program is sponsored by St. Jude Medical.

**Number awarded** 1 each year.

**Deadline** March of each year.

## [611]
## STEPHANIE HUSEK SCHOLARSHIP

First Catholic Slovak Union of the United States and
  Canada
Jednota Benevolent Foundation, Inc.
Attn: Scholarship Program
6611 Rockside Road, Suite 300
Independence, OH 44131
(216) 642-9406          Toll Free: (800) JEDNOTA
Fax: (216) 642-4310          E-mail: FCSU@aol.com
Web: www.fcsu.com/scholarships

**Summary** To provide financial assistance for college to female high school seniors who are of Slovak descent and the Catholic faith.

**Eligibility** This program is open to women graduating from high schools in the United States and Canada and planning to attend an approved institution of higher education. Applicants must be of Slovak descent and the Catholic faith. They must have had at least $5,000 of reserve insurance with the sponsoring organization for at least 4 years. Along with their application, they must submit 1) a transcript of grades that includes ACT or SAT scores; 2) a list of volunteer community activities in which they have participated; 3) a list of awards received for academic excellence and leadership ability; 4) a description of their career objectives; 5) an essay on why they think they should receive this scholarship; and 6) information on their financial need.

**Financial data** The stipend is $1,000. The winner also receives a $3,000 single premium life insurance policy upon proof of graduation from college.

**Duration** 1 year; nonrenewable.

**Number awarded** 1 each year.

**Deadline** March of each year.

## [612]
## STEPHEN BUFTON MEMORIAL EDUCATION FUND OUTRIGHT GRANTS PROGRAM

American Business Women's Association
Attn: Stephen Bufton Memorial Educational Fund
11050 Roe Avenue, Suite 200
Overland Park, KS 66211
Toll Free: (800) 228-0007
Web: www.sbmef.org/Opportunities.cfm

**Summary** To provide financial assistance to women undergraduate and graduate students in any field who are sponsored by a chapter of the American Business Women's Association (ABWA).

**Eligibility** This program is open to women who are at least juniors at an accredited college or university. Applicants must be working on an undergraduate or graduate degree and have a GPA of 2.5 or higher. They are not required to be ABWA members, but they must be sponsored by an ABWA chapter that has contributed to the fund in the previous chapter year. U.S. citizenship is required.

**Financial data** The maximum grant is $1,500. Funds are paid directly to the recipient's institution to be used only for tuition, books, and fees.

**Duration** 1 year. Grants are not automatically renewed, but recipients may reapply.

**Additional information** This program began in 1953. The ABWA does not provide the names and addresses of local chapters; it recommends that applicants check with their local Chamber of Commerce, library, or university to see if any chapter has registered a contact's name and number.

**Number awarded** Varies each year; since the inception of this program, it has awarded more than $14 million to more than 14,000 students.

**Deadline** May of each year.

## [613]
## SUE AND VIRGINIA HESTER SPECIAL EDUCATION SCHOLARSHIP

Alabama Federation of Women's Clubs
Attn: Scholarship Chair
2728 Niazuma Avenue
Birmingham, AL 35205
(205) 323-2392          Fax: (205) 323-8443
Web: www.gfwc-alabama.org/Scholarships.html

**Summary** To provide financial assistance to women who are residents of Alabama and interested in studying special education at a public university in the state.

**Eligibility** This program is open to female residents of Alabama who are attending or planning to attend a public university in the state. Applicants must be interested in majoring in special education. Along with their application, they must submit a personal letter on their educational goals, 3 letters of recommendation, and transcripts. Financial need is not considered in the selection process.

**Financial data** The stipend is $1,000.
**Duration** 1 year.
**Number awarded** 1 each year.
**Deadline** Deadline not specified.

## [614]
## SUSAN BURDETT SCHOLARSHIP

American Legion Auxiliary
Department of Washington
3600 Ruddell Road S.E.
P.O. Box 5867
Lacey, WA 98509-5867
(360) 456-5995                     Fax: (360) 491-7442
E-mail: secretary@walegion-aux.org
Web: www.walegion-aux.org/EducationScholarships.html

**Summary** To provide financial assistance to delegates to Evergreen Girls State in Washington who are interested in attending college in any state.

**Eligibility** This program award is open to former Evergreen Girls State citizens. Applicants must be attending or planning to attend a college or university in any state. Along with their application, they must submit a 500-word essay on "How I Benefited from Attending Evergreen Girls State." Selection is based on character, leadership, scholarship, the essay, and financial need.

**Financial data** The stipend is $1,000.
**Duration** 1 year.
**Number awarded** 1 each year.
**Deadline** April of each year.

## [615]
## SUSAN EKDALE MEMORIAL SCHOLARSHIP

Association for Women Geoscientists
Attn: AWG Foundation
12000 North Washington Street, Suite 285
Thornton, CO 80241
(303) 412-6219                     Fax: (303) 253-9220
E-mail: office@awg.org
Web: www.awg.org/EAS/scholarships.html

**Summary** To provide financial assistance for a summer field camp to women who have a Utah connection and are majoring in geoscience.

**Eligibility** This program is open to women majoring in geoscience at a college or university in Utah who must attend a summer field camp as part of their graduation requirements. Women geoscience students from Utah attending college in other states are also eligible. Applicants must submit a 1- to 2-page essay in which they describe their personal and academic highlights, their reasons for applying for the scholarship, and what they, as women, can contribute to the geosciences. Selection is based on merit and need.

**Financial data** The stipend is $2,000. Funds must be used to help pay field camp expenses.
**Duration** Summer months.
**Additional information** This program is sponsored by the Salt Lake Chapter of the Association for Women Geoscientists.

**Number awarded** 1 each year.
**Deadline** March of each year.

## [616]
## SUSAN GLOVER HITCHCOCK SCHOLARSHIPS

Madeline H. Soren Trust
c/o BNY Mellon, N.A.
201 Washington Street
AIM: 024-0092
Boston, MA 02108-4402
(617) 722-3891                     Fax: (617) 722-6826

**Summary** To provide financial assistance to women who are residents of Massachusetts and working on a college degree in music.

**Eligibility** This program is open to women who are residents of Massachusetts and working on a college degree in music in any state. Students must apply through their college. Along with their application, they must submit a statement on their plans for studying and preparing for a career in music, along with information on their musical accomplishments and extracurricular activities. Selection is based on academic performance; character, abilities, and talents in music; and financial need.

**Financial data** The stipend is $2,000. Funds must be used to cover tuition, room and board, and other expenses related to the recipient's college education.
**Duration** 1 year.
**Additional information** This program was formerly called the Young Artists Award Program. It was originally established in 1934 by Madeline Soren and named the Susan Glover Hitchcock Scholarship Award in honor of her mother.
**Number awarded** Varies; approximately 15 each year.
**Deadline** June of each year.

## [617]
## SUSAN MISZKOWICZ MEMORIAL SCHOLARSHIP

Society of Women Engineers
Attn: Scholarship Selection Committee
203 North LaSalle Street, Suite 1675
Chicago, IL 60601-1269
(312) 596-5223                     Toll Free: (877) SWE-INFO
Fax: (312) 644-8557          E-mail: scholarships@swe.org
Web: societyofwomenengineers.swe.org

**Summary** To provide financial assistance to undergraduate women majoring in computer science or engineering.

**Eligibility** This program is open to women who are entering their sophomore, junior, or senior year at a 4-year ABET-accredited college or university. Applicants must be working full time on a degree in computer science or engineering and have a GPA of 3.0 or higher. Selection is based on merit.

**Financial data** The stipend is $1,500.
**Duration** 1 year.
**Additional information** This program began in 2002 to honor a member of the Society of Women Engineers who was killed in the New York World Trade Center on September 11, 2001.
**Number awarded** 1 each year.
**Deadline** February of each year.

## [618]
## SUSAN STEIN SCHOLARSHIP

American College of Nurse-Midwives
Attn: ACNM Foundation, Inc.
8403 Colesville Road, Suite 1550
Silver Spring, MD 20910-6374
(240) 485-1850                    Fax: (240) 485-1818
E-mail: fdn@acnm.org
Web: www.midwife.org

**Summary** To provide financial assistance for midwifery education to student members of the American College of Nurse-Midwives (ACNM) who have had a personal experience with breast cancer.

**Eligibility** This program is open to ACNM members who are currently enrolled in an accredited basic midwife education program and have successfully completed 1 academic or clinical semester/quarter or clinical module. Applicants must have had or currently have a personal experience with breast cancer, either their own or a family member's. Along with their application, they must submit a 150-word essay on their midwifery career plans; a 100-word essay on their intended future participation in the local, regional, and/or national activities of the ACNM; and a 300-word essay on the effect of breast cancer in themselves or a close family member on their choice of midwifery. Selection is based primarily on the quality of the application, although leadership potential, financial need, academic achievement, and personal goals may also be considered.

**Financial data** The stipend is $3,000.

**Duration** 1 year.

**Additional information** This program began in 2010.

**Number awarded** 1 each year.

**Deadline** March of each year.

## [619]
## SUSIE HOLMES MEMORIAL SCHOLARSHIP

International Order of Job's Daughters
c/o Betty Klotz, Educational Scholarships Committee
   Chair
1228 Moss Rock Court
Santa Rosa, CA 95404
(707) 462-6834              E-mail: bettyklotz@gmail.com
Web: www.jobsdaughtersinternational.org

**Summary** To provide financial assistance for college to members of Job's Daughters.

**Eligibility** This program is open to high school graduates who are members of Job's Daughters. Applicants must be able to demonstrate dedicated, continuous, and joyful service to Job's Daughters; regular attendance at Supreme and/or Grand Sessions; participation in competitions at Supreme and/or Grand Sessions; friendship and impartiality in their Bethel; good character and integrity; and a GPA of 2.5 or higher.

**Financial data** The stipend is $1,000.

**Duration** 1 year.

**Number awarded** 1 or more each year.

**Deadline** April of each year.

## [620]
## SWE/ACCENTURE SCHOLARSHIPS

Society of Women Engineers
Attn: Scholarship Selection Committee
203 North LaSalle Street, Suite 1675
Chicago, IL 60601-1269
(312) 596-5223                Toll Free: (877) SWE-INFO
Fax: (312) 644-8557        E-mail: scholarships@swe.org
Web: societyofwomenengineers.swe.org

**Summary** To provide financial assistance to undergraduate women majoring in designated engineering specialties.

**Eligibility** This program is open to women who are entering their sophomore or junior year at a 4-year ABET-accredited college or university. Applicants must be working full time on a degree in computer science or chemical, civil, computer, electrical, industrial, or mechanical engineering and have a GPA of 3.2 or higher. They must be U.S. citizens or permanent residents. Selection is based on merit.

**Financial data** The stipend is $2,000.

**Duration** 1 year.

**Additional information** This program is sponsored by Accenture.

**Number awarded** 5 each year: 2 to sophomores and 3 to juniors.

**Deadline** February of each year.

## [621]
## SYLVIA FORMAN PRIZE COMPETITION

American Anthropological Association
Attn: Association for Feminist Anthropology
2200 Wilson Boulevard, Suite 600
Arlington, VA 22201-3357
(703) 528-1902                    Fax: (703) 528-3546
Web: www.aaanet.org/sections/afa/?page_id=103

**Summary** To recognize and reward the best student essays in feminist anthropology.

**Eligibility** This award is available to graduate and undergraduate students who submit essays (up to 35 pages) in any subfield of anthropology that focus on such topics as feminist analysis of women's work, reproduction, sexuality, religion, language and expressive culture, family and kin relations, economic development, gender and material culture, gender and biology, women and development, globalization, or race and class. Essays that have been submitted for publication but have not yet been accepted may be eligible as entries. Already accepted or published articles may not be submitted. Only 1 submission per student is accepted. Selection is based on the use of feminist theory to analyze a particular issue; organization, quality, and clarity of writing; effective use of both theory and data; significance to feminist scholarship; timeliness and relevance of the topic; and originality of research topic.

**Financial data** The prize is $1,000 for a graduate student or $500 for an undergraduate.

**Duration** The competition is held annually.

**Additional information** The winning essays are published in the association's *Anthropology Newsletter*. This competition began in 1995.

**Number awarded** At least 2 each year: 1 for an undergraduate and 1 for a graduate student.

**Deadline** May of each year.

## [622]
## T & T HIKE SCHOLARSHIP

International Order of Job's Daughters
c/o Betty Klotz, Educational Scholarships Committee
  Chair
1228 Moss Rock Court
Santa Rosa, CA 95404
(707) 462-6834          E-mail: bettyklotz@gmail.com
Web: www.jobsdaughtersinternational.org

**Summary**  To provide financial assistance to members of Job's Daughters who are working on a degree related to speech disabilities.

**Eligibility**  This program is open to Job's Daughters in good standing in their Bethels and unmarried majority members under 30 years of age. Applicants must be entering their junior year of college or higher in audiology, speech pathology, or deaf education. Selection is based on scholastic standing, Job's Daughters activities, recommendation by the Executive Bethel Guardian Council, faculty recommendations, and achievements outside Job's Daughters.

**Financial data**  The stipend is $1,000.

**Duration**  1 year.

**Number awarded**  1 or more each year.

**Deadline**  April of each year.

## [623]
## TALL CEDARS OF LEBANON SCHOLARSHIPS

Tall Cedars of Lebanon of North America
Attn: Supreme Forest
2609 North Front Street
Harrisburg, PA 17110
(717) 232-5991                    Fax: (717) 232-5997
E-mail: tclsf@verizon.net
Web: www.tallcedars.org/Forms/FormsIndex.htm

**Summary**  To provide financial assistance for college to members of Masonic-affiliated youth organizations.

**Eligibility**  This program is open to high school seniors who are a member of Rainbow Girls, Job's Daughters, or DeMolay or the child or grandchild of a member of Tall Cedars of Lebanon. Applicants must be residents of a state with a Tall Cedars Forest and accepted as a full-time student in an associate, baccalaureate, technical, or vocational program.

**Financial data**  The stipend is $1,000. Funds are paid directly to the recipient's institution.

**Duration**  1 year.

**Number awarded**  3 each year.

**Deadline**  February of each year.

## [624]
## TEEN LATINA WORLD

Dawn Rochelle Models Agency
129 South Tennessee Street
McKinney, TX 75069
(469) 396-5670          E-mail: contact@dawnrochelle.com
Web: www.misslatina.com

**Summary**  To recognize and reward teen-aged Latinas who compete in a national beauty pageant.

**Eligibility**  This program is open to girls between 13 and 17 years of age who are at least 25% Hispanic. Applicants must be single and they may not have children. They appear in a nationally-televised pageant where selection is based on 3 categories: beauty/evening gown, fashion wear, and photogenic. Judges also interview each participant; the interview score may replace the fashion wear score. Height and weight are not factors, but contestants should be proportionate. Pageant experience and fluency in Spanish are not required.

**Financial data**  Each year, prizes vary. The overall winner receives a $5,000 cash award.

**Duration**  The pageant is held annually.

**Number awarded**  1 overall winner is selected each year.

**Deadline**  April of each year.

## [625]
## TENNESSEE ACTEENS SCHOLARSHIP

Tennessee Baptist Convention
Attn: WMU Scholarships
5001 Maryland Way
P.O. Box 728
Brentwood, TN 37024-9728
(615) 371-7923          Toll Free: (800) 558-2090, ext. 7923
Fax: (615) 371-2014          E-mail: lrader@tnbaptist.org
Web: www.tnbaptist.org/page.asp?page=92

**Summary**  To provide financial assistance to members of Baptist churches in Tennessee who have been active in the Acteens program for girls and plan to attend college in any state.

**Eligibility**  This program is open to high school seniors who are members and active participants in mission programs and ministry of a Tennessee Baptist church. Applicants must be able to demonstrate active involvement in Acteens in at least 2 of the following ways: 1) participation in local ministry for at least 2 years; 2) completion of at least 2 levels of MissionsQuest or an approved individual achievement plan; 3) selection as a state or national Acteen advisory panelist or Top Teen; or 4) service for 2 summers as an Acteens Activator. They must have a GPA of 2.6 or higher and be planning to enroll full time at a college or university in any state.

**Financial data**  The stipend is $2,500.

**Duration**  1 year.

**Number awarded**  1 each year.

**Deadline**  January of each year.

## [626]
## TESA SCHOLARSHIP PROGRAM

Texas Elks State Association
c/o Jim Nephew, Scholarship Chair
534 Woodcreek Circle
McQueeney, TX 78123
E-mail: jnephew1@satx.rr.com
Web: www.texaselks.org/Scholarships.html

**Summary**  To provide financial assistance to high school seniors in Texas who are not at the top of their class and plan to attend college in the state (females and males are considered separately).

**Eligibility**  This program is open to seniors at high schools in Texas who are not in the top 5% of their class. Candidates are nominated by their high school counselors; up to 3 boys and 3 girls may be nominated per school. Nominees must be U.S. citizens, residents of Texas, and planning to enroll full time at an accredited junior college, college, or university in the state. The names of these nominees are submitted to the local lodge; each lodge then selects 1 boy and 1 girl and submits their applications to the state scholarship chair. Those students must submit 1) a 300-word statement on their professional goals and how their past, present, and future activities make attainment of those goals probable; 2) a transcript; 3) a 200-word parent statement on the family's financial situation; and 4) SAT and/or ACT scores. Females and males compete separately. Final selection at the state level is based on leadership and extracurricular activities (200 points), character (200 points), scholarship (300 points), and financial need (300 points).

**Financial data** The stipend is $1,250 per year.

**Duration** 4 years.

**Number awarded** 6 each year: 3 boys and 3 girls.

**Deadline** School nominations must be submitted to the local lodges by February of each year.

## [627]
## TESA TEENAGER OF THE YEAR CONTEST

Texas Elks State Association
c/o Charles S. Page, Youth Activities Committee
1911 Palo Duro Road
Austin, TX 78757
E-mail: charles@austinairbalancing.com
Web: www.texaselks.org/Scholarships.html

**Summary** To provide financial assistance to seniors at high schools in Texas who plan to attend college in the state (females and males are selected separately).

**Eligibility** This program is open to seniors at high schools in Texas who are U.S. citizens. Applicants must be planning to enroll full time an accredited college or university in the state. Each Elks lodge in the state may submit the application of 1 boy and 1 girl. Selection is based on SAT or ACT scores; participation, leadership, honors, and awards in academic organizations; participation, leadership, honors, and awards in extracurricular activities; participation, leadership, honors, and awards in civic organizations; part-time employment; future plans; and overall appearance of the application. Boys and girls compete separately.

**Financial data** Stipends are $1,500, $1,000, or $500.

**Duration** 1 year.

**Number awarded** 6 each year: 2 each (1 each for a boy and 1 each for a girl) at $1,500, $1,000, and $500.

**Deadline** Students must submit applications to local lodges by February of each year.

## [628]
## TEXAS COLLEGIATE CATTLEWOMEN SCHOLARSHIP

Texas CattleWomen, Inc.
Attn: Erin Worrell, Scholarship Chair
657 Blue Oak Trail
Harper, TX 78631-6371
(830) 864-5161  E-mail: erin@theranchersresource.com
Web: www.txcattlewomen.org/programsactivities.html

**Summary** To provide financial assistance to members of Texas CattleWomen who are majoring in an agriculture-related field at a college in the state.

**Eligibility** This program is open to members of Texas CattleWomen who are currently enrolled at the sophomore through senior level at a 4-year college or university in the

state. They must have a GPA of 3.0 or higher and be majoring in an agricultural field. Selection is based on evidence of potential for continuing education, participation in student activities, evidence of leadership qualities, ability to relate well with others, financial need, and interest in and willingness to support the production and consumption of beef.

**Financial data** The stipend is $1,000 per year. Funds may be used for any educational expense.

**Duration** 1 year; recipients may reapply.

**Number awarded** 1 each year.

**Deadline** January of each year.

## [629]
## TEXAS ELKS STATE ASSOCIATION GIRL SCOUT GOLD AWARD SCHOLARSHIP

Texas Elks State Association
c/o Norma Williams, Gold Award Scholarship Committee
1501 North Loop 499, Suite 614
Harlingen, TX 78550
E-mail: normarupert@yahoo.com
Web: www.texaselks.org/Scholarships.html

**Summary** To provide financial assistance to high school seniors in Texas who earned the Girl Scout Gold Award and plan to attend college in the state.

**Eligibility** This program is open to seniors at high schools in Texas who have earned a Girl Scout Gold Award. Applicants must be planning to attend a college, university, or trade/vocational school in the state. Selection is based on leadership, achievement, recommendations, and financial need.

**Financial data** The stipend is $2,500. Funds are paid directly to the recipient's school.

**Duration** 1 year.

**Number awarded** 1 each year.

**Deadline** Applications must be submitted to the state chairperson by April of each year.

## [630]
## TEXAS FEDERATION OF REPUBLICAN WOMEN STATE SCHOLARSHIPS

Texas Federation of Republican Women
515 Capital of Texas Highway, Suite 133
Austin, TX 78746
(512) 477-1615  E-mail: tfrw@tfrw.org
Web: www.tfrw.org/Scholarships.aspx

**Summary** To provide financial assistance to women in Texas who are registered Republicans and attending college in any state.

**Eligibility** This program is open to women who have been residents of Texas for at least 2 years and have completed at least 12 hours of undergraduate study at an institution of higher learning in any state. Applicants must be U.S. citizens who are registered to vote and have a record of Republican party activity. They must have a GPA of 2.5 or higher. Financial need is not considered in the selection process.

**Financial data** A stipend is awarded (amount not specified).

**Duration** 1 year.

**Number awarded** 1 or more each year.

**Deadline** September of each year.

## [631]
## TEXAS KAPPA DELTA ALUMNAE SCHOLARSHIP

Kappa Delta Sorority
Attn: Foundation Project Manager
3205 Players Lane
Memphis, TN 38125
(901) 748-1897, ext. 203          Toll Free: (800) 536-1897
Fax: (901) 748-0949
E-mail: caroline.cullum@kappadelta.org
Web: www.kappadelta.org/scholarshipapplications_1

**Summary**   To provide financial assistance for undergraduate education to members of Kappa Delta Sorority at chapters in Texas.

**Eligibility**   This program is open to full-time undergraduate members of Kappa Delta Sorority at chapters in Texas. Applicants must submit a personal statement giving their reasons for applying for this scholarship, an official undergraduate transcript, and 2 letters of recommendation. They must have a GPA of 3.0 or higher. Selection is based on academic excellence; service to the chapter, alumnae association, or national Kappa Delta; service to the campus and community; personal objectives and goals; potential; recommendations; and financial need.

**Financial data**   The stipend is $1,000. Funds may be used only for tuition, fees, and books, not for room and board.

**Duration**   1 year.

**Number awarded**   1 each year.

**Deadline**   November of each year.

## [632]
## TEXAS RURAL ELECTRIC WOMEN'S ASSOCIATION SCHOLARSHIPS

Texas Rural Electric Women's Association
c/o Lynne Erickson, Scholarship Chair
Houston County Electric Cooperative
P.O. Box 52
Crockett, TX 75835
(800) 657-2445, ext. 224
E-mail: lynne@houstoncountyelec.com
Web: www.trewa.org

**Summary**   To provide financial assistance to members and children of members of the Texas Rural Electric Women's Association (TREWA) who plan to study a field related to energy or electricity at a college in any state.

**Eligibility**   This program is open to current members of the association and their children who are graduating high school seniors, current college students, or adults. Applicants may be enrolled or planning to enroll full time at an accredited college, university, junior or community college, trade/technical school, or business school in any state to work on a degree, certificate, diploma, or license. Along with their application, they must submit a 250-word essay on their planned field of study and how it relates to energy or electricity, their goals (educational, professional, and personal), their plans for the future, and why they have chosen their particular field of study. Grades received in high school are not the deciding factor in the selection process; leadership qualities, career focus, energy awareness, the essay, general knowledge of the rural electric program, and financial need are considered.

**Financial data**   The stipend is $1,500. Funds are paid directly to the recipient's institution, half at the beginning of

the first semester and half upon verification of completion of the first semester with passing grades.

**Duration**   1 year; nonrenewable.

**Additional information**   This scholarship is sponsored by TREWA and administered by Texas Electric Cooperatives, Inc. Membership in TREWA is open to rural electric employees, directors, and co-op members. The organization is run by women, but men are also eligible to join.

**Number awarded**   15 each year.

**Deadline**   March of each year.

## [633]
## TEXAS STATE FIRE FIGHTERS COLLEGE SCHOLARSHIP FUND

Texas State Association of Fire Fighters
Attn: Emergency Relief and College Scholarship Fund
627 Radam Lane
Austin, TX 78745-1121
(512) 326-5050                    Fax: (512) 326-5040
Web: www.tsaff.org

**Summary**   To provide financial assistance to dependent children of certified Texas firefighters who plan to attend college in any state (females and males are considered separately).

**Eligibility**   This program is open to dependents under 24 years of age of current, retired, or deceased certified firefighters in Texas. Applicants must be first-time students enrolled full time at an accredited college, university, or junior college in any state. Along with their application, they must submit a brief essay about their life and school years. Financial need is considered in the selection process. Males and females compete separately for scholarships.

**Financial data**   The stipend is at least $500 per term for the first 2 terms or semesters of college (a total of $1,000). Funds are paid directly to the recipient's school.

**Duration**   1 year.

**Additional information**   This fund was established in 1997.

**Number awarded**   At least 2 each year: 1 is set aside specifically for a female and 1 for a male. If additional funds are available, the program may award additional scholarships to equal numbers of female and male applicants.

**Deadline**   April of each year.

## [634]
## THADDEUS COLSON AND ISABELLE SAALWAECHTER FITZPATRICK MEMORIAL SCHOLARSHIP

Community Foundation of Louisville
Attn: Community Leadership Officer
Waterfront Plaza, Suite 1110
325 West Main Street
Louisville, KY 40202-4251
(502) 585-4649                    Fax: (502) 587-7484
E-mail: info@cflouisville.org
Web: scholarship.cflouisville.org/all_scholarships

**Summary**   To provide financial assistance to women from Kentucky studying fields related to the environment at colleges and universities in the state.

**Eligibility**   This program is open to female residents of Kentucky who are entering their sophomore, junior, or senior year at a 4-year public college or university in the state. Applicants must be majoring in an environmentally-related program (e.g., agriculture, biology, horticulture, environmental studies, environmental engineering). They must be enrolled full time with a GPA of 3.0 or higher. Along with their application, they must submit a 200-word essay describing their interest, leadership, volunteer efforts, and work experience in the environmental field; their future plans and goals in the environmental field; and what they hope to accomplish with their college degree. Financial need is also considered in the selection process.

**Financial data** The stipend ranges up to $5,000. Funds are paid directly to the college or university.

**Duration** 1 year; nonrenewable.

**Number awarded** 1 each year.

**Deadline** March of each year.

## [635]
## THEODORE AND MARY JANE RICH MEMORIAL SCHOLARSHIPS

Slovak Catholic Sokol
Attn: Membership Memorial Scholarship Fund
205 Madison Street
P.O. Box 899
Passaic, NJ 07055-0899
(973) 777-2605 Toll Free: (800) 886-7656
Fax: (973) 779-8245 E-mail: life@slovakcatholicsokol.org
Web: www.slovakcatholicsokol.org/grantsscholarships.asp

**Summary** To provide financial assistance to female and male members (judged separately) of the Slovak Catholic Sokol who are working on a medically-related degree at a college or graduate school in any state.

**Eligibility** This program is open to members of the Slovak Catholic Sokol who have completed at least 1 semester of college and are currently enrolled full time as an undergraduate or graduate student at an accredited college, university, or professional school in any state. Applicants must have been a member for at least 5 years, have at least $3,000 permanent life insurance coverage, and have at least 1 parent who is a member and is of Slovak ancestry. They must be studying a medical program. Males and females compete for scholarships separately.

**Financial data** The stipend is $2,500 per year.

**Duration** 1 year; may be renewed 1 additional year.

**Additional information** Slovak Catholic Sokol was founded as a fraternal benefit society in 1905. It is licensed to operate in the following states: Connecticut, Illinois, Indiana, Massachusetts, Michigan, New Jersey, New York, Ohio, Pennsylvania, and Wisconsin. This program was established in 2003.

**Number awarded** 2 each year: 1 for a male and 1 for a female.

**Deadline** March of each year.

## [636]
## THOMAS A. BRADY, MD COMEBACK AWARDS

Methodist Sports Medicine/The Orthopedic Specialists
Attn: Research and Education Foundation
201 Pennsylvania Parkway, Suite 100
Indianapolis, IN 46280
(317) 817-1258 Fax: (317) 817-1220
E-mail: dthornton@methodistsports.com
Web: www.methodistsports.com

**Summary** To recognize and reward, with scholarships, high school and college athletes in Indiana who have overcome adversity or injury and returned to excel in competition in their respective sport (females and males are judged separately).

**Eligibility** This award is available to student athletes who are nominated by a high school, college, or university in Indiana. Each school may nominate 1 male and 1 female athlete. Nominees must have distinguished themselves by overcoming adversity or injury and returned and excelled beyond expectations in their respective sport. They must have demonstrated good sportsmanship and ethical behavior on and off the playing field.

**Financial data** The award is a $1,000 college scholarship.

**Duration** The awards are presented annually.

**Additional information** This program began in 2006.

**Number awarded** 4 each year: 2 high school athletes (1 male and 1 female) and 2 college athletes (1 male and 1 female).

**Deadline** February of each year.

## [637]
## THORNBERG/HAVENS SCHOLARSHIP

Delta Zeta Sorority
Attn: Foundation Coordinator
202 East Church Street
Oxford, OH 45056
(513) 523-7597 Fax: (513) 523-1921
E-mail: DZFoundation@dzshq.com
Web: www.deltazeta.org

**Summary** To provide financial assistance for continued undergraduate or graduate study to members of Delta Zeta Sorority.

**Eligibility** This program is open to undergraduate and graduate members of the sorority who have a GPA of 3.0 or higher. Applicants must submit an official transcript, a statement of their career goals, information on their service to the sorority, documentation of campus activities and/or community involvement, a list of academic honors, and an explanation of their financial need.

**Financial data** The stipend ranges from $500 to $2,500 for undergraduates or from $1,000 to $15,000 for graduate students, depending on the availability of funds.

**Duration** 1 year; nonrenewable.

**Number awarded** 1 each year.

**Deadline** February of each year.

## [638]
## TIFFANY PHILLIPS SCHOLAR-ATHLETE AWARD

Miss America Pageant
Attn: Scholarship Department
222 New Road, Suite 700
Linwood, NJ 08221
(609) 653-8700, ext. 127　　　　　Fax: (609) 653-8740
E-mail: info@missamerica.org
Web: www.missamerica.org/scholarships

**Summary** To provide financial assistance to female scholar-athletes who are interested in working on an undergraduate degree and who competed at some level in the Miss America competition during the current year.

**Eligibility** This program is open to women who have competed at the local, state, or national level in the Miss America competition of the current year, regardless of whether or not they won a title, and are attending or planning to attend a college or university. Applicants must 1) be a participant in and demonstrate good sportsmanship in an athletic sport at the high school or university they attend; 2) have a GPA of 3.5 or higher; and 3) be involved in an activity that benefits their community or campus. Along with their application, they must submit brief statements on their greatest achievement as an athlete and a synopsis of their extracurricular or community service activities. Financial need is not considered in the selection process.

**Financial data** The stipend is $2,000.

**Duration** 1 year; renewable.

**Additional information** This scholarship was established in 1998.

**Number awarded** 1 each year.

**Deadline** June of each year.

## [639]
## TRAUB-DICKER RAINBOW SCHOLARSHIPS

Stonewall Community Foundation
Attn: Bee's Fund
446 West 33rd Street, Sixth Floor
New York, NY 10001
(212) 367-1155　　　　　　　Fax: (212) 367-1157
E-mail: grants@stonewallfoundation.org
Web: stonewallfoundation.org/grants/scholarships

**Summary** To provide financial assistance to undergraduate and graduate students who identify as lesbians.

**Eligibility** This program is open to lesbian-identified students who are 1) graduating high school seniors planning to attend a recognized college or university; 2) currently-enrolled undergraduates; and 3) graduate students. Applicants must submit 400-word essays on 1) their personal history, including a significant challenge or achievement in terms of community service, academic excellence, or dynamic leadership; 2) a particularly important experience they have had as a lesbian and how it has affected them; and 3) their plans or goals to give back to or focus on the lesbian, gay, bisexual, and transgender (LGBT) community while in school or after graduating. Selection is based on academic excellence, community service, and commitment to impacting LGBT issues. Financial need is not considered.

**Financial data** The stipend is $3,000. Funds are paid directly to the recipient's school, to be used for tuition, books, or room and board.

**Duration** 1 year.

**Additional information** This program began in 2004.

**Number awarded** 3 each year.

**Deadline** April of each year.

## [640]
## TULSA AREA COUNCIL ENDOWMENT SCHOLARSHIP

Epsilon Sigma Alpha International
Attn: ESA Foundation
363 West Drake Road
Fort Collins, CO 80526
(970) 223-2824　　　　　　　Fax: (970) 223-4456
E-mail: esainfo@epsilonsigmaalpha.org
Web: www.epsilonsigmaalpha.org/scholarships-and-grants

**Summary** To provide financial assistance to women in Oklahoma who plan to attend college in the state.

**Eligibility** This program is open to female residents of Oklahoma who are 1) graduating high school seniors with a GPA of 3.0 or higher or with minimum scores of 22 on the ACT or 1030 on the combined critical reading and mathematics SAT; 2) enrolled in college with a GPA of 3.0 or higher; 3) enrolled at a technical school or returning to school after an absence for retraining of job skills or obtaining a degree; or 4) engaged in online study through an accredited college, university, or vocational school. Applicants may be attending or planning to attend a school in Oklahoma and major in any field. Selection is based on service and leadership (20 points), financial need (35 points), and scholastic ability (35 points). A $5 processing fee is required.

**Financial data** The stipend is $1,000.

**Duration** 1 year; may be renewed.

**Additional information** Epsilon Sigma Alpha (ESA) is a women's service organization. This program began in 2004. Completed applications must be submitted to the ESA state counselor who then verifies the information before forwarding them to the scholarship director.

**Number awarded** 1 each year.

**Deadline** January of each year.

## [641]
## TWEET COLEMAN AVIATION SCHOLARSHIP

American Association of University Women-Honolulu Branch
Attn: Scholarship Committee
1802 Ke'eaumoku Street
Honolulu, HI 96822
(808) 537-4702　　　　　　　Fax: (808) 537-4702
E-mail: aauwhnb@hawaii.rr.com
Web: honolulu-hi.aauw.net/scholarships

**Summary** To provide financial assistance to women in Hawaii who are interested in a career in aviation.

**Eligibility** This program is open to women who are residents of Hawaii, at least 17 years of age, and attending an accredited college in the state. Applicants must be interested in obtaining a private pilot license. They must be able to pass a First Class FAA medical examination and to speak, read, write, and understand the English language. Along with their application, they must include a 1-page statement about themselves and their involvement in aviation. Selection is based on the merit of the applicant and a personal interview.

**Financial data** The stipend is $2,000. Funds may be used for flight training, ground school training, and aviation study manuals.

**Duration** 1 year.

**Additional information** This program began in 1990.

**Number awarded** 1 each year.

**Deadline** January of each year.

## [642]
## TWISTER SCHOLARSHIP

Women in Technology of Tennessee
c/o Barbara Webb
330 Franklin Road, Suite 135A-538
Brentwood, TN 37027
(615) 202-5840    E-mail: barbara.webb@level3.com
Web: www.wittn.org/outreach/technology-scholarships

**Summary** To provide financial assistance to female high school seniors in Tennessee who are interested in attending college in any state to prepare for a career in science, technology, engineering, or research.

**Eligibility** This program (Tennessee Women in Science, Technology, Engineering & Research) is open to women who are graduating from a Tennessee public high school, approved private high school, or home school. Applicants must be interested in attending college in any state to prepare for a career in science, technology, engineering, or research. They must have a GPA of 3.0 or higher. Along with their application, they must submit a 2-page essay on a topic that changes annually but relates to science, technology, or engineering. Financial need is not considered in the selection process.

**Financial data** Stipends are $2,500 and $1,000.

**Duration** 1 year.

**Additional information** This program, established in 2006, is offered in partnership with the Adventure Science Center of Nashville.

**Number awarded** 2 each year: 1 at $2,500 and 1 at $1,000.

**Deadline** February of each year.

## [643]
## UNITED PARCEL SERVICE SCHOLARSHIP FOR FEMALE STUDENTS

Institute of Industrial Engineers
Attn: Scholarship Coordinator
3577 Parkway Lane, Suite 200
Norcross, GA 30092
(770) 449-0461, ext. 105    Toll Free: (800) 494-0460
Fax: (770) 441-3295    E-mail: bcameron@iienet.org
Web: www.iienet2.org/Details.aspx?id=857

**Summary** To provide financial assistance to female undergraduates who are studying industrial engineering at a school in the United States, Canada, or Mexico.

**Eligibility** Eligible to be nominated are female undergraduate students enrolled at any school in the United States or its territories, Canada, or Mexico, provided the school's engineering program is accredited by an agency recognized by the Institute of Industrial Engineers (IIE) and the student is pursuing a full-time course of study in industrial engineering with a GPA of at least 3.4. Nominees must have at least 5 full quarters or 3 full semesters remaining until graduation. Stu-

dents may not apply directly for these awards; they must be nominated by the head of their industrial engineering department. Nominees must be IIE members. Selection is based on scholastic ability, character, leadership, and potential service to the industrial engineering profession.

**Financial data** The stipend is $4,000.

**Duration** 1 year.

**Additional information** Funding for this program is provided by the UPS Foundation.

**Number awarded** 1 each year.

**Deadline** Schools must submit nominations by November of each year.

## [644]
## UNITED STATES STEEL CORPORATION SCHOLARSHIPS

Society of Women Engineers
Attn: Scholarship Selection Committee
203 North LaSalle Street, Suite 1675
Chicago, IL 60601-1269
(312) 596-5223    Toll Free: (877) SWE-INFO
Fax: (312) 644-8557    E-mail: scholarships@swe.org
Web: societyofwomenengineers.swe.org

**Summary** To provide financial assistance to members of the Society of Women Engineers (SWE) majoring in computer science or engineering at designated universities.

**Eligibility** This program is open to members of the society who are entering their junior year or fourth year of a 5-year program at a designated ABET-accredited college or university. Applicants must be U.S. citizens or permanent residents who are working full time on a degree in computer science or engineering and have a GPA of 3.0 or higher. Selection is based on merit and interest in manufacturing.

**Financial data** The stipend is $5,000.

**Duration** 1 year.

**Additional information** This program is supported by the United States Steel Corporation. For a list of the designated universities, check the SWE web site.

**Number awarded** 6 each year.

**Deadline** February of each year.

## [645]
## U.S. ARMY WOMEN'S FOUNDATION LEGACY SCHOLARSHIPS

U.S. Army Women's Foundation
Attn: Scholarship Committee
P.O. Box 5030
Fort Lee, VA 23801-0030
(804) 734-3078    E-mail: info@awfdn.org
Web: www.awfdn.org/programs/legacyscholarships.shtml

**Summary** To provide financial assistance for college to women who are serving or have served in the Army and their children.

**Eligibility** This program is open to 1) women who have served or are serving honorably in the U.S. Army, U.S. Army Reserve, or Army National Guard; and 2) children of women who served honorably in the U.S. Army, U.S. Army Reserve, or Army National Guard. Applicants must be 1) upper-division students at an accredited college or university and have a GPA of 3.0 or higher; or 2) high school graduates or GED recipients enrolled at a community college and have a GPA of

2.5 or higher. Along with their application, they must submit a 2-page essay on why they should be considered for this scholarship, their future plans as related to their program of study, and information about their community service, activities, and work experience. Selection is based on merit, academic potential, community service, and financial need.

**Financial data**   The stipend is $2,500 for college and university students or $1,000 for community college students.

**Duration**   1 year.

**Number awarded**   5 to 10 each year.

**Deadline**   January of each year.

## [646]
## USBC YOUTH AMBASSADOR OF THE YEAR AWARDS

United States Bowling Congress
Attn: Youth Department
621 Six Flags Drive
Arlington, TX 76011
Toll Free: (800) 514-BOWL, ext. 3168
Fax: (817) 385-8262
E-mail: usbcyouth@bowl.com
Web: www.bowl.com

**Summary**   To recognize and reward, with college scholarships, outstanding young bowlers (females and males are considered separately).

**Eligibility**   These awards are presented to members of the United States Bowling Congress (USBC) who are 18 years of age or older. Males and females are considered in separate competitions. Selection is based on contributions to the sport of bowling (excluding league or tournament play), academic accomplishment, and community involvement.

**Financial data**   The awards consist of $1,500 college scholarships and an all-expense paid trip to the awards ceremony.

**Duration**   The awards are presented annually.

**Additional information**   The winners may also be selected to serve on the USBC Youth Committee for 3 years. This program was formerly named the USBC Youth Leader of the Year Awards.

**Number awarded**   2 each year: 1 for a female and 1 for a male.

**Deadline**   Nominations must be submitted by November of each year.

## [647]
## VANGUARD WOMEN IN INFORMATION TECHNOLOGY SCHOLARSHIP PROGRAM

Scholarship America
Attn: Scholarship Management Services
One Scholarship Way
P.O. Box 297
St. Peter, MN 56082
(507) 931-1682          Toll Free: (800) 537-4180
Fax: (507) 931-9168
Web: sms.scholarshipamerica.org

**Summary**   To provide financial assistance to women working on an undergraduate degree in fields related to information technology.

**Eligibility**   This program is open to women who are U.S. citizens or permanent residents. Applicants must be entering

their junior or senior year as a full-time student at an accredited 4-year college or university in the United States and have a GPA of 3.0 or higher. They must be working on a degree in computer science, computer engineering, web design, or other field related to information technology. Selection is based on academic record, demonstrated leadership and participation in school and community activities, honors, work experience, a statement of goals and aspirations, unusual personal or family circumstances, recommendations, and a resume; financial need is not considered.

**Financial data**   The stipend ranges up to $10,000.

**Duration**   1 year; nonrenewable.

**Additional information**   This program, established in 2004, is sponsored by Vanguard Group, Inc.

**Number awarded**   Up to 10 each year.

**Deadline**   November of each year.

## [648]
## VERIZON SCHOLARSHIPS OF THE SOCIETY OF WOMEN ENGINEERS

Society of Women Engineers
Attn: Scholarship Selection Committee
203 North LaSalle Street, Suite 1675
Chicago, IL 60601-1269
(312) 596-5223          Toll Free: (877) SWE-INFO
Fax: (312) 644-8557     E-mail: scholarships@swe.org
Web: societyofwomenengineers.swe.org

**Summary**   To provide financial assistance to women working on an undergraduate or graduate degree in designated engineering specialties.

**Eligibility**   This program is open to women who are enrolling as sophomores, juniors, seniors, or graduate students at an ABET-accredited 4-year college or university. Applicants must be working full time on a degree in computer science or computer, electrical, industrial, or mechanical engineering and have a GPA of 3.0 or higher. Preference is given to students attending specified colleges and universities, to students enrolled in an ROTC program, and to disabled veterans. Selection is based on merit. U.S. citizenship or permanent resident status is required.

**Financial data**   The stipend is $3,000.

**Duration**   1 year.

**Additional information**   This program is sponsored by Verizon. For a list of the specified colleges and universities, check the web site of the Society of Women Engineers.

**Number awarded**   10 each year.

**Deadline**   February of each year.

## [649]
## VHSL-ALLSTATE ACHIEVEMENT AWARDS

Virginia High School League
1642 State Farm Boulevard
Charlottesville, VA 22911
(434) 977-8475          Fax: (434) 977-5943
E-mail: info@vhsl.org
Web: www.vhsl.org/about/scholarships

**Summary**   To provide financial assistance to high school seniors who have participated in activities of the Virginia High School League (VHSL) and plan to attend college in any state (females and males are considered separately).

**Eligibility** This program is open to seniors graduating from high schools that are members of the VHSL and planning to attend a college or university in any state. Applicants must have participated in 1 or more VHSL athletic activities (baseball, basketball, cheer, cross country, field hockey, football, golf, gymnastics, lacrosse, soccer, softball, swimming, tennis, indoor and outdoor track, volleyball, wrestling) and/or academic activities (student publications, creative writing, drama, forensics, debate, scholastic bowl). They must have a GPA of 3.0 or higher. Each school may nominate up to 4 students: 1 female athlete, 1 male athlete, 1 academic participant, and 1 courageous achievement candidate. The courageous achievement category is reserved for students who have overcome serious obstacles to make significant contributions to athletic and/or academic activities. The obstacles may include a serious illness, injury, or disability; a challenging social or home situation; or another extraordinary situation where the student has displayed tremendous courage against overwhelming odds. Along with their application, students must submit a 500-word essay describing how extracurricular activities have enhanced their educational experience. Candidates are judged separately in the 3 VHSL groups (A, AA, and AAA). Selection is based on the essay; involvement in other school-sponsored activities; involvement in activities outside of school; and 2 letters of support.

**Financial data** The stipend is $1,000.

**Duration** 1 year.

**Additional information** This program, which began in 1992, is currently supported by the Allstate Foundation. The courageous achievement category, designated the Andrew Mullins Courageous Achievement Award, was added in 2002.

**Number awarded** 10 each year. For each of the 3 groups (A, AA, and AAA), 1 female athlete, 1 male athlete, and 1 academic participant are selected. In addition, 1 courageous achievement candidate is selected statewide.

**Deadline** March of each year.

## [650]
## VIASAT SOFTWARE ENGINEERING SCHOLARSHIP

Society of Women Engineers
Attn: Scholarship Selection Committee
203 North LaSalle Street, Suite 1675
Chicago, IL 60601-1269
(312) 596-5223            Toll Free: (877) SWE-INFO
Fax: (312) 644-8557      E-mail: scholarships@swe.org
Web: societyofwomenengineers.swe.org

**Summary** To provide financial assistance to women from specified states who are members of the Society of Women Engineers (SWE) and working on an undergraduate or graduate degree in software engineering.

**Eligibility** This program is open to SWE members who will be juniors, seniors, or graduate students at ABET-accredited colleges and universities and have a GPA of 3.2 or higher. Applicants must reside in or attend school in California, Maryland, Massachusetts, or Washington, D.C. They must be U.S. citizens or permanent residents working full time on a degree in computer science or software engineering. Selection is based on merit.

**Financial data** The stipend is $2,200.

**Duration** 1 year.

**Additional information** This program is sponsored by ViaSat, Inc.

**Number awarded** 1 each year.

**Deadline** February of each year.

## [651]
## VICKIE CLARK-FLAHERTY SCHOLARSHIP

North Carolina Restaurant and Lodging Association
Attn: NC Hospitality Education Foundation
6036 Six Forks Road
Raleigh, NC 27609
(919) 844-0098            Toll Free: (800) 582-8750
Fax: (919) 844-0190      E-mail: alyssab@ncrla.biz
Web: www.ncrla.biz

**Summary** To provide financial assistance to female residents of North Carolina who are interested in attending college in any state to major in a hospitality-related field.

**Eligibility** This program is open to female residents of North Carolina who are high school seniors, high school graduates, or undergraduates enrolled or planning to enroll full time at an accredited 2- or 4-year college, university, or vocational/technical school in the United States. Preference is given to students majoring in a hospitality-related field. Selection is based on academic achievement, community involvement, student leadership, extracurricular activities, employment and/or school references, and financial need.

**Financial data** The stipend ranges from $1,500 to $2,500 per year.

**Duration** 1 year; recipients may reapply.

**Number awarded** 1 or more each year.

**Deadline** February of each year.

## [652]
## VICTORIA ALEGRIA TRACY SCHOLARSHIP

Great Minds in STEM
Attn: HENAAC Scholars Program
602 Monterey Pass Road
Monterey Park, CA 91754
(323) 262-0997            Fax: (323) 262-0946
E-mail: gcruz@greatmindsinstem.org
Web: www.greatmindsinstem.org

**Summary** To provide financial assistance to Hispanic women from any state who are enrolled at universities in southern California and majoring in a field of science, technology, engineering, or mathematics (STEM).

**Eligibility** This program is open to female Hispanic undergraduate students from any state who are working on a degree in a field of STEM at colleges and universities in southern California. Applicants must be of Hispanic origin and/or must significantly participate in and promote organizations and activities in the Hispanic community. They must have a GPA of 2.5 or higher. Along with their application, they must submit a 700-word essay on a topic that changes annually. Selection is based on leadership, academic achievements, and campus and community activities; financial need is not considered.

**Financial data** Stipends range from $500 to $10,000.

**Duration** 1 year; recipients may reapply.

**Additional information** The Hispanic Engineer National Achievement Awards Conference (HENAAC) was established in 1989 and initiated a scholarship program in 2000. In

2010, the sponsoring organization officially adopted its current name, but it continues to hold the annual HENAAC conference, at which the scholarships are presented. This program was first offered in 2008. Recipients must attend the conference to accept their scholarship.

**Number awarded** Varies each year; recently, 5 of these scholarships were awarded.

**Deadline** April of each year.

## [653]
## VICTORY FOR WOMEN ACADEMIC SCHOLARSHIP FOR WOMEN WITH BLEEDING DISORDERS

National Hemophilia Foundation
Attn: Manager of Education
P.O. Box 971483
Ypsilanti, MI 48197
(734) 890-2504          E-mail: pflax@hemophilia.org
Web: www.hemophilia.org

**Summary** To provide financial assistance for college or graduate school to women who have a bleeding disorder.

**Eligibility** This program is open to women who are entering or already enrolled in an undergraduate or graduate program at a university, college, or accredited vocational school. Applicants must have von Willebrand Disease, hemophilia or other clotting factor deficiency, or carrier status. Along with their application, they must submit a 250-word essay that describes how their education and future career plans will benefit others in the bleeding disorders community. Selection is based on that essay, achievements, and community service to the bleeding disorders community.

**Financial data** The stipend is $2,500.

**Duration** 1 year.

**Additional information** The program, known also as V4W, was established in 2005 as the Project Red Flag Academic Scholarship for Women with Bleeding Disorders.

**Number awarded** 2 each year.

**Deadline** May of each year.

## [654]
## VINCENT J. DOOLEY AWARDS

Athletes for a Better World
Attn: Program Director
1401 Peachtree Street N.E., Suite 500
Atlanta, GA 30309
(404) 892-2328          E-mail: sajigirvan@abw.org
Web: www.abw.org/awards

**Summary** To recognize and reward, with scholarships for college study in any field, high school senior athletes in Georgia who demonstrate outstanding sportsmanship (females and males are considered separately).

**Eligibility** All high schools in Georgia are invited to nominate 2 of their senior athletes (1 male and 1 female) on the basis of character, teamwork, and citizenship. A selection committee then chooses 10 males and 10 females as finalists and invites them to a banquet at Turner Field in Atlanta, where they are interviewed and winners are selected.

**Financial data** The award is a scholarship of $1,000 per year.

**Duration** 4 years.

**Additional information** This program, which began in 2008, is co-sponsored by the Georgia High School Association.

**Number awarded** 2 each year: 1 male and 1 female.

**Deadline** Schools must submit their nominations by March of each year.

## [655]
## VIP WOMEN IN TECHNOLOGY SCHOLARSHIPS

Visionary Integration Professionals
80 Iron Point Circle, Suite 100
Folsom, CA 95630
(916) 985-9625          Toll Free: (800) 434-2673
Fax: (916) 985-9632     E-mail: WITS@vipconsulting.com
Web: www.vipconsulting.com

**Summary** To provide financial assistance to women preparing for a career in information technology.

**Eligibility** This program is open to women who are enrolled at or accepted into a 2- or 4-year college or university to prepare for a career in information technology or a related field. Applicants must have a cumulative GPA of 3.0 or higher. Along with their application, they must submit a 1,000-word essay in which they define a specific problem that they see in their community related to information technology and recommend a solution that is thoughtful and likely to make an impact on the problem. Selection is based on that essay, academic performance, and participation in community service and/or extracurricular activities.

**Financial data** The stipend is $2,500.

**Duration** 1 year.

**Number awarded** Varies each year; recently, 9 of these scholarships were awarded.

**Deadline** April of each year.

## [656]
## VIRGINIA GOLF FOUNDATION SCHOLARSHIP PROGRAM

Virginia Golf Association
Attn: Virginia Golf Foundation, Inc.
600 Founders Bridge Boulevard, Third Floor
Midlothian, VA 23113
(804) 378-2300, ext. 11          Fax: (804) 378-8216
E-mail: info@vsga.org
Web: www.vsga.org/about/scholarship-program

**Summary** To provide financial assistance to high school seniors in Virginia who have an interest in golf and plan to attend college in the state (some scholarships are set aside just for females).

**Eligibility** This program is open to high school seniors in Virginia who are interested in golf and wish to attend a college or university in the state. Applicants must submit an essay of 500 words or less on how golf has influenced their life, the role it will play in their future plans, why they are applying for this scholarship, and their career plans following graduation. Selection is based on the essay, interest in golf (excellence and ability are not considered), academic achievement, citizenship, character, and financial need. Applications must be made on behalf of the candidate by a member club of the Virginia State Golf Association (VSGA). Some scholarships are reserved for women, for men, and for students working on graduate degrees in turfgrass management at Virginia Polytechnic Institute and State University.

**Financial data** Stipends range from $1,000 to $7,000. Funds may be used only for tuition, room, and other approved educational expenses.

**Duration** The program includes 4-year scholarships and 1-year merit awards.

**Additional information** This program began in 1984. It includes the following named awards: the C. Dan Keffer Award (for the highest ranked applicant), the David A. King Merit Award, the Red Speigle Award, and the Spencer-Wilkinson Awards (presented by the Women's Division).

**Number awarded** Varies each year; recently, 33 of these scholarships were awarded: 13 for 4 years (with a total value of $66,000), 18 merit awards for 1 year each (with a total value of $26,000), and 2 at $2,500 each for turfgrass management graduate students at Virginia Tech. Since the program began, it has awarded more than $1.85 million to more than 800 students.

**Deadline** February of each year.

## [657]
## VIRGINIA M. WAGNER EDUCATIONAL GRANT

Soroptimist International of the Americas-Midwestern
  Region
c/o Alexandra Nicholis
2117 Quayle Drive
Akron, OH 44312-2332
(330) 524-7113          E-mail: soroptimist@simwr.org
Web: simwr.org/#!virginia-wagner-award/c1vsh

**Summary** To provide financial assistance to women working on an undergraduate or graduate degree at a college or university in the Midwest.

**Eligibility** This program is open to women who reside in Illinois, Indiana, Kentucky, Michigan, Ohio, or Wisconsin and are attending college or graduate school in any state. Applicants must be working on a bachelor's, master's, or doctoral degree in the field of their choice. Awards are first presented at the club level, then in districts, and finally for the entire region. Selection is based on the effort toward education by the applicant and her family, cumulative GPA, extracurricular activities, general impression, and financial need.

**Financial data** Club level awards vary at the discretion of the club. District finalists receive a $500 award and are then judged at the regional level. The regional winner receives a $2,500 award.

**Duration** 1 year.

**Additional information** This program began in 1972 and given its current name in 2004.

**Number awarded** 4 district winners are selected each year; 1 of those receives the regional award.

**Deadline** January of each year.

## [658]
## VIRGINIA PEACE MACKEY-ALTHOUSE VOICE AWARD

National Federation of Music Clubs
1646 Smith Valley Road
Greenwood, IN 46142
(317) 882-4003          Fax: (317) 882-4019
E-mail: info@nfmc-music.org
Web: nfmc-music.org

**Summary** To recognize and reward outstanding female student singers who are members of the National Federation of Music Clubs (NFMC).

**Eligibility** This award is presented to female singers between 19 and 26 years of age. Student membership in the federation and U.S. citizenship are required. Candidates for the NFMC Biennial Student/Collegiate Audition Awards competition are automatically considered for this award; no separate application is necessary.

**Financial data** The prize is $1,750.

**Duration** The competition is held biennially, in odd-numbered years.

**Additional information** The entry fee is $30.

**Number awarded** 1 every other year.

**Deadline** January of odd-numbered years.

## [659]
## VIVIAN D. TILLMAN SCHOLARSHIP

Sigma Gamma Rho Sorority, Inc.
Attn: National Education Fund
1000 Southhill Drive, Suite 200
Cary, NC 27513
(919) 678-9720          Toll Free: (888) SGR-1922
Fax: (919) 678-9721          E-mail: info@sgrho1922.org
Web: www.sgrho1922.org/nef

**Summary** To provide financial assistance to African American females and other undergraduate students working on a degree in journalism or communications.

**Eligibility** This program is open to undergraduates working on a degree in journalism or communications. The sponsor is a traditionally African American sorority. Applicants must have a GPA of "C" or higher and be able to demonstrate financial need. Along with their application, they must submit a 500-word essay on how they will use their communication or journalism skills for the betterment of the country.

**Financial data** A stipend is awarded (amount not specified).

**Duration** 1 year.

**Additional information** A processing fee of $20 is required.

**Number awarded** 1 each year.

**Deadline** April of each year.

## [660]
## WALTER REED SMITH SCHOLARSHIP PROGRAM

United Daughters of the Confederacy
Attn: Second Vice President General
328 North Boulevard
Richmond, VA 23220-4008
(804) 355-1636          Fax: (804) 353-1396
E-mail: jamieretired@sbcglobal.net
Web: www.hqudc.org/Scholarships/index.htm

**Summary** To provide financial assistance to mature women who are lineal descendants of Confederate veterans and plan to major in selected fields in college.

**Eligibility** Eligible to apply for these scholarships are women over the age of 30 who are lineal descendants of worthy Confederates or collateral descendants and members of the Children of the Confederacy or the United Daughters of the Confederacy. Applicants must intend to study business administration, computer science, home economics, nutrition, or nursing. They must submit certified proof of the Confederate record of 1 ancestor, with the company and regiment in which he served, and must have had at least a 3.0 GPA in high school.

**Financial data** The amount of this scholarship depends on the availability of funds.

**Duration** 1 year; may be renewed.

**Number awarded** 1 each year.

**Deadline** April of each year.

## [661]
## WANDA MUNN SCHOLARSHIP

Society of Women Engineers
Attn: Scholarship Selection Committee
203 North LaSalle Street, Suite 1675
Chicago, IL 60601-1269
(312) 596-5223          Toll Free: (877) SWE-INFO
Fax: (312) 644-8557     E-mail: scholarships@swe.org
Web: societyofwomenengineers.swe.org

**Summary** To provide financial assistance to women from selected northwestern states, particularly those who have worked in the engineering field, who are interested in returning to college or graduate school to continue their study of engineering or computer science.

**Eligibility** This program is open to women who are planning to enroll at an ABET-accredited 4-year college or university. Applicants must have been out of the engineering workforce and school for at least 2 years and must be planning to return as an undergraduate or graduate student to work on a degree in computer science or engineering. They must be residents of are attending school in Alaska, Idaho, Montana, Oregon, or Washington and have a GPA of 3.0 or higher. Selection is based on merit. Preference is given to engineers who already have a degree and are planning to reenter the engineering workforce after a period of temporary retirement.

**Financial data** The stipend is $1,500.

**Duration** 1 year.

**Additional information** This program is sponsored by the Eastern Washington Section of the Society of Women Engineers.

**Number awarded** 1 each year.

**Deadline** February of each year.

## [662]
## WASHINGTON DC ALUMNAE CHAPTER SCHOLARSHIPS

Delta Sigma Theta Sorority, Inc.-Washington DC Alumnae Chapter
Attn: Scholarship Committee
P.O. Box 90202
Washington, DC 20090-0202
Toll Free: (201) 388-1912
E-mail: scholarship@wdcac.org
Web: www.wdcac.org/scholarship

**Summary** To provide financial assistance to high school seniors (especially female African Americans) in Washington, D.C. who plan to attend college in any state.

**Eligibility** This program is open to seniors graduating from public, charter, parochial, and private high schools in Washington, D.C. and planning to enroll full time at a 2- or 4-year college or university in any state. Applicants must submit an official high school transcript, a copy of their SAT or ACT scores, documentation of financial need, 2 letters of recommendation, and a 1-page autobiographical essay including their academic and career goals, community service involvement, why the scholarship is important, and its expected benefit.

**Financial data** Stipends range from $1,050 to $2,500 per year.

**Duration** 1 year; may be renewed.

**Additional information** The sponsor is the local alumnae chapter of a traditionally African American social sorority.

**Number awarded** Varies each year.

**Deadline** February of each year.

## [663]
## WASHINGTON STATE BUSINESS AND PROFESSIONAL WOMEN'S FOUNDATION SINGLE PARENT SCHOLARSHIP

Washington State Business and Professional Women's Foundation
Attn: Virginia Murphy, Scholarship Committee Chair
P.O. Box 631
Chelan, WA 98816-0631
(509) 682-4747          E-mail: vamurf@nwi.net
Web: www.bpwwa.org/foundation_apps.htm

**Summary** To provide financial assistance to women from Washington who are single parents interested in returning to college to continue their education.

**Eligibility** This program is open to women of any age who have been residents of Washington for at least 2 years. Applicants must have at least 1 dependent child, under 18 years of age, living at home. They must be interested in returning to school in the state to continue their education beyond the high school level. Along with their application, they must submit a 500-word essay on their specific short-term goals and how the proposed training will help them accomplish those goals and make a difference in their professional career. Financial need is considered in the selection process. U.S. citizenship is required.

**Financial data** The stipend is $1,000.

**Duration** 1 year.

**Number awarded** 1 or more each year.

**Deadline** April of each year.

## [664]
## WASHINGTON WOMEN IN NEED EDUCATIONAL GRANTS

Washington Women in Need
700 108th Avenue, N.E., Suite 207
Bellevue, WA 98004
(425) 451-8838          Toll Free: (888) 440-WWIN
Fax: (425) 451-8845     E-mail: wwininfo@wwin.org
Web: www.wwin.org/how-to-apply/programs

**Summary** To provide financial assistance to low-income women who reside in Washington and are interested in attending college in the state.

**Eligibility** This program is open to low-income women who are at least 18 years of age and residents of Washington. Applicants must be interested in attending an accredited institution in the state. They must first apply for all available federal and private grants and scholarships. If all available assistance does not fully cover the costs of tuition and books, they may apply for these grants. Any field of study is eligible, at any level of degree or vocational certification through a bachelor's degree, including GED completion and college transfer.

**Financial data** Stipends range up to $5,000 per year.

**Duration** 1 year; renewal is possible if the recipient maintains a GPA of 2.5 or higher and remains eligible for in-state tuition at their institution.

**Number awarded** Varies each year.

**Deadline** Deadline not specified.

## [665]
## WASHINGTON ZONTA CLUB SCHOLARSHIPS

Zonta Club of Washington, D.C.
c/o Merilyn D. Francis, Scholarship Committee
P.O. Box 9753
Washington, DC 20016
(202) 380-5222
Web: www.zontawashingtondc.org/projects.html

**Summary** To provide financial assistance to women from any state who are attending college in Washington, D.C.

**Eligibility** This program is open to women undergraduates from any state who are enrolled full or part time at universities in the Washington, D.C. area. Applicants must have completed at least 15 semester hours and have a GPA of 3.0 or higher. Selection is based on GPA, community involvement and leadership, relevant personal circumstances, an essay on academic and career interests, letters of recommendation, commitment to professional excellence in future career, and financial need.

**Financial data** The amount awarded varies; recently, stipends averaged $4,400.

**Duration** 1 year.

**Number awarded** Varies each year; recently, 5 of these scholarships were awarded.

**Deadline** March of each year.

## [666]
## WATSON MIDWIVES OF COLOR SCHOLARSHIP

American College of Nurse-Midwives
Attn: ACNM Foundation, Inc.
8403 Colesville Road, Suite 1550
Silver Spring, MD 20910-6374
(240) 485-1850          Fax: (240) 485-1818
E-mail: fdn@acnm.org
Web: www.midwife.org

**Summary** To provide financial assistance for midwifery education to students of color who belong to the American College of Nurse-Midwives (ACNM).

**Eligibility** This program is open to ACNM members of color who are currently enrolled in an accredited basic midwife education program and have successfully completed 1 academic or clinical semester/quarter or clinical module. Applicants must submit a 150-word essay on their 5-year midwifery career plans and a 100-word essay on their intended future participation in the local, regional, and/or national activities of the ACNM. Selection is based on leadership potential, financial need, academic history, and potential for future professional contribution to the organization.

**Financial data** The stipend is $3,000.

**Duration** 1 year.

**Number awarded** Varies each year; recently, 3 of these scholarships were awarded.

**Deadline** March of each year.

## [667]
## WELLS FARGO CITIZENSHIP AWARDS

Virginia High School League
1642 State Farm Boulevard
Charlottesville, VA 22911
(434) 977-8475          Fax: (434) 977-5943
E-mail: info@vhsl.org
Web: www.vhsl.org/about/scholarships

**Summary** To provide financial assistance to high school seniors who have participated in activities of the Virginia High School League (VHSL) and plan to attend college in any state (females and males are considered separately).

**Eligibility** This program is open to seniors graduating from high schools that are members of the VHSL and planning to attend a college or university in any state. Applicants must have participated in 1 or more of the following VHSL activities: baseball, basketball, cheer, creative writing, cross country, debate, drama, field hockey, football, forensics, golf, gymnastics, lacrosse, leaders conference, magazines, newspapers/newsmagazines, scholastic bowl, soccer, softball, sportsmanship summit/committee, swimming and diving, tennis, track (indoor and outdoor), volleyball, wrestling, or yearbook. They must submit an essay (from 500 to 1,000 words) on what they have done that meets a definition of citizenship and how others have benefited. Each school may nominate 1 female and 1 male. Candidates are judged separately in the 3 VHSL groups (A, AA, and AAA). Selection is based on the essay; contributions to family, school, and community; promotion of good citizenship and sportsmanship; and 2 letters of support.

**Financial data** The stipend is $1,000.

**Duration** 1 year.

**Additional information** This program is supported by Wells Fargo Bank.

**Number awarded** 6 each year: 1 female and 1 male in each of the 3 VHSL groups.

**Deadline** March of each year.

## [668]
## WETV SCHOLARSHIP OF NEW YORK WOMEN IN COMMUNICATIONS

New York Women in Communications, Inc.
Attn: NYWICI Foundation
355 Lexington Avenue, 15th Floor
New York, NY 10017-6603
(212) 297-2133                    Fax: (212) 370-9047
E-mail: nywicipr@nywici.org
Web: www.nywici.org/foundation/scholarships

**Summary** To provide financial assistance to female residents of designated eastern states who are enrolled at a college in any state and preparing for a career in broadcast production.

**Eligibility** This program is open to women who are residents of New York, New Jersey, Connecticut, or Pennsylvania and currently enrolled as undergraduate or graduate students at a college or university in any state. Graduate students must be members of New York Women in Communications, Inc. (NYWICI). Also eligible are women who reside outside the 4 states but are currently enrolled at a college or university within 1 of the 5 boroughs of New York City. Applicants must be able to demonstrate a commitment to a career in broadcast production. They must have a GPA of 3.2 or higher. Along with their application, they must submit a 2-page resume; a personal essay of 300 words on an assigned topic that changes annually; 2 letters of recommendation; and an official transcript. Selection is based on academic record, need, demonstrated leadership, participation in school and community activities, honors and other awards or recognition, work experience, goals and aspirations, and unusual personal and/or family circumstances. U.S. citizenship is required.

**Financial data** The stipend ranges up to $10,000.

**Duration** 1 year.

**Additional information** This program is sponsored by WEtv.

**Number awarded** 1 each year.

**Deadline** January of each year.

## [669]
## WICHITA CHAPTER AFWA SCHOLARSHIPS

Accounting and Financial Women's Alliance-Wichita
    Chapter
c/o Terra Eck, Scholarship Chair
5320 Tenpoint
Andale, KS 67001
(316) 828-5084
Web: www.wichitaaswa.org

**Summary** To provide financial assistance to women working on an undergraduate or graduate degree in accounting or finance at a college or university in Kansas.

**Eligibility** This program is open to women working full or part time on an associate, bachelor's, or master's degree in accounting or finance at a college or university in Kansas.

Applicants must have completed at least 15 semester hours in a 2-year program or 60 semester hours in a 4-year program. They must have a cumulative GPA of 3.0 or higher. Membership in the Accounting and Financial Women's Alliance (AFWA) is not required. Along with their application, they must submit an essay of 150 to 250 words on their career goals and objectives, the impact they want to have on the accounting world, community involvement, and leadership examples. Selection is based on leadership, character, communication skills, GPA, and financial need.

**Financial data** The stipend is $1,000.

**Duration** 1 year.

**Additional information** The highest-ranked recipient is entered into the national competition for scholarships that range from $1,500 to $4,500.

**Number awarded** Varies each year; recently, 4 of these scholarships were awarded.

**Deadline** February of each year.

## [670]
## WILLIAM BRIDGE SCHOLARSHIP

Ninety-Nines, Inc.-Eastern New England Chapter
c/o Olga Mitchell
10 Glory Lane
East Falmouth, MA 02536
E-mail: ene99s@comcast.net
Web: womenpilotsene.org/scholarships.html

**Summary** To provide financial assistance to female residents of New England who are interested in preparing for a career in aviation.

**Eligibility** This program is open to women who are at least of high school age and reside or study in 1 of the following states: Maine, New Hampshire, Rhode Island, Vermont, Massachusetts, or Connecticut. Applicants must be studying or planning to study in an area of aviation at an accredited college or university, at a college or other flight school, or with a private instructor. They must have at least a private pilot certificate. Along with their application, they must submit a personal letter describing their reasons for choosing an aviation career, including descriptions of all their aviation-related activities. Selection is based on academic achievement, interest and dedication to a career in aviation, recommendations, involvement in aviation activities (e.g., flying, aviation employment, model airplane building, science fair projects), and financial need.

**Financial data** The stipend is $1,500.

**Duration** 1 year.

**Number awarded** 1 each year.

**Deadline** January of each year.

## [671]
## WILLIAM RUCKER GREENWOOD SCHOLARSHIP

Association for Women Geoscientists
Attn: AWG Foundation
12000 North Washington Street, Suite 285
Thornton, CO 80241
(303) 412-6219                    Fax: (303) 253-9220
E-mail: office@awg.org
Web: www.awg.org/members/po_scholarships.html

**Summary** To provide financial assistance to minority women from any state working on an undergraduate or graduate degree in the geosciences at a college in the Potomac Bay region.

**Eligibility** This program is open to minority women who are residents of any state and currently enrolled as full-time undergraduate or graduate geoscience majors at an accredited, degree-granting college or university in Delaware, the District of Columbia, Maryland, Virginia, or West Virginia. Selection is based on the applicant's 1) participation in geoscience or earth science educational activities; and 2) potential for leadership as a future geoscience professional.

**Financial data** The stipend is $1,000. The recipient also is granted a 1-year membership in the Association for Women Geoscientists (AWG).

**Duration** 1 year.

**Additional information** This program is sponsored by the AWG Potomac Area Chapter.

**Number awarded** 1 each year.

**Deadline** April of each year.

## [672]
## WISCONSIN LEGION AUXILIARY DEPARTMENT PRESIDENT'S SCHOLARSHIP

American Legion Auxiliary
Department of Wisconsin
Attn: Education Chair
2930 American Legion Drive
P.O. Box 140
Portage, WI 53901-0140
(608) 745-0124          Toll Free: (866) 664-3863
Fax: (608) 745-1947     E-mail: alawi@amlegionauxwi.org
Web: www.amlegionauxwi.org/Scholarships.htm

**Summary** To provide financial assistance to Wisconsin residents who are members or children of members of the American Legion Auxiliary and interested in attending college in any state.

**Eligibility** This program is open to members and children of members of the American Legion Auxiliary in Wisconsin. Applicants must be high school seniors or graduates and attending or planning to attend a college or university in any state. They must have a GPA of 3.5 or higher and be able to demonstrate financial need. Along with their application, they must submit a 300-word essay on "Education—An Investment in the Future."

**Financial data** The stipend is $1,000.

**Duration** 1 year.

**Number awarded** 3 each year.

**Deadline** March of each year.

## [673]
## WISCONSIN LEGION AUXILIARY MERIT AND MEMORIAL SCHOLARSHIPS

American Legion Auxiliary
Department of Wisconsin
Attn: Education Chair
2930 American Legion Drive
P.O. Box 140
Portage, WI 53901-0140
(608) 745-0124          Toll Free: (866) 664-3863
Fax: (608) 745-1947     E-mail: alawi@amlegionauxwi.org
Web: www.amlegionauxwi.org/Scholarships.htm

**Summary** To provide financial assistance to Wisconsin residents who are related to veterans or members of the American Legion Auxiliary and interested in working on an undergraduate degree at a school in any state.

**Eligibility** This program is open to the children, wives, and widows of veterans who are high school seniors or graduates and have a GPA of 3.5 or higher. Grandchildren and great-grandchildren of members of the American Legion Auxiliary are also eligible. Applicants must be residents of Wisconsin and interested in working on an undergraduate degree at a school in any state. Along with their application, they must submit a 300-word essay on "Education—An Investment in the Future." Financial need is considered in the selection process.

**Financial data** The stipend is $1,000.

**Duration** 1 year; nonrenewable.

**Additional information** This program includes the following named scholarships: the Harriet Hass Scholarship, the Adalin Macauley Scholarship, the Eleanor Smith Scholarship, the Pearl Behrend Scholarship, the Barbara Kranig Scholarship, and the Jan Pulvermacher-Ryan Scholarship.

**Number awarded** 7 each year.

**Deadline** March of each year.

## [674]
## WISCONSIN LEGION AUXILIARY PAST PRESIDENTS PARLEY HEALTH CAREER SCHOLARSHIPS

American Legion Auxiliary
Department of Wisconsin
Attn: Education Chair
2930 American Legion Drive
P.O. Box 140
Portage, WI 53901-0140
(608) 745-0124          Toll Free: (866) 664-3863
Fax: (608) 745-1947     E-mail: alawi@amlegionauxwi.org
Web: www.amlegionauxwi.org/Scholarships.htm

**Summary** To provide financial assistance for health-related education at a school in any state to the dependents and descendants of veterans in Wisconsin.

**Eligibility** This program is open to the children, wives, and widows of veterans who are attending or entering a hospital, university, or technical school in any state to prepare for a health-related career. Grandchildren and great-grandchildren of veterans are eligible if they are members of the American Legion Auxiliary. Applicants must be residents of Wisconsin and have a GPA of 3.5 or higher. Along with their application, they must submit a 300-word essay on "The Importance of Health Careers Today." Financial need is considered in the selection process.

**Financial data** The stipend is $1,000.

**Duration** 1 year; nonrenewable.

**Number awarded** 2 each year.

**Deadline** March of each year.

## [675]
## WISCONSIN LEGION AUXILIARY PAST PRESIDENTS PARLEY REGISTERED NURSE SCHOLARSHIPS

American Legion Auxiliary
Department of Wisconsin
Attn: Education Chair
2930 American Legion Drive
P.O. Box 140
Portage, WI 53901-0140
(608) 745-0124       Toll Free: (866) 664-3863
Fax: (608) 745-1947    E-mail: alawi@amlegionauxwi.org
Web: www.amlegionauxwi.org/Scholarships.htm

**Summary** To provide financial assistance to the dependents and descendants of Wisconsin veterans who are interested in studying nursing at a school in any state.

**Eligibility** This program is open to the wives, widows, and children of Wisconsin veterans who are enrolled or have been accepted in an accredited school of nursing in any state to prepare for a career as a registered nurse. Grandchildren and great-grandchildren of veterans are also eligible if they are American Legion Auxiliary members. Applicants must be Wisconsin residents and have a GPA of 3.5 or higher. Along with their application, they must submit a 300-word essay on "The Need for Trained Nurses Today." Financial need is considered in the selection process.

**Financial data** The stipend is $1,000.

**Duration** 1 year.

**Number awarded** 2 each year.

**Deadline** March of each year.

## [676]
## WISCONSIN TOWNS ASSOCIATION SCHOLARSHIPS

Wisconsin Towns Association
Attn: Scholarship Program
W7686 County Road MMM
Shawano, WI 54166-6086
(715) 526-3157       Fax: (715) 524-3917
E-mail: wtowns@frontiernet.net
Web: www.wisctowns.com/home/scholarship-program

**Summary** To provide financial assistance to high school seniors in Wisconsin (females and males are judged separately) who submit outstanding essays on town government and plan to attend college in the state.

**Eligibility** This program is open to seniors graduating from high schools in Wisconsin who plan to attend a college, university, or vocational/technical institute in the state. Applicants must submit an essay of 500 to 1,000 words on a topic that changes annually but relates to local government in Wisconsin; recently, students were asked to write on "Should state funds be used to assist in the maintenance and construction of local roads, and if so, from what types of funding sources?" Selection is based primarily on the essay's originality and subject matter in relationship to the topic; financial need is not considered. Boys and girls are judged separately.

**Financial data** The stipend is $1,000.

**Duration** 1 year.

**Additional information** This program is supported by Rural Mutual Insurance Company and by Scott Construction, Inc.

**Number awarded** 5 each year: 2 to boys, 2 to girls, and 1 to a boy or girl who has the next highest ranking.

**Deadline** May of each year.

## [677]
## WISCONSIN WOMEN IN GOVERNMENT UNDERGRADUATE SCHOLARSHIPS

Wisconsin Women in Government, Inc.
Attn: Scholarship Committee
P.O. Box 2543
Madison, WI 53701
(608) 848-2321
E-mail: info@wiscwomeningovernment.org
Web: www.wiscwomeningovernment.org/scholarships.cfm

**Summary** To provide financial assistance to women in Wisconsin interested in attending a college or university in the state to prepare for a career in public service.

**Eligibility** This program is open to women in Wisconsin who are enrolled full or part time at an institution that is a member of the University of Wisconsin system, the Wisconsin Technical College System, or the Wisconsin Association of Independent Colleges and Universities. Applicants must have a grade average of "C" or higher and be able to demonstrate financial need. They must possess leadership potential, initiative, and excellent communication skills and have an interest in public service, government, and the political process. Juniors and seniors must have declared a major. Selection is based on leadership, demonstrated ability to handle responsibility, initiative, communication skills, academic achievement, community involvement, and commitment to public service.

**Financial data** The stipend is $3,000 per year. Funds may be used for tuition, school supplies, child care, or to reduce loan burden.

**Duration** 1 year; may be renewed.

**Number awarded** Varies each year; recently, 3 of these scholarships were awarded.

**Deadline** April of each year.

## [678]
## WISCONSIN WOMEN'S ALLIANCE FOUNDATION SCHOLARSHIP

Community Foundation for the Fox Valley Region, Inc.
Attn: Scholarships
4455 West Lawrence Street
P.O. Box 563
Appleton, WI 54912-0563
(920) 830-1290       Fax: (920) 830-1293
E-mail: scholarships@cffoxvalley.org
Web: www.cffoxvalley.org/page.aspx?pid=246

**Summary** To provide financial assistance to mature women in Wisconsin who are working on an undergraduate or graduate degree at a school in any state.

**Eligibility** This program is open to Wisconsin women who are 25 years of age or older. Applicants must be attending an accredited 2- or 4-year college, university, or technical college to work on an undergraduate or graduate degree. They must submit a personal statement of their reasons for working on a degree in their chosen field, including their special professional interests, goals, and purposes within that field. Selection is based on that statement, employment history, volunteer activities, professional and community activities, and financial need.

**Financial data** The stipend ranges up to $1,000.

**Duration** 1 year.

**Number awarded** Normally, 3 each year.

**Deadline** February of each year.

## [679]
## WOKSAPE OYATE: "WISDOM OF THE PEOPLE" KEEPERS OF THE NEXT GENERATION AWARD

American Indian College Fund
Attn: Scholarship Department
8333 Greenwood Boulevard
Denver, CO 80221
(303) 426-8900            Toll Free: (800) 776-FUND
Fax: (303) 426-1200
E-mail: scholarships@collegefund.org
Web: www.collegefund.org

**Summary** To provide financial assistance to Native Americans who are single parents and attending or planning to attend a Tribal College or University (TCU).

**Eligibility** This program is open to American Indians or Alaska Natives who are single parents and enrolled or planning to enroll full time at an eligible TCU. Applicants must have a GPA of 2.0 or higher. Applications are available only online and include required essays on specified topics. Selection is based on exceptional academic achievement. U.S. citizenship is required.

**Financial data** The stipend is $8,000.

**Duration** 1 year.

**Additional information** This program began in 2006 with an endowment grant from the Lilly Foundation.

**Number awarded** 1 each year.

**Deadline** May of each year.

## [680]
## WOMEN CHEFS & RESTAURATEURS SCHOLARSHIP PROGRAM

Women Chefs & Restaurateurs
Attn: Scholarship Program Coordinator
115 South Patrick Street, Suite 101
Alexandria, VA 22314
(630) 396-8339            Toll Free: (877) 927-7787
E-mail: Scholarship@womenchefs.org
Web: www.womenchefs.org

**Summary** To provide financial assistance to members of Women Chefs & Restaurateurs (WCR) who are interested in preparing for a culinary or related career.

**Eligibility** This program is open to women who are members of WCR, interested in attending a culinary or related school, and at least 18 years of age (21 for the wine scholarships). Recently, support was offered at the Tante Marie Cooking School in San Francisco; the Italian culinary experience, the classic culinary arts program, the classic pastry arts program, and the intensive sommelier program at the International Culinary Center (New York, New York); the Italian Culinary Experience, the classic pastry arts program, and the intensive sommelier program at the International Culinary Center (Campbell, California); and the pastry and baking diploma program and the culinary management diploma program at the Institute of Culinary Education (New York, New

York). Applicants must submit a 1-page essay about their food service career, their culinary interests, what inspires them professionally, and how the scholarship will contribute to their career.

**Financial data** In general, scholarships provide payment of full or partial tuition, or stipends of $5,000 or $7,500 per year.

**Duration** Program lengths vary; scholarships must be used during the calendar year in which they are awarded.

**Additional information** Students may apply for only 1 program on a single application; the fee is $25 for the first application $40 for multiple applications (to a maximum of 3).

**Number awarded** Varies each year; recently, 18 of these scholarships were awarded.

**Deadline** July of each year.

## [681]
## WOMEN IN AVIATION, INTERNATIONAL GENERAL SCHOLARSHIPS

Women in Aviation, International
Attn: Scholarships
Morningstar Airport
3647 State Route 503 South
West Alexandria, OH 45381-9354
(937) 839-4647            Fax: (937) 839-4645
E-mail: scholarships@wai.org
Web: www.wai.org/education/scholarships.cfm

**Summary** To provide financial assistance for college to members of Women in Aviation, International (WAI).

**Eligibility** This program is open to WAI members who are undergraduate or graduate students working on a degree in a field related to aviation or aerospace. Applicants must have earned a GPA of 3.0 or higher and be able to demonstrate leadership potential. Along with their application, they must submit a 500-word essay on their career aspirations and other topics that depend on the requirements of specific scholarships. Selection is based on achievements, attitude toward self and others, commitment to success, dedication to career, financial need, motivation, reliability, responsibility, and teamwork.

**Financial data** Stipends range from $1,000 to $5,000.

**Duration** 1 year.

**Additional information** WAI is a nonprofit professional organization dedicated to encouraging women to consider an aviation career and to providing educational outreach activities and networking resources to women active in the industry. Among its general programs for women working on degree in an aviation-related field are the Airbus Leadership Grant, the Boeing Company Career Enhancement Scholarship (sponsored by Boeing), the Candi Chamberlin Kubeck Award, the Changing the World Scholarship (established in 2014), the Janet Clark Memorial Scholarship, the Signature Flight Support Scholarship (established in 2014 by Signature Flight Support Corporation), and the Women in Aviation, International Achievement Awards.

**Number awarded** Varies each year.

**Deadline** November of each year.

**[682]**
## WOMEN IN AVIATION, INTERNATIONAL MAINTENANCE SCHOLARSHIPS

Women in Aviation, International
Attn: Scholarships
Morningstar Airport
3647 State Route 503 South
West Alexandria, OH 45381-9354
(937) 839-4647          Fax: (937) 839-4645
E-mail: scholarships@wai.org
Web: www.wai.org/education/scholarships.cfm

**Summary**   To provide financial assistance to members of Women in Aviation, International (WAI) who are interested in a career in aviation maintenance.

**Eligibility**   This program is open to WAI members who are full-time students with at least 2 semesters of study remaining. Applicants must be preparing for an aviation maintenance technician license (A&P) or a degree in aviation maintenance technology. They must have a cumulative GPA of 3.0 or higher and be U.S. citizens or eligible noncitizens. Along with their application, they must submit an essay of 500 to 1,000 words on who or what inspired them to prepare for a career in aviation maintenance technology, their greatest life challenge, their greatest strength and strongest characteristic, their most memorable academic experience, and why they are the most qualified candidate for this scholarship. Selection is based on achievements, attitude toward self and others, commitment to success, dedication to career, financial need, motivation, reliability, responsibility, and teamwork.

**Financial data**   The stipend ranges up to $5,000.

**Duration**   1 year.

**Additional information**   WAI is a nonprofit professional organization dedicated to encouraging women to consider an aviation career and to providing educational outreach activities and networking resources to women active in the industry. This program includes the American Airlines Maintenance Technology Scholarship, the AtP General Aviation Maintenance Scholarship (established by AtP in 2014), and the Delta Air Lines Aircraft Maintenance Technology Scholarships.

**Number awarded**   3 each year.

**Deadline**   November of each year.

**[683]**
## WOMEN IN FEDERAL LAW ENFORCEMENT MEMBERS-ONLY SCHOLARSHIP

Women in Federal Law Enforcement
Attn: Scholarship Coordinator
2200 Wilson Boulevard, Suite 102
PMB 204
Arlington, VA 22201-3324
(301) 805-2180          Fax: (301) 560-8836
E-mail: WIFLE@comcast.net
Web: wifle.wildapricot.org/Default.aspx?pageId=1491217

**Summary**   To provide financial assistance for college or graduate school to women who are interested in preparing for a career in law enforcement and are members of Women in Federal Law Enforcement (WIFLE) or sponsored by a member.

**Eligibility**   This program is open to women who are members of WIFLE or sponsored by a member and have completed at least 1 academic year of full-time study at an accredited 4-year college or university (or at a community college with the intention of transferring to a 4-year school). Applicants must be majoring in criminal justice or a related field (e.g., social sciences, public administration, computer science, finance, linguistic arts, chemistry, physics). They must have a GPA of 3.0 or higher. Students in graduate and postgraduate programs are also eligible, but those working on an associate degree are not. Along with their application, they must submit a letter demonstrating their financial need and describing their career objectives. U.S. citizenship is required.

**Financial data**   The stipend is $1,500 per year.

**Duration**   1 year; may be renewed automatically for 1 additional year.

**Number awarded**   1 each year.

**Deadline**   April of each year.

**[684]**
## WOMEN IN FEDERAL LAW ENFORCEMENT SCHOLARSHIP

Women in Federal Law Enforcement
Attn: Scholarship Coordinator
2200 Wilson Boulevard, Suite 102
PMB 204
Arlington, VA 22201-3324
(301) 805-2180          Fax: (301) 560-8836
E-mail: WIFLE@comcast.net
Web: wifle.wildapricot.org/Default.aspx?pageId=1491217

**Summary**   To provide financial assistance for college or graduate school to women interested in preparing for a career in law enforcement.

**Eligibility**   This program is open to women who have completed at least 1 academic year of full-time study at an accredited 4-year college or university (or at a community college with the intention of transferring to a 4-year school). Applicants must be majoring in criminal justice or a related field (e.g., social sciences, public administration, computer science, finance, linguistic arts, chemistry, physics). They must have a GPA of 3.0 or higher. Students in graduate and postgraduate programs are also eligible, but those working on an associate degree are not. Along with their application, they must submit a 500-word essay describing a community project in which they have been involved and the results or impact to the community. Selection is based on academic potential, achievement, and commitment to serving communities in the field of law enforcement. U.S. citizenship is required.

**Financial data**   The stipend is $2,500.

**Duration**   1 year; may be renewed.

**Number awarded**   Varies each year; recently, 6 of these scholarships were awarded.

**Deadline**   April of each year.

**[685]**
## WOMEN IN FILM AND TELEVISION ATLANTA

Women in Film and Television Atlanta
P.O. Box 52726
Atlanta, GA 30355
(770) 621-5071
Web: www.wifta.org/student_scholarship

**Summary**   To provide financial assistance to members of Women in Film and Television Atlanta (WIFTA) who are working on an undergraduate degree in film or video at a college in Georgia.

**Eligibility** This program is open to women who are members of WIFTA and majoring in (or having a primary field of study in) film or video at an accredited 4-year college or university in Georgia. Applicants must have a GPA of 2.75 or higher. Along with their application, they must submit a 5-minute sample of their work on DVD and a 1,000-word essay highlighting their accomplishments and explaining their career goals. Selection is based on academic standing, artistic talents, and commitment to a film-based curriculum.

**Financial data** The stipend is $1,500.

**Duration** 1 year.

**Number awarded** 1 or more each year.

**Deadline** May of each year.

## [686]
## WOMEN IN FILM/DALLAS COLLEGE/ UNIVERSITY STUDENT TUITION SCHOLARSHIP

Women in Film/Dallas
Attn: Scholarships and Grants
5930 Royal Lane, Suite E
PMB 236
Dallas, TX 75230
(214) 379-1171          Toll Free: (800) 724-0767
Fax: (214) 379-1172     E-mail: education@wifdallas.org
Web: www.wifdallas.org/Default.aspx?pageId=950618

**Summary** To provide financial assistance to women from any state who are studying film and video at colleges and universities in north Texas.

**Eligibility** This program is open to women who are residents of any state majoring or with a primary field of study in film or video at an accredited college or university in the north Texas area. Applicants must have consistently maintained a GPA of 3.0 or higher. Along with their application, they must submit a 3-page essay on what inspired them to study film or video, 2 letters of recommendation, a letter from the college or university verifying their enrollment, and a short sample of their work. Financial need is not considered in the selection process.

**Financial data** The stipend is $2,500.

**Duration** 1 year.

**Number awarded** 1 each year.

**Deadline** June of each year.

## [687]
## WOMEN IN PUBLIC FINANCE SCHOLARSHIP PROGRAM

Women in Public Finance
Attn: Scholarship Committee
P.O. Box 1195
Chicago, IL 60690-1195
(312) 402-7788          E-mail: scholarship@wpfc.com
Web: www.wpfc.com/?page_id=774

**Summary** To provide financial assistance to women who are high school seniors and interested in attending college to prepare for a career in public finance or related fields.

**Eligibility** This program is open to female graduating high school seniors who have exhibited academic achievement, preferably with a demonstrated aptitude in mathematics and demonstrated leadership skills. Applicants must be planning

to enroll in college to prepare for a career in finance, especially public finance, or related fields (e.g., government, nonprofits, law). Along with their application, they must submit 1) a 250-word essay on their favorite subjects in school and why those are their favorites; and 2) an essay of 350 to 500 words on their choice of 5 topics related to their interests and goals. Financial need is not considered in the selection process.

**Financial data** Stipends range from $1,000 to $2,000.

**Duration** 1 year.

**Number awarded** Up to 10 each year.

**Deadline** August of each year.

## [688]
## WOMEN MILITARY AVIATORS DREAM OF FLIGHT SCHOLARSHIP

Women in Aviation, International
Attn: Scholarships
Morningstar Airport
3647 State Route 503 South
West Alexandria, OH 45381-9354
(937) 839-4647          Fax: (937) 839-4645
E-mail: scholarships@wai.org
Web: www.wai.org/education/scholarships.cfm

**Summary** To provide financial assistance to members of Women in Aviation, International (WAI) who are interested in academic study or flight training.

**Eligibility** This program is open to WAI members who are students in high school, an accredited flight program, or an accredited college or university. Applicants must submit 2 letters of recommendation, a 500-word essay on their aviation history and goals, a resume, copies of all aviation licenses and medical certificates, and the last 3 pages of their pilot logbook (if applicable). Selection is based on the applicant's ambition to further women in aviation, demonstrated persistence and determination, financial need, ability to complete training, and ability to bring honor to the women of Women Military Aviators, Inc. (WMA).

**Financial data** The stipend is $2,500.

**Duration** Recipients must be able to complete training within 1 year.

**Additional information** WAI is a nonprofit professional organization dedicated to encouraging women to consider an aviation career and to providing educational outreach activities and networking resources to women active in the industry. WMA established this program in 2005 to honor the women aviators who are serving or have served in Iraq and Afghanistan.

**Number awarded** 1 each year.

**Deadline** November of each year.

## [689]
## WOMEN OF THE ELCA SCHOLARSHIP PROGRAM

Women of the Evangelical Lutheran Church in America
Attn: Scholarships
8765 West Higgins Road
Chicago, IL 60631-4101
(773) 380-2741          Toll Free: (800) 638-3522, ext. 2741
Fax: (773) 380-2419     E-mail: valora.starr@elca.org
Web: www.womenoftheelca.org

**Summary** To provide financial assistance to lay women who are members of Evangelical Lutheran Church of America (ELCA) congregations and who wish to take classes on the undergraduate, graduate, professional, or vocational school level.

**Eligibility** This program is open to ELCA lay women who are at least 21 years of age and have experienced an interruption of at least 2 years in their education since high school. Applicants must have been admitted to an educational institution to prepare for a career in other than the ordained ministry. They may be working on an undergraduate, graduate, professional, or vocational school degree. U.S. citizenship is required.

**Financial data** The average stipend is $1,000.

**Duration** Up to 2 years.

**Additional information** These scholarships are supported by several endowment funds: the Cronk Memorial Fund, the First Triennial Board Scholarship Fund, the General Scholarship Fund, the Mehring Fund, the Paepke Scholarship Fund, the Piero/Wade/Wade Fund, and the Edwin/Edna Robeck Scholarship.

**Number awarded** Varies each year; recently, 15 of these scholarships were awarded.

**Deadline** February of each year.

## [690]
## WOMEN SOAR SCHOLARSHIP FOR INNOVATION

Experimental Aircraft Association
Attn: Scholarship Department
3000 Poberezny Road
P.O. Box 3086
Oshkosh, WI 54903-3086
(920) 426-6823          Toll Free: (800) 236-1025
Fax: (920) 426-6887     E-mail: scholarships@eaa.org
Web: www.youngeagles.org

**Summary** To provide financial assistance to female members of the Experimental Aircraft Association (EAA) who are high school students and interested in studying the sciences, engineering, or aviation in college.

**Eligibility** This program is open to female EAA members who are juniors or seniors in high school and planning to enroll in an academic program at a college or university. Applicants must be planning to major in the sciences, engineering, or aviation to help solve the technology problems of the future. Selection is based on 1) a 1,500-word essay on the subject of the environmental impact of aviation, summarizing the current issue and impact and discussing potential technological solutions to reduce the impact on the environment (60%); 2) a brief synopsis of their current accomplishments at the high school level, including GPA for 2 years, major focus of studies, and description of extracurricular activities (20%); and 3) a written description of their plans for the future, including colleges of interest, professional aspirations, and "passion for becoming one of society's innovators."

**Financial data** The stipend is $1,000.

**Duration** 1 year.

**Number awarded** 1 each year.

**Deadline** February of each year.

## [691]
## WOMEN@MICROSOFT HOPPERS SCHOLARSHIP

Fargo-Moorhead Area Foundation
Attn: Finance/Program Assistant
502 First Avenue North, Suite 202
Fargo, ND 58102-4804
(701) 234-0756          Fax: (701) 234-9724
E-mail: Cher@areafoundation.org
Web: areafoundation.org/index.php/scholarships

**Summary** To provide financial assistance to women who are interested in studying computer science at a college or university in Minnesota or the Dakotas.

**Eligibility** This program is open to women who are accepted or enrolled at a college or university in Minnesota, North Dakota, or South Dakota. Applicants must be undergraduates with a declared major in computer science or a related discipline and a GPA of 3.0 or higher. Along with their application, they must submit essays, up to 500 words each, on 2 of the following topics: 1) What they see as the computer industry's primary shortcomings? If they were a leader in the technical world today, how would they take the shortcomings and turn them to positive attributes? 2) Describe examples of their leadership experience in which they significantly influenced others, helped resolve disputes, or contributed to group efforts over time; 3) What guidance do they have for organizations in the technology industry as they respond to the social media wave; or 4) What they think the computer/software industry will be like in the next 10 years. Selection is based on the essays, academic achievement, character, qualities of leadership, and financial need.

**Financial data** The stipend is $1,500.

**Duration** 1 year.

**Additional information** This program began in 1990 as part of an effort to make Microsoft a great place for women. In addition to scholarships, other Hoppers committees deal with outreach, technical women, mentoring, program, career development, and diversity. The program is named for Grace Hopper, a computer science pioneer.

**Number awarded** 1 each year.

**Deadline** May of each year.

## [692]
## WOMEN'S BUSINESS ALLIANCE SCHOLARSHIP PROGRAM

Choice Hotels International
Attn: Women's Business Alliance
4225 East Windrose Drive
Phoenix, AZ 85032
(602) 953-4478
Web: www.choicehotels.com/en/about-choice/wba

**Summary** To provide financial assistance to women interested in preparing for a career in the hospitality industry.

**Eligibility** This program is open to female high school seniors, undergraduates, and graduate students. Applicants must be U.S. citizens or permanent residents interested in preparing for a career in the hospitality industry. They must submit an essay of 500 words or less on why they are interested in a career in the hospitality industry, the area of the industry that appeals to them the most, and some of their major accomplishments and/or personal characteristics that will benefit their work in the hospitality industry. Selection is based on that essay, academic record, and 2 letters of recommendation.

**Financial data** The stipend is $2,000.

**Duration** 1 year; recipients may reapply.

**Additional information** This program began in 2004.

**Number awarded** 2 or more each year.

**Deadline** January of each year.

## [693]
## WOMEN'S CAMPAIGN FUND FELLOWSHIP PROGRAM

Women's Campaign Fund
Attn: Political Director
1900 L Street, N.W., Suite 500
Washington, DC 20036
(202) 393-8164     Toll Free: (800) 446-8170
Fax: (202) 393-0649     E-mail: info@wcfonline.org
Web: www.wcfonline.org

**Summary** To provide an opportunity for young women to gain work experience within a national political organization.

**Eligibility** This program is open to female students and recent graduates who have a strong interest in protecting women's reproductive choices and options. Applicants must be interested in working at the Women's Campaign Fund in the areas of communications, development, political, and programs. They must have excellent research, writing, and communications skills as well as the ability to work independently and in a small group setting.

**Financial data** The stipend is $500 per month for full-time fellows or $250 per month for part-time fellows.

**Duration** 14 weeks during spring or fall; 10 weeks during summer.

**Additional information** The Women's Campaign Fund is the first national non-partisan committee founded in America dedicated to the election of pro-choice women to public office. This program includes 2 endowed fellowships: the Bertha Wurmser Herz Fellowship and the Annie Kahn Feinsod Fellowship.

**Number awarded** Approximately 7 each term.

**Deadline** November of each year for spring; March of each year for summer; July of each year for fall.

## [694]
## WOMEN'S ECONOMIC COUNCIL FOUNDATION SCHOLARSHIP AWARDS FOR NON-TRADITIONAL STUDENTS

Tennessee Economic Council on Women
Attn: Women's Economic Council Foundation
405 Westland Drive
Lebanon, TN 37087
(615) 969-2857
Web: www.womenseconomicfoundation.org

**Summary** To provide financial assistance to women in Tennessee who plan to return to college in any state to improve their economic autonomy after an absence.

**Eligibility** This program is open to women who are residents of Tennessee and have been out of high school or received a GED 5 years previously or longer. Applicants must be enrolled or planning to enroll as an undergraduate at a college or university in any state. Along with their application, they must submit a summary of their personal education

goals. Selection is based on that summary, participation in community activities, work history, letters of recommendation, and financial need.

**Financial data** The stipend is $1,000.

**Duration** 1 year.

**Number awarded** 3 each year: 1 to a woman in each division of the state (western, central, and eastern).

**Deadline** September of each year.

## [695]
## WOMEN'S ECONOMIC COUNCIL FOUNDATION SCHOLARSHIP AWARDS FOR TRADITIONAL HIGH SCHOOL SENIORS

Tennessee Economic Council on Women
Attn: Women's Economic Council Foundation
405 Westland Drive
Lebanon, TN 37087
(615) 969-2857
Web: www.womenseconomicfoundation.org

**Summary** To provide financial assistance to female high school seniors in Tennessee who plan to attend college in any state to improve their economic autonomy.

**Eligibility** This program is open to women graduating from high schools in Tennessee and planning to enroll at a college or university in any state. Applicants must submit a copy of their high school transcript that includes their ACT/SAT scores, a description of participation in school and community activities, a general description of employment positions held, 2 letters of recommendation, and a summary of personal education goals. Financial need is not considered in the selection process. The program includes 1 scholarship reserved for a Girl Scout Gold Award recipient.

**Financial data** The stipend is $1,000.

**Duration** 1 year.

**Number awarded** 3 each year, included 1 for an applicant who has received the Girl Scout Gold Award.

**Deadline** September of each year.

## [696]
## WOMEN'S ENVIRONMENTAL COUNCIL SCHOLARSHIPS

Women's Environmental Council
Attn: Scholarships
P.O. Box 882744
San Diego, CA 92168
E-mail: kellyn.lupfer@gmail.com
Web: www.wecweb.org/scholarships.html

**Summary** To provide financial assistance to women from any state working on an undergraduate or graduate degree in an environmental field at colleges and universities in southern California.

**Eligibility** This program is open to female undergraduate and graduate students from any state who are enrolled at colleges and universities in Los Angeles, Orange, and San Diego counties in California. Applicants must be studying such environmental fields as architecture, biology, chemistry, environmental science, ecology, environmental engineering, forestry, geography, geology/hydrology, marine studies, or urban planning. They must have a GPA of 3.0 or higher. Along with their application, they must submit a personal statement that includes a description of their academic professional, and environmental achievements and goals; how they became interested in preparing for a career in the environmental field; and how this scholarship will help them achieve their professional and personal goals. Selection is based on that statement (50%); personal incentive, volunteerism, and extracurricular activities (20%); grades and course work (10%); a letter of reference (15%); and thoroughness and presentation of the application packet (5%).

**Financial data** The stipend is $1,000. Recipients are also given a 1-year membership in the Women's Environmental Council (WEC).

**Duration** 1 year.

**Additional information** The WEC, founded in 1993, currently has chapters in Los Angeles, Orange County, and San Diego. Recipients are expected to attend the WEC annual meeting in the spring to receive their awards.

**Number awarded** Varies each year; recently, 5 of these scholarships were awarded.

**Deadline** January of each year.

## [697]
## WOMEN'S INDEPENDENCE SCHOLARSHIP PROGRAM

Women's Independence Scholarship Program, Inc.
Attn: WISP Program
4900 Randall Parkway, Suite H
Wilmington, NC 28403
(910) 397-7742          Toll Free: (866) 255-7742
Fax: (910) 397-0023     E-mail: nancy@wispinc.org
Web: www.wispinc.org

**Summary** To provide financial assistance for college or graduate school to women who are victims of partner abuse.

**Eligibility** This program is open to women who are victims of partner abuse and have worked for at least 6 months with a nonprofit domestic violence victim services provider that is willing to sponsor them. Applicants must be interested in attending a vocational school, community college, 4-year college or university, or (in exceptional circumstances) graduate school as a full- or part-time student. They should have left an abusive partner at least 1 year previously; women who have been parted from their batterer for more than 5 years are also eligible, but funding for such applicants may be limited. Preference is given to single mothers with young children. Special consideration is given to applicants who plan to use their education to further the rights of, and options for, women and girls. Selection is based primarily on financial need. U.S. citizenship or permanent resident status is required.

**Financial data** Stipends depend on the need of the recipient, but they are at least $250 and average $2,000 per academic term. First priority is given to funding for direct educational expenses (tuition, books, and fees), which is paid directly to the educational institution. Second priority is for assistance in reducing indirect financial barriers to education (e.g., child care, transportation), which is paid directly to the sponsoring agency.

**Duration** 1 year; may be renewed if the recipient maintains a GPA of 2.75 or higher.

**Additional information** This program began in 1999 when the sponsor was known as the Sunshine Lady Foundation.

**Number awarded** Varies each year. Since the program began, it has awarded more than $16 million in scholarships to approximately 2,000 women.

**Deadline** Applications may be submitted at any time, but they must be received at least 2 months before the start of the intended program.

## [698]
## WOMEN'S JEWELRY ASSOCIATION SCHOLARSHIPS

Women's Jewelry Association
Attn: Scholarship Chair
52 Vanderbilt Avenue, 19th Floor
New York, NY 10017-3827
(212) 687-2722          Toll Free: (877) 224-5421
Fax: (212) 355-0219     E-mail: lisa@lisaslovis.com
Web: wjamarion.memberlodge.com

**Summary** To provide financial assistance for college to women who are interested in careers in jewelry.

**Eligibility** This program is open to women who are enrolled at a college or university and taking classes in fine jewelry and watch design. Applicants in the designer category must submit images (e.g., CAD, drawings of finished work they have created. Applicants in the designer/creator category must submit images of finished pieces that they have designed and created. Applicants in the non-designer category must be interested in preparing for a career as a bench jeweler, appraiser, gemologist, watch-maker, or retailer; they must submit a 2-page essay on the program for which they are applying, what motivated them to attend this program, why they think they deserve a scholarship, why they wish to prepare for a career in jewelry or watches, their goals and aspirations for the future, and how the jewelry industry will benefit from their receiving this scholarship. Financial need is not considered in the selection process.

**Financial data** Stipends range from $500 to $7,000.

**Duration** 1 year.

**Number awarded** Varies each year; recently, 10 of these scholarships, with a total value of $19,300, were awarded.

**Deadline** April of each year.

## [699]
## WOMEN'S MUSIC COMMISSION

Broadcast Music Inc.
Attn: BMI Foundation, Inc.
7 World Trade Center
250 Greenwich Street
New York, NY 10007-0030
(212) 220-3000          E-mail: info@bmifoundation.org
Web: www.bmifoundation.org

**Summary** To recognize and reward, with a commission for production of a new work, outstanding young female composers.

**Eligibility** This competition is open to women between 20 and 30 years of age who are citizens or permanent residents of the United States. Applicants must submit samples of their original compositions.

**Financial data** The winner receives a $5,000 commission to create a new work.

**Duration** The competition is held annually.

**Additional information** This program began in 2006. Each year, the sponsor partners with a different world-class performer, ensemble, or presenter to present the premier performance.

**Number awarded** 1 each year.

**Deadline** May of each year.

## [700]
## WOMEN'S OPPORTUNITY AWARDS PROGRAM

Soroptimist International of the Americas
Attn: Program Department
1709 Spruce Street
Philadelphia, PA 19103-6103
(215) 893-9000    Fax: (215) 893-5200
E-mail: siahq@soroptimist.org
Web: www.soroptimist.org/awards/awards.html

**Summary** To provide financial assistance to women reentering the job market to upgrade their employment status through education.

**Eligibility** This program is open to women who provide the primary financial support for their family. Applicants must have been accepted to a vocational/skills training program or an undergraduate degree program. They must reside in 1 of the 20 countries or territories (divided into 28 regions) that are part of Soroptimist International of the Americas. Along with their application, they must submit 1) a 300-word description of their career goals and how their education and/or skills training support those goals; 2) a 750-word essay on the economic and personal hardships they have faced and their plans to gain additional skills, training, and education; and 3) documentation of financial need.

**Financial data** Each region grants an award of $5,000; most regions grant additional $3,000 awards. From among the regional winners, additional awards of $10,000 are presented to the most outstanding applicants.

**Duration** The awards are issued each year and are nonrenewable.

**Additional information** This program, established in 1972, was formerly known as the Training Awards Program. The awards may not be used for graduate study or international travel. Applications are to be processed through the local Soroptimist club. Countries that are part of Soroptimist International of the Americas include Argentina, Bolivia, Brazil, Canada, Chile, Colombia, Costa Rica, Ecuador, Guam, Japan, Republic of Korea, Mexico, Panama, Paraguay, Peru, Philippines, Puerto Rico, Taiwan, United States, and Venezuela.

**Number awarded** Awards are presented in each of the 28 regions. From among the regional winners, 3 receive an additional award from Soroptimist International of the Americas. Since the program was established, it has awarded approximately $30 million in scholarships to more than 30,000 women.

**Deadline** Applications must be submitted to regional contacts by November of each year.

## [701]
## WOMEN'S OVERSEAS SERVICE LEAGUE SCHOLARSHIPS FOR WOMEN

Women's Overseas Service League
Attn: Scholarship Committee
P.O. Box 124
Cedar Knolls, NJ 07927-0124
E-mail: kelsey@openix.com
Web: www.wosl.org/scholarships.htm

**Summary** To provide financial assistance for college to women who are committed to a military or other public service career.

**Eligibility** This program is open to women who are committed to a military or other public service career. Applicants must have completed at least 12 semester or 18 quarter hours of postsecondary study with a GPA of 2.5 or higher. They must be working on an academic degree (the program may be professional or technical in nature) and must agree to enroll for at least 6 semester or 9 quarter hours of study each academic period. Along with their application, they must submit a 250-word essay on their career goals. Financial need is considered in the selection process.

**Financial data** Stipends range from $500 to $1,000 per year.

**Duration** 1 year; may be renewed 1 additional year.

**Additional information** The Women's Overseas Service League is a national organization of women who have served overseas in or with the armed forces.

**Number awarded** Varies each year.

**Deadline** February of each year.

## [702]
## WOMEN'S RE-ENTRY SCHOLARSHIPS

American GI Forum of the United States
2870 North Speer Boulevard, Suite 103
Denver, CO 80211
(303) 458-1700    Toll Free: (866) 244-3628
Fax: (303) 458-1634    E-mail: agifnat@gmail.com
Web: www.agifusa.org/women

**Summary** To provide financial assistance to mature women who are members of the American GI Forum and interested in returning to college.

**Eligibility** This program is open to women who have been members of a women's chapter of the American GI Forum for at least 2 years. Applicants must be at least 25 years of age and enrolled or planning to enroll at a college or university as a full- or part-time student. Along with their application, they must submit transcripts, 3 letters of recommendation, proof of income, and a biographical essay.

**Financial data** A stipend is awarded (amount not specified).

**Duration** 1 year; recipients may reapply.

**Additional information** The American GI Forum is the largest federally-charter Hispanic veterans organization in the United States.

**Number awarded** 1 or more each year.

**Deadline** Deadline not specified.

## [703]
## WOMEN'S SECOND CHANCE COLLEGE SCHOLARSHIP

Community Foundation of Louisville
Attn: Community Leadership Officer
Waterfront Plaza, Suite 1110
325 West Main Street
Louisville, KY 40202-4251
(502) 585-4649 Fax: (502) 587-7484
E-mail: info@cflouisville.org
Web: scholarship.cflouisville.org/all_scholarships

**Summary** To provide financial assistance for college to mature female residents of Kentucky and southern Indiana.

**Eligibility** This program is open to women between 25 and 40 years of age who reside in Kentucky or the Indiana counties of Clark, Crawford, Floyd, Harrison, Scott, or Washington. Applicants must have a high school diploma or GED certificate and may have some college credits. They must commit to attend a participating college or university and complete a baccalaureate degree within an agreed upon period of time. Selection is based on financial need and desire to learn.

**Financial data** The stipend is at least $1,000 per year.

**Duration** 1 year; renewable until completion of a baccalaureate degree if the recipient maintains a GPA of 2.5 or higher.

**Number awarded** 1 or more each year.

**Deadline** March of each year.

## [704]
## WOMEN'S SOUTHERN GOLF ASSOCIATION SCHOLARSHIP

Women's Southern Golf Association
c/o Janie Carpenter, Scholarship Committee Chair
3225 Laurel Oaks Court
Garland, TX 75044
(972) 495-8322
E-mail: scholarship@womens-southerngolfassociation.
org
Web: www.womens-southerngolfassociation.org

**Summary** To provide financial assistance to women golfers in the southern states who plan to attend college in any state.

**Eligibility** This program is open to amateur female golfers who are residents of 1 of the 15 southern states (Alabama, Arkansas, Florida, Georgia, Kentucky, Louisiana, Maryland, Mississippi, North Carolina, Oklahoma, South Carolina, Tennessee, Texas, Virginia, and West Virginia) or the District of Columbia. Applicants must be graduating high school seniors planning to work on an undergraduate degree at an accredited institution of higher learning in any state. Along with their application, they must submit a 200-word personal statement on their goals for college and their future. Selection is based on academic excellence, citizenship, sportsmanship, and financial need. U.S. citizenship is required.

**Financial data** The stipend is $3,500 per year. Funds are paid directly to the recipient's college.

**Duration** 1 year; may be renewed up to 3 additional years, provided the recipient maintains a GPA of 3.0 or higher.

**Additional information** This program began in 1973.

**Number awarded** 1 each year.

**Deadline** April of each year.

## [705]
## WOMEN'S TRANSPORTATION SEMINAR JUNIOR COLLEGE SCHOLARSHIP

Women's Transportation Seminar
Attn: WTS Foundation
1701 K Street, N.W., Suite 800
Washington, DC 20006
(202) 955-5085 Fax: (202) 955-5088
E-mail: wts@wtsinternational.org
Web: www.wtsinternational.org/education/scholarships

**Summary** To provide financial assistance to women enrolled at a community college or trade school to prepare for a career in transportation.

**Eligibility** This program is open to women who are working on an associate or technical degree in transportation or a transportation-related field (e.g., transportation engineering, planning, finance, or logistics). Applicants must have a GPA of 3.0 or higher. Along with their application, they must submit a 500-word statement about their career goals after graduation and why they think they should receive the scholarship award. Applications must be submitted first to a local chapter; the chapters forward selected applications for consideration on the national level. Minority women are especially encouraged to apply. Selection is based on transportation involvement and goals, job skills, academic record, and leadership potential; financial need is not considered.

**Financial data** The stipend is $1,000.

**Duration** 1 year.

**Additional information** Local chapters may also award additional funding to winners for their area.

**Number awarded** 1 each year.

**Deadline** Applications must be submitted by November to a local WTS chapter.

## [706]
## WOMEN'S WESTERN GOLF FOUNDATION SCHOLARSHIP

Women's Western Golf Foundation
c/o Mrs. Richard Willis, Scholarship Selection Director
393 Ramsay Road
Deerfield, IL 60015
Web: www.wwga.org

**Summary** To provide financial assistance to high school senior girls who are interested in the sport of golf and plan to attend college.

**Eligibility** Applicants must be high school senior girls who intend to graduate in the year they submit their application. They must meet entrance requirements of, and plan to enroll at, an accredited college or university. Selection is based on academic achievement, financial need, excellence of character, and involvement with the sport of golf. Skill or excellence in the game is not a criterion. U.S. citizenship is required.

**Financial data** The stipend is $2,000 per year. The funds are to be used to pay for room, board, tuition, and other university fees or charges.

**Duration** 1 year; may be renewed up to 3 additional years if the recipient maintains a GPA of 3.0 or higher.

**Additional information** This program began in 1971.

**Number awarded** 15 each year. Since this program began, it has awarded more than $3.5 million to more than 530 undergraduates.

**Deadline** Preliminary applications must be submitted by February of each year.

## [707]
## WOMEN'S WILDLIFE MANAGEMENT/ CONSERVATION SCHOLARSHIP

National Rifle Association of America
Attn: Women's Policy Committee
11250 Waples Mill Road
Fairfax, VA 22030-7400
(703) 267-1399            Toll Free: (800) 861-1166
E-mail: grantprogram@nrahq.org
Web: wwmcs.nra.org

**Summary** To provide financial assistance to women who are upper-division students working on a degree in wildlife management or conservation.

**Eligibility** This program is open to women currently enrolled full time as college juniors or seniors. Applicants must be working on a degree in wildlife management or conservation. They must have a GPA of 3.0 or higher. Financial need is not considered in the selection process.

**Financial data** The stipend is $1,000 per year.

**Duration** 1 year; may be renewed 1 additional year.

**Additional information** This program began in 2006.

**Number awarded** 1 each year.

**Deadline** October of each year.

## [708]
## XI PSI OMEGA CHAPTER SCHOLARSHIPS

Alpha Kappa Alpha Sorority, Inc.-Xi Psi Omega Chapter
Attn: President
P.O. Box 140894
Anchorage, AK 99514
(907) 346-3998            E-mail: akaxpo@gmail.com
Web: xipsiomega.com/scholarship.html

**Summary** To provide financial assistance to high school seniors (especially African American women) from Alaska who plan to attend college in any state.

**Eligibility** This program is open to seniors graduating from high schools in Alaska who are planning to attend a 2- or 4-year accredited college or university in any state. Applicants must have a GPA of 2.5 or higher and a record of active participation in school and community activities. Alpha Kappa Alpha (AKA) is currently 1 of the largest social sororities whose membership is predominantly African American women.

**Financial data** A stipend is awarded (amount not specified).

**Duration** 1 year; nonrenewable.

**Additional information** The Xi Psi Omega chapter of AKA serves alumnae members in Alaska.

**Number awarded** 1 or more each year.

**Deadline** March of each year.

## [709]
## YASUKO ASADA MEMORIAL COLLEGE SCHOLARSHIP FUND

David S. Ishii Foundation
Attn: College Scholarship Committee Chair
P.O. Box 2927
Aiea, HI 96701
(808) 478-6440        E-mail: info@davidsishiifoundation.org
Web: www.davidsishiifoundation.org/scholarships

**Summary** To provide financial assistance to high school seniors in Hawaii who have played on their school golf team and plan to attend college in any state (females and males are considered separately).

**Eligibility** This program is open to seniors graduating from high schools in Hawaii who have been active members of their high school golf team. Applicants must be planning to enroll full time at an accredited 4-year college or university in any state. They must have a GPA of 2.0 or higher and be able to demonstrate financial need. Along with their application, they must submit a 250-word essay about the influence of golf in their life. Females and males are considered separately.

**Financial data** The stipend is $1,000 per year.

**Duration** 4 years.

**Number awarded** 4 each year: 2 to females and 2 to males.

**Deadline** April of each year.

## [710]
## YOUNG LADIES' RADIO LEAGUE SCHOLARSHIPS

Foundation for Amateur Radio, Inc.
Attn: Scholarship Committee
P.O. Box 911
Columbia, MD 21044-0911
(410) 552-2652            Fax: (410) 981-5146
E-mail: dave.prestel@gmail.com
Web: www.farweb.org/scholarships

**Summary** To provide funding to female licensed radio amateurs who are interested in earning a bachelor's or graduate degree in the United States.

**Eligibility** This program is open to female radio amateurs who have at least an FCC Technician Class license or equivalent foreign authorization. Applicants must intend to work full time on a bachelor's or graduate degree at a college or university in the United States. There are no restrictions on the course of study or residency location. Non-U.S. amateurs are eligible. Preference is given to students working on a degree in communications, electronics, or related arts and sciences. Financial need is considered in the selection process.

**Financial data** The stipend is $1,500.

**Duration** 1 year.

**Additional information** This program is sponsored by the Young Ladies' Radio League. It includes the following named scholarships: the Ethel Smith, K4LMB, Memorial Scholarship and the Mary Lou Brown, NM7N Memorial, Scholarship.

**Number awarded** 2 each year.

**Deadline** April of each year.

## [711]
## YOUNG WOMEN IN PUBLIC AFFAIRS AWARDS

Zonta International
Attn: Foundation
1211 West 22nd Street, Suite 900
Oak Brook, IL 60523-3384
(630) 928-1400                     Fax: (630) 928-1559
E-mail: programs@zonta.org
Web: www.zonta.org

**Summary** To recognize and reward women in secondary schools who are interested in a career in fields related to public affairs.

**Eligibility** This program is open to young women, 16 to 19 years of age, who are currently living or studying in a district or region of Zonta International. Applicants must be interested in preparing for a career in government, public policy, or volunteer organizations. Along with their application, they must submit essays on their student activities and leadership roles (200 words), their community service activities (200 words), their efforts to understand other countries (150 words), and the status of women in their country and worldwide (300 words). Selection is based on commitment to volunteerism, experience in local or student government, volunteer leadership achievements, knowledge of Zonta International and its programs, and advocating in Zonta International's mission of advancing the status of women worldwide. Winners are selected at the club level and forwarded for a district competition; district winners are entered in the international competition.

**Financial data** District awardees receive $1,000 and international awardees receive an additional $3,000.

**Duration** The competition is held annually.

**Additional information** This program began in 1990.

**Number awarded** Varies each year; recently, 32 district winners were selected. of whom 10 were chosen as international awardees. Since the program began, it has presented 637 awards to 565 young women from 50 countries.

**Deadline** Clubs set their own deadlines but must submit their winners to the district governor by March of each year.

## [712]
## YOUTH PARTNERS ACCESSING CAPITAL SCHOLARSHIPS

Alpha Kappa Alpha Sorority, Inc.
Attn: Educational Advancement Foundation
5656 South Stony Island Avenue
Chicago, IL 60637
(773) 947-0026                     Toll Free: (800) 653-6528
Fax: (773) 947-0277          E-mail: akaeaf@akaeaf.net
Web: www.akaeaf.org/undergraduate_scholarships.htm

**Summary** To provide financial assistance to undergraduate members of Alpha Kappa Alpha sorority who demonstrate outstanding community service.

**Eligibility** This program is open to members of the organization, a traditionally African American women's sorority, who are working at least as sophomores on an undergraduate degree at an accredited degree-granting institution. Applicants must have a GPA of 3.0 or higher and a record of demonstrated participation in leadership, volunteer, civic, or campus activities. They must be able to demonstrate exceptional academic achievement or extreme financial need.

**Financial data** Stipends vary; recently, they averaged $1,300.

**Duration** 1 year.

**Number awarded** Varies each year; recently, 10 of these scholarships were awarded.

**Deadline** April of each year.

## [713]
## YOUTH PARTNERS ACCESSING CAPITAL SERVICE AWARDS

Alpha Kappa Alpha Sorority, Inc.
Attn: Educational Advancement Foundation
5656 South Stony Island Avenue
Chicago, IL 60637
(773) 947-0026                     Toll Free: (800) 653-6528
Fax: (773) 947-0277          E-mail: akaeaf@akaeaf.net
Web: www.akaeaf.org/undergraduate_scholarships.htm

**Summary** To provide funding to undergraduate members of Alpha Kappa Alpha sorority interested in conducting a community service project to support the platform of the sorority.

**Eligibility** This program is open to members of the organization, a traditionally African American women's sorority, who are working at least as sophomores on an undergraduate degree at an accredited degree-granting institution. Applicants must have a GPA of 3.0 or higher and a record of demonstrated participation in leadership, volunteer, civic, or campus activities. They must be proposing to conduct a community service project that will implement 1 of the platforms of the sorority: emerging young leaders, health, global poverty, economic security, social justice and human rights, or internal leadership training for external service. Along with their application, they must submit a personal goal statement on how they promote healing, nurturing, learning, and uplifting of youth by assisting in developing lifelong learning skills.

**Financial data** Grants range from $500 to $1,000.

**Duration** 1 year; nonrenewable.

**Additional information** This program began in 1997.

**Number awarded** Varies each year; recently, 13 of these grants were awarded.

**Deadline** April of each year.

## [714]
## YUKIKO HOWELL MEMORIAL S.T.E.M. SCHOLARSHIP

Women in Aviation, International
Attn: Scholarships
Morningstar Airport
3647 State Route 503 South
West Alexandria, OH 45381-9354
(937) 839-4647                     Fax: (937) 839-4645
E-mail: scholarships@wai.org
Web: www.wai.org/education/scholarships.cfm

**Summary** To provide financial assistance to members of Women in Aviation, International (WAI) who are working on a college degree in a field related to science, technology, engineering, or mathematics (STEM).

**Eligibility** This program is open to WAI members who are currently enrolled at an accredited 2- or 4-year college or university, technical institute, or certificate program. Applicants must be preparing for a career in a field of STEM or taking

STEM continuing education classes. They must have experience volunteering in STEM or aviation-related events and/or activities in the previous year. Along with their application, they must submit an essay that includes explanations of their career plans, goals, and volunteer experiences. Selection is based on achievements, attitude toward self and others, commitment to success, dedication to career, financial need, motivation, reliability, responsibility, and teamwork.

**Financial data** The stipend is $1,500.

**Duration** 1 year.

**Additional information** WAI is a nonprofit professional organization dedicated to encouraging women to consider an aviation career and to providing educational outreach activities and networking resources to women active in the industry. This program began in 2014. The sponsor defines STEM fields to include air traffic controller, avionics technician, dispatch certification, aircraft mechanic, meteorologist, or educator for STEM.

**Number awarded** 1 each year.

**Deadline** November of each year.

## [715]
## YWCA HARRIET M. HEATHERINGTON SCHOLARSHIP

Arizona Community Foundation
Attn: Education and Scholarships Manager
2201 East Camelback Road, Suite 405B
Phoenix, AZ 85016
(602) 682-2040          Toll Free: (800) 222-8221
Fax: (602) 381-1575    E-mail: jmedina@azfoundation.org
Web: azfoundation.academicworks.com

**Summary** To provide financial assistance to women, especially those with dependents, who are residents of Arizona and interested in attending college in the state.

**Eligibility** This program is open to female residents of Arizona who are U.S. citizens or legal immigrants. Preference is given to women who have dependents. Applicants must be enrolled or planning to enroll at a college, university, community college, or vocational school in the state. They must be 1) high school graduates who had a GPA of 2.0 or higher or GED score of 460 or higher; or 2) students who have already completed at least 12 credits of college work with a GPA of 2.0 or higher. Financial need is considered in the selection process. Preference is given to current or former residents of YWCA Haven House and to women in refugee status.

**Financial data** The stipend is $1,500 per year.

**Duration** 1 year; recipients may reapply for up to 3 additional years.

**Number awarded** Varies each year.

**Deadline** February of each year.

## [716]
## ZANNONI INDIVIDUAL SUMMER UNDERGRADUATE RESEARCH FELLOWSHIPS

American Society for Pharmacology and Experimental
  Therapeutics
9650 Rockville Pike
Bethesda, MD 20814-3995
(301) 634-7060          Fax: (301) 634-7061
E-mail: djordan@aspet.org
Web: www.aspet.org/awards/SURF

**Summary** To provide funding to undergraduate students (particularly women and underrepresented minorities) who are interested in participating in a summer research project at a laboratory affiliated with the American Society for Pharmacology and Experimental Therapeutics (ASPET).

**Eligibility** This program is open to undergraduate students interested in working during the summer in the laboratory of a society member who must agree to act as a sponsor. Applications must be submitted jointly by the student and the sponsor, and they must include 1) a letter from the sponsor with a brief description of the proposed research, a statement of the qualifications of the student, the degree of independence the student will have, a description of complementary activities available to the student, and a description of how the student will report on the research results; 2) a letter from the student indicating the nature of his or her interest in the project and a description of future plans; 3) a copy of the sponsor's updated curriculum vitae; and 4) copies of all the student's undergraduate transcripts. Selection is based on the nature of the research opportunities provided, student and sponsor qualifications, and the likelihood the student will prepare for a career in pharmacology. Applications from underrepresented minorities and women are particularly encouraged.

**Financial data** The stipend is $2,800. Funds are paid directly to the institution but may be used only for student stipends.

**Duration** 10 weeks during the summer.

**Additional information** Some of these awards are funded through the Glenn E. Ullyot Fund; those recipients are designated as the Ullyot Fellows.

**Number awarded** Varies each year; recently, 4 of these fellowships were awarded.

**Deadline** February of each year.

## [717]
## ZETA TAU ALPHA ACHIEVEMENT SCHOLARSHIPS

Zeta Tau Alpha Foundation, Inc.
Attn: Director of Foundation Administration
3450 Founders Road
Indianapolis, IN 46268
(317) 872-0540          Fax: (317) 876-3948
E-mail: zetataualpha@zetataualpha.org
Web: www.zetataualpha.org

**Summary** To provide financial assistance for college or graduate school to women who are members of Zeta Tau Alpha.

**Eligibility** This program is open to undergraduate and graduate women who are enrolled at a 4-year college or university and student members of the school's Zeta Tau Alpha chapter. Applicants must demonstrate leadership qualities within their chapter or in campus activities while maintaining a high scholastic average. Selection is based on academic achievement (GPA of 2.9 or higher), involvement in campus and community activities, recommendations, current class status, and financial need.

**Financial data** The stipend is at least $1,000.

**Duration** 1 year; renewable.

**Number awarded** Varies each year; recently, the foundation awarded a total of more than $620,000 to 279 undergraduate and graduate members for all of its scholarship programs.

**Deadline** February of each year.

## [718]
## ZETA TAU ALPHA ENDOWED SCHOLARSHIPS

Zeta Tau Alpha Foundation, Inc.
Attn: Director of Foundation Administration
3450 Founders Road
Indianapolis, IN 46268
(317) 872-0540                    Fax: (317) 876-3948
E-mail: zetataualpha@zetataualpha.org
Web: www.zetataualpha.org

**Summary** To provide financial assistance to undergraduate women who are members of Zeta Tau Alpha.

**Eligibility** This program is open to undergraduate women who are enrolled at a 4-year college or university and student members of the school's Zeta Tau Alpha chapter. These scholarships have been established for specific chapters, with preference for the award going to a member of that particular chapter. Selection is based on academic achievement (GPA of 2.9 or higher), involvement in campus and community activities, recommendations, current class status, and financial need.

**Financial data** The stipend is at least $1,000.

**Duration** 1 year; renewable.

**Number awarded** Varies each year; recently, the foundation awarded a total of more than $620,000 to 279 undergraduate and graduate members for all of its scholarship programs.

**Deadline** February of each year.

## [719]
## ZETA TAU ALPHA RECOGNITION SCHOLARSHIPS

Zeta Tau Alpha Foundation, Inc.
Attn: Director of Foundation Administration
3450 Founders Road
Indianapolis, IN 46268
(317) 872-0540                    Fax: (317) 876-3948
E-mail: zetataualpha@zetataualpha.org
Web: www.zetataualpha.org

**Summary** To provide financial assistance for college to women who are members of Zeta Tau Alpha.

**Eligibility** This program is open to undergraduate women who are enrolled at a 4-year college or university and student members of the school's Zeta Tau Alpha chapter. These scholarships have been established with endowment monies and annual gifts in memory or honor of a member of the sorority. Selection is based on academic achievement (GPA of 2.9 or higher), involvement in campus and community activities, recommendations, current class status, and financial need.

**Financial data** The stipend is $1,800.

**Duration** 1 year; renewable.

**Number awarded** Varies each year; recently, the foundation awarded a total of more than $620,000 to 279 undergraduate and graduate members for all of its scholarship programs.

**Deadline** February of each year.

## [720]
## ZOE CAVALARIS OUTSTANDING FEMALE ATHLETE AWARD

Daughters of Penelope
1909 Q Street, N.W., Suite 500
Washington, DC 20009-1007
(202) 234-9741                    Fax: (202) 483-6983
E-mail: dophq@ahepa.org
Web: daughtersofpenelope.org

**Summary** To recognize and reward women of Greek descent who demonstrate excellence in high school or college athletics.

**Eligibility** This award is presented to a young woman of Hellenic descent who has unusually high quality athletic ability and a record of accomplishment in any sport or any series of sports. Nominees must be outstanding high school or college amateur female athletes recognized for their accomplishments during their high school and/or college years. Along with a letter of nomination from a sponsoring chapter of Daughters of Penelope, they must submit documentation of their current overall GPA, academic honors, other honors, participation in sports activities, extracurricular activities (other than sports), church and/or community activities, and special achievements (other than sports).

**Financial data** The award includes a college scholarship (amount not specified), an engraved plaque, public recognition through Daughters of Penelope events and publications, and reimbursement of transportation and hotel accommodations to attend the organization's national convention.

**Duration** The award is presented annually.

**Number awarded** 1 each year.

**Deadline** May of each year.

## [721]
## ZONTA CLUB OF BANGOR SCHOLARSHIPS

Zonta Club of Bangor
c/o Barbara A. Cardone
P.O. Box 1904
Bangor, ME 04402-1904
Web: www.zontaclubofbangor.org/?area=scholarship

**Summary** To provide financial assistance to women attending or planning to attend college in Maine and major in any field.

**Eligibility** This program is open to women who are attending or planning to attend an accredited 2- or 4-year college in Maine. Applicants may major in any field. Along with their application, they must submit brief essays on 1) their goals in seeking higher education and their plans for the future; and 2) any school and community activities that have been of particular importance to them and why they found them worthwhile. Financial need may be considered in the selection process.

**Financial data** The stipend is $1,000.

**Duration** 1 year.

**Number awarded** 2 each year.

**Deadline** March of each year.

## [722]
## ZONTA CLUB OF MILWAUKEE TECHNICAL SPECIALTY SCHOLARSHIP AWARD

Zonta Club of Milwaukee
Attn: Scholarship Team
P.O. Box 1494
Milwaukee, WI 53201
E-mail: zcscholarship@zontamilwaukee.org
Web: www.zontamilwaukee.org/OurScholarships.htm

**Summary**  To provide financial assistance to women, especially residents of Wisconsin, who are interested in working on an associate degree or certificate at a technical college or institute in any state.

**Eligibility**  This program is open to women who are interested in working on an associate degree or certificate in a health care or nontraditional technical field. Preference is given to residents of Wisconsin and to low income or otherwise disadvantaged women. Applicants must be currently enrolled at an accredited technical college or institute in any state. They must have a GPA of 2.5 or higher. Along with their application, they must submit a description of their anticipated course of study and current career interests, including how they plan to continue to advance the status of women through their career.

**Financial data**  The stipend is $1,000.

**Duration**  1 year.

**Number awarded**  1 or more each year.

**Deadline**  July of each year.

## [723]
## ZONTA CLUB OF MILWAUKEE WOMEN IN SCIENCE SCHOLARSHIP

Zonta Club of Milwaukee
Attn: Scholarship Team
P.O. Box 1494
Milwaukee, WI 53201
E-mail: zcscholarship@zontamilwaukee.org
Web: www.zontamilwaukee.org/OurScholarships.htm

**Summary**  To provide financial assistance to women, especially residents of Wisconsin, who are upper-division students working on a degree in a field of science, technology, engineering or mathematics (STEM) at a college in any state.

**Eligibility**  This program is open to women who are entering the third or fourth year of an undergraduate degree program in a STEM-related field at a college, university, or institute in any state. Preference is given to residents of Wisconsin. Applicants must submit a 300-word essay that describes their academic and professional goals, the relevance of their program of study to STEM, and how the scholarship will assist them in reaching their goals. Financial need is not considered in the selection process.

**Financial data**  The stipend is $1,000.

**Duration**  1 year.

**Additional information**  This program began in 2005.

**Number awarded**  1 each year.

**Deadline**  July of each year.

# Graduate Students

Listed alphabetically by program title and described in detail here are 485 fellowships, grants, awards, internships, and other sources of "free money" set aside for women who are incoming, continuing, or returning graduate students working on a master's. doctoral, or professional degree. This funding is available to support study, training, research, and/or creative activities in the United States.

## [724]
## AAJUW SCHOLARSHIP PROGRAM

American Association of Japanese University Women
Attn: Scholarship Committee
3543 West Boulevard
Los Angeles, CA 90016
E-mail: scholarship@aajuw.org
Web: www.aajuw.org/scholarship.php

**Summary** To provide financial assistance to female students (any ethnicity) currently enrolled in upper-division or graduate classes in California.

**Eligibility** This program is open to women enrolled at accredited colleges or universities in California as juniors, seniors, or graduate students. Applicants must be involved in U.S.-Japan relations, cultural exchanges, and leadership development in the areas of their designated field of study. Along with their application, they must submit a current resume, an official transcript of the past 2 years of college work, 2 letters of recommendation, and an essay (up to 2 pages in English or 1,200 characters in Japanese) on what they hope to accomplish in their field of study and how that will contribute to better U.S.-Japan relations.

**Financial data** The stipend is $2,000.

**Duration** 1 year.

**Additional information** The association was founded in 1970 to promote the education of women as well as to contribute to U.S.-Japan relations, cultural exchanges, and leadership development.

**Number awarded** 1 to 3 each year. Since this program was established, it has awarded more than $100,000 worth of scholarships to nearly 100 women.

**Deadline** October of each year.

## [725]
## AAUW CAREER DEVELOPMENT GRANTS

American Association of University Women
Attn: AAUW Educational Foundation
301 ACT Drive, Department 60
P.O. Box 4030
Iowa City, IA 52243-4030
(319) 337-1716, ext. 60          Fax: (319) 337-1204
E-mail: aauw@act.org
Web: www.aauw.org

**Summary** To provide financial assistance to women who are seeking career advancement, career change, or reentry into the workforce.

**Eligibility** This program is open to women who are U.S. citizens or permanent residents, have earned a bachelor's degree, received their most recent degree more than 4 years ago, and are making career changes, seeking to advance in current careers, or reentering the workforce. Applicants must be interested in working toward a master's degree, second bachelor's or associate degree, professional degree (e.g., M.D., J.D.), certification program, or technical school certificate. They must be planning to undertake course work at an accredited 2- or 4-year college or university (or a technical school that is licensed, accredited, or approved by the U.S. Department of Education). Primary consideration is given to women of color and women pursuing their first advanced degree or credentials in nontraditional fields. Support is not provided for prerequisite course work or for Ph.D. course

work or dissertations. Selection is based on demonstrated commitment to education and equity for women and girls, reason for seeking higher education or technical training, degree to which study plan is consistent with career objectives, potential for success in chosen field, documentation of opportunities in chosen field, feasibility of study plans and proposed time schedule, validity of proposed budget and budget narrative (including sufficient outside support), and quality of written proposal.

**Financial data** Grants range from $2,000 to $12,000. Funds may be used for tuition, fees, books, supplies, local transportation, dependent child care, or purchase of a computer required for the study program.

**Duration** 1 year, beginning in July; nonrenewable.

**Additional information** The filing fee is $35.

**Number awarded** Varies each year; recently, 63 of these grants, with a value of $670,000, were awarded.

**Deadline** December of each year.

## [726]
## ACNM FOUNDATION FELLOWSHIP FOR GRADUATE EDUCATION

American College of Nurse-Midwives
Attn: ACNM Foundation, Inc.
8403 Colesville Road, Suite 1550
Silver Spring, MD 20910-6374
(240) 485-1850          Fax: (240) 485-1818
E-mail: fdn@acnm.org
Web: www.midwife.org

**Summary** To provide financial assistance for midwifery education at the doctoral or postdoctoral level to members of the American College of Nurse-Midwives (ACNM).

**Eligibility** This program is open to ACNM members who are currently enrolled in a doctoral or postdoctoral midwife education program. Applicants must be a certified nurse midwife (CNM) or a certified midwife (CM). Along with their application, they must submit a curriculum vitae; a sample of up to 30 pages of scholarly work; and brief essays on their 5-year academic career plans, intended use of the fellowship money, and intended future participation in the local, regional, and/or national activities of ACNM or other activities that contribute to midwifery research, education, or practice.

**Financial data** A stipend is awarded (amount not specified).

**Duration** 1 year.

**Additional information** This program began in 1997.

**Number awarded** 1 each year.

**Deadline** March of each year.

## [727]
## ADA I. PRESSMAN SCHOLARSHIP

Society of Women Engineers
Attn: Scholarship Selection Committee
203 North LaSalle Street, Suite 1675
Chicago, IL 60601-1269
(312) 596-5223          Toll Free: (877) SWE-INFO
Fax: (312) 644-8557          E-mail: scholarships@swe.org
Web: societyofwomenengineers.swe.org

**Summary** To provide financial assistance to women working on an undergraduate or graduate degree in engineering or computer science.

**Eligibility** This program is open to women who will be sophomores, juniors, seniors, or graduate students at ABET-accredited colleges and universities. Applicants must be U.S. citizens or permanent residents working full time on a degree in computer science or engineering and have a GPA of 3.0 or higher. Selection is based on merit.

**Financial data** The stipend is $5,000.

**Duration** 1 year.

**Number awarded** 7 each year.

**Deadline** February of each year.

## [728]
## ADULT WOMEN SEMINARY SCHOLARSHIP

American Baptist Women's Ministries of Wisconsin
c/o Nancy Byleen, Scholarship Committee Chair
9322 West Garden Court
Hales Corners, WI 53130
Web: www.abcofwi.org/abwinfo.htm

**Summary** To provide financial assistance to female members of American Baptist Churches in Wisconsin who are interested in attending a seminary in any state that is affiliated with the denomination.

**Eligibility** This program is open to adult women who are residents of Wisconsin and attending or planning to attend an American Baptist seminary in any state. Applicants must have been an active member of an American Baptist Church in Wisconsin for the preceding 3 years. They must have graduated from a college affiliated with the American Baptist Churches USA. Financial need is considered in the selection process.

**Financial data** A stipend is awarded (amount not specified).

**Duration** 1 year.

**Number awarded** 1 or more each year.

**Deadline** February.

## [729]
## ADVANCING WOMEN IN ACCOUNTING SCHOLARSHIP

Illinois CPA Society
Attn: CPA Endowment Fund of Illinois
550 West Jackson, Suite 900
Chicago, Il 60661-5716
(312) 993-0407      Toll Free: (800) 993-0407 (within IL)
Fax: (312) 993-9954
Web: www.icpas.org/hc-students.aspx?id=2724

**Summary** To provide financial assistance to female residents of Illinois who will be enrolled as seniors or graduate students in an accounting program in the state.

**Eligibility** This program is open to women in Illinois who plan to enroll as seniors or graduate students in an accounting program at a college or university in the state. Applicants must be planning to complete the educational requirements needed to sit for the C.P.A. examination in Illinois. They must have at least a 3.0 GPA and be able to demonstrate financial need or special circumstances; the society is especially interested in assisting students who, because of limited options or opportunities, may not have alternative means of support. U.S. citizenship or permanent resident status is required. Selection is based on academic achievement and financial need.

**Financial data** The maximum stipend is $4,000 for payment of tuition and fees. Awards include up to $500 in expenses for books and required classroom materials.

**Duration** 1 year (fifth year for accounting students planning to become a C.P.A.).

**Additional information** This program was established by the Women's Executive Committee of the Illinois CPA Society. The scholarship does not cover the cost of C.P.A. examination review courses. Recipients may not receive a full graduate assistantship, fellowship, or scholarship from a college or university, participate in a full-tuition reimbursement cooperative education or internship program, or participate in an employee full-tuition reimbursement program during the scholarship period.

**Number awarded** Varies each year; recently, 3 of these scholarships were awarded.

**Deadline** March of each year.

## [730]
## AEPHI FOUNDATION SCHOLARSHIPS

Alpha Epsilon Phi
Attn: AEPhi Foundation
11 Lake Avenue Extension, Suite 1A
Danbury, CT 06811
(203) 748-0029      Fax: (203) 748-0039
E-mail: aephifoundation@aephi.org
Web: www.aephi.org/foundation/scholarships

**Summary** To provide financial assistance for undergraduate or graduate education to Alpha Epsilon Phi members or alumnae.

**Eligibility** This program is open to active and alumnae members of the sorority who are either full-time rising juniors or seniors or graduate students who have completed at least 1 year of graduate study. Applicants must have a GPA of 3.0 or higher. Along with their application, they must submit a letter describing 1) their activities in their chapter, on campus, and in the general community; 2) what they have done to supplement their parents' contribution toward their education; and 3) their need for scholarship consideration.

**Financial data** Stipends range from $1,000 to $2,000 per year.

**Duration** 1 year; may be renewed.

**Additional information** This program includes the following named scholarships: the 1909 Scholarships (established in 2009 to celebrate the sorority's centennial), the Anne Klauber Berson Memorial Scholarship, the Edith Hirsch Miller Memorial Scholarship (preference to Jewish applicants who are members of Nu Chapter at the University of Pittsburgh or residents of Pittsburgh), the Irma Loeb Cohen Scholarship (preference to members of Rho Chapter at Ohio State University), the Constance Bauman Abraham Scholarship (preference to members of Eta Chapter at SUNY Albany or at universities in other northeastern states), and the Shonnette Meyer Kahn Scholarship (preference to members of Rho Chapter at Ohio State University or Epsilon Chapter at Tulane University). Recipients must be willing to remain active in the sorority and live in the sorority house (if any) for the entire year the scholarship covers.

**Number awarded** Several each year.

**Deadline** March of each year.

**[731]**
## AFRL/DAGSI OHIO STUDENT-FACULTY RESEARCH FELLOWSHIP PROGRAM

Dayton Area Graduate Studies Institute
3155 Research Boulevard, Suite 205
Kettering, OH 45420
(937) 781-4001                    Fax: (937) 781-4005
E-mail: kelam@dagsi.org
Web: www.dagsi.org/pages/osrfp_proinforeq.html

**Summary** To provide funding to women and other faculty and graduate students from any state at designated universities in Ohio who are interested in conducting research in aerospace technologies of interest to the U.S. Air Force.

**Eligibility** This program is open to research teams of full-time graduate students and faculty at 18 designated Ohio universities. Applicants must be interested in conducting research that will utilize the facilities of the Air Force Research Laboratory (AFRL) at Wright-Patterson Air Force Base. All 6 directorates at the AFRL (air vehicles, propulsion, sensors, materials and manufacturing, human effectiveness, and information) participate in this program. Applications from Ph.D. candidates must be developed and written largely by the student, with support, guidance, and input as necessary from the faculty partner. For master's projects, the proposal can be developed and written jointly by the faculty member and the student. All participants (faculty and student) must be U.S. citizens. Underrepresented minorities, women, and persons with disabilities are strongly urged to apply.

**Financial data** Grants provide stipends of $23,500 for students who have a master's degree and are working on a Ph.D. or $18,500 for students who have a bachelor's degree and are working on a master's; student's tuition for 1 academic year; a faculty stipend of $11,000; student and faculty allowances of $3,000 each for program-related travel or other approved expenses; and overhead at a maximum off-campus rate of 26% of student and faculty stipends and miscellaneous allowances.

**Duration** 1 year; may be renewed for 1 additional year by master's students and for 2 additional years by Ph.D. candidates. Students are expected to spend 8 consecutive weeks conducting research at AFRL and faculty members are expected to spend at least 1 month conducting research at AFRL.

**Additional information** DAGSI was established in 1994 as a consortium of graduate engineering schools at the University of Dayton, Wright State University, and the Air Force Institute of Technology. The Ohio State University and the University of Cincinnati joined as affiliated members in 1996 and Miami University and Ohio University joined as associate members in 2001. Students from the following universities are also eligible to participate in this program: University of Akron, Bowling Green State University, Central State University, Cleveland State University, Kent State University, Shawnee State University, University of Toledo, Youngstown State University, Medical College of Ohio, Northeastern Ohio Universities College of Medicine, and Case Western Reserve University.

**Number awarded** At least 20 each year.

**Deadline** January of each year.

**[732]**
## AGI/AAPG SEMESTER INTERNSHIPS IN GEOSCIENCE PUBLIC POLICY

American Geological Institute
Attn: Government Affairs Program
4220 King Street
Alexandria, VA 22302-1502
(703) 379-2480                    Fax: (703) 379-7563
E-mail: govt@agiweb.org
Web: www.agiweb.org/gap/interns/index.html

**Summary** To provide work experience to women, minority, and other geoscience students who have a strong interest in federal science policy.

**Eligibility** This program is open to geoscience undergraduate and master's degree students who are interested in working with Congress and federal agencies to promote sound public policy in areas that affect geoscientists, including water, energy, and mineral resources; geologic hazards; environmental protection, and federal funding for geoscience research and education. Applicants must submit official copies of college transcripts, a resume with the names and contact information for 2 references, and a statement of their science and policy interests and what they feel they can contribute to the program. Women and minorities are especially encouraged to apply.

**Financial data** The stipend is $5,000.

**Duration** 14 weeks, during the fall or spring semester.

**Additional information** This program is jointly funded by the American Geological Institute (AGI) and the American Association of Petroleum Geologists (AAPG). Activities for the interns include monitoring and analyzing geoscience-related legislation in Congress, updating legislative and policy information on AGI's web site, attending House and Senate hearings and preparing summaries, responding to information requests from AGI's member societies, and attending meetings with policy-level staff members in Congress, federal agencies, and non-governmental organizations. The sponsor also offers a similar internship program for 12 weeks during the summer (with a $5,000 stipend).

**Number awarded** 1 each semester.

**Deadline** April of each year for fall internships; October of each year for spring internships.

**[733]**
## AGU GRADUATE FELLOWSHIP IN THE HISTORY OF SCIENCE

American Geophysical Union
Attn: History of Geophysics
2000 Florida Avenue, N.W.
Washington, DC 20009-1277
(202) 462-6900                    Toll Free: (800) 966-2481
Fax: (202) 328-0566
E-mail: HistoryofGeophysics@agu.org
Web: www.agu.org/about/history/fellowship.shtml

**Summary** To provide funding to doctoral candidates (particularly women, minorities, and individuals with disabilities) who are conducting dissertation research in the history of geophysics.

**Eligibility** This program is open to doctoral candidates at U.S. institutions who have passed all preliminary examinations. Applicants must be completing a dissertation in the history of the geophysical sciences, including topics related to atmospheric sciences, bio geosciences, geodesy, geomagnetism and paleomagnetism, hydrology, ocean sciences, planetary sciences, seismology, space physics, aeronomy, tectonophysics, volcanology, geochemistry, and petrology. They must submit a cover letter with a vita, undergraduate and graduate transcripts, a 10-page description of the dissertation topic and proposed research plan, and 3 letters of recommendation. U.S. citizenship or permanent resident status is required. Applications are encouraged from women, minorities, and students with disabilities who are traditionally underrepresented in the geophysical sciences.

**Financial data** The grant is $5,000; funds are to be used to assist with the costs of travel to obtain archival or research materials.

**Duration** Up to 1 year.

**Number awarded** 1 each year.

**Deadline** August of each year.

## [734]
## AHIMA FOUNDATION DIVERSITY SCHOLARSHIPS

American Health Information Management Association
Attn: AHIMA Foundation
233 North Michigan Avenue, 21st Floor
Chicago, IL 60601-5809
(312) 233-1175                    Fax: (312) 233-1475
E-mail: info@ahimafoundation.org
Web: www.ahimafoundation.org

**Summary** To provide financial assistance to women and other members of the American Health Information Management Association (AHIMA) who are interested in working on an undergraduate or graduate degree in health information management (HIM) or health information technology (HIT) and will contribute to diversity in the profession.

**Eligibility** This program is open to AHIMA members who are enrolled at least half time in a program accredited by the Commission on Accreditation for Health Informatics and Information Management Education (CAHIM). Applicants must be working on a degree in HIM or HIT at the associate, bachelor's, post-baccalaureate, master's, or doctoral level. They must have a GPA of 3.5 or higher and at least 1 full semester remaining after the date of the award. To qualify for this support, applicants must demonstrate how they will contribute to diversity in the health information management profession; diversity is defined as differences in race, ethnicity, nationality, gender, sexual orientation, socioeconomic status, age, physical capabilities, and religious beliefs. Selection is based on GPA and academic achievement, volunteer and work experience, commitment to the HIM profession, quality and relevance of references, and completeness and clarity of thought.

**Financial data** Stipends are $1,000 for associate degree students, $1,500 for bachelor's degree or post-baccalaureate certificate students, $2,000 for master's degree students, or $2,500 for doctoral degree students.

**Duration** 1 year.

**Number awarded** Varies each year; recently, 9 of these scholarships were awarded: 6 to undergraduates and 3 to graduate students.

**Deadline** September of each year.

## [735]
## AKA ENDOWMENT AWARDS

Alpha Kappa Alpha Sorority, Inc.
Attn: Educational Advancement Foundation
5656 South Stony Island Avenue
Chicago, IL 60637
(773) 947-0026                    Toll Free: (800) 653-6528
Fax: (773) 947-0277              E-mail: akaeaf@akaeaf.net
Web: www.akaeaf.org/fellowships_endowments.htm

**Summary** To provide financial assistance to undergraduate and graduate students (especially African American women) who meet designated requirements.

**Eligibility** This program is open to undergraduate and graduate students who are enrolled full time as sophomores or higher in an accredited degree-granting institution and are planning to continue their program of education. Applicants may apply for scholarships that include specific requirements established by the donor of the endowment that supports it. Along with their application, they must submit 1) a list of honors, awards, and scholarships received; 2) a list of organizations in which they have memberships, especially minority organizations; and 3) a statement of their personal and career goals, including how this scholarship will enhance their ability to attain those goals. The sponsor is a traditionally African American women's sorority.

**Financial data** Award amounts are determined by the availability of funds from the particular endowment. Recently, stipends averaged more than $1,700 per year.

**Duration** 1 year or longer.

**Additional information** Each endowment establishes its own requirements. Examples of requirements include residence of the applicant, major field of study, minimum GPA, attendance at an Historically Black College or University (HBCU) or member institution of the United Negro College Fund (UNCF), or other personal feature. For further information on all endowments, contact the sponsor.

**Number awarded** Varies each year; recently, 32 of these scholarships, with a total value of nearly $76,00, were awarded.

**Deadline** April of each year.

## [736]
## AKA GRADUATE SCHOLARSHIPS

Alpha Kappa Alpha Sorority, Inc.
Attn: Educational Advancement Foundation
5656 South Stony Island Avenue
Chicago, IL 60637
(773) 947-0026                    Toll Free: (800) 653-6528
Fax: (773) 947-0277              E-mail: akaeaf@akaeaf.net
Web: www.akaeaf.org/graduate_scholarships.htm

**Summary** To provide financial assistance for study or research to graduate students (especially African American women).

**Eligibility** This program is open to students who are working full time on a graduate degree in any state. Applicants may apply either for a scholarship based on merit (requires a GPA of 3.0 or higher) or on financial need (requires a GPA of 2.5 or higher). Along with their application, they must submit 1) a list of honors, awards, and scholarships received; 2) a list of organizations in which they have memberships, especially minority organizations; 3) a description of the project or research on which they are currently working, or (if they are not involved in a project or research) the aspects of their field that interest them; and 4) a statement of their personal and career goals, including how this scholarship will enhance their ability to attain those goals. The sponsor is a traditionally African American women's sorority.

**Financial data** Stipends range up to $3,000.

**Duration** 1 year; nonrenewable.

**Number awarded** Varies each year; recently, 74 of these scholarships, with a total value of $62,050, were awarded.

**Deadline** August of each year.

## [737]
## ALPHA CHI OMEGA EDUCATIONAL ASSISTANCE GRANTS

Alpha Chi Omega Foundation
Attn: Educational Assistance Grants Committee
5939 Castle Creek Parkway North Drive
Indianapolis, IN 46250-4343
(317) 579-5050, ext. 265     Fax: (317) 579-5051
E-mail: alatta@alphachiomega.org
Web: www.alphachiomega.org/index.aspx?id=1031

**Summary** To provide financial assistance to members of Alpha Chi Omega sorority who are interested in continuing education, including study abroad.

**Eligibility** This program is open to members of the sorority at the undergraduate and graduate school levels. Applicants must be seeking funding for continuing education and related expenses. They may be interested in studying abroad if the credits earned will be included with credits needed to earn a degree. Along with their application, they must submit documentation of financial need, an outline of their future career goals, a description of their participation in sorority activities, transcripts, and (if studying abroad) confirmation that credits earned will be included with credits needed to earn a degree.

**Financial data** Grants range from $500 to $2,000.

**Duration** 1 year.

**Additional information** This program includes the Alpha Zeta Undergraduate Member Assistance Grant in Memory of Kay Roh, the Anne Folrath Gerhart/Carla Henke Mattson Educational Assistance Grant the Carol Edmundson Hutcheson Education Assistance Fund, the Florence Staiger Lonn Educational Grants, the Lisa Hancock Rehrig Educational Assistance Grants, and the Mary Frances-Guilbert Mariani-Bigler Continuing Education Grant.

**Number awarded** Varies each year; recently, 30 of these grants, worth $19,621, were awarded.

**Deadline** April of each year for spring applications; September of each year for fall applications.

## [738]
## ALPHA CHI OMEGA FOUNDATION SCHOLARSHIPS

Alpha Chi Omega Foundation
Attn: Assistant Director-Grants and Stewardship
5939 Castle Creek Parkway North Drive
Indianapolis, IN 46250-4343
(317) 579-5050, ext. 265     Fax: (317) 579-5051
E-mail: alatta@alphachiomega.org
Web: www.alphachiomega.org/index.aspx?id=1030

**Summary** To provide financial assistance for college to undergraduate and graduate members of Alpha Chi Omega.

**Eligibility** This program is open to women attending college full time who are members of Alpha Chi Omega. Applicants must be sophomores, juniors, seniors, or graduate students working on a degree in any field. Selection is based on academic achievement, chapter involvement, campus and community service, and financial need.

**Financial data** A stipend is awarded (amount not specified).

**Duration** 1 year.

**Additional information** This program includes more than 80 separate funds, many of which give preference to members of specified chapters of the sorority or are limited to students majoring in specified fields.

**Number awarded** Varies each year; recently, 111 of these scholarships, worth $103,581, were awarded.

**Deadline** February of each year.

## [739]
## ALPHA CHI OMEGA FOUNDERS FELLOWSHIP

Alpha Chi Omega Foundation
Attn: Assistant Director-Grants and Stewardship
5939 Castle Creek Parkway North Drive
Indianapolis, IN 46250-4343
(317) 579-5050, ext. 265     Fax: (317) 579-5051
E-mail: alatta@alphachiomega.org
Web: www.alphachiomega.org/index.aspx?id=1030

**Summary** To provide financial assistance to graduating Alpha Chi Omega members who are interested in studying on the graduate school level.

**Eligibility** This program is open to women college seniors or graduates who are members of the sorority. Applicants must be interested in attending graduate school. They may study any field. Financial need is considered in the selection process.

**Financial data** A stipend is awarded (amount not specified).

**Duration** 1 year.

**Number awarded** 1 each year.

**Deadline** February of each year.

## [740]
## ALPHA EPSILON IOTA SCHOLARSHIP FUND

Alpha Epsilon Iota
Scholarship Fund
c/o Key Bank Trust Client Services Center
P.O. Box 94605
Cleveland, OH 44114-1717
Toll Free: (800) 999-9658

**Summary** To provide financial assistance to women enrolled or accepted at an accredited school or college of medicine in the United States.

**Eligibility** This program is open to women who are candidates for degrees in accredited schools or colleges of medicine or osteopathy in the United States. Selection is based on scholastic merit, work experience, scholarly publication, research experience, and financial need (last year's income cannot exceed $15,000 and assets cannot exceed $10,000). Race, age, religion, political affiliation, or national origin are not considered in awarding the fellowships. Priority is given to applicants in their first year of medical school. An interview may be required.

**Financial data** Awards range from $3,000 to $4,000 each year. Funds may be used for tuition-related fees, books, materials, food, clothing, housing, transportation, medical and dental expenses, insurance, and child care.

**Duration** 1 year; renewal is possible.

**Number awarded** 2 each year.

**Deadline** May of each year.

## [741]
## ALPHA GAMMA DELTA FOUNDATION SCHOLARSHIPS

Alpha Gamma Delta Foundation, Inc.
Attn: Scholarship Committee
8710 North Meridian Street
Indianapolis, IN 46260
(317) 663-4242     Fax: (317) 663-4244
E-mail: jmores@alphagammadeltafoundation.org
Web: alphagammadelta.org

**Summary** To provide financial assistance to members of Alpha Gamma Delta who are interested in continuing undergraduate or graduate study.

**Eligibility** This program is open to 1) collegiate members of Alpha Gamma Delta who are entering their junior or senior year of full-time undergraduate study; and 2) alumnae members entering or enrolled in a full-time graduate program. Applicants must submit a 1-page narrative on their reasons for requesting a scholarship, why they have chosen their field of study, and their special qualifications for it. Financial need is considered in the selection process.

**Financial data** A stipend is awarded (amount not specified).

**Duration** 1 year.

**Number awarded** Varies each year.

**Deadline** February of each year.

## [742]
## ALPHA OMICRON PI ALUMNAE CHAPTER HONOR SCHOLARSHIP

Alpha Omicron Pi Foundation
Attn: Scholarship Committee
5390 Virginia Way
Brentwood, TN 37027
(615) 370-0920     Fax: (615) 370-4424
E-mail: foundation@alphaomicronpi.org
Web: www.alphaomicronpi.org

**Summary** To provide financial assistance to alumnae members of Alpha Omicron Pi interested in returning to graduate school after an absence.

**Eligibility** This program is open to alumnae chapter members of Alpha Omicron Pi who wish to return to school to work full time on a graduate degree after an absence of 3 or more years. If no alumnae chapter member applies or is eligible, then the award is available to at-large alumnae members. If no at-large alumnae member applies or is eligible, then the award is available to a collegiate member. Applicants must submit brief essays about themselves. Selection is based on those essays, academic achievement, Alpha Omicron Pi leadership and honors, campus and community involvement, letters of recommendation, and financial need.

**Financial data** Stipend amounts vary; recently, the average value of each scholarship provided by this foundation was approximately $1,200.

**Duration** 1 year.

**Number awarded** 1 each year.

**Deadline** February of each year.

## [743]
## ALPHA OMICRON PI DIAMOND JUBILEE FOUNDATION SCHOLARSHIPS

Alpha Omicron Pi Foundation
Attn: Scholarship Committee
5390 Virginia Way
Brentwood, TN 37027
(615) 370-0920     Fax: (615) 370-4424
E-mail: foundation@alphaomicronpi.org
Web: www.alphaomicronpi.org

**Summary** To provide financial assistance for college or graduate school to collegiate and alumnae members of Alpha Omicron Pi.

**Eligibility** This program is open to members of Alpha Omicron Pi who are 1) full-time undergraduates entering their sophomore, junior, or senior year; 2) seniors applying to graduate school or alumnae of 2 years or less already enrolled in graduate school; or 3) returning alumnae reentering college after an absence of 3 or more years. Applicants must submit brief essays about themselves. Selection is based on those essays, academic achievement, Alpha Omicron Pi leadership and honors, campus and community involvement, letters of recommendation, and financial need.

**Financial data** Stipend amounts vary; recently, the average value of each scholarship provided by this foundation was approximately $1,200.

**Duration** 1 year.

**Additional information** This program began in 1962. It includes the Muriel T. McKinney Scholarship, awarded to the top-ranked undergraduate applicant.

**Number awarded** Varies each year; recently, 20 of these scholarships were awarded (11 to undergraduates, 7 to graduate students, and 2 to a returning alumna).

**Deadline** February of each year.

## [744]
## ALPHA SIGMA TAU SCHOLARSHIPS

Alpha Sigma Tau National Foundation
Attn: Scholarships
3334 Founders Road
Indianapolis, IN 46268
(317) 613-7575     Fax: (317) 613-7111
E-mail: melinda@alphasigmataufoundation.org
Web: www.alphasigmataufoundation.org/scholarships

**Summary** To provide financial assistance to members of Alpha Sigma Tau sorority interested in continuing undergraduate or graduate study.

**Eligibility** This program is open to members of Alpha Sigma Tau who are sophomores, juniors, seniors, or graduate students. Applicants must have a GPA of 3.0 or higher. Along with their application, they must submit a 1-page essay on how their involvement in the sorority has impacted them personally and professionally. Selection is based on academic achievement, service to Alpha Sigma Tau, academic honors, university or community service, and financial need.

**Financial data** Stipends range from $200 to $2,550.

**Duration** 1 year.

**Number awarded** Varies each year; recently, 26 of these scholarships were awarded.

**Deadline** January of each year.

## [745]
## ALPHA TAU CHAPTER SCHOLARSHIP

Alpha Omicron Pi Foundation
Attn: Scholarship Committee
5390 Virginia Way
Brentwood, TN 37027
(615) 370-0920                    Fax: (615) 370-4424
E-mail: foundation@alphaomicronpi.org
Web: www.alphaomicronpi.org

**Summary** To provide financial assistance to alumnae members of Alpha Omicron Pi interested in returning to graduate school after an absence.

**Eligibility** This program is open to alumnae members of Alpha Omicron Pi who wish to return to school and work full time on a graduate degree after an absence of 3 or more years. Preference is given to legacies; if no legacy qualifies, the award is available to any alumna. Applicants must submit brief essays about themselves. Selection is based on those essays, academic achievement, Alpha Omicron Pi leadership and honors, campus and community involvement, letters of recommendation, and financial need.

**Financial data** Stipend amounts vary; recently, the average value of each scholarship provided by this foundation was approximately $1,200.

**Duration** 1 year.

**Number awarded** 1 each year.

**Deadline** February of each year.

## [746]
## ALUMNA CIRCLE KEY GRANTS FOR CONTINUING EDUCATION

Kappa Kappa Gamma Fraternity
Attn: Foundation Administrator
530 East Town Street
P.O. Box 38
Columbus, OH 43216-0038
(614) 228-6515                    Toll Free: (866) KKG-1870
Fax: (614) 228-6303               E-mail: kkghq@kappa.org
Web: www.kappakappagamma.org

**Summary** To assist alumna members of Kappa Kappa Gamma who wish to pursue additional education.

**Eligibility** This program is open to Kappa Kappa Gamma alumnae who have found it necessary to interrupt their education or need financial assistance for part-time educational programs related to career opportunities. The grants are awarded on the basis of need, merit, and individual goals for study at a college, university, or vocational/technical school.

**Financial data** Grants range up to $1,000.

**Duration** Up to 1 year.

**Additional information** The Rose McGill Fund was established in 1922 to provide confidential aid to Kappa Kappa Gamma members. These funds are to be used to continue, not to start, a course of study. Requests for applications

must be accompanied by a self-addressed stamped envelope and chapter membership identification.

**Number awarded** Varies each year; in a recent biennium, Rose McGill programs provided $696,424 in support.

**Deadline** April, July, or November of each year.

## [747]
## AMELIA EARHART FELLOWSHIP AWARDS

Zonta International
Attn: Foundation
1211 West 22nd Street, Suite 900
Oak Brook, IL 60523-3384
(630) 928-1400                    Fax: (630) 928-1559
E-mail: programs@zonta.org
Web: www.zonta.org

**Summary** To provide financial assistance to women interested in doctoral study in scientific or engineering areas related to aerospace.

**Eligibility** This program is open to women who have a bachelor's degree in an area of science or engineering related to aerospace. Applicants must be registered as a full-time student at an accredited Ph.D. program at a recognized institution of higher learning and be able to provide evidence of a well-defined research and development program. They may be citizens of any country and studying in any country. Along with their application, they must submit a 500-word statement on their academic research program, their professional goals, and the relevance of their research program to aerospace-related sciences or engineering.

**Financial data** The stipend is $10,000, paid in 2 installments. Funds may be used for tuition, books, and fees.

**Duration** 1 year; renewable.

**Additional information** The fellowship may be used at any institution offering accredited courses in the applicant's field of study in the United States or abroad. Fellows may receive financial assistance from other programs. This program, established in 1938, is named for Amelia Earhart, famed air pioneer and Zontian, who disappeared over the Pacific in 1937.

**Number awarded** 35 each year. Since the program began, it has awarded more than 1,400 of these fellowships, worth $8.3 million, to women from 68 countries.

**Deadline** November of each year.

## [748]
## AMELIA EARHART MEMORIAL ACADEMIC SCHOLARSHIPS

Ninety-Nines, Inc.
4300 Amelia Earhart Road, Suite A
Oklahoma City, OK 73159
(405) 685-7969                    Toll Free: (800) 994-1929
Fax: (405) 685-7985   E-mail: AEChair@ninety-nines.org
Web: www.ninety-nines.org/index.cfm/scholarships.htm

**Summary** To provide funding to members of the Ninety-Nines (an organization of women pilots) who are enrolled in academic study related to aviation or aerospace.

**Eligibility** This program is open to women from any country who have been members of the organization for at least 1 year. Applicants must be currently enrolled at an accredited college or university and working on an associate, bachelor's, master's, or doctoral degree in such fields as aerospace engineering, aviation technology, aviation business management, air traffic management, or professional pilot. They must have a GPA of 3.0 or higher and be able to demonstrate financial need.

**Financial data**  The stipend is $5,000 per year.

**Duration**  1 year; may be renewed.

**Additional information**  This program began in 1941.

**Number awarded**  Varies each year; recently, 7 of these scholarships were awarded: 5 to undergraduates and 2 to graduate students.

**Deadline**  Applications must be submitted to the chapter scholarship chair by November of each year; those chairs must forward the applications from their chapter to the designated trustee by January of each year. At-large numbers (those who do not belong to a specific chapter) must submit their application to their section by December of each year.

## [749]
## AMELIA EARHART RESEARCH SCHOLAR GRANT

Ninety-Nines, Inc.
Attn: Chair, Research Scholar Grants
4300 Amelia Earhart Road, Suite A
Oklahoma City, OK 73159
(405) 685-7969          Toll Free: (800) 994-1929
Fax: (405) 685-7985    E-mail: AEChair@ninety-nines.org
Web: www.ninety-nines.org/index.cfm/scholarships.htm

**Summary**  To provide funding to scholars interested in expanding knowledge about women in aviation and space.

**Eligibility**  This program is open to scholars who are conducting research on the role of women in aviation and space. Disciplines may include, but are not limited to, biology, business administration, economics, ergonomics, history, human engineering, psychology, or sociology. Applicants may be seeking funding to be used in conjunction with other research activities, such as completion of requirements for an advanced degree or matching funds with other grants to support a program larger than either grant could sponsor independently.

**Financial data**  The amount awarded varies; generally, the grant is at least $1,000.

**Duration**  The grant is awarded periodically.

**Number awarded**  1 each granting period.

**Deadline**  Deadline not specified.

## [750]
## AMELIA KEMP MEMORIAL SCHOLARSHIP

Women of the Evangelical Lutheran Church in America
Attn: Scholarships
8765 West Higgins Road
Chicago, IL 60631-4101
(773) 380-2741          Toll Free: (800) 638-3522, ext. 2741
Fax: (773) 380-2419    E-mail: valora.starr@elca.org
Web: www.womenoftheelca.org

**Summary**  To provide financial assistance to lay women of color who are members of Evangelical Lutheran Church of America (ELCA) congregations and who wish to study on the undergraduate, graduate, professional, or vocational school level.

**Eligibility**  This program is open to ELCA lay women of color who are at least 21 years of age and have experienced

an interruption of at least 2 years in their education since high school. Applicants must have been admitted to an educational institution to prepare for a career in other than ordained ministry. U.S. citizenship is required.

**Financial data**  The maximum stipend is $1,000.

**Duration**  Up to 2 years.

**Number awarded**  1 or more each year.

**Deadline**  February of each year.

## [751]
## AMERICAN ASSOCIATION OF UNIVERSITY WOMEN DISSERTATION FELLOWSHIPS

American Association of University Women
Attn: AAUW Educational Foundation
301 ACT Drive, Department 60
P.O. Box 4030
Iowa City, IA 52243-4030
(319) 337-1716, ext. 60          Fax: (319) 337-1204
E-mail: aauw@act.org
Web: www.aauw.org

**Summary**  To provide funding to women in the final year of writing their dissertation.

**Eligibility**  This program is open to U.S. citizens and permanent residents who are women and intend to pursue professional careers in the United States. They should have successfully completed all required course work for their doctorate, passed all preliminary examinations, and received written acceptance of their prospectus. Applicants may propose research in any field. Selection is based on scholarly excellence, quality of project design, originality of project, scholarly significance of project to discipline, feasibility of project and proposed schedule, qualifications of applicant, potential of applicant to make a significant contribution to field, applicant's teaching experience, applicant's commitment to women's issues in profession and community, and applicant's mentoring of other women.

**Financial data**  The stipend is $20,000.

**Duration**  1 year, beginning in July.

**Additional information**  The filing fee is $40. It is expected that the fellowship will be used for the final year of doctoral work and that the degree will be received at the end of the fellowship year. The fellowship is not intended to fund extended field research. The recipient should be prepared to devote full time to the dissertation during the fellowship year.

**Number awarded**  Varies each year; recently, 60 of these fellowships were awarded.

**Deadline**  November of each year.

## [752]
## AMERICAN BAPTIST WOMEN'S MINISTRIES OF COLORADO STUDENT GRANTS

American Baptist Churches of the Rocky Mountains
Attn: American Baptist Women's Ministries
9085 East Mineral Circle, Suite 170
Centennial, CO 80112
(303) 988-3900          E-mail: web@abcrm.org
Web: www.abcrm.org

**Summary**  To provide financial assistance to women who are members of churches affiliated with the American Baptist Churches (ABC) USA in Colorado, New Mexico, and Utah and interested in attending an ABC college or seminary in any state.

**Eligibility** This program is open to women older than 26 years of age who are active members of churches cooperating with ABC in Colorado, New Mexico, or Utah. Applicants must be enrolled or planning to enroll at an ABC college, university, or seminary in any state. Along with their application, they must submit a personal letter describing their Christian experience; their participation in the life of their church, school, and community; and their goals for the future. Selection is based on academic performance, Christian participation in church and school, and financial need.

**Financial data** A stipend is awarded (amount not specified). Funds are sent directly to the recipient's school.

**Duration** 1 year; recipients may reapply.

**Number awarded** 1 or more each year.

**Deadline** March of each year.

## [753]
## AMERICAN BAPTIST WOMEN'S MINISTRIES OF NEW YORK STATE SCHOLARSHIPS

American Baptist Women's Ministries of New York State
c/o Rebecca Walters, Scholarship Committee
7 Sealy Drive
Potsdam, NY 13676
(315) 265-5309          E-mail: ontiptoe20@gmail.com
Web: www.abwm-nys.org/scholarship

**Summary** To provide financial assistance to women who are members of American Baptist Churches in New York and interested in attending college in any state.

**Eligibility** This program is open to women who are residents of New York and active members of an American Baptist Church. Applicants must be enrolled or planning to enroll full time at a college or university in any state. While in college, they must maintain Christian fellowship, preferably with the American Baptist Church (although any Protestant church or campus ministry is acceptable). Along with their application, they must submit a 1-page essay on an event that occurred in their life during the past year and how it has impacted their faith. Women may be of any age; graduate students are considered on an individual basis. Financial need is considered in the selection process.

**Financial data** A stipend is awarded (amount not specified).

**Duration** 1 year.

**Number awarded** Varies each year.

**Deadline** February of each year.

## [754]
## AMERICAN BUSINESS WOMEN'S ASSOCIATION PRESIDENT'S SCHOLARSHIP

American Business Women's Association
Attn: Stephen Bufton Memorial Educational Fund
11050 Roe Avenue, Suite 200
Overland Park, KS 66211
Toll Free: (800) 228-0007
Web: www.sbmef.org/Scholarships.cfm

**Summary** To provide financial assistance to female graduate students who are working on a degree in a specified field (the field changes each year).

**Eligibility** This program is open to women who are working on a graduate degree and have a cumulative GPA of 3.0 or higher. Applicants are not required to be members of the American Business Women's Association. Along with their application, they must submit a 250-word biographical sketch that includes information about their background, activities, honors, work experience, and long-term educational and professional goals. Financial need is not considered in the selection process. Each year, the trustees designate an academic discipline for which the scholarship will be presented that year. U.S. citizenship is required.

**Financial data** The stipend is $3,000. Funds are paid directly to the recipient's institution to be used only for tuition, books, and fees.

**Duration** 1 year.

**Additional information** This program was created in 1969 as part of ABWA's Stephen Bufton Memorial Education Fund. The ABWA does not provide the names and addresses of local chapters; it recommends that applicants check with their local Chamber of Commerce, library, or university to see if any chapter has registered a contact's name and number.

**Number awarded** 1 each year.

**Deadline** May of each year.

## [755]
## AMERICAN NUCLEAR SOCIETY DELAYED EDUCATION SCHOLARSHIP FOR WOMEN

American Nuclear Society
Attn: Scholarship Coordinator
555 North Kensington Avenue
La Grange Park, IL 60526-5535
(708) 352-6611          Toll Free: (800) 323-3044
Fax: (708) 352-0499          E-mail: outreach@ans.org
Web: www.new.ans.org/honors/scholarships

**Summary** To provide financial assistance to mature women whose formal studies in nuclear science or nuclear engineering have been delayed or interrupted.

**Eligibility** Applicants must be mature women who have experienced at least a 1-year delay or interruption of their undergraduate studies and are returning to school to work on an undergraduate or graduate degree in nuclear science or nuclear engineering. They must be members of the American Nuclear Society (ANS), but they may be citizens of any country. Along with their application, they must submit an essay on their academic and professional goals, experiences that have affected those goals, and other relevant information. Selection is based on that essay, academic achievement, letters of recommendation, and financial need.

**Financial data** The stipend is $5,000. Funds may be used by the student to cover any educational expense, including tuition, books, room, and board.

**Duration** 1 year; nonrenewable.

**Number awarded** 1 each year.

**Deadline** January of each year.

## [756]
## AMS GRADUATE FELLOWSHIP IN THE HISTORY OF SCIENCE

American Meteorological Society
Attn: Development and Student Program Manager
45 Beacon Street
Boston, MA 02108-3693
(617) 227-2426, ext. 3907          Fax: (617) 742-8718
E-mail: dFernandez@ametsoc.org
Web: www.ametsoc.org

**Summary**  To provide funding to graduate students (particularly women, minorities, and persons with disabilities) who are members of the American Meteorological Society (AMS) and interested in conducting dissertation research on the history of meteorology.

**Eligibility**  This program is open to AMS members and student members who are planning to complete a doctoral dissertation on the history of the atmospheric or related oceanic or hydrologic sciences. Applicants must be U.S. citizens or permanent residents and working on a degree at a U.S. institution. Fellowships may be used to support research at a location away from the student's institution, provided the plan is approved by the student's thesis adviser. In such an instance, an effort is made to place the student into a mentoring relationship with a member of the society at an appropriate institution. The sponsor specifically encourages applications from women, minorities, and students with disabilities who are traditionally underrepresented in the atmospheric and related oceanic sciences.

**Financial data**  The stipend is $15,000.

**Duration**  1 year.

**Number awarded**  1 each year.

**Deadline**  February of each year.

## [757]
## AMS GRADUATE FELLOWSHIPS

American Meteorological Society
Attn: Development and Student Program Manager
45 Beacon Street
Boston, MA 02108-3693
(617) 227-2426, ext. 3907          Fax: (617) 742-8718
E-mail: dFernandez@ametsoc.org
Web: www.ametsoc.org

**Summary**  To encourage students (particularly women, minorities, and persons with disabilities) who are entering their first year of graduate school to work on an advanced degree in the atmospheric and related oceanic and hydrologic sciences.

**Eligibility**  This program is open to students entering their first year of graduate study and planning to work on an advanced degree in the atmospheric or related oceanic or hydrologic sciences. Applicants must be U.S. citizens or permanent residents and have a GPA of 3.25 or higher. Along with their application, they must submit 200-word essays on 1) their most important achievements that qualify them for this scholarship; and 2) their career goals in the atmospheric or related sciences. Selection is based on academic record as an undergraduate. The sponsor specifically encourages applications from women, minorities, and students with disabilities who are traditionally underrepresented in the atmospheric and related sciences.

**Financial data**  The stipend is $24,000 per academic year.

**Duration**  9 months.

**Additional information**  This program was initiated in 1991. It is funded by high-technology firms and government agencies.

**Number awarded**  Varies each year; recently, 13 of these scholarships were awarded.

**Deadline**  January of each year.

## [758]
## AMWA SCHOLARSHIPS

American Medical Women's Association
Attn: National Student Leadership
100 North 20th Street, Fourth Floor
Philadelphia, PA 19103
(215) 320-3716          Toll Free: (866) 564-2483
Fax: (215) 564-2175  E-mail: awards@amwa-student.org
Web: www.amwa-doc.org/students/awards-scholarships

**Summary**  To provide financial assistance for medical education to student members of the American Medical Women's Association (AMWA).

**Eligibility**  This program is open to student members of the association currently enrolled in medical school. Applicants must submit brief statements on a situation in which they demonstrated leadership, their involvement in AMWA, their plans for future AMWA involvement, and their goals for women in medicine. Financial need is considered but is not required.

**Financial data**  The stipend is $1,000.

**Duration**  1 year.

**Number awarded**  4 each year.

**Deadline**  January or September of each year.

## [759]
## ANITA BENEDETTI MEMORIAL SCHOLARSHIP

Spencer Educational Foundation, Inc.
c/o Risk Insurance and Management Society
1065 Avenue of the Americas, 13th Floor
New York, NY 10018
(212) 286-9292          E-mail: asabatino@spencered.org
Web: www.spencered.org

**Summary**  To provide financial assistance to female full-time graduate students who are preparing for a career in risk management.

**Eligibility**  This program is open to women who are enrolled as a full-time master's degree candidate or a teaching-oriented pre-dissertation Ph.D. candidate. Applicants must be working on a degree in a risk management discipline and be preparing for a career in that field. They must have a GPA of 3.0 or higher and relevant work experience. Along with their application, they must submit a 500-word essay on their chosen career path and goals. Selection is based on merit.

**Financial data**  The stipend is $10,000.

**Duration**  1 year.

**Number awarded**  1 or more each year.

**Deadline**  January of each year.

## [760]
## ANITA BORG MEMORIAL SCHOLARSHIPS

Google Inc.
Attn: Scholarships
1600 Amphitheatre Parkway
Mountain View, CA 94043-8303
(650) 253-0000          Fax: (650) 253-0001
E-mail: anitaborgscholarship@google.com
Web: www.google.com/anitaborg/us

**Summary**   To provide financial assistance to women working on a bachelor's or graduate degree in a computer-related field.

**Eligibility**   This program is open to women who are entering their senior year of undergraduate study or are enrolled in a graduate program in computer science, computer engineering, or a closely-related field. Applicants must be full-time students at a university in the United States and have a GPA of 3.5 or higher. They must submit essays of 400 to 600 words on 1) a significant technical project on which they have worked; 2) their leadership abilities; 3) what they would do if someone gave them the funding and resources for a 3- to 12-month project to investigate a technical topic of their choice; and 4) what they would do if someone gave them $1,000 to plan an event or project to benefit women in technical fields. Citizens, permanent residents, and international students are eligible. Selection is based on academic background and demonstrated leadership.

**Financial data**   The stipend is $10,000 per year.

**Duration**   1 year; recipients may reapply.

**Additional information**   These scholarships were first offered in 2004.

**Number awarded**   Varies each year; recently, 25 of these scholarships were awarded.

**Deadline**   February of each year.

## [761]
## ANL LABORATORY–GRADUATE RESEARCH APPOINTMENTS

Argonne National Laboratory
Division of Educational Programs
Attn: Graduate Student Program Office
9700 South Cass Avenue/DEP 223
Argonne, IL 60439-4845
(630) 252-3366          Fax: (630) 252-3193
E-mail: lisareed@anl.gov
Web: www.dep.anl.gov/p_graduate/labgrad.htm

**Summary**   To offer opportunities for qualified graduate students (particularly women and underrepresented minorities) who are interested in carrying out their master's or doctoral thesis research at the Argonne National Laboratory (ANL).

**Eligibility**   Appointments are available for graduate students at U.S. universities who wish to carry out their thesis research under the co-sponsorship of an Argonne National Laboratory staff member and a faculty member. Research may be conducted in the basic physical and life sciences, mathematics, computer science, and engineering, as well as in a variety of applied areas relating to energy, conservation, environmental impact and technology, nanomaterials, and advanced nuclear energy systems. Applicants must be U.S. citizens or permanent residents. The laboratory encourages applications from all qualified persons, especially women and members of underrepresented minority groups.

**Financial data**   Support consists of a stipend, tuition payments up to $5,000 per year, and payment of certain travel expenses. In addition, the student's faculty sponsor may receive payment for limited travel expenses.

**Duration**   1 year; may be renewed.

**Additional information**   This program, which is also referred to as the Lab–Grad Program, is sponsored by the U.S. Department of Energy. In certain cases, students may be awarded support for pre-thesis studies on campus, provided that they intend to carry out their thesis research at Argonne.

**Number awarded**   Varies each year.

**Deadline**   Applications may be submitted at any time, but a complete application should be submitted at least 2 months prior to the proposed starting date.

## [762]
## ANN E. DICKERSON SCHOLARSHIPS

Christian Church (Disciples of Christ)
Attn: Higher Education and Leadership Ministries
11477 Olde Cabin Road, Suite 310
St. Louis, MO 63141-7130
(314) 991-3000          Fax: (314) 991-2957
E-mail: helm@helmdisciples.org
Web: www.helmdisciples.org/aid/graduate.htm

**Summary**   To provide financial assistance to female members of the Christian Church (Disciples of Christ) who are working on a Ph.D. degree in religion.

**Eligibility**   This program is open to women working on a Ph.D. degree in religion. Applicants must members of the Christian Church (Disciples of Christ). Along with their application, they must submit a 300-word essay describing their vocational goals, their academic interests, and how they envision being of service to the church.

**Financial data**   The stipend is $2,000.

**Duration**   1 year.

**Number awarded**   3 each year.

**Deadline**   April of each year.

## [763]
## ANNALEY NAEGLE REDD STUDENT AWARD IN WOMEN'S HISTORY

Brigham Young University
Attn: Charles Redd Center for Western Studies
366 Spencer W. Kimball Tower
Provo, UT 84602
(801) 422-4048          Fax: (801) 422-0035
E-mail: redd_center@byu.edu
Web: reddcenter.byu.edu/Pages/Apply-for-an-Award.aspx

**Summary**   To provide funding to undergraduate and graduate students interested in conducting research on women in the West.

**Eligibility**   This program is open to undergraduate and graduate students who are interested in conducting a research project related to women in the American West (defined as west of the Mississippi). Applicants may be proposing any kind of project, including seminar papers, theses, or dissertations. Along with their application, they must submit brief statements on the central research question and conceptual framework, how the project will increase understanding of the American West, where they plan to conduct research and the resources available there, other research that has been conducted on the topic, what makes this study and approach unique and important, the planned use of the research, and a detailed budget.

**Financial data** The grant is $1,500. Funds may be used for research support (supplies, travel, etc.) but not for salary or capital equipment.

**Duration** Normally work is to be undertaken during the summer.

**Number awarded** 1 each year.

**Deadline** March of each year.

## [764]
## ANNE C. CARTER STUDENT LEADERSHIP AWARD

American Medical Women's Association
Attn: National Student Leadership
100 North 20th Street, Fourth Floor
Philadelphia, PA 19103
(215) 320-3716                    Toll Free: (866) 564-2483
Fax: (215) 564-2175   E-mail: awards@amwa-student.org
Web: www.amwa-doc.org/students/awards-scholarships

**Summary** To recognize and reward student members of the American Medical Women's Association (AMWA) who have demonstrated exceptional leadership skills.

**Eligibility** This program is open to student members of the association who are nominated by their chapter. Nominees must have demonstrated exceptional leadership skills through vision, inspiration, innovation, and coordination of local projects that further the mission of AMWA by improving women's health and/or supporting women in medicine.

**Financial data** The award is $1,000. The nominating chapter also receives an award of $500 to be used at its discretion.

**Duration** The award is presented annually.

**Additional information** This award was first presented in 2004.

**Number awarded** 1 each year.

**Deadline** January of each year.

## [765]
## APF/COGDOP GRADUATE RESEARCH SCHOLARSHIPS

American Psychological Foundation
750 First Street, N.E.
Washington, DC 20002-4242
(202) 336-5843                    Fax: (202) 336-5812
E-mail: foundation@apa.org
Web: www.apa.org/apf/funding/cogdop.aspx

**Summary** To provide funding to graduate students (particularly women, minorities, and persons with disabilities) who are interested in conducting psychological research.

**Eligibility** Each department of psychology that is a member in good standing of the Council of Graduate Departments of Psychology (COGDOP) may nominate up to 3 candidates for these scholarships. Nominations must include a completed application form, a letter of nomination from the department chair or director of graduate studies, a letter of recommendation from the nominee's graduate research

adviser, a transcript of all graduate course work completed by the nominee, a curriculum vitae, and a brief outline of the nominee's thesis or dissertation research project. Selection is based on the context for the research, the clarity and comprehensibility of the research question, the appropriateness of the research design, the general importance of the research, and the use of requested funds. The sponsor encourages applications from individuals who represent diversity in race, ethnicity, gender, age, disability, and sexual orientation.

**Financial data** Awards range from $1,000 to $5,000 per year. A total of $28,000 is available for these scholarships each year.

**Duration** 1 year.

**Additional information** The highest rated nominees receive the Harry and Miriam Levinson Scholarship of $5,000 and the William and Dorothy Bevan Scholarship of $5,000. The next highest rated nominee receives the Ruth G. and Joseph D. Matarazzo Scholarship of $3,000. The next highest rated nominee receives the Clarence Rosecrans Scholarship of $2,000. The next highest rated nominees receive the William C. Howell Scholarship and the Peter and Malina James and Dr. Louis P. James Legacy Scholarship of $1,000 each. Another 9 scholarships of $1,000 each are also awarded.

**Number awarded** 15 each year: 2 at $5,000, 1 at $3,000, 1 at $2,000, and 11 at $1,000.

**Deadline** June of each year.

## [766]
## APPLIED COMPUTER SECURITY ASSOCIATES CYBERSECURITY SCHOLARSHIP

Society of Women Engineers
Attn: Scholarship Selection Committee
203 North LaSalle Street, Suite 1675
Chicago, IL 60601-1269
(312) 596-5223                    Toll Free: (877) SWE-INFO
Fax: (312) 644-8557        E-mail: scholarships@swe.org
Web: societyofwomenengineers.swe.org

**Summary** To provide financial assistance to women working on an undergraduate or graduate degree in a field of engineering related to cybersecurity.

**Eligibility** This program is open to women who will be juniors, seniors, or graduate students at ABET-accredited colleges and universities. Applicants must be U.S. citizens or permanent residents working full time on a degree in computer science, cybersecurity, computer security, or software engineering. They must have a GPA of 3.0 or higher and a demonstrated interest in security, as evidenced by course work, outside study, and work experience. Selection is based on merit.

**Financial data** The stipend is $10,000.

**Duration** 1 year.

**Additional information** This program, which began in 2011, is sponsored by Applied Computer Security Associates.

**Number awarded** 1 each year.

**Deadline** February of each year.

## [767]
## ARMENIAN INTERNATIONAL WOMEN'S ASSOCIATION SCHOLARSHIPS

Armenian International Women's Association
65 Main Street, Room 3A
Watertown, MA 02472
(617) 926-0171                E-mail: aiwainc@aol.com
Web: aiwainternational.org/initiatives/scholarships

**Summary**  To provide financial assistance to Armenian women who are upper-division and graduate students.

**Eligibility**  This program is open to full-time women students of Armenian descent attending an accredited college or university. Applicants must be full-time juniors, seniors, or graduate students with a GPA of 3.2 or higher. They must submit an essay, up to 500 words, describing their planned academic program, their career goals, and the reasons why they believe they should be awarded this scholarship. Selection is based on financial need and merit.

**Financial data**  Stipends are $1,000 or $500.

**Duration**  1 year.

**Additional information**  This program includes the following named scholarships: the Ethel Jafarian Duffett Scholarships, the Zarouhi Y. Getsoyan Scholarship, the Rose "Azad" Hovannesian Scholarship, the Agnes Missirian Scholarship, and the Dr. Carolann S. Najarian Scholarships.

**Number awarded**  Varies each year; recently, 15 of these scholarships were awarded: 12 at $1,000 and 3 at $500.

**Deadline**  April of each year.

## [768]
## ARMY JUDGE ADVOCATE GENERAL CORPS SUMMER INTERN PROGRAM

U.S. Army
Attn: Judge Advocate Recruiting Office
1777 North Kent Street, Suite 5200
Rosslyn, VA 22209-2194
(703) 696-2822                Toll Free: (866) ARMY-JAG
Fax: (703) 588-0100
Web: www.goarmy.com/jag/summer_intern_program.html

**Summary**  To provide law students (particularly women and minorities) with an opportunity to gain work experience during the summer in Army legal offices throughout the United States and overseas.

**Eligibility**  This program is open to full-time students enrolled in law schools accredited by the American Bar Association. Applications are accepted both from students who are completing the first year of law school and those completing the second year. Students must be interested in a summer internship with the Army Judge Advocate General's Corps (JAGC). U.S. citizenship is required. The program actively seeks applications from women and minority group members. Selection is based on academic ability and demonstrated leadership potential.

**Financial data**  Interns who have completed the first year of law school are paid at the GS-5 scale, starting at $527 per week. Interns who have completed the second year of law school are paid at the GS-7 scale, starting at $653 per week.

**Duration**  Approximately 60 days, beginning in May or June.

**Additional information**  Interns work under the supervision of an attorney and perform legal research, write briefs and opinions, conduct investigations, interview witnesses, and otherwise assist in preparing civil or criminal cases. Positions are available at Department of the Army legal offices in Washington, D.C. and at Army installations throughout the United States and overseas. These are not military positions. No military obligation is incurred by participating in the summer intern program.

**Number awarded**  100 per year: 25 first-year students and 75 second-year students.

**Deadline**  February of each year for first-year students; October of each year for second-year students.

## [769]
## ARNE ADMINISTRATIVE LEADERSHIP SCHOLARSHIP

Women of the Evangelical Lutheran Church in America
Attn: Scholarships
8765 West Higgins Road
Chicago, IL 60631-4101
(773) 380-2741                Toll Free: (800) 638-3522, ext. 2741
Fax: (773) 380-2419          E-mail: women.elca@elca.org
Web: www.womenoftheelca.org/scholarships-pages-57.php

**Summary**  To provide financial assistance to women members of congregations of the Evangelical Lutheran Church of America (ELCA) who wish to train for administrative positions.

**Eligibility**  This program is open to women members of the ELCA who have completed a bachelor's degree or its equivalent and have taken some academic or professional courses since completing that degree. Applicants must have been admitted to an academic institution as a full-time student to take regular classes, night courses, or summer session. U.S. citizenship is required. Selection is based on records of graduate academic or professional courses, examples of being a decision-maker, and evidence of ability and willingness to study.

**Financial data**  The maximum stipend is $2,000.

**Duration**  Up to 2 years.

**Additional information**  This program began in 1998.

**Number awarded**  Varies each year.

**Deadline**  February of each year.

## [770]
## ARTTABLE MENTORED INTERNSHIPS FOR DIVERSITY IN THE VISUAL ARTS PROFESSIONS

ArtTable Inc.
137 Varick Street, Suite 402
New York, NY 10013
(212) 343-1735, ext. 24          Fax: (866) 363-4188
E-mail: ebround@arttable.org
Web: www.arttable.org

**Summary**  To provide an opportunity for women who are from diverse backgrounds to gain mentored work experience during the summer and to prepare for a career as an art professional.

**Eligibility**  This program is open to women who are college seniors, recent graduates, or graduate students and interested in preparing for a career as a visual arts professional (including administrative director, art adviser, art appraiser, art critic, art dealer, art librarian, arts funder, arts lawyer, conservator, curator, editor, educator, fundraiser, management consultant, public relations consultant, writer). Applicants must be from a cultural or ethnic background that is underrepresented in the field. They must be interested in working during the summer with a mentor at an art museum or similar facility. U.S. citizenship or permanent resident status is required.

**Financial data** The stipend is $3,000. The hosting institution or mentor receives $500 for administrative and other costs.

**Duration** 8 weeks during the summer.

**Additional information** This program began in 2000.

**Number awarded** Varies each year; recently, 4 of these internships were awarded.

**Deadline** February of each year.

## [771]
## ASME GRADUATE TEACHING FELLOWSHIP

ASME International
Attn: Centers Administrator
Two Park Avenue
New York, NY 10016-5675
(212) 591-8131          Toll Free: (800) THE-ASME
Fax: (212) 591-7143      E-mail: LefeverB@asme.org
Web: www.asme.org

**Summary** To provide funding to members of the American Society of Mechanical Engineers (ASME), particularly women and minorities, who are working on a doctorate in mechanical engineering.

**Eligibility** This program is open to U.S. citizens or permanent residents who have an undergraduate degree from an ABET-accredited program, belong to the society as a student member, are currently employed as a teaching assistant with lecture responsibility, and are working on a Ph.D. in mechanical engineering. Along with their application, they must submit a statement about their interest in a faculty career. Applications from women and minorities are particularly encouraged.

**Financial data** Fellowship stipends are $5,000 per year.

**Duration** Up to 2 years.

**Additional information** Recipients must teach at least 1 lecture course.

**Number awarded** Up to 4 each year.

**Deadline** February of each year.

## [772]
## ASPA SPECIAL FUND FOR THE STUDY OF WOMEN AND POLITICS

American Political Science Association
Attn: Centennial Center Visiting Scholars Program
1527 New Hampshire Avenue, N.W.
Washington, DC 20036-1206
(202) 483-2512          Fax: (202) 483-2657
E-mail: center@apsanet.org
Web: www.apsanet.org/content_3471.cfm

**Summary** To provide funding to members of the American Political Science Association (APSA) who are interested in conducting research on women and politics at the Centennial Center for Political Science and Public Affairs.

**Eligibility** This program is open to members of the association who are interested in conducting research on women and politics while in residence at the center. Junior faculty

members, postdoctoral fellows, and advanced graduate students are strongly encouraged to apply, but scholars at all stages of their careers are eligible. International applicants are also welcome if they have demonstrable command of spoken English. Non-resident scholars may also be eligible.

**Financial data** Grants provide supplemental financial support to resident scholars.

**Duration** 2 weeks to 12 months.

**Additional information** The APSA launched its Centennial Center for Political Science and Public Affairs in 2003 to commemorate the centennial year of the association.

**Number awarded** 1 or more each year.

**Deadline** February, June, or October of each year.

## [773]
## ASSE DIVERSITY COMMITTEE SCHOLARSHIP

American Society of Safety Engineers
Attn: ASSE Foundation
Scholarship Award Program
1800 East Oakton Street
Des Plaines, IL 60018
(847) 699-2929          Fax: (847) 768-3434
E-mail: bzylstra@asse.org
Web: www.asse.org

**Summary** To provide financial assistance to women and other upper-division and graduate students working on a degree related to occupational safety who come from diverse groups.

**Eligibility** This program is open to students who are working on an undergraduate or graduate degree in occupational safety, health, environment, industrial hygiene, occupational health nursing, or a closely-related field (e.g., industrial or environmental engineering). Applicants must be full-time students who have completed at least 60 semester hours with a GPA of 3.0 or higher as undergraduates or at least 9 semester hours as graduate students. A goal of this program is to encourage diversity within the field. U.S. citizenship is not required. Membership in the American Society of Safety Engineers (ASSE) is not required, but preference is given to members.

**Financial data** The stipend is $1,000 per year.

**Duration** 1 year; recipients may reapply.

**Number awarded** 1 each year.

**Deadline** November of each year.

## [774]
## ASSOCIATION FOR FEMINIST ANTHROPOLOGY DISSERTATION AWARD

American Anthropological Association
Attn: Association for Feminist Anthropology
2200 Wilson Boulevard, Suite 600
Arlington, VA 22201-3357
(703) 528-1902          Fax: (703) 528-3546
Web: www.aaanet.org/sections/afa/?page_id=111

**Summary** To provide funding to doctoral candidates completing a dissertation on a topic related to feminist anthropology.

**Eligibility** This program is open to doctoral candidates who are in the writing phase of a dissertation that makes a significant contribution to feminist anthropology. Applicants must be members of the Association for Feminist Anthropology (AFA) of the American Anthropological Association. They may be working in any of the subfields of anthropology (archaeology, biological anthropology, cultural anthropology, or linguistics).

**Financial data** The grant is $2,000.

**Duration** 1 year.

**Number awarded** 1 each year.

**Deadline** April of each year.

## [775]
## ASSOCIATION FOR WOMEN IN SPORTS MEDIA SCHOLARSHIP/INTERNSHIP PROGRAM

Association for Women in Sports Media
Attn: Scholarship and Internship Coordinator
161 West Sylvania Avenue
Neptune City, NJ 07753
E-mail: lindsay.jones@awsmonline.org
Web: awsmonline.org/internship-scholarship

**Summary** To provide financial assistance and work experience to women undergraduate and graduate students who are interested in preparing for a career in sports writing.

**Eligibility** This program is open to women who are enrolled in college or graduate school full time and preparing for a career in sports writing, sports copy editing, sports broadcasting, or sports public relations. Applicants must submit a 750-word essay describing their most memorable experience in sports or sports media, a 1-page resume highlighting their journalism experience, a letter of recommendation, up to 5 samples of their work, and a $20 application fee. They must apply for and accept an internship with a sports media organization.

**Financial data** Winners receive a stipend up to $1,000 and placement in a paid internship.

**Duration** 1 year; nonrenewable.

**Additional information** This program, which began in 1990, includes the Jackie and Gene Autry Memorial Scholarship, the Jim Brennan Scholarship, the Betty Brennan Scholarship, the Mike Roberts Memorial Scholarship, the Katie Jackson Morrison Memorial Scholarship, and the Leah Siegel Scholarship.

**Number awarded** Varies each year; recently, 6 students received support from this program.

**Deadline** October of each year.

## [776]
## ASSOCIATION FOR WOMEN LAWYERS FOUNDATION SCHOLARSHIPS

Association for Women Lawyers
Attn: AWL Foundation
3322 North 92nd Street
Milwaukee, WI 53222
(414) 750-4404                    Fax: (414) 255-3615
E-mail: associationforwomenlawyers@gmail.com
Web: awl.memberlodge.org/scholarships

**Summary** To provide financial assistance to women who are attending law school in Wisconsin.

**Eligibility** This program is open to women from any state currently enrolled at law schools in Wisconsin. Applicants must be able to demonstrate academic achievement, service to others, diversity, unique life experience or circumstance, commitment to advancement of women in the profession, and financial need.

**Financial data** The stipend varies; recently, awards averaged $2,500.

**Duration** 1 year.

**Additional information** This program began in 1998.

**Number awarded** Varies each year; recently, 2 of these scholarships were awarded.

**Deadline** June of each year.

## [777]
## AUTOMOTIVE WOMEN'S ALLIANCE FOUNDATION SCHOLARSHIPS

Automotive Women's Alliance Foundation
Attn: Scholarship
P.O. Box 4305
Troy, MI 48099
Toll Free: (877) 393-AWAF          Fax: (248) 239-0291
E-mail: admin@AWAFoundation.org
Web: www.awafoundation.org/pages/Scholarships

**Summary** To provide financial assistance to women who are interested in attending college or graduate school to prepare for a career in the automotive industry.

**Eligibility** This program is open to women who are entering or enrolled in an undergraduate or graduate program that will prepare them for a career in the automotive industry. Applicants must be citizens of Canada or the United States. They must have a GPA of 3.0 or higher. Along with their application, they must submit a 1-page cover letter explaining their automotive-related career aspirations.

**Financial data** The stipend is $2,500.

**Duration** 1 year.

**Additional information** This program began in 2001.

**Number awarded** Varies each year; recently, 5 of these scholarships were awarded.

**Deadline** Deadline not specified.

## [778]
## BANNER ENGINEERING MINNESOTA SWE SCHOLARSHIP

Society of Women Engineers-Minnesota Section
Attn: Scholarship Committee
P.O. Box 582813
Minneapolis, MN 55458-2813
E-mail: scholarships@swe-mn.org
Web: www.swe-mn.org/scholarships.html

**Summary** To provide financial assistance to women from any state working on an undergraduate or graduate degree in electrical or mechanical engineering at colleges and universities in Minnesota, North Dakota, and South Dakota.

**Eligibility** This program is open to female undergraduate and graduate students at ABET-accredited engineering programs in Minnesota, North Dakota, or South Dakota. Applicants must be working full time on a degree in electrical or mechanical engineering. Along with their application, they must submit a short paragraph describing how they plan to utilize their engineering skills after they graduate. Selection is based on potential to succeed as an engineer (20 points), communication skills (10 points), extracurricular or community involvement and leadership skills (10 points), demonstrated successful work experience (10 points), and academic success (5 points).

**Financial data** The stipend is $2,000.

**Duration**   1 year.

**Additional information**   This program is sponsored by Banner Engineering Corporation.

**Number awarded**   1 each year.

**Deadline**   March of each year.

## [779]
## BAPTIST WOMEN IN MINISTRY OF NORTH CAROLINA STUDENT SCHOLARSHIPS

Baptist Women in Ministry of North Carolina
c/o Luelle Crumpler
1808 Ellison Creek Road
Lewisville, NC 27023
Web: www.bwimnc.org/Scholarships.html

**Summary**   To provide financial assistance to women ministerial students enrolled at a North Carolina Baptist institution.

**Eligibility**   This program is open to women working on a graduate degree in theological education at North Carolina Baptist institutions. Applicants must be able to demonstrate a clear call and commitment to vocational Christian ministry, academic excellence, leadership skills, and expressed support of inclusiveness in all dimensions of life.

**Financial data**   The stipend is $1,000.

**Duration**   1 year.

**Additional information**   The eligible schools include Duke Divinity School, Campbell University Divinity School, M. Christopher White School of Divinity at Gardner-Webb University, and the Wake Forest University Divinity School.

**Number awarded**   4 each year: 1 at each of the eligible schools.

**Deadline**   Deadline not specified.

## [780]
## BARBARA ALICE MOWER MEMORIAL SCHOLARSHIP

Barbara Alice Mower Memorial Scholarship Committee
c/o Nancy A. Mower
1536 Kamole Street
Honolulu, HI 96821-1424
(808) 373-2901          E-mail: nmower@hawaii.edu

**Summary**   To provide financial assistance to female residents of Hawaii who are interested in women's studies and are attending college on the undergraduate or graduate level in the United States or abroad.

**Eligibility**   This program is open to female residents of Hawaii who are at least juniors in college, are interested in and committed to women's studies, and have worked or studied in the field. Selection is based on interest in studying about and commitment to helping women, previous work and/or study in that area, previous academic performance, character, personality, and future plans to help women (particularly women in Hawaii). If there are several applicants who meet all these criteria, then financial need may be taken into consideration.

**Financial data**   The stipend ranges from $1,000 to $3,500.

**Duration**   1 year; may be renewed.

**Additional information**   Recipients may use the scholarship at universities in Hawaii, on the mainland, or in foreign countries. They must focus on women's studies or topics that relate to women in school.

**Number awarded**   1 or more each year.

**Deadline**   April of each year.

## [781]
## BARBARA GIBSON FROEMMING SCHOLARSHIP

Kappa Delta Sorority
Attn: Foundation Project Manager
3205 Players Lane
Memphis, TN 38125
(901) 748-1897, ext. 203          Toll Free: (800) 536-1897
Fax: (901) 748-0949
E-mail: caroline.cullum@kappadelta.org
Web: www.kappadelta.org/scholarshipapplications_1

**Summary**   To provide financial assistance to members of Kappa Delta Sorority who are working on a graduate degree in education.

**Eligibility**   This program is open to graduate members of Kappa Delta Sorority. Applicants must submit a personal statement giving their reasons for applying for this scholarship, official undergraduate and graduate transcripts, and 2 letters of recommendation. They must be working on a graduate degree in education. Selection is based on academic excellence; service to the chapter, alumnae association, or national Kappa Delta; service to the campus and community; personal objectives and goals; potential; recommendations; and financial need.

**Financial data**   The stipend is $2,000 per year. Funds may be used only for tuition, fees, and books, not for room and board.

**Duration**   1 year; may be renewed.

**Additional information**   This program began in 2007.

**Number awarded**   1 each year.

**Deadline**   November of each year.

## [782]
## BARBARA MCBRIDE SCHOLARSHIP

Society of Exploration Geophysicists
Attn: SEG Foundation
8801 South Yale, Suite 500
P.O. Box 702740
Tulsa, OK 74170-2740
(918) 497-5500          Fax: (918) 497-5557
E-mail: scholarships@seg.org
Web: www.seg.org/web/foundation/programs/scholarship

**Summary**   To provide financial assistance to women who are interested in studying applied geophysics or a related field on the undergraduate or graduate school level.

**Eligibility**   This program is open to women who are 1) high school students planning to enter college in the fall; or 2) undergraduate or graduate students whose grades are above average. Applicants must intend to work on a degree directed toward a career in applied geophysics or a closely-related field (e.g., energy, environmental sciences, geology, geoscience, mathematics, physics, or seismology). Along with their application, they must submit a 150-word essay on how they plan to use geophysics in their future. Financial need is not considered in the selection process.

**Financial data**   Stipends provided by this sponsor average $3,000 per year.

**Duration** 1 academic year; may be renewable, based on scholastic standing, availability of funds, and continuance of a course of study leading to a career in applied geophysics.

**Number awarded** 1 each year.

**Deadline** February of each year.

## [783]
## BARBARA ROSENBLUM CANCER DISSERTATION SCHOLARSHIP

Sociologists for Women in Society
Attn: Executive Officer
Southern Connecticut State University
Department of Sociology
501 Crescent Street
New Haven, CT 06515
(203) 392-7714                    Fax: (203) 392-7715
E-mail: swseo@socwomen.org
Web: www.socwomen.org/awards.html

**Summary** To provide funding to women interested in conducting doctoral research on the social science aspects of women and cancer.

**Eligibility** This program is open to women doctoral students with a feminist orientation who are interested in studying breast cancer and its impact on diverse groups of women, including those of diverse social classes and cultural backgrounds, socioeconomic status, sexual orientation, language, religion, geographical area, and other cultural perspectives. The research may be conducted in the areas of sociology, anthropology, psychology, or other social science fields concerned with women's experiences with breast cancer and the prevention of breast cancer. Priority is given to research that is not only useful academically but will have pragmatic and practical applications.

**Financial data** The grant is $1,500.

**Duration** 1 year.

**Additional information** This program began in 1991.

**Number awarded** 1 each year.

**Deadline** March of each year.

## [784]
## BASIC MIDWIFERY STUDENT SCHOLARSHIPS

American College of Nurse-Midwives
Attn: ACNM Foundation, Inc.
8403 Colesville Road, Suite 1550
Silver Spring, MD 20910-6374
(240) 485-1850                    Fax: (240) 485-1818
E-mail: fdn@acnm.org
Web: www.midwife.org

**Summary** To provide financial assistance for midwifery education to student members of the American College of Nurse-Midwives (ACNM).

**Eligibility** This program is open to ACNM members who are currently enrolled in an accredited basic midwife education program and have successfully completed 1 academic or clinical semester/quarter or clinical module. Applicants must submit a 150-word essay on their midwifery career plans and a 100-word essay on their intended future participation in the local, regional, and/or national activities of the ACNM. Selection is based on leadership potential, financial need, academic history, and potential for future professional contribution to the organization.

**Financial data** The stipend is $3,000.

**Duration** 1 year.

**Number awarded** Varies each year; recently, 4 of these scholarships were awarded.

**Deadline** March of each year.

## [785]
## BENTON-MEIER NEUROPSYCHOLOGY SCHOLARSHIPS

American Psychological Foundation
750 First Street, N.E.
Washington, DC 20002-4242
(202) 336-5843                    Fax: (202) 336-5812
E-mail: foundation@apa.org
Web: www.apa.org/apf/funding/benton-meier.aspx

**Summary** To provide research funding to graduate students (particularly women, minorities, and persons with disabilities) who are completing a dissertation related to neuropsychology.

**Eligibility** This program is open to students who have been admitted to candidacy for a doctoral degree in the area of neuropsychology. Applicants must submit statements documenting their research competence and area commitment, a budget and justification, and how the scholarship money will be used. Selection is based on conformance with stated program goals and the applicant's demonstrated scholarship and research competence. The sponsor encourages applications from individuals who represent diversity in race, ethnicity, gender, age, disability, and sexual orientation.

**Financial data** The grant is $2,500.

**Duration** 1 year.

**Additional information** This program replaces the Henry Hécaen Scholarship, first awarded in 1994, and the Manfred Meier Scholarship, first awarded in 1997.

**Number awarded** 2 each year.

**Deadline** May of each year.

## [786]
## BERKSHIRE CONFERENCE OF WOMEN HISTORIANS GRADUATE STUDENT FELLOWSHIP

Coordinating Council for Women in History
c/o Sandra Dawson, Executive Director
Northern Illinois University
Department of History and Women's Studies
715 Zulauf Hall
DeKalb, IL 60115
(815) 895-2624                    E-mail: execdir@theccwh.org
Web: theccwh.org/ccwh-awards

**Summary** To provide funding to women graduate students in history for completion of their doctoral dissertations.

**Eligibility** This program is open to women graduate students in history departments at U.S. institutions who are members of the Coordinating Council for Women in History (CCWH). Applicants must have passed to A.B.D. status. They may be specializing in any field of history.

**Financial data** The grant is $1,000.

**Duration** 1 year.

**Additional information** This program, established in 1991, is administered by the CCWH and the Berkshire Conference of Women Historians. The award is presented at the CCWH luncheon at the annual meeting of the American Historical Association, although the recipient does not need to be present to accept the award.

**Number awarded** 1 each year.

**Deadline** September of each year.

## [787]
## BERNICE F. ELLIOTT MEMORIAL SCHOLARSHIP

Baptist Convention of New Mexico
Attn: Missions Mobilization Team WMU
5325 Wyoming Boulevard, N.E.
P.O. Box 94485
Albuquerque, NM 87199-4485
(505) 924-2316          Toll Free: (800) 898-8544
Fax: (505) 924-2320          E-mail: ktreece@bcnm.com
Web: www.bcnm.com

**Summary** To provide financial assistance to women who are Southern Baptists from New Mexico and interested in attending a college or seminary in any state.

**Eligibility** This program is open to women college and seminary students who are members of churches affiliated with the Baptist Convention of New Mexico. Preference is given to applicants who are committed to full-time Christian service, have a background in the Woman's Missionary Union, and can demonstrate financial need.

**Financial data** A stipend is awarded (amount not specified).

**Duration** 1 year; may be renewed.

**Number awarded** 1 or more each year.

**Deadline** March of each year.

## [788]
## BESSIE BELLAMY PARKER SCHOLARSHIPS

South Carolina United Methodist Foundation
P.O. Box 5087
Columbia, SC 29250-5087
(803) 771-9125          Fax: (803) 771-9135
E-mail: scumf@bellsouth.net
Web: www.umcsc.org

**Summary** To provide financial assistance to female Methodist seminary students from South Carolina.

**Eligibility** This program is open to women from South Carolina who are certified candidates for ministry in the United Methodist Church. Applicants must have completed at least 1 year of full-time enrollment in an approved United Methodist seminary with a grade average of "C" or higher. They must be planning to work in a local church setting. Selection is based (in descending order of importance) on self-understanding of ministry and intended future direction, promise for ministry, financial need, and academic performance in seminary.

**Financial data** A stipend is awarded (amount not specified).

**Duration** 1 year.

**Additional information** This scholarship was established by the South Carolina Conference of the United Methodist Church in 1986.

**Number awarded** 1 or more each year.

**Deadline** March of each year.

## [789]
## BETSY B. AND GAROLD A. LEACH
## SCHOLARSHIP FOR MUSEUM STUDIES

Delta Zeta Sorority
Attn: Foundation Coordinator
202 East Church Street
Oxford, OH 45056
(513) 523-7597          Fax: (513) 523-1921
E-mail: DZFoundation@dzshq.com
Web: www.deltazeta.org

**Summary** To provide financial assistance to members of Delta Zeta Sorority working on an undergraduate or graduate degree to prepare for a career in museum work.

**Eligibility** This program is open to upper-division and graduate members of the sorority who have a GPA of 3.0 or higher. Applicants must be working on a degree in a field that will prepare them for a career in museum work, including library science, archaeology, geology, or art history. Along with their application, they must submit an official transcript, a statement of their career goals, information on their service to the sorority, documentation of campus activities and/or community involvement, a list of academic honors, and an explanation of their financial need.

**Financial data** The stipend ranges from $500 to $2,500 for undergraduates or from $1,000 to $15,000 for graduate students, depending on the availability of funds.

**Duration** 1 year; nonrenewable.

**Number awarded** 1 each year.

**Deadline** February of each year.

## [790]
## BETTY HANSEN NATIONAL SCHOLARSHIPS

Danish Sisterhood of America
c/o Connie Schell, Scholarship Chair
246 Foster Road
Fort Covington, NY 12937
(518) 358-4686          E-mail: cschell4dss@aol.com
Web: www.danishsisterhood.org/DanishHTML/rschol.asp

**Summary** To provide financial assistance for educational purposes in the United States or Denmark to members or relatives of members of the Danish Sisterhood of America.

**Eligibility** This program is open to members or the family of members of the sisterhood who are interested in attending an accredited 4-year college or university as a full-time undergraduate or graduate student. Members must have belonged to the sisterhood for at least 1 year. They must have a GPA of 2.5 or higher. Selection is based on academics (including ACT or SAT scores), academic awards or honors, other special recognition and awards, employment record, special talents or hobbies, and participation in Danish Sisterhood and other civic activities. Upon written request, the scholarship may be used for study in Denmark.

**Financial data** The stipend is $1,000.

**Duration** 1 year; nonrenewable.

**Number awarded** Up to 8 each year.

**Deadline** February of each year.

## [791]
## BETTY LOU BAILEY SWE REGION F SCHOLARSHIP

Society of Women Engineers
Attn: Scholarship Selection Committee
203 North LaSalle Street, Suite 1675
Chicago, IL 60601-1269
(312) 596-5223                    Toll Free: (877) SWE-INFO
Fax: (312) 644-8557          E-mail: scholarships@swe.org
Web: societyofwomenengineers.swe.org

**Summary**   To provide financial assistance to members of the Society of Women Engineers (SWE) working on an undergraduate or graduate degree in engineering or computer science at a school in its Region F (states in New England and upstate New York).

**Eligibility**   This program is open to members of the society who will be sophomores, juniors, seniors, or graduate students at ABET-accredited colleges and universities. First preference is given to applicants who attend college or graduate school in the New England states or upstate New York; second preference is given to students who reside in New England or upstate New York. Applicants must be working full time on a degree in computer science or engineering and have a GPA of 3.0 or higher. Financial need is considered in the selection process. U.S. citizenship or permanent resident status is required.

**Financial data**   The stipend is $1,500.

**Duration**   1 year.

**Number awarded**   1 each year.

**Deadline**   February of each year.

## [792]
## BISHOP FRANK MURPHY SCHOLARSHIP FOR WOMEN IN MINISTRY

Women's Ordination Conference
Attn: Scholarship Committee
P.O. Box 15057
Washington, DC 20003
(202) 675-1006                         Fax: (202) 675-1008
E-mail: woc@womensordination.org
Web: www.womensordination.org/content/view/38/66

**Summary**   To provide financial assistance to members of the Women's Ordination Conference (WOC) who are working on a graduate degree to prepare for Catholic ministry.

**Eligibility**   This program is open to women who are members of the WOC. Applicants must be enrolled or accepted in a graduate program at a seminary or a diocesan certificate program preparing for Catholic priestly ministry. They must submit a letter of recommendation from a mentor who can testify to their commitment to WOC's goals, a personal statement of how their future ministry supports WOC's mission, a resume or curriculum vitae, and proof of enrollment.

**Financial data**   The stipend is $1,000. Funds must be used for educational expenses.

**Duration**   1 year.

**Additional information**   The WOC is an organization "working locally and nationally in collaboration with the worldwide movement for women's ordination." In pursuit of its goals, it "works for justice and equality for women in our church; strives to eliminate all forms of domination and discrimination in the Catholic church; advocates inclusive church structures; supports and affirms women's talents, gifts and calls to ministry." Recipients are required to submit a report at the end of the grant period explaining how the award impacted their study and growth.

**Number awarded**   1 or 2 each year.

**Deadline**   January of each year.

## [793]
## B.J. DEAN SCHOLARSHIP

Community Foundation of Middle Tennessee
Attn: Scholarship Committee
3833 Cleghorn Avenue, Suite 400
Nashville, TN 37215-2519
(615) 321-4939                    Toll Free: (888) 540-5200
Fax: (615) 327-2746          E-mail: grants@cfmt.org
Web: www.cfmt.org/request/scholarships/allscholarships

**Summary**   To provide financial assistance to women from Tennessee or Texas preparing for a career in the ministry at a seminary in any state.

**Eligibility**   This program is open to women from Tennessee or Texas interested in entering the ministry; students enrolled at Yale Divinity School are also eligible. Applicants must be preparing for full-time ministry but not necessarily seeking ordination. They must be planning to enroll full time at a seminary in any state. There are no denominational restrictions. Along with their application, they must submit an essay describing their educational plans and how those plans will help them reach their career goals. Financial need is considered in the selection process.

**Financial data**   Stipends range from $500 to $2,500 per year. Funds are paid to the recipient's school and must be used for tuition, fees, books, supplies, room, board, or miscellaneous expenses.

**Duration**   1 year; recipients may reapply.

**Additional information**   This program began in 1995.

**Number awarded**   1 or more each year.

**Deadline**   March of each year.

## [794]
## B.K. KRENZER MEMORIAL REENTRY SCHOLARSHIP

Society of Women Engineers
Attn: Scholarship Selection Committee
203 North LaSalle Street, Suite 1675
Chicago, IL 60601-1269
(312) 596-5223                    Toll Free: (877) SWE-INFO
Fax: (312) 644-8557          E-mail: scholarships@swe.org
Web: societyofwomenengineers.swe.org

**Summary**   To provide financial assistance to women interested in returning to college or graduate school to study engineering or computer science.

**Eligibility**   This program is open to women who are planning to enroll at an ABET-accredited 4-year college or university. Applicants must have been out of the engineering workforce and school for at least 2 years and must be planning to return as an undergraduate or graduate student to work on a degree in computer science or engineering. They must have a GPA of 3.0 or higher. Selection is based on merit. Preference is given to engineers who already have a degree and are planning to reenter the engineering workforce after a period of temporary retirement.

**Financial data**   The stipend is $2,000.

**Duration**   1 year.

**Additional information**   This program began in 1996.

**Number awarded**   1 each year.

**Deadline**   February of each year.

## [795]
## BLACK WOMEN IN ENTERTAINMENT LAW STUDENT SCHOLARSHIP

Black Women in Entertainment Law
Attn: Monica Andralliski
110 West 40th Street, Suite 900
New York, NY 10018
(212) 986-6262
Web: www.bwelfoundation.org/scholarships.html

**Summary**   To provide financial assistance to women of color who are enrolled in law school and have an interest in entertainment law.

**Eligibility**   This program is open to women of color who have completed at least 1 semester of law school as a full- or part-time student. Applicants must list the entertainment law courses they have taken and write a 1,500-word essay on a question related to entertainment law. They must have a GPA of 2.5 or higher. Financial need is considered in the selection process.

**Financial data**   Stipends are $4,000 and $2,000.

**Duration**   1 year.

**Number awarded**   2 each year: 1 at $4,000 and 1 at $2,000.

**Deadline**   April of each year.

## [796]
## BOBBIE BURK CONDUCTING SCHOLARSHIP FOR GRADUATE STUDENTS

Sigma Alpha Iota Philanthropies, Inc.
One Tunnel Road
Asheville, NC 28805
(828) 251-0606                Fax: (828) 251-0644
E-mail: nh@sai-national.org
Web: www.sai-national.org

**Summary**   To provide financial assistance to members of Sigma Alpha Iota (an organization of women musicians) who are working on a graduate degree in conducting.

**Eligibility**   This program is open to members of the organization who are currently enrolled in a graduate degree program with an emphasis on conducting. Applicants must include a videotape of a performance they conducted.

**Financial data**   The stipend is $2,500.

**Duration**   1 year.

**Number awarded**   1 each year.

**Deadline**   March of each year.

## [797]
## BOSTON AFFILIATE AWSCPA SCHOLARSHIP

American Woman's Society of Certified Public
  Accountants-Boston Affiliate
c/o Andrea Costantino
Oxford Bioscience Partners
222 Berkeley Street, Suite 1650
Boston, MA 02116
(617) 357-7474                E-mail: acostantino@oxbio.com
Web: www.awscpa.org/affiliate_scholarships/boston.html

**Summary**   To provide financial assistance to women from any state who are working on an undergraduate or graduate degree in accounting at a college or university in New England.

**Eligibility**   This program is open to women from any state who are attending a college in New England and majoring in accounting. Applicants must have completed at least 12 semester hours of accounting or tax courses and have a cumulative GPA of 3.0 or higher. They must be planning to graduate between May of next year and May of the following year or, for the 15-month graduate program, before September of the current year. Along with their application, they must submit a brief essay on why they feel they would be a good choice for this award. Selection is based on that essay, academic achievement, work experience, extracurricular activities, scholastic honors, career plans, and financial need.

**Financial data**   The stipend is $1,000.

**Duration**   1 year.

**Number awarded**   2 each year.

**Deadline**   September of each year.

## [798]
## BOSTON CHAPTER/CLAIRE BARRETT MEMORIAL SCHOLARSHIP

Women's Transportation Seminar-Boston Chapter
c/o Denise Bartone
CDW Consultants, Inc.
40 Speen Street, Suite 301
Framingham, MA 01701
(508) 875-2657   E-mail: dbartone@cdwconsultants.com
Web: www.wtsinternational.org/boston/scholarships

**Summary**   To provide financial assistance to women from any state who have an interest in public policy issues and are working on a transportation-related graduate degree at a college or university in Massachusetts.

**Eligibility**   This program is open to women enrolled at colleges and universities in Massachusetts who are working on a graduate degree in a transportation-related field, including transportation engineering, planning, finance, or logistics. Applicants must be able to demonstrate 1) plans to prepare for a career in a transportation-related field; 2) excellent communication skills; 3) a belief in the power of public dialogue in communicating and improving the goals of public institutions and public projects; and 4) current involvement in a research or thesis project that incorporates use of public transportation, environmental awareness, use of public art, awareness of diversity, and use of landscape architecture. Along with their application, they must submit a 750-word personal statement about their career goals after graduation and why they think they should receive this scholarship. Selection is based on the applicant's specific transportation involvement and goals, job skills, and academic record. Minority women are especially encouraged to apply.

**Financial data** The stipend is $4,000.

**Duration** 1 year.

**Additional information** This program began in 2005.

**Number awarded** 1 or more each year.

**Deadline** November of each year.

## [799]
## C200 SCHOLAR AWARDS

Committee of 200
Attn: C200 Foundation
980 North Michigan Avenue, Suite 1575
Chicago, IL 60611-7540
(312) 255-0296                    Fax: (312) 255-0789
E-mail: info@c200.org
Web: www.c200.org/foundation/scholarOutreach.aspx

**Summary** To provide financial assistance to women working on an M.B.A. degree at universities that host outreach seminars conducted by the Committee of 200 (C200).

**Eligibility** Twice each year, C200 co-sponsors 1-day outreach seminars for women M.B.A. students. Seminars rotate among the outstanding business schools in the country. These scholarships are available to first-year women students at each of the schools where a seminar is held. The schools select finalists on the basis of work experience, GPA, recommendations, and essays. Members of C200 interview the finalists and select the winners.

**Financial data** The stipend is $10,000.

**Duration** 1 year.

**Additional information** Scholars also receive an internship at a C200 member's company.

**Number awarded** 3 each year.

**Deadline** Deadline not specified.

## [800]
## CALIFORNIA P.E.O. SELECTED SCHOLARSHIPS

P.E.O. Foundation-California State Chapter
c/o Lynne Miller, Scholarship Committee Chair
1875 Los Altos
Clovis, CA 93611
(559) 709-6123                    E-mail: peoca.rgw@gmail.com
Web: www.peocalifornia.org

**Summary** To provide financial assistance to female residents of California attending college or graduate school in any state.

**Eligibility** This program is open to female residents of California who have completed 4 years of high school (or the equivalent); are enrolled at or accepted by an accredited college, university, vocational school, or graduate school in any state; and have an excellent academic record. Selection is based on financial need, character, academic ability, and school and community activities. Some awards include additional requirements.

**Financial data** Stipends recently ranged from $400 to $2,500.

**Duration** 1 year; may be renewed for up to 3 additional years.

**Additional information** This program includes the following named scholarships: the Barbara Furse Mackey Scholar-

ship (for women whose education has been interrupted); the Beverly Dye Anderson Scholarship (for the fields of teaching or health care); the Marjorie M. McDonald P.E.O. Scholarship (for women who are continuing their education after a long hiatus from school); the Ora Keck Scholarship (for women who are preparing for a career in music or the fine arts); the Phyllis J. Van Deventer Scholarship (for women who are preparing for a career in music performance or music education); the Jean Gower Scholarship (for women preparing for a career in education); the Helen D. Thompson Memorial Scholarship (for women studying music or fine arts); the Stella May Nau Scholarship (for women who are interested in reentering the job market); the Linda Jones Memorial Fine Arts Scholarship (for women studying fine arts); the Polly Thompson Memorial Music Scholarship (for women studying music); the Ruby W. Henry Scholarship; the Jean W. Gratiot Scholarship; the Pearl Prime Scholarship; the Helen Beardsley Scholarship; the Chapter GA Scholarship; and the Nearly New Scholarship.

**Number awarded** Varies each year; recently, 43 of these scholarships were awarded.

**Deadline** January of each year.

## [801]
## CAROL STEPHENS REGION F SCHOLARSHIP

Society of Women Engineers
Attn: Scholarship Selection Committee
203 North LaSalle Street, Suite 1675
Chicago, IL 60601-1269
(312) 596-5223                    Toll Free: (877) SWE-INFO
Fax: (312) 644-8557               E-mail: scholarships@swe.org
Web: societyofwomenengineers.swe.org

**Summary** To provide financial assistance to members of the Society of Women Engineers (SWE) working on an undergraduate or graduate degree in engineering or computer science at a school in its Region F (New England states and eastern New York).

**Eligibility** This program is open to members of the society who will be sophomores, juniors, seniors, or graduate students at ABET-accredited colleges and universities. First preference is given to applicants who attend college or graduate school in the New England states or upstate New York; second preference is given to students who reside in New England or upstate New York. Applicants must be working full time on a degree in computer science or engineering and have a GPA of 3.0 or higher. Financial need is considered in the selection process. U.S. citizenship or permanent resident status is required.

**Financial data** The stipend is $1,000.

**Duration** 1 year.

**Number awarded** 1 each year.

**Deadline** February of each year.

## [802]
## CAROL TYLER AWARD

International Precious Metals Institute
5101 North 12th Avenue, Suite C
Pensacola, FL 32504
(850) 476-1156                    Fax: (850) 476-1548
E-mail: mail@ipmi.org
Web: www.ipmi.org/awards/index.cfm

**Summary** To recognize and reward women graduate students, professionals, and postdoctorates who have a record of outstanding achievement in the science and technology of precious metals.

**Eligibility** This award is available to women who are graduate students or currently employed in industry or academia. Nominees must have made outstanding theoretical and experimental contributions to the science and technology of precious metals. They may be residents of any country.

**Financial data** The award is $5,000 and a certificate.

**Duration** The award is presented annually.

**Additional information** This award was first presented in 2011.

**Number awarded** 1 each year.

**Deadline** January of each year.

## [803]
## CAROL WILLIAMS-NICKELSON AWARD FOR WOMEN'S LEADERSHIP AND SCHOLARSHIP IN WOMEN'S ISSUES

American Psychological Association
Attn: American Psychological Association of Graduate
  Students
750 First Street, N.E.
Washington, DC 20002-4242
(202) 336-6014          Fax: (202) 336-5694
E-mail: apags@apa.org
Web: www.apa.org

**Summary** To recognize and reward female psychology doctoral students who are members of the American Psychological Association of Graduate Students (APAGS) and have advanced women's issues.

**Eligibility** This program is open to women who are working on a doctoral degree in psychology and are members of APAGS. Applicants must have demonstrated exceptional leadership by serving in 1 or more leadership roles locally, regionally, and/or nationally while also advancing women's issues through their writing, publications, research, advocacy, or other scholarly activities. Examples of relevant issues include personal and professional balance, barriers to women's achievement, challenges to advancement in academia or other environments, inequities in pay, different career opportunities, health disparities, dual-career family issues, combining family and child-rearing with a career, mentoring, or other issues that are important to or impact women. Along with their application, they must submit a 1,500-word essay that describes their future educational and professional goals and how their research, advocacy, or other scholarly work advances women and women's issues.

**Financial data** The award is $1,500.

**Duration** 1 year.

**Additional information** This program began in 2008.

**Number awarded** 1 each year.

**Deadline** April of each year.

## [804]
## CAROLYN WEATHERFORD SCHOLARSHIP FUND

Woman's Missionary Union
Attn: WMU Foundation
100 Missionary Ridge
Birmingham, AL 35242
(205) 408-5525          Toll Free: (877) 482-4483
Fax: (205) 408-5508     E-mail: wmufoundation@wmu.org
Web: www.wmufoundation.com

**Summary** To provide an opportunity for women to work on a graduate degree or an internship so they can engage in activities of the Woman's Missionary Union (WMU).

**Eligibility** This program is open to women who are members of the Baptist Church and are attending or planning to attend a Southern Baptist seminary or divinity school at the graduate level or participate in an internship. Applicants must be interested in 1) field work experience as interns or in women's missionary work in the United States; or 2) service in women's missionary work in the United States. They must arrange for 3 letters of endorsement, from a recent professor, a state or associational WMU official, and a recent pastor. Selection is based on current active involvement in WMU, previous activity in WMU, plans for long-term involvement in WMU and/or home missions, academic strength, leadership skills, and personal and professional characteristics.

**Financial data** A stipend is awarded (amount not specified).

**Duration** 1 year.

**Number awarded** 1 or more each year.

**Deadline** February of each year.

## [805]
## CARRIE CHAPMAN CATT PRIZE FOR RESEARCH ON WOMEN AND POLITICS

Iowa State University
Attn: Carrie Chapman Catt Center for Women and Politics
309 Carrie Chapman Catt Hall
Ames, IA 50011-1305
(515) 294-3181          Fax: (515) 294-3741
E-mail: cattcntr@iastate.edu
Web: cattcenter.las.iastate.edu/catt-research/catt-prize

**Summary** To recognize and reward outstanding research in the area of women and politics.

**Eligibility** This competition is open to scholars at all levels, including graduate students and junior faculty, who are planning to conduct research in the area of women and politics. Applicants must submit a detailed description of their research project, including 1) its purpose and content; 2) a discussion of relevant theory, contributions to literature in the field, and methodology; 3) a statement on how this prize will contribute to the research project; and 4) a timetable for completion of the project. They also must submit a 1-page biographical statement. Research projects can address the annual conference theme or any other topic related to women and politics.

**Financial data** Prizes are $1,500 for winners or $500 for honorable mention. All prize-winners may also receive travel expenses to Des Moines, Iowa, where awards are presented at the annual conference of the Carrie Chapman Catt Center for Women and Politics.

**Duration** The prizes are awarded annually.

**Number awarded** Up to 4 winners and up to 2 honorable mentions are selected each year.

**Deadline** November of each year.

## [806]
## CATERPILLAR SWE SCHOLARSHIPS

Society of Women Engineers
Attn: Scholarship Selection Committee
203 North LaSalle Street, Suite 1675
Chicago, IL 60601-1269
(312) 596-5223              Toll Free: (877) SWE-INFO
Fax: (312) 644-8557       E-mail: scholarships@swe.org
Web: societyofwomenengineers.swe.org

**Summary** To provide financial assistance to women who are working on an undergraduate or graduate degree in selected fields of engineering or computer science.

**Eligibility** This program is open to women who are sophomores, juniors, seniors, or graduate students at ABET-accredited 4-year colleges and universities. Applicants must be working full time on a degree in computer science or agricultural, chemical, electrical, industrial, manufacturing, materials, or mechanical engineering. They must be U.S. citizens or authorized to work in the United States and have a GPA of 3.0 or higher. Selection is based on merit.

**Financial data** The stipend is $2,400.

**Duration** 1 year.

**Additional information** This program is sponsored by Caterpillar, Inc.

**Number awarded** 3 each year.

**Deadline** February of each year.

## [807]
## CATHERINE PRELINGER AWARD

Coordinating Council for Women in History
c/o Sandra Dawson, Executive Director
Northern Illinois University
Department of History and Women's Studies
715 Zulauf Hall
DeKalb, IL 60115
(815) 895-2624              E-mail: execdir@theccwh.org
Web: theccwh.org/ccwh-awards

**Summary** To provide funding to members of the Coordinating Council for Women in History (CCWH) for a project that focuses on women's roles in history.

**Eligibility** This program is open to members of CCWH whose academic path has not followed the traditional pattern of uninterrupted study. Applicants must hold either A.B.D. status or a Ph.D. and be engaged in scholarship that is historical in nature, although their degree may be in related fields. They must submit a description of a project they propose to undertake with this award, including the work they intend to complete, the schedule they have developed, the sources they intend to use, and the contribution the work will make to women in history. Independent and non-academic scholars are encouraged to apply.

**Financial data** The grant is $20,000.

**Duration** 1 year.

**Additional information** This program began in 1998.

**Number awarded** 1 each year.

**Deadline** September of each year.

## [808]
## CELIA M. HOWARD FELLOWSHIP

Illinois Federation of Business Women's Clubs
c/o Fayrene Wright, Howard Fellowship Fund Committee Chair
804 East Locust Street
Robinson, IL 62454
(618) 546-1233
E-mail: info@celiamhowardfellowship.com
Web: www.celiamhowardfellowship.com

**Summary** To provide funding to women in Illinois who are interested in working on a graduate degree in specified fields at eligible universities.

**Eligibility** This program is open to Illinois women who are U.S. citizens; have been Illinois residents for at least the past 2 years; have earned a bachelor's degree with at least 12 hours of undergraduate work in economics, history, and/or political science; and have a GPA of 3.0 or higher. A personal interview may be required. Applicants must be planning to study for a master's degree in administration of justice at Southern Illinois University at Carbondale or Edwardsville, a J.D. degree at the University of Illinois College of Law at Urbana-Champaign, a master's degree in diplomacy at the Fletcher School of Law and Diplomacy in Medford, Massachusetts, or a master's degree in international management at the Garvin School of International Management in Glendale, Arizona. Selection is based on financial need, previous graduate study, practical business experience in government, and leadership experience.

**Financial data** Awards normally pay full tuition, to a maximum of $10,000 per year. Funds are paid directly to the recipient's school.

**Duration** 1 year; renewable.

**Additional information** This program began in 1948.

**Number awarded** Varies each year; recently, 3 of these fellowships were awarded.

**Deadline** November of each year.

## [809]
## CENTRAL NEW MEXICO RE-ENTRY SCHOLARSHIP

Society of Women Engineers
Attn: Scholarship Selection Committee
203 North LaSalle Street, Suite 1675
Chicago, IL 60601-1269
(312) 596-5223              Toll Free: (877) SWE-INFO
Fax: (312) 644-8557       E-mail: scholarships@swe.org
Web: societyofwomenengineers.swe.org

**Summary** To provide financial assistance to members of the Society of Women Engineers (SWE) from any state who are reentering college or graduate school in New Mexico to work on a degree in engineering or computer science.

**Eligibility** This program is open to members of the society who are sophomores, juniors, seniors, or graduate students at an ABET-accredited college, university, or 4-year engineering technology program in New Mexico. Applicants must be returning to college or graduate school after an absence of several years to work on a degree in computer science or engineering. They must have a GPA of 3.0 or higher. Selection is based on merit. U.S. citizenship or permanent resident status is required.

**Financial data**   The stipend is $1,250 per year.

**Duration**   1 year; may be renewed up to 5 additional years.

**Additional information**   This program began in 2005 by the Central New Mexico section of SWE.

**Number awarded**   1 each year.

**Deadline**   February of each year.

## [810]
## CH2M HILL PARTNERSHIP SCHOLARSHIP

Women's Transportation Seminar
Attn: WTS Foundation
1701 K Street, N.W., Suite 800
Washington, DC 20006
(202) 955-5085          Fax: (202) 955-5088
E-mail: wts@wtsinternational.org
Web: www.wtsinternational.org/education/scholarships

**Summary**   To provide financial assistance to women graduate students interested in preparing for a career in transportation.

**Eligibility**   This program is open to women who are enrolled in a graduate degree program in a transportation-related field (e.g., transportation engineering, planning, finance, or logistics). Applicants must have at least a 3.0 GPA and be interested in a career in transportation. Along with their application, they must submit a 750-word statement about their career goals after graduation and why they think they should receive the scholarship award. Applications must be submitted first to a local chapter; the chapters forward selected applications for consideration on the national level. Minority women are particularly encouraged to apply. Selection is based on transportation involvement and goals, job skills, and academic record.

**Financial data**   The stipend is $10,000.

**Duration**   1 year.

**Additional information**   This program is sponsored by CH2M Hill. Local chapters may also award additional funding to winners in their area.

**Number awarded**   1 each year.

**Deadline**   Applications must be submitted by November to a local WTS chapter.

## [811]
## CHARLES T. STONER LAW SCHOLARSHIP AWARD

Women's Basketball Coaches Association
Attn: Manager of Events, Awards and Office
   Administration
4646 Lawrenceville Highway
Lilburn, GA 30047-3620
(770) 279-8027, ext. 110        Fax: (770) 279-8473
E-mail: dtrujillo@wbca.org
Web: www.wbca.org

**Summary**   To provide financial assistance for law school to women's basketball players.

**Eligibility**   This program is open to women's college basketball players who are seniors planning to attend law school. Applicants must be nominated by a member of the Women's Basketball Coaches Association (WBCA). Selection is based on a letter of recommendation, academic major and GPA, basketball statistics for all 4 years of college, academic and athletic honors, and campus activities.

**Financial data**   The stipend is $1,000.

**Duration**   1 year; nonrenewable.

**Additional information**   This program began in 2001.

**Number awarded**   1 each year.

**Deadline**   Deadline not specified.

## [812]
## CHARLINE CHILSON SCHOLARSHIPS

Delta Zeta Sorority
Attn: Foundation Coordinator
202 East Church Street
Oxford, OH 45056
(513) 523-7597          Fax: (513) 523-1921
E-mail: DZFoundation@dzshq.com
Web: www.deltazeta.org

**Summary**   To provide financial assistance to members of Delta Zeta Sorority working on an undergraduate or graduate degree in science.

**Eligibility**   This program is open to upper-division and graduate members of the sorority who have a high GPA in their major. Applicants must be working on a degree in science. Along with their application, they must submit an official transcript, a statement of their career goals, information on their service to the sorority, documentation of campus activities and/or community involvement, a list of academic honors, and an explanation of their financial need.

**Financial data**   The stipend ranges from $500 to $2,500 for undergraduates or from $1,000 to $15,000 for graduate students, depending on the availability of funds.

**Duration**   1 year; nonrenewable.

**Number awarded**   Varies each year; recently, 12 of these scholarships were awarded: 6 to undergraduates and 6 to graduate students.

**Deadline**   February of each year.

## [813]
## CHARLOTTE BRENT MEMORIAL SCHOLARSHIP

United Methodist Church-Louisiana Conference
Attn: Coordinator, Conference Board of Ordained Ministry
527 North Boulevard
Baton Rouge, LA 70802-5700
(225) 346-1646, ext. 230
Toll Free: (888) 239-5286, ext. 230
Fax: (225) 383-2652
E-mail: JohnEdddHarper@la-umc.org
Web: www.la-umc.org/pages/detail/1595

**Summary**   To provide financial assistance to women from Louisiana who are attending a Methodist seminary in any state to prepare for a career in ordained ministry.

**Eligibility**   This program is open to female members of United Methodist Churches in Louisiana who are enrolled or planning to enroll full time at a Methodist seminary in any state. Applicants must be beginning a second career as an ordained minister. Along with their application, they must submit an essay on their vocational goals and plans for ministry.

**Financial data**   The stipend is $1,000.

**Duration**   1 year.

**Number awarded**   1 each year.

**Deadline**   February of each year.

## [814]
## CHARLOTTE FIELDS SILVERSTEEN SCHOLARSHIP

Delta Zeta Sorority
Attn: Foundation Coordinator
202 East Church Street
Oxford, OH 45056
(513) 523-7597          Fax: (513) 523-1921
E-mail: DZFoundation@dzshq.com
Web: www.deltazeta.org

**Summary** To provide financial assistance to members of Delta Zeta Sorority working on a graduate degree in education.

**Eligibility** This program is open to graduate members of the sorority who are working on a degree in education. Applicants must submit an official transcript, a statement of their career goals, information on their service to the sorority, documentation of campus activities and/or community involvement, a list of academic honors, and an explanation of their financial need. Preference is given to applicants from the Delta Tau chapter at Temple University.

**Financial data** The stipend ranges from $1,000 to $15,000, depending on the availability of funds.

**Duration** 1 year; nonrenewable.

**Number awarded** 1 each year.

**Deadline** February of each year.

## [815]
## CHERYL A. RUGGIERO SCHOLARSHIP

Rhode Island Society of Certified Public Accountants
45 Royal Little Drive
Providence, RI 02904
(401) 331-5720          Fax: (401) 454-5780
E-mail: info@riscpa.org
Web: student.riscpa.org

**Summary** To provide financial assistance to female undergraduate and graduate students from Rhode Island who are working on a degree in accounting at a school in any state.

**Eligibility** This program is open to female residents of Rhode Island who are working on an undergraduate or graduate degree in public accounting at a school in any state. Applicants must be U.S. citizens who have a GPA of 3.0 or higher. Selection is based on demonstrated potential to become a valued member of the public accounting profession. Finalists are interviewed.

**Financial data** The stipend is $1,250.

**Duration** 1 year.

**Additional information** This program began in 2005.

**Number awarded** 1 each year.

**Deadline** January of each year.

## [816]
## CHI OMEGA FOUNDATION ALUMNAE EDUCATIONAL GRANTS

Chi Omega Fraternity
Attn: Chi Omega Foundation
3395 Players Club Parkway
Memphis, TN 38125
(901) 748-8600          Fax: (901) 748-8686
E-mail: foundation@chiomega.com
Web: www.chiomega.com/wemakeadifference/scholarships

**Summary** To provide funding for graduate school to women who are members of Chi Omega Fraternity and have been out of college for a period of time.

**Eligibility** This program is open to women over 24 years of age who are alumnae members of Chi Omega Fraternity. Applicants must be planning to enter graduate school as a full- or part-time student for career qualification or advancement. Along with their application, they must submit a personal letter describing their reasons and need for the grant. Selection is based on academic achievement, aptitude, service to Chi Omega, contributions to the university and community, personal and professional goals, and financial need.

**Financial data** The stipend is $1,000.

**Duration** 1 year.

**Additional information** This program began in 1997.

**Number awarded** 10 each year.

**Deadline** February of each year.

## [817]
## CHRYSALIS SCHOLARSHIP

Association for Women Geoscientists
Attn: AWG Foundation
12000 North Washington Street, Suite 285
Thornton, CO 80241
(303) 412-6219          Fax: (303) 253-9220
E-mail: chrysalis@awg.org
Web: www.awg.org/EAS/scholarships.html

**Summary** To provide assistance to women who have returned to graduate school to earn a degree in the geosciences and need funding to complete their thesis.

**Eligibility** This program is open to women geoscience graduate students whose education has been interrupted for at least 1 year for personal or financial reasons. Applicants must submit a letter describing their background, career goals and objectives, how the scholarship will be used, and nature and length of the interruption to their education.

**Financial data** The stipend is $2,000. The funds may be used for typing, drafting, child care, or anything necessary to allow a degree candidate to finish her thesis and enter a geoscience profession.

**Duration** 1 year.

**Number awarded** 1 or more each year.

**Deadline** March of each year.

## [818]
## CHURCH TRAINING AND DEACONESS HOUSE SCHOLARSHIP

Episcopal Diocese of Pennsylvania
Attn: Church Training and Deaconess House Scholarship
Fund
240 South Fourth Street
Philadelphia, PA 19106
(215) 627-6434, ext. 101          Fax: (215) 627-7550
E-mail: nevin-field@stpetersphila.org
Web: www.diopa.org/deaconess-training

**Summary** To provide financial assistance for graduate school to women preparing for a career in religious or benevolent work for the Episcopal Church.

**Eligibility** This program is open to women who are seeking to be ordained to the ministry of the Episcopal Church or to work on a graduate degree that would further their lay ministry. Preference is given to women in the Diocese of Pennsylvania. Applicants must submit a 250-word essay on how they expect to use this graduate educational training to advance their ordained or lay ministry within the Episcopal Church or the church at large. Selection is based on the quality of the essay, academic record, and financial need.

**Financial data** Stipends range from $2,000 to $3,000.

**Duration** 1 year; may be renewed up to 2 additional years.

**Number awarded** 1 or more each year.

**Deadline** March of each year.

## [819]
## CLARE BOOTH LUCE GRADUATE FELLOWSHIP

Society of Women Engineers
Attn: Scholarship Selection Committee
203 North LaSalle Street, Suite 1675
Chicago, IL 60601-1269
(312) 596-5223          Toll Free: (877) SWE-INFO
Fax: (312) 644-8557          E-mail: scholarships@swe.org
Web: societyofwomenengineers.swe.org

**Summary** To provide financial assistance to women who are members of the Society of Women Engineers (SWE) and working on a graduate degree in engineering or computer science.

**Eligibility** This program is open to SWE members who will be full-time graduate students at ABET-accredited colleges and universities. Applicants must be working on a doctoral degree in computer science or engineering with career plans to teach at the college or university level. They must have a GPA of 3.5 or higher. Selection is based on merit.

**Financial data** The stipend is $20,000.

**Duration** 1 year.

**Additional information** This program, which began in 2011, is sponsored by the Henry Luce Foundation.

**Number awarded** 1 each year.

**Deadline** February of each year.

## [820]
## CLAUDIA STEELE BAKER GRADUATE FELLOWSHIP

Alpha Chi Omega Foundation
Attn: Assistant Director-Grants and Stewardship
5939 Castle Creek Parkway North Drive
Indianapolis, IN 46250-4343
(317) 579-5050, ext. 265          Fax: (317) 579-5051
E-mail: alatta@alphachiomega.org
Web: www.alphachiomega.org/index.aspx?id=1030

**Summary** To provide financial assistance to Alpha Chi Omega members who are interested in studying social services in graduate school.

**Eligibility** Women college seniors and graduates who are members of the sorority are eligible to apply if they have majored in a social service field, are committed to peace and understanding, and plan to attend graduate school. Selection is based on campus, community, and chapter service.

**Financial data** A stipend is awarded (amount not specified).

**Duration** 1 year.

**Number awarded** 1 each year.

**Deadline** February of each year.

## [821]
## COLDER PRODUCTS COMPANY MINNESOTA SWE SCHOLARSHIP

Society of Women Engineers-Minnesota Section
Attn: Scholarship Committee
P.O. Box 582813
Minneapolis, MN 55458-2813
E-mail: scholarships@swe-mn.org
Web: www.swe-mn.org/scholarships.html

**Summary** To provide financial assistance to women from any state working on an undergraduate or graduate degree in mechanical engineering at colleges and universities in Minnesota, North Dakota, and South Dakota.

**Eligibility** This program is open to female undergraduate and graduate students at ABET-accredited engineering programs in Minnesota, North Dakota, or South Dakota. Applicants must be working full time on a degree in mechanical engineering. Along with their application, they must submit a short paragraph describing how they plan to utilize their engineering skills after they graduate. Selection is based on potential to succeed as an engineer (20 points), communication skills (10 points), extracurricular or community involvement and leadership skills (10 points), demonstrated successful work experience (10 points), and academic success (5 points).

**Financial data** The stipend is $1,000.

**Duration** 1 year.

**Additional information** This program is sponsored by Colder Products Company.

**Number awarded** 1 each year.

**Deadline** March of each year.

## [822]
## CONGRESSIONAL FELLOWSHIPS ON WOMEN AND PUBLIC POLICY

Women's Research and Education Institute
Attn: Education and Training Programs
714 G Street, S.E., Suite 200
Washington, DC 20003
(202) 280-2720          E-mail: wrei@wrei.org
Web: www.wrei.org

**Summary** To provide graduate students and young professionals with an opportunity to work as a Congressional aide on policy issues affecting women.

**Eligibility** This program is open to women and men who are currently enrolled in a master's or doctoral program at an accredited institution in the United States or who have completed such a program within the past 18 months. Applicants should have completed at least 9 hours of graduate course work or the equivalent and have a demonstrated interest in research or political activity relating to women's social and political status. They may be of any age, gender, race, religion, sexual orientation, experience, or academic field, but they must be articulate and adaptable and have strong writing skills. Selection is based on academic competence and demonstrated interest in the public policy process. Interviews are required of semifinalists.

**Financial data** Fellows receive a stipend of $1,450 per month, $500 for health insurance, and up to $1,500 for reimbursement of 3 hours of tuition at their home institutions.

**Duration** 8 months, from January through August; nonrenewable.

**Additional information** This program began in 1977. Fellows are assigned to Congressional or committee offices to work for at least 30 hours per week as a legislative assistant monitoring, researching, and providing information on policy issues affecting women.

**Number awarded** At least 5 each year; since the program began, 277 fellows (all women) have been appointed to these positions.

**Deadline** June of each year.

## [823]
## COOLEY DIVERSITY FELLOWSHIP PROGRAM

Cooley LLP
Attn: Attorney Recruiting Manager
4401 Eastgate Mall
San Diego, CA 92121-1909
(858) 550-6474   E-mail: diversityfellowship@cooley.com
Web: www.cooley.com/diversityfellowship

**Summary** To provide financial assistance and work experience to female and other law students who are committed to promoting diversity in their community and are interested in summer associateships and employment at an office of Cooley LLP.

**Eligibility** This program is open to students enrolled full time at an ABA-accredited law school and planning to graduate 2 years after applying. Applicants must submit a 3-page personal statement describing their demonstrated commitment to promoting diversity (e.g., ethnicity, gender, physical disability, and/or sexual orientation) in their community. They must be interested in a summer associateship. Selection is based on undergraduate and law school academic performance, personal achievements, leadership abilities, community service, and demonstrated commitment to promoting diversity.

**Financial data** The award includes a stipend of $10,000 after completing a summer associateship after the first year of law school, another stipend of $10,000 after completing another summer associateship after the second year of law school, and another stipend of $10,000 after graduating from law school and joining the firm as a full-time associate.

**Duration** 3 years.

**Additional information** Summer associates may work in any of the firm's offices in California (Palo Alto, San Diego, or San Francisco), Colorado (Broomfield), Massachusetts (Boston), New York (New York), Virginia (Reston), Washington (Seattle), or Washington, D.C.

**Number awarded** 1 or more each year.

**Deadline** June of each year.

## [824]
## CREW NETWORK SCHOLARSHIPS

Commercial Real Estate Women (CREW) Network
1201 Wakarusa Drive, Suite C3
Lawrence, KS 66049
(785) 832-1808          Fax: (785) 832-1551
E-mail: crewnetwork@crewnetwork.org
Web: crewnetwork.org/CZ_scholarships.aspx?id=257

**Summary** To provide financial assistance to women who are attending college to prepare for a career in commercial real estate.

**Eligibility** This program is open to women who are enrolled as full-time juniors, seniors, or graduate students at a college or university that has an accredited real estate program. If their institution does not have a real estate program, they may be studying another field, as long as they are preparing for a career in commercial real estate. They must have a GPA of 3.0 or higher and be U.S. or Canadian citizens. Along with their application, undergraduates must submit a brief statement about their interest in commercial real estate and their career objectives; graduate students must submit a statement that explains why they are interested in the commercial real estate industry, their experiences and insights into that industry and how those have impacted them, the impact they expect to make in the commercial real estate industry, and how their long-term career objectives make them uniquely qualified for this scholarship. Financial need is not considered in the selection process.

**Financial data** The stipend is $5,000.

**Duration** 1 year.

**Number awarded** 10 each year.

**Deadline** April of each year.

## [825]
## CUMMINS SCHOLARSHIPS

Society of Women Engineers
Attn: Scholarship Selection Committee
203 North LaSalle Street, Suite 1675
Chicago, IL 60601-1269
(312) 596-5223          Toll Free: (877) SWE-INFO
Fax: (312) 644-8557          E-mail: scholarships@swe.org
Web: societyofwomenengineers.swe.org

**Summary** To provide financial assistance to women working on an undergraduate or graduate degree in computer science or designated engineering specialties.

**Eligibility** This program is open to women who are sophomores, juniors, seniors, or graduate students at 4-year ABET-accredited colleges and universities. Applicants must be working full time on a degree in computer science or automotive, chemical, computer, electrical, industrial, manufacturing, materials, or mechanical engineering and have a GPA of 3.5 or higher. Preference is given to members of groups underrepresented in engineering or computer science. Selection is based on merit. U.S. citizenship or permanent resident status is required.

**Financial data** The stipend is $1,000.

**Duration** 1 year.

**Additional information** This program is sponsored by Cummins, Inc.

**Number awarded** 2 each year.

**Deadline** February of each year.

## [826]
## CYNTHIA HUNT-LINES SCHOLARSHIP

Minnesota Nurses Association
Attn: Minnesota Nurses Association Foundation
345 Randolph Avenue, Suite 200
St. Paul, MN 55102-3610
(651) 414-2822      Toll Free: (800) 536-4662, ext. 122
Fax: (651) 695-7000   E-mail: linda.owens@mnnurses.org
Web: www.mnnurses.org

**Summary** To provide financial assistance to members of the Minnesota Nurses Association (MNA) and the Minnesota Student Nurses Association (MSNA) who are single parents and interested in working on a baccalaureate or master's degree in nursing.

**Eligibility** This program is open to MNA and MSNA members who are enrolled or entering a baccalaureate or master's program in nursing in Minnesota or North Dakota. Applicants must be single parents, at least 21 years of age, with at least 1 dependent. Along with their application, they must submit: a current transcript; a short essay describing their interest in nursing, their long-range career goals, and how their continuing education will have an impact on the profession of nursing in Minnesota; a description of their financial need; and 2 letters of support.

**Financial data** The stipend is $2,000 per year.

**Duration** 1 year; may be renewed.

**Number awarded** 1 each year.

**Deadline** May of each year.

## [827]
## D. ANITA SMALL SCIENCE AND BUSINESS SCHOLARSHIP

Business and Professional Women of Maryland
Attn: BPW Foundation of Maryland
c/o Joyce Draper, Chief Financial Officer
615 Fairview Avenue
Frederick, MD 21701
Web: bpwmd2.timberlakepublishing.com

**Summary** To provide financial assistance to women in Maryland who are interested in working on an undergraduate or graduate degree in a science or business-related field.

**Eligibility** This program is open to women who are at least 21 years of age and have been accepted to a bachelor's or advanced degree program at an accredited Maryland academic institution. Applicants must be preparing for a career in 1 of the following or a related field: business administration, computer sciences, engineering, mathematics, medical sciences (including nursing, laboratory technology, therapy, etc.), or physical sciences. They must have a GPA of 3.0 or higher and be able to demonstrate financial need.

**Financial data** The stipend is $1,500.

**Duration** 1 year.

**Number awarded** 1 or more each year.

**Deadline** April of each year.

## [828]
## DASSAULT FALCON JET CORPORATION SCHOLARSHIP

Women in Aviation, International
Attn: Scholarships
Morningstar Airport
3647 State Route 503 South
West Alexandria, OH 45381-9354
(937) 839-4647                    Fax: (937) 839-4645
E-mail: scholarships@wai.org
Web: www.wai.org/education/scholarships.cfm

**Summary** To provide financial assistance to women who are working on an undergraduate or graduate degree in a field related to aviation.

**Eligibility** This program is open to women who are working on an undergraduate or graduate degree in an aviation-related field. Applicants must be U.S. citizens, be fluent in English, and have a GPA of 3.0 or higher. Along with their application, they must submit 2 letters of recommendation; a 1-page essay on their current educational status, what they hope to achieve by working on a degree in aviation, and their aspirations in the field; a resume; copies of all aviation licenses and medical certificates; and the last 3 pages of their pilot logbook (if applicable). Selection is based on achievements, attitude toward self and others, commitment to success, dedication to career, financial need, motivation, reliability, responsibility, and teamwork.

**Financial data** The stipend is $1,000.

**Duration** 1 year.

**Additional information** WAI is a nonprofit professional organization dedicated to encouraging women to consider an aviation career and to providing educational outreach activities and networking resources to women active in the industry. This program is sponsored by Dassault Falcon Jet Corporation.

**Number awarded** 1 each year.

**Deadline** November of each year.

## [829]
## DAUGHTERS OF PENELOPE GRADUATE STUDENT SCHOLARSHIPS

Daughters of Penelope
Attn: Daughters of Penelope Foundation, Inc.
1909 Q Street, N.W., Suite 500
Washington, DC 20009-1007
(202) 234-9741                Fax: (202) 483-6983
E-mail: president@dopfoundationinc.com
Web: dopfoundationinc.com/scholarships/apply

**Summary**  To provide financial assistance for graduate school to women of Greek descent.

**Eligibility**  This program is open to women who have been members of the Daughters of Penelope or the Maids of Athena for at least 2 years, or whose parents or grandparents have been members of the Daughters of Penelope or the Order of AHEPA for at least 2 years. Applicants must be accepted or currently enrolled for a minimum of 9 units per academic year in an M.A., M.S., M.B.A., Ph.D., D.D.S., M.D., or other graduate degree program. They must have taken the GRE or other entrance examination (or Canadian, Greek, or Cypriot equivalent) and must write an essay (in English) about their educational and vocational goals. Selection is based on academic merit.

**Financial data**  Stipends are $2,500 or $1,000.

**Duration**  1 year; nonrenewable.

**Additional information**  This program includes the Dorothy Lillian Quincey Memorial Graduate Scholarship, the Big Five Graduate Scholarship, and the Sonja Stefanadis Graduate Scholarship.

**Number awarded**  Varies each year; recently, 3 of these scholarships (1 at $2,500 and 2 at $1,000) were awarded.

**Deadline**  May of each year.

## [830]
## DAVID HILLIARD EATON SCHOLARSHIP

Unitarian Universalist Association
Attn: Ministerial Credentialing Office
25 Beacon Street
Boston, MA 02108-2800
(617) 948-6403                Fax: (617) 742-2875
E-mail: mcoadministrator@uua.org
Web: www.uua.org

**Summary**  To provide financial assistance to minority women preparing for the Unitarian Universalist (UU) ministry.

**Eligibility**  This program is open to women from historically marginalized groups who are currently enrolled or planning to enroll full or at least half time in a UU ministerial training program with aspirant or candidate status. Applicants must be citizens of the United States or Canada. Priority is given first to those who have demonstrated outstanding ministerial ability and secondarily to students with the greatest financial need (especially women of color).

**Financial data**  The stipend ranges from $1,000 to $11,000 per year.

**Duration**  1 year.

**Number awarded**  1 or 2 each year.

**Deadline**  April of each year.

## [831]
## DEALER DEVELOPMENT SCHOLARSHIP PROGRAM

General Motors Corporation
Women's Retail Network
c/o Charitable Management Systems, Inc.
P.O. Box 648
Naperville, IL 60566
(630) 428-2412                Fax: (630) 428-2695
E-mail: wrnscholarshipinfo@gmsac.com
Web: www.gmsac.com

**Summary**  To provide financial assistance to women attending college or graduate school to prepare for a retail automotive career.

**Eligibility**  This program is open to women who are enrolled full time in undergraduate, graduate, and nontraditional continuing education institutions that offer degrees in the automotive retail and/or automotive service field. Applicants must be interested in preparing for a career in automotive retail and/or service management. They must be citizens of the United States or have the ability to accept permanent employment in the United States without the need for visa sponsorship now or in the future. Along with their application, they must submit an essay of 500 to 750 words on their interest and motivation for a career in the automotive retail and/or automotive service sector. Selection is based on that statement, academic performance, leadership and participation in school and community activities, work experience, career and educational aspirations, and financial need.

**Financial data**  The stipend is $5,000 per year.

**Duration**  1 year; recipients may reapply.

**Additional information**  This program began in 2011.

**Number awarded**  Varies each year; recently, 6 of these scholarships were awarded.

**Deadline**  April of each year.

## [832]
## DELTA DELTA DELTA UNRESTRICTED GRADUATE SCHOLARSHIPS

Delta Delta Delta
Attn: Tri Delta Foundation
2331 Brookhollow Plaza Drive
P.O. Box 5987
Arlington, TX 76005-5987
(817) 633-8001                Fax: (817) 652-0212
E-mail: fdnscholarship@trideltaeo.org
Web: www.tridelta.org/Foundation/Scholarships

**Summary**  To provide financial assistance for graduate study to women students who are members of Delta Delta Delta.

**Eligibility**  This program is open to members of the sorority who are entering or already engaged in graduate study. Applicants must submit a personal statement outlining their educational and vocational goals, 2 academic recommendations, a Tri Delta recommendation, academic transcripts, and documentation of financial need. Selection is based on academic merit, chapter and campus activities, and community activities.

**Financial data**  The stipend is $3,000.

**Duration**  1 year.

**Additional information** This program, originally established in 1938, includes the following named awards: the Mary Margaret Hafter Fellowship, the Luella Akins Key Graduate Scholarship, the Second Century Graduate Scholarship, the Margaret Stafford Memorial Scholarship, and the Sarah Shinn Marshall Graduate Scholarship.

**Number awarded** Varies each year; recently, a total of 21 graduate scholarships were awarded.

**Deadline** February of each year.

## [833]
## DELTA GAMMA FELLOWSHIPS

Delta Gamma Foundation
Attn: Director of Scholarships, Fellowships and Loans
3250 Riverside Drive
P.O. Box 21397
Columbus, OH 43221-0397
(614) 481-8169          Toll Free: (800) 644-5414
Fax: (614) 481-0133
E-mail: scholarshipfellowship@deltagamma.org
Web: www.deltagamma.org

**Summary** To provide financial assistance to members of Delta Gamma sorority who are interested in working on a graduate degree.

**Eligibility** This program is open to dues-paying members of Delta Gamma who are currently enrolled in graduate school or will have completed their undergraduate work by June 30 of the year in which the fellowship is granted and will begin graduate study in the following fall. Applicants may attend an accredited university in the United States or Canada and work on a degree in any field. Along with their application, they must submit a 1- to 2-page essay in which they introduce themselves, including their career goals, their reasons for applying, and the impact Delta Gamma has had upon their life. Selection is based on scholastic excellence, contributions to their chosen field, past and current Delta Gamma activities, and campus and community involvement.

**Financial data** The stipend is $2,500.

**Duration** 1 year.

**Number awarded** Varies each year; recently, 26 of these fellowships were awarded.

**Deadline** March of each year.

## [834]
## DELTA KAPPA GAMMA NATIVE AMERICAN PROJECT GRANTS

Delta Kappa Gamma Society International-Mu State
    Organization
c/o Joann Higgins, Native American Project
1386 Craleigh Street
North Port, FL 34288
E-mail: charlygrll496@yahoo.com
Web: dkgmustateflorida.weebly.com

**Summary** To provide financial assistance to female Native Americans from Florida who are working on a degree in education or conducting research into the history of Native Americans at a college or university in the state.

**Eligibility** This program is open to women who are members of a recognized Native American tribe in Florida. Applicants must be enrolled at an accredited college or university in the state and either working on a degree in education or

conducting research into the history of Native Americans in Florida. Along with their application, they must submit a brief statement with details of the purpose of the grant, a letter of recommendation from a tribal official, and a copy of high school or college transcripts.

**Financial data** The stipend is $1,000.

**Duration** 1 year.

**Number awarded** 6 each year: 1 in each of the districts of the sponsoring organization in Florida.

**Deadline** May of each year.

## [835]
## DELTA KAPPA GAMMA SCHOLARSHIP PROGRAM

Delta Kappa Gamma Society International
Attn: Scholarships Committee
416 West 12th Street
P.O. Box 1589
Austin, TX 78767-1589
(512) 478-5748          Toll Free: (888) 762-4685
Fax: (512) 478-3961     E-mail: societyoper@dkg.org
Web: www.dkg.org

**Summary** To provide financial assistance to members of Delta Kappa Gamma Society International from any country interested in graduate study or research.

**Eligibility** Applicants must have been members in good standing of the Delta Kappa Gamma Society International (an honorary society of women educators) for at least 3 years, have completed a bachelor's degree or equivalent, and have been accepted and enrolled in a graduate program at a nationally accredited institution of higher education, preferably working on a doctoral degree. Along with their application, they must submit a 500-word impact statement that describes the area of their intended study or major interest, the potential benefits of the degree to them professionally, and the potential benefits of the degree to Delta Kappa Gamma. Selection is based on that statement (30 points), active participation and demonstrated leadership in Delta Kappa Gamma (20 points), recognitions for achievement (10 points), professional work experience (10 points), current status of program (10 points), prior education (10 points), and recommendations (10 points).

**Financial data** The stipend is $6,000 for master's degree students or $10,000 for doctoral students.

**Duration** 1 year.

**Additional information** Delta Kappa Gamma Society International has 170,000 members in 13 countries and is the largest organization of its kind. This program includes the following named awards: the Marjorie Jeanne Allen Scholarship, the Mamie Sue Bastian Scholarship, the Dr. Annie Webb Blanton Scholarship, the Blanton Centennial Scholarship, the A. Margaret Boyd Scholarship, the Edna McGuire Boyd Scholarship, the Dr. Eula Lee Carter Scholarship, the Delta Kappa Gamma Founders Scholarship, the Delta Kappa Gamma Golden Anniversary Scholarship, the Delta Kappa Gamma 60th Anniversary Scholarship, the Delta Kappa Gamma 70th Anniversary Scholarship, the Zora Ellis Scholarship, the Emma Giles Scholarship, the Carolyn Guss Scholarship, the Dr. Ola B. Hiller Scholarship, the Eunah Temple Holden Scholarship, the Hazel Johnson Memorial Scholarship, the Dr. Evelyn L. Milam Scholarships, the Berneta Minkwitz Scholarship, the Lois and Marguerite Morse Scholarship, the Dr. Catherine Nutterville Scholarship, the Alida W. Parker Scholarship, the J. Maria Pierce Scholarship, the Dr. Emma Reinhart Scholarship, the Norma Bristow Salter Scholarship, the Dr. Maycie K. Southall Scholarship, the M. Margaret Stroh Scholarship, the Letti P. Trefz Scholarship, and the Dr. Mary Frances White Scholarship. Recipients must remain active members of Delta Kappa Gamma, work full time on the study or research outlined in their applications, submit reports requested by the society, and acknowledge assistance of the society in any publication that results from data gathered while the award was being used.

**Number awarded** Up to 30 each year.

**Deadline** January of each year.

## [836]
## DELTA PHI EPSILON GRADUATE SCHOLARSHIPS

Delta Phi Epsilon Educational Foundation
Attn: Executive Director
251 South Carnac Street
Philadelphia, PA 19107
(215) 732-5901                    Fax: (215) 732-5906
E-mail: info@dphie.org
Web: www.dphie.org

**Summary** To provide financial assistance for graduate school to Delta Phi Epsilon Sorority alumnae.

**Eligibility** This program is open to undergraduate Delta Phi Epsilon sorority sisters (not pledges) and alumnae who are returning to college or graduate school. Applicants must submit a 250-word essay on how this scholarship will benefit the continuation of their educational pursuits. Selection is based on service and involvement, academics, and financial need.

**Financial data** The stipend is $1,000.

**Duration** 1 year or longer, depending upon the scholarship awarded.

**Number awarded** Varies each year; recently, 6 of these scholarships were awarded.

**Deadline** March of each year.

## [837]
## DELTA SIGMA THETA SORORITY GENERAL SCHOLARSHIPS

Delta Sigma Theta Sorority, Inc.
Attn: Scholarship and Standards Committee Chair
1707 New Hampshire Avenue, N.W.
Washington, DC 20009
(202) 986-2400                    Fax: (202) 986-2513
E-mail: dstemail@deltasigmatheta.org
Web: www.deltasigmatheta.org

**Summary** To provide financial assistance to members of Delta Sigma Theta who are working on an undergraduate or graduate degree in any field.

**Eligibility** This program is open to active, dues-paying members of Delta Sigma Theta who are currently enrolled in college or graduate school. Applicants must submit an essay on their major goals and educational objectives, including realistic steps they foresee as necessary for the fulfillment of their plans. Financial need is considered in the selection process.

**Financial data** The stipends range from $1,000 to $2,000. The funds may be used to cover tuition, fees, and living expenses.

**Duration** 1 year; may be renewed for 1 additional year.

**Additional information** This sponsor is a traditionally-African American social sorority. The application fee is $20.

**Number awarded** Varies each year.

**Deadline** April of each year.

## [838]
## DESK AND DERRICK EDUCATION TRUST SCHOLARSHIPS

Association of Desk and Derrick Clubs
Attn: Desk and Derrick Educational Trust
3930 Waverly Bend
Katy, TX 77450
(281) 392-7181                    Fax: (318) 671-8887
E-mail: info@theeducationaltrust.org
Web: www.theeducationaltrust.org/scholarships

**Summary** To provide funding (some just for women) to currently-enrolled college students who are planning a career in the petroleum or an allied industry.

**Eligibility** This program is open to full-time undergraduate and graduate students who have completed at least 2 years of college or are currently enrolled in the second year of undergraduate study. Applicants must have a GPA of 3.2 or higher and be able to demonstrate financial need. They must be preparing for a career in the petroleum, energy, or an allied industry; qualifying majors include geology, geophysics, petroleum engineering, chemical engineering, mechanical engineering, nuclear engineering, and energy management. Students working on degrees in research and development of alternate energy sources (e.g., coal, electric, solar, wind, hydroelectric, nuclear, ethanol) are also eligible. U.S. or Canadian citizenship is required. Some of the awards are designated for women.

**Financial data** Stipends range from $1,000 to $1,500.

**Duration** 1 year.

**Additional information** This program, established in 1982, includes the following named awards designated for women: the Bettie Conley Helis Scholarship, the Lois G. Johnston Scholarship, the Edith Snizek Scholarship, the Gladys Watford Scholarship, and the Paula Mace Scholarship.

**Number awarded** Varies each year; recently, 12 of these scholarships (including 9 designated for women) were awarded.

**Deadline** March of each year.

## [839]
## DETTRE ARCHIVAL INTERNSHIP

National Museum of Women in the Arts
Attn: Director of the Library and Research Center
1250 New York Avenue, N.W.
Washington, DC 20005-3920
(202) 783-5000                    Toll Free: (800) 222-7270
E-mail: internship@nmwa.org
Web: nmwa.org

**Summary** To provide work experience at the National Museum of Women in the Arts (NMWA) to students and recent graduates interested in a career in archives.

**Eligibility**    This program is open to students enrolled in, or recently graduated from, an ALA-accredited library school or accredited archives program. Applicants must be interested in performing various tasks related to the archives of the NMWA. They must be familiar with Microsoft Office software. Familiarity with principals of archival and records management, knowledge of art history and/or museum studies, and excellent communication skills are preferred. Along with their application, they must submit a letter that includes information on prior experience working with archival collections, relevant classes related to archives, and background and interest in art and art history.

**Financial data**    The stipend is $10,000.

**Duration**    12 months.

**Additional information**    This program began in 2011.

**Number awarded**    1 each year.

**Deadline**    June of each year.

## [840]
## DISABLED AMERICAN VETERANS AUXILIARY NATIONAL EDUCATION SCHOLARSHIP FUND

Disabled American Veterans Auxiliary
Attn: National Education Scholarship Fund
3725 Alexandria Pike
Cold Spring, KY 41076
(859) 441-7300        Toll Free: (877) 426-2838, ext. 4020
Fax: (859) 442-2095        E-mail: dava@davmail.org
Web: auxiliary.dav.org/membership/Programs.aspx

**Summary**    To provide financial assistance to members of the Disabled American Veterans (DAV) Auxiliary who are interested in attending college or graduate school.

**Eligibility**    This program is open to paid life members of the auxiliary who are attending or planning to attend a college, university, or vocational school as a full- or part-time undergraduate or graduate student. Applicants must be at least seniors in high school, but there is no maximum age limit. Selection is based on academic achievement; participation in DAV activities; participation in other activities for veterans in their school, community, or elsewhere; volunteer work; membership in clubs or organizations; honors and awards; a statement of academic goals; and financial need.

**Financial data**    Stipends are $1,500 per year for full-time students or $750 per year for part-time students.

**Duration**    1 year; may be renewed for up to 4 additional years, provided the recipient maintains a GPA of 2.5 or higher.

**Additional information**    Membership in the DAV Auxiliary is available to extended family members of veterans eligible for membership in Disabled American Veterans (i.e., any man or woman who served in the armed forces during a period of war or under conditions simulating war and was wounded, disabled to any degree, or left with long-term illness as a result of military service and was discharged or retired from military service under honorable conditions). This program was established in September 2010 as a replacement for the educational loan program that the DAV Auxiliary operated from 1931 until August 2010.

**Number awarded**    Varies each year.

**Deadline**    March of each year.

## [841]
## DIVISION I-AAA ATHLETICS DIRECTORS ASSOCIATION POSTGRADUATE SCHOLARSHIPS

National Association of Collegiate Directors of Athletics
Attn: Division I-AAA Athletics Directors Association
24651 Detroit Road
P.O. Box 16428
Cleveland, OH 44116-0426
(440) 892-4000        Fax: (440) 892-4007
E-mail: bhorning@nacda.com
Web: www.nacda.com/div1aaaada/nacda-div1aaaada.html

**Summary**    To provide financial assistance for graduate school to college basketball players on teams in Division I-AAA (females and males compete separately).

**Eligibility**    This program is open to basketball players at colleges and universities that are members of NCAA Division I-AAA (the 99 Division I institutions that do not sponsor football). Nominees must have a GPA of 3.2 or higher and have participated in at least 50% of the team's games. They must be completing their eighth semester of undergraduate study and be planning to enroll in graduate school. Along with their application, they must submit a brief essay on how their experience as a student-athlete has prepared them to be a future leader of our society.

**Financial data**    The stipend is $5,000.

**Duration**    1 year.

**Number awarded**    2 each year: 1 female and 1 male.

**Deadline**    March of each year.

## [842]
## DOE/MICKEY LELAND ENERGY FELLOWSHIPS

Department of Energy
Office of Fossil Energy
1000 Independence Avenue, S.W., FE-6
Washington, DC 20585
(202) 586-4484        E-mail: alan.perry@hq.doe.gov
Web: energy.gov/fe/mickey-leland-energy-fellowship

**Summary**    To provide summer work experience at fossil energy sites of the Department of Energy (DOE) to female and underrepresented minority students or postdoctorates.

**Eligibility**    This program is open to U.S. citizens currently enrolled full time at an accredited college or university. Applicants must be undergraduate, graduate, or postdoctoral students in fields of science, technology (IT), engineering, or mathematics (STEM) and have a GPA of 3.0 or higher. They must be interested in a summer work experience at a DOE fossil energy research facility. Along with their application, they must submit a 100-word statement on why they want to participate in this program. A goal of the program is to recruit women and underrepresented minorities into careers related to fossil energy, although all qualified students are encouraged to apply.

**Financial data**    Weekly stipends are $600 for undergraduates, $750 for master's degree students, or $850 for doctoral and postdoctoral students. Travel costs for a round trip to and from the site and for a trip to a designated place for technical presentations are also paid.

**Duration**    10 weeks during the summer.

**Additional information**    This program began as 3 separate activities: the Historically Black Colleges and Universities Internship Program established in 1995, the Hispanic Internship Program established in 1998, and the Tribal Colleges and Universities Internship Program, established in 2000. Those 3 programs were merged into the Fossil Energy Minority Education Initiative, renamed the Mickey Leland Energy Fellowship Program in 2000. Sites to which interns may be assigned include the Albany Research Center (Albany, Oregon), the National Energy Technology Laboratory (Morgantown, West Virginia and Pittsburgh, Pennsylvania), Pacific Northwest National Laboratory (Richland, Washington), Rocky Mountain Oilfield Testing Center (Casper, Wyoming), Strategic Petroleum Reserve Project Management Office (New Orleans, Louisiana), or U.S. Department of Energy Headquarters (Washington, D.C.).

**Number awarded** Varies each year; recently, 30 students participated in this program.

**Deadline** January of each year.

## [843]
## DONALD W. BANNER DIVERSITY SCHOLARSHIP

Banner & Witcoff, Ltd.
Attn: Christopher Hummel
1100 13th Street, N.W., Suite 1200
Washington, DC 20005-4051
(202) 824-3000                    Fax: (202) 824-3001
E-mail: chummel@bannerwitcoff.com
Web: www.bannerwitcoff.com/about/diversity

**Summary** To provide financial assistance to female law students and others who come from groups historically underrepresented in intellectual property law.

**Eligibility** This program is open to students enrolled in the first or second year of a J.D. program at an ABA-accredited law school in the United States. Applicants must come from a group historically underrepresented in intellectual property law; that underrepresentation may be the result of race, sex, ethnicity, sexual orientation, disability, education, culture, religion, age, or socioeconomic background. Selection is based on academic merit, commitment to the pursuit of a career in intellectual property law, written communication skills, oral communication skills (determined through an interview), leadership qualities, and community involvement.

**Financial data** The stipend is $5,000 per year.

**Duration** 1 year (the second or third year of law school); students who accept and successfully complete the firm's summer associate program may receive an additional $5,000 for a subsequent semester of law school.

**Number awarded** 2 each year.

**Deadline** October of each year.

## [844]
## DONNA HEIKEN DOCTORAL GRANT

Sigma Alpha Iota Philanthropies, Inc.
One Tunnel Road
Asheville, NC 28805
(828) 251-0606                    Fax: (828) 251-0644
E-mail: nh@sai-national.org
Web: www.sai-national.org

**Summary** To provide funding for doctoral research in music to members of Sigma Alpha Iota (an organization of women musicians).

**Eligibility** This program is open to members of the organization who are enrolled in a program leading to a doctoral degree. They must be conducting doctoral research on music education, music therapy, musicology, ethnomusicology, music theory, psychology of music, or applied research (including performance or pedagogy).

**Financial data** The grant is $2,500 per year.

**Duration** 1 year.

**Number awarded** 1 each year.

**Deadline** March of each year.

## [845]
## DONNA REIFSCHNEIDER SCHOLARSHIP

Delta Zeta Sorority
Attn: Foundation Coordinator
202 East Church Street
Oxford, OH 45056
(513) 523-7597                    Fax: (513) 523-1921
E-mail: DZFoundation@dzshq.com
Web: www.deltazeta.org

**Summary** To provide financial assistance for continued undergraduate or graduate study in music or music education to members of Delta Zeta Sorority.

**Eligibility** This program is open to upper-division and graduate members of the sorority who have a GPA of 3.0 or higher. Applicants must be working on a degree in music or music education. Along with their application, they must submit an official transcript, a statement of their career goals, information on their service to the sorority, documentation of campus activities and/or community involvement, a list of academic honors, and an explanation of their financial need. Preference is given to members of the Iota Upsilon chapter at California State University at Fullerton or Iota Iota chapter at Middle Tennessee State University.

**Financial data** The stipend ranges from $500 to $2,500 for undergraduates or from $1,000 to $15,000 for graduate students, depending on the availability of funds.

**Duration** 1 year; nonrenewable.

**Number awarded** 1 each year.

**Deadline** February of each year.

## [846]
## DORIS BALLANCE ORMAN, '25, FELLOWSHIP

Gallaudet University Alumni Association
Attn: Graduate Fellowship Fund Committee
Peikoff Alumni House
Gallaudet University
800 Florida Avenue, N.E.
Washington, DC 20002-3695
(202) 651-5060                    Fax: (202) 651-5062
TDD: (202) 651-5060
E-mail: alumni.relations@gallaudet.edu
Web: www.gallaudet.edu/gff_info.xml

**Summary** To provide financial assistance to deaf women who wish to work on a graduate degree at universities for people who hear normally.

**Eligibility** This program is open to deaf or hard of hearing women graduates of Gallaudet University or other accredited academic institutions who have been accepted for graduate study at colleges or universities for people who hear normally. Applicants must be working full time on a doctorate or other terminal degree. They must have a particular interest in the arts, the humanities, or community leadership. Financial need is considered in the selection process.

**Financial data**   The amount awarded varies, depending upon the needs of the recipient and the availability of funds.

**Duration**   1 year; may be renewed.

**Additional information**   This program is 1 of 12 designated funds within the Graduate Fellowship Fund of the Gallaudet University Alumni Association.

**Number awarded**   Up to 1 each year.

**Deadline**   April of each year.

## [847]
## DORIS HERTSGAARD SCHOLARSHIP

Fargo-Moorhead Area Foundation
Attn: Finance/Program Assistant
502 First Avenue North, Suite 202
Fargo, ND 58102-4804
(701) 234-0756            Fax: (701) 234-9724
E-mail: Cher@areafoundation.org
Web: areafoundation.org/index.php/scholarships

**Summary**   To provide financial assistance to women from any state who are working on an undergraduate or graduate degree in a mathematics-related field at specified colleges and universities in Minnesota or North Dakota.

**Eligibility**   This program is open to women from any state who are currently enrolled at Concordia University, Minnesota State University at Moorhead, or North Dakota State University. Applicants must be working on an undergraduate or graduate degree with a mathematics component (e.g., computer science, engineering, mathematics, physical science, statistics). Along with their application, they must submit a 2-page essay on their professional goals and how those relate to their academic interest in their mathematical field of study. Financial need is considered in the selection process, but greater emphasis is placed on academic achievement. Preference is given to women who are single parents with pre-teenage children.

**Financial data**   A stipend is awarded (amount not specified).

**Duration**   1 year.

**Number awarded**   1 or more each year.

**Deadline**   April of each year.

## [848]
## DOROTHY E. SCHOELZEL MEMORIAL SCHOLARSHIP

General Federation of Women's Clubs of Connecticut
c/o Nancy Kalyan, President
4 Mulberry Lane
Enfield, CT 06082
E-mail: KalyanGFWCC@aol.com
Web: www.gfwcct.org

**Summary**   To provide financial assistance to women in Connecticut who are working on an undergraduate or graduate degree in education.

**Eligibility**   This program is open to female residents of Connecticut who have completed at least 3 years of college. Applicants must have a GPA of 3.0 or higher and be working on a bachelor's or master's degree in education. They must be U.S. citizens. Selection is based on academic ability, future promise, and financial need.

**Financial data**   The stipend is $2,000.

**Duration**   1 year.

**Number awarded**   1 each year.

**Deadline**   February of each year.

## [849]
## DOROTHY L. WELLER PEO SCHOLARSHIP

P.E.O. Foundation-California State Chapter
c/o Lynne Miller, Scholarship Committee Chair
1875 Los Altos
Clovis, CA 93611
(559) 709-6123         E-mail: peoca.rgw@gmail.com
Web: www.peocalifornia.org

**Summary**   To provide financial assistance for law school or paralegal studies to women in California.

**Eligibility**   This program is open to female residents of California who have been admitted to an accredited law school or a licensed paralegal school. Applicants must have completed 4 years of high school and be able to demonstrate excellence in academic ability, character, integrity, and school activities. Financial need is also considered in the selection process.

**Financial data**   Recently, the stipend was $2,500.

**Duration**   1 year.

**Number awarded**   Varies each year; recently, 4 of these scholarships were awarded.

**Deadline**   January of each year.

## [850]
## DOROTHY WORDEN RONKEN SCHOLARSHIP

Delta Zeta Sorority
Attn: Foundation Coordinator
202 East Church Street
Oxford, OH 45056
(513) 523-7597         Fax: (513) 523-1921
E-mail: DZFoundation@dzshq.com
Web: www.deltazeta.org

**Summary**   To provide financial assistance to members of Delta Zeta Sorority working on a graduate degree in education or business.

**Eligibility**   This program is open to graduate members of the sorority who are working on a degree in education or business. Applicants must be preparing for a career in the purchase of academic books. Along with their application, they must submit an official transcript, a statement of their career goals, information on their service to the sorority, documentation of campus activities and/or community involvement, a list of academic honors, and an explanation of their financial need. Preference is given to applicants from the Alpha Alpha chapter at Northwestern University.

**Financial data**   The stipend ranges from $1,000 to $15,000, depending on the availability of funds.

**Duration**   1 year; nonrenewable.

**Number awarded**   1 each year.

**Deadline**   February of each year.

## [851]
## DOT SUMMER TRANSPORTATION INTERNSHIP PROGRAM FOR DIVERSE GROUPS

Department of Transportation
Attn: Summer Transportation Internship Program for
  Diverse Groups
HAHR-40, Room E63-433
1200 New Jersey Avenue, S.E.
Washington, DC 20590
(202) 366-2907          E-mail: lafayette.melton@dot.gov
Web: www.fhwa.dot.gov/education/stipdg.cfm

**Summary** To enable female, minority, and disabled undergraduate, graduate, and law students to gain work experience during the summer at facilities of the U.S. Department of Transportation (DOT).

**Eligibility** This program is open to all qualified applicants, but it is designed to provide women, persons with disabilities, and members of diverse social and ethnic groups with summer opportunities in transportation. Applicants must be U.S. citizens currently enrolled in a degree-granting program of study at an accredited institution of higher learning at the undergraduate (community or junior college, university, college, or Tribal College or University) or graduate level. Undergraduates must be entering their junior or senior year; students attending a Tribal or community college must have completed their first year of school; law students must be entering their second or third year of school. Students who will graduate during the spring or summer are not eligible unless they have been accepted for enrollment in graduate school. The program accepts applications from students in all majors who are interested in working on transportation-related topics and issues. Preference is given to students with a GPA of 3.0 or higher. Undergraduates must submit a 1-page essay on their transportation interests and how participation in this program will enhance their educational and career plans and goals. Graduate students must submit a writing sample representing their educational and career plans and goals. Law students must submit a legal writing sample.

**Financial data** The stipend is $4,000 for undergraduates or $5,000 for graduate and law students. The program also provides housing and reimbursement of travel expenses from interns' homes to their assignment location.

**Duration** 10 weeks during the summer.

**Additional information** Assignments are at the DOT headquarters in Washington, D.C., a selected modal administration, or selected field offices around the country.

**Number awarded** 80 to 100 each year.

**Deadline** December of each year.

## [852]
## DOYNE M. GREEN SCHOLARSHIP

Seattle Foundation
Attn: Scholarship Administrator
1200 Fifth Avenue, Suite 1300
Seattle, WA 98101-3151
(206) 622-2294                    Fax: (206) 622-7673
E-mail: scholarships@seattlefoundation.org
Web: www.seattlefoundation.org

**Summary** To provide financial assistance to women in Washington working on a graduate degree in law, medicine, or social and public services in any state.

**Eligibility** This program is open to female residents of Washington who have completed the first year of a graduate program in law, medicine, or social and public services. Applicants must be able to demonstrate financial need. Along with their application, they must submit a brief statement on their plans as they relate to their educational and career objectives and long-term goals.

**Financial data** The stipend is $4,000.

**Duration** 1 year; nonrenewable.

**Additional information** This program is administered by Scholarship Management Services, a division of Scholarship America.

**Number awarded** 6 each year.

**Deadline** February of each year.

## [853]
## DR. ALEXANDRA KIRKLEY TRAVELING FELLOWSHIP

Ruth Jackson Orthopaedic Society
6300 North River Road, Suite 727
Rosemont, IL 60018-4226
(847) 698-1626                    Fax: (847) 823-0536
E-mail: rjos@aaos.org
Web: www.rjos.org/web/awards/index.htm

**Summary** To provide funding to female orthopedic medical students who are interested in traveling to enrich their academic career.

**Eligibility** This program is open to female medical students who are members of the Ruth Jackson Orthopaedic Society (RJOS). Applicants must be Board Eligible orthopedic surgeons and citizens of the United States or Canada. They must be interested in a program of travel to enrich their academic career.

**Financial data** Grants up to $6,000 are available.

**Duration** UP to 1 year.

**Additional information** Funding for this program is provided by Zimmer, Inc.

**Number awarded** 1 each year.

**Deadline** September of each year.

## [854]
## DR. AND MRS. DAVID B. ALLMAN MEDICAL SCHOLARSHIPS

Miss America Pageant
Attn: Scholarship Department
222 New Road, Suite 700
Linwood, NJ 08221
(609) 653-8700, ext. 127          Fax: (609) 653-8740
E-mail: info@missamerica.org
Web: www.missamerica.org

**Summary** To provide financial assistance to medical students who have competed or are competing in the Miss America contest at any level.

**Eligibility** This program is open to women who have competed in the Miss America competition at least once, at any level of competition, within the past 10 years. Applicants do not have to apply during the year they competed; they may apply any year following as long as they are attending or accepted by a medical school and plan to become a medical doctor. They must submit an essay, up to 500 words, on why they wish to become a medical doctor and how this scholarship can help them attain that goal. Selection is based on GPA, class rank, MCAT score, extracurricular activities, financial need, and level of participation within the system.

**Financial data** The stipend is $4,500.

**Duration** 1 year.

**Additional information** This scholarship was established in 1974.

**Number awarded** 1 each year.

**Deadline** June of each year.

## [855]
## DR. B. OLIVE COLE GRADUATE EDUCATIONAL GRANT

Lambda Kappa Sigma Pharmacy Fraternity
Attn: Executive Director
S77 W16906 Casey Drive
P.O. Box 570
Muskego, WI 53150-0570
Toll Free: (800) LKS-1913          Fax: (262) 679-4558
E-mail: lks@lks.org
Web: www.lks.org

**Summary** To provide financial assistance to members of Lambda Kappa Sigma who are interested in working on an advanced degree.

**Eligibility** This program is open to members of Lambda Kappa Sigma who are enrolled in a program of graduate study and research that will advance their career. Eligible programs include master's or doctoral degrees (e.g., M.S., M.A., M.B.A., M.P.H., Ph.D., J.D., Dr.P.H.) as well as joint degree programs that combine the Pharm.D. degree with master's or doctoral studies. Applicants must have an initial degree in pharmacy. They must rank in the upper half of their class and be able to demonstrate financial need. Studies may be at institutions that do not offer the Pharm.D. or have a chapter of Lambda Kappa Sigma.

**Financial data** The stipend is $1,000.

**Duration** 1 year.

**Additional information** This program began in 1972. Lambda Kappa Sigma was founded in 1913 to promote the profession of pharmacy among women. Although some of its chapters are now coeducational, it still emphasizes women's health issues.

**Number awarded** 1 each year.

**Deadline** October of each year.

## [856]
## DR. BESSIE ELIZABETH DELANEY FELLOWSHIP

National Dental Association
Attn: National Dental Association Foundation, Inc.
3517 16th Street, N.W.
Washington, DC 20010
(202) 588-1697          Fax: (202) 588-1244
E-mail: admin@ndaonline.org
Web: www.ndafoundation.org/NDAF/Scholarships.html

**Summary** To provide financial assistance to female dental postdoctoral students who are members of minority groups.

**Eligibility** This program is open to female members of minority groups who are working on a postdoctoral degree in subspecialty areas of dentistry, public health, administration, pediatrics, research, or law. Students working on a master's degree beyond their residency may be considered. Appli-

cants must be members of the National Dental Association (NDA) and U.S. citizens or permanent residents. Along with their application, they must submit a letter explaining why they should be considered for this scholarship, 2 letters of recommendation, a curriculum vitae, a description of the program, nomination by their program director, and documentation of financial need.

**Financial data** The stipend is $10,000.

**Duration** 1 year.

**Additional information** This program, established in 1990, is supported by the Colgate-Palmolive Company.

**Number awarded** 1 each year.

**Deadline** May of each year.

## [857]
## DR. DORRI PHIPPS FELLOWSHIPS

Alpha Kappa Alpha Sorority, Inc.
Attn: Educational Advancement Foundation
5656 South Stony Island Avenue
Chicago, IL 60637
(773) 947-0026          Toll Free: (800) 653-6528
Fax: (773) 947-0277          E-mail: akaeaf@akaeaf.net
Web: www.akaeaf.org/fellowships_endowments.htm

**Summary** To provide financial assistance to students (especially African American women) working on a degree in medicine or conducting research related to lupus.

**Eligibility** This program is open to students currently enrolled in a medical or related program in any state. Applicants must be working on a degree in medicine or conducting research related to lupus. Along with their application, they must submit 1) a list of honors, awards, and scholarships received; 2) a list of organizations in which they have memberships, especially minority organizations; 3) a description of the project or research on which they are currently working, of (if they are not involved in a project or research) the aspects of their field that interest them; and 4) a statement of their personal and career goals, including how this scholarship will enhance their ability to attain those goals. The sponsor is a traditionally African American women's sorority.

**Financial data** A stipend is awarded (amount not specified).

**Duration** 1 year.

**Number awarded** Varies each even-numbered year; recently, 5 of these fellowships were awarded.

**Deadline** April of each even-numbered year.

## [858]
## DR. MARIE E. ZAKRZEWSKI MEDICAL SCHOLARSHIP

Kosciuszko Foundation
Attn: Grants Department
15 East 65th Street
New York, NY 10021-6595
(212) 734-2130, ext. 210          Fax: (212) 628-4552
E-mail: addy@thekf.org
Web: www.thekf.org/scholarships/about

**Summary** To provide financial assistance to women of Polish ancestry studying medicine.

**Eligibility** This program is open to young women of Polish ancestry entering their first, second, or third year of study at an accredited medical school in the United States. Applicants must be U.S. citizens of Polish descent or Polish citizens with permanent resident status in the United States. They must have a GPA of 3.0 or higher. First preference is given to residents of Massachusetts. If no candidates from Massachusetts apply, qualified residents of New England are considered. Selection is based on academic excellence; the applicant's academic achievements, interests, and motivation; the applicant's interest in Polish subjects or involvement in the Polish American community; and financial need.

**Financial data** The stipend is $3,000.

**Duration** 1 year; nonrenewable.

**Additional information** This program is funded by the Massachusetts Federation of Polish Women's Clubs but administered by the Kosciuszko Foundation.

**Number awarded** 1 each year.

**Deadline** January of each year.

## [859]
## DR. MARY FEENEY BONAWITZ SCHOLARSHIP

Accounting and Financial Women's Alliance
Attn: Educational Foundation
1760 Old Meadow Road, Suite 500
McLean, VA 22102
(703) 506-3265　　　　　　Toll Free: (800) 326-2163
Fax: (703) 506-3266　　　　E-mail: foundation@afwa.org
Web: www.afwa.org/PageDisplay.asp?p1=1386

**Summary** To provide funding for research to members of the Accounting and Financial Women's Alliance (AFWA) working on a doctoral degree in accounting.

**Eligibility** This program is open to AFWA members who are currently enrolled in an AASCB-accredited Ph.D. program in accounting. Applicants must be seeking funding for research costs (such as measurement instruments and analysis, uses of financial databases, copying, and telecommunications expenses). Along with their application, they must submit an essay of 150 to 250 words on their reasons for working on a Ph.D. in accounting and how they would advocate for women in the accounting profession if they receive this scholarship. Selection is based on leadership, character, communication skills, scholastic average, and financial need. Applications must be submitted to a local AFWA chapter.

**Financial data** The grant is $1,000.

**Duration** 1 year.

**Number awarded** Varies each year.

**Deadline** Local chapters must submit their candidates to the national office by February of each year.

## [860]
## DR. NANCY FOSTER SCHOLARSHIP PROGRAM

National Oceanic and Atmospheric Administration
Attn: Office of Education
1315 East-West Highway
SSMC3, Room 11146
Silver Spring, MD 20910
(301) 713-9437, ext. 150　　　　　Fax: (301) 713-9465
E-mail: fosterscholars@noaa.gov
Web: fosterscholars.noaa.gov

**Summary** To provide financial assistance to graduate students, especially women and minorities, who are interested in working on a degree in fields related to marine sciences.

**Eligibility** This program is open to U.S. citizens, particularly women and members of minority groups, currently working on or intending to work on a master's or doctoral degree in oceanography, marine biology, or maritime archaeology, including all science, engineering, and resource management of ocean and coastal areas. Applicants must submit a description of their academic, research, and career goals, and how their proposed course of study or research will help them to achieve those goals. They must be enrolled full time and have a GPA of 3.0 or higher. As part of their program, they must be interested in participating in a summer research collaboration at a facility of the National Oceanic and Atmospheric Administration (NOAA). Selection is based on academic record and the statement of career goals and objectives (25%); quality of project and applicability to program priorities (35%); recommendations and/or endorsements (15%); additional relevant experience related to diversity of education, extracurricular activities, honors and awards, written and oral communication skills, and interpersonal skills (15%); and financial need (10%).

**Financial data** The program provides a stipend of $30,000 per academic year, a tuition allowance of up to $12,000 per academic year, and up to $10,000 of support for a 4- to 6-week research collaboration at a NOAA facility is provided.

**Duration** Master's degree students may receive up to 2 years of stipend and tuition support and 1 research collaboration (for a total of $94,000). Doctoral students may receive up to 4 years of stipend and tuition support and 2 research collaborations (for a total of $188,000).

**Additional information** This program began in 2001.

**Number awarded** Varies each year; recently, 3 of these fellowships were awarded.

**Deadline** February of each year.

## [861]
## DR. PRENTICE GAUTT POSTGRADUATE SCHOLARSHIPS

Big 12 Conference
400 East John Carpenter Freeway
Irving, TX 75062
(469) 524-1000
Web: www.big12sports.com

**Summary** To provide financial assistance for graduate school to student athletes who complete their undergraduate study at a Big 12 university (females and males are judged separately).

**Eligibility** This program is open to students graduating from a Big 12 university who have participated in at least 2 years of intercollegiate athletics. Applicants must have a GPA of 3.5 or higher and be planning to enroll full time in a program of professional or graduate study. Male and female athletes are considered separately.

**Financial data** The stipend is $9,000. Funds are paid directly to the student.

**Duration** 1 year.

**Additional information** This program began with the inception of the league in 1996-97. Members of the Big 12 include Baylor, Iowa State, Kansas, Kansas State, Oklahoma, Oklahoma State, Texas, Texas Christian, Texas Tech, and West Virginia. Recipients must graduate from their Big 12 university within 15 months of their selection for this scholarship and must enroll in a graduate or professional school within 2 years of graduation.

**Number awarded** 20 each year: 2 (1 male and 1 female) at each member institution.

**Deadline** Deadline not specified.

## [862]
## DRI LAW STUDENT DIVERSITY SCHOLARSHIP

DRI-The Voice of the Defense Bar
Attn: Deputy Executive Director
55 West Monroe Street, Suite 2000
Chicago, IL 60603
(312) 795-1101                     Fax: (312) 795-0747
E-mail: dri@dri.org
Web: www.dri.org/About

**Summary** To provide financial assistance to female and minority law students.

**Eligibility** This program is open to full-time students entering their second or third year of law school who are African American, Hispanic, Asian, Native American, or women. Applicants must submit an essay, up to 1,000 words, on a topic that changes annually but relates to the work of defense attorneys. Selection is based on that essay, demonstrated academic excellence, service to the profession, service to the community, and service to the cause of diversity. Students affiliated with the American Association for Justice as members, student members, or employees are not eligible. Finalists are invited to participate in personal interviews.

**Financial data** The stipend is $10,000.

**Duration** 1 year.

**Additional information** This program began in 2004.

**Number awarded** 2 each year.

**Deadline** May of each year.

## [863]
## DURNING SISTERS FELLOWSHIP

Delta Delta Delta
Attn: Tri Delta Foundation
2331 Brookhollow Plaza Drive
P.O. Box 5987
Arlington, TX 76005-5987
(817) 633-8001                     Fax: (817) 652-0212
E-mail: fdnscholarship@trideltaeo.org
Web: www.tridelta.org/Foundation/Scholarships

**Summary** To provide financial assistance for graduate study to unmarried women who are members of Delta Delta Delta.

**Eligibility** This program is open to members of the sorority who have completed at least 12 hours of graduate study. Applicants must be unmarried. Along with their application, they must submit a personal statement outlining their educational and vocational goals, 2 academic recommendations, a Tri Delta recommendation, academic transcripts, and documentation of financial need. Selection is based on academic merit, chapter and campus activities, and community activities.

**Financial data** The stipend is $3,000.

**Duration** 1 year.

**Number awarded** 1 each year.

**Deadline** February of each year.

## [864]
## EDITH B. WONNELL SCHOLARSHIP

American College of Nurse-Midwives
Attn: ACNM Foundation, Inc.
8403 Colesville Road, Suite 1550
Silver Spring, MD 20910-6374
(240) 485-1850                     Fax: (240) 485-1818
E-mail: fdn@acnm.org
Web: www.midwife.org

**Summary** To provide financial assistance for midwifery education to student members of the American College of Nurse-Midwives (ACNM) who plan to work in a home or birth center midwifery practice after graduation.

**Eligibility** This program is open to ACNM members who are currently enrolled in an accredited basic midwife education program and have successfully completed 1 academic or clinical semester/quarter or clinical module. Applicants must be planning to work in an out-of-hospital setting, either in a birth center or home birth practice. Along with their application, they must submit a 150-word essay on their midwifery career plans; a 100-word essay on their intended future participation in the local, regional, and/or national activities of the ACNM; and a 300-word statement about their goals in choosing to work in a home or birth center as a midwife. Selection is based on leadership potential, financial need, academic history, and potential for future professional contribution to the organization.

**Financial data** A stipend is awarded (amount not specified).

**Duration** 1 year.

**Number awarded** 1 or more each year.

**Deadline** March of each year.

## [865]
## EDITH HEAD SCHOLARSHIP

Delta Zeta Sorority
Attn: Foundation Coordinator
202 East Church Street
Oxford, OH 45056
(513) 523-7597                     Fax: (513) 523-1921
E-mail: DZFoundation@dzshq.com
Web: www.deltazeta.org

**Summary** To provide financial assistance for continued undergraduate or graduate study in fashion design to members of Delta Zeta Sorority.

**Eligibility** This program is open to upper-division and graduate members of the sorority who have a GPA of 3.0 or higher. Applicants must be juniors, seniors, graduate students, or students at a professional school that offers fashion merchandising, textiles, and clothing and costume design. Along with their application, they must submit an official transcript, a statement of their career goals, information on their service to the sorority, documentation of campus activities and/or community involvement, a list of academic honors, and an explanation of their financial need.

**Financial data** The stipend ranges from $500 to $2,500 for undergraduates or from $1,000 to $15,000 for graduate students, depending on the availability of funds.

**Duration** 1 year; nonrenewable.

**Number awarded** 1 each year.

**Deadline** February of each year.

## [866]
## EDITH HUNTINGTON ANDERSON SCHOLARSHIP

Alpha Omicron Pi Foundation
Attn: Scholarship Committee
5390 Virginia Way
Brentwood, TN 37027
(615) 370-0920          Fax: (615) 370-4424
E-mail: foundation@alphaomicronpi.org
Web: www.alphaomicronpi.org

**Summary** To provide financial assistance to alumnae members of Alpha Omicron Pi who are interested in preparing for a medical career.

**Eligibility** This program is open to alumnae members of Alpha Omicron Pi who have a bachelor's degree and are preparing for a career in medicine or a medical-related field. Applicants must be enrolled full time. Along with their application, they must submit brief essays about themselves. Selection is based on those essays, academic achievement, Alpha Omicron Pi leadership and honors, campus and community involvement, letters of recommendation, and financial need.

**Financial data** Stipend amounts vary; recently, the average value of each scholarship provided by this foundation was approximately $1,200.

**Duration** 1 year.

**Number awarded** 1 each odd-numbered year.

**Deadline** February of each odd-numbered year.

## [867]
## EDITH SEVILLE COALE SCHOLARSHIPS

Zonta Club of Washington, D.C.
c/o Merilyn D. Francis, Scholarship Committee
P.O. Box 9753
Washington, DC 20016
(202) 380-5222
Web: www.zontawashingtondc.org/projects.html

**Summary** To provide financial assistance to women who have completed the first year of medical school in the Washington, D.C. area.

**Eligibility** This program is open to women from any state who are in the second, third, or fourth year of medical school in the Washington, D.C. area. Selection is based on financial need and scholastic achievement.

**Financial data** The amount awarded varies; recently, stipends averaged $8,405.

**Duration** 1 year.

**Additional information** The trust fund contains limited funds. Awards are not made for the first year of medical school. Preference is given to women students nominated by medical school faculty members.

**Number awarded** Varies each year; recently, 4 of these scholarships were awarded.

**Deadline** March of each year.

## [868]
## EDUCATIONAL FOUNDATION FOR WOMEN IN ACCOUNTING IMA GRADUATE SCHOLARSHIP

Educational Foundation for Women in Accounting
Attn: Foundation Administrator
136 South Keowee Street
Dayton, OH 45402
(937) 424-3391          Fax: (937) 222-5749
E-mail: info@efwa.org
Web: www.efwa.org/scholarships.php

**Summary** To provide financial support to women who are entering a graduate program in accounting.

**Eligibility** This program is open to women who are entering a master's degree program in accounting at an accredited college or university. Selection is based on aptitude for accounting and business, commitment to the goal of working on a degree in accounting (including evidence of continued commitment after receiving this award), clear evidence that the candidate has established goals and a plan for achieving those goals (both personal and professional), and financial need. U.S. citizenship is required.

**Financial data** The stipend is $1,000. Winners also receive a CMA Learning System kit (worth $745) and a complimentary 1-year students membership to the Institute of Management Accountants (IMA).

**Duration** 1 year.

**Additional information** This program is funded by the IMA.

**Number awarded** 1 each year.

**Deadline** April of each year.

## [869]
## E.K. WISE SCHOLARSHIP FUND

American Occupational Therapy Association
Attn: Membership Department
4720 Montgomery Lane, Suite 200
Bethesda, MD 20824-3449
(301) 652-2682, ext. 2769          Fax: (301) 652-7711
TDD: (800) 377-8555          E-mail: ekwise@aota.org
Web: www.aota.org

**Summary** To provide financial assistance to female members of the American Occupational Therapy Association (AOTA) who are working on a professional master's degree in occupational therapy.

**Eligibility** This program is open to women who are AOTA members working full time on a professional post-baccalaureate occupational therapy degree. Applicants must be able to demonstrate a sustained record of outstanding scholastic performance, demonstrated leadership, and community service. Along with their application, they must submit an essay (up to 1,000 words) on how they can contribute to meeting the AOTA objective of developing a well-prepared, diverse workforce. Financial need is considered in the selection process. U.S. citizenship or permanent resident status is required.

**Financial data** The stipend is $5,000 per year.

**Duration** 1 year; may be renewed 1 additional year.

**Additional information** This fund was established in 1969 as the E.K. Wise Loan Program. In 2008, the AOTA converted it to a scholarship program.

**Number awarded** 2 each year.

**Deadline** May of each year.

## [870]
## ELI LILLY TRAVEL AWARDS

American Chemical Society
Attn: Department of Diversity Programs
1155 16th Street, N.W.
Washington, DC 20036
(202) 872-6334          Toll Free: (800) 227-5558, ext. 6334
Fax: (202) 776-8003          E-mail: diversity@acs.org
Web: www.acs.org

**Summary**   To provide funding to women chemists interested in traveling to scientific meetings.

**Eligibility**   This program is open to women chemists (students, professionals, and postdoctorates) who wish to travel to scientific meetings to present the results of their research. Only U.S. citizens and permanent residents are eligible. Awards are made on the basis of scientific merit and financial need. Preference is given to those who have not made a previous presentation at a national or major meeting. Women who have received a prior award under this program are ineligible.

**Financial data**   Awards range up to $1,000 and may be used for registration, travel, and accommodations only.

**Additional information**   Funding for this program is provided by Eli Lilly and Company. Grants are restricted to travel within the United States.

**Number awarded**   Varies each year.

**Deadline**   September of each year for meetings between January and June; February of each year for meetings between July and December.

## [871]
## ELIZABETH FURBUR FELLOWSHIP

American Indian Graduate Center
Attn: Executive Director
3701 San Mateo Boulevard, N.E., Suite 200
Albuquerque, NM 87110-1249
(505) 881-4584          Toll Free: (800) 628-1920
Fax: (505) 884-0427          E-mail: fellowships@aigc.com
Web: www.aigcs.com/scholarships/graduate-fellowships

**Summary**   To provide financial assistance to female Native American graduate students interested in working on a degree related to the arts.

**Eligibility**   This program is open to women who are enrolled members of federally-recognized American Indian tribes and Alaska Native groups or who can document one-fourth degree federally-recognized Indian blood. Applicants must be enrolled full time in a graduate program in the creative fine arts, visual works, crafts, music, performing, dance, literary arts, creative writing, or poetry. Along with their application, they must submit a 500-word essay on how receiving this fellowship will enable them to continue to build, promote, and honor self-sustaining American Indian and Alaska Native communities. Financial need is also considered in the selection process.

**Financial data**   Stipends range from $500 to $5,000 per academic year, depending on the availability of funds and the recipient's unmet financial need.

**Duration**   1 year; may be renewed.

**Number awarded**   1 each year.

**Deadline**   May of each year.

## [872]
## ELIZABETH M. GRUBER SCHOLARSHIPS

Delta Zeta Sorority
Attn: Foundation Coordinator
202 East Church Street
Oxford, OH 45056
(513) 523-7597          Fax: (513) 523-1921
E-mail: DZFoundation@dzshq.com
Web: www.deltazeta.org

**Summary**   To provide financial assistance to members of Delta Zeta Sorority working on a graduate degree in the liberal arts.

**Eligibility**   This program is open to graduate members of the sorority who are working on a degree in the liberal arts. Applicants must have a GPA of 3.0 or higher. Along with their application, they must submit an official transcript, a statement of their career goals, information on their service to the sorority, documentation of campus activities and/or community involvement, a list of academic honors, and an explanation of their financial need. Preference is given to applicants from the Alpha Beta chapter at the University of Illinois at Urbana-Champaign or at a university in the Midwest, in that order.

**Financial data**   The stipend ranges from $1,000 to $15,000, depending on the availability of funds.

**Duration**   1 year; nonrenewable.

**Number awarded**   Varies each year; recently, 3 of these scholarships were awarded.

**Deadline**   February of each year.

## [873]
## ELIZABETH MUNSTERBERG KOPPITZ CHILD PSYCHOLOGY GRADUATE FELLOWSHIPS

American Psychological Foundation
750 First Street, N.E.
Washington, DC 20002-4242
(202) 336-5843          Fax: (202) 336-5812
E-mail: foundation@apa.org
Web: www.apa.org/apf/funding/koppitz.aspx

**Summary**   To provide funding to doctoral students (particularly women and members of other underrepresented groups) who are interested in conducting research in child psychology.

**Eligibility**   This program is open to graduate students who have progressed academically through the qualifying examinations, usually after the third or fourth year of doctoral study. Applicants must be interested in conducting psychological research that promotes the advancement of knowledge and learning in the field of child psychology. Selection is based on conformance with stated program goals, magnitude of incremental contribution, quality of proposed work, and applicant's demonstrated scholarship and research competence. The sponsor encourages applications from individuals who represent diversity in race, ethnicity, gender, age, disability, and sexual orientation.

**Financial data**   The grant is $25,000 for fellows or $5,000 for runners-up.

**Duration**   1 year.

**Additional information**   This fellowship was first awarded in 2003.

**Number awarded** Varies each year; recently, 6 fellows and 2 runners-up were selected.

**Deadline** November of each year.

## [874]
## ELLEN CUSHING SCHOLARSHIPS

American Baptist Churches USA
National Ministries
Attn: Office of Financial Aid for Studies
P.O. Box 851
Valley Forge, PA 19482-0851
(610) 768-2067 Toll Free: (800) ABC-3USA, ext. 2067
Fax: (610) 768-2453
E-mail: Financialaid.Web@abc-usa.org
Web: www.nationalministries.org

**Summary** To provide financial assistance to Baptist women interested in working on a graduate degree in human service fields.

**Eligibility** This program is open to female Baptists in graduate programs who are preparing for a human service career in the secular world. Applicants must be U.S. citizens who have been a member of a church affiliated with American Baptist Churches USA for at least 1 year. M.Div. and D.Min. students are not eligible. Preference is given to students active in their school, church, or region.

**Financial data** The stipend is $2,000.

**Duration** 1 year.

**Number awarded** Up to 3 each year.

**Deadline** May of each year.

## [875]
## ELSA LUDEKE GRADUATE SCHOLARSHIPS

Delta Zeta Sorority
Attn: Foundation Coordinator
202 East Church Street
Oxford, OH 45056
(513) 523-7597 Fax: (513) 523-1921
E-mail: DZFoundation@dzshq.com
Web: www.deltazeta.org

**Summary** To provide financial assistance for graduate school to members of Delta Zeta Sorority.

**Eligibility** This program is open to members of the sorority who are working on a graduate degree. Applicants may be either continuing students who are entering graduate school immediately after completing their bachelor's degree or alumnae returning to graduate school after an absence of more than 3 years. They must have a GPA of 3.0 or higher. Along with their application, they must submit an official transcript, a statement of their career goals, information on their service to the sorority, documentation of campus activities and/or community involvement, a list of academic honors, and an explanation of their financial need.

**Financial data** The stipend ranges from $1,000 to $15,000, depending on the availability of funds.

**Duration** 1 year; nonrenewable.

**Number awarded** 2 each year: 1 to a continuing student and 1 to a returning alumna.

**Deadline** February of each year.

## [876]
## ELSIE G. RIDDICK SCHOLARSHIP

North Carolina Federation of Business and Professional Women's Club, Inc.
Attn: BPW/NC Foundation
175 BPW Club Road
P.O. Box 276
Carrboro, NC 27510
Web: www.bpw-nc.org/Default.aspx?pageId=837230

**Summary** To provide financial assistance to women attending North Carolina colleges, community colleges, or graduate schools.

**Eligibility** This program is open to women who are currently enrolled in a community college, 4-year college, or graduate school in North Carolina. Applicants must be endorsed by a local BPW unit. Along with their application, they must submit a 1-page statement that summarizes their career goals, previous honors, or community activities and justifies their need for this scholarship. U.S. citizenship is required.

**Financial data** The stipend is $1,000. Funds are paid directly to the recipient's school.

**Duration** 1 year; recipients may reapply.

**Additional information** This program began in 1925 as a loan fund. Since 1972 it has been administered as a scholarship program.

**Number awarded** 1 each year.

**Deadline** April of each year.

## [877]
## EMERGE SCHOLARSHIPS

Emerge Scholarships, Inc.
3525 Piedmont Road
Building Five, Suite 30305
Atlanta, GA 30305
(404) 477-5808 E-mail: info@emergescholarships.org
Web: www.emergescholarships.org

**Summary** To provide financial assistance to women interested in returning to college or graduate school after a delay or interruption.

**Eligibility** This program is open to women who are at least 25 years of age and who have interrupted or delayed their education because they are changing careers, seeking advancement in their career or work life, looking for personal growth, or returning to school after caring for children. Applicants must have been accepted as an undergraduate or graduate student at an educational institution. They must be current residents of the United States or Puerto Rico (including foreign nationals who plan to study in the United States) or U.S. citizens living abroad applying to study in the United States. Along with their application, they must submit a 2-page essay on how beginning or continuing their education will positively impact their life. Selection is based on that essay, leadership and participation in community activities, honors and awards received, career and life goals, financial need, and other funding received. Preference is given to women pursuing their education in Georgia.

**Financial data** Stipends range from $2,000 to $5,000. funds may be used only for tuition, books, and fees at the recipient's educational institution.

**Duration** 1 year.

**Additional information** This program began in 2001. Winners are invited to Atlanta to accept their scholarships; the sponsor pays all travel expenses.

**Number awarded** Varies each year; recently, 13 of these scholarships were awarded.

**Deadline** October of each year.

## [878]
## EMIL SLAVIK MEMORIAL SCHOLARSHIPS

Slovak Catholic Sokol
Attn: Membership Memorial Scholarship Fund
205 Madison Street
P.O. Box 899
Passaic, NJ 07055-0899
(973) 777-2605          Toll Free: (800) 886-7656
Fax: (973) 779-8245   E-mail: life@slovakcatholicsokol.org
Web: www.slovakcatholicsokol.org/grantsscholarships.asp

**Summary** To provide financial assistance to female and male members (judged separately) of the Slovak Catholic Sokol who are working on a degree in specified fields at a college or graduate school in any state.

**Eligibility** This program is open to members of the Slovak Catholic Sokol who have completed at least 1 semester of college and are currently enrolled full time as an undergraduate or graduate student at an accredited college, university, or professional school in any state with a GPA of 2.5 or higher. Applicants must have been a member for at least 5 years, have at least $3,000 permanent life insurance coverage, have both parents who are members, and have at least 1 parent who is of Slovak descent. They must be working on a degree in the liberal arts, the sciences, pre-law, pre-medicine, or business. Males and females are judged separately.

**Financial data** The stipend is $2,500 per year.

**Duration** 1 year; may be renewed 1 additional year.

**Additional information** Slovak Catholic Sokol was founded as a fraternal benefit society in 1905. It is licensed to operate in the following states: Connecticut, Illinois, Indiana, Massachusetts, Michigan, New Jersey, New York, Ohio, Pennsylvania, and Wisconsin.

**Number awarded** 2 each year: 1 for a male and 1 for a female.

**Deadline** March of each year.

## [879]
## EMILY SCHOENBAUM RESEARCH AND COMMUNITY DEVELOPMENT GRANTS

Tulane University
Newcomb College Institute
Attn: Assistant Director for Administration and Programs
200 Caroline Richardson Hall
62 Newcomb Place
New Orleans, LA 70118
(504) 314-2721          Toll Free: (888) 327-0009
Fax: (504) 862-8589      E-mail: lwolford@tulane.edu
Web: tulane.edu/newcomb/grants.cfm

**Summary** To provide funding to scholars and students in Louisiana interested in conducting research or other projects related to women and girls.

**Eligibility** This program is open to students, faculty, and staff of primary and secondary schools, colleges, and universities in Louisiana, as well as community scholars and activ-

ists. Applicants must be interested in conducting a project with potential to bring about change in women's lives or effect public policy so as to improve the well-being of women and girls, particularly those in the New Orleans area.

**Financial data** The grant is $2,000.

**Duration** 1 year.

**Additional information** This program began in 1999.

**Number awarded** 1 or 2 each year.

**Deadline** April of each year.

## [880]
## ERIN MARIE EMERINE MEMORIAL SCHOLARSHIP

Columbus Foundation
Attn: Scholarship Manager
1234 East Broad Street
Columbus, OH 43205-1453
(614) 251-4000          Fax: (614) 251-4009
E-mail: dhigginbotham@columbusfoundation.org
Web: tcfapp.org

**Summary** To provide financial assistance to women working on an undergraduate or graduate degree at a college or university in Ohio.

**Eligibility** This program is open to women currently attending an accredited 4-year college or university in Ohio. Applicants may be residents of any state, although preference may be given to Ohio residents. They must meet 1 of the following stipulations: 1) returned to college as an undergraduate or graduate student after an extended absence of at least 2 years; 2) 23 years of age or older and in college for the first time or applying for graduate school for the first time with a GPA of 3.0 or higher; or 3) has completed the freshman year with a GPA of 3.0 or higher. Along with their application, they must submit their most recent transcript, 2 letters of recommendation, a list of volunteer activities, a list of extracurricular activities, a personal essay on how volunteering has impacted their life, and information on financial need.

**Financial data** The stipend is $1,500.

**Duration** 1 year.

**Number awarded** 1 or more each year.

**Deadline** April of each year.

## [881]
## ESPERANZA SCHOLARSHIP

New York Women in Communications, Inc.
Attn: NYWICI Foundation
355 Lexington Avenue, 15th Floor
New York, NY 10017-6603
(212) 297-2133          Fax: (212) 370-9047
E-mail: nywicipr@nywici.org
Web: www.nywici.org/foundation/scholarships

**Summary** To provide financial assistance to Hispanic women who are residents of designated eastern states and interested in preparing for a career in communications at a college or graduate school in any state.

**Eligibility** This program is open to Hispanic women who are seniors graduating from high schools in New York, New Jersey, Connecticut, or Pennsylvania or undergraduate or graduate students who are permanent residents of those states; they must be attending or planning to attend a college or university in any state. Graduate students must be members of New York Women in Communications, Inc. (NYWICI). Also eligible are Hispanic women who reside outside the 4 states but are currently enrolled at a college or university within 1 of the 5 boroughs of New York City. All applicants must be working on a degree in a communications-related field (e.g., advertising, broadcasting, communications, English, film, journalism, marketing, digital media, public relations) and have a GPA of 3.2 or higher. Along with their application, they must submit a 2-page resume; a personal essay of 300 words on an assigned topic that changes annually; 2 letters of recommendation; and an official transcript. Selection is based on academic record, need, demonstrated leadership, participation in school and community activities, honors and other awards or recognition, work experience, goals and aspirations, and unusual personal and/or family circumstances. U.S. citizenship is required.

**Financial data** The stipend ranges up to $10,000.

**Duration** 1 year.

**Additional information** This program is funded by Macy's and Bloomingdale's.

**Number awarded** 1 each year.

**Deadline** January of each year.

## [882]
## ESTHER EDWARDS GRADUATE SCHOLARSHIP

United Methodist Church
Attn: General Board of Higher Education and Ministry
Office of Loans and Scholarships
1001 19th Avenue South
P.O. Box 340007
Nashville, TN 37203-0007
(615) 340-7344                    Fax: (615) 340-7367
E-mail: umscholar@gbhem.org
Web: www.gbhem.org

**Summary** To provide financial assistance to female graduate students who are working on a degree in higher education administration to prepare for a career with a United Methodist school.

**Eligibility** This program is open to women who are working on a graduate degree to prepare for an executive management career in higher education administration with a United Methodist school, college, or university. Applicants must have been active, full members of a United Methodist Church for at least 1 year prior to applying. They must have a GPA of 3.0 or higher. First preference is given to students currently employed by a United Methodist school, college, or university and to full-time students.

**Financial data** The stipend is $5,000.

**Duration** 1 year; nonrenewable.

**Number awarded** 1 each year.

**Deadline** February of each year.

## [883]
## ESTHER KATZ ROSEN GRADUATE STUDENT FELLOWSHIPS

American Psychological Foundation
750 First Street, N.E.
Washington, DC 20002-4242
(202) 336-5843                    Fax: (202) 336-5812
E-mail: foundation@apa.org
Web: www.apa.org/apf/funding/rosen.aspx

**Summary** To provide funding to graduate students (particularly women, minorities, and persons with disabilities) who are interested in conducting research on psychological issues relevant to giftedness in children.

**Eligibility** This program is open to graduate students at universities in the United States and Canada who have advanced to candidacy. Applicants must be interested in conducting research on the psychological understanding of gifted and talented children and adolescents. Selection is based on conformance with stated program goals, magnitude of incremental contribution, quality of proposed work, and applicant's demonstrated scholarship and research competence. The sponsor encourages applications from individuals who represent diversity in race, ethnicity, gender, age, disability, and sexual orientation.

**Financial data** The grant is $20,000. The fellow's home institution is expected to provide a tuition waiver.

**Duration** 1 year.

**Additional information** This fund was established in 1974.

**Number awarded** 1 each year.

**Deadline** April of each year.

## [884]
## ESTHER NGAN-LING CHOW AND MAREYJOYCE GREEN SCHOLARSHIP

Sociologists for Women in Society
Attn: Executive Officer
Southern Connecticut State University
Department of Sociology
501 Crescent Street
New Haven, CT 06515
(203) 392-7714                    Fax: (203) 392-7715
E-mail: swseo@socwomen.org
Web: www.socwomen.org/awards.html

**Summary** To provide funding to women of color who are conducting dissertation research in sociology.

**Eligibility** This program is open to women from a racial/ethnic group that faces discrimination in the United States. Applicants must be in the early stages of writing a doctoral dissertation in sociology on a topic relating to the concerns that women of color face domestically and/or internationally. They must be able to demonstrate financial need. Both domestic and international students are eligible to apply. Along with their application, they must submit a personal statement that details their short- and long-term career and research goals; a resume or curriculum vitae; 2 letters of recommendation; and a 5-page dissertation proposal that includes the purpose of the research, the work to be accomplished through support from this scholarship, and a time line for completion.

**Financial data** The stipend is $15,000. An additional grant of $500 is provided to enable the recipient to attend the winter meeting of Sociologists for Women in Society (SWS), and travel expenses to attend the summer meeting are reimbursed.

**Duration** 1 year.

**Additional information** This program began in 2007 and originally named the Women of Color Dissertation Scholarship.

**Number awarded** 1 each year.

**Deadline** March of each year.

## [885]
## ETHEL F. LORD AWARD

Soroptimist International of the Americas-North Atlantic Region
c/o Deborah R. Cook, Governor
1713 Glen Savage Road
Fairhope, PA 15538
E-mail: governor@soroptimistnar.org
Web: www.soroptimistnar.org

**Summary** To provide financial assistance to women who reside in the north Atlantic region and are working on a graduate degree in gerontology at a university in the region.

**Eligibility** This program is open to female residents of Delaware, New Jersey, New York, Pennsylvania, and the panhandle area of West Virginia who are enrolled full time at a college or university in the region. Applicants must be working on a master's or doctoral degree in gerontology. Selection is based on academic excellence and financial need.

**Financial data** The stipend is $5,000.

**Duration** 1 year.

**Number awarded** 1 each odd-numbered year.

**Deadline** November of each even-numbered year.

## [886]
## ETHEL O. GARDNER PEO SCHOLARSHIP

P.E.O. Foundation-California State Chapter
c/o Lynne Miller, Scholarship Committee Chair
1875 Los Altos
Clovis, CA 93611
(559) 709-6123          E-mail: peoca.rgw@gmail.com
Web: www.peocalifornia.org

**Summary** To provide financial assistance to women from California who are upper-division or graduate students at a school in any state.

**Eligibility** This program is open to female residents of California who have completed at least 2 years at a college or university in any state. Applicants must be enrolled as full-time undergraduate or graduate students. Selection is based on financial need, character, and a record of academic and extracurricular activities achievement.

**Financial data** Stipends range from $500 to $1,500.

**Duration** 1 year.

**Number awarded** Varies each year; recently, 69 of these scholarships were awarded.

**Deadline** January of each year.

## [887]
## EUGENIA VELLNER FISCHER AWARD FOR THE PERFORMING ARTS

Miss America Pageant
Attn: Scholarship Department
222 New Road, Suite 700
Linwood, NJ 08221
(609) 653-8700, ext. 127          Fax: (609) 653-8740
E-mail: info@missamerica.org
Web: www.missamerica.org/scholarships/eugenia.aspx

**Summary** To provide financial assistance to women who are working on an undergraduate or graduate degree in the performing arts and who, in the past, competed at some level in the Miss America competition.

**Eligibility** This program is open to women who are working on an undergraduate, master's, or higher degree in the performing arts and who competed at the local, state, or national level in a Miss America competition within the past 10 years. Applicants may be studying dance, instrumental, monologue, or vocal. They must submit an essay, up to 500 words, on the factors that influenced their decision to enter the field of performing arts, what they consider to be their major strengths in the field, and how they plan to use their degree in the field. Selection is based on GPA, class rank, extracurricular activities, financial need, and level of participation within the system.

**Financial data** The stipend is $2,000.

**Duration** 1 year; renewable.

**Additional information** This scholarship was established in 1999.

**Number awarded** 1 each year.

**Deadline** June of each year.

## [888]
## FEDERATION OF HOUSTON PROFESSIONAL WOMEN EDUCATIONAL FOUNDATION SCHOLARSHIPS

Federation of Houston Professional Women
Attn: Educational Foundation
P.O. Box 27621
Houston, TX 77227-7621
E-mail: educationalfoundation@fhpw.org
Web: www.fhpw.org/the_foundation.html

**Summary** To provide financial assistance for college or graduate school to women from Texas.

**Eligibility** This program is open to women who are residents of Texas and have completed at least 30 semesters hours of work on an associate, bachelor's, or graduate degree at an accredited college or university in the state. Applicants must be U.S. citizens or permanent residents and have a GPA of 3.0 or higher. Along with their application, they must submit 1) a 200-word statement on their short- and long-term goals; 2) a 400-word essay on either the experiences that have helped determine their goals or the avenues that can help determine their goals; and 3) a 100-word biographical sketch. Financial need is considered in the selection process.

**Financial data** Stipends are $2,000 for students at 4-year colleges and universities or $1,000 for students at community colleges. Funds are issued payable jointly to the student and the educational institution.

**Duration** 1 year.

**Additional information** This program began in 2000.

**Number awarded** Varies each year; recently, 18 of these scholarships were awarded. Since this program began, it has awarded more than $275,000 in scholarships.

**Deadline** March of each year.

## [889]
## FELLOWSHIP ON WOMEN AND PUBLIC POLICY

University at Albany
Center for Women in Government and Civil Society
Attn: Fellowship Program Coordinator
135 Western Avenue, Draper 302
Albany, NY 12222
(518) 442-3986                    Fax: (518) 442-3877
E-mail: cwgcs@albany.edu
Web: www.albany.edu/womeningov

**Summary** To provide an opportunity for women graduate students in New York to contribute to the improvement of the status of women and underrepresented populations through work experience and course work.

**Eligibility** This program is open to women graduate students at all accredited colleges and universities within New York who have completed 12 graduate credit hours with a GPA of 3.0 or higher. Applicant must have demonstrated an interest in studies, research, employment, or voluntary activities designed to improve the status of women and underrepresented populations. They must be available to accept an assignment to a policy-making office, such as the legislature, a state agency, or a nonprofit organization, while earning graduate credits from the Rockefeller College of Public Affairs and Policy at the University at Albany, SUNY. Along with their application, they must submit a 1,500-word essay on why they are interested in becoming a fellow.

**Financial data** Fellows receive a $10,000 stipend plus free tuition for 9 graduate credits of related academic work.

**Duration** 7 months.

**Additional information** This program was initiated in 1983. Fellows work 30 hours a week at their assignment and complete 3 graduate courses.

**Number awarded** Varies each year; recently, 11 of these fellows were appointed.

**Deadline** August of each year.

## [890]
## FELLOWSHIPS IN SCIENCE AND INTERNATIONAL AFFAIRS

Harvard University
John F. Kennedy School of Government
Belfer Center for Science and International Affairs
Attn: Fellowship Coordinator
79 John F. Kennedy Street, Mailbox 53
Cambridge, MA 02138
(617) 495-8806                    Fax: (617) 495-8963
E-mail: bcsia_fellowships@hks.harvard.edu
Web: belfercenter.ksg.harvard.edu/fellowships

**Summary** To provide funding to professionals, postdoctorates, and doctoral students (particularly women and minorities) who are interested in conducting research in areas of concern to the Belfer Center for Science and International Affairs at Harvard University in Cambridge, Massachusetts.

**Eligibility** The postdoctoral fellowship is open to recent recipients of the Ph.D. or equivalent degree, university faculty members, and employees of government, military, international, humanitarian, and private research institutions who have appropriate professional experience. Applicants for predoctoral fellowships must have passed their general examinations. Lawyers, economists, political scientists, those

in the natural sciences, and others of diverse disciplinary backgrounds are also welcome to apply. The program especially encourages applications from women, minorities, and citizens of all countries. All applicants must be interested in conducting research in 1 of the 2 major program areas of the center: 1) the International Security Program (ISP), which addresses U.S. defense and foreign policy, security policy, nuclear proliferation, terrorism, internal and ethnic conflict, and related topics; and 2) the Science, Technology, and Public Policy Program (STPP), including technology and innovation, information and communications technology, water-energy nexus, managing the atom, energy technology innovation policy, China and environmental sustainability, geoengineering and climate policy, geopolitics of energy, and geospatial policy and management.

**Financial data** The stipend is $34,000 for postdoctoral research fellows or $20,000 for predoctoral research fellows. Health insurance is also provided.

**Duration** 10 months.

**Number awarded** A limited number each year.

**Deadline** January of each year.

## [891]
## FINANCIAL WOMEN INTERNATIONAL OF HAWAII SCHOLARSHIP

Hawai'i Community Foundation
Attn: Scholarship Department
827 Fort Street Mall
Honolulu, HI 96813
(808) 566-5570                    Toll Free: (888) 731-3863
Fax: (808) 521-6286
E-mail: scholarships@hcf-hawaii.org
Web: www.hawaiicommunityfoundation.org/scholarships

**Summary** To provide financial assistance to women in Hawaii who are studying business on the upper-division or graduate school level at a school in any state.

**Eligibility** This program is open to female residents of Hawaii who are working on a degree in business or a business-related field as a junior, senior, or graduate student at a school in any state. Applicants must be able to demonstrate academic achievement (GPA of 3.5 or higher), good moral character, and financial need. Along with their application, they must submit a short statement indicating their reasons for attending college, their planned course of study, their career goals, and what community service means to them.

**Financial data** The amounts of the awards depend on the availability of funds and the need of the recipient. Recently, the average value of each of the scholarships awarded by the foundation was more than $2,000.

**Duration** 1 year.

**Additional information** This program was established in 1992 by the Hawaii chapter of Financial Women International.

**Number awarded** 1 or more each year.

**Deadline** February of each year.

## [892]
## F.J. MCGUIGAN DISSERTATION AWARD

American Psychological Foundation
750 First Street, N.E.
Washington, DC 20002-4242
(202) 336-5843                     Fax: (202) 336-5812
E-mail: foundation@apa.org
Web: www.apa.org/apf/funding/mcguigan-dissertation.aspx

**Summary**   To provide funding to doctoral candidates (especially women, minorities, and individuals with disabilities) who are interested in conducting research on the materialistic understanding of the human mind.

**Eligibility**   This program is open to graduate students enrolled full time in a psychology program at an accredited college or university in the United States or Canada. Applicants must be interested in conducting dissertation research that addresses an aspect of mental function (e.g., cognition, affect, motivation) and should utilize behavioral and/or neuroscientific methods. Selection is based on conformance with stated program goals, quality of proposed work, and applicant's demonstrated scholarship and research competence. The sponsor encourages applications from individuals who represent diversity in race, ethnicity, gender, age, disability, and sexual orientation.

**Financial data**   The grant is $2,000.

**Duration**   1 year.

**Additional information**   This grant was first awarded in 2009.

**Number awarded**   1 each year.

**Deadline**   May of each year.

## [893]
## FLETCHER MAE HOWELL SCHOLARSHIP

Woman's Missionary Union of Virginia
2828 Emerywood Parkway
Richmond, VA 23294
(804) 915-5000, ext. 8267
Toll Free: (800) 255-2428 (within VA)
Fax: (804) 672-8008              E-mail: wmuv@wmuv.org
Web: wmuv.org/developing-future-leaders/scholarships

**Summary**   To provide financial assistance to African American women from Virginia who are working on a graduate degree in Christian education.

**Eligibility**   This program is open to African American women from Virginia who are interested in full-time graduate study in Christian education. An interview is required.

**Financial data**   The stipend is $1,000.

**Duration**   1 year.

**Number awarded**   Up to 2 each year.

**Deadline**   January of each year.

## [894]
## FLORENCE SMALL GAYNOR AWARD

National Association of Health Services Executives
Attn: Educational Assistance Program
1050 Connecticut Avenue, N.W., Tenth Floor
Washington, DC 20036
(202) 772-1030                     Fax: (202) 772-1072
E-mail: nahsehg@nahse.org
Web: netforum.avectra.com

**Summary**   To provide financial assistance to African American women who are members of the National Association of Health Services Executives (NAHSE) and interested in preparing for a career in health care administration.

**Eligibility**   This program is open to African American women who are either enrolled or accepted at an accredited college or university to work on a master's or doctoral degree in health care administration. Applicants must be members of NAHSE and able to demonstrate financial need. They must have a GPA of 2.5 or higher as undergraduates or 3.0 or higher as graduate students. Along with their application, they must submit a 3-page essay that describes themselves and their career goals, commitment and interest in health care management, and financial need.

**Financial data**   The stipend is $2,500. Funds are sent to the recipient's institution.

**Duration**   1 year.

**Number awarded**   1 each year.

**Deadline**   May of each year.

## [895]
## FLORIDA LEGION AUXILIARY MASTER'S PROGRAM GRANT

American Legion Auxiliary
Department of Florida
1912A Lee Road
P.O. Box 547917
Orlando, FL 32854-7917
(407) 293-7411                     Toll Free: (866) 710-4192
Fax: (407) 299-6522                E-mail: contact@alafl.org
Web: alafl.org/index.php/scholarships

**Summary**   To provide financial assistance to members of the Florida American Legion Auxiliary who are interested in working on a master's degree in any field at a university in any state.

**Eligibility**   This program is open to residents of Florida who have been members of the American Legion Auxiliary for at least 5 consecutive years. Applicants must be planning to enroll in an accredited master's degree program in any field at a college or university in any state. They must be sponsored by the local American Legion Auxiliary unit. Selection is based on academic record and financial need.

**Financial data**   The stipend is $2,500 per year. All funds are paid directly to the institution.

**Duration**   1 year; may be renewed 1 additional year if the recipient needs further financial assistance and has maintained at least a 2.5 GPA.

**Number awarded**   1 each year.

**Deadline**   January of each year.

**[896]**
## FORT WORTH CHAPTER/WANDA J. SCHAFER GRADUATE SCHOLARSHIP

Women's Transportation Seminar-Greater Dallas/Fort
  Worth Chapter
c/o Amanda Wilson, Scholarship Chair
North Central Texas Council of Governments
616 Six Flags Drive
P.O. Box 5888
Arlington, TX 76005-5888
(817) 695-9284                    Fax: (817) 640-3028
E-mail: awilson@nctcog.org
Web: www.wtsinternational.org/greaterdallas/scholarships

**Summary**   To provide financial assistance to women from any state working on a graduate degree in a field related to transportation at specified colleges and universities in Oklahoma or Texas.

**Eligibility**   This program is open to women from any state who are enrolled at a college or university in Oklahoma or Texas that has been selected to participate. Applicants must be working on an graduate degree in a transportation-related field, such as transportation engineering, planning, finance, or logistics and have a GPA of 3.0 or higher. They must be preparing for a career in a transportation-related field. Along with their application, they must submit a 750-word statement about their career goals after graduation and why they think they should receive this scholarship. Selection is based on transportation involvement and goals, job skills, and academic record. Minority women are especially encouraged to apply.

**Financial data**   The stipend is $1,500.

**Duration**   1 year; nonrenewable.

**Additional information**   This program began in 2002. The winner is also nominated for scholarships offered by the national organization of the Women's Transportation Seminar. For a list of the eligible Oklahoma and Texas schools, contact the sponsor.

**Number awarded**   1 each year.

**Deadline**   October of each year.

**[897]**
## FOUNDATION FOR THE HISTORY OF WOMEN IN MEDICINE FELLOWSHIPS

Foundation for the History of Women in Medicine
P.O. Box 543
Pottstown, PA 19464
(610) 970-9143                    Fax: (610) 970-7520
Web: www.fhwim.org/programs/fellowships.php

**Summary**   To provide funding to students and scholars interested in short-term use of resources in the Boston area to conduct research on the history of women and medicine.

**Eligibility**   This program is open to doctoral candidates and other advanced scholars interested in using the Archives for Women in Medicine at the Countway Library's Center for the History of Medicine in Boston. Applicants must be interested in conducting research on the history of women in medicine. Preference is given to projects that deal specifically with women as physicians or other health workers, but proposals dealing with the history of women's health issues are also considered. Preference is given to applicants who live beyond commuting distance of the Countway.

**Financial data**   The grant is $5,000.

**Duration**   Recipients may conduct research on a flexible schedule during 1 academic year.

**Additional information**   The Francis A. Countway Library of Medicine, the largest academic medical library in the United States, was established in 1960 as the result of an alliance between the Boston Medical Library and the Harvard Medical School Library.

**Number awarded**   1 or 2 each year.

**Deadline**   February of each year.

**[898]**
## FOUNDER REGION SOROPTIMIST FELLOWSHIPS

Soroptimist International of the Americas-Founder Region
c/o Linda Sue Hansen, President Founder Region
  Fellowship
1466 Ash Street
Napa, CA 94559
(707) 815-0500                    Fax: (707) 252-4522
E-mail: lshansen50@sbcglobal.net
Web: www.founderregionellowship.org

**Summary**   To provide financial assistance to women from any state who are completing a doctoral degree at a university in the Founder Region of Soroptimist International of the Americas.

**Eligibility**   This program is open to women from any state who are attending graduate school in the Founder Region of Soroptimist International of the Americas (which includes designated counties in northern California, the state of Hawaii, and the U.S. possessions of Guam and the Marianas). Applicants must have been advanced to candidacy for a doctoral degree and should be entering the final year of their program. Along with their application, they must submit a statement of purpose that includes how their area of study improves the lives of women and girls or contributes to the welfare of humanity. A personal interview is required.

**Financial data**   Recently, stipends have been approximately $10,000.

**Duration**   1 year.

**Additional information**   This program began in 1948. The designated northern California counties are Alameda, Contra Costa, Del Norte, Humboldt, Lake, Marin, Mendocino, Napa, Solano, and Sonoma.

**Number awarded**   Varies each year; recently, 5 of these fellowships have been awarded.

**Deadline**   January of each year.

**[899]**
## FRAMELINE COMPLETION FUND

Frameline
Attn: Completion Fund
145 Ninth Street, Suite 300
San Francisco, CA 94103
(415) 703-8650                    Fax: (415) 861-1404
E-mail: info@frameline.org
Web: www.frameline.org/filmmaker-support

**Summary**   To provide funding to lesbian, gay, bisexual, and transgender (LGBT) film/video artists (priority is given to women and people of color).

**Eligibility** This program is open to LGBT artists who are in the last stages of the production of documentary, educational, narrative, animated, or experimental projects about or of interest to LGBT people and their communities. Applicants may be independent artists, students, producers, or nonprofit corporations. They must be interested in completion work and must have 90% of the production completed; projects in development, script-development, pre-production, or production are not eligible. Student projects are eligible only if the student maintains artistic and financial control of the project. Women and people of color are especially encouraged to apply. Selection is based on financial need, the contribution the grant will make to completing the project, assurances that the project will be completed, and the statement the project makes about LGBT people and/or issues of concern to them and their communities.

**Financial data** Grants range from $1,000 to $5,000.

**Duration** These are 1-time grants.

**Additional information** This program began in 1990.

**Number awarded** Varies each year; recently, 5 of these grants were awarded. Since this program was established, it has provided $389,200 in support to 118 films.

**Deadline** October of each year.

## [900]
## FRANCES C. ALLEN FELLOWSHIPS
Newberry Library
Attn: Committee on Awards
60 West Walton Street
Chicago, IL 60610-3305
(312) 255-3666        Fax: (312) 255-3513
E-mail: research@newberry.org
Web: www.newberry.org/short-term-fellowships

**Summary** To provide funding to Native American women graduate students who wish to use the resources of the D'Arcy McNickle Center for the History of the American Indian at the Newberry Library.

**Eligibility** This program is open to women of American Indian heritage who are interested in using the library for a project appropriate to its collections. Applicants must be enrolled in a graduate or pre-professional program, especially in the humanities or social sciences. Recommendations are required; at least 2 must come from academic advisers or instructors who can comment on the significance of the applicant's proposed project and explain how it will help in the achievement of professional goals.

**Financial data** The basic stipend is $2,000 per month; supplemental funding may be available on a case by case basis.

**Duration** From 1 month to 1 year.

**Additional information** These grants were first awarded in 1983. Fellows must spend a significant portion of their time at the library's D'Arcy McNickle Center.

**Number awarded** Varies each year; recently, 2 of these fellowships were awarded.

**Deadline** January of each year.

## [901]
## FRANCES LEWIS FELLOWSHIPS
Virginia Historical Society
Attn: Chair, Research Fellowships and Awards Committee
428 North Boulevard
P.O. Box 7311
Richmond, VA 23221-0311
(804) 342-9686        Fax: (804) 355-2399
E-mail: fpollard@vahistorical.org
Web: www.vahistorical.org/research/fellowships.htm

**Summary** To offer short-term financial assistance to pre- and postdoctoral scholars interested in conducting research in women's studies at the Virginia Historical Society.

**Eligibility** This program is open to doctoral candidates, faculty, or independent scholars interested in conducting research in women's studies. Applicants whose research promises to result in a significant publication, such as in the society's documents series of edited texts or in the *Virginia Magazine of History and Biography,* receive primary consideration. Along with their application, they must submit a resume, 2 letters of recommendation, a description of the research project (up to 2 pages), and a cover letter. Because the program is designed to help defray research travel expenses, residents of the Richmond metropolitan area are not eligible. Also ineligible are undergraduates, master's students, and graduate students not yet admitted to Ph.D. candidacy. Selection is based on the applicants' scholarly qualifications, the merits of their research proposals, and the appropriateness of their topics to the holdings of the Virginia Historical Society.

**Financial data** A few small grants (up to $150 per week) are awarded for mileage to researchers who live at least 50 miles from Richmond. The majority of the awards are $500 per week and go to researchers who live further away and thus incur greater expenses.

**Duration** Up to 3 weeks a year. Recipients may reapply in following years up to these limits: a maximum of 3 weeks in a 5-year period for doctoral candidates; a maximum of 6 weeks in a 5-year period for faculty or independent scholars.

**Additional information** The society's library contains 7 million manuscripts and thousands of books, maps, broadsides, newspapers, and historical objects. This program was formerly known as the Sydney and Frances Lewis Fellowships. Recipients are expected to work on a regular basis in the society's reading room during the period of the award.

**Number awarded** Varies each year; recently, the society awarded a total of 28 research fellowships.

**Deadline** January of each year.

## [902]
## FRANCIS M. KEVILLE MEMORIAL SCHOLARSHIP
Construction Management Association of America
Attn: CMAA Foundation
7926 Jones Branch Drive, Suite 800
McLean, VA 22101-3303
(703) 356-2622        Fax: (703) 356-6388
E-mail: foundation@cmaanet.org
Web: www.cmaafoundation.org

**Summary** To provide financial assistance to female and minority undergraduate and graduate students working on a degree in construction management.

**Eligibility** This program is open to women and members of minority groups who are enrolled as full-time undergraduate or graduate students. Applicants must have completed at least 1 year of study and have at least 1 full year remaining for a bachelor's or master's degree in construction management or a related field. Along with their application, they must submit essays on why they are interested in a career in construction management and why they should be awarded this scholarship. Selection is based on that essay (20%), academic performance (40%), recommendation of the faculty adviser (15%), and extracurricular activities (25%); a bonus of 5% is given to student members of the Construction Management Association of America (CMAA).

**Financial data** The stipend is $3,000. Funds are disbursed directly to the student's university.

**Duration** 1 year.

**Number awarded** 1 each year.

**Deadline** June of each year.

## [903]
## GABWA FOUNDATION SCHOLARSHIPS

Georgia Association of Black Women Attorneys
Attn: GABWA Foundation
P.O. Box 7381
Atlanta, GA 30309-9998
(678) 825-5675          E-mail: contact@gabwa.org
Web: www.gabwa.org/foundation.php

**Summary** To provide financial assistance to Black women from any state enrolled at law schools in Georgia.

**Eligibility** This program is open to Black women from any state enrolled in the second or third year at a law school in Georgia. Applicants must be able to demonstrate academic achievement, leadership, and commitment to the profession and their community. Along with their application, they must submit a 300-word personal statement that discusses their experience as a Black woman law student, how they expect their legal career to benefit the community at large, and how this scholarship will benefit their quest for a legal education and future career goals. Financial need is considered in the selection process but is not required.

**Financial data** Stipend amounts vary, depending on the availability of funds; recently, they averaged $5,000.

**Duration** 1 year.

**Additional information** This program began in 2002.

**Number awarded** Varies each year. Since the program was established, it has awarded nearly $200,000 to more than 50 African American women law students.

**Deadline** October of each year.

## [904]
## GAIL PATRICK CHARITABLE TRUST "WOMEN OF DISTINCTION" SCHOLARSHIPS

Delta Zeta Sorority
Attn: Foundation Coordinator
202 East Church Street
Oxford, OH 45056
(513) 523-7597          Fax: (513) 523-1921
E-mail: DZFoundation@dzshq.com
Web: www.deltazeta.org

**Summary** To provide financial assistance for graduate school to alumnae members of Delta Zeta Sorority.

**Eligibility** This program is open to alumnae members of the sorority who are returning to graduate school after an absence of up to 10 years. Applicants must have an undergraduate GPA of 3.1 or higher. Along with their application, they must submit an official transcript, a statement of their career goals, information on their service to the sorority, documentation of campus activities and/or community involvement, a list of academic honors, and an explanation of their financial need.

**Financial data** The stipend ranges from $15,000 to $20,000.

**Duration** 1 year; nonrenewable.

**Number awarded** 2 each year.

**Deadline** February of each year.

## [905]
## GAIUS CHARLES BOLIN DISSERTATION AND POST-MFA FELLOWSHIPS

Williams College
Attn: Dean of the Faculty
880 Main Street
Hopkins Hall, Third Floor
P.O. Box 141
Williamstown, MA 01267
(413) 597-4351          Fax: (413) 597-3553
E-mail: gburda@williams.edu
Web: dean-faculty.williams.edu

**Summary** To provide financial assistance to women and members of other underrepresented groups who are interested in teaching courses at Williams College while working on their doctoral dissertation or building their post-M.F.A. professional portfolio.

**Eligibility** This program is open to members of underrepresented groups, including ethnic minorities, first-generation college students, women in predominantly male fields, and scholars with disabilities. Applicants must be 1) doctoral candidates in any field who have completed all work for a Ph.D. except for the dissertation; or 2) artists who completed an M.F.A. degree within the past 2 years and are building their professional portfolio. They must be willing to teach a course at Williams College. Along with their application, they must submit a full curriculum vitae, a graduate school transcript, 3 letters of recommendation, a copy of their dissertation prospectus or samples of their artistic work, and a description of their teaching interests within a department or program at Williams College. U.S. citizenship or permanent resident status is required.

**Financial data** Fellows receive $36,000 for the academic year, plus housing assistance, office space, computer and library privileges, and a research allowance of up to $4,000.

**Duration** 2 years.

**Additional information** Bolin fellows are assigned a faculty adviser in the appropriate department. This program was established in 1985. Fellows are expected to teach a 1-semester course each year. They must be in residence at Williams College for the duration of the fellowship.

**Number awarded** 3 each year.

**Deadline** November of each year.

## [906]
## GE WOMEN'S NETWORK MINNESOTA SWE SCHOLARSHIP

Society of Women Engineers-Minnesota Section
Attn: Scholarship Committee
P.O. Box 582813
Minneapolis, MN 55458-2813
E-mail: scholarships@swe-mn.org
Web: www.swe-mn.org/scholarships.html

**Summary** To provide financial assistance to women from any state working on an undergraduate or graduate degree in biomedical engineering at colleges and universities in Minnesota, North Dakota, and South Dakota.

**Eligibility** This program is open to female undergraduate and graduate students at ABET-accredited engineering programs in Minnesota, North Dakota, or South Dakota. Applicants must be working full time on a degree in biomedical engineering. Along with their application, they must submit a short paragraph describing how they plan to utilize their engineering skills after they graduate. Selection is based on potential to succeed as an engineer (20 points), communication skills (10 points), extracurricular or community involvement and leadership skills (10 points), demonstrated successful work experience (10 points), and academic success (5 points).

**Financial data** The stipend is $1,500.

**Duration** 1 year.

**Additional information** This program is sponsored by the General Electric Women's Network.

**Number awarded** 2 each year.

**Deadline** March of each year.

## [907]
## GEIS MEMORIAL AWARD

American Psychological Association
Attn: Division 35 (Psychology of Women)
750 First Street, N.E.
Washington, DC 20002-4242
(202) 216-7602                Fax: (202) 336-5953
TDD: (202) 336-6123          E-mail: kcooke@apa.org
Web: www.apadivisions.org/division-35/awards/index.aspx

**Summary** To provide funding to psychology doctoral students interested in conducting feminist research.

**Eligibility** This program is open to advanced doctoral students interested in conducting dissertation research on the psychology of women. The research must be feminist, address a feminist/womanist issue, use social psychology research methods, and make a significant contribution to social psychology theory and practice. Selection is based on suitability, feasibility, merit of the research, and potential of the student to have a career as a feminist researcher in social psychology.

**Financial data** The grant is $15,000.

**Duration** 1 academic year.

**Number awarded** 1 each year.

**Deadline** April of each year.

## [908]
## GEORGIA ASSOCIATION FOR WOMEN LAWYERS SCHOLARSHIPS

Georgia Association for Women Lawyers
Attn: GAWL Foundation, Inc.
3855 Spalding Bluff Drive
Norcross, GA 30092
(770) 446-1517                Fax: (770) 446-7721
E-mail: gawlscholarships@gmail.com
Web: www.gawl.org/page/foundation_scholarships

**Summary** To provide financial assistance to women enrolled at law schools in Georgia.

**Eligibility** This program is open to women enrolled in the second or third year at a law school in Georgia. Applicants must submit a 200-word statement describing their career objectives and expectations with respect to the practice of law. Selection is based on academic achievement, leadership, participation in community outreach activities and/or philanthropic endeavors, and commitment to the legal profession. Students who can demonstrate involvement in programs that affect and/or promote the advancement of women in the profession and in the community receive particular consideration.

**Financial data** The stipend is generally $2,000.

**Duration** 1 year.

**Number awarded** Varies each year; recently, 3 of these scholarships were awarded.

**Deadline** February of each year.

## [909]
## GEORGIA HARKNESS SCHOLARSHIP AWARDS

United Methodist Higher Education Foundation
Attn: Scholarships Administrator
60 Music Square East, Suite 350
P.O. Box 340005
Nashville, TN 37203-0005
(615) 649-3990                Toll Free: (800) 811-8110
Fax: (615) 649-3980
E-mail: umhefscholarships@umhef.org
Web: www.umhef.org

**Summary** To provide financial assistance to women over 35 years of age who are preparing for a second career in ordained ministry as an elder in the United Methodist Church.

**Eligibility** This program is open to women over 35 years of age who have a bachelor's degree. Applicants must be enrolled full time in a school of theology approved by the University Senate of the United Methodist Church and working on an M.Div. degree. They must be currently certified as candidates for ordained ministry as an elder in the United Methodist Church. The award is not available for undergraduate, D.Min., or Ph.D. work. Selection is based on financial need, academic scholarship, spiritual leadership, and commitment to social justice.

**Financial data** The stipend is $5,000.

**Duration** 1 year; recipients may reapply.

**Additional information** This program is supported by the Division of Ordained Ministry of the General Board of Higher Education and Ministry.

**Number awarded** Varies each year; recently, 11 of these scholarships were awarded.

**Deadline** February of each year.

## [910]
## GERTRUDE BOYD CRANE SCHOLARSHIP

United Methodist Church-Oregon-Idaho Conference
Attn: United Methodist Women
1505 S.W. 18th Avenue
Portland, OR 97201-2524
(503) 226-7031          Toll Free: (800) J-WESLEY
E-mail: cjoh1@frontier.com
Web: www.umoi.org/pages/detail/45

**Summary** To provide financial assistance to female Methodists from Oregon and Idaho who are interested in attending graduate school or seminary in any state to prepare for a church-related career.

**Eligibility** This program is open to women who are members of congregations affiliated with the Oregon-Idaho Conference of the United Methodist Church (UMC). Applicants must be enrolled or planning to enroll at an accredited graduate school or seminary in any state to prepare for a church-related vocation within the Conference. Selection is based primarily on financial need.

**Financial data** The stipend, which depends on the availability of funds, has ranged from $200 to $1,900.

**Duration** 1 year.

**Number awarded** Varies each year; recently, 4 of these scholarships were awarded.

**Deadline** April of each year.

## [911]
## GERTRUDE M. COX SCHOLARSHIP IN STATISTICS

American Statistical Association
Attn: Awards Liaison
732 North Washington Street
Alexandria, VA 22314-1914
(703) 684-1221, ext. 1860     Toll Free: (888) 231-3473
Fax: (703) 684-2037          E-mail: pamela@amstat.org
Web: www.amstat.org/awards/awardsscholarships.cfm

**Summary** To provide funding to women who wish to earn a graduate degree in order to enter statistically-oriented professions.

**Eligibility** This program is open to women who are citizens or permanent residents of the United States or Canada and admitted to full-time study in a graduate statistics (including biostatistics and other statistical sciences) program. Women in or entering the early stages of graduate training are especially encouraged to apply. Applicants must submit a 1-page personal essay on why they are enrolled in their present academic program and how they intend to use their technical training, along with examples of acts of leadership, community service, and/or mentoring they have performed. Selection is based on academic record, employment history, references, and a personal statement of interest.

**Financial data** The stipend is $2,000.

**Duration** 1 year.

**Additional information** This program began in 1989.

**Number awarded** 2 each year: 1 to a woman in or entering the early stages of graduate training and 1 to a woman in a more advanced stage of training.

**Deadline** March of each year.

## [912]
## GFWC-MFWC HEBRON MEMORIAL SCHOLARSHIP

GFWC/Mississippi Federation of Women's Clubs, Inc.
c/o Ione Bond, Scholarship Committee Chair
224 Beverly Hills Loop
Petal, MS 39465
E-mail: info@gfwc-mfwc.org
Web: www.gfwc-mfwc.org

**Summary** To provide financial assistance to women in Mississippi who are interested in attending college or graduate school in the state.

**Eligibility** This program is open to women who are residents of Mississippi and are high school seniors, high school graduates, or graduates of a college in the state. Applicants must be planning to enroll at a Mississippi institution of higher learning as an undergraduate or graduate student. They may be planning to work on a degree in any field, but preference is given to applicants in areas of service where it is felt there is a need in the state.

**Financial data** The stipend is $1,000. Funds are sent directly to the recipient's institution.

**Duration** 1 year.

**Number awarded** 1 each year.

**Deadline** January of each year.

## [913]
## GLADYS C. ANDERSON MEMORIAL SCHOLARSHIP

American Foundation for the Blind
Attn: Scholarship Committee
2 Penn Plaza, Suite 1102
New York, NY 10121
(212) 502-7661          Toll Free: (800) AFB-LINE
Fax: (888) 545-8331       E-mail: afbinfo@afb.net
Web: www.afb.org/Section.asp?Documentid=2962

**Summary** To provide financial assistance to legally blind women who are studying classical or religious music on the undergraduate or graduate school level.

**Eligibility** This program is open to women who are legally blind, U.S. citizens, and enrolled in an undergraduate or graduate degree program in classical or religious music. Along with their application, they must submit 200-word essays on 1) their past and recent achievements and accomplishments; 2) their intended field of study and why they have chosen it; and 3) the role their visual impairment has played in shaping their life. They must also submit a sample performance tape or CD of up to 30 minutes. Financial need is considered in the selection process.

**Financial data** The stipend is $1,000.

**Duration** 1 academic year.

**Number awarded** 1 each year.

**Deadline** April of each year.

**[914]**
## GLORINE TUOHEY MEMORIAL SCHOLARSHIP

American Business Women's Association
Attn: Stephen Bufton Memorial Educational Fund
11050 Roe Avenue, Suite 200
Overland Park, KS 66211
Toll Free: (800) 228-0007
Web: www.sbmef.org/Scholarships.cfm

**Summary** To provide financial assistance to female graduate students who are working on a degree in a specified field (the field changes each year).

**Eligibility** This program is open to women who are working on a graduate degree and have a cumulative GPA of 3.0 or higher. Applicants are not required to be members of the American Business Women's Association. Along with their application, they must submit a 250-word biographical sketch that includes information about their background, activities, honors, work experience, and long-term educational and professional goals. Financial need is not considered in the selection process. Annually, the trustees designate an academic discipline for which the scholarship will be presented that year. U.S. citizenship is required.

**Financial data** The stipend is $3,000. Funds are paid directly to the recipient's institution to be used only for tuition, books, and fees.

**Duration** 1 year.

**Additional information** This program was created in 1997 as part of ABWA's Stephen Bufton Memorial Education Fund.

**Number awarded** 1 each year.

**Deadline** May of each year.

**[915]**
## GRACE LEGENDRE FELLOWSHIP FOR ADVANCED GRADUATE STUDY

Grace LeGendre Endowment Fund, Inc.
Attn: Fellowship Committee Chair
901 East Lake Road
Dundee, NY 14837
(315) 536-8440 E-mail: fellowships@gracelegendre.org
Web: www.gracelegendre.org

**Summary** To provide financial assistance to women in New York who wish to continue their education on the graduate level.

**Eligibility** This program is open to women who are permanent residents of New York and citizens of the United States, have a bachelor's degree, and are currently registered full time or have completed 1 year in an advanced graduate degree program at a recognized college or university in New York. Applicants must show evidence of scholastic ability and need for financial assistance. They should be within 2 years of completing their degree.

**Financial data** The stipend is $1,500.

**Duration** 1 year; recipients may reapply.

**Additional information** This program began in 1969.

**Number awarded** Varies each year; recently, 4 of these fellowships were awarded.

**Deadline** February of each year.

**[916]**
## GRADUATE PERFORMANCE AWARDS

Sigma Alpha Iota Philanthropies, Inc.
One Tunnel Road
Asheville, NC 28805
(828) 251-0606 Fax: (828) 251-0644
E-mail: nh@sai-national.org
Web: www.sai-national.org

**Summary** To recognize and reward outstanding performances in vocal and instrumental categories by graduate student members of Sigma Alpha Iota (an organization of women musicians).

**Eligibility** This program is open to college and alumna members of the organization who are working on a graduate degree in the field of performance. Competitions are held in 4 categories: voice, piano or percussion, strings or harp, and woodwinds or brass.

**Financial data** Awards are $2,000 for first place or $1,500 for second place. Funds must be used for graduate study in the field of performance.

**Duration** The competition is held triennially.

**Additional information** The awards for piano or percussion and for woodwinds or brass are designated as the Mary Ann Starring Memorial Awards. The awards for strings or harp are designated as the Dorothy E. Morris Memorial Awards. The awards for vocalists are designated the Blanche Z. Hoffman Memorial Awards.

**Number awarded** 8 every 3 years: 1 first place and 1 second place in each of the 4 categories.

**Deadline** March of the year of the awards (2015, 2018, etc.).

**[917]**
## GRADUATE RESEARCH FELLOWSHIP PROGRAM OF THE NATIONAL SCIENCE FOUNDATION

National Science Foundation
Directorate for Education and Human Resources
Attn: Division of Graduate Education
4201 Wilson Boulevard, Room 875S
Arlington, VA 22230
(703) 292-8694 Toll Free: (866) NSF-GRFP
Fax: (703) 292-9048 E-mail: info@nsfgrfp.org
Web: www.nsf.gov/funding/pgm_summ.jsp?pims_id=6201

**Summary** To provide financial assistance to graduate students (particularly women and other members of underrepresented groups) who are interested in working on a master's or doctoral degree in fields supported by the National Science Foundation (NSF).

**Eligibility** This program is open to U.S. citizens, nationals, and permanent residents who wish to work on research-based master's or doctoral degrees in a field of science, technology, engineering, or mathematics (STEM) supported by NSF (including astronomy, chemistry, computer and information sciences and engineering, geosciences, engineering, life sciences, materials research, mathematical sciences, physics, psychology, social sciences, or STEM education and learning). Other work in medical, dental, law, public health, or practice-oriented professional degree programs, or in joint science-professional degree programs, such as M.D./Ph.D. and J.D./Ph.D. programs, is not eligible. Applications normally should be submitted during the senior year in college or in the first year of graduate study; eligibility is limited to those who have completed no more than 12 months of graduate study since completion of a baccalaureate degree. Applicants who have already earned an advanced degree in science, engineering, or medicine (including an M.D., D.D.S., or D.V.M.) are ineligible. Selection is based on 1) intellectual merit of the proposed activity: strength of the academic record, proposed plan of research, previous research experience, references, appropriateness of the choice of institution; and 2) broader impacts of the proposed activity: how well does the activity advance discovery and understanding, how well does it broaden the participation of underrepresented groups (e.g., women, minorities, persons with disabilities, veterans), to what extent will it enhance the infrastructure for research and education, will the results be disseminated broadly to enhance scientific and technological understanding, what may be the benefits of the proposed activity to society).

**Financial data** The stipend is $30,000 per year; an additional $12,000 cost-of-education allowance is provided to the recipient's institution.

**Duration** Up to 3 years, usable over a 5-year period.

**Number awarded** Approximately 2,000 each year.

**Deadline** November of each year.

## [918]
## GRETCHEN L. BLECHSCHMIDT AWARD

Geological Society of America
Attn: Program Officer-Grants, Awards and Recognition
3300 Penrose Place
P.O. Box 9140
Boulder, CO 80301-9140
(303) 357-1028     Toll Free: (800) 472-1988, ext. 1028
Fax: (303) 357-1070     E-mail: awards@geosociety.org
Web: www.geosociety.org/grants/gradgrants.htm

**Summary** To provide support to female members of the Geological Society of America (GSA) interested in conducting doctoral research in geology.

**Eligibility** This program is open to GSA members working on a doctoral degree at a university in the United States, Canada, Mexico, or Central America. Applicants must be women interested in a career in academic research. Their proposals must be in the fields of 1) biostratigraphy and/or paleoceanography; or 2) sequence stratigraphy analysis, particularly in conjunction with research into deep-sea sedimentology. Disabled and minority women are particularly encouraged to submit research proposals. Selection is based on the scientific merits of the proposal, the capability of the investigator, and the reasonableness of the budget.

**Financial data** Grants range up to $4,000. Funds can be used for the cost of travel, room and board in the field, services of a technician or field assistant, funding of chemical and isotope analyses, or other expenses directly related to the fulfillment of the research contract. Support is not provided for the purchase of ordinary field equipment, for maintenance of the families of the grantees and their assistants, as reimbursement for work already accomplished, for institutional overhead, for adviser participation, or for tuition costs.

**Duration** 1 year.

**Number awarded** 1 each year.

**Deadline** January of each year.

## [919]
## GROTTO/JOB'S DAUGHTERS SCHOLARSHIP

International Order of Job's Daughters
c/o Betty Klotz, Educational Scholarships Committee
  Chair
1228 Moss Rock Court
Santa Rosa, CA 95404
(707) 462-6834     E-mail: bettyklotz@gmail.com
Web: www.jobsdaughtersinternational.org

**Summary** To provide financial assistance to members of Job's Daughters who are working on an undergraduate or graduate degree in a dental field.

**Eligibility** This program is open to high school seniors and graduates; students in early graduation programs; junior college, technical, and vocational students; and college and graduate students. Applicants must be Job's Daughters in good standing in their Bethels; unmarried majority members under 30 years of age are also eligible. They must be working on a degree in a dental field, preferably with some training in the field of disabilities. Selection is based on scholastic standing, Job's Daughters activities, recommendation by the Executive Bethel Guardian Council, faculty recommendations, and achievements outside Job's Daughters.

**Financial data** The stipend is $1,500.

**Duration** 1 year.

**Number awarded** 1 or more each year.

**Deadline** April of each year.

## [920]
## HADASSAH-BRANDEIS INSTITUTE GRADUATE INTERNSHIPS

Brandeis University
Hadassah-Brandeis Institute
Attn: Program Manager
515 South Street
Mailstop 079
Waltham, MA 02454-9110
(781) 736-8113     Fax: (781) 736-2078
E-mail: dolins@brandeis.edu
Web: www.brandeis.edu/hbi/internship/graduate.html

**Summary** To provide summer work experience to graduate students in the field of Jewish women's studies at the Hadassah-Brandeis Institute of Brandeis University.

**Eligibility** This program is open to graduate students attending universities in the United States and abroad. Applicants must have a demonstrated interest in women's studies, Jewish women's studies, or issues relating to Jewish women around the world. They must be interested in working at the institute with Brandeis staff and scholars on new and established research projects. Applicants must select 2 of the supervised projects operating each year and write a brief explanation for their interest in it. They must also submit a 1-page essay explaining their interest in Jewish gender studies and 1 or 2 ideas for an independent project. Selection is based on intellectual promise, independence, originality, initiative, capacity for growth, enthusiasm, unique skills, and strengths and weaknesses.

**Financial data** Interns receive subsidized housing on the Brandeis campus and a weekly stipend.

**Duration** 8 weeks during the summer.

**Additional information** The Hadassah-Brandeis Institute was formerly the Hadassah International Research Institute on Jewish Women at Brandeis University.

**Number awarded** Varies each year.

**Deadline** March of each year.

## [921]
## HADASSAH-BRANDEIS INSTITUTE RESEARCH AWARDS

Brandeis University
Hadassah-Brandeis Institute
Attn: Program Manager
515 South Street
Mailstop 079
Waltham, MA 02454-9110
(781) 736-8113                    Fax: (781) 736-2078
E-mail: dolins@brandeis.edu
Web: www.brandeis.edu/hbi/grants/research.html

**Summary** To provide funding to scholars, graduate students, writers, activists, and artists conducting research in the field of Jewish women's studies.

**Eligibility** This program offers senior grants (for established scholars and professionals) and junior grants (for graduate students and scholars within 3 years of receiving a Ph.D.). All applicants must be interested in conducting interdisciplinary research on Jewish women and gender issues. Graduate students in recognized master's and Ph.D. programs are encouraged to apply. Applications from outside the United States are welcome. Grants are awarded in 10 categories: history; the Yishuv and Israel; Diaspora studies; families, children, and the Holocaust; gender, culture, religion, and the law; women's health; Judaism; biography; the arts (performance arts, visual arts, creative writing); and film and video. Applications must specify the category and may be for only 1 category. Selection is based on excellence.

**Financial data** Senior grants are $5,000 and junior grants are $2,000.

**Duration** 1 year.

**Additional information** The Hadassah-Brandeis Institute was formerly the Hadassah International Research Institute on Jewish Women at Brandeis University.

**Number awarded** Between 20 and 30 each year.

**Deadline** September of each year.

## [922]
## HARRIET EVELYN WALLACE SCHOLARSHIP

American Geological Institute
Attn: Outreach and Scholarships
4220 King Street
Alexandria, VA 22302-1502
(703) 379-2480, ext. 227          Fax: (703) 379-7563
E-mail: wallacescholarship@agiweb.org
Web: www.agiweb.org/scholarships/wallace

**Summary** To provide financial assistance to women interested in working on a graduate degree in the geosciences.

**Eligibility** This program is open to women who are entering or currently enrolled in a graduate program in the geosciences. Applications must have at least 1 year remaining in their graduate program and be members of at least 1 of the 49 professional member societies of the American Geological Institute. They must have an undergraduate GPA of 3.25 or

higher and a graduate GPA of 3.0 or higher. Along with their application, they must submit a 500-word abstract about their research interests. Selection is based solely on merit.

**Financial data** The stipend is $5,000 per year.

**Duration** 1 year; may be renewed 1 additional year.

**Additional information** This program began in 2013.

**Number awarded** 1 each year.

**Deadline** March of each year.

## [923]
## HARRIETT G. JENKINS PREDOCTORAL FELLOWSHIP PROGRAM

United Negro College Fund Special Programs
  Corporation
6402 Arlington Boulevard, Suite 600
Falls Church, VA 22042
(703) 205-7625                    Toll Free: (800) 530-6232
Fax: (703) 205-7645
E-mail: sheryl.karpowicz@uncfsp.org
Web: www.uncfsp.org

**Summary** To provide financial assistance and work experience to women, minorities, and people with disabilities who are working on a graduate degree in a field of interest to the National Aeronautics and Space Administration (NASA).

**Eligibility** This program is open to members of groups underrepresented in science, technology, engineering, or mathematics (STEM), including women, minorities, and people with disabilities. Applicants must be full-time graduate students entering or in the first 3 years of a program leading to a master's or doctoral degree in a NASA-related discipline (aeronautics, aerospace engineering, astronomy, atmospheric science, bioengineering, biology, chemistry, computer science, earth sciences, engineering, environmental sciences, life sciences, materials sciences, mathematics, meteorology, neuroscience, physics, or robotics). They must be U.S. citizens and have a GPA of 3.0 or higher. Doctoral students who have advanced to candidacy are ineligible.

**Financial data** The stipend is $24,000 per year for doctoral fellows or $18,000 per year for master's degree students. The tuition offset is at least $8,500. Fellows who are also selected for a mini research award at a NASA Center or the Jet Propulsion Laboratory receive an additional grant of $8,000.

**Duration** 3 years.

**Additional information** This program, established in 2001, is funded by NASA and administered by the United Negro College Fund Special Programs Corporation. Fellows may also compete for a mini research award to engage in a NASA research experience that is closely aligned with the research conducted at the fellow's institution. The participating NASA facilities are Ames Research Center (Moffett Field, California), Jet Propulsion Laboratory (Pasadena, California), Dryden Flight Research Center (Edwards, California), Johnson Space Center (Houston, Texas), Stennis Space Center (Stennis Space Center, Mississippi), Marshall Space Flight Center (Marshall Space Flight Center, Alabama), Glenn Research Center (Cleveland, Ohio), Kennedy Space Center (Kennedy Space Center, Florida), Langley Research Center (Hampton, Virginia), and Goddard Space Flight Center (Greenbelt, Maryland).

**Number awarded** Approximately 20 each year.

**Deadline** April of each year.

## [924]
## HAZEL BEARD LEASE SCHOLARSHIP

Kappa Alpha Theta Foundation
Attn: Manager of Programs
8740 Founders Road
Indianapolis, IN 46268-1337
(317) 876-1870          Toll Free: (800) KAO-1870
Fax: (317) 876-1925
E-mail: gmerritt@kappaalphatheta.org
Web: www.kappaalphathetafoundation.org

**Summary** To provide financial assistance to members of Kappa Alpha Theta who are working on an undergraduate or graduate degree in speech therapy or speech communication.

**Eligibility** This program is open to members of Kappa Alpha Theta who are full-time sophomores, juniors, seniors, or graduate students at a college or university in Canada or the United States. Applicants must be working on a degree in speech therapy or speech communication. Along with their application, they must submit an official transcript, personal essays on assigned topics related to their involvement in Kappa Alpha Theta, and 2 letters of reference. Financial need is not considered in the selection process.

**Financial data** The stipend is $1,940.

**Duration** 1 year.

**Number awarded** 1 each year.

**Deadline** January of each year.

## [925]
## HEALTH SCIENCES STUDENT FELLOWSHIPS IN EPILEPSY

Epilepsy Foundation
Attn: Research Department
8301 Professional Place
Landover, MD 20785-2353
(301) 459-3700          Toll Free: (800) EFA-1000
Fax: (301) 577-2684          TDD: (800) 332-2070
E-mail: grants@efa.org
Web: www.epilepsyfoundation.org

**Summary** To provide financial assistance to medical and health science graduate students (especially women, minorities, and persons with disabilities) who are interested in working on an epilepsy project during the summer.

**Eligibility** This program is open to students enrolled, or accepted for enrollment, in a medical school, a doctoral program, or other graduate program. Applicants must have a defined epilepsy-related study or research plan to be carried out under the supervision of a qualified mentor. Because the program is designed as a training opportunity, the quality of the training plans and environment are considered in the selection process. Other selection criteria include the quality of the proposed project, the relevance of the proposed work to epilepsy, the applicant's interest in the field of epilepsy, the applicant's qualifications, the mentor's qualifications (including his or her commitment to the student and the project), and the quality of the training environment for research related to epilepsy. U.S. citizenship is not required, but the project must be conducted in the United States. Applications from women, members of minority groups, and people with disabilities are especially encouraged. The program is not intended for students working on a dissertation research project.

**Financial data** Stipends are $3,000.

**Duration** 3 months during the summer.

**Additional information** Support for this program is provided by many individuals, families, and corporations, especially the American Epilepsy Society, Abbott Laboratories, Ortho-McNeil Pharmaceutical, and Pfizer Inc.

**Number awarded** Varies each year; recently, 3 of these fellowships were awarded.

**Deadline** March of each year.

## [926]
## HELEN ANN MINS ROBBINS FELLOWSHIP

University of Rochester
Attn: Rossell Hope Robbins Library
Rush Rhees 416
Rochester, NY 14627-0055
(585) 275-0110          E-mail: alupack@library.rochester.edu
Web: www.library.rochester.edu/robbins/fellowship

**Summary** To provide funding to women interested in using the resources of the Rossell Hope Robbins Library at the University of Rochester to conduct research for a dissertation in medieval studies.

**Eligibility** This program is open to women working on a doctoral dissertation in medieval studies, especially English literature, British history and culture, and the relations between England and France in the Middle Ages. Applicants must be interested in using the resources of the Rossell Hope Robbins Library while remaining in residence in Rochester, New York for the academic year. Along with their application, they must submit a narrative of 750 to 1,000 words describing their dissertation, outlining the appropriateness of the library to the work they are doing, and commenting on the benefit of the period of research free of other obligations that the fellowship would allow.

**Financial data** The grant is $20,000.

**Duration** 1 academic year (up to 12 months).

**Additional information** The fellow is expected to engage in the academic life of the university and, towards the end of her residency, to give a lecture based on her research.

**Number awarded** 1 each even-numbered year.

**Deadline** March of each even-numbered year.

## [927]
## HELEN HALLER SCHOLARSHIP

Alpha Omicron Pi Foundation
Attn: Scholarship Committee
5390 Virginia Way
Brentwood, TN 37027
(615) 370-0920          Fax: (615) 370-4424
E-mail: foundation@alphaomicronpi.org
Web: www.alphaomicronpi.org

**Summary** To provide financial assistance for graduate school to alumnae members of Alpha Omicron Pi.

**Eligibility** This program is open to members of Alpha Omicron Pi who are seniors applying to graduate school or alumnae of 2 years or less currently enrolled in graduate school. Applicants must be enrolled full time. Along with their application, they must submit brief essays about themselves. Selection is based on those essays, academic achievement, Alpha Omicron Pi leadership and honors, campus and community involvement, letters of recommendation, and financial need. This award is presented to the highest-ranked graduate applicant.

**Financial data** Stipend amounts vary; recently, the average value of each scholarship provided by this foundation was approximately $1,200.

**Duration** 1 year.

**Number awarded** 1 each year.

**Deadline** February of each year.

## [928]
## HELEN W. NIES SCHOLARSHIP

Federal Circuit Bar Association
1620 I Street, N.W., Suite 900
Washington, DC 20006
(202) 466-3923                    Fax: (202) 833-1061
Web: www.fedcirbar.org

**Summary** To provide financial assistance to female law students who are interested in intellectual property law.

**Eligibility** This program is open to women who are currently enrolled in ABA-accredited law schools and are interested in intellectual property law. Applicants must submit a 450-word essay on their financial need, interest in particular areas of the law, and any other qualifications for this particular scholarship. Selection is based on academic excellence, financial need, and interest in intellectual property law.

**Financial data** The stipend is $10,000.

**Duration** 1 year.

**Additional information** This scholarship was first presented in 2007.

**Number awarded** 1 each year.

**Deadline** April of each year.

## [929]
## HELEN WOODRUFF NOLOP SCHOLARSHIP IN AUDIOLOGY AND ALLIED FIELDS

Delta Zeta Sorority
Attn: Foundation Coordinator
202 East Church Street
Oxford, OH 45056
(513) 523-7597                    Fax: (513) 523-1921
E-mail: DZFoundation@dzshq.com
Web: www.deltazeta.org

**Summary** To provide financial assistance to women who are working on a graduate degree in audiology or a related field.

**Eligibility** This program is open to women working on a graduate degree in audiology or a related field of speech and hearing. Membership in Delta Zeta Sorority is not required. Applicants must submit an official transcript, a statement of their career goals, documentation of campus activities and/or community involvement, a list of academic honors, and an explanation of their financial need.

**Financial data** The stipend ranges from $1,000 to $15,000, depending on the availability of funds.

**Duration** 1 year; nonrenewable.

**Number awarded** 1 each year.

**Deadline** February of each year.

## [930]
## HELENE M. OVERLY MEMORIAL GRADUATE SCHOLARSHIP

Women's Transportation Seminar
Attn: WTS Foundation
1701 K Street, N.W., Suite 800
Washington, DC 20006
(202) 955-5085                    Fax: (202) 955-5088
E-mail: wts@wtsinternational.org
Web: www.wtsinternational.org/education/scholarships

**Summary** To provide financial assistance to women graduate students interested in preparing for a career in transportation.

**Eligibility** This program is open to women who are enrolled in a graduate degree program in a transportation-related field (e.g., transportation engineering, planning, finance, or logistics). Applicants must have at least a 3.0 GPA and be interested in a career in transportation. Along with their application, they must submit a 750-word statement about their career goals after graduation and why they think they should receive the scholarship award. Applications must be submitted first to a local chapter; the chapters forward selected applications for consideration on the national level. Minority women are particularly encouraged to apply. Selection is based on transportation involvement and goals, job skills, and academic record.

**Financial data** The stipend is $10,000.

**Duration** 1 year.

**Additional information** This program began in 1981. Local chapters may also award additional funding to winners in their area.

**Number awarded** 1 each year.

**Deadline** Applications must be submitted by November to a local WTS chapter.

## [931]
## HENRY DAVID RESEARCH GRANT IN HUMAN REPRODUCTIVE BEHAVIOR AND POPULATION STUDIES

American Psychological Foundation
750 First Street, N.E.
Washington, DC 20002-4242
(202) 336-5843                    Fax: (202) 336-5812
E-mail: foundation@apa.org
Web: www.apa.org/apf/funding/david.aspx

**Summary** To provide funding to young psychologists (particularly women, minorities, and individuals with disabilities) who are interested in conducting research on reproductive behavior.

**Eligibility** This program is open to doctoral students in psychology working on a dissertation and young psychologists who have no more than 7 years of postgraduate experience. Applicants must be interested in conducting research on human reproductive behavior or an area related to population concerns. Along with their application, they must submit a current curriculum vitae, 2 letters of recommendation, and an essay of 1 to 2 pages on their interest in human reproductive behavior or in population studies. The sponsor encourages applications from individuals who represent diversity in race, ethnicity, gender, age, disability, and sexual orientation.

**Financial data** The grant is $1,500.

**Duration** The grant is presented annually.

**Number awarded** 1 each year.

**Deadline** February of each year.

## [932]
## HERBERT AND BETTY CARNES FUND

American Ornithologists' Union
c/o Executive Officer
5405 Villa View Drive
Farmington, NM 87402
(505) 326-1579          E-mail: aou@aou.org
Web: www.aou.org/awards/research

**Summary** To provide funding to female graduate students and scholars who are members of the American Ornithologists' Union (AOU) and interested in conducting research on avian biology.

**Eligibility** This program is open to female AOU members who are graduate students, postdoctorates, or other researchers without access to major funding agencies. Applicants must be interested in conducting research on avian biology. They must be nonsmokers (have not smoked in at least the previous 6 months). Along with their application, they should send a cover letter (about 5 pages) describing their proposed project, a budget, and 1 letter of reference. Selection is based on significance and originality of the research question, clarity of the objectives, feasibility of the plan of research, and appropriateness of the budget.

**Financial data** The maximum award is $2,500 per year.

**Duration** 1 year; recipients may reapply for 1 additional award.

**Number awarded** The sponsor awards a total of 28 to 30 grants each year.

**Deadline** January of each year.

## [933]
## HERBERT W. AND CORRINE CHILSTROM SCHOLARSHIP

Women of the Evangelical Lutheran Church in America
Attn: Scholarships
8765 West Higgins Road
Chicago, IL 60631-4101
(773) 380-2741          Toll Free: (800) 638-3522, ext. 2741
Fax: (773) 380-2419          E-mail: women.elca@elca.org
Web: www.womenoftheelca.org

**Summary** To provide financial assistance to mature women who are studying for a second career in the ordained ministry in the Evangelical Lutheran Church of America (ELCA).

**Eligibility** Applicants for this scholarship must be women who have experienced an interruption of at least 5 years in their education since college graduation and are currently entering the final year of an M.Div. program at an ELCA seminary. They must have been endorsed by the Synodical Candidacy Committee. Selection is based on academic achievement, personal commitment and determination to serve as a pastor in the ELCA, and financial need. U.S. citizenship is required.

**Financial data** The maximum stipend is $1,000.

**Duration** 1 year.

**Additional information** This scholarship was established in 1996 to honor Rev. Herbert W. Chilstrom and Rev. Corrine

Chilstrom during the 25th anniversary year of the ordination of women in the predecessor bodies of the ELCA. Recipients must agree to serve for at least 3 years as an ELCA pastor after graduation from seminary.

**Number awarded** 1 each year.

**Deadline** February of each year.

## [934]
## HERMINE DALKOWITZ TOBOLOWSKY SCHOLARSHIP

Texas Business Women
Attn: Texas Business and Professional Women's
  Foundation
2637 Pine Springs Drive
Plano, TX 75093
(972) 822-1173     E-mail: info@texasbusinesswomen.org
Web: www.texasbpwfoundation.org/scholarships.php

**Summary** To provide financial assistance to women from any state who are attending college in Texas to prepare for a career in selected professions.

**Eligibility** This program is open to women from any state who are interested in preparing for a career in law, public service, government, political science, or women's history. Applicants must have completed at least 2 semesters of study at an accredited college or university in Texas, have a GPA of 3.0 or higher, and be U.S. citizens. Selection is based on academic achievement and financial need.

**Financial data** A stipend is awarded (amount not specified).

**Duration** 1 year.

**Additional information** This program began in 1995 when Texas Business Women was named Texas Federation of Business and Professional Women's Clubs.

**Number awarded** 1 or more each year.

**Deadline** December of each year.

## [935]
## HILARY A. BUFTON JR. SCHOLARSHIP

American Business Women's Association
Attn: Stephen Bufton Memorial Educational Fund
11050 Roe Avenue, Suite 200
Overland Park, KS 66211
Toll Free: (800) 228-0007
Web: www.sbmef.org/Scholarships.cfm

**Summary** To provide financial assistance to female graduate students who are working on a degree in a specified field (the field changes each year).

**Eligibility** This program is open to women who are working on a graduate degree and have a cumulative GPA of 3.0 or higher. Applicants are not required to be members of the American Business Women's Association. Along with their application, they must submit a 250-word biographical sketch that includes information about their background, activities, honors, work experience, and long-term educational and professional goals. Financial need is not considered in the selection process. Annually, the trustees designate an academic discipline for which the scholarship will be presented that year. U.S. citizenship is required.

**Financial data** The stipend is $10,000 (paid over a 2-year period). Funds are paid directly to the recipient's institution to be used only for tuition, books, and fees.

**Duration** 2 years.

**Additional information** This program was created in 1986 as part of ABWA's Stephen Bufton Memorial Education Fund. The ABWA does not provide the names and addresses of local chapters; it recommends that applicants check with their local Chamber of Commerce, library, or university to see if any chapter has registered a contact's name and number.

**Number awarded** 1 each even-numbered year.

**Deadline** May of each even-numbered year.

## [936]
## HOLLAND & HART SUMMER ASSOCIATES PROGRAM DIVERSITY INITIATIVE

Holland & Hart LLP
Attn: Manager of Recruitment and Professional
  Development
555 17th Street, Suite 3200
Denver, CO 80202
(303) 295-8509                    Fax: (303) 295-8261
E-mail: mnishikura@hollandhart.com
Web: www.hhjobs.com/diversityinitiative.html

**Summary** To provide summer work experience at Holland & Hart in Denver, Colorado to female and minority law students.

**Eligibility** This program is open to second-year students at top-tier law schools who are interested in a summer clerkship at the firm. Applicants must be women or people of color. They must submit a resume, transcript, and cover letter.

**Financial data** The current stipend is $2,308 per week.

**Duration** Summer months.

**Number awarded** 1 each year.

**Deadline** August of each year.

## [937]
## HOLLY A. CORNELL SCHOLARSHIP

American Water Works Association
Attn: Scholarship Coordinator
6666 West Quincy Avenue
Denver, CO 80235-3098
(303) 794-7771              Toll Free: (800) 926-7337
Fax: (303) 347-0804        E-mail: lmoody@awwa.org
Web: www.awwa.org

**Summary** To provide financial assistance to outstanding female and minority students interested in working on an master's degree in the field of water supply and treatment.

**Eligibility** <EG>This program is open to female and minority students working on a master's degree in the field of water supply and treatment at a college or university in Canada, Guam, Mexico, Puerto Rico, or the United States. Students who have been accepted into graduate school but have not yet begun graduate study are encouraged to apply. Applicants must submit a 2-page resume, official transcripts, 3 letters of recommendation, a proposed curriculum of study, a 1-page statement of educational plans and career objectives demonstrating an interest in the drinking water field, and a 3-page proposed plan of research. Selection is based on academic record and potential to provide leadership in the field of water supply and treatment.

**Financial data** The stipend is $7,500.

**Duration** 1 year; nonrenewable.

**Additional information** Funding for this program comes from the consulting firm CH2M Hill.

**Number awarded** 1 each year.

**Deadline** January of each year.

## [938]
## HON. GERALDINE A. FERRARO ENDOWED SCHOLARSHIP

National Organization of Italian American Women
25 West 43rd Street, Suite 1005
New York, NY 10036
(212) 642-2003                    Fax: (212) 642-2006
E-mail: noiaw@noiaw.org
Web: www.noiaw.org

**Summary** To provide financial assistance for law school to women of Italian descent.

**Eligibility** This program is open to women who have at least 1 parent of Italian American descent and are working on a law degree. Applicants must be enrolled full time and have a GPA of 3.5 or higher. Along with their application, they must submit a 2-page essay on how being an Italian American has impacted them personally and professionally. Financial need is considered in the selection process.

**Financial data** The stipend is $2,000.

**Duration** 1 year; nonrenewable.

**Additional information** A processing fee of $25 must accompany the application.

**Number awarded** 1 each year.

**Deadline** March of each year.

## [939]
## HONOLULU BRANCH AAUW POSTGRADUATE SCHOLARSHIP

American Association of University Women-Honolulu
  Branch
Attn: Scholarship Committee
1802 Ke'eaumoku Street
Honolulu, HI 96822
(808) 537-4702                    Fax: (808) 537-4702
E-mail: aauwhnb@hawaii.rr.com
Web: honolulu-hi.aauw.net/scholarships

**Summary** To provide financial assistance to women in Hawaii who are working on an advanced degree in any field at a school in the state.

**Eligibility** This program is open to female residents of Hawaii who are currently enrolled at an accredited university in the state. Applicants must be working on a graduate degree in any field. Along with their application, they must submit a biographical statement that includes information on the importance of their study or research with respect to their career path. Financial need is considered in the selection process.

**Financial data** Stipends range up to $10,000.

**Duration** 1 year.

**Number awarded** 1 or more each year.

**Deadline** April of each year.

## [940]
## HONORABLE HARRISON W. EWING FELLOWSHIPS

Alpha Chi Omega Foundation
Attn: Assistant Director-Grants and Stewardship
5939 Castle Creek Parkway North Drive
Indianapolis, IN 46250-4343
(317) 579-5050, ext. 265          Fax: (317) 579-5051
E-mail: alatta@alphachiomega.org
Web: www.alphachiomega.org/index.aspx?id=1030

**Summary**   To provide financial assistance to graduating Alpha Chi Omega members who are interested in attending law school.

**Eligibility**   Women college seniors or college graduates who are members of the sorority are eligible to apply if they are interested in attending law school. Selection is based on academic achievement, chapter involvement, campus and community service, and financial need.

**Financial data**   A stipend is awarded (amount not specified).

**Duration**   1 year.

**Number awarded**   Up to 5 each year.

**Deadline**   February of each year.

## [941]
## HORIZONS FOUNDATION SCHOLARSHIP PROGRAM

Women in Defense
c/o National Defense Industrial Association
2111 Wilson Boulevard, Suite 400
Arlington, VA 22201-3061
(703) 247-2552          Fax: (703) 522-1885
E-mail: wid@ndia.org
Web: wid.ndia.org/horizons/Pages/default.aspx

**Summary**   To provide financial assistance to women who are upper-division or graduate students engaged in or planning careers related to the national security interests of the United States.

**Eligibility**   This program is open to women who are already working in national security fields as well as women planning such careers. Applicants must 1) be currently enrolled at an accredited college or university, either full time or part time, as graduate students or upper-division undergraduates; 2) demonstrate financial need; 3) be U.S. citizens; 4) have a GPA of 3.25 or higher; and 5) demonstrate interest in preparing for a career related to national security. The preferred fields of study include business (as it relates to national security or defense), computer science, cyber security, economics, engineering, government relations, international relations, law (as it relates to national security or defense), mathematics, military history, political science, physics, and security studies; others are considered if the applicant can demonstrate relevance to a career in national security or defense. Selection is based on academic achievement, participation in defense and national security activities, field of study, work experience, statements of objectives, recommendations, and financial need.

**Financial data**   The stipend ranges up to $10,000.

**Duration**   1 year; renewable.

**Additional information**   This program began in 1988.

**Number awarded**   Varies each year; recently, 6 of these scholarships were awarded: 1 at $10,000, 1 at $7,000, 1 at $5,000, 1 at $3,000, and 2 at $2,500. Since the program was established, 116 women have received more than $180,000 in support.

**Deadline**   June of each year.

## [942]
## HORIZONS-MICHIGAN SCHOLARSHIP

Women in Defense-Michigan Chapter
Attn: Scholarship Director
P.O. Box 4744
Troy, MI 48099
E-mail: scholarships@wid-mi.org
Web: www.wid-mi.org/scholarships.aspx

**Summary**   To provide financial assistance to women in Michigan who are upper-division or graduate students working on a degree related to national defense.

**Eligibility**   This program is open to women who are residents of Michigan and enrolled either full or part time at a college or university in the state. Applicants must be juniors, seniors, or graduate students and have a GPA of 3.25 or higher. They must be interested in preparing for a career related to national security or defense. Relevant fields of study include security studies, military history, government relations, engineering, computer science, physics, mathematics, business (as related to national security or defense), law (as related to national security or defense), international relations, political science, or economics; other fields may be considered if the applicant can demonstrate relevance to a career in national security or defense. Along with their application, they must submit brief statements on their interest in a career in national security or defense, the principal accomplishments in their life that relate to their professional goals, and the objectives of their educational program. Selection is based on those statements, academic achievement, participation in defense and national security activities, field of study, work experience, recommendations, and financial need. U.S. citizenship is required.

**Financial data**   Stipends have averaged at least $3,000.

**Duration**   1 year.

**Additional information**   This program began in 2009.

**Number awarded**   Varies each year; recently, 6 of these scholarships were awarded.

**Deadline**   August of each year.

## [943]
## H.S. AND ANGELINE LEWIS SCHOLARSHIPS

American Legion Auxiliary
Department of Wisconsin
Attn: Education Chair
2930 American Legion Drive
P.O. Box 140
Portage, WI 53901-0140
(608) 745-0124          Toll Free: (866) 664-3863
Fax: (608) 745-1947   E-mail: alawi@amlegionauxwi.org
Web: www.amlegionauxwi.org/Scholarships.htm

**Summary**   To provide financial assistance for college or graduate study in any state to the wives, widows, and children of Wisconsin residents who are veterans or members of the American Legion Auxiliary.

**Eligibility** This program is open to the children, wives, and widows of veterans who are high school seniors or graduates and have a GPA of 3.5 or higher. Grandchildren and great-grandchildren of members of the American Legion Auxiliary are also eligible. Applicants must be residents of Wisconsin and interested in working on an undergraduate or graduate degree at a school in any state. Along with their application, they must submit a 300-word essay on "Education—An Investment in the Future." Financial need is considered in the selection process.

**Financial data** The stipend is $1,000.

**Duration** 1 year; nonrenewable.

**Number awarded** 6 each year: 1 to a graduate student and 5 to undergraduates.

**Deadline** March of each year.

## [944]
## HUMBLE ARTESIAN CHAPTER ABWA SCHOLARSHIP GRANTS

American Business Women's Association-Humble
 Artesian Chapter
c/o Caroline Smith, Education Committee
1702 Baldsprings Trail
Kingwood, TX 77345-1997
(281) 360-6226     E-mail: californiasmith@earthlink.net
Web: abwahumble.org/scholarship

**Summary** To provide financial assistance to women from any state who have completed at least the sophomore year of college.

**Eligibility** This program is open to all women who are U.S. citizens. Applicants must be enrolled as juniors, seniors, or graduate students at a college or university in any state and have a GPA of 2.5 or higher.

**Financial data** The stipend is $2,000.

**Duration** 1 year.

**Number awarded** 1 each year.

**Deadline** January of each year.

## [945]
## IADES FELLOWSHIP AWARD

International Alumnae of Delta Epsilon Sorority
c/o Virginia Borggaard
2453 Bear Den Road
Frederick, MD 21701-9321
Fax: (301) 663-3231     TDD: (301) 663-9235
E-mail: vborggaard@juno.com

**Summary** To provide financial assistance to deaf women who are working on a doctoral degree.

**Eligibility** This program is open to deaf women who have completed 12 or more units in a doctoral-level program and have a GPA of 3.0 or more. They need not be members of Delta Epsilon. Along with their application, they must submit official transcripts, a recent copy of their audiogram, and 2 letters of recommendation.

**Financial data** The stipend is $2,000.

**Duration** 1 year.

**Number awarded** 1 or more each year.

**Deadline** September of each year.

## [946]
## IBM PHD FELLOWSHIP PROGRAM

IBM Corporation
Attn: University Relations
1133 Westchester Avenue
White Plains, NY 10604
Toll Free: (800) IBM-4YOU     TDD: (800) IBM-3383
E-mail: phdfellow@us.ibm.com
Web: www.research.ibm.com

**Summary** To provide funding and work experience to students from any country working on a Ph.D. in a research area of broad interest to IBM.

**Eligibility** Students nominated for this fellowship should be enrolled full time at an accredited college or university in any country and should have completed at least 1 year of graduate study in computer science or engineering, electrical or mechanical engineering, physical sciences (chemistry, material sciences, physics), mathematical sciences, public sector and business sciences, or service science, management, and engineering (SSME). Focus areas that receive special consideration include technology that creates new business or social value, innovative software, new types of computers, or interdisciplinary projects that create social and business value. Applicants should be planning a career in research. Nominations must be made by a faculty member and endorsed by the department head. The program values diversity, and encourages nominations of women, minorities, and others who contribute to that diversity. Selection is based on the applicants' potential for research excellence, the degree to which their technical interests align with those of IBM, and academic progress to date. Preference is given to students who have had an IBM internship or have closely collaborated with technical or services people from IBM.

**Financial data** Fellowships pay tuition, fees, and a stipend of $17,500 per year.

**Duration** 1 year; may be renewed up to 2 additional years, provided the recipient is renominated, interacts with IBM's technical community, and demonstrates continued progress and achievement.

**Additional information** Recipients are offered an internship at 1 of the IBM Research Division laboratories and are given an IBM computer.

**Number awarded** Varies each year; recently, 57 of these scholarships were awarded.

**Deadline** October of each year.

## [947]
## IDA B. WELLS GRADUATE STUDENT FELLOWSHIP

Coordinating Council for Women in History
c/o Sandra Dawson, Executive Director
Northern Illinois University
Department of History and Women's Studies
715 Zulauf Hall
DeKalb, IL 60115
(815) 895-2624     E-mail: execdir@theccwh.org
Web: theccwh.org/ccwh-awards

**Summary** To provide funding to women graduate students for completion of their doctoral dissertations on an historical topic.

**Eligibility** This program is open to women graduate students in history departments at U.S. institutions who are members of the Coordinating Council for Women in History (CCWH). Applicants must have passed to A.B.D. status. They may be specializing in any field, but they must be working on an historical project. Preference is given to applicants working on a project involving issues of race.

**Financial data** The grant is $1,000.

**Duration** 1 year.

**Additional information** This program, established in 1999, is administered by the CCWH and the Berkshire Conference of Women Historians. The award is presented at the CCWH luncheon at the annual meeting of the American Historical Association, although the recipient does not need to be present to accept the award.

**Number awarded** 1 each year.

**Deadline** September of each year.

## [948]
## IDA M. POPE MEMORIAL SCHOLARSHIPS

Hawai'i Community Foundation
Attn: Scholarship Department
827 Fort Street Mall
Honolulu, HI 96813
(808) 566-5570          Toll Free: (888) 731-3863
Fax: (808) 521-6286
E-mail: scholarships@hcf-hawaii.org
Web: www.hawaiicommunityfoundation.org/scholarships

**Summary** To provide financial assistance to Native Hawaiian women who are interested in working on an undergraduate or graduate degree in designated fields at a school in any state.

**Eligibility** This program is open to female residents of Hawaii who are Native Hawaiian, defined as a descendant of the aboriginal inhabitants of the Hawaiian islands prior to 1778. Applicants must be enrolled at a school in any state in an accredited associate, bachelor's, or graduate degree program and working on a degree in health, science, mathematics, or education (including counseling and social work). They must be able to demonstrate academic achievement (GPA of 3.5 or higher), good moral character, and financial need. Along with their application, they must submit a short statement indicating their reasons for attending college, their planned course of study, their career goals, and what community service means to them.

**Financial data** The amounts of the awards depend on the availability of funds and the need of the recipient. Recently, the average value of each of the scholarships awarded by the foundation was more than $2,000.

**Duration** 1 year; may be renewed.

**Number awarded** Varies each year; recently, 61 of these scholarships were awarded.

**Deadline** February of each year.

## [949]
## INGEBORG HASELTINE SCHOLARSHIP FUND FOR WOMEN

Unitarian Universalist Association
Attn: Ministerial Credentialing Office
25 Beacon Street
Boston, MA 02108-2800
(617) 948-6403          Fax: (617) 742-2875
E-mail: mcoadministrator@uua.org
Web: www.uua.org

**Summary** To provide financial assistance to women preparing for the Unitarian Universalist (UU) ministry.

**Eligibility** This program is open to women currently enrolled or planning to enroll full time in a UU ministerial training program with aspirant or candidate status. Financial need is considered in the selection process.

**Financial data** The stipend ranges from $1,000 to $11,000 per year.

**Duration** 1 year.

**Number awarded** Varies each year; recently, 5 of these scholarships were awarded.

**Deadline** April of each year.

## [950]
## INSTITUTE FOR SUPPLY MANAGEMENT DOCTORAL DISSERTATION GRANT PROGRAM

Institute for Supply Management
Attn: Director, Education and Training
2055 East Centennial Circle
P.O. Box 22160
Tempe, AZ 85285-2160
(480) 752-6276, ext. 3092
Toll Free: (800) 888-6276, ext. 3092
Fax: (480) 752-7890          E-mail: cmendoza@ism.ws
Web: www.ism.ws

**Summary** To provide financial support to female, minority, and other doctoral candidates who are conducting dissertation research in purchasing or related fields.

**Eligibility** This program is open to doctoral candidates who are working on a Ph.D. or D.B.A. in supply management, supply chain management, business, management, logistics, economics, industrial engineering, or a related field at an accredited university in the United States. International applicants are accepted. Examples of research projects that could be funded include: purchasing and supply management models, methodologies, measurement, supply networks, operations and logistics integration, produce/service innovation, supply relationships, supply's role in corporate success, or strategic development of supply. The research proposal (up to 25 pages) must discuss hypotheses, significance of the study, research methodology, and value of the research to the field of purchasing. The program encourages applications from a diverse population, regardless of gender, race, creed, age, ethnic or national origin, sexual orientation, or disability.

**Financial data** Grants range up to $6,000.

**Duration** 1 year.

**Additional information** The sponsoring organization was previously known as the National Association of Purchasing Management.

**Number awarded** Up to 4 each year.

**Deadline** January of each year.

## [951]
## INTEL CORPORATION SCHOLARSHIPS

Society of Women Engineers
Attn: Scholarship Selection Committee
203 North LaSalle Street, Suite 1675
Chicago, IL 60601-1269
(312) 596-5223          Toll Free: (877) SWE-INFO
Fax: (312) 644-8557     E-mail: scholarships@swe.org
Web: societyofwomenengineers.swe.org

**Summary**  To provide financial assistance to women who are members of the Society of Women Engineers (SWE) and working on a graduate degree in computer science or specified fields of engineering.

**Eligibility**  This program is open to SWE members working full time on a graduate degree in computer science or chemical, computer, electrical, industrial, manufacturing, materials, or mechanical engineering. Applicants must have a GPA of 3.5 or higher. Selection is based on merit and financial need. Preference is given to members of groups underrepresented in computer science and engineering and to residents of Arizona, California, Colorado, Massachusetts, New Mexico, Oregon, and Washington. U.S. citizenship or permanent residents status is required.

**Financial data**  The stipend is $5,000.

**Duration**  1 year.

**Additional information**  This program is sponsored by Intel Corporation.

**Number awarded**  2 each year.

**Deadline**  February of each year.

## [952]
## INTELLECTUAL PROPERTY LAW SECTION WOMEN AND MINORITY SCHOLARSHIP

State Bar of Texas
Attn: Intellectual Property Law Section
c/o Syed K. Fareed, Scholarship Selection Committee
Vinson & Elkins LLP
2801 Via Fortuna, Suite 100
Austin, TX 78746
(512) 542-8400          Fax: (512) 542-8612
E-mail: sfareed@velaw.com
Web: texasbariplaw.org

**Summary**  To provide financial assistance to female and minority students at law schools in Texas who plan to practice intellectual property law.

**Eligibility**  This program is open to women and members of minority groups (African Americans, Hispanics, Asian Americans, and Native Americans) from any state who are currently enrolled at an ABA-accredited law school in Texas. Applicants must be planning to practice intellectual property law in Texas. Along with their application, they must submit a 2-page essay explaining why they plan to prepare for a career in intellectual property law in Texas, any qualifications they believe are relevant for their consideration for this scholarship, and (optionally) any issues of financial need they wish to have considered.

**Financial data**  The stipend is $2,500.

**Duration**  1 year.

**Number awarded**  2 each year: 1 to a women and 1 to a minority.

**Deadline**  April of each year.

## [953]
## IOTA SIGMA PI MEMBERS-AT-LARGE REENTRY AWARD

Iota Sigma Pi
c/o Gail Blaustein, MAL National Coordinator
West Liberty University
208 University Drive
College Union Box 139
West Liberty, WV 26074
(304) 336-8539     E-mail: gail.blaustein@westliberty.edu
Web: www.iotasigmapi.info

**Summary**  To provide financial assistance to women who are reentering college to work on an undergraduate or graduate degree in chemistry.

**Eligibility**  This program is open to women who have returned to academic studies after an absence of 3 or more years and have completed at least 1 academic year of college chemistry since returning. Students must be working on an undergraduate or graduate degree in chemistry or a related field at a 4-year college or university. They must be nominated by a member of Iota Sigma Pi or by a member of the faculty at their institution. Nominees must submit a short essay describing their goals, pertinent experiences that influenced their choice of major, any interests or talents that will assist them in succeeding in their professional career, and how the scholarship will benefit them in meeting their goals. Financial need is not considered in the selection process.

**Financial data**  The winner receives a stipend of $1,500, a certificate, and a 1-year waiver of Iota Sigma Pi dues.

**Duration**  1 year.

**Additional information**  This award was first presented in 1991.

**Number awarded**  1 each year.

**Deadline**  March of each year.

## [954]
## IRENE AND DAISY MACGREGOR MEMORIAL SCHOLARSHIP

Daughters of the American Revolution-National Society
Attn: Committee Services Office, Scholarships
1776 D Street, N.W.
Washington, DC 20006-5303
(202) 628-1776
Web: www.dar.org/natsociety/edout_scholar.cfm

**Summary**  To provide financial assistance to graduate students (preference give to women) who are working on a degree in medicine or psychiatric nursing.

**Eligibility**  This program is open to students who have been accepted into or are enrolled in an approved program of graduate psychiatric nursing or medicine. Applicants must be U.S. citizens and attend an accredited medical school, college, or university in the United States. They must obtain a letter of sponsorship from a local Daughters of the American Revolution (DAR) chapter. Preference is given to women applicants, provided they are "equally qualified." Selection is based on academic excellence, commitment to the field of study, and financial need.

**Financial data**  The stipend is $5,000 per year.

**Duration**  1 year; may be renewed for up to 3 additional years, provided the recipient maintains a GPA of 3.25 or higher.

**Number awarded** 1 or more each year.

**Deadline** February of each year.

## [955]
## IRENE DRINKALL FRANKE/MARY SEELEY KNUDSTRUP SCHOLARSHIP

Women of the Evangelical Lutheran Church in America
Attn: Scholarships
8765 West Higgins Road
Chicago, IL 60631-4101
(773) 380-2741          Toll Free: (800) 638-3522, ext. 2741
Fax: (773) 380-2419          E-mail: valora.starr@elca.org
Web: www.womenoftheelca.org

**Summary** To provide financial assistance to lay women who are members of Evangelical Lutheran Church of America (ELCA) congregations and who wish to pursue graduate studies.

**Eligibility** This program is open to ELCA lay women who are at least 21 years of age and have experienced an interruption of at least 2 years in their education since high school. Applicants must have been admitted to a graduate program at an academic institution to prepare for a career of Christian service but not in the ordained ministry. U.S. citizenship is required.

**Financial data** The maximum stipend is $1,000.

**Duration** Up to 2 years.

**Number awarded** 1 or more each year.

**Deadline** February of each year.

## [956]
## ISAAC J. "IKE" CRUMBLY MINORITIES IN ENERGY GRANT

American Association of Petroleum Geologists
  Foundation
Attn: Grants-in-Aid Program
1444 South Boulder Avenue
P.O. Box 979
Tulsa, OK 74101-0979
(918) 560-2644          Toll Free: (855) 302-2743
Fax: (918) 560-2642          E-mail: foundation@aapg.org
Web: foundation.aapg.org/gia/crumbly.cfm

**Summary** To provide funding to female and minority graduate students who are interested in conducting research related to earth science aspects of the petroleum industry.

**Eligibility** This program is open to women and ethnic minorities (Black, Hispanic, Asian, or Native American, including American Indian, Eskimo, Hawaiian, or Samoan) who are working on a master's or doctoral degree. Applicants must be interested in conducting research related to the search for and development of petroleum and energy-minerals resources and to related environmental geology issues. Selection is based on student's academic and employment history (10 points), scientific merit of proposal (30 points), suitability to program objectives (30 points), financial merit of proposal (20 points), and endorsement by faculty or department adviser (10 points).

**Financial data** Grants range from $500 to $3,000. Funds are to be applied to research-related expenses (e.g., a summer of field work). They may not be used to purchase capital equipment or to pay salaries, tuition, room, or board.

**Duration** 1 year. Doctoral candidates may receive a 1-year renewal.

**Number awarded** 1 each year.

**Deadline** February of each year.

## [957]
## J. FRANCES ALLEN SCHOLARSHIP AWARD

American Fisheries Society
Attn: Equal Opportunities Section
5410 Grosvenor Lane, Suite 110
Bethesda, MD 20814-2199
(301) 897-8616          Fax: (301) 897-8096
E-mail: main@fisheries.org
Web: fisheries.org/awards_call

**Summary** To provide financial assistance for doctoral studies to female members of the American Fisheries Society (AFS).

**Eligibility** This program is open to women Ph.D. students who are AFS members. Applicants must be studying a branch of fisheries science, including but not limited to aquatic biology, engineering, fish culture, limnology, oceanography, or sociology. Selection is based on research promise, scientific merit, and academic achievement.

**Financial data** The stipend is $2,500, paid directly to the student. Funds may be used for any aspect of doctoral education, including tuition, textbooks, equipment, travel, or living expenses.

**Duration** 1 year; nonrenewable.

**Additional information** This program began in 1986.

**Number awarded** 1 each year.

**Deadline** March of each year.

## [958]
## JANE M. KLAUSMAN WOMEN IN BUSINESS SCHOLARSHIPS

Zonta International
Attn: Foundation
1211 West 22nd Street, Suite 900
Oak Brook, IL 60523-3384
(630) 928-1400          Fax: (630) 928-1559
E-mail: programs@zonta.org
Web: www.zonta.org

**Summary** To provide financial assistance to women working on an undergraduate or master's degree in business at a school in any country.

**Eligibility** This program is open to women who are working on a business-related degree at a college or university anywhere in the world at the level of the second year of an undergraduate program through the final year of a master's degree program. Applicants first compete at the club level, and then advance to district and international levels. Along with their application, they must submit a 500-word essay that describes their academic and professional goals, the relevance of their program to the business field, and how this scholarship will assist them in reaching their goals. Selection is based on that essay, academic record, demonstrated intent to complete a program in business, achievement in business-related subjects, and 2 letters of recommendation.

**Financial data** District winners receive a $1,000 scholarship; the international winners receive a $7,000 scholarship.

**Duration** 1 year.

**Additional information**   This program began in 1998.

**Number awarded**   The number of district winners varies each year; recently, 12 international winners (including 5 from the United States) were selected. Since this program was established, it has awarded more than 300 of these scholarships to women from 44 countries.

**Deadline**   Clubs set their own deadlines but must submit their winners to the district governor by May of each year.

## [959]
## JANE WALKER SCHOLARSHIP

United Methodist Church-Alabama-West Florida
   Conference
Attn: Commission on the Status and Role of Women
100 Interstate Park Drive, Suite 120
Montgomery, AL 36109
(334) 356-8014                    Toll Free: (888) 873-3127
Fax: (334) 356-8029          E-mail: awfcrc@awfumc.org
Web: www.awfumc.org/news/detail/547

**Summary**   To provide financial assistance to female residents of the Alabama-West Florida Conference of the United Methodist Church (UMC) who are undergraduate or seminary students preparing for a church-related career.

**Eligibility**   This program is open to women who are residents of the Alabama-West Florida Conference of the UMW and who affirm, represent, and advocate women's leadership in the church. Applicants must be accepted or enrolled at an approved UMC seminary or working on an undergraduate degree in Christian education at an approved UMC institution in any state. They must be a candidate for ministry or preparing for a UMC church-related career. Along with their application, they must submit a 500-word essay on why they are preparing for full-time Christian ministry and how they can promote the cause of women through this ministry. Financial need is considered in the selection process.

**Financial data**   The stipend is $1,000.

**Duration**   1 year.

**Number awarded**   1 each year.

**Deadline**   May of each year.

## [960]
## JANET H. GRISWOLD PEO SCHOLARSHIP

P.E.O. Foundation-California State Chapter
c/o Lynne Miller, Scholarship Committee Chair
1875 Los Altos
Clovis, CA 93611
(559) 709-6123              E-mail: peoca.rgw@gmail.com
Web: www.peocalifornia.org

**Summary**   To provide financial assistance to women from California who are undergraduate or graduate students at a school in any state.

**Eligibility**   This program is open to female residents of California who are attending an accredited college or university in any state. Applicants must be enrolled as full-time undergraduate or graduate students. Selection is based on financial need, character, and a record of academic and extracurricular activities achievement.

**Financial data**   Stipends range from $500 to $1,500.

**Duration**   1 year.

**Number awarded**   Varies each year.

**Deadline**   January of each year.

## [961]
## JANICE E. ARNETT CONTINUING EDUCATION SCHOLARSHIP

Kappa Delta Sorority
Attn: Foundation Project Manager
3205 Players Lane
Memphis, TN 38125
(901) 748-1897, ext. 203          Toll Free: (800) 536-1897
Fax: (901) 748-0949
E-mail: caroline.cullum@kappadelta.org
Web: www.kappadelta.org/scholarshipapplications_1

**Summary**   To provide financial assistance to members of Kappa Delta Sorority who are interested in returning to school to continue their education at the graduate level.

**Eligibility**   This program is open to graduate members of Kappa Delta Sorority who have been out of school for at least 5 years and are returning to further their education at the graduate level. Applicants must submit a personal statement giving their reasons for applying for this scholarship, official undergraduate and graduate transcripts, and 2 letters of recommendation. Selection is based on academic excellence; service to the chapter, alumnae association, or national Kappa Delta; service to the campus and community; personal objectives and goals; potential; recommendations; and financial need.

**Financial data**   The stipend is $2,000 per year. Funds may be used only for tuition, fees, and books, not for room and board.

**Duration**   1 year; may be renewed.

**Additional information**   This program began in 2009.

**Number awarded**   1 each year.

**Deadline**   November of each year.

## [962]
## JANICE E. ARNETT SCHOLARSHIP FOR LEADERSHIP AND VOLUNTEERISM

Kappa Delta Sorority
Attn: Foundation Project Manager
3205 Players Lane
Memphis, TN 38125
(901) 748-1897, ext. 203          Toll Free: (800) 536-1897
Fax: (901) 748-0949
E-mail: caroline.cullum@kappadelta.org
Web: www.kappadelta.org/scholarshipapplications_1

**Summary**   To provide financial assistance to members of Kappa Delta Sorority who are interested in continuing their education at the graduate level and have an outstanding record of leadership and volunteerism.

**Eligibility**   This program is open to graduate members of Kappa Delta Sorority. Applicants must submit a personal statement giving their reasons for applying for this scholarship, official undergraduate and graduate transcripts, and 2 letters of recommendation. Selection is based primarily on community leadership and volunteerism, although academic excellence, service to the sorority, service to the campus and community, personal objectives and goals, potential, recommendations, and financial need.

**Financial data**   The stipend is $1,500 per year. Funds may be used only for tuition, fees, and books, not for room and board.

**Duration**   1 year; may be renewed.

**Additional information** This program began in 2009.

**Number awarded** 1 each year.

**Deadline** November of each year.

## [963]
## JAZZ PERFORMANCE AWARDS

Sigma Alpha Iota Philanthropies, Inc.
One Tunnel Road
Asheville, NC 28805
(828) 251-0606 Fax: (828) 251-0644
E-mail: nh@sai-national.org
Web: www.sai-national.org

**Summary** To provide financial assistance to members of Sigma Alpha Iota (an organization of women musicians) who are interested in working on an undergraduate or graduate degree in jazz performance.

**Eligibility** This program is open to members of the organization who are enrolled in an undergraduate or graduate degree program in jazz performance or studies. Applicants must be younger than 32 years of age. Along with their application, they must submit a CD recording of a performance "set" of 30 to 45 minutes.

**Financial data** Stipends are $2,000 for the winner or $1,500 for the runner-up.

**Duration** 1 year.

**Additional information** These awards were first presented in 2006.

**Number awarded** 2 every 3 years.

**Deadline** March of the year of the awards (2015, 2018, etc.).

## [964]
## JEANNE ROSS MILLER SCHOLARSHIP

Kappa Alpha Theta Foundation
Attn: Manager of Programs
8740 Founders Road
Indianapolis, IN 46268-1337
(317) 876-1870 Toll Free: (800) KAO-1870
Fax: (317) 876-1925
E-mail: gmerritt@kappaalphatheta.org
Web: www.kappaalphathetafoundation.org

**Summary** To provide financial assistance to alumnae members of Kappa Alpha Theta who are enrolled in medical school.

**Eligibility** This program is open to members of Kappa Alpha Theta who are currently enrolled full time at a medical school in Canada or the United States. Along with their application, they must submit an official transcript, personal essays on assigned topics related to their involvement in Kappa Alpha Theta, and 2 letters of reference. Financial need is not considered in the selection process.

**Financial data** The stipend is $3,000.

**Duration** 1 year.

**Number awarded** 1 each year.

**Deadline** February of each year.

## [965]
## JENNY LIND COMPETITION FOR SOPRANOS

Barnum Festival Foundation
Attn: Director
1070 Main Street
Bridgeport, CT 06604
(203) 367-8495 Toll Free: (866) 867-8495
Fax: (203) 367-0212 E-mail: barnumfestival@aol.com
Web: barnumfestival.com

**Summary** To recognize and reward outstanding young female singers who have not yet reached professional status.

**Eligibility** This program is open to sopranos between 20 and 30 years of age who have not yet attained professional status. They must be U.S. citizens. Past finalists may reapply, but former first-place winners and mezzo-sopranos are not eligible. Applicants must submit a CD or audio cassette tape with 2 contrasting arias and 1 art song. Based on the CD or tape, 12 semifinalists are selected for an audition at the Barnum Festival in Bridgeport, Connecticut every April. From that audition, 6 finalists are chosen. Selection of the winner is based on technique, musicianship, diction, interpretation, and stage presence.

**Financial data** The winner receives a $2,000 cash prize and is featured in a concert in June with the Swedish Jenny Lind. The runner-up receives a $500 prize.

**Duration** The competition is held annually.

**Additional information** The winner of this competition serves as the American Jenny Lind, a 21st-century counterpart of the Swedish Nightingale brought to the United States for a successful concert tour in 1850 by P.T. Barnum. There is a $35 application fee.

**Number awarded** 2 each year: 1 winner and 1 runner-up.

**Deadline** April of each year.

## [966]
## JIM MCKAY SCHOLARSHIP PROGRAM

National Collegiate Athletic Association
Attn: Jim McKay Scholarship Program Staff Liaison
700 West Washington Street
P.O. Box 6222
Indianapolis, IN 46206-6222
(317) 917-6222 Fax: (317) 917-6888
E-mail: lthomas@ncaa.org
Web: www.ncaa.org

**Summary** To provide financial assistance to student-athletes (especially women and minorities) who are interested in attending graduate school to prepare for a career in sports communications.

**Eligibility** This program is open to college seniors planning to enroll full time in a graduate degree program and to students already enrolled full time in graduate study at an institution that is a member of the National Collegiate Athletic Association (NCAA). Applicants must have competed in intercollegiate athletics as a member of a varsity team at an NCAA member institution and have an overall undergraduate cumulative GPA of 3.5 or higher. They must be preparing for a career in the sports communications industry. Women and minorities are especially encouraged to apply. Neither financial need nor U.S. citizenship are required. Nominations must be submitted by the faculty athletics representative or chief academic officer at the institution in which the student is or was an undergraduate.

**Financial data**   The stipend is $10,000.

**Duration**   1 year; nonrenewable.

**Additional information**   This program began in 2008.

**Number awarded**   2 each year: 1 female and 1 male.

**Deadline**   January of each year.

## [967]
## JOAN F. GIAMBALVO MEMORIAL SCHOLARSHIP

American Medical Association
Attn: AMA Foundation
515 North State Street
Chicago, IL 60610
(312) 464-4743                    Fax: (312) 464-4142
E-mail: wpc@ama-assn.org
Web: www.ama-assn.org

**Summary**   To provide funding to physicians and medical students who are interested in conducting a research project related to women in the medical profession.

**Eligibility**   This program is open to investigators or teams of investigators of whom at least 1 member is a medical student or physician. Applicants must be interested in conducting a research project that will advance the progress of women in the medical profession and strengthen the ability of the American Medical Association (AMA) to identify and address the needs of women physicians and medical students.

**Financial data**   The grant is $10,000.

**Duration**   1 year.

**Additional information**   This program is offered by the AMA Foundation in collaboration with the AMA Women Physicians Congress (WPC) and with support from Pfizer.

**Number awarded**   2 each year.

**Deadline**   February of each year.

## [968]
## JOHN AND MURIEL LANDIS SCHOLARSHIPS

American Nuclear Society
Attn: Scholarship Coordinator
555 North Kensington Avenue
La Grange Park, IL 60526-5535
(708) 352-6611                    Toll Free: (800) 323-3044
Fax: (708) 352-0499              E-mail: outreach@ans.org
Web: www.new.ans.org/honors/scholarships

**Summary**   To provide financial assistance to undergraduate or graduate students (especially women and minorities) who are interested in preparing for a career in nuclear-related fields and can demonstrate financial need.

**Eligibility**   This program is open to undergraduate and graduate students at colleges or universities located in the United States who are preparing for, or planning to prepare for, a career in nuclear science, nuclear engineering, or a nuclear-related field. Qualified high school seniors are also eligible. Applicants must have greater than average financial need and have experienced circumstances that render them disadvantaged. Along with their application, they must submit an essay on their academic and professional goals, experiences that have affected those goals, etc. Selection is based on that essay, academic achievement, letters of recommendation, and financial need. Women and members of minority

groups are especially urged to apply. U.S. citizenship is not required.

**Financial data**   The stipend is $5,000, to be used to cover tuition, books, fees, room, and board.

**Duration**   1 year; nonrenewable.

**Number awarded**   Up to 9 each year.

**Deadline**   January of each year.

## [969]
## JOHN RAINER GRADUATE FELLOWSHIP

American Indian Graduate Center
Attn: Executive Director
3701 San Mateo Boulevard, N.E., Suite 200
Albuquerque, NM 87110-1249
(505) 881-4584                    Toll Free: (800) 628-1920
Fax: (505) 884-0427              E-mail: fellowships@aigc.com
Web: www.aigcs.com/scholarships/graduate-fellowships

**Summary**   To provide financial assistance to Native American students interested in working on a graduate degree in any field (females and males are considered separately).

**Eligibility**   This program is open to enrolled members of federally-recognized American Indian tribes and Alaska Native groups and students who can document one-fourth degree federally-recognized Indian blood. Applicants must be enrolled full time at a graduate school in the United States. Along with their application, they must submit a 500-word essay on how receiving this fellowship will enable them to continue to build, promote, and honor self-sustaining American Indian and Alaska Native communities. Financial need is also considered in the selection process. Males and females are considered separately.

**Financial data**   The stipend is $1,000, of which $500 may be applied to the cost of education and $500 must be used to support participation in volunteer activities that afford an opportunity to develop leadership skills.

**Duration**   1 year; nonrenewable.

**Number awarded**   2 each year: 1 to a male and 1 to a female.

**Deadline**   May of each year.

## [970]
## JOSEPH B. GITTLER AWARD

American Psychological Foundation
750 First Street, N.E.
Washington, DC 20002-4242
(202) 336-5843                    Fax: (202) 336-5812
E-mail: foundation@apa.org
Web: www.apa.org/apf/funding/gittler.aspx

**Summary**   To recognize and reward scholars and graduate students in psychology (particularly women and members of other diverse groups) who have made outstanding contributions to the philosophical foundations of the discipline.

**Eligibility**   This award is available to scholars and graduate students whose body of work or whose individual work has transformed the philosophical foundations of psychological knowledge. Self-nominations are welcome. Selection is based on conformance with stated program goals and magnitude of contributions The sponsor encourages nominations of individuals who represent diversity in race, ethnicity, gender, age, disability, and sexual orientation.

**Financial data**   The award is $10,000.

**Duration** The award is presented annually.

**Additional information** This award was first presented in 2008.

**Number awarded** 1 each year.

**Deadline** Nominations must be submitted by May of each year.

## [971]
## JOSEPH H. FICHTER RESEARCH GRANT COMPETITION

Association for the Sociology of Religion
Attn: Executive Officer
University of South Florida
Department of Sociology
4202 East Fowler Avenue, CPR 107
Tampa, FL 33620
(813) 974-2633                    Fax: (813) 974-6455
E-mail: jcavendi@usf.edu
Web: www.sociologyofreligion.com

**Summary** To provide funding to scholars interested in conducting research on women and religion.

**Eligibility** This program is open to scholars involved in research on women and religion or on the intersection between religion and gender or religion and sexualities. Scholars at the beginning of their careers are particularly encouraged to apply; dissertation research qualifies for funding. Applicants must be members of the association at the time the application is submitted. The proposal should outline the rationale and plan of the research, previous research, methodology proposed, timeline, and budget; a curriculum vitae should also be included. Simultaneous submissions to other grant competitions are permissible if the applicant is explicit about which budget items in the Fichter grant proposal do not overlap items in other submitted proposals.

**Financial data** Each year, a total of $24,000 is available to be awarded.

**Duration** 1 year.

**Number awarded** Varies each year; recently, 6 of these grants were awarded.

**Deadline** April of each year.

## [972]
## JOSEPH L. FISHER DOCTORAL DISSERTATION FELLOWSHIPS

Resources for the Future
Attn: Coordinator for Academic Programs
1616 P Street, N.W., Suite 600
Washington, DC 20036-1400
(202) 328-5020                    Fax: (202) 939-3460
E-mail: fisher-award@rff.org
Web: www.rff.org

**Summary** To provide funding to female, minority, and other doctoral candidates in economics interested in conducting dissertation research on issues related to the environment, natural resources, or energy.

**Eligibility** This program is open to graduate students in their final year of research on a dissertation related to the environment, natural resources, or energy. Applicants must submit a brief letter of application and a curriculum vitae, a graduate transcript, a 1-page abstract of the dissertation, a technical summary of the dissertation (up to 2,500 words), a letter from their department chair, and 2 letters of recommendation from faculty members on the student's dissertation committee. The technical summary should describe clearly the aim of the dissertation, its significance in relation to the existing literature, and the research methods to be used. Women and minority candidates are strongly encouraged to apply. Non-citizens are eligible if they have proper work and residency documentation.

**Financial data** The stipend is $18,000.

**Duration** 1 academic year.

**Additional information** It is expected that recipients will not hold other employment during the fellowship period. Recipients must notify Resources for the Future of any financial assistance they receive from any other source for support of doctoral work.

**Number awarded** 1 to 3 each year.

**Deadline** February of each year.

## [973]
## JOSEPHINE AND BENJAMIN WEBBER TRUST SCHOLARSHIPS

Arizona Association of Family and Consumer Sciences
Attn: Webber Educational Grant Committee
Kathryn L. Hatch
4843 North Via Sonrisa
Tucson, AZ 85718-5724
(502) 577-6109                    E-mail: klhatch@u.arizona.edu
Web: ag.arizona.edu/webbertrusts

**Summary** To provide financial assistance to Hispanic women from mining towns in Arizona who are interested in working on an undergraduate or graduate degree in a field related to family and consumer sciences at a school in the state.

**Eligibility** This program is open to Hispanic women who reside in the following Arizona mining towns: Ajo, Arizona City, Bisbee, Clifton, Douglas, Duncan, Globe, Green Valley, Hayden, Kingman, Kearny, Mammoth, Morenci, Prescott, Safford, Sahuarita, San Manuel, Seligman, Superior, or Winkelman. If too few female Hispanic residents of those towns apply, the program may be open to 1) non-Hispanic women who live in those towns, and/or 2) Hispanic women who currently live elsewhere in Arizona and whose parents or grandparents had lived or continue to live in those communities. Applicants must be enrolled or planning to enroll at a college or university in Arizona to work on an undergraduate or graduate degree. Eligible fields of study include those in the following categories: foods, nutrition, and/or dietetics; restaurant and food service management; culinary arts; family studies; interior design; family and consumer science education; dietetic education; early childhood education; or apparel and clothing. Financial need is considered in the selection process.

**Financial data** Funding at public colleges and universities provides for payment of tuition and fees, books, educational supplies, housing, food, and transportation to and from campus. At private institutions, stipend amounts are equivalent to those at public schools.

**Duration** 1 year; may be renewed for a total of 8 semesters and 2 summers of undergraduate study or 4 semesters and 2 summers of graduate study.

**Additional information** This program began in 1980.

**Number awarded** Varies each year; recently, 5 of these scholarships were awarded.

**Deadline** March of each year.

## [974]
## JOSEPHINE CARROLL NORWOOD MEMORIAL SCHOLARSHIPS

Baptist Convention of Maryland/Delaware
Attn: United Baptist Women of Maryland, Inc.
10255 Old Columbia Road
Columbia, MD 21046
(410) 290-5290          Toll Free: (800) 466-5290
E-mail: gparker@bcmd.org
Web: www.bcmd.org/wmu

**Summary** To provide financial assistance to women who are members of Baptist churches associated with an affiliate of United Baptist Women of Maryland and interested in attending seminary or graduate school in any state to prepare for a Christian vocation.

**Eligibility** This program is open to women who are enrolled or planning to enroll full time at a seminary or graduate school in any state to prepare for a Christian vocation. Applicants must be a member in good standing of a Baptist church associated with an affiliate of United Baptist Women of Maryland. They must have a grade average of "C" or higher and be able to demonstrate financial need. Along with their application, they must submit brief statements on their Christian experience, school activities, church and community activities, and career goals.

**Financial data** A stipend is awarded (amount not specified).

**Duration** 1 year.

**Number awarded** Varies each year.

**Deadline** June of each year.

## [975]
## JUDITH MCMANUS PRICE SCHOLARSHIPS

American Planning Association
Attn: Leadership Affairs Associate
205 North Michigan Avenue, Suite 1200
Chicago, IL 60601
(312) 431-9100          Fax: (312) 786-6700
E-mail: fellowship@planning.org
Web: www.planning.org/scholarships/apa

**Summary** To provide financial assistance to women and underrepresented minority students enrolled in undergraduate or graduate degree programs at recognized planning schools.

**Eligibility** This program is open to undergraduate and graduate students in urban and regional planning who are women or members of the following minority groups: African American, Hispanic American, or Native American. Applicants must be citizens of the United States and able to document financial need. They must intend to work as practicing planners in the public sector. Along with their application, they must submit a 2-page personal and background statement describing how their education will be applied to career goals and why they chose planning as a career path. Selection is based (in order of importance), on: 1) commitment to planning as reflected in their personal statement and on their resume; 2) academic achievement and/or improvement dur-

ing the past 2 years; 3) letters of recommendation; 4) financial need; and 5) professional presentation.

**Financial data** Stipends range from $2,000 to $4,000 per year. The money may be applied to tuition and living expenses only. Payment is made to the recipient's university and divided by terms in the school year.

**Duration** 1 year; recipients may reapply.

**Additional information** This program began in 2002.

**Number awarded** Varies each year; recently, 3 of these scholarships were awarded.

**Deadline** April of each year.

## [976]
## JUDITH RESNIK MEMORIAL SCHOLARSHIP

Alpha Epsilon Phi
Attn: AEPhi Foundation
11 Lake Avenue Extension, Suite 1A
Danbury, CT 06811
(203) 748-0029          Fax: (203) 748-0039
E-mail: aephifoundation@aephi.org
Web: www.aephi.org/foundation/scholarships

**Summary** To provide financial assistance to Alpha Epsilon Phi members or alumnae who are working on an undergraduate or graduate degree, especially in science, engineering, or a related field.

**Eligibility** This program is open to active and alumnae members of the sorority who are either full-time rising juniors or seniors or graduate students who have completed at least 1 year of graduate study. Preference is given to applicants who are working on a degree in science, engineering, or a related field and have a GPA of 3.5 or higher. Along with their application, they must submit a letter describing 1) their activities in their chapter, on campus, and in the general community; 2) what they have done to supplement their parents' contribution toward their education; and 3) their need for scholarship consideration.

**Financial data** Stipends range from $1,000 to $2,000 per year.

**Duration** 1 year; may be renewed.

**Additional information** Recipients must be willing to remain active in the sorority and live in the sorority house (if any) for the entire year the scholarship covers.

**Number awarded** 1 or more each year.

**Deadline** March of each year.

## [977]
## JUDY CORMAN MEMORIAL SCHOLARSHIP AND INTERNSHIP

New York Women in Communications, Inc.
Attn: NYWICI Foundation
355 Lexington Avenue, 15th Floor
New York, NY 10017-6603
(212) 297-2133          Fax: (212) 370-9047
E-mail: nywicipr@nywici.org
Web: www.nywici.org/foundation/scholarships

**Summary** To provide financial assistance and work experience to female residents of designated eastern states who are interested in preparing for a career in communications and media relations at a college or graduate school in any state.

**Eligibility** This program is open to women who are seniors graduating from high schools in New York, New Jersey, Connecticut, or Pennsylvania or undergraduate or graduate students who are permanent residents of those states; they must be attending or planning to attend a college or university in any state. Graduate students must be members of New York Women in Communications, Inc. (NYWICI). Also eligible are women who reside outside the 4 states but are currently enrolled at a college or university within 1 of the 5 boroughs of New York City. Applicants must be preparing for a career in communications and media relations and be interested in a summer internship with Scholastic. They must have a GPA of 3.2 or higher. Along with their application, they must submit a 2-page resume; a personal essay of 300 words on an assigned topic that changes annually; 2 letters of recommendation; and an official transcript. Selection is based on academic record, need, demonstrated leadership, participation in school and community activities, honors and other awards or recognition, work experience, goals and aspirations, and unusual personal and/or family circumstances. U.S. citizenship is required.

**Financial data** The scholarship stipend ranges up to $10,000; the internship is salaried (amount not specified).

**Duration** 1 year.

**Additional information** This program is sponsored by Scholastic, Inc.

**Number awarded** 1 each year.

**Deadline** January of each year.

## [978]
## JULIA BUMRY JONES SCHOLARSHIP PROGRAM

Delta Sigma Theta Sorority, Inc.
Attn: Scholarship and Standards Committee Chair
1707 New Hampshire Avenue, N.W.
Washington, DC 20009
(202) 986-2400                Fax: (202) 986-2513
E-mail: dstemail@deltasigmatheta.org
Web: www.deltasigmatheta.org

**Summary** To provide financial assistance to members of Delta Sigma Theta who are interested in working on a graduate degree in journalism or another area of communications.

**Eligibility** This program is open to graduating college seniors and graduate students who are interested in preparing for a career in journalism or another area of communications. Applicants must be active, dues-paying members of Delta Sigma Theta. Selection is based on meritorious achievement.

**Financial data** The stipends range from $1,000 to $2,000. The funds may be used to cover tuition, fees, and living expenses.

**Duration** 1 year; may be renewed for 1 additional year.

**Additional information** This sponsor is a traditionally-African American social sorority. The application fee is $20.

**Number awarded** 1 or more each year.

**Deadline** April of each year.

## [979]
## JULIETTE DERRICOTTE SCHOLARSHIP

Delta Sigma Theta Sorority, Inc.
Attn: Scholarship and Standards Committee Chair
1707 New Hampshire Avenue, N.W.
Washington, DC 20009
(202) 986-2400                Fax: (202) 986-2513
E-mail: dstemail@deltasigmatheta.org
Web: www.deltasigmatheta.org

**Summary** To provide financial assistance to members of Delta Sigma Theta who are interested in preparing for a career in social work.

**Eligibility** This program is open to graduating college seniors or graduate students who are interested in preparing for a career in social work. Applicants must be active, dues-paying members of Delta Sigma Theta. Selection is based on meritorious achievement.

**Financial data** The stipends range from $1,000 to $2,000 per year. The funds may be used to cover tuition, school, and living expenses.

**Duration** 1 year; may be renewed for 1 additional year.

**Additional information** This sponsor is a traditionally-African American social sorority. The application fee is $20.

**Number awarded** 1 or more each year.

**Deadline** April of each year.

## [980]
## JULIETTE MATHER SCHOLARSHIP

Woman's Missionary Union
Attn: WMU Foundation
100 Missionary Ridge
Birmingham, AL 35242
(205) 408-5525                Toll Free: (877) 482-4483
Fax: (205) 408-5508        E-mail: wmufoundation@wmu.org
Web: www.wmufoundation.com

**Summary** To provide financial assistance to female Southern Baptist undergraduate or graduate students preparing for a career in Christian ministry.

**Eligibility** This program is open to female Southern Baptist undergraduate and graduate students who are preparing for a career in Christian ministry and service. They must be interested in preparing to become the Baptist leaders of the future.

**Financial data** A stipend is awarded (amount not specified).

**Duration** 1 year.

**Number awarded** Varies each year.

**Deadline** January of each year.

## [981]
## JUSTICE JANIE L. SHORES SCHOLARSHIP

Alabama Law Foundation
415 Dexter Avenue
P.O. Box 4129
Montgomery, AL 36101
(334) 269-1515                Fax: (334) 261-6310
E-mail: info@alfinc.org
Web: www.alfinc.org/janieShores.cfm

**Summary** To provide financial assistance to female residents of Alabama who are attending law school in the state.

**Eligibility** This program is open to women who are residents of Alabama and enrolled at a law school in the state. Applicants must submit documentation of financial need and an essay on their career plans.

**Financial data** A stipend is awarded (amount not specified).

**Duration** 1 year.

**Additional information** This program began in 2006.

**Number awarded** 1 or more each year.

**Deadline** June of each year.

## [982]
## JUSTICE PAULINE DAVIS HANSON SCHOLARSHIP

Fresno County Women Lawyers
c/o Nancy J. Stegall, Scholarship Committee
2445 Capitol Street, Suite 140
Fresno, CA 93721-2267
(559) 237-6800                    Fax: (559) 237-6807
E-mail: nstegall@cv-familylaw.com
Web: www.fcwl.org/fcwl_scholarships.htm

**Summary** To provide financial assistance to female law students in selected areas of California.

**Eligibility** This program is open to women from California who have completed their first year of law school. Preference is given to current or former residents of Fresno, Kings, Madera, and Tulare counties, especially if they intend to practice in those counties. Selection is based on academic achievement, extracurricular and community activities, demonstrated leadership capabilities, and financial need. Finalists are interviewed.

**Financial data** The stipend is $2,000.

**Duration** 1 year.

**Number awarded** 1 each year.

**Deadline** May of each year.

## [983]
## KAFI WILFORD CONSTANTINE FELLOWSHIP

Alpha Kappa Alpha Sorority, Inc.
Attn: Educational Advancement Foundation
5656 South Stony Island Avenue
Chicago, IL 60637
(773) 947-0026                    Toll Free: (800) 653-6528
Fax: (773) 947-0277          E-mail: akaeaf@akaeaf.net
Web: www.akaeaf.org/fellowships_endowments.htm

**Summary** To provide financial assistance to undergraduates (especially African American women) who are working on a law degree.

**Eligibility** This program is open to full-time law students who are enrolled at a school in any state. Applicants must submit 1) a list of honors, awards, and scholarships received; 2) a list of organizations in which they have memberships, especially minority organizations; and 3) a statement of their personal and career goals, including how this scholarship will enhance their ability to attain those goals. The sponsor is a traditionally African American women's sorority.

**Financial data** A stipend is awarded (amount not specified).

**Duration** 1 year.

**Number awarded** 1 or more each even-numbered year.

**Deadline** April of each even-numbered year.

## [984]
## KAILASH, MONA, AND ANILA JAIN SCHOLARSHIP

Kappa Delta Sorority
Attn: Foundation Project Manager
3205 Players Lane
Memphis, TN 38125
(901) 748-1897, ext. 203          Toll Free: (800) 536-1897
Fax: (901) 748-0949
E-mail: caroline.cullum@kappadelta.org
Web: www.kappadelta.org/scholarshipapplications_1

**Summary** To provide financial assistance to members of Kappa Delta Sorority who are working on a graduate degree in health care.

**Eligibility** This program is open to graduate members of Kappa Delta Sorority. Applicants must submit a personal statement giving their reasons for applying for this scholarship, official undergraduate and graduate transcripts, and 2 letters of recommendation. They must be working on a graduate degree in a field related to health care. Selection is based on academic excellence; service to the chapter, alumnae association, or national Kappa Delta; service to the campus and community; personal objectives and goals; potential; recommendations; and financial need.

**Financial data** The stipend is $2,000 per year. Funds may be used only for tuition, fees, and books, not for room and board.

**Duration** 1 year; may be renewed.

**Additional information** This program began in 2001.

**Number awarded** 1 each year.

**Deadline** November of each year.

## [985]
## KAPPA ALPHA THETA ALUMNAE SCHOLARSHIPS

Kappa Alpha Theta Foundation
Attn: Manager of Programs
8740 Founders Road
Indianapolis, IN 46268-1337
(317) 876-1870                    Toll Free: (800) KAO-1870
Fax: (317) 876-1925
E-mail: gmerritt@kappaalphatheta.org
Web: www.kappaalphathetafoundation.org

**Summary** To provide financial assistance to members of Kappa Alpha Theta (the first Greek letter fraternity for women) who are working on advanced degrees in North America or abroad.

**Eligibility** This program is open to members of Kappa Alpha Theta who are enrolled as graduate students at a university in Canada or the United States. Along with their application, they must submit an official transcript, personal essays on assigned topics related to their involvement in Kappa Alpha Theta, and 2 letters of reference. Financial need is not considered in the selection process.

**Financial data** Stipends range from $1,000 to $12,000. Recently, the average was $4,760.

**Duration** 1 year. Recipients may reapply, but they may not receive a maximum lifetime amount of more than $20,000 from the foundation.

**Additional information** Recipients may study abroad, provided they do so as part of a program leading to a degree from an institution in the United States or Canada.

**Number awarded** Varies each year; recently, the organization awarded scholarships to 90 graduate student members.

**Deadline** February of each year.

## [986]
## KAPPA DELTA SORORITY GRADUATE SCHOLARSHIPS

Kappa Delta Sorority
Attn: Foundation Project Manager
3205 Players Lane
Memphis, TN 38125
(901) 748-1897, ext. 203          Toll Free: (800) 536-1897
Fax: (901) 748-0949
E-mail: caroline.cullum@kappadelta.org
Web: www.kappadelta.org/scholarshipapplications_1

**Summary** To provide financial assistance to members of Kappa Delta Sorority who are interested in continuing their education at the graduate level.

**Eligibility** This program is open to graduate members of Kappa Delta Sorority. Applicants must submit a personal statement giving their reasons for applying for this scholarship, official undergraduate and graduate transcripts, and 2 letters of recommendation. Most scholarships are available to all graduate members, but some have additional restrictions. Selection is based on academic excellence; service to the chapter, alumnae association, or national Kappa Delta; service to the campus and community; personal objectives and goals; potential; recommendations; and financial need.

**Financial data** Stipends range from $1,000 to $5,000 per year. Funds may be used only for tuition, fees, and books, not for room and board.

**Duration** 1 year; may be renewed.

**Additional information** This program includes the following named scholarships that have no additional restrictions: the Dorothea B. Cavin Scholarship, the Helen A. Snyder Scholarship, the Minnie Mae Prescott Scholarship, the Muriel Johnstone Scholarship, the Herff Jones Graduate Fellowship, the Janice E. Arnett Graduate Scholarship and the Alumna Grant for Continuing Education.

**Number awarded** Varies each year; recently, the sorority awarded a total of 15 graduate scholarships: 1 at $5,000, 3 at $2,500, 8 at $2,000, 1 at $1,500, and 2 at $1,000.

**Deadline** November of each year.

## [987]
## KAPPA KAPPA GAMMA GRADUATE FELLOWSHIP AWARDS

Kappa Kappa Gamma Fraternity
Attn: Foundation Administrator
530 East Town Street
P.O. Box 38
Columbus, OH 43216-0038
(614) 228-6515          Toll Free: (866) KKG-1870
Fax: (614) 228-6303          E-mail: kkghq@kappa.org
Web: www.kappakappagamma.org

**Summary** To provide financial assistance for graduate school to members of Kappa Kappa Gamma.

**Eligibility** This program is open to members of Kappa Kappa Gamma who are full-time graduate students with a GPA of 3.0 or higher. Applicants must be initiated members who were in good standing as undergraduates. Along with their application, they must submit a personal essay or letter describing their educational and career goals and financial need. Selection is based on merit, academic achievement, participation in sorority activities, and financial need.

**Financial data** Stipends average $3,000.

**Duration** 1 year; nonrenewable.

**Number awarded** Varies each year; recently, the foundation awarded a total of 152 undergraduate and graduate scholarships with a value of $466,812.

**Deadline** January of each year.

## [988]
## KATE GLEASON SCHOLARSHIP

ASME International
Attn: Centers Administrator
Two Park Avenue
New York, NY 10016-5675
(212) 591-8131          Toll Free: (800) THE-ASME
Fax: (212) 591-7143          E-mail: LefeverB@asme.org
Web: www.asme.org

**Summary** To provide financial assistance to female undergraduate and graduate students from any country who are working on a degree in mechanical engineering.

**Eligibility** This program is open to women who are enrolled in an ABET-accredited or equivalent mechanical engineering, mechanical engineering technology, or related undergraduate or graduate program. Applicants must submit a nomination from their department head, a recommendation from a faculty member, and an official transcript. Only 1 nomination may be submitted per department. There are no citizenship requirements, but study must be conducted in the United States. Selection is based on academic ability and potential contribution to the mechanical engineering profession.

**Financial data** The stipend is $3,000.

**Duration** 1 year.

**Number awarded** 1 each year.

**Deadline** February of each year.

**[989]**
## KATHARINE C. BRYAN GRADUATE SCHOLARSHIP

Tennessee Baptist Convention
Attn: WMU Scholarships
5001 Maryland Way
P.O. Box 728
Brentwood, TN 37024-9728
(615) 371-7923          Toll Free: (800) 558-2090, ext. 7923
Fax: (615) 371-2014          E-mail: lrader@tnbaptist.org
Web: www.tnbaptist.org/page.asp?page=92

**Summary**   To provide financial assistance to female members of Baptist churches in Tennessee who are interested in attending graduate school in any state.

**Eligibility**   This program is open to women who are members of Tennessee Baptist churches or have Tennessee Baptist ties. Applicants must be active in missions and ministries of their local church. They must be enrolled in full-time graduate study in any state and have a GPA of 2.6 or higher. Financial need is not considered in the selection process.

**Financial data**   A stipend is awarded (amount not specified).

**Duration**   1 year; may be renewed if the recipient maintains a GPA of 3.5 or higher.

**Number awarded**   1 or more each year.

**Deadline**   January of each year.

**[990]**
## KATHERINE J. SCHUTZE MEMORIAL SCHOLARSHIP

Christian Church (Disciples of Christ)
Attn: Disciples Home Missions
130 East Washington Street
P.O. Box 1986
Indianapolis, IN 46206-1986
(317) 713-2652          Toll Free: (888) DHM-2631
Fax: (317) 635-4426          E-mail: mail@dhm.disciples.org
Web: www.discipleshomemissions.org

**Summary**   To provide financial assistance to female seminary students affiliated with the Christian Church (Disciples of Christ).

**Eligibility**   This program is open to female seminary students who are members of a Christian Church (Disciples of Christ) congregation in the United States or Canada. Applicants must plan to prepare for the ordained ministry, be working on an M.Div. or equivalent degree, provide evidence of financial need, be enrolled full time in an accredited school or seminary, provide a transcript of academic work, and be under the care of a regional Commission on the Ministry or in the process of coming under care.

**Financial data**   A stipend is awarded (amount not specified).

**Duration**   1 year; recipients may reapply.

**Number awarded**   1 or more each year.

**Deadline**   March of each year.

**[991]**
## KATHY KARDISH WILSON MEMORIAL EDUCATIONAL FUND

Chautauqua Region Community Foundation
Attn: Scholarship Coordinator
418 Spring Street
Jamestown, NY 14701
(716) 661-3394          Fax: (716) 488-0387
E-mail: llynde@crcfonline.org
Web: www.crcfonline.org

**Summary**   To provide financial assistance to married women in New York, Ohio, and Pennsylvania who are interested in returning to school to complete an undergraduate or graduate degree.

**Eligibility**   This program is open to women who live and attend college or graduate school in New York, Ohio, or Pennsylvania. Applicants must be mothers of school-aged children, part of a 2-income family in which tuition would be a burden on the family, able to complete the educational and career goals set for themselves, community-minded and considerably involved in at least 1 community organization, and giving of themselves and their talents to help others reach their potential. Along with their application, they must submit a 1-page essay describing their past achievements, career goals, and reasons for returning to school or training.

**Financial data**   A stipend is awarded (amount not specified).

**Duration**   1 year.

**Number awarded**   1 or more each year.

**Deadline**   May of each year.

**[992]**
## KATHY LOUDAT MUSIC SCHOLARSHIP

New Mexico Baptist Foundation
5325 Wyoming Boulevard, N.E.
P.O. Box 16560
Albuquerque, NM 87191-6560
(505) 332-3777          Toll Free: (877) 841-3777
Fax: (505) 332-2777          E-mail: foundation@nmbf.com
Web: www.bcnm.com

**Summary**   To provide financial assistance to female members of Southern Baptist churches in New Mexico who are attending college in any state to prepare for a career in church music.

**Eligibility**   This program is open to full-time female college, university, and seminary students who are preparing for a career in church music. Applicants must have a GPA of 3.0 or higher and be able to demonstrate financial need. They must be members of Southern Baptist churches in New Mexico or former members in good standing with the Southern Baptist Convention.

**Financial data**   A stipend is awarded (amount not specified).

**Duration**   1 year.

**Number awarded**   1 or more each year.

**Deadline**   April of each year.

## [993]
## KENTUCKY WOMEN IN AGRICULTURE SCHOLARSHIP

Kentucky Women in Agriculture
Attn: Scholarship
P.O. Box 4409
Lexington, KY 40544-4409
Toll Free: (877) 266-8823
E-mail: info@kywomeninag.com
Web: www.kywomeninag.com/scholarship.php

**Summary** To provide financial assistance to female residents of Kentucky enrolled as upper-division or graduate students at colleges in the state and working on a degree in agriculture.

**Eligibility** This program is open to women who are residents of Kentucky and enrolled full time as juniors, seniors, or graduate students at a college or university in the state. Applicants must be working on a degree in a field related to agriculture and have a GPA of 2.5 or higher. Along with their application, they must submit a 500-word essay on their career goals for working in agriculture and how this scholarship will support them in their academic pursuits. Selection is based on desire to work in the field of agriculture (40 points), financial need (30 points), academic record (20 points), and extracurricular activities (10 points).

**Financial data** The stipend is $1,000 per year.

**Duration** 1 year.

**Number awarded** 1 each year.

**Deadline** May of each year.

## [994]
## KITTY STONE GRADUATE SCHOLARSHIP

Alabama Federation of Women's Clubs
Attn: Scholarship Chair
2728 Niazuma Avenue
Birmingham, AL 35205
(205) 323-2392                Fax: (205) 323-8443
Web: www.gfwc-alabama.org/Scholarships.html

**Summary** To provide financial assistance to women who are residents of Alabama and interested in working on a graduate degree at a public university in the state.

**Eligibility** This program is open to female residents of Alabama who are attending or planning to attend a public university in the state. Applicants must be interested in working on a graduate degree in any field. Along with their application, they must submit a personal letter on their educational goals, 3 letters of recommendation, and transcripts. Financial need is not considered in the selection process.

**Financial data** The stipend is $1,500.

**Duration** 1 year.

**Number awarded** 1 each year.

**Deadline** Deadline not specified.

## [995]
## LAMBDA KAPPA SIGMA GRANTS

Lambda Kappa Sigma Pharmacy Fraternity
Attn: Executive Director
S77 W16906 Casey Drive
P.O. Box 570
Muskego, WI 53150-0570
Toll Free: (800) LKS-1913        Fax: (262) 679-4558
E-mail: lks@lks.org
Web: www.lks.org

**Summary** To provide financial assistance to members of Lambda Kappa Sigma who are interested in working on a Pharm.D. degree and can demonstrate leadership.

**Eligibility** This program is open to collegiate or alumnae members of Lambda Kappa Sigma who are enrolled in a licensure-eligible pharmacy degree program. (In the United States, the Pharm.D. degree is the only qualifying program at schools or colleges of pharmacy recognized by the Accreditation Council on Pharmacy Education.) Applicants must rank in the top half of their class and be able to demonstrate financial need. Along with their application, they must submit a brief essay on their leadership qualities and the importance of leadership.

**Financial data** The stipend is $1,000.

**Duration** 1 year.

**Additional information** Lambda Kappa Sigma was founded in 1913 to promote the profession of pharmacy among women. Although some of its chapters are now coeducational, it still emphasizes women's health issues. This program includes the following named awards: the Cora E. Craven Educational Grant, the Mary Connolly Livingston Educational Grant, the Adele Lobracio Lowe Leadership Grant, and the Norma Chipman Wells Loyalty Grant.

**Number awarded** Varies each year.

**Deadline** October of each year.

## [996]
## LAURELS FUND SCHOLARSHIPS

Educational Foundation for Women in Accounting
Attn: Foundation Administrator
136 South Keowee Street
Dayton, OH 45402
(937) 424-3391                Fax: (937) 222-5749
E-mail: info@efwa.org
Web: www.efwa.org/scholarships_laurels_fund.php

**Summary** To provide financial support to women working on a doctoral degree in accounting.

**Eligibility** This program is open to women who are working on a Ph.D. degree in accounting and have completed their comprehensive examinations. Applicants must submit a statement of personal and career goals and objectives. Selection is based on 1) scholarship, including academic achievements in course work and research activities; 2) service, including volunteer work to which the applicant has made significant or long-term commitments; and 3) financial need. U.S. citizenship is required.

**Financial data** The stipend ranges from $1,000 to $5,000.

**Duration** 1 year; nonrenewable.

**Additional information** This program began in 1978.

**Number awarded** Varies each year.

**Deadline** May of each year.

## [997]
## LEADERSHIP LEGACY SCHOLARSHIP FOR GRADUATES

Women's Transportation Seminar
Attn: WTS Foundation
1701 K Street, N.W., Suite 800
Washington, DC 20006
(202) 955-5085            Fax: (202) 955-5088
E-mail: wts@wtsinternational.org
Web: www.wtsinternational.org/education/scholarships

**Summary** To provide financial assistance to graduate women interested in a career in transportation.

**Eligibility** This program is open to women who are working on a graduate degree in transportation or a transportation-related field (e.g., transportation engineering, planning, business management, finance, or logistics). Applicants must have a GPA of 3.0 or higher and be interested in a career in transportation. Along with their application, they must submit a 1,000-word statement about their vision of how their education will give them the tools to better serve their community's needs and transportation issues. Applications must be submitted first to a local chapter; the chapters forward selected applications for consideration on the national level. Minority women are especially encouraged to apply. Selection is based on transportation involvement and goals, job skills, and academic record; financial need is not considered.

**Financial data** The stipend is $5,000.

**Duration** 1 year.

**Additional information** This program began in 2008. Each year, it focuses on women with a special interest; recently, it was reserved for women who have a specific interest in addressing the impact of transportation on sustainability, land use, environmental impact, security, and quality of life issues internationally.

**Number awarded** 1 each year.

**Deadline** Applications must be submitted by November to a local WTS chapter.

## [998]
## LEAH J. DICKSTEIN, M.D. AWARD

Association of Women Psychiatrists
Attn: Executive Director
P.O. Box 570218
Dallas, TX 75357-0218
(972) 613-0985            Fax: (972) 613-5532
E-mail: womenpsych@aol.com
Web: www.associationofwomenpsychiatrists.com

**Summary** To recognize and reward outstanding female medical students.

**Eligibility** This award is available to female medical students who demonstrate superior academic achievement, creativity, and leadership. Activities that may be recognized include service or clinical aspects of medicine, science research, or excellence in art, music, or literature.

**Financial data** The award consists of $1,000 and a plaque. Funds may be used to attend the annual meeting of the Association of Women Psychiatrists, with the balance at the discretion of the recipient.

**Duration** The award is presented annually.

**Additional information** The awardee is invited to join the award committee for the following year.

**Number awarded** 1 each year.

**Deadline** February of each year.

## [999]
## LESLIE S. PARKER MEMORIAL SCHOLARSHIP

Order of the Eastern Star-Grand Chapter of Oregon
c/o Marymargaret Holstein, Scholarship Committee Chair
161 S.E. 118th Street
South Beach, OR 97366-9732
E-mail: mholstein@charter.net
Web: www.oregonoes.org/scholarships/index.html

**Summary** To provide financial assistance to women who are residents of Oregon and attending college or graduate school in the state.

**Eligibility** This program is open to female residents of Oregon who have completed at least 2 years of undergraduate or graduate study at an accredited non-sectarian college or university in the state. Applicants must be able to demonstrate financial need.

**Financial data** Stipends are approximately $1,000. Funds are sent directly to the recipient's college or university to be used for books, tuition, room and board, clothing, or medical aid.

**Duration** 1 year.

**Number awarded** 1 or more each year.

**Deadline** April of each year.

## [1000]
## LIBRARY OF CONGRESS JUNIOR FELLOWS PROGRAM

Library of Congress
Library Services
Attn: Junior Fellows Program Coordinator
101 Independence Avenue, S.E., Room LM-642
Washington, DC 20540-4600
(202) 707-6610            Fax: (202) 707-6269
E-mail: jrfell@loc.gov
Web: www.loc.gov/hr/jrfellows/index.html

**Summary** To provide summer work experience at the Library of Congress (LC) to upper-division students, graduate students, and recent graduates (particularly women, minorities, and persons with disabilities).

**Eligibility** This program is open to U.S. citizens with subject expertise in the following areas: collections preservation; geography and maps; humanities, art, and culture; information technology; library science; or chemistry and science. Applicants must 1) be juniors or seniors at an accredited college or university; 2) be graduate students; or 3) have completed their degree in the past year. Women, minorities, and persons with disabilities are strongly encouraged to apply. Selection is based on academic achievement, letters of recommendation, and an interview.

**Financial data** Fellows are paid a taxable stipend of $3,000.

**Duration** 10 weeks, beginning in either May or June. Fellows work a 40-hour week.

**Additional information** Fellows work with primary source materials and assist selected divisions at LC in the organization and documentation of archival collections, production of finding aids and bibliographic records, preparation of materials for preservation and service, completion of bibliographical research, and digitization of LC's historical collections.

**Number awarded** Varies each year; recently, 38 of these internships were awarded.

**Deadline** January of each year.

## [1001]
## LINCOLN COMMUNITY FOUNDATION MEDICAL RESEARCH SCHOLARSHIP

Lincoln Community Foundation
215 Centennial Mall South, Suite 100
Lincoln, NE 68508
(402) 474-2345          Toll Free: (888) 448-4668
Fax: (402) 476-8532          E-mail: lcf@lcf.org
Web: www.lcf.org/page.aspx?pid=477

**Summary** To provide financial assistance to residents of Nebraska (preference given to women) who are interested in working on an advanced degree in a medical field at a school in any state.

**Eligibility** This program is open to residents of Nebraska who are working on an advanced degree in a medical field (nursing students may apply as undergraduates or graduate students). Applicants must submit an essay explaining their progress toward completing their education, why they have chosen to prepare for a career in a medical field, and their future career goals once they complete their degree. Preference is given to 1) female applicants; 2) students preparing for careers as physicians and nurses; and 3) applicants who demonstrate financial need.

**Financial data** The stipend is $2,000.

**Duration** 1 year; may be renewed up to 3 additional years.

**Additional information** This program began in 2005.

**Number awarded** 2 each year.

**Deadline** March of each year.

## [1002]
## LINDA J. MURPHY SCHOLARSHIPS

Women Lawyers' Association of Greater St. Louis
c/o Jennifer Gustafson, Scholarship Committee Chair
Lewis, Rice & Fingersh, L.C.
600 Washington, Suite 2500
St. Louis, MO 63101
(314) 444-7600          E-mail: jgustafson@lewisrice.com
Web: wlastl.org/scholarships

**Summary** To provide financial assistance to women from any state who are attending law school in Missouri.

**Eligibility** This program is open to women attending law school in Missouri on a part-time or full-time basis. Applicants must submit a 2-page personal statement on events, decisions, or individuals that have helped to shape their life; short-term and long-term career goals; and/or contributions they would like to make to society in general, their community, women, or the legal profession. Selection is based on commitment to causes that are consistent with the mission of the sponsoring association or the advancement of women, academic achievement, and financial need.

**Financial data** Stipends range from $1,000 to $6,000.

**Duration** 1 year.

**Additional information** This program began in 1996.

**Number awarded** Varies each year; recently, 3 of these scholarships were awarded.

**Deadline** April of each year.

## [1003]
## LIZETTE PETERSON-HOMER INJURY PREVENTION RESEARCH GRANT

American Psychological Foundation
750 First Street, N.E.
Washington, DC 20002-4242
(202) 336-5843          Fax: (202) 336-5812
E-mail: foundation@apa.org
Web: www.apa.org/apf/funding/peterson-homer.aspx

**Summary** To provide funding to women and other graduate students and faculty from diverse groups who interested in conducting research related to the prevention of injuries in children.

**Eligibility** This program is open to graduate students and faculty interested in conducting research that focuses on the prevention of physical injury in children and young adults through accidents, violence, abuse, or suicide. Applicants must submit a 100-word abstract, description of the project, detailed budget, curriculum vitae, and letter from the supporting faculty supervisor (if the applicant is a student). Selection is based on conformance with stated program goals, magnitude of incremental contribution, quality of proposed work, and applicant's demonstrated scholarship and research competence. The sponsor encourages applications from individuals who represent diversity in race, ethnicity, gender, age, disability, and sexual orientation.

**Financial data** Grants up to $5,000 are available.

**Duration** 1 year.

**Additional information** This program began in 1999 as the Rebecca Routh Coon Injury Research Award. The current name was adopted in 2003. It is supported by Division 54 (Society of Pediatric Psychology) of the American Psychological Association and the American Psychological Foundation.

**Number awarded** 1 each year.

**Deadline** September of each year.

## [1004]
## LORAM MINNESOTA SWE SCHOLARSHIP

Society of Women Engineers-Minnesota Section
Attn: Scholarship Committee
P.O. Box 582813
Minneapolis, MN 55458-2813
E-mail: scholarships@swe-mn.org
Web: www.swe-mn.org/scholarships.html

**Summary** To provide financial assistance to women from any state working on an undergraduate or graduate degree in mechanical engineering at colleges and universities in Minnesota, North Dakota, and South Dakota.

**Eligibility** This program is open to female undergraduate and graduate students at ABET-accredited engineering programs in Minnesota, North Dakota, or South Dakota. Applicants must be working full time on a degree in mechanical engineering. Along with their application, they must submit a short paragraph describing how they plan to utilize their engineering skills after they graduate. Selection is based on potential to succeed as an engineer (20 points), communication skills (10 points), extracurricular or community involvement and leadership skills (10 points), demonstrated successful work experience (10 points), and academic success (5 points).

**Financial data** The stipend is $1,000.

**Duration** 1 year.

**Additional information** This program is sponsored by Loram Maintenance of Way.

**Number awarded** 1 each year.

**Deadline** March of each year.

## [1005]
## LOUISIANA WMU SCHOLARSHIP FOR WOMEN SEMINARY STUDENTS

Louisiana Baptist Convention
Attn: Woman's Missionary Union
1250 MacArthur Drive
P.O. Box 311
Alexandria, LA 71309-0311
(318) 448-3402          Toll Free: (800) 622-6549
E-mail: wmu@lbc.org
Web: www.lbc.org/Women/Interior.aspx?id=3400

**Summary** This provide financial assistance to women from Louisiana who are working on a master's degree at a Southern Baptist seminary.

**Eligibility** This program is open to women who are active members of a Southern Baptist church in Louisiana and have been long-term residents of the state. Applicants must be enrolled full time at 1 of the 6 Southern Baptist seminaries, have a GPA of 2.5 or higher, and be working on a master's degree. They must participate in activities of the Woman's Missionary Union (WMU) and be actively involved in missions education with the church or on campus. Along with their application, they must submit evidence of "their devotion to the Lord and their call to ministry.".

**Financial data** The stipend is $1,600 per year.

**Duration** Up to 3 years.

**Additional information** The eligible seminaries are Southeastern Baptist Theological Seminary (Wake Forest, North Carolina); Southern Baptist Theological Seminary (Louisville, Kentucky); Southwestern Baptist Theological Seminary (Fort Worth, Texas); New Orleans Baptist Theological Seminary (New Orleans, Louisiana); Midwestern Baptist Theological Seminary (Kansas City, Missouri); or Golden Gate Baptist Theological Seminary (Mill Valley, California).

**Number awarded** 1 or more each year.

**Deadline** June of each year.

## [1006]
## LUCY KASPARIAN AHARONIAN SCHOLARSHIPS

Armenian International Women's Association
65 Main Street, Room 3A
Watertown, MA 02472
(617) 926-0171          E-mail: aiwainc@aol.com
Web: aiwainternational.org/initiatives/scholarships

**Summary** To provide financial assistance to Armenian women who are upper-division or graduate students working on a degree in specified fields.

**Eligibility** This program is open to full-time women students of Armenian descent attending an accredited college or university. Applicants must be full-time juniors, seniors, or graduate students with a GPA of 3.2 or higher. They must be

working on a degree in architecture, computer science, engineering, mathematics, science, or technology. Selection is based on financial need and merit.

**Financial data** Stipends are $4,000 or $1,000.

**Duration** 1 year.

**Additional information** This program, established in 2008, is offered in conjunction with the Boston Section of the Society of Women Engineers.

**Number awarded** Varies each year; recently, 4 of these scholarships were awarded: 2 at $4,000 and 2 at $1,000.

**Deadline** April of each year.

## [1007]
## LYDIA I. PICKUP MEMORIAL SCHOLARSHIP

Society of Women Engineers
Attn: Scholarship Selection Committee
203 North LaSalle Street, Suite 1675
Chicago, IL 60601-1269
(312) 596-5223          Toll Free: (877) SWE-INFO
Fax: (312) 644-8557          E-mail: scholarships@swe.org
Web: societyofwomenengineers.swe.org

**Summary** To provide financial assistance to women working on a graduate degree in engineering or computer science.

**Eligibility** This program is open to women who will be full-time graduate students at ABET-accredited colleges and universities. Applicants must be working on a degree in computer science or engineering and have a GPA of 3.0 or higher. Selection is based on merit.

**Financial data** The stipend is $3,000.

**Duration** 1 year.

**Additional information** This program began in 2000.

**Number awarded** 1 each year.

**Deadline** February of each year.

## [1008]
## LYDIA SCHOLARSHIP

Presbyterians for Renewal
Scholarship Coordinator
8134 New LaGrange Road, Suite 227
Louisville, KY 40222-4679
(502) 425-4630          E-mail: npwl@pfrenewal.org
Web: www.pfrenewal.org/ministries/npwl

**Summary** To provide financial assistance to women who are interested in preparing for a career in the Presbyterian Church (USA) ordained pastoral ministry.

**Eligibility** This program is open to women who are interested in preparing for ordained pastoral ministry in the PC (USA). Applicants must be working on an M.Div. degree at an accredited seminary. Along with their application, they must submit essays on their education and work history, faith story, personal theology, and call to ministry. Those essays should demonstrate their desire to serve as an evangelical missionary within the PCUSA in cooperation with Presbyterians for Renewal.

**Financial data** The stipend is $2,500 per year.

**Duration** 2 years; may be renewed for 1 additional year, provided the student has participated in a pastoral ministry internship and is still enrolled full time in an M.Div. program.

**Number awarded** 1 each year.

**Deadline** April of each year.

**[1009]**
## M. LOUISE CARPENTER GLOECKNER, M.D. SUMMER RESEARCH FELLOWSHIP

Drexel University College of Medicine
Attn: Archives and Special Collections
2900 West Queen Lane
Philadelphia, PA 19129
(215) 991-8340                    Fax: (215) 991-8172
E-mail: archives@drexelmed.edu
Web: archives.drexelmed.edu/fellowship.php

**Summary** To provide funding to scholars and students interested in conducting research during the summer on the history of women in medicine at the Archives and Special Collections on Women in Medicine at Drexel University in Philadelphia.

**Eligibility** This program is open to students at all levels, scholars, and general researchers. Applicants must be interested in conducting research utilizing the archives, which emphasize the history of women in medicine, nursing, medical missionaries, the American Medical Women's Association, American Women's Hospital Service, and other women in medical organizations. Selection is based on research background of the applicant, relevance of the proposed research project to the goals of the applicant, overall quality and clarity of the proposal, appropriateness of the proposal to the holdings of the collection, and commitment of the applicant to the project.

**Financial data** The grant is $4,000.

**Duration** 4 to 6 weeks during the summer.

**Number awarded** 1 each year.

**Deadline** February of each year.

**[1010]**
## M.A. CARTLAND SHACKFORD MEDICAL FELLOWSHIP

Wellesley College
Center for Work and Service
Attn: Extramural Graduate Fellowships and Scholarships
106 Central Street
Wellesley, MA 02181-8203
(781) 283-3525                    Fax: (781) 283-3674
E-mail: cws-fellowships@wellesley.edu
Web: www.wellesley.edu/cws/fellowships/wellesley

**Summary** To provide financial assistance to women for graduate study in the medical fields.

**Eligibility** This program is open to women who have graduated from an American academic institution and are interested in general medical practice (but not psychiatry).

**Financial data** The fellowship of at least $10,000 is tenable at any institution of the recipient's choice.

**Duration** 1 year.

**Additional information** The recipient must pursue full-time graduate study.

**Number awarded** 1 each year.

**Deadline** January of each year.

**[1011]**
## MABEL BIEVER MUSIC EDUCATION SCHOLARSHIP FOR GRADUATE STUDENTS

Sigma Alpha Iota Philanthropies, Inc.
One Tunnel Road
Asheville, NC 28805
(828) 251-0606                    Fax: (828) 251-0644
E-mail: nh@sai-national.org
Web: www.sai-national.org

**Summary** To provide financial assistance for graduate study in music education to members of Sigma Alpha Iota (an organization of women musicians).

**Eligibility** This program is open to alumnae members of the organization who have completed an undergraduate degree in music education and are accepted into or currently enrolled in a program leading to a master's or doctoral degree in that field. Applicants should have had at least 1 year of teaching experience in a private or public school. If they do not have teaching experience, they must include a video of student teaching experience and references from their major professor and their student teacher adviser.

**Financial data** The stipend is $1,500.

**Duration** 1 year.

**Additional information** This program is sponsored by the Oak Park Alumnae Chapter of Sigma Alpha Iota.

**Number awarded** 1 each year.

**Deadline** March of each year.

**[1012]**
## MABEL HEIL SCHOLARSHIP

United Methodist Church-Wisconsin Conference
Attn: United Methodist Women
750 Windsor Street
P.O. Box 620
Sun Prairie, WI 53590-0620
(608) 837-7328                    Toll Free: (888) 240-7328
Fax: (608) 837-8547
Web: www.wisconsinumc.org

**Summary** To provide financial assistance to United Methodist women from Wisconsin who are interested in attending college or graduate school in any state.

**Eligibility** This program is open to women who are members of congregations affiliated with the Wisconsin Conference of the United Methodist Church and attending or planning to attend college or graduate school in any state. Applicants must submit an essay on why they consider themselves a worthy student and a letter of recommendation from their pastor or the president of the local United Methodist Women. Preference is given to women who are responsible for others and are returning to the employment field.

**Financial data** A stipend is awarded (amount not specified).

**Duration** 1 semester; recipients may reapply.

**Number awarded** 1 or more each year.

**Deadline** April of each year for the first semester; September of each year for the second semester.

## [1013]
## MAIDS OF ATHENA SCHOLARSHIPS

Maids of Athena
1909 Q Street, N.W., Suite 500
Washington, DC 20009-1007
(202) 232-6300             Fax: (202) 232-2145
E-mail: MOAHeadquarters@gmail.com
Web: www.maidsofathena.org

**Summary**   To provide financial assistance for undergraduate and graduate education to women of Greek descent.

**Eligibility**   This program is open to women who are members of the Maids of Athena. Applicants may be a graduating high school senior, an undergraduate student, or a graduate student. Selection is based on academic merit, financial need, and participation in the organization.

**Financial data**   The stipend is $1,000.

**Duration**   1 year.

**Additional information**   Membership in Maids of Athena is open to unmarried women between 14 and 24 years of age who are of Greek descent from either parent.

**Number awarded**   At least 2 each year.

**Deadline**   May of each year.

## [1014]
## MALENA RANCE SCHOLARSHIP FUND

Black Entertainment and Sports Lawyers Association
Attn: Scholarships
P.O. Box 230794
New York, NY 10023
E-mail: scholarship@besla.org
Web: www.besla.org/#!scholarship/cfvg

**Summary**   To provide financial assistance to African American women who are interested in the fields of entertainment and/or sports law.

**Eligibility**   This program is open to African American women who have completed at least 1 year of full-time study at an accredited law school. Applicants must be able to demonstrate an interest in entertainment or sports law by 1 or more of the following: 1) completing an entertainment law or sports law related course; 2) internship or clerkship in the entertainment or sports law field; 3) current job in the field of entertainment or sports; 4) current membership in an entertainment or sports law society or association; or 5) attendance at an entertainment law or sports law seminar or conference since enrolling in law school. They must have a GPA of 3.0 or higher. Along with their application, they must submit a 5-page legal memorandum on an issue facing the entertainment or sports industry.

**Financial data**   The stipend is at least $1,500.

**Duration**   1 year.

**Number awarded**   1 or more each year.

**Deadline**   July of each year.

## [1015]
## MANAHAN-BOHAN AWARD

Philanthrofund Foundation
Attn: Scholarship Committee
1409 Willow Street, Suite 109
Minneapolis, MN 55403-2241
(612) 870-1806          Toll Free: (800) 435-1402
Fax: (612) 871-6587       E-mail: info@PfundOnline.org
Web: www.pfundonline.org/scholarships.html

**Summary**   To provide financial assistance to lesbian students from rural Minnesota.

**Eligibility**   This program is open to residents of Madelia, Minnesota; if no resident of Madelia applies, the award is available to residents of any rural area in Minnesota. Applicants must be self-identified as lesbian. They may be attending or planning to attend trade school, technical college, college, or university in any state (as an undergraduate or graduate student). Selection is based on the applicant's 1) affirmation of GLBT or allied identity; 2) evidence of experience and skills in service and leadership; and 3) evidence of service, leading, and working for change in GLBT communities, including serving as a role model, mentor, and/or adviser.

**Financial data**   The stipend is $1,000. Funds must be used for tuition, books, fees, or dissertation expenses.

**Duration**   1 year.

**Number awarded**   1 each year.

**Deadline**   January of each year.

## [1016]
## MARGARET ABEL SCHOLARSHIP

Delta Kappa Gamma Society International-Alpha Zeta
    State Organization
c/o Marilyn Gonyo, State Scholarship Chair
22 Chichester Road
Monroe Township, NJ 08831
E-mail: mgony1063@aol.com
Web: www.deltakappagamma.org/NJ/scholarships.html

**Summary**   To provide financial assistance to women who are residents of New Jersey working on an undergraduate or graduate degree in education at a school in the state.

**Eligibility**   This program is open to women who residents of New Jersey and enrolled as juniors, seniors, or graduate students at a 4-year college or university in the state. Applicants must be preparing for a career as a teacher and have a GPA of 3.0 or higher. They must be U.S. citizens. Along with their application, they must submit a 500-word essay and their desire to become a teacher and the attributes that make them worthy to receive this scholarship.

**Financial data**   The stipend is $1,000.

**Duration**   1 year; recipients may reapply.

**Number awarded**   1 or more each year.

**Deadline**   November of each year.

## [1017]
## MARGARET KELDIE SCHOLARSHIP

Accounting and Financial Women's Alliance-Chicago
    Chapter
c/o Pamela Metz, Scholarship Fund Secretary
1957 North Dayton Street, Number 1
Chicago, IL 60614
(312) 480-8566         E-mail: MKSF_aswa@yahoo.com

**Summary** To provide financial assistance to women from any state working on an undergraduate or graduate degree in accounting at a college or university in Illinois.

**Eligibility** This program is open to women from any state who are currently enrolled full or part time at an accredited 4-year college or university in Illinois. Applicants must be working on an undergraduate or graduate degree in accounting and have a cumulative grade average of "B" or higher. They must have indicated an intention to prepare for an accounting career. Undergraduates must have completed at least 60 semester hours. Financial need is not considered in the selection process.

**Financial data** Stipends are $1,500 for full-time students or $800 for part-time students.

**Duration** 1 year.

**Additional information** This program began in 1956.

**Number awarded** 1 or more each year. Since the program was established, it has awarded nearly $135,000 in scholarships to more than 250 women.

**Deadline** February of each year.

## [1018]
## MARGARET MORSE NICE FUND

American Ornithologists' Union
c/o Executive Officer
5405 Villa View Drive
Farmington, NM 87402
(505) 326-1579          E-mail: aou@aou.org
Web: www.aou.org/awards/research/index.php

**Summary** To provide funding to female graduate students who are members of the American Ornithologists' Union (AOU) and interested in conducting research related to ornithology.

**Eligibility** This program is open to female graduate students who are AOU members. Applicants must be interested in conducting research related to ornithology. They should send a cover letter (about 5 pages) describing their proposed project, a budget, and 1 letter of reference. Selection is based on significance and originality of the research question, clarity of the objectives, feasibility of the plan of research, appropriateness of the budget, and the letter of recommendation.

**Financial data** The maximum award is $2,500 per year.

**Duration** 1 year; recipients may reapply for 1 additional award.

**Number awarded** The sponsor awards a total of 28 to 30 grants each year.

**Deadline** January of each year.

## [1019]
## MARGARET YARDLEY FELLOWSHIP

New Jersey State Federation of Women's Clubs
Attn: Fellowship Chair
55 Labor Center Way
New Brunswick, NJ 08901-1593
(732) 249-5474          Toll Free: (800) 465-7392
E-mail: njsfwc@njsfwc.org
Web: www.njsfwc.org/index.php/article/sub/9

**Summary** To provide financial assistance to women from New Jersey interested in graduate studies in any state.

**Eligibility** This program is open to women from New Jersey who are enrolled full time in a master's or doctoral program at a college or university in the United States. Applicants must submit a 2-page essay describing their charitable endeavors, future goals, and financial need.

**Financial data** The stipend is $1,000.

**Duration** 1 year.

**Additional information** This program began in 1930. Award recipients must give written assurance of an uninterrupted year of study at an American college of their choice.

**Number awarded** 6 to 8 each year.

**Deadline** February of each year.

## [1020]
## MARGERY DICK MILLER MEMORIAL SCHOLARSHIPS

Kappa Alpha Theta Foundation
Attn: Manager of Programs
8740 Founders Road
Indianapolis, IN 46268-1337
(317) 876-1870          Toll Free: (800) KAO-1870
Fax: (317) 876-1925
E-mail: gmerritt@kappaalphatheta.org
Web: www.kappaalphathetafoundation.org

**Summary** To provide financial assistance for graduate school to members of Kappa Alpha Theta.

**Eligibility** This program is open to members of Kappa Alpha Theta who are full-time graduate students at a college or university in Canada or the United States. Applicants may be working on a degree in any field. Along with their application, they must submit an official transcript, personal essays on assigned topics related to their involvement in Kappa Alpha Theta, and 2 letters of reference. Financial need is not considered in the selection process.

**Financial data** The stipend is $4,525.

**Duration** 1 year.

**Number awarded** 1 each year.

**Deadline** February of each year.

## [1021]
## MARIAM K. CHAMBERLAIN FELLOWSHIP IN WOMEN AND PUBLIC POLICY

Institute for Women's Policy Research
Attn: Fellowship Coordinator
1200 18th Street, N.W., Suite 301
Washington, DC 20036
(202) 785-5100          Fax: (202) 833-4362
E-mail: yi@iwpr.org
Web: www.iwpr.org/about/fellowships

**Summary** To provide work experience at the Institute for Women's Policy Research (IWPR) to college graduates and graduate students who are interested in economic justice for women.

**Eligibility** Applicants for this internship should have at least a bachelor's degree in social science, statistics, or women's studies. Graduate work is desirable but not required. They should have strong quantitative and library research skills and knowledge of women's issues. Familiarity with Microsoft Word and Excel is required; knowledge of STATA, SPSS, SAS, or graphics software is a plus.

**Financial data** The stipend is $27,000 and includes health insurance and a public transportation stipend.

**Duration** 9 months, beginning in September.

**Additional information** The institute is a nonprofit, scientific research organization that works primarily on issues related to equal opportunity and economic and social justice for women. Research topics vary each year but relate to women and public policy.

**Number awarded** 1 each year.

**Deadline** February of each year.

## [1022]
## MARIAN J. WETTRICK CHARITABLE FOUNDATION MEDICAL SCHOLARSHIPS

Marian J. Wettrick Charitable Foundation
c/o Citizens & Northern Bank
C&N Trust and Financial Management Group
10 North Main Street
P.O. Box 229
Coudersport, PA 16915-0229
(814) 274-1927          Toll Free: (800) 921-9150
Fax: (814) 274-0297     E-mail: eileenb@cnbankpa.com
Web: www.cnbankpa.com

**Summary** To provide financial assistance to women who graduated from a college in Pennsylvania and are interested in attending a medical school in the state.

**Eligibility** This program is open to women who graduated from a college or university in Pennsylvania with a recognized pre-medical major. They must be interested in attending a medical school in the state. Priority is given to applicants who are interested in practicing medicine at Charles Cole Medical Center in Coudersport (although this is not a binding requirement). A personal interview may be required. Financial need is considered in the selection process.

**Financial data** Stipends range from $5,000 to $35,000 per year.

**Duration** 1 year; may be renewed.

**Additional information** This program began in 1996.

**Number awarded** Up to 6 each year. Since the program was established, it has awarded more than $1 million in scholarships to more than 30 female medical students.

**Deadline** March of each year.

## [1023]
## MARIE MORISAWA RESEARCH AWARD

Geological Society of America-Quaternary Geology and
   Geomorphology Division
c/o Jim O'Connor, Second Vice Chair
U.S. Geological Survey
2130 S.W. Fifth Avenue
Portland, OR 97201
(503) 251-3222          Fax: (503) 251-3470
E-mail: oconnor@usgs.gov
Web: rock.geosociety.org/qgg

**Summary** To provide support to female graduate student members of the Geological Society of America (GSA) interested in conducting research on quaternary geology or geomorphology.

**Eligibility** This program is open to women who are GSA members working on a master's or doctoral degree at a university in any state. Applicants must be interested in conducting research on quaternary geology or geomorphology. Selection is based on quality of the proposed research.

**Financial data** The grant is $1,000.

**Duration** 1 year.

**Additional information** This program, established in 2008, is sponsored by the Geological Society of America's Quaternary Geology and Geomorphology Division.

**Number awarded** 1 each year.

**Deadline** January of each year.

## [1024]
## MARILYNNE GRABOYS WOOL SCHOLARSHIP

Rhode Island Foundation
Attn: Funds Administrator
One Union Station
Providence, RI 02903
(401) 427-4017          Fax: (401) 331-8085
E-mail: lmonahan@rifoundation.org
Web: www.rifoundation.org

**Summary** To provide financial assistance to women who are residents of Rhode Island and interested in studying law at a school in any state.

**Eligibility** This program is open to female residents of Rhode Island who are planning to enroll or are registered in an accredited law school in any state. Applicants must be able to demonstrate financial need. Along with their application, they must submit an essay (up to 300 words) on the impact they would like to have on the legal field.

**Financial data** The stipend is $2,000.

**Duration** 1 year; nonrenewable.

**Number awarded** 1 each year.

**Deadline** June of each year.

## [1025]
## MARJORIE BOWENS-WHEATLEY SCHOLARSHIPS

Unitarian Universalist Association
Attn: UU Women's Federation
25 Beacon Street
Boston, MA 02108-2800
(617) 948-4692          Fax: (617) 742-2402
E-mail: uuwf@uua.org
Web: www.uuwf.org

**Summary** To provide financial assistance to women of color who are working on an undergraduate or graduate degree to prepare for Unitarian Universalist ministry or service.

**Eligibility** This program is open to women of color who are either 1) aspirants or candidates for the Unitarian Universalist ministry; or 2) candidates in the Unitarian Universalist Association's professional religious education or music leadership credentialing programs. Applicants must submit a 1- to 2-page narrative that covers their call to UU ministry, religious education, or music leadership; their passions; how their racial/ethnic/cultural background influences their goals for their calling; and how the work of the program's namesake relates to their dreams and plans for their UU service.

**Financial data** Stipends from $1,500 to $2,000.

**Duration** 1 year.

**Additional information** This program began in 2009.

**Number awarded** Varies each year; recently, 4 of these scholarships were awarded.

**Deadline** March of each year.

## [1026]
## MARJORIE COOK SCHOLARS PROGRAM

Central Scholarship Bureau
1700 Reisterstown Road, Suite 220
Baltimore, MD 21208
(410) 415-5558 Toll Free: (855) 276-0239
Fax: (410) 415-5501
E-mail: gohigher@central-scholarship.org
Web: www.central-scholarship.org/scholarships/overview

**Summary** To provide financial assistance to women in Maryland who are interested in working on a graduate degree in law or public policy at a school in any state.

**Eligibility** This program is open to female residents of Maryland who are working on a graduate degree in public policy or law at a college or university in any state. Applicants must be able to demonstrate a passion for and commitment to women's rights and equality, as evidenced by volunteerism, internships, dedicated research, or prior work experience related to advancing women's social and political status. They must have a GPA of 3.0 or higher and a family income of less than $90,000 per year. Selection is based on academic achievement, extracurricular activities, and financial need. U.S. citizenship or permanent resident status is required.

**Financial data** Stipends range up to $5,000.

**Duration** 1 year.

**Additional information** This program began in 2008.

**Number awarded** 1 or more each year.

**Deadline** March of each year.

## [1027]
## MARK T. BANNER SCHOLARSHIP FOR LAW STUDENTS

Richard Linn American Inn of Court
c/o Matthew Walch, Scholarship Chair
Latham & Watkins LLP
233 South Wacker Drive, Suite 5800
Chicago, IL 60606
(312) 876-7603 E-mail: matthew.walch@lw.com
Web: www.linninn.org/marktbanner.htm

**Summary** To provide financial assistance to women and other law students who are members of a group historically underrepresented in intellectual property law.

**Eligibility** This program is open to students at ABA-accredited law schools in the United States who are members of groups historically underrepresented (by gender, race, ethnicity, sexual orientation, or disability) in intellectual property law. Applicants must submit a 3-page statement on how they have focused on ethics, civility, and professionalism have been their focus; how diversity has impacted them; and their commitment to a career in intellectual property law.

**Financial data** The stipend is $5,000.

**Duration** 1 year.

**Number awarded** 1 each year.

**Deadline** November of each year.

## [1028]
## MARTHA GAVRILA SCHOLARSHIP FOR WOMEN

Association of Romanian Orthodox Ladies Auxiliaries of North America
Attn: Scholarship Committee
222 Orchard Park Drive
New Castle, PA 16105
(724) 652-4313 E-mail: adelap@verizon.net
Web: www.arfora.org/scholarships.htm

**Summary** To provide financial assistance to women who are members of a parish of the Romanian Orthodox Episcopate of America and interested in working on a graduate degree.

**Eligibility** This program is open to women who have been voting communicant members of a parish of the Romanian Orthodox Episcopate of America for at least 1 year. Applicants must have completed a baccalaureate degree and been accepted as a graduate student at a college or university in any state. Along with their application, they must submit a 300-word statement describing their personal goals; high school, university, church, and community involvement; honors and awards; and why they should be considered for this award. Selection is based on academic achievement, character, worthiness, and participation in religious life.

**Financial data** The stipend is $1,000.

**Duration** 1 year.

**Additional information** This program began in 1985. The Association of Romanian Orthodox Ladies Auxiliaries (ARFORA) was established in 1938 as a women's organization within the Romanian Orthodox Episcopate of America.

**Number awarded** 1 each year.

**Deadline** May of each year.

## [1029]
## MARY BALL CARRERA SCHOLARSHIP

National Medical Fellowships, Inc.
Attn: Scholarship Program
347 Fifth Avenue, Suite 510
New York, NY 10016
(212) 483-8880 Toll Free: (877) NMF-1DOC
Fax: (212) 483-8897 E-mail: info@nmfonline.org
Web: www.nmfonline.org/page.aspx?pid=485

**Summary** To provide financial assistance to Native American women who are attending medical school.

**Eligibility** This program is open to Native American women who are enrolled in the first or second year of an accredited medical school in the United States. Applicants must be able to demonstrate academic achievement, leadership, and community service, but selection is based primarily on financial need.

**Financial data** The stipend is $2,500.

**Duration** 1 year; nonrenewable.

**Number awarded** 1 or more each year.

**Deadline** August of each year.

## [1030]
## MARY BLACKWELL BARNES MEMORIAL SCHOLARSHIPS

Women in Public Finance-Virginia Chapter
Attn: Scholarship Committee
P.O. Box 129
Richmond, VA 23219
E-mail: info@virginiawpf.org
Web: www.virginiawpf.org/?page_id=202

**Summary** To provide financial assistance to women from any state who are working on an undergraduate or graduate degree in a field related to public finance at a college in Virginia or Washington, D.C.

**Eligibility** This program is open to women from any state who are enrolled at a college or university in Virginia or Washington, D.C. as a sophomore or higher undergraduate or a graduate student. Applicants must be preparing for a career in public finance, including work in government, nonprofits, law, or finance. Along with their application, they must submit essays on 1) their interested in preparing for a career in public finance, government, or public service; 2) their career goals and what has influenced those goals; and 3) their personal interests, activities, and achievements. Financial need is not considered.

**Financial data** Stipends range from $1,000 to $3,000.

**Duration** 1 year.

**Additional information** This program began in 2009.

**Number awarded** Up to 5 each year.

**Deadline** August of each year.

## [1031]
## MARY ISABEL SIBLEY FELLOWSHIP FOR FRENCH STUDIES

Phi Beta Kappa Society
Attn: Director of Society Affairs
1606 New Hampshire Avenue, N.W.
Washington, DC 20009
(202) 745-3287                    Fax: (202) 986-1601
E-mail: awards@pbk.org
Web: www.pbk.org/infoview/PBK_InfoView.aspx?t=&id=28

**Summary** To provide funding to women involved in dissertation or advanced research or writing projects dealing with French studies.

**Eligibility** This program is open to unmarried women between 25 and 35 years of age who have demonstrated their ability to conduct original research. Applicants must be planning to conduct a research project dealing with French language or literature. They must hold the doctorate or have fulfilled all the requirements for the doctorate except the dissertation, and they must be planning to devote full time to their research during the fellowship year. Along with their application, they must submit a statement that includes a description of the project, the present state of the project, where the study would be carried out, and expectations regarding publication of the results of the study. Eligibility is not restricted to members of Phi Beta Kappa or to U.S. citizens.

**Financial data** The stipend is $20,000.

**Duration** 1 year (the fellowship is offered in even-numbered years only).

**Additional information** Periodic progress reports are not required, but they are welcomed. It is the hope of the committee that the results of the year of research will be made available in some form, although no pressure for publication will be put on the recipient.

**Number awarded** 1 every other year.

**Deadline** January of even-numbered years.

## [1032]
## MARY ISABEL SIBLEY FELLOWSHIP FOR GREEK STUDIES

Phi Beta Kappa Society
Attn: Director of Society Affairs
1606 New Hampshire Avenue, N.W.
Washington, DC 20009
(202) 745-3287                    Fax: (202) 986-1601
E-mail: awards@pbk.org
Web: www.pbk.org/infoview/PBK_InfoView.aspx?t=&id=28

**Summary** To provide funding to women involved in dissertation or advanced research or writing projects dealing with Greek studies.

**Eligibility** This program is open to unmarried women between 25 and 35 years of age who have demonstrated their ability to conduct original research. Applicants must be planning to conduct a research project dealing with Greek language, literature, history, or archaeology. They must hold the doctorate or have fulfilled all the requirements for the doctorate except the dissertation, and they must be planning to devote full time to their research during the fellowship year. Along with their application, they must submit a statement that includes a description of the project, the present state of the project, where the study would be carried out, and expectations regarding publication of the results of the study. Eligibility is not restricted to members of Phi Beta Kappa or to U.S. citizens.

**Financial data** The stipend is $20,000.

**Duration** 1 year (the fellowship is offered in odd-numbered years only).

**Additional information** Periodic progress reports are not required, but they are welcomed. It is the hope of the committee that the results of the year of research will be made available in some form, although no pressure for publication will be put on the recipient.

**Number awarded** 1 every other year.

**Deadline** January of odd-numbered years.

## [1033]
## MARY LILY RESEARCH GRANTS

Duke University
David M. Rubenstein Rare Book and Manuscript Library
Attn: Sallie Bingham Center for Women's History and
      Culture
P.O. Box 90185
Durham, NC 27708-0185
(919) 660-5828                    Fax: (919) 660-5934
E-mail: cwhc@duke.edu
Web: library.duke.edu

**Summary** To provide funding to scholars at all levels who wish to use the resources of the Sallie Bingham Center for Women's History and Culture in the Special Collections Library at Duke University.

**Eligibility** This program is open to undergraduates, graduate students, faculty members, and independent scholars in any academic field who wish to use the resources of the center for their research in women's studies. Applicants must reside outside a 100-mile radius of Durham, North Carolina. Undergraduate and graduate students must be currently enrolled, be working on a degree, and enclose a letter of recommendation from their adviser or thesis director. Faculty members must be working on a research project and enclose a curriculum vitae. Independent scholars must be working on a nonprofit project and enclose a curriculum vitae. Research topics should be strongly supported by the collections of the center.

**Financial data** Grants up to $1,000 are available; funds may be used for travel, accommodations, meals, and photocopying and reproduction expenses.

**Duration** Up to 1 year.

**Additional information** The library's collections are especially strong in the history of feminist activism and theory, prescriptive literature, girls' literature, artists' books by women, lay and ordained church women, gender expression, women's sexuality, and the history and culture of women in the South. A number of prominent women writers have placed their personal and professional papers in the collections.

**Number awarded** Varies each year; recently, 8 of these grants were awarded.

**Deadline** January of each year.

## [1034]
## MARY LOVE COLLINS MEMORIAL SCHOLARSHIP

Chi Omega Fraternity
Attn: Chi Omega Foundation
3395 Players Club Parkway
Memphis, TN 38125
(901) 748-8600                    Fax: (901) 748-8686
E-mail: foundation@chiomega.com
Web: www.chiomega.com/wemakeadifference/scholarships

**Summary** To provide financial assistance to women who are members of Chi Omega Fraternity entering graduate school.

**Eligibility** This program is open to women who are members of Chi Omega Fraternity planning to enter graduate school as a full-time student. Applicants must submit an essay, from 200 to 500 words in length, on 1) why they want to pursue graduate study; 2) what they hope to gain from it; and 3) why they feel they are particularly qualified for a scholarship designed to honor Mary Love Collins. Selection is based on the essay; academic achievement; aptitude; contributions and service to Chi Omega, the university, and the community; and professional and personal goals.

**Financial data** The stipend is $1,700.

**Duration** 1 year.

**Additional information** This program began in 1972.

**Number awarded** 5 each year.

**Deadline** March of each year.

## [1035]
## MARY MCEWEN SCHIMKE SCHOLARSHIP

Wellesley College
Center for Work and Service
Attn: Extramural Graduate Fellowships and Scholarships
106 Central Street
Wellesley, MA 02181-8203
(781) 283-3525                    Fax: (781) 283-3674
E-mail: cws-fellowships@wellesley.edu
Web: www.wellesley.edu/CWS/students/wellfs.html

**Summary** To provide financial assistance to women working on a graduate degree who need relief from household or child care responsibilities.

**Eligibility** Women who have graduated from an American academic institution, are over 30 years of age, are currently engaged in graduate study in literature and/or history (preference is given to American studies), and need relief from household or child care responsibilities while pursuing graduate studies may apply. The award is made on the basis of scholarly ability and financial need.

**Financial data** The fellowship awards range up to $1,500 and are tenable at the institution of the recipient's choice.

**Duration** 1 year.

**Number awarded** 1 each year.

**Deadline** January of each year.

## [1036]
## MARY PAOLOZZI MEMBER'S SCHOLARSHIP

Navy Wives Clubs of America
c/o NSA Mid-South
P.O. Box 54022
Millington, TN 38054-0022
Toll Free: (866) 511-NWCA
E-mail: nwca@navywivesclubsofamerica.org
Web: www.navywivesclubsofamerica.org/scholarships

**Summary** To provide financial assistance for undergraduate or graduate study to members of the Navy Wives Clubs of America (NWCA).

**Eligibility** This program is open to NWCA members who can demonstrate financial need. Applicants must be 1) a high school graduate or senior planning to attend college full time next year; 2) currently enrolled in an undergraduate program and planning to continue as a full-time undergraduate; 3) a college graduate or senior planning to be a full-time graduate student next year; or 4) a high school graduate or GED recipient planning to attend vocational or business school next year. Along with their application, they must submit a brief statement on why they feel they should be awarded this scholarship and any special circumstances (financial or other) they wish to have considered. Financial need is also considered in the selection process.

**Financial data** Stipends range from $500 to $1,000 each year (depending upon the donations from the NWCA chapters).

**Duration** 1 year.

**Additional information** Membership in the NWCA is open to spouses of enlisted personnel serving in the Navy, Marine Corps, Coast Guard, and the active Reserve units of those services; spouses of enlisted personnel who have been honorably discharged, retired, or transferred to the Fleet

Reserve on completion of duty; and widows of enlisted personnel in those services.

**Number awarded** 1 or more each year.

**Deadline** May of each year.

## [1037]
## MARY R. NORTON MEMORIAL SCHOLARSHIP AWARD

ASTM International
100 Barr Harbor Drive
P.O. Box C700
West Conshohocken, PA 19428-2959
(610) 832-9500
Web: www.astm.org/studentmember/Student_Awards.html

**Summary** To provide financial assistance to female undergraduate and graduate students working on a degree related to physical metallurgy.

**Eligibility** This program is open to women entering their senior year of college or first year of graduate study. Applicants must be working on a degree in physical metallurgy or materials science, with an emphasis on relationship of microstructure and properties.

**Financial data** The stipend is $1,000.

**Duration** 1 year.

**Additional information** This program, established in 1975, is administered by ASTM Committee C04 on Metallography. ASTM International was formerly the American Society for Testing and Materials.

**Number awarded** 1 or more each year.

**Deadline** Deadline not specified.

## [1038]
## MCCONNEL FAMILY SCHOLARSHIP

Epsilon Sigma Alpha International
Attn: ESA Foundation
363 West Drake Road
Fort Collins, CO 80526
(970) 223-2824          Fax: (970) 223-4456
E-mail: esainfo@epsilonsigmaalpha.org
Web: www.epsilonsigmaalpha.org/scholarships-and-grants

**Summary** To provide financial assistance to women interested in studying veterinary medicine.

**Eligibility** This program is open to female residents of any state who are interested in studying veterinary medicine. Applicants may be attending school in any state. They must have a GPA of 3.0 or higher. Selection is based on service and leadership (20 points), financial need (35 points), and scholastic ability (35 points). A $5 processing fee is required.

**Financial data** The stipend is $1,000.

**Duration** 1 year; may be renewed.

**Additional information** Epsilon Sigma Alpha (ESA) is a women's service organization. This program began in 2002. Completed applications must be submitted to the ESA state counselor who then verifies the information before forwarding them to the scholarship director.

**Number awarded** 2 each year.

**Deadline** January of each year.

## [1039]
## MCGRAW-HILL COMPANIES SCHOLARSHIP OF NEW YORK WOMEN IN COMMUNICATIONS

New York Women in Communications, Inc.
Attn: NYWICI Foundation
355 Lexington Avenue, 15th Floor
New York, NY 10017-6603
(212) 297-2133          Fax: (212) 370-9047
E-mail: nywicipr@nywici.org
Web: www.nywici.org/foundation/scholarships

**Summary** To provide financial assistance to female residents of designated eastern states who are enrolled at a college in any state and preparing for a career in corporate communications and public relations.

**Eligibility** This program is open to women who are residents of New York, New Jersey, Connecticut, or Pennsylvania and currently enrolled as undergraduate or graduate students at a college or university in any state. Graduate students must be members of New York Women in Communications, Inc. (NYWICI). Also eligible are women who reside outside the 4 states but are currently enrolled at a college or university within 1 of the 5 boroughs of New York City. Applicants must be able to demonstrate a commitment to a career in corporate communications and public relations. They must have a GPA of 3.2 or higher. Along with their application, they must submit a 2-page resume; a personal essay of 300 words on an assigned topic that changes annually; 2 letters of recommendation; and an official transcript. Selection is based on academic record, need, demonstrated leadership, participation in school and community activities, honors and other awards or recognition, work experience, goals and aspirations, and unusual personal and/or family circumstances. U.S. citizenship is required.

**Financial data** The stipend ranges up to $10,000.

**Duration** 1 year.

**Additional information** This program is sponsored by McGraw-Hill Companies.

**Number awarded** 1 each year.

**Deadline** January of each year.

## [1040]
## MEDTRONIC SWENET SCHOLARSHIP

Society of Women Engineers-Minnesota Section
Attn: Scholarship Committee
P.O. Box 582813
Minneapolis, MN 55458-2813
E-mail: scholarships@swe-mn.org
Web: www.swe-mn.org/scholarships.html

**Summary** To provide financial assistance to women from any state working on an undergraduate or graduate degree in specified fields of engineering at colleges and universities in Minnesota, North Dakota, and South Dakota.

**Eligibility** This program is open to female undergraduate and graduate students at ABET-accredited engineering programs in Minnesota, North Dakota, or South Dakota. Applicants must be working full time on a degree in biomedical, chemical, electrical, or mechanical engineering. Along with their application, they must submit a short paragraph describing how they plan to utilize their engineering skills after they graduate. Selection is based on potential to succeed as an engineer (20 points), communication skills (10 points), extracurricular or community involvement and leadership skills (10 points), demonstrated successful work experience (10 points), and academic success (5 points).

**Financial data**  The stipend is $1,000.

**Duration**  1 year.

**Additional information**  This program is sponsored by Medtronic, Inc.

**Number awarded**  3 each year.

**Deadline**  March of each year.

## [1041]
## MEMORIAL EDUCATION FUND FELLOWSHIPS

General Federation of Women's Clubs of Massachusetts
Attn: Scholarship Chair
245 Dutton Road
P.O. Box 679
Sudbury, MA 01776-0679
(781) 891-1326          E-mail: Karen-ibew1@excite.com
Web: www.gfwcma.org/scholarships.html

**Summary**  To provide financial assistance to Massachusetts women interested in working on a graduate degree in designated fields at a school in any state.

**Eligibility**  This program is open to women college graduates who have resided in Massachusetts for at least 5 years. Applicants must be planning to work on a graduate degree in a designated field of study that changes annually. Along with their application, they must submit college and graduate school transcripts, a letter of reference from college department chair or recent employer, and a personal statement of no more than 500 words addressing their professional goals and financial need. An interview is required.

**Financial data**  The stipend is $3,000. Funds are paid directly to the recipient's college or university for tuition only.

**Duration**  1 year; nonrenewable.

**Number awarded**  2 each year.

**Deadline**  February of each year.

## [1042]
## MEREDITH CORPORATION SCHOLARSHIP AND INTERNSHIP

New York Women in Communications, Inc.
Attn: NYWICI Foundation
355 Lexington Avenue, 15th Floor
New York, NY 10017-6603
(212) 297-2133          Fax: (212) 370-9047
E-mail: nywicipr@nywici.org
Web: www.nywici.org/foundation/scholarships

**Summary**  To provide financial assistance and work experience to female residents of designated eastern states who are interested in preparing for a career in publishing at a college or graduate school in any state.

**Eligibility**  This program is open to women who are residents of New York, New Jersey, Connecticut, or Pennsylvania and enrolled as sophomores, juniors, seniors, or graduate students at a college or university in any state. Graduate students must be members of New York Women in Communications, Inc. (NYWICI). Also eligible are women who reside outside the 4 states but are currently enrolled at a college or university within 1 of the 5 boroughs of New York City. Applicants must be preparing for a career in publishing (print, digital, and/or marketing) and be interested in a summer internship

with Meredith Corporation. They must have a GPA of 3.2 or higher. Along with their application, they must submit a 2-page resume; a personal essay of 300 words on an assigned topic that changes annually; 2 letters of recommendation; and an official transcript. Selection is based on academic record, need, demonstrated leadership, participation in school and community activities, honors and other awards or recognition, work experience, goals and aspirations, and unusual personal and/or family circumstances. U.S. citizenship is required.

**Financial data**  The scholarship stipend ranges up to $10,000; the internship is salaried (amount not specified).

**Duration**  1 year.

**Additional information**  This program is sponsored by Meredith Corporation.

**Number awarded**  1 each year.

**Deadline**  January of each year.

## [1043]
## MICHELLE JACKSON SCHOLARSHIP FUND

Christian Church (Disciples of Christ)
Attn: Disciples Home Missions
130 East Washington Street
P.O. Box 1986
Indianapolis, IN 46206-1986
(317) 713-2652          Toll Free: (888) DHM-2631
Fax: (317) 635-4426          E-mail: mail@dhm.disciples.org
Web: www.discipleshomemissions.org

**Summary**  To provide financial assistance to African American women interested in preparing for a career in the ministry of the Christian Church (Disciples of Christ).

**Eligibility**  This program is open to female African American ministerial students who are members of a Christian Church (Disciples of Christ) congregation in the United States or Canada. Applicants must plan to prepare for the ordained ministry, be working on an M.Div. or equivalent degree, provide evidence of financial need, be enrolled full time in an accredited school or seminary, provide a transcript of academic work, and be under the care of a regional Commission on the Ministry or in the process of coming under care.

**Financial data**  A stipend is awarded (amount not specified).

**Duration**  1 year; recipients may reapply.

**Number awarded**  1 each year.

**Deadline**  March of each year.

## [1044]
## MICHIGAN COUNCIL OF WOMEN IN TECHNOLOGY FOUNDATION SCHOLARSHIPS

Michigan Council of Women in Technology Foundation
Attn: Scholarship Committee
19011 Norwich Road
Livonia, MI 48152
(248) 654-3697          Fax: (248) 281-5391
E-mail: info@mcwtf.org
Web: www.mcwt.org/Scholarships_196.html

**Summary**  To provide financial assistance to women from Michigan who are interested in working on an undergraduate or graduate degree in a field related to information technology at a school in any state.

**Eligibility** This program is open to female residents of Michigan who are graduating high school seniors, current undergraduates, or graduate students. Applicants must be planning to work on a degree in business applications, computer science, computer engineering, graphics design, health technology, information security, information systems, instructional technology, music technology, or software engineering at a college or university in any state. They must have a GPA of 2.8 or higher. Along with their application, they must submit an essay of 200 to 400 words on why they are preparing for a career in information technology, the accomplishments in which they take the most pride, why they should be selected for this scholarship, and what constitutes success for them in this program and/or their future career and life mission. Selection is based on that essay, GPA, technology related activities, community service, letters of recommendation, and completeness of the application. U.S. citizenship is required.

**Financial data** The stipend is $5,000 per year; funds are sent directly to the financial aid office at the college or university where the recipient is enrolled.

**Duration** 1 year; may be renewed for up to 3 additional years for high school seniors or 2 additional years for undergraduate and graduate students.

**Number awarded** 3 or more each year: at least each to a high school senior, an undergraduate, and a graduate student.

**Deadline** January of each year.

## [1045]
## MIKE EIDSON SCHOLARSHIP

American Association for Justice
Attn: Scholarships
777 Sixth Street, N.W., Suite 200
Washington, DC 20001
(202) 965-3500, ext. 2834
Toll Free: (800) 424-2725, ext. 2834
Fax: (202) 965-0355
E-mail: catherine.rodman@justice.org
Web: www.justice.org/cps/rde/xchg/justice/hs.xsl/648.htm

**Summary** To provide financial assistance to female law students who are interested in a career as a trial lawyer.

**Eligibility** This program is open to women entering their third year of law school (or fourth year in a night program). Applicants must submit a brief letter explaining their interest in a career as a trial lawyer, dedication to upholding the principles of the Constitution, and commitment to the concept of a fair trial, the adversary system, and a just result for the injured, the accused, and those whose rights are jeopardized.

**Financial data** The stipend is $5,000.

**Duration** 1 year.

**Additional information** This program began in 2008. The American Association for Justice was formerly the Association of Trial Lawyers of America.

**Number awarded** 1 or 2 each year.

**Deadline** April of each year.

## [1046]
## MIKE SHINN DISTINGUISHED MEMBER OF THE YEAR AWARDS

National Society of Black Engineers
Attn: Programs Department
205 Daingerfield Road
Alexandria, VA 22314
(703) 549-2207          Fax: (703) 683-5312
E-mail: scholarships@nsbe.org
Web: www.nsbe.org/Programs/Scholarships.aspx

**Summary** To provide financial assistance to male and female members of the National Society of Black Engineers (NSBE) who are working on a degree in engineering.

**Eligibility** This program is open to members of the society who are undergraduate or graduate engineering students. Applicants must have a GPA of 3.2 or higher. Selection is based on an essay; NSBE and university academic achievement; professional development; service to the society at the chapter, regional, and/or national level; and campus and community activities. The male and female applicants for the NSBE Fellows Scholarship Program who are judged most outstanding receive these awards.

**Financial data** The stipend is $7,500. Travel, hotel accommodations, and registration to the national convention are also provided.

**Duration** 1 year.

**Number awarded** 2 each year: 1 male and 1 female.

**Deadline** November of each year.

## [1047]
## MILDRED CATER BRADHAM SOCIAL WORK FELLOWSHIP

Zeta Phi Beta Sorority, Inc.
Attn: National Education Foundation
1734 New Hampshire Avenue, N.W.
Washington, DC 20009
(202) 387-3103          Fax: (202) 232-4593
E-mail: scholarship@ZPhiBNEF.org
Web: www.zphib1920.org/nef

**Summary** To provide financial assistance to members of Zeta Phi Beta Sorority who are interested in studying social work on the graduate level.

**Eligibility** This program is open to members of Zeta Phi Beta who are interested in working full time on a graduate or professional degree in social work. Applicants must have shown scholarly distinction or unusual ability in their chosen field. Along with their application, they must submit a 150-word essay on their educational goals and professional aspirations, how this award will help them to achieve those goals, and why they should receive the award. Financial need is not considered in the selection process.

**Financial data** The stipend ranges from $500 to $1,000 per year; funds are paid directly to the college or university.

**Duration** 1 academic year; may be renewed.

**Number awarded** 1 each year.

**Deadline** January of each year.

## [1048]
## MILDRED RICHARDS TAYLOR MEMORIAL SCHOLARSHIP

United Daughters of the Confederacy
Attn: Second Vice President General
328 North Boulevard
Richmond, VA 23220-4008
(804) 355-1636 Fax: (804) 353-1396
E-mail: jamieretired@sbcglobal.net
Web: www.hqudc.org/Scholarships/index.htm

**Summary** To provide financial assistance to female lineal descendants of Confederate veterans who are interested in working on a graduate degree in business.

**Eligibility** Eligible to apply for these scholarships are female lineal descendants of worthy Confederates or collateral descendants who intend to study business or a business-related field at the graduate level. Applicants must submit certified proof of the Confederate record of 1 ancestor, with the company and regiment in which he served. Preference is given to former members of Children of the Confederacy. They must have a GPA of 3.0 or higher.

**Financial data** The amount of this scholarship depends on the availability of funds.

**Duration** 1 year; may be renewed up to 2 additional years.

**Number awarded** 1 each year.

**Deadline** April of each year.

## [1049]
## MINDY SOPHER SCHOLARSHIP

Kappa Delta Sorority
Attn: Foundation Project Manager
3205 Players Lane
Memphis, TN 38125
(901) 748-1897, ext. 203 Toll Free: (800) 536-1897
Fax: (901) 748-0949
E-mail: caroline.cullum@kappadelta.org
Web: www.kappadelta.org/scholarshipapplications_1

**Summary** To provide financial assistance to members of Kappa Delta Sorority who are working on a graduate degree in higher education or student personnel.

**Eligibility** This program is open to graduate members of Kappa Delta Sorority. Applicants must submit a personal statement giving their reasons for applying for this scholarship, official undergraduate and graduate transcripts, and 2 letters of recommendation. They must be working on a graduate degree in higher education or student personnel. Selection is based on academic excellence; service to the chapter, alumnae association, or national Kappa Delta; service to the campus and community; personal objectives and goals; potential; recommendations; and financial need.

**Financial data** The stipend is $1,000 per year. Funds may be used only for tuition, fees, and books, not for room and board.

**Duration** 1 year; may be renewed.

**Number awarded** 1 each year.

**Deadline** November of each year.

## [1050]
## MINNIE L. MAFFETT FELLOWSHIPS

Texas Business Women
Attn: Texas Business and Professional Women's Foundation
2637 Pine Springs Drive
Plano, TX 75093
(972) 822-1173 E-mail: info@texasbusinesswomen.org
Web: www.texasbpwfoundation.org/scholarships.php

**Summary** To provide financial assistance to women in Texas interested in studying or conducting research in a medical field.

**Eligibility** This program is open to 1) female graduates of Texas medical schools interested in postgraduate or research work; 2) women who have been awarded a Ph.D. degree from a Texas university and are doing research in a medical field; 3) women who need financial aid for the first year in establishing a family practice in a rural area of Texas with a population of less than 5,000; and 4) fourth-year female medical students who are completing an M.D. or D.O. degree at an accredited medical school in Texas.

**Financial data** The stipend recently was $1,500.

**Duration** 1 year; nonrenewable.

**Additional information** This program began in 1948 when Texas Business Women was named Texas Federation of Business and Professional Women's Clubs.

**Number awarded** Varies each year; recently, 3 of these fellowships were awarded.

**Deadline** December of each year.

## [1051]
## MORGAN STANLEY MBA FELLOWSHIP

Morgan Stanley
Attn: Diversity Recruiting
1585 Broadway
New York, NY 10036
(212) 762-0211 Toll Free: (888) 454-3965
Fax: (212) 507-4972
E-mail: mbafellowship@morganstanley.com
Web: www.morganstanley.com

**Summary** To provide financial assistance and work experience to female and other members of underrepresented groups who are working on an M.B.A. degree.

**Eligibility** This program is open to full-time M.B.A. students who are women, African Americans, Hispanics, Native Americans, or lesbian/gay/bisexual/transgender. Selection is based on assigned essays, academic achievement, recommendations, extracurricular activities, leadership qualities, and on-site interviews.

**Financial data** The program provides full payment of tuition and fees and a paid summer internship.

**Duration** 1 year; may be renewed for a second year, providing the student remains enrolled full time in good academic standing and completes the summer internship following the first year.

**Additional information** The paid summer internship is offered within Morgan Stanley institutional securities (equity research, fixed income, institutional equity, investment banking), investment management, or private wealth management. This program was established in 1999.

**Number awarded** 1 or more each year.

**Deadline** December of each year.

## [1052]
## MOSS ADAMS FOUNDATION SCHOLARSHIP

Educational Foundation for Women in Accounting
Attn: Foundation Administrator
136 South Keowee Street
Dayton, OH 45402
(937) 424-3391                      Fax: (937) 222-5749
E-mail: info@efwa.org
Web: www.efwa.org/scholarships_MossAdams.php

**Summary** To provide financial support to women, including minority women, who are working on an accounting degree.

**Eligibility** This program is open to women who are enrolled in an accounting degree program at an accredited college or university. Applicants must meet 1 of the following criteria: 1) women pursuing a fifth-year requirement either through general studies or within a graduate program; 2) women returning to school as current or reentry juniors or seniors; or 3) minority women. Selection is based on aptitude for accounting and business, commitment to the goal of working on a degree in accounting (including evidence of continued commitment after receiving this award), clear evidence that the candidate has established goals and a plan for achieving those goals (both personal and professional), financial need, and a demonstration of how the scholarship will impact her life. U.S. citizenship is required.

**Financial data** The stipend is $1,000.

**Duration** 1 year.

**Additional information** This program was established by Rowling, Dold & Associates LLP, a woman-owned C.P.A. firm based in San Diego. It was renamed when that firm merged with Moss Adams LLP.

**Number awarded** 1 each year.

**Deadline** April of each year.

## [1053]
## MSCPA WOMEN IN ACCOUNTING SCHOLARSHIP

Massachusetts Society of Certified Public Accountants
Attn: MSCPA Educational Foundation
105 Chauncy Street, Tenth Floor
Boston, MA 02111
(617) 556-4000                    Toll Free: (800) 392-6145
Fax: (617) 556-4126        E-mail: info@mscpaonline.org
Web: www.cpatrack.com/scholarships

**Summary** To provide financial assistance to women from Massachusetts working on an undergraduate or graduate degree in accounting at a college or university in the state.

**Eligibility** This program is open to female Massachusetts residents enrolled at a college or university in the state. Applicants must be undergraduates who have completed the first semester of their junior year or graduate students. They must be able to demonstrate financial need, academic excellence, and an intention to prepare for a career as a Certified Public Accountant (C.P.A.) at a firm in Massachusetts.

**Financial data** The stipend is $2,500.

**Duration** 1 year.

**Additional information** This program is sponsored by the Women's Golf Committee of the Massachusetts Society of Certified Public Accountants (MSCPA).

**Number awarded** Varies each year; recently, 4 of these scholarships were awarded.

**Deadline** March of each year.

## [1054]
## MTS SYSTEMS CORPORATION SCHOLARSHIP

Society of Women Engineers-Minnesota Section
Attn: Scholarship Committee
P.O. Box 582813
Minneapolis, MN 55458-2813
E-mail: scholarships@swe-mn.org
Web: www.swe-mn.org/scholarships.html

**Summary** To provide financial assistance to women from any state working on an undergraduate or graduate degree in software or mechanical engineering at colleges and universities in Minnesota, North Dakota, and South Dakota.

**Eligibility** This program is open to female undergraduate and graduate students at ABET-accredited engineering programs in Minnesota, North Dakota, or South Dakota. Applicants must be working full time on a degree in software or mechanical engineering. Along with their application, they must submit a short paragraph describing how they plan to utilize their engineering skills after they graduate. Selection is based on potential to succeed as an engineer (20 points), communication skills (10 points), extracurricular or community involvement and leadership skills (10 points), demonstrated successful work experience (10 points), and academic success (5 points).

**Financial data** The stipend is $1,500.

**Duration** 1 year.

**Additional information** This program is sponsored by MTS Systems Corporation.

**Number awarded** 1 each year.

**Deadline** March of each year.

## [1055]
## MUSIC THERAPY SCHOLARSHIP

Sigma Alpha Iota Philanthropies, Inc.
One Tunnel Road
Asheville, NC 28805
(828) 251-0606                      Fax: (828) 251-0644
E-mail: nh@sai-national.org
Web: www.sai-national.org

**Summary** To provide financial assistance to members of Sigma Alpha Iota (an organization of women musicians) who are working on an undergraduate or graduate degree in music therapy.

**Eligibility** This program is open to members of the organization who have completed at least 2 years of study for an undergraduate or graduate degree in music therapy. Applicants must submit an essay that includes their personal definition of music therapy, their career plans and professional goals as a music therapist, and why they feel they are deserving of this scholarship. Selection is based on music therapy skills, musicianship, fraternity service, community service, leadership, self-reliance, and dedication to the field of music therapy as a career.

**Financial data** The stipend is $1,500.

**Duration** 1 year.

**Number awarded** 1 each year.

**Deadline** March of each year.

## [1056]
## MUSICIANS WITH SPECIAL NEEDS SCHOLARSHIP

Sigma Alpha Iota Philanthropies, Inc.
One Tunnel Road
Asheville, NC 28805
(828) 251-0606                    Fax: (828) 251-0644
E-mail: nh@sai-national.org
Web: www.sai-national.org

**Summary** To provide financial assistance for college or graduate school to members of Sigma Alpha Iota (an organization of women musicians) who have a disability and are working on a degree in music.

**Eligibility** This program is open to members of the organization who either 1) have a sensory or physical impairment and are enrolled in a graduate or undergraduate degree program in music; or 2) are preparing to become a music teacher or therapist for people with disabilities. Performance majors must submit a 15-minute DVD of their work; non-performance majors must submit evidence of work in their area of specialization, such as composition, musicology, or research.

**Financial data** The stipend is $1,500.

**Duration** 1 year.

**Number awarded** 1 each year.

**Deadline** March of each year.

## [1057]
## MYRA DAVIS HEMMINGS SCHOLARSHIP

Delta Sigma Theta Sorority, Inc.
Attn: Scholarship and Standards Committee Chair
1707 New Hampshire Avenue, N.W.
Washington, DC 20009
(202) 986-2400                    Fax: (202) 986-2513
E-mail: dstemail@deltasigmatheta.org
Web: www.deltasigmatheta.org

**Summary** To provide financial assistance to members of Delta Sigma Theta who are interested in working on a graduate degree in the performing or creative arts.

**Eligibility** This program is open to graduating college seniors and graduate students who are interested in preparing for a career in the performing or creative arts. Applicants must be active, dues-paying members of Delta Sigma Theta. Selection is based on meritorious achievement.

**Financial data** The stipends range from $1,000 to $2,000 per year. The funds may be used to cover tuition and living expenses.

**Duration** 1 year; may be renewed for 1 additional year.

**Additional information** This sponsor is a traditionally-African American social sorority. The application fee is $20.

**Number awarded** 1 or more each year.

**Deadline** April of each year.

## [1058]
## MYRNA F. BERNATH FELLOWSHIP AWARD

Society for Historians of American Foreign Relations
c/o Ohio State University
Department of History
106 Dulles Hall
230 West 17th Avenue
Columbus, OH 43210
(614) 292-1951                    Fax: (614) 292-2282
E-mail: shafr@osu.edu
Web: www.shafr.org/members/fellowships-grants

**Summary** To provide funding to women who are members of the Society for Historians of American Foreign Relations (SHAFR) and interested in conducting research on the history of U.S. foreign relations.

**Eligibility** This program is open to women at U.S. universities who wish to conduct historically-based research in the United States or abroad and to women from other countries who wish to conduct research in the United States. The proposed study should focus on U.S. foreign relations, transnational history, international history, peace studies, cultural interchange, or defense or strategic studies. Preference is given to applications from graduate students and those who completed their Ph.D. within the past 5 years. Applicants must submit a curriculum vitae, a letter of intent, and a detailed research proposal that discusses the sources to be consulted and their value, the funds needed, and the plan for spending those funds.

**Financial data** The grant is $5,000.

**Duration** The grant is presented biennially, in odd-numbered years.

**Additional information** This grant was first presented in 1992.

**Number awarded** 1 each odd-numbered year.

**Deadline** September of each even-numbered year.

## [1059]
## NABA 20 PEARLS SCHOLARSHIP

National Association of Black Accountants
Attn: National Scholarship Program
7474 Greenway Center Drive, Suite 1120
Greenbelt, MD 20770
(301) 474-NABA                    Fax: (301) 474-3114
E-mail: scholarships@nabainc.org
Web: www.nabainc.org

**Summary** To provide financial assistance to student members of the National Association of Black Accountants (NABA) who are also members of Alpha Kappa Alpha sorority and working on an undergraduate or graduate degree in a field related to accounting.

**Eligibility** This program is open to NABA members who are also Alpha Kappa Alpha members and enrolled full time as 1) an undergraduate freshman, sophomore, junior, or first-semester senior majoring in accounting, business, or finance at a 4-year college or university; or 2) a graduate student working on a master's degree in accounting. High school seniors are not eligible. Applicants must have a GPA of 3.5 or higher in their major and 3.3 or higher overall. Selection is based on grades, financial need, and a 500-word description of their involvement in NABA.

**Financial data** The stipend is $1,500.

**Duration** 1 year.

**Number awarded** 1 each year.

**Deadline** January of each year.

## [1060]
## NANCY B. WOOLRIDGE MCGEE GRADUATE FELLOWSHIP

Zeta Phi Beta Sorority, Inc.
Attn: National Education Foundation
1734 New Hampshire Avenue, N.W.
Washington, DC 20009
(202) 387-3103                    Fax: (202) 232-4593
E-mail: scholarship@ZPhiBNEF.org
Web: www.zphib1920.org/nef

**Summary** To provide financial assistance for graduate school to members of Zeta Phi Beta Sorority.

**Eligibility** This program is open to members of Zeta Phi Beta Sorority who are working on or are interested in working full time on a graduate or professional degree. Applicants must have shown scholarly distinction or unusual ability in their chosen profession. Along with their application, they must submit a 150-word essay on their educational goals and professional aspirations, how this award will help them to achieve those goals, and why they should receive the award. Financial need is not considered in the selection process.

**Financial data** The stipend ranges from $500 to $1,000 per year; funds are paid to the college or university.

**Duration** 1 academic year; may be renewed.

**Number awarded** 1 each year.

**Deadline** January of each year.

## [1061]
## NANCY KELLY FEMALE WRITER AWARD

Philanthrofund Foundation
Attn: Scholarship Committee
1409 Willow Street, Suite 109
Minneapolis, MN 55403-2241
(612) 870-1806              Toll Free: (800) 435-1402
Fax: (612) 871-6587      E-mail: info@PfundOnline.org
Web: www.pfundonline.org/scholarships.html

**Summary** To provide financial assistance to female Minnesota students who have supported gay, lesbian, bisexual, and transgender (GLBT) activities and are interested in studying writing.

**Eligibility** This program is open to female residents of Minnesota and students attending a Minnesota educational institution. Applicants must be self-identified as GLBT or from a GLBT family. They may be attending or planning to attend trade school, technical college, college, or university (as an undergraduate or graduate student) to study writing. Selection is based on the applicant's 1) affirmation of GLBT or allied identity; 2) evidence of experience and skills in service and leadership; and 3) evidence of service, leading, and working for change in GLBT communities, including serving as a role model, mentor, and/or adviser.

**Financial data** The stipend is $2,000. Funds must be used for tuition, books, fees, or dissertation expenses.

**Duration** 1 year.

**Number awarded** 1 each year.

**Deadline** January of each year.

## [1062]
## NATIONAL ASSOCIATION OF UNIVERSITY WOMEN FELLOWSHIPS

National Association of University Women
Attn: Fellowship Chair
1001 E Street, S.E.
Washington, DC 20003
(202) 547-3967                    Fax: (202) 547-5226
E-mail: info@nauw1910.org
Web: www.nauw1910.org

**Summary** To provide financial assistance to members of the National Association of University Women (NAUW) and other women who are working on a doctoral degree.

**Eligibility** This program is open to women who already have a master's degree and are enrolled in a program leading to a doctoral degree. They should be close to completing their degree. Preference is given to members of NAUW, an organization that historically has served African American women.

**Financial data** The stipend is $3,000.

**Duration** 1 year; nonrenewable.

**Number awarded** 3 each year: 2 to members of NAUW and 1 to a non-member.

**Deadline** April of each year.

## [1063]
## NATIONAL COLLEGIATE ATHLETIC ASSOCIATION POSTGRADUATE SCHOLARSHIP PROGRAM

National Collegiate Athletic Association
Attn: Postgraduate Scholarship Program
700 West Washington Street
P.O. Box 6222
Indianapolis, IN 46206-6222
(317) 917-6650                    Fax: (317) 917-6888
E-mail: lthomas@ncaa.org
Web: www.ncaa.org

**Summary** To provide financial support for graduate education in any field to student-athletes (females and males are considered separately).

**Eligibility** Eligible are student-athletes who have excelled academically and athletically and who are in their final year of intercollegiate athletics competition at member schools of the National Collegiate Athletic Association (NCAA). Candidates must be nominated by the faculty athletic representative or director of athletics and must have a GPA of 3.2 or higher. Nominees must be planning full- or part-time graduate study. Foreign student-athletes are also eligible. For the fall term, scholarships are presented to athletes who participated in men's and women's cross country, men's football, men's and women's soccer, men's water polo, women's volleyball, women's field hockey, women's equestrian, and women's rugby. For the winter term, scholarships are presented to athletes who participated in men's and women's basketball, men's and women's fencing, men's and women's gymnastics, men's and women's ice hockey, men's and women's rifle, men's and women's skiing, men's and women's swimming and diving, men's and women's indoor track and field, men's wrestling, women's bowling, and women's squash. For the spring term, scholarships are presented to athletes who participated in men's baseball, men's and women's golf, men's and women's lacrosse, women's rowing, women's softball, men's and women's tennis, men's volleyball, men's and women's outdoor track and field, women's water polo, and women's sand volleyball. Financial need is not considered in the selection process.

**Financial data** The stipend is $7,500.

**Duration** These are 1-time, nonrenewable awards.

**Number awarded** 174 each year: 87 for women and 87 for men. Each term, 29 scholarships are awarded to men and 29 to women.

**Deadline** January of each year for fall sports; March of each year for winter sports; May of each year for spring sports.

## [1064]
## NATIONAL DEFENSE SCIENCE AND ENGINEERING GRADUATE FELLOWSHIP PROGRAM

American Society for Engineering Education
Attn: NDSEG Fellowship Program
1818 N Street, N.W., Suite 600
Washington, DC 20036-2479
(202) 649-3831                    Fax: (202) 265-8504
E-mail: ndseg@asee.org
Web: ndseg.asee.org

**Summary** To provide financial assistance to doctoral students (particularly women, minorities, and persons with disabilities) who are specializing in areas of science and engineering that are of potential military importance.

**Eligibility** This program is open to U.S. citizens and nationals entering or enrolled in the early stages of a doctoral program in aeronautical and astronautical engineering; biosciences, including toxicology; chemical engineering; chemistry; civil engineering; cognitive, neural, and behavioral sciences; computer and computational sciences; electrical engineering; geosciences, including terrain, water, and air; materials science and engineering; mathematics; mechanical engineering; naval architecture and ocean engineering; oceanography; or physics, including optics. Applicants must be enrolled or planning to enroll as full-time students. Applications are particularly encouraged from women, members of ethnic minority groups (American Indians, African Americans, Hispanics or Latinos, Native Hawaiians, Alaska Natives, Asians, and Pacific Islanders), and persons with disabilities. Selection is based on all available evidence of ability, including academic records, letters of recommendation, and GRE scores.

**Financial data** The annual stipend is $30,500 for the first year, $31,000 for the second year; and $31,500 for the third year; the program also pays the recipient's institution full tuition and required fees (not to include room and board). Medical insurance is covered up to $1,000 per year.

**Duration** 3 years, as long as satisfactory academic progress is maintained.

**Additional information** This program is sponsored by the High Performance Computing Modernization Program within the Department of Defense, the Army Research Office, the Air Force Office of Scientific Research, and the Office of Naval Research. Recipients do not incur any military or other service obligation.

**Number awarded** Approximately 200 each year.

**Deadline** December of each year.

## [1065]
## NATIONAL HISPANIC BUSINESS WOMEN ASSOCIATION EDUCATIONAL SCHOLARSHIPS

National Hispanic Business Women Association
2024 North Broadway, Suite 100
Santa Ana, CA 92706
(714) 836-4042
Web: nationalhbwa.com/main/?page_id=367

**Summary** To provide financial assistance to women in California who are working on an undergraduate or graduate degree at a school in any state and submit an essay related to Latinas in education.

**Eligibility** This program is open to female residents of California who are currently enrolled as undergraduate or graduate students at a school in any state. Applicants must have a GPA of 3.0 or higher and be able to demonstrate financial need. They must also have a record of participation in some form of community service. Along with their application, they must submit 2 essays of 2 pages each on 1) their academic and professional goals; and 2) the importance or value of obtaining a higher education, the potential impacts or influences of a growing Latino population in relation to their field of interest, or the specific challenges faced by Latinas in pursuit of higher education.

**Financial data** Stipends range from $500 to $1,000.

**Duration** 1 year.

**Number awarded** Varies each year; recently, 13 of these scholarships were awarded.

**Deadline** March of each year.

## [1066]
## NATIONAL ORGANIZATION OF ITALIAN AMERICAN WOMEN SCHOLARSHIPS

National Organization of Italian American Women
25 West 43rd Street, Suite 1005
New York, NY 10036
(212) 642-2003                    Fax: (212) 642-2006
E-mail: noiaw@noiaw.org
Web: www.noiaw.org

**Summary** To provide financial assistance for college or graduate school to women of Italian descent.

**Eligibility** This program is open to women who have at least 1 parent of Italian American descent and are working on an associate, bachelor's, or master's degree. Applicants must be enrolled full time and have a GPA of 3.5 or higher. Along with their application, they must submit a 2-page essay on how being an Italian American has impacted them personally and professionally. Financial need is considered in the selection process.

**Financial data** The stipend is $2,000.

**Duration** 1 year; nonrenewable.

**Additional information** A processing fee of $25 must accompany the application.

**Number awarded** 5 each year, including 1 reserved for an undergraduate or graduate student at the City University of New York system.

**Deadline** March of each year.

## [1067]
## NATIONAL PATHFINDER SCHOLARSHIPS

National Federation of Republican Women
Attn: Scholarships and Internships
124 North Alfred Street
Alexandria, VA 22314-3011
(703) 548-9688                    Fax: (703) 548-9836
E-mail: mail@nfrw.org
Web: www.nfrw.org/programs/scholarships.htm

**Summary** To provide financial assistance for college or graduate school to Republican women.

**Eligibility** This program is open to women currently enrolled as college sophomores, juniors, seniors, or master's degree students. Recent high school graduates and first-year college women are not eligible. Applicants must submit 3 letters of recommendation, an official transcript, a 1-page essay on why they should be considered for the scholarship, and a 1-page essay on career goals. Applications must be submitted to the Republican federation president in the applicant's state. Each president chooses 1 application from her state to submit for scholarship consideration. Financial need is not a factor in the selection process. U.S. citizenship is required.

**Financial data** The stipend is $2,500.

**Duration** 1 year; nonrenewable.

**Additional information** This program, previously named the Nancy Reagan Pathfinder Scholarships, was established in 1985.

**Number awarded** 3 each year.

**Deadline** Applications must be submitted to the state federation president by May of each year.

## [1068]
## NATIONAL PHYSICAL SCIENCE CONSORTIUM GRADUATE FELLOWSHIPS

National Physical Science Consortium
c/o University of Southern California
3716 South Hope Street, Suite 348
Los Angeles, CA 90007-4344
(213) 821-2409                    Toll Free: (800) 854-NPSC
Fax: (213) 821-2407               E-mail: npschq@npsc.org
Web: www.npsc.org

**Summary** To provide financial assistance and summer work experience to women and underrepresented minorities who are interested in working on a Ph.D. in designated science and engineering fields.

**Eligibility** This program is open to U.S. citizens who are seniors graduating from college with a GPA of 3.0 or higher, enrolled in the first year of a doctoral program, completing a terminal master's degree, or returning from the workforce and holding no more than a master's degree. Students currently in the third or subsequent year of a Ph.D. program or who already have a doctoral degree in any field (Ph.D., M.D., J.D., Ed.D.) are ineligible. Applicants must be interested in working on a Ph.D. in fields that vary but emphasize astronomy, chemistry, computer science, engineering (chemical, computer, electrical, environmental, or mechanical), geology, materials science, mathematical sciences, or physics. The program welcomes applications from all qualified students and continues to emphasize the recruitment of underrepresented minority (African American, Hispanic, Native American Indian, Eskimo, Aleut, and Pacific Islander) and women physical sci-

ence and engineering students. Fellowships are provided to students at more than 100 universities that are members of the consortium. Selection is based on academic standing (GPA), course work taken in preparation for graduate school, university and/or industry research experience, letters of recommendation, and GRE scores.

**Financial data** The fellowship pays tuition and fees plus an annual stipend of $20,000. It also provides on-site paid summer employment to enhance technical experience. The exact value of the fellowship depends on academic standing, summer employment, and graduate school attended; the total amount generally exceeds $200,000.

**Duration** Support is initially provided for 2 or 3 years, depending on the employer-sponsor. If the fellow makes satisfactory progress and continues to meet the conditions of the award, support may continue for a total of up to 6 years or completion of the Ph.D., whichever comes first.

**Additional information** This program began in 1989. Tuition and fees are provided by the participating universities. Stipends and summer internships are provided by sponsoring organizations. Students must submit separate applications for internships, which may have additional eligibility requirements. Internships are currently available at Lawrence Livermore National Laboratory in Livermore, California (astronomy, chemistry, computer science, geology, materials science, mathematics, and physics); National Institute of Standards and Technology in Gaithersburg, Maryland (various fields of STEM); National Security Agency in Fort Meade, Maryland (astronomy, chemistry, computer science, geology, materials science, mathematics, and physics); Sandia National Laboratory in Livermore, California (biology, chemistry, computer science, environmental science, geology, materials science, mathematics, and physics); and Sandia National Laboratory in Albuquerque, New Mexico (chemical engineering, chemistry, computer science, materials science, mathematics, mechanical engineering, and physics). Fellows must submit a separate application for dissertation support in the year prior to the beginning of their dissertation research program, but not until they can describe their intended research in general terms.

**Number awarded** Varies each year; recently, 11 of these fellowships were awarded.

**Deadline** November of each year.

## [1069]
## NATIONAL SPACE GRANT COLLEGE AND FELLOWSHIP PROGRAM

National Aeronautics and Space Administration
Attn: Office of Education
300 E Street, S.W.
Mail Suite 6M35
Washington, DC 20546-0001
(202) 358-1069                    Fax: (202) 358-7097
E-mail: Diane.D.DeTroye@nasa.gov
Web: www.nasa.gov

**Summary** To provide financial assistance to undergraduate and graduate students (particularly women, underrepresented minorities, and persons with disabilities) interested in preparing for a career in a space-related field.

**Eligibility** This program is open to undergraduate and graduate students at colleges and universities that participate in the National Space Grant program of the U.S. National

Aeronautics and Space Administration (NASA) through their state consortium. Applicants must be interested in a program of study and/or research in a field of science, technology, engineering, or mathematics (STEM) related to space. A specific goal of the program is to recruit and train U.S. citizens, especially underrepresented minorities, women, and persons with disabilities, for careers in aerospace science and technology. Financial need is not considered in the selection process.

**Financial data** Each consortium establishes the terms of the fellowship program in its state.

**Duration** 1 year; may be renewed.

**Additional information** NASA established the Space Grant program in 1989. It operates through 52 consortia in each state, the District of Columbia, and Puerto Rico. Each consortium includes selected colleges and universities in that state as well as other affiliates from industry, museums, science centers, and state and local agencies.

**Number awarded** Varies each year.

**Deadline** Each consortium sets its own deadlines.

## [1070]
## NATIONAL STRENGTH AND CONDITIONING ASSOCIATION WOMEN'S SCHOLARSHIPS

National Strength and Conditioning Association
Attn: Grants and Scholarships Program
1885 Bob Johnson Drive
Colorado Springs, CO 80906-4000
(719) 632-6722, ext. 152        Toll Free: (800) 815-6826
Fax: (719) 632-6367        E-mail: foundation@nsca-lift.org
Web: www.nsca-lift.org/Foundation/grants-and-scholarships

**Summary** To provide financial assistance to women who are interested in working on an undergraduate or graduate degree in strength training and conditioning.

**Eligibility** This program is open to women who are 17 years of age or older. Applicants must have been accepted into an accredited postsecondary institution to work on an undergraduate or graduate degree in the strength and conditioning field. Along with their application, they must submit a 500-word essay on their personal and professional goals and how receiving this scholarship will assist them in achieving those goals. Selection is based on that essay, academic achievement, strength and conditioning experience, honors and awards, community involvement, letters of recommendation, and involvement in the National Strength and Conditioning Association (NSCA).

**Financial data** The stipend is $1,500.

**Duration** 1 year.

**Additional information** The NSCA is a nonprofit organization of strength and conditioning professionals, including coaches, athletic trainers, physical therapists, educators, researchers, and physicians. This program was first offered in 2003.

**Number awarded** Varies each year; recently, 12 of these scholarships were awarded.

**Deadline** March of each year.

## [1071]
## NATIONAL URBAN FELLOWS PROGRAM

National Urban Fellows, Inc.
Attn: Program Director
989 Avenue of the Americas, Suite 400
New York, NY 10018
(212) 730-1700        Fax: (212) 730-1823
E-mail: info@nuf.org
Web: www.nuf.org/fellows-overview

**Summary** To provide mid-career public sector professionals, especially women and minorities, with an opportunity to strengthen leadership skills through a master's degree program coupled with a mentorship.

**Eligibility** This program is open to U.S. citizens who have a bachelor's degree, have at least 3 years of administrative or managerial experience, have demonstrated exceptional ability and leadership potential, meet academic admission requirements, have a high standard of integrity and work ethic, and are committed to the solution of urban problems. Applicants must a 1,000-word autobiographical statement and a 1,000-word statement on their career goals. They may be of any racial or ethnic background, but the program's goal is to increase the number of competent administrators from underrepresented ethnic and cultural groups at all levels of public and private urban management organizations. Semifinalists are interviewed.

**Financial data** The stipend is $25,000. The program also provides full payment of tuition, a relocation allowance of $500, a book allowance of $500, and reimbursement for program-related travel.

**Duration** 14 months.

**Additional information** The program begins with a summer semester of study at Bernard M. Baruch College of the City University of New York. Following this, fellows spend 9 months in mentorship assignments with a senior administrator in a government agency, a major nonprofit, or a foundation. The final summer is spent in another semester of study at Baruch College. Fellows who successfully complete all requirements are granted a master's of public administration from that college. A $75 processing fee must accompany each application.

**Number awarded** Varies; approximately 40 each year.

**Deadline** February of each year.

## [1072]
## NAVY/MARINE CORPS/COAST GUARD ENLISTED DEPENDENT SPOUSE SCHOLARSHIP

Navy Wives Clubs of America
c/o NSA Mid-South
P.O. Box 54022
Millington, TN 38054-0022
Toll Free: (866) 511-NWCA
E-mail: nwca@navywivesclubsofamerica.org
Web: www.navywivesclubsofamerica.org/scholarships

**Summary** To provide financial assistance for undergraduate or graduate study to spouses of naval personnel.

**Eligibility** This program is open to the spouses of active-duty Navy, Marine Corps, or Coast Guard members who can demonstrate financial need. Applicants must be 1) a high school graduate or senior planning to attend college full time next year; 2) currently enrolled in an undergraduate program and planning to continue as a full-time undergraduate; 3) a college graduate or senior planning to be a full-time graduate student next year; or 4) a high school graduate or GED recipient planning to attend vocational or business school next year. Along with their application, they must submit a brief statement on why they feel they should be awarded this scholarship and any special circumstances (financial or other) they wish to have considered. Financial need is also considered in the selection process.

**Financial data** The stipends range from $500 to $1,000 each year (depending upon the donations from chapters of the Navy Wives Clubs of America).

**Duration** 1 year.

**Number awarded** 1 or more each year.

**Deadline** May of each year.

## [1073]
## NCAA WOMEN'S ENHANCEMENT SCHOLARSHIP PROGRAM

National Collegiate Athletic Association
Attn: Office for Diversity and Inclusion
700 West Washington Street
P.O. Box 6222
Indianapolis, IN 46206-6222
(317) 917-6222                    Fax: (317) 917-6888
E-mail: tstrum@ncaa.org
Web: www.ncaa.org

**Summary** To provide funding to women who are interested in working on a graduate degree in athletics.

**Eligibility** This program is open to women who have been accepted into a program at a National Collegiate Athletic Association (NCAA) member institution that will prepare them for a career in intercollegiate athletics (athletics administrator, coach, athletic trainer, or other career that provides a direct service to intercollegiate athletics). Applicants must be U.S. citizens, have performed with distinction as a student body member at their respective undergraduate institution, and be entering the first semester or term of full-time postgraduate study. Selection is based on the applicant's involvement in extracurricular activities, course work, commitment to preparing for a career in intercollegiate athletics, and promise for success in that career. Financial need is not considered.

**Financial data** The stipend is $6,000; funds are paid to the college or university of the recipient's choice.

**Duration** 1 year; nonrenewable.

**Number awarded** 13 each year.

**Deadline** November of each year.

## [1074]
## NELL I. MONDY FELLOWSHIP

Sigma Delta Epsilon-Graduate Women in Science, Inc.
c/o Laurie B. Cook, Fellowships Coordinator
The College at Brockport, State University of New York
Biology Department, 217 Lennon Hall
350 New Campus Drive
Brockport, NY 14420
(585) 395-5757    E-mail: fellowshipsquestions@gwis.org
Web: gwis.org/national-fellowships-program

**Summary** To provide funding to women interested in conducting research anywhere in the world in food science or nutrition.

**Eligibility** This program is open to women from any country currently enrolled as a graduate student, engaged in postdoctoral research, or holding a junior faculty position. Applicants must be interested in conducting research anywhere in the world in food science or nutrition. Along with their application, they must submit 2-paragraph essays on 1) how the proposed research relates to their degree program and/or career development; 2) initiatives in which they are participating to promote the careers of scientists, particularly women, within their institution, program, or peer group; and 3) relevant personal factors, including financial need, that should be considered in evaluating their proposal. Appointments are made without regard to race, religion, nationality, creed, national origin, sexual orientation, or age. Membership in Sigma Delta Epsilon-Graduate Women in Science (SDE-GWIS) is encouraged.

**Financial data** The maximum grant is $10,000. Funds may be used for such research expenses as expendable supplies, small equipment, publication of research findings, travel and subsistence while performing field studies, or travel to another laboratory for collaborative research. They may not be used for tuition, child care, travel to professional meetings or to begin a new appointment, administrative overhead or indirect costs, personal computers, living allowances, or equipment for general use.

**Duration** 1 year.

**Additional information** This fellowship was first awarded in 2002. Non-members of SDE-GWIS must pay an application fee of $50.

**Number awarded** Varies each year; recently, 2 of these grants were awarded.

**Deadline** January of each year.

## [1075]
## NELLIE YEOH WHETTEN AWARD

AVS-Science and Technology of Materials, Interfaces, and Processing
Attn: Scholarship Committee
125 Maiden Lane, 15th Floor
New York, NY 10038
(212) 248-0200, ext. 221          Fax: (212) 248-0245
E-mail: angela@avs.org
Web: avs.org/About/Awards-Recognition

**Summary** To provide financial assistance to women interested in studying vacuum science and technology on the graduate school level.

**Eligibility** This program is open to women of any nationality who are accepted at or enrolled in a graduate school in North America and studying vacuum science and technology. Applicants are normally expected not to graduate before the award selection. They must submit a description of their current research, including its goals and objectives, the scientific and/or technological reasons that motivate the work, their approach for achieving the goals, progress (if any), program plans, and impact the results might have in the advancement of the area of research. Selection is based on research and academic excellence.

**Financial data** The stipend is $1,500; the winner also receives reimbursement of travel costs to attend the society's international symposium.

**Duration** 1 year.

**Additional information** This award was established in 1989. AVS-Science and Technology of Materials, Interfaces, and Processing was formerly the American Vacuum Society.

**Number awarded** 1 each year.

**Deadline** April of each year.

## [1076]
## NESBITT MEDICAL STUDENT FOUNDATION SCHOLARSHIP

Nesbitt Medical Student Foundation
c/o National Bank & Trust Company of Sycamore
230 West State Street
Sycamore, IL 60178
(815) 895-2125, ext. 228

**Summary** To provide financial assistance to needy medical students (especially women) residing in Illinois and to encourage their entry into general practice in the state.

**Eligibility** Applicants must be U.S. citizens, residents of Illinois, and either accepted for enrollment or a regular full-time student in good standing at an approved college of medicine. Applicants must be interested in entry into general practice either in DeKalb County or in any county in Illinois having a population of less than 50,000 residents. Preference is given to women, persons who are or have been residents of DeKalb County, and students already attending an approved medical school in Illinois. Financial need must be demonstrated.

**Financial data** The maximum stipend is $2,000 per year, depending upon the needs of the recipient.

**Duration** 1 academic year; renewable.

**Number awarded** Approximately 20 each year.

**Deadline** May of each year.

## [1077]
## NETWORK OF EXECUTIVE WOMEN SCHOLARSHIP

Network of Executive Women
c/o Nathalia Granger, Director of Operations
Accenture
161 North Clark Street, 38th Floor
Chicago, IL 60601
(312) 693-6855                    Fax: (312) 726-4704
E-mail: ngranger@newonline.org
Web: www.newonline.org

**Summary** To provide financial assistance to upper-division and graduate student women preparing for a career in the consumer products and retail industry.

**Eligibility** This program is open to women enrolled full time as juniors, seniors, or graduate students in a retail, food, or consumer packaged goods-related program at a U.S. college or university. Applicants must have a GPA of 3.0 or higher. Along with their application, they must submit a 1-page essay explaining why they merit this scholarship and outlining their food, retail, or consumer packaged goods industry interests. Selection is based on that essay, a current resume, a transcript, and 2 letters of recommendation; financial need is not considered. U.S. citizenship is required.

**Financial data** The stipend is $5,000.

**Duration** 1 year.

**Number awarded** Varies each year; recently, 5 of these scholarships were awarded.

**Deadline** April of each year.

## [1078]
## NEW MEXICO MINORITY DOCTORAL LOAN-FOR-SERVICE PROGRAM

New Mexico Higher Education Department
Attn: Financial Aid Division
2048 Galisteo Street
Santa Fe, NM 87505-2100
(505) 476-8411                    Toll Free: (800) 279-9777
Fax: (505) 476-8454    E-mail: feliz.romero1@state.nm.us
Web: hed.state.nm.us/MinDoc.aspx

**Summary** To provide loans-for-service to women and underrepresented minorities who reside in New Mexico and are interested in working on a doctoral degree in selected fields.

**Eligibility** This program is open to ethnic minorities and women who are residents of New Mexico and have received a baccalaureate degree from a public 4-year college or university in the state in mathematics, engineering, the physical or life sciences, or any other academic discipline in which ethnic minorities and women are demonstrably underrepresented in New Mexico academic institutions. Applicants must have been admitted as a full-time doctoral student at an approved university in any state. They must be sponsored by a New Mexico institution of higher education which has agreed to employ them in a tenure-track faculty position after they obtain their degree. U.S. citizenship is required.

**Financial data** Loans average $15,000. This is a loan-for-service program; for every year of service as a college faculty member in New Mexico, a portion of the loan is forgiven. If the entire service agreement is fulfilled, 100% of the loan is eligible for forgiveness. Penalties may be assessed if the service agreement is not satisfied.

**Duration** 1 year; may be renewed up to 3 additional years.

**Number awarded** Up to 12 each year.

**Deadline** March of each year.

## [1079]
## NFMC BIENNIAL STUDENT/COLLEGIATE AUDITION AWARDS

National Federation of Music Clubs
1646 Smith Valley Road
Greenwood, IN 46142
(317) 882-4003                    Fax: (317) 882-4019
E-mail: info@nfmc-music.org
Web: nfmc-music.org

**Summary** To recognize and reward outstanding student musicians (some awards are only for women) who are members of the National Federation of Music Clubs (NFMC).

**Eligibility** This competition is open to instrumentalists and vocalists between 19 and 26 years of age. Student membership in the federation and U.S. citizenship are required. Competition categories include: women's voice, men's voice, piano, organ, harp, classical guitar, violin, viola, cello, double bass, orchestral woodwinds, orchestral brass, and percussion. Awards are presented at the national level after auditions at the state and district levels.

**Financial data** The winner in each category is awarded $1,100.

**Duration** The competition is held biennially, in odd-numbered years.

**Additional information**   Students who enter this competition are also automatically considered for a number of supplemental awards. The entry fee is $30 for each category.

**Number awarded**   13 each year: 1 in each category.

**Deadline**   January of odd-numbered years.

## [1080]
## NINA BELLE REDDITT MEMORIAL SCHOLARSHIP

American Business Women's Association-Pirate Charter
   Chapter
Attn: Scholarship Program
P.O. Box 20498
Greenville, NC 27858
E-mail: pirateabwascholarship@yahoo.com
Web: pirateabwa.org/scholarship.html

**Summary**   To provide financial assistance to female residents of North Carolina interested in working on an undergraduate or graduate degree at a school in the state.

**Eligibility**   This program is open to women who are residents of North Carolina and U.S. citizens. Applicants must be graduating high school seniors, undergraduates, or graduate students and have a GPA of 2.5 or higher. They must be attending or planning to attend an accredited college, university, community college, or technical/vocational school in North Carolina. Along with their application, they must submit a 2-page biographical sketch that includes information about their background, school activities, outside interests, honors and awards, work experience, community service, and long-term goals. Financial need is not considered in the selection process.

**Financial data**   The stipend is $5,000.

**Duration**   1 year.

**Additional information**   This program began in 1978.

**Number awarded**   2 each year.

**Deadline**   May of each year.

## [1081]
## NORMAN'S ORCHIDS MASTERS SCHOLARSHIP

American Orchid Society
c/o Fairchild Tropical Botanic Garden
10901 Old Cutler Road
Coral Gables, FL 33156
(305) 740-2010                   Fax: (305) 740-2011
E-mail: TheAOS@aos.org
Web: www.aos.org/Default.aspx?id=545

**Summary**   To provide funding for research to students (particularly women, minorities, and persons with disabilities) who are working on a master's degree in a field related to orchids.

**Eligibility**   This program is open to students working on a master's degree at an accredited institution. Applicants must have a thesis project that deals with an aspect of orchid education, applied science, or orchid biology in the disciplines of physiology, molecular biology, structure, systematics, cytology, ecology, or evolution. They must submit a current curriculum vitae, transcripts of all college course work, a synopsis of the proposed project or research, a 1-page statement of the value of their project and importance to the future of orchid education or orchidology, and a letter of recommendation from their chairperson. Women, minorities, and persons with disabilities are especially encouraged to apply.

**Financial data**   The grant is $5,000 per year. Funds are paid through the recipient's college or university, but institutional overhead is not allowed.

**Duration**   2 years.

**Additional information**   This program, established in 2005, is supported by Norman's Orchids of Montclair, California.

**Number awarded**   1 each year.

**Deadline**   March of each year.

## [1082]
## NORTH CAROLINA BUSINESS AND PROFESSIONAL WOMEN'S FOUNDATION SCHOLARSHIPS

North Carolina Federation of Business and Professional
   Women's Club, Inc.
Attn: BPW/NC Foundation
175 BPW Club Road
P.O. Box 276
Carrboro, NC 27510
Web: www.bpw-nc.org/Default.aspx?pageId=837230

**Summary**   To provide financial assistance to women attending North Carolina colleges, community colleges, or graduate schools.

**Eligibility**   This program is open to women who are currently enrolled in a community college, 4-year college, or graduate school in North Carolina. Applicants must be endorsed by a local BPW unit. Along with their application, they must submit a 1-page statement that summarizes their career goals, previous honors, or community activities and justifies their need for this scholarship. U.S. citizenship is required.

**Financial data**   The stipend is $1,000. Funds are paid directly to the recipient's school.

**Duration**   1 year; recipients may reapply.

**Additional information**   This program began in 1996.

**Number awarded**   2 each year: 1 for an undergraduate and 1 for a graduate student.

**Deadline**   April of each year.

## [1083]
## NORTHWESTERN REGION FELLOWSHIP AWARD

Soroptimist International of the Americas-Northwestern
   Region
c/o Kathy A. King
22330 Drazil Road
Malin, OR 97632-9722
E-mail: info@soroptimistnwr.org
Web: soroptimistnwr.org/what-we-do/fellowship-award

**Summary**   To provide financial assistance for graduate study in any state to women who reside in the Northwestern Region of Soroptimist International of the Americas.

**Eligibility**   This program is open to women who reside in the Northwestern Region of Soroptimist International of the Americas. Applicants must be established in business or a profession and have a bachelor's or master's degree from an accredited university. They must present a plan of graduate study at an accredited college or university in any state that leads to an advanced degree or enhanced standing or competence in their business or profession.

**Financial data**   The stipend is $4,000.

**Duration** 1 year.

**Additional information** The Northwestern Region includes Alaska, designated counties in Idaho (Benewah, Bonner, Boundary, Clearwater, Idaho, Kootenai, Latah, Lewis, Nez Perce, and Shoshone), Montana, Oregon (except Malheur County), and Washington.

**Number awarded** 1 each year.

**Deadline** The application must be submitted to the sponsoring Soroptimist Club by January of each year.

## [1084]
## NOVICE RESEARCHER AWARD

Association of Women's Health, Obstetric and Neonatal
  Nurses
Attn: Research Grants Program
2000 L Street, N.W., Suite 740
Washington, DC 20036
(202) 261-2431         Toll Free: (800) 673-8499, ext. 2431
Fax: (202) 728-0575
E-mail: ResearchPrograms@awhonn.org
Web: www.awhonn.org

**Summary** To provide funding for small research projects to members of the Association of Women's Health, Obstetric and Neonatal Nurses (AWHONN) who qualify as novice researchers.

**Eligibility** This program is open to members of the association who have at least a master's degree or are currently enrolled in a master's program and completing a thesis or clinical research project. Applicants must be interested in beginning areas of study, investigating clinical issues, and/or launching a pilot study. They must identify a senior researcher who has agreed to serve as mentor and who submits a letter of support describing the role he or she will be implementing.

**Financial data** The grant is $5,000. Funds may not be used for indirect costs, tuition, computer hardware or printers, conference attendance, or salary for the principal investigator or other investigators.

**Duration** 1 year.

**Number awarded** 1 each year.

**Deadline** November of each year.

## [1085]
## NWSA GRADUATE SCHOLARSHIP AWARD

National Women's Studies Association
11 East Mount Royal Avenue, Suite 100
Baltimore, MD 21202
(410) 528-0355         Fax: (410) 528-0357
E-mail: awards@nwsa.org
Web: www.nwsa.org/content.asp?pl=16&contentid=16

**Summary** To provide funding to members of the National Women's Studies Association (NWSA) working on a graduate thesis in women's studies.

**Eligibility** This program is open to association members engaged in the research or writing stages of a master's thesis or Ph.D. dissertation in the interdisciplinary field of women's studies. The research project must focus on women and must enhance the NWSA mission. Applicants must submit brief statements on their financial need, feminist or community activities, and relevance of research to NWSA goals.

**Financial data** The grant is $1,000.

**Duration** 1 year.

**Number awarded** 1 each year.

**Deadline** May of each year.

## [1086]
## NYWICI FOUNDATION SCHOLARSHIPS

New York Women in Communications, Inc.
Attn: NYWICI Foundation
355 Lexington Avenue, 15th Floor
New York, NY 10017-6603
(212) 297-2133         Fax: (212) 370-9047
E-mail: nywicipr@nywici.org
Web: www.nywici.org/foundation/scholarships

**Summary** To provide financial assistance to female residents of designated eastern states who are interested in preparing for a career in communications at a college or graduate school in any state.

**Eligibility** This program is open to women who are seniors graduating from high schools in New York, New Jersey, Connecticut, or Pennsylvania or undergraduate or graduate students who are permanent residents of those states; they must be attending or planning to attend a college or university in any state. Graduate students must be members of New York Women in Communications, Inc. (NYWICI). Also eligible are women who reside outside the 4 states but are currently enrolled at a college or university within 1 of the 5 boroughs of New York City. All applicants must be working on a degree in a communications-related field (e.g., advertising, broadcasting, communications, English, film, journalism, marketing, new media, public relations) and have a GPA of 3.2 or higher. Along with their application, they must submit a 2-page resume; a personal essay of 300 words on an assigned topic that changes annually; 2 letters of recommendation; and an official transcript. Selection is based on academic record, need, demonstrated leadership, participation in school and community activities, honors and other awards or recognition, work experience, goals and aspirations, and unusual personal and/or family circumstances. U.S. citizenship is required.

**Financial data** The maximum stipend is $10,000.

**Duration** 1 year; recipients may reapply.

**Number awarded** Varies each year; recently, 9 of these scholarships were awarded.

**Deadline** January of each year.

## [1087]
## OKLAHOMA BW FOUNDATION SCHOLARSHIPS

Oklahoma Federation of Business Women, Inc.
Attn: Oklahoma Business Women's Foundation
P.O. Box 160
Maud, OK 74854-0160
(405) 374-2866         Fax: (405) 374-2316
E-mail: askkathy@oklahomabusinesswomen.org
Web: www.oklahomabusinesswomen/obw_foundation.htm

**Summary** To provide financial assistance to women from any state who are working on an undergraduate or graduate degree in any field at a school in Oklahoma.

**Eligibility** This program is open to women from any state who are working on an undergraduate or graduate degree at a college, university, or technical school in Oklahoma. Applicants must submit a 500-word essay on their career goals and how receiving this scholarship will help them to accomplish those goals and make a difference in their professional career. Selection is based on that essay, academic record, employment and volunteer record, and financial need.

**Financial data**　Stipends are $1,000, $750, or $500.

**Duration**　1 year.

**Additional information**　This program includes the following named scholarships: the Jewell Russell Mann Scholarship, the Dorothy Dickerson Scholarship, the Ann Garrison/Delores Schofield Scholarship, and the Dr. Ann Marie Benson Scholarship.

**Number awarded**　Varies each year; recently, 9 of these scholarships were awarded.

**Deadline**　February of each year.

## [1088]
## OKLAHOMA CITY CHAPTER AWC SCHOLARSHIPS

Association for Women in Communications-Oklahoma City Chapter
c/o Sunny Cearley, Scholarship Committee Chair
2728 Orlando Road
Oklahoma City, OK 73120
Web: www.awcokc.org/events-programs

**Summary**　To provide financial assistance to women from any state working on an undergraduate or graduate degree in communications or a related field at a school in Oklahoma.

**Eligibility**　This program is open to women who are residents of any state working full time on an undergraduate or graduate degree in a communications-related field (e.g., public relations, journalism, advertising, photography) at a 2- or 4-year college or university in Oklahoma. Applicants must submit a 250-word statement explaining why they are applying for the scholarship, why they chose to study communications, their goals after graduation, and related topics. Selection is based on aptitude, interest in a communications-related career, academic achievement, community service, and financial need.

**Financial data**　Stipends range from $1,000 to $1,500.

**Duration**　1 year.

**Additional information**　Recipients must enroll full time.

**Number awarded**　Varies each year; recently, 5 of these scholarships were awarded: 1 at $1,500, 2 at $1,250, and 2 at $1,000.

**Deadline**　March of each year.

## [1089]
## OLIVE LYNN SALEMBIER MEMORIAL REENTRY SCHOLARSHIP

Society of Women Engineers
Attn: Scholarship Selection Committee
203 North LaSalle Street, Suite 1675
Chicago, IL 60601-1269
(312) 596-5223　　　　　Toll Free: (877) SWE-INFO
Fax: (312) 644-8557　　　E-mail: scholarships@swe.org
Web: societyofwomenengineers.swe.org

**Summary**　To provide financial assistance to women interested in returning to college or graduate school to study engineering or computer science.

**Eligibility**　This program is open to women who are planning to enroll at an ABET-accredited 4-year college or university. Applicants must have been out of the engineering workforce and school for at least 2 years and must be planning to return as an undergraduate or graduate student to major in computer science or engineering. They must have a GPA of 3.0 or higher. Selection is based on merit.

**Financial data**　The award is $1,500.

**Duration**　1 year; may be renewed up to 3 additional years.

**Additional information**　This program began in 1978.

**Number awarded**　1 each year.

**Deadline**　February of each year.

## [1090]
## OMAHA CHAPTER AFWA SCHOLARSHIPS

Accounting and Financial Women's Alliance-Omaha Chapter
Attn: Scholarship Committee
P.O. Box 540345
Omaha, NE 68154
E-mail: aswaomaha@gmail.com
Web: www.aswaomaha.org

**Summary**　To provide financial assistance to women from any state working on an undergraduate or graduate degree in accounting at a school in Nebraska.

**Eligibility**　This program is open to women from any state enrolled part or full time in a bachelor's or master's degree program in accounting or finance at a college or university in Nebraska. Applicants must have completed at least 60 semester hours of a 4- or 5-year program. They must have a GPA of 3.0 or higher. Membership in the Accounting and Financial Women's Alliance (AFWA) is not required. Along with their application, they must submit an essay of 150 to 250 words on their career goals and objectives, the impact they want to have on the accounting world, community involvement, and leadership examples. Selection is based on leadership, character, communication skills, scholastic average, and financial need.

**Financial data**　The stipend is $2,000.

**Duration**　1 year.

**Number awarded**　Varies each year; recently, 3 of these scholarships (2 for undergraduates and 1 for a graduate student) were awarded.

**Deadline**　March of each year.

## [1091]
## ORGANIC CHEMISTRY GRADUATE STUDENT FELLOWSHIPS

American Chemical Society
Division of Organic Chemistry
1155 16th Street, N.W.
Washington, DC 20036
(202) 872-4401　　　　Toll Free: (800) 227-5558, ext. 4401
E-mail: division@acs.org
Web: www.organicdivision.org/?nd=graduate_fellowship

**Summary**　To provide funding for research to members of the Division of Organic Chemistry of the American Chemical Society (ACS), particular women and minorities, who are working on a doctoral degree in organic chemistry.

**Eligibility**　This program is open to members of the division who are entering the third or fourth year of a Ph.D. program in organic chemistry. Applicants must submit 3 letters of recommendation, a resume, and a short essay on a research area of their choice. U.S. citizenship or permanent resident status is required. Selection is based primarily on evidence of research accomplishment. Applications from women and minorities are especially encouraged.

**Financial data** The stipend is $26,000; that includes $750 for travel support to present a poster of their work at the National Organic Symposium.

**Duration** 1 year.

**Additional information** This program began in 1982. It includes the Emmanuil Troyansky Fellowship. Current corporate sponsors include Genentech, Organic Syntheses, Boehringer Ingelheim, and Amgen.

**Number awarded** Varies each year; recently, 8 of these fellowships were awarded.

**Deadline** May of each year.

## [1092]
## OUTPUTLINKS WOMAN OF DISTINCTION AWARD

Electronic Document Systems Foundation
Attn: EDSF Scholarship Awards
1845 Precinct Line Road, Suite 212
Hurst, TX 76054
(817) 849-1145                    Fax: (817) 849-1185
E-mail: info@edsf.org
Web: www.edsf.org/what_we_do/scholarships/index.html

**Summary** To provide financial assistance to female undergraduate and graduate students from any country interested in preparing for a career in document management and graphic communications.

**Eligibility** This program is open to full-time female undergraduate and graduate students from any country who demonstrate a strong interest in preparing for a career in the document management and graphic communications industry, including computer science and engineering (e.g., web design, webmaster, software development, materials engineer, applications specialist, information technology designer, systems analyst); graphic and media communications (e.g., graphic designer, illustrator, color scientist, print production, prepress imaging specialist, workflow specialist, document preparation, production and/or document distribution, content management, e-commerce, imaging science, printing, web authoring, electronic publishing, archiving, security); or business (e.g., sales, marketing, trade shows, customer service, project or product development, management). Preference is given to graduate students and upper-division undergraduates, but freshmen and sophomores who can show interest, experience, and/or commitment to the document management and graphic communication industry are encouraged to apply. Applicants must have a GPA of 3.0 or higher. Along with their application, they must submit 2 essays on assigned topics that change annually but relate to the document management and graphic communication industries. Selection is based on the essays, academic excellence, participation in school activities, community service, honors and organizational affiliations, education goals, and recommendations; financial need is not considered.

**Financial data** The stipend is $5,000.

**Duration** 1 year.

**Additional information** This program is sponsored by OutputLinks Communications Group.

**Number awarded** 1 each year.

**Deadline** April of each year.

## [1093]
## PATSY TAKEMOTO MINK EDUCATION FOUNDATION EDUCATION SUPPORT AWARD

Patsy Takemoto Mink Education Foundation for Low-Income Women and Children
P.O. Box 769
Granby, MA 01033
Web: www.patsyminkfoundation.org/edsupport.html

**Summary** To provide financial assistance for college or graduate school to low-income mothers.

**Eligibility** This program is open to women who are at least 17 years of age and are from a low-income family (less than $18,000 annually for a family of 2, $24,000 for a family of 3, or $27,000 for a family of 4). Applicants must be mothers with minor children. They must be 1) enrolled in a skills training, ESL, or GED program; or 2) working on a technical/vocational, associate, bachelor's, master's, professional, or doctoral degree. Along with their application, they must submit brief essays on what this award will help them accomplish, the program in which they are or will be enrolled, how they decided on that educational pursuit, their educational goals, their educational experience, and their personal and educational history.

**Financial data** The stipend is $3,000.

**Duration** 1 year.

**Additional information** This program began in 2003.

**Number awarded** Up to 6 each year.

**Deadline** July of each year.

## [1094]
## PEDRO ZAMORA PUBLIC POLICY FELLOWSHIP

AIDS United
Attn: Fellowship Coordinator
1424 K Street, N.W., Suite 200
Washington, DC 20005
(202) 408-4848, ext. 248                    Fax: (202) 408-1818
E-mail: Zamora@aidsunited.org
Web: www.aidsunited.org/about/jobs

**Summary** To provide work experience at AIDS United to female, minority, and other undergraduate and graduate students from diverse backgrounds who are interested in public policy.

**Eligibility** This program is open to undergraduate and graduate students who can demonstrate strong research, writing, and organizational skills and a willingness to work in a professional office. Familiarity with HIV-related issues and the legislative process is preferred. Applicants must 1) describe their participation in school or extracurricular activities related to HIV and AIDS (e.g., peer prevention programs, volunteer activities); 2) describe their participation in any school, work, or extracurricular activities related to advocacy (e.g., lobbying, political campaigns); 3) explain why they would be the best candidate for this fellowship; and 4) explain how they would use the skills they acquire from the fellowship. People of color, women, gay, lesbian, bisexual, transgender, and HIV-positive individuals are encouraged to apply.

**Financial data** A stipend is provided (amount not specified).

**Duration** From 8 to 26 weeks.

**Additional information** Responsibilities include assisting in researching a variety of public health and civil rights issues related to HIV prevention, treatment, and care; attending Congressional hearings and coalition meetings; monitoring voting records; reviewing the Federal Register and Congressional Record; and preparing correspondence, mailings, and briefing materials. AIDS United was formerly named AIDS Action. Fellows must commit to a minimum of 30 hours per week at AIDS United in Washington, D.C.

**Number awarded** Varies each year.

**Deadline** March of each year for summer; July of each year for fall; October of each year for spring.

## [1095]
## P.E.O. SCHOLAR AWARDS

P.E.O. Sisterhood
Attn: Scholar Awards Office
3700 Grand Avenue
Des Moines, IA 50312-2899
(515) 255-3153                    Fax: (515) 255-3820
E-mail: psa@peodsm.org
Web: www.peointernational.org/peo-projectsphilanthropies

**Summary** To provide funding for doctoral study in any field to women in the United States or Canada.

**Eligibility** This program is open to women who are working full time on a doctoral degree at universities in the United States or Canada. Students in master's degree, certificate, residency, specialization, or postdoctoral programs are not eligible. Applicants must be within 2 years of achieving their educational goal but have at least 1 full academic year remaining. They must be sponsored by a local P.E.O. chapter. Selection is based on academic record, academic awards and honors, scholarly activities, and recommendations; financial need is not considered. U.S. or Canadian citizenship is required.

**Financial data** The stipend is $15,000.

**Duration** 1 year; nonrenewable.

**Additional information** This program was established in 1991 by the Women's Philanthropic Educational Organization (P.E.O.).

**Number awarded** Varies each year.

**Deadline** November of each year.

## [1096]
## PETER B. WAGNER MEMORIAL AWARD FOR WOMEN IN ATMOSPHERIC SCIENCES

Desert Research Institute
Attn: Selection Committee, Wagner Award
2215 Raggio Parkway
Reno, NV 89512-1095
(702) 673-7300                    Fax: (702) 673-7397
E-mail: vera.samburova@dri.edu
Web: www.dri.edu

**Summary** To recognize and reward outstanding research papers written by women graduate students on atmospheric sciences.

**Eligibility** Women working on a master's or doctoral degree in atmospheric sciences or a related field are invited to submit a research paper for consideration. The applicants may be enrolled at a university anywhere in the United States. They must submit a paper, up to 15 pages in length, based on original research directly related to the identification, clarification, and/or resolution of an atmospheric/climatic problem. Selection is based on the originality of ideas expressed, presentation of concept, how well the subject matter relates to real-world atmospheric/climatic problems or their resolution, and how well the research is defined by the introduction, methods, results, and conclusions of the manuscript.

**Financial data** The award is $1,500.

**Duration** The award is presented annually.

**Additional information** This award was first presented in 1998.

**Number awarded** 1 each year.

**Deadline** April of each year.

## [1097]
## PHIPPS MEMORIAL SCHOLARSHIP

General Federation of Women's Clubs of Connecticut
c/o Nancy Kalyan, President
4 Mulberry Lane
Enfield, CT 06082
E-mail: KalyanGFWCC@aol.com
Web: www.gfwcct.org

**Summary** To provide financial assistance to women in Connecticut who are working on an undergraduate or graduate degree.

**Eligibility** This program is open to female residents of Connecticut who have completed at least 2 years of college. Applicants must have a GPA of 3.0 or higher and be working on a bachelor's or master's degree. They must be U.S. citizens. Selection is based on academic ability, future promise, and financial need.

**Financial data** The stipend is $1,000.

**Duration** 1 year.

**Number awarded** 1 each year.

**Deadline** February of each year.

## [1098]
## PHYLLIS V. ROBERTS SCHOLARSHIP

General Federation of Women's Clubs of Virginia
Attn: Scholarship Committee
513 Forest Avenue
P.O. Box 8750
Richmond, VA 23226
(804) 288-3724                    Toll Free: (800) 699-8392
Fax: (804) 288-0341
E-mail: scholarships@gfwcvirginia.org
Web: www.gfwcvirginia.org/forms.htm

**Summary** To provide financial assistance to women residents of Virginia who are working on a graduate degree in a designated field.

**Eligibility** This program is open to women residents of Virginia who are working on a graduate degree at a college or university in the state. The field of study varies each year. Applicants must have an undergraduate GPA of 3.0 or higher. Along with their application, they must submit 1) a short statement of their reason for choosing a graduate degree in the designated field; and 2) a resume that includes educational and employment history, community service, and awards received.

**Financial data** The stipend is $1,000. Funds are paid directly to the recipient's college or university.
**Duration** 1 year.
**Number awarded** 3 each year.
**Deadline** March of each year.

## [1099]
## PI BETA PHI ALUMNAE CONTINUING EDUCATION SCHOLARSHIPS

Pi Beta Phi
Attn: Pi Beta Phi Foundation
1154 Town and Country Commons Drive
Town and Country, MO 63017
(636) 256-1357          Fax: (636) 256-8124
E-mail: fndn@pibetaphi.org
Web: www.pibetaphifoundation.org/programs/scholarships

**Summary** To provide financial assistance for graduate school or continuing education to alumnae of Pi Beta Phi.
**Eligibility** This program is open to women who are members of Pi Beta Phi in good standing and have paid their alumnae dues for the current year. Applicants must have been out of undergraduate school for at least 2 years and have a GPA of 3.0 or higher for all undergraduate and graduate study. Advanced work at a college or university is encouraged, but advanced study at a career, vocational, or technical school will also be considered. Along with their application, they must submit documentation of financial need, an employment history, a record of volunteer service, a description of the proposed program of study, transcripts, and recommendations. Selection is based on financial need, academic record, alumnae service, community service, and how the proposed course of study relates to future career development.
**Financial data** Stipends range from $1,200 to $1,800.
**Duration** 1 year.
**Additional information** This program began in 1982.
**Number awarded** Varies each year; recently, 4 of these scholarships were awarded.
**Deadline** February of each year.

## [1100]
## PI BETA PHI GRADUATE FELLOWSHIPS

Pi Beta Phi
Attn: Pi Beta Phi Foundation
1154 Town and Country Commons Drive
Town and Country, MO 63017
(636) 256-1357          Fax: (636) 256-8124
E-mail: fndn@pibetaphi.org
Web: www.pibetaphifoundation.org/programs/scholarships

**Summary** To provide financial assistance for graduate school to members of Pi Beta Phi.
**Eligibility** This program is open to women who are dues-paying members in good standing of Pi Beta Phi (as a graduating senior or alumna) and graduated no more than 4 years previously. Applicants must be planning full-time graduate work at an accredited college, university, or technical professional school. They must have a GPA of 3.0 or higher for all undergraduate and graduate study. Selection is based on financial need, academic record, and service to the sorority, campus, and community.
**Financial data** Stipends range from $1,500 to $6,500.
**Duration** 1 year.

**Additional information** This program began in 1909. It includes the Past Grand Presidents Memorial Graduate Fellowship, the Corrine Hammond Gray Graduate Fellowship, the Joanie Arnold Graduate Fellowship, and the Elsie Lantz St. Cyr Graduate Fellowship.
**Number awarded** Varies each year; recently, 15 of these fellowships were awarded.
**Deadline** February of each year.

## [1101]
## PI STATE NATIVE AMERICAN GRANTS-IN-AID

Delta Kappa Gamma Society International-Pi State Organization
c/o Deborah Packard, Native American Committee Chair
232 Evergreen Road
Brockport, NY 14420-1140
(315) 657-2373          E-mail: dpackard@bataviacsd.org
Web: www.deltakappagamma.org/NY/ASaGiA.html

**Summary** To provide funding to Native American women from New York who plan to work in education or another service field.
**Eligibility** This program is open to Native American women from New York who are attending a 2- or 4-year college in the state. Applicants must be planning to work in education or another service field, but preference is given to those majoring in education. Both undergraduate and graduate students are eligible.
**Financial data** The grant is $500 per semester ($1,000 per year). Funds may be used for any career-related purpose, including purchase of textbooks.
**Duration** 1 semester; may be renewed for a total of 5 years and a total of $5,000 over a recipient's lifetime.
**Number awarded** Up to 5 each year.
**Deadline** February of each year.

## [1102]
## PREDOCTORAL RESEARCH TRAINING FELLOWSHIPS IN EPILEPSY

Epilepsy Foundation
Attn: Research Department
8301 Professional Place
Landover, MD 20785-2353
(301) 459-3700          Toll Free: (800) EFA-1000
Fax: (301) 577-2684          TDD: (800) 332-2070
E-mail: grants@efa.org
Web: www.epilepsyfoundation.org

**Summary** To provide funding to doctoral candidates (especially women, minorities, and persons with disabilities) in designated fields who are interested in conducting dissertation research on a topic related to epilepsy.
**Eligibility** This program is open to full-time graduate students working on a Ph.D. in biochemistry, genetics, neuroscience, nursing, pharmacology, pharmacy, physiology, or psychology. Applicants must be conducting dissertation research on a topic relevant to epilepsy under the guidance of a mentor with expertise in the area of epilepsy investigation. Applications from women, members of minority groups, and people with disabilities are especially encouraged. U.S. citizenship is not required, but the project must be conducted in the United States. Selection is based on the relevance of the proposed work to epilepsy, the applicant's qualifications, the mentor's

qualifications, the scientific quality of the proposed dissertation research, the quality of the training environment for research related to epilepsy, and the adequacy of the facility.

**Financial data** The grant is $20,000, consisting of $19,000 for a stipend and $1,000 to support travel to attend the annual meeting of the American Epilepsy Society.

**Duration** 1 year.

**Additional information** Support for this program, which began in 1998, is provided by many individuals, families, and corporations, especially the American Epilepsy Society, Abbott Laboratories, Ortho-McNeil Pharmaceutical, and Pfizer Inc.

**Number awarded** Varies each year.

**Deadline** August of each year.

## [1103]
## PUGET SOUND BUSINESS JOURNAL'S WOMEN OF INFLUENCE-LYTLE ENTERPRISES SCHOLARSHIP

Seattle Foundation
Attn: Scholarship Administrator
1200 Fifth Avenue, Suite 1300
Seattle, WA 98101-3151
(206) 622-2294                    Fax: (206) 622-7673
E-mail: scholarships@seattlefoundation.org
Web: www.seattlefoundation.org

**Summary** To provide financial assistance to women from any state working on a graduate business degree at a university in Washington.

**Eligibility** This program is open to women from any state who are working on a master's degree in business at an accredited college or university in Washington. Applicants must be able to demonstrate financial need. Along with their application, they must submit a 250-word essay about themselves, their educational and career achievements, and their goals. Nontraditional students, including returning students and older adults, are strongly encouraged to apply.

**Financial data** The stipend is $5,000.

**Duration** 1 year; nonrenewable.

**Additional information** This program began in 2006 with support from the Puget Sound Business Journal and Chuck and Karen Lytel. The recipient must attend the annual "Women of Influence" event in November.

**Number awarded** 1 or more each year.

**Deadline** March of each year.

## [1104]
## RACHEL ROYSTON PERMANENT SCHOLARSHIP

Delta Kappa Gamma Society International-Alpha Sigma
   State Organization
c/o Billie Hilton, Chair
Royston Scholarship Foundation
1825 South 68th Avenue
Yakima, WA 98908
E-mail: roystonscholarship@yahoo.com
Web: www.deltakappagamma.org/WA/rachel.html

**Summary** To provide financial assistance to women in Washington who are interested in working on a graduate degree in education at a university in any state.

**Eligibility** This program is open to women who are Washington residents doing graduate work in education at an

approved institution of higher learning in any state, working on either a master's or doctoral degree or in a field of special interest. Applicants must submit 300-word essays on 1) their long-term professional goal and its significance to the field of education; 2) the steps toward their goal they will complete during the scholarship time period; and 3) anything else they wish the committee to know. Selection is based on scholarship, professional service, potential for future service in education, and promise of distinction. A personal interview is required of all finalists.

**Financial data** The amount of each award is set at the discretion of the foundation's board of trustees. Awards generally range from $500 to $2,000.

**Duration** Awards may be made for 1 quarter, semester, or academic year. A recipient may, upon fulfilling certain conditions, reapply for a second award.

**Additional information** This program became operational in 1967.

**Number awarded** Varies each year; recently, 6 of these scholarships, with a value of $10,000, were awarded. Since the program began, 285 scholarships worth $534,640 have been awarded.

**Deadline** November of each year.

## [1105]
## RALPH W. SHRADER DIVERSITY SCHOLARSHIPS

Armed Forces Communications and Electronics
   Association
Attn: AFCEA Educational Foundation
4400 Fair Lakes Court
Fairfax, VA 22033-3899
(703) 631-6138          Toll Free: (800) 336-4583, ext. 6138
Fax: (703) 631-4693   E-mail: scholarshipsinfo@afcea.org
Web: www.afcea.org

**Summary** To provide financial assistance to female, minority, and other master's degree students in fields related to communications and electronics.

**Eligibility** This program is open to U.S. citizens working on a master's degree at an accredited college or university in the United States. Applicants must be enrolled full time and studying computer science, computer technology, engineering (chemical, electrical, electronic, communications, or systems), mathematics, physics, management information systems, or a field directly related to the support of U.S. national security or intelligence enterprises. At least 1 of these scholarships is set aside for a woman or a minority. Selection is based primarily on academic excellence.

**Financial data** The stipend is $3,000. Funds are paid directly to the recipient.

**Duration** 1 year.

**Additional information** This program is sponsored by Booz Allen Hamilton.

**Number awarded** Up to 5 each year, at least 1 of which is for a woman or minority candidate.

**Deadline** February of each year.

## [1106]
## RANDY GERSON MEMORIAL GRANT

American Psychological Foundation
750 First Street, N.E.
Washington, DC 20002-4242
(202) 336-5843                    Fax: (202) 336-5812
E-mail: foundation@apa.org
Web: www.apa.org/apf/funding/gerson.aspx

**Summary** To provide funding to graduate students (particularly women, minorities, and individuals with disabilities) who are interested in conducting research in the psychology of couple and/or family dynamics and/or multi-generational processes.

**Eligibility** This program is open to full-time graduate students in psychology. Applicants must be proposing a project that advances the systemic understanding of couple and/or family dynamics and/or multi-generational processes. Work that advances theory, assessment, or clinical practice in those areas is eligible. Preference is given to projects that use or contribute to the development of Bowen family systems. Selection is based on conformance with stated program goals, magnitude of incremental contribution, quality of proposed work, and applicant's demonstrated scholarship and research competence. The sponsor encourages applications from individuals who represent diversity in race, ethnicity, gender, age, disability, and sexual orientation.

**Financial data** The grant is $6,000.

**Duration** The grant is presented annually.

**Additional information** This grant was first awarded in 1998.

**Number awarded** 1 each year.

**Deadline** January of each year.

## [1107]
## REGION H SCHOLARSHIP

Society of Women Engineers
Attn: Scholarship Selection Committee
203 North LaSalle Street, Suite 1675
Chicago, IL 60601-1269
(312) 596-5223                    Toll Free: (877) SWE-INFO
Fax: (312) 644-8557        E-mail: scholarships@swe.org
Web: societyofwomenengineers.swe.org

**Summary** To provide financial assistance to members of the Society of Women Engineers (SWE) working on an undergraduate or graduate degree in engineering or computer science at a school in the upper Midwest (Region H).

**Eligibility** This program is open to members of the society who will be sophomores, juniors, seniors, or graduate students at ABET-accredited colleges and universities in Illinois, Indiana, Iowa, Michigan, Minnesota, North Dakota, South Dakota, or Wisconsin. Applicants must have a record of active involvement in SWE, based on the amount of time spent volunteering, level of commitment, and years of service. They must be working full time on a degree in computer science or engineering and have a GPA of 3.0 or higher. Selection is based on merit and participation in SWE activities.

**Financial data** The stipend is $1,500 or $1,000.

**Duration** 1 year.

**Number awarded** 2 each year: 1 at $1,500 and 1 at $1,000.

**Deadline** February of each year.

## [1108]
## REGIONAL SUMMER MUSIC SCHOLARSHIPS

Sigma Alpha Iota Philanthropies, Inc.
One Tunnel Road
Asheville, NC 28805
(828) 251-0606                    Fax: (828) 251-0644
E-mail: nh@sai-national.org
Web: www.sai-national.org

**Summary** To provide financial assistance for summer study in music, in the United States or abroad, to members of Sigma Alpha Iota (an organization of women musicians).

**Eligibility** This program is open to undergraduate and graduate student members of the organization who are planning to study at a summer music program in the United States or abroad. Applicants must submit a complete resume (including musical studies and activities, academic GPA, community service record, and record of participation in Sigma Alpha Iota), supporting materials (recital and concert programs, reviews, repertoire list, etc.), a statement of why they chose this program and how it will aid their musical growth, a full brochure of information on the program (including cost and payment due dates), a copy of the completed summer school application and acceptance letter (when available), and a letter of recommendation from their major teacher.

**Financial data** The stipend is $1,000.

**Duration** Summer months.

**Number awarded** 10 each year: 2 from each region of Sigma Alpha Iota.

**Deadline** March of each year.

## [1109]
## RESEARCH PROGRAM AT EARTHWATCH

Earthwatch Institute
Attn: Director of Research
114 Western Avenue
Boston, MA 02134
(978) 461-0081                    Toll Free: (800) 776-0188
Fax: (978) 461-2332     E-mail: research@earthwatch.org
Web: www.earthwatch.org/aboutus/research

**Summary** To support field research anywhere in the world by pre- and postdoctoral scientists (especially women) who are working to investigate and/or preserve our physical, biological, and cultural heritage.

**Eligibility** This program is open to doctoral and postdoctoral researchers and researchers with equivalent scholarship or life experience. Applicants must be interested in conducting field research worldwide in the sponsor's topic areas of 1) ecosystem services, including biodiversity conservation, sustainable agriculture, sustainable forestry, and freshwater; 2) climate change, including adaptation and mitigation; 3) oceans, including coastal ecosystems and marine biodiversity conservation; and 4) cultural heritage, including sacred landscapes and indigenous knowledge systems. They may be of any nationality and interested in conducting research in any geographic region, as long as the research design integrates non-specialist volunteers into the field research agenda. Applicants intending to conduct research in foreign countries are strongly encouraged to include host-country nationals in their research staffs. Early career scientists, women in science, and developing country nationals are especially encouraged to apply.

**Financial data** Grants are awarded on a per capita basis, determined by multiplying the per capita grant by the number of volunteers on the project. Per capita grants average $850; total project grants range from $17,000 to $51,000. Grants cover all expenses for food, accommodations, and in-field transportation for the research team (principal investigator, research staff, and volunteers); principal investigator travel to and from the field; leased or rented field equipment; insurance; support of staff and visiting scientists; and support for associates from the host country. Funds are not normally provided for capital equipment, principal investigator salaries, university overhead or indirect costs, or preparation of results for publication. Volunteers donate time, services, and skills to the research endeavor in the field and pay their own travel expenses to and from the research site.

**Duration** 1 year; may be renewed. Projects typically involve from 30 to 60 total volunteers, with 5 to 12 volunteers each on 4 to 5 sequential teams. Each team normally spends 8 to 15 days in the field.

**Additional information** Earthwatch was established in 1971 to support the efforts of scholars to preserve the world's endangered habitats and species, to explore the vast heritage of its peoples, and to promote world health and international cooperation. Its research program was formerly known as the Center for Field Research. Earthwatch also recruits and screens volunteers; in the past, 20% of these have been students, 20% educators, and 60% non-academic professionals.

**Number awarded** Varies each year; recently, 108 of these grants were awarded.

**Deadline** January of each year.

## [1110]
## RESOURCES FOR THE FUTURE SUMMER INTERNSHIPS

Resources for the Future
Attn: Internship Coordinator
1616 P Street, N.W., Suite 600
Washington, DC 20036-1400
(202) 328-5020          Fax: (202) 939-3460
E-mail: IC@rff.org
Web: www.rff.org

**Summary** To provide internships to undergraduate and graduate students (especially women and minorities) who are interested in working on research projects in public policy during the summer.

**Eligibility** This program is open to undergraduate and graduate students (with priority to graduate students) interested in an internship at Resources for the Future (RFF). Applicants must be working on a degree in the social and natural sciences and have training in economics and quantitative methods or an interest in public policy. They should display strong writing skills and a desire to analyze complex environmental policy problems amenable to interdisciplinary methods. The ability to work without supervision in a careful and conscientious manner is essential. Women and minority candidates are strongly encouraged to apply. Both U.S. and non-

U.S. citizens are eligible, if the latter have proper work and residency documentation.

**Financial data** The stipend is $375 per week for graduate students or $350 per week for undergraduates. Housing assistance is not provided.

**Duration** 10 weeks during the summer; beginning and ending dates can be adjusted to meet particular student needs.

**Number awarded** Varies each year.

**Deadline** February of each year.

## [1111]
## REV. MARTHA SINGLETARY SCHOLARSHIP FUND

United Methodist Church-New Mexico Conference
Attn: Board of Ordained Ministry
11816 Lomas Boulevard, N.E.
Albuquerque, NM 87112
(505) 255-8786, ext. 101          Toll Free: (800) 678-8786
Fax: (505) 265-6184  E-mail: mridgeway@nmconfum.com
Web: www.nmconfum.com

**Summary** To provide financial assistance to female Methodists from New Mexico who are interested in attending seminary in any state to prepare for a career in ordained ministry.

**Eligibility** This program is open to women who are enrolled or planning to enroll at a seminary in any state and who have an affiliation with a congregation of the New Mexico Conference of the United Methodist Church (UMC). Applicants must be preparing for a career in ordained ministry to local churches in the New Mexico Conference. Along with their application, they must submit brief essays on their current financial situation, how their sense of calling to ministry has changed or grown during the past year, the areas of ministry in which they are currently interested, what they believe to be their greatest spiritual gifts, and how they believe God is calling them to use those gifts in the local church.

**Financial data** A stipend is awarded (amount not specified).

**Duration** 1 year.

**Number awarded** 1 or more each year.

**Deadline** April of each year.

## [1112]
## RHODA D. HOOD MEMORIAL SCHOLARSHIP

Northwest Baptist Convention
Attn: Woman's Missionary Union
3200 N.E. 109th Avenue
Vancouver, WA 98682-7749
(360) 882-2100          Fax: (360) 882-2295
Web: www.nwbaptist.org

**Summary** To provide financial assistance to women from the Northwest who are attending college or seminary in any state to prepare for a career in vocational ministry, preferably with a Southern Baptist Convention church.

**Eligibility** This program is open to women who have been active members of a church affiliated with the Northwest Baptist Convention and a member of the Woman's Missionary Union within their church. Special consideration is given to women who are the children of ministers from the Northwest. Applicants must be attending or planning to attend an accredited college, university, or Southern Baptist seminary in any

state with the intention of serving in a vocational ministry position through a church or denomination; priority is given to applicants going into a mission vocation affiliated with the Southern Baptist Convention. Along with their application, they must submit 1) a written account of their conversion experience and their call to vocational ministry; and 2) a written endorsement from their church.

**Financial data** A stipend is awarded (amount not specified).

**Duration** 1 year; may be renewed if the recipient maintains a GPA of 2.5 or higher.

**Additional information** The Northwest Baptist Convention serves Oregon, Washington, and northern Idaho.

**Number awarded** 1 or more each year.

**Deadline** May of each year for fall term; October of each year for spring term.

## [1113]
## RHONDA J.B. O'LEARY MEMORIAL SCHOLARSHIP

Educational Foundation for Women in Accounting
Attn: Foundation Administrator
136 South Keowee Street
Dayton, OH 45402
(937) 424-3391                     Fax: (937) 222-5749
E-mail: info@efwa.org
Web: www.efwa.org/scholarships.php

**Summary** To provide financial support to women who are enrolled in an undergraduate or graduate accounting degree program at a school in Washington.

**Eligibility** This program is open to women from any state who are working on a bachelor's or master's degree in accounting at an accredited school in Washington. Selection is based on aptitude for accounting and business, commitment to the goal of working on a degree in accounting (including evidence of continued commitment after receiving this award), clear evidence that the candidate has established goals and a plan for achieving those goals (both personal and professional), and financial need. U.S. citizenship is required.

**Financial data** The stipend is $2,000 per year.

**Duration** 1 year; may be renewed 1 additional year if the recipient completes at least 12 hours each semester.

**Additional information** This program began in 2007 with funds provided by the Seattle Chapter of the American Society of Women Accountants (ASWA).

**Number awarded** 1 each year.

**Deadline** April of each year.

## [1114]
## RITA MAE KELLY ENDOWMENT FELLOWSHIP

American Political Science Association
Attn: Centennial Center Visiting Scholars Program
1527 New Hampshire Avenue, N.W.
Washington, DC 20036-1206
(202) 483-2512                     Fax: (202) 483-2657
E-mail: center@apsanet.org
Web: www.apsanet.org/content_3471.cfm

**Summary** To provide funding to women, minority, and other members of the American Political Science Association (APSA) who are interested in conducting research on the intersection of gender, race, ethnicity, and political power at the Centennial Center for Political Science and Public Affairs.

**Eligibility** This program is open to members of the association who are interested in conducting research on the intersection of gender, race, ethnicity, and political power while in residence at the center. Support is available to pre-dissertation graduate students as well as for an award or public presentation. Non-resident scholars may also be eligible.

**Financial data** Grants provide supplemental financial support to resident scholars.

**Duration** 2 weeks to 12 months.

**Additional information** The APSA launched its Centennial Center for Political Science and Public Affairs in 2003 to commemorate the centennial year of the association. This program was established in affiliation with the Women's Caucus for Political Science, the Latina Caucus for Political Science, the Committee for the Status of Latino/Latinas in the Profession, the Women and Politics Research Organized Section, and the Race, Ethnicity and Politics Organized Section.

**Number awarded** 1 or more each year.

**Deadline** February, June, or October of each year.

## [1115]
## ROBIN ROBERTS/WBCA BROADCASTING SCHOLARSHIP

Women's Basketball Coaches Association
Attn: Manager of Events, Awards and Office
  Administration
4646 Lawrenceville Highway
Lilburn, GA 30047-3620
(770) 279-8027, ext. 110              Fax: (770) 279-8473
E-mail: dtrujillo@wbca.org
Web: www.wbca.org/robertsaward.asp

**Summary** To provide financial assistance for graduate study in sports communications to women's basketball players.

**Eligibility** This program is open to women's college basketball players who are seniors planning to work on a graduate degree in sports communication and journalism. Applicants must be nominated by a member of the Women's Basketball Coaches Association (WBCA). Selection is based on a letter of recommendation, academic major and GPA, basketball statistics for all 4 years of college, and campus activities.

**Financial data** The stipend is $4,000.

**Duration** 1 year.

**Additional information** This program began in 2001.

**Number awarded** 1 each year.

**Deadline** Deadline not specified.

## [1116]
## ROCKY MOUNTAIN SECTION COLLEGE SCHOLARSHIPS

Society of Women Engineers-Rocky Mountain Section
Attn: Collegiate Scholarship Committee Chair
P.O. Box 260692
Lakewood, CO 80226-0692
(303) 751-0741                     Fax: (303) 751-2581
E-mail: christi.wisleder@gmail.copm
Web: www.societyofwomenengineers.org

**Summary**   To provide financial assistance to women from any state who are working on an undergraduate or graduate degree in engineering at colleges and universities in Colorado and Wyoming.

**Eligibility**   This program is open to women from any state who are enrolled as an undergraduate or graduate engineering student in an ABET-accredited engineering or computer science program in Colorado or Wyoming (excluding zip codes 80800-81599). Applicants must have a GPA of 3.0 or higher. Along with their application, they must submit an essay on why they have chosen an engineering major, what they will accomplish or how they believe they will make a difference as an engineer, and who or what influenced them to study engineering. Selection is based on merit.

**Financial data**   The stipend is $1,250.

**Duration**   1 year.

**Additional information**   This program includes the following named scholarships: the Dorolyn Lines Scholarship, the Lottye Miner Scholarship, and the Rocky Mountain Section Pioneer Scholarship.

**Number awarded**   3 each year.

**Deadline**   January of each year.

## [1117]
## ROWDY AND LUCKY SHAIN SCHOLARSHIP

Chi Omega Fraternity
Attn: Chi Omega Foundation
3395 Players Club Parkway
Memphis, TN 38125
(901) 748-8600                    Fax: (901) 748-8686
E-mail: foundation@chiomega.com
Web: www.chiomega.com/wemakeadifference/scholarships

**Summary**   To provide financial assistance to women who are collegian or alumnae members of Chi Omega Fraternity studying animal welfare or veterinary medicine.

**Eligibility**   This program is open to women who are collegian or alumnae members of Chi Omega Fraternity. Applicants must be working on an undergraduate or graduate degree in animal welfare or veterinary medicine. Selection is based on an essay, academic aptitude, service to Chi Omega, contributions to the university and community, personal and professional goals, and financial need.

**Financial data**   The stipend is $1,000.

**Duration**   1 year.

**Additional information**   This program began in 2012 with a gift from foundation trustee Melanie Maxwell Shain and her husband John who wished to honor their 2 cats.

**Number awarded**   1 each year.

**Deadline**   April of each year.

## [1118]
## ROY SCRIVNER MEMORIAL RESEARCH GRANTS

American Psychological Foundation
750 First Street, N.E.
Washington, DC 20002-4242
(202) 336-5843                    Fax: (202) 336-5812
E-mail: foundation@apa.org
Web: www.apa.org/apf/funding/scrivner.aspx

**Summary**   To provide funding to graduate students interested in conducting dissertation research on lesbian, gay, bisexual, and transgender (LGBT) family psychology and therapy.

**Eligibility**   This program is open to doctoral candidates who are interested in conducting empirical research in all fields of the behavioral and social sciences that focus on LGBT family psychology and LGBT family therapy. Proposals are especially encouraged for empirical studies that address the following: problems faced by LGBT families such as those associated with cultural, racial, socioeconomic, and family structure diversity; successful coping mechanisms such as sources of support and resilience for family members; and clinical issues and interventions in the domain of LGBT. Selection is based on conformance with stated program goals, magnitude of incremental contribution, quality of proposed work, and applicant's demonstrated scholarship and research competence. The sponsor encourages applications from individuals who represent diversity in race, ethnicity, gender, age, disability, and sexual orientation.

**Financial data**   The grant is $12,000.

**Duration**   1 year.

**Number awarded**   1 each year.

**Deadline**   October of each year.

## [1119]
## RUKMINI AND JOYCE VASUDEVAN SCHOLARSHIP

Wisconsin Medical Society
Attn: Wisconsin Medical Society Foundation
330 East Lakeside Street
Madison, WI 53715
(608) 442-3789          Toll Free: (866) 442-3800, ext. 3789
Fax: (608) 442-3851 E-mail: elizabeth.ringle@wismed.org
Web: www.wisconsinmedicalsociety.org

**Summary**   To provide financial assistance to female students enrolled at medical schools in Wisconsin.

**Eligibility**   This program is open to women who are entering their third or fourth year of full-time study at a medical school in Wisconsin. Applicants must submit a personal statement of 1 to 2 pages on their family background, achievements, current higher educational status, career goals, and financial need; their statement should include examples of their compassion, caring, and courage or hard work despite adversity or obstacles in life. Preference is given to residents of Wisconsin, those close to completing their degree, and those who demonstrate ties to their community and a desire to practice in Wisconsin. U.S. citizenship is required. Selection is based on financial need, academic achievement, personal qualities and strengths, and letters of recommendation.

**Financial data**   A stipend is awarded (amount not specified).

**Duration**   1 year.

**Number awarded**   1 each year.

**Deadline**   January of each year.

## [1120]
## RUTH AND LINCOLN EKSTROM FELLOWSHIP

Brown University
John Carter Brown Library
Attn: Fellowships Coordinator
P.O. Box 1894
Providence, RI 02912
(401) 863-5010          Fax: (401) 863-3477
E-mail: Valerie_Andrews@Brown.edu
Web: www.brown.edu

**Summary**  To support scholars and graduate students interested in conducting research on the history of women at the John Carter Brown Library, which is renowned for its collection of historical sources pertaining to the Americas prior to 1830.

**Eligibility**  This fellowship is open to U.S-based and foreign graduate students, scholars, and independent researchers. Graduate students must have passed their preliminary or general examinations. Applicants must be proposing to conduct research on the history of women and the family in the Americas prior to 1825, including the question of cultural influences on gender formation. Selection is based on the applicant's scholarly qualifications, the merits and significance of the project, and the particular need that the holdings of the John Carter Brown Library will fill in the development of the project.

**Financial data**  The stipend is $2,100 per month.

**Duration**  From 2 to 4 months.

**Additional information**  Fellows are expected to be in regular residence at the library and to participate in the intellectual life of Brown University for the duration of the program.

**Number awarded**  1 or more each year.

**Deadline**  December of each year.

## [1121]
## RUTH BADER GINSBURG SCHOLARSHIP

Alpha Epsilon Phi
Attn: AEPhi Foundation
11 Lake Avenue Extension, Suite 1A
Danbury, CT 06811
(203) 748-0029          Fax: (203) 748-0039
E-mail: aephifoundation@aephi.org
Web: www.aephi.org/foundation/scholarships

**Summary**  To provide financial assistance to Alpha Epsilon Phi alumnae, especially those entering the second year of law school.

**Eligibility**  This program is open to alumnae members of the sorority, preferably those entering their second year of law school. Applicants must have a GPA of 3.0 or higher. They must be able to demonstrate academic excellence and financial need.

**Financial data**  Stipends range from $1,000 to $2,000 per year.

**Duration**  1 year; may be renewed.

**Number awarded**  1 or more each year.

**Deadline**  March of each year.

## [1122]
## RUTH G. WHITE P.E.O. SCHOLARSHIP

P.E.O. Foundation-California State Chapter
c/o Lynne Miller, Scholarship Committee Chair
1875 Los Altos
Clovis, CA 93611
(559) 709-6123          E-mail: peoca.rgw@gmail.com
Web: www.peocalifornia.org

**Summary**  To provide financial assistance to women from California who are interested in working on a medical-related degree at a graduate school in any state.

**Eligibility**  This program is open to female residents of California who have completed their first year of graduate work in the field of medicine. Applicants may be studying in any state. They must submit a personal narrative that describes their background, interests, scholastic achievements, extracurricular activities, service, talents, and goals. Selection is based on character, integrity, academic excellence, and financial need.

**Financial data**  Stipends recently averaged $4,320.

**Duration**  1 year; recipients may reapply.

**Additional information**  This fund was established in 1957.

**Number awarded**  Varies each year; recently, 12 of these scholarships were awarded.

**Deadline**  January of each year.

## [1123]
## RUTH H. BUFTON SCHOLARSHIP

American Business Women's Association
Attn: Stephen Bufton Memorial Educational Fund
11050 Roe Avenue, Suite 200
Overland Park, KS 66211
Toll Free: (800) 228-0007
Web: www.sbmef.org/Scholarships.cfm

**Summary**  To provide financial assistance to female graduate students who are working on a degree in a specified field (the field changes each year).

**Eligibility**  This program is open to women who are working on a graduate degree and have a cumulative GPA of 3.0 or higher. Applicants are not required to be members of the American Business Women's Association. Along with their application, they must submit a 250-word biographical sketch that includes information about their background, activities, honors, work experience, and long-term educational and professional goals. Financial need is not considered in the selection process. Annually, the trustees designate an academic discipline for which the scholarship will be presented that year. U.S. citizenship is required.

**Financial data**  The stipend is $10,000 (paid over a 2-year period). Funds are paid directly to the recipient's institution to be used only for tuition, books, and fees.

**Duration**  2 years.

**Additional information**  This program was created in 1986 as part of ABWA's Stephen Bufton Memorial Education Fund. The ABWA does not provide the names and addresses of local chapters; it recommends that applicants check with their local Chamber of Commerce, library, or university to see if any chapter has registered a contact's name and number.

**Number awarded**  1 each odd-numbered year.

**Deadline**  May of each odd-numbered year.

## [1124]
## RUTH R. AND ALYSON R. MILLER FELLOWSHIPS

Massachusetts Historical Society
Attn: Short-Term Fellowships
1154 Boylston Street
Boston, MA 02215-3695
(617) 646-0568          Fax: (617) 859-0074
E-mail: fellowships@masshist.org
Web: www.masshist.org/research/fellowships/short-term

**Summary** To fund research visits to the Massachusetts Historical Society for graduate students and other scholars interested in women's history.

**Eligibility** This program is open to advanced graduate students, postdoctorates, and independent scholars who are conducting research in women's history and need to use the resources of the Massachusetts Historical Society. Applicants must be U.S. citizens or foreign nationals holding appropriate U.S. government documents. Along with their application, they must submit a curriculum vitae and a proposal describing the project and indicating collections at the society to be consulted. Graduate students must also arrange for a letter of recommendation from a faculty member familiar with their work and with the project being proposed. Preference is given to candidates who live 50 or more miles from Boston.

**Financial data** The grant is $2,000.

**Duration** 4 weeks.

**Additional information** This fellowship was first awarded in 1998.

**Number awarded** 1 or more each year.

**Deadline** February of each year.

## [1125]
## RUTH ROSENBAUM GOLDFEDER MEMORIAL SCHOLARSHIP

Alpha Epsilon Phi
Attn: AEPhi Foundation
11 Lake Avenue Extension, Suite 1A
Danbury, CT 06811
(203) 748-0029          Fax: (203) 748-0039
E-mail: aephifoundation@aephi.org
Web: www.aephi.org/foundation/scholarships

**Summary** To provide financial assistance for undergraduate or graduate education to Alpha Epsilon Phi members or alumnae, especially those at California universities.

**Eligibility** This program is open to active and alumnae members of the sorority who are either full-time rising juniors or seniors or graduate students who have completed at least 1 year of graduate study. Preference is given to members at universities in California. Applicants must have a GPA of 3.0 or higher. Along with their application, they must submit a letter describing 1) their activities in their chapter, on campus, and in the general community; 2) what they have done to supplement their parents' contribution toward their education; and 3) their need for scholarship consideration.

**Financial data** Stipends range from $1,000 to $2,000 per year.

**Duration** 1 year; may be renewed.

**Additional information** Recipients must be willing to remain active in the sorority and live in the sorority house (if any) for the entire year the scholarship covers.

**Number awarded** 1 or more each year.

**Deadline** March of each year.

## [1126]
## RUTH WHITNEY SCHOLARSHIP

New York Women in Communications, Inc.
Attn: NYWICI Foundation
355 Lexington Avenue, 15th Floor
New York, NY 10017-6603
(212) 297-2133          Fax: (212) 370-9047
E-mail: nywicipr@nywici.org
Web: www.nywici.org/foundation/scholarships

**Summary** To provide financial assistance to female residents of designated eastern states who are interested in preparing for a career in magazine journalism or publishing at a college or graduate school in any state.

**Eligibility** This program is open to women who are residents of New York, New Jersey, Connecticut, or Pennsylvania and enrolled as undergraduate or graduate students at a college or university in any state. Graduate students must be members of New York Women in Communications, Inc. (NYWICI). Also eligible are women who reside outside the 4 states but are currently enrolled at a college or university within 1 of the 5 boroughs of New York City. Applicants must have some experience in writing, reporting, or design and be preparing for a career in magazine journalism or publishing. Along with their application, they must submit a 2-page resume; a personal essay of 300 words on an assigned topic that changes annually; 2 letters of recommendation; and an official transcript. Selection is based on academic record, need, demonstrated leadership, participation in school and community activities, honors and other awards or recognition, work experience, goals and aspirations, and unusual personal and/or family circumstances. U.S. citizenship is required.

**Financial data** The stipend ranges up to $10,000.

**Duration** 1 year.

**Additional information** This program is sponsored by *Glamour* magazine, which invites the recipient to visit its offices and spend a week with its editorial team.

**Number awarded** 1 each year.

**Deadline** January of each year.

## [1127]
## RUTHANN FAIRBAIRN SCHOLARSHIP

Oklahoma Society of Certified Public Accountants
Attn: OSCPA Educational Foundation
1900 N.W. Expressway, Suite 910
Oklahoma City, OK 73118-1898
(405) 841-3811
Toll Free: (800) 522-8261, ext. 3811 (within OK)
Fax: (405) 841-3801          E-mail: hjared@oscpa.com
Web: www.oscpa.com/?524

**Summary** To provide financial assistance to female members of the Oklahoma Society of Certified Public Accountants (OSCPA) working on a bachelor's or advanced degree in accounting in Oklahoma.

**Eligibility** This program is open to female OSCPA members who are nominated by an accounting program at an Oklahoma college or university. Nominees must be working on a bachelor's or advanced degree in accounting and have successfully completed at least 6 hours of principles of accounting. As part of the selection process, they must submit a resume, a transcript, standardized test scores, and 3 letters of reference.

**Financial data** The stipend ranges from $250 to $1,500.

**Duration** 1 year.

**Number awarded** 1 each year.

**Deadline** March of each year.

## [1128]
## S. EVELYN LEWIS MEMORIAL SCHOLARSHIP IN MEDICAL HEALTH SCIENCES

Zeta Phi Beta Sorority, Inc.
Attn: National Education Foundation
1734 New Hampshire Avenue, N.W.
Washington, DC 20009
(202) 387-3103                    Fax: (202) 232-4593
E-mail: scholarship@ZPhiBNEF.org
Web: www.zphib1920.org/nef

**Summary** To provide financial assistance to women interested in studying medicine or health sciences on the undergraduate or graduate school level.

**Eligibility** This program is open to women enrolled full time in a program on the undergraduate or graduate school level leading to a degree in medicine or health sciences. Proof of enrollment is required. Applicants need not be members of Zeta Phi Beta Sorority. Along with their application, they must submit a 150-word essay on their educational goals and professional aspirations, how this award will help them to achieve those goals, and why they should receive the award. Financial need is not considered in the selection process.

**Financial data** The stipend ranges from $500 to $1,000. Funds are paid directly to the college or university.

**Duration** 1 academic year.

**Number awarded** 1 or more each year.

**Deadline** January of each year.

## [1129]
## SADIE T.M. ALEXANDER SCHOLARSHIP

Delta Sigma Theta Sorority, Inc.
Attn: Scholarship and Standards Committee Chair
1707 New Hampshire Avenue, N.W.
Washington, DC 20009
(202) 986-2400                    Fax: (202) 986-2513
E-mail: dstemail@deltasigmatheta.org
Web: www.deltasigmatheta.org

**Summary** To provide financial assistance to members of Delta Sigma Theta who are interested in preparing for a career in law.

**Eligibility** This program is open to graduating college seniors and students who are currently enrolled in law school. Applicants must be active, dues-paying members of Delta Sigma Theta. Selection is based on meritorious achievement.

**Financial data** The stipends range from $1,000 to $2,000 per year. The funds may be used to cover tuition and living expenses.

**Duration** 1 year; may be renewed for 1 additional year.

**Additional information** This sponsor is a traditionally African American social sorority. The application fee is $20.

**Number awarded** 1 or more each year.

**Deadline** April of each year.

## [1130]
## SARA OWEN ETHERIDGE STUDENT SCHOLARSHIP

Baptist Women in Ministry of Georgia
c/o Darlene Flaming, Scholarship Committee Chair
1400 Coleman Avenue
Macon, GA 31207
E-mail: rachel.heaven0784@gmail.com
Web: www.bwimga.org/scholarship-info.asp

**Summary** To provide financial assistance to Baptist women from Georgia who are working on a graduate degree in theology at a seminary in any state.

**Eligibility** This program is open to women who are, or have been, residents of Georgia. Applicants must be Baptists who have completed at least 30 hours of study for a master's or doctoral degree at a seminary in any state. Along with their application, they must submit a brief narrative that includes a summary of their call to ministry, plans for carrying out their ministry, an autobiography, and a description of any ministry experience that illustrate their gifts for ministry.

**Financial data** The stipend is $1,500.

**Duration** 1 year.

**Number awarded** 1 or 2 each year.

**Deadline** February of each year.

## [1131]
## SARAH BRADLEY TYSON MEMORIAL FELLOWSHIP

Woman's National Farm and Garden Association, Inc.
Attn: Vice President and Communications Director
505 East Willow Grove Avenue
Wyndmoor, PA 19038
E-mail: matynjm@att.net
Web: www.wnfga.org/scholarships/fellowships

**Summary** To provide funding to women with prior work experience who are interested in working on an advanced study in agriculture, horticulture, and allied subjects.

**Eligibility** The fellowship is open to women interested in working on an advanced degree in the fields of agriculture, horticulture, or allied subjects at educational institutions of recognized standing within the United States. Applicants must have several years of experience. There are no application forms. Interested women should send a letter of application that contains an account of their educational training, a plan of study, references, samples of publishable papers, and a health certificate.

**Financial data** The fellowship award is $1,000 and is tenable at an American institution of higher learning chosen by the candidate with the approval of the fellowship committee.

**Duration** 1 year.

**Additional information** This program began in 1928. Students who accept the fellowships must agree to devote themselves to the study outlined in their application and to submit any proposed change in their plan to the committee for approval. They must send the committee at least 2 reports on their work, 1 at the end of the first semester and another upon completion of the year's work.

**Number awarded** Varies each year.

**Deadline** April of each year.

## [1132]
## SBE DOCTORAL DISSERTATION RESEARCH IMPROVEMENT GRANTS

National Science Foundation
Attn: Directorate for Social, Behavioral, and Economic Sciences
4201 Wilson Boulevard, Room 905N
Arlington, VA 22230
(703) 292-8700                    Fax: (703) 292-9083
TDD: (800) 281-8749
Web: www.nsf.gov/funding/pgm_summ.jsp?pims_id=13453

**Summary** To provide partial support to doctoral candidates (especially women, minorities, and persons with disabilities) who are conducting dissertation research in areas of interest to the Directorate for Social, Behavioral, and Economic Sciences (SBE) of the National Science Foundation (NSF).

**Eligibility** Applications may be submitted through regular university channels by dissertation advisers on behalf of graduate students who have advanced to candidacy and have begun or are about to begin dissertation research. Students must be enrolled at U.S. institutions, but they need not be U.S. citizens. The proposed research must relate to SBE's Division of Behavioral and Cognitive Sciences (archaeology, cultural anthropology, documenting endangered languages, geography and spatial sciences, linguistics, or biological anthropology); Division of Social and Economic Sciences (decision, risk, and management science; economics; law and social science; methodology, measurement, and statistics; political science; sociology; or science, technology, and society); National Center for Science and Engineering Statistics (science and technology surveys and statistics); or Office of Multidisciplinary Activities (science and innovation policy). Women, minorities, and persons with disabilities are strongly encouraged to apply.

**Financial data** Grants have the limited purpose of providing funds to enhance the quality of dissertation research. They are to be used exclusively for necessary expenses incurred in the actual conduct of the dissertation research, including (but not limited to) conducting field research in settings away from campus that would not otherwise be possible, data collection and sample survey costs, payments to subjects or informants, specialized research equipment, analysis and services not otherwise available, supplies, travel to archives, travel to specialized facilities or field research locations, and partial living expenses for conducting necessary research away from the student's U.S. academic institution. Funding is not provided for stipends, tuition, textbooks, journals, allowances for dependents, travel to scientific meetings, publication costs, dissertation preparation or reproduction, or indirect costs.

**Duration** Up to 2 years.

**Number awarded** 200 to 300 each year. Approximately $2.5 million is available for this program annually.

**Deadline** Deadline dates for the submission of dissertation improvement grant proposals differ by program within the divisions of the SBE Directorate; applicants should obtain information regarding target dates for proposals from the relevant program.

## [1133]
## SCHLESINGER LIBRARY DOCTORAL DISSERTATION GRANTS

Radcliffe Institute for Advanced Study at Harvard University
Attn: Arthur and Elizabeth Schlesinger Library
10 Garden Street
Cambridge, MA 02138
(617) 495-8647                    Fax: (617) 496-8340
E-mail: slgrants@radcliffe.harvard.edu
Web: www.radcliffe.harvard.edu/schlesinger-library/grants

**Summary** To provide funding to doctoral students who need to use the holdings of the Arthur and Elizabeth Schlesinger Library on the History of Women in America to complete their dissertation.

**Eligibility** Applicants must be enrolled in a doctoral program in a relevant field, have completed their course work toward the doctoral degree, and have an approved dissertation topic by the time application is made. Priority is given to those whose projects require use of materials available nowhere else but the Schlesinger Library. The project description should indicate the purpose of the research, the Schlesinger Library holdings to be consulted, and the significance of those holdings to the project overall. Selection is based on the significance of the research, the project's potential contribution to the advancement of knowledge, and its creativity in using the library's holdings.

**Financial data** Grants range up to $3,000. Funds must be used to cover travel, living expenses, photocopying, and other incidental research expenses.

**Duration** Up to 1 year.

**Additional information** The Schlesinger Library is a non-circulating research library that documents the history of women in the United States during the 19th and 20th centuries. Recipients must present the results of their research in a colloquium at the library, give the library a copy of the completed dissertation, and acknowledge the program's support in the dissertation and any resulting publications.

**Number awarded** Varies each year; recently, 11 of these grants were awarded.

**Deadline** March of each year.

## [1134]
## SCHOLARSHIPS FOR WOMEN RESIDENTS OF THE STATE OF DELAWARE

American Association of University Women-Wilmington Branch
Attn: Scholarship Committee
1800 Fairfax Boulevard
Wilmington, DE 19803-3106
(302) 737-6447                    E-mail: aauwwilm@gmail.com
Web: www.aauwwilmington.org/procedure.html

**Summary** To provide financial assistance to female residents of Delaware who plan to attend college in any state.

**Eligibility** This program is open to women who are U.S. citizens and 1) a Delaware resident and a high school graduate; 2) a Delaware resident and a senior at a high school in New Castle County; or 3) a resident of New Castle County, Delaware and a home-schooled student who can meet the admission requirements of the University of Delaware. Applicants must be attending or planning to attend a college or university in any state. Along with their application, they must submit a 150-word essay on what they plan to study and why. High school seniors must also submit a 150-word essay on either 1) what they would do and where they would do it if they had 4 hours to spend any place, either now or in history; or 2) the famous person, past or present, they would like to meet and why. Selection is based on scholastic standing, contributions to school and community, SAT scores, and financial need. An interview is required.

**Financial data** A stipend is awarded (amount not specified).

**Duration** 1 year.

**Number awarded** Varies each year; recently, 17 of these scholarships, worth $55,000, were awarded.

**Deadline** February of each year.

## [1135]
## SCHOLARSHIPS SUPPORTING POST-SECONDARY EDUCATION FOR A CAREER IN THE AUDIOVISUAL INDUSTRY

InfoComm International
International Communications Industries Foundation
11242 Waples Mill Road, Suite 200
Fairfax, VA 22030
(703) 273-7200             Toll Free: (800) 659-7469
Fax: (703) 278-8082     E-mail: jhardwick@infocomm.org
Web: www.infocomm.org

**Summary** To provide financial assistance to undergraduate and graduate students (especially women and minorities) who are interested in preparing for a career in the audiovisual (AV) industry.

**Eligibility** This program is open to second-year students at 2-year colleges, juniors and seniors at 4-year institutions, and graduate students. Applicants must have a GPA of 2.75 or higher and be majoring or planning to major in audiovisual subjects or related fields, including audio, video, audiovisual, radio/television/film, or other field related to a career in the audiovisual industry. Students in other programs, such as journalism, may be eligible if they can demonstrate a relationship to career goals in the AV industry. Along with their application, they must submit 1) an essay of 150 to 200 words on the career path they plan to pursue in the audiovisual industry in the next 5 years; and 2) an essay of 250 to 300 words on the experience or person influencing them the most in selecting the audiovisual industry as their career of choice. Minority and women candidates are especially encouraged to apply. Selection is based on the essays, presentation of the application, GPA, AV-related experience, work experience, and letters of recommendation.

**Financial data** The stipend is $4,000. Funds are sent directly to the school.

**Duration** 1 year.

**Additional information** InfoComm International, formerly the International Communications Industries Association, established the International Communications Industries Foundation (ICIF) to manage its charitable and educational activities.

**Number awarded** Varies each year.

**Deadline** April of each year.

## [1136]
## SCOTT AND PAUL PEARSALL SCHOLARSHIP

American Psychological Foundation
750 First Street, N.E.
Washington, DC 20002-4242
(202) 336-5843                              Fax: (202) 336-5812
E-mail: foundation@apa.org
Web: www.apa.org/apf/funding/pearsall.aspx

**Summary** To provide funding to graduate students (particularly women and others with diverse backgrounds) who are interested in conducting research on the psychological effect of stigma on people with disabilities.

**Eligibility** This program is open to full-time graduate students at accredited universities in the United States and Canada. Applicants must be interested in conducting research that seeks to increase the public's understanding of the psychological pain and stigma experiences by adults living with physical disabilities, such as cerebral palsy. Selection is based on conformance with stated program goals and the quality of proposed work. The sponsor encourages applications from individuals who represent diversity in race, ethnicity, gender, age, disability, and sexual orientation.

**Financial data** The grant is $10,000.

**Duration** 1 year.

**Additional information** This program began in 2013.

**Number awarded** 1 each year.

**Deadline** September of each year.

## [1137]
## SEATTLE CHAPTER AFWA SCHOLARSHIPS

Accounting and Financial Women's Alliance-Seattle
  Chapter
Attn: Scholarships
800 Fifth Avenue, Suite 101
PMB 237
Seattle, WA 98104-3191
(206) 467-8645       E-mail: scholarship@aswaseattle.com
Web: www.aswaseattle.com/scholarships.cfm

**Summary** To provide financial assistance to women from any state working on an undergraduate or graduate degree in accounting at a college or university in Washington.

**Eligibility** This program is open to female residents of any state who are working part time or full time on an associate, bachelor's, or master's degree in accounting at a college or university in Washington. Applicants must have completed at least 30 semester hours and have maintained a GPA of at least 2.5 overall and 3.0 in accounting. Membership in the Accounting and Financial Women's Alliance (AFWA) is not required. Selection is based on career goals, communication skills, GPA, personal circumstances, and financial need.

**Financial data** Stipends range from $1,500 to $5,000.

**Duration** 1 year.

**Additional information** This program began in 1962.

**Number awarded** Varies each year; recently, 8 of these scholarships were awarded: 1 at $5,000, 2 at $3,000, and 5 at $2,000. Since the program began, it has awarded nearly $250,000 in scholarships.

**Deadline** June of each year.

## [1138]
## SEATTLE PROFESSIONAL CHAPTER AWC SCHOLARSHIPS

Association for Women in Communications-Seattle
  Professional Chapter
Attn: Tina Christiansen, Vice-president of Student Affairs
P.O. Box 60262
Seattle, WA 98160
E-mail: tina@writeasrain.com
Web: www.seattleawc.org

**Summary** To provide financial assistance to female upper-division and graduate students in Washington who are preparing for a career in the communications industry.

**Eligibility** This program is open to female Washington state residents who are enrolled at a 4-year college or university in the state as a junior, senior, or graduate student (sophomores at 2-year colleges applying to a 4-year institution are also eligible). Applicants must be working on or planning to work on a degree in a communications program, including print and broadcast journalism, television and radio production, film, advertising, public relations, marketing, graphic design, multimedia design, photography, or technical communication. Selection is based on demonstrated excellence in communications, contributions made to communications on campus and/or in the community, scholastic achievement, financial need, and work samples.

**Financial data** The stipend is $1,500. Funds are paid directly to the recipient's school and must be used for tuition and fees.

**Duration** 1 year.

**Number awarded** 2 each year.

**Deadline** April of each year.

## [1139]
## SECTION OF BUSINESS LAW DIVERSITY CLERKSHIP PROGRAM

American Bar Association
Attn: Section of Business Law
321 North Clark Street
Chicago, IL 60654-7598
(312) 988-6398                    Fax: (312) 988-5578
E-mail: businesslaw@abanet.org
Web: www.americanbar.org

**Summary** To provide summer work experience in business law to female and other student members of the American Bar Association (ABA) and its Section of Business Law who will help the section to fulfill its goal of promoting diversity.

**Eligibility** This program is open to first- and second-year students at ABA-accredited law schools who are interested in a summer business court clerkship. Applicants must 1) be a member of an underrepresented group (student of color, woman, student with disabilities, gay, lesbian, bisexual, or transgender); or 2) have overcome social or economic disadvantages, such as a physical disability, financial constraints, or cultural impediments to becoming a law student. They must be able to demonstrate financial need. Along with their application, they must submit a 500-word essay that covers why they are interested in this clerkship program, what they would gain from the program, how it would positively influence their future professional goals as a business lawyer, and how they meet the program's criteria. Membership in the ABA and its Section of Business Law are required.

**Financial data** The stipend is $6,000.

**Duration** Summer months.

**Additional information** This program began in 2008. Assignments vary, but have included business courts in Delaware, Illinois, Maryland, Pennsylvania, and South Carolina.

**Number awarded** 9 each year.

**Deadline** December of each year.

## [1140]
## SELECTED PROFESSIONS FELLOWSHIPS

American Association of University Women
Attn: AAUW Educational Foundation
301 ACT Drive, Department 60
P.O. Box 4030
Iowa City, IA 52243-4030
(319) 337-1716, ext. 60          Fax: (319) 337-1204
E-mail: aauw@act.org
Web: www.aauw.org

**Summary** To aid women who are working on a master's degree in the fields of architecture, computer science, information science, engineering, mathematics, or statistics.

**Eligibility** This program is open to women who are U.S. citizens or permanent residents and who intend to pursue their professional careers in the United States. Applicants must be working full time on a master's degree in architecture, computer and information science, engineering, mathematics, or statistics. They must be students in an accredited U.S. institution of higher learning enrolled in any year of study. Special consideration is given to applicants who 1) demonstrate their intent to enter professional practice in disciplines in which women are underrepresented, to serve underserved populations and communities, or to pursue public interest areas; and 2) are nontraditional students. Selection is based on professional promise and personal attributes (50%), academic excellence and related academic success indicators (40%), and financial need (10%).

**Financial data** Stipends range from $5,000 to $18,000.

**Duration** 1 academic year, beginning in September.

**Additional information** The filing fee is $35.

**Number awarded** Varies each year; recently, a total of 25 Selected Professions Fellowships were awarded.

**Deadline** January of each year.

## [1141]
## SELECTED PROFESSIONS FELLOWSHIPS FOR WOMEN OF COLOR

American Association of University Women
Attn: AAUW Educational Foundation
301 ACT Drive, Department 60
P.O. Box 4030
Iowa City, IA 52243-4030
(319) 337-1716, ext. 60          Fax: (319) 337-1204
E-mail: aauw@act.org
Web: www.aauw.org

**Summary** To aid women of color who are in their final year of graduate training in the fields of business administration, law, or medicine.

**Eligibility** This program is open to women who are working full time on a degree in fields in which women of color have been historically underrepresented: business administration (M.B.A.), law (J.D.), or medicine (M.D., D.O.). They must be

African Americans, Mexican Americans, Puerto Ricans and other Hispanics, Native Americans, Alaska Natives, Asian Americans, or Pacific Islanders. U.S. citizenship or permanent resident status is required. Applicants in business administration must be entering their second year of study; applicants in law must be entering their third year of study; applicants in medicine may be entering their third or fourth year of study. Special consideration is given to applicants who 1) demonstrate their intent to enter professional practice in disciplines in which women are underrepresented, to serve underserved populations and communities, or to pursue public interest areas; and 2) are nontraditional students. Selection is based on professional promise and personal attributes (50%), academic excellence and related academic success indicators (40%), and financial need (10%).

**Financial data** Stipends range from $5,000 to $18,000.

**Duration** 1 academic year, beginning in September.

**Additional information** The filing fee is $35.

**Number awarded** Varies each year; recently, a total of 25 Selected Professions Fellowships were awarded.

**Deadline** January of each year.

## [1142]
## SEMICONDUCTOR RESEARCH CORPORATION MASTER'S SCHOLARSHIP PROGRAM

Semiconductor Research Corporation
Attn: Global Research Collaboration
1101 Slater Road, Suite 120
P.O. Box 12053
Research Triangle Park, NC 27709-2053
(919) 941-9400                    Fax: (919) 941-9450
E-mail: students@src.org
Web: www.src.org/student-center/fellowship

**Summary** To provide financial assistance to women and minorities who are interested in working on a master's degree in a field of microelectronics relevant to the Semiconductor Research Corporation (SRC).

**Eligibility** This program is open to women and members of underrepresented minority groups (African Americans, Hispanics, and Native Americans). Applicants must be U.S. citizens or have permanent resident, refugee, or political asylum status in the United States. They must be admitted to an SRC participating university to work on a master's degree in a field relevant to microelectronics under the guidance of an SRC-sponsored faculty member and under an SRC-funded contract. Selection is based on academic achievement.

**Financial data** The fellowship provides full tuition and fee support, a competitive stipend (recently, $2,186 per month), an annual grant of $2,000 to the university department with which the student recipient is associated, and travel expenses to the Graduate Fellowship Program Annual Conference.

**Duration** Up to 2 years.

**Additional information** This program began in 1997 for underrepresented minorities and expanded to include women in 1999.

**Number awarded** Approximately 12 each year.

**Deadline** February of each year.

## [1143]
## SENATOR SCOTT WHITE MEMORIAL SCHOLARSHIP

Women's Transportation Seminar-Puget Sound Chapter
c/o Jennifer Barnes, Scholarship Co-Chair
Heffron Transportation, Inc.
532 27th Avenue
Seattle, WA 98122
(206) 324-3623                    Fax: (877) 314-9959
E-mail: jennifer@hefftrans.com
Web: www.wtsinternational.org

**Summary** To provide financial assistance to women undergraduate and graduate students from Washington enrolled in a college in the state and working on a degree related to public policy or public administration in transportation.

**Eligibility** This program is open to women who are residents of Washington, studying at a college in the state, or working as an intern in the state. Applicants must be currently enrolled in an undergraduate or graduate degree program in public policy or public administration in a transportation-related field. They must have a GPA of 3.0 or higher and plans to prepare for a career in their field of study. Minority women are especially encouraged to apply. Along with their application, they must submit a 500-word statement about their career goals after graduation, how their goals are related to public policy or public administration, and why they think they should receive this scholarship award. Selection is based on that statement, academic record, financial need, and transportation-related activities or job skills.

**Financial data** The stipend is $2,500.

**Duration** 1 year.

**Number awarded** 1 each year.

**Deadline** November of each year.

## [1144]
## SIGMA ALPHA IOTA/KENNEDY CENTER INTERNSHIP

Sigma Alpha Iota Philanthropies, Inc.
One Tunnel Road
Asheville, NC 28805
(828) 251-0606                    Fax: (828) 251-0644
E-mail: nh@sai-national.org
Web: www.sai-national.org

**Summary** To provide summer internships at the Kennedy Center to members of Sigma Alpha Iota (an organization of women musicians).

**Eligibility** This program is open to student members of the organization who are interested in a summer internship at the Institute for Arts Management at the John F. Kennedy Center for the Performing Arts in Washington, D.C. Applicants must be juniors, seniors, graduate students, or graduates out of school for less than 2 years.

**Financial data** The stipend is $2,400.

**Duration** 10 weeks during the summer.

**Additional information** Assignments are full time, with possible college credit available.

**Number awarded** 1 or more each year.

**Deadline** February of each year.

**[1145]**
## SIGMA DELTA EPSILON FELLOWSHIPS

Sigma Delta Epsilon-Graduate Women in Science, Inc.
c/o Laurie B. Cook, Fellowships Coordinator
The College at Brockport, State University of New York
Biology Department, 217 Lennon Hall
350 New Campus Drive
Brockport, NY 14420
(585) 395-5757     E-mail: fellowshipsquestions@gwis.org
Web: gwis.org/national-fellowships-program

**Summary**   To provide funding to women interested in conducting research anywhere in the world in the natural sciences.

**Eligibility**   This program is open to women from any country currently enrolled as a graduate student, engaged in postdoctoral research, or holding a junior faculty position. Applicants must be interested in conducting research anywhere in the world in the natural sciences (including physical, environmental, mathematical, computer, or life sciences), anthropology, psychology, or statistics. Along with their application, they must submit 2-paragraph essays on 1) how the proposed research relates to their degree program and/or career development; 2) initiatives in which they are participating to promote the careers of scientists, particularly women, within their institution, program, or peer group; and 3) relevant personal factors, including financial need, that should be considered in evaluating their proposal. Appointments are made without regard to race, religion, nationality, creed, national origin, sexual orientation, or age. Membership in Sigma Delta Epsilon-Graduate Women in Science (SDE-GWIS) is encouraged.

**Financial data**   The maximum grant is $10,000. Funds may be used for such research expenses as expendable supplies, small equipment, publication of research findings, travel and subsistence while performing field studies, or travel to another laboratory for collaborative research. They may not be used for tuition, child care, travel to professional meetings or to begin a new appointment, administrative overhead or indirect costs, personal computers, living allowances, or equipment for general use.

**Duration**   1 year.

**Additional information**   This program includes the Adele Lewis Fellowship, the Hartley Corporation Fellowship, the Ethel K. Allen Fellowship, the Eloise Gerry Fellowships, and the Vessa Notchev Fellowship. Non-members of SDE-GWIS must pay an application fee of $50.

**Number awarded**   Varies each year; recently, 8 of these grants were awarded.

**Deadline**   January of each year.

**[1146]**
## SIGMA GAMMA RHO SCHOLARSHIPS/ FELLOWSHIPS

Sigma Gamma Rho Sorority, Inc.
Attn: National Education Fund
1000 Southhill Drive, Suite 200
Cary, NC 27513
(919) 678-9720            Toll Free: (888) SGR-1922
Fax: (919) 678-9721       E-mail: info@sgrho1922.org
Web: www.sgrho1922.org/nef

**Summary**   To provide financial assistance for undergraduate or graduate study to African American women and other applicants who can demonstrate financial need.

**Eligibility**   This program is open to high school seniors, undergraduates, and graduate students who can demonstrate financial need. The sponsor is a traditionally African American sorority. Applicants must have a GPA of "C" or higher.

**Financial data**   A stipend is awarded (amount not specified).

**Duration**   1 year.

**Additional information**   This program includes the following named awards: the Lorraine A. Williams Scholarship, the Philo Sallie A. Williams Scholarship, the Cleo W. Higgins Scholarship (limited to doctoral students), the Angela E. Randall Scholarship, the Inez Colson Memorial Scholarship (limited to students majoring in education or mathematics at Savannah State University), and the Philo Geneva Young Scholarship. A processing fee of $20 is required.

**Number awarded**   Varies each year.

**Deadline**   April of each year.

**[1147]**
## SIGMA KAPPA ALUMNAE CONTINUING EDUCATION SCHOLARSHIPS

Sigma Kappa Foundation Inc.
Attn: Scholarship Committee
8733 Founders Road
Indianapolis, IN 46268
(317) 872-3275                    Fax: (317) 872-0716
E-mail: foundationscholarships@sigmakappa.org
Web: www.sigmakappafoundation.org/scholarships

**Summary**   To provide financial assistance to alumnae members of Sigma Kappa sorority who are working on a graduate degree.

**Eligibility**   This program is open to alumnae members of the sorority who have an undergraduate degree from a 4-year institution and are entering or continuing in a graduate degree program. Applicants must have an undergraduate GPA of 3.0 or higher. Along with their application, they must submit an essay describing themselves, their future career goals after graduation, and why they are qualified for this scholarship. Financial need is considered in the selection process.

**Financial data**   The stipend is $1,000.

**Duration**   1 year.

**Number awarded**   4 each year.

**Deadline**   March of each year.

**[1148]**
## SOCIETY OF WOMEN ENGINEERS MID-HUDSON SECTION SCHOLARSHIP

Society of Women Engineers
Attn: Scholarship Selection Committee
203 North LaSalle Street, Suite 1675
Chicago, IL 60601-1269
(312) 596-5223                Toll Free: (877) SWE-INFO
Fax: (312) 644-8557           E-mail: scholarships@swe.org
Web: societyofwomenengineers.swe.org

**Summary**   To provide financial assistance to women, especially those from New York, who are working on an undergraduate or graduate degree in engineering or computer science.

**Eligibility** This program is open to women who will be full-time sophomores, juniors, seniors, or graduate students at ABET-accredited colleges and universities. Applicants must be working on a degree in computer science or engineering and have a GPA of 3.0 or higher. Selection is based on merit. Preference is given to applicants who reside and attend school in New York.

**Financial data** The stipend is $1,000.

**Duration** 1 year.

**Additional information** This program is supported by the Mid-Hudson Section of the Society of Women Engineers.

**Number awarded** 1 each year.

**Deadline** February of each year.

## [1149]
## SOCIETY OF WOMEN ENGINEERS PAST PRESIDENTS SCHOLARSHIPS

Society of Women Engineers
Attn: Scholarship Selection Committee
203 North LaSalle Street, Suite 1675
Chicago, IL 60601-1269
(312) 596-5223          Toll Free: (877) SWE-INFO
Fax: (312) 644-8557     E-mail: scholarships@swe.org
Web: societyofwomenengineers.swe.org

**Summary** To provide financial assistance to women working on an undergraduate or graduate degree in engineering or computer science.

**Eligibility** This program is open to women who will be sophomores, juniors, seniors, or graduate students at ABET-accredited colleges and universities. Applicants must be U.S. citizens or permanent residents working full time on a degree in computer science or engineering and have a GPA of 3.0 or higher. Along with their application, they must submit a 1-page essay on why they want to be an engineer or computer scientist, how they believe they will make a difference as an engineer or computer scientist, and what influenced them to study engineering or computer science. Selection is based on merit.

**Financial data** The stipend is $1,500.

**Duration** 1 year.

**Additional information** This program began in 1999 by an anonymous donor to honor the commitment and accomplishments of past presidents of the Society of Women Engineers (SWE).

**Number awarded** 2 each year.

**Deadline** February of each year.

## [1150]
## SPIE SCHOLARSHIP PROGRAM

SPIE-The International Society for Optical Engineering
Attn: Scholarship Committee
1000 20th Street
P.O. Box 10
Bellingham, WA 98227-0010
(360) 676-3290          Toll Free: (888) 504-8171
Fax: (360) 647-1445     E-mail: scholarships@spie.org
Web: spie.org/x7236.xml

**Summary** To provide financial assistance to entering or continuing undergraduate and graduate student members of

SPIE-The International Society for Optical Engineering who are preparing for a career in optical science or engineering (particularly women, minorities, and veterans).

**Eligibility** This program is open to high school seniors planning to attend college, current undergraduate students, and current graduate students. Applicants must be society members majoring or planning to enroll full or part time and major in optics, optoelectronics, photonics, imaging, or a related discipline (e.g., physics, electrical engineering) at a college or university anywhere in the world. Along with their application, they must submit a 500-word essay on their academic work, career objectives, how this scholarship would help them attain their goals, and what they have achieved and learned through their studies and activities. Financial need is not considered in the selection process. Women, minorities, and veterans are encouraged to apply.

**Financial data** Stipends range from $2,000 to $11,000. Special awards include the D.J. Lovell Scholarship at $11,000; the John Kiel Scholarship at $10,000; the Laser Technology, Engineering, and Applications Scholarship at $5,000; the Optical Design and Engineering Scholarship at $5,000, and the BACUS Scholarship at $5,000.

**Duration** 1 year.

**Additional information** The International Society for Optical Engineering was founded in 1955 as the Society of Photo-Optical Instrumentation Engineers (SPIE). This program includes the following special named scholarships: the D.J. Lovell Scholarship, sponsored by SPIE (the most prestigious of the scholarships); the John Kiel Scholarship, awarded for a student's potential for long-term contribution to the field of optics and optical engineering; the Optical Design and Engineering Scholarship in Optical Engineering, established to honor Bill Price and Warren Smith and awarded to a full-time graduate or undergraduate student in the field of optical design and engineering; the Laser Technology, Engineering, and Applications Scholarship (formerly the F-MADE Scholarship), sponsored by the Forum for Military Applications of Directed Energy (F-MADE) in recognition of a student's scholarly achievement in laser technology, engineering, or applications; and the BACUS Scholarship, awarded to a full-time undergraduate or graduate student in the field of microlithography with an emphasis on optical tooling and/or semiconductor manufacturing technologies, sponsored by BACUS (SPIE's photomask international technical group).

**Number awarded** Varies each year; recently, this program awarded 140 scholarships with a value of $353,000. Since the program was established, it has awarded more than $3.8 million to nearly 2,000 students in 86 countries.

**Deadline** February of each year.

## [1151]
## ST. JUDE MEDICAL MINNESOTA SWE SCHOLARSHIP

Society of Women Engineers-Minnesota Section
Attn: Scholarship Committee
P.O. Box 582813
Minneapolis, MN 55458-2813
E-mail: scholarships@swe-mn.org
Web: www.swe-mn.org/scholarships.html

**Summary** To provide financial assistance to women from any state working on an undergraduate or graduate degree in biomedical engineering at colleges and universities in Minnesota, North Dakota, and South Dakota.

**Eligibility** This program is open to female undergraduate and graduate students at ABET-accredited engineering programs in Minnesota, North Dakota, or South Dakota. Applicants must be working full time on a degree in biomedical engineering. Along with their application, they must submit a short paragraph describing how they plan to utilize their engineering skills after they graduate. Selection is based on potential to succeed as an engineer (20 points), communication skills (10 points), extracurricular or community involvement and leadership skills (10 points), demonstrated successful work experience (10 points), and academic success (5 points).

**Financial data** The stipend is $1,000.

**Duration** 1 year.

**Additional information** This program is sponsored by St. Jude Medical.

**Number awarded** 1 each year.

**Deadline** March of each year.

## [1152]
## STEPHEN BUFTON MEMORIAL EDUCATION FUND OUTRIGHT GRANTS PROGRAM

American Business Women's Association
Attn: Stephen Bufton Memorial Educational Fund
11050 Roe Avenue, Suite 200
Overland Park, KS 66211
Toll Free: (800) 228-0007
Web: www.sbmef.org/Opportunities.cfm

**Summary** To provide financial assistance to women undergraduate and graduate students in any field who are sponsored by a chapter of the American Business Women's Association (ABWA).

**Eligibility** This program is open to women who are at least juniors at an accredited college or university. Applicants must be working on an undergraduate or graduate degree and have a GPA of 2.5 or higher. They are not required to be ABWA members, but they must be sponsored by an ABWA chapter that has contributed to the fund in the previous chapter year. U.S. citizenship is required.

**Financial data** The maximum grant is $1,500. Funds are paid directly to the recipient's institution to be used only for tuition, books, and fees.

**Duration** 1 year. Grants are not automatically renewed, but recipients may reapply.

**Additional information** This program began in 1953. The ABWA does not provide the names and addresses of local chapters; it recommends that applicants check with their local Chamber of Commerce, library, or university to see if any chapter has registered a contact's name and number.

**Number awarded** Varies each year; since the inception of this program, it has awarded more than $14 million to more than 14,000 students.

**Deadline** May of each year.

## [1153]
## STUDENT FELLOWSHIP AWARDS FOR FEMALE SCHOLARS IN VISION RESEARCH

Prevent Blindness Ohio
Attn: Investigator Award
1500 West Third Avenue, Suite 200
Columbus, OH 43212
(614) 464-2020          Toll Free: (800) 301-2020, ext. 112
Fax: (614) 481-9670          E-mail: info@pbohio.org
Web: ohio.preventblindness.org

**Summary** To provide funding for research to women from any state working on a graduate degree in a field related to prevention of blindness at a university in Ohio.

**Eligibility** This program is open to women who are residents of any state working on a master's or doctoral degree at a recognized academic institution in Ohio. Applicants must be working on a biomedical, behavioral, or clinical degree and conducting research related to the prevention of blindness and preservation of sight. Preference is given to research topics that investigate public health issues related to the burden of eye-related health and safety topics. Appropriate fields in the health sciences include, but are not limited to, ophthalmology, optometry, nursing, genetics, public health, nutrition, gerontology, and bioengineering. U.S. citizenship or permanent resident status is required.

**Financial data** Grants range from $3,000 to $5,000.

**Duration** 1 year.

**Additional information** This program is supported by the Sarah E. Slack Prevention of Blindness Fund at the Muskingum County Community Foundation and The Reinberger Foundation.

**Number awarded** 1 or more each year.

**Deadline** February of each year.

## [1154]
## SUSAN E. STUTZ-MCDONALD FOUNDATION SCHOLARSHIP

Society of Women Engineers
Attn: Scholarship Selection Committee
203 North LaSalle Street, Suite 1675
Chicago, IL 60601-1269
(312) 596-5223          Toll Free: (877) SWE-INFO
Fax: (312) 644-8557          E-mail: scholarships@swe.org
Web: societyofwomenengineers.swe.org

**Summary** To provide financial assistance to women who are members of the Society of Women Engineers (SWE) and working on a graduate degree in specified fields of engineering or computer science.

**Eligibility** This program is open to SWE members who will be full-time graduate students at ABET-accredited colleges and universities. Applicants must be working on a degree in computer science or chemical, civil, or environmental engineering and have a GPA of 3.0 or higher. Preference is given to students whose emphasis is on water or wastewater engineering. Selection is based on merit. U.S. citizenship or permanent resident status is required.

**Financial data** The stipend is $2,500.

**Duration** 1 year.

**Number awarded** 1 each year.

**Deadline** February of each year.

## [1155]
## SUSAN STEIN SCHOLARSHIP

American College of Nurse-Midwives
Attn: ACNM Foundation, Inc.
8403 Colesville Road, Suite 1550
Silver Spring, MD 20910-6374
(240) 485-1850                          Fax: (240) 485-1818
E-mail: fdn@acnm.org
Web: www.midwife.org

**Summary** To provide financial assistance for midwifery education to student members of the American College of Nurse-Midwives (ACNM) who have had a personal experience with breast cancer.

**Eligibility** This program is open to ACNM members who are currently enrolled in an accredited basic midwife education program and have successfully completed 1 academic or clinical semester/quarter or clinical module. Applicants must have had or currently have a personal experience with breast cancer, either their own or a family member's. Along with their application, they must submit a 150-word essay on their midwifery career plans; a 100-word essay on their intended future participation in the local, regional, and/or national activities of the ACNM; and a 300-word essay on the effect of breast cancer in themselves or a close family member on their choice of midwifery. Selection is based primarily on the quality of the application, although leadership potential, financial need, academic achievement, and personal goals may also be considered.

**Financial data** The stipend is $3,000.

**Duration** 1 year.

**Additional information** This program began in 2010.

**Number awarded** 1 each year.

**Deadline** March of each year.

## [1156]
## SYLVIA FORMAN PRIZE COMPETITION

American Anthropological Association
Attn: Association for Feminist Anthropology
2200 Wilson Boulevard, Suite 600
Arlington, VA 22201-3357
(703) 528-1902                          Fax: (703) 528-3546
Web: www.aaanet.org/sections/afa/?page_id=103

**Summary** To recognize and reward the best student essays in feminist anthropology.

**Eligibility** This award is available to graduate and undergraduate students who submit essays (up to 35 pages) in any subfield of anthropology that focus on such topics as feminist analysis of women's work, reproduction, sexuality, religion, language and expressive culture, family and kin relations, economic development, gender and material culture, gender and biology, women and development, globalization, or race and class. Essays that have been submitted for publication but have not yet been accepted may be eligible as entries. Already accepted or published articles may not be submitted. Only 1 submission per student is accepted. Selection is based on the use of feminist theory to analyze a particular issue; organization, quality, and clarity of writing; effective use of both theory and data; significance to feminist scholarship; timeliness and relevance of the topic; and originality of research topic.

**Financial data** The prize is $1,000 for a graduate student or $500 for an undergraduate.

**Duration** The competition is held annually.

**Additional information** The winning essays are published in the association's *Anthropology Newsletter.* This competition began in 1995.

**Number awarded** At least 2 each year: 1 for an undergraduate and 1 for a graduate student.

**Deadline** May of each year.

## [1157]
## SYLVIA LANE MENTOR FELLOWSHIP

Agricultural and Applied Economics Association
Attn: Trust Committee
555 East Wells Street, Suite 1100
Milwaukee, WI 53202
(414) 918-3190                          Fax: (414) 276-3349
E-mail: info@aaea.org
Web: www.aaea.org/trust/special-purpose-funds

**Summary** To provide funding to young female scholars who are working on food, agricultural, or resource issues and interested in relocating in order to conduct research with an established expert at another university, institution, or firm.

**Eligibility** These fellowships are awarded to mentee/mentor pairs of individuals. Mentees must have completed at least 1 year in residence in an accredited American graduate degree program in agricultural economics or a closely-related discipline; women with Ph.D. degrees and advanced graduate students are encouraged to apply. Mentors must have a Ph.D. and established expertise in an area of food, agriculture, or natural resources. The goal is to enable female scholars to relocate in order to conduct research with an established expert at another university, institution, or firm, even though they may reside in different parts of the country or the world. Selection is based on the relevance of the research problem, potential for generating output, synergy of the mentor/mentee pairing, and opportunity for advancing the mentee's research skills beyond her graduate studies and current position.

**Financial data** Awards may be used to cover direct research costs, travel, and temporary relocation expenses for the mentee.

**Duration** Several weeks.

**Additional information** This program was established by the Committee on Women in Agricultural Economics of the Agricultural and Applied Economics Association.

**Number awarded** 1 each year.

**Deadline** September of each year.

## [1158]
## T & T HIKE SCHOLARSHIP

International Order of Job's Daughters
c/o Betty Klotz, Educational Scholarships Committee
  Chair
1228 Moss Rock Court
Santa Rosa, CA 95404
(707) 462-6834                          E-mail: bettyklotz@gmail.com
Web: www.jobsdaughtersinternational.org

**Summary** To provide financial assistance to members of Job's Daughters who are working on a degree related to speech disabilities.

**Eligibility**   This program is open to Job's Daughters in good standing in their Bethels and unmarried majority members under 30 years of age. Applicants must be entering their junior year of college or higher in audiology, speech pathology, or deaf education. Selection is based on scholastic standing, Job's Daughters activities, recommendation by the Executive Bethel Guardian Council, faculty recommendations, and achievements outside Job's Daughters.

**Financial data**   The stipend is $1,000.

**Duration**   1 year.

**Number awarded**   1 or more each year.

**Deadline**   April of each year.

## [1159]
## TEXAS YOUNG LAWYERS ASSOCIATION MINORITY SCHOLARSHIP PROGRAM

Texas Young Lawyers Association
Attn: Minority Involvement Committee
1414 Colorado, Suite 502
P.O. Box 12487
Austin, TX 78711-2487
(512) 427-1529        Toll Free: (800) 204-2222, ext. 1529
Fax: (512) 427-4117        E-mail: btrevino@texasbar.com
Web: www.tyla.org

**Summary**   To provide financial assistance to minorities and women residents of any state who are attending law school in Texas.

**Eligibility**   This program is open to members of recognized minority groups, including students of varying gender, national origin, racial and ethnic backgrounds, sexual orientation and gender identity, and of disability status. Applicants must be attending an ABA-accredited law school in Texas. Along with their application, they must submit a 2-page essay on either 1) the role the minority attorney should play in the community and profession; or 2) how attorneys, specifically minority attorneys, can improve the image of the legal profession. Selection is based on academic performance, merit, participation in extracurricular activities inside and outside law school, and financial need.

**Financial data**   The stipend is $1,000.

**Duration**   1 year.

**Number awarded**   9 each year: 1 at each accredited law school in Texas.

**Deadline**   October of each year.

## [1160]
## THEODORE AND MARY JANE RICH MEMORIAL SCHOLARSHIPS

Slovak Catholic Sokol
Attn: Membership Memorial Scholarship Fund
205 Madison Street
P.O. Box 899
Passaic, NJ 07055-0899
(973) 777-2605        Toll Free: (800) 886-7656
Fax: (973) 779-8245  E-mail: life@slovakcatholicsokol.org
Web: www.slovakcatholicsokol.org/grantsscholarships.asp

**Summary**   To provide financial assistance to female and male members (judged separately) of the Slovak Catholic Sokol who are working on a medically-related degree at a college or graduate school in any state.

**Eligibility**   This program is open to members of the Slovak Catholic Sokol who have completed at least 1 semester of college and are currently enrolled full time as an undergraduate or graduate student at an accredited college, university, or professional school in any state. Applicants must have been a member for at least 5 years, have at least $3,000 permanent life insurance coverage, and have at least 1 parent who is a member and is of Slovak ancestry. They must be studying a medical program. Males and females compete for scholarships separately.

**Financial data**   The stipend is $2,500 per year.

**Duration**   1 year; may be renewed 1 additional year.

**Additional information**   Slovak Catholic Sokol was founded as a fraternal benefit society in 1905. It is licensed to operate in the following states: Connecticut, Illinois, Indiana, Massachusetts, Michigan, New Jersey, New York, Ohio, Pennsylvania, and Wisconsin. This program was established in 2003.

**Number awarded**   2 each year: 1 for a male and 1 for a female.

**Deadline**   March of each year.

## [1161]
## THOMPSON SCHOLARSHIP FOR WOMEN IN SAFETY

American Society of Safety Engineers
Attn: ASSE Foundation
Scholarship Award Program
1800 East Oakton Street
Des Plaines, IL 60018
(847) 699-2929        Fax: (847) 768-3434
E-mail: bzylstra@asse.org
Web: www.asse.org

**Summary**   To provide financial assistance to graduate students, especially women, working on a degree in safety-related fields.

**Eligibility**   This program is open to students working on a graduate degree in occupational safety, health, environment, industrial hygiene, occupational health nursing, or a closely-related field (e.g., industrial or environmental engineering). Priority is given to women. Applicants must be full-time students who have completed at least 9 semester hours and had an undergraduate GPA of 3.0 or higher. U.S. citizenship is not required. Membership in the American Society of Safety Engineers (ASSE) is not required, but preference is given to members.

**Financial data**   The stipend is $1,000 per year.

**Duration**   1 year; recipients may reapply.

**Number awarded**   1 each year.

**Deadline**   November of each year.

## [1162]
## THORNBERG/HAVENS SCHOLARSHIP

Delta Zeta Sorority
Attn: Foundation Coordinator
202 East Church Street
Oxford, OH 45056
(513) 523-7597        Fax: (513) 523-1921
E-mail: DZFoundation@dzshq.com
Web: www.deltazeta.org

**Summary** To provide financial assistance for continued undergraduate or graduate study to members of Delta Zeta Sorority.

**Eligibility** This program is open to undergraduate and graduate members of the sorority who have a GPA of 3.0 or higher. Applicants must submit an official transcript, a statement of their career goals, information on their service to the sorority, documentation of campus activities and/or community involvement, a list of academic honors, and an explanation of their financial need.

**Financial data** The stipend ranges from $500 to $2,500 for undergraduates or from $1,000 to $15,000 for graduate students, depending on the availability of funds.

**Duration** 1 year; nonrenewable.

**Number awarded** 1 each year.

**Deadline** February of each year.

## [1163]
## TRAUB-DICKER RAINBOW SCHOLARSHIPS

Stonewall Community Foundation
Attn: Bee's Fund
446 West 33rd Street, Sixth Floor
New York, NY 10001
(212) 367-1155                    Fax: (212) 367-1157
E-mail: grants@stonewallfoundation.org
Web: stonewallfoundation.org/grants/scholarships

**Summary** To provide financial assistance to undergraduate and graduate students who identify as lesbians.

**Eligibility** This program is open to lesbian-identified students who are 1) graduating high school seniors planning to attend a recognized college or university; 2) currently-enrolled undergraduates; and 3) graduate students. Applicants must submit 400-word essays on 1) their personal history, including a significant challenge or achievement in terms of community service, academic excellence, or dynamic leadership; 2) a particularly important experience they have had as a lesbian and how it has affected them; and 3) their plans or goals to give back to or focus on the lesbian, gay, bisexual, and transgender (LGBT) community while in school or after graduating. Selection is based on academic excellence, community service, and commitment to impacting LGBT issues. Financial need is not considered.

**Financial data** The stipend is $3,000. Funds are paid directly to the recipient's school, to be used for tuition, books, or room and board.

**Duration** 1 year.

**Additional information** This program began in 2004.

**Number awarded** 3 each year.

**Deadline** April of each year.

## [1164]
## UNESCO-L'OREAL INTERNATIONAL FELLOWSHIPS

United Nations Educational, Scientific, and Cultural Organization
Attn: Fellowships Section
7, place de Fontenoy
75352 Paris 07 SP
France
33 1 45 68 15 49                    Fax: 33 1 45 68 55 03
E-mail: a.zaid@unesco.org
Web: www.unesco.org/en/fellowships/loreal

**Summary** To provide funding to women from UNESCO member countries (including the United States) who are conducting pre- or postdoctoral research in the life sciences.

**Eligibility** Eligible to apply are women from UNESCO member countries who are conducting research in life sciences, including biology, biochemistry, biotechnology, agriculture, medicine, pharmacy, and physiology. Applicants must be younger than 35 years of age. They must have already distinguished themselves by their talent and commitment. Preference is given to applicants who already have a Ph.D. degree, but applications from students pursuing study or research leading to a Ph.D. are also accepted. Special attention is given to candidates from the least developed countries. Each UNESCO member state may nominate 4 candidates. Applications must be submitted first to the national commission for UNESCO in the candidate's country (no application without this endorsement will be considered).

**Financial data** The maximum grant is $20,000 per year. Funds may not be used for computer or equipment purchases, publication costs, or attendance at conferences (unless a case can be made that such attendance is an integral part of the research and would make a direct and significant contribution to the outcome of the development of life sciences). Fellows also receive funding for airfare, meals, lodging, and pocket money to travel to UNESCO headquarters in Paris to attend an awards ceremony and visit there for 5 days.

**Duration** 2 years.

**Additional information** This program, which began in 1998, is sponsored by L'Oréal.

**Number awarded** 15 each year (3 in each of the 5 areas designated by UNESCO: Europe and North America, Asia and the Pacific, Africa, Latin America and the Caribbean, and Arab states).

**Deadline** July of each year.

## [1165]
## UNITED METHODIST WOMEN OF COLOR SCHOLARS PROGRAM

United Methodist Church
Attn: General Board of Higher Education and Ministry
Office of Loans and Scholarships
1001 19th Avenue South
P.O. Box 340007
Nashville, TN 37203-0007
(615) 340-7344                    Fax: (615) 340-7367
E-mail: umscholar@gbhem.org
Web: www.gbhem.org

**Summary** To provide financial assistance to Methodist women of color who are working on a doctoral degree to prepare for a career as an educator at a United Methodist seminary.

**Eligibility** This program is open to women of color (have at least 1 parent who is African American, African, Hispanic, Asian, Native American, Alaska Native, or Pacific Islander) who have an M.Div. degree. Applicants must have been active, full members of a United Methodist Church for at least 3 years prior to applying. They must be enrolled full time in a degree program at the Ph.D. or Th.D. level to prepare for a career teaching at a United Methodist seminary.

**Financial data** The maximum stipend is $10,000 per year.

**Duration** 1 year; may be renewed up to 3 additional years.

**Number awarded** Varies each year; recently, 10 of these scholarships were awarded.

**Deadline** January of each year.

## [1166]
## VASHTI TURLEY MURPHY SCHOLARSHIP PROGRAM

Delta Sigma Theta Sorority, Inc.
Attn: Scholarship and Standards Committee Chair
1707 New Hampshire Avenue, N.W.
Washington, DC 20009
(202) 986-2400 Fax: (202) 986-2513
E-mail: dstemail@deltasigmatheta.org
Web: www.deltasigmatheta.org

**Summary** To provide financial assistance to members of Delta Sigma Theta who are interested in working on a graduate degree to prepare for a career in ministry.

**Eligibility** This program is open to graduating college seniors and graduate students who are interested in working on a master's or doctoral degree to prepare for a career in ministry. Applicants must be active, dues-paying members of Delta Sigma Theta. Selection is based on meritorious achievement.

**Financial data** The stipends range from $1,000 to $2,000. The funds may be used to cover tuition, fees, and living expenses.

**Duration** 1 year; may be renewed for 1 additional year.

**Additional information** This sponsor is a traditionally-African American social sorority. The application fee is $20.

**Number awarded** 1 or more each year.

**Deadline** April of each year.

## [1167]
## VERIZON SCHOLARSHIPS OF THE SOCIETY OF WOMEN ENGINEERS

Society of Women Engineers
Attn: Scholarship Selection Committee
203 North LaSalle Street, Suite 1675
Chicago, IL 60601-1269
(312) 596-5223 Toll Free: (877) SWE-INFO
Fax: (312) 644-8557 E-mail: scholarships@swe.org
Web: societyofwomenengineers.swe.org

**Summary** To provide financial assistance to women working on an undergraduate or graduate degree in designated engineering specialties.

**Eligibility** This program is open to women who are enrolling as sophomores, juniors, seniors, or graduate students at an ABET-accredited 4-year college or university. Applicants must be working full time on a degree in computer science or

computer, electrical, industrial, or mechanical engineering and have a GPA of 3.0 or higher. Preference is given to students attending specified colleges and universities, to students enrolled in an ROTC program, and to disabled veterans. Selection is based on merit. U.S. citizenship or permanent resident status is required.

**Financial data** The stipend is $3,000.

**Duration** 1 year.

**Additional information** This program is sponsored by Verizon. For a list of the specified colleges and universities, check the web site of the Society of Women Engineers.

**Number awarded** 10 each year.

**Deadline** February of each year.

## [1168]
## VIASAT SOFTWARE ENGINEERING SCHOLARSHIP

Society of Women Engineers
Attn: Scholarship Selection Committee
203 North LaSalle Street, Suite 1675
Chicago, IL 60601-1269
(312) 596-5223 Toll Free: (877) SWE-INFO
Fax: (312) 644-8557 E-mail: scholarships@swe.org
Web: societyofwomenengineers.swe.org

**Summary** To provide financial assistance to women from specified states who are members of the Society of Women Engineers (SWE) and working on an undergraduate or graduate degree in software engineering.

**Eligibility** This program is open to SWE members who will be juniors, seniors, or graduate students at ABET-accredited colleges and universities and have a GPA of 3.2 or higher. Applicants must reside in or attend school in California, Maryland, Massachusetts, or Washington, D.C. They must be U.S. citizens or permanent residents working full time on a degree in computer science or software engineering. Selection is based on merit.

**Financial data** The stipend is $2,200.

**Duration** 1 year.

**Additional information** This program is sponsored by ViaSat, Inc.

**Number awarded** 1 each year.

**Deadline** February of each year.

## [1169]
## VICTORIA NAMAN GRADUATE SCHOOL SCHOLARSHIP

Delta Sigma Theta Sorority, Inc.-Denver Alumnae
Chapter
Attn: Scholarship Committee
P.O. Box 7432
Denver, CO 80207
(303) 858-9972 E-mail: info@milehighdst.org
Web: denverdeltas.org/programs/scholarship

**Summary** To provide financial assistance to female African American residents of Colorado who are interested in attending graduate school in any state.

**Eligibility** This program is open to African American women who are residents of Colorado and enrolled or planning to enroll at a graduate school in any state. Applicants must have a GPA of 3.0 or higher. They must submit an essay of at least 200 words on their personal goals, academic achievements, and plans for making a difference in their community. Selection is based on the essay, financial need, scholastic record, 2 letters of recommendation, and an interview.

**Financial data** Stipends range from $1,000 to $3,000.

**Duration** 1 year.

**Number awarded** 1 or more each year.

**Deadline** March of each year.

## [1170]
## VICTORY FOR WOMEN ACADEMIC SCHOLARSHIP FOR WOMEN WITH BLEEDING DISORDERS

National Hemophilia Foundation
Attn: Manager of Education
P.O. Box 971483
Ypsilanti, MI 48197
(734) 890-2504          E-mail: pflax@hemophilia.org
Web: www.hemophilia.org

**Summary** To provide financial assistance for college or graduate school to women who have a bleeding disorder.

**Eligibility** This program is open to women who are entering or already enrolled in an undergraduate or graduate program at a university, college, or accredited vocational school. Applicants must have von Willebrand Disease, hemophilia or other clotting factor deficiency, or carrier status. Along with their application, they must submit a 250-word essay that describes how their education and future career plans will benefit others in the bleeding disorders community. Selection is based on that essay, achievements, and community service to the bleeding disorders community.

**Financial data** The stipend is $2,500.

**Duration** 1 year.

**Additional information** The program, known also as V4W, was established in 2005 as the Project Red Flag Academic Scholarship for Women with Bleeding Disorders.

**Number awarded** 2 each year.

**Deadline** May of each year.

## [1171]
## VIOLET AND CYRIL FRANKS SCHOLARSHIP

American Psychological Foundation
750 First Street, N.E.
Washington, DC 20002-4242
(202) 336-5843          Fax: (202) 336-5812
E-mail: foundation@apa.org
Web: www.apa.org/apf/funding/franks.aspx

**Summary** To provide funding to doctoral students (particularly women and members of other groups that represent diversity) who are interested in conducting research related to mental illness.

**Eligibility** This program is open to full-time graduate students who are interested in conducting a research project that uses a psychological perspective to help understand and reduce stigma associated with mental illness. Applicants must identify the project's goal, the prior research that has been conducted in the area, whom the project will serve, the in intended outcomes and how the project will achieve those, and the total cost of the project. Selection is based on conformance with stated program goals and quality of proposed work. The sponsor encourages applications from individuals

who represent diversity in race, ethnicity, gender, age, disability, and sexual orientation.

**Financial data** The grant is $5,000.

**Duration** 1 year.

**Additional information** This grant was first awarded in 2007.

**Number awarded** 1 each year.

**Deadline** May of each year.

## [1172]
## VIRGINIA A. POMEROY SCHOLARSHIPS

Association for Women Lawyers
Attn: AWL Foundation
3322 North 92nd Street
Milwaukee, WI 53222
(414) 750-4404          Fax: (414) 255-3615
E-mail: associationforwomenlawyers@gmail.com
Web: awl.memberlodge.org/scholarships

**Summary** To provide financial assistance to women who are attending law school in Wisconsin and have demonstrated an interest in service to the disadvantaged.

**Eligibility** This program is open to women from any state currently enrolled at law schools in Wisconsin. Applicants must have demonstrated a special interest in service to the vulnerable or disadvantaged, civil rights law, appellate practice, public service, public policy, or public interest law. Selection is based on academic achievement, service to others, unique life experience or circumstance, and financial need.

**Financial data** The stipend varies; recently, awards averaged $2,500.

**Duration** 1 year.

**Additional information** This program began in 1998.

**Number awarded** Varies each year; recently, 2 of these scholarships were awarded.

**Deadline** June of each year.

## [1173]
## VIRGINIA BURNS BOYNTON SCHOLARSHIP

Kappa Alpha Theta Foundation
Attn: Manager of Programs
8740 Founders Road
Indianapolis, IN 46268-1337
(317) 876-1870          Toll Free: (800) KAO-1870
Fax: (317) 876-1925
E-mail: gmerritt@kappaalphatheta.org
Web: www.kappaalphathetafoundation.org

**Summary** To provide financial assistance to alumnae members of Kappa Alpha Theta who are working on a graduate degree in medicine or the sciences.

**Eligibility** This program is open to members of Kappa Alpha Theta who are currently enrolled full time at a graduate or medical school in Canada or the United States. Applicants must be working on a degree in the sciences, medicine, or medical research. Along with their application, they must submit an official transcript, personal essays on assigned topics related to their involvement in Kappa Alpha Theta, and 2 letters of reference. Financial need is not considered in the selection process.

**Financial data** The stipend is approximately $2,500.

**Duration** 1 year.

**Number awarded** 2 each year.

**Deadline** February of each year.

## [1174]
## VIRGINIA M. WAGNER EDUCATIONAL GRANT

Soroptimist International of the Americas-Midwestern
Region
c/o Alexandra Nicholis
2117 Quayle Drive
Akron, OH 44312-2332
(330) 524-7113          E-mail: soroptimist@simwr.org
Web: simwr.org/#!virginia-wagner-award/c1vsh

**Summary** To provide financial assistance to women working on an undergraduate or graduate degree at a college or
university in the Midwest.

**Eligibility** This program is open to women who reside in
Illinois, Indiana, Kentucky, Michigan, Ohio, or Wisconsin and
are attending college or graduate school in any state. Applicants must be working on a bachelor's, master's, or doctoral
degree in the field of their choice. Awards are first presented
at the club level, then in districts, and finally for the entire
region. Selection is based on the effort toward education by
the applicant and her family, cumulative GPA, extracurricular
activities, general impression, and financial need.

**Financial data** Club level awards vary at the discretion of
the club. District finalists receive a $500 award and are then
judged at the regional level. The regional winner receives a
$2,500 award.

**Duration** 1 year.

**Additional information** This program began in 1972 and
given its current name in 2004.

**Number awarded** 4 district winners are selected each
year; 1 of those receives the regional award.

**Deadline** January of each year.

## [1175]
## VIRGINIA PEACE MACKEY-ALTHOUSE VOICE AWARD

National Federation of Music Clubs
1646 Smith Valley Road
Greenwood, IN 46142
(317) 882-4003          Fax: (317) 882-4019
E-mail: info@nfmc-music.org
Web: nfmc-music.org

**Summary** To recognize and reward outstanding female
student singers who are members of the National Federation
of Music Clubs (NFMC).

**Eligibility** This award is presented to female singers
between 19 and 26 years of age. Student membership in the
federation and U.S. citizenship are required. Candidates for
the NFMC Biennial Student/Collegiate Audition Awards competition are automatically considered for this award; no separate application is necessary.

**Financial data** The prize is $1,750.

**Duration** The competition is held biennially, in odd-numbered years.

**Additional information** The entry fee is $30.

**Number awarded** 1 every other year.

**Deadline** January of odd-numbered years.

## [1176]
## WALTER BYERS POSTGRADUATE SCHOLARSHIP PROGRAM

National Collegiate Athletic Association
Attn: Walter Byers Scholarship Committee Staff Liaison
700 West Washington Street
P.O. Box 6222
Indianapolis, IN 46206-6222
(317) 917-6477          Fax: (317) 917-6888
E-mail: lthomas@ncaa.org
Web: www.ncaa.org

**Summary** To provide financial assistance for graduate education in any field to student-athletes with outstanding academic records (females and males are selected separately).

**Eligibility** This program is open to student-athletes who
are seniors or already enrolled in graduate school while completing their final year of athletics eligibility at a member institution of the National Collegiate Athletic Association (NCAA).
Men and women compete for scholarships separately. Applicants must be planning to work full time on a graduate degree
or post-baccalaureate professional degree. They must have a
GPA of 3.5 or higher, have evidenced superior character and
leadership, and have demonstrated that participation in athletics and community service has been a positive influence
on their personal and intellectual development. Candidates
must be nominated by their institution's faculty athletic representative or chief academic officer. Financial need is not considered in the selection process.

**Financial data** The stipend is $24,000 per year.

**Duration** 2 years.

**Additional information** This program began in 1988 in
honor of the former executive director of the NCAA.

**Number awarded** 2 each year: 1 is set aside for a female
and 1 for a male.

**Deadline** January of each year.

## [1177]
## WALTER O. SPOFFORD, JR. MEMORIAL INTERNSHIP

Resources for the Future
Attn: Coordinator for Academic Programs
1616 P Street, N.W., Suite 600
Washington, DC 20036-1400
(202) 328-5020          Fax: (202) 939-3460
E-mail: spofford-award@rff.org
Web: www.rff.org

**Summary** To provide summer internships to graduate students (especially women and minorities) who are interested
in working on Chinese environmental issues at Resources for
the Future (RFF).

**Eligibility** This program is open to first- or second-year
graduate students in the social or natural sciences. Applicants must have a special interest in Chinese environmental
issues and outstanding policy analysis and writing skills.
They must be interested in an internship in Washington, D.C.
at RFF. Women and minority candidates are strongly encouraged to apply. Both U.S. and non-U.S. citizens (especially
Chinese students) are eligible, if the latter have proper work
and residency documentation.

**Financial data** The stipend is $375 per week. Housing
assistance is not provided.

**Duration** The duration of the internship depends on the intern's situation.

**Number awarded** 1 each year.

**Deadline** February of each year.

## [1178]
## WANDA MUNN SCHOLARSHIP

Society of Women Engineers
Attn: Scholarship Selection Committee
203 North LaSalle Street, Suite 1675
Chicago, IL 60601-1269
(312) 596-5223          Toll Free: (877) SWE-INFO
Fax: (312) 644-8557     E-mail: scholarships@swe.org
Web: societyofwomenengineers.swe.org

**Summary** To provide financial assistance to women from selected northwestern states, particularly those who have worked in the engineering field, who are interested in returning to college or graduate school to continue their study of engineering or computer science.

**Eligibility** This program is open to women who are planning to enroll at an ABET-accredited 4-year college or university. Applicants must have been out of the engineering workforce and school for at least 2 years and must be planning to return as an undergraduate or graduate student to work on a degree in computer science or engineering. They must be residents of are attending school in Alaska, Idaho, Montana, Oregon, or Washington and have a GPA of 3.0 or higher. Selection is based on merit. Preference is given to engineers who already have a degree and are planning to reenter the engineering workforce after a period of temporary retirement.

**Financial data** The stipend is $1,500.

**Duration** 1 year.

**Additional information** This program is sponsored by the Eastern Washington Section of the Society of Women Engineers.

**Number awarded** 1 each year.

**Deadline** February of each year.

## [1179]
## WASHINGTON EPISCOPAL CHURCH WOMEN MEMORIAL SCHOLARSHIP FUND

Episcopal Diocese of Washington
Attn: Episcopal Church Women
Episcopal Church House
Mount St. Alban
Washington, DC 20016-5094
(202) 537-6530          Toll Free: (800) 642-4427
Fax: (202) 364-6605     E-mail: ecw@edow.org
Web: www.edow.org

**Summary** To provide financial assistance for graduate school to women who are members of Episcopal churches in Washington, D.C.

**Eligibility** This program is open to women members of the Episcopal Church who have been a canonical member of the Diocese of Washington for at least 1 year prior to application. Priority is given to members who reside in the Diocese of Washington. Applicants must be enrolled in graduate or professional study and their course of study must be related to church work or activity in preparation for some pertinent field of Christian endeavor. Along with their application, they must submit a statement of purpose for working on a graduate

degree and how they plan to use it, letters of recommendation (including 1 from their vicar or rector), financial information, and (if seeking ordination) a letter from their parish intern committee.

**Financial data** A stipend is awarded (amount not specified); funds are sent directly to the recipient's school.

**Duration** 1 year; may be renewed.

**Additional information** This program began in 1925. The Episcopal Diocese of Washington serves the District of Columbia and the Maryland counties of Charles, St. Mary's, Prince George's, and Montgomery.

**Number awarded** 1 or more each year.

**Deadline** May of each year.

## [1180]
## WATSON MIDWIVES OF COLOR SCHOLARSHIP

American College of Nurse-Midwives
Attn: ACNM Foundation, Inc.
8403 Colesville Road, Suite 1550
Silver Spring, MD 20910-6374
(240) 485-1850          Fax: (240) 485-1818
E-mail: fdn@acnm.org
Web: www.midwife.org

**Summary** To provide financial assistance for midwifery education to students of color who belong to the American College of Nurse-Midwives (ACNM).

**Eligibility** This program is open to ACNM members of color who are currently enrolled in an accredited basic midwife education program and have successfully completed 1 academic or clinical semester/quarter or clinical module. Applicants must submit a 150-word essay on their 5-year midwifery career plans and a 100-word essay on their intended future participation in the local, regional, and/or national activities of the ACNM. Selection is based on leadership potential, financial need, academic history, and potential for future professional contribution to the organization.

**Financial data** The stipend is $3,000.

**Duration** 1 year.

**Number awarded** Varies each year; recently, 3 of these scholarships were awarded.

**Deadline** March of each year.

## [1181]
## WAWH FOUNDERS DISSERTATION FELLOWSHIP

Western Association of Women Historians
c/o Amy Essington, Executive Director
3242 Petaluma Avenue
Long Beach, CA 90808-4249
E-mail: amyessington@wawh.org
Web: www.wawh.org/awards/currentinfo.html

**Summary** To provide dissertation funding to graduate students who are members of the Western Association of Women Historians (WAWH).

**Eligibility** This program is open to graduate students who are members of WAWH, have advanced to candidacy, are writing their dissertation at the time of application, and are expecting to receive their Ph.D. no earlier than December of the calendar year in which the award is made. Selection is based on scholarly potential of the student, significance of the dissertation project for historical scholarship, and progress already made towards completing the necessary research.

**Financial data** The grant is $1,000. Funds may be used for any expenses related to the dissertation.

**Duration** 1 year.

**Additional information** This fellowship was first awarded in 1986.

**Number awarded** 1 each year.

**Deadline** January of each year.

## [1182]
## WAYNE F. PLACEK GRANTS

American Psychological Foundation
750 First Street, N.E.
Washington, DC 20002-4242
(202) 336-5843　　　　　　　Fax: (202) 336-5812
E-mail: foundation@apa.org
Web: www.apa.org/apf/funding/placek.aspx

**Summary** To provide funding to pre- and postdoctoral scholars (particularly women, minorities, and individuals with disabilities) who are interested in conducting research that will increase the general public's understanding of homosexuality and alleviate the stress experienced by gay men and lesbians.

**Eligibility** This program is open to scholars who have a doctoral degree (e.g., Ph.D., Psy.D., M.D.) and to graduate students in all fields of the behavioral and social sciences. Applicants must be interested in conducting empirical studies that address the following topics: prejudice, discrimination, and violence based on sexual orientation, including heterosexuals' attitudes and behaviors toward lesbian, gay, bisexual, and transgender (LGBT) people; family and workplace issues relevant to LGBT people; and subgroups of the LGBT population that have been historically underrepresented in scientific research. Selection is based on conformance with stated program goals, magnitude of incremental contribution, quality of proposed work, and applicant's demonstrated scholarship and research competence. The sponsor encourages applications from individuals who represent diversity in race, ethnicity, gender, age, disability, and sexual orientation.

**Financial data** The grant is $15,000.

**Duration** 1 year.

**Additional information** This program began in 1995.

**Number awarded** 1 or 2 each year.

**Deadline** February of each year.

## [1183]
## WBF SCHOLARSHIP AWARDS

Women's Bar Association of Illinois
Attn: Women's Bar Foundation
321 South Plymouth Court, Suite 4S
P.O. Box 641068
Chicago, IL 60664-1068
(312) 341-8530　　　　　　E-mail: illinoiswbf@aol.com
Web: www.illinoiswbf.org/?page_id=19

**Summary** To provide financial assistance to women from any state attending law school in Illinois.

**Eligibility** This program is open to female residents of any state enrolled at accredited law schools in Illinois.

**Financial data** The stipend is $10,000.

**Duration** 1 year.

**Additional information** This program began in 1966. It includes the Chief Justice Mary Ann G. McMorrow Scholarship, first presented in 2004, and the Esther Rothstein Scholarship, first awarded in 2002.

**Number awarded** Varies each year; recently, 9 of these scholarships were awarded. Since the program was established, it has awarded more than 280 scholarships worth more than $1.1 million.

**Deadline** Deadline not specified.

## [1184]
## WETV SCHOLARSHIP OF NEW YORK WOMEN IN COMMUNICATIONS

New York Women in Communications, Inc.
Attn: NYWICI Foundation
355 Lexington Avenue, 15th Floor
New York, NY 10017-6603
(212) 297-2133　　　　　　Fax: (212) 370-9047
E-mail: nywicipr@nywici.org
Web: www.nywici.org/foundation/scholarships

**Summary** To provide financial assistance to female residents of designated eastern states who are enrolled at a college in any state and preparing for a career in broadcast production.

**Eligibility** This program is open to women who are residents of New York, New Jersey, Connecticut, or Pennsylvania and currently enrolled as undergraduate or graduate students at a college or university in any state. Graduate students must be members of New York Women in Communications, Inc. (NYWICI). Also eligible are women who reside outside the 4 states but are currently enrolled at a college or university within 1 of the 5 boroughs of New York City. Applicants must be able to demonstrate a commitment to a career in broadcast production. They must have a GPA of 3.2 or higher. Along with their application, they must submit a 2-page resume; a personal essay of 300 words on an assigned topic that changes annually; 2 letters of recommendation; and an official transcript. Selection is based on academic record, need, demonstrated leadership, participation in school and community activities, honors and other awards or recognition, work experience, goals and aspirations, and unusual personal and/or family circumstances. U.S. citizenship is required.

**Financial data** The stipend ranges up to $10,000.

**Duration** 1 year.

**Additional information** This program is sponsored by WEtv.

**Number awarded** 1 each year.

**Deadline** January of each year.

## [1185]
## WHOI GEOPHYSICAL FLUID DYNAMICS FELLOWSHIPS

Woods Hole Oceanographic Institution
Attn: Academic Programs Office
Clark Laboratory, MS 31
266 Woods Hole Road
Woods Hole, MA 02543-1541
(508) 289-2950　　　　　　Fax: (508) 457-2188
E-mail: gfd@whoi.edu
Web: www.whoi.edu/gfd

**Summary** To provide summer research and study opportunities at Woods Hole Oceanographic Institution (WHOI) to pre- and postdoctoral scholars (particularly women and members of underrepresented groups) who are interested in geophysical fluid dynamics.

**Eligibility** This program is open to pre- and postdoctorates who are interested in pursuing research or study opportunities in a field that involves non-linear dynamics of rotating, stratified fluids. Fields of specialization include classical fluid dynamics, physical oceanography, meteorology, geophysical fluid dynamics, astrophysics, planetary atmospheres, hydromagnetics, physics, and applied mathematics. Applications from women and members of underrepresented groups are particularly encouraged.

**Financial data** Participants receive a stipend of $5,600 and an allowance for travel expenses within the United States.

**Duration** 10 weeks during the summer.

**Additional information** Each summer, the program at WHOI revolves around a central theme. A recent theme related to shear turbulence. The main components of the summer program are a series of principal lectures, a set of supplementary research seminars, and research projects conducted by the student fellows with the active support of the staff. Funding for this program, which began in 1959, is provided by the National Science Foundation and Office of Naval Research.

**Number awarded** Up to 10 graduate students are supported each year.

**Deadline** February of each year.

## [1186]
## WICHITA CHAPTER AFWA SCHOLARSHIPS

Accounting and Financial Women's Alliance-Wichita
  Chapter
c/o Terra Eck, Scholarship Chair
5320 Tenpoint
Andale, KS 67001
(316) 828-5084
Web: www.wichitaaswa.org

**Summary** To provide financial assistance to women working on an undergraduate or graduate degree in accounting or finance at a college or university in Kansas.

**Eligibility** This program is open to women working full or part time on an associate, bachelor's, or master's degree in accounting or finance at a college or university in Kansas. Applicants must have completed at least 15 semester hours in a 2-year program or 60 semester hours in a 4-year program. They must have a cumulative GPA of 3.0 or higher. Membership in the Accounting and Financial Women's Alliance (AFWA) is not required. Along with their application, they must submit an essay of 150 to 250 words on their career goals and objectives, the impact they want to have on the accounting world, community involvement, and leadership examples. Selection is based on leadership, character, communication skills, GPA, and financial need.

**Financial data** The stipend is $1,000.

**Duration** 1 year.

**Additional information** The highest-ranked recipient is entered into the national competition for scholarships that range from $1,500 to $4,500.

**Number awarded** Varies each year; recently, 4 of these scholarships were awarded.

**Deadline** February of each year.

## [1187]
## WILLIAM RUCKER GREENWOOD SCHOLARSHIP

Association for Women Geoscientists
Attn: AWG Foundation
12000 North Washington Street, Suite 285
Thornton, CO 80241
(303) 412-6219                    Fax: (303) 253-9220
E-mail: office@awg.org
Web: www.awg.org/members/po_scholarships.html

**Summary** To provide financial assistance to minority women from any state working on an undergraduate or graduate degree in the geosciences at a college in the Potomac Bay region.

**Eligibility** This program is open to minority women who are residents of any state and currently enrolled as full-time undergraduate or graduate geoscience majors at an accredited, degree-granting college or university in Delaware, the District of Columbia, Maryland, Virginia, or West Virginia. Selection is based on the applicant's 1) participation in geoscience or earth science educational activities; and 2) potential for leadership as a future geoscience professional.

**Financial data** The stipend is $1,000. The recipient also is granted a 1-year membership in the Association for Women Geoscientists (AWG).

**Duration** 1 year.

**Additional information** This program is sponsored by the AWG Potomac Area Chapter.

**Number awarded** 1 each year.

**Deadline** April of each year.

## [1188]
## WINIFRED HILL BOYD GRADUATE SCHOLARSHIP

Kappa Delta Sorority
Attn: Foundation Project Manager
3205 Players Lane
Memphis, TN 38125
(901) 748-1897, ext. 203          Toll Free: (800) 536-1897
Fax: (901) 748-0949
E-mail: caroline.cullum@kappadelta.org
Web: www.kappadelta.org/scholarshipapplications_1

**Summary** To provide financial assistance to members of Kappa Delta Sorority who are working on a graduate degree in science or mathematics.

**Eligibility** This program is open to graduate members of Kappa Delta Sorority. Applicants must submit a personal statement giving their reasons for applying for this scholarship, official undergraduate and graduate transcripts, and 2 letters of recommendation. They must be working on a graduate degree in science or mathematics. Selection is based on academic excellence; service to the chapter, alumnae association, or national Kappa Delta; service to the campus and community; personal objectives and goals; potential; recommendations; and financial need.

**Financial data** The stipend is $5,000 per year. Funds may be used only for tuition, fees, and books, not for room and board.

**Duration** 1 year; may be renewed.

**Additional information** This program began in 2002.

**Number awarded** 1 each year.

**Deadline** November of each year.

## [1189]
## WISCONSIN LEGION AUXILIARY CHILD WELFARE SCHOLARSHIP

American Legion Auxiliary
Department of Wisconsin
Attn: Education Chair
2930 American Legion Drive
P.O. Box 140
Portage, WI 53901-0140
(608) 745-0124                    Toll Free: (866) 664-3863
Fax: (608) 745-1947       E-mail: alawi@amlegionauxwi.org
Web: www.amlegionauxwi.org/Scholarships.htm

**Summary** To provide financial assistance for graduate training in special education at a school in any state to dependents and descendants of veterans in Wisconsin.

**Eligibility** This program is open to the children, wives, and widows of veterans who are college graduates and have a GPA of 3.5 or higher. Grandchildren and great-grandchildren of members of the American Legion Auxiliary are also eligible. Applicants must be residents of Wisconsin and interested in working on a graduate degree in special education at a school in any state. Along with their application, they must submit a 300-word essay on "Education—An Investment in the Future." Financial need is considered in the selection process.

**Financial data** The stipend is $1,000.

**Duration** 1 year; nonrenewable.

**Number awarded** 1 each year.

**Deadline** March of each year.

## [1190]
## WISCONSIN WOMEN'S ALLIANCE FOUNDATION SCHOLARSHIP

Community Foundation for the Fox Valley Region, Inc.
Attn: Scholarships
4455 West Lawrence Street
P.O. Box 563
Appleton, WI 54912-0563
(920) 830-1290                    Fax: (920) 830-1293
E-mail: scholarships@cffoxvalley.org
Web: www.cffoxvalley.org/page.aspx?pid=246

**Summary** To provide financial assistance to mature women in Wisconsin who are working on an undergraduate or graduate degree at a school in any state.

**Eligibility** This program is open to Wisconsin women who are 25 years of age or older. Applicants must be attending an accredited 2- or 4-year college, university, or technical college to work on an undergraduate or graduate degree. They must submit a personal statement of their reasons for working on a degree in their chosen field, including their special professional interests, goals, and purposes within that field. Selection is based on that statement, employment history, volunteer activities, professional and community activities, and financial need.

**Financial data** The stipend ranges up to $1,000.

**Duration** 1 year.

**Number awarded** Normally, 3 each year.

**Deadline** February of each year.

## [1191]
## WLAM FOUNDATION SCHOLARS

Women Lawyers Association of Michigan Foundation
3150 Livernois, Suite 235
Troy, MI 48083
E-mail: wlamfmi@gmail.com
Web: www.wlamfoundation.org

**Summary** To provide financial assistance to women from any state enrolled at law schools in Michigan.

**Eligibility** This program is open to women from any state enrolled full or part time and in good academic standing at accredited law schools in Michigan. Applicants must be able to demonstrate leadership capabilities in advancing the position of women in society, including service in such areas as social justice, equality, family law, child advocacy, domestic violence, or work on behalf of underserved areas of populations. Along with their application, they must submit law school transcripts, a detailed letter of interest explaining how they meet the award criteria, a resume, and up to 3 letters of recommendation.

**Financial data** The stipend is $3,000.

**Duration** 1 year.

**Additional information** The accredited law schools are the University of Michigan Law School, Wayne State University Law School, University of Detroit Mercy School of Law, Thomas M. Cooley Law School, and Michigan State University-Detroit College of Law. This program includes the Kimberly M. Cahill Scholarship (for a student at the University of Michigan Law School) and the Dickinson Wright Women's Network Scholarship (for a student at Wayne State University Law School).

**Number awarded** 10 each year: 2 at each participating law school.

**Deadline** October of each year.

## [1192]
## WOMAN'S MISSIONARY UNION OF VIRGINIA SEMINARY SCHOLARSHIP

Woman's Missionary Union of Virginia
2828 Emerywood Parkway
Richmond, VA 23294
(804) 915-5000, ext. 8267
Toll Free: (800) 255-2428 (within VA)
Fax: (804) 672-8008              E-mail: wmuv@wmuv.org
Web: wmuv.org/developing-future-leaders/scholarships

**Summary** To provide financial assistance to women from Virginia who are interested in attending a Baptist seminary.

**Eligibility** This program is open to women from Virginia who are interested in attending a seminary supported through the Baptist General Association of Virginia (BGAV). Applicants must be seeking career missions appointments and/or professional ministry positions in churches, associations, states, or the world. An interview is required.

**Financial data** The stipend is $1,500 per year.

**Duration** 1 year; may be renewed up to 2 additional years.

**Number awarded** Up to 3 each year.

**Deadline** June of each year.

## [1193]
## WOMEN CHEFS & RESTAURATEURS SCHOLARSHIP PROGRAM

Women Chefs & Restaurateurs
Attn: Scholarship Program Coordinator
115 South Patrick Street, Suite 101
Alexandria, VA 22314
(630) 396-8339          Toll Free: (877) 927-7787
E-mail: Scholarship@womenchefs.org
Web: www.womenchefs.org

**Summary** To provide financial assistance to members of Women Chefs & Restaurateurs (WCR) who are interested in preparing for a culinary or related career.

**Eligibility** This program is open to women who are members of WCR, interested in attending a culinary or related school, and at least 18 years of age (21 for the wine scholarships). Recently, support was offered at the Tante Marie Cooking School in San Francisco; the Italian culinary experience, the classic culinary arts program, the classic pastry arts program, and the intensive sommelier program at the International Culinary Center (New York, New York); the Italian Culinary Experience, the classic pastry arts program, and the intensive sommelier program at the International Culinary Center (Campbell, California); and the pastry and baking diploma program and the culinary management diploma program at the Institute of Culinary Education (New York, New York). Applicants must submit a 1-page essay about their food service career, their culinary interests, what inspires them professionally, and how the scholarship will contribute to their career.

**Financial data** In general, scholarships provide payment of full or partial tuition, or stipends of $5,000 or $7,500 per year.

**Duration** Program lengths vary; scholarships must be used during the calendar year in which they are awarded.

**Additional information** Students may apply for only 1 program on a single application; the fee is $25 for the first application $40 for multiple applications (to a maximum of 3).

**Number awarded** Varies each year; recently, 18 of these scholarships were awarded.

**Deadline** July of each year.

## [1194]
## WOMEN IN AVIATION, INTERNATIONAL GENERAL SCHOLARSHIPS

Women in Aviation, International
Attn: Scholarships
Morningstar Airport
3647 State Route 503 South
West Alexandria, OH 45381-9354
(937) 839-4647          Fax: (937) 839-4645
E-mail: scholarships@wai.org
Web: www.wai.org/education/scholarships.cfm

**Summary** To provide financial assistance for college to members of Women in Aviation, International (WAI).

**Eligibility** This program is open to WAI members who are undergraduate or graduate students working on a degree in a field related to aviation or aerospace. Applicants must have earned a GPA of 3.0 or higher and be able to demonstrate leadership potential. Along with their application, they must submit a 500-word essay on their career aspirations and other topics that depend on the requirements of specific scholarships. Selection is based on achievements, attitude toward self and others, commitment to success, dedication to career, financial need, motivation, reliability, responsibility, and teamwork.

**Financial data** Stipends range from $1,000 to $5,000.

**Duration** 1 year.

**Additional information** WAI is a nonprofit professional organization dedicated to encouraging women to consider an aviation career and to providing educational outreach activities and networking resources to women active in the industry. Among its general programs for women working on degree in an aviation-related field are the Airbus Leadership Grant, the Boeing Company Career Enhancement Scholarship (sponsored by Boeing), the Candi Chamberlin Kubeck Award, the Changing the World Scholarship (established in 2014), the Janet Clark Memorial Scholarship, the Signature Flight Support Scholarship (established in 2014 by Signature Flight Support Corporation), and the Women in Aviation, International Achievement Awards.

**Number awarded** Varies each year.

**Deadline** November of each year.

## [1195]
## WOMEN IN FEDERAL LAW ENFORCEMENT MEMBERS-ONLY SCHOLARSHIP

Women in Federal Law Enforcement
Attn: Scholarship Coordinator
2200 Wilson Boulevard, Suite 102
PMB 204
Arlington, VA 22201-3324
(301) 805-2180          Fax: (301) 560-8836
E-mail: WIFLE@comcast.net
Web: wifle.wildapricot.org/Default.aspx?pageId=1491217

**Summary** To provide financial assistance for college or graduate school to women who are interested in preparing for a career in law enforcement and are members of Women in Federal Law Enforcement (WIFLE) or sponsored by a member.

**Eligibility** This program is open to women who are members of WIFLE or sponsored by a member and have completed at least 1 academic year of full-time study at an accredited 4-year college or university (or at a community college with the intention of transferring to a 4-year school). Applicants must be majoring in criminal justice or a related field (e.g., social sciences, public administration, computer science, finance, linguistic arts, chemistry, physics). They must have a GPA of 3.0 or higher. Students in graduate and postgraduate programs are also eligible, but those working on an associate degree are not. Along with their application, they must submit a letter demonstrating their financial need and describing their career objectives. U.S. citizenship is required.

**Financial data** The stipend is $1,500 per year.

**Duration** 1 year; may be renewed automatically for 1 additional year.

**Number awarded** 1 each year.

**Deadline** April of each year.

## [1196]
## WOMEN IN FEDERAL LAW ENFORCEMENT SCHOLARSHIP

Women in Federal Law Enforcement
Attn: Scholarship Coordinator
2200 Wilson Boulevard, Suite 102
PMB 204
Arlington, VA 22201-3324
(301) 805-2180                    Fax: (301) 560-8836
E-mail: WIFLE@comcast.net
Web: wifle.wildapricot.org/Default.aspx?pageId=1491217

**Summary**  To provide financial assistance for college or graduate school to women interested in preparing for a career in law enforcement.

**Eligibility**  This program is open to women who have completed at least 1 academic year of full-time study at an accredited 4-year college or university (or at a community college with the intention of transferring to a 4-year school). Applicants must be majoring in criminal justice or a related field (e.g., social sciences, public administration, computer science, finance, linguistic arts, chemistry, physics). They must have a GPA of 3.0 or higher. Students in graduate and postgraduate programs are also eligible, but those working on an associate degree are not. Along with their application, they must submit a 500-word essay describing a community project in which they have been involved and the results or impact to the community. Selection is based on academic potential, achievement, and commitment to serving communities in the field of law enforcement. U.S. citizenship is required.

**Financial data**  The stipend is $2,500.

**Duration**  1 year; may be renewed.

**Number awarded**  Varies each year; recently, 6 of these scholarships were awarded.

**Deadline**  April of each year.

## [1197]
## WOMEN IN TOXICOLOGY SPECIAL INTEREST GROUP VERA W. HUDSON AND ELIZABETH K. WEISBURGER SCHOLARSHIP FUND

Society of Toxicology
Attn: Women in Toxicology Special Interest Group
1821 Michael Faraday Drive, Suite 300
Reston, VA 20190-5348
(703) 438-3115                    Fax: (703) 438-3113
E-mail: sothq@toxicology.org
Web: www.toxicology.org/ai/af/awards.aspx

**Summary**  To provide funding to members of the Society of Toxicology (SOT), especially its Women in Toxicology Special Interest Group (WIT), who are conducting doctoral research in the field.

**Eligibility**  This program is open to full-time graduate student members of the society who have been advanced to candidacy for a Ph.D. in toxicology. Students who are not WIT members are strongly encouraged to join. Along with their application, they must submit a narrative of 1 to 2 pages describing their graduate research hypothesis, background, and significance. Selection is based on relevance of the research to toxicology, scholastic achievement, demonstrated leadership (professionally and/or in the community), and letters of recommendation.

**Financial data**  The grant is $2,000. Funds are paid to the recipient's university to be used for a tuition payment and/or other education and research-related expenses, including travel.

**Duration**  1 year.

**Number awarded**  1 each year.

**Deadline**  December of each year.

## [1198]
## WOMEN OF THE ELCA SCHOLARSHIP PROGRAM

Women of the Evangelical Lutheran Church in America
Attn: Scholarships
8765 West Higgins Road
Chicago, IL 60631-4101
(773) 380-2741        Toll Free: (800) 638-3522, ext. 2741
Fax: (773) 380-2419        E-mail: valora.starr@elca.org
Web: www.womenoftheelca.org

**Summary**  To provide financial assistance to lay women who are members of Evangelical Lutheran Church of America (ELCA) congregations and who wish to take classes on the undergraduate, graduate, professional, or vocational school level.

**Eligibility**  This program is open to ELCA lay women who are at least 21 years of age and have experienced an interruption of at least 2 years in their education since high school. Applicants must have been admitted to an educational institution to prepare for a career in other than the ordained ministry. They may be working on an undergraduate, graduate, professional, or vocational school degree. U.S. citizenship is required.

**Financial data**  The average stipend is $1,000.

**Duration**  Up to 2 years.

**Additional information**  These scholarships are supported by several endowment funds: the Cronk Memorial Fund, the First Triennial Board Scholarship Fund, the General Scholarship Fund, the Mehring Fund, the Paepke Scholarship Fund, the Piero/Wade/Wade Fund, and the Edwin/Edna Robeck Scholarship.

**Number awarded**  Varies each year; recently, 15 of these scholarships were awarded.

**Deadline**  February of each year.

## [1199]
## WOMEN'S BUSINESS ALLIANCE SCHOLARSHIP PROGRAM

Choice Hotels International
Attn: Women's Business Alliance
4225 East Windrose Drive
Phoenix, AZ 85032
(602) 953-4478
Web: www.choicehotels.com/en/about-choice/wba

**Summary**  To provide financial assistance to women interested in preparing for a career in the hospitality industry.

**Eligibility**  This program is open to female high school seniors, undergraduates, and graduate students. Applicants must be U.S. citizens or permanent residents interested in preparing for a career in the hospitality industry. They must submit an essay of 500 words or less on why they are interested in a career in the hospitality industry, the area of the industry that appeals to them the most, and some of their major accomplishments and/or personal characteristics that will benefit their work in the hospitality industry. Selection is based on that essay, academic record, and 2 letters of recommendation.

**Financial data** The stipend is $2,000.

**Duration** 1 year; recipients may reapply.

**Additional information** This program began in 2004.

**Number awarded** 2 or more each year.

**Deadline** January of each year.

## [1200]
## WOMEN'S ENVIRONMENTAL COUNCIL SCHOLARSHIPS

Women's Environmental Council
Attn: Scholarships
P.O. Box 882744
San Diego, CA 92168
E-mail: kellyn.lupfer@gmail.com
Web: www.wecweb.org/scholarships.html

**Summary** To provide financial assistance to women from any state working on an undergraduate or graduate degree in an environmental field at colleges and universities in southern California.

**Eligibility** This program is open to female undergraduate and graduate students from any state who are enrolled at colleges and universities in Los Angeles, Orange, and San Diego counties in California. Applicants must be studying such environmental fields as architecture, biology, chemistry, environmental science, ecology, environmental engineering, forestry, geography, geology/hydrology, marine studies, or urban planning. They must have a GPA of 3.0 or higher. Along with their application, they must submit a personal statement that includes a description of their academic professional, and environmental achievements and goals; how they became interested in preparing for a career in the environmental field; and how this scholarship will help them achieve their professional and personal goals. Selection is based on that statement (50%); personal incentive, volunteerism, and extracurricular activities (20%); grades and course work (10%); a letter of reference (15%); and thoroughness and presentation of the application packet (5%).

**Financial data** The stipend is $1,000. Recipients are also given a 1-year membership in the Women's Environmental Council (WEC).

**Duration** 1 year.

**Additional information** The WEC, founded in 1993, currently has chapters in Los Angeles, Orange County, and San Diego. Recipients are expected to attend the WEC annual meeting in the spring to receive their awards.

**Number awarded** Varies each year; recently, 5 of these scholarships were awarded.

**Deadline** January of each year.

## [1201]
## WOMEN'S INDEPENDENCE SCHOLARSHIP PROGRAM

Women's Independence Scholarship Program, Inc.
Attn: WISP Program
4900 Randall Parkway, Suite H
Wilmington, NC 28403
(910) 397-7742          Toll Free: (866) 255-7742
Fax: (910) 397-0023     E-mail: nancy@wispinc.org
Web: www.wispinc.org

**Summary** To provide financial assistance for college or graduate school to women who are victims of partner abuse.

**Eligibility** This program is open to women who are victims of partner abuse and have worked for at least 6 months with a nonprofit domestic violence victim services provider that is willing to sponsor them. Applicants must be interested in attending a vocational school, community college, 4-year college or university, or (in exceptional circumstances) graduate school as a full- or part-time student. They should have left an abusive partner at least 1 year previously; women who have been parted from their batterer for more than 5 years are also eligible, but funding for such applicants may be limited. Preference is given to single mothers with young children. Special consideration is given to applicants who plan to use their education to further the rights of, and options for, women and girls. Selection is based primarily on financial need. U.S. citizenship or permanent resident status is required.

**Financial data** Stipends depend on the need of the recipient, but they are at least $250 and average $2,000 per academic term. First priority is given to funding for direct educational expenses (tuition, books, and fees), which is paid directly to the educational institution. Second priority is for assistance in reducing indirect financial barriers to education (e.g., child care, transportation), which is paid directly to the sponsoring agency.

**Duration** 1 year; may be renewed if the recipient maintains a GPA of 2.75 or higher.

**Additional information** This program began in 1999 when the sponsor was known as the Sunshine Lady Foundation.

**Number awarded** Varies each year. Since the program began, it has awarded more than $16 million in scholarships to approximately 2,000 women.

**Deadline** Applications may be submitted at any time, but they must be received at least 2 months before the start of the intended program.

## [1202]
## WOMEN'S MUSIC COMMISSION

Broadcast Music Inc.
Attn: BMI Foundation, Inc.
7 World Trade Center
250 Greenwich Street
New York, NY 10007-0030
(212) 220-3000          E-mail: info@bmifoundation.org
Web: www.bmifoundation.org

**Summary** To recognize and reward, with a commission for production of a new work, outstanding young female composers.

**Eligibility** This competition is open to women between 20 and 30 years of age who are citizens or permanent residents of the United States. Applicants must submit samples of their original compositions.

**Financial data** The winner receives a $5,000 commission to create a new work.

**Duration** The competition is held annually.

**Additional information** This program began in 2006. Each year, the sponsor partners with a different world-class performer, ensemble, or presenter to present the premier performance.

**Number awarded** 1 each year.

**Deadline** May of each year.

## [1203]
## WORKSHOPS FOR WOMEN GRADUATE STUDENTS AND RECENT PH.D.S

Association for Women in Mathematics
11240 Waples Mill Road, Suite 200
Fairfax, VA 22030
(703) 934-0163                        Fax: (703) 359-7562
E-mail: awm@awm-math.org
Web: sites.google.com/site/awmmath/programs/workshops

**Summary** To enable women graduate students and recent Ph.D.s in mathematics to participate in workshops in conjunction with major meetings.

**Eligibility** Eligible for funding are women graduate students who have begun work on a thesis problem in mathematics and women mathematicians who received their Ph.D.s within the preceding 5 years. Applicants must wish to participate in workshops held in conjunction with major mathematics meetings at which each participating graduate student presents a poster on her thesis problem and each postdoctorate presents a talk on her research.

**Financial data** Funding covers travel and subsistence.

**Duration** Funding for 2 days is provided.

**Additional information** Participants have the opportunity to present and discuss their research and to meet with other women mathematicians at all stages of their careers. The workshop also includes a panel discussion on issues of career development and a luncheon. This program is supported by the Office of Naval Research, the Department of Energy, and the National Security Agency.

**Number awarded** Up to 20 at each of 2 workshops each year.

**Deadline** October or August of each year.

## [1204]
## YOUNG LADIES' RADIO LEAGUE SCHOLARSHIPS

Foundation for Amateur Radio, Inc.
Attn: Scholarship Committee
P.O. Box 911
Columbia, MD 21044-0911
(410) 552-2652                        Fax: (410) 981-5146
E-mail: dave.prestel@gmail.com
Web: www.farweb.org/scholarships

**Summary** To provide funding to female licensed radio amateurs who are interested in earning a bachelor's or graduate degree in the United States.

**Eligibility** This program is open to female radio amateurs who have at least an FCC Technician Class license or equivalent foreign authorization. Applicants must intend to work full

time on a bachelor's or graduate degree at a college or university in the United States. There are no restrictions on the course of study or residency location. Non-U.S. amateurs are eligible. Preference is given to students working on a degree in communications, electronics, or related arts and sciences. Financial need is considered in the selection process.

**Financial data** The stipend is $1,500.

**Duration** 1 year.

**Additional information** This program is sponsored by the Young Ladies' Radio League. It includes the following named scholarships: the Ethel Smith, K4LMB, Memorial Scholarship and the Mary Lou Brown, NM7N Memorial, Scholarship.

**Number awarded** 2 each year.

**Deadline** April of each year.

## [1205]
## ZETA PHI BETA GENERAL GRADUATE FELLOWSHIPS

Zeta Phi Beta Sorority, Inc.
Attn: National Education Foundation
1734 New Hampshire Avenue, N.W.
Washington, DC 20009
(202) 387-3103                        Fax: (202) 232-4593
E-mail: scholarship@ZPhiBNEF.org
Web: www.zphib1920.org/nef

**Summary** To provide financial assistance to women who are working on a professional degree, master's degree, doctorate, or postdoctorate.

**Eligibility** Women graduate or postdoctoral students are eligible to apply if they have achieved distinction or shown promise of distinction in their chosen fields. Applicants need not be members of Zeta Phi Beta. They must be enrolled full time in a professional, graduate, or postdoctoral program. Along with their application, they must submit a 150-word essay on their educational goals and professional aspirations, how this award will help them to achieve those goals, and why they should receive the award. Financial need is not considered in the selection process.

**Financial data** The stipend ranges up to $2,500, paid directly to the recipient.

**Duration** 1 academic year; may be renewed.

**Number awarded** 1 or more each year.

**Deadline** January of each year.

## [1206]
## ZETA TAU ALPHA ACHIEVEMENT SCHOLARSHIPS

Zeta Tau Alpha Foundation, Inc.
Attn: Director of Foundation Administration
3450 Founders Road
Indianapolis, IN 46268
(317) 872-0540                        Fax: (317) 876-3948
E-mail: zetataualpha@zetataualpha.org
Web: www.zetataualpha.org

**Summary** To provide financial assistance for college or graduate school to women who are members of Zeta Tau Alpha.

**Eligibility** This program is open to undergraduate and graduate women who are enrolled at a 4-year college or university and student members of the school's Zeta Tau Alpha chapter. Applicants must demonstrate leadership qualities within their chapter or in campus activities while maintaining a high scholastic average. Selection is based on academic achievement (GPA of 2.9 or higher), involvement in campus and community activities, recommendations, current class status, and financial need.

**Financial data** The stipend is at least $1,000.

**Duration** 1 year; renewable.

**Number awarded** Varies each year; recently, the foundation awarded a total of more than $620,000 to 279 undergraduate and graduate members for all of its scholarship programs.

**Deadline** February of each year.

## [1207]
## ZETA TAU ALPHA FOUNDERS GRANTS

Zeta Tau Alpha Foundation, Inc.
Attn: Director of Foundation Administration
3450 Founders Road
Indianapolis, IN 46268
(317) 872-0540          Fax: (317) 876-3948
E-mail: zetataualpha@zetataualpha.org
Web: www.zetataualpha.org

**Summary** To provide financial assistance to graduate women who are alumnae of Zeta Tau Alpha.

**Eligibility** This program is open to graduate students who have been members of Zeta Tau Alpha. Applicants must be able to demonstrate leadership abilities, academic achievement, and financial need. Selection is based on academic achievement (GPA of 2.9 or higher), involvement in campus and community activities, recommendations, current class status, and financial need.

**Financial data** The stipend is $9,000.

**Duration** 1 year; renewable.

**Number awarded** 9 each year.

**Deadline** February of each year.

## [1208]
## ZETA TAU ALPHA SERVICE SCHOLARSHIPS

Zeta Tau Alpha Foundation, Inc.
Attn: Director of Foundation Administration
3450 Founders Road
Indianapolis, IN 46268
(317) 872-0540          Fax: (317) 876-3948
E-mail: zetataualpha@zetataualpha.org
Web: www.zetataualpha.org

**Summary** To provide financial assistance for graduate study in specified fields to women who are alumnae of Zeta Tau Alpha.

**Eligibility** This program is open to graduate students who have been members of Zeta Tau Alpha. Applicants must be studying special education, social work, or other health-related professions. Selection is based on academic achievement (GPA of 2.9 or higher), involvement in campus and community activities, recommendations, current class status, and financial need.

**Financial data** The stipend is at least $1,000.

**Duration** 1 year; renewable.

**Number awarded** Varies each year; recently, the foundation awarded a total of more than $620,000 to 279 undergraduate and graduate members for all of its scholarship programs.

**Deadline** February of each year.

# Professionals/ Postdoctorates

Listed alphabetically by program title and described in detail here are 278 grants, awards, educational support programs, residencies, and other sources of "free money" available to women who are professionals and post-doctorates. This funding can be used to support research, creative activities, formal academic classes, training courses, and/or residencies in the United States.

## [1209]
## AAUW CAREER DEVELOPMENT GRANTS

American Association of University Women
Attn: AAUW Educational Foundation
301 ACT Drive, Department 60
P.O. Box 4030
Iowa City, IA 52243-4030
(319) 337-1716, ext. 60          Fax: (319) 337-1204
E-mail: aauw@act.org
Web: www.aauw.org

**Summary**  To provide financial assistance to women who are seeking career advancement, career change, or reentry into the workforce.

**Eligibility**  This program is open to women who are U.S. citizens or permanent residents, have earned a bachelor's degree, received their most recent degree more than 4 years ago, and are making career changes, seeking to advance in current careers, or reentering the workforce. Applicants must be interested in working toward a master's degree, second bachelor's or associate degree, professional degree (e.g., M.D., J.D.), certification program, or technical school certificate. They must be planning to undertake course work at an accredited 2- or 4-year college or university (or a technical school that is licensed, accredited, or approved by the U.S. Department of Education). Primary consideration is given to women of color and women pursuing their first advanced degree or credentials in nontraditional fields. Support is not provided for prerequisite course work or for Ph.D. course work or dissertations. Selection is based on demonstrated commitment to education and equity for women and girls, reason for seeking higher education or technical training, degree to which study plan is consistent with career objectives, potential for success in chosen field, documentation of opportunities in chosen field, feasibility of study plans and proposed time schedule, validity of proposed budget and budget narrative (including sufficient outside support), and quality of written proposal.

**Financial data**  Grants range from $2,000 to $12,000. Funds may be used for tuition, fees, books, supplies, local transportation, dependent child care, or purchase of a computer required for the study program.

**Duration**  1 year, beginning in July; nonrenewable.

**Additional information**  The filing fee is $35.

**Number awarded**  Varies each year; recently, 63 of these grants, with a value of $670,000, were awarded.

**Deadline**  December of each year.

## [1210]
## ACNM FOUNDATION FELLOWSHIP FOR GRADUATE EDUCATION

American College of Nurse-Midwives
Attn: ACNM Foundation, Inc.
8403 Colesville Road, Suite 1550
Silver Spring, MD 20910-6374
(240) 485-1850          Fax: (240) 485-1818
E-mail: fdn@acnm.org
Web: www.midwife.org

**Summary**  To provide financial assistance for midwifery education at the doctoral or postdoctoral level to members of the American College of Nurse-Midwives (ACNM).

**Eligibility**  This program is open to ACNM members who are currently enrolled in a doctoral or postdoctoral midwife education program. Applicants must be a certified nurse midwife (CNM) or a certified midwife (CM). Along with their application, they must submit a curriculum vitae; a sample of up to 30 pages of scholarly work; and brief essays on their 5-year academic career plans, intended use of the fellowship money, and intended future participation in the local, regional, and/or national activities of ACNM or other activities that contribute to midwifery research, education, or practice.

**Financial data**  A stipend is awarded (amount not specified).

**Duration**  1 year.

**Additional information**  This program began in 1997.

**Number awarded**  1 each year.

**Deadline**  March of each year.

## [1211]
## AERA-ETS FELLOWSHIP PROGRAM IN MEASUREMENT

American Educational Research Association
1430 K Street, N.W., Suite 1200
Washington, DC 20005
(202) 238-3200          Fax: (202) 238-3250
E-mail: fellowships@aera.net
Web: www.aera.net

**Summary**  To provide an opportunity for junior scholars (particularly women and minorities) in the field of education to engage in a program of research and advanced training while in residence at Educational Testing Service (ETS) in Princeton, New Jersey.

**Eligibility**  This program is open to junior scholars and early career research scientists in fields and disciplines related to education research. Applicants must have completed their Ph.D. or Ed.D. degree within the past 3 years. They must be proposing a program of intensive research and training at the ETS campus in Princeton, New Jersey in such areas as educational measurement, assessment design, psychometrics, statistical analyses, large-scale evaluations, and other studies directed to explaining student progress and achievement. A particular goal of the program is to increase the involvement of women and underrepresented minority professionals in measurement, psychometrics, assessment, and related fields. U.S. citizenship or permanent resident status is required.

**Financial data**  The stipend is $55,000 per year. Fellows also receive relocation expenses and ETS employee benefits.

**Duration**  Up to 2 years.

**Additional information**  This program is jointly sponsored by the American Educational Research Association (AERA) and ETS.

**Number awarded**  Up to 2 each year.

**Deadline**  November of each year.

## [1212]
## AFRL/DAGSI OHIO STUDENT-FACULTY RESEARCH FELLOWSHIP PROGRAM

Dayton Area Graduate Studies Institute
3155 Research Boulevard, Suite 205
Kettering, OH 45420
(937) 781-4001                    Fax: (937) 781-4005
E-mail: kelam@dagsi.org
Web: www.dagsi.org/pages/osrfp_proinforeq.html

**Summary**   To provide funding to women and other faculty and graduate students from any state at designated universities in Ohio who are interested in conducting research in aerospace technologies of interest to the U.S. Air Force.

**Eligibility**   This program is open to research teams of full-time graduate students and faculty at 18 designated Ohio universities. Applicants must be interested in conducting research that will utilize the facilities of the Air Force Research Laboratory (AFRL) at Wright-Patterson Air Force Base. All 6 directorates at the AFRL (air vehicles, propulsion, sensors, materials and manufacturing, human effectiveness, and information) participate in this program. Applications from Ph.D. candidates must be developed and written largely by the student, with support, guidance, and input as necessary from the faculty partner. For master's projects, the proposal can be developed and written jointly by the faculty member and the student. All participants (faculty and student) must be U.S. citizens. Underrepresented minorities, women, and persons with disabilities are strongly urged to apply.

**Financial data**   Grants provide stipends of $23,500 for students who have a master's degree and are working on a Ph.D. or $18,500 for students who have a bachelor's degree and are working on a master's; student's tuition for 1 academic year; a faculty stipend of $11,000; student and faculty allowances of $3,000 each for program-related travel or other approved expenses; and overhead at a maximum off-campus rate of 26% of student and faculty stipends and miscellaneous allowances.

**Duration**   1 year; may be renewed for 1 additional year by master's students and for 2 additional years by Ph.D. candidates. Students are expected to spend 8 consecutive weeks conducting research at AFRL and faculty members are expected to spend at least 1 month conducting research at AFRL.

**Additional information**   DAGSI was established in 1994 as a consortium of graduate engineering schools at the University of Dayton, Wright State University, and the Air Force Institute of Technology. The Ohio State University and the University of Cincinnati joined as affiliated members in 1996 and Miami University and Ohio University joined as associate members in 2001. Students from the following universities are also eligible to participate in this program: University of Akron, Bowling Green State University, Central State University, Cleveland State University, Kent State University, Shawnee State University, University of Toledo, Youngstown State University, Medical College of Ohio, Northeastern Ohio Universities College of Medicine, and Case Western Reserve University.

**Number awarded**   At least 20 each year.

**Deadline**   January of each year.

## [1213]
## AGA RESEARCH SCHOLAR AWARDS

American Gastroenterological Association
Attn: AGA Research Foundation
Research Awards Manager
4930 Del Ray Avenue
Bethesda, MD 20814-2512
(301) 222-4012                    Fax: (301) 654-5920
E-mail: awards@gastro.org
Web: www.gastro.org/aga-foundation/grants

**Summary**   To provide research funding to women, minorities, and other young investigators developing an independent career in an area of gastroenterology, hepatology, or related fields.

**Eligibility**   Applicants must hold full-time faculty positions at North American universities or professional institutes at the time of application. They should be early in their careers (fellows and established investigators are not appropriate candidates). Candidates with an M.D. degree must have completed clinical training within the past 5 years and those with a Ph.D. must have completed their degree within the past 5 years. Membership in the American Gastroenterological Association (AGA) is required. Selection is based on significance, investigator, innovation, approach, environment, relevance to AGA mission, and evidence of institutional commitment. Women, minorities, and physician/scientist investigators are strongly encouraged to apply.

**Financial data**   The grant is $90,000 per year. Funds are to be used for project costs, including salary, supplies, and equipment but excluding travel. Indirect costs are not allowed.

**Duration**   2 years.

**Additional information**   At least 70% of the recipient's research effort should relate to the gastrointestinal tract or liver.

**Number awarded**   4 each year.

**Deadline**   October of each year.

## [1214]
## ALEXANDER GRALNICK RESEARCH INVESTIGATOR PRIZE

American Psychological Foundation
750 First Street, N.E.
Washington, DC 20002-4242
(202) 336-5843                    Fax: (202) 336-5812
E-mail: foundation@apa.org
Web: www.apa.org/apf/funding/gralnick.aspx

**Summary**   To recognize and reward women, minority, and other psychologists conducting exceptional research on serious mental illness.

**Eligibility**   This program is open to psychologists who have a doctoral degree, have a record of significant research productivity, and are able to demonstrate evidence on continuing creativity in the area of research on serious mental illness (including, but not limited to, schizophrenia, bipolar disorder, and paranoia). Nominees must also have significant involvement in training and development of younger investigators. They must have an affiliation with an accredited college, university, or other treatment or research institution. The sponsor encourages nominations of individuals who represent diversity in race, ethnicity, gender, age, disability, and sexual orientation.

**Financial data** The award is $20,000.

**Duration** The award is presented biennially, in even-numbered years.

**Additional information** This award was first presented in 2002.

**Number awarded** 1 each even-numbered year.

**Deadline** April of each even-numbered year.

## [1215]
## ALFRED P. SLOAN FOUNDATION RESEARCH FELLOWSHIPS

Alfred P. Sloan Foundation
630 Fifth Avenue, Suite 2550
New York, NY 10111-0242
(212) 649-1649                     Fax: (212) 757-5117
E-mail: researchfellows@sloan.org
Web: www.sloan.org/sloan-research-fellowships

**Summary** To provide funding for research in selected fields of science to recent doctorates, particularly women and underrepresented minorities.

**Eligibility** This program is open to scholars who are no more than 6 years from completion of the most recent Ph.D. or equivalent in computational and evolutionary molecular biology, chemistry, computer science, economics, mathematics, ocean sciences (including marine biology), neuroscience, physics, or a related interdisciplinary field. Applicants must have a tenure track position at a college or university in the United States or Canada. Direct applications are not accepted; candidates must be nominated by department heads or other senior scholars. Although fellows must be at an early stage of their research careers, they should give strong evidence of independent research accomplishments and creativity. The sponsor strongly encourages the participation of women and members of underrepresented minority groups.

**Financial data** The stipend is $25,000 per year. Funds are paid directly to the fellow's institution to be used by the fellow for equipment, technical assistance, professional travel, trainee support, or any other research-related expense; they may not be used to augment an existing full-time salary.

**Duration** 2 years; may be extended if unexpended funds still remain.

**Additional information** This program began in 1955, when it awarded $235,000 to 22 chemists, physicists, and pure mathematicians. Neuroscience was added in 1972, economics and applied mathematics in 1980, computer science in 1993, computational and evolutionary molecular biology in 2002, and ocean sciences in 2012. Currently, the program awards more than $5.5 million in grants annually.

**Number awarded** 126 each year: 23 in chemistry, 12 in computational and evolutionary molecular biology, 16 in computer science, 8 in economics, 20 in mathematics, 16 in neuroscience, 8 in ocean sciences, and 23 in physics.

**Deadline** September of each year.

## [1216]
## AMBER GRANTS

WomensNet.Net
c/o Christina Lambert
61 Falling Brook Road
Fairport, NY 14450-8961
E-mail: womensnetnet@gmail.com
Web: www.womensnet.net/AmberGrants.aspx

**Summary** To provide funding to women entrepreneurs who start a new business.

**Eligibility** This funding is available to women who are trying to start small businesses, home-based or online. Applicants must be seeking funds to upgrade equipment, pay for a web site, or meet other small but essential expenses necessary to get a new business off the ground. Selection is based on merit, potential success of the idea, and impact of the grant on the business; formal business plans are not required.

**Financial data** Grants are $500 or $1,000.

**Duration** These are 1-time grants.

**Additional information** This program began in 1998.

**Number awarded** Grants are awarded periodically, but at least quarterly and as often as monthly.

**Deadline** Applications may be submitted at any time and will be considered when the next grant is awarded.

## [1217]
## AMELIA EARHART MEMORIAL SCHOLARSHIPS

Ninety-Nines, Inc.
4300 Amelia Earhart Road, Suite A
Oklahoma City, OK 73159
(405) 685-7969                 Toll Free: (800) 994-1929
Fax: (405) 685-7985    E-mail: AEChair@ninety-nines.org
Web: www.ninety-nines.org/index.cfm/scholarships.htm

**Summary** To provide funding to members of the Ninety-Nines (an organization of women pilots) who are interested in advanced flight training or other technical study related to aviation.

**Eligibility** This program is open to women from any country who have been members of the organization for at least 1 year. They must be interested in 1 of the following 3 types of scholarships: 1) flight training, to complete an additional pilot certificate or rating or pilot training course; 2) jet type rating, to complete type rating certification in any jet; 3) technical training, to complete an aviation or aerospace technical training or certification course. Applicants for flight training scholarships must be a current pilot with the appropriate medical certification and approaching the flight time requirement for the rating or certificate. Applicants for jet type rating scholarships must be a current airline transport pilot with a first-class medical certificate and at least 100 hours of multi-engine flight time or combined multi-engine and turbine time. Applicants for technical training scholarships must be enrolled in a course that is not part of a college degree program. Financial need is considered in the selection process.

**Financial data** These scholarships provide payment of all costs to complete the appropriate rating or certificate.

**Duration** Support is provided until completion of the rating or certificate.

**Additional information** This program began in 1941.

**Number awarded** Varies each year; recently, 24 of these scholarships were awarded.

**Deadline** Applications must be submitted to the chapter scholarship chair by November of each year; those chairs must forward the applications from their chapter to the designated trustee by January of each year. At-large numbers (those who do not belong to a specific chapter) must submit their application to their section by December of each year.

## [1218]
## AMELIA EARHART RESEARCH SCHOLAR GRANT

Ninety-Nines, Inc.
Attn: Chair, Research Scholar Grants
4300 Amelia Earhart Road, Suite A
Oklahoma City, OK 73159
(405) 685-7969        Toll Free: (800) 994-1929
Fax: (405) 685-7985    E-mail: AEChair@ninety-nines.org
Web: www.ninety-nines.org/index.cfm/scholarships.htm

**Summary** To provide funding to scholars interested in expanding knowledge about women in aviation and space.

**Eligibility** This program is open to scholars who are conducting research on the role of women in aviation and space. Disciplines may include, but are not limited to, biology, business administration, economics, ergonomics, history, human engineering, psychology, or sociology. Applicants may be seeking funding to be used in conjunction with other research activities, such as completion of requirements for an advanced degree or matching funds with other grants to support a program larger than either grant could sponsor independently.

**Financial data** The amount awarded varies; generally, the grant is at least $1,000.

**Duration** The grant is awarded periodically.

**Number awarded** 1 each granting period.

**Deadline** Deadline not specified.

## [1219]
## AMERICAN ASSOCIATION OF OBSTETRICIANS AND GYNECOLOGISTS FOUNDATION SCHOLARSHIPS

American Association of Obstetricians and Gynecologists
  Foundation
2105 Laurel Bush Road, Suite 201
Bel Air, MD 21015
(443) 640-1051        Fax: (443) 640-1031
E-mail: info@aaogf.org
Web: www.aaogf.org/scholarship.asp

**Summary** To provide funding to physicians (particularly women and minorities) who are interested in a program of research training in obstetrics and gynecology.

**Eligibility** Applicants must have an M.D. degree and be eligible for the certification process of the American Board of Obstetrics and Gynecology (ABOG). They must be interested in participating in research training conducted by 1 or more faculty mentors at an academic department of obstetrics and gynecology in the United States or Canada. The research training may be either laboratory-based or clinical, and should focus on fundamental biology, disease mechanisms, interventions or diagnostics, epidemiology, or translational research. Applicants for the scholarship co-sponsored by the Society for Maternal-Fetal Medicine (SMFM) must also be members or associate members of the SMFM. Women and minority candidates are strongly encouraged to apply. Selection is based on the scholarly, clinical, and research qualifications of the candidate; evidence of the candidate's commitment to an investigative career in academic obstetrics and gynecology in the United States or Canada; qualifications of the sponsoring department and mentor; overall quality of the mentoring plan; and quality of the research project.

**Financial data** The grant is $120,000 per year. Sufficient funds to support travel to the annual fellows' retreat must be set aside. The balance of the funds may be used for salary, technical support, and supplies.

**Duration** 1 year; may be renewed for 2 additional years, based on satisfactory progress of the scholar.

**Additional information** Scholars must devote at least 75% of their effort to the program of research training.

**Number awarded** 2 each year: 1 co-sponsored by ABOG and 1 co-sponsored by SMFM.

**Deadline** June of each year.

## [1220]
## AMERICAN LEGION AUXILIARY EMERGENCY FUND

American Legion Auxiliary
Attn: AEF Program Case Manager
8945 North Meridian Street
Indianapolis, IN 46260
(317) 569-4544        Fax: (317) 569-4502
E-mail: aef@alaforveterans.org
Web: www.alaforveterans.org

**Summary** To provide funding to members of the American Legion Auxiliary who need educational training or are facing temporary emergency needs.

**Eligibility** This program is open to members of the American Legion Auxiliary who have maintained their membership for the immediate past 2 consecutive years and have paid their dues for the current year. Applicants must need emergency assistance for the following purposes: 1) food, shelter, and utilities during a time of financial crisis; 2) food and shelter because of weather-related emergencies and natural disasters; or 3) educational training for eligible members who lack the necessary skills for employment or to upgrade competitive workforce skills. They must have exhausted all other sources of financial assistance, including funds and/or services available through the local Post and/or Unit, appropriate community welfare agencies, or state and federal financial aid for education. Grants are not available to settle already existing or accumulated debts, handle catastrophic illness, resettle disaster victims, or other similar problems.

**Financial data** The maximum grant is $2,400. Payments may be made directly to the member or to the mortgage company or utility. Educational grants may be paid directly to the educational institution.

**Duration** Grants are expended over no more than 3 months.

**Additional information** This program began in 1969. In 1981, it was expanded to include the Displaced Homemaker Fund (although that title is no longer used).

**Number awarded** Varies each year.

**Deadline** Applications may be submitted at any time.

## [1221]
## AMERICAN PSYCHOLOGICAL FOUNDATION VISIONARY GRANTS

American Psychological Foundation
750 First Street, N.E.
Washington, DC 20002-4242
(202) 336-5843                    Fax: (202) 336-5812
E-mail: foundation@apa.org
Web: www.apa.org/apf/funding/vision-weiss.aspx

**Summary**   To provide funding to professionals (especially women, minorities, and individuals with disabilities) who are interested in conducting projects that use psychology to solve social problems related to the priorities of the American Psychological Foundation (APF).

**Eligibility**   This program is open to professionals at nonprofit organizations engaged in research, education, and intervention projects and programs. Applicants must be interested in conducting an activity that uses psychology to solve social problems in the following priority areas: understanding and fostering the connection between mental and physical health; reducing stigma and prejudice; understanding and preventing all forms of violence; or addressing the long-term psychological needs of individuals and communities in the aftermath of disaster. Selection is based on the criticality of the proposed funding for the proposed work; conformance with stated program goals and requirements; innovative and potential impact qualities; quality, viability, and promise of proposed work, and competence and capability of project leaders. The sponsor encourages applications from individuals who represent diversity in race, ethnicity, gender, age, disability, and sexual orientation.

**Financial data**   Grants range from $2,500 to $20,000.

**Duration**   1 year; nonrenewable.

**Additional information**   This program began in 2003.

**Number awarded**   1 or more each year.

**Deadline**   March of each year.

## [1222]
## ANN E. KAMMER MEMORIAL FELLOWSHIP FUND

Marine Biological Laboratory
Attn: Chief Academic and Scientific Officer
7 MBL Street
Woods Hole, MA 02543-1015
(508) 289-7173                    Fax: (508) 457-1924
E-mail: casoofice@mbl.edu
Web: hermes.mbl.edu

**Summary**   To provide funding to women who have faculty positions and wish to conduct summer research at the Marine Biological Laboratory (MBL) in Woods Hole, Massachusetts.

**Eligibility**   This program is open to female faculty members who are interested in conducting summer research at the MBL. Applicants must submit a statement of the potential impact of this award on their career development. Preference is given to investigators working in the neurosciences.

**Financial data**   Grants range from $5,000 to $25,000, typically to cover laboratory rental and/or housing costs. Awardees are responsible for other costs, such as supplies, shared resource usage, affiliated staff who accompany them, or travel.

**Duration**   8 to 10 weeks during the summer.

**Number awarded**   1 each year.

**Deadline**   December of each year.

## [1223]
## ANNIE JUMP CANNON AWARD IN ASTRONOMY

American Astronomical Society
Attn: Secretary
2000 Florida Avenue, N.W., Suite 400
Washington, DC 20009-1231
(202) 328-2010                    Fax: (202) 234-2560
E-mail: aassec@aas.org
Web: aas.org

**Summary**   To recognize and reward female postdoctoral scholars for significant research in astronomy.

**Eligibility**   This award is available to North American female astronomers who completed their Ph.D. within the past 5 years. Self-nominations are allowed. Selection is based on completed research and promise for future research.

**Financial data**   The award is $1,500.

**Duration**   The award is presented annually.

**Additional information**   This award was established in 1934 by the American Astronomical Society (AAS). From 1974 through 2004, it was awarded by the American Association of University Women (AAUW) Educational Foundation with the advice of the AAS. Effective in 2005, the AAS resumed administration of the award.

**Number awarded**   1 each year.

**Deadline**   June of each year.

## [1224]
## ART MEETS ACTIVISM GRANT PROGRAM

Kentucky Foundation for Women
Heyburn Building
332 West Broadway, Suite 1215-A
Louisville, KY 40202-2184
(502) 562-0045                    Toll Free: (866) 654-7564
Fax: (502) 561-0420               E-mail: team@kfw.org
Web: www.kfw.org/artact.html

**Summary**   To support women and organizations in Kentucky wishing to conduct artistic activities that will benefit women and girls in the state.

**Eligibility**   This program is open to women artists who have resided in Kentucky for at least 1 year and whose work is feminist in nature and is intentionally focused on social change outcomes. Nonprofit organizations are also eligible if their proposed project is artist driven. Applicants may be seeking funding for a range of artistic activities, including arts education programs focused on women or girls, community participation in the creation of new art forms, community based projects involving new partnerships between artists and activists, and arts-based community projects with social change themes or contents. In the selection process, the following criteria are considered: artwork in the sample is strong, highly original, and reflects feminism and social change; the proposed activities will directly benefit women and girls in Kentucky; application and work sample demonstrate applicant's understanding and practice of feminism; application and work sample demonstrate a clear understanding of the relationship between art and social change; work plan, timeline, and budget are clear, detailed, and realistic; and applicant's ability to complete the proposed activities in clearly shown. If applications are of equal artistic merit, priority is given to first-time applicants and those from underrepresented demographic populations (such as lesbians, African Americans, and women with disabilities).

**Financial data** Grants may range from $1,000 to $7,500, but most average between $3,000 and $5,000.

**Duration** Up to 1 year.

**Additional information** The foundation was established in 1985. Funding is not provided for general operating costs for organizations; for-profit organizations; tuition costs or living expenses while working toward a degree; endowment or capital campaigns; activities that do not focus on changing the lives of women in Kentucky; the promotion of religious doctrines; non-art related expenses, such as overdue bills or taxes; or work conducted by artists or organizations that have not resided in Kentucky for at least 1 year.

**Number awarded** Varies each year; recently, 32 of these grants were awarded. A total of $100,000 is available annually.

**Deadline** February of each year.

## [1225]
## ART STUDIO INTERNSHIPS

Women's Studio Workshop
722 Binnewater Lane
P.O. Box 489
Rosendale, NY 12472
(845) 658-9133                    Fax: (845) 658-9031
E-mail: info@wsworkshop.org
Web: www.wsworkshop.org/program/internships

**Summary** To provide internship opportunities in the arts at the Women's Studio Workshop (WSW) in Rosendale, New York.

**Eligibility** This program is open to young women artists interested in working with the staff at the studio on projects including papermaking, book arts, and arts administration. Applicants should send a resume, 10 to 20 images of recent works, 3 letters of reference, and a letter of interest. They should have studio experience, be hard-working, and have a desire and ability to live in a close-knit community of women artists. Along with their application, they must submit a letter of interest explaining why an internship at WSW is important to them and why type of experiences they would bring to the position, 3 letters of reference, a resume, and a CD with 10 images of recent work.

**Financial data** Interns receive on-site housing and a stipend of $250 per month.

**Duration** Approximately 6 months, either as winter-spring interns (beginning in January) or as summer-fall interns (beginning in June). Interns may reapply for a second 6-month assignment.

**Additional information** Tasks include (but are not limited to) maintaining the studios; assisting in the production of artists' books; administrative duties (including data entry and web maintenance); designing, printing, and distributing brochures and posters; assisting in all aspects of the exhibition program; preparing the apartments for visiting artists; setting up evening programs; managing the set up and break down of lunch each day; and working as studio assistants in all classes.

**Number awarded** 2 to 3 each term (winter-spring or summer-fall).

**Deadline** October of each year for winter-spring internships; February of each year for summer-fall internships.

## [1226]
## ART-IN-EDUCATION RESIDENCY GRANTS

Women's Studio Workshop
722 Binnewater Lane
P.O. Box 489
Rosendale, NY 12472
(845) 658-9133                    Fax: (845) 658-9031
E-mail: info@wsworkshop.org
Web: www.wsworkshop.org/program/residency-grants

**Summary** To provide a residency and financial support to women interested in producing a limited edition artist's book and working with young people.

**Eligibility** This program is open to emerging artists who come from different regions of the country and/or diverse cultural backgrounds. Applicants must be interested in spending half their time involved with the design and production of a limited edition artist's book, and the other half working with young people in an arts-in-education program. Along with their application, they must submit a 1-page description of the proposed project; a 1-page history of their relevant experience working with youth; a structural dummy of the project; a materials budget; and a resume.

**Financial data** The program provides a stipend of $400 per week, a $750 materials grant, travel costs up to $250 within the continental United States, and housing while in residence.

**Duration** Up to 10 weeks (between February and May with elementary school students or between October and December with high school students).

**Number awarded** 2 each year.

**Deadline** November of each year.

## [1227]
## ARTIST ENRICHMENT GRANT PROGRAM

Kentucky Foundation for Women
Heyburn Building
332 West Broadway, Suite 1215-A
Louisville, KY 40202-2184
(502) 562-0045                    Toll Free: (866) 654-7564
Fax: (502) 561-0420              E-mail: team@kfw.org
Web: www.kfw.org/artenr.html

**Summary** To support women in Kentucky who wish to promote positive social change through feminist expression in the arts.

**Eligibility** This program is open to women who have resided in Kentucky for at least 1 year and are artists at any stage in their career able to demonstrate potential in terms of quality of work and an understanding of the power of art for social change. Applicants must be seeking funding for a range of activities, including artistic development, artist residencies, the exploration of new areas or techniques, or building a body of work. In the selection process, the following criteria are considered: artwork in the sample is strong, highly original, and reflects feminism and social change; the proposed activities will further the applicant's development as a feminist social change artist; application and work sample demonstrate applicant's understanding and practice of feminism; application and work sample demonstrate a clear understanding of the relationship between art and social change; work plan, timeline, and budget are clear, detailed, and realistic; and applicant's ability to complete the proposed activities in clearly shown. If applications are of equal artistic merit, priority is given to first-time applicants and those from underrepresented demographic populations (such as lesbians, African Americans, and women with disabilities).

**Financial data** Grants may range from $1,000 to $7,500, but most average between $2,000 and $4,000.

**Duration** Up to 1 year.

**Additional information** The foundation was established in 1985. Funding is not provided for general operating costs for organizations; for-profit organizations; tuition costs or living expenses while working toward a degree; endowment or capital campaigns; projects that do not focus on changing the lives of women in Kentucky; the promotion of religious doctrines; non-art related expenses, such as overdue bills or taxes; or work conducted by artists or organizations that have not resided in Kentucky for at least 1 year.

**Number awarded** Varies each year; recently, 35 of these grants were awarded. A total of $100,000 is available annually.

**Deadline** September of each year.

## [1228]
## ARTISTS' BOOK RESIDENCY GRANTS

Women's Studio Workshop
722 Binnewater Lane
P.O. Box 489
Rosendale, NY 12472
(845) 658-9133                    Fax: (845) 658-9031
E-mail: info@wsworkshop.org
Web: www.wsworkshop.org/program/residency-grants

**Summary** To provide funding and a residency at the Women's Studio Workshop (WSW) to female artists who are interested in producing a book.

**Eligibility** This program is open to female artists who are interested in producing new books that will have a press run of 50 to 100 copies. Applicants must submit a 1-page description of the proposed project, a description of the media/studios they will need to print the book, a structural dummy, a materials budget, a resume, and 10 images of recent work.

**Financial data** The program provides a stipend of $350 per week, a $750 materials grant, travel costs up to $250 within the continental United States, and housing while in residence.

**Duration** 6 to 8 weeks.

**Additional information** This program provides an opportunity for book artists to come and work in residency at WSW in Rosendale, New York. Selected artists are involved in all aspects of the design and production of their new books. The studio provides technical advice and, when possible, help with editing. Assistance with marketing is also available. The contract requires that 10% of the published books go to the sponsor for archives, exhibition, and display copies; 10% to the artist; and 80% for general marketing.

**Number awarded** Varies each year.

**Deadline** November of each year.

## [1229]
## ARTTABLE MENTORED INTERNSHIPS FOR DIVERSITY IN THE VISUAL ARTS PROFESSIONS

ArtTable Inc.
137 Varick Street, Suite 402
New York, NY 10013
(212) 343-1735, ext. 24          Fax: (866) 363-4188
E-mail: ebround@arttable.org
Web: www.arttable.org

**Summary** To provide an opportunity for women who are from diverse backgrounds to gain mentored work experience during the summer and to prepare for a career as an art professional.

**Eligibility** This program is open to women who are college seniors, recent graduates, or graduate students and interested in preparing for a career as a visual arts professional (including administrative director, art adviser, art appraiser, art critic, art dealer, art librarian, arts funder, arts lawyer, conservator, curator, editor, educator, fundraiser, management consultant, public relations consultant, writer). Applicants must be from a cultural or ethnic background that is underrepresented in the field. They must be interested in working during the summer with a mentor at an art museum or similar facility. U.S. citizenship or permanent resident status is required.

**Financial data** The stipend is $3,000. The hosting institution or mentor receives $500 for administrative and other costs.

**Duration** 8 weeks during the summer.

**Additional information** This program began in 2000.

**Number awarded** Varies each year; recently, 4 of these internships were awarded.

**Deadline** February of each year.

## [1230]
## ASPA SPECIAL FUND FOR THE STUDY OF WOMEN AND POLITICS

American Political Science Association
Attn: Centennial Center Visiting Scholars Program
1527 New Hampshire Avenue, N.W.
Washington, DC 20036-1206
(202) 483-2512                    Fax: (202) 483-2657
E-mail: center@apsanet.org
Web: www.apsanet.org/content_3471.cfm

**Summary** To provide funding to members of the American Political Science Association (APSA) who are interested in conducting research on women and politics at the Centennial Center for Political Science and Public Affairs.

**Eligibility** This program is open to members of the association who are interested in conducting research on women and politics while in residence at the center. Junior faculty members, postdoctoral fellows, and advanced graduate students are strongly encouraged to apply, but scholars at all stages of their careers are eligible. International applicants are also welcome if they have demonstrable command of spoken English. Non-resident scholars may also be eligible.

**Financial data** Grants provide supplemental financial support to resident scholars.

**Duration** 2 weeks to 12 months.

**Additional information** The APSA launched its Centennial Center for Political Science and Public Affairs in 2003 to commemorate the centennial year of the association.

**Number awarded** 1 or more each year.

**Deadline** February, June, or October of each year.

## [1231]
## ASSOCIATION FOR WOMEN IN SPORTS MEDIA MEMBER TRAINING GRANTS

Association for Women in Sports Media
Attn: Chair of the Board
161 West Sylvania Avenue
Neptune City, NJ 07753
E-mail: training@awsmonline.org
Web: awsmonline.org/?s=training+grant

**Summary** To provide funding to members of the Association for Women in Sports Media (AWSM) who are interested in additional training.

**Eligibility** This program is open to AWSM members who are interested in obtaining additional training (e.g., an on online journalism seminar or video production class). Applicants must submit a resume that includes their professional experience, formal education, professional development seminars or workshops, or other relevant training experiences; a 500-word statement on how this grant would help them; and a description of how the grant would be used.

**Financial data** Grants range from $500 to $1,500.

**Duration** These are 1-time grants.

**Additional information** This program began in 2008 with funding from the Ethics and Excellence in Journalism Foundation.

**Number awarded** Up to 5 each year.

**Deadline** November of each year.

## [1232]
## ASTRAEA VISUAL ARTS FUND

Astraea Lesbian Foundation for Justice
Attn: Program Director
116 East 16th Street, Seventh Floor
New York, NY 10003
(212) 529-8021                    Fax: (212) 982-3321
E-mail: grants@astraeafoundation.org
Web: www.astraeafoundation.org

**Summary** To provide funding for additional work to lesbian artists.

**Eligibility** This program is open to U.S. residents who agree to be acknowledged publicly as lesbian artists in the following categories: sculpture, painting in any medium, prints, drawing, work on paper, and mixed media (traditional or nontraditional materials). Students currently enrolled in an arts degree-granting program or its equivalent are not eligible. Applicants must submit slides of their original works of art, a current resume, and a 250-word statement responding to the goal of the fund.

**Financial data** The award is $2,500.

**Duration** The awards are presented annually.

**Additional information** This program began in 2002. An application fee of $5 must be included.

**Number awarded** 3 each year.

**Deadline** October of each year.

## [1233]
## ATHENA LECTURER AWARD

Association for Computing Machinery
Attn: Awards Committee Liaison
2 Penn Plaza, Suite 701
New York, NY 10121-0701
(212) 626-0561                    Toll Free: (800) 342-6626
Fax: (212) 944-1318          E-mail: mcguinness@acm.org
Web: awards.acm.org/homepage.cfm?srt=all&awd=166

**Summary** To recognize and reward, with a lectureship, women researchers who have made outstanding contributions to computer science.

**Eligibility** This award is presented to women who have made outstanding contributions to research on computer science. Nominees must be available to deliver a lecture at the Symposium on the Theory of Computing sponsored by the Special Interest Group on Algorithms and Computation Theory (SIGACT) of the Association for Computing Machinery (ACM).

**Financial data** The award is $10,000.

**Duration** The award is presented annually.

**Additional information** This award was established in 2006 by the ACM-W Council, originally known as the Committee on Women in Computing of ACM. Financial support is provided by Google, Inc.

**Number awarded** 1 each year.

**Deadline** November of each year.

## [1234]
## B. JUNE WEST RECRUITMENT GRANT

Delta Kappa Gamma Society International-Theta State
   Organization
c/o Sharron Stepro, Committee on Professional Affairs
   Chair
10038 San Marcos Court
Las Cruces, NM 88007-8954
Web: thetastatenmdkg.weebly.com/award-forms-html

**Summary** To provide financial assistance to women in New Mexico who are interested in preparing for a career as a teacher.

**Eligibility** This program is open to women residents of New Mexico who are 1) graduating high school seniors planning to go into education; 2) college students majoring in education; or 3) teachers needing educational assistance. Applicants must submit a list of activities in which they are involved, 3 letters of recommendation, a list of achievements and awards, and a statement of their educational goal and how this grant would be of assistance to them. Financial need is not considered in the selection process.

**Financial data** A stipend is awarded (amount not specified).

**Duration** 1 year.

**Number awarded** 1 or more each year.

**Deadline** February of each year.

## [1235]
## BARNARD WOMEN POETS PRIZE

Barnard College
Attn: Department of English
417 Barnard Hall
3009 Broadway
New York, NY 10027-6598
(212) 854-2116          Fax: (212) 854-9498
E-mail: english@barnard.edu
Web: english.barnard.edu/women-poets/contest

**Summary** To recognize and reward outstanding unpublished poetry written by American women.

**Eligibility** This program is open to women writers who have already published 1 book of poetry (in an edition of 500 copies or more) and are seeking a publisher for a second collection. Manuscripts that are under option to another publisher are not eligible. Applicants should submit 3 copies of a book-length manuscript (the page limit is not specified).

**Financial data** The prize is $1,500 and publication of the manuscript.

**Duration** The prize is awarded biennially.

**Additional information** This prize was first awarded in 2003. Winning submissions are published by W.W. Norton & Co. The entry fee is $20.

**Number awarded** 1 each odd-numbered year.

**Deadline** October of each even-numbered year.

## [1236]
## BEHAVIORAL SCIENCES POSTDOCTORAL FELLOWSHIPS IN EPILEPSY

Epilepsy Foundation
Attn: Research Department
8301 Professional Place
Landover, MD 20785-2353
(301) 459-3700          Toll Free: (800) EFA-1000
Fax: (301) 577-2684          TDD: (800) 332-2070
E-mail: grants@efa.org
Web: www.epilepsyfoundation.org

**Summary** To provide funding to postdoctorates (especially women, minorities, and persons with disabilities) in the behavioral sciences who wish to pursue research training in an area related to epilepsy.

**Eligibility** Applicants must have received a Ph.D. or equivalent degree in a field of social science, including (but not limited to) sociology, social work, anthropology, nursing, or economics. They must be interested in receiving additional research training to prepare for a career in clinical behavioral aspects of epilepsy. Academic faculty holding the rank of instructor or above are not eligible, nor are graduate or medical students, medical residents, permanent government employees, or employees in private industry. Because these fellowships are designed as training opportunities, the quality of the training plans and environment are considered in the selection process. Other selection criteria include the scientific quality of the proposed research, a statement regarding the relevance of the research to epilepsy, the applicant's qualifications, the preceptor's qualifications, adequacy of the facility, and related epilepsy programs at the institution. Applications from women, members of minority groups, and people with disabilities are especially encouraged. U.S. citizenship is not required, but the research must be conducted in the United States.

**Financial data** Grants up to $40,000 are available.

**Duration** 1 year.

**Number awarded** Varies each year.

**Deadline** March of each year.

## [1237]
## BERKSHIRE CONFERENCE FIRST BOOK PRIZES

Berkshire Conference of Women Historians
c/o Serena Zabin
Carleton College
History Department, Leighton Hall 210
1 North College Street
Northfield, MN 55057
(507) 222-7160          E-mail: szabin@carleton.edu
Web: berksconference.org/prizes-awards

**Summary** To recognize and reward women who have written outstanding first books in history.

**Eligibility** This prize is awarded for the best first book written by a woman normally resident in North America during the preceding year. Prizes are awarded in 2 categories: 1) books in any historical field; and 2) books that deal substantially with the history of women, gender, and/or sexuality. Textbooks, juveniles, fiction, poetry, collections of essays, and documentary collections are not eligible.

**Financial data** Amount varies. In the past, this prize has been $1,000 per year.

**Duration** The prize is awarded annually.

**Number awarded** 2 each year: 1 in each category.

**Deadline** January of each year.

## [1238]
## BILL WHITEHEAD AWARD FOR LIFETIME ACHIEVEMENT

Publishing Triangle
332 Bleecker Street, D36
New York, NY 10014
E-mail: publishingtriangle@gmail.com
Web: www.publishingtriangle.org/awards.asp

**Summary** To recognize and reward female and male writers (judged separately) who have dealt openly with gay or lesbian issues.

**Eligibility** This is a lifetime achievement award. It is presented to writers whose body of work makes a significant contribution to gay and lesbian literature. The award alternates between women (in even-numbered years) and men (in odd-numbered years). Only members of the Publishing Triangle may nominate candidates for the award.

**Financial data** The award is $3,000.

**Duration** The award is presented annually.

**Additional information** The Publishing Triangle is an association of lesbians and gay men in publishing. This award was first presented in 1989.

**Number awarded** 1 each year.

**Deadline** November of each year.

## [1239]
## B.K. KRENZER MEMORIAL REENTRY SCHOLARSHIP

Society of Women Engineers
Attn: Scholarship Selection Committee
203 North LaSalle Street, Suite 1675
Chicago, IL 60601-1269
(312) 596-5223          Toll Free: (877) SWE-INFO
Fax: (312) 644-8557     E-mail: scholarships@swe.org
Web: societyofwomenengineers.swe.org

**Summary** To provide financial assistance to women interested in returning to college or graduate school to study engineering or computer science.

**Eligibility** This program is open to women who are planning to enroll at an ABET-accredited 4-year college or university. Applicants must have been out of the engineering workforce and school for at least 2 years and must be planning to return as an undergraduate or graduate student to work on a degree in computer science or engineering. They must have a GPA of 3.0 or higher. Selection is based on merit. Preference is given to engineers who already have a degree and are planning to reenter the engineering workforce after a period of temporary retirement.

**Financial data** The stipend is $2,000.

**Duration** 1 year.

**Additional information** This program began in 1996.

**Number awarded** 1 each year.

**Deadline** February of each year.

## [1240]
## BORIS CHRISTOFF INTERNATIONAL COMPETITION FOR YOUNG OPERA SINGERS

International Competition for Young Opera Singers
Attn: Secretariat
41 Tzar Boris III Boulevard
1612 Sofia
Bulgaria
359 2 951 5903          Fax: 359 2 952 1558
E-mail: borischristoff@yahoo.com
Web: www.borischristoff.dir.bg/index.htm

**Summary** To recognize and reward outstanding young opera singers (females and males are judged separately) at a competition in Bulgaria.

**Eligibility** The competition is open to singers from all countries who are younger than 33 years of age. Competitors select their program, consisting of 4 major arias, 1 song, and 1 central opera part, from specified categories.

**Financial data** The best singer of either sex receives the Grand Prix of Sofia, of $7,000, a gold medal, a gold ring, and a diploma. The prizes in each of the 2 classes (female and male) are: first prize—$5,000, a gold medal, and a diploma; second prize—$3,000, a silver medal, and a diploma; third prize—$2,000, a bronze medal, and a diploma. All singers who reach the finals but do not receive a prize are awarded $500 and a diploma. In addition, there are various token and special awards. The organizing committee defrays all expenses associated with accommodations and subsistence for all competitors and their accompanists.

**Duration** The competition is held every 4 years (2016, 2020, etc.).

**Additional information** The organizing committee secures an accompanist free of charge for all competitors. Competitors can take part in the competition with their own pianos. The 1996 competition was the 11th in the series that began in 1961 and the first to bear the name of Boris Christoff, the renowned Bulgarian opera singer. There is an entry fee of 100 Euros.

**Deadline** April of the years in which the competition is held.

## [1241]
## BROOKHAVEN NATIONAL LABORATORY PROFESSIONAL ASSOCIATES PROGRAM FOR WOMEN AND MINORITIES

Brookhaven National Laboratory
Attn: Diversity Office, Human Resources Division
Building 400B
P.O. Box 5000
Upton, New York 11973-5000
(631) 344-2703          Fax: (631) 344-5305
E-mail: palmore@bnl.gov
Web: www.bnl.gov/diversity/programs.asp

**Summary** To provide professional experience in scientific areas at Brookhaven National Laboratory (BNL) to women and members of other underrepresented groups.

**Eligibility** This program is open to underrepresented minorities (African Americans, Hispanics, or Native Americans), people with disabilities, and women. Applicants must have earned at least a bachelor's degree and be seeking professional experience in fields of science, engineering, or administration. They must plan to attend a graduate or professional school and express an interest in long-term employment at BNL. U.S. citizenship or permanent resident status is required.

**Financial data** Participants receive a competitive salary.

**Duration** 1 year.

**Additional information** Interns work in a goal-oriented on-the-job training program under the supervision of employees who are experienced in their areas of interest.

**Number awarded** Varies each year.

**Deadline** Applications may be submitted at any time.

## [1242]
## BURROUGHS WELLCOME FUND/CAREER AWARDS FOR MEDICAL SCIENTISTS

Burroughs Wellcome Fund
21 T.W. Alexander Drive, Suite 100
P.O. Box 13901
Research Triangle Park, NC 27709-3901
(919) 991-5100          Fax: (919) 991-5160
E-mail: info@bwfund.org
Web: www.bwfund.org

**Summary** To provide funding to biomedical scientists in the United States and Canada (priority given to women and minorities) who require assistance to make the transition from postdoctoral training to faculty appointment.

**Eligibility** This program is open to citizens and permanent residents of the United States and Canada who have an M.D., D.D.S., or D.V.M. degree and from 2 to 10 years of postdoctoral research experience. Candidates who work in reproductive science are encouraged to apply. Applicants must be interested in a program of research training in the area of basic biomedical, disease-oriented, or translational research. Training must take place at a degree-granting medical school, graduate school, hospital, or research institute in the United States or Canada. Each U.S. and Canadian institution may nominate up to 5 candidates. The sponsor encourages institutions to nominate women and underrepresented minorities (African Americans, Hispanics, or Native Americans); if a woman or underrepresented minority is among the initial 5 candidates, the institution may nominate a sixth candidate who is a woman or underrepresented minority.

**Financial data** The stipend is $140,000 per year.

**Duration** 5 years.

**Additional information** This program began in 1995 as Career Awards in the Biomedical Sciences (CABS). It was revised to its current format in 2006 as a result of the NIH K99/R00 Pathway to Independence program. As the CABS, the program provided more than $100 million in support to 241 U.S. and Canadian scientists. Awardees are required to devote at least 75% of their time to research-related activities.

**Number awarded** Varies each year: recently, 10 of these awards were granted.

**Deadline** September of each year.

## [1243]
## BURROUGHS WELLCOME FUND INVESTIGATORS IN PATHOGENESIS OF INFECTIOUS DISEASE

Burroughs Wellcome Fund
21 T.W. Alexander Drive, Suite 100
P.O. Box 13901
Research Triangle Park, NC 27709-3901
(919) 991-5112                    Fax: (919) 991-5160
E-mail: info@bwfund.org
Web: www.bwfund.org

**Summary** To provide funding to physician/scientists (particularly women and underrepresented minorities) who wish to conduct research on pathogenesis, with a focus on the intersection of human and pathogen biology.

**Eligibility** This program is open to established independent physician/scientists who are citizens or permanent residents of the United States or Canada and affiliated with accredited degree-granting U.S. or Canadian medical schools. Applicants must be interested in conducting research projects related to the fungal, metazoan, and protozoan pathogens. Candidates must have an M.D., D.V.M., or Ph.D. degree and be tenure-track investigators as an assistant professor or equivalent at a degree-granting institution. Each institution (including its medical school, graduate schools, and all affiliated hospitals and research institutes) may nominate up to 2 candidates. Institutions that nominate a researcher who has a D.V.M. are allowed 3 nominations. The sponsor also encourages institutions to nominate underrepresented minorities and women. Selection is based on qualifications of the candidate and potential to conduct innovative research; demonstration of an established record of independent research; and quality and originality of the proposed research and its potential to advance understanding of fundamental issues of how infectious agents and human hosts interact.

**Financial data** The grant provides $100,000 per year. No more than $20,000 of the grant may be used for salary sup-

port, but institutions may supplement the award to a level consistent with its own scale.

**Duration** 5 years.

**Additional information** This program began in 2001 as a replacement for several former programs: New Investigator and Scholar Awards in Molecular Pathogenic Mycology, New Investigator and Scholar Awards in Molecular Parasitology, and New Initiatives in Malaria Awards. Awardees are required to devote at least 75% of their time to research-related activities.

**Number awarded** Varies each year; recently, 9 of these grants were awarded.

**Deadline** October of each year.

## [1244]
## CAREER DEVELOPMENT AWARDS IN DIABETES RESEARCH

Juvenile Diabetes Research Foundation International
Attn: Grant Administrator
26 Broadway, 14th Floor
New York, NY 10004
(212) 479-7572                    Toll Free: (800) 533-CURE
Fax: (212) 785-9595                E-mail: info@jdrf.org
Web: jdrf.org

**Summary** To encourage young scientists (particularly women, minorities, and persons with disabilities) to develop into independent investigators in diabetes-related research.

**Eligibility** This program is open to postdoctorates early in their faculty careers who show promise as diabetes researchers. Applicants must have received their first doctoral (M.D., Ph.D., D.M.D., D.V.M., or equivalent) degree at least 3 but not more than 7 years previously. They may not have an academic position at the associate professor, professor, or equivalent level, but they must be a faculty member (instructor or assistant professor) at a university, health science center, or comparable institution with strong, well-established research and training programs. The proposed research must relate to Type 1 diabetes, but it may be basic or clinical. There are no citizenship requirements. Applications are encouraged from women, members of minority groups underrepresented in the sciences, and people with disabilities. The proposed research may be conducted at foreign or domestic, for-profit or non-profit, or public or private institutions, including universities, colleges, hospitals, laboratories, units of state or local government, or eligible agencies of the federal government. Selection is based on the applicant's perceived ability and potential for a career in Type 1 diabetes research, the caliber of the proposed research, and the quality and commitment of the host institution.

**Financial data** The total award may be up to $150,000 each year. Indirect costs cannot exceed 10%.

**Duration** Up to 5 years.

**Additional information** Fellows must spend up to 75% of their time in research.

**Number awarded** Varies each year.

**Deadline** August of each year.

## [1245]
## CAREER DEVELOPMENT GRANTS FOR POSTDOCTORAL WOMEN

American Society for Microbiology
Attn: Membership Board
1752 N Street, N.W.
Washington, DC 20036-2804
(202) 942-9253                      Fax: (202) 942-9346
E-mail: adempsey@asmusa.org
Web: www.asm.org/index.php/fellowships-2

**Summary**  To provide funding for career development activities to postdoctoral female members of the American Society for Microbiology (ASM).

**Eligibility**  This program is open to women who have a doctoral degree, are currently performing postdoctoral work in microbiology at an institution in the United States, have no more than 5 years of relevant research experience since completing their doctorate, and are ASM members. Applicants must be seeking funding to travel to a meeting, visit another laboratory, take a course in a geographically distant place, or other purpose to advance their career. Along with their application, they must submit a statement that describes their academic accomplishments, career goals, and intended use of the grant to aid their career.

**Financial data**  The grant is $1,200.

**Duration**  Grants are awarded annually.

**Additional information**  This program began in 2006.

**Number awarded**  3 each year.

**Deadline**  January of each year.

## [1246]
## CAROL TYLER AWARD

International Precious Metals Institute
5101 North 12th Avenue, Suite C
Pensacola, FL 32504
(850) 476-1156                      Fax: (850) 476-1548
E-mail: mail@ipmi.org
Web: www.ipmi.org/awards/index.cfm

**Summary**  To recognize and reward women graduate students, professionals, and postdoctorates who have a record of outstanding achievement in the science and technology of precious metals.

**Eligibility**  This award is available to women who are graduate students or currently employed in industry or academia. Nominees must have made outstanding theoretical and experimental contributions to the science and technology of precious metals. They may be residents of any country.

**Financial data**  The award is $5,000 and a certificate.

**Duration**  The award is presented annually.

**Additional information**  This award was first presented in 2011.

**Number awarded**  1 each year.

**Deadline**  January of each year.

## [1247]
## CAROLINE CRAIG AUGUSTYN AND DAMIAN AUGUSTYN AWARD IN DIGESTIVE CANCER

American Gastroenterological Association
Attn: AGA Research Foundation
Research Awards Manager
4930 Del Ray Avenue
Bethesda, MD 20814-2512
(301) 222-4012                      Fax: (301) 654-5920
E-mail: awards@gastro.org
Web: www.gastro.org/aga-foundation/grants

**Summary**  To provide funding to junior investigators (especially women and minorities) who are interested in conducting research related to digestive cancer.

**Eligibility**  Applicants must have an M.D., Ph.D., or equivalent degree and a full-time faculty position at an accredited North American institution. They must have received an NIH K series or other federal or non-federal career development award of at least 4 years duration, but may not have received an R01 or equivalent award. For M.D. applicants, no more than 7 years may have elapsed following the completion of clinical training, and for Ph.D. applicants no more than 7 years may have elapsed since the completion of their degree. Individual membership in the American Gastroenterology Association (AGA) is required. The proposal must relate to the pathogenesis, prevention, diagnosis, or treatment of digestive cancer. Women and minority investigators are strongly encouraged to apply. Selection is based on the qualifications of the candidate and the novelty, feasibility, and significance of their research.

**Financial data**  The grant is $40,000. Funds may be used for salary, supplies, or equipment. Indirect costs are not allowed.

**Duration**  1 year.

**Number awarded**  1 each year.

**Deadline**  January of each year.

## [1248]
## CARRIE CHAPMAN CATT PRIZE FOR RESEARCH ON WOMEN AND POLITICS

Iowa State University
Attn: Carrie Chapman Catt Center for Women and Politics
309 Carrie Chapman Catt Hall
Ames, IA 50011-1305
(515) 294-3181                      Fax: (515) 294-3741
E-mail: cattcntr@iastate.edu
Web: cattcenter.las.iastate.edu/catt-research/catt-prize

**Summary**  To recognize and reward outstanding research in the area of women and politics.

**Eligibility**  This competition is open to scholars at all levels, including graduate students and junior faculty, who are planning to conduct research in the area of women and politics. Applicants must submit a detailed description of their research project, including 1) its purpose and content; 2) a discussion of relevant theory, contributions to literature in the field, and methodology; 3) a statement on how this prize will contribute to the research project; and 4) a timetable for completion of the project. They also must submit a 1-page biographical statement. Research projects can address the annual conference theme or any other topic related to women and politics.

**Financial data** Prizes are $1,500 for winners or $500 for honorable mention. All prize-winners may also receive travel expenses to Des Moines, Iowa, where awards are presented at the annual conference of the Carrie Chapman Catt Center for Women and Politics.

**Duration** The prizes are awarded annually.

**Number awarded** Up to 4 winners and up to 2 honorable mentions are selected each year.

**Deadline** November of each year.

## [1249]
## CATHARINE STIMPSON PRIZE FOR OUTSTANDING FEMINIST SCHOLARSHIP

*Signs: Journal of Women in Culture and Society*
Rutgers University
Voorhees Chapel, Room 8
5 Chapel Drive
New Brunswick, NJ 08901
(832) 932-2842          E-mail: signs@signs.rutgers.edu
Web: signsjournal.org

**Summary** To recognize and reward authors of outstanding papers in feminist scholarship.

**Eligibility** This competition is open to feminist scholars who are less than 7 years since receipt of their terminal degree. Applicants must submit a paper, up to 10,000 words in length, on a topic in the field of interdisciplinary feminist scholarship.

**Financial data** The prize is $1,000.

**Duration** The prize is presented biennially, in odd-numbered years.

**Number awarded** 1 each odd-numbered year.

**Deadline** February of each even-numbered year.

## [1250]
## CATHERINE PRELINGER AWARD

Coordinating Council for Women in History
c/o Sandra Dawson, Executive Director
Northern Illinois University
Department of History and Women's Studies
715 Zulauf Hall
DeKalb, IL 60115
(815) 895-2624          E-mail: execdir@theccwh.org
Web: theccwh.org/ccwh-awards

**Summary** To provide funding to members of the Coordinating Council for Women in History (CCWH) for a project that focuses on women's roles in history.

**Eligibility** This program is open to members of CCWH whose academic path has not followed the traditional pattern of uninterrupted study. Applicants must hold either A.B.D. status or a Ph.D. and be engaged in scholarship that is historical in nature, although their degree may be in related fields. They must submit a description of a project they propose to undertake with this award, including the work they intend to complete, the schedule they have developed, the sources they intend to use, and the contribution the work will make to women in history. Independent and non-academic scholars are encouraged to apply.

**Financial data** The grant is $20,000.

**Duration** 1 year.

**Additional information** This program began in 1998.

**Number awarded** 1 each year.

**Deadline** September of each year.

## [1251]
## CELIA M. HOWARD FELLOWSHIP

Illinois Federation of Business Women's Clubs
c/o Fayrene Wright, Howard Fellowship Fund Committee Chair
804 East Locust Street
Robinson, IL 62454
(618) 546-1233
E-mail: info@celiamhowardfellowship.com
Web: www.celiamhowardfellowship.com

**Summary** To provide funding to women in Illinois who are interested in working on a graduate degree in specified fields at eligible universities.

**Eligibility** This program is open to Illinois women who are U.S. citizens; have been Illinois residents for at least the past 2 years; have earned a bachelor's degree with at least 12 hours of undergraduate work in economics, history, and/or political science; and have a GPA of 3.0 or higher. A personal interview may be required. Applicants must be planning to study for a master's degree in administration of justice at Southern Illinois University at Carbondale or Edwardsville, a J.D. degree at the University of Illinois College of Law at Urbana-Champaign, a master's degree in diplomacy at the Fletcher School of Law and Diplomacy in Medford, Massachusetts, or a master's degree in international management at the Garvin School of International Management in Glendale, Arizona. Selection is based on financial need, previous graduate study, practical business experience in government, and leadership experience.

**Financial data** Awards normally pay full tuition, to a maximum of $10,000 per year. Funds are paid directly to the recipient's school.

**Duration** 1 year; renewable.

**Additional information** This program began in 1948.

**Number awarded** Varies each year; recently, 3 of these fellowships were awarded.

**Deadline** November of each year.

## [1252]
## CHARLES L. BREWER DISTINGUISHED TEACHING OF PSYCHOLOGY AWARD

American Psychological Foundation
750 First Street, N.E.
Washington, DC 20002-4242
(202) 336-5843          Fax: (202) 336-5812
E-mail: foundation@apa.org
Web: www.apa.org/apf/funding/brewer.aspx

**Summary** To recognize and reward distinguished career contributions to the teaching of psychology by women, minorities, and others.

**Eligibility** This award is available to psychologists who demonstrate outstanding teaching. Selection is based on evidence of influence as a teacher of students who become psychologists, research on teaching, development of effective teaching methods and/or materials, development of innovation curricula and courses, performance as a classroom teacher, demonstrated training of teachers of psychology, teaching of advanced research methods and practice in psychology, and/or administrative facilitation of teaching. Nominators must complete an application form, write a letter of support, and submit the nominee's current vitae and bibliography. The sponsor encourages nominations of individuals who represent diversity in race, ethnicity, gender, age, disability, and sexual orientation.

**Financial data** Awardees receive a plaque, a $2,000 honorarium, and an all-expense paid trip to the annual convention where the award is presented.

**Duration** The award is presented annually.

**Additional information** This award, originally named the Distinguished Teaching in Psychology Award, was first presented in 1970.

**Number awarded** 1 each year.

**Deadline** Nominations must be submitted by November of each year.

## [1253]
## CHURCH TRAINING AND DEACONESS HOUSE SCHOLARSHIP

Episcopal Diocese of Pennsylvania
Attn: Church Training and Deaconess House Scholarship
   Fund
240 South Fourth Street
Philadelphia, PA 19106
(215) 627-6434, ext. 101       Fax: (215) 627-7550
E-mail: nevin-field@stpetersphila.org
Web: www.diopa.org/deaconess-training

**Summary** To provide financial assistance for graduate school to women preparing for a career in religious or benevolent work for the Episcopal Church.

**Eligibility** This program is open to women who are seeking to be ordained to the ministry of the Episcopal Church or to work on a graduate degree that would further their lay ministry. Preference is given to women in the Diocese of Pennsylvania. Applicants must submit a 250-word essay on how they expect to use this graduate educational training to advance their ordained or lay ministry within the Episcopal Church or the church at large. Selection is based on the quality of the essay, academic record, and financial need.

**Financial data** Stipends range from $2,000 to $3,000.

**Duration** 1 year; may be renewed up to 2 additional years.

**Number awarded** 1 or more each year.

**Deadline** March of each year.

## [1254]
## COMMUNITY ACTION GRANTS

American Association of University Women
Attn: AAUW Educational Foundation
301 ACT Drive, Department 60
P.O. Box 4030
Iowa City, IA 52243-4030
(319) 337-1716, ext. 60       Fax: (319) 337-1204
E-mail: aauw@act.org
Web: www.aauw.org

**Summary** To provide seed money to branches or divisions of the American Association of University Women (AAUW) or to individual women for projects or non-degree research that promote education and equity for women and girls.

**Eligibility** This program is open to individual women who are U.S. citizens or permanent residents, AAUW branches,

AAUW state organizations, and local community-based non-profit organizations. Applicants must be proposing projects that have direct public impact, are non-partisan, and take place within the United States or its territories. Grants for 1 year provide seed money for new projects; topic areas are unrestricted but should include a clearly defined activity that promotes education and equity for women and girls. Grants for 2 years provide start-up funds for longer-term programs that address the particular needs of the community and develop girls' sense of efficacy through leadership or advocacy opportunities; funds support planning activities, coalition building, implementation, and evaluation. Special consideration is given to 1) AAUW branch and state projects that seek community partners (e.g., local schools or school districts, businesses, other community-based organizations); and 2) projects focused on K-14 girls' achievement in mathematics, science, and/or technology. Selection is based on relevance of the proposed project to education and equity for women and girls, strength of the project rationale, clarity and creativity of the project design, feasibility of the project, strength of the evaluation plan, strength of the dissemination plan, impact of the project, overall quality of the proposal, and potential for and/or commitment of additional funds and involvement from community organizations and/or businesses.

**Financial data** Grants for 1 year range from $2,000 to $7,000. Grants for 2 years range from $5,000 to $10,000. Funds are to be used for such project-related expenses as office supplies, mailing, photocopying, honoraria, and transportation. Funds cannot cover salaries for project directors or regular, ongoing overhead costs for any organization.

**Duration** 1 or 2 years.

**Additional information** The filing fee is $35.

**Number awarded** Varies each year; recently, 15 1-year grants and 17 2-year grants, with a total value of $258,561, were awarded.

**Deadline** January of each year.

## [1255]
## CONGRESSIONAL FELLOWSHIPS ON WOMEN AND PUBLIC POLICY

Women's Research and Education Institute
Attn: Education and Training Programs
714 G Street, S.E., Suite 200
Washington, DC 20003
(202) 280-2720       E-mail: wrei@wrei.org
Web: www.wrei.org

**Summary** To provide graduate students and young professionals with an opportunity to work as a Congressional aide on policy issues affecting women.

**Eligibility** This program is open to women and men who are currently enrolled in a master's or doctoral program at an accredited institution in the United States or who have completed such a program within the past 18 months. Applicants should have completed at least 9 hours of graduate course work or the equivalent and have a demonstrated interest in research or political activity relating to women's social and political status. They may be of any age, gender, race, religion, sexual orientation, experience, or academic field, but they must be articulate and adaptable and have strong writing skills. Selection is based on academic competence and demonstrated interest in the public policy process. Interviews are required of semifinalists.

**Financial data** Fellows receive a stipend of $1,450 per month, $500 for health insurance, and up to $1,500 for reimbursement of 3 hours of tuition at their home institutions.

**Duration** 8 months, from January through August; nonrenewable.

**Additional information** This program began in 1977. Fellows are assigned to Congressional or committee offices to work for at least 30 hours per week as a legislative assistant monitoring, researching, and providing information on policy issues affecting women.

**Number awarded** At least 5 each year; since the program began, 277 fellows (all women) have been appointed to these positions.

**Deadline** June of each year.

## [1256]
## COUNSELING PSYCHOLOGY GRANTS

American Psychological Foundation
750 First Street, N.E.
Washington, DC 20002-4242
(202) 336-5843          Fax: (202) 336-5812
E-mail: foundation@apa.org
Web: www.apa.org/apf/funding/counseling.aspx

**Summary** To provide funding to women, minority, and other psychologists who wish to conduct a project related to counseling psychology.

**Eligibility** This program is open to psychologists who wish to conduct a project to enhance the science and practice of counseling psychology, including basic and applied research, literary, and educational activities. Applicants must be members of Division 17 (Society of Counseling Psychotherapy) of the American Psychological Association, members of an educational institution or nonprofit organization, or affiliate of an educational institution or nonprofit organization. Selection is based on conformance with stated program goals, magnitude of incremental contribution in specified activity area, quality of proposed work, and applicant's demonstrated competence and capability to execute the proposed work. The sponsor encourages applications from individuals who represent diversity in race, ethnicity, gender, age, disability, and sexual orientation.

**Financial data** Grants range up to $5,000.

**Duration** 1 year.

**Additional information** These grants were first awarded in 2007.

**Number awarded** Varies each year; recently, 2 of these grants were awarded.

**Deadline** March of each year.

## [1257]
## CYNOSURE SCREENWRITING AWARDS

BroadMind Entertainment
3699 Wilshire Boulevard, Suite 850
Los Angeles, CA 90010
(310) 855-8730     E-mail: cynosure@broadmindent.com
Web: www.broadmindent.com/id10.html

**Summary** To recognize and reward outstanding unpublished screenplays with 1) a female protagonist or 2) a minority protagonist.

**Eligibility** Writers in any country are eligible to submit unpublished feature-length scripts (90-130 pages) with either a female protagonist or with a minority protagonist (either male or female). Scripts may be submitted under 1 category only. Scripts by multiple authors are acceptable. More than 1 script may be submitted, provided the signed entry/release form and an application fee accompany each submission. Scripts must be registered with the WGA or with the U.S. Copyright Office. Screenplays must be in English and may be of any genre.

**Financial data** The prize is $3,000.

**Duration** The competition is held annually.

**Additional information** This competition began in 1999. The fee is $50 for early entries, $60 for regular entries, or $70 for late entries.

**Number awarded** 2 each year: 1 for scripts with female protagonists and 1 for scripts with a minority protagonist.

**Deadline** Deadlines are March of each year for early, May of each year for regular, or July of each year for late entries.

## [1258]
## DANIEL H. EFRON RESEARCH AWARD

American College of Neuropsychopharmacology
Attn: Executive Office
5034-A Thoroughbred Lane
Brentwood, TN 37027
(615) 324-2360          Fax: (615) 523-1715
E-mail: acnp@acnp.org
Web: www.acnp.org/programs/awards.aspx

**Summary** To recognize and reward young scientists (priority is given to women and minorities) who have conducted outstanding basic or translational research to neuropsychopharmacology.

**Eligibility** This award is available to scientists who are younger than 50 years of age. Nominees must have made an outstanding basic or translational contribution to neuropsychopharmacology. The contribution may be preclinical or work that emphasizes the relationship between basic and clinical research. Selection is based on the quality of the contribution and its impact on advancing neuropsychopharmacology. Membership in the American College of Neuropsychopharmacology (ACNP) is not required. Nomination of women and minorities is highly encouraged.

**Financial data** The award consists of an expense-paid trip to the ACNP annual meeting, a monetary honorarium, and a plaque.

**Duration** The award is presented annually.

**Additional information** This award was first presented in 1974.

**Number awarded** 1 each year.

**Deadline** Nominations must be submitted by June of each year.

## [1259]
## DARLENE CLARK HINE AWARD

Organization of American Historians
Attn: Award and Committee Coordinator
112 North Bryan Street
Bloomington, IN 47408-4141
(812) 855-7311                    Fax: (812) 855-0696
E-mail: khamm@oah.org
Web: www.oah.org/awards/awards.hine.index.html

**Summary**   To recognize and reward authors of outstanding books dealing with African American women's and gender history.

**Eligibility**   This award is presented to the author of the outstanding book in African American women's and gender history. Entries must have been published during the current calendar year.

**Financial data**   The award is $1,000.

**Duration**   The award is presented annually.

**Additional information**   This award was first presented in 2010.

**Number awarded**   1 each year.

**Deadline**   September of each year.

## [1260]
## DELTA KAPPA GAMMA SOCIETY INTERNATIONAL EDUCATOR'S AWARD

Delta Kappa Gamma Society International
Attn: Educator's Award Committee
416 West 12th Street
P.O. Box 1589
Austin, TX 78767-1589
(512) 478-5748                    Toll Free: (888) 762-4685
Fax: (512) 478-3961               E-mail: soceditr@dkg.org
Web: www.dkg.org

**Summary**   To recognize women's contributions to education that may influence future directions in the profession; these contributions may be in research, philosophy, or any other area of learning that is stimulating and creative.

**Eligibility**   Any published book in research, philosophy, or another area of learning that stimulates the intellect and imagination may be submitted for consideration if it is written by 1 or 2 women in Canada, Costa Rica, El Salvador, Finland, Germany, Guatemala, Iceland, Mexico, the Netherlands, Norway, Puerto Rico, Sweden, the United Kingdom, or the United States and copyrighted (in its first edition or the first English translation) during the preceding calendar year. Contributions should possess excellence in style, be well-edited and attractive in format, and be of more than local interest. Ineligible are methods books, skill books, textbooks, and unpublished manuscripts.

**Financial data**   The award is $1,500. In the case of dual authorship, the prize is divided in the same manner as royalties are divided by the awardees' publisher.

**Duration**   The award is granted annually.

**Additional information**   This award was first presented in 1946.

**Number awarded**   1 each year.

**Deadline**   February of each year.

## [1261]
## DENHAM FELLOWSHIP

Stage Directors and Choreographers Society
Attn: Stage Directors and Choreographers Foundation
1501 Broadway, Suite 1701
New York, NY 10036
(646) 524-2226                    Fax: (212) 302-6195
E-mail: Foundation@SDCweb.org
Web: www.sdcweb.org

**Summary**   To provide an opportunity for aspiring young directors, especially women, to develop their directing skills.

**Eligibility**   This program is open to young directors, especially women, who are interested in developing a program to improve their skills. Applicants may be proposing either 1) fee enhancement, for which they are seeking funding to augment a fee offered by a theater or director; or 2) self-producing, for which they are seeking funding for a directorial project they will develop themselves. Along with their application, they must submit 1) a 1-page resume; 2) 2 letters of recommendation (including 1 from the producing theater's artistic or producing director for a fee enhancement award); 3) for applicants for self-producing awards, verification that the production will occur (e.g., agreement with theater); and 4) a 2-page letter of intent, including the challenges posed by the proposed project, their goals and how they will achieve them, and the potential impact of both the project and the fellowship on their craft and career.

**Financial data**   The stipend is $2,500.

**Duration**   1 year.

**Additional information**   This program began in 2006.

**Number awarded**   1 each year.

**Deadline**   July of each year.

## [1262]
## DEPARTMENT OF DEFENSE SMALL BUSINESS INNOVATION RESEARCH GRANTS

Department of Defense
Attn: Office of Small Business Programs
4800 Mark Center Drive, Suite 15G13
Alexandria, VA 22530
Toll Free: (866) SBIR-HLP
E-mail: administrator.dodsbir@osd.mil
Web: www.acq.osd.mil/osbp/sbir

**Summary**   To support small businesses (especially those owned by women and minorities) that have the technological expertise to contribute to the research and development mission of various agencies within the Department of Defense.

**Eligibility**   For the purposes of this program, a "small business" is defined as a firm that is organized for profit with a location in the United States; is in the legal form of an individual proprietorship, partnership, limited liability company, corporation, joint venture, association, trust, or cooperative; is at least 51% owned and controlled by 1 or more individuals who are citizens or permanent residents of the United States; and has (including its affiliates) fewer than 500 employees. The primary employment of the principal investigator must be with the firm at the time of award and during the conduct of the proposed project. Applications are encouraged from 1) women-owned small business concerns, defined as those that are at least 51% owned by a woman or women who also control and operate them; and 2) socially and economically disadvantaged small business concerns that are at least 51% owned by an Indian tribe, a Native Hawaiian organization, or 1 or more socially and economically disadvantaged individuals (African Americans, Hispanic Americans, Native Americans, Asian Pacific Americans, or subcontinent Asian Americans). Agencies that offer Department of Defense Small Business Innovation Research (SBIR) programs are the Department of the Army, Department of the Navy, Department of the Air Force, Defense Advanced Research Projects Agency (DARPA), Defense Threat Reduction Agency (DTRA), Chemical and Biological Defense (CBD), Defense Health Program (DHP), Defense Logistics Agency (DLA), Special Operations Command (SOCOM), Missile Defense Agency (MDA), National Geospatial-Intelligence Agency (NGA), Defense Microelectronics Activity (DMEA), and Office of Secretary of Defense (OSD). Selection is based on the soundness, technical merit, and innovation of the proposed approach and its incremental progress toward topic or subtopic solution; the qualifications of the principal investigator, supporting staff, and consultants; and the potential for commercial application and the benefits expected to accrue from this commercialization.

**Financial data** Grants are offered in 2 phases. In phase 1, awards normally range from $70,000 to $150,000 (for both direct and indirect costs); in phase 2, awards normally range from $500,000 to $1,000,000 (including both direct and indirect costs).

**Duration** Phase 1 awards may extend up to 6 months; phase 2 awards may extend up to 2 years.

**Number awarded** Varies each year; recently, 1,816 Phase 1 awards were granted: 582 for Department of the Navy, 295 for Department of the Army, 480 for Department of the Air Force, 68 for DARPA, 17 for DTRA, 16 for CBD, 16 for SOCOM, 122 for MDA, 7 for DLA, 40 for DHP, 4 for NGA, and 160 for OSD. The number of Phase 2 awards was 938, including 321 for Department of the Navy, 190 for Department of the Army, 207 for Department of the Air Force, 60 for DARPA, 4 for DTRA, 12 for CBD, 8 for SOCOM, 67 for MDA, 2 for DLA, 1 for DMEA, 27 for DHP, and 39 for OSD. Total funding was approximately $1.04 billion.

**Deadline** September of each year.

## [1263]
## DEPARTMENT OF DEFENSE SMALL BUSINESS TECHNOLOGY TRANSFER GRANTS

Department of Defense
Attn: Office of Small Business Programs
4800 Mark Center Drive, Suite 15G13
Alexandria, VA 22530
Toll Free: (866) SBIR-HLP
E-mail: administrator.dodsbir@osd.mil
Web: www.acq.osd.mil/osbp/sbir

**Summary** To provide financial support to cooperative research and development projects carried out between small women-owned or other business concerns and research institutions in areas of interest to various agencies within the Department of Defense.

**Eligibility** For the purposes of this program, a "small business" is defined as a firm that is organized for profit with a location in the United States; is in the legal form of an individual proprietorship, partnership, limited liability company, corporation, joint venture, association, trust, or cooperative; is at least 51% owned and controlled by 1 or more individuals who are citizens or permanent residents of the United States; and has (including its affiliates) fewer than 500 employees. Unlike the Department of Defense Small Business Innovation Research Grants, the primary employment of the principal investigator does not need to be with the business concern. This program, however, requires that the small business apply in collaboration with a nonprofit research institution for conduct of a project that has potential for commercialization. At least 40% of the work must be performed by the small business and at least 30% of the work must be performed by the research institution. Principal investigators from the nonprofit research institution must commit at least 10% of their effort to the project. Applications are encouraged from 1) women-owned small business concerns, defined as those that are at least 51% owned by a woman or women who also control and operate them; and 2) socially and economically disadvantaged small business concerns that are at least 51% owned by an Indian tribe, a Native Hawaiian organization, or 1 or more socially and economically disadvantaged individuals (African Americans, Hispanic Americans, Native Americans, Asian Pacific Americans, or subcontinent Asian Americans). Partnerships between small businesses and Historically Black Colleges and Universities (HBCUs) and Minority Institutions (MIs) are especially encouraged. Agencies of the Department of Defense currently participating in this program are the Department of the Army, Department of the Navy, Department of the Air Force, Defense Advanced Research Projects Agency (DARPA), Missile Defense Agency (MDA), and Office of Secretary of Defense (OSD). Selection is based on the soundness, technical merit, and innovation of the proposed approach and its incremental progress toward topic or subtopic solution; the qualifications of the proposed principal investigators, supporting staff, and consultants; and the potential for commercial application and the benefits expected to accrue from this commercialization.

**Financial data** In the first phase, annual awards range from $70,000 to $150,000 for direct costs, indirect costs, and negotiated fixed fees. In the second phase, awards from $500,000 to $1,000,000 for the full period are available.

**Duration** Generally 1 year for the first phase and 2 years for the second phase.

**Additional information** Grants in the first phase are to determine the scientific, technical, and commercial merit and feasibility of the proposed cooperative effort and the quality of performance of the small business concern. In the second phase, the research and development efforts continue, depending on the results of the first phase.

**Number awarded** Varies each year; recently, 309 Phase 1 awards were granted: 63 for Department of the Army, 117 for Department of the Navy, 87 for Department of the Air Force, 23 for OSD, and 19 for MDA. The number of Phase 2 awards was 127, including 31 for Department of the Army, 54 for Department of the Navy, 28 for Department of the Air Force, 5 for DARPA, 3 for OSD, and 6 for MDA. Total funding was approximately $117 million.

**Deadline** April of each year.

## [1264]
## DEPARTMENT OF EDUCATION SMALL BUSINESS INNOVATION RESEARCH GRANTS

Department of Education
Attn: Institute of Education Sciences
555 New Jersey Avenue, N.W., Room 608D
Washington, DC 20208-5544
(202) 208-1983                    Fax: (202) 219-2030
E-mail: Edward.metz@ed.gov
Web: www2.ed.gov/programs/sbir/index.html

**Summary**  To support small businesses (especially those owned by minorities and women) that have the technological expertise to contribute to the research and development mission of the Department of Education.

**Eligibility**  For the purposes of this program, a "small business" is defined as a firm that is organized for profit with a location in the United States; is in the legal form of an individual proprietorship, partnership, limited liability company, corporation, joint venture, association, trust, or cooperative; is at least 51% owned and controlled by 1 or more individuals who are citizens or permanent residents of the United States; and has (including its affiliates) fewer than 500 employees. The primary employment of the principal investigator must be with the firm at the time of award and during the conduct of the proposed project. Applications are encouraged from 1) women-owned small business concerns, defined as those that are at least 51% owned by a woman or women who also control and operate them; and 2) socially and economically disadvantaged small business concerns that are at least 51% owned by an Indian tribe, a Native Hawaiian organization, or 1 or more socially and economically disadvantaged individuals (African Americans, Hispanic Americans, Native Americans, Asian Pacific Americans, or subcontinent Asian Americans). Firms with strong research capabilities in science, engineering, or educational technology in any of the topic areas are encouraged to participate. Recently, the program operated in 2 branches of the Department of Education: 1) the National Institute on Disability and Rehabilitations Research (NIDRR) within the Office of Special Education and Rehabilitative Services (OSERS); and 2) the Institute of Education Sciences (IES), formerly the Office of Educational Research and Improvement (OERI). Selection is based on quality of project design (45 points), significance (25 points), quality of project personnel (20 points), and adequacy of resources (10 points).

**Financial data**  Grants are offered in 2 phases. Phase 1 awards normally do not exceed $150,000; phase 2 awards normally do not exceed $750,000 for IES programs or $500,000 for OSERS/NIDRR programs.

**Duration**  Phase 1 awards may extend up to 6 months; phase 2 awards may extend up to 2 years.

**Additional information**  Information on the NIDRR program is available from the Office of Special Education and Rehabilitative Services, Potomac Center Plaza, 550 12th Street, Room 5140, Washington, DC 20202-2700, (202) 245-7338, E-mail: Lynn.Medley@ed.gov.

**Number awarded**  Varies each year; recently, 25 Phase 1 awards (9 for IES and 16 for NIDRR) and 21 Phase 1 awards (16 for IES and 5 for NIDRR) were granted.

**Deadline**  February of each year for IES proposals; June of each year for NIDRR proposals.

## [1265]
## DEPARTMENT OF HOMELAND SECURITY SMALL BUSINESS INNOVATION RESEARCH GRANTS

Department of Homeland Security
Homeland Security Advanced Research Projects Agency
Attn: SBIR Program Manager
Washington, DC 20528
(202) 254-6768                    Toll Free: (800) 754-3043
Fax: (202) 254-7170   E-mail: elissa.sobolewski@dhs.gov
Web: www.dhs.gov/files/grants/gc_1247254058883.shtm

**Summary**  To support small businesses (especially those owned by women, minorities, and disabled veterans) that have the technological expertise to contribute to the research and development mission of the Department of Homeland Security (DHS).

**Eligibility**  For the purposes of this program, a "small business" is defined as a firm that is organized for profit with a location in the United States; is in the legal form of an individual proprietorship, partnership, limited liability company, corporation, joint venture, association, trust, or cooperative; is at least 51% owned and controlled by 1 or more individuals who are citizens or permanent residents of the United States; and has (including its affiliates) fewer than 500 employees. The primary employment of the principal investigator must be with the firm at the time of award and during the conduct of the proposed project. Applications are encouraged from 1) women-owned small business concerns, defined as those that are at least 51% owned by a woman or women who also control and operate them; 2) socially and economically disadvantaged small business concerns that are at least 51% owned by an Indian tribe, a Native Hawaiian organization, or 1 or more socially and economically disadvantaged individuals (African Americans, Hispanic Americans, Native Americans, Asian Pacific Americans, or subcontinent Asian Americans); and 3) service-disabled veteran small business concerns that are at least 51% owned by a service-disabled veteran and controlled by such a veteran or (for veterans with permanent and severe disability) the spouse or permanent caregiver of such a veteran. Each year, DHS identifies specialized topics for investigation. Selection is based on the soundness, technical merit, and innovation of the proposed approach and its incremental progress toward topic or subtopic solution; the qualifications of the proposed principal investigators, supporting staff, and consultants; the potential for commercial application and the benefits expected to accrue from this commercialization; and the realism and reasonableness of the cost proposal.

**Financial data**  Grants are offered in 2 phases. In phase 1, awards normally range up to $100,000; in phase 2, awards normally range up to $750,000.

**Duration**  Phase 1 awards may extend up to 6 months; phase 2 awards may extend up to 2 years.

**Number awarded**  Varies each year; recently, 61 Phase 1 awards were granted.

**Deadline**  January and July of each year.

## [1266]
## DETTRE ARCHIVAL INTERNSHIP

National Museum of Women in the Arts
Attn: Director of the Library and Research Center
1250 New York Avenue, N.W.
Washington, DC 20005-3920
(202) 783-5000                    Toll Free: (800) 222-7270
E-mail: internship@nmwa.org
Web: nmwa.org

**Summary**  To provide work experience at the National Museum of Women in the Arts (NMWA) to students and recent graduates interested in a career in archives.

**Eligibility**  This program is open to students enrolled in, or recently graduated from, an ALA-accredited library school or accredited archives program. Applicants must be interested in performing various tasks related to the archives of the NMWA. They must be familiar with Microsoft Office software. Familiarity with principals of archival and records management, knowledge of art history and/or museum studies, and excellent communication skills are preferred. Along with their application, they must submit a letter that includes information on prior experience working with archival collections, relevant classes related to archives, and background and interest in art and art history.

**Financial data**  The stipend is $10,000.

**Duration**  12 months.

**Additional information**  This program began in 2011.

**Number awarded**  1 each year.

**Deadline**  June of each year.

## [1267]
## DIANE J. WILLIS EARLY CAREER AWARD

American Psychological Foundation
750 First Street, N.E.
Washington, DC 20002-4242
(202) 336-5843                    Fax: (202) 336-5812
E-mail: foundation@apa.org
Web: www.apa.org/apf/funding/div-37-willis.aspx

**Summary**  To provide funding to women, minority, and other young psychologists interested in conducting research or other projects related to children and families.

**Eligibility**  This program is open to young psychologists who completed a doctoral degree (Ed.D., Psy.D., Ph.D.) within the past 7 years. Applicants must be interested in conducting research or other projects that inform, advocate for, and improve the mental health and well-being of children and families, particularly through public policy. The sponsor encourages applications from individuals who represent diversity in race, ethnicity, gender, age, disability, and sexual orientation.

**Financial data**  The grant is $2,000.

**Duration**  1 year.

**Additional information**  This program, sponsored by Division 37 (Child and Family Policy and Practice) of the American Psychological Association (APA), began in 2013.

**Number awarded**  1 each year.

**Deadline**  January of each year.

## [1268]
## DIFFUSION OF RESEARCH-BASED INNOVATIONS GRANTS OF THE RESEARCH ON GENDER IN SCIENCE AND ENGINEERING PROGRAM

National Science Foundation
Directorate for Education and Human Resources
Attn: Division of Human Resource Development
4201 Wilson Boulevard, Room 815N
Arlington, VA 22230
(703) 292-7303                    Fax: (703) 292-9018
TDD: (800) 281-8749               E-mail: jjesse@nsf.gov
Web: www.nsf.gov/funding/pgm_summ.jsp?pims_id=5475

**Summary**  To provide funding to scholars interested in conducting activities designed to engage a wider audience of practitioners with research findings and strategies for changing educational practice relative to the underrepresentation of girls and women in science, technology, engineering, or mathematics (STEM) education.

**Eligibility**  This program is open to scholars interested in engaging in activities designed to engage a wider audience of practitioners (e.g., teachers, faculty, guidance counselors, parents, policy makers) with research findings and strategies for changing educational practice to address gender-related issues. Applicants may be interested in conducting 1) pilot projects, to provide funds for small-scale development of materials and/or piloting of promising practices; 2) scale up projects, to reach broader regional or national audiences one proof of concept is established; or 3) dissemination of outcomes projects, to communicate the findings from currently- or previously-funded research of this program. Priority is given to proposals that are collaborative in nature and that focus on populations underrepresented across STEM fields (especially underrepresented minority, first-generation, or disability communities). Proposals that involve partnerships with minority-serving institutions, community colleges, or K-12 school districts are encouraged.

**Financial data**  Pilot projects may request $125,000 per year; scale up projects may request $200,000 per year; and dissemination of outcomes projects may request $125,000 per year.

**Duration**  Support for pilot projects is available for 1 to 3 years, for scale up projects for 3 to 5 years, or for dissemination of outcomes projects for 1 to 3 years.

**Additional information**  The National Science Foundation (NSF) established the Research on Gender in Science and Engineering (GSE) program in 1993 under the name "Program for Women and Girls." That was replaced with the "Program for Gender Equity in Science, Mathematics, Engineering and Technology," and then in the 2003 fiscal year by "Gender Diversity in STEM Education." The current title became effective in the 2007 fiscal year.

**Number awarded**  7 to 10 each year. The GSE program plans to award 15 to 22 grants per year for all of its activities. A total of $5,000,000 is available for the program annually.

**Deadline**  October of each year.

## [1269]
## DOE/MICKEY LELAND ENERGY FELLOWSHIPS

Department of Energy
Office of Fossil Energy
1000 Independence Avenue, S.W., FE-6
Washington, DC 20585
(202) 586-4484　　　　E-mail: alan.perry@hq.doe.gov
Web: energy.gov/fe/mickey-leland-energy-fellowship

**Summary**　To provide summer work experience at fossil energy sites of the Department of Energy (DOE) to female and underrepresented minority students or postdoctorates.

**Eligibility**　This program is open to U.S. citizens currently enrolled full time at an accredited college or university. Applicants must be undergraduate, graduate, or postdoctoral students in fields of science, technology (IT), engineering, or mathematics (STEM) and have a GPA of 3.0 or higher. They must be interested in a summer work experience at a DOE fossil energy research facility. Along with their application, they must submit a 100-word statement on why they want to participate in this program. A goal of the program is to recruit women and underrepresented minorities into careers related to fossil energy, although all qualified students are encouraged to apply.

**Financial data**　Weekly stipends are $600 for undergraduates, $750 for master's degree students, or $850 for doctoral and postdoctoral students. Travel costs for a round trip to and from the site and for a trip to a designated place for technical presentations are also paid.

**Duration**　10 weeks during the summer.

**Additional information**　This program began as 3 separate activities: the Historically Black Colleges and Universities Internship Program established in 1995, the Hispanic Internship Program established in 1998, and the Tribal Colleges and Universities Internship Program, established in 2000. Those 3 programs were merged into the Fossil Energy Minority Education Initiative, renamed the Mickey Leland Energy Fellowship Program in 2000. Sites to which interns may be assigned include the Albany Research Center (Albany, Oregon), the National Energy Technology Laboratory (Morgantown, West Virginia and Pittsburgh, Pennsylvania), Pacific Northwest National Laboratory (Richland, Washington), Rocky Mountain Oilfield Testing Center (Casper, Wyoming), Strategic Petroleum Reserve Project Management Office (New Orleans, Louisiana), or U.S. Department of Energy Headquarters (Washington, D.C.).

**Number awarded**　Varies each year; recently, 30 students participated in this program.

**Deadline**　January of each year.

## [1270]
## DOE SMALL BUSINESS INNOVATION RESEARCH GRANTS

Department of Energy
Attn: SBIR/STTR Program, SC-29
Germantown Building
1000 Independence Avenue, S.W.
Washington, DC 20585-1290
(301) 903-5707　　　　　　　Fax: (301) 903-5488
E-mail: sbir-sttr@science.doe.gov
Web: science.energy.gov/sbir

**Summary**　To support small businesses (especially those owned by women and minorities) that have the technological expertise to contribute to the research and development mission of the Department of Energy (DOE).

**Eligibility**　For the purposes of this program, a "small business" is defined as a firm that is organized for profit with a location in the United States; is in the legal form of an individual proprietorship, partnership, limited liability company, corporation, joint venture, association, trust, or cooperative; is at least 51% owned and controlled by 1 or more individuals who are citizens or permanent residents of the United States; and has (including its affiliates) fewer than 500 employees. The primary employment of the principal investigator must be with the firm at the time of award and during the conduct of the proposed project. Applications are encouraged from 1) women-owned small business concerns, defined as those that are at least 51% owned by a woman or women who also control and operate them; and 2) socially and economically disadvantaged small business concerns that are at least 51% owned by an Indian tribe, a Native Hawaiian organization, or 1 or more socially and economically disadvantaged individuals (African Americans, Hispanic Americans, Native Americans, Asian Pacific Americans, or subcontinent Asian Americans). Each office within DOE defines technical topics eligible for research.

**Financial data**　Support is offered in 2 phases: in phase 1, awards normally do not exceed $150,000 (for both direct and indirect costs); in phase 2, awards normally do not exceed $1,000,000 (including both direct and indirect costs).

**Duration**　Phase 1: up to 9 months; phase 2: up to 2 years.

**Additional information**　The objectives of this program include increasing private sector commercialization of technology developed through research and development supported by the Department of Energy, stimulating technological innovation in the private sector, strengthening the role of small business in meeting federal research and development needs, and improving the return on investment from federally-funded research for economic and social benefits to the nation.

**Number awarded**　Varies each year; recently 279 Phase 1 and 113 Phase 2 grants were awarded.

**Deadline**　November of each year.

## [1271]
## DOE SMALL BUSINESS TECHNOLOGY TRANSFER GRANTS

Department of Energy
Attn: SBIR/STTR Program, SC-29
Germantown Building
1000 Independence Avenue, S.W.
Washington, DC 20585-1290
(301) 903-5707　　　　　　　Fax: (301) 903-5488
E-mail: sbir-sttr@science.doe.gov
Web: science.energy.gov/sbir

**Summary**　To provide financial support to cooperative research and development projects carried out between small women-owned or other business concerns and research institutions in areas of interest to the Department of Energy.

**Eligibility**　For the purposes of this program, a "small business" is defined as a firm that is organized for profit with a location in the United States; is in the legal form of an individual proprietorship, partnership, limited liability company, corporation, joint venture, association, trust, or cooperative; is at least 51% owned and controlled by 1 or more individuals who are citizens or permanent residents of the United States; and has (including its affiliates) fewer than 500 employees. Unlike the Department of Energy Small Business Innovation Research Grants, the primary employment of the principal investigator does not need to be with the business concern. This program, however, requires that the small business apply in collaboration with a nonprofit research institution for conduct of a project that has potential for commercialization. At least 40% of the work must be performed by the small business and at least 30% of the work must be performed by the research institution. Principal investigators from the nonprofit research institution must commit at least 10% of their effort to the project. Applications are encouraged from 1) women-owned small business concerns, defined as those that are at least 51% owned by a woman or women who also control and operate them; and 2) socially and economically disadvantaged small business concerns that are at least 51% owned by an Indian tribe, a Native Hawaiian organization, or 1 or more socially and economically disadvantaged individuals (African Americans, Hispanic Americans, Native Americans, Asian Pacific Americans, or subcontinent Asian Americans). Each office within DOE defines technical topics eligible for research.

**Financial data** In the first phase, annual awards do not exceed $150,000 for direct costs, indirect costs, and negotiated fixed fees. In the second phase, awards up to $1,000,000 are available.

**Duration** Generally 9 months for the first phase and 2 years for the second phase.

**Additional information** Grants in the first phase are to determine the scientific, technical, and commercial merit and feasibility of the proposed cooperative effort and the quality of performance of the small business concern. In the second phase, the research and development efforts continue, depending on the results of the first phase.

**Number awarded** Varies each year; recently 39 Phase 1 and 15 Phase 2 grants were awarded.

**Deadline** January of each year.

## [1272]
## DOROTHEA M. LANG PIONEER AWARD

American College of Nurse-Midwives
Attn: ACNM Foundation, Inc.
8403 Colesville Road, Suite 1550
Silver Spring, MD 20910-6374
(240) 485-1850                     Fax: (240) 485-1818
E-mail: fdn@acnm.org
Web: www.midwife.org

**Summary** To recognize and reward members of the American College of Nurse-Midwives (ACNM) who have made outstanding contributions to the profession of midwifery.

**Eligibility** Nominees for this award must have been ACNM members for at least 10 years. They must have demonstrated vision and leadership in 1 of the following categories: pioneering midwives who, after 1958, demonstrated what midwifery care could and should be on the health team; pioneering efforts to integrate midwives and midwifery into the health care system of the United States or internationally; unsung heroes who initiated, rescued, enhanced, or saved midwifery

services or educational programs or are working to accomplish those goals; visionaries who encouraged or created open-minded pathways in education for professional midwives or are working to accomplish that goal; energetic anticipants who have furthered or are furthering the legislative agenda for certified midwives; or have contributed other pioneering activities.

**Financial data** The award includes a cash honorarium and a necklace.

**Duration** The award is presented annually.

**Additional information** This program began in 2002.

**Number awarded** Varies each year; recently, 3 of these awards were presented.

**Deadline** April of each year.

## [1273]
## DR. BESSIE ELIZABETH DELANEY FELLOWSHIP

National Dental Association
Attn: National Dental Association Foundation, Inc.
3517 16th Street, N.W.
Washington, DC 20010
(202) 588-1697                     Fax: (202) 588-1244
E-mail: admin@ndaonline.org
Web: www.ndafoundation.org/NDAF/Scholarships.html

**Summary** To provide financial assistance to female dental postdoctoral students who are members of minority groups.

**Eligibility** This program is open to female members of minority groups who are working on a postdoctoral degree in subspecialty areas of dentistry, public health, administration, pediatrics, research, or law. Students working on a master's degree beyond their residency may be considered. Applicants must be members of the National Dental Association (NDA) and U.S. citizens or permanent residents. Along with their application, they must submit a letter explaining why they should be considered for this scholarship, 2 letters of recommendation, a curriculum vitae, a description of the program, nomination by their program director, and documentation of financial need.

**Financial data** The stipend is $10,000.

**Duration** 1 year.

**Additional information** This program, established in 1990, is supported by the Colgate-Palmolive Company.

**Number awarded** 1 each year.

**Deadline** May of each year.

## [1274]
## DRS. ROSALEE G. AND RAYMOND A. WEISS RESEARCH AND PROGRAM INNOVATION GRANT

American Psychological Foundation
750 First Street, N.E.
Washington, DC 20002-4242
(202) 336-5843                     Fax: (202) 336-5812
E-mail: foundation@apa.org
Web: www.apa.org/apf/funding/vision-weiss.aspx

**Summary** To provide funding to professionals (particularly women, minorities, and individuals with disabilities) who are interested in conducting projects that use psychology to solve social problems related to the priorities of the American Psychological Foundation (APF).

**Eligibility** This program is open to professionals at non-profit organizations engaged in research, education, and intervention projects and programs. Applicants must be interested in conducting an activity that uses psychology to solve social problems in the following priority areas: understanding and fostering the connection between mental and physical health; reducing stigma and prejudice; understanding and preventing violence to create a safer, more humane world; or addressing the long-term psychological needs of individuals and communities in the aftermath of disaster. Selection is based on the criticality of the proposed funding for the proposed work; conformance with stated program goals and requirements; innovative and potential impact qualities; quality, viability, and promise of proposed work, and competence and capability of project leaders. The sponsor encourages applications from individuals who represent diversity in race, ethnicity, gender, age, disability, and sexual orientation.

**Financial data** The grant is $2,500.

**Duration** 1 year; nonrenewable.

**Additional information** This program began in 2003.

**Number awarded** 1 each year.

**Deadline** March of each year.

## [1275]
## DUPONT MINORITIES IN ENGINEERING AWARD

American Society for Engineering Education
Attn: Awards Administration
1818 N Street, N.W., Suite 600
Washington, DC 20036-2479
(202) 331-3550        Fax: (202) 265-8504
E-mail: board@asee.org
Web: www.asee.org/member-resources/awards

**Summary** To recognize and reward outstanding achievements by engineering educators to increase diversity by gender or ethnicity in science, engineering, and technology.

**Eligibility** Eligible for nomination are engineering or engineering technology educators who, as part of their educational activity, either assume or are charged with the responsibility of motivating underrepresented students to enter and continue in engineering or engineering technology curricula at the college or university level, graduate or undergraduate. Nominees must demonstrate leadership in the conception, organization, and operation of pre-college and college activities designed to increase participation by underrepresented students in engineering and engineering technology.

**Financial data** The award consists of $1,500, a certificate, and a grant of $500 for travel expenses to the ASEE annual conference.

**Duration** The award is granted annually.

**Additional information** Funding for this award is provided by DuPont. It was originally established in 1956 as the Vincent Bendix Minorities in Engineering Award.

**Number awarded** 1 each year.

**Deadline** January of each year.

## [1276]
## EARLY CAREER AWARD

American Psychological Foundation
750 First Street, N.E.
Washington, DC 20002-4242
(202) 336-5843        Fax: (202) 336-5812
E-mail: foundation@apa.org
Web: www.apa.org/apf/funding/div-29.aspx

**Summary** To recognize and reward women, minority, and other young psychologists who have made outstanding contributions to psychotherapy.

**Eligibility** This award is available to psychologists who are no more than 7 years past completion of their doctoral degree. Nominees must have demonstrated promising professional achievement related to psychotherapy theory, practice, research, or training. They must be members of Division 29 (Psychotherapy) of the American Psychological Association. Self-nominations are not accepted. Selection is based on conformance with stated program goals and qualifications and applicant's demonstrated accomplishments and promise. The sponsor encourages nominations of individuals who represent diversity in race, ethnicity, gender, age, disability, and sexual orientation.

**Financial data** The award is $2,500.

**Duration** The award is presented annually.

**Additional information** This award was established in 1981 and named the Jack D. Krasner Memorial Award. It was renamed in 2007.

**Number awarded** 1 each year.

**Deadline** Nominations must be submitted by December of each year.

## [1277]
## EARLY CAREER PATIENT-ORIENTED DIABETES RESEARCH AWARD

Juvenile Diabetes Research Foundation International
Attn: Grant Administrator
26 Broadway, 14th Floor
New York, NY 10004
(212) 479-7572        Toll Free: (800) 533-CURE
Fax: (212) 785-9595        E-mail: info@jdrf.org
Web: jdrf.org

**Summary** To provide funding to physician scientists (particularly women, minorities, and persons with disabilities) who are interested in pursuing a program of clinical diabetes-related research training.

**Eligibility** This program is open to investigators in diabetes-related research who have an M.D. or M.D./Ph.D. degree and a faculty appointment at the late training or assistant professor level. Applicants must be sponsored by an investigator who is affiliated full time with an accredited institution, who pursues patient-oriented clinical research, and who agrees to supervise the applicant's training. There are no citizenship requirements. Applications are encouraged from women, members of minority groups underrepresented in the sciences, and people with disabilities. Areas of relevant research can include: mechanisms of human disease, therapeutic interventions, clinical trials, and the development of new technologies. The proposed research may be conducted at foreign or domestic, for-profit or nonprofit, or public or private institutions, including universities, colleges, hospitals, laboratories, units of state or local government, or eligible agencies of the federal government.

**Financial data** The total award may be up to $150,000 each year, up to $75,000 of which may be requested for research (including a technician, supplies, equipment, and travel). The salary request must be consistent with the established salary structure of the applicant's institution. Equipment purchases in years other than the first must be strongly justified. Indirect costs may not exceed 10%.

**Duration** The award is for 5 years and is generally nonrenewable.

**Number awarded** Varies each year.

**Deadline** August of each year.

## [1278]
## EINSTEIN POSTDOCTORAL FELLOWSHIP PROGRAM

Smithsonian Astrophysical Observatory
Attn: Chandra X-Ray Center
Einstein Fellowship Program Office
60 Garden Street, MS4
Cambridge, MA 02138
(617) 496-7941                      Fax: (617) 495-7356
E-mail: fellows@head.cfa.harvard.edu
Web: cxc.harvard.edu/fellows

**Summary** To provide funding to recent postdoctoral scientists (especially women and minorities) who are interested in conducting research related to high energy astrophysics missions of the National Aeronautics and Space Administration (NASA).

**Eligibility** This program is open to postdoctoral scientists who completed their Ph.D., Sc.D., or equivalent doctoral degree within the past 3 years in astronomy, physics, or related disciplines. Applicants must be interested in conducting research related to NASA Physics of the Cosmos program missions: Chandra, Fermi, XMM-Newton and International X-Ray Observatory, cosmological investigations relevant to the Planck and JDEM missions, and gravitational astrophysics relevant to the LISA mission. They must be citizens of the United States or English-speaking citizens of other countries who have valid visas. Women and minorities are strongly encouraged to apply.

**Financial data** Stipends are approximately $66,500 per year. Fellows may also receive health insurance, relocation costs, and moderate support (up to $16,000 per year) for research-related travel, computing services, publications, and other direct costs.

**Duration** 3 years (depending on a review of scientific activity).

**Additional information** This program, which began in 2009 with funding from NASA, incorporates the former Chandra and GLAST Fellowship programs.

**Number awarded** Up to 10 each year.

**Deadline** November of each year.

## [1279]
## ELEANOR ROOSEVELT FUND AWARD

American Association of University Women
Attn: AAUW Educational Foundation
1111 16th Street, N.W.
Washington, DC 20036-4873
(202) 785-7624                      Toll Free: (800) 326-AAUW
Fax: (202) 872-1425                 TDD: (202) 785-7777
E-mail: fellowships@aauw.org
Web: www.aauw.org

**Summary** To recognize and reward individuals, organizations, institutions, or projects that provide an equitable school environment for women and girls.

**Eligibility** Nominations for this award are not solicited from the general public. The goals of the Eleanor Roosevelt Fund are to 1) remove barriers to women's and girls' participation in education; 2) promote the value of diversity and cross-cultural communication; and 3) develop greater understanding of the ways women learn, think, work, and play. Individuals, organizations, institutions, or projects that work for those goals are eligible to be nominated for this award. Their activities may include classroom teaching, educational and research contributions, or legal and legislative work that contributes to equity for women and girls. Although the award focuses on education, the nominee need not be an educator.

**Financial data** The award is $5,000.

**Duration** The award is presented biennially.

**Additional information** This award was established in 1989.

**Number awarded** 1 each odd-numbered year.

**Deadline** Nominations must be submitted by October of even-numbered years.

## [1280]
## ELI LILLY TRAVEL AWARDS

American Chemical Society
Attn: Department of Diversity Programs
1155 16th Street, N.W.
Washington, DC 20036
(202) 872-6334          Toll Free: (800) 227-5558, ext. 6334
Fax: (202) 776-8003               E-mail: diversity@acs.org
Web: www.acs.org

**Summary** To provide funding to women chemists interested in traveling to scientific meetings.

**Eligibility** This program is open to women chemists (students, professionals, and postdoctorates) who wish to travel to scientific meetings to present the results of their research. Only U.S. citizens and permanent residents are eligible. Awards are made on the basis of scientific merit and financial need. Preference is given to those who have not made a previous presentation at a national or major meeting. Women who have received a prior award under this program are ineligible.

**Financial data** Awards range up to $1,000 and may be used for registration, travel, and accommodations only.

**Additional information** Funding for this program is provided by Eli Lilly and Company. Grants are restricted to travel within the United States.

**Number awarded** Varies each year.

**Deadline** September of each year for meetings between January and June; February of each year for meetings between July and December.

## [1281]
## ELSEVIER GUT MICROBIOME PILOT RESEARCH AWARD

American Gastroenterological Association
Attn: AGA Research Foundation
Research Awards Manager
4930 Del Ray Avenue
Bethesda, MD 20814-2512
(301) 222-4012                    Fax: (301) 654-5920
E-mail: awards@gastro.org
Web: www.gastro.org/aga-foundation/grants

**Summary** To provide funding to new or established gastro-enterologists (particularly women and minorities) who need funding for pilot research projects in areas related to the gut microbiome.

**Eligibility** Applicants must have an M.D., Ph.D., or equivalent degree and a full-time faculty position at an accredited North American institution. They may not hold grants for projects on a similar topic from other agencies. Individual membership in the American Gastroenterology Association (AGA) is required. The proposal must enable investigators to obtain new data on the relationships of the gut microbiota to digestive health and disease that can ultimately lead to subsequent grant applications for more substantial funding and duration. Women and minority investigators are strongly encouraged to apply. Selection is based on novelty, importance, feasibility, environment, commitment of the institution, and overall likelihood that the project will lead to more substantial grants in gut microbiome research.

**Financial data** The grant is $25,000. Funds may be used for salary, supplies, or equipment. Indirect costs are not allowed.

**Duration** 1 year.

**Additional information** This award is sponsored by Elsevier Science.

**Number awarded** 1 each year.

**Deadline** January of each year.

## [1282]
## ELSEVIER PILOT RESEARCH AWARDS

American Gastroenterological Association
Attn: AGA Research Foundation
Research Awards Manager
4930 Del Ray Avenue
Bethesda, MD 20814-2512
(301) 222-4012                    Fax: (301) 654-5920
E-mail: awards@gastro.org
Web: www.gastro.org/aga-foundation/grants

**Summary** To provide funding to new or established investigators (particularly women and minorities) for pilot research projects in areas related to gastroenterology or hepatology.

**Eligibility** Applicants must have an M.D., Ph.D., or equivalent degree and a full-time faculty position at an accredited North American institution. They may not hold grants for projects on a similar topic from other agencies. Individual membership in the American Gastroenterology Association (AGA)

is required. The proposal must involve obtaining new data that can ultimately provide the basis for subsequent grant applications for more substantial funding and duration in gastroenterology- or hepatology-related areas. Women and minority investigators are strongly encouraged to apply. Selection is based on novelty, importance, feasibility, environment, commitment of the institution, and overall likelihood that the project will lead to more substantial grant applications.

**Financial data** The grant is $25,000. Funds may be used for salary, supplies, or equipment. Indirect costs are not allowed.

**Duration** 1 year.

**Additional information** This award is sponsored by Elsevier Science.

**Number awarded** 3 each year.

**Deadline** January of each year.

## [1283]
## EMILY SCHOENBAUM RESEARCH AND COMMUNITY DEVELOPMENT GRANTS

Tulane University
Newcomb College Institute
Attn: Assistant Director for Administration and Programs
200 Caroline Richardson Hall
62 Newcomb Place
New Orleans, LA 70118
(504) 314-2721              Toll Free: (888) 327-0009
Fax: (504) 862-8589        E-mail: lwolford@tulane.edu
Web: tulane.edu/newcomb/grants.cfm

**Summary** To provide funding to scholars and students in Louisiana interested in conducting research or other projects related to women and girls.

**Eligibility** This program is open to students, faculty, and staff of primary and secondary schools, colleges, and universities in Louisiana, as well as community scholars and activists. Applicants must be interested in conducting a project with potential to bring about change in women's lives or effect public policy so as to improve the well-being of women and girls, particularly those in the New Orleans area.

**Financial data** The grant is $2,000.

**Duration** 1 year.

**Additional information** This program began in 1999.

**Number awarded** 1 or 2 each year.

**Deadline** April of each year.

## [1284]
## EMMA HARPER TURNER FUND

Pi Beta Phi
Attn: Pi Beta Phi Foundation
1154 Town and Country Commons Drive
Town and Country, MO 63017
(636) 256-1357                    Fax: (636) 256-8124
E-mail: fndn@pibetaphi.org
Web: www.pibetaphifoundation.org/emma-harper-turner

**Summary** To provide assistance to alumnae of Pi Beta Phi Sorority who are in extreme need of college funding or personal financial assistance.

**Eligibility** Any member of Pi Beta Phi needing financial assistance is eligible to be considered for this funding. Each potential recipient must be sponsored by 3 Pi Beta Phi alumnae who are aware of the candidate's need and are personally acquainted with her. Applicants must submit a confidential financial information form to validate their need. The program includes 3 types of grants: collegian (for college students who have experienced a life change that jeopardizes their ability to stay in school), alumna (for college graduates who are experiencing financial difficulties), and immediate needs (for alumnae who are victims of a natural disaster).

**Financial data** Small monthly gifts are awarded.

**Duration** Awards are provided for 1 year; the recipient's application is then reviewed to determine if the "gifts of love" should continue.

**Additional information** This fund was established in 1946.

**Number awarded** Varies each year. A total of $100,000 is available for these grants annually.

**Deadline** Applications may be submitted at any time.

## [1285]
## ENID A. NEIDLE SCHOLAR-IN-RESIDENCE PROGRAM FOR WOMEN

American Dental Education Association
Attn: ADEA Access, Diversity, and Inclusion, Policy Center
1400 K Street, N.W., Suite 1100
Washington, DC 20005
(202) 289-7201, ext. 197          Fax: (202) 289-7204
E-mail: dabreuk@adea.org
Web: www.adea.org

**Summary** To provide funding to women dental faculty members who are interested in a residency at the American Dental Education Association (ADEA) in Washington, D.C.

**Eligibility** This program is open to full-time female faculty with primary teaching appointments in predoctoral and advanced dental education programs at ADEA-member institutions; female junior dental and dental hygiene faculty members are particularly encouraged to apply. Candidates must belong to ADEA. They must be interested in concentrating on issues that affect women faculty during a 3 month residency at ADEA in Washington, D.C. Interested faculty members should submit the following: a completed application form, a personal statement on their general interests and expectations for the residency, a letter of recommendation from their dean or chief administrative officer, a current curriculum vitae, and a formal letter of support from a colleague or mentor.

**Financial data** Scholars receive a $6,000 stipend to cover travel and living expenses while at the residency in Washington, D.C. It is a requirement of the program that the fellow's institution continue to provide salary support and fringe benefits for the duration of the experience.

**Duration** At least 3-months.

**Additional information** This program, established in 1994, is sponsored by the ADEA and Johnson & Johnson Healthcare Products. While in Washington, D.C., it is expected that the scholar will gain perspectives on issues facing women faculty, including promotion, advancement, and tenure policies; entry and reentry into the workforce; child care and elder care; women's health; work patterns; advanced education and research opportunities; and other gender-related issues. The scholar is assigned to a senior ADEA staff member and will have the opportunity to be involved in a range of activities there, in addition to her own project.

**Number awarded** 1 each year.

**Deadline** January of each year.

## [1286]
## EPILEPSY FOUNDATION RESEARCH GRANTS PROGRAM

Epilepsy Foundation
Attn: Research Department
8301 Professional Place
Landover, MD 20785-2353
(301) 459-3700          Toll Free: (800) EFA-1000
Fax: (301) 577-2684          TDD: (800) 332-2070
E-mail: grants@efa.org
Web: www.epilepsyfoundation.org

**Summary** To provide funding to junior investigators (especially women, minorities, and persons with disabilities) who are interested in conducting research that will advance the understanding, treatment, and prevention of epilepsy.

**Eligibility** Applicants must have a doctoral degree and an academic appointment at the level of assistant professor in a university or medical school (or equivalent standing at a research institution or medical center). They must be interested in conducting basic or clinical research to advance understanding of the behavioral and psychosocial aspects of having epilepsy. Faculty with appointments at the level of associate professor or higher are not eligible. Applications from women, members of minority groups, and people with disabilities are especially encouraged. U.S. citizenship is not required, but the research must be conducted in the United States. Selection is based on the scientific quality of the research plan, the relevance of the proposed research to epilepsy, the applicant's qualifications, and the adequacy of the institution and facility where research will be conducted.

**Financial data** The grant is $50,000 per year.

**Duration** 1 year; recipients may reapply for 1 additional year of funding.

**Additional information** Support for this program is provided by many individuals, families, and corporations, especially the American Epilepsy Society, Abbott Laboratories, Ortho-McNeil Pharmaceutical, and Pfizer Inc.

**Number awarded** Varies each year.

**Deadline** August of each year.

## [1287]
## EPILEPSY RESEARCH RECOGNITION AWARDS PROGRAM

American Epilepsy Society
342 North Main Street
West Hartford, CT 06117-2507
(860) 586-7505          Fax: (860) 586-7550
E-mail: ctubby@aesnet.org
Web: www.aesnet.org/research/research-awards

**Summary** To provide funding to women, minority, and other investigators anywhere in the world interested in conducting research related to epilepsy.

**Eligibility** This program is open to active scientists and clinicians working in any aspect of epilepsy. Candidates must be nominated by their home institution and be at the level of associate professor or professor. There are no geographic restrictions; nominations from outside the United States and North America are welcome. Nominations of women and members of minority groups are especially encouraged. Selection is based on pioneering research, originality of research, quality of publications, research productivity, relationship of the candidate's work to problems in epilepsy, training activities, other contributions in epilepsy, and productivity over the next decade; all criteria are weighted equally.

**Financial data** The grant is $10,000. No institutional overhead is allowed.

**Additional information** This program began in 1991.

**Number awarded** 2 each year.

**Deadline** August of each year.

## [1288]
## EQUALITY AWARD

American Library Association
Attn: Governance Office, Awards Program
50 East Huron Street
Chicago, IL 60611-2795
(312) 280-3247    Toll Free: (800) 545-2433, ext. 3247
Fax: (312) 280-3256    TDD: (888) 814-7692
E-mail: awards@ala.org
Web: www.ala.org/awardsgrants/awards/129/detail

**Summary** To recognize and reward the person or group that best promotes equality in librarianship.

**Eligibility** This program is open to librarians and other people who work in a library, are a trustee, work in a library-related institution, work in an organization, work in an association, or work in a subdivision of any of those. Nominees must have contributed significantly to promoting equality in the library profession, either through a sustained contribution or a single outstanding accomplishment. The award may be given for an activist or scholarly contribution in such areas as pay equity, affirmative action, legislative work, or non-sexist education.

**Financial data** The award is $1,000 and a citation.

**Duration** The award is presented annually.

**Additional information** The award, first presented in 1984, is funded by Scarecrow Press and administered by the American Library Association.

**Number awarded** 1 each year.

**Deadline** November of each year.

## [1289]
## ERIC AND BARBARA DOBKIN NATIVE ARTIST FELLOWSHIP FOR WOMEN

School for Advanced Research
Attn: Indian Arts Research Center
660 Garcia Street
P.O. Box 2188
Santa Fe, NM 87504-2188
(505) 954-7205    Fax: (505) 954-7207
E-mail: iarc@sarsf.org
Web: sarweb.org/?artists

**Summary** To provide an opportunity for Native American women artists to improve their skills through a spring residency at the Indian Arts Research Center in Santa Fe, New Mexico.

**Eligibility** This program is open to Native American women who excel in the arts, including sculpture, perfor-

mance, basketry, painting, printmaking, digital art, mixed media, photography, pottery, writing, and filmmaking. Applicants should be attempting to explore new avenues of creativity, grapple with new ideas to advance their work, and strengthen existing talents. Along with their application, they must submit a current resume, examples of their current work, and a 2-page statement that explains why they are applying for this fellowship, how it will help them realize their professional and/or personal goals as an artist, and the scope of the project they plan to complete during the residency.

**Financial data** The fellowship provides a stipend of $3,000 per month, housing, studio space, supplies allowance, and travel reimbursement to and from the center.

**Duration** 3 months, beginning in March.

**Additional information** Fellows work with the staff and research curators at the Indian Arts Research Center, an academic division of the School of American Research that is devoted solely to Native American art scholarship. The center has a significant collection of Pueblo pottery, Navajo and Pueblo Indian textiles, and early 20th-century Indian paintings, as well as holdings of jewelry and silverwork, basketry, clothing, and other ethnological materials. This fellowship was established in 2001.

**Number awarded** 1 each year.

**Deadline** January of each year.

## [1290]
## EUDORA WELTY PRIZE

Mississippi University for Women
Attn: Department of Languages, Literature, and
    Philosophy
Painter Hall, Room 111
P.O. Box MUW-1634
Columbus, MS 39701
(662) 329-7386    Fax: (662) 329-7387
E-mail: info@humanities.muw.edu
Web: www.muw.edu/welty/weltyprize.php

**Summary** To recognize and reward original works of interpretive scholarship from disciplines within the humanities and related to women's studies, Southern studies, or modern letters.

**Eligibility** Eligible to be submitted are unpublished book-length manuscripts (80,000 to 100,000 words) complete at the time of submission and not under consideration by any other press. Submissions must be original works of interpretive scholarship and from disciplines within the humanities related to women's studies, Southern studies, or modern literature. Collections of essays, bibliographies, translations, and unrevised theses or dissertations are not eligible.

**Financial data** The prize consists of a cash award of $1,500 and publication of the winning manuscript by the University Press of Mississippi.

**Duration** The prize is presented annually.

**Additional information** This prize, established in 1989, is jointly sponsored by Mississippi University for Women and the University Press of Mississippi.

**Number awarded** 1 each year.

**Deadline** April of each year.

## [1291]
## EVA KING KILLAM RESEARCH AWARD

American College of Neuropsychopharmacology
Attn: Executive Office
5034-A Thoroughbred Lane
Brentwood, TN 37027
(615) 324-2360          Fax: (615) 523-1715
E-mail: acnp@acnp.org
Web: www.acnp.org/programs/awards.aspx

**Summary** To recognize and reward young scientists (particularly women and minorities) who have contributed outstanding translational research to neuropsychopharmacology.

**Eligibility** This award is available to scientists who are younger than 50 years of age. Nominees must have made an outstanding translational research contribution to neuropsychopharmacology. The contributions should focus on translating advances from basic science to human investigations. Selection is based on the quality of the contribution and its impact in advancing neuropsychopharmacology. Neither membership in the American College of Neuropsychopharmacology (ACNP) nor U.S. citizenship are required. Nomination of women and minorities is highly encouraged.

**Financial data** The award consists of an expense-paid trip to the ACNP annual meeting, a monetary honorarium, and a plaque.

**Duration** The award is presented annually.

**Additional information** This award was first presented in 2011.

**Number awarded** 1 each year.

**Deadline** Nominations must be submitted by June of each year.

## [1292]
## EXCELLENCE IN SCIENCE AWARD

Federation of American Societies for Experimental
  Biology
Attn: Excellence in Science Award
9650 Rockville Pike
Bethesda, MD 20814-3998
(301) 634-7092          Fax: (301) 634-7049
E-mail: info@faseb.org
Web: www.faseb.org

**Summary** To recognize and reward women whose research in experimental biology has contributed significantly to our understanding of their discipline.

**Eligibility** Nominations for this award may be submitted by members of the component societies of the Federation of American Societies for Experimental Biology (FASEB). Nominees must be women who are senior in their field and have a national reputation for outstanding contributions in research, leadership, and mentorship. They must also be members of 1 or more of the 27 societies of FASEB. Letters of nomination should identify the nominee's contributions to the field that represents her outstanding achievement in science, leadership and mentorship, evidence of national recognition, honors and awards, and a selected bibliography. Self-nominations are not accepted.

**Financial data** The award consists of a $10,000 unrestricted research grant, travel expenses to the annual meeting, complimentary registration at the meeting, and a plaque.

**Duration** This award is presented annually.

**Additional information** This award was first presented in 1989. Member societies of FASEB include the American Physiological Society (APS), American Society for Biochemistry and Molecular Biology (ASBMB), American Society for Pharmacology and Experimental Therapeutics (ASPET), American Society for Investigative Pathology (ASIP), American Society for Nutrition (ASN), American Association of Immunologists (AAI), American Association of Anatomists (AAA), The Protein Society, American Society for Bone and Mineral Research (ASBMR), American Society for Clinical Investigation (ASCI), The Endocrine Society, American Society of Human Genetics (ASHG), Society for Developmental Biology (SDB), American Peptide Society (APEPS), Association of Biomolecular Resource Facilities (ABRF), Society for the Study of Reproduction (SSR), Teratology Society, Environmental Mutagen Society (EMS), International Society for Computational Biology (ISCB), American College of Sports Medicine (ACSM), Biomedical Engineering Society (BMES), Genetics Society of America, American Federation for Medical Research (AFMR), The Histochemical Society (HCS) Society for Pediatric Research (SPR), Society for Glycobiology (SFG), and Association for Molecular Pathology (AMP).

**Number awarded** 1 each year.

**Deadline** Nominations must be submitted by February of each year.

## [1293]
## EXTENSION SERVICES GRANTS OF THE RESEARCH ON GENDER IN SCIENCE AND ENGINEERING PROGRAM

National Science Foundation
Directorate for Education and Human Resources
Attn: Division of Human Resource Development
4201 Wilson Boulevard, Room 815N
Arlington, VA 22230
(703) 292-7303          Fax: (703) 292-9018
TDD: (800) 281-8749     E-mail: jjesse@nsf.gov
Web: www.nsf.gov/funding/pgm_summ.jsp?pims_id=5475

**Summary** To provide funding to professionals interested in providing consulting services to educators and institutions, to enable them to adopt policies and programs related to the underrepresentation of girls and women in science, technology, engineering, or mathematics (STEM) education.

**Eligibility** This program is open to anyone with professional skills that will enable them to 1) integrate various findings about gender in science and engineering into a comprehensive program of change or to facilitate the interpretation of research knowledge into practice; 2) show educators how to adapt exemplary projects, research-based learning tools, pedagogical approaches, and service or support programs; 3) communicate to researchers the problems that practicing educators find most urgent or troublesome in adopting the new methods or tools; or 4) provide training and consulting services that will develop a cadre of extension service agents that will reach significant practitioner communities in a train-the-trainer model. The target community may be a mix of teachers, counselors, parents, community leaders, administrators, faculty, and others.

**Financial data** Grants up to $500,000 per year are available.

**Duration** Up to 5 years; support in years 4 and 5 depends upon performance.

**Additional information** The National Science Foundation (NSF) established the Research on Gender in Science and Engineering (GSE) program in 1993 under the name "Program for Women and Girls." That was replaced with the "Program for Gender Equity in Science, Mathematics, Engineering and Technology," and then in the 2003 fiscal year by "Gender Diversity in STEM Education." The current title became effective in the 2007 fiscal year.

**Number awarded** 1 to 2 each year. The GSE program plans to award 15 to 22 grants per year for research, outreach and communication, and extension service activities. A total of $5,000,000 is available for the program annually.

**Deadline** Letters of intent must be submitted in September of each year; full proposals are due in October.

## [1294]
## FACULTY EARLY CAREER DEVELOPMENT PROGRAM

National Science Foundation
Directorate for Education and Human Resources
Senior Staff Associate for Cross Directorate Programs
4201 Wilson Boulevard, Room 805
Arlington, VA 22230
(703) 292-8600          TDD: (800) 281-8749
E-mail: info@nsf.gov
Web: www.nsf.gov

**Summary** To provide funding to outstanding new faculty (particularly women, minorities, and individuals with disabilities) who are working in science and engineering fields of interest to the National Science Foundation (NSF) and intend to develop academic careers involving both research and education.

**Eligibility** This program, identified as the CAREER program, is open to faculty members who meet all of the following requirements: 1) be employed in a tenure-track (or equivalent) position at an institution in the United States, its territories or possessions, or the Commonwealth of Puerto Rico that awards degrees in a field supported by NSF or that is a nonprofit, non-degree granting organization, such as a museum, observatory, or research laboratory; 2) have a doctoral degree in a field of science or engineering supported by NSF: 3) not have competed more than 3 times in this program; 4) be untenured; and 5) not be a current or former recipient of a Presidential Early Career Award for Scientists and Engineers (PECASE) or CAREER award. Applicants are not required to be U.S. citizens or permanent residents. They must submit a career development plan that indicates a description of the proposed research project, including preliminary supporting data (if appropriate), specific objectives, methods, procedures to be used, and expected significance of the results; a description of the proposed educational activities, including plans to evaluate their impact; a description of how the research and educational activities are integrated with each other; and results of prior NSF support (if applicable). Proposals from women, underrepresented minorities, and persons with disabilities are especially encouraged.

**Financial data** The grant is at least $80,000 per year (or $100,000 per year for the Directorate of Biological Sciences or the Office of Polar Programs), including indirect costs or overhead.

**Duration** 5 years.

**Additional information** This program is operated by various disciplinary divisions within the NSF; for a list of the participating divisions and their telephone numbers, contact the sponsor. Outstanding recipients of these grants are nominated for the NSF component of the PECASE awards, which are awarded to 20 recipients of these grants as an honorary award.

**Number awarded** Approximately 600 each year.

**Deadline** July of each year.

## [1295]
## FELLOWSHIPS IN SCIENCE AND INTERNATIONAL AFFAIRS

Harvard University
John F. Kennedy School of Government
Belfer Center for Science and International Affairs
Attn: Fellowship Coordinator
79 John F. Kennedy Street, Mailbox 53
Cambridge, MA 02138
(617) 495-8806          Fax: (617) 495-8963
E-mail: bcsia_fellowships@hks.harvard.edu
Web: belfercenter.ksg.harvard.edu/fellowships

**Summary** To provide funding to professionals, postdoctorates, and doctoral students (particularly women and minorities) who are interested in conducting research in areas of concern to the Belfer Center for Science and International Affairs at Harvard University in Cambridge, Massachusetts.

**Eligibility** The postdoctoral fellowship is open to recent recipients of the Ph.D. or equivalent degree, university faculty members, and employees of government, military, international, humanitarian, and private research institutions who have appropriate professional experience. Applicants for predoctoral fellowships must have passed their general examinations. Lawyers, economists, political scientists, those in the natural sciences, and others of diverse disciplinary backgrounds are also welcome to apply. The program especially encourages applications from women, minorities, and citizens of all countries. All applicants must be interested in conducting research in 1 of the 2 major program areas of the center: 1) the International Security Program (ISP), which addresses U.S. defense and foreign policy, security policy, nuclear proliferation, terrorism, internal and ethnic conflict, and related topics; and 2) the Science, Technology, and Public Policy Program (STPP), including technology and innovation, information and communications technology, water-energy nexus, managing the atom, energy technology innovation policy, China and environmental sustainability, geoengineering and climate policy, geopolitics of energy, and geospatial policy and management.

**Financial data** The stipend is $34,000 for postdoctoral research fellows or $20,000 for predoctoral research fellows. Health insurance is also provided.

**Duration** 10 months.

**Number awarded** A limited number each year.

**Deadline** January of each year.

## [1296]
## FEMINIST LECTURER AWARD

Sociologists for Women in Society
Attn: Executive Officer
Southern Connecticut State University
Department of Sociology
501 Crescent Street
New Haven, CT 06515
(203) 392-7714                    Fax: (203) 392-7715
E-mail: swseo@socwomen.org
Web: www.socwomen.org/awards.html

**Summary** To bring major feminist scholars to campuses that do not have the funds to do so on their own.

**Eligibility** Feminists scholars (with advanced degrees or the equivalent experience) are eligible to be nominated. They must be interested in delivering a lecture at 2 college campuses that are rural, isolated, or not located in or near major metropolitan centers.

**Financial data** The society pays the recipient $1,000 as an honorarium and provides travel funds (up to $750) to visit each site; the host college pays the remainder of the travel expenses and other direct costs.

**Duration** The award is presented annually.

**Additional information** This program began in 1985. The lecture may be published in the association's journal, *Gender and Society.*

**Number awarded** 1 lecturer is selected each year; 2 institutions are selected to host her.

**Deadline** Nominations for the lecturer and applications from institutions interested in serving as a host are due by March of each year.

## [1297]
## F.J. MCGUIGAN EARLY CAREER INVESTIGATOR RESEARCH PRIZE

American Psychological Foundation
750 First Street, N.E.
Washington, DC 20002-4242
(202) 336-5843                    Fax: (202) 336-5812
E-mail: foundation@apa.org
Web: www.apa.org/apf/funding/mcguigan-prize.aspx

**Summary** To provide funding to young psychologists (especially women, minorities, and individuals with disabilities) who are interested in conducting research related to the human mind.

**Eligibility** This program is open to investigators who have earned a doctoral degree in psychology or in a related field within the past 9 years. Nominees must have an affiliation with an accredited college, university, or other research institution. They must be engaged in research that seeks to explicate the concept of the human mind. The approach must be materialistic and should be primarily psychophysiological, but physiological and behavioral research may also qualify. Self-nominations are not accepted; candidates must be nominated by a senior colleague. The sponsor encourages nominations of individuals who represent diversity in race, ethnicity, gender, age, disability, and sexual orientation.

**Financial data** The grant is $25,000.

**Duration** These grants are awarded biennially, in even-numbered years.

**Additional information** The first grant under this program was awarded in 2002.

**Number awarded** 1 every other year.

**Deadline** February of even-numbered years.

## [1298]
## FLORENCE NIGHTINGALE DAVID AWARD

Committee of Presidents of Statistical Societies
c/o Nancy Reid, David Award Committee Chair
University of Toronto
Department of Statistics
Sidney Smith Hall, Room 6002A
100 St. George Street
Toronto, ON M5S 3G3
Canada
(416) 978-5046                    Fax: (416) 978-5133
E-mail: reid@utstate.utoronto.ca
Web: nisla05.niss.org/copss/?q=copss

**Summary** To recognize and reward female statisticians who have made notable contributions to the field.

**Eligibility** This program is open to women who have demonstrated excellence as a role model to women in statistical research, leadership of multidisciplinary collaborative groups, statistics education, or service to the statistics profession. Nominees may be of any age, race, sexual orientation, nationality, or citizenship, but they must be living at the time of their nomination.

**Financial data** The award consists of a plaque and a cash honorarium of $1,000.

**Duration** The award is presented biennially, in odd-numbered years.

**Additional information** The award was established in 2001.

**Number awarded** 1 every other year.

**Deadline** January of odd-numbered years.

## [1299]
## FOUNDATION FOR THE HISTORY OF WOMEN IN MEDICINE FELLOWSHIPS

Foundation for the History of Women in Medicine
P.O. Box 543
Pottstown, PA 19464
(610) 970-9143                    Fax: (610) 970-7520
Web: www.fhwim.org/programs/fellowships.php

**Summary** To provide funding to students and scholars interested in short-term use of resources in the Boston area to conduct research on the history of women and medicine.

**Eligibility** This program is open to doctoral candidates and other advanced scholars interested in using the Archives for Women in Medicine at the Countway Library's Center for the History of Medicine in Boston. Applicants must be interested in conducting research on the history of women in medicine. Preference is given to projects that deal specifically with women as physicians or other health workers, but proposals dealing with the history of women's health issues are also considered. Preference is given to applicants who live beyond commuting distance of the Countway.

**Financial data** The grant is $5,000.

**Duration** Recipients may conduct research on a flexible schedule during 1 academic year.

**Additional information** The Francis A. Countway Library of Medicine, the largest academic medical library in the United States, was established in 1960 as the result of an alliance between the Boston Medical Library and the Harvard Medical School Library.

**Number awarded** 1 or 2 each year.

**Deadline** February of each year.

## [1300]
## FRAMELINE COMPLETION FUND

Frameline
Attn: Completion Fund
145 Ninth Street, Suite 300
San Francisco, CA 94103
(415) 703-8650                    Fax: (415) 861-1404
E-mail: info@frameline.org
Web: www.frameline.org/filmmaker-support

**Summary** To provide funding to lesbian, gay, bisexual, and transgender (LGBT) film/video artists (priority is given to women and people of color).

**Eligibility** This program is open to LGBT artists who are in the last stages of the production of documentary, educational, narrative, animated, or experimental projects about or of interest to LGBT people and their communities. Applicants may be independent artists, students, producers, or nonprofit corporations. They must be interested in completion work and must have 90% of the production completed; projects in development, script-development, pre-production, or production are not eligible. Student projects are eligible only if the student maintains artistic and financial control of the project. Women and people of color are especially encouraged to apply. Selection is based on financial need, the contribution the grant will make to completing the project, assurances that the project will be completed, and the statement the project makes about LGBT people and/or issues of concern to them and their communities.

**Financial data** Grants range from $1,000 to $5,000.

**Duration** These are 1-time grants.

**Additional information** This program began in 1990.

**Number awarded** Varies each year; recently, 5 of these grants were awarded. Since this program was established, it has provided $389,200 in support to 118 films.

**Deadline** October of each year.

## [1301]
## FRANCES LEWIS FELLOWSHIPS

Virginia Historical Society
Attn: Chair, Research Fellowships and Awards Committee
428 North Boulevard
P.O. Box 7311
Richmond, VA 23221-0311
(804) 342-9686                    Fax: (804) 355-2399
E-mail: fpollard@vahistorical.org
Web: www.vahistorical.org/research/fellowships.htm

**Summary** To offer short-term financial assistance to pre- and postdoctoral scholars interested in conducting research in women's studies at the Virginia Historical Society.

**Eligibility** This program is open to doctoral candidates, faculty, or independent scholars interested in conducting research in women's studies. Applicants whose research promises to result in a significant publication, such as in the

society's documents series of edited texts or in the *Virginia Magazine of History and Biography,* receive primary consideration. Along with their application, they must submit a resume, 2 letters of recommendation, a description of the research project (up to 2 pages), and a cover letter. Because the program is designed to help defray research travel expenses, residents of the Richmond metropolitan area are not eligible. Also ineligible are undergraduates, master's students, and graduate students not yet admitted to Ph.D. candidacy. Selection is based on the applicants' scholarly qualifications, the merits of their research proposals, and the appropriateness of their topics to the holdings of the Virginia Historical Society.

**Financial data** A few small grants (up to $150 per week) are awarded for mileage to researchers who live at least 50 miles from Richmond. The majority of the awards are $500 per week and go to researchers who live further away and thus incur greater expenses.

**Duration** Up to 3 weeks a year. Recipients may reapply in following years up to these limits: a maximum of 3 weeks in a 5-year period for doctoral candidates; a maximum of 6 weeks in a 5-year period for faculty or independent scholars.

**Additional information** The society's library contains 7 million manuscripts and thousands of books, maps, broadsides, newspapers, and historical objects. This program was formerly known as the Sydney and Frances Lewis Fellowships. Recipients are expected to work on a regular basis in the society's reading room during the period of the award.

**Number awarded** Varies each year; recently, the society awarded a total of 28 research fellowships.

**Deadline** January of each year.

## [1302]
## FRANK NELSON DOUBLEDAY MEMORIAL AWARD

Wyoming Arts Council
2320 Capitol Avenue
Cheyenne, WY 82002
(307) 777-5234                    Fax: (307) 777-5499
TDD: (307) 777-5964              E-mail: mike.shaw@wyo.gov
Web: wyoarts.state.wy.us/wac-program/test-grant-5

**Summary** To recognize and reward outstanding female writers (in any genre) who live in Wyoming.

**Eligibility** This program is open to female writers who live in Wyoming for at least 10 months of the year, are older than 18 years of age, and are not full-time students or faculty members. Writers are eligible if they have never published a book; if they have published only 1 full-length book of fiction, poetry, or nonfiction; of if they have published no more than 1 book of poetry, 1 of fiction, and 1 of nonfiction. They are invited to submit manuscripts of poetry (up to 10 printed pages with no more than 1 poem per page), fiction or creative nonfiction (up to 25 pages), or drama and screenplays (up to 25 pages).

**Financial data** The award is $1,000.

**Duration** The award is presented annually.

**Number awarded** 1 each year.

**Deadline** October of each year.

## [1303]
## FUTURAMA FOUNDATION CAREER ADVANCEMENT SCHOLARSHIP

Maine Federation of Business and Professional Women's Clubs
Attn: BPW/Maine Futurama Foundation
c/o Marilyn V. Ladd, Office Manager
103 County Road
Oakland, ME 04963
Web: www.bpwmefoundation.org/files/index.php?id=10

**Summary** To provide financial assistance to Maine women over 30 years of age who are continuing a program of higher education.

**Eligibility** This program is open to women who are older than 30 years of age and residents of Maine. Applicants must be continuing in, or returning to, an accredited program of higher education or job-related training, either full or part time. They must have a definite plan to use the desired training in a practical and immediate way to improve chances for advancement, train for a new career field, or enter or reenter the job market. Along with their application, they must submit a statement describing their educational, personal, and career goals, including financial need, expectations of training, and future plans for using this educational program. Preference is given to members of Maine Federation of Business and Professional Women's Clubs.

**Financial data** The stipend is $1,200. Funds are paid directly to the school.

**Duration** 1 year.

**Number awarded** 1 or more each year.

**Deadline** April of each year.

## [1304]
## GAIUS CHARLES BOLIN DISSERTATION AND POST-MFA FELLOWSHIPS

Williams College
Attn: Dean of the Faculty
880 Main Street
Hopkins Hall, Third Floor
P.O. Box 141
Williamstown, MA 01267
(413) 597-4351                     Fax: (413) 597-3553
E-mail: gburda@williams.edu
Web: dean-faculty.williams.edu

**Summary** To provide financial assistance to women and members of other underrepresented groups who are interested in teaching courses at Williams College while working on their doctoral dissertation or building their post-M.F.A. professional portfolio.

**Eligibility** This program is open to members of underrepresented groups, including ethnic minorities, first-generation college students, women in predominantly male fields, and scholars with disabilities. Applicants must be 1) doctoral candidates in any field who have completed all work for a Ph.D. except for the dissertation; or 2) artists who completed an M.F.A. degree within the past 2 years and are building their professional portfolio. They must be willing to teach a course at Williams College. Along with their application, they must submit a full curriculum vitae, a graduate school transcript, 3 letters of recommendation, a copy of their dissertation prospectus or samples of their artistic work, and a description of their teaching interests within a department or program at

Williams College. U.S. citizenship or permanent resident status is required.

**Financial data** Fellows receive $36,000 for the academic year, plus housing assistance, office space, computer and library privileges, and a research allowance of up to $4,000.

**Duration** 2 years.

**Additional information** Bolin fellows are assigned a faculty adviser in the appropriate department. This program was established in 1985. Fellows are expected to teach a 1-semester course each year. They must be in residence at Williams College for the duration of the fellowship.

**Number awarded** 3 each year.

**Deadline** November of each year.

## [1305]
## GEORGIA HARKNESS SCHOLARSHIP AWARDS

United Methodist Higher Education Foundation
Attn: Scholarships Administrator
60 Music Square East, Suite 350
P.O. Box 340005
Nashville, TN 37203-0005
(615) 649-3990                     Toll Free: (800) 811-8110
Fax: (615) 649-3980
E-mail: umhefscholarships@umhef.org
Web: www.umhef.org

**Summary** To provide financial assistance to women over 35 years of age who are preparing for a second career in ordained ministry as an elder in the United Methodist Church.

**Eligibility** This program is open to women over 35 years of age who have a bachelor's degree. Applicants must be enrolled full time in a school of theology approved by the University Senate of the United Methodist Church and working on an M.Div. degree. They must be currently certified as candidates for ordained ministry as an elder in the United Methodist Church. The award is not available for undergraduate, D.Min., or Ph.D. work. Selection is based on financial need, academic scholarship, spiritual leadership, and commitment to social justice.

**Financial data** The stipend is $5,000.

**Duration** 1 year; recipients may reapply.

**Additional information** This program is supported by the Division of Ordained Ministry of the General Board of Higher Education and Ministry.

**Number awarded** Varies each year; recently, 11 of these scholarships were awarded.

**Deadline** February of each year.

## [1306]
## GERTRUDE AND MAURICE GOLDHABER DISTINGUISHED FELLOWSHIPS

Brookhaven National Laboratory
Attn: Bill Bookless
Building 460
40 Brookhaven Avenue
Upton, NY 11973
(631) 344-5734                     E-mail: wbookless@bnl.gov
Web: www.bnl.gov/hr/goldhaber.asp

**Summary** To provide funding to women, minority, and other postdoctoral scientists interested in conducting research at Brookhaven National Laboratory (BNL).

**Eligibility** This program is open to scholars who are no more than 3 years past receipt of the Ph.D. and are interested in working at BNL. Candidates must be interested in working in close collaboration with a member of the BNL scientific staff and qualifying for a scientific staff position at BNL upon completion of the appointment. The sponsoring scientist must have an opening and be able to support the candidate at the standard starting salary for postdoctoral research associates. The program especially encourages applications from minorities and women.

**Financial data** The program provides additional funds to bring the salary to $75,000 per year.

**Duration** 3 years.

**Additional information** This program is funded by Battelle Memorial Institute and the State University of New York at Stony Brook.

**Number awarded** Up to 2 each year.

**Deadline** June of each year.

## [1307]
## GILBERT F. WHITE POSTDOCTORAL FELLOWSHIP PROGRAM

Resources for the Future
Attn: Coordinator for Academic Programs
1616 P Street, N.W., Suite 600
Washington, DC 20036-1400
(202) 328-5020 Fax: (202) 939-3460
E-mail: white-award@rff.org
Web: www.rff.org

**Summary** To provide funding to women, minority, and other postdoctoral researchers who wish to devote a year to scholarly work at Resources for the Future (RFF) in Washington, D.C.

**Eligibility** This program is open to individuals in any discipline who have completed their doctoral requirements and are interested in conducting scholarly research at RFF in social or policy science areas that relate to natural resources, energy, or the environment. Teaching and/or research experience at the postdoctoral level is preferred but not essential. Individuals holding positions in government as well as at academic institutions are eligible. Women and minority candidates are strongly encouraged to apply. Non-citizens are eligible if they have proper work and residency documentation.

**Financial data** Fellows receive an annual stipend (based on their academic salary) plus research support, office facilities at RFF, and an allowance of up to $1,000 for moving or living expenses. Fellowships do not provide medical insurance or other RFF fringe benefits.

**Duration** 11 months.

**Additional information** Fellows are assigned to an RFF research division: the Energy and Natural Resources division, the Quality of the Environment division, or the Center for Risk, Resource, and Environmental Management. Fellows are expected to be in residence at Resources for the Future for the duration of the program.

**Number awarded** 1 each year.

**Deadline** February of each year.

## [1308]
## GIRLS WITH WINGS PRIVATE PILOT SCHOLARSHIPS

Girls With Wings
Attn: Executive Director
1275 Andrews Avenue
Lakewood, OH 44107-3922
(216) 228-0856 E-mail: scholarship@girlswithwings.com
Web: www.girlswithwings.com/scholarshipmain.html

**Summary** To provide financial assistance to young women who are interested in earning a private pilot certificate.

**Eligibility** This program is open to female U.S. citizens who are at least 16 years of age and working on a private pilot certificate. Applicants must have completed a solo flight and hold a current medical certificate. Along with their application, they must submit an essay that includes 1) their plan for pursuing a private pilot certificate; 2) reasons and vision for becoming a role model for the Girls With Wings organization; 3) their motivation and inspiration for involvement in aviation; 4) achievements and participation in other organizations and related events; 5) how the scholarship would improve their ability to obtain a private pilot certificate; and 6) their financial need.

**Financial data** The stipend is $1,000. Funds are paid directly to the flight school or Certified Flight Instructor (CFI). Support is not provided for flying club dues or membership, ground school fees, books, or other pilot supplies.

**Duration** Training must be completed within 1 year.

**Number awarded** Varies each year; recently, 3 of these scholarships were awarded.

**Deadline** June of each year.

## [1309]
## GITA CHUADHURI PRIZE

Western Association of Women Historians
c/o Amy Essington, Executive Director
3242 Petaluma Avenue
Long Beach, CA 90808-4249
E-mail: amyessington@wawh.org
Web: www.wawh.org/awards/currentinfo.html

**Summary** To recognize and reward outstanding books on rural women published by members of the Western Association of Women Historians (WAWH).

**Eligibility** Members of the WAWH are eligible to submit their books for consideration if they were published any time during the preceding 3 years. The entry must be a single-authored monograph based on original research that relates to rural women, from any era and any place in the world. Anthologies and edited works are not eligible for consideration.

**Financial data** The award is $1,000.

**Duration** The award is presented annually.

**Additional information** This award was first presented in 2009.

**Number awarded** 1 each year.

**Deadline** January of each year.

## [1310]
## GLORIA E. ANZALDUA BOOK PRIZE

National Women's Studies Association
Attn: Book Prizes
11 East Mount Royal Avenue, Suite 100
Baltimore, MD 21202
(410) 528-0355                     Fax: (410) 528-0357
E-mail: awards@nwsa.org
Web: www.nwsa.org/content.asp?pl=16&contentid=16

**Summary** To recognize and reward members of the National Women's Studies Association (NWSA) who have written outstanding books on women of color and transnational issues.

**Eligibility** This award is available to NWSA members who submit a book that was published during the preceding year. Entries must present groundbreaking scholarship in women's studies and make a significant multicultural feminist contribution to women of color and/or transnational studies.

**Financial data** The award provides an honorarium of $1,000 and lifetime membership in NWSA.

**Duration** The award is presented annually.

**Additional information** This award was first presented in 2008.

**Number awarded** 1 each year.

**Deadline** April of each year.

## [1311]
## HADASSAH-BRANDEIS INSTITUTE RESEARCH AWARDS

Brandeis University
Hadassah-Brandeis Institute
Attn: Program Manager
515 South Street
Mailstop 079
Waltham, MA 02454-9110
(781) 736-8113                     Fax: (781) 736-2078
E-mail: dolins@brandeis.edu
Web: www.brandeis.edu/hbi/grants/research.html

**Summary** To provide funding to scholars, graduate students, writers, activists, and artists conducting research in the field of Jewish women's studies.

**Eligibility** This program offers senior grants (for established scholars and professionals) and junior grants (for graduate students and scholars within 3 years of receiving a Ph.D.). All applicants must be interested in conducting interdisciplinary research on Jewish women and gender issues. Graduate students in recognized master's and Ph.D. programs are encouraged to apply. Applications from outside the United States are welcome. Grants are awarded in 10 categories: history; the Yishuv and Israel; Diaspora studies; families, children, and the Holocaust; gender, culture, religion, and the law; women's health; Judaism; biography; the arts (performance arts, visual arts, creative writing); and film and video. Applications must specify the category and may be for only 1 category. Selection is based on excellence.

**Financial data** Senior grants are $5,000 and junior grants are $2,000.

**Duration** 1 year.

**Additional information** The Hadassah-Brandeis Institute was formerly the Hadassah International Research Institute on Jewish Women at Brandeis University.

**Number awarded** Between 20 and 30 each year.

**Deadline** September of each year.

## [1312]
## HARVARD DIVINITY SCHOOL/WOMEN'S STUDIES IN RELIGION PROGRAM

Harvard Divinity School
Attn: Director of Women's Studies in Religion Program
45 Francis Avenue
Cambridge, MA 02138
(617) 495-5705                     Fax: (617) 496-8564
E-mail: wsrp@hds.harvard.edu
Web: www.hds.harvard.edu/wsrp

**Summary** To encourage and support research at Harvard Divinity School's Women's Studies in Religion Program (WSRP) on the relationship between gender, religion, and culture.

**Eligibility** This program is open to scholars who have a Ph.D. in the field of religion. Candidates with primary competence in other humanities, social sciences, and public policy fields who have a serious interest in religion and religious professionals with equivalent achievements are also eligible. Applicants should be proposing to conduct research projects at Harvard Divinity School's Women's Studies in Religion Program on topics related to the history and function of gender in religious traditions, the institutionalization of gender roles in religious communities, or the interaction between religion and the personal, social, and cultural situations of women. Appropriate topics include feminist theology, biblical studies, ethics, women's history, and interdisciplinary scholarship on women in world religions. Selection is based on the quality of the applicant's research prospectus, outlining objectives and methods; its fit with the program's research priorities; the significance of the contribution of the proposed research to the study of religion, gender, and culture, and to its field; and agreement to produce a publishable piece of work by the end of the appointment.

**Financial data** The stipend is $55,000; health insurance and reimbursement of some expenses are also provided.

**Duration** 1 academic year, from September to June.

**Additional information** This program was founded in 1973. Fellows at the WSRP devote the majority of their appointments to individual research projects in preparation for publication, meeting together regularly for discussion of research in process. They also design and teach new courses related to their research projects and offer a series of lectures in the spring. Recipients are required to be in full-time residence at the school while carrying out their research project.

**Number awarded** 5 each year. The group each year usually includes at least 1 international scholar, 1 scholar working on a non-western tradition, 1 scholar of Judaism, and 1 minority scholar.

**Deadline** October of each year.

## [1313]
## HARVARD–NEWCOMEN POSTDOCTORAL FELLOWSHIP IN BUSINESS HISTORY

Harvard Business School
Attn: Fellowships
Rock Center 104
Boston, MA 02163
(617) 495-1003                    Fax: (617) 495-0594
E-mail: wfriedman@hbs.edu
Web: www.hbs.edu/businesshistory/fellowships.html

**Summary** To provide residencies for study and research at Harvard Business School to women, minorities, and other scholars in history, economics, or a related field.

**Eligibility** This program is open to scholars who, within the last 10 years, have received a Ph.D. degree in history, economics, or a related field. Applicants must be proposing to engage in research that would benefit from the resources at the Harvard Business School and the larger Boston scholarly community. In addition, they must be interested in participating in the school's business history courses, seminars, and case development activities. Along with their application, they must submit concise statements and descriptions of academic research undertaken in the past and a detailed description of the research they wish to undertake at Harvard. Women and minorities are especially encouraged to apply.

**Financial data** The stipend is $46,000. In addition, a travel fund, a book fund, and administrative support are provided.

**Duration** 12 months, beginning in July.

**Additional information** This program began in 1949. Fellows spend approximately two-thirds of their time conducting research of their own choosing. The remainder of their time is devoted to participating in activities of the school, including attendance at the business history seminar and working with faculty teaching the business history courses offered in the M.B.A. program. Fellows are strongly encouraged to submit an article to *Business History Review* during their year at the school. Support for this fellowship is provided by the Newcomen Society of the United States.

**Deadline** October of each year.

## [1314]
## HATTIE HEMSCHEMEYER AWARD

American College of Nurse-Midwives
Attn: Associate Director
8403 Colesville Road, Suite 1550
Silver Spring, MD 20910-6374
(240) 485-1800                    Fax: (240) 485-1818
Web: www.midwife.org/index.asp?bid=363

**Summary** To recognize and reward long-time members of the American College of Nurse-Midwives (ACNM) who have made outstanding contributions to midwifery.

**Eligibility** Nominees for this award must be ACNM members who have been certified nurse midwives (CNMs) or certified midwives (CMs) for at least 10 years. They must have demonstrated 1) continuous outstanding contributions or distinguished service to midwifery and/or MCH; or 2) contributions of historical significance to the development and advancement of midwifery, ACNM, or MCH.

**Financial data** A monetary award is presented.

**Duration** The award is presented annually.

**Additional information** This award was first presented in 1977.

**Number awarded** 1 each year.

**Deadline** January of each year.

## [1315]
## HEATHER WESTPHAL MEMORIAL SCHOLARSHIP AWARD

International Association of Fire Chiefs
Attn: IAFC Foundation
4025 Fair Ridge Drive, Suite 300
Fairfax, VA 22033-2868
(703) 896-4822                    Fax: (703) 273-9363
E-mail: Sbaroncelli@iafc.org
Web: www.iafcf.org/Scholarship.htm

**Summary** To provide financial assistance to female firefighters, especially members of the International Association of Fire Chiefs, who wish to further their academic education.

**Eligibility** This program is open to women who are active members of state, county, provincial, municipal, community, industrial, or federal fire departments in the United States or Canada and have demonstrated proficiency as members for at least 2 years of paid or 3 years of volunteer service. Dependents of members are not eligible. Applicants must be planning to attend a recognized institution of higher education. Along with their application, they must submit a 250-word essay that includes a brief description of the course work, how the course work will benefit their fire service career and department and improve the fire service, and their financial need. Preference is given to members of the International Association of Fire Chiefs (IAFC).

**Financial data** A stipend is awarded (amount not specified).

**Duration** Up to 1 year.

**Additional information** This program began in 2009 with support from the International Association of Women in Fire and Emergency Service.

**Number awarded** 1 each year.

**Deadline** May of each year.

## [1316]
## HECKSEL-SUTHERLAND SCHOLARSHIP

Ninety-Nines, Inc.-Michigan Chapter
c/o Rosemary Sieracki, Administrator
41490 Hanford Road
Canton, MI 48187-3512
(734) 981-4787                    E-mail: sierackr@att.net
Web: michigan99s.info/node/4

**Summary** To provide financial assistance to women in Michigan who are interested in attending a school in any state to prepare for a career in aviation.

**Eligibility** This program is open to women who live in Michigan and are interested in preparing for a career in aviation or aeronautics. Applicants must be enrolled or planning to enroll in private pilot training, additional pilot certificate or rating, college education in aviation, technical training in aviation, or other aviation-related training. Along with their application, they must submit 1) a 1-page essay on how the money will be used; 2) documentation from the training or academic institution verifying the cost of the training; 3) copies of all aviation and medical certificates and the last 3 pages of the pilot logbook (if applicable); and 4) an essay that covers their aviation history, short- and long-term goals, how the scholarship will help them achieve those goals, any educational awards and honors they have received, their significant or unique achievements, where training would be received and the costs involved, their involvement in aviation activities, and their community involvement. Selection is based on motivation, willingness to accept responsibility, reliability, and commitment to success.

**Financial data** The stipend is $1,500.

**Duration** 1 year.

**Additional information** This program began in 2012.

**Number awarded** 1 each year.

**Deadline** October of each year.

## [1317]
## HELEN GARTNER HAMMER SCHOLAR-IN-RESIDENCE PROGRAM

Brandeis University
Hadassah-Brandeis Institute
Attn: Program Manager
515 South Street
Mailstop 079
Waltham, MA 02454-9110
(781) 736-8113                         Fax: (781) 736-2078
E-mail: dolins@brandeis.edu
Web: www.brandeis.edu/hbi/residencies/scholar.html

**Summary** To provide an opportunity for scholars, artists, writers, and communal professionals to conduct research in the field of Jewish women's studies while in residence at the Hadassah-Brandeis Institute of Brandeis University.

**Eligibility** This program is open to scholars, artists, writers, and communal professionals who are working in the area of Jewish women's and gender studies. Applicants must be interested in taking time from their regular institutional duties to work at the institute. Scholars outside the United States and those with an international research focus are especially encouraged to apply.

**Financial data** Scholars receive a stipend of $3,000 per month and office space at the Brandeis University Women's Studies Research Center.

**Duration** 1 month to 1 semester.

**Additional information** The Hadassah-Brandeis Institute was formerly the Hadassah International Research Institute on Jewish Women at Brandeis University.

**Number awarded** Varies each year; recently, 12 of these residencies were awarded.

**Deadline** January of each year.

## [1318]
## HENRY DAVID RESEARCH GRANT IN HUMAN REPRODUCTIVE BEHAVIOR AND POPULATION STUDIES

American Psychological Foundation
750 First Street, N.E.
Washington, DC 20002-4242
(202) 336-5843                         Fax: (202) 336-5812
E-mail: foundation@apa.org
Web: www.apa.org/apf/funding/david.aspx

**Summary** To provide funding to young psychologists (particularly women, minorities, and individuals with disabilities) who are interested in conducting research on reproductive behavior.

**Eligibility** This program is open to doctoral students in psychology working on a dissertation and young psychologists who have no more than 7 years of postgraduate experience. Applicants must be interested in conducting research on human reproductive behavior or an area related to population concerns. Along with their application, they must submit a current curriculum vitae, 2 letters of recommendation, and an essay of 1 to 2 pages on their interest in human reproductive behavior or in population studies. The sponsor encourages applications from individuals who represent diversity in race, ethnicity, gender, age, disability, and sexual orientation.

**Financial data** The grant is $1,500.

**Duration** The grant is presented annually.

**Number awarded** 1 each year.

**Deadline** February of each year.

## [1319]
## HERBERT AND BETTY CARNES FUND

American Ornithologists' Union
c/o Executive Officer
5405 Villa View Drive
Farmington, NM 87402
(505) 326-1579                         E-mail: aou@aou.org
Web: www.aou.org/awards/research

**Summary** To provide funding to female graduate students and scholars who are members of the American Ornithologists' Union (AOU) and interested in conducting research on avian biology.

**Eligibility** This program is open to female AOU members who are graduate students, postdoctorates, or other researchers without access to major funding agencies. Applicants must be interested in conducting research on avian biology. They must be nonsmokers (have not smoked in at least the previous 6 months). Along with their application, they should send a cover letter (about 5 pages) describing their proposed project, a budget, and 1 letter of reference. Selection is based on significance and originality of the research question, clarity of the objectives, feasibility of the plan of research, and appropriateness of the budget.

**Financial data** The maximum award is $2,500 per year.

**Duration** 1 year; recipients may reapply for 1 additional award.

**Number awarded** The sponsor awards a total of 28 to 30 grants each year.

**Deadline** January of each year.

## [1320]
## HERBERT W. AND CORRINE CHILSTROM SCHOLARSHIP

Women of the Evangelical Lutheran Church in America
Attn: Scholarships
8765 West Higgins Road
Chicago, IL 60631-4101
(773) 380-2741        Toll Free: (800) 638-3522, ext. 2741
Fax: (773) 380-2419        E-mail: women.elca@elca.org
Web: www.womenoftheelca.org

**Summary** To provide financial assistance to mature women who are studying for a second career in the ordained ministry in the Evangelical Lutheran Church of America (ELCA).

**Eligibility** Applicants for this scholarship must be women who have experienced an interruption of at least 5 years in their education since college graduation and are currently entering the final year of an M.Div. program at an ELCA seminary. They must have been endorsed by the Synodical Candidacy Committee. Selection is based on academic achievement, personal commitment and determination to serve as a pastor in the ELCA, and financial need. U.S. citizenship is required.

**Financial data** The maximum stipend is $1,000.

**Duration** 1 year.

**Additional information** This scholarship was established in 1996 to honor Rev. Herbert W. Chilstrom and Rev. Corrine Chilstrom during the 25th anniversary year of the ordination of women in the predecessor bodies of the ELCA. Recipients must agree to serve for at least 3 years as an ELCA pastor after graduation from seminary.

**Number awarded** 1 each year.

**Deadline** February of each year.

## [1321]
## HIGH PRIORITY, SHORT-TERM BRIDGE AWARDS IN DIABETES RESEARCH

Juvenile Diabetes Research Foundation International
Attn: Grant Administrator
26 Broadway, 14th Floor
New York, NY 10004
(212) 479-7572          Toll Free: (800) 533-CURE
Fax: (212) 785-9595          E-mail: info@jdrf.org
Web: jdrf.org

**Summary** To provide funding to scientists (particularly women, minorities, and persons with disabilities) who are interested in conducting diabetes-related research but have not yet received any support.

**Eligibility** Applicants must have an M.D., D.M.D., D.V.M., Ph.D., or equivalent degree and have a full-time faculty position or equivalent at a college, university, medical school, or other research facility. They must have applied for grants previously and scored within 10% of the funding payline of a research funding agency but failed to receive support. Awards must be used to obtain new data to support the feasibility or validity of the research, address reviewers' concerns, or revise approaches to the research. There are no citizenship requirements. Applications are encouraged from women, members of minority groups underrepresented in the sciences, and people with disabilities. The proposed research may be conducted at foreign or domestic, for-profit or non-profit, or public or private institutions, including universities, colleges, hospitals, laboratories, units of state or local government, or eligible agencies of the federal government.

**Financial data** Awards are limited to $55,000 plus 10% indirect costs.

**Duration** 1 year; generally nonrenewable.

**Number awarded** Varies each year.

**Deadline** February, May, or October of each year.

## [1322]
## HILL–ROM, CELESTE PHILLIPS FAMILY-CENTERED MATERNITY CARE AWARD

Association of Women's Health, Obstetric and Neonatal Nurses
Attn: Research Grants Program
2000 L Street, N.W., Suite 740
Washington, DC 20036
(202) 261-2431          Toll Free: (800) 673-8499, ext. 2431
Fax: (202) 728-0575
E-mail: ResearchPrograms@awhonn.org
Web: www.awhonn.org

**Summary** To provide funding for small research projects to members of the Association of Women's Health, Obstetric and Neonatal Nurses (AWHONN).

**Eligibility** This program is open to members of the association who are interested in conducting research related to women's health, obstetric, or neonatal nursing. Researchers who are currently principal investigators on a federally-funded grant, or who have already received an AWHONN-funded research grant within the past 5 years, are not eligible.

**Financial data** The grant is $10,000. Funds may not be used for indirect costs, tuition, computer hardware or printers, conference attendance, or salary for the principal investigator or other investigators.

**Duration** 1 year.

**Additional information** This program is funded by Hill-Rom.

**Number awarded** 1 each year.

**Deadline** November of each year.

## [1323]
## HORIZONS FOUNDATION SCHOLARSHIP PROGRAM

Women in Defense
c/o National Defense Industrial Association
2111 Wilson Boulevard, Suite 400
Arlington, VA 22201-3061
(703) 247-2552          Fax: (703) 522-1885
E-mail: wid@ndia.org
Web: wid.ndia.org/horizons/Pages/default.aspx

**Summary** To provide financial assistance to women who are upper-division or graduate students engaged in or planning careers related to the national security interests of the United States.

**Eligibility** This program is open to women who are already working in national security fields as well as women planning such careers. Applicants must 1) be currently enrolled at an accredited college or university, either full time or part time, as graduate students or upper-division undergraduates; 2) demonstrate financial need; 3) be U.S. citizens; 4) have a GPA of 3.25 or higher; and 5) demonstrate interest in preparing for a career related to national security. The preferred fields of study include business (as it relates to national security or defense), computer science, cyber security, economics, engineering, government relations, international relations, law (as it relates to national security or defense), mathematics, military history, political science, physics, and security studies; others are considered if the applicant can demonstrate relevance to a career in national security or defense. Selection is based on academic achievement, participation in defense and national security activities, field of study, work experience, statements of objectives, recommendations, and financial need.

**Financial data**  The stipend ranges up to $10,000.

**Duration**  1 year; renewable.

**Additional information**  This program began in 1988.

**Number awarded**  Varies each year; recently, 6 of these scholarships were awarded: 1 at $10,000, 1 at $7,000, 1 at $5,000, 1 at $3,000, and 2 at $2,500. Since the program was established, 116 women have received more than $180,000 in support.

**Deadline**  June of each year.

## [1324]
## HUBBLE FELLOWSHIPS

Space Telescope Science Institute
Attn: Hubble Fellowship Program Office
3700 San Martin Drive
Baltimore, MD 21218
(410) 338-5079                          Fax: (410) 338-4211
E-mail: hfinquiry@stsci.edu
Web: www.stsci.edu/institute/smo/fellowships/hubble

**Summary**  To provide funding to recent postdoctoral scientists (particularly women and minorities) who are interested in conducting research related to the Hubble Space Telescope or related missions of the National Aeronautics and Space Administration (NASA).

**Eligibility**  This program is open to postdoctoral scientists who completed their doctoral degree within the past 3 years in astronomy, physics, or related disciplines. Applicants must be interested in conducting research related to NASA Cosmic Origins missions: the Hubble Space Telescope, Herschel Space Observatory, James Webb Space Telescope, Stratospheric Observatory for Infrared Astronomy, or the Spitzer Space Telescope. They may U.S. citizens or English-speaking citizens of other countries with valid visas. Research may be theoretical, observational, or instrumental. Women and members of minority groups are strongly encouraged to apply.

**Financial data**  Stipends are approximately $66,500 per year. Other benefits may include health insurance, relocation costs, and support for travel, equipment, and other direct costs of research.

**Duration**  3 years: an initial 1-year appointment and 2 annual renewals, contingent on satisfactory performance and availability of funds.

**Additional information**  This program, funded by NASA, began in 1990 and was limited to work with the Hubble Space Telescope. A parallel program, called the Spitzer Fellowship, began in 2002 and was limited to work with the Spitzer Space Telescope. In 2009, those programs were combined into this single program, which was also broadened to include the other NASA Cosmic Origins missions. Fellows are required to be in residence at their host institution engaged in full-time research for the duration of the grant.

**Number awarded**  Varies each year; recently, 17 of these fellowships were awarded.

**Deadline**  October of each year.

## [1325]
## IOTA SIGMA PI NATIONAL HONORARY MEMBER

Iota Sigma Pi
c/o Nancy Hopkins, National Director for Professional
  Awards
Tulane University School of Science and Engineering
Cell and Molecular Biology
2000 Percival Stern Hall
New Orleans, LA 70118
(504) 865-5546                    E-mail: nhopkins@tulane.edu
Web: www.iotasigmapi.info

**Summary**  To recognize exceptional and significant achievement by women working in chemistry or allied fields.

**Eligibility**  Nominees for the award must be outstanding women chemists. They may be from any country and need not be members of Iota Sigma Pi. Each active chapter is entitled to make only 1 nomination, but individual members, individual chemists, or groups of chemists may make independent nominations if properly documented. The nomination dossier must contain the candidate's name and address, educational and professional background, membership in professional societies, area of specialization or research, honors, awards, citations, publications, and letters of recommendation.

**Financial data**  The award consists of $1,500, a certificate, and a lifetime waiver of Iota Sigma Pi dues.

**Duration**  The award is granted triennially (2017, 2020, etc.).

**Additional information**  This award was first presented in 1921.

**Number awarded**  1 every 3 years.

**Deadline**  Nominations must be submitted by February of the year of award.

## [1326]
## IRVING AND YVONNE TWINING HUMBER AWARD FOR LIFETIME ARTISTIC ACHIEVEMENT

Artist Trust
Attn: Director of Grant Programs
1835 12th Avenue
Seattle, WA 98122-2437
(206) 467-8734                      Toll Free: (866) 21-TRUST
Fax: (206) 467-9633                 E-mail: info@artisttrust.org
Web: www.artisttrust.org/index.php/for-artists/money

**Summary**  To recognize and reward the artistic achievements of older women artists in Washington.

**Eligibility**  Eligible to be nominated for this award are women visual artists over 60 years of age from Washington state. Nominees must have devoted at least 25 years of their lives to creating art. Selection is based on creative excellence, professional accomplishment, and dedication to the visual arts.

**Financial data**  The award is $10,000.

**Duration**  The award is presented annually.

**Number awarded**  At least 1 each year.

**Deadline**  December of each year.

## [1327]
## J. CORDELL BREED AWARD FOR WOMEN LEADERS

Society of Automotive Engineers
Attn: Award Program Staff
400 Commonwealth Drive
Warrendale, PA 15096-0001
(724) 776-4970     Toll Free: (877) 606-7323
Fax: (724) 776-0790     E-mail: awards@sae.org
Web: www.sae.org/news/awards/list/wec

**Summary** To recognize and reward female members of the Society of Automotive Engineering (SAE) who have been active in the mobility industry.

**Eligibility** This award is presented to women who participate in and are involved in SAE activities. Nominees must 1) exhibit outstanding service to their company and community; 2) demonstrate excellent leadership as a supervisor, manager, or member in a team environment; 3) display innovation and uniqueness in achieving corporate and personal goals; 4) provide important engineering or technical contributions to the mobility industry; 5) demonstrate strong interpersonal skills; and 6) have overcome adversity.

**Financial data** The award consists of an engraved plaque and an honorarium of $2,000.

**Duration** The award is presented annually.

**Additional information** This award was established in 1999 by the SAE Women Engineers Committee (WEC).

**Number awarded** 1 each year.

**Deadline** Nominations must be submitted by July of each year.

## [1328]
## JAN JONES MEMORIAL SCHOLARSHIP

International Council of Air Shows
Attn: ICAS Foundation
750 Miller Drive, S.E., Suite F-3
Leesburg, VA 20175
(703) 779-8510     Fax: (703) 779-8511
E-mail: scholarships@icasfoundation.org
Web: www.icasfoundation.org/scholarship-jones

**Summary** To provide financial assistance to women interested in aerobatic flight training.

**Eligibility** This program is open to women who have a private pilot certificate. Applicants must be interested in beginning or continuing aerobatic flight training. Along with their application, they must submit a 1-page essay on why they want to receive this scholarship, how the funds will be used, their goals, and why they wish to learn aerobatics.

**Financial data** The stipend is $2,000.

**Duration** 1 year.

**Number awarded** 1 or more each year.

**Deadline** December of each year.

## [1329]
## JOAN F. GIAMBALVO MEMORIAL SCHOLARSHIP

American Medical Association
Attn: AMA Foundation
515 North State Street
Chicago, IL 60610
(312) 464-4743     Fax: (312) 464-4142
E-mail: wpc@ama-assn.org
Web: www.ama-assn.org

**Summary** To provide funding to physicians and medical students who are interested in conducting a research project related to women in the medical profession.

**Eligibility** This program is open to investigators or teams of investigators of whom at least 1 member is a medical student or physician. Applicants must be interested in conducting a research project that will advance the progress of women in the medical profession and strengthen the ability of the American Medical Association (AMA) to identify and address the needs of women physicians and medical students.

**Financial data** The grant is $10,000.

**Duration** 1 year.

**Additional information** This program is offered by the AMA Foundation in collaboration with the AMA Women Physicians Congress (WPC) and with support from Pfizer.

**Number awarded** 2 each year.

**Deadline** February of each year.

## [1330]
## JOAN KELLY MEMORIAL PRIZE IN WOMEN'S HISTORY

American Historical Association
Attn: Book Prize Administrator
400 A Street, S.E.
Washington, DC 20003-3889
(202) 544-2422     Fax: (202) 544-8307
E-mail: info@historians.org
Web: www.historians.org

**Summary** To recognize and reward outstanding works in women's history and/or feminist theory that were published during the previous year.

**Eligibility** The prize is open to works in any chronological period, any geographical location, or any area of feminist theory that incorporate an historical perspective. Preference is given to books that demonstrate originality of research, creativity of insight, graceful stylistic presentation, analytical skills, and recognition of the important role of sex and gender in the historical process.

**Financial data** The prize is $1,000.

**Duration** The award is granted annually.

**Additional information** This prize was established in 1984 by the Coordinating Committee on Women in the Historical Profession and the Conference Group on Women's History (now the Coordinating Council for Women in History) and is administered by the American Historical Association.

**Number awarded** 1 each year.

**Deadline** May of each year.

## [1331]
## JOEL ELKES RESEARCH AWARD

American College of Neuropsychopharmacology
Attn: Executive Office
5034-A Thoroughbred Lane
Brentwood, TN 37027
(615) 324-2360                    Fax: (615) 523-1715
E-mail: acnp@acnp.org
Web: www.acnp.org/programs/awards.aspx

**Summary**  To recognize and reward women, minority, and other young scientists who have contributed outstanding clinical or translational research to neuropsychopharmacology.

**Eligibility**  This award is available to scientists who are younger than 50 years of age. Nominees must have made an outstanding clinical or translational contribution to neuropsychopharmacology. The contribution may be based on a single discovery or a cumulative body of work. Emphasis is placed on contributions that further understanding of self-regulatory processes as they affect mental function and behavior in disease and well-being. Membership in the American College of Neuropsychopharmacology (ACNP) is not required. Nomination of women and minorities is highly encouraged.

**Financial data**  The award consists of an expense-paid trip to the ACNP annual meeting, a monetary honorarium, and a plaque.

**Duration**  The award is presented annually.

**Additional information**  This award was first presented in 1986.

**Number awarded**  1 each year.

**Deadline**  Nominations must be submitted by June of each year.

## [1332]
## JOHN AND POLLY SPARKS EARLY CAREER GRANT

American Psychological Foundation
750 First Street, N.E.
Washington, DC 20002-4242
(202) 336-5843                    Fax: (202) 336-5812
E-mail: foundation@apa.org
Web: www.apa.org/apf/funding/sparks-early-career.aspx

**Summary**  To provide funding to young psychologists (particularly women, minorities, and persons with disabilities) who are interested in conducting research on serious emotional disturbance in children.

**Eligibility**  This program is open to young psychologists who completed a doctoral degree (Ed.D., Psy.D., Ph.D.) within the past 7 years. Applicants must be interested in conducting research in the area of early intervention and treatment for serious emotional disturbance in children. The sponsor encourages applications from individuals who represent diversity in race, ethnicity, gender, age, disability, and sexual orientation.

**Financial data**  The grant is $10,000.

**Duration**  1 year.

**Additional information**  This program began in 2013.

**Number awarded**  1 each year.

**Deadline**  May of each year.

## [1333]
## JOHN V. KRUTILLA RESEARCH STIPEND

Resources for the Future
Attn: Coordinator for Academic Programs
1616 P Street, N.W., Suite 600
Washington, DC 20036-1400
(202) 328-5020                    Fax: (202) 939-3460
E-mail: krutilla-award@rff.org
Web: www.rff.org

**Summary**  To provide funding for research related to environmental and resource economics to young scholars (particularly women and minorities).

**Eligibility**  This program is open to scholars who received their doctoral degree within the past 5 years. Applicants must be interested in conducting research related to environmental and resource economics. They must submit a short description of the proposed research, a curriculum vitae, and a letter of recommendation. Women and minority candidates are strongly encouraged to apply. Non-citizens are eligible if they have proper work and residency documentation.

**Financial data**  The grant is $5,500.

**Duration**  1 year.

**Additional information**  This award was first presented in 2006.

**Number awarded**  1 each year.

**Deadline**  February of each year.

## [1334]
## JONATHAN REICHERT AND BARBARA WOLFF-REICHERT AWARD FOR EXCELLENCE IN ADVANCED LABORATORY INSTRUCTION

American Physical Society
Attn: Honors Program
One Physics Ellipse
College Park, MD 20740-3844
(301) 209-3268                    Fax: (301) 209-0865
E-mail: honors@aps.org
Web: www.aps.org/programs/honors/awards/lab.cfm

**Summary**  To recognize and reward physicists (particularly women and underrepresented minorities) who have made outstanding achievements in teaching undergraduate laboratory courses.

**Eligibility**  This award is available to individuals or teams of individuals who have taught, developed, and sustained advanced undergraduate physics laboratory courses for at least 4 years at an institution in the United States. Nominations should present evidence of the dissemination of the laboratory work to the broader physics community. Nominations of qualified women and members of underrepresented minority groups are especially encouraged.

**Financial data**  The award consists of $5,000 as an honorarium, a certificate citing the accomplishments of the recipient, and an allowance up to $2,000 for travel expenses to the meeting where the award is presented.

**Duration**  The award is presented annually.

**Additional information**  This award was established in 2012.

**Number awarded**  1 each year.

**Deadline**  June of each year.

## [1335]
## JOSEPH B. GITTLER AWARD

American Psychological Foundation
750 First Street, N.E.
Washington, DC 20002-4242
(202) 336-5843                     Fax: (202) 336-5812
E-mail: foundation@apa.org
Web: www.apa.org/apf/funding/gittler.aspx

**Summary**   To recognize and reward scholars and graduate students in psychology (particularly women and members of other diverse groups) who have made outstanding contributions to the philosophical foundations of the discipline.

**Eligibility**   This award is available to scholars and graduate students whose body of work or whose individual work has transformed the philosophical foundations of psychological knowledge. Self-nominations are welcome. Selection is based on conformance with stated program goals and magnitude of contributions The sponsor encourages nominations of individuals who represent diversity in race, ethnicity, gender, age, disability, and sexual orientation.

**Financial data**   The award is $10,000.

**Duration**   The award is presented annually.

**Additional information**   This award was first presented in 2008.

**Number awarded**   1 each year.

**Deadline**   Nominations must be submitted by May of each year.

## [1336]
## JOSEPH H. FICHTER RESEARCH GRANT COMPETITION

Association for the Sociology of Religion
Attn: Executive Officer
University of South Florida
Department of Sociology
4202 East Fowler Avenue, CPR 107
Tampa, FL 33620
(813) 974-2633                     Fax: (813) 974-6455
E-mail: jcavendi@usf.edu
Web: www.sociologyofreligion.com

**Summary**   To provide funding to scholars interested in conducting research on women and religion.

**Eligibility**   This program is open to scholars involved in research on women and religion or on the intersection between religion and gender or religion and sexualities. Scholars at the beginning of their careers are particularly encouraged to apply; dissertation research qualifies for funding. Applicants must be members of the association at the time the application is submitted. The proposal should outline the rationale and plan of the research, previous research, methodology proposed, timeline, and budget; a curriculum vitae should also be included. Simultaneous submissions to other grant competitions are permissible if the applicant is explicit about which budget items in the Fichter grant proposal do not overlap items in other submitted proposals.

**Financial data**   Each year, a total of $24,000 is available to be awarded.

**Duration**   1 year.

**Number awarded**   Varies each year; recently, 6 of these grants were awarded.

**Deadline**   April of each year.

## [1337]
## JUDY GRAHN AWARD FOR LESBIAN NONFICTION

Publishing Triangle
332 Bleecker Street, D36
New York, NY 10014
E-mail: publishingtriangle@gmail.com
Web: www.publishingtriangle.org/awards.asp

**Summary**   To recognize and reward outstanding lesbian nonfiction writers or writings.

**Eligibility**   This award is presented to authors of books that have had significant influence on lesbians. For the purposes of this award, "lesbian nonfiction" is defined as nonfiction affecting lesbian lives. The book may be written by a lesbian, or about lesbians or lesbian culture, or both. It must have been published in the United States or Canada.

**Financial data**   The award is $1,000.

**Duration**   The award is presented annually.

**Additional information**   The Publishing Triangle is an association of lesbians and gay men in publishing. This award was first presented in 1997. Current members of the Publishing Triangle may nominate authors for free; all others must pay a $35 nomination fee.

**Number awarded**   1 each year.

**Deadline**   November of each year.

## [1338]
## JULIUS AXELROD MENTORSHIP AWARD

American College of Neuropsychopharmacology
Attn: Executive Office
5034-A Thoroughbred Lane
Brentwood, TN 37027
(615) 324-2360                     Fax: (615) 523-1715
E-mail: acnp@acnp.org
Web: www.acnp.org/programs/awards.aspx

**Summary**   To recognize and reward women, minority, and other members of the American College of Neuropsychopharmacology (ACNP) who have demonstrated outstanding mentoring of young scientists.

**Eligibility**   This award is available to ACNP members who have made an outstanding contribution to neuropsychopharmacology by mentoring and developing young scientists into leaders in the field. Nominations must be accompanied by letters of support from up to 3 people who have been mentored by the candidate. Nomination of women and minorities is highly encouraged.

**Financial data**   The award consists of a monetary honorarium and a plaque.

**Duration**   The award is presented annually.

**Additional information**   This award was first presented in 2004.

**Number awarded**   1 each year.

**Deadline**   Nominations must be submitted by June of each year.

## [1339]
## JUVENILE DIABETES RESEARCH FOUNDATION INNOVATIVE GRANTS

Juvenile Diabetes Research Foundation International
Attn: Grant Administrator
26 Broadway, 14th Floor
New York, NY 10004
(212) 479-7572 Toll Free: (800) 533-CURE
Fax: (212) 785-9595 E-mail: info@jdrf.org
Web: jdrf.org

**Summary** To provide funding to scientists (particularly women, minorities, and persons with disabilities) who are interested in conducting innovative diabetes-related research.

**Eligibility** Applicants must have an M.D., D.M.D., D.V.M., Ph.D., or equivalent degree and have a full-time faculty position or equivalent at a college, university, medical school, or other research facility. They must be seeking "seed" money for investigative work based on a sound hypothesis for which preliminary data are insufficient for a regular research grant but that are likely to lead to important results for the treatment of diabetes and its complications. Applicants must specifically explain how the proposal is innovative. Selection is based on whether 1) the proposed research is innovative; 2) the underlying premise, goal, or hypothesis is plausible; 3) the proposed research can be completed in 1 year; and 4) the proposed research is relevant to the mission of the Juvenile Diabetes Research Foundation and its potential impact. There are no citizenship requirements. Applications are encouraged from women, members of minority groups underrepresented in the sciences, and people with disabilities. The proposed research may be conducted at foreign or domestic, for-profit or nonprofit, or public or private institutions, including universities, colleges, hospitals, laboratories, units of state or local government, or eligible agencies of the federal government.

**Financial data** Awards are limited to $110,000 plus 10% indirect costs.

**Duration** 1 year; nonrenewable.

**Number awarded** Varies each year.

**Deadline** August of each year.

## [1340]
## KATE GLEASON AWARD

ASME International
Attn: Committee on Honors
Three Park Avenue
New York, NY 10016-5990
(212) 591-7094 Toll Free: (800) THE-ASME
Fax: (212) 591-8080 E-mail: mckivorf@asme.org
Web: www.asme.org

**Summary** To recognize and reward distinguished female leaders in engineering.

**Eligibility** This award is available to women who are highly successful entrepreneurs in a field of engineering or who had a lifetime of achievement in the engineering profession.

**Financial data** The award consists of $10,000, travel support to attend the meeting where the award is presented, a bronze medal, and a certificate.

**Duration** The award is presented annually.

**Additional information** This award was established in 2011.

**Number awarded** 1 each year.

**Deadline** January of each year.

## [1341]
## KATHERINE E. WEIMER AWARD

American Physical Society
Attn: Division of Plasma Physics
One Physics Ellipse
College Park, MD 20740-3844
(301) 209-3200 Fax: (301) 209-0865
Web: www.aps.org

**Summary** To recognize and reward women who have made outstanding contributions to plasma science research.

**Eligibility** This award is available to female plasma scientists who received their Ph.D. within the previous 10 years. Nominees must have made outstanding achievements in plasma science research.

**Financial data** The award consists of $2,000, a certificate citing the contributions of the recipient, and an allowance for travel to the meeting of the American Physical Society (APS) at which the award is presented.

**Duration** The award is presented triennially (2014, 2017, etc.).

**Additional information** This prize was established in 2001.

**Number awarded** 1 every 3 years.

**Deadline** March of the year of the award.

## [1342]
## KENTUCKY UNIVERSITY RESEARCH POSTDOCTORAL FELLOWSHIP

University of Kentucky
Attn: Vice President for Research
201 Main Building
Lexington, KY 40506-0032
(859) 257-5090 Fax: (859) 323-2800
E-mail: vprgrants@uky.edu
Web: www.research.uky.edu

**Summary** To provide an opportunity for recent postdoctorates, especially women, to conduct research at the University of Kentucky (UK).

**Eligibility** This program is open to U.S. citizens and permanent residents who have completed a doctoral degree within the past 2 years. Applicants must be interested in conducting an individualized research program under the mentorship of 1 or more U.K. professors. Special consideration is given to women interested in conducting research in fields in which they can contribute to diversity at U.K., including, but not limited to, engineering, life sciences, and physical sciences. Selection is based on evidence of scholarship with competitive potential for a tenure-track faculty appointment at a research university, compatibility of specific research interests with those in doctorate-granting units at U.K., quality of the research proposal, support from mentor and references, and effect of the appointment on the educational benefit of diversity within the research or professional area.

**Financial data** The fellowship provides a stipend of $35,000 plus $5,000 for support of research activities.

**Duration** Up to 2 years.

**Additional information** Fellows actively participate in research and teaching as well as service to the university, their profession, and the community. This program began in 1992.

**Number awarded** 2 each year.

**Deadline** October of each year.

## [1343]
## KITTY ERNST AWARD

American College of Nurse-Midwives
Attn: Associate Director
8403 Colesville Road, Suite 1550
Silver Spring, MD 20910-6374
(240) 485-1800                    Fax: (240) 485-1818
Web: www.midwife.org/index.asp?bid=363

**Summary** To recognize and reward recent members of the American College of Nurse-Midwives (ACNM) who have made outstanding contributions to midwifery.

**Eligibility** Nominees for this award must be ACNM members who have been certified nurse midwives (CNMs) or certified midwives (CMs) for less than 10 years. They must have demonstrated innovative, creative endeavors in midwifery and/or women's health clinical practice, education, administration, or research.

**Financial data** A monetary award is presented.

**Duration** The award is presented annually.

**Additional information** This award was first presented in 1998.

**Number awarded** 1 each year.

**Deadline** January of each year.

## [1344]
## KPMG BEST PAPER AWARD GENDER SECTION

American Accounting Association
Attn: Gender Issues and Worklife Balance Section
5717 Bessie Drive
Sarasota, FL 34233-2399
(941) 921-7747                    Fax: (941) 923-4093
E-mail: info@aaahq.org
Web: aaahq.org/awards/GenderIssuesAwards.htm

**Summary** To recognize and reward outstanding papers on gender issues presented at the annual meeting of the American Accounting Association (AAA).

**Eligibility** This competition is open to authors of papers presented at the AAA annual meeting. At least 1 of the authors must be a member of the Gender Issues and Worklife Balance section.

**Financial data** The award is $1,000.

**Duration** The award is presented annually.

**Additional information** This award is supported by the KPMG Foundation.

**Number awarded** 1 each year.

**Deadline** February of each year.

## [1345]
## KPMG OUTSTANDING DISSERTATION AWARD GENDER SECTION

American Accounting Association
Attn: Gender Issues and Worklife Balance Section
5717 Bessie Drive
Sarasota, FL 34233-2399
(941) 921-7747                    Fax: (941) 923-4093
E-mail: info@aaahq.org
Web: aaahq.org/awards/GenderIssuesAwards.htm

**Summary** To recognize and reward outstanding dissertations on gender issues in accounting.

**Eligibility** This competition is open to authors of dissertations completed in the prior calendar year. Manuscripts need not be focused solely on gender issues and worklife balance, but they must include some consideration of those topics.

**Financial data** The award is $1,000.

**Duration** The award is presented annually.

**Additional information** This award is supported by the KPMG Foundation.

**Number awarded** 1 each year.

**Deadline** February of each year.

## [1346]
## KPMG OUTSTANDING PUBLISHED MANUSCRIPT AWARD GENDER SECTION

American Accounting Association
Attn: Gender Issues and Worklife Balance Section
5717 Bessie Drive
Sarasota, FL 34233-2399
(941) 921-7747                    Fax: (941) 923-4093
E-mail: info@aaahq.org
Web: aaahq.org/awards/GenderIssuesAwards.htm

**Summary** To recognize and reward outstanding research publications on gender issues in accounting.

**Eligibility** This competition is open to authors of articles published in the prior calendar year. Manuscripts need not be focused solely on gender issues and worklife balance, but they must include some consideration of those topics. At least 1 of the authors must be a member of the Gender Issues and Worklife Balance section of the American Accounting Association.

**Financial data** The award is $1,000.

**Duration** The award is presented annually.

**Additional information** This award is supported by the KPMG Foundation.

**Number awarded** 1 each year.

**Deadline** February of each year.

## [1347]
## LEGACY ARTISTS RESIDENCY GRANT

Women's Studio Workshop
722 Binnewater Lane
P.O. Box 489
Rosendale, NY 12472
(845) 658-9133                    Fax: (845) 658-9031
E-mail: info@wsworkshop.org
Web: www.wsworkshop.org/program/residency-grants

**Summary** To provide a residency and financial support at the Women's Studio Workshop (WSW) to women interested in printmaking or papermaking.

**Eligibility** This program is open to women who are interested in working in the printmaking or hand papermaking studios while in residence at the WSW. They must provide a 1-page summary of their proposed project, a resume, and a CD with 10 images of their recent work.

**Financial data** The program provides a stipend of $2,100, a $250 travel stipend, a materials budget of $500, unlimited studio use, and housing while in residence.

**Duration** 6 weeks.

**Number awarded** 1 each year.

**Deadline** March of each year.

## [1348]
## LEO GOLDBERG FELLOWSHIPS

National Optical Astronomy Observatories
Attn: Human Resources Office
950 North Cherry Avenue
P.O. Box 26732
Tucson, AZ 85726-6732
(520) 318-8000                Fax: (520) 318-8494
E-mail: hrnoao@noao.edu
Web: ast.noao.edu/opportunities/post-doc-programs

**Summary** To provide an opportunity for women, underrepresented minorities, and other postdoctorates in astronomy to conduct research at the facilities of the National Optical Astronomy Observatories (NOAO) in Arizona or Chile.

**Eligibility** This program is open to recent Ph.D. recipients in observational astronomy, astronomical instrumentation, or theoretical astrophysics. Applicants must be interested in conducting a research program of their own choosing or participating in a current NOAO initiative at Kitt Peak National Observatory (KPNO) near Tucson, Arizona or Cerro Tololo Inter-American Observatory (CTIO) in La Serena, Chile. Women and candidates from underrepresented minorities are particularly encouraged to apply. Preference is given to Native Americans living on or near the Tohono O'Odham Reservation in Arizona. Selection is based on the applicant's promise for an outstanding career in astronomy, their proposed use of KPNO or CTIO facilities, the relationship of their research to a proposed interaction with NOAO programs to develop community facilities, and the relationship of their research to programs conducted by NOAO staff.

**Financial data** A competitive salary is paid. Additional support is provided to fellows and their families in Chile.

**Duration** 5 years. The first 4 years are spent either at Kitt Peak or in La Serena; the final year is spent at an U.S. university or astronomical institute willing to host the fellow.

**Additional information** NOAO is supported under a contract between the National Science Foundation and the Association of Universities for Research in Astronomy, Inc. This program, which began in 2002, was formerly known as the NOAO 5-Year Science Fellowship.

**Number awarded** 1 each year.

**Deadline** November of each year.

## [1349]
## LEO SZILARD LECTURESHIP AWARD

American Physical Society
Attn: Honors Program
One Physics Ellipse
College Park, MD 20740-3844
(301) 209-3268                Fax: (301) 209-0865
E-mail: honors@aps.org
Web: www.aps.org/programs/honors/awards/szilard.cfm

**Summary** To recognize and reward women, minority, and other physicists for their work in areas of benefit to society.

**Eligibility** This program is open to living physicists who have promoted the use of physics for the benefit of society in such areas as the environment, arms control, and science policy. Nominations of qualified women, members of underrepresented minority groups, and scientists from outside the United States are especially encouraged.

**Financial data** The award consists of $1,000, a certificate citing the contributions of the recipient, and a $2,000 allowance to pay for travel expenses for lectures given by the recipient at an American Physical Society meeting and at 2 or more educational institutions or research laboratories in the year following the award.

**Duration** The award is presented annually.

**Additional information** This award was established in 1974. Since 1998 it has been supported by donations from the John D. and Catherine T. MacArthur Foundation, the Energy Foundation, the David and Lucile Packard Foundation, and individuals.

**Number awarded** 1 each year.

**Deadline** June of each year.

## [1350]
## LESBIAN WRITERS FUND AWARDS

Astraea Lesbian Foundation for Justice
Attn: Program Director
116 East 16th Street, Seventh Floor
New York, NY 10003
(212) 529-8021                Fax: (212) 982-3321
E-mail: grants@astraeafoundation.org
Web: www.astraeafoundation.org

**Summary** To provide funding for additional work to emerging lesbian writers.

**Eligibility** These grants are presented to emerging lesbian writers of poetry and fiction who reside in the United States. Applicants must have published at least 1 piece of their writing (in any genre) in a newspaper, magazine, journal, or anthology, but no more than 1 book. Their work must include some lesbian content. Submissions may consist of up to 20 pages of fiction (a novel or collection of short stories) or at least 10 but no more than 15 pages of poetry.

**Financial data** Grants are either $10,000 or $1,500; honorable mentions are $100.

**Additional information** This fund was established in 1991. Requests for applications must be accompanied by a self-addressed stamped envelope.

**Number awarded** Varies each year; recently, 12 of these grants were awarded: 2 at $10,000 (1 for fiction and 1 for poetry), 4 at $1,500 (2 for fiction and 2 for poetry), and 6 honorable mentions (3 for fiction and 3 for poetry).

**Deadline** February of each year.

## [1351]
## LIBRARY OF CONGRESS JUNIOR FELLOWS PROGRAM

Library of Congress
Library Services
Attn: Junior Fellows Program Coordinator
101 Independence Avenue, S.E., Room LM-642
Washington, DC 20540-4600
(202) 707-6610                     Fax: (202) 707-6269
E-mail: jrfell@loc.gov
Web: www.loc.gov/hr/jrfellows/index.html

**Summary** To provide summer work experience at the Library of Congress (LC) to upper-division students, graduate students, and recent graduates (particularly women, minorities, and persons with disabilities).

**Eligibility** This program is open to U.S. citizens with subject expertise in the following areas: collections preservation; geography and maps; humanities, art, and culture; information technology; library science; or chemistry and science. Applicants must 1) be juniors or seniors at an accredited college or university; 2) be graduate students; or 3) have completed their degree in the past year. Women, minorities, and persons with disabilities are strongly encouraged to apply. Selection is based on academic achievement, letters of recommendation, and an interview.

**Financial data** Fellows are paid a taxable stipend of $3,000.

**Duration** 10 weeks, beginning in either May or June. Fellows work a 40-hour week.

**Additional information** Fellows work with primary source materials and assist selected divisions at LC in the organization and documentation of archival collections, production of finding aids and bibliographic records, preparation of materials for preservation and service, completion of bibliographical research, and digitization of LC's historical collections.

**Number awarded** Varies each year; recently, 38 of these internships were awarded.

**Deadline** January of each year.

## [1352]
## LINDA FENNER YOUNG WOMEN'S SCHOLARSHIP

Allied Jewish Federation of Colorado
Attn: Donor Relationship Manager
300 South Dahlia Street, Suite 300
Denver, CO 80246-8118
(303) 321-3399                     Fax: (303) 322-8328
E-mail: federation@ajfcolorado.org
Web: www.jewishcolorado.org/page.aspx?id=196980

**Summary** To provide funding for professional development activities to young Jewish women in Colorado.

**Eligibility** This program is open to female residents of Colorado between 21 and 45 years of age. Applicants must have been identified as a leader or someone with leadership potential in the Jewish community. They must be interested in attending nonprofit Jewish conferences, missions to Israel, or other young adult program that will develop their leadership skills in order to better the Jewish community.

**Financial data** The grant is $2,500.

**Duration** These are 1-time grants.

**Additional information** This program is supported by the Jewish Community Foundation, (303) 316-6469.

**Number awarded** 1 or more each year.

**Deadline** April of each year.

## [1353]
## LIZETTE PETERSON-HOMER INJURY PREVENTION RESEARCH GRANT

American Psychological Foundation
750 First Street, N.E.
Washington, DC 20002-4242
(202) 336-5843                     Fax: (202) 336-5812
E-mail: foundation@apa.org
Web: www.apa.org/apf/funding/peterson-homer.aspx

**Summary** To provide funding to women and other graduate students and faculty from diverse groups who interested in conducting research related to the prevention of injuries in children.

**Eligibility** This program is open to graduate students and faculty interested in conducting research that focuses on the prevention of physical injury in children and young adults through accidents, violence, abuse, or suicide. Applicants must submit a 100-word abstract, description of the project, detailed budget, curriculum vitae, and letter from the supporting faculty supervisor (if the applicant is a student). Selection is based on conformance with stated program goals, magnitude of incremental contribution, quality of proposed work, and applicant's demonstrated scholarship and research competence. The sponsor encourages applications from individuals who represent diversity in race, ethnicity, gender, age, disability, and sexual orientation.

**Financial data** Grants up to $5,000 are available.

**Duration** 1 year.

**Additional information** This program began in 1999 as the Rebecca Routh Coon Injury Research Award. The current name was adopted in 2003. It is supported by Division 54 (Society of Pediatric Psychology) of the American Psychological Association and the American Psychological Foundation.

**Number awarded** 1 each year.

**Deadline** September of each year.

## [1354]
## LONE STAR RISING CAREER SCHOLARSHIP

Association for Women Geoscientists
Attn: AWG Foundation
12000 North Washington Street, Suite 285
Thornton, CO 80241
(303) 412-6219                     Fax: (303) 253-9220
E-mail: chrysalis@awg.org
Web: www.awg.org/EAS/scholarships.html

**Summary** To provide assistance to female geoscientists who have been out of the workforce and need funding to resume their career.

**Eligibility** This program is open to women in the geoscience profession who wish to resume their career after having been out of the workforce. Applicants must be seeking funding for such professional development costs as enrollment in geoscience training courses or workshops, fees for certifications and licensing, professional membership fees, or any other costs to help them reenter the workforce. Along with their application, they must submit a 1-page personal statement describing their academic qualifications, professional work history, and any recent volunteer or home activities relevant to their area of expertise.

**Financial data** A total of $1,000 is available for this program each year.

**Duration** 1 year.

**Additional information** This program is sponsored by the Lone Star Chapter of the Association for Women Geoscientists (AWG), but neither Texas residency nor AWG membership are required.

**Number awarded** 1 or more each year.

**Deadline** December of each year.

## [1355]
## L'OREAL USA FELLOWSHIPS FOR WOMEN IN SCIENCE

L'Oréal USA
c/o American Association for the Advancement of Science
Education and Human Resources
1200 New York Avenue, Sixth Floor
Washington, DC 20005
(202) 326-6677    E-mail: lorealusafellowships@aaas.org
Web: www.aaas.org/programs/education/loreal.shtml

**Summary** To provide research funding to postdoctoral women scientists.

**Eligibility** This program is open to women who have a Ph.D. in the life sciences, physical or material sciences, engineering, technology, computer science, or mathematics. Additional areas of study include immunology, all areas of chemistry, earth science, and medical research. Women who have an M.D. or whose work is in psychology, science education, or social science are not eligible. Applicants must be planning to conduct a research project in their field of specialization at an institution in the United States or Puerto Rico. They must be U.S. citizens or permanent residents.

**Financial data** The grant is $60,000.

**Duration** 1 year.

**Additional information** This program, established in 2003, is sponsored by L'Oréal USA and administered by the American Association for the Advancement of Science (AAAS).

**Number awarded** 5 each year.

**Deadline** December of each year.

## [1356]
## L'OREAL-UNESCO FOR WOMEN IN SCIENCE AWARDS

United Nations Educational, Scientific, and Cultural
    Organization
Attn: Fellowships Section
7, place de Fontenoy
75352 Paris 07 SP
France
33 1 45 68 15 49                Fax: 33 1 45 68 55 03
E-mail: a.zaid@unesco.org
Web: www.unesco.org

**Summary** To recognize and reward women from any country who have contributed outstanding research in the physical or life sciences.

**Eligibility** This award is presented to women who have contributed outstanding research in the physical (in odd-num-

bered years) or life (in even-numbered years) sciences. Candidates are nominated by a jury of international scientists, and winners are selected on the basis of their research, the strength of their commitments, and their impact on society.

**Financial data** The award is $100,000.

**Duration** The awards are presented annually.

**Additional information** This program, which began in 1998, is sponsored by L'Oréal.

**Number awarded** 5 each year (1 in each of the 5 continents: Europe, North America, Asia and the Pacific, Africa and the Arab States, and Latin America).

**Deadline** Deadline not specified.

## [1357]
## LOREEN ARBUS DISABILITY AWARENESS GRANTS

New York Women in Film & Television
6 East 39th Street, Suite 1200
New York, NY 10016-0112
(212) 679-0870, ext. 39         Fax: (212) 679-0899
E-mail: development@nywift.org
Web: www.nywift.org/article.aspx?id=LAS

**Summary** To provide funding to women filmmakers who are interested in making a film on disability issues.

**Eligibility** This program is open to women who are interested in making a film on physical or developmental disability issues. The film must be a work-in-progress of any length or genre but may not be a finished film. Applicants must submit a 2- to 4-page description of the project, a budget indicating amount raised to date, a list of key creative personnel with 1-paragraph bios, and a DVD of the work-in-progress.

**Financial data** The grant is $7,500. Funds may be used only for completion work.

**Duration** These grants are provided annually.

**Number awarded** 1 or more each year.

**Deadline** June of each year.

## [1358]
## M. CAREY THOMAS AWARD

Alumnae Association of Bryn Mawr College
Wyndham Alumnae House
101 North Merion Avenue
Bryn Mawr, PA 19010-2899
(610) 526-5227                Toll Free: (800) BMC-ALUM
Fax: (610) 526-5228    E-mail: bmcalum@brynmawr.edu
Web: www.brynmawr.edu/alumnae

**Summary** To recognize and reward unusual achievement on the part of distinguished American women.

**Eligibility** Applications are not accepted. Recipients are chosen by a special committee that is formed several months prior to the presentation of the award. Selection is based on eminent and outstanding achievement. Recipients may be affiliated with Bryn Mawr College.

**Financial data** The award is $10,000.

**Duration** The award is granted periodically.

**Additional information** Past recipients have included Martha Graham and Georgia O'Keefe.

**Number awarded** 1 whenever a suitable candidate is identified.

**Deadline** Deadline not specified.

## [1359]
## M. HILDRED BLEWETT SCHOLARSHIP

American Physical Society
Attn: Committee on the Status of Women in Physics
One Physics Ellipse, Fourth Floor
College Park, MD 20740-3844
(301) 209-3231                    Fax: (301) 209-0865
E-mail: blewett@aps.org
Web: www.aps.org

**Summary**   To provide funding to early-career women interested in returning to physics research after interrupting those careers for family reasons.

**Eligibility**   This program is open to women who have completed work toward a Ph.D. in physics and currently have an affiliation with a research-active educational institution or national laboratory in Canada or the United States. Applicants must be interested in conducting a research project after interrupting their career for family reasons. They must currently reside in the United States or Canada and be citizens or legal residents of those countries. No matching contribution from the institution is required, but institutional support is considered as evidence of support for the applicant.

**Financial data**   The grant is $45,000. Funds may be used for dependent care (limited to 50% of the award), salary, travel, equipment, and tuition and fees.

**Duration**   1 year.

**Additional information**   This program began in 2005.

**Number awarded**   2 each year.

**Deadline**   May of each year.

## [1360]
## M. LOUISE CARPENTER GLOECKNER, M.D. SUMMER RESEARCH FELLOWSHIP

Drexel University College of Medicine
Attn: Archives and Special Collections
2900 West Queen Lane
Philadelphia, PA 19129
(215) 991-8340                    Fax: (215) 991-8172
E-mail: archives@drexelmed.edu
Web: archives.drexelmed.edu/fellowship.php

**Summary**   To provide funding to scholars and students interested in conducting research during the summer on the history of women in medicine at the Archives and Special Collections on Women in Medicine at Drexel University in Philadelphia.

**Eligibility**   This program is open to students at all levels, scholars, and general researchers. Applicants must be interested in conducting research utilizing the archives, which emphasize the history of women in medicine, nursing, medical missionaries, the American Medical Women's Association, American Women's Hospital Service, and other women in medical organizations. Selection is based on research background of the applicant, relevance of the proposed research project to the goals of the applicant, overall quality and clarity of the proposal, appropriateness of the proposal to the holdings of the collection, and commitment of the applicant to the project.

**Financial data**   The grant is $4,000.

**Duration**   4 to 6 weeks during the summer.

**Number awarded**   1 each year.

**Deadline**   February of each year.

## [1361]
## MARA CRAWFORD PERSONAL DEVELOPMENT SCHOLARSHIP

Kansas Federation of Business & Professional Women's Clubs, Inc.
Attn: Kansas BPW Educational Foundation, Inc.
c/o Kathy Niehoff, Executive Secretary
605 East 15th
Ottawa, KS 66067
(785) 242-9319                    Fax: (785) 242-1047
E-mail: kathyniehoff@sbcglobal.net
Web: kansasbpw.memberlodge.org

**Summary**   To provide financial assistance to women in Kansas who are already in the workforce but are interested in pursuing additional education.

**Eligibility**   This program is open to women residents of Kansas who graduated from high school more than 5 years previously and are already in the workforce. Applicants may be seeking a degree in any field of study and may be attending a 2-year, 4-year, vocational, or technological program. They must submit a 3-page personal biography in which they express their career goals, the direction they want to take in the future, their proposed field of study, their reason for selecting that field, the institutions they plan to attend and why, their circumstances for reentering school (if a factor), and what makes them uniquely qualified for this scholarship. Preference is given to applicants who demonstrate they have serious family responsibilities and obligations. Applications must be submitted through a local unit of the sponsor.

**Financial data**   A stipend is awarded (amount not specified).

**Duration**   1 year.

**Number awarded**   1 or more each year.

**Deadline**   December of each year.

## [1362]
## MARCH OF DIMES COMERFORD FREDA "SAVING BABIES, TOGETHER" AWARD

Association of Women's Health, Obstetric and Neonatal Nurses
Attn: Research Grants Program
2000 L Street, N.W., Suite 740
Washington, DC 20036
(202) 261-2431        Toll Free: (800) 673-8499, ext. 2431
Fax: (202) 728-0575
E-mail: ResearchPrograms@awhonn.org
Web: www.awhonn.org

**Summary**   To provide funding for small research projects to members of the Association of Women's Health, Obstetric and Neonatal Nurses (AWHONN).

**Eligibility**   This program is open to members of the association who are interested in conducting research related to women's health, obstetric, or neonatal nursing. Researchers who are currently principal investigators on a federally-funded grant, or who have already received an AWHONN-funded research grant within the past 5 years, are not eligible.

**Financial data**   The grant is $9,000. Funds may not be used for indirect costs, tuition, computer hardware or printers, conference attendance, or salary for the principal investigator or other investigators.

**Duration**   1 year.

**Additional information** This program is funded by the March of Dimes and named in honor of long-time AWHONN member, Dr. Margaret Comerford Freda.

**Number awarded** 1 each year.

**Deadline** November of each year.

## [1363]
## MARCIA FEINBERG AWARD

Association of Jewish Women Publishers
3160 Wedgewood Court
Reno, NV 89509-7103

**Summary** To recognize and reward Jewish women who have made outstanding contributions to careers in library science and publishing.

**Eligibility** This award is presented to Jewish women who received a library science doctoral degree from a university in the upper Midwest (Montana, South Dakota, North Dakota, or Minnesota). Nominees must have spent a portion of their career working as a librarian, and then changed careers to enter the field of publishing. They may currently reside in any state except Nebraska or Rhode Island. Selection is based on service to the library profession, awards received for librarianship, innovativeness, and loyalty to colleagues.

**Financial data** The award includes an honorarium of $10,000 and a gold engraved plaque.

**Duration** The award is presented annually.

**Additional information** This award, named in honor of a well-known 19th-century Jewish woman librarian and publisher, has been presented annually since 1923. Self-nominations are not accepted. Only professional colleagues may nominate a candidate.

**Number awarded** 1 each year.

**Deadline** August of each year.

## [1364]
## MARGARET FULLER AWARDS PROGRAM

Unitarian Universalist Association
Attn: UU Women's Federation
25 Beacon Street
Boston, MA 02108-2800
(617) 948-4692                    Fax: (617) 742-2402
E-mail: uuwf@uua.org
Web: www.uuwf.org

**Summary** To provide funding to Unitarian Universalists working on projects that promote feminist theology.

**Eligibility** This program is open to Unitarian Universalist (UU) women interested in working on a scholarly project that relates to any of the thematic strands of UU feminist theology. The project should result in a product that can be shared widely with UU women, such as a book, curriculum materials, program outlines or descriptions, DVDs, audio-tapes, workshop templates, or publishable articles. Examples of appropriate projects include poetry, drama, ritual, song, curricula for youth or adults, historical or theological analyses of the lives and writings of early feminists, or scholarly descriptions of feminist theories and theologies. Grants are generally made to individuals, although group projects may be eligible.

**Financial data** Grants range from $500 to $5,000.

**Duration** Proposed projects should take not more than 1 to 2 years to complete.

**Additional information** This program originated as the Feminist Theology Award program in 1989. That program ended in 1997 and was succeeded by this in 2002. Funds are not available for graduate school or to support dissertations. Funding is no longer available for computer hardware.

**Number awarded** Varies each year; recently, 2 of these grants were awarded.

**Deadline** March of each year.

## [1365]
## MARGARET OAKLEY DAYHOFF AWARD

Biophysical Society
Attn: Awards Committee
11400 Rockville Pike, Suite 800
Rockville, MD 20852
(240) 290-5600                    Fax: (240) 290-5555
E-mail: society@biophysics.org
Web: www.biophysics.org

**Summary** To recognize and reward outstanding junior women scientists in fields of interest to the Biophysical Society.

**Eligibility** This program is open to junior women scientists whose writings have made substantial contributions to scientific fields within the range of interest of the society but who have not yet attained university tenure. Candidates who have a Ph.D. or equivalent degree remain eligible until they have completed 10 years of full-time work following the degree. Candidates with a baccalaureate degree but without a Ph.D. have 12 years of eligibility. Time taken off for child rearing is not counted. Candidates who work in non-academic environments are eligible if their work is published and meets academic standards, and if they do not have tenure equivalency. Membership is the society is required. Nominations may be submitted by any member of the society in good standing, but self-nominations are not accepted.

**Financial data** The award is $2,000.

**Duration** The award is presented annually.

**Additional information** This award was established in 1984.

**Number awarded** 1 each year.

**Deadline** April of each year.

## [1366]
## MARGARET W. ROSSITER HISTORY OF WOMEN IN SCIENCE PRIZE

History of Science Society
Attn: Nominations
University of Notre Dame
440 Geddes Hall
Notre Dame, IN 46556
(574) 631-1194                    Fax: (574) 631-1533
E-mail: prizes@hssonline.org
Web: www.hssonline.org/about/society_awards.html

**Summary** To recognize and reward scholars who publish outstanding work in the specialty field of women in the history of science.

**Eligibility** Books and articles published during the last 4 years are eligible for consideration, provided they deal with a topic related to women in science, including discussions of women's activities in science, analyses of past scientific practices that deal explicitly with gender, and investigations regarding women as viewed by scientists. Entries may take a biographical, institutional, theoretical, or other approach to the topic. They may relate to medicine, technology, and the social sciences as well as the natural sciences.

**Financial data** The prize is $1,000.

**Duration** This is an annual award, presented in alternate years to the most outstanding article (even-numbered years) and the most outstanding book (odd-numbered years).

**Additional information** This award was established in 1987 and given its current name in 2004.

**Number awarded** 1 each year.

**Deadline** March of each year.

## [1367]
## MARIA GOEPPERT-MAYER AWARD

American Physical Society
Attn: Honors Program
One Physics Ellipse
College Park, MD 20740-3844
(301) 209-3268                          Fax: (301) 209-0865
E-mail: honors@aps.org
Web: www.aps.org

**Summary** To recognize the achievements of outstanding female physicists and to offer them an opportunity to share these achievements by delivering public lectures.

**Eligibility** This award is available to women who are working in a field of physics and are in the early stages of their careers. They must have received their doctorates no more than 10 years ago. Nominations of members of underrepresented minority groups and scientists from outside the United States are especially encouraged.

**Financial data** The award is $2,500 plus a $4,000 travel allowance to cover the costs of providing lectures at 4 institutions of the recipient's choice.

**Duration** The lectures must be given within 2 years after the award is presented.

**Additional information** The lectures may be given at 4 institutions of the recipient's choice within the United States or its possessions, and at the meeting of the American Physical Society at which the award is presented. The award was established by the General Electric Foundation (now the GE Fund) in 1985.

**Number awarded** 1 each year.

**Deadline** June of each year.

## [1368]
## MARIAM K. CHAMBERLAIN FELLOWSHIP IN WOMEN AND PUBLIC POLICY

Institute for Women's Policy Research
Attn: Fellowship Coordinator
1200 18th Street, N.W., Suite 301
Washington, DC 20036
(202) 785-5100                          Fax: (202) 833-4362
E-mail: yi@iwpr.org
Web: www.iwpr.org/about/fellowships

**Summary** To provide work experience at the Institute for Women's Policy Research (IWPR) to college graduates and graduate students who are interested in economic justice for women.

**Eligibility** Applicants for this internship should have at least a bachelor's degree in social science, statistics, or women's studies. Graduate work is desirable but not required. They should have strong quantitative and library research skills and knowledge of women's issues. Familiarity with Microsoft Word and Excel is required; knowledge of STATA, SPSS, SAS, or graphics software is a plus.

**Financial data** The stipend is $27,000 and includes health insurance and a public transportation stipend.

**Duration** 9 months, beginning in September.

**Additional information** The institute is a nonprofit, scientific research organization that works primarily on issues related to equal opportunity and economic and social justice for women. Research topics vary each year but relate to women and public policy.

**Number awarded** 1 each year.

**Deadline** February of each year.

## [1369]
## MARIAN NORBY SCHOLARSHIP

Society for Technical Communication
Attn: Scholarships
9401 Lee Highway, Suite 904
Fairfax, VA 22031-1822
(703) 522-4114                          Fax: (703) 522-2075
E-mail: stc@stc.org
Web: www.stc.org

**Summary** To provide financial assistance to female employees of the federal government who are interested in additional study related to technical communications.

**Eligibility** This program is open to women who working full or part time for the federal government as a secretary or administrative assistant. Applicants must be interested in enrolling in a training or academic class related to technical communication, including technical writing, editing, graphical design, interface design, or web design. Along with their application, they must submit a 1- to 3-page description of their career goals and significant achievements to date. Financial need is not considered in the selection process.

**Financial data** The stipend is $2,500.

**Duration** 1 academic year.

**Number awarded** 1 each year.

**Deadline** May of each year.

## [1370]
## MARY ISABEL SIBLEY FELLOWSHIP FOR FRENCH STUDIES

Phi Beta Kappa Society
Attn: Director of Society Affairs
1606 New Hampshire Avenue, N.W.
Washington, DC 20009
(202) 745-3287                          Fax: (202) 986-1601
E-mail: awards@pbk.org
Web: www.pbk.org/infoview/PBK_InfoView.aspx?t=&id=28

**Summary** To provide funding to women involved in dissertation or advanced research or writing projects dealing with French studies.

**Eligibility** This program is open to unmarried women between 25 and 35 years of age who have demonstrated their ability to conduct original research. Applicants must be planning to conduct a research project dealing with French language or literature. They must hold the doctorate or have fulfilled all the requirements for the doctorate except the dissertation, and they must be planning to devote full time to their research during the fellowship year. Along with their application, they must submit a statement that includes a description of the project, the present state of the project, where the study would be carried out, and expectations regarding publication of the results of the study. Eligibility is not restricted to members of Phi Beta Kappa or to U.S. citizens.

**Financial data** The stipend is $20,000.

**Duration** 1 year (the fellowship is offered in even-numbered years only).

**Additional information** Periodic progress reports are not required, but they are welcomed. It is the hope of the committee that the results of the year of research will be made available in some form, although no pressure for publication will be put on the recipient.

**Number awarded** 1 every other year.

**Deadline** January of even-numbered years.

## [1371]
## MARY ISABEL SIBLEY FELLOWSHIP FOR GREEK STUDIES

Phi Beta Kappa Society
Attn: Director of Society Affairs
1606 New Hampshire Avenue, N.W.
Washington, DC 20009
(202) 745-3287          Fax: (202) 986-1601
E-mail: awards@pbk.org
Web: www.pbk.org/infoview/PBK_InfoView.aspx?t=&id=28

**Summary** To provide funding to women involved in dissertation or advanced research or writing projects dealing with Greek studies.

**Eligibility** This program is open to unmarried women between 25 and 35 years of age who have demonstrated their ability to conduct original research. Applicants must be planning to conduct a research project dealing with Greek language, literature, history, or archaeology. They must hold the doctorate or have fulfilled all the requirements for the doctorate except the dissertation, and they must be planning to devote full time to their research during the fellowship year. Along with their application, they must submit a statement that includes a description of the project, the present state of the project, where the study would be carried out, and expectations regarding publication of the results of the study. Eligibility is not restricted to members of Phi Beta Kappa or to U.S. citizens.

**Financial data** The stipend is $20,000.

**Duration** 1 year (the fellowship is offered in odd-numbered years only).

**Additional information** Periodic progress reports are not required, but they are welcomed. It is the hope of the committee that the results of the year of research will be made available in some form, although no pressure for publication will be put on the recipient.

**Number awarded** 1 every other year.

**Deadline** January of odd-numbered years.

## [1372]
## MARY JANE OESTMANN PROFESSIONAL WOMEN'S ACHIEVEMENT AWARD

American Nuclear Society
Attn: Honors and Awards
555 North Kensington Avenue
La Grange Park, IL 60526-5535
(708) 352-6611          Toll Free: (800) 323-3044
Fax: (708) 352-0499     E-mail: honors@ans.org
Web: www.new.ans.org/honors

**Summary** To recognize and reward women who have made outstanding contributions to the field of nuclear science.

**Eligibility** This award is presented to women who have contributed outstanding personal dedication and technical achievement in the fields of nuclear science, engineering, research, or education. Nominees need not be a member of the American Nuclear Society (ANS), but they should be affiliated with the nuclear community in some manner. The award may be given for lifetime achievement or for a singular outstanding contribution to the technical community.

**Financial data** The award consists of an honorarium of $1,000 and an engraved plaque.

**Duration** The award is presented annually.

**Additional information** This award was first presented in 1991.

**Number awarded** 1 each year.

**Deadline** June of each year.

## [1373]
## MARY LILY RESEARCH GRANTS

Duke University
David M. Rubenstein Rare Book and Manuscript Library
Attn: Sallie Bingham Center for Women's History and
    Culture
P.O. Box 90185
Durham, NC 27708-0185
(919) 660-5828          Fax: (919) 660-5934
E-mail: cwhc@duke.edu
Web: library.duke.edu

**Summary** To provide funding to scholars at all levels who wish to use the resources of the Sallie Bingham Center for Women's History and Culture in the Special Collections Library at Duke University.

**Eligibility** This program is open to undergraduates, graduate students, faculty members, and independent scholars in any academic field who wish to use the resources of the center for their research in women's studies. Applicants must reside outside a 100-mile radius of Durham, North Carolina. Undergraduate and graduate students must be currently enrolled, be working on a degree, and enclose a letter of recommendation from their adviser or thesis director. Faculty members must be working on a research project and enclose a curriculum vitae. Independent scholars must be working on a nonprofit project and enclose a curriculum vitae. Research topics should be strongly supported by the collections of the center.

**Financial data** Grants up to $1,000 are available; funds may be used for travel, accommodations, meals, and photocopying and reproduction expenses.

**Duration** Up to 1 year.

**Additional information**   The library's collections are especially strong in the history of feminist activism and theory, prescriptive literature, girls' literature, artists' books by women, lay and ordained church women, gender expression, women's sexuality, and the history and culture of women in the South. A number of prominent women writers have placed their personal and professional papers in the collections.

**Number awarded**   Varies each year; recently, 8 of these grants were awarded.

**Deadline**   January of each year.

## [1374]
## MATHEMATICS EDUCATION RESEARCH MENTORING TRAVEL GRANTS FOR WOMEN

Association for Women in Mathematics
11240 Waples Mill Road, Suite 200
Fairfax, VA 22030
(703) 934-0163                           Fax: (703) 359-7562
E-mail: awm@awm-math.org
Web: sites.google.com

**Summary**   To provide funding to female postdoctorates in mathematics who wish to travel to develop a long-term working and mentoring relationship with an educational researcher.

**Eligibility**   This program is open to women holding a doctorate or with equivalent experience and with a work address in the United States (or home address if unemployed). The applicant's research may be in any field that is funded by the Division of Mathematical Sciences (DMS) of the National Science Foundation (NSF). The proposed travel must be to collaborate with a mentor who holds a doctorate in mathematics education or in a related field, such as psychology or curriculum and instruction.

**Financial data**   These grants provide full or partial support for travel, subsistence, and other required expenses, to a maximum of $5,000.

**Duration**   The proposed visit may last up to 1 month.

**Additional information**   Funding for this program is provided by the DMS of the NSF. For foreign travel, U.S. carriers must be used whenever possible.

**Number awarded**   Up to 7 each year.

**Deadline**   January of each year.

## [1375]
## MATHEMATICS EDUCATION RESEARCH TRAVEL GRANTS FOR WOMEN RESEARCHERS

Association for Women in Mathematics
11240 Waples Mill Road, Suite 200
Fairfax, VA 22030
(703) 934-0163                           Fax: (703) 359-7562
E-mail: awm@awm-math.org
Web: sites.google.com

**Summary**   To enable women mathematicians to attend research conferences related to education.

**Eligibility**   This program is open to women who wish to attend a research conference on mathematics or mathematics education. They may be mathematicians attending a mathematics education research conference or mathematics education researchers attending a mathematics conference. Applicants must be women holding a doctorate (or equiva-

lent) and with a work address in the United States (or home address, in the case of unemployed mathematicians). Women who have been awarded this grant in the past 2 years or who have other sources of external funding (e.g., a regular NSF grant) are ineligible. Partial institutional support does not, however, make the applicant ineligible. Interested applicants must use an online registration system that will call for 1) a description of their current research and how the proposed travel would benefit their research program; 2) their curriculum vitae; 3) a budget for the proposed travel; and 4) information about all other sources of travel funding available to the applicant.

**Financial data**   These grants provide full or partial support for travel and subsistence for a meeting or conference in the applicant's field of specialization. A maximum of $1,750 for domestic travel or of $2,300 for foreign travel may be awarded.

**Duration**   There are 3 award periods each year.

**Additional information**   Funding for this program, established in 2006, is provided by the Division of Mathematical Sciences of the National Science Foundation. For foreign travel, U.S. carriers must be used whenever possible.

**Number awarded**   Varies each year.

**Deadline**   January, April, or September of each year.

## [1376]
## MATHEMATICS MENTORING TRAVEL GRANTS FOR WOMEN

Association for Women in Mathematics
11240 Waples Mill Road, Suite 200
Fairfax, VA 22030
(703) 934-0163                           Fax: (703) 359-7562
E-mail: awm@awm-math.org
Web: sites.google.com

**Summary**   To provide funding to junior female postdoctorates in mathematics who wish to travel to develop a long-term working and mentoring relationship with a senior mathematician.

**Eligibility**   This program is open to women holding a doctorate or with equivalent experience and with a work address in the United States. They must be untenured. The applicant's research may be in any field that is funded by the Division of Mathematical Sciences (DMS) of the National Science Foundation (NSF). The proposed travel must be to an institute or a department (in the United States or abroad) to do research with a senior mathematician so the applicant can establish her research program and eventually receive tenure.

**Financial data**   These grants provide full or partial support for travel, subsistence, and other required expenses, to a maximum of $5,000.

**Duration**   The proposed visit may last up to 1 month.

**Additional information**   Funding for this program is provided by the DMS of the NSF. For foreign travel, U.S. carriers must be used whenever possible.

**Number awarded**   Up to 7 each year.

**Deadline**   January of each year.

## [1377]
## MATHEMATICS TRAVEL GRANTS FOR WOMEN RESEARCHERS

Association for Women in Mathematics
11240 Waples Mill Road, Suite 200
Fairfax, VA 22030
(703) 934-0163 Fax: (703) 359-7562
E-mail: awm@awm-math.org
Web: sites.google.com

**Summary** To enable women mathematicians to attend research conferences in their fields.

**Eligibility** This program is open to women who wish to attend a research conference on a topic sponsored by the Division of Mathematical Sciences (DMS) of the National Science Foundation (NSF). The proposed research conference must be in an area supported by the DMS. That includes certain areas of statistics but excludes most mathematics education and the history of mathematics. Applicants must be women holding a doctorate (or equivalent) and with a work address in the United States (or home address, in the case of unemployed mathematicians). Women who have been awarded this grant in the past 2 years or who have other sources of external funding (e.g., a regular NSF grant) are ineligible. Partial institutional support does not, however, make the applicant ineligible. Interested applicants must use an online registration system that will call for 1) a description of their current research and how the proposed travel would benefit their research program; 2) their curriculum vitae; 3) a budget for the proposed travel; and 4) information about all other sources of travel funding available to the applicant.

**Financial data** These grants provide full or partial support for travel and subsistence for a meeting or conference in the applicant's field of specialization. A maximum of $1,750 for domestic travel or of $2,300 for foreign travel may be awarded.

**Duration** There are 3 award periods each year.

**Additional information** Funding for this program is provided by the Division of Mathematical Sciences of the National Science Foundation. For foreign travel, U.S. carriers must be used whenever possible.

**Number awarded** Varies each year; recently, 36 of these grants were awarded.

**Deadline** January, April, or September of each year.

## [1378]
## MATURE WOMAN EDUCATIONAL SCHOLARSHIP

Washington State Business and Professional Women's
  Foundation
Attn: Virginia Murphy, Scholarship Committee Chair
P.O. Box 631
Chelan, WA 98816-0631
(509) 682-4747 E-mail: vamurf@nwi.net
Web: www.bpwwa.org/foundation_apps.htm

**Summary** To provide financial assistance to mature women from Washington interested in attending postsecondary school in the state for retraining or continuing education.

**Eligibility** This program is open to women over 30 years of age who have been residents of Washington for at least 2 years. Applicants must be planning to enroll at a college or university in the state for a program of retraining or continuing education. Along with their application, they must submit a 500-word essay on their specific short-term goals and how the proposed training will help them accomplish those goals and make a difference in their professional career. Financial need is considered in the selection process. U.S. citizenship is required.

**Financial data** The stipend is $1,000.

**Duration** 1 year.

**Number awarded** 1 or more each year.

**Deadline** April of each year.

## [1379]
## MCNEILL-NOTT AWARD

American Alpine Club
Attn: Grants Manager
710 Tenth Street, Suite 100
Golden, CO 80401
(303) 384-0110, ext. 15 Fax: (303) 384-0111
E-mail: grants@americanalpineclub.org
Web: www.americanalpineclub.org/grants

**Summary** To provide funding to mountain climbers (especially all-women teams) interested in attempting new and difficult climbs.

**Eligibility** This program is open to amateur climbers exploring new routes or unclimbed peaks with small and lightweight teams. Preference is given to projects that have strong exploratory and adventuresome mountaineering components and to all-women teams. Grant applicants must be U.S. citizens, although team members may be foreign citizens. All participants must be at least 18 years of age. Membership in the American Alpine Club is required. Selection is based on the remoteness and exploratory nature of the objective, planned climbing style, and relevance of the team's experience to the objective.

**Financial data** A total of $7,000 is available for this program each year.

**Duration** Climbs must be completed within 1 year of the award of the grant.

**Additional information** This program began in 2007 to honor Karen McNeill and Sue Nott, who had died during a climb in the previous year. Funding is provided by Mountain Hardwear.

**Number awarded** 2 or 3 each year.

**Deadline** December of each year.

## [1380]
## MEDTRONIC PRIZE FOR SCIENTIFIC CONTRIBUTIONS TO WOMEN'S HEALTH

Society for Women's Health Research
Attn: Prize
1025 Connecticut Avenue, N.W., Suite 701
Washington, DC 20036
(202) 496-5001 Fax: (202) 833-3472
E-mail: aaron@swhr.org
Web: www.womenshealthresearch.org

**Summary** To recognize and reward women scientists and engineers who have made outstanding contributions to women's health.

**Eligibility** This award is available to women scientists and engineers in mid-career whose work has led or will lead directly to the improvement of women's health. Nominees should have devoted a significant part of their careers to the area of women's health, especially to work on sex differences. They must be U.S. citizens who completed their first graduate degree within the past 15 years. They must have a demonstrated interest in teaching and mentorship.

**Financial data** The award is $75,000.

**Duration** The award is presented annually.

**Additional information** This award, first presented in 2006, is sponsored by Medtronic.

**Number awarded** 1 each year.

**Deadline** February of each year.

## [1381]
## MEERSBURGER DROSTE-PREIS

Kulturamt der Stadt Meersburg
Postfach 1140
D-88701 Meersburg
Germany
49 7532 440 260          Fax: 49 7532 440 264
E-mail: kulturamt@meersburg.de

**Summary** To recognize and reward women poets from any country who write in the German language.

**Eligibility** The competition is open to women poets of any nationality writing in German. Self-nominations are not accepted.

**Financial data** The prize is 6,000 Euros.

**Duration** The competition is held every 3 years (2015, 2018, etc.).

**Additional information** This prize was first awarded in 1957.

**Number awarded** 1 every 3 years.

**Deadline** Deadline not specified.

## [1382]
## MICROBIOLOGY OF THE BUILT ENVIRONMENT PROGRAM FELLOWSHIPS

Alfred P. Sloan Foundation
630 Fifth Avenue, Suite 2550
New York, NY 10111-0242
(212) 649-1649          Fax: (212) 757-5117
E-mail: olsiewski@sloan.org
Web: www.sloan.org

**Summary** To provide funding to recent doctorates (particularly women and members of other underrepresented groups) who are interested in conducting research on the microbiology of the build environment.

**Eligibility** This program is open to early stage Ph.D. scientists and engineers in laboratories engaged in research on the microbiology of the build environment in the United States or Canada. Cross-disciplinary studies in microbial biology and engineering are encouraged. Applications may be submitted by graduate students if accompanied by a letter of commitment from a potential postdoctoral adviser. Members of underrepresented groups in science and engineering are especially encouraged to apply. Selection is based on an assessment of the proposed research, the arrangements for the interdisciplinary educational broadening of the fellow, and the previous research records of the potential fellow and adviser.

**Financial data** The grant is $60,000 per year, including $48,000 as a stipend (may be supplemented by institutional or other sources), $2,000 for travel or research expenses, and $10,000 for fringe benefits.

**Duration** 2 years.

**Additional information** This program began in 2013.

**Number awarded** 8 each year.

**Deadline** September of each year.

## [1383]
## MID KOLSTAD SCHOLARSHIP

Women Soaring Pilots Association
c/o Phyllis Wells
P.O. Box 278
Aguila, AZ 85320
(719) 429-4999 E-mail: scholarships@womensoaring.org
Web: www.womensoaring.org/?p=info

**Summary** To provide financial assistance to mature women interested in obtaining their private glider license.

**Eligibility** This program is open to women over 25 years of age who are student glider pilots or licensed airplane pilots. Applicants must be members of the Women Soaring Pilots Association (WSPA). They must be interested in a program of training for a private glider certificate or add-on rating. Along with their application, they must submit a 500-word essay explaining their goals and previous experiences as they relate to gliders and how this scholarship will help them meet their goals.

**Financial data** The stipend is $1,500.

**Duration** 1 year.

**Number awarded** 1 or more each year.

**Deadline** May of each year.

## [1384]
## MINISTRY TO WOMEN AWARD

Unitarian Universalist Association
Attn: UU Women's Federation
25 Beacon Street
Boston, MA 02108-2800
(617) 948-4692          Fax: (617) 742-2402
E-mail: uuwf@uua.org
Web: www.uuwf.org

**Summary** To recognize and reward significant actions that have improved the lot of women.

**Eligibility** Individuals or organizations that have ministered to women in an outstanding manner are considered for this award. Originally, only non-Unitarian Universalists were eligible, but currently women who are UU members may be nominated.

**Financial data** The prize is a $1,000 honorarium, a citation, and travel expenses to the awards presentation.

**Duration** The award is presented annually.

**Additional information** This award was established in 1974.

**Number awarded** 1 each year.

**Deadline** Deadline not specified.

## [1385]
## MINNIE L. MAFFETT FELLOWSHIPS

Texas Business Women
Attn: Texas Business and Professional Women's
  Foundation
2637 Pine Springs Drive
Plano, TX 75093
(972) 822-1173    E-mail: info@texasbusinesswomen.org
Web: www.texasbpwfoundation.org/scholarships.php

**Summary** To provide financial assistance to women in Texas interested in studying or conducting research in a medical field.

**Eligibility** This program is open to 1) female graduates of Texas medical schools interested in postgraduate or research work; 2) women who have been awarded a Ph.D. degree from a Texas university and are doing research in a medical field; 3) women who need financial aid for the first year in establishing a family practice in a rural area of Texas with a population of less than 5,000; and 4) fourth-year female medical students who are completing an M.D. or D.O. degree at an accredited medical school in Texas.

**Financial data** The stipend recently was $1,500.

**Duration** 1 year; nonrenewable.

**Additional information** This program began in 1948 when Texas Business Women was named Texas Federation of Business and Professional Women's Clubs.

**Number awarded** Varies each year; recently, 3 of these fellowships were awarded.

**Deadline** December of each year.

## [1386]
## MISS LATINA WORLD

Dawn Rochelle Models Agency
129 South Tennessee Street
McKinney, TX 75069
(469) 396-5670    E-mail: contact@dawnrochelle.com
Web: www.misslatina.com

**Summary** To recognize and reward young Latina women who compete in a national beauty pageant.

**Eligibility** This program is open to women between 18 and 28 years of age who are at least 25% Hispanic. Applicants may be single, married, or divorced, and they may have children. They appear in a nationally-televised pageant where selection is based on 3 categories: beauty/evening gown, fashion wear, and photogenic. Judges also interview each participant; the interview score may replace the fashion wear score. Height and weight are not factors, but contestants should be proportionate. Pageant experience and fluency in Spanish are not required.

**Financial data** Each year, prizes vary. The overall winner receives a $5,000 cash award.

**Duration** The pageant is held annually.

**Number awarded** 1 overall winner is selected each year.

**Deadline** April of each year.

## [1387]
## MONTICELLO COLLEGE FOUNDATION FELLOWSHIP FOR WOMEN

Newberry Library
Attn: Committee on Awards
60 West Walton Street
Chicago, IL 60610-3305
(312) 255-3666              Fax: (312) 255-3513
E-mail: research@newberry.org
Web: www.newberry.org/long-term-fellowships

**Summary** To provide funding to women who wish to conduct postdoctoral research at the Newberry Library.

**Eligibility** This program is open to women at the early stages (pre-tenure) of their academic career. Applicants must be interested in conducting research in a field appropriate to the collections of the library. Preference is given to proposals particularly concerned with the study of women.

**Financial data** The maximum stipend is $4,200 per month.

**Duration** 4 to 6 months.

**Additional information** Nearly all of the Newberry's 1 million volumes and 5 million manuscripts relate to the history of western Europe and the Americas. Fellows are expected to participate actively in the Newberry's scholarly community.

**Number awarded** 1 or more each year.

**Deadline** November of each year.

## [1388]
## MYRNA F. BERNATH BOOK AWARD

Society for Historians of American Foreign Relations
c/o Ohio State University
Department of History
106 Dulles Hall
230 West 17th Avenue
Columbus, OH 43210
(614) 292-1951              Fax: (614) 292-2282
E-mail: shafr@osu.edu
Web: www.shafr.org/members/prizes

**Summary** To recognize and reward outstanding books written by women on U.S. foreign relations.

**Eligibility** Eligible to be considered for this award are books written by women on U.S. foreign relations, transnational history, international history, peace studies, cultural interchange, and defense or strategic studies that were published during the previous 2 years. Authors or publishers should submit 5 copies of books that meet these requirements. Nominees must be members of the Society for Historians of American Foreign Relations. Selection is based on the book's contribution to scholarship.

**Financial data** The award is $2,500.

**Duration** The award is offered biennially.

**Additional information** This award was first presented in 1991.

**Number awarded** 1 each even-numbered year.

**Deadline** November of each odd-numbered year.

## [1389]
## MYRNA F. BERNATH FELLOWSHIP AWARD

Society for Historians of American Foreign Relations
c/o Ohio State University
Department of History
106 Dulles Hall
230 West 17th Avenue
Columbus, OH 43210
(614) 292-1951                    Fax: (614) 292-2282
E-mail: shafr@osu.edu
Web: www.shafr.org/members/fellowships-grants

**Summary**   To provide funding to women who are members of the Society for Historians of American Foreign Relations (SHAFR) and interested in conducting research on the history of U.S. foreign relations.

**Eligibility**   This program is open to women at U.S. universities who wish to conduct historically-based research in the United States or abroad and to women from other countries who wish to conduct research in the United States. The proposed study should focus on U.S. foreign relations, transnational history, international history, peace studies, cultural interchange, or defense or strategic studies. Preference is given to applications from graduate students and those who completed their Ph.D. within the past 5 years. Applicants must submit a curriculum vitae, a letter of intent, and a detailed research proposal that discusses the sources to be consulted and their value, the funds needed, and the plan for spending those funds.

**Financial data**   The grant is $5,000.

**Duration**   The grant is presented biennially, in odd-numbered years.

**Additional information**   This grant was first presented in 1992.

**Number awarded**   1 each odd-numbered year.

**Deadline**   September of each even-numbered year.

## [1390]
## NATIONAL CENTER FOR ATMOSPHERIC RESEARCH POSTDOCTORAL APPOINTMENTS

National Center for Atmospheric Research
Attn: Advanced Study Program
3090 Center Green Drive
P.O. Box 3000
Boulder, CO 80307-3000
(303) 497-1601                    Fax: (303) 497-1646
E-mail: paulad@ucar.edu
Web: www.asp.ucar.edu/pdfp/pd_announcement.php

**Summary**   To provide funding to recent Ph.D.s (especially women and minorities) who wish to conduct research at the National Center for Atmospheric Research (NCAR) in Boulder, Colorado.

**Eligibility**   This program is open to recent Ph.D.s and Sc.D.s in applied mathematics, chemistry, engineering, and physics as well as specialists in atmospheric sciences from such disciplines as biology, economics, geography, geology, and science education. Applicants must be interested in conducting research at the center in atmospheric sciences and global change. Selection is based on the applicant's scientific capability and potential, originality and independence, and the match between their interests and the research opportu-

nities at the center. Applications from women and minorities are encouraged.

**Financial data**   The stipend is $57,500 in the first year and $60,500 in the second year. Fellows also receive life and health insurance, an allowance of $750 for moving and storing personal belongings, and at least $3,500 for annual scientific travel support. a.

**Duration**   2 years.

**Additional information**   NCAR is operated by the University Corporation for Atmospheric Research (a consortium of 70 universities and research institutes) and sponsored by the National Science Foundation.

**Number awarded**   Varies; currently, up to 9 each year.

**Deadline**   January of each year.

## [1391]
## NATIONAL FEDERATION OF MUSIC CLUBS BIENNIAL YOUNG ARTIST AWARDS

National Federation of Music Clubs
1646 Smith Valley Road
Greenwood, IN 46142
(317) 882-4003                    Fax: (317) 882-4019
E-mail: info@nfmc-music.org
Web: nfmc-music.org

**Summary**   To recognize and reward outstanding young musicians (female singers are considered separately) who are members of the National Federation of Music Clubs (NFMC).

**Eligibility**   Vocalists must be between 25 and 36 years of age; instrumentalists must be between 18 and 29. Competitions are held in 4 categories: women's voice, men's voice, piano, and strings. Membership in the federation and U.S. citizenship are required.

**Financial data**   Awards are $15,000 for first, $2,000 for second, and $1,000 for third in each category.

**Duration**   The competition is held biennially, in odd-numbered years.

**Additional information**   Musicians who enter this competition are also automatically considered for a number of supplemental awards. There is a $50 entry fee for each category.

**Number awarded**   12 every other year: 3 in each of the 4 categories.

**Deadline**   January of odd-numbered years.

## [1392]
## NATIONAL URBAN FELLOWS PROGRAM

National Urban Fellows, Inc.
Attn: Program Director
989 Avenue of the Americas, Suite 400
New York, NY 10018
(212) 730-1700                    Fax: (212) 730-1823
E-mail: info@nuf.org
Web: www.nuf.org/fellows-overview

**Summary**   To provide mid-career public sector professionals, especially women and minorities, with an opportunity to strengthen leadership skills through a master's degree program coupled with a mentorship.

**Eligibility**   This program is open to U.S. citizens who have a bachelor's degree, have at least 3 years of administrative or managerial experience, have demonstrated exceptional ability and leadership potential, meet academic admission requirements, have a high standard of integrity and work ethic, and are committed to the solution of urban problems. Applicants must a 1,000-word autobiographical statement and a 1,000-word statement on their career goals. They may be of any racial or ethnic background, but the program's goal is to increase the number of competent administrators from underrepresented ethnic and cultural groups at all levels of public and private urban management organizations. Semifinalists are interviewed.

**Financial data** The stipend is $25,000. The program also provides full payment of tuition, a relocation allowance of $500, a book allowance of $500, and reimbursement for program-related travel.

**Duration** 14 months.

**Additional information** The program begins with a summer semester of study at Bernard M. Baruch College of the City University of New York. Following this, fellows spend 9 months in mentorship assignments with a senior administrator in a government agency, a major nonprofit, or a foundation. The final summer is spent in another semester of study at Baruch College. Fellows who successfully complete all requirements are granted a master's of public administration from that college. A $75 processing fee must accompany each application.

**Number awarded** Varies; approximately 40 each year.

**Deadline** February of each year.

## [1393]
## NCAA ETHNIC MINORITY AND WOMEN'S INTERNSHIP GRANT PROGRAM

National Collegiate Athletic Association
Attn: Office for Diversity and Inclusion
700 West Washington Street
P.O. Box 6222
Indianapolis, IN 46206-6222
(317) 917-6222          Fax: (317) 917-6888
E-mail: kdavis@ncaa.org
Web: www.ncaa.org

**Summary** To provide work experience at Division III institutions of the National Collegiate Athletic Association (NCAA) to women or minority college graduates.

**Eligibility** This program is open to women and ethnic minorities who have completed the requirements for an undergraduate degree. Applicants must have demonstrated a commitment to prepare for a career in intercollegiate athletics and the ability to succeed in such a career. They must be selected by an NCAA Division III college or university to work full time in athletics administration.

**Financial data** Grants provide $20,100 per year as a stipend for the intern and $3,000 to cover the cost of attendance at professional development activities.

**Duration** 2 years.

**Number awarded** Up to 15 each year.

**Deadline** February of each year.

## [1394]
## NELL I. MONDY FELLOWSHIP

Sigma Delta Epsilon-Graduate Women in Science, Inc.
c/o Laurie B. Cook, Fellowships Coordinator
The College at Brockport, State University of New York
Biology Department, 217 Lennon Hall
350 New Campus Drive
Brockport, NY 14420
(585) 395-5757     E-mail: fellowshipsquestions@gwis.org
Web: gwis.org/national-fellowships-program

**Summary** To provide funding to women interested in conducting research anywhere in the world in food science or nutrition.

**Eligibility** This program is open to women from any country currently enrolled as a graduate student, engaged in postdoctoral research, or holding a junior faculty position. Applicants must be interested in conducting research anywhere in the world in food science or nutrition. Along with their application, they must submit 2-paragraph essays on 1) how the proposed research relates to their degree program and/or career development; 2) initiatives in which they are participating to promote the careers of scientists, particularly women, within their institution, program, or peer group; and 3) relevant personal factors, including financial need, that should be considered in evaluating their proposal. Appointments are made without regard to race, religion, nationality, creed, national origin, sexual orientation, or age. Membership in Sigma Delta Epsilon-Graduate Women in Science (SDE-GWIS) is encouraged.

**Financial data** The maximum grant is $10,000. Funds may be used for such research expenses as expendable supplies, small equipment, publication of research findings, travel and subsistence while performing field studies, or travel to another laboratory for collaborative research. They may not be used for tuition, child care, travel to professional meetings or to begin a new appointment, administrative overhead or indirect costs, personal computers, living allowances, or equipment for general use.

**Duration** 1 year.

**Additional information** This fellowship was first awarded in 2002. Non-members of SDE-GWIS must pay an application fee of $50.

**Number awarded** Varies each year; recently, 2 of these grants were awarded.

**Deadline** January of each year.

## [1395]
## NEW PILOT AWARDS

Ninety-Nines, Inc.
4300 Amelia Earhart Road, Suite A
Oklahoma City, OK 73159
(405) 685-7969          Toll Free: (800) 994-1929
Fax: (405) 685-7985     E-mail: AEChair@ninety-nines.org
Web: www.ninety-nines.org/index.cfm/scholarships.htm

**Summary** To provide financial support to associate members of the Ninety-Nines (an organization of women pilots) who are interested in earning a private pilot certificate.

**Eligibility** This program is open to women who are associate members of the organization, have a current medical certificate, have log book entries showing at least 20 hours of flight time, have soloed, have passed the private pilot written test, meet all requirements specific to the country where training will occur, and are able to demonstrate financial need. Applicants must be interested in taking flight training for a private pilot certificate. They must be nominated by their chapter. Each chapter is allowed 1 applicant and an alternate.

**Financial data**   The maximum stipend is $2,000.

**Duration**   The training must be completed within 1 year.

**Additional information**   Recipients must agree to become a full member of the Ninety-Nines upon earning their private pilot certificate.

**Number awarded**   Varies each year; recently, 5 of these scholarships were awarded.

**Deadline**   Applications must be submitted to the chapter scholarship chair by November of each year.

## [1396]
## NOAA SMALL BUSINESS INNOVATION RESEARCH GRANTS

National Oceanic and Atmospheric Administration
Office of Research and Technology Applications
Attn: SBIR Program Manager
1335 East-West Highway, SSMC1, Room 106
Silver Spring, MD 20910-3284
(301) 713-3565                    Fax: (301) 713-4100
E-mail: Kelly.Wright@noaa.gov
Web: www.oar.noaa.gov/orta

**Summary**   To support small businesses (especially those owned by women and minorities) that have the technological experience to contribute to the research and development mission of the National Oceanic and Atmospheric Administration (NOAA).

**Eligibility**   For the purposes of this program, a "small business" is defined as a firm that is organized for profit with a location in the United States; is in the legal form of an individual proprietorship, partnership, limited liability company, corporation, joint venture, association, trust, or cooperative; is at least 51% owned and controlled by 1 or more individuals who are citizens or permanent residents of the United States; and has (including its affiliates) fewer than 500 employees. The primary employment of the principal investigator must be with the firm at the time of award and during the conduct of the proposed project. Applications are encouraged rom 1) women-owned small business concerns, defined as those that are at least 51% owned by a woman or women who also control and operate them; and 2) socially and economically disadvantaged small business concerns that are at least 51% owned by an Indian tribe, a Native Hawaiian organization, or 1 or more socially and economically disadvantaged individuals (African Americans, Hispanic Americans, Native Americans, Asian Pacific Americans, or subcontinent Asian Americans). Current priority areas of research include: 1) resilient coastal communities and economics; 2) healthy oceans; 3) climate adaptation and mitigation; or 4) weather-ready nation. Selection is based on the technical approach and anticipated agency and commercial benefits that may be derived from the research (25 points); the adequacy of the proposed effort and its relationship to the fulfillment of the requirements of the research topic (20 points); the soundness and technical merit of the proposed approach and its incremental progress towards topic solution (20 points); qualifications of the principal investigators, supporting staff, and consultants (15 points); and the proposal's commercial potential (20 points).

**Financial data**   Grants are offered in 2 phases. In phase 1, awards normally do not exceed $95,000 (for both direct and indirect costs); in phase 2, awards normally do not exceed $400,000 (including both direct and indirect costs).

**Duration**   Phase 1 awards may extend up to 6 months; phase 2 awards may extend up to 2 years.

**Number awarded**   Varies each year; recently, NOAA planned to award 15 Phase 1 contracts. Approximately half of Phase 1 awardees receive Phase 2 awards.

**Deadline**   January of each year.

## [1397]
## NOVICE RESEARCHER AWARD

Association of Women's Health, Obstetric and Neonatal Nurses
Attn: Research Grants Program
2000 L Street, N.W., Suite 740
Washington, DC 20036
(202) 261-2431          Toll Free: (800) 673-8499, ext. 2431
Fax: (202) 728-0575
E-mail: ResearchPrograms@awhonn.org
Web: www.awhonn.org

**Summary**   To provide funding for small research projects to members of the Association of Women's Health, Obstetric and Neonatal Nurses (AWHONN) who qualify as novice researchers.

**Eligibility**   This program is open to members of the association who have at least a master's degree or are currently enrolled in a master's program and completing a thesis or clinical research project. Applicants must be interested in beginning areas of study, investigating clinical issues, and/or launching a pilot study. They must identify a senior researcher who has agreed to serve as mentor and who submits a letter of support describing the role he or she will be implementing.

**Financial data**   The grant is $5,000. Funds may not be used for indirect costs, tuition, computer hardware or printers, conference attendance, or salary for the principal investigator or other investigators.

**Duration**   1 year.

**Number awarded**   1 each year.

**Deadline**   November of each year.

## [1398]
## NSF SMALL BUSINESS INNOVATION RESEARCH GRANTS

National Science Foundation
Directorate for Engineering
Attn: Division of Industrial Innovation and Partnerships
4201 Wilson Boulevard, Room 590 N
Arlington, VA 22230
(703) 292-8050                    Fax: (703) 292-9057
TDD: (800) 281-8749
Web: www.nsf.gov/eng/iip/spir

**Summary**   To provide funding to small and creative engineering, science, education, and technology-related firms (particularly those that are owned by women or minorities) to conduct innovative, high-risk research on scientific and technical problems.

**Eligibility**   For the purposes of this program, a "small business" is defined as a firm that is organized for profit with a location in the United States; is in the legal form of an individual proprietorship, partnership, limited liability company, corporation, joint venture, association, trust, or cooperative; is at least 51% owned and controlled by 1 or more individuals who are citizens or permanent residents of the United States; and has (including its affiliates) fewer than 500 employees. The primary employment of the principal investigator must be with the firm at the time of award and during the conduct of the proposed project. Applications are encouraged from 1) women-owned small business concerns, defined as those that are at least 51% owned by a woman or women who also control and operate them; and 2) socially and economically disadvantaged small business concerns that are at least 51% owned by an Indian tribe, a Native Hawaiian organization, or 1 or more socially and economically disadvantaged individuals (African Americans, Hispanic Americans, Native Americans, Asian Pacific Americans, or subcontinent Asian Americans). Current priorities for critical technology areas of national importance include 1) biological and chemical technologies; 2) education applications; 3) electronics, information and communication technologies; and 4) nanotechnology, advanced materials, and manufacturing. Selection is based on the intellectual merit and the broader impacts of the proposed activity.

**Financial data**  Support is offered in 2 phases. In phase 1, awards normally may not exceed $150,000 (for both direct and indirect costs); in phase 2, awards normally may not exceed $500,000 (including both direct and indirect costs).

**Duration**  Phase 1 awards may extend up to 6 months; phase 2 awards may extend up to 2 years.

**Number awarded**  Depends on the availability of funds; the National Science Foundation (NSF) plans to award approximately 100 phase 1 grants each year; recently, $15 million was budgeted for this program.

**Deadline**  June of each year.

## [1399]
## NSF SMALL BUSINESS TECHNOLOGY TRANSFER GRANTS

National Science Foundation
Directorate for Engineering
Attn: Division of Industrial Innovation and Partnerships
4201 Wilson Boulevard, Room 590 N
Arlington, VA 22230
(703) 292-8050                          Fax: (703) 292-9057
TDD: (800) 281-8749
Web: www.nsf.gov/eng/iip/spir

**Summary**  To provide financial support to cooperative research and development projects carried out between small business concerns (particularly those owned by women or minorities) and research institutions in areas of concern to the National Science Foundation (NSF).

**Eligibility**  For the purposes of this program, a "small business" is defined as a firm that is organized for profit with a location in the United States; is in the legal form of an individual proprietorship, partnership, limited liability company, corporation, joint venture, association, trust, or cooperative; is at least 51% owned and controlled by 1 or more individuals who are citizens or permanent residents of the United States; and has (including its affiliates) fewer than 500 employees. Unlike the NSF Small Business Innovation Research Grants, the primary employment of the principal investigator does not need

to be with the business concern. This program, however, requires that the small business apply in collaboration with a nonprofit research institution for conduct of a project that has potential for commercialization. Principal investigators from the nonprofit research institution must commit at least 10% of their effort to the project. At least 40% of the work must be performed by the small business and at least 30% of the work must be performed by the research institution. Applications are encouraged from 1) women-owned small business concerns, defined as those that are at least 51% owned by a woman or women who also control and operate them; and 2) socially and economically disadvantaged small business concerns that are at least 51% owned by an Indian tribe, a Native Hawaiian organization, or 1 or more socially and economically disadvantaged individuals (African Americans, Hispanic Americans, Native Americans, Asian Pacific Americans, or subcontinent Asian Americans). Recently, the program was accepting applications only for the topic area of enhancing access to the radio spectrum; previous topics have included 1) advanced materials, chemical technology and manufacturing; 2) biotechnology; 3) electronics; 4) information technology; and 5) emerging opportunities (projects with a focus on near-term commercialization). Selection is based on the intellectual merit and the broader impacts of the proposed activity.

**Financial data**  In the first phase, annual awards may not exceed $150,000 for direct costs, indirect costs, and negotiated fixed fees. In the second phase, awards up to $500,000 are available.

**Duration**  Normally, 12 months for phase 1 and 2 years for phase 2.

**Additional information**  Grants in the first phase are to determine the scientific, technical, and commercial merit and feasibility of the proposed cooperative effort and the quality of performance of the small business concern. In the second phase, the research and development efforts continue, depending on the results of the first phase.

**Number awarded**  35 phase 1 grants are awarded each year. Approximately one-third of phase 1 awardees receive phase 2 grants. Approximately $5,250,000 is budgeted for this program each year.

**Deadline**  December of each year.

## [1400]
## NUPUR CHAUDHURI FIRST ARTICLE PRIZE

Coordinating Council for Women in History
c/o Sandra Dawson, Executive Director
Northern Illinois University
Department of History and Women's Studies
715 Zulauf Hall
DeKalb, IL 60115
(815) 895-2624                  E-mail: execdir@theccwh.org
Web: theccwh.org/ccwh-awards

**Summary**  To recognize and reward members of the Coordinating Council for Women in History (CCWH) who have published outstanding first articles in an historical journal.

**Eligibility**  This award is available to CCWH members who have published an article in a refereed journal during the preceding 2 years. The article must be the first published by the candidate and must have full scholarly apparatus. All fields of history are eligible.

**Financial data**  The award is $1,000.

**Duration**  The award is presented annually.

**Additional information** This award was established in 2010.

**Number awarded** 1 each year.

**Deadline** September of each year.

## [1401]
## NWSA/UNIVERSITY OF ILLINOIS PRESS FIRST BOOK PRIZE

National Women's Studies Association
Attn: Book Prizes
11 East Mount Royal Avenue, Suite 100
Baltimore, MD 21202
(410) 528-0355                 Fax: (410) 528-0357
E-mail: awards@nwsa.org
Web: www.nwsa.org/content.asp?pl=16&contentid=16

**Summary** To recognize and reward members of the National Women's Studies Association (NWSA) who submit outstanding manuscripts in the field of women's and gender studies.

**Eligibility** This award is available to NWSA members who submit a manuscript of a dissertation or first book. Entries should reflect cutting-edge intersectional feminist scholarship, whether historical or contemporary.

**Financial data** The award includes publication by the University of Illinois Press and a $1,000 advance against royalties.

**Duration** The award is presented annually.

**Additional information** This award was first presented in 2011.

**Number awarded** 1 each year.

**Deadline** May of each year.

## [1402]
## OHIO STATE UNIVERSITY BYRD FELLOWSHIP PROGRAM

Ohio State University
Byrd Polar Research Center
Attn: Fellowship Committee
Scott Hall Room 108
1090 Carmack Road
Columbus, OH 43210-1002
(614) 292-6531                 Fax: (614) 292-4697
Web: bprc.osu.edu/byrdfellow

**Summary** To provide funding to postdoctorates (particularly women and others from diverse backgrounds) who are interested in conducting research on the Arctic or Antarctic areas at Ohio State University.

**Eligibility** This program is open to postdoctorates of superior academic background who are interested in conducting advanced research on either Arctic or Antarctic problems at the Byrd Polar Research Center at Ohio State University. Applicants must have received their doctorates within the past 5 years. Along with their application, they must submit a description of the specific research to be conducted during the fellowship and a curriculum vitae. Women, minorities, Vietnam-era veterans, disabled veterans, and individuals with disabilities are particularly encouraged to apply.

**Financial data** The stipend is $42,000 per year; an allowance of $5,000 for research and travel is also provided.

**Duration** 18 months.

**Additional information** This program was established by a major gift from the Byrd Foundation in memory of Rear Admiral Richard Evelyn Byrd and Marie Ames Byrd, his wife. Except for field work or other research activities requiring absence from campus, fellows are expected to be in residence at the university for the duration of the program.

**Deadline** March of each year.

## [1403]
## ONLINE BIBLIOGRAPHIC SERVICES/ TECHNICAL SERVICES JOINT RESEARCH GRANT

American Association of Law Libraries
Attn: Online Bibliographic Services Special Interest
  Section
105 West Adams Street, Suite 3300
Chicago, IL 60603
(312) 939-4764                 Fax: (312) 431-1097
E-mail: aallhq@aall.org
Web: www.aallnet.org/sis/obssis/research/funding.htm

**Summary** To provide funding to members of the American Association of Law Libraries (AALL), particularly women and minorities, who are interested in conducting a research project related to technical services.

**Eligibility** This program is open to AALL members who are technical services law librarians. Preference is given to members of the Online Bibliographic Services and Technical Services Special Interest Sections, although members of other special interest sections are eligible if their work relates to technical services law librarianship. Applicants must be interested in conducting research that will enhance technical services law librarianship. Women and minorities are especially encouraged to apply. Preference is given to projects that can be completed in the United States or Canada, although foreign research projects are given consideration.

**Financial data** Grants range up to $1,000.

**Duration** 1 year.

**Number awarded** 1 or more each year.

**Deadline** March or September of each year.

## [1404]
## OREGON LITERARY FELLOWSHIPS TO WOMEN WRITERS

Literary Arts, Inc.
Attn: Oregon Book Awards and Fellowships Program
  Coordinator
925 S.W. Washington Street
Portland, OR 97205
(503) 227-2583                 Fax: (503) 243-1167
E-mail: susan@literary-arts.org
Web: www.literary-arts.org/oba-home

**Summary** To provide funding to women writers in Oregon interested in working on a literary project.

**Eligibility** This program is open to women who are residents of Oregon and interested in initiating, developing, or completing a literary project in the areas of poetry, fiction, literary nonfiction, drama, or young readers' literature. Priority is given to women whose writing explores race, ethnicity, class, physical disability, and/or sexual orientation. Writers in the early stages of their careers are especially encouraged to apply. Selection is based primarily on literary merit.

**Financial data** Grants are at least $2,500.

**Duration** The grants are presented annually.

**Additional information** Funding for this program is provided by the Ralph L. Smith Foundation.

**Number awarded** 1 each year.

**Deadline** June of each year.

## [1405]
## OTTOLINE MORRELL PRIZE

Fence Books
Attn: Prizes
University at Albany
Science Library 320
1400 Washington Avenue
Albany, NY 12222-0100
(518) 591-8162                 E-mail: fence@albany.edu
Web: www.fenceportal.org/?page_id=44

**Summary** To recognize and reward outstanding books of poetry by women.

**Eligibility** Women who are writing poetry in English are invited to submit an unpublished manuscript (48 to 80 pages). They must have published 1 or more books of poetry previously. Translations are not accepted.

**Financial data** The prize has been $5,000 and publication of the winning manuscript by Fence Books.

**Duration** The competition is held annually.

**Additional information** This prize was known from 2001 through 2006 as the Alberta Prize and from 2008 through 2013 as the Motherwell Prize. Its current name became effective in 2014. There is a $25 entry fee.

**Number awarded** 1 each year.

**Deadline** November of each year.

## [1406]
## PAUL HOCH DISTINGUISHED SERVICE AWARD

American College of Neuropsychopharmacology
Attn: Executive Office
5034-A Thoroughbred Lane
Brentwood, TN 37027
(615) 324-2360                 Fax: (615) 523-1715
E-mail: acnp@acnp.org
Web: www.acnp.org/programs/awards.aspx

**Summary** To recognize and reward female, minority, and other members of the American College of Neuropsychopharmacology (ACNP) who have contributed outstanding service to the organization.

**Eligibility** This award is available to ACNP members who have made unusually significant contributions to the College. The emphasis of the award is on service to the organization, not on teaching, clinical, or research accomplishments. Any member or fellow of ACNP may nominate another member. Nomination of women and minorities is highly encouraged.

**Financial data** The award consists of an expense-paid trip to the ACNP annual meeting, a monetary honorarium, and a plaque.

**Duration** The award is presented annually.

**Additional information** This award was first presented in 1965.

**Number awarded** 1 each year.

**Deadline** Nominations must be submitted by June of each year.

## [1407]
## PAULA DE MERIEUX RHEUMATOLOGY FELLOWSHIP AWARD

American College of Rheumatology
Attn: Research and Education Foundation
2200 Lake Boulevard N.E.
Atlanta, GA 30319
(404) 633-3777                 Fax: (404) 633-1870
E-mail: ref@rheumatology.org
Web: www.rheumatology.org/ref/awards/index.asp

**Summary** To provide funding to women and underrepresented minorities interested in a program of training for a career providing clinical care to people affected by rheumatic diseases.

**Eligibility** This program is open to trainees at ACGME-accredited institutions. Applications must be submitted by the training program director at the institution who is responsible for selection and appointment of trainees. The program must train and prepare fellows to provide clinical care to those affected by rheumatic diseases. Trainees must be women or members of underrepresented minority groups, defined as Black Americans, Hispanics, and Native Americans (Native Hawaiians, Alaska Natives, and American Indians). They must be U.S. citizens, nationals, or permanent residents. Selection is based on the institution's pass rate of rheumatology fellows, publication history of staff and previous fellows, current positions of previous fellows, and status of clinical faculty.

**Financial data** The grant is $25,000 per year, to be used as salary for the trainee. Other trainee costs (e.g., fees, health insurance, travel, attendance at scientific meetings) are to be incurred by the recipient's institutional program. Supplemental or additional support to offset the cost of living may be provided by the grantee institution.

**Duration** Up to 1 year.

**Additional information** This fellowship was first awarded in 2005.

**Number awarded** 1 each year.

**Deadline** July of each year.

## [1408]
## PEARSON EARLY CAREER GRANT

American Psychological Foundation
750 First Street, N.E.
Washington, DC 20002-4242
(202) 336-5843                 Fax: (202) 336-5812
E-mail: foundation@apa.org
Web: www.apa.org/apf/funding/pearson.aspx

**Summary** To provide funding to early career psychologists (especially women, minorities, and individuals with disabilities) who are interested in conducting a project in an area of critical society need.

**Eligibility** This program is open to psychologists who have an Ed.D., Psy.D., or Ph.D. from an accredited experience and no more than 7 years of postdoctoral experience. Applicants must be interested in conducting a project to improve areas of critical need in society, including (but not limited to) innovative scientifically-based clinical work with serious mental illness, serious emotional disturbance, incarcerated or homeless individuals, children with serious emotional disturbance (SED), or adults with serious mental illness (SMI). The sponsor encourages applications from individuals who represent diversity in race, ethnicity, gender, age, disability, and sexual orientation.

**Financial data**  The grant is $12,000.

**Duration**  1 year.

**Additional information**  This grant was first awarded in 2010.

**Number awarded**  1 each year.

**Deadline**  December of each year.

## [1409]
## PEMBROKE CENTER POSTDOCTORAL FELLOWSHIPS

Brown University
Attn: Pembroke Center for Teaching and Research on Women
172 Meeting Street
Box 1958
Providence, RI 02912
(401) 863-2643                    Fax: (401) 863-1298
E-mail: Pembroke_Center@brown.edu
Web: www.brown.edu

**Summary**  To provide funding to postdoctoral scholars interested in conducting research on the cross-cultural study of gender at Brown University's Pembroke Center for Teaching and Research on Women.

**Eligibility**  Fellowships are open to scholars in relevant fields who have completed their Ph.D. but do not have a tenured position at an American college or university. Applicants must be willing to spend a year in residence at the Pembroke Center for Teaching and Research on Women and participate in a research project related to gender and/or sexuality. The project focuses on a theme that changes annually (recently: "Aesthetics and the Question of Beauty"). The center encourages underrepresented minority and international scholars to apply.

**Financial data**  The stipend is $50,000. Health insurance is also provided.

**Duration**  1 academic year.

**Additional information**  Postdoctoral fellows in residence participate in weekly seminars and present at least 2 public papers during the year, as well as conduct an individual research project. Supplementary funds are available for assistance with travel expenses from abroad. This program includes the following named fellowships: the Nancy L. Buc Postdoctoral Fellowship, the Artemis A.W. and Martha Joukowsky Postdoctoral Fellowship, and the Carol G. Lederer Postdoctoral Fellowship.

**Number awarded**  3 or 4 each year.

**Deadline**  December of each year.

## [1410]
## P.E.O. PROGRAM FOR CONTINUING EDUCATION

P.E.O. Sisterhood
Attn: Executive Office
3700 Grand Avenue
Des Moines, IA 50312-2899
(515) 255-3153                    Fax: (515) 255-3820
Web: www.peointernational.org/peo-projectsphilanthropies

**Summary**  To provide financial assistance to mature women interested in resuming or continuing their academic or technical education.

**Eligibility**  This program is open to mature women who are citizens of the United States or Canada and have experienced an interruption in their education that has lasted at least 24 consecutive months during their adult life. Applicants are frequently single parents who must acquire marketable skills to support their families. They must be within 2 years of completing an academic or technical course of study and be sponsored by a local P.E.O. chapter. Students enrolled in a doctoral degree program are not eligible.

**Financial data**  The maximum stipend is $3,000.

**Duration**  1 year; nonrenewable.

**Additional information**  This program was established in 1973 by the Women's Philanthropic Educational Organization (P.E.O.).

**Number awarded**  Varies each year; for a recent biennium, 3,242 of these awards, with a total value of nearly $4.3 million, were granted.

**Deadline**  Applications may be submitted at any time.

## [1411]
## PI BETA PHI ALUMNAE CONTINUING EDUCATION SCHOLARSHIPS

Pi Beta Phi
Attn: Pi Beta Phi Foundation
1154 Town and Country Commons Drive
Town and Country, MO 63017
(636) 256-1357                    Fax: (636) 256-8124
E-mail: fndn@pibetaphi.org
Web: www.pibetaphifoundation.org/programs/scholarships

**Summary**  To provide financial assistance for graduate school or continuing education to alumnae of Pi Beta Phi.

**Eligibility**  This program is open to women who are members of Pi Beta Phi in good standing and have paid their alumnae dues for the current year. Applicants must have been out of undergraduate school for at least 2 years and have a GPA of 3.0 or higher for all undergraduate and graduate study. Advanced work at a college or university is encouraged, but advanced study at a career, vocational, or technical school will also be considered. Along with their application, they must submit documentation of financial need, an employment history, a record of volunteer service, a description of the proposed program of study, transcripts, and recommendations. Selection is based on financial need, academic record, alumnae service, community service, and how the proposed course of study relates to future career development.

**Financial data**  Stipends range from $1,200 to $1,800.

**Duration**  1 year.

**Additional information**  This program began in 1982.

**Number awarded** Varies each year; recently, 4 of these scholarships were awarded.

**Deadline** February of each year.

## [1412]
## POSTDOCTORAL FELLOWSHIP IN THE HISTORY OF MODERN SCIENCE AND TECHNOLOGY IN EAST ASIA

Harvard University
Attn: Department of East Asian Languages and
 Civilizations
2 Divinity Avenue
Cambridge, MA 02138
(617) 495-2754                    Fax: (617) 496-6040
E-mail: ealc@fas.harvard.edu
Web: harvardealc.org/postdoc.html

**Summary** To provide funding to postdoctoral scholars (particularly women and minorities) who wish to conduct research at Harvard University on a topic related to the history of science and technology in east Asia.

**Eligibility** This program is open to junior scholars who completed a Ph.D. within the past 5 years. Applicants must be interested in conducting research in residence at Harvard University to revise their dissertation and prepare it for publication. Preference is given to research projects exploring the understudied histories of modern science and technology in Korea and Japan, but all proposals concerning the development of science and technology in post-19th century east Asia are eligible. Applicants from women and minority candidates are strongly encouraged.

**Financial data** The stipend is $43,000.

**Duration** 1 academic year.

**Additional information** Fellows are provided with office space and access to the libraries and resources of Harvard University. They are invited to participate in the academic life of the Departments of East Asian Languages and Civilizations and the History of Science. Fellows are expected to reside in the Cambridge/Boston area during the term of the fellowship; work on revising their dissertation for publication; teach or collaborate on a course related to the history of modern science and/or technology in east Asia; and give at least 1 presentation of research to faculty and graduate students in East Asian Languages and Civilizations and the History of Science.

**Number awarded** 1 each year.

**Deadline** February of each year.

## [1413]
## POSTDOCTORAL FELLOWSHIPS IN DIABETES RESEARCH

Juvenile Diabetes Research Foundation International
Attn: Grant Administrator
26 Broadway, 14th Floor
New York, NY 10004
(212) 479-7572              Toll Free: (800) 533-CURE
Fax: (212) 785-9595          E-mail: info@jdrf.org
Web: jdrf.org

**Summary** To provide research training to scientists (particularly women, underrepresented minorities, and persons with disabilities) who are beginning their professional careers and are interested in participating in research training on the causes, treatment, prevention, or cure of diabetes or its complications.

**Eligibility** This program is open to postdoctorates who are interested in a career in Type 1 diabetes-relevant research. Applicants must have received their first doctoral degree (M.D., Ph.D., D.M.D., or D.V.M.) within the past 5 years and may not have a faculty appointment. There are no citizenship requirements. Applications are encouraged from women, members of minority groups underrepresented in the sciences, and people with disabilities. The proposed research training may be conducted at foreign or domestic, for-profit or nonprofit, or public or private institutions, including universities, colleges, hospitals, laboratories, units of state or local government, or eligible agencies of the federal government. Applicants must be sponsored by an investigator who is affiliated full time with an accredited institution and who agrees to supervise the applicant's training. Selection is based on the applicant's previous experience and academic record; the caliber of the proposed research; and the quality of the mentor, training program, and environment.

**Financial data** Stipends range from $44,764 to $59,680 per year (depending upon years of experience). In any case, the award may not exceed the salary the recipient is currently earning. Fellows also receive a research allowance of $5,500 per year.

**Duration** 3 years.

**Additional information** Fellows must devote 100% of their effort to the fellowship project.

**Number awarded** Varies each year.

**Deadline** August of each year.

## [1414]
## POSTDOCTORAL RESEARCH LEAVE FELLOWSHIPS

American Association of University Women
Attn: AAUW Educational Foundation
301 ACT Drive, Department 60
P.O. Box 4030
Iowa City, IA 52243-4030
(319) 337-1716, ext. 60            Fax: (319) 337-1204
E-mail: aauw@act.org
Web: www.aauw.org

**Summary** To enable American women who have achieved distinction or promise of distinction in their fields of scholarly work to engage in additional research.

**Eligibility** This program is open to women who have a research doctorate (e.g., Ph.D., Ed.D., D.B.A., D.M.) or an M.F.A. degree as of the application deadline. Applicants must be interested in conducting independent research; preference is given to projects that are not simply a revision of a doctoral dissertation. Fields of study include the arts and humanities, social sciences, and natural sciences. Selection is based on scholarly excellence, quality of project design, originality of project, scholarly significance of project to discipline, feasibility of project and proposed schedule, qualifications of applicant, potential of applicant to make a significant contribution to field, applicant's commitment to women's issues in profession and community, applicant's teaching experience, and applicant's mentoring of other women. U.S. citizenship or permanent resident status is required.

**Financial data** The stipend is $30,000. Funding is not provided for laboratory supplies and equipment, research assistants, publication costs, travel to professional meetings or seminars, tuition for additional course work, repayment of loans or other personal obligations, or tuition for a dependent's education.

**Duration** 1 year, beginning in July.

**Additional information** The filing fee is $45.

**Number awarded** Varies each year; recently, 12 of these fellowships were awarded.

**Deadline** November of each year.

## [1415]
## POSTDOCTORAL RESEARCH TRAINING FELLOWSHIPS IN EPILEPSY

Epilepsy Foundation
Attn: Research Department
8301 Professional Place
Landover, MD 20785-2353
(301) 459-3700                Toll Free: (800) EFA-1000
Fax: (301) 577-2684           TDD: (800) 332-2070
E-mail: grants@efa.org
Web: www.epilepsyfoundation.org

**Summary** To provide funding for a program of postdoctoral training to academic physicians and scientists (especially women, minorities, and persons with disabilities) who are committed to epilepsy research.

**Eligibility** Applicants must have a doctoral degree (M.D., Sc.D., Ph.D., or equivalent) and be a clinical or postdoctoral fellow at a university, medical school, research institution, or medical center. They must be interested in participating in a training experience and research project that has potential significance for understanding the causes, treatment, or consequences of epilepsy. The program is geared toward applicants who will be trained in research in epilepsy rather than those who use epilepsy as a tool for research in other fields. Equal consideration is given to applicants interested in acquiring experience either in basic laboratory research or in the conduct of human clinical studies. Academic faculty holding the rank of instructor or higher are not eligible, nor are graduate or medical students, medical residents, permanent government employees, or employees of private industry. Applications from women, members of minority groups, and people with disabilities are especially encouraged. U.S. citizenship is not required, but the project must be conducted in the United States. Selection is based on scientific quality of the proposed research, a statement regarding its relevance to epilepsy, the applicant's qualifications, the preceptor's qualifications, and the adequacy of facility and related epilepsy programs at the institution.

**Financial data** The grant is $45,000. No indirect costs are covered.

**Duration** 1 year.

**Additional information** Support for this program is provided by many individuals, families, and corporations, especially the American Epilepsy Society, Abbott Laboratories, Ortho-McNeil Pharmaceutical, and Pfizer Inc. The fellowship must be carried out at a facility in the United States where there is an ongoing epilepsy research program.

**Number awarded** Varies each year.

**Deadline** August of each year.

## [1416]
## PRACTICE ENRICHMENT TRAVELING FELLOWSHIP

Ruth Jackson Orthopaedic Society
6300 North River Road, Suite 727
Rosemont, IL 60018-4226
(847) 698-1626                Fax: (847) 823-0536
E-mail: rjos@aaos.org
Web: www.rjos.org/web/awards/index.htm

**Summary** To provide funding to female orthopedic surgeons who are interested in traveling to enhance their practice.

**Eligibility** This program is open to women who are members of the Ruth Jackson Orthopaedic Society (RJOS). Applicants must be Board Eligible orthopedic surgeons and citizens of the United States or Canada. They must be interested in a program of travel to learn new techniques or expand their sub-specialty interests.

**Financial data** Grants up to $6,000 are available.

**Additional information** Funding for this program is provided by Zimmer, Inc.

**Number awarded** 1 each year.

**Deadline** September of each year.

## [1417]
## PRIZE FOR A FACULTY MEMBER FOR RESEARCH IN AN UNDERGRADUATE INSTITUTION

American Physical Society
Attn: Honors Program
One Physics Ellipse
College Park, MD 20740-3844
(301) 209-3268                Fax: (301) 209-0865
E-mail: honors@aps.org
Web: www.aps.org

**Summary** To recognize and reward physics faculty (particularly women and underrepresented minorities) at undergraduate institutions.

**Eligibility** Nominees for this prize must be members of the physics faculty at undergraduate institutions. They must have contributed substantially to physics research and provided inspirational guidance and encouragement to undergraduate students participating in that research. Nominations of qualified women and members of underrepresented minority groups are especially encouraged.

**Financial data** The prize consists of a stipend of $5,000 to the recipient, a grant of $5,000 to the recipient's institution for research, a certificate citing the accomplishments of the recipient, and an allowance for travel expenses to the meeting of the American Physical Society (APS) at which the prize is presented.

**Duration** The prize is presented annually.

**Additional information** This prize was established in 1984 by a grant from the Research Corporation.

**Number awarded** 1 each year.

**Deadline** June of each year.

**[1418]**
## R. ROBERT & SALLY D. FUNDERBURG RESEARCH AWARD IN GASTRIC CANCER

American Gastroenterological Association
Attn: AGA Research Foundation
Research Awards Manager
4930 Del Ray Avenue
Bethesda, MD 20814-2512
(301) 222-4012                    Fax: (301) 654-5920
E-mail: awards@gastro.org
Web: www.gastro.org/aga-foundation/grants

**Summary**   To provide funding to established investigators (especially women and minorities) who are working on research that enhances fundamental understanding of gastric cancer pathobiology.

**Eligibility**   This program is open to faculty at accredited North American institutions who have established themselves as independent investigators in the field of gastric biology, pursuing novel approaches to gastric mucosal cell biology, including the fields of gastric mucosal cell biology, regeneration and regulation of cell growth, inflammation as precancerous lesions, genetics of gastric carcinoma, oncogenes in gastric epithelial malignancies, epidemiology of gastric cancer, etiology of gastric epithelial malignancies, or clinical research in diagnosis or treatment of gastric carcinoma. Applicants must be individual members of the American Gastroenterological Association (AGA). Women and minority investigators are strongly encouraged to apply. Selection is based on the novelty, feasibility, and significance of the proposal. Preference is given to novel approaches.

**Financial data**   The grant is $50,000 per year. Funds are to be used for the salary of the investigator. Indirect costs are not allowed.

**Duration**   2 years.

**Number awarded**   1 each year.

**Deadline**   August of each year.

**[1419]**
## RADCLIFFE INSTITUTE FELLOWSHIPS

Radcliffe Institute for Advanced Study at Harvard
  University
Attn: Fellowships Office
8 Garden Street
Cambridge, MA 02138
(617) 496-1324                    Fax: (617) 495-8136
E-mail: fellowships@radcliffe.edu
Web: www.radcliffe.harvard.edu

**Summary**   To provide funding to scholars, professionals, writers, and artists from around the world who are interested in working at the Radcliffe Institute for Advanced Study at Harvard University and are committed to the study of women, gender, and society.

**Eligibility**   These fellowships are open to scholars, professionals, artists, and writers of exceptional promise and demonstrated accomplishment who wish to pursue independent work in academic and professional fields and in the creative arts. Applicants must have received their doctorate or appropriate terminal degree at least 2 years prior to appointment or have achieved comparable professional achievement. Academicians must be working in the humanities, social sciences, natural sciences, or mathematics. Artists and writers may be working in fiction or nonfiction, poetry, playwriting, musical composition or performance, visual arts, or filmmaking. All applicants must submit supporting materials.

**Financial data**   The stipend is $70,000 per year. Fellows receive office or studio space and access to libraries and other resources of Harvard University.

**Duration**   1 academic year.

**Additional information**   This program began in 1960 as the Radcliffe Institute for Independent Study, a multidisciplinary program for women scholars, scientists, artists, and writers. That institute became the Mary Ingraham Bunting Institute within Radcliffe College in 1978 When that college officially merged with Harvard University in 1999, the Radcliffe Institute for Advanced Study was founded as a component of Harvard and remains 1 of the major postdoctoral research centers in the country. Although men are also eligible to apply for its fellowships, in recognition of Radcliffe's historic contributions to the education of women and to the study of issues related to women, it sustains a continuing commitment to the study of women, gender, and society. The fellows must be in residence in the Boston area during the fellowship year. They are expected to present their work-in-progress at a public colloquium, performance, or exhibition, and to attend other fellows' events.

**Number awarded**   Varies each year; recently, 52 of these fellowships were granted.

**Deadline**   September of each year for the humanities, social sciences, and creative arts; October of each year for natural science and mathematics.

**[1420]**
## RESEARCH AND TRAINING FELLOWSHIPS IN EPILEPSY FOR CLINICIANS

Epilepsy Foundation
Attn: Research Department
8301 Professional Place
Landover, MD 20785-2353
(301) 459-3700                    Toll Free: (800) EFA-1000
Fax: (301) 577-2684              TDD: (800) 332-2070
E-mail: grants@efa.org
Web: www.epilepsyfoundation.org

**Summary**   To provide funding to clinically-trained professionals (especially women, minorities, and persons with disabilities) who are interested in gaining additional training in order to develop an epilepsy research program.

**Eligibility**   Applicants must have an M.D., D.O., Ph.D., D.Sc., or equivalent degree and be a clinical or postdoctoral fellow at a university, medical school, or other appropriate research institution. Holders of other doctoral-level degrees (e.g., Pharm.D., D.S.N.) may also be eligible. Candidates must be interested in a program of research training that may include mechanisms of epilepsy, novel therapeutic approaches, clinical trials, development of new technologies, or behavioral and psychosocial impact of epilepsy. The training program may consist of both didactic training and a supervised research experience that is designed to develop the necessary knowledge and skills in the chosen area of research and foster the career goals of the candidate. Academic faculty holding the rank of instructor or higher are not eligible, nor are graduate or medical students, medical residents, permanent government employees, or employees of private industry. Applications from women, members of minority groups, and people with disabilities are especially encouraged. U.S. citizenship is not required, but the project must be conducted in the United States. Selection is based on the quality of the proposed research training program, the applicant's qualifications, the preceptor's qualifications, and the adequacy of clinical training, research facilities, and other epilepsy-related programs at the institution.

**Financial data**   The grant is $50,000 per year. No indirect costs are provided.

**Duration**   Up to 2 years.

**Additional information**   Support for this program is provided by many individuals, families, and corporations, especially the American Epilepsy Society, Abbott Laboratories, Ortho-McNeil Pharmaceutical, and Pfizer Inc. Grantees are expected to dedicate at least 50% of their time to research training and conducting research.

**Number awarded**   Varies each year.

**Deadline**   September of each year.

## [1421]
## RESEARCH GRANTS OF THE RESEARCH ON GENDER IN SCIENCE AND ENGINEERING PROGRAM

National Science Foundation
Directorate for Education and Human Resources
Attn: Division of Human Resource Development
4201 Wilson Boulevard, Room 815N
Arlington, VA 22230
(703) 292-7303                    Fax: (703) 292-9018
TDD: (800) 281-8749        E-mail: jjesse@nsf.gov
Web: www.nsf.gov/funding/pgm_summ.jsp?pims_id=5475

**Summary**   To provide funding to investigators interested in conducting research related to the underrepresentation of girls and women in science, technology, engineering, or mathematics (STEM) education.

**Eligibility**   This program is open to investigators interested in conducting research designed to 1) discover and describe gender-based differences and preferences in learning STEM at the K-16 levels and factors that affect interest, performance, and choice of STEM study and careers in fields where there are significant gender gaps; 2) discover and describe how experiences and interactions in informal and formal educational settings inhibit or encourage interest and performance of students based on gender; 3) increase the knowledge about organizational models that lead to more equitable and inviting STEM educational environments at the K-16 levels; or 4) increase knowledge of the process of institutional change required to achieve more equitable and inviting STEM educational environments at the K-16 levels. Behavioral, cognitive, affective, learning, and social differences may be investigated, using methods of sociology, psychology, anthropology, economics, statistics or other social and behavioral science and education disciplines. Gender should be the major variable in the analysis.

**Financial data**   Grants up to a total of $525,000 are available.

**Duration**   Up to 3 years.

**Additional information**   The National Science Foundation (NSF) established the Research on Gender in Science and Engineering (GSE) program in 1993 under the name "Program for Women and Girls." That was replaced with the "Program for Gender Equity in Science, Mathematics, Engineering and Technology," and then in the 2003 fiscal year by "Gender Diversity in STEM Education." The current title became effective in the 2007 fiscal year.

**Number awarded**   7 to 10 each year. The GSE program plans to award 15 to 22 grants per year for research, outreach and communication, and extension service activities. A total of $5,000,000 is available for the program annually.

**Deadline**   Letters of intent must be submitted in February of each year; full proposals are due in March.

## [1422]
## RESEARCH PROGRAM AT EARTHWATCH

Earthwatch Institute
Attn: Director of Research
114 Western Avenue
Boston, MA 02134
(978) 461-0081                      Toll Free: (800) 776-0188
Fax: (978) 461-2332      E-mail: research@earthwatch.org
Web: www.earthwatch.org/aboutus/research

**Summary**   To support field research anywhere in the world by pre- and postdoctoral scientists (especially women) who are working to investigate and/or preserve our physical, biological, and cultural heritage.

**Eligibility**   This program is open to doctoral and postdoctoral researchers and researchers with equivalent scholarship or life experience. Applicants must be interested in conducting field research worldwide in the sponsor's topic areas of 1) ecosystem services, including biodiversity conservation, sustainable agriculture, sustainable forestry, and freshwater; 2) climate change, including adaptation and mitigation; 3) oceans, including coastal ecosystems and marine biodiversity conservation; and 4) cultural heritage, including sacred landscapes and indigenous knowledge systems. They may be of any nationality and interested in conducting research in any geographic region, as long as the research design integrates non-specialist volunteers into the field research agenda. Applicants intending to conduct research in foreign countries are strongly encouraged to include host-country nationals in their research staffs. Early career scientists, women in science, and developing country nationals are especially encouraged to apply.

**Financial data**   Grants are awarded on a per capita basis, determined by multiplying the per capita grant by the number of volunteers on the project. Per capita grants average $850; total project grants range from $17,000 to $51,000. Grants cover all expenses for food, accommodations, and in-field transportation for the research team (principal investigator, research staff, and volunteers); principal investigator travel to and from the field; leased or rented field equipment; insurance; support of staff and visiting scientists; and support for associates from the host country. Funds are not normally provided for capital equipment, principal investigator salaries, university overhead or indirect costs, or preparation of results for publication. Volunteers donate time, services, and skills to the research endeavor in the field and pay their own travel expenses to and from the research site.

**Duration**   1 year; may be renewed. Projects typically involve from 30 to 60 total volunteers, with 5 to 12 volunteers each on 4 to 5 sequential teams. Each team normally spends 8 to 15 days in the field.

**Additional information**   Earthwatch was established in 1971 to support the efforts of scholars to preserve the world's endangered habitats and species, to explore the vast heritage of its peoples, and to promote world health and international cooperation. Its research program was formerly known as the Center for Field Research. Earthwatch also recruits and screens volunteers; in the past, 20% of these have been students, 20% educators, and 60% non-academic professionals.

**Number awarded** Varies each year; recently, 108 of these grants were awarded.

**Deadline** January of each year.

## [1423]
## RITA MAE KELLY ENDOWMENT FELLOWSHIP

American Political Science Association
Attn: Centennial Center Visiting Scholars Program
1527 New Hampshire Avenue, N.W.
Washington, DC 20036-1206
(202) 483-2512                    Fax: (202) 483-2657
E-mail: center@apsanet.org
Web: www.apsanet.org/content_3471.cfm

**Summary** To provide funding to women, minority, and other members of the American Political Science Association (APSA) who are interested in conducting research on the intersection of gender, race, ethnicity, and political power at the Centennial Center for Political Science and Public Affairs.

**Eligibility** This program is open to members of the association who are interested in conducting research on the intersection of gender, race, ethnicity, and political power while in residence at the center. Support is available to pre-dissertation graduate students as well as for an award or public presentation. Non-resident scholars may also be eligible.

**Financial data** Grants provide supplemental financial support to resident scholars.

**Duration** 2 weeks to 12 months.

**Additional information** The APSA launched its Centennial Center for Political Science and Public Affairs in 2003 to commemorate the centennial year of the association. This program was established in affiliation with the Women's Caucus for Political Science, the Latina Caucus for Political Science, the Committee for the Status of Latino/Latinas in the Profession, the Women and Politics Research Organized Section, and the Race, Ethnicity and Politics Organized Section.

**Number awarded** 1 or more each year.

**Deadline** February, June, or October of each year.

## [1424]
## RJOS RESEARCH GRANT IN WOMEN'S MUSCULOSKELETAL HEALTH

Orthopaedic Research and Education Foundation
Attn: Vice President, Grants
6300 North River Road, Suite 700
Rosemont, IL 60018-4261
(847) 698-9980                    Fax: (847) 698-7806
E-mail: communications@oref.org
Web: www.oref.org

**Summary** To provide funding to female orthopedic surgeons who are interested in a program of research training in women's musculoskeletal health.

**Eligibility** This program is open to female orthopedic surgeons who are members of the Ruth Jackson Orthopaedic Society (RJOS). Applicants must be interested in participat-

ing in a program of training to enhance their understanding of gender and diversity differences in the outcomes of orthopedic procedures.

**Financial data** The grant is $25,000.

**Duration** 1 year.

**Number awarded** 1 each year.

**Deadline** September of each year.

## [1425]
## ROBERT L. FANTZ MEMORIAL AWARD

American Psychological Foundation
750 First Street, N.E.
Washington, DC 20002-4242
(202) 336-5843                    Fax: (202) 336-5812
E-mail: foundation@apa.org
Web: www.apa.org/apf/funding/fantz.aspx

**Summary** To provide funding to promising young investigators in psychology, particularly women, minorities, and individuals with disabilities.

**Eligibility** This program is open to young investigators in psychology or related disciplines. Candidates must show 1) evidence of basic scientific research or scholarly writing in perceptual-cognitive development and the development of selection attention; and 2) research and writing on the development of individuality, creativity, and free-choice of behavior. The sponsor encourages applications from individuals who represent diversity in race, ethnicity, gender, age, disability, and sexual orientation.

**Financial data** The award is $2,000. Funds are paid directly to the recipient's institution for equipment purchases, travel, computer resources, or other expenses related to the work recognized by the award.

**Duration** The award is presented annually.

**Additional information** This award was first presented in 1992.

**Number awarded** 1 each year.

**Deadline** Deadline not specified.

## [1426]
## RONA JAFFE FOUNDATION WRITERS' AWARDS

Rona Jaffe Foundation
c/o Beth McCabe
Digitas New York
355 Park Avenue South
New York, NY 10010
(212) 610-5000          E-mail: Jaffemedia@fairpoint.net
Web: www.ronajaffefoundation.org

**Summary** To recognize and reward outstanding women writers.

**Eligibility** These awards are presented to women who have written outstanding fiction, poetry, and creative nonfiction. Authors are normally in the early stages of their writing careers, and awards are intended to make writing time available and provide assistance for such specific purposes as child care, research, and related travel activities. Application and nominations are not accepted; the foundation identifies writers through its internal processes.

**Financial data** The awards are $30,000.

**Duration** The awards are presented annually.

**Additional information** This program began in 1995.

**Number awarded** 6 each year.

**Deadline** Deadline not specified.

## [1427]
## ROSE MARY CRAWSHAY PRIZES

British Academy
Attn: Chief Executive and Secretary
10-11 Carlton House Terrace
London SW1Y 5AH
England
44 20 7969 5255          Fax: 44 20 7969 5300
E-mail: chiefexec@britac.ac.uk
Web: www.britac.ac.uk

**Summary** To recognize and reward women who have written or published outstanding historical or critical works on any subject connected with English literature.

**Eligibility** Women of any nationality are eligible to be nominated if within the preceding 3 years they have written an historical or critical work on any subject connected with English literature. Preference is given to works on Byron, Shelley, or Keats. Submissions are invited from publishing houses only.

**Financial data** The prize is 500 pounds.

**Duration** The prize is awarded each year.

**Additional information** The prize was established by Rose Mary Crawshay in 1888.

**Number awarded** 1 or 2 each year.

**Deadline** December of each year.

## [1428]
## RUTH AND LINCOLN EKSTROM FELLOWSHIP

Brown University
John Carter Brown Library
Attn: Fellowships Coordinator
P.O. Box 1894
Providence, RI 02912
(401) 863-5010          Fax: (401) 863-3477
E-mail: Valerie_Andrews@Brown.edu
Web: www.brown.edu

**Summary** To support scholars and graduate students interested in conducting research on the history of women at the John Carter Brown Library, which is renowned for its collection of historical sources pertaining to the Americas prior to 1830.

**Eligibility** This fellowship is open to U.S-based and foreign graduate students, scholars, and independent researchers. Graduate students must have passed their preliminary or general examinations. Applicants must be proposing to conduct research on the history of women and the family in the Americas prior to 1825, including the question of cultural influences on gender formation. Selection is based on the applicant's scholarly qualifications, the merits and significance of the project, and the particular need that the holdings of the John Carter Brown Library will fill in the development of the project.

**Financial data** The stipend is $2,100 per month.

**Duration** From 2 to 4 months.

**Additional information** Fellows are expected to be in regular residence at the library and to participate in the intellectual life of Brown University for the duration of the program.

**Number awarded** 1 or more each year.

**Deadline** December of each year.

## [1429]
## RUTH ANDERSON PRIZE

International Alliance for Women in Music
c/o Pamela Marshall, Search for New Music Competition
  Coordinator
38 Dexter Road
Lexington, MA 02420
E-mail: snm@iawm.org
Web: iawm.org

**Summary** To recognize and reward members of the International Alliance for Women (IAWM) who are commissioned to compose a new sound installation for electro-acoustic music.

**Eligibility** This award is presented to an IAWM member who is commissioned to compose a new sound installation for electro-acoustic music. Applicants must submit a detailed proposal of the sound installation. The location of the installation may be, but is not restricted to, an IAWM annual concert or congress.

**Financial data** The prize is $1,000. The prize is presented to the recipient after submitting a report to IAWM following the public showing of the completed installation.

**Duration** The project must be completed within 12 months.

**Number awarded** 1 each year.

**Deadline** March of each year.

## [1430]
## RUTH I. MICHLER MEMORIAL PRIZE

Association for Women in Mathematics
11240 Waples Mill Road, Suite 200
Fairfax, VA 22030
(703) 934-0163          Fax: (703) 359-7562
E-mail: michlerprize@awm-math.org
Web: sites.google.com

**Summary** To recognize and reward, with a fellowship at Cornell University, outstanding women mathematicians.

**Eligibility** This prize is available to women recently promoted to associate professor or equivalent position in the mathematical sciences at an institution of higher learning other than Cornell University. Applicants may be of any nationality and hold a position in any country. They must submit a proposal describing a research or book project to be undertaken during the fellowship period and explaining how the semester in the mathematics department at Cornell University will enhance their project or research career. Selection is based on the excellence of the applicant's research and the potential benefit to her of a semester in the mathematics department at Cornell.

**Financial data** The prize is $47,000. A supplemental housing and subsistence award of $3,000 is also provided.

**Duration** The prize is presented annually. The recipient may spend a semester of her choice in residence at Cornell.

**Additional information** This prize was first presented in 2007.

**Number awarded** 1 each year.

**Deadline** October of each year.

## [1431]
## RUTH JACKSON ORTHOPAEDIC SOCIETY/ ZIMMER RESEARCH GRANT

Ruth Jackson Orthopaedic Society
6300 North River Road, Suite 727
Rosemont, IL 60018-4226
(847) 698-1626                    Fax: (847) 823-0536
E-mail: rjos@aaos.org
Web: www.rjos.org/web/awards/index.htm

**Summary**  To provide funding to members of the Ruth Jackson Orthopaedic Society (RJOS) who are interested in conducting pilot research.

**Eligibility**  This program is open to women who are board certified or board eligible orthopaedic surgeons and RJOS members. Applicants must be seeking seed and start-up funding for promising research projects. Clinical or basic science projects are encouraged. Preference is given to grants with a focus on women's musculoskeletal health.

**Financial data**  The grant is a $30,000.

**Duration**  1 year; nonrenewable.

**Additional information**  Funding for this program is provided by Zimmer, Inc.

**Number awarded**  2 each year.

**Deadline**  September of each year.

## [1432]
## RUTH LYTTLE SATTER PRIZE IN MATHEMATICS

American Mathematical Society
Attn: Prizes and Awards
201 Charles Street
Providence, RI 02904-2294
(401) 455-4107                    Toll Free: (800) 321-4AMS
Fax: (401) 455-4046
Web: www.ams.org/profession/prizes-awards/prizes

**Summary**  To recognize and reward women who have made outstanding contributions to mathematics.

**Eligibility**  This program is open to female mathematicians who have made outstanding contributions to research in the field. The work must have been completed within the past 6 years.

**Financial data**  The prize is $5,000.

**Duration**  The prize is awarded biennially, in odd-numbered years.

**Additional information**  This prize was first awarded in 1991.

**Number awarded**  1 every other year.

**Deadline**  June of each even-numbered year.

## [1433]
## RUTH P. MORGAN FELLOWSHIP

Southern Methodist University
Clements Center for Southwest Studies
Attn: Russell Martin, Director
DeGolyer Library
P.O. Box 750396
Dallas, TX 75275-0396
(214) 768-0829                    E-mail: swcenter@smu.edu
Web: www.smu.edu

**Summary**  To provide funding to advanced scholars interested in using the Archives of Women of the Southwest at DeGolyer Library, Southern Methodist University (Dallas, Texas).

**Eligibility**  This program is open to advanced scholars interested in conducting research at the DeGolyer Library using the Archives of Women of the Southwest. Applicants must live outside the Dallas and Fort Worth metropolitan areas. They should submit an outline of the project, an explanation of how work in the DeGolyer Library collections will enhance it, length of time expected to be spent there, a curriculum vitae, and 2 letters of reference.

**Financial data**  The grant is $700 per week. Funds are intended to help pay the costs of travel, lodging, and research materials.

**Duration**  From 1 to 4 weeks.

**Additional information**  The Archives of Women of the Southwest includes papers of leaders in women's organizations and social and political reform movements, papers of outstanding women in the professions, the arts, and voluntary service; papers of families and of women in private life; records of women's organizations and organizations concerned with women's issues; and oral history interviews.

**Number awarded**  1 each year.

**Deadline**  Applications may be submitted at any time.

## [1434]
## RUTH R. AND ALYSON R. MILLER FELLOWSHIPS

Massachusetts Historical Society
Attn: Short-Term Fellowships
1154 Boylston Street
Boston, MA 02215-3695
(617) 646-0568                    Fax: (617) 859-0074
E-mail: fellowships@masshist.org
Web: www.masshist.org/research/fellowships/short-term

**Summary**  To fund research visits to the Massachusetts Historical Society for graduate students and other scholars interested in women's history.

**Eligibility**  This program is open to advanced graduate students, postdoctorates, and independent scholars who are conducting research in women's history and need to use the resources of the Massachusetts Historical Society. Applicants must be U.S. citizens or foreign nationals holding appropriate U.S. government documents. Along with their application, they must submit a curriculum vitae and a proposal describing the project and indicating collections at the society to be consulted. Graduate students must also arrange for a letter of recommendation from a faculty member familiar with their work and with the project being proposed. Preference is given to candidates who live 50 or more miles from Boston.

**Financial data**  The grant is $2,000.

**Duration**  4 weeks.

**Additional information**  This fellowship was first awarded in 1998.

**Number awarded**  1 or more each year.

**Deadline**  February of each year.

## [1435]
## SARA WHALEY BOOK PRIZE

National Women's Studies Association
Attn: Book Prizes
11 East Mount Royal Avenue, Suite 100
Baltimore, MD 21202
(410) 528-0355                    Fax: (410) 528-0357
E-mail: awards@nwsa.org
Web: www.nwsa.org/content.asp?pl=16&contentid=16

**Summary** To recognize and reward members of the National Women's Studies Association (NWSA) who have written outstanding books on topics related to women and labor.

**Eligibility** This award is available to NWSA members who submit a book manuscript that relates to women and labor, including migration and women's paid jobs, illegal immigration and women's work, impact of AIDS on women's employment, trafficking of women and women's employment, women and domestic work, or impact of race on women's work. Both senior scholars (who have issued at least 2 books and published the entry within the past year) and junior scholars (who have a publication contract or a book in production) are eligible. Women of color of U.S. or international origin are encouraged to apply.

**Financial data** The award is $2,000.

**Duration** The awards are presented annually.

**Additional information** This award was first presented in 2008.

**Number awarded** 2 each year: 1 to a senior scholar and 1 to a junior scholar.

**Deadline** April of each year.

## [1436]
## SARAH BRADLEY TYSON MEMORIAL FELLOWSHIP

Woman's National Farm and Garden Association, Inc.
Attn: Vice President and Communications Director
505 East Willow Grove Avenue
Wyndmoor, PA 19038
E-mail: matynjm@att.net
Web: www.wnfga.org/scholarships/fellowships

**Summary** To provide funding to women with prior work experience who are interested in working on an advanced study in agriculture, horticulture, and allied subjects.

**Eligibility** The fellowship is open to women interested in working on an advanced degree in the fields of agriculture, horticulture, or allied subjects at educational institutions of recognized standing within the United States. Applicants must have several years of experience. There are no application forms. Interested women should send a letter of application that contains an account of their educational training, a plan of study, references, samples of publishable papers, and a health certificate.

**Financial data** The fellowship award is $1,000 and is tenable at an American institution of higher learning chosen by the candidate with the approval of the fellowship committee.

**Duration** 1 year.

**Additional information** This program began in 1928. Students who accept the fellowships must agree to devote themselves to the study outlined in their application and to submit any proposed change in their plan to the committee for approval. They must send the committee at least 2 reports on their work, 1 at the end of the first semester and another upon completion of the year's work.

**Number awarded** Varies each year.

**Deadline** April of each year.

## [1437]
## SCHLESINGER LIBRARY ORAL HISTORY GRANTS

Radcliffe Institute for Advanced Study at Harvard University
Attn: Arthur and Elizabeth Schlesinger Library
10 Garden Street
Cambridge, MA 02138
(617) 495-8647                    Fax: (617) 496-8340
E-mail: slgrants@radcliffe.harvard.edu
Web: www.radcliffe.harvard.edu/schlesinger-library/grants

**Summary** To provide funding to scholars who are conducting oral history interviews related to the history of women.

**Eligibility** This program is open to scholars who are conducting oral history interviews relevant to the history of women or gender in the United States. The interviews must take place in accordance with guidelines of the Oral History Association, that consent is obtained from interviewees for their words to be viewed by researchers worldwide, and that copies or transcripts of the interviews be deposited in the Schlesinger Library. Selection is based on the significance of the research and the project's potential contribution to the advancement of knowledge.

**Financial data** Grants range up to $3,000. Funds must be used to cover travel, living expenses, photocopying, and other incidental research expenses.

**Duration** This are 1-time grants.

**Additional information** The Schlesinger Library is a non-circulating research library that documents the history of women in the United States during the 19th and 20th centuries. These grants were first awarded in 2012.

**Number awarded** Varies each year; recently, 4 of these grants were awarded.

**Deadline** March of each year.

## [1438]
## SCHLESINGER LIBRARY RESEARCH SUPPORT GRANTS

Radcliffe Institute for Advanced Study at Harvard University
Attn: Arthur and Elizabeth Schlesinger Library
10 Garden Street
Cambridge, MA 02138
(617) 495-8647                    Fax: (617) 496-8340
E-mail: slgrants@radcliffe.harvard.edu
Web: www.radcliffe.harvard.edu/schlesinger-library/grants

**Summary** To provide funding to faculty and unaffiliated scholars who are actively pursuing research that requires or will benefit from access to the holdings of the Schlesinger Library on the History of Women in America.

**Eligibility** Eligible to apply are scholars who have a doctoral degree or equivalent research and writing experience. Priority is given to those whose projects require use of materials available nowhere else but the Schlesinger Library. The project description should indicate the purpose of the research, the Schlesinger Library holdings to be consulted, and the significance of those holdings to the project overall. Selection is based on the significance of the research, the project's potential contribution to the advancement of knowledge, and its creativity in using the library's holdings.

**Financial data** Grants range up to $3,000. Funds must be used to cover travel, living expenses, photocopying, and other incidental research expenses.

**Duration** Summer months or the academic year.

**Additional information** The Schlesinger Library is a non-circulating research library that documents the history of women in the United States during the 19th and 20th centuries.

**Number awarded** Varies each year; recently, 11 of these grants were awarded.

**Deadline** March of each year.

## [1439]
## SCHMIEDER LEADERSHIP SCHOLARSHIP

Women of the Evangelical Lutheran Church in America
Attn: Scholarships
8765 West Higgins Road
Chicago, IL 60631-4101
(773) 380-2741          Toll Free: (800) 638-3522, ext. 2741
Fax: (773) 380-2419          E-mail: valora.starr@elca.org
Web: www.womenoftheelca.org

**Summary** To provide financial assistance to female faculty members at Evangelical Lutheran Church of America (ELCA) institutions who wish to participate in a leadership and management summer training institute.

**Eligibility** This program is open to female faculty at ELCA colleges, universities, and seminaries. Applicants must be interested in enrolled at a summer institute of their choice, provided that the program includes work in governance, financial management, administration, and professional development. They must be nominated by the president of their institution, which also must agree to provide partial assistance for the program.

**Financial data** The program provides a grant of $2,000 to $4,000; additional funding must be provided by the recipient's institution.

**Duration** Recipients are eligible for support for a maximum of 2 years.

**Additional information** Recipients are expected to submit an evaluation of the institute experience to the sponsor within 3 months of the training and to share learning experiences with colleagues at their home institution and, if requested, at Women of the ELCA events.

**Number awarded** Varies each year, depending upon the funds available. Since the program was established, it has awarded scholarships to 22 women.

**Deadline** February of each year.

## [1440]
## SCHOLARS IN HEALTH POLICY RESEARCH PROGRAM

Robert Wood Johnson Foundation
c/o Boston University Health Policy Institute
53 Bay State Road
Boston, MA 02215-2197
(617) 353-9220          Fax: (617) 353-9227
E-mail: rwjf@bu.edu
Web: healthpolicyscholars.org

**Summary** To provide support for postdoctoral training in health policy to scholars (particularly women and underrepresented minorities) in economics, political science, and sociology.

**Eligibility** This program is open to scholars who have a doctoral degree in economics, political science, or sociology. Applicants must have earned their degree during the past 5 years and be U.S. citizens or permanent residents. They need not have worked previously in the health policy field or have produced a health-oriented dissertation in order to apply. Selection is based on the applicant's commitment to a health policy career, quality of the past research, capability to undertake this challenging program, recommendations, and potential to contribute creatively to future U.S. health policies. The program embraces racial, ethnic, and gender diversity and encourages applications from candidates from groups that historically have been underrepresented in the 3 disciplines of interest.

**Financial data** The stipend is $89,000 per year.

**Duration** 2 years.

**Additional information** Fellows train at 1 of 3 nationally prominent academic institutions: University of California at Berkeley (in collaboration with the University of California at San Francisco), Harvard University, or the University of Michigan. There, they have the opportunity to work closely with faculty from the social sciences, as well as from medicine, public health, and public policy. Specific activities vary by institution but generally include seminars, workshops, tutorials, independent research projects, and policy placements in local or state government. The sponsor also offers 2 other programs which encourage applications from women and minorities: the Robert Wood Johnson Clinical Scholars Program and the Robert Wood Johnson Foundation Health and Society Scholars Program.

**Number awarded** Up to 9 each year.

**Deadline** October of each year.

## [1441]
## SHARON KEILLOR AWARD FOR WOMEN IN ENGINEERING EDUCATION

American Society for Engineering Education
Attn: Awards Administration
1818 N Street, N.W., Suite 600
Washington, DC 20036-2479
(202) 331-3550          Fax: (202) 265-8504
E-mail: board@asee.org
Web: www.asee.org/member-resources/awards

**Summary** To recognize and reward outstanding women engineering educators.

**Eligibility** This award is presented to a woman engineering educator who has an outstanding record in teaching engineering students and reasonable performance histories of research and service within an engineering school. Nominees must have an earned doctoral degree in an engineering discipline and have at least 5 years of teaching experience in an engineering school.

**Financial data** The award consists of a $2,000 honorarium and an inscribed plaque.

**Duration** The award is granted annually.

**Number awarded** 1 each year.

**Deadline** January of each year.

## [1442]
## SHIRLEY HOLDEN HELBERG ART GRANTS FOR MATURE WOMEN

National League of American Pen Women
1300 17th Street, N.W.
Washington, DC 20036-1973
(202) 785-1997          Fax: (202) 452-8868
E-mail: contact@nlapw.org
Web: www.nlapw.org/competitions

**Summary** To recognize and reward, with funding for additional education, mature women artists.

**Eligibility** Women artists or photographers who are 35 years of age or older are eligible to apply if neither they nor members of their immediate family are members of the league. They must submit 3 color prints (4 by 6 inches) of any media (oil, water color, original works on paper, acrylic, or sculpture) or 3 color or black-and-white prints (8 by 10 inches) of photographic works. U.S. citizenship is required.

**Financial data** The award is $1,000. Funds are to be used for education or other goals that affect their creative efforts.

**Duration** The award is granted biennially.

**Additional information** An entry fee of $35 must accompany each application.

**Number awarded** 1 each even-numbered year.

**Deadline** October of odd-numbered years.

## [1443]
## SHIRLEY HOLDEN HELBERG LETTERS GRANTS FOR MATURE WOMEN

National League of American Pen Women
1300 17th Street, N.W.
Washington, DC 20036-1973
(202) 785-1997          Fax: (202) 452-8868
E-mail: contact@nlapw.org
Web: www.nlapw.org/competitions

**Summary** To recognize and reward, with funding for additional education, mature women writers.

**Eligibility** Women writers who are 35 years of age or older are eligible to apply if they (or their immediate family) are not affiliated with the league. They must submit an unpublished manuscript of an article or short story, up to 2,500 words in length, or the first chapter of a novel or nonfiction book, up to 4,000 words in length. U.S. citizenship is required.

**Financial data** The award is $1,000. Funds are to be used for education or other goals that affect their creative efforts.

**Duration** The award is granted biennially.

**Additional information** An entry fee of $35 must accompany each application.

**Number awarded** 1 each even-numbered year.

**Deadline** October of odd-numbered years.

## [1444]
## SHIRLEY HOLDEN HELBERG MUSIC GRANTS FOR MATURE WOMEN

National League of American Pen Women
1300 17th Street, N.W.
Washington, DC 20036-1973
(202) 785-1997          Fax: (202) 452-8868
E-mail: contact@nlapw.org
Web: www.nlapw.org/competitions

**Summary** To recognize and reward, with funding for additional education, mature women composers.

**Eligibility** Women composers who are 35 years of age or older are eligible to apply if they (or their immediate family) are not affiliated with the sponsor. They must submit 2 published or unpublished compositions with performance times of 10 to 15 minutes. At least 1 of the scores must have been composed in the last 5 years. U.S. citizenship is required.

**Financial data** The award is $1,000. Funds are to be used for education or other goals that affect their creative efforts.

**Duration** The award is granted biennially.

**Additional information** An entry fee of $35 must accompany each application.

**Number awarded** 1 each even-numbered year.

**Deadline** October of odd-numbered years.

## [1445]
## SHOOTING STAR GRANTS

Montana Federation of Business and Professional
  Women's Organizations
Attn: Montana BPW Foundation, Inc.
P.O. Box 303
Great Falls, MT 59403
E-mail: mtbpwfoundation@gmail.com
Web: sites.google.com/mtbpwfoundation/home

**Summary** To provide funding to Montana women interested in personal or professional development.

**Eligibility** This program is open to women in Montana seeking funding for self-sufficiency, professional development, acquisition of skills, or business start-up and expansion. Funding is not available for scholarships, religious purposes, veteran or fraternal organizations, general endowment funds, or fundraising. Applicants must submit brief statements that 1) describe the project, business, or professional opportunity for which they are requesting funds; 2) describe how the opportunity will help them in their professional development; 3) identify the timeline for the project; 4) list other programs or funding they have requested for this project; 5) describe the projected outcomes of the project and the methods that will be used to measure those; and 6) discuss their goals and objectives once this project is completed.

**Financial data** Grants up to $1,000 are available.

**Number awarded** Varies each year; recently, 4 of these grants were awarded.

**Deadline** January of each year.

## [1446]
## SIGMA ALPHA IOTA/KENNEDY CENTER INTERNSHIP

Sigma Alpha Iota Philanthropies, Inc.
One Tunnel Road
Asheville, NC 28805
(828) 251-0606                    Fax: (828) 251-0644
E-mail: nh@sai-national.org
Web: www.sai-national.org

**Summary** To provide summer internships at the Kennedy Center to members of Sigma Alpha Iota (an organization of women musicians).

**Eligibility** This program is open to student members of the organization who are interested in a summer internship at the Institute for Arts Management at the John F. Kennedy Center for the Performing Arts in Washington, D.C. Applicants must be juniors, seniors, graduate students, or graduates out of school for less than 2 years.

**Financial data** The stipend is $2,400.

**Duration** 10 weeks during the summer.

**Additional information** Assignments are full time, with possible college credit available.

**Number awarded** 1 or more each year.

**Deadline** February of each year.

## [1447]
## SIGMA DELTA EPSILON FELLOWSHIPS

Sigma Delta Epsilon-Graduate Women in Science, Inc.
c/o Laurie B. Cook, Fellowships Coordinator
The College at Brockport, State University of New York
Biology Department, 217 Lennon Hall
350 New Campus Drive
Brockport, NY 14420
(585) 395-5757    E-mail: fellowshipsquestions@gwis.org
Web: gwis.org/national-fellowships-program

**Summary** To provide funding to women interested in conducting research anywhere in the world in the natural sciences.

**Eligibility** This program is open to women from any country currently enrolled as a graduate student, engaged in postdoctoral research, or holding a junior faculty position. Applicants must be interested in conducting research anywhere in the world in the natural sciences (including physical, environmental, mathematical, computer, or life sciences), anthropology, psychology, or statistics. Along with their application, they must submit 2-paragraph essays on 1) how the proposed research relates to their degree program and/or career development; 2) initiatives in which they are participating to promote the careers of scientists, particularly women, within their institution, program, or peer group; and 3) relevant personal factors, including financial need, that should be considered in evaluating their proposal. Appointments are made without regard to race, religion, nationality, creed, national origin, sexual orientation, or age. Membership in Sigma Delta Epsilon-Graduate Women in Science (SDE-GWIS) is encouraged.

**Financial data** The maximum grant is $10,000. Funds may be used for such research expenses as expendable supplies, small equipment, publication of research findings, travel and subsistence while performing field studies, or travel to another laboratory for collaborative research. They may not be used for tuition, child care, travel to professional meetings or to begin a new appointment, administrative overhead or indirect costs, personal computers, living allowances, or equipment for general use.

**Duration** 1 year.

**Additional information** This program includes the Adele Lewis Fellowship, the Hartley Corporation Fellowship, the Ethel K. Allen Fellowship, the Eloise Gerry Fellowships, and the Vessa Notchev Fellowship. Non-members of SDE-GWIS must pay an application fee of $50.

**Number awarded** Varies each year; recently, 8 of these grants were awarded.

**Deadline** January of each year.

## [1448]
## SOCIOLOGISTS FOR WOMEN IN SOCIETY FEMINIST ACTIVISM AWARD

Sociologists for Women in Society
Attn: Executive Officer
Southern Connecticut State University
Department of Sociology
501 Crescent Street
New Haven, CT 06515
(203) 392-7714                    Fax: (203) 392-7715
E-mail: swseo@socwomen.org
Web: www.socwomen.org/awards.html

**Summary** To recognize and reward members of Sociologists for Women in Society (SWS) who have used sociology to improve conditions for women in society.

**Eligibility** This program is open to SWS members who have notably and consistently used sociology to better the lives of women. The award honors outstanding feminist advocacy efforts that embody the goal of service to women and that have identifiably improved women's lives. Selection is based on activist contributions, rather than occupational and academic achievements.

**Financial data** The award includes an honorarium of $1,000 and a travel budget of $1,500 for presentations (lectures, workshops, or training sessions) related to the recipient's field of activism at 2 selected campus sites.

**Duration** The award is presented annually.

**Additional information** This award was first presented in 1995.

**Number awarded** 1 each year.

**Deadline** Nominations must be submitted by February of each year.

## [1449]
## SONIA KOVALEVSKY HIGH SCHOOL MATHEMATICS DAYS GRANTS

Association for Women in Mathematics
11240 Waples Mill Road, Suite 200
Fairfax, VA 22030
(703) 934-0163                    Fax: (703) 359-7562
E-mail: awm@awm-math.org
Web: sites.google.com

**Summary** To provide funding to women, minority, and other faculty at colleges and universities who wish to conduct Sonia Kovalevsky High School and Middle School Mathematics Days.

**Eligibility** Faculty and staff at universities and colleges may apply for these grants to support Sonia Kovalevsky High School and Middle School Mathematics Days; staff at Historically Black Colleges and Universities are particularly encouraged to apply. Programs targeted towards inner-city or rural high schools are especially welcomed. The proposed activity should consist of workshops, talks, and problem-solving competitions for female high school or middle school students and their teachers (both women and men).

**Financial data** The maximum grant is $3,000; most range from $1,500 to $2,200. Funds must be used for direct costs for the activity. Stipends and personnel costs are not permitted for organizers. Reimbursement for indirect costs or fringe benefits is not allowed.

**Duration** The grants are awarded annually.

**Additional information** This program is supported by grants from the National Science Foundation.

**Number awarded** 12 to 20 each year.

**Deadline** August or February of each year.

## [1450]
## STUDIO RESIDENCIES

Women's Studio Workshop
722 Binnewater Lane
P.O. Box 489
Rosendale, NY 12472
(845) 658-9133          Fax: (845) 658-9031
E-mail: info@wsworkshop.org
Web: www.wsworkshop.org/program/residency-grants

**Summary** To provide a residency and financial support at the Women's Studio Workshop (WSW) to women artists.

**Eligibility** This program is open to artists in all stages of their careers and working in intaglio, hand papermaking, letterpress printing, screen printing, book arts, or ceramics. Applicants must be interested in creating a new body of work while in residence at the WSW. They must provide a 1-page summary of their proposed project, a resume, and a CD with 10 images of their recent work.

**Financial data** The program provides a stipend of $350 per week, a $500 materials grant, a travel stipend up to $250 within the continental United States, unlimited studio use, and housing while in residence.

**Duration** 6 to 8 weeks.

**Number awarded** Varies each year.

**Deadline** March of each year.

## [1451]
## SUBARU OUTSTANDING WOMAN IN SCIENCE AWARD

Geological Society of America
Attn: Program Officer-Grants, Awards and Recognition
3300 Penrose Place
P.O. Box 9140
Boulder, CO 80301-9140
(303) 357-1028     Toll Free: (800) 472-1988, ext. 1028
Fax: (303) 357-1070     E-mail: awards@geosociety.org
Web: www.geosociety.org/awards

**Summary** To recognize and reward women who have exerted a major impact on the field of geosciences through their Ph.D. research.

**Eligibility** This program is open to women geoscientists who are within 3 years of completion of their Ph.D. degree. Nominations should include a letter that describes how the Ph.D. research has impacted geosciences in a major way, a short summary of the research, a short resume with a list of publications, and a copy of the dissertation abstract, published abstracts, and/or reprints if available.

**Financial data** The award is $2,500.

**Duration** The award is presented annually.

**Additional information** This award, first presented in 2001, is sponsored by Subaru of America, Inc. It was formerly named the Doris M. Curtis Memorial Fund for Women in Science Award.

**Number awarded** 1 each year.

**Deadline** January of each year.

## [1452]
## SUMMER/SHORT-TERM RESEARCH PUBLICATION GRANTS

American Association of University Women
Attn: AAUW Educational Foundation
301 ACT Drive, Department 60
P.O. Box 4030
Iowa City, IA 52243-4030
(319) 337-1716, ext. 60          Fax: (319) 337-1204
E-mail: aauw@act.org
Web: www.aauw.org

**Summary** To provide summer or short-term fellowships to women scholars interested in conducting postdoctoral research.

**Eligibility** This program is open to women who are interested in preparing research manuscripts for publication (but not to undertake new research). Applicants may be tenure-track, part-time, or temporary faculty or may be independent scholars or researchers, either new or established. They must have completed a doctoral or M.F.A. degree. U.S. citizenship or permanent resident status is required. Scholars with strong publishing records are discouraged from applying. Selection is based on scholarly excellence, quality of project design, originality of project, scholarly significance of project to discipline, feasibility of project and proposed schedule, qualifications of applicant, potential of applicant to make a significant contribution to field, applicant's commitment to women's issues in profession and community, applicant's teaching experience, and applicant's mentoring of other women.

**Financial data** The grant is $6,000. Funds may be used for stipends for recipient, clerical and technical support, research assistance related to verification (not basic research), supplies, and expenses. Grants do not cover travel, purchase of equipment, indirect costs, salary increase, or doctoral dissertation research or writing.

**Duration** 8 weeks; most recipients, especially full-time faculty, use the awards during the summer, but the research may be conducted at any time during the year.

**Additional information** The filing fee is $40.

**Number awarded** Varies each year; recently, 17 of these grants were awarded.

**Deadline** November of each year.

## [1453]
## SUSAN SMITH BLACKBURN PRIZE

Susan Smith Blackburn Prize, Inc.
c/o Leslie Swackhamer, Chair
Sam Houston State University
Department of Theatre and Musical Theatre
UTC 112
Huntsville, TX 77341-2297
(936) 294-1333                    Fax: (936) 294-3898
E-mail: las056@shsu.edu
Web: www.blackburnprize.org

**Summary**   To recognize and reward women who have written works of outstanding quality for the English-speaking theater.

**Eligibility**   This award is available to women who have written a full-length play in English. Playwrights may not submit their work directly. Each year, prominent professionals (directors or literary managers) are asked to nominate plays from the United States, United Kingdom, Ireland, Canada, South Africa, Australia, and New Zealand for consideration. Plays are eligible whether or not they have been produced, but any premier production must have taken place within the preceding 12 months. Each script is read by at least 3 members of a screening committee in order to select 10 finalists. All final nominations are read by all 6 judges.

**Financial data**   The prizes are $25,000 to the winner, $5,000 for special commendation, and $2,500 to each of the other finalists.

**Duration**   The prizes are awarded annually.

**Additional information**   The prizes are administered in Houston, London, and New York by a board of directors who choose 6 judges each year, 3 in the United States and 3 in the United Kingdom. The prize was established in 1978 by the friends and family of Susan Smith Blackburn, the American writer/actress who spent the last 15 years of her life in London.

**Number awarded**   1 winner, 1 special commendation recipient, and 8 other finalists are chosen each year.

**Deadline**   September of each year.

## [1454]
## SUSIE PRYOR AWARD IN ARKANSAS WOMEN'S HISTORY

Arkansas Women's History Institute
c/o Kristin Dutcher Mann
University of Arkansas at Little Rock
History Department
2801 South University Avenue
Little Rock, AR 72204
(501) 569-8152                    E-mail: kdmann@ualr.edu
Web: www.h-net.org/announce/show.cgi?ID=200522

**Summary**   To recognize and reward the best unpublished essay or article on topics related to Arkansas women's history.

**Eligibility**   This competition is open to authors at any academic level from any state. Applicants must submit manuscripts, from 20 to 35 pages in length, on a topic related to the history of women in Arkansas. Entries are judged on the basis of contributions to knowledge of women in Arkansas history, use of primary and secondary materials, and analytic and stylistic excellence.

**Financial data**   The prize is $1,000.

**Duration**   The prize is awarded annually.

**Additional information**   This prize was first awarded in 1986 as a feature of Arkansas' sesquicentennial celebration.

**Number awarded**   1 each year.

**Deadline**   February of each year.

## [1455]
## SYLVIA LANE MENTOR FELLOWSHIP

Agricultural and Applied Economics Association
Attn: Trust Committee
555 East Wells Street, Suite 1100
Milwaukee, WI 53202
(414) 918-3190                    Fax: (414) 276-3349
E-mail: info@aaea.org
Web: www.aaea.org/trust/special-purpose-funds

**Summary**   To provide funding to young female scholars who are working on food, agricultural, or resource issues and interested in relocating in order to conduct research with an established expert at another university, institution, or firm.

**Eligibility**   These fellowships are awarded to mentee/mentor pairs of individuals. Mentees must have completed at least 1 year in residence in an accredited American graduate degree program in agricultural economics or a closely-related discipline; women with Ph.D. degrees and advanced graduate students are encouraged to apply. Mentors must have a Ph.D. and established expertise in an area of food, agriculture, or natural resources. The goal is to enable female scholars to relocate in order to conduct research with an established expert at another university, institution, or firm, even though they may reside in different parts of the country or the world. Selection is based on the relevance of the research problem, potential for generating output, synergy of the mentor/mentee pairing, and opportunity for advancing the mentee's research skills beyond her graduate studies and current position.

**Financial data**   Awards may be used to cover direct research costs, travel, and temporary relocation expenses for the mentee.

**Duration**   Several weeks.

**Additional information**   This program was established by the Committee on Women in Agricultural Economics of the Agricultural and Applied Economics Association.

**Number awarded**   1 each year.

**Deadline**   September of each year.

## [1456]
## THEODORE BLAU EARLY CAREER AWARD FOR OUTSTANDING CONTRIBUTION TO PROFESSIONAL CLINICAL PSYCHOLOGY

American Psychological Foundation
750 First Street, N.E.
Washington, DC 20002-4242
(202) 336-5843                    Fax: (202) 336-5812
E-mail: foundation@apa.org
Web: www.apa.org/apf/funding/blau.aspx

**Summary**   To recognize and reward young clinical psychologists (particularly women, minorities, and individuals with disabilities) who have a record of outstanding professional accomplishments.

**Eligibility** This award is available to clinical psychologists who are no more than 7 years past completion of their doctoral degree. Nominees must have a record of accomplishments that may include promoting the practice of clinical psychology through professional service; innovation in service delivery; novel application of applied research methodologies to professional practice; positive impact on health delivery systems; development of creative educational programs for practice; or other novel or creative activities advancing the service of the profession. Self-nominations are accepted. The sponsor encourages nominations of individuals who represent diversity in race, ethnicity, gender, age, disability, and sexual orientation.

**Financial data** The award is $4,000.

**Duration** The award is presented annually.

**Additional information** This award, first presented in 1998, is sponsored by Division 12 (Society of Clinical Psychology) of the American Psychological Association.

**Number awarded** 1 each year.

**Deadline** Nominations must be submitted by October of each year.

## [1457]
## THEODORE MILLON AWARD IN PERSONALITY PSYCHOLOGY

American Psychological Foundation
750 First Street, N.E.
Washington, DC 20002-4242
(202) 336-5843                          Fax: (202) 336-5812
E-mail: foundation@apa.org
Web: www.apa.org/apf/funding/millon.aspx

**Summary** To recognize and reward psychologists (especially women, minorities, and individuals with disabilities) who have made outstanding contributions to the science of personality psychology.

**Eligibility** This award is available to psychologists engaged in advancing the science of personality psychology, including the areas of personology, personality theory, personality disorders, and personality measurement. Nominees should be between 8 and 20 years past completion of their doctoral degree. The sponsor encourages nominations of individuals who represent diversity in race, ethnicity, gender, age, disability, and sexual orientation.

**Financial data** The award is $1,000.

**Duration** The award is presented annually.

**Additional information** This award, established in 2004, is sponsored by Division 12 (Society of Clinical Psychology) of the American Psychological Association.

**Number awarded** 1 each year.

**Deadline** Nominations must be submitted by October of each year.

## [1458]
## TIMOTHY JEFFREY MEMORIAL AWARD IN CLINICAL HEALTH PSYCHOLOGY

American Psychological Foundation
750 First Street, N.E.
Washington, DC 20002-4242
(202) 336-5843                          Fax: (202) 336-5812
E-mail: foundation@apa.org
Web: www.apa.org/apf/funding/jeffrey.aspx

**Summary** To recognize and reward psychologists (especially women, minorities, and individuals with disabilities) who have made outstanding contributions to clinical health psychology.

**Eligibility** This award is available to full-time providers of direct clinical services who demonstrate an outstanding commitment to clinical health psychology. Nominees must be members of Division 38 (Health Psychology) of the American Psychological Association. They must have a full and unrestricted license to practice psychology and typically spend 15 to 20 hours per week in direct patient care. Letters of nomination should be accompanied by a curriculum vitae, at least 1 letter of support from a non-psychologist professional colleague, and another letter of support from a psychologist colleague. The sponsor encourages nominations of individuals who represent diversity in race, ethnicity, gender, age, disability, and sexual orientation.

**Financial data** The award is $3,000.

**Duration** The award is presented annually.

**Additional information** This award is sponsored by Division 38.

**Number awarded** 1 each year.

**Deadline** April of each year.

## [1459]
## TRAVEL AND TRAINING FUND

Women's Sports Foundation
Attn: Award and Grant Programs Manager
Eisenhower Park
1899 Hempstead Turnpike, Suite 400
East Meadow, NY 11554-1000
(516) 307-3915                          Toll Free: (800) 227-3988
E-mail: lflores@womenssportsfoundation.org
Web: www.womenssportsfoundation.org

**Summary** To provide funding for travel and training activities to women athletes (both individuals and teams).

**Eligibility** This program is open to women who are amateur athletes and U.S. citizens or legal residents. Applicants must demonstrate the ability, based on competitive record and years in training, to reach and compete at an elite level; they should have competed regionally (outside their state), nationally, or internationally and/or be ranked by a national governing body. Athletes may apply as individuals or as a team consisting of 2 or more women. High school, college, university, and community recreation sports teams are not eligible.

**Financial data** Grants range from $2,500 to $10,000.

**Duration** Individuals and teams may receive only 1 grant per calendar year and 3 grants in a lifetime.

**Additional information** This program, established in 1984, is currently funded by the Gatorade Company.

**Number awarded** Varies each year; recently, 26 of these grants (23 to individuals and 3 to teams) with a total value of $100,000 were awarded. Since the program was established, it has awarded grants to more than 1,300 individuals and teams.

**Deadline** May of each year.

## [1460]
## UNESCO-L'OREAL INTERNATIONAL FELLOWSHIPS

United Nations Educational, Scientific, and Cultural
  Organization
Attn: Fellowships Section
7, place de Fontenoy
75352 Paris 07 SP
France
33 1 45 68 15 49                    Fax: 33 1 45 68 55 03
E-mail: a.zaid@unesco.org
Web: www.unesco.org/en/fellowships/loreal

**Summary** To provide funding to women from UNESCO member countries (including the United States) who are conducting pre- or postdoctoral research in the life sciences.

**Eligibility** Eligible to apply are women from UNESCO member countries who are conducting research in life sciences, including biology, biochemistry, biotechnology, agriculture, medicine, pharmacy, and physiology. Applicants must be younger than 35 years of age. They must have already distinguished themselves by their talent and commitment. Preference is given to applicants who already have a Ph.D. degree, but applications from students pursuing study or research leading to a Ph.D. are also accepted. Special attention is given to candidates from the least developed countries. Each UNESCO member state may nominate 4 candidates. Applications must be submitted first to the national commission for UNESCO in the candidate's country (no application without this endorsement will be considered).

**Financial data** The maximum grant is $20,000 per year. Funds may not be used for computer or equipment purchases, publication costs, or attendance at conferences (unless a case can be made that such attendance is an integral part of the research and would make a direct and significant contribution to the outcome of the development of life sciences). Fellows also receive funding for airfare, meals, lodging, and pocket money to travel to UNESCO headquarters in Paris to attend an awards ceremony and visit there for 5 days.

**Duration** 2 years.

**Additional information** This program, which began in 1998, is sponsored by L'Oréal.

**Number awarded** 15 each year (3 in each of the 5 areas designated by UNESCO: Europe and North America, Asia and the Pacific, Africa, Latin America and the Caribbean, and Arab states).

**Deadline** July of each year.

## [1461]
## UNIVERSITY OF CALIFORNIA PRESIDENT'S POSTDOCTORAL FELLOWSHIP PROGRAM FOR ACADEMIC DIVERSITY

University of California at Berkeley
Attn: Office of Equity and Inclusion
102 California Hall
Berkeley, CA 94720-1508
(510) 643-6566              E-mail: ppfpinfo@berkeley.edu
Web: ppfp.ucop.edu/info/uc_ppfp.html

**Summary** To provide an opportunity to conduct research at campuses of the University of California to recent postdoctorates (particularly women and members of other underrepre-sented groups) who are committed to careers in university teaching and research and who will contribute to diversity.

**Eligibility** This program is open to U.S. citizens or permanent residents who have a Ph.D. from an accredited university. Applicants must be proposing to conduct research at a branch of the university under the mentorship of a faculty or laboratory sponsor. Preference is given to applicants 1) with the potential to bring to their academic careers the critical perspective that comes from their nontraditional educational background or their understanding of the experiences of groups historically underrepresented in higher education; 2) who have the communications skill and cross-cultural abilities to maximize effective collaboration with a diverse cross-section of the academic community; 3) who have demonstrated significant academic achievement by overcoming barriers such as economic, social, or educational disadvantage; and 4) who have the potential to contribute to higher education through their understanding of the barriers facing women, domestic minorities, students with disabilities, and other members of groups underrepresented in higher education careers, as evidenced by life experiences and educational background.

**Financial data** The stipend ranges from $41,000 to $50,000, depending on the field and level of experience. The program also offers health benefits and up to $4,000 for supplemental and research-related expenses.

**Duration** Appointments are for 1 academic year, with possible renewal for a second year.

**Additional information** Research may be conducted at any of the University of California's 10 campuses (Berkeley, Davis, Irvine, Los Angeles, Merced, Riverside, San Diego, San Francisco, Santa Barbara, or Santa Cruz). The program provides mentoring and guidance in preparing for an academic career. This program was established in 1984 to encourage applications from minority and women scholars in fields where they were severely underrepresented; it is now open to all qualified candidates whose research, teaching, and service will contribute to diversity and equal opportunity at the University of California.

**Number awarded** Varies each year; recently, 30 of these fellows were selected.

**Deadline** October of each year.

## [1462]
## UNIVERSITY OF ILLINOIS AT CHICAGO ACADEMIC RESIDENT LIBRARIAN PROGRAM

University of Illinois at Chicago
Attn: Library Human Resources
801 South Morgan
MC 234
Chicago, IL 60607
(312) 996-7353
Web: library.uic.edu/about/employment

**Summary** To provide a residency at the University of Illinois at Chicago (UIC) to librarians (particularly women, minorities, and persons with disabilities) who are interested in preparing for a career in academic librarianship.

**Eligibility** This program is open to librarians who graduated within the past year with a master's degree from an ALA-accredited program. Applicants must be interested in preparing for a career as an academic librarian through a residency at (UIC). Preference is given to applicants who can demonstrate an interest in 1 or more of the following areas: 1) technical services, with an emphasis on development and assessment of library discovery tools; 2) outreach, with an emphasis on initiatives to rural and underserved users; 3) reference and instruction, with an emphasis on instructional technical design and the development of multimedia learning objects; 4) E-science, with an emphasis on data curation in support of university-wide data management and preservation initiatives; 5) digital preservation, with an emphasis on preservation architectures, standards, and workflows; or 7) digital image collections, with an emphasis on mapping using GIS technologies. A goal of the program is to increase diversity within the profession of academic librarianship; applications are especially welcome from women, underrepresented minority group members, persons with disabilities, members of sexual minority groups, and others whose background, education, experience, and academic interests would enrich the diversity of the profession.

**Financial data**   The stipend is at least $42,000.

**Duration**   1 year; may be renewed 1 additional year.

**Number awarded**   2 or more each year.

**Deadline**   June of each year.

## [1463]
## UNIVERSITY OF MICHIGAN/CENTER FOR THE EDUCATION OF WOMEN VISITING SCHOLAR PROGRAM

University of Michigan
Attn: Center for the Education of Women
330 East Liberty Street
Ann Arbor, MI 48104-2289
(734) 764-6343                              Fax: (734) 998-6203
E-mail: contactcew@umich.edu
Web: www.cew.umich.edu/research/vs

**Summary**   To provide funding to scholars from any country (including the United States) who are interested in conducting research on women at the University of Michigan's Center for the Education of Women.

**Eligibility**   This program is open to scholars from the United States and abroad who have a Ph.D. or equivalent degree. Applicants must be interested in utilizing the resources of the center to explore the following or related issues: women in nontraditional fields, leadership, women and work, gender and poverty, women in higher education, women of color in the academy, or gender equity in education and employment.

**Financial data**   Scholars receive office space, full access to University of Michigan facilities and programs (including library and computing resources), and stipends up to $7,500. An additional $1,000 is paid upon receipt of the scholar's paper.

**Duration**   From 2 to 12 months.

**Additional information**   Visiting scholars must be in residence at the center for the duration of the program. They are expected to prepare a working paper on the basis of their research.

**Number awarded**   Varies each year.

**Deadline**   February of each year.

## [1464]
## USDA SMALL BUSINESS INNOVATION RESEARCH PROGRAM

Department of Agriculture
National Institute of Food and Agriculture
Attn: Director, SBIR Program
1400 Independence Avenue, S.W.
Stop 2201
Washington, DC 20250-2201
(202) 401-4002                              Fax: (202) 401-6070
E-mail: sbir@nifa.usda.gov
Web: www.csrees.usda.gov/funding/sbir/sbir.html

**Summary**   To stimulate technological innovation related to agriculture in the private sector by small business firms, especially those owned by women or members of socially and economically disadvantaged groups.

**Eligibility**   For the purposes of this program, a "small business" is defined as a firm that is organized for profit with a location in the United States; is in the legal form of an individual proprietorship, partnership, limited liability company, corporation, joint venture, association, trust, or cooperative; is at least 51% owned and controlled by 1 or more individuals who are citizens or permanent residents of the United States; and has (including its affiliates) fewer than 500 employees. The primary employment of the principal investigator must be with the firm at the time of award and during the conduct of the proposed project. Applications are encouraged from 1) women-owned small business concerns, defined as those that are at least 51% owned by a woman or women who also control and operate them; and 2) socially and economically disadvantaged small business concerns that are at least 51% owned by an Indian tribe, a Native Hawaiian organization, or 1 or more socially and economically disadvantaged individuals (African Americans, Hispanic Americans, Native Americans, Asian Pacific Americans, or subcontinent Asian Americans). Proposals are accepted in 10 topic areas: forests and related resources; plant production and protection (biology); animal production and protection; air, water, and soils; food science and nutrition; rural development; aquaculture; biofuels and biobased products; small and mid-sized farms; and plant production and protection (engineering). Selection is based on scientific and technical feasibility of the project, importance of the problem, qualifications of the investigator and research facilities, appropriateness of the budget, and extent of duplication of the project with other ongoing or previous research.

**Financial data**   Support is offered in 2 phases. In phase 1, awards normally do not exceed $100,000 (for both direct and indirect costs); in phase 2, awards normally do not exceed $450,000 (including both direct and indirect costs).

**Duration**   Phase 1 awards may extend up to 8 months; phase 2 awards may extend up to 2 years.

**Additional information**   Phase 1 is to determine the scientific or technical feasibility of ideas submitted by the applicants on research topic areas. Phase 2 awards are made to firms with approaches that appear sufficiently promising as a result of phase 1 studies.

**Number awarded**   Recently, the department granted 80 phase 1 awards and 32 phase 2 awards. Total program funding was approximately $19 million.

**Deadline**   September of each year for phase 1 awards; February of each year for phase 2 awards.

## [1465]
## VERNA ROSS ORNDORFF CAREER PERFORMANCE AWARD

Sigma Alpha Iota Philanthropies, Inc.
One Tunnel Road
Asheville, NC 28805
(828) 251-0606                    Fax: (828) 251-0644
E-mail: nh@sai-national.org
Web: www.sai-national.org

**Summary** To provide funding for advanced study, coaching, or other activities directly related to the development of a musical career to members of Sigma Alpha Iota (an organization of women musicians).

**Eligibility** This program is open to members of the organization who are preparing for a concert career. Singers may not be older than 35 years of age and instrumentalists may not be older than 32. Applicants may not have professional management, but they must have had considerable performing experience outside the academic environment.

**Financial data** The grant is $5,000; funds must be used for advanced study, coaching, or other purposes directly related to the development of a professional performing career.

**Duration** 1 year.

**Additional information** The area supported rotates annually among strings, woodwinds, and brass (2014); piano, harpsichord, organ, and percussion (2015); and voice (2016).

**Number awarded** 1 each year.

**Deadline** March of each year.

## [1466]
## VICTORIA SCHUCK AWARD

American Political Science Association
1527 New Hampshire Avenue, N.W.
Washington, DC 20036-1206
(202) 483-2512                    Fax: (202) 483-2657
E-mail: apsa@apsanet.org
Web: www.apsanet.org/content_4129.cfm?navID=756

**Summary** To recognize and reward outstanding scholarly books on women and politics.

**Eligibility** Eligible to be nominated (by publishers or individuals) are scholarly political science books issued the previous year on women and politics.

**Financial data** The award is $1,000.

**Duration** The award is presented annually.

**Additional information** This award was first presented in 1988.

**Number awarded** 1 each year.

**Deadline** January of each year for nominations from individuals; February of each year for nominations from publishers.

## [1467]
## VIOLET DILLER PROFESSIONAL EXCELLENCE AWARD

Iota Sigma Pi
c/o Nancy Hopkins, National Director for Professional Awards
Tulane University School of Science and Engineering
Cell and Molecular Biology
2000 Percival Stern Hall
New Orleans, LA 70118
(504) 865-5546                    E-mail: nhopkins@tulane.edu
Web: www.iotasigmapi.info

**Summary** To recognize exceptional and significant achievement by women working in chemistry or allied fields.

**Eligibility** Nominees for the award must be women chemists who have made significant contributions to academic, governmental, or industrial chemistry; in education; in administration; or in a combination of those areas. They may be from any country and need not be members of Iota Sigma Pi. Each active chapter is entitled to make only 1 nomination, but individual members, individual chemists, or groups of chemists may make independent nominations if properly documented. Contributions may include innovation design, development, application, or promotion of a principle or practice that has widespread significance to the scientific community or society on a national level.

**Financial data** The award consists of $1,000, a certificate, and a lifetime waiver of Iota Sigma Pi dues.

**Duration** The award is granted triennially (2017, 2020, etc.).

**Additional information** This award was first presented in 1984.

**Number awarded** 1 every 3 years.

**Deadline** Nominations must be submitted by February of the year of award.

## [1468]
## W. NEWTON LONG AWARD

American College of Nurse-Midwives
Attn: ACNM Foundation, Inc.
8403 Colesville Road, Suite 1550
Silver Spring, MD 20910-6374
(240) 485-1850                    Fax: (240) 485-1818
E-mail: fdn@acnm.org
Web: www.midwife.org

**Summary** To provide funding to midwives who are interested in conducting a research or other project in the United States or abroad.

**Eligibility** This program is open to midwives, including certified nurse midwives (CNMs) and certified midwives (CMs). Applicants must be seeking funding for a project that relates to 1 or more of the following areas: advancement of nurse-midwifery clinical skills; advancement of nurse-midwifery through research; dissemination of nurse-midwifery research; promotion of professional nurse-midwifery; presentations by nurse midwives at medical or midwifery conferences; establishment of new nurse-midwifery practice or service; or study of different aspects of nurse-midwifery practice in the United States and abroad.

**Financial data** The maximum grant is $1,000.

**Duration** The grants are presented annually.

**Number awarded** 1 or 2 each year.

**Deadline** March of each year.

## [1469]
## WANDA MUNN SCHOLARSHIP

Society of Women Engineers
Attn: Scholarship Selection Committee
203 North LaSalle Street, Suite 1675
Chicago, IL 60601-1269
(312) 596-5223          Toll Free: (877) SWE-INFO
Fax: (312) 644-8557          E-mail: scholarships@swe.org
Web: societyofwomenengineers.swe.org

**Summary** To provide financial assistance to women from selected northwestern states, particularly those who have worked in the engineering field, who are interested in returning to college or graduate school to continue their study of engineering or computer science.

**Eligibility** This program is open to women who are planning to enroll at an ABET-accredited 4-year college or university. Applicants must have been out of the engineering workforce and school for at least 2 years and must be planning to return as an undergraduate or graduate student to work on a degree in computer science or engineering. They must be residents of are attending school in Alaska, Idaho, Montana, Oregon, or Washington and have a GPA of 3.0 or higher. Selection is based on merit. Preference is given to engineers who already have a degree and are planning to reenter the engineering workforce after a period of temporary retirement.

**Financial data** The stipend is $1,500.

**Duration** 1 year.

**Additional information** This program is sponsored by the Eastern Washington Section of the Society of Women Engineers.

**Number awarded** 1 each year.

**Deadline** February of each year.

## [1470]
## WAYNE F. PLACEK GRANTS

American Psychological Foundation
750 First Street, N.E.
Washington, DC 20002-4242
(202) 336-5843          Fax: (202) 336-5812
E-mail: foundation@apa.org
Web: www.apa.org/apf/funding/placek.aspx

**Summary** To provide funding to pre- and postdoctoral scholars (particularly women, minorities, and individuals with disabilities) who are interested in conducting research that will increase the general public's understanding of homosexuality and alleviate the stress experienced by gay men and lesbians.

**Eligibility** This program is open to scholars who have a doctoral degree (e.g., Ph.D., Psy.D., M.D.) and to graduate students in all fields of the behavioral and social sciences. Applicants must be interested in conducting empirical studies that address the following topics: prejudice, discrimination, and violence based on sexual orientation, including heterosexuals' attitudes and behaviors toward lesbian, gay, bisexual, and transgender (LGBT) people; family and workplace issues relevant to LGBT people; and subgroups of the LGBT population that have been historically underrepresented in scientific research. Selection is based on conformance with

stated program goals, magnitude of incremental contribution, quality of proposed work, and applicant's demonstrated scholarship and research competence. The sponsor encourages applications from individuals who represent diversity in race, ethnicity, gender, age, disability, and sexual orientation.

**Financial data** The grant is $15,000.

**Duration** 1 year.

**Additional information** This program began in 1995.

**Number awarded** 1 or 2 each year.

**Deadline** February of each year.

## [1471]
## WHIRLY-GIRLS MEMORIAL FLIGHT TRAINING SCHOLARSHIP

Whirly-Girls International
c/o Bev Haug-Schaffter, Vice President Scholarships
3996 Zapotec Way
Las Vegas, NV 89103-2232
E-mail: wgvpsch@whirlygirls.org
Web: www.whirlygirls.org

**Summary** To provide financial assistance to members of Whirly-Girls International who are interested in obtaining an additional helicopter rating.

**Eligibility** This program is open to women who have been members of Whirly-Girls International for at least 1 year. Applicants must be interested in advanced helicopter flight training to upgrade their current rating (typically toward commercial, instrument, instructor, ATP, long line or turbine transition training). Along with their application, they must submit information on honors or awards they have received, organizations with which they are affiliated, activities or hobbies they pursue, involvement in aviation-related activities, achievements and contributions in aviation, what originally sparked their interest in the helicopter industry, how they have helped other women become interested in aviation, their personal experiences in aviation, and why they need this financial assistance.

**Financial data** The stipend is $8,000.

**Duration** Training must be completed within 1 year.

**Additional information** This program combines the former Phelan International Flight Training Scholarship and Doris Mullen Flight Training Scholarship. Completed applications must include $45 to cover the cost of processing and mailing.

**Number awarded** 1 each year.

**Deadline** September of each year.

## [1472]
## WHOI GEOPHYSICAL FLUID DYNAMICS FELLOWSHIPS

Woods Hole Oceanographic Institution
Attn: Academic Programs Office
Clark Laboratory, MS 31
266 Woods Hole Road
Woods Hole, MA 02543-1541
(508) 289-2950          Fax: (508) 457-2188
E-mail: gfd@whoi.edu
Web: www.whoi.edu/gfd

**Summary** To provide summer research and study opportunities at Woods Hole Oceanographic Institution (WHOI) to pre- and postdoctoral scholars (particularly women and members of underrepresented groups) who are interested in geophysical fluid dynamics.

**Eligibility** This program is open to pre- and postdoctorates who are interested in pursuing research or study opportunities in a field that involves non-linear dynamics of rotating, stratified fluids. Fields of specialization include classical fluid dynamics, physical oceanography, meteorology, geophysical fluid dynamics, astrophysics, planetary atmospheres, hydromagnetics, physics, and applied mathematics. Applications from women and members of underrepresented groups are particularly encouraged.

**Financial data** Participants receive a stipend of $5,600 and an allowance for travel expenses within the United States.

**Duration** 10 weeks during the summer.

**Additional information** Each summer, the program at WHOI revolves around a central theme. A recent theme related to shear turbulence. The main components of the summer program are a series of principal lectures, a set of supplementary research seminars, and research projects conducted by the student fellows with the active support of the staff. Funding for this program, which began in 1959, is provided by the National Science Foundation and Office of Naval Research.

**Number awarded** Up to 10 graduate students are supported each year.

**Deadline** February of each year.

## [1473]
## WIF FILM FINISHING FUND GRANTS

Women in Film/Los Angeles
Attn: Film Finishing Fund
6100 Wilshire Boulevard, Suite 710
Los Angeles, CA 90048
(323) 935-2211                    Fax: (323) 935-2212
E-mail: foundation@wif.org
Web: www.wif.org/foundation/film-finishing-fund

**Summary** To provide funding to women from any country for the completion of films of any length or genre.

**Eligibility** This program is open to female filmmakers who have completed principal photography and can submit a complete rough cut of an edited film (narrative feature length films are accepted if at least 90% of the film is complete). Projects in all genres (narrative, documentary, educational, animated, and experimental) and all lengths are eligible. No student projects, including thesis projects and films initiated while the applicant was a student, are considered. Applicants do not need to be members of Women in Film, although they are encouraged to join. Applications are accepted from filmmakers worldwide, but projects must be accessible to English-speaking audiences or at least have English subtitles. Selection is based on a demonstration that this grant will make a critical contribution to the completion of the film, the number of women involved in key creative personnel, and the film's positive statement about women and/or the way in which it deals with issues relevant to women.

**Financial data** Grants provide cash (up to $15,000) and in-kind services.

**Additional information** This program, which began in 1985, currently receives support from Netflix. A $75 processing fee is charged.

**Number awarded** Varies each year; recently, 7 of these grants were awarded. Since the program began, it has awarded more than $2 million in cash and in-kind services to 170 films.

**Deadline** May of each year.

## [1474]
## WILLIAM L. FISHER CONGRESSIONAL GEOSCIENCE FELLOWSHIP

American Geological Institute
Attn: Government Affairs Program
4220 King Street
Alexandria, VA 22302-1502
(703) 379-2480, ext. 212          Fax: (703) 379-7563
E-mail: govt@agiweb.org
Web: www.agiweb.org/gap/csf/index.html

**Summary** To provide women, minority, and other members of an American Geological Institute (AGI) component society with an opportunity to gain professional experience in the office of a member of Congress or a Congressional committee.

**Eligibility** This program is open to members of 1 of AGI's 49 member societies who have a master's degree and at least 3 years of post-degree work experience or a Ph.D. Applicants should have a broad geoscience background and excellent written and oral communications skills. They must be interested in working with Congress. Although prior experience in public policy is not required, a demonstrated interest in applying science to the solution of public problems is desirable. Applications from women and minorities are especially encouraged. U.S. citizenship or permanent resident status is required.

**Financial data** Fellows receive a stipend of up to $65,000 plus allowances for health insurance, relocation, and travel.

**Duration** 12 months, beginning in September.

**Additional information** This program is 1 of more than 20 Congressional Science Fellowships operating in affiliation with the American Association for the Advancement of Science (AAAS), which provides a 2-week orientation on Congressional and executive branch operations.

**Number awarded** 1 each year.

**Deadline** January of each year.

## [1475]
## WOMEN IN AVIATION, INTERNATIONAL FLIGHT SCHOLARSHIPS

Women in Aviation, International
Attn: Scholarships
Morningstar Airport
3647 State Route 503 South
West Alexandria, OH 45381-9354
(937) 839-4647                    Fax: (937) 839-4645
E-mail: scholarships@wai.org
Web: www.wai.org/education/scholarships.cfm

**Summary** To provide funding to members of Women in Aviation, International (WAI) who are interested in obtaining an additional rating or certificate.

**Eligibility** This program is open to women who are WAI members and interested in furthering their career in aviation. Applicants must be interested in working on an additional license, rating, or certificate. Most programs require applicants to have an academic GPA of 3.0 or higher. They must submit 2 letters of recommendation (including 1 from a pilot who has flown with them), a 500-word essay on their aviation history and goals, a resume, copies of all aviation licenses and medical certificates, and the last 3 pages of their pilot logbook. Selection is based on achievements, attitude toward self and others, commitment to success, dedication to career, financial need, motivation, reliability, responsibility, and teamwork.

**Financial data** Stipends range from $1,000 to $5,000. Funds are paid directly to the flight school.

**Duration** Training must be completed within 1 year.

**Additional information** WAI is a nonprofit professional organization dedicated to encouraging women to consider an aviation career and to providing educational outreach activities and networking resources to women active in the industry. Among the scholarships for women interested in flight training are the Aircraft Owners and Pilots Association Student Pilot Scholarship (sponsored by AOPA), the Anne Bridge Baddour Aviation Scholarship, the Bunny M. Connors Memorial Scholarship, the Christine Reed Memorial Flight Scholarship, the Dare to Dream Scholarship, the Jeppesen Flight Training Scholarship, the Keep Flying Scholarship, the Kelsey A. Meyer Memorial Scholarship, and the Sporty's Foundation Flight Training Scholarship.

**Number awarded** Varies each year.

**Deadline** November of each year.

## [1476]
## WOMEN IN AVIATION INTERNATIONAL MANAGEMENT SCHOLARSHIP

Women in Aviation, International
Attn: Scholarships
Morningstar Airport
3647 State Route 503 South
West Alexandria, OH 45381-9354
(937) 839-4647                    Fax: (937) 839-4645
E-mail: scholarships@wai.org
Web: www.wai.org/education/scholarships.cfm

**Summary** To provide financial assistance to members of Women in Aviation, International (WAI) who are in an aviation management field and interested in attending leadership-related courses or seminars.

**Eligibility** This program is open to WAI members in an aviation management field who have exemplified the traits of leadership, community spirit, and volunteerism. They must be interested in attending a leadership-related course or seminar or participating in some other means of advancing their managerial position. Along with their application, they must submit 2 letters of recommendation, a 500-word essay on their aviation history and goals, a resume, copies of all aviation licenses and medical certificates, and the last 3 pages of their pilot logbook (if applicable). Selection is based on achievements, attitude toward self and others, commitment to success, dedication to career, financial need, motivation, reliability, responsibility, and teamwork.

**Financial data** The stipend is $1,000.

**Additional information** WAI is a nonprofit professional organization dedicated to encouraging women to consider an aviation career and to providing educational outreach activities and networking resources to women active in the industry.

**Number awarded** 1 each year.

**Deadline** November of each year.

## [1477]
## WOMEN IN UNITED METHODIST HISTORY RESEARCH GRANT

United Methodist Church
General Commission on Archives and History
Attn: General Secretary
36 Madison Avenue
P.O. Box 127
Madison, NJ 07940
(973) 408-3189                    Fax: (973) 408-3909
E-mail: gcah@gcah.org
Web: www.gcah.org

**Summary** To support research related to the history of women in the United Methodist Church.

**Eligibility** Proposed research projects must deal specifically with the history of women in the United Methodist Church or its antecedents. Proposals on women of color and on history at the grassroots level are especially encouraged. Applicants must submit a description of the project, including its significance, format, timetable, budget, and how the results will be disseminated.

**Financial data** The grant is at least $1,000. Grant funds are not to be used for equipment, publication costs, or researcher's salary.

**Duration** These grants are awarded annually.

**Number awarded** Varies each year. A total of $2,500 is available for this program annually.

**Deadline** December of each year.

## [1478]
## WOMEN MILITARY AVIATORS DREAM OF FLIGHT SCHOLARSHIP

Women in Aviation, International
Attn: Scholarships
Morningstar Airport
3647 State Route 503 South
West Alexandria, OH 45381-9354
(937) 839-4647                    Fax: (937) 839-4645
E-mail: scholarships@wai.org
Web: www.wai.org/education/scholarships.cfm

**Summary** To provide financial assistance to members of Women in Aviation, International (WAI) who are interested in academic study or flight training.

**Eligibility** This program is open to WAI members who are students in high school, an accredited flight program, or an accredited college or university. Applicants must submit 2 letters of recommendation, a 500-word essay on their aviation history and goals, a resume, copies of all aviation licenses and medical certificates, and the last 3 pages of their pilot logbook (if applicable). Selection is based on the applicant's ambition to further women in aviation, demonstrated persistence and determination, financial need, ability to complete training, and ability to bring honor to the women of Women Military Aviators, Inc. (WMA).

**Financial data** The stipend is $2,500.

**Duration** Recipients must be able to complete training within 1 year.

**Additional information** WAI is a nonprofit professional organization dedicated to encouraging women to consider an aviation career and to providing educational outreach activities and networking resources to women active in the industry. WMA established this program in 2005 to honor the women aviators who are serving or have served in Iraq and Afghanistan.

**Number awarded** 1 each year.

**Deadline** November of each year.

## [1479]
## WOMEN'S CAMPAIGN FUND FELLOWSHIP PROGRAM

Women's Campaign Fund
Attn: Political Director
1900 L Street, N.W., Suite 500
Washington, DC 20036
(202) 393-8164                    Toll Free: (800) 446-8170
Fax: (202) 393-0649           E-mail: info@wcfonline.org
Web: www.wcfonline.org

**Summary** To provide an opportunity for young women to gain work experience within a national political organization.

**Eligibility** This program is open to female students and recent graduates who have a strong interest in protecting women's reproductive choices and options. Applicants must be interested in working at the Women's Campaign Fund in the areas of communications, development, political, and programs. They must have excellent research, writing, and communications skills as well as the ability to work independently and in a small group setting.

**Financial data** The stipend is $500 per month for full-time fellows or $250 per month for part-time fellows.

**Duration** 14 weeks during spring or fall; 10 weeks during summer.

**Additional information** The Women's Campaign Fund is the first national non-partisan committee founded in America dedicated to the election of pro-choice women to public office. This program includes 2 endowed fellowships: the Bertha Wurmser Herz Fellowship and the Annie Kahn Feinsod Fellowship.

**Number awarded** Approximately 7 each term.

**Deadline** November of each year for spring; March of each year for summer; July of each year for fall.

## [1480]
## WOMEN'S CAUCUS EDITING AND TRANSLATION FELLOWSHIP

American Society for Eighteenth-Century Studies
c/o Wake Forest University
P.O. Box 7867
Winston-Salem, NC 27109
(336) 727-4694                    Fax: (336) 727-4697
E-mail: asecs@wfu.edu
Web: asecs.press.jhu.edu

**Summary** To provide funding to postdoctoral scholars working on an editing or translating project that deals with women's issues in the 18th century.

**Eligibility** This program is open to members of the American Society for Eighteenth-Century Studies (ASECS) who are working on an editing or translating project. Applicants must have a Ph.D. or be an emeritae/i faculty who does not

already have professional support for the project. The project must translate and/or edit works by 18th century writers or works that significantly advance understanding of women's experiences in the 18th century or offer a feminist analysis of an aspect of 18th-century culture and/or society.

**Financial data** The grant is $1,000.

**Duration** The grant is offered annually.

**Additional information** This award, offered by the Women's Caucus of the ASECS, was first presented in 2004. The recipient is asked to submit a brief written report on the progress of the project 1 year after receiving the award and, wherever possible, will serve on the award committee in the following year.

**Number awarded** 1 each year.

**Deadline** January of each year.

## [1481]
## WOMEN'S FILM PRESERVATION FUND GRANTS

New York Women in Film & Television
6 East 39th Street, Suite 1200
New York, NY 10016-0112
(212) 679-0870, ext. 39           Fax: (212) 679-0899
E-mail: info@nywift.org
Web: www.nywift.org/article.aspx?id=4121

**Summary** To provide funding to restore and preserve films in which women have had significant creative roles.

**Eligibility** Eligible to apply for this funding are individuals and nonprofit organizations who are interested in preserving films in which women had key creative roles, as directors, writers, producers, editors, or performers. Films may be of any length, on any subject matter, and in any film format or base. Selection is based on the artistic, historic, cultural, and/or educational importance of the film, especially in relation to the role of women in film history; significance of the key creative women in the production; evidence of the artistic and technical expertise of those planning and executing the project; urgency of the need to preserve the film; appropriateness of the budget for the proposed work; and realism of the plan for making the film available to professionals, scholars, and interested audiences.

**Financial data** The maximum grant is $10,000. Funds may be used only for actual costs connected with restoration and preservation, not for salaries or general administrative costs. In addition to cash grants, the fund also awards approximately $25,000 worth of in-kind post-production services for films created by or related to women.

**Duration** These grants are provided annually.

**Number awarded** Varies each year; recently, 3 of these grants were awarded.

**Deadline** September of each year.

## [1482]
## WOMEN'S LAW AND PUBLIC POLICY FELLOWSHIP PROGRAM

Georgetown University Law Center
Attn: Women's Law and Public Policy Fellowship Program
600 New Jersey Avenue, N.W., H5024A
Washington, DC 20001
(202) 662-9650                    Fax: (202) 662-9117
E-mail: wlppfp@law.georgetown.edu
Web: www.law.georgetown.edu

**Summary** To provide an opportunity for recently-graduated public interest lawyers in the Washington D.C. area to work on women's rights issues.

**Eligibility** This program is open to recent graduates of law schools accredited by the American Bar Association. Applicants must be interested in working on women's rights issues in the Washington, D.C. area (e.g., at the Georgetown University School of Law, the National Partnership for Women and Families, and the National Women's Law Center).

**Financial data** The stipend is approximately $41,000 per year.

**Duration** The fellowships at Georgetown Law are 2-year teaching assignments; other fellowships are for 1 year.

**Additional information** This program includes 2 named fellowships: the Rita Charmatz Davidson Fellowship (to work on issues primarily affecting poor women) and the Harriet R. Burg Fellowship (to work primarily on issues affecting women with disabilities). In addition, the Ford Foundation supports fellowships at organizations focusing on issues concerning women and AIDS/HIV. Fellows are supervised by attorneys at the participating organizations.

**Number awarded** Approximately 6 each year.

**Deadline** November of each year.

## [1483]
## WOMEN'S MUSIC COMMISSION

Broadcast Music Inc.
Attn: BMI Foundation, Inc.
7 World Trade Center
250 Greenwich Street
New York, NY 10007-0030
(212) 220-3000          E-mail: info@bmifoundation.org
Web: www.bmifoundation.org

**Summary** To recognize and reward, with a commission for production of a new work, outstanding young female composers.

**Eligibility** This competition is open to women between 20 and 30 years of age who are citizens or permanent residents of the United States. Applicants must submit samples of their original compositions.

**Financial data** The winner receives a $5,000 commission to create a new work.

**Duration** The competition is held annually.

**Additional information** This program began in 2006. Each year, the sponsor partners with a different world-class performer, ensemble, or presenter to present the premier performance.

**Number awarded** 1 each year.

**Deadline** May of each year.

## [1484]
## WOMEN'S PRIZE FOR FICTION

Booktrust
45 East Hill
London SW18 2QZ
England
44 20 8516 2977          Fax: 44 20 8516 2978
E-mail: womensprize@booktrust.org.uk
Web: www.womensprizeforfiction.co.uk

**Summary** To recognize and reward the most outstanding novels by women from any country that are written in English and published in the United Kingdom.

**Eligibility** Eligible to be considered for this prize are novels written by women (of any nationality) in English and published in the United Kingdom during the 12 months prior to March 31 of the year of the award. Submissions may also have been published in other countries, including the United States, as long as their first U.K. publication was within the prescribed time period. Ineligible works include books of short stories, novellas (stories between 12,000 and 30,000 words), and translations of books originally written in other languages.

**Financial data** The prize is 30,000 pounds and a bronze figurine known as the "Bessie."

**Duration** The prize is awarded annually.

**Additional information** This prize, first awarded in 1996, is the United Kingdom's largest annual literary award for a single novel. It was formerly known as the Orange Broadband Prize for Fiction.

**Number awarded** 1 each year.

**Deadline** Deadline not specified.

## [1485]
## WORKSHOPS FOR WOMEN GRADUATE STUDENTS AND RECENT PH.D.S

Association for Women in Mathematics
11240 Waples Mill Road, Suite 200
Fairfax, VA 22030
(703) 934-0163          Fax: (703) 359-7562
E-mail: awm@awm-math.org
Web: sites.google.com/site/awmmath/programs/workshops

**Summary** To enable women graduate students and recent Ph.D.s in mathematics to participate in workshops in conjunction with major meetings.

**Eligibility** Eligible for funding are women graduate students who have begun work on a thesis problem in mathematics and women mathematicians who received their Ph.D.s within the preceding 5 years. Applicants must wish to participate in workshops held in conjunction with major mathematics meetings at which each participating graduate student presents a poster on her thesis problem and each postdoctorate presents a talk on her research.

**Financial data** Funding covers travel and subsistence.

**Duration** Funding for 2 days is provided.

**Additional information** Participants have the opportunity to present and discuss their research and to meet with other women mathematicians at all stages of their careers. The workshop also includes a panel discussion on issues of career development and a luncheon. This program is supported by the Office of Naval Research, the Department of Energy, and the National Security Agency.

**Number awarded** Up to 20 at each of 2 workshops each year.

**Deadline** October or August of each year.

**[1486]**
## ZETA PHI BETA GENERAL GRADUATE FELLOWSHIPS

Zeta Phi Beta Sorority, Inc.
Attn: National Education Foundation
1734 New Hampshire Avenue, N.W.
Washington, DC 20009
(202) 387-3103          Fax: (202) 232-4593
E-mail: scholarship@ZPhiBNEF.org
Web: www.zphib1920.org/nef

**Summary**  To provide financial assistance to women who are working on a professional degree, master's degree, doctorate, or postdoctorate.

**Eligibility**  Women graduate or postdoctoral students are eligible to apply if they have achieved distinction or shown promise of distinction in their chosen fields. Applicants need not be members of Zeta Phi Beta. They must be enrolled full time in a professional, graduate, or postdoctoral program. Along with their application, they must submit a 150-word essay on their educational goals and professional aspirations, how this award will help them to achieve those goals, and why they should receive the award. Financial need is not considered in the selection process.

**Financial data**  The stipend ranges up to $2,500, paid directly to the recipient.

**Duration**  1 academic year; may be renewed.

**Number awarded**  1 or more each year.

**Deadline**  January of each year.

# Indexes

- Program Title Index ●
- Sponsoring Organization Index ●
- Residency Index ●
- Tenability Index ●
- Subject Index ●
- Calendar Index ●

# Program Title Index

If you know the name of a particular funding program open to women and want to find out where it is covered in the directory, use the Program Title Index. Here, program titles are arranged alphabetically, word by word. To assist you in your search, every program is listed by all its known names or abbreviations. In addition, we've used an alphabetical code (within parentheses) to help you determine if the program is aimed at you: U = Undergraduates; G = Graduate Students; P = Professionals/Postdoctorates. Here's how the code works: if a program is followed by (U) 241, the program is described in the Undergraduates chapter, in entry 241. If the same program title is followed by another entry number—for example, (P) 1370—the program is also described in the Professionals/Postdoctorates chapter, in entry 1370. Remember: the numbers cited here refer to program entry numbers, not to page numbers in the book.

## A

A. Margaret Boyd Scholarship. *See* Delta Kappa Gamma Scholarship Program, entry (G) 835

AAJUW Scholarship Program, (U) 1, (G) 724

AAPG Semester Internships in Geoscience Public Policy. *See* AGI/AAPG Semester Internships in Geoscience Public Policy, entries (U) 12, (G) 732

AAU High School Sullivan Scholarship Award, (U) 2

AAUW Career Development Grants, (U) 3, (G) 725, (P) 1209

AAUW Postdoctoral Research Leave Fellowships. *See* Postdoctoral Research Leave Fellowships, entry (P) 1414

Abel Scholarship. *See* Margaret Abel Scholarship, entries (U) 397, (G) 1016

Abraham Scholarship. *See* AEPhi Foundation Scholarships, entries (U) 11, (G) 730

Abrahim Ekramullah Zafar Foundation Scholarship. *See* Sehar Saleha Ahmad and Abrahim Ekramullah Zafar Foundation Scholarship, entry (U) 582

Academic Excellence Scholarships, (U) 4

Accelerator Applications Division Scholarship, (U) 5

Accenture Scholarships. *See* SWE/Accenture Scholarships, entry (U) 620

ACNM Foundation Fellowship for Graduate Education, (G) 726, (P) 1210

Ada I. Pressman Scholarship, (U) 6, (G) 727

Adair Scholarship. *See* Native Daughters of the Golden West Scholarship Program, entry (U) 471

Adalin Macauley Scholarship. *See* Wisconsin Legion Auxiliary Merit and Memorial Scholarships, entry (U) 673

Adams Endowed Student Scholarships. *See* Charlie Adams Endowed Student Scholarships, entry (U) 118

Adams Memorial Scholarship. *See* Dixie Softball Scholarships, entry (U) 176

Adele Lewis Fellowship. *See* Sigma Delta Epsilon Fellowships, entries (G) 1145, (P) 1447

Adele Lobracio Lowe Leadership Grant. *See* Lambda Kappa Sigma Grants, entry (G) 995

Adkins Memorial Scholarship. *See* Dixie Softball Scholarships, entry (U) 176

Admiral Grace Murray Hopper Memorial Scholarships, (U) 7

Adult Students in Scholastic Transition (ASIST) Program, (U) 8

Adult Women Seminary Scholarship, (G) 728

Advancing Aspirations Global Scholarships, (U) 9

Advancing Women in Accounting Scholarship, (U) 10, (G) 729

AEPhi Foundation Scholarships, (U) 11, (G) 730

AERA-ETS Fellowship Program in Measurement, (P) 1211

AFRL/DAGSI Ohio Student-Faculty Research Fellowship Program, (G) 731, (P) 1212

AGA Research Scholar Awards, (P) 1213

AGI/AAPG Semester Internships in Geoscience Public Policy, (U) 12, (G) 732

Agnes Missirian Scholarship. *See* Armenian International Women's Association Scholarships, entries (U) 53, (G) 767

AGU Graduate Fellowship in the History of Science, (G) 733

Aharonian Scholarships. *See* Lucy Kasparian Aharonian Scholarships, entries (U) 384, (G) 1006

AHIMA Foundation Diversity Scholarships, (U) 13, (G) 734

Ahmad and Abrahim Ekramullah Zafar Foundation Scholarship. *See* Sehar Saleha Ahmad and Abrahim Ekramullah Zafar Foundation Scholarship, entry (U) 582

Air Force Research Laboratory/Dayton Area Graduate Studies Institute Ohio Student-Faculty Research Fellowship Program. *See* AFRL/DAGSI Ohio Student-Faculty Research Fellowship Program, entries (G) 731, (P) 1212

Airbus Leadership Grant. *See* Women in Aviation, International General Scholarships, entries (U) 681, (G) 1194

Aircraft Electronics Association Avionics Technician Scholarship. *See* Association for Women in Aviation Maintenance Scholarship Program, entry (U) 60

Aircraft Owners and Pilots Association Student Pilot Scholarship. *See* Women in Aviation, International Flight Scholarships, entry (P) 1475

AKA Endowment Awards, (U) 14, (G) 735

AKA Graduate Scholarships, (G) 736

Bolin Dissertation and Post-MFA Fellowships. *See* Gaius Charles Bolin Dissertation and Post-MFA Fellowships, entries (G) 905, (P) 1304

Bonawitz Scholarship. *See* Dr. Mary Feeney Bonawitz Scholarship, entry (G) 859

Boney Memorial Scholarships. *See* New Mexico Elks Association Charitable and Benevolent Trust Scholarships, entry (U) 482

Borg Memorial Scholarships. *See* Anita Borg Memorial Scholarships, entries (U) 40, (G) 760

Borg Memorial Scholarships for First Years. *See* Google Anita Borg Memorial Scholarships for First Years, entry (U) 267

Boris Christoff International Competition for Young Opera Singers, (P) 1240

Boston Affiliate AWSCPA Scholarship, (U) 94, (G) 797

Boston Chapter/Claire Barrett Memorial Scholarship, (G) 798

Boston Scientific Scholarships, (U) 95

Bowens-Wheatley Scholarships. *See* Marjorie Bowens-Wheatley Scholarships, entries (U) 402, (G) 1025

Boyd Graduate Scholarship. *See* Winifred Hill Boyd Graduate Scholarship, entry (G) 1188

Boynton Scholarship. *See* Virginia Burns Boynton Scholarship, entry (G) 1173

BPW/WA Past President Memorial Scholarship, (U) 96

Bradford Grant-in-Aid, (U) 97

Bradham Social Work Fellowship. *See* Mildred Cater Bradham Social Work Fellowship, entry (G) 1047

Brady, MD Comeback Awards. *See* Thomas A. Brady, MD Comeback Awards, entry (U) 636

Breed Award for Women Leaders. *See* J. Cordell Breed Award for Women Leaders, entry (P) 1327

Brennan Scholarship. *See* Association for Women in Sports Media Scholarship/Internship Program, entries (U) 61, (G) 775

Brent Memorial Scholarship. *See* Charlotte Brent Memorial Scholarship, entry (G) 813

Brewer Distinguished Teaching of Psychology Award. *See* Charles L. Brewer Distinguished Teaching of Psychology Award, entry (P) 1252

Bridge Scholarship. *See* William Bridge Scholarship, entry (U) 670

Brill Family Scholarship, (U) 98

Brookhaven National Laboratory Professional Associates Program for Women and Minorities, (P) 1241

Brookhaven National Laboratory Science and Engineering Programs for Women and Minorities, (U) 99

Brown, NM7N, Memorial Scholarship. *See* Young Ladies' Radio League Scholarships, entries (U) 710, (G) 1204

Brown Scholarship. *See* Erma Metz Brown Scholarship, entry (U) 221

Bryan Graduate Scholarship. *See* Katharine C. Bryan Graduate Scholarship, entry (G) 989

Buc Postdoctoral Fellowship. *See* Pembroke Center Postdoctoral Fellowships, entry (P) 1409

Buddy Wade Memorial Scholarship. *See* Dixie Softball Scholarships, entry (U) 176

Bufton Jr. Scholarship. *See* Hilary A. Bufton Jr. Scholarship, entry (G) 935

Bufton Memorial Education Fund Outright Grants Program. *See* Stephen Bufton Memorial Education Fund Outright Grants Program, entries (U) 612, (G) 1152

Bufton Scholarship. *See* Ruth H. Bufton Scholarship, entry (G) 1123

Buick Achievers Scholarship Program, (U) 100

Bunny M. Connors Memorial Scholarship. *See* Women in Aviation, International Flight Scholarships, entry (P) 1475

Burdett Scholarship. *See* Susan Burdett Scholarship, entry (U) 614

Burg Fellowship. *See* Women's Law and Public Policy Fellowship Program, entry (P) 1482

Burk Conducting Scholarship for Graduate Students. *See* Bobbie Burk Conducting Scholarship for Graduate Students, entry (G) 796

Burns-Smith "Dare to Dream" Scholarships. *See* Gail Burns-Smith "Dare to Dream" Scholarships, entry (U) 251

Burroughs Wellcome Fund/Career Awards for Medical Scientists, (P) 1242

Burroughs Wellcome Fund Investigators in Pathogenesis of Infectious Disease, (P) 1243

Business and Professional Women of Iowa Foundation Educational Scholarship, (U) 101

Business and Professional Women of Washington Past President Memorial Scholarship. *See* BPW/WA Past President Memorial Scholarship, entry (U) 96

Business and Professional Women's Foundation of Maryland Scholarship, (U) 102

Business Women in Missouri General Scholarships, (U) 103

Byers Postgraduate Scholarship Program. *See* Walter Byers Postgraduate Scholarship Program, entry (G) 1176

Byrd Fellowship Program. *See* Ohio State University Byrd Fellowship Program, entry (P) 1402

## C

C. Dan Keffer Award. *See* Virginia Golf Foundation Scholarship Program, entry (U) 656

C200 Scholar Awards, (G) 799

Cady McDonnell Memorial Scholarship, (U) 104

Cahill Scholarship. *See* WLAM Foundation Scholars, entry (G) 1191

Calder Summer Undergraduate Research Program, (U) 105

California Legion Auxiliary Past Department President's Junior Scholarship, (U) 106

California P.E.O. Selected Scholarships, (U) 107, (G) 800

Callahan Scholar Athlete. *See* Lindy Callahan Scholar Athlete, entry (U) 372

Cammer-Hill Grant, (U) 108

Campbell Memorial Scholarship. *See* Dorothy Campbell Memorial Scholarship, entry (U) 184

Campbell Scholarship Program. *See* Bertha Pitts Campbell Scholarship Program, entry (U) 79

Candi Chamberlin Kubeck Award. *See* Women in Aviation, International General Scholarships, entries (U) 681, (G) 1194

Candon Scholarship. *See* Sister Elizabeth Candon Scholarship, entry (U) 595

Cannon Award in Astronomy. *See* Annie Jump Cannon Award in Astronomy, entry (P) 1223

Captain Sally Tompkins Nursing and Applied Health Sciences Scholarship, (U) 109

Capture the Dream Single Parent Scholarship, (U) 110

Career Advancement Scholarships, (U) 111

Career Awards for Medical Scientists. *See* Burroughs Wellcome Fund/Career Awards for Medical Scientists, entry (P) 1242

Career Awards in the Biomedical Sciences. *See* Burroughs Wellcome Fund/Career Awards for Medical Scientists, entry (P) 1242

Career Development Awards in Diabetes Research, (P) 1244

Career Development Grants. *See* AAUW Career Development Grants, entries (U) 3, (G) 725, (P) 1209

Career Development Grants for Postdoctoral Women, (P) 1245

Harriet M. Heatherington Scholarship. *See* YWCA Harriet M. Heatherington Scholarship, entry (U) 715

Harriet R. Burg Fellowship. *See* Women's Law and Public Policy Fellowship Program, entry (P) 1482

Harriett G. Jenkins Predoctoral Fellowship Program, (G) 923

Harris Math and Science Scholarships. *See* ExxonMobil Bernard Harris Math and Science Scholarships, entry (U) 231

Harrod Scholarships. *See* B.J. Harrod Scholarships, entry (U) 90

Harry and Miriam Levinson Scholarship. *See* APF/COGDOP Graduate Research Scholarships, entry (G) 765

Hartley Corporation Fellowship. *See* Sigma Delta Epsilon Fellowships, entries (G) 1145, (P) 1447

Harvard Divinity School/Women's Studies in Religion Program, (P) 1312

Harvard–Newcomen Postdoctoral Fellowship in Business History, (P) 1313

Harvard-Smithsonian Center for Astrophysics Solar REU Program, (U) 273

Haseltine Scholarship Fund for Women. *See* Ingeborg Haseltine Scholarship Fund for Women, entry (G) 949

Hasmik Mgrdichian Scholarship, (U) 274

Hass Scholarship. *See* Wisconsin Legion Auxiliary Merit and Memorial Scholarships, entry (U) 673

Hattie Hemschemeyer Award, (P) 1314

Hattie J. Hilliard Scholarship, (U) 275

Hayden W. Wagner Memorial Fund. *See* Society of Daughters of the United States Army Scholarships, entry (U) 597

Hazel Beard Lease Scholarship, (U) 276, (G) 924

Hazel Johnson Memorial Scholarship. *See* Delta Kappa Gamma Scholarship Program, entry (G) 835

Hazel Palmer General Scholarship. *See* Judge Hazel Palmer General Scholarship, entry (U) 333

Head Scholarship. *See* Edith Head Scholarship, entries (U) 204, (G) 865

Health and Society Scholars Program. *See* Scholars in Health Policy Research Program, entry (P) 1440

Health Sciences Student Fellowships in Epilepsy, (G) 925

Hearst Scholarship of New York Women in Communications, (U) 277

Heather Westphal Memorial Scholarship Award, (U) 278, (P) 1315

Heatherington Scholarship. *See* YWCA Harriet M. Heatherington Scholarship, entry (U) 715

Hécaen Scholarship. *See* Benton-Meier Neuropsychology Scholarships, entry (G) 785

Hecksel-Sutherland Scholarship, (U) 279, (P) 1316

Heflin Scholarship. *See* Linly Heflin Scholarship, entry (U) 373

Heiken Doctoral Grant. *See* Donna Heiken Doctoral Grant, entry (G) 844

Heil Scholarship. *See* Mabel Heil Scholarship, entries (U) 389, (G) 1012

Helberg Art Grants for Mature Women. *See* Shirley Holden Helberg Art Grants for Mature Women, entry (P) 1442

Helberg Letters Grants for Mature Women. *See* Shirley Holden Helberg Letters Grants for Mature Women, entry (P) 1443

Helberg Music Grants for Mature Women. *See* Shirley Holden Helberg Music Grants for Mature Women, entry (P) 1444

Helen A. Snyder Scholarship. *See* Kappa Delta Sorority Graduate Scholarships, entry (G) 986

Helen Ann Mins Robbins Fellowship, (G) 926

Helen Beardsley Scholarship. *See* California P.E.O. Selected Scholarships, entries (U) 107, (G) 800

Helen D. Thompson Memorial Scholarship. *See* California P.E.O. Selected Scholarships, entries (U) 107, (G) 800

Helen Gartner Hammer Scholar-in-Residence Program, (P) 1317

Helen Haller Scholarship, (G) 927

Helen J. Beldecos Scholarship. *See* Daughters of Penelope Undergraduate Scholarships, entry (U) 147

Helen Louise Jordan Memorial Scholarship. *See* Dixie Softball Scholarships, entry (U) 176

Helen Muntean Education Scholarship for Women, (U) 280

Helen Trueheart Cox Art Scholarship, (U) 281

Helen W. Nies Scholarship, (G) 928

Helen Woodruff Nolop Scholarship in Audiology and Allied Fields, (G) 929

Helene M. Overly Memorial Graduate Scholarship, (G) 930

Helis Scholarship. *See* Desk and Derrick Education Trust Scholarships, entries (U) 167, (G) 838

Heloise Werthan Kuhn Scholarship, (U) 282

"Helping Hand" from Rice Family Scholarships. *See* Association for Women in Aviation Maintenance Scholarship Program, entry (U) 60

Helping Hands of WSC Endowment Scholarship, (U) 283

Hemmings Scholarship. *See* Myra Davis Hemmings Scholarship, entry (G) 1057

Hemschemeyer Award. *See* Hattie Hemschemeyer Award, entry (P) 1314

Hennesy Scholarship. *See* Cheryl Dant Hennesy Scholarship, entry (U) 121

Henry David Research Grant in Human Reproductive Behavior and Population Studies, (G) 931, (P) 1318

Henry Hécaen Scholarship. *See* Benton-Meier Neuropsychology Scholarships, entry (G) 785

Henry Scholarship. *See* California P.E.O. Selected Scholarships, entries (U) 107, (G) 800

Herbert and Betty Carnes Fund, (G) 932, (P) 1319

Herbert W. and Corrine Chilstrom Scholarship, (G) 933, (P) 1320

Herff Jones Graduate Fellowship. *See* Kappa Delta Sorority Graduate Scholarships, entry (G) 986

Hermine Dalkowitz Tobolowsky Scholarship, (U) 284, (G) 934

Hertsgaard Scholarship. *See* Doris Hertsgaard Scholarship, entries (U) 181, (G) 847

Herz Fellowship. *See* Women's Campaign Fund Fellowship Program, entries (U) 693, (P) 1479

Hester Special Education Scholarship. *See* Sue and Virginia Hester Special Education Scholarship, entry (U) 613

Higgins Scholarship. *See* Sigma Gamma Rho Scholarships/ Fellowships, entries (U) 591, (G) 1146

High Priority, Short-Term Bridge Awards in Diabetes Research, (P) 1321

Hilary A. Bufton Jr. Scholarship, (G) 935

Hiller Scholarship. *See* Delta Kappa Gamma Scholarship Program, entry (G) 835

Hilliard Scholarship. *See* Hattie J. Hilliard Scholarship, entry (U) 275

Hill–Rom, Celeste Phillips Family-Centered Maternity Care Award, (P) 1322

Hine Award. *See* Darlene Clark Hine Award, entry (P) 1259

History of Women in Science Prize. *See* Margaret W. Rossiter History of Women in Science Prize, entry (P) 1366

Hitchcock Scholarships. *See* Susan Glover Hitchcock Scholarships, entry (U) 616

Hoch Distinguished Service Award. *See* Paul Hoch Distinguished Service Award, entry (P) 1406

Hodge Scholarship. *See* New Jersey Schoolwomen's Club Scholarships, entry (U) 478

---

    **U–Undergraduates**          **G–Graduate Students**          **P–Professionals/Postdoctorates**

**U–Undergraduates**　　　　**G–Graduate Students**　　　　**P–Professionals/Postdoctorates**

**U–Undergraduates**     **G–Graduate Students**     **P–Professionals/Postdoctorates**

Minnesota Child Care Grant Program, (U) 430

Minnesota Legion Auxiliary Past Presidents Parley Health Care Scholarship, (U) 431

Minnesota Section SWE Scholarship, (U) 432

Minnie L. Maffett Fellowships, (G) 1050, (P) 1385

Minnie Mae Prescott Kappa Delta Staff Risk Management Scholarship. *See* Kappa Delta Sorority Undergraduate Scholarships, entry (U) 343

Minnie Mae Prescott Scholarship. *See* Kappa Delta Sorority Graduate Scholarships, entry (G) 986

Miracle Maker Award. *See* Miss America Competition Awards, entry (U) 434

Miriam Levinson Scholarship. *See* APF/COGDOP Graduate Research Scholarships, entry (G) 765

Miss America Community Service Scholarships, (U) 433

Miss America Competition Awards, (U) 434

Miss America Scholar Awards, (U) 435

Miss Congeniality Award. *See* Miss America Competition Awards, entry (U) 434

Miss Indian USA Scholarship Program, (U) 436

Miss Latina World, (U) 437, (P) 1386

Miss Teen America, (U) 438

Miss Teen USA, (U) 439

Miss USA, (U) 440

Missirian Scholarship. *See* Armenian International Women's Association Scholarships, entries (U) 53, (G) 767

Missouri State Knights of Columbus Ladies Auxiliary Scholarship, (U) 441

Missouri Women's Golf Education Association Scholarships, (U) 442

Miszkowicz Memorial Scholarship. *See* Susan Miszkowicz Memorial Scholarship, entry (U) 617

Mock Scholarship. *See* Kappa Delta Sorority Undergraduate Scholarships, entry (U) 343

Moldovan Scholarship. *See* Peppy Moldovan Scholarship, entry (U) 518

Molitoris Leadership Award. *See* Louise Moritz Molitoris Leadership Award, entry (U) 378

Mona and Anila Jain Scholarship. *See* Kailash, Mona, and Anila Jain Scholarship, entry (G) 984

Mondy Fellowship. *See* Nell I. Mondy Fellowship, entries (G) 1074, (P) 1394

Monticello College Foundation Fellowship for Women, (P) 1387

Moore-Velez Woman of Substance Scholarship. *See* Dr. Blanca Moore-Velez Woman of Substance Scholarship, entry (U) 193

Morgan Fellowship. *See* Ruth P. Morgan Fellowship, entry (P) 1433

Morgan Stanley MBA Fellowship, (G) 1051

Morgan Stanley Sophomore Internship Program, (U) 443

Morisawa Research Award. *See* Marie Morisawa Research Award, entry (G) 1023

Morrell Prize. *See* Ottoline Morrell Prize, entry (P) 1405

Morris Memorial Award for Strings or Harp. *See* Awards for Undergraduate Performance, entry (U) 67

Morris Memorial Awards. *See* Graduate Performance Awards, entry (G) 916

Morris Scholarship. *See* Dorothy P. Morris Scholarship, entry (U) 190, 358

Morrison Memorial Scholarship. *See* Association for Women in Sports Media Scholarship/Internship Program, entries (U) 61, (G) 775

Morse Scholarship. *See* Delta Kappa Gamma Scholarship Program, entry (G) 835

Mosley Scholarships. *See* Dwight Mosley Scholarships, entry (U) 199

Moss Adams Foundation Scholarship, (U) 444, (G) 1052

Motherwell Prize. *See* Ottoline Morrell Prize, entry (P) 1405

Mower Memorial Scholarship. *See* Barbara Alice Mower Memorial Scholarship, entries (U) 71, (G) 780

Mrs. Dexter Otis Arnold Scholarship, (U) 445

MSCPA Women in Accounting Scholarship, (U) 446, (G) 1053

MTS Systems Corporation Scholarship, (U) 447, (G) 1054

Mueller Scholarships. *See* Elizabeth Banta Mueller Scholarships, entry (U) 208

Mullen Flight Training Scholarship. *See* Whirly-Girls Memorial Flight Training Scholarship, entry (P) 1471

Mullins Courageous Achievement Award. *See* VHSL-Allstate Achievement Awards, entry (U) 649

Mullins Scholarship. *See* Marion Day Mullins Scholarship, entry (U) 401

Munger Memorial Scholarship. *See* Mary V. Munger Memorial Scholarship, entry (U) 414

Munn Scholarship. *See* Wanda Munn Scholarship, entries (U) 661, (G) 1178, (P) 1469

Muntean Education Scholarship for Women. *See* Helen Muntean Education Scholarship for Women, entry (U) 280

Muriel Johnstone Scholarship. *See* Kappa Delta Sorority Graduate Scholarships, entry (G) 986

Muriel Johnstone Scholarships. *See* Kappa Delta Sorority Undergraduate Scholarships, entry (U) 343

Muriel Landis Scholarships. *See* John and Muriel Landis Scholarships, entries (U) 329, (G) 968

Muriel Lothrop-Ely Endowment. *See* Arizona BPW Foundation Scholarships, entry (U) 49

Muriel T. McKinney Scholarship. *See* Alpha Omicron Pi Diamond Jubilee Foundation Scholarships, entries (U) 24, (G) 743

Murphy Scholarship for Women in Ministry. *See* Bishop Frank Murphy Scholarship for Women in Ministry, entry (G) 792

Murphy Scholarship Program. *See* Vashti Turley Murphy Scholarship Program, entry (G) 1166

Murphy Scholarships. *See* Linda J. Murphy Scholarships, entry (G) 1002

Murray Scholarship. *See* Bernice Murray Scholarship, entry (U) 77

Musemeche Scholarship Program, (U) 448

Music Business/Technology Scholarship. *See* Dorothy Cooke Whinery Music Business/Technology Scholarship, entry (U) 185

Music Education Scholarship for Graduate Students. *See* Mabel Biever Music Education Scholarship for Graduate Students, entry (G) 1011

Music Therapy Scholarship, (U) 449, (G) 1055

Musical Theater Scholarship, (U) 450

Musicians with Special Needs Scholarship, (U) 451, (G) 1056

Myra Davis Hemmings Scholarship, (G) 1057

Myrna F. Bernath Book Award, (P) 1388

Myrna F. Bernath Fellowship Award, (G) 1058, (P) 1389

Myrt Willey Scholarship, (U) 452

## N

NABA 20 Pearls Scholarship, (U) 453, (G) 1059

NACOPRW Scholarship Award, (U) 454

NAHB Women's Council Strategies for Success Scholarship, (U) 455

Najarian Scholarships. *See* Armenian International Women's Association Scholarships, entries (U) 53, (G) 767

Naman Graduate School Scholarship. *See* Victoria Naman Graduate School Scholarship, entry (G) 1169

Nancy Anne Weinstein Scholarship, (U) 456

Nancy B. Woolridge McGee Graduate Fellowship, (G) 1060

Nancy Foster Scholarship Program. *See* Dr. Nancy Foster Scholarship Program, entry (G) 860

Nancy Holliman Scholarship. *See* Houston/Nancy Holliman Scholarship, entry (U) 293

Nancy Kelly Female Writer Award, (U) 457, (G) 1061

Nancy L. Buc Postdoctoral Fellowship. *See* Pembroke Center Postdoctoral Fellowships, entry (P) 1409

Nancy Lorraine Jensen Memorial Scholarship Fund, (U) 458

Nancy Reagan Pathfinder Scholarships. *See* National Pathfinder Scholarships, entries (U) 466, (G) 1067

Nannie W. Norfleet Scholarship, (U) 459

NASA Undergraduate Student Research Program, (U) 460

Nathalie A. Price Memorial Scholarship, (U) 461

National Aeronautics and Space Administration Undergraduate Student Research Program. *See* NASA Undergraduate Student Research Program, entry (U) 460

National Association of Black Accountants 20 Pearls Scholarship. *See* NABA 20 Pearls Scholarship, entries (U) 453, (G) 1059

National Association of Home Builders Women's Council Strategies for Success Scholarship. *See* NAHB Women's Council Strategies for Success Scholarship, entry (U) 455

National Association of Purchasing Management Doctoral Dissertation Grant Program. *See* Institute for Supply Management Doctoral Dissertation Grant Program, entry (G) 950

National Association of University Women Fellowships, (G) 1062

National Center for Atmospheric Research Postdoctoral Appointments, (P) 1390

National Collegiate Athletic Association Ethnic Minority and Women's Internship Grant Program. *See* NCAA Ethnic Minority and Women's Internship Grant Program, entry (P) 1393

National Collegiate Athletic Association Postgraduate Scholarship Program, (G) 1063

National Collegiate Athletic Association Women's Enhancement Postgraduate Scholarship Program. *See* NCAA Women's Enhancement Scholarship Program, entry (G) 1073

National Conference of Puerto Rican Women Scholarship Award. *See* NACOPRW Scholarship Award, entry (U) 454

National Co-op Scholarship Program, (U) 462

National Defense Science and Engineering Graduate Fellowship Program, (G) 1064

National Federation of Music Clubs Biennial Student Audition Awards. *See* NFMC Biennial Student/Collegiate Audition Awards, entries (U) 484, (G) 1079

National Federation of Music Clubs Biennial Young Artist Awards, (P) 1391

National Foundation for Women Legislators/NRA Bill of Rights Essay Contest. *See* NFWL/NRA Bill of Rights Essay Contest, entry (U) 485

National Hispanic Business Women Association Educational Scholarships, (U) 463, (G) 1065

National Network of Presbyterian College Women Scholarship, (U) 464

National Oceanic and Atmospheric Administration Small Business Innovation Research Grants. *See* NOAA Small Business Innovation Research Grants, entry (P) 1396

National Optical Astronomy Observatories 5-Year Science Fellowship. *See* Leo Goldberg Fellowships, entry (P) 1348

National Organization of Italian American Women Scholarships, (U) 465, (G) 1066

National Pathfinder Scholarships, (U) 466, (G) 1067

National Physical Science Consortium Graduate Fellowships, (G) 1068

National Press Club Scholarship for Journalism Diversity, (U) 467

National Rifle Association Bill of Rights Essay Contest. *See* NFWL/NRA Bill of Rights Essay Contest, entry (U) 485

National Science Foundation Graduate Research Fellowships. *See* Graduate Research Fellowship Program of the National Science Foundation, entry (G) 917

National Science Foundation Small Business Innovation Research Grants. *See* NSF Small Business Innovation Research Grants, entry (P) 1398

National Science Foundation Small Business Technology Transfer Grants. *See* NSF Small Business Technology Transfer Grants, entry (P) 1399

National Society of Professional Engineers Auxiliary Legacy Scholarship. *See* NSPE Auxiliary Legacy Scholarship, entry (U) 493

National Sorority of Phi Delta Kappa Scholarships, (U) 468

National Space Grant College and Fellowship Program, (U) 469, (G) 1069

National Strength and Conditioning Association Women's Scholarships, (U) 470, (G) 1070

National Urban Fellows Program, (G) 1071, (P) 1392

National Women's Studies Association Graduate Scholarship Award. *See* NWSA Graduate Scholarship Award, entry (G) 1085

National Women's Studies Association/University of Illinois Press First Book Prize. *See* NWSA/University of Illinois Press First Book Prize, entry (P) 1401

Native Daughters of the Golden West Scholarship Program, (U) 471

Nau Scholarship. *See* California P.E.O. Selected Scholarships, entries (U) 107, (G) 800

Navy/Marine Corps/Coast Guard Enlisted Dependent Spouse Scholarship, (U) 472, (G) 1072

NCAA Ethnic Minority and Women's Internship Grant Program, (P) 1393

NCAA Women's Enhancement Scholarship Program, (G) 1073

NCAIAW Scholarship, (U) 473

Nearly New Scholarship. *See* California P.E.O. Selected Scholarships, entries (U) 107, (G) 800

Nebraska Rural Community Schools Association Scholarships, (U) 474

Neely Memorial Scholarship. *See* Dixie Softball Scholarships, entry (U) 176

Neely-Gary Memorial Scholarship. *See* Aura Neely-Gary Memorial Scholarship, entry (U) 64

Neidle Scholar-in-Residence Program for Women. *See* Enid A. Neidle Scholar-in-Residence Program for Women, entry (P) 1285

Nell I. Mondy Fellowship, (G) 1074, (P) 1394

Nellie Yeoh Whetten Award, (G) 1075

Nesbitt Medical Student Foundation Scholarship, (G) 1076

Network of Executive Women Scholarship, (U) 475, (G) 1077

New Horizons Leader Scholarship, (U) 476

New Immigrant Scholarships, (U) 477

New Initiatives in Malaria Awards. *See* Burroughs Wellcome Fund Investigators in Pathogenesis of Infectious Disease, entry (P) 1243

---

**U–Undergraduates**          **G–Graduate Students**          **P–Professionals/Postdoctorates**

New Investigator and Scholar Awards in Molecular Parasitology. *See* Burroughs Wellcome Fund Investigators in Pathogenesis of Infectious Disease, entry (P) 1243

New Investigator and Scholar Awards in Molecular Pathogenic Mycology. *See* Burroughs Wellcome Fund Investigators in Pathogenesis of Infectious Disease, entry (P) 1243

New Jersey Schoolwomen's Club Scholarships, (U) 478

New Jersey State Elks Special Children's Scholarship, (U) 479

New Jersey SWE Scholarship, (U) 480

New Jersey Utilities Association Excellence in Diversity Scholarships, (U) 481

New Mexico Elks Association Charitable and Benevolent Trust Scholarships, (U) 482

New Mexico Federation of Republican Women Scholarships, (U) 483

New Mexico Minority Doctoral Loan-for-Service Program, (G) 1078

New Pilot Awards, (P) 1395

New York Women in Communications, Inc. Foundation Scholarships. *See* NYWICI Foundation Scholarships, entries (U) 494, (G) 1086

Newcomen Postdoctoral Fellowship in Business History. *See* Harvard–Newcomen Postdoctoral Fellowship in Business History, entry (P) 1313

Newman Scholarship. *See* Kappa Delta Sorority Undergraduate Scholarships, entry (U) 343

NFMC Biennial Student/Collegiate Audition Awards, (U) 484, (G) 1079

NFMC Biennial Young Artist Awards. *See* National Federation of Music Clubs Biennial Young Artist Awards, entry (P) 1391

NFWL/NRA Bill of Rights Essay Contest, (U) 485

Nice Fund. *See* Margaret Morse Nice Fund, entry (G) 1018

Nies Scholarship. *See* Helen W. Nies Scholarship, entry (G) 928

Nina Belle Redditt Memorial Scholarship, (U) 486, (G) 1080

NOAA Small Business Innovation Research Grants, (P) 1396

NOAO 5-Year Science Fellowship. *See* Leo Goldberg Fellowships, entry (P) 1348

Nolop Scholarship in Audiology and Allied Fields. *See* Helen Woodruff Nolop Scholarship in Audiology and Allied Fields, entry (G) 929

Norby Scholarship. *See* Marian Norby Scholarship, entries (U) 399, (P) 1369

Norfleet Scholarship. *See* Nannie W. Norfleet Scholarship, entry (U) 459

Norma Bristow Salter Scholarship. *See* Delta Kappa Gamma Scholarship Program, entry (G) 835

Norma Chipman Wells Loyalty Grant. *See* Lambda Kappa Sigma Grants, entry (G) 995

Norma Ross Walter Scholarship Program, (U) 487

Norman's Orchids Masters Scholarship, (G) 1081

North Carolina Association of Intercollegiate Athletics for Women Scholarship. *See* NCAIAW Scholarship, entry (U) 473

North Carolina Business and Professional Women's Foundation Scholarships, (U) 488, (G) 1082

North Dakota Women's Opportunity Scholarship Fund, (U) 489

North Pointe Junior Gold Championships, (U) 490

Northrop Grumman Foundation Scholarship, (U) 491

Northwest Women in Educational Administration Scholarship, (U) 492

Northwestern Region Fellowship Award, (G) 1083

Norton Memorial Scholarship Award. *See* Mary R. Norton Memorial Scholarship Award, entries (U) 412, (G) 1037

Norwood Memorial Scholarships. *See* Josephine Carroll Norwood Memorial Scholarships, entry (G) 974

Notchev Fellowship. *See* Sigma Delta Epsilon Fellowships, entries (G) 1145, (P) 1447

Novice Researcher Award, (G) 1084, (P) 1397

NRA Bill of Rights Essay Contest. *See* NFWL/NRA Bill of Rights Essay Contest, entry (U) 485

NSF Small Business Innovation Research Grants, (P) 1398

NSF Small Business Technology Transfer Grants, (P) 1399

NSPE Auxiliary Legacy Scholarship, (U) 493

Nupur Chaudhuri First Article Prize, (P) 1400

Nursing and Applied Health Sciences Scholarship. *See* Captain Sally Tompkins Nursing and Applied Health Sciences Scholarship, entry (U) 109

Nutterville Scholarship. *See* Delta Kappa Gamma Scholarship Program, entry (G) 835

NWSA Graduate Scholarship Award, (G) 1085

NWSA/University of Illinois Press First Book Prize, (P) 1401

NYWICI Foundation Scholarships, (U) 494, (G) 1086

## O

Oestmann Professional Women's Achievement Award. *See* Mary Jane Oestmann Professional Women's Achievement Award, entry (P) 1372

Ohio Council 8 AFSCME Scholarships, (U) 495

Ohio State University Byrd Fellowship Program, (P) 1402

Oklahoma BW Foundation Scholarships, (U) 496, (G) 1087

Oklahoma City Chapter AWC Scholarships, (U) 497, (G) 1088

Okwu Girl Scout Gold Award Scholarship. *See* Dr. Bea Okwu Girl Scout Gold Award Scholarship, entry (U) 192

Ola B. Hiller Scholarship. *See* Delta Kappa Gamma Scholarship Program, entry (G) 835

O'Leary Memorial Scholarship. *See* Rhonda J.B. O'Leary Memorial Scholarship, entries (U) 548, (G) 1113

Olive Lynn Salembier Memorial Reentry Scholarship, (U) 498, (G) 1089

Omaha Chapter AFWA Scholarships, (U) 499, (G) 1090

One Family Scholars Program, (U) 500

O'Neil Arts Award. *See* M. Josephine O'Neil Arts Award, entry (U) 387

Onipa'a Chapter ABWA Scholarships, (U) 501

Online Bibliographic Services/Technical Services Joint Research Grant, (P) 1403

Optical Design and Engineering Scholarship. *See* SPIE Scholarship Program, entries (U) 605, (G) 1150

Optimist International Oratorical Contest, (U) 502

Ora Keck Scholarship. *See* California P.E.O. Selected Scholarships, entries (U) 107, (G) 800

Orange Broadband Prize for Fiction. *See* Women's Prize for Fiction, entry (P) 1484

Order of the Eastern Star of Pennsylvania Scholarships, (U) 503

Oregon Legion Auxiliary Department Nurses Scholarship for Dependents of Disabled Veterans, (U) 504

Oregon Legion Auxiliary Department Nurses Scholarship for Widows, (U) 505

Oregon Legion Auxiliary Department Scholarships for Dependents of Disabled Veterans, (U) 506

Oregon Legion Auxiliary Department Scholarships for Widows of Veterans, (U) 507

Oregon Literary Fellowships to Women Writers, (P) 1404

Organic Chemistry Graduate Student Fellowships, (G) 1091

Poll-Ette Founders Scholarships, (U) 529

Polly Sparks Early Career Grant. *See* John and Polly Sparks Early Career Grant, entry (P) 1332

Polly Thompson Memorial Music Scholarship. *See* California P.E.O. Selected Scholarships, entries (U) 107, (G) 800

Pomeroy Scholarships. *See* Virginia A. Pomeroy Scholarships, entry (G) 1172

Pompa Memorial Endowed Scholarship. *See* Gilbert G. Pompa Memorial Endowed Scholarship, entry (U) 258

Pope Memorial Scholarships. *See* Ida M. Pope Memorial Scholarships, entries (U) 298, (G) 948

Postdoctoral Fellowship in the History of Modern Science and Technology in East Asia, (P) 1412

Postdoctoral Fellowships in Diabetes Research, (P) 1413

Postdoctoral Research Leave Fellowships, (P) 1414

Postdoctoral Research Training Fellowships in Epilepsy, (P) 1415

Practice Enrichment Traveling Fellowship, (P) 1416

Praxair Scholarships, (U) 530

Predoctoral Research Training Fellowships in Epilepsy, (G) 1102

Prelinger Award. *See* Catherine Prelinger Award, entries (G) 807, (P) 1250

Prentice Gautt Postgraduate Scholarships. *See* Dr. Prentice Gautt Postgraduate Scholarships, entry (G) 861

Prescott Kappa Delta Staff Risk Management Scholarship. *See* Kappa Delta Sorority Undergraduate Scholarships, entry (U) 343

Prescott Scholarship. *See* Kappa Delta Sorority Graduate Scholarships, entry (G) 986

Pressman Scholarship. *See* Ada I. Pressman Scholarship, entries (U) 6, (G) 727

Price Memorial Scholarship. *See* Nathalie A. Price Memorial Scholarship, entry (U) 461

Price Scholarships. *See* Judith McManus Price Scholarships, entries (U) 334, (G) 975

Prickett Scholarship Fund. *See* Society of Daughters of the United States Army Scholarships, entry (U) 597

Prime Scholarship. *See* California P.E.O. Selected Scholarships, entries (U) 107, (G) 800

Prince Scholarship. *See* Scholarships for ELCA Service Abroad, entry (U) 577

Priscilla Carney Jones Scholarship, (U) 531

Priscilla Maxwell Endicott Scholarships, (U) 532

Prize for a Faculty Member for Research in an Undergraduate Institution, (P) 1417

Professional Business Women of California Academic Scholarships, (U) 533

Project Red Flag Academic Scholarship for Women with Bleeding Disorders. *See* Victory for Women Academic Scholarship for Women with Bleeding Disorders, entries (U) 653, (G) 1170

Providence Alumnae Chapter Scholastic Achievement Award, (U) 534

Providence Alumnae Memorial Award, (U) 535

Pryor Award in Arkansas Women's History. *See* Susie Pryor Award in Arkansas Women's History, entry (P) 1454

Puget Sound Business Journal's Women of Influence-Lytle Enterprises Scholarship, (G) 1103

Pulvermacher-Ryan Scholarship. *See* Wisconsin Legion Auxiliary Merit and Memorial Scholarships, entry (U) 673

Putnam Prize. *See* Elizabeth Lowell Putnam Prize, entry (U) 209

**Q**

Quality of Life Awards, (U) 536

Quick/Gamma Phi Beta Scholarship. *See* Elizabeth Ahlemeyer Quick/Gamma Phi Beta Scholarship, entry (U) 207

Quincey Memorial Graduate Scholarship. *See* Daughters of Penelope Graduate Student Scholarships, entry (G) 829

**R**

R. Robert & Sally D. Funderburg Research Award in Gastric Cancer, (P) 1418

Rachel Royston Permanent Scholarship, (G) 1104

Radcliffe Institute Fellowships, (P) 1419

Rainer Graduate Fellowship. *See* John Rainer Graduate Fellowship, entry (G) 969

Ralph W. Shrader Diversity Scholarships, (G) 1105

Ramage Scholarship. *See* Kappa Delta Sorority Undergraduate Scholarships, entry (U) 343

Rance Scholarship Fund. *See* Malena Rance Scholarship Fund, entry (G) 1014

Randall Scholarship. *See* Sigma Gamma Rho Scholarships/ Fellowships, entries (U) 591, (G) 1146

Randy Gerson Memorial Grant, (G) 1106

Rankin Award. *See* Jeannette Rankin Award, entry (U) 324

Rapp Memorial ASA Scholarship. *See* Bob Rapp Memorial ASA Scholarship, entry (U) 92

Rayam Prize in Sacred Music. *See* Grady-Rayam Prize in Sacred Music, entry (U) 268

Raymond A. Weiss Research and Program Innovation Grant. *See* Drs. Rosalee G. and Raymond A. Weiss Research and Program Innovation Grant, entry (P) 1274

Reagan Pathfinder Scholarships. *See* National Pathfinder Scholarships, entries (U) 466, (G) 1067

Ream's Food Stores Scholarships, (U) 537

Rebecca Routh Coon Injury Research Award. *See* Lizette Peterson-Homer Injury Prevention Research Grant, entries (G) 1003, (P) 1353

Red Speigle Award. *See* Virginia Golf Foundation Scholarship Program, entry (U) 656

Redd Student Award in Women's History. *See* Annaley Naegle Redd Student Award in Women's History, entries (U) 42, (G) 763

Redditt Memorial Scholarship. *See* Nina Belle Redditt Memorial Scholarship, entries (U) 486, (G) 1080

Reed and Gloria Pennington Scholarship, (U) 538

Reed Memorial Flight Scholarship. *See* Women in Aviation, International Flight Scholarships, entry (P) 1475

Region F Scholarship. *See* Carol Stephens Region F Scholarship, entries (U) 113, (G) 801

Region H Scholarship, (U) 539, (G) 1107

Regional Summer Music Scholarships, (U) 540, (G) 1108

Reichert and Barbara Wolff-Reichert Award for Excellence in Advanced Laboratory Instruction. *See* Jonathan Reichert and Barbara Wolff-Reichert Award for Excellence in Advanced Laboratory Instruction, entry (P) 1334

Reifschneider Scholarship. *See* Donna Reifschneider Scholarship, entries (U) 180, (G) 845

Reinhart Scholarship. *See* Delta Kappa Gamma Scholarship Program, entry (G) 835

Rejesta V. Perry Scholarship, (U) 541

Rendel Scholarships. *See* Betty Rendel Scholarships, entry (U) 86

Research and Engineering Apprenticeship Program (REAP) for High School Students, (U) 542

Research and Training Fellowships in Epilepsy for Clinicians, (P) 1420

**U–Undergraduates**  **G–Graduate Students**  **P–Professionals/Postdoctorates**

**U–Undergraduates**          **G–Graduate Students**          **P–Professionals/Postdoctorates**

**U–Undergraduates**        **G–Graduate Students**        **P–Professionals/Postdoctorates**

Wichita Chapter AFWA Scholarships, (U) 669, (G) 1186

WIF Film Finishing Fund Grants, (P) 1473

Wilder Educational Fund Scholarship. *See* Fannie Wilder Educational Fund Scholarship, entry (U) 232

WILL Scholarship. *See* Fran O'Sullivan Women in Lenovo Leadership (WILL) Scholarship, entry (U) 247

Willey Scholarship. *See* Myrt Willey Scholarship, entry (U) 452

William Bridge Scholarship, (U) 670

William C. Howell Scholarship. *See* APF/COGDOP Graduate Research Scholarships, entry (G) 765

William L. Fisher Congressional Geoscience Fellowship, (P) 1474

William Rucker Greenwood Scholarship, (U) 671, (G) 1187

Williams Scholarship. *See* Sigma Gamma Rho Scholarships/ Fellowships, entries (U) 591, (G) 1146

Williams-Nickelson Award for Women's Leadership and Scholarship in Women's Issues. *See* Carol Williams-Nickelson Award for Women's Leadership and Scholarship in Women's Issues, entry (G) 803

Willis Early Career Award. *See* Diane J. Willis Early Career Award, entry (P) 1267

Wilson Memorial Educational Fund. *See* Kathy Kardish Wilson Memorial Educational Fund, entries (U) 347, (G) 991

Winifred Hill Boyd Graduate Scholarship, (G) 1188

Wisconsin Legion Auxiliary Child Welfare Scholarship, (G) 1189

Wisconsin Legion Auxiliary Department President's Scholarship, (U) 672

Wisconsin Legion Auxiliary Merit and Memorial Scholarships, (U) 673

Wisconsin Legion Auxiliary Past Presidents Parley Health Career Scholarships, (U) 674

Wisconsin Legion Auxiliary Past Presidents Parley Registered Nurse Scholarships, (U) 675

Wisconsin Towns Association Scholarships, (U) 676

Wisconsin Women in Government Undergraduate Scholarships, (U) 677

Wisconsin Women's Alliance Foundation Scholarship, (U) 678, (G) 1190

"Wisdom of the People" Keepers of the Next Generation Award. *See* Woksape Oyate: "Wisdom of the People" Keepers of the Next Generation Award, entry (U) 679

Wise Loan Program. *See* E.K. Wise Scholarship Fund, entry (G) 869

Wise Scholarship Fund. *See* E.K. Wise Scholarship Fund, entry (G) 869

Wisner Scholarship. *See* Dorothy C. Wisner Scholarship, entry (U) 183

WLAM Foundation Scholars, (G) 1191

Woksape Oyate: "Wisdom of the People" Keepers of the Next Generation Award, (U) 679

Wolff-Reichert Award for Excellence in Advanced Laboratory Instruction. *See* Jonathan Reichert and Barbara Wolff-Reichert Award for Excellence in Advanced Laboratory Instruction, entry (P) 1334

Woman's Missionary Union of Virginia Seminary Scholarship, (G) 1192

Women Chefs & Restaurateurs Scholarship Program, (U) 680, (G) 1193

Women in Aviation, International Achievement Awards. *See* Women in Aviation, International General Scholarships, entries (U) 681, (G) 1194

Women in Aviation, International Flight Scholarships, (P) 1475

Women in Aviation, International General Scholarships, (U) 681, (G) 1194

Women in Aviation, International Maintenance Scholarships, (U) 682

Women in Aviation International Management Scholarship, (P) 1476

Women in Federal Law Enforcement Members-Only Scholarship, (U) 683, (G) 1195

Women in Federal Law Enforcement Scholarship, (U) 684, (G) 1196

Women in Film and Television Atlanta, (U) 685

Women in Film/Dallas College/University Student Tuition Scholarship, (U) 686

Women in Film Finishing Fund Grants. *See* WIF Film Finishing Fund Grants, entry (P) 1473

Women in Lenovo Leadership (WILL) Scholarship. *See* Fran O'Sullivan Women in Lenovo Leadership (WILL) Scholarship, entry (U) 247

Women in Public Finance Scholarship Program, (U) 687

Women in Toxicology Special Interest Group Vera W. Hudson and Elizabeth K. Weisburger Scholarship Fund, (G) 1197

Women in United Methodist History Research Grant, (P) 1477

Women Lawyers Association of Michigan Foundation Scholars. *See* WLAM Foundation Scholars, entry (G) 1191

Women Military Aviators Dream of Flight Scholarship, (U) 688, (P) 1478

Women of Color Dissertation Scholarship. *See* Esther Ngan-ling Chow and Mareyjoyce Green Scholarship, entry (G) 884

Women of Influence-Lytle Enterprises Scholarship. *See* Puget Sound Business Journal's Women of Influence-Lytle Enterprises Scholarship, entry (G) 1103

Women of the ELCA Scholarship Program, (U) 689, (G) 1198

Women Soar Scholarship for Innovation, (U) 690

Women@Microsoft Hoppers Scholarship, (U) 691

Women's Art Studio Internships. *See* Art Studio Internships, entries (U) 54, (P) 1225

Women's Bar Foundation Scholarship Awards. *See* WBF Scholarship Awards, entry (G) 1183

Women's Basketball Coaches Association Sports Communication Scholarship Award. *See* Robin Roberts/ WBCA Broadcasting Scholarship, entry (G) 1115

Women's Business Alliance Scholarship Program, (U) 692, (G) 1199

Women's Campaign Fund Fellowship Program, (U) 693, (P) 1479

Women's Caucus Editing and Translation Fellowship, (P) 1480

Women's Economic Council Foundation Scholarship Awards for Non-Traditional Students, (U) 694

Women's Economic Council Foundation Scholarship Awards for Traditional High School Seniors, (U) 695

Women's Environmental Council Scholarships, (U) 696, (G) 1200

Women's Film Preservation Fund Grants, (P) 1481

Women's Independence Scholarship Program, (U) 697, (G) 1201

Women's Jewelry Association Scholarships, (U) 698

Women's Law and Public Policy Fellowship Program, (P) 1482

Women's Music Commission, (U) 699, (G) 1202, (P) 1483

Women's Opportunity Awards Program, (U) 700

Women's Overseas Service League Scholarships for Women, (U) 701

Women's Prize for Fiction, (P) 1484

Women's Re-Entry Scholarships, (U) 702

Women's Second Chance College Scholarship, (U) 703

Women's Southern Golf Association Scholarship, (U) 704

Women's Studies in Religion Program. *See* Harvard Divinity School/Women's Studies in Religion Program, entry (P) 1312

---

**U–Undergraduates**　　　　**G–Graduate Students**　　　　**P–Professionals/Postdoctorates**

# Sponsoring Organization Index

The Sponsoring Organization Index makes it easy to identify agencies that offer financial aid primarily or exclusively to women. In this index, the sponsoring organizations are listed alphabetically, word by word. In addition, we've used an alphabetical code (within parentheses) to help you identify the intended recipients of the funding offered by the organizations: U = Undergraduates; G = Graduate Students; P = Professionals/Postdoctorates. For example, if the name of a sponsoring organization is followed by (U) 241, a program sponsored by that organization is described in the Undergraduates chapter, in entry 241. If that sponsoring organization's name is followed by another entry number—for example, (G) 1370—the same or a different program sponsored by that organization is described in the Professionals/Postdoctorates chapter, in entry 1370. Remember: the numbers cited here refer to program entry numbers, not to page numbers in the book.

American Association of University Women. Honolulu Branch, (U)
288, 641, (G) 939

American Association of University Women. Northern Ocean
County Branch, (U) 346

American Association of University Women. Wilmington Branch,
(U) 578, (G) 1134

American Astronomical Society, (P) 1223

American Baptist Churches of the Rocky Mountains, (U) 31, 201,
312, (G) 752

American Baptist Churches USA, (G) 874

American Baptist Women's Ministries of New Jersey, (U) 154

American Baptist Women's Ministries of New York State, (U) 32,
(G) 753

American Baptist Women's Ministries of Wisconsin, (U) 138, (G)
728

American Bar Association. Section of Business Law, (G) 1139

American Board of Obstetrics and Gynecology, (P) 1219

American Business Women's Association, (U) 114, 612, (G) 754,
914, 935, 1123, 1152

American Business Women's Association. Humble Artesian
Chapter, (U) 296, (G) 944

American Business Women's Association. Onipa'a Chapter, (U)
501

American Business Women's Association. Pirate Charter Chapter,
(U) 486, (G) 1080

American Chemical Society. Department of Diversity Programs,
(U) 531, (G) 870, (P) 1280

American Chemical Society. Division of Organic Chemistry, (G)
1091

American College of Neuropsychopharmacology, (P) 1258, 1291,
1331, 1338, 1406

American College of Nurse-Midwives, (U) 74, 202, 618, 666, (G)
726, 784, 864, 1155, 1180, (P) 1210, 1272, 1314, 1343, 1468

American College of Rheumatology, (P) 1407

American Dental Education Association, (P) 1285

American Educational Research Association, (P) 1211

American Epilepsy Society, (G) 925, 1102, (P) 1286-1287, 1415,
1420

American Eurocopter, (U) 60

American Federation of State, County and Municipal Employees.
Ohio Council 8, (U) 495

American Fisheries Society, (G) 957

American Foundation for the Blind, (U) 262, 550, (G) 913

American Gastroenterological Association, (P) 1213, 1247, 1281-
1282, 1418

American Geological Institute, (U) 12, (G) 732, 922, (P) 1474

American Geophysical Union, (G) 733

American GI Forum of the United States, (U) 702

American Health Information Management Association, (U) 13, (G)
734

American Heart Association, (U) 265

American Hereford Association, (U) 529

American Historical Association, (P) 1330

American Indian College Fund, (U) 679

American Indian Graduate Center, (G) 871, 969

American Indian Heritage Foundation, (U) 436

American Legion Auxiliary, (U) 33, 606, (P) 1220

American Legion. California Auxiliary, (U) 106

American Legion. Colorado Auxiliary, (U) 132

American Legion. Florida Auxiliary, (U) 241, (G) 895

American Legion. Illinois Auxiliary, (U) 299

American Legion. Indiana Department, (U) 300-301

American Legion. Kentucky Auxiliary, (U) 405

American Legion. Maryland Auxiliary, (U) 415-416

American Legion. Minnesota Auxiliary, (U) 431

American Legion. Missouri Department, (U) 368

American Legion. New York Auxiliary, (U) 237

American Legion. North Carolina Auxiliary, (U) 459

American Legion. Oregon Auxiliary, (U) 504-507

American Legion. Virginia Auxiliary, (U) 41

American Legion. Washington Auxiliary, (U) 614

American Legion. Wisconsin Auxiliary, (U) 156, 294, 672-675, (G)
943, 1189

American Library Association. Governance Office, (P) 1288

American Mathematical Society, (P) 1432

American Medical Association, (G) 967, (P) 1329

American Medical Women's Association, (G) 758, 764

American Meteorological Society, (U) 34, 37, (G) 756-757

American Nuclear Society, (U) 5, 35, 329, (G) 755, 968, (P) 1372

American Occupational Therapy Association, (G) 869

American Orchid Society, (G) 1081

American Ornithologists' Union, (G) 932, 1018, (P) 1319

American Physical Society, (U) 46, 361, (P) 1334, 1341, 1349,
1359, 1367, 1417

American Planning Association, (U) 334, (G) 975

American Political Science Association, (G) 772, 1114, (P) 1230,
1423, 1466

American Psychological Association. American Psychological
Association of Graduate Students, (G) 803

American Psychological Association. Division 12, (P) 1456-1457

American Psychological Association. Division 17, (P) 1256

American Psychological Association. Division 29, (P) 1276

American Psychological Association. Division 35, (G) 907

American Psychological Association. Division 37, (P) 1267

American Psychological Association. Division 38, (P) 1458

American Psychological Association. Division 54, (G) 1003, (P)
1353

American Psychological Foundation, (G) 765, 785, 873, 883, 892,
931, 970, 1003, 1106, 1118, 1136, 1171, 1182, (P) 1214, 1221,
1252, 1256, 1267, 1274, 1276, 1297, 1318, 1332, 1335, 1353,
1408, 1425, 1456-1458, 1470

American Railway Engineering and Maintenance-of-Way
Association, (U) 47

American Society for Eighteenth-Century Studies, (P) 1480

American Society for Engineering Education, (G) 1064, (P) 1275,
1441

American Society for Microbiology, (P) 1245

American Society for Pharmacology and Experimental
Therapeutics, (U) 716

American Society of Safety Engineers, (U) 59, (G) 773, 1161

American Society of Women Accountants. Albuquerque Chapter,
(U) 425

American Society of Women Accountants. Seattle Chapter, (U)
548, (G) 1113

American Statistical Association, (G) 911

American Water Works Association, (G) 937

American Woman's Society of Certified Public Accountants.
Boston Affiliate, (U) 94, (G) 797

America's National Teenager Scholarship Organization, (U) 36

Amgen Inc., (G) 1091

AMVETS National Ladies Auxiliary, (U) 38

Applied Computer Security Associates, (U) 44, (G) 766

Appraisal Institute, (U) 45

**U–Undergraduates**          **G–Graduate Students**          **P–Professionals/Postdoctorates**

**U–Undergraduates**   **G–Graduate Students**   **P–Professionals/Postdoctorates**

Paul and Phyllis Fireman Charitable Foundation, (U) 500

Pennsylvania Federation of Democratic Women, (U) 515

Pennsylvania Masonic Youth Foundation, (U) 503

P.E.O. Foundation. California State Chapter, (U) 107, 183, 187, 225, 317, (G) 800, 849, 886, 960, 1122

P.E.O. Sisterhood, (U) 516-517, (G) 1095, (P) 1410

P.E.O. Sisterhood. Florida Chapters, (U) 242

PepsiCo, Inc., (U) 519

Pfizer Inc., (G) 925, 967, 1102, (P) 1286, 1329, 1415, 1420

PG&E Women's Network Employee Association, (U) 110

Phi Beta Kappa Society, (G) 1031-1032, (P) 1370-1371

Philanthrofund Foundation, (U) 395, 457, (G) 1015, 1061

Pi Beta Phi, (U) 219, 524-525, 593, (G) 1099-1100, (P) 1284, 1411

Pittsburgh Institute of Aeronautics, (U) 60

PNC Bank, (U) 527

Pratt & Whitney Company, (U) 60

Praxair, Inc., (U) 530

Presbyterian Church (USA), (U) 464, 477

Presbyterians for Renewal, (G) 1008

Prevent Blindness Ohio, (G) 1153

Professional Business Women of California, (U) 533

Publishing Triangle, (P) 1238, 1337

Puget Sound Business Journal, (G) 1103

## R

The Race for Education, (U) 57

Ralph L. Smith Foundation, (P) 1404

The Reinberger Foundation, (G) 1153

Research Corporation, (P) 1417

Resources for the Future, (U) 544, (G) 972, 1110, 1177, (P) 1307, 1333

Rhode Island Commission on Women, (U) 546

Rhode Island Foundation, (U) 546, (G) 1024

Rhode Island Society of Certified Public Accountants, (U) 120, (G) 815

Rhode Island Women's Golf Association, (U) 547

Richard Linn American Inn of Court, (G) 1027

Robert Wood Johnson Foundation, (P) 1440

Rockwell Automation, Inc., (U) 553

Rockwell Collins, Inc., (U) 554

Rolls-Royce Corporation, (U) 116

Rona Jaffe Foundation, (P) 1426

Royal Neighbors of America, (U) 393, 476

Rural Mutual Insurance Company, (U) 563, 676

Ruth Jackson Orthopaedic Society, (G) 853, (P) 1416, 1424, 1431

## S

St. Jude Medical, Inc., (U) 610, (G) 1151

San Antonio Area Foundation, (U) 327

San Diego Foundation, (U) 55

Sandia National Laboratories, (G) 1068

Scarecrow Press, (P) 1288

Scholarship America, (U) 100, 314, 433, 435, 647, (G) 852

Scholastic, Inc., (U) 337, (G) 977

School for Advanced Research, (P) 1289

Scott Construction, Inc., (U) 676

Seattle Foundation, (U) 93, (G) 852, 1103

Seattle Post-Intelligencer, (U) 93

Semiconductor Research Corporation, (G) 1142

ServiceMaster Company, (U) 135

Shepherd Foundation, (U) 442

Siemens Foundation, (U) 588

Sigma Alpha Iota Philanthropies, Inc., (U) 67, 185, 318-319, 449-451, 521, 540, 589-590, (G) 796, 844, 916, 963, 1011, 1055-1056, 1108, 1144, (P) 1446, 1465

Sigma Delta Epsilon-Graduate Women in Science, Inc., (G) 1074, 1145, (P) 1394, 1447

Sigma Gamma Rho Sorority, Inc., (U) 358, 541, 591, 659, (G) 1146

Sigma Kappa Foundation Inc., (U) 592, (G) 1147

Signature Flight Support Corporation, (U) 681, (G) 1194

Signs: Journal of Women in Culture and Society, (P) 1249

Slovak Catholic Sokol, (U) 216, 635, (G) 878, 1160

Smithsonian Astrophysical Observatory, (U) 572, (P) 1278

Society for Historians of American Foreign Relations, (G) 1058, (P) 1388-1389

Society for Maternal-Fetal Medicine, (P) 1219

Society for Technical Communication, (U) 399, (P) 1369

Society for Women's Health Research, (P) 1380

Society of Automotive Engineers, (U) 570, (P) 1327

Society of Daughters of the United States Army, (U) 597

Society of Exploration Geophysicists, (U) 73, (G) 782

Society of Manufacturing Engineers, (U) 382

Society of Toxicology, (G) 1197

Society of Women Engineers, (U) 6-7, 43-44, 75, 78, 83, 90-91, 95, 98, 113, 115, 126, 142, 155, 188-190, 194, 197, 211, 229, 244, 247, 253, 266, 285, 297, 309, 328, 336, 351, 365-366, 375, 408, 414, 417, 422, 491, 498, 530, 539, 553-554, 599-600, 617, 620, 644, 648, 650, (G) 727, 766, 791, 794, 801, 806, 819, 825, 951, 1007, 1089, 1107, 1149, 1154, 1167-1168, (P) 1239

Society of Women Engineers. Birmingham Section, (U) 89

Society of Women Engineers. Boston Section, (U) 384, (G) 1006

Society of Women Engineers. Central Indiana Section, (U) 116

Society of Women Engineers. Central New Mexico Section, (U) 117, 131, (G) 809

Society of Women Engineers. DelMar Section, (U) 157

Society of Women Engineers. Detroit Section, (U) 168

Society of Women Engineers. Eastern Washington Section, (U) 661, (G) 1178, (P) 1469

Society of Women Engineers. Greatland Section, (U) 270

Society of Women Engineers. Houston Section, (U) 292

Society of Women Engineers. Mid-Hudson Section, (U) 598, (G) 1148

Society of Women Engineers. Minnesota Section, (U) 70, 129, 252, 377, 420, 432, 447, 610, (G) 778, 821, 906, 1004, 1040, 1054, 1151

Society of Women Engineers. New Jersey Section, (U) 480

Society of Women Engineers. Pacific Northwest Section, (U) 386, 407

Society of Women Engineers. Rocky Mountain Section, (U) 555, (G) 1116

Society of Women Engineers. Southwest Idaho Section, (U) 604

Sociologists for Women in Society, (G) 783, 884, (P) 1296, 1448

Sons of Norway, (U) 458

Soroptimist International of the Americas, (U) 700

Soroptimist International of the Americas. Founder Region, (G) 898

Soroptimist International of the Americas. Midwestern Region, (U) 657, (G) 1174

Soroptimist International of the Americas. North Atlantic Region, (G) 885

Soroptimist International of the Americas. Northwestern Region, (G) 1083

South Carolina Coaches Association of Women's Sports, (U) 601

**U–Undergraduates**      **G–Graduate Students**      **P–Professionals/Postdoctorates**

# Residency Index

Some programs listed in this book are set aside for women who are residents of a particular state, region, or other geographic location. Others are open to applicants wherever they may live. The Residency Index will help you pinpoint programs available in your area as well as programs that have no residency restrictions at all (these are listed under the term "United States"). To use this index, look up the geographic areas that apply to you (always check the listings under "United States"), jot down the entry numbers listed for the recipient level that applies to you (Undergraduates, Graduate Students, or Professionals/Postdoctorates), and use those numbers to find the program descriptions in the directory. To help you in your search, we've provided some "see" and "see also" references in the index entries. Remember: the numbers cited here refer to program entry numbers, not to page numbers in the book.

# Tenability Index

Some programs listed in this book can be used only in specific cities, counties, states, or regions. Others may be used anywhere in the United States. The Tenability Index will help you locate funding that is restricted to a specific area as well as funding that has no tenability restrictions (these are listed under the term "United States"). To use this index, look up the geographic areas where you'd like to go (always check the listings under "United States"), jot down the entry numbers listed for the recipient group that represents you (Undergraduates, Graduate Students, Professionals/Postdoctorates), and use those numbers to find the program descriptions in the directory. To help you in your search, we've provided some "see" and "see also" references in the index entries. Remember: the numbers cited here refer to program entry numbers, not to page numbers in the book.

## A

Alabama: **Undergraduates,** 17, 89, 373, 603, 613; **Graduate Students,** 981, 994. *See also* United States; names of specific cities and counties

Alameda County, California: **Graduate Students,** 898. *See also* California

Alaska: **Undergraduates,** 586, 661; **Graduate Students,** 1178; **Professionals/Postdoctorates,** 1469. *See also* United States; names of specific cities

Albany, New York: **Graduate Students,** 889. *See also* New York

Albany, Oregon: **Undergraduates,** 177; **Graduate Students,** 842; **Professionals/Postdoctorates,** 1269. *See also* Oregon

Albuquerque, New Mexico: **Graduate Students,** 1068. *See also* New Mexico

Ann Arbor, Michigan: **Professionals/Postdoctorates,** 1440, 1463. *See also* Michigan

Argonne, Illinois: **Graduate Students,** 761. *See also* Illinois

Arizona: **Undergraduates,** 49, 55, 149, 331, 715; **Graduate Students,** 973; **Professionals/Postdoctorates,** 1348. *See also* United States; names of specific cities and counties

Arkansas: **Undergraduates,** 561. *See also* United States; names of specific cities and counties

Armonk, New York: **Undergraduates,** 105. *See also* New York

Austin, Texas: **Undergraduates,** 46, 233. *See also* Texas

## B

Berkeley, California: **Professionals/Postdoctorates,** 1440, 1461. *See also* California

Boiling Springs, North Carolina: **Graduate Students,** 779. *See also* North Carolina

Boston, Massachusetts: **Graduate Students,** 823, 897, 1124; **Professionals/Postdoctorates,** 1299, 1313, 1419, 1434. *See also* Massachusetts

Boulder, Colorado: **Undergraduates,** 543, 594; **Professionals/Postdoctorates,** 1390. *See also* Colorado

Broomfield, Colorado: **Graduate Students,** 823. *See also* Colorado

Buies Creek, North Carolina: **Graduate Students,** 779. *See also* North Carolina

## C

California: **Undergraduates,** 1, 55, 66, 106, 149, 245, 471, 564; **Graduate Students,** 724, 982, 1125. *See also* United States; names of specific cities and counties

California, southern: **Undergraduates,** 652. *See also* California

Cambridge, Massachusetts: **Undergraduates,** 273, 572; **Graduate Students,** 890, 1133; **Professionals/Postdoctorates,** 1295, 1312, 1412, 1419, 1438, 1440. *See also* Massachusetts

Campbell, California: **Undergraduates,** 680; **Graduate Students,** 1193. *See also* California

Carbondale, Illinois: **Undergraduates,** 518; **Graduate Students,** 808; **Professionals/Postdoctorates,** 1251. *See also* Illinois

Casper, Wyoming: **Undergraduates,** 177; **Graduate Students,** 842; **Professionals/Postdoctorates,** 1269. *See also* Wyoming

Champaign, Illinois: **Undergraduates,** 518; **Graduate Students,** 808, 872; **Professionals/Postdoctorates,** 1251. *See also* Illinois

Charleston, South Carolina: **Undergraduates,** 462

Charlotte, North Carolina: **Undergraduates,** 462. *See also* North Carolina

Chicago, Illinois: **Graduate Students,** 900; **Professionals/Postdoctorates,** 1387, 1462. *See also* Illinois

Cincinnati, Ohio: **Undergraduates,** 462. *See also* Ohio

Cleveland, Ohio: **Undergraduates,** 460; **Graduate Students,** 923. *See also* Ohio

College Station, Texas: **Undergraduates,** 233. *See also* Texas

Colorado: **Undergraduates,** 132-133, 149, 166, 201, 555; **Graduate Students,** 1116; **Professionals/Postdoctorates,** 1352. *See also* United States; names of specific cities and counties

# Subject Index

There are hundreds of specific subject fields covered in this directory. Use the Subject Index to identify these topics, as well as the recipient level supported (Undergraduates, Graduate Students, or Professionals/Postdoctorates) by the available funding programs. To help you pinpoint your search, we've included many "see" and "see also" references. Since a large number of programs are not restricted by subject, be sure to check the references listed under the "General programs" heading in the subject index (in addition to the specific terms that directly relate to your interest areas); hundreds of funding opportunities are listed there that can be used to support activities in any subject area (although the programs may be restricted in other ways). Remember: the numbers cited in this index refer to program entry numbers, not to page numbers in the book.

Urban affairs: **Graduate Students,** 1071; **Professionals/Postdoctorates,** 1392. *See also* Community development; General programs; Urban and regional planning

Urban and regional planning: **Undergraduates,** 63, 66, 334, 696; **Graduate Students,** 798, 896, 975, 1071, 1200; **Professionals/Postdoctorates,** 1392. *See also* Community development; General programs; Urban affairs

Urban development. *See* Community development

Utilities: **Undergraduates,** 632. *See also* Energy; General programs

## V

Vacuum sciences: **Graduate Students,** 1075. *See also* General programs; Sciences

Veteran law. *See* Military law

Veterans. *See* Military affairs

Veterinary sciences: **Undergraduates,** 57, 562; **Graduate Students,** 1038, 1117. *See also* Animal science; General programs; Sciences

Video. *See* Filmmaking; Television

Violence: **Professionals/Postdoctorates,** 1221, 1274. *See also* General programs; Rape

Visual arts: **Undergraduates,** 56, 387; **Graduate Students,** 770, 871, 921; **Professionals/Postdoctorates,** 1229, 1232, 1311, 1326, 1419. *See also* General programs; Humanities; names of specific visual arts

Visual impairments: **Graduate Students,** 1153. *See also* Disabilities; General programs; Health and health care

Voice: **Undergraduates,** 67, 226, 268, 325, 387, 484, 658; **Graduate Students,** 887, 916, 965, 1079, 1175; **Professionals/Postdoctorates,** 1240, 1391, 1465. *See also* General programs; Music; Performing arts

## W

Water resources: **Undergraduates,** 12, 587; **Graduate Students,** 732, 937, 1109; **Professionals/Postdoctorates,** 1422. *See also* Environmental sciences; General programs; Natural resources

Weather. *See* Climatology

Web design. *See* Internet design and development

Web journalism. *See* Journalism, online

Welfare. *See* Social services

Wildlife management: **Undergraduates,** 586, 707. *See also* Environmental sciences; General programs

Wine industry. *See* Beer and wine industries

Women's history. *See* History, women's

Women's studies and programs: **Undergraduates,** 9, 71, 218, 251, 272, 284, 388, 409, 621; **Graduate Students,** 772, 774, 780, 803, 805, 822, 879, 889, 901, 907, 920-921, 934, 971, 1009, 1021, 1033, 1085, 1114, 1133, 1156; **Professionals/Postdoctorates,** 1230, 1248-1249, 1254-1255, 1257, 1259, 1279, 1283, 1290, 1296, 1301, 1310-1312, 1317, 1336, 1344-1346, 1360, 1364, 1366, 1368, 1373, 1380, 1384, 1401, 1423, 1433, 1435, 1437-1438, 1448, 1463, 1466, 1473, 1477, 1481-1482. *See also* Discrimination, sex; General programs

Work. *See* Employment

World literature. *See* Literature

## Y

Youth. *See* Child development

# Calendar Index

Since most funding programs have specific deadline dates, some may have already closed by the time you begin to look for money. You can use the Calendar Index to identify which programs are still open. To do that, go to the recipient category (Undergraduates, Graduate Students, or Professionals/Postdoctorates) that interests you, think about when you'll be able to complete your application forms, go to the appropriate months, jot down the entry numbers listed there, and use those numbers to find the program descriptions in the directory. Keep in mind that the numbers cited here refer to program entry numbers, not to page numbers in the book.